EIGHTH EDITION

the LABOR RELATIONS PROCESS

William H. Holley, Jr.
Auburn University

Kenneth M. Jennings

Roger S. Wolters
Auburn University

THOMSON

SOUTH-WESTERN

Australia · Canada · Mexico · Singapore · Spain · United Kingdom · United States

THOMSON

SOUTH-WESTERN

This book is dedicated to all those individuals

who work hard for the money.

The Labor Relations Process, 8e

William H. Holley, Jr., Kenneth M. Jennings, Roger S. Wolters

VP/Editorial Director:
Jack W. Calhoun

VP/Editor-in-Chief:
Michael P. Roche

Senior Publisher:
Melissa Acuña

Acquisitions Editor:
Joe Sabatino

Senior Developmental Editor:
Mardell Toomey

Production Editor:
Tamborah E. Moore

Marketing Manager:
Jacquelyn Carrillo

Manager of Technology:
Vicky True

Technology Project Editor:
Kristen Meere

Media Editor:
Karen Schaffer

Manufacturing Coordinator:
Rhonda Utley

Production House:
Graphic World, Inc.

Printer:
QuebecorWorld, Taunton, MA

Design Project Manager:
Stacy Jenkins Shirley

Cover and Internal Designer:
Lou Ann Thesing

Cover Image:
© Getty Images

For permission to use material
from this text or product, submit
a request online at
http://www.thomsonrights.com.

For more information
contact South-Western,
5191 Natorp Boulevard,
Mason, Ohio 45040.
Or you can visit our Internet site
at: http://www.swlearning.com

Preface

This text book is a culmination of almost a hundred years of classroom teaching to approximately ten thousand undergraduate and graduate college students. The eighth edition of *The Labor Relations Process* reflects our original objective in writing the book: to provide students with a textbook that will generate an understanding of and appreciation for core elements of union-management relationships. We have attempted to involve the student with the subject matter and to create an interest in related issues that will continue after the student completes the course. A model of the labor relations process (Exhibit 1.2) is presented in the first chapter and expanded in subsequent chapters through extensive references to academics and practitioners that focus on real-world situations and concerns. This provides a balance between concepts and applications for the reader.

As with the first edition and all subsequent editions, the eighth edition of *The Labor Relations Process* continues to be the most comprehensive text on the market.

Features of the Eighth Edition

The eighth edition approaches our student involvement objective by enhancing our commitment to application, an emphasis that is unmatched by other textbooks in this area. We believe that application generates student interest in the subject matter while enabling students to demonstrate their understanding of concepts and principles and apply this information to real-world situations. These opportunities and related efforts should sharpen readers' communication skills, a desirable skill for any student, regardless of his or her academic major or intended occupation.

Application has been enhanced through new "Labor Relations in Action" features, National Labor Relations Board, court, or arbitration case studies at the end of most chapters, and some new "class activity" experiential exercises designed to promote active student participation in the learning process. There are updated Internet exercises called "Exploring the Web" at the end of each chapter to enhance student learning and application and to create interest in independent research. The negotiation exercise with computer applications and the arbitration cases have been prepared for role-playing experience to promote the reality of union-management relations. The book has also maintained many of the previous edition's features: a focus on currency, ethics, international issues, and the "Labor Relations in Action" boxes:

- *Currency.* This edition offers many opportunities for readers to become involved with the current applications of the labor relations process. For example, recent collective bargaining occurred with management and union officials in the auto industry and recent bargaining subjects such as health care costs and technological change are given expanded coverage in the eighth edition.
- *Ethics.* Ethical issues concerning such topics as bargaining behavior, union organizing, employee empowerment, and termination for union activities are addressed throughout the book.
- *International Labor.* Chapter 14 has been updated and expanded to include changes that have occurred in Canada, Mexico, China, Western Europe, Cuba, Korea, Australia, the North American Free Trade Agreement and the European Community.

- *Labor Relations in Action.* The "Labor Relations in Action" boxes integrate current events in labor relations and have been updated with several new applications, discussed further in the next section.

Key Chapter-by-Chapter Changes in the Eighth Edition

Each chapter has been extensively updated with current research, laws and judicial decisions, studies, and statistics. Additional attention has been given to explaining the labor relations process and influences in Chapter 1 and indicating how this process operates in subsequent chapters. Following are some of the key features and additions to the seventh edition:

- *Chapter 1.* Updated union membership data and "Getting Online with Labor Relations Research" (introducing students to computerized search possibilities on current labor relations topics), which is supplemented by Internet exercises in every chapter.
- *Chapter 2.* New labor history timeline feature chronicling important dates and events in labor history and expanded coverage of the unions' role in politics and campaign finance reform.
- *Chapter 3.* Recent key decisions of the NLRB and courts affecting labor relations such as the reclassification of hospital interns and residents and graduate students in academic institutions as "employees" subject to coverage under the Labor Management Relations Act. Expanded coverage of the NLRB's unfair labor practice procedure and the concept of concerted and protected activity under the LMRA.
- *Chapter 4.* Updates on union mergers; coverage of the possible merger between the National Education Association and the American Federation of Teachers; expanded coverage of "financial core" membership rights; and "right-to-work" legislation.
- *Chapter 5.* Coverage of new union organizing tactics, like union salting and renewed emphasis on union organizing led by AFL-CIO President John Sweeney.
- *Chapter 6.* Expanded coverage of collective bargaining preparation and behavior, including a comparison of distributive bargaining versus mutual gain (interest-based) bargaining approaches.
- *Chapter 7.* Updates on wage and benefit trends, expanded coverage of wage incentive pay plans such as skill based pay, health care cost containment, and pension plans.
- *Chapter 8.* Expanded coverage of technological change issues, efforts to foster more cooperative labor-management relationships, and updates on safety and health issues and the Americans with Disabilities Act.
- *Chapter 9.* Role of the mediator as viewed through the eyes of one of the nation's prominent labor mediators. Coverage of trends in strike activity, legal decisions affecting employees' and employers' rights during a work stoppage, and expanded coverage of secondary strike, picket, and boycott activity.
- *Chapter 10.* Grievance mediation and updates on a union's legal duty of fair representation.
- *Chapter 11.* Exploration of employment arbitration, its advantages and shortcomings; controversy over mandated employment arbitration (as a condition of employment); Due Process Protocol; and arbitrator decision's potential conflict and accommodation with public policy.

- *Chapter 12*. Guidelines used by arbitrators in determining "just cause"; updates on *Weingarten* rights, such as its extension to nonunion (unrepresented) employees.
- *Chapter 13*. Updates on public sector bargaining rights, dispute resolution, privatization of public services, and homeland security issues.
- *Chapter 14*. Updates on labor relations systems of America's major trading partners including: the North American Free Trade Agreement and European Union countries, new coverage of labor relations in China, and coverage of major developments in Australia.

Supplementary Materials

Instructor's Manual with Test Bank, Transparency Masters, and Video Guide
(ISBN 0-324-22599-7)

This supplement includes chapter outlines, answers to end-of-chapter discussion questions, case notes, suggested student readings and term projects, and both instructors' and students' instructions for the Collective Bargaining Negotiations Exercise (available on our product support website). The instructor's manual will also include a video guide for the CNN® video on labor relations that accompanies this text. The video guide consists of a description of all video content, suggestions for incorporating the video content into classroom lectures, and discussion questions designed to generate an exciting learning environment. The *Test Bank* has been revised, updated, and expanded. The number of transparency masters has been increased.

ExamView Testing Software
(ISBN: 0-324-23630-1)

ExamView Testing Software contains all of the questions in the printed test bank. This program is an easy-to-use test creation software compatible with Microsoft® Windows. Instructors can add or edit questions, instructions, and answers; and select questions by previewing them on the screen, choosing them randomly, or selecting them by number. Instructors can also create and administer quizzes online, whether over the Internet, a local area network (LAN), or a wide area network (WAN).

"Labor Relations" CNN® Videos
(ISBN: 0-324-23629-8)

CNN® video segments are available on DVD or VHS. The video segments show recent workplace issues for union employees and managers on topics ranging from the exportation of North American jobs, to strikes at Wal-Mart, to Ergonomics.

Instructor's Resource CD-ROM
(ISBN: 0-324-22600-4)

Instructor's Resource CD-ROM contains all instructor materials cited previously: Instructor's Manual, Test Bank and ExamView® plus a complete PowerPoint® slide presentation (new to this edition).

Holley/Wolters Product Support Website

Our product support website, http://holley.swlearning.com, is a robust learning and resource center for both instructors and students. New to this edition are Self-Assessment Exercises that include:

- An Industrial Relations Orientation Self-Assessment that measures the degree of one's pro-union or anti-union sentiment.

- Bargaining Strategy Orientation Self-Assessment that measures one's preference in using various bargaining strategies (e.g., hard vs. soft and win-lose vs. win-win) under negotiation scenarios reflecting equal and unequal bargaining power between the negotiating parties.
- Mediator Effectiveness Potential Self-Assessment measures the degree to which one possesses the personal characteristics attributed to successful mediators.

Interactive Quizzes presented as multiple-choice and true-false questions allow self-assessments by students in understanding material related to each chapter's key terms and concepts.

ACKNOWLEDGMENTS

We are especially grateful to the following professors for their reviews and suggestions on this revision:

Gene Brady, *Southern Connecticut State University*
James Chambers, *Florida Gulf Coast University*
Satish Desphande, *Western Michigan University*
Art Finkle, *Rider University*
Thomas Hyclak, *Lehigh University*
Eugene Lorge, *Old Dominion University*
Douglas McCabe, *Georgetown University*
Frank Milman
Lou Parrotta, *Utica School of Commerce*

We also extend our appreciation to those who made valuable suggestions for previous editions: John Kilgour, Douglas McCabe, Patrick McHugh, Sue Schaefer, Todd Baker, John C. Bird, Mollie Bowers, James F. Byers, Joseph M. Cambridge, Anthony Campagna, William Chase, Boyd Childress, Milton Derber, Satish P. Deshpande, James B. Dworkin, Geraldine Ellerbrock, Paul Gerhart, Dennis W. Gibson, Carol L. Gilmore, Thomas P. Gilroy, David Gray, Charles R. Greer, Marvin Hill, Jr., Wayne Hochwarter, Janis Holden, Denise Tanguay Hoyer, H. Roy Kaplan, Zeinrab A. Karake, Katherine Karl, Philip Kienast, Kenneth A. Kovach, Charles Krider, Thomas W. Lloyd, Howard T. Ludlow, Karl O. Magnusen, Marick Masters, William Maloney, Pamela Marett, Jonathan Monat, Roy Moore, William L. Moore, Thomas Noble, Dane M. Partridge, Robert Penfield, Alex Pomnichowski, Roy R. Reynolds, Robert Rodgers, Richard L. Rowan, Peter Sherer, David Shulenberger, Herman A. Theeke, Peter A. Veglahn, Suzanne M. Vest, William Werther, Elizabeth Wesman, and Carolyn Wiley.

We also wish to thank Sarah M. Philips for her aid in the preparation of this book.

Finally, we would like to thank Thomson South-Western Publishing Company for its fine work on this book. We are especially grateful to our developmental editor Mardell Toomey and production editors Carol O'Connell and Tamborah Moore. Without Mardell, Carol, and Tammy, this edition would be a year or more away.

William H. Holley, Jr.
Auburn University
Kenneth M. Jennings
Roger S. Wolters
Auburn University

About the Authors

William H. Holley, Jr., taught labor relations, collective bargaining, and arbitration for 32 years at Auburn University. He received his B.S. and M.B.A. from Mississippi State University and his Ph.D. from the University of Alabama. He has been active in the Southern Management Association, a division of the Academy of Management, where he has served as Secretary and President, and on the editorial board of the *Journal of Management* for three terms. He is a coauthor of *Personnel/Human Resource Management* with Ken Jennings and of *Labor Relations: An Experiential and Case Approach* with Roger Wolters. His research has been published in a wide range of journals, such as the *Academy of Management Journal, Labor Law Journal, Personnel Psychology,* and others. He is an active labor and employment arbitrator; he is a member of the National Academy of Arbitrators and served as its Executive Secretary-Treasurer; he now serves on the Board of Governors.

Kenneth M. Jennings, Jr., was the Richard de Raismes Professor of Industrial Relations at the University of North Florida, where he taught undergraduate and graduate courses in labor relations and human resource management. After receiving his B.S. from Knox College and M.S. from the University of Illinois, he spent four years with Union Carbide in various industrial relations assignments. He received a Ph.D. from the University of Illinois, and was a faculty member at the University of North Florida for over 20 years. Ken was a prolific scholar and had the reputation among his students as an exciting and engaging teacher. He has written numerous books (*Balls and Strikes: The Money Game in Professional Baseball* and *Labor Relations at the New York Daily News*) and articles in journals such as *Industrial and Labor Relations Review, Industrial Management, Personnel Journal, Employee Relations Law Journal,* and *Transportation Journal.* As a lifelong Chicago Cubs fan, he firmly believed that one day the Cubbies would win the World Series. He was a collector of jazz recordings and baseball cards.

Roger S. Wolters, is an Associate Professor in the Department of Management at Auburn University. Dr. Wolters received his B.B.A. and M.A. from the University of North Florida and his Ph.D. from the University of Illinois in Labor and Industrial Relations. Wolters' primary teaching interests include labor law, collective bargaining, and dispute resolution. He is the co-author of *Labor Relations: An Experiential and Case Approach* with William H. Holley, Jr. His research has been published in a variety of journals including *Labor Law Journal, Arbitration Journal, Employee Responsibilities and Rights Journal, Journal of Construction Engineering and Management, Industrial Relations,* and others. He has engaged in consulting with private and public organizations and served as an Administrative Hearing Officer in the grievance procedure of the City of Auburn, Alabama. Dr. Wolters is a member of the Industrial Relations Research Association. Outside interests include golf and motorcycling.

Brief Contents

Contents

PART 1

Recognizing Rights and Responsibilities of Unions and Management

Part 1 introduces the labor relations process that will be discussed throughout the book, placing it in historical and legal perspectives. It also examines differences in union and management organization and labor relations strategies.

CHAPTER 1

Union–Management Relationships in Perspective

T his chapter first defines the three phases of the labor relations process and then places this process into an analytical perspective. It introduces the activities, focal point, participants, and influences of the labor relations process, which are discussed in detail in subsequent chapters. The chapter ends with a discussion of the current status of union membership and explanations for decline in union membership as a percentage of the total labor force.

Phases in the Labor Relations Process

The **labor relations process** occurs when management and the exclusive bargaining agent for the employees (the union) jointly determine and administer work rules. It is neither automatically nor uniformly applied across public and private sector organizations in the United States. The labor relations process includes the following three phases:

1. **Recognition of the legitimate rights and responsibilities of union and management representatives.** This phase includes the legal right of employees to join unions (see Chapter 3), union organizing drives (see Chapter 5), and the rights of management and union officials, as well as their responsibilities to abide by related laws and labor agreement provisions.

2. **Negotiation of the labor agreement, including appropriate strategies and tactics and impasse-resolution techniques.** Strikes and mediation are examples of the latter (discussed in Chapter 9). This phase is usually the most publicized by the media, even though phases 1 and 3 are equally essential.

3. **Administration of the negotiated labor agreement—applying and enforcing the terms of the agreement on a daily basis.** This phase of the process (discussed in detail in Chapters 10 and 11) accounts for the most time and en-

ergy spent by union and management officials and usually involves a larger number of these officials than the preceding phases.

Clearly, the sequence of the labor relations process is cumulative. Formal negotiations seldom occur if the parties have not first recognized each other's legitimate rights and responsibilities. Similarly, the first two phases are necessary for the existence of the third phase—administration of the labor agreement. This sequence is applied to an increasingly significant topic, employee drug testing, in the "Labor Relations in Action" box.

Of course, not all labor-management relationships have focused on these three phases. Indeed, employees and their representative unions at some public and private sector facilities are still striving to accomplish the first phase of the process.[1]

The phases of the labor relations process are subject to qualitative variation as well. In the first phase, for example, organizations vary in the amount of respect union and management officials have for each other's goals. In the second phase, negotiations are carried out with different levels of intelligence, preparation, and sincere desire to achieve results. The third phase may vary as to how well the negotiated labor agreement is understood and effectively administered in good faith by both parties. There are probably as many different relationships as there are union and management officials negotiating labor agreements.

Elements in the Labor Relations Process

Exhibit 1.2 provides a framework for the labor relations process. The elements shown can be applied to the labor relations activities at a single manufacturing facility, at some or all of the facilities owned by a single company, or in an entire industry. The exhibit cites three major categories: (1) the focal point of labor relations, which is the work rules; (2) the participants in the process, which are the union and management organizations, employees, third-party neutrals, and the government; and (3) constraints or influences affecting the parties in their negotiation and administration of the work rules.

Focal Point of Labor Relations: Work Rules

Any academic discipline needs a focal point so that research, investigation, and commentary can generate applicable insights. "Labor" or "industrial" relations can become a very broad topic including many academic concerns. Sociologists have examined employee alienation, psychologists have investigated causes of job satisfaction, economists have studied wage determination, and political scientists have assessed the structural relationships for the internal union organization and its members and leaders.

In 1958 John Dunlop's book *Industrial Relations Systems* provided a useful focal point for the diverse academic approaches. Dunlop suggested that the center of attention in labor relations should be the work rules negotiated between management and union officials. It is important to understand the influences determining whether a work rule exists and, if so, its particular content.[2] **Work rules** can be placed in two general categories: (1) rules governing compensation in all its forms—wages, overtime payments, vacations, holidays, shift premiums,

LABOR RELATIONS IN ACTION

Drug Testing and the Labor Relations Process

Drug testing has been called the "Jar Wars" of the 1980s and 1990s. A nationwide concern over drug use and its accompanying problems has resulted in many businesses taking measures against drug use. In 1982, only 3 percent of *Fortune* 500 companies were involved in employee drug testing. Ten years later, a 1992 American Medical Association survey found 75 percent of the responding firms testing for employee drug use.

Whether for altruistic reasons—social responsibility or concern for employee welfare—or for monetary advantages—lower insurance rates, increased productivity, or reduction of property damage—concern has been translated into controversy, which illustrates the three phases of the labor relations process.

Recognition of the Legitimate Rights of Union and Employer Organizations

The desire for a drug-free workplace appears to be a legitimate one, which would attract opposition only from drug users, pushers, or radical subversives. Yet organized labor is one of the most formidable opponents of the current drug-testing movement, contending that random or mandatory testing assumes its members are guilty and must prove their innocence.

The government has partially resolved the first phase. Unions have contended in various legal suits that management's unilateral imposition of employee drug testing ignores the legal rights of their members and organizations and violates the Fourth Amendment prohibitions against suspicionless search and seizure.

The Supreme Court has not held private sector employers accountable to constitutional restraints.[a] However, government agencies have formulated guidelines that can apply to both private and public sector employees. A Supreme Court decision, *Skinner v. Railway Labor Executives' Association*, ruled that post-accident drug and alcohol testing required by the Federal Railroad Administration did not violate rail employees' Fourth Amendment rights even though the regulations did not "individualize" suspicion of drug or alcohol use prior to testing.[b] The court contended that the government's compelling public safety interest in ensuring that rail workers are not impaired on the job outweighed the "minimal" employee rights intrusion.

Another Supreme Court decision, *National Treasury Employees Union* v. *Von Raab*, upheld the U.S. Custom Service's policy of testing applicants for promotion for illegal drug use. The majority contended, "Employees involved in drug interdiction reasonably should expect effective inquiry into their fitness and probity."

Negotiation of the Labor Agreement

Unions want to subject drug testing to the second phase of the labor relations process although related efforts in the railroad and airline industries do not come under the Labor Management Relations Act (LMRA; discussed more in Chapter 3). The Supreme Court in *Consolidated Rail Corp.* v. *Railway Labor Executives' Association* indicated that companies in these industries may add drug screening to periodic physical examinations without having to bargain with unions over this practice.

This situation is not the case for most unionized, private-sector companies that are covered by the LMRA and the National Labor Relations Board (NLRB; also discussed more in Chapter 3), a government agency charged with overseeing this labor legislation. The NLRB has made it clear that employee drug testing is a mandatory bargaining issue (discussed more in Chapter 6) where the details of such a program should be negotiated with the union until agreement or impasse. In the case of impasse, an employer may proceed with implementation of the program unless limited by other contract language.

The past practice of "for-cause" drug testing, also, does not give management the go-ahead to implement a change in the existing program such as a switch to random testing or testing as an addition to routine physicals. Unions must protest at the outset of such a program, however, or their lack of immediate response may be interpreted as a waiver of their rights. Even when a current program for routine physicals includes urinalysis, any change in the use of the samples should be an immediate matter of union interest.

Management also cannot assume that an agreement in principle with the union on drug testing constitutes any waiver of the union's right to be included in outlining the specifics of the actual program.

Unions might seek to bargain over who will be tested and under what conditions; the type of test (hair follicles versus urinalysis, for example); and what procedures will be used to ensure accurate results (possibly including retests). In their negotiations, unions will question the existence of any hard evidence that employees who occasionally use marijuana have higher accident rates and litigation claims.

Two unions, the United Auto Workers (UAW) and the American Federation of State, County, and Municipal Employees (AFSCME), have negotiated labor agreement language that stresses that management should emphasize prevention, education, and rehabilitation through counseling as the major aspects of any drug-screening program. The first drug-testing program approved under a UAW labor agreement stressed that testing will be solely on a for-cause basis determined by a supervisor and confirmed by a medical professional. No random drug testing is allowed except for employees in safety-sensitive jobs such as commercial drivers, large crane operators, and top-security personnel. The employee would not receive discipline for failing the test on two occasions; he or she would presumably be discharged for the third occasion of failing the test established for one of nine drugs. AFSCME stresses in its contract negotiations and labor-agreement language that drug tests should not be required without clear evidence that the affected employee is "impaired by the use of alcohol or controlled substances."

Administering the Labor Agreement on a Daily Basis

Unions might protest management's administration of employee drug testing through grievances, and possibly arbitration,[c] (discussed in Chapters 10 and 11) for three general reasons:

1. The labor agreement did not specify drug testing; therefore, a unilaterally established management policy on the subject is a possible invasion of employee privacy rights[d] and is subject to defamation charges in state courts.[e]
2. Testing may be challenged unless there is a demonstrated employee drug problem and/or job performance (e.g., product damage or accidents) is adversely affected.
3. Management did not administer related labor-agreement provisions correctly (e.g., did not ensure that the evidence belonged to the accused employee or misinterpreted the drug tests: see Exhibit 1.1 for related procedures involving flight attendants). ■

SOURCES: [a] "Supreme Court Declines to Review Legality of Private-Sector Drug Tests," Bureau of National Affairs, Inc., *Daily Labor Report*, no. 218 (November 10, 1992), pp. A-4, A-5.
[b] For related and additional considerations, see Thomas H. Christopher, "Employee Drug Testing: A Constitutional Perspective," *Employee Responsibilities and Rights Journal* 4, no. 1 (1991), pp. 311–328, and Barbara Noble, "The New Deal on Drug Testing," *New York Times*, January 8, 1995, which discuss the Omnibus Transportation Employee Testing Act of 1991. See also Bureau of National Affairs, Inc., *Daily Labor Report*, no. 41 (March 3, 1998) where the Supreme Court let a lower court decision stand because it upheld random drug testing of employees working at the Office of Management and Budget, who have frequent access to the president and vice-president of the United States.
[c] Charles L. Redel and Augustus Abbey, "Arbitration of Drug Use and Testing in the Work Place," *Arbitration Journal* 48 (March 1993), pp. 80–85; and Steven M. Crow and Lillian Y. Fok, "Drug Testing at a Labor Arbitration—Friend or Foe?" *Dispute Resolution Journal* (January 1995), pp. 37–43.
[d] John M. Norwood, "Drug Testing in the Private Sector and Its Impact on Employees' Right to Privacy," *Labor Law Journal* 45 (December 1994), pp. 731–748. For possible evidential problems in drug testing see "Hair, Saliva Testing under Consideration to Replace Urinalysis, Ease Alcohol Tests," Bureau of National Affairs, Inc., *Daily Labor Report*, no. 126 (July 5, 1994), pp. C-1–C-4.
[e] "Supreme Court Leaves Intact NLRB Ruling: No Review of Defamation-Drug Testing Case," Bureau of National Affairs, Inc. *Daily Labor Report*, no. 232 (December 3, 1996), pp. AA-1.

Exhibit 1.1

Rights and Responsibilities of Flight Attendants in Two Drug and Alcohol Testing Situations

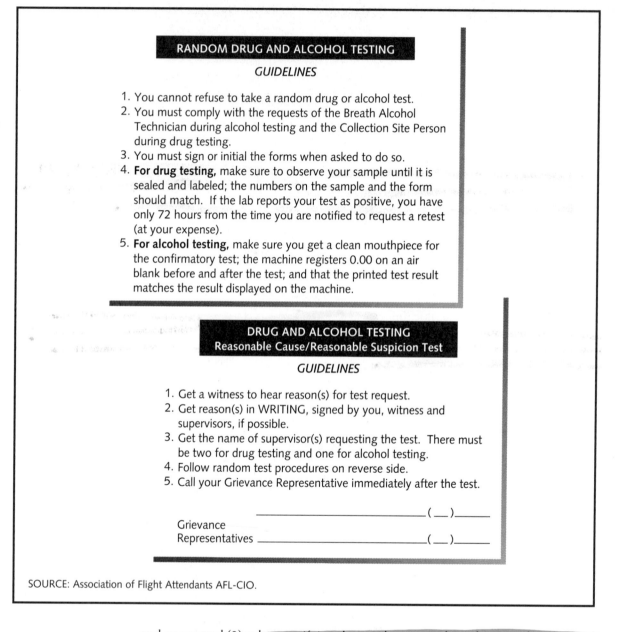

RANDOM DRUG AND ALCOHOL TESTING

GUIDELINES

1. You cannot refuse to take a random drug or alcohol test.
2. You must comply with the requests of the Breath Alcohol Technician during alcohol testing and the Collection Site Person during drug testing.
3. You must sign or initial the forms when asked to do so.
4. **For drug testing,** make sure to observe your sample until it is sealed and labeled; the numbers on the sample and the form should match. If the lab reports your test as positive, you have only 72 hours from the time you are notified to request a retest (at your expense).
5. **For alcohol testing,** make sure you get a clean mouthpiece for the confirmatory test; the machine registers 0.00 on an air blank before and after the test; and that the printed test result matches the result displayed on the machine.

DRUG AND ALCOHOL TESTING
Reasonable Cause/Reasonable Suspicion Test

GUIDELINES

1. Get a witness to hear reason(s) for test request.
2. Get reason(s) in WRITING, signed by you, witness and supervisors, if possible.
3. Get the name of supervisor(s) requesting the test. There must be two for drug testing and one for alcohol testing.
4. Follow random test procedures on reverse side.
5. Call your Grievance Representative immediately after the test.

Grievance
Representatives _____ (__) _____

_____ (__) _____

SOURCE: Association of Flight Attendants AFL-CIO.

and so on, and (2) rules specifying the employees' and employers' job rights and obligations, such as no employee strike or employer lockout during the term of the labor agreement, performance standards, promotion qualifications and procedures, job specifications, and layoff procedures. Additional examples of work rules are furnished in Exhibit 1.3.

Compensation work rules such as negotiated wages are often publicized because they are easily understood by the public. Union and management officials, however, can attach equal or greater significance to the second work-rule

Exhibit 1.2

Elements in the Labor Relations Process

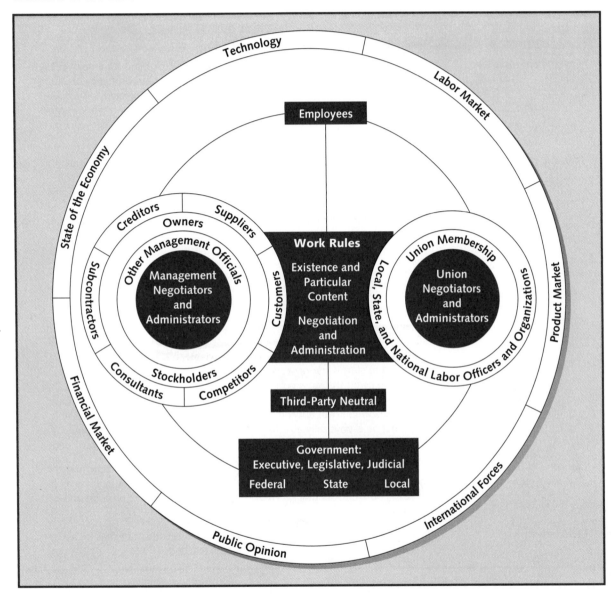

category, job rights and obligations. Managers, for example, might be most concerned with obtaining a contract provision whereby production employees can be required to perform "minor repairs," instead of requiring higher-paid maintenance employees to do them. Many unions have sought work rules that would give members the rights to refuse overtime or even to work less than 40 hours a week while maintaining the original wages and benefits.[3]

Work rules can vary in three characteristics: They can be *common or unique,* they can be *vague or specific,* and they can *change over time.* Some work rules, such as the first one in Exhibit 1.3, are common to many occupations or industries.

Exhibit 1.3

Examples of Work Rules

Job or Industry Classification	Work Rule
Government Installation	The Employer agrees to furnish adequate protective clothing for employees required to work outside during rain, sleet, hail, or other atmospheric conditions detrimental to health or safety, provided the employee subjected to such assignments normally and historically performs the majority of his work assignment indoors. Employees who normally perform a majority of their work outdoors shall furnish their own protective clothing . . .
Professional Baseball	The Player and the Club recognize and agree that the Player's participation in certain other sports may impair or destroy his ability and skill as a baseball player. Accordingly, the Player agrees that he will not engage in professional boxing or wrestling and that except with the written consent of the club, he will not engage in skiing, auto racing, motorcycle racing, sky diving or in any game or exhibition of football, soccer, professional league basketball, ice hockey, or other sport involving a substantial risk of personal injury.
Television	The latest version of the script will be made accessible to the Player in the casting office 24 hours in advance of a scheduled reading or immediately after the scheduling of the interview, whichever last occurs.
Steel Industry	An employee reporting to work on his regularly scheduled shift, unless he is notified by the Company not to report at least 16 hours before the scheduled starting time, shall be given work that is available, but in the event he is not permitted to start work, or works less than 1 hour, he shall be given 4 hours' pay. In the event that an employee works more than 1 hour of his regular shift before being sent home because of lack of work, he will receive 8 hours pay. This provision shall not apply in the event that an employee refused available work that he is physically able to perform or in the event that catastrophes, failures of utilities, or acts of a public enemy interfere with work being provided.
Clerical and Technical Employees at a College	The Board and the Union recognize and agree that while democratic principles should prevail in every American school system, urban colleges in a city as diverse in population as Chicago must be exemplary in their expression and practice of the democratic ideal.
Cemeteries	In all cases where a grave is dug straight down, a second man shall be assigned to assist the digger after a depth of 5 feet is reached.

Others may be unique to a particular job classification, such as those for baseball players and cemetery employees. Work rules likewise may vary in vagueness or specificity: for example, consider the provision for "Clerical and Technical Employees at a College" cited in Exhibit 1.3. This rule at first appears rather insignificant; yet unions and management could easily become heatedly involved over the meaning and intent of the work *democracy*. For example, a professor, discharged because of poor teaching evaluations, might contend this decision violated the "democratic ideal" cited in the labor agreement because he or she also supported an unpopular political cause.

An analysis of work rules helps us understand the complex output of the labor relations process. The formal labor agreement in this sense represents a compilation of jointly negotiated work rules. However, as discussed in Chapter 10, labor relations activities are not limited to those involving the establishment and content of the work rule; it is also appropriate to examine how the particular rule is administered between union and management officials.

Work rules also change over time as a response to changing workplace conditions and societal values. For example, the contemporary work rules for airline flight attendants would most certainly differ from the following three work requirements formulated in the 1930s: (1) swat flies in the cabin after takeoff, (2) prevent passengers from throwing lighted cigar butts out the windows, and (3) carry a railroad timetable in case of plane trouble. Today, the flight attendants' union is concerned with too much luggage stuffed into overhead compartments that may fall and hit a passenger.[4]

Acquired Immune Deficiency Syndrome, or AIDS AIDS represents a relatively new working condition that has commanded employer and union concern and shaped work rules. Almost 99 percent of hospitals recently surveyed by the Occupational Safety and Health Administration have written policies regarding occupational exposure to blood-borne infectious diseases such as AIDS. One nurses' union recently negotiated a contract containing "precedent-setting" health and safety provisions aimed at protecting members from occupational exposure to the virus that causes AIDS.[5]

Smoking "No-smoking" rules have also been relatively recent in their formulation and application. In 1908 a Columbia University professor insisted that "the deleterious effects of tobacco are greatly exaggerated," a belief that prevailed for the next 70 years.[6] Now, union and management officials and possibly arbitrators at thousands of facilities jointly determine whether the issuance of a no-smoking policy is reasonable and whether an employee was properly disciplined or discharged for violating the rule.

Workplace Violence A recent report indicated that nearly 1 million employees each year are injured on the job, and the second-leading cause of workplace deaths is homicide. Fifteen unions have formed the Inter-Union Workplace Assault Coalition to combat this problem.[7]

Electronic Monitoring Electronic monitoring of employee work performance has become a recent and widespread issue affecting factory and an estimated 6 million office employees, particularly in the service industries. New technology such as computers, bar code scanners, and pressure-sensitive plates has enabled management to monitor employee performance in various ways, such as counting the number of keystrokes made on computer keyboards and listening to employees' telephone conversations with customers.

The U.S. Postal Service has adopted one of the more recent forms of electronic monitoring in its nationwide installation of a computer chip in a mail collection box that, when activated by a letter carrier at a mail pickup, will record the time and location. This work issue is not opposed by the union, as one official contends customer allegations about poor service will be resolved efficiently.

Participants in the Labor Relations Process

Management Officials Through the corporate structure, managers represent the stockholders. The negotiated and administered work rules involve managers at several organizational levels and functions. Labor relations managers and representatives are typically found at corporate, divisional, and plant levels. Related objectives are developed at the upper levels and coordinated at the corporate and divisional levels to ensure that a particular work rule at one location, such as a wage rate for a particular job classification, does not adversely alter precedents or conditions at another production facility.

Plant-level labor relations representatives implement these directives, but they must also deal with other managers at the location, particularly production and maintenance managers and first-line supervisors, who direct the daily work activities of hourly employees. As will be further discussed in Chapter 10, management's first-line supervisors typically hear and attempt to resolve employees' grievances on the production floor. In some cases, they are surprised to learn that higher-level management officials have overturned their decisions. Alert union leaders may use dissension among management officials to influence labor relations activities and the company's position toward unions.

Management consultants' activities in the labor relations process are varied, ranging from restructuring personnel practices in nonunion firms (without any organizing campaign) to designing and presenting the employer's response throughout the campaign and representation election. Controversy occurs over the consultants' effectiveness and ethics. One union estimate found that consultants were involved in more than 90 percent of the representational elections lost by unions.[8] However, another research effort found that the impact of consultants on union victories in representation elections was not very great.[9] Seventy-five percent of employers hire consultants to help them fight union organizing drives. It is estimated that unionization rates would more than triple (to about 44 percent) if employers were forced to stay out of the unionization process.

Employers spend hundreds of millions of dollars per year hiring professional "union avoidance" experts. In fact, union organizers routinely see levels of union support in the 60 to 75 percent range melt to less than 50 percent in the face of an employer anti-union campaign, which usually crests just before the date of the NLRB election. It is estimated that approximately 40 percent of the decline in union success in NLRB elections is due to employer opposition.

Management must be conscious of its competitors, who may challenge the company's product in quality, price, and/or service. A company must consider its competitors when negotiating terms of the labor agreement. In some cases (the airline industry, for example) a strike can result in customers and revenues being transferred to competitors.

An advertisement of Ford Motor Products stressed that its particular labor-management relationship gives it a competitive edge. The advertisement was titled, "A Breakthrough in Labor Relations Has Helped Create the Highest Quality Vehicles Made in America." It referred to a new era of commitment and mutual respect between union and management.

Union Officials Union leaders, usually elected by the members, represent the membership, but they, like their management counterparts, do not necessarily represent a consensual group because unions experience internal differences of view. Members and officers do not completely agree on priorities; sometimes conflict occurs over specific tactics to be used in accomplishing commonly shared bargaining objectives.

Union and management officials are subjected to their own pressures, which can either brighten labor relations differences or blur their organizational distinctions when joint problem resolution is sought and obtained. Union officials who are involved in negotiations have to accommodate the interests of members who have a multitude of individual interests. For example, in the 2003 negotiations between the United Auto Workers and Ford, DaimlerChrysler, and General Motors, the parties at the bargaining table addressed wages and performance bonuses, the amount of co-pay for insurance, pensions for current retirees and for surviving spouses, future retirement benefits and credited service, a retirement benefit package for members who take the "30-and-out" package, employment protections for less senior employees who may be laid off or for employees who may lose their jobs when a plant is closed, and wages for new hires.

Employees Perhaps the most significant participant category is employees because they often determine whether a union is even present in an organization (representation elections and union organizing drives are discussed in Chapter 5); whether a negotiated labor agreement is accepted or rejected; and the extent to which a threatened strike is actually carried out (see Chapter 9).

Employees are treated here as a separate category because they may have loyalties to both management and union organizations.[11] This situation is found in both the private and public sectors: for example, public employees such as firefighters, police, and teachers may feel torn between the critical or professional nature of their jobs and the strategic advantages of a strike. Employees want their organizations to thrive and prosper; at the same time, they want to share in the rewards of success. Because their desires may shape the existence and content of particular work rules, employees can be considered the third participant in the labor relations process.

Employees may choose to form a union or choose not to be represented. Typically, when a union represents the employees, it negotiates a collective-bargaining agreement that governs the working relationship for a specific period of time. Any changes in the content of the agreement must be renegotiated with the union and approved by the membership. Employees not represented by a union and not covered under a collective bargaining agreement are not protected from unilateral work-rule changes by companies. As flight attendants of Delta Air Lines discovered in October 2003, Delta announced that new rules for flight attendant pay would be an hourly wage and the removal of caps on how many hours flight attendants were allowed to work. Since there was no collective bargaining agreement between Delta and the flight attendants, the company was not required to negotiate these work-rule changes prior to implementation. Needless to say, even though the flight attendants rejected union representation in 2002 when only 29 percent voted to be represented by the Association of Flight Attendants, meetings of pro-union flight attendants were held at Delta bases immediately after the company's announcement.[12]

The Government The government participates through three branches—executive, legislative, and judicial, occurring at federal, state, and local levels (discussed Chapter 3). In the public sector, government officials also serve as management officials in the labor relations process (discussed in Chapter 13).

In the private sector the federal government has traditionally played an indirect role at the bargaining table. A mediator from the Federal Mediation and Conciliation Service can assist union and management officials in reaching an agreement. The mediator's advice, however, can be refused; this individual can also be asked by one or both parties to leave the negotiations. The federal government's hands-off approach in most private-sector bargaining situations is based on the belief that most management and union officials are better equipped than their government counterparts to assess their needs and limitations and reach a mutually acceptable labor agreement.

Although the federal government does not dictate the terms of a negotiated labor agreement, laws, judicial decisions, and administrative agencies can influence or restrict work rules. For example, legislation to deregulate the trucking industry has contributed to a reduction in union membership and strength.[13]

Union and management officials cannot negotiate a mandatory retirement age of 60 years because this would conflict with the Age Discrimination in Employment Act. Or, although coal miners have long believed that if females worked in the mines, bad luck would result, union and management officials would be violating sexual discrimination aspects of the Civil Rights Act if they negotiated a provision prohibiting female employees from working in the mines. Perhaps more widespread is the controversy over negotiated seniority provisions that are used for administration decisions, such as promotions and layoffs, and affirmative action programs monitored by the government. (This will be discussed in Chapter 8).

Third-Party Neutrals Differences between union and management officials that arise in negotiating the labor agreement or administering its provisions are often resolved by third-party neutrals. **Mediators** (discussed in Chapters 9 and 13) are the most frequently used third-party neutrals in contract negotiations. The mediator assists the union and management officials in resolving their differences themselves. He or she only offers advice and does not have binding decision-making authority.

An **arbitrator** is a third-party neutral hired by union and management officials to make a final and binding decision on a disputed issue. This participant sometimes becomes involved in the second phase of the labor relations process, resolving a negotiations impasse, but is far less used in this capacity than a mediator. The arbitrator's most frequent efforts pertain to the third phase of the labor relations process, resolving a grievance, which is further discussed in Chapter 11.

Neutrals play an important role in the labor relations process. A recent arbitrator's decision reinstated 3,400 employees with back pay from December 2002 to August 2003, which amounted to tens of millions of dollars. The arbitrator was asked to determine whether Verizon had violated its contract with the Communication Workers of America, which had contained a no-layoff provision since 1994. The contract provision stated that the company could not lay off employees for reasons of "process change" having to do with technological or various business changes; layoffs could occur only as a result of special conditions caused by an "external event." The arbitrator agreed with the union position that an "external event" did not cause the 3,400 employees to be laid off.[14]

Constraints or Influences Affecting Participants' Negotiation and Administration of Work Rules

The labor relations participants who affect the development of work rules are in turn influenced by external variables or constraints in their labor relations activities (see the outer circle of Exhibit 1.2). These constraints/influences can sometimes affect one another and may relate to the particular firm, the local community, or society in general. The following discussion furnishes a few illustrations of how these constraints/influences can affect the existence and content of work rules.

State of the Economy: National, Industrial, and Firm-Specific Indicators The state of the economy is usually referred to by indicating movement among such quantitative indicators as inflation, unemployment, and productivity. During the 1980s, the United States witnessed a rising inflation rate, which influenced the negotiation of work rules—notably, union insistence that a labor agreement include provisions to increase wages if increases occur in the cost of living (see Chapter 7). In the early 1990s, the focus of negotiations returned to wage increases, employee benefits, and health-care costs. However, in the late 1990s and the early 2000s, with a slow economy, low rate of inflation, and loss of jobs, the parties returned to an emphasis on job security and other job protection issues.

Two other economic indicators that can affect work rules are interest and unemployment rates. An increase in interest rates could retard home and industrial construction projects. Under these circumstances, work rules might be negotiated to ensure that construction workers are not laid off or that they receive some compensation for the reduced work load.

The unemployment rate affects work rules providing job protection. Chapter 6 discusses ways in which the unemployment rate can affect the bargaining power of union and management officials. If this and other economic measures pertaining to the gross national product, productivity, cost of living, compensation at all employee levels, and exports and imports are unfavorable, unions will be more likely to accept bargaining concessions.

Between March 2001 and August 2003, 2.8 millions jobs were lost in America, and economists estimated that between 600,000 and 995,000 jobs have been lost overseas. Estimates suggest that the work sent overseas has been enough to raise the unemployment rate four-tenths of a percentage point to 6.1 percent. Most of these jobs have been in manufacturing or in telephone call centers; however, the jobs have recently climbed up the skills ladder to include aeronautical engineers, software designers, and the like. These jobs have moved to such countries as China, Russia, and India, where there are a large number of educated workers. As an example, Boeing now employs aeronautical engineers at a design center in Moscow, while it has reduced its engineering staff in Seattle. It is estimated that an American company can save as much as 50 percent for each job shifted, even after transportation, communication, and other costs are included. One estimate for the period of 2000 to 2015 has as many as 3.3 million jobs eliminated at home due to the globalization of American production.[15]

With the loss of jobs after 2001, job security issues became the focus of most contract negotiations. The Steelworkers-Goodyear negotiations yielded several important job security measures. Twelve Goodyear plants were identified as Protected Plants that must remain open during the terms of their collective bargaining agreement, except for the most extreme circumstances. Transfer of production from a Protected Plant to a non-USWA plant would be restricted. Protected Plants would be given "meaningful and significant first consideration and preference" for all new products developed for sale in North America.[16]

Labor Market The skills and wage levels of employees in the relevant labor market can affect negotiated work rules. Management is often concerned with the skill level of employees in the particular community. For example, a firm needing skilled employees from a relatively unskilled labor market would probably wish to negotiate work rules regarding apprenticeship programs. Management would also consider negotiating a 90-day probationary period within which it could terminate the employment of an employee who cannot learn the job and perform adequately, and the union could not protest the action through the grievance procedure.

Both management and union representatives are also interested in the compensation rates for comparably skilled employees in the labor market. Certainly, the wages paid by other companies in the local area affect negotiated wage rates. In some cases, particularly in the construction trades, some unions have had to reduce their wages to counter nonunion competition.

The demand for labor is an important influence in the labor relations process. Although labor market conditions change over time in accordance with the overall economic conditions of the country, there are examples of how the labor market influences such data as employment, wages, types of jobs, and the like. In September 2003, the Department of Labor announced a gain of 57,000 jobs; however, employment must grow by roughly 150,000 jobs per month to keep pace with the increase in population of those older than 16 years of age. The service sector showed gain of 74,000 jobs in September 2003. However, manufacturing showed a loss of 29,000 jobs, which brought the job loss to more than 450,000 for the first eight months of 2003. Then, in October 2003, manufacturing employment showed its highest monthly increase in over three years. This increase was due to a recovering economy and a weakened dollar in the international markets.

In September 2003, the makers of computers and other electronic equipment eliminated 3,800 jobs, their 32nd consecutive month of cutting jobs. Ford Motor Company, which just had completed negotiations with the United Auto Workers, announced that it would lay off 1,700 workers and eliminate 1,300 vacant positions. Verizon Communications offered voluntary buyouts to 74,000 employees in hopes of reducing its payroll. With an economy that had lost 2.8 million jobs since the beginning of 2001, employees continued to lose bargaining power, and the average weekly earnings for rank-and-file workers actually fell in September of 2003. The number of people who had been out of work for at least 27 weeks and continued to look for employment increased from 1.9 in August 2003 to 2.1 million in September.[17]

One effort being taken to assist employees in adjusting to changes in labor market forces is training. As far back as 1986, the Alliance for Employee Growth and Development, Inc., was created as a joint enterprise by AT&T, the CWA, and the IBEW to help displaced workers. By 1989, the focus had changed to preparing workers to handle new technologies. The Alliance set up Technicians for Tomorrow to train employees to qualify for future jobs with the company. Other outstanding examples include the UAW/General Motors Skills Centers and the joint training programs of Ford Motor and the UAW. In the building trades, unions have played a major role in training skilled workers. Because workers moved from employer to employer on a regular basis, single construction companies have no financial incentive to train employees who may end up working for a competitor. Therefore, the unions through their training and apprenticeship programs provide an obvious contribution to the general national welfare. In fact, unions and their contractors outspend their nonunion counterparts by a ratio of 50 to 1 in training investments.[18]

Product Market The labor relations process can be affected by the **product market**, where the company either sells its product or purchases key elements for manufacture of its product. Management would be more vulnerable if a strike occurred at a time when major customer sales were anticipated. For example, management at a brewery would prefer to avoid a labor agreement expiring, possibly leading to a strike, during the summer months. Indeed, one major brewery has been successful in changing the contract expiration date from June 1 to March 1.

The second dimension of the product market, the source of key elements for product manufacture, is illustrated by the UAW's deep concern over the fact that many of the parts for U.S. automobiles are being manufactured in other countries and that it is often difficult to determine which parts on "American" cars are foreign made.[19]

Financial Market An element of important consideration in the labor relations process is the **financial market**, the arena in which the employers (and unions) seek to borrow funds to develop their investment strategies. Companies also consider exchange rates between countries to determine plant location for producing and trading. When a company wants to expand its plant capacity and increase jobs, it often has to borrow money in the financial markets at the same time as it may request wage concessions from the union (see Chapter 7) and/or request elimination of work-rule restrictions to productivity (see Chapter 8). A union must also enter the financial markets to support an employee stock option plan (ESOP) (see Chapter 7) while it agrees to wage concessions to support the stock purchase.

Exchange rates between countries (see Chapter 14) can alter companies' investment strategies because exchange rates affect the comparative wage rates and, consequently, the comparative labor costs of production. As an example, when the peso in Mexico was devalued by as much as 50 percent of the U.S. dollar, the labor costs of production in Mexico declined dramatically and made producing goods in Mexico more attractive and economical for multinational corporations. Thus, products were made in Mexico at lower wage rates and shipped to the United States and elsewhere at comparatively lower prices. As well, in 2001, when the euro was strong in comparison with the U.S. dollar and wage rates in Germany were higher (18 percent—see Chapter 14), firms such as Mercedes-Chrysler determined that producing automobiles in the United States was more attractive and located a plant in the United States. Mercedes-Chrysler announced plans to expand production in China.

Financial circumstances may present major obstacles to contract negotiations. In the Steelworkers-Goodyear negotiations in 2003, the company had initially planned to reduce its North America production substantially by closing a number of plants and downsizing others. That production was scheduled for transfer offshore with capital investments earmarked for foreign and nonunion domestic facilities. The Steelworkers employed a team of Wall Street experts to work with its own financial and legal experts to analyze Goodyear's finances, operations, and business strategy. The union's strategy focused on restructuring the company by improving production efficiencies, managing health-care costs, and eliminating excessive layers of management. Its goal was to achieve a contract that would keep existing plants open with sufficient capital expenditures to enable them to remain competitive in a global market.[20]

Labor unions have been able to use their financial resources and become active in the financial markets. The United Steelworkers have created a regional investment fund of $100 million called the Heartland Labor Capital Project, which has the following objectives:

1. invest in regional business and protect jobs;
2. promote economic awareness as well as training workers and unions and raising the level of influence on economic development;
3. stimulate regional economies;
4. encourage regional business enterprises by involving both labor and its allies to support institutional development;
5. provide capital to enterprises where unions have created more democratic and sustainable practices, and
6. provide prudent returns to investors.

Others unions, including the AFL-CIO, have similar programs to promote jobs for union members.[21]

Technology   Perhaps the most immediate and persistent influence on work rules is the technology of the particular workplace. **Technology** has four dimensions: (1) equipment used in the operation; (2) the pace and scheduling of work; (3) characteristics of the work environment and tasks to be performed; and (4) information exchange. Consider, for example, the major equipment found at a steel mill, blast furnaces, which require very high temperatures for operation. These furnaces cannot be simply turned on and off like a household oven. Often several days are required for either reaching these high temperatures or for cooling the furnaces for repairs. This equipment characteristic affects the facility's work rules. In essence, steel mills must be operated 24 hours a day, 7 days a week— a situation prompting related work rules such as wage premiums for working the night shift, weekends, and holidays.

In some cases the introduction of equipment reduces or eliminates employees in a particular job classification. This situation occurs when industrial robots handle tasks formerly performed by employees. A rather common application occurs in the auto industry, where mechanically joined arms perform spot welding, spraying, machine unloading, and assembly. Unions faced with having membership replaced by robots have increased related bargaining demands (such as more paid time off and the 4-day week) for their members' job security.

Changes in technology have raised the skill requirements for workers. Firms that are able to more fully utilize the skills and brainpower of their employees have a competitive advantage. This change has created a greater demand for more highly skilled workers who are able to assume multiple responsibilities and a lower demand for manual workers. While average real hourly compensation for American workers has not changed over the last 20 years, low-wage workers are actually worse off than comparable workers in other advanced countries and high-wage workers are better off than workers anywhere else in the world. Thus, there appears to be an economic bifurcation of the American labor force.[22]

Even less managerial enthusiasm for automation has been generated by the U.S. Postal Service experience, where a $5 billion automation program featuring bar coding has fallen short of its projected workforce reduction of 87,000 full-time employees. The program has also not significantly reduced expenses because of higher costs and operating inefficiencies.

There is, however, a possibility in some organizations that highly automated equipment can threaten union members' job security, a situation that can affect their bargaining goals and behavior. In the supermarket industry, electronic scanners are used to change item prices, record customer purchases, and maintain products' inventory counts. These activities result in fewer stockhands and reduced skills and compensation of cashiers.

The pace and scheduling of the workday also affect the work rules of certain occupations. For example, bus companies optimizing their productivity and revenue would concentrate on rush-hour traffic (6:00–9:00 A.M., 3:00–7:00 P.M.) when buses would be likely to be filled with passengers. However, problems would remain in scheduling work because many bus drivers might have a daily work schedule of 3 hours on, 3 hours off, 1 hour on, 2 hours off, 4 hours on. Because of the nature of the work, most labor agreements in related industries have provisions pertaining to the permissible number, length, and possible compensation of intervals (times off) between daily work assignments.

Computer operations can help both union and management officials in their daily labor relations activities. Union officers can use computer applications to maintain membership and dues records, as well as word processing for communication to the membership. Union and management officials can also use computer applications in the areas of contract negotiations (costing the various proposals) and administration (maintenance and research of grievances and arbitration decisions).[23] Union officers can use computer applications to maintain and train membership and dues records as well as word processing for communication to the membership.[24] E-mail, Internet, and Web pages are used to keep employees and union members informed of progress during negotiations. Also, both unions and management are frequently using these communication tools during union organizing campaigns. (See Chapter 4, which discusses how unions are using computer technology.)

The American Federation of Labor–Congress of Industrial Organizations (AFL-CIO) has introduced two computer information networks, Labor-NET (for members only) and Labor-WEB (public access), the organization's new "home page" on the Internet's World Wide Web that will enable practitioners and students of industrial relations to become well informed on current developments.[25] One AFL-CIO official contends that labor's message will be communicated to more people because most American families have computers at home or have access to computers at their work site. Many students needing to research a current labor relations topic for a class assignment may find available sources somewhat dated. The following "Labor Relations in Action" box should help

LABOR RELATIONS IN ACTION

Getting Online with Labor Relations Research

The number of electronic sources for locating information on collective bargaining and labor relations is constantly increasing. The most efficient method for finding reports in journals, magazines, newspapers, and other periodical literature is through the use of online research databases, which are offered by most university and college libraries to their students, faculty and staff members. You will choose your sources depending on the time period you want to cover, the amount of information you need and the availability of resources in your area. Libraries still maintain a collection of print indexes, but most of these are being replaced by online versions, which allow for faster searching and less maintenance by the library.

Online databases have several advantages over print indexes, including currency, the ability to print in a variety of formats, the ability to combine terms and other qualifiers (e.g., date, language, and publication title), to broaden or narrow a search, the ability to email or download articles and availability by remote access. A few disadvantages are the commitment of time to become skilled in their use, the availability of only selected content in some databases, and overlapping titles from database to database.

Subscriptions to online databases that provide access to indexing or the full text of articles on business topics are being sold by a number of vendors, including Lexis/Nexis, ProQuest (formerly University Microfilms or UMI), OCLC (FirstSearch), Gale (part of the Thomson Company), EBSCO, and H. W. Wilson. Databases specifically devoted to labor relations cases and issues are provided by the Bureau of National Affairs (BNA) and Commerce Clearing House (CCH). Most of these databases are provided through the Web, although there are a few that are still available electronically only on CD-ROM.

Online databases that can be searched from university and college libraries also can usually be searched from a dorm room, home, or office with appropriate user authentication. Until a few years ago, the content of many of these databases was available only through mediated searches requested by a student or faculty member and performed by a librarian who would then pass on the cost of the search to the requestor. These costs included a connection fee, ranging from $1.60 to $2.20 per connect minute, and charges for each record displayed, ranging from $.50 per record to $1.40 per record. Web-based electronic resources have virtually eliminated the need for mediated searches and allow students to perform free searches with or without the assistance of a librarian.

General business indexes are extremely useful in locating articles on collective bargaining. *Business Periodicals Index*, published by the H. W. Wilson Company, is a print index that is still found in most libraries and, for many years, was the only business index in a small library. The online version of the index is *Wilson Business Abstracts*, which includes indexing and abstracting of the *Wall Street Journal* and the business section of *The New York Times*, as well as more than 600 publications back to 1952. *Wilson Business Full Text* provides access to full text articles in more than 350 publications back to 1995.

Other general business periodical databases that are useful for finding trade publications are *ABI/INFORM Trade and Industry* (ProQuest), *Business and Industry* (Gale RDS), *Business and Management Practices* (FirstSearch), and the Business News portion of Lexis/Nexis Academic. Trade journals such as *Automotive News, Supermarket News, Editor & Publisher,* and *Modern Healthcare* can provide related insights into labor issues and unions such as the United Autoworkers (UAW), United Food and Commercial Workers (UFCW), Newspaper Guild, and American Nurses Association, respectively.

ABI/INFORM Global, produced by ProQuest, was one of the first electronic databases to provide an index to the scholarly literature of business, although coverage is not limited to scholarly titles. Coverage also includes general business magazines and trade periodicals. *ABI/INFORM* contains abstracts and full-text articles published from 1971 to the present. Recently, ProQuest began to offer *ABI/INFORM Archive,* which provides full-text articles published from 1918 to 1986. EBSCO *Business Source Premier* is another comprehensive business periodical database that offers scholarly journals and general business periodicals, including *Business Week, Forbes, Fortune, American Banker,* and many others. EBSCO has exclusive rights to the electronic version of *Harvard Business Review.*

Newspapers are an excellent source of business information because of the detailed analysis of events not often found in other periodical literature. Because they are often published daily, they offer the latest news of labor negotiations. Citations to articles in leading newspapers may be found in print indexes, while a rapidly increasing number of electronic indexes provides the complete text and indexing of national and regional newspapers. The major publishers of online full-text newspapers include Knight-Ridder, Lexis/Nexis, Newsbank, and ProQuest. The text of *The Wall Street Journal* is offered by several sources, and students can also sign up for a subscription to the online WSJ, which includes articles not found in the print copy of the newspaper. WSJ offers a special subscription for professors and students, which can be found on the Web site at http://www.wsj.com.

Lexis/Nexis Academic and *Business Newsbank Plus* are reliable sources to consult for articles from regional newspapers about a particular event published in the city or region where the event took place. The regional publications often offer a different perspective from that of a national newspaper. For example, articles retrieved from *Business Newsbank* on the Bridgestone/Firestone strike, which lasted from July 1, 1994, through May 30, 1995, were published in regional newspapers such as the *Des Moines Register,* the *Akron Beacon* Journal, the *Daily Oklahoman,* and the *Indianapolis Star.*

The *Daily Labor Report,* published by The Bureau of National Affairs in both print and online versions, is extremely useful in researching current labor relations topics. Coverage includes legislation pending in Congress, discussion of court cases, bargaining settlements, statistical information, and other items relating to labor. BNA also publishes the Labor and Employment Law Library, providing the full text of labor and employment cases and manuals for answering day-to-day labor and employment law questions.

Consider a search through electronic databases for articles on the negotiations for a labor agreement between Verizon Communications and Communications Workers of America in 2003. The following search was used to retrieve citations from several databases:

verizon and communications workers and (agreement or contract) and date=2003

The databases searched and the number of citations found are: ABI/INFORM, 32; Lexis/Nexis Academic, 60; Wilson Business Abstracts, 17; Gale Business and Industry, 62; Business Newsbank, 31; and EBSCO Business Source Elite, 8. ∎

students who are researching current labor relations topics. Appendix B, "Internet Possibilities for the Labor Relations Process" and Internet exercises at the end of each chapter will be helpful as well.

International Forces The war in Iraq affected thousands of Americans, including union members called up as reservists. Although companies were required to retain the reservists' positions, the companies were reluctant to hire and train new employees who may have to be laid off upon return of the reservists. Instead, companies required other employees to work more overtime and were required to temporarily reclassify employees (through promotions or transfers) to fill the positions left vacant by the call-up of the reservists.

Unions have been concerned about competitive labor costs generated by the North American Free-Trade Agreement (NAFTA; discussed more in Chapters 2 and 14), which involves the United States, Canada, and Mexico and some $6 trillion worth of goods and services a year. Whether NAFTA will increase or decrease jobs in the long run is unknown. However, NAFTA will have a significant impact on work rules.[26] It would, for example, make it possible for a Mexican trucker earning $7 a day to drive an eighteen-wheeler loaded with auto parts from Mexico to Detroit. Before the agreement, that driver would have to stop at the Rio Grande, where the goods would be loaded onto an American truck. More recently, unions have been actively campaigning against the entry of China to the World Trade Organization.

International trade is a major influence in the labor relations process. Imports/exports, trade deficits, exchange rates, capital investments, and jobs are interconnected. As an example, Chinese exports to the United States have risen from $39 billion in 1994 to about $137 billion in 2003, a trade imbalance of over $100 billion. Some economists claim that China's currency is undervalued by 15 to 25 percent. Coupled with a low-wage workforce, China has a competitive advantage in trade with the United States. At the same time, 65 percent of the rise in Chinese exports has come from foreign companies, including those from the United States that have located plants in China. Of China's 40 top exporters, 10 are companies from the United States, including Motorola and Dell. Major retailers, like Target and Wal-Mart, depend on low-priced imports from China. Wal-Mart alone imports $12 billion worth of products from China annually, accounting for nearly 10 percent of all Chinese imports to the United States. These imports help to keep inflation rates low and allows the Federal Reserve to keep interest rates in the United States at the lowest levels in four decades. In addition, China helps keep U.S. interest rates low and by 2003 had invested $126 billion in U.S. Treasury securities, up from $60 billion in 2000.[27]

Globalization has been characterized as free-market capitalism, which places enormous competitive pressures on all firms that become part of the global economy. Multinational firms that sell globally are pressured to produce globally by slicing their production chains and outsourcing each segment to the country that can produce cheapest and most efficiently. Newly industrialized countries are able to compete in price-conscious markets by paying lower wages than those paid in the United States. In addition, due to the diversity and customization made possible by computer-based technology, the cost advantages of American-style mass production have been lost.[28]

Labor unions have been active in the international arena since their beginning. American labor unions have a long history of resisting the importation of foreign products. Over the last two centuries, organized labor has been one of the more protectionist institutions in America. This position should not be a surprise because unions are democratic organizations that must reflect the needs of their members, who believe that their jobs are endangered by foreign imports. Most union members have little inclination to accept assurances that they will find another job or that in the long run, everyone will be better off. Therefore, organized labor unsuccessfully opposed the North American Free-Trade Agreement and attempted to stop the "fast-track" authority of the president to open up trade with other countries. However, organized labor was not successful because Congress passed legislation to authorize President George W. Bush to open normal trading relationships with China and other countries. American unions continue to support positions of the International Labor Organization, which has adopted "core labor standards" such as freedom of association and collective bargaining, rights to a living wage and a safe workplace, prevention of forced child labor, and the like. Organized labor continues to engage in pressure tactics before the World Trade Organization and the International Monetary Fund to forge links between international trading rights and labor standards.[29]

Public Opinion The two general dimensions of **public opinion** are (1) influential individuals and organizations within the community, and (2) attitudes and traditions held by community residents. The mass media represent an important influence within the community, serving as both generator and conduit of community opinion. The media are profit-making businesses, and at least one prominent union official contends that this orientation biases the reporting of labor relations activities:

> The media tend to cover collective bargaining as if it were a pier six brawl. The intricate moves and trade-offs that really make up bargaining aren't as newsy as impassioned rhetoric or a picket line confrontation.
>
> Reporters are given little training in covering collective bargaining. They are told to look for the "news"—the fist fight, the walkout, the heated exchange— and, as a result, frequently miss the "story," which is the settlement. . . .
>
> Every union proposal is a "demand," every management proposal is an "offer."[30]

An analysis of 40 years of *The New York Times* columns concerning labor unions agreed with the preceding quotation as it found that the newspaper had become increasingly concentrated on strike activities and had exaggerated the frequency of strikes.[31]

Even though union membership has fallen from 34 percent of the labor force in 1956 to less than 14 percent in 2002, public support for labor unions has remained steadfast. A 2003 Gallup survey showed that nearly two-thirds of Americans approve of labor unions. Most Americans believe that unions are helpful to their members, to the companies where workers are organized, and to the overall economy. Only when it comes to the interests of the employees who are not union members do Americans tend to believe that unions are not beneficial.[32]

A 2001 national poll conducted for the Associated Press by ICR of Media PA found that the American public sided with unions in labor disputes by a margin of 2 to 1. In 1999, support for unions was much smaller, with only a 10 percent difference between union support and support for the companies. Young adults were more likely to side with unions than those over 65. Residents in the Northwest and Midwest were more likely than residents in the South and West to support unions during a labor dispute. Republicans were split in their support, while Democrats sided with unions by 3 to 1 and independents by 2 to 1.[33]

Unions' only solace regarding public opinion statistics is that a majority of the public currently has confidence in only 4 out of 13 various American institutions (e.g., the military, organized religion, the Supreme Court, and the police), and organized labor currently fares better than big business and Congress.

The attitudes and traditions dimension of public opinion can pertain to the local municipality or to a broader geographical region. It can even be extended to include societal differences in labor relations patterns, such as those affecting U.S. trade with Japan, the European Community, and Eastern Europe (covered in Chapter 14).

Public opinion, like the other external influences, can affect one or more phases of the labor relations process, as well as the content of negotiated work rules. This influence can affect the first phase of the labor relations process—determining whether employers locate in a community and/or accept unions at their facilities. After experiencing a bitter, well-publicized strike between Caterpillar and the UAW, the mayor of Peoria, Illinois, feared employers would not locate in his community:

> We had worked so hard to make this a city with the image of having a cohesive relationship between labor and management, a place that people should think about expanding their businesses or opening new ones. Now comes this strike, which is going to damage our reputation.[34]

In some cases, communities stress the nonexistence of unions and/or their populations' antiunion attitudes as a benefit for organizations during expansion or relocation. For example, the Economic Development Council of Richmond, Virginia, placed a full-page ad in *The Wall Street Journal* that urged firms to relocate and join Richmond's 14 corporate headquarters. Among the sales points: "There isn't a single office union in the Richmond area. In fact, there haven't been any attempts to organize one."[35]

Community opposition to unions might be based on moral values. Union officials attempt to counter this obstacle when attempting to organize employees who contend that their religious beliefs prevent them from joining a union. For example, the Communications Workers of America has published a pamphlet, "The Church Believes in Unions," which features the endorsements of prominent representatives of the Catholic, Jewish, and Protestant religions. The AFL-CIO has similarly reported in its national publication, *AFL-CIO News*, Pope John Paul II's endorsement of unions as playing a "decisive role" in negotiating minimum wages and in helping employees to "share in a fully human way" in determining other workplace conditions.

Union officials are aware of the significant influence that public opinion can have on the three phases of the labor relations process. Albert Shanker, former president of the American Federation of Teachers, indicated why he wrote the first of 1,000 columns entitled "Where We Stand." After strikes were conducted by his union, Shanker reflected,

> I became one of the best-known figures in New York City, but people saw me only as a militant union leader—urging teachers to strike, refusing to settle, going to jail. In late 1968, I became convinced that I had been dead wrong in believing that the public's opinion of me didn't matter. Public schools depend on public support. And the public was not likely to support the schools for long if they thought teachers were led by a powerful madman. . . .
>
> I decided to devote some time and energy to letting the public know that the union's president was someone who read books and had ideals and ideas about how to fix the schools.[36]

Union officials seek to enhance public opinion in three general ways: *monitoring and reacting to negative comments made in the media; getting organized labor's positive message out to the community;* and *forming alliances with various groups in the community.* An example of monitoring and reacting to media comments occurred when some members of Local 44 of the International Association of Theatrical Stage Employees booed and spilled water on Bruce Willis when he visited the movie set of *Hook.* This event occurred a few months after Willis stated in an interview, "Unions are the number one cost in making films." A union official, aware that Willis's salary for *The Last Boy Scout* approximated $14 million, justified his organization's protest by saying, "After what [Willis] has taken out of the industry, he's an idiot to make statements like that."[37]

Public opinion can also affect the second phase of the labor relations process, negotiating the labor agreement and work rules. For example, teachers desiring limits on the number of students allowed in a classroom might stress to the community that increased class size would lower educational quality. Educational administrators, on the other hand, would probably indicate to the community that a teachers' strike over this issue would place educational funding in jeopardy.[38]

Perhaps the most vivid example of public opinion affecting the third phase of the labor relations process, administering the labor agreement, occurred in Milwaukee, Wisconsin. The Milwaukee Police Association (MPA) called for Police Chief Philip Arreola's resignation because he suspended and subsequently dismissed two of its members, who allowed a Laotian youth to return to a serial killer's apartment, where he was eventually murdered. The MPA claimed that Arreola was pressured by the public to take disciplinary action against the officers, who had fine work records, and urged the chief to step down because 98 percent of the MPA's 1,570 members believed he mishandled the discipline and 93.6 percent of the members indicated they had no confidence in the chief. Arreola then informed a cheering rally led by Jesse Jackson that he would not step down. Arreola remained in his position, and a subsequent vote by the civilian Milwaukee Fire and Police Commission upheld the dismissals of the two police officers.

Some 30 labor groups, including the AFL-CIO Labor Institute of Public Affairs (LIPA), have recently used public access and cable television channels to indicate union perspectives and accomplishments. LIPA has produced many programs for public access television, including "Working in America," which won an Emmy Award.

The third related topic involves cultivating alliances with groups such as clergy, students, and educators, which are more numerous and active today than since the early 1970s and perhaps the Depression. They have currently worked together to renounce sweatshops, back a higher minimum wage, and help organize janitors and poultry workers. Alliances can also be formed with community subgroups, such as civil rights groups and feminist organizations.[39] They can appeal on the basis of common goals, a sense of fair play, or reciprocity (where the union has previously built up a reservoir of goodwill and credibility). Citizens may be asked to help the union by supporting boycotts of a product, providing direct assistance to strikers (such as support of local merchants or local welfare), pressuring local government agencies to censure or control the employer's actions, supporting a corporate campaign, or backing the union in an organizing drive.[40]

Labor unions should also consider cultivating high school students to influence union membership in the future. A study confirmed that high school students, while lacking a basic knowledge of labor history and collective bargaining, share relatively little antilabor bias and appear more receptive than adults to advantages of unionization.[41]

In some cases, organized labor has cultivated alliances with business organizations. A recent example, "Stand up for Steel," involved the AFL-CIO, United Steelworkers of America, and leading American steel companies. It urged the public to ensure a "fair global trade environment" by swiftly and effectively dealing with foreign governments and companies that illegally or unfairly dump their steel into U.S. markets.[42]

Current Status of Labor Unions

Labor unions' status can be assessed from both statistical and general or philosophical standpoints. Unions have shown a steady decline in membership as a proportion of the total labor force since 1945, when union membership was about 36 percent of the labor force. Exhibit 1.4 shows that union density declined to 13.2 percent of the labor force in 2002. With an estimated workforce growth of about 1 million per year, unions will have to gain over 140,000 new members each year just to maintain about 14 percent.[43]

This reduction has three general explanations: structural changes in the labor force, organizational practices, and companies' use of current laws governing the workplace. Of these three explanations, research suggests that changes in the structure of the labor force is the most important.[44]

Employment has shifted from traditionally unionized industries (manufacturing, railroads, mining) to high-technology industries (computers, scientific instruments) that are difficult to organize. A shift has also occurred in the occupational mix toward more professional, technical, and service (white-collar) employees, who are also traditionally difficult to organize. Employment has also been growing faster in small businesses than in larger ones. Data show that 80 percent of new jobs have been created in firms with 100 or fewer employees, where fewer than 9 percent of the employees are members of unions.[45] There has also been a demographic shift of those who are employed. Many new entrants are female, better educated, and younger employees who have traditionally been more difficult to organize.

Growth in part-time and temporary employment helps explain some of this decline. Part-time employment is now over 20 percent of the total labor force,

Exhibit 1.4

Union Membership Trends, 1960–2002

Year	Union Membership	Total Employed	
		Number	Percentage
1960	17,049,000	72,142,000	23.6%
1970	19,381,000	85,903,000	22.6
1978	20,238,000	102,537,000	19.7
1985	16,996,000	94,521,000	18.0
1990	16,740,000	103,905,000	16.1
1992	16,390,000	103,688,000	15.8
1994	16,748,000	107,989,000	15.5
1996	16,289,000	111,960,000	14.5
1998	16,211,000	116,730,000	13.9
1999	16,477,000	118,963,000	13.9
2001	16,387,000	122,482,000	13.4
2002	16,107,000	122,007,000	13.2

SOURCE: Updated from "Union Membership in 2002" (Washington, DC. Bureau of Labor Statistics, U.S. Department of Labor, updated annually).
http://www.stats.bls.gov/news.release/February 25, 2003.

and only 6.9 percent of part-time employees are union members. Also, over 2.2 million work as temporary employees today, whereas just 417,000 worked as temporary employees in 1982.[46]

NLRB, the Internal Revenue Service (IRS), the Department of Labor, and other federal agencies are keeping a watchful eye on this increasing percentage of the total labor force. Once limited to clerical employees, temporary agencies now provide the services of factory employees, engineers, architects, computer programmers, lawyers, and physicists. When they work, they are actually employed by the temporary agency or they are self-employed. Often, their employment usually does not extend beyond the probationary period; therefore, they do not qualify for union membership. Moreover, if they are considered temporary employees or if they are considered independent contractors, they are not part of the bargaining unit.

Some employers, such as Microsoft and Time-Warner, consider many of its temporaries as independent contractors who are not entitled to any employee benefits, such as credits toward pensions, hospitalization insurance, and so on. However, many times this temporary work turns into multiyear employment, with workers becoming "permatemps." The past NLRB Chairman William Gould stated that employers have expanded their definition of "contract workers" in an attempt to circumvent the labor laws.[47]

In addition, union membership declines during economic recessions through layoffs and permanent job loss. Individual unions may suffer more dramatically. For example, the United Steelworkers lost more than half its membership due to plant closings and cuts in the workforce in the last 12 years. The Amalgamated Clothing and Textile Workers Union (now UNITE) has lost over 100,000 members, 45 percent of its total membership, since 1980. During this time the proportion of foreign-made apparel grew to about 60 percent of the total apparel consumption, and foreign-made shoes increased from 50 to 84 percent.

More organizations are learning how to operate their businesses on a nonunion basis. Sometimes this entails moving some or all operations to less unionized sections of the United States (the West and South). Managers are also adopting human resource management practices, including antiunion campaigns (see Chapter 5), to keep their firms nonunion. They have become more sophisticated in understanding the reasons employees organize unions and more aggressive in presenting their firms' viewpoints to the employees.

Some union officials indicate that employers often use labor law loopholes to forestall or negate free employee union choices through secret-ballot elections. For example, preelection time delays, contested elections, lengthy appeals, and stalled labor agreement negotiations are possible under the LMRA (see Chapter 3).

Another factor in the decline of union membership is the unfavorable legal climate for organized labor. One analyst makes a comparison with the political process:

> Suppose U.S. political elections were legally structured so access to the electorate is denied one political party (analogous to the union), while it is granted the other one for eight hours a day at one's place of work. The second political party (analogous to management) could force the electorate to listen to campaign speeches (captive audience meetings), while the opposing party was denied access.[48]

Legal alterations that have expanded employees' legal rights through the Americans with Disabilities Act, Equal Employment Opportunity Act, Occupational Safety and Health Act, Employee Retirement and Income Security Act, and other legislation have helped make union organizing more difficult. These legal rights give employees a "free ride" in areas for which the union once was the primary protector and provider, and the increasing costs of these programs to employers have caused them to stiffen their resistance to unions, to be more cost conscious, and to increase their managerial sophistication in personnel practices.

Indeed, many unions appear to be committing more of their resources to serving the needs of their current members rather than to organizing new members. As unions mature and have organized a major portion of the workers within their jurisdictions, their expenditures, time, and efforts focus on representation services, such as negotiating contracts, researching wages and benefits, preparing for arbitration, processing grievances, and so on. In fact, organizing new employees may not be in the interests of the present union membership if these efforts would siphon funds earmarked for present members' services. Because unions are political organizations and the leaders are elected by the current membership, the incentive to organize new members is often less than the incentive to provide services to current members.[49]

Unions were devoting less than 5 percent of their resources to organizing new unions in 1995. This complacency led to a contested election for the presidency of the AFL-CIO. John Sweeney, then president of the successful Service Employees International Union, which had grown rather rapidly due to its organizing efforts, was elected. In 2000, 10 percent of the AFL-CIO unions were doing 90 percent of the organizing, and the vast bulk of labor's resources still went into servicing union contracts, such as grievance handling, arbitration, and the like.[50]

Although union membership has continued to decline as a percentage of the total labor force and declined in total numbers from 2001 to 2002, labor unions have responded by increasing their union organizing activities. For example, the AFL-CIO held a two-day Organizing Summit in January 2003 for more than 250 union organizers to meet and exchange innovative strategies to help workers gain a voice on the job. Greater emphasis was placed on the AFL-CIO Organizing Institute, which recruits, trains, and places talented individuals in positions so they will be able to help workers who want to form and join unions. The AFL-CIO sponsors the Union Summer program, which is an intensive, five-week educational internship for individuals who develop skills for leading union organizing drives and participating in other campaigns to promote workers' rights and social justice.[51]

Unions' social significance can also be assessed in general terms by considering what the consequences would be if unions were absent from our society. Some would argue that unions' previous bargaining gains, coupled with current legislation aimed at protecting employees' welfare, make unions obsolete. Others have suggested that unions must remain to ensure that employers do not reduce previously negotiated working conditions. This belief likens organized labor to the military in peacetime—a strong countervailing power needed to preserve the existing situation. In other words, unions are necessary to maintain some balance between employer and employee rights and responsibilities.

SUMMARY

Although unique to the particular labor-management activities, attitudes, and relationships at each organization (discussed more in Chapter 4), the labor relations process includes the following three phases: recognition of the legitimate rights and responsibilities of union and management representatives, negotiation of the labor agreement, and administration of the terms of the negotiated labor agreement on a daily basis.

The labor relations process focuses on jointly negotiated and administered work rules that pertain to compensation and employees' and employers' job rights and obligations. These rules can vary to the extent that they are unique to a particular job classification or industry and are vague or specific. They can also reflect the dynamic nature of labor relations by changing over time.

Union and management officials represent two participant categories in the labor relations process. Neither grouping is consensual, however, because different perspectives occur between and within organizations. Employees represent perhaps the most significant participant category because they can have loyalties to both union and management officials and because they determine whether a union receives representation at an organization and whether a strike is taken and successfully completed. Other participants are third-party neutrals (mediators and arbitrators) and the government, with its executive decisions, legislative action, and judicial decisions.

These participants are influenced in their rule-making efforts by several variables such as technology (equipment, pace and scheduling of work, the work environment and tasks to be performed, and information exchange); labor and product markets; international forces such as the North American Free Trade Agreement (NAFTA); public opinion; financial market; and the state of the economy.

The current status of labor unions can be assessed from both statistical and general standpoints. A nearly 50-year drop in the proportion of unionized employees has occurred in the United States. However, this change and related general explanations (employment shifts, organizational practices, and legal alterations) do not indicate that unions have lost their societal significance.

KEY TERMS

labor relations process	labor markets
work rules	product markets
mediator	financial markets
arbitrator	technology
economy	public opinion

DISCUSSION QUESTIONS

1. Exhibit 1.2 illustrates the focal point of the labor relations process and many variables that affect the process. Select an academic discipline such as political science, economics, or sociology, and indicate three specific ways the discipline could add insights into the labor relations process.

2. Discuss the different dimensions of technology, indicating how this variable might contribute to two unique and specific work rules for unionized employees at a grocery store. Also indicate with examples how two other external constraints or influences (see the outer circle of Exhibit 1.2) could affect the work rules at a grocery store.

3. "The 'Labor Relations in Action' concerning employee drug testing illustrates the focal point but not the phases of the labor relations process." Is this statement true or false? Explain your answer.

EXPLORING THE WEB

Labor Relations from Several Points of View

1. The Gallup Poll   Chapter 1 discusses the effect that public opinion may have on the labor relations process. Public opinion polls provide an indication of the backing or support by the public during a strike. The Gallup Organization's Web page, which requires a subscription to read most of the full reports, provides abstracts to the results of public opinion polls conducted by the organization as well as articles that present poll analyses. Go to the Gallup Organization's Web page and use the search block to locate Daniel Cornfield's article, "Shift in Public Approval of Labor Unions in the United States, 1936–1999." Comment on the author's discussion of trends in public approval of labor unions.

http://www.gallup.com

See a summary, presented by the United Steelworkers of America, of the 2003 Gallup poll on public opinion and labor unions.

http://www.uswa.org/uswa/program/content/604.php

2. Reports from Labor and Management Web Sites   Good sources of information on strikes and labor relations can be found by searching the Web pages of both labor unions and management as well as reports from newspapers and newswires. This will allow you to see examples of the reporting of the strike from both sides. Go to the Web site maintained by the Communication Workers of America and search for news articles on Verizon's alleged "antiunion campaign."

http://cwa-union.org

Looking at a strike through articles published by the management side may give a different perspective. Read news releases from the Web site for Northwest Airlines on the 1998 strike by pilots represented by the Air Line Pilots Association labor union. Scroll down to articles published in July through September.

http://www.nwa.com/corpinfo/newsc/1998

3. Newspapers   Search newspaper archives to find actual articles that were published in reporting news of the UPS strike in 1997. Some newspapers offer free searching for titles and then require a subscription fee or charge for each article requested. Good sources for links to homepages of newspapers are:

Newspaper Association of America: Newspaper links

http://www.newspaperlinks.com

NewsLink: Newspapers on the Web arranged by state and country

http://newslink.org/news.html

Library of Congress Newspaper and Current Periodical Reading Room:
News and periodicals resources on the Web

http://www.loc.gov/rr/news/lists.html

REFERENCES

1. See, for example, William N. Cooke, "The Failure to Negotiate First Contracts: Determinants and Policy Implications," *Industrial and Labor Relations Review* 38 (January 1985), pp. 162–178.

2. John Dunlop, *Industrial Relations Systems*, rev. ed. (Boston: Harvard Business School Press, 1993), pp. 13–16.

3. Peter T. Kilborn, "Labor Wants Shorter Hours to Make Up for Job Losses," *New York Times*, October 11, 1993, p. A-7; See for example, "Bell Atlantic Reaches Pact with Union," *New York Times*, August 13, 1998, p. C-20.

4. Nancy Keates, "Rising Concern: Falling Luggage Inside Airplanes," *Wall Street Journal*, November 10, 1997, pp. B-1, B-10.

5. Bureau of National Affairs Inc., *Daily Labor Report,* September 10, 1992, p. A-12.

6. Mollie H. Bowers, "What Labor and Management Need to Know about Workplace Smoking Cases," *Labor Law Journal,* January 1992, pp. 40–49.

7. Sharolyn A. Rosier, "Assaults at the Workplace," *AFL-CIO News,* December 12, 1994, p. 5. For related concerns and considerations see John R. Aiello and Kathryn Kolb, "Electronic Performance Monitoring and Social Context: Impact on Productivity and Stress," *Journal of Applied Psychology* (June 1995), pp. 339–353.

8. Bureau of National Affairs Inc., *Daily Labor Report,* no. 37 (February 25, 1985), p. F-1; Jules Bernstein, "The Evolution of the Use of Management Consultants in Labor Relations: A Labor Perspective," *Labor Law Journal* 36 (May 1985), p. 296.

9. John J. Lawler, "The Influence of Management Consultants on the Outcome of Union Certification Elections," *Industrial and Labor Relations Review* 38 (October 1984), pp. 38–51. See also Bureau of National Affairs Inc., Special Report, *Labor Relations Consultants: Issues, Trends, and Controversies* (Washington, D.C.: Bureau of National Affairs Inc., 1985); and Terry A. Bethel, "Profiting from Unfair Labor Practices: A Proposal to Regulate Management Representatives," *Northwestern University Law Review* 79 (1984), pp. 506–565; Bruce E. Kaufman and Paula E. Stephan, "The Role of Management Attorneys in Union Organizing Campaigns," *Journal of Labor Research,* Fall 1995, pp. 439–455.

10. "UAW News," http://www.uaw.org/news/news/ (accessed December 2, 2003).

11. For an early study of employee dual loyalty, see Theodore V. Purcell, *Blue Collar Man: Patterns of Dual Allegiance in Industry* (Cambridge: Harvard University Press, 1960). See also Michael E. Gordon and Robert T. Ladd, "Dual Allegiance: Renewal, Reconsideration, and Recantation," *Personnel Psychology* 43 (1990); Julian Barling, Bill Wade, and Clive Fullagar, "Predicting Employee Commitment to Company and Union: Divergent Models," *Journal of Occupational Psychology* 63 (1990), pp. 49–61; and Clive J. A. Fullagar, Daniel G. Gallagher, Michael E. Gordon, and Paul F. Clark, "Impact of Early Socialization on Union Commitment and Participation: A Longitudinal Study," *Journal of Applied Psychology* 80 (February 1995), pp. 147–157; Brian Bemmels, "Dual Commitment: Unique Construct or Epiphenomenon?" *Journal of Labor Research,* Fall 1995, pp. 401–423.

12. Evan Perez, "Delta Readies Work-Rule Changes," *The Wall Street Journal,* October 10, 2003, p. A8.

13. Michael H. Belzer, "Collective Bargaining after Deregulation: Do the Teamsters Still Count?" *Industrial and Labor Relations Review,* July 1995, pp. 636–655.

14. "Arbitration Win Means Jobs, Back Pay for 3,4000 at Verizon," http://www.cwapunion.org/news,CWANewsDisplay.asp?ID=1274.

15. Louis Uchitelle, "A Missing Statistic: U.S. Jobs That have Moved Overseas," *New York Times,* October 3, 2003, p. 21. For a more thorough discussion, see: Erica L. Groshen and Simon Porter, "Has Structural Change Contributed to a Jobless Recovery?" *Report of the Federal Reserve Bank of New York,* August 2003, vol. 9, Number 8, http://www.ny.frb.org/research.

16. "Steelworkers Ratify Goodyear Contract,": http://www.uswa.org/uswa/program/content/537.php, September 15, 2003.

17. David Leonhardt, "Employment Rises for the First Time in Seven Months," *New York Times,* October 4, 2003, pp. A-1 and B-3; Michael Schroeder, "U.S. Manufacturing Activity Surges," *The Wall Street Journal,* December 2, 2003, p. A-2.

18. Hoyt N. Wheeler, *The Future of the American Labor Movement* (Cambridge, U.K.: Cambridge University Press, 2002), pp. 80–81.

19. James R. Healey, "Tangled Web of Rules Obscures Autos' Origins," *USA Today,* March 2, 1992, pp. 1 and 3B.

20. "Steelworkers Ratify Goodyear Contract": http://www.uswa.org/uswa/program/content/537.php, September 15, 2003.

21. Wheeler, *The Future of the American Labor Movement*, pp. 176–177.

22. Ibid., pp. 25–27.

23. Neil De Clercq, Alec Meiklejohn, and Ken Mericle, "The Use of Microcomputers in Local Union Administration," *Labor Studies Journal* 10 (Spring 1985), pp. 3–45.

24. John Lund, "Using Microcomputer Spreadsheets to Teach Industrial and Labor Relations Applications," *Labor Studies Journal*, Summer 1995, pp. 22–38.

25. For related considerations, see "AFL-CIO Goes On-Line with New Labor NET," *AFL-CIO News*, July 26, 1993, p. 6; "Labor Unions Are Getting off to a Slow Start in Cyberspace," *The Wall Street Journal*, May 30, 1995, p. A-1; and Montieth M. Illingworth, "Workers on the Net, Unite!" *Information Week*, August 22, 1994, pp. 27–36.

26. For a somewhat detailed account of this situation at one company, see Ron Suskind, "Tough Vote: Threat of Cheap Labor Abroad Complicates Decisions to Unionize," *The Wall Street Journal*, July 28, 1992, pp. A-1, A-8.

27. Rich Miller, Pete Engardio, Dexter Roberts, and Michael Arndt, "Is It China's Fault?" *Business Week*, October 13, 2003, pp. 32–35.

28. Wheeler, *The Future of the American Labor Movement*, p. 25.

29. Ibid., pp. 81–82.

30. Lane Kirkland, "Labor and the Press," *American Federationist* 82 (December 1975), p. 3. See also John A. Grimes, "Are the Media Short Changing Organized Labor?" *Monthly Labor Review* 110 (August 1987), pp. 53–54.

31. Diane E. Schmidt, "Public Opinion and Media Coverage of Labor Unions," *Journal of Labor Research* 13 (Summer 1992), pp. 151–165. See also William J. Puette, *Through Jaundiced Eyes: How the Media View Organized Labor* (Ithaca, NY: ILR Press, 1992); and Paul Jarley and Sarosh Kuruvilla, "American Trade Unions and Public Approval: Can Unions Please People All of the Time," *Journal of Labor Research* 15 (Spring 1994), pp. 97–117.

32. "Poll Analyses: Labor Unions Broadly Supported," http://www.gallup.com/ (accessed August 29, 2003).

33. "A New Poll for Labor Day: Labor Unions Gain Sympathy," http://civic.net/civic-values.archives/200108/msg00084.html (accessed November 4, 2003).

34. Jonathan P. Hicks, "Dreams and City Image Put at Stake in Strike," *New York Times*, April 10, 1992, p. A-31.

35. *The Wall Street Journal*, October 18, 1988, p. A-13.

36. Albert Shanker, "Where We Stand," *New York Times*, December 16, 1990, p. 7; Sandra Feldman, "The Big Lie," *New York Times*, June 7, 1998, p. 7.

37. "Bad Feelings by Movie Unions toward Willis Could Die Hard," *Florida Times-Union*, July 13, 1991, p. D-5.

38. Albert Shanker, "Blaming Unions," *New York Times*, September 8, 1998, p. E-7.

39. Steve Early and Larry Cohen, "Jobs with Justice: Mobilizing Labor Community Coalitions," *Working USA*, 1, no. 4 (November–December 1997), pp. 49–57.

40. James Craft, "The Community as a Source of Union Power," *Journal of Labor Research* 11 (Spring 1990), p. 149. This article discusses several examples of working with the community. For a detailed account of a community effort involving religious institutions in an attempt to restore closed steel mills as a community and employee owned enterprise, see Thomas G. Fuechtmann, *Steeples and Stacks: Religion and Steel Crisis in Youngstown* (New York: Cambridge University Press, 1989).

41. Tom Juravich, "Anti-Union or Unaware? Work and Labor as Understood by High School Students," *Labor Studies Journal* 16 (Fall 1991), pp. 16–32.

42. "Take the Pledge," *New York Times*, October 1, 1998, p. A-19.

43. "Union members in 2002," http://stats.bls.gov/newsrels.htm.

44. C. Timothy Koeller, "Union Activity and the Decline in American Trade Union Membership," *Journal of Labor Research* 15 (Winter 1994), pp. 19–31.

45. *The State of Small Business* (Washington, D.C.: U.S. Government Printing Office, 1984), pp. xv, 9.

46. http://www.bls.gov/.

47. Glenn Burkins, "Temp Workers May Be Able to Join Unions," *The Wall Street Journal*, December 2, 1996, p. A-3.

48. Bruce Nissen, "The Recent Past and Near Future of Private Sector Unionism in the U.S.: An Appraisal," *Journal of Labor Research* 26, no. 2 (Spring 2001), p. 325.

49. Joseph B. Rose and Gary N. Chiason, "New Measures of Union Organizing Effectiveness," *Industrial Relations* 29 (Fall 1990), pp. 457–468.

50. Ibid.

51. http://www.aflcio.org/aboutunions/.

Discharge for Whistleblower Activity

Janet Broom and Darla Miller were employed as a certified medication aide and cook, respectively, at the employer's residential care facility located in Norman, Oklahoma. Both employees suspected another employee of stealing and using drugs intended for use by residents of the facility from the facility's medication room. Broom and Miller decided to report the suspected employee based on their observation that she had falsified medical drug log books to conceal her theft from facility managers.

The Facility's Employee Handbook clearly outlined a procedure employees were to follow when making complaints involving other employees. The Employee Handbook called for the initial complaint to be filed with the accused employee's immediate supervisor. Because the two employees making the complaint believed that the immediate supervisor in this case, Sarah Dutton, was a close personal friend of the accused, Broom and Miller chose to make their complaint to another manager, who was the medication consultant at the facility. Upon learning of the complaint from the medication consultant, supervisor Dutton discharged Broom and Miller for "not following the proper chain of command in raising an issue about another employee."

Both Broom and Miller are nonunion employees unrepresented by a union. After being discharged, Broom and Miller's only recourse was to file a wrongful discharge state court claim arguing that they were engaged in internal whistleblowing activity and thus protected from discharge as a matter of Oklahoma public policy. The employer argued that Broom and Miller were subject to the Oklahoma common law **employment-at-will** doctrine, which permits an employer to discharge an at-will employee at any time for any or no stated reason. The employer sought and received a summary judgment in state district court declaring Broom and Miller's discharge to be lawful under the state's common law employment-at-will doctrine. Broom and Miller appealed the state district court's decision to a federal Court of Appeals, seeking to reverse the district court's decision.

In *Groce v. Foster*, 880 P.2d902 (Okla. 1994), the Oklahoma Supreme Court recognized five types of public policy exceptions to the common law employment-at-will doctrine. Under Oklahoma law, an at-will employee may not be lawfully discharged for (1) refusing to participate in an illegal activity; (2) performing an important public service (e.g. jury duty); (3) exercising a legal right or interest of the employee; (4) exposing some wrongdoing by his or her employer; and (5) performing an act that public policy would encourage or refusing to perform an act public policy would discourage, when the discharge action is coupled with a showing of bad faith, malice, or retaliation.

Broom and Miller argued that their discharge fell under the fifth public policy exception to the employment-at-will doctrine. By reporting to management a co-worker who they honestly believed was engaged in stealing drugs intended for administration to residents of the facility, Broom and Miller believed they were engaging in conduct that Oklahoma public policy encourages. The Oklahoma Supreme Court mandates that to be recognized and enforced, public policy exceptions must be clearly stated in state constitutional, regulatory, or case decision law. To that end, Broom and Miller cited three statutory laws that they believed provided a clear statement of public policy supporting their action.

The first law is the *Nursing Home Care Act,* which governs safeguards and procedures for the storage, safekeeping, monitoring, dispensing, and, when necessary, destruction of patient prescription drugs. The employer argued that the act specifically applies only to licensed nursing homes operating within the state. The employer's facility is licensed as a residential care

Continued

facility and thus is excluded from coverage under the *Nursing Home Care Act*. The state of Oklahoma grants operating licenses for several different types of elder-care facilities, including nursing homes, assisted living homes, and residential care facilities.

The second law is the *Residential Care Act*, which the employer admitted does apply to the facility in this case. Broom and Miller noted that the law authorizes the Oklahoma State Department of Health to "develop and enforce rules and regulations . . . to implement the provisions of the *Residential Care Act*. Such rules and regulations shall include but not be limited to governing temperature limits, lighting, ventilation, and other physical conditions which shall protect the health, safety, and welfare of the residents in the home."

The employer argued that Broom and Miller did not raise the issue of the *Residential Care Act*'s applicability to their case when the case was before the district court and therefore could not legally raise it as a supporting argument on appeal. It is a well-settled legal principle that issues or arguments not clearly presented and considered at a prior legal proceeding cannot be subsequently raised as a legal basis for argument on appeal. The employer also noted that the language referred to by Broom and Miller in the *Residential Care Act* is very general and not specific enough to rise to the level of a clear statement of public policy supporting intent to make an exception to the prevailing Oklahoma employment-at-will doctrine.

The third law cited by Broom and Miller as a basis for their appeal is the *Uniform Controlled Dangerous Substances Act*. Although this law does make it a criminal offense to steal a controlled dangerous substance, Broom and Miller made no specific argument as to how this law established a clear mandate of public policy applicable to their discharge case. The employer argued that Broom and Miller again failed to meet the required showing of a clear and compelling public policy in favor of restricting an employer's right to discharge an at-will employee for failing to follow the established procedure for bringing a serious complaint against a co-worker.

QUESTIONS

1. Should the federal appeals court deny Broom and Miller's appeal and enforce the decision of the state district court finding upholding the discharge of the two whistleblowers? Explain your reasoning.
2. How might this case have been handled differently if Broom and Miller had been members of a bargaining unit represented by a union for purposes of collective bargaining?

Work Rules

Directions

This activity can be performed as an individual or group assignment using either an oral or written report format. Select a recent (not more than one year old) news story or article and explain how the information in the story could affect the negotiation or administration of a particular work rule. An appropriate news story or article should contain information on one or more of the possible constraints or influences affecting the negotiation or administration of work rules identified in the text (e.g., state of the economy, labor market conditions, product market conditions, financial market conditions, technology, and international forces or events).

Union Membership Trend

Directions

This activity can be performed as an individual or group assignment using either an oral or written report format. Select a recent (not more than one year old) news story or article and explain how the information in the story could affect future union membership growth in a positive or negative manner. Your explanation should clearly indicate why or how you think the information in your story will have the predicted effect on future union membership growth.

Word Association

Directions

Divide the class into groups of 3–5 students. Presented below are several words or phrases. Each group member should indicate, *using the appropriate letter*, beside each word whether he or she would strongly associate that word or phrase with the word *UNION* (U) or *MANAGEMENT* (M), or *BOTH* U & M (B), or *NEITHER* U nor M (N). Group members should compare their results and discuss their reasoning for associating particular words or phrases with the term **Union** or **Management**.

1. POWERFUL
2. EDUCATED
3. DEMOCRATIC
4. PROFIT-ORIENTED
5. PRODUCTIVITY
6. FAIR
7. VIOLENCE
8. TRUSTWORTHY
9. JOB SECURITY
10. HONEST
11. POLITICAL
12. AUTHORITY
13. REASONABLE
14. STRIKE
15. PROFESSIONAL
16. EMPLOYEE COMPENSATION
17. ETHICAL
18. INNOVATIVE
19. FLEXIBLE
20. CREATIVE
21. RISK TAKER
22. NECESSARY
23. JOB SAFETY & HEALTH
24. WORK RULES
25. GROWTH-ORIENTED

Please list any additional terms or phrases that you strongly identify with the term **UNION** or **MANAGEMENT** or **BOTH** U & M.

CHAPTER 2

Evolution of Labor–Management Relationships

The American labor movement as we know it has adjusted to changing social events, employers' attitudes and actions, and employee preferences for more than 100 years. A historical perspective is necessary to better understand current labor relations issues and trends as well as make reasonable predictions about future changes.

There is no best way to obtain this perspective.[1] Insights from many academic disciplines (sociology, economics, political science, and so forth) have to be considered, and many focal points can be assessed. Our discussion focuses on what has worked and not worked for organized labor through two interrelated historical dimensions: (1) relationships between labor and management organizations and (2) organizational characteristics of labor organizations.

This second dimension is important to labor relations students and practitioners because the current American Federation of Labor–Congress of Industrial Organizations (AFL-CIO, which represents 64 national and international unions and over 13 million affiliated union members) has been historically affected by four major labor organizations: the Knights of Labor, the Industrial Workers of the World, the American Federation of Labor, and the Congress of Industrial Organizations.

The strength of any labor organization depends on four criteria:

- Its structural and financial stability.
- Its ability to work within established political and economic systems, particularly the wage system.
- Supportive or disruptive features of the broader social environment such as legislation, media, and public opinion.
- The ability of union leaders to identify and satisfy members' goals and interests.

Readers can use these criteria to assess why some labor organizations failed in the past and to predict the likelihood of current unions posing a strong challenge to management.

The historical dimensions are organized into three time periods: 1869 to World War I, World War I to World War II, and World War II to the present.

1869 to World War I

Unions as we know them today did not exist before 1800. There were small local guilds, joint associations of employers and craftspeople that pressed for professional standards and restrictions on outside competitors.[2] These interests typically benefited employees and employers alike. By 1820 there had been only a few scattered strikes, usually over wages, because only two industries, shoemaking and printing, had even the semblance of collective bargaining. There was also no general labor philosophy or national labor movement in the United States at this time.[3]

The 1850s heralded the arrival of the Industrial Revolution, which utilized new production technologies and improved rail and road transportation to expand local markets into regional and national markets. For example, the advent of mass-production techniques in a larger factory system permitted an employer to produce shoes at lower wages in Baltimore and ship them to Boston, where they could be sold at a higher price. Expanding product markets created more competition among employers, increasing pressure to minimize production costs in order to meet competitors' selling prices and still remain profitable. Minimizing labor costs became an important competitive strategy for employers.

The Civil War (1861–1865) refined and encouraged mass-production techniques, concentrating large numbers of semi-skilled and unskilled employees under one factory roof—a situation that attracted organized labor. Workers migrated from rural to urban areas, attracted by employment opportunities in the new industrial economy. Competition among workers for available jobs helped to ensure low wage rates and minimal employee benefits. Few legal rights existed for hourly wage earners, and employment gains were solely dependent upon the employer's willingness to voluntarily provide them. Competition among employers for market share and profits made many employers reluctant to improve wages or working conditions beyond the minimum required to attract and retain sufficient numbers of employees required to operate.

The emergence of national labor organizations can be viewed as a realization on the part of some workers that larger, more powerful labor organizations were necessary to balance the increasing power of the corporate form of ownership if labor's interests were to receive a higher priority in determining work rules. "The contemporary union may be viewed primarily as a response to modern industrialism. . . . Central to modern industrialism is the principle of rationality in the planning of enterprise decisions according to some cost-output standard. The application of this principle introduces tensions and strains in the management-worker relationship whenever it leads to decisions which in the eyes of the workers conflict with their interest in job security, work satisfaction, and sense of equity."[4] Four important national labor organizations are examined in this chapter to provide insight into the development of the current U.S. labor movement: the Knights of Labor (KOL), the American Federation of Labor (AFL), the Industrial Workers of the World (IWW), and the Congress of Industrial Organizations (CIO). By focusing on each labor organization's goals, structure, and strategies and tactics, one can better understand why some labor organizations succeed while others fail. Three prominent labor events of the late 1800s are also discussed: the drive for an 8-hour workday (including the Haymarket Riot of 1886), the Homestead strike (1892), and the Pullman strike (1894) to provide some sense of the economic, social, legal, and political environments in which labor organizations seek to succeed.

The Knights of Labor (KOL)

Founded by Uriah S. Stephens as a secret society in 1869, the **Knights of Labor (KOL)** maintained secrecy regarding their membership and activities until 1882 to protect members from discharge by their employers for participating in a labor organization. As the union gradually gained strength, its activities became more public and union members were more willing to risk openly acknowledging their labor organization affiliation.

There are two major reasons for discussing the KOL. First, the KOL had more members than any previous union in American history, making it the first union with a membership base that was national in scope. In the early 1880s, the KOL experienced steady growth, reaching a membership of more than 100,000 in 1885. Between 1885 and 1886, the organization's membership increased sharply, to 700,000, due in large part to favorable media publicity concerning the KOL's involvement in persuading managers of railroads owned by prominent entrepreneur Jay Gould to rescind an announced 10-percent wage cut after local KOL members began an unauthorized wildcat strike that lasted for almost one month.[5] Many workers rushed to join the KOL in the belief that the labor organization could stand up to the strength of their employer and advance employees' interests. Second, the KOL achieved more power, prestige, and notoriety than any other previous labor organization.[6] However, the KOL's goals and strategies also contributed to its demise as an effective organization, providing an important negative lesson to the American Federation of Labor and more contemporary labor organizations that would follow.

The Knights strongly objected to the adverse impacts that the Industrial Revolution entailed for many workers' lives. Long work hours under difficult, often dangerous, working conditions for minimal pay made it very difficult for many workers to improve their educational, spiritual, or economic status. Time and energy for social pursuits with family or friends were scarce for many workers. These concerns led the KOL to focus on two major long-term economic and social reform goals: (1) change existing labor-management relationships to minimize the adverse impact of the depersonalized and narrow, specialized focus of mass production and (2) strive for the attainment of the moral betterment of employees and society. To accomplish these broad goals the KOL advocated policies such as educating employers and employees to each other's needs and interests; eliminating the use of child and convict labor; equal pay for women; and pubic control over firms providing essential services such as water or energy utilities.

The KOL's goals were greatly influenced by the personal philosophy of **Terence V. Powderly,** its leader and chief spokesman from 1879 to 1883. Powderly felt that mass production reduced employees' feelings of pride and personal accomplishment.[7] In the previous agricultural economy, employees learned and used all the skills necessary to produce a particular product, providing employees with pride in their craftsmanship and a sense of skilled accomplishment in producing high-quality products from beginning to end. Mass-production techniques encouraged job specialization, creating several different employee classifications, each contributing some portion of the final product but reducing the breadth or depth of skills required of each individual employee. Powderly placed this situation in perspective by considering changes in the shoemakers' craft: "The man who was called a shoemaker 30 years ago made shoes; the man who claims to be a shoemaker today makes only part of a shoe.

What was once a trade in itself is a multiplicity of trades. Once there were shoe-makers, now we have Beaters, Binders, Bottomers, Buffers, Burnishers, Chan-nellers, Crimpers, Cutters, Dressers, Edge Setters . . . and several other workers at the shoe trade, and they all consider themselves shoemakers."[8]

The Knights didn't seek to stop the Industrial Revolution, merely to reform some of its harsher elements. Minimizing the negative effects of the new industrial system would help accomplish the KOL's second major goal, moral betterment and increased dignity for their members. Powderly claimed that members must place their concerns on a "higher" ground than material working conditions, as these physical effects were but stepping stones to "a higher cause, of a nobler nature . . . the more exalted and divine nature of man, his high and noble capabilities for good."[9] The leadership of the KOL was continually concerned that its members would devote too much attention to improving working conditions and ignore the long-term goal of moral betterment—to make every man his own master.[10]

The moralistic overtones of the Knights guided their membership policies, organizational structure, and strategies and tactics. Because moral betterment affected all members of society and all workers were viewed as being similarly affected by the Industrial Revolution, the Knights adopted a **one big union** mem-bership philosophy, which encouraged all types of workers regardless of occu-pation or skill level to join their labor organization. The only exceptions were professional gamblers, stockbrokers, lawyers, bankers, and those who lived in whole or in part by the sale or manufacture of intoxicating liquors.[11] The KOL even encouraged employers to join based on the rationale that employers along with employees were being duped by financiers and lawyers to focus only on short-term economic gains. Once educated to the adverse impacts of industrial society, employers would work cooperatively with employees to improve society.

The **local assembly**, the basic unit within the KOL's structure, could con-sist of employers and employees from several trades (mixed) or of a single craft (intended to encourage already existing local unions of skilled craft workers to join the KOL). This often presented problems in setting union priorities for tar-geting scarce resources where the highly diversified membership often experi-enced different working conditions or concerns. There were 1,100 KOL local as-semblies in 1886 whose principal function was to educate members on the KOL's principles. The authority and power within the KOL was centralized in the Gen-eral Executive Board headed by Powderly.[12] This created a classic pyramid-style organizational structure that featured primarily one-way communication travel-ing from the top (Powderly and the General Executive Board) to the bottom (lo-cal assembly members) of the organization.

Strategies to Accomplish the KOL's Goals The Knights used at least four strategies to accomplish their goals. First, political action was viewed as impor-tant, particularly because the Knights felt that previous legislation had led soci-ety down the wrong road. The Knights believed that politicians were often moti-vated by self-interest and therefore required careful watching, although Powderly himself was elected mayor of Scranton, Pennsylvania. The KOL also actively lob-bied against importation of foreign labor and for appropriations to support pub-lic school systems.

A second strategy was the encouragement of producer and consumer co-operatives. Unlike the socialists, the Knights did not want the cooperatives to be owned by the state. Instead, the KOL wanted current employees to save enough from their wages to either purchase the operation or establish a new cooperative. Because factories would then be employee owned, conflict between labor and capital would cease to occur.[13] Establishing such cooperatives would enable employees to become their own masters, granting them a voice in decision making, including the determination of a fair distribution of the profits. KOL leaders' rhetoric apparently exceeded their capacity for action, as they made little attempt to establish new cooperatives or to financially aid the approximately 100 cooperatives established by local or district KOL assemblies during the mid-1880s. Most of these cooperatives failed because of "inefficient managers, squabbles among shareholders, lack of capital, and injudicious borrowing of money at high rates of interest."[14]

The KOL pursued a third strategy when it actively avoided the use of strikes to obtain its goals. Indeed, the national union leadership often discouraged strikes and, in some cases, demoralized strikers with their statements.[15] Some KOL leaders viewed strikes as a last resort, feeling they would distract members from the major goal of moral betterment and make it more difficult for employers and employees to focus on their common interests. An additional concern was the risk that strike action could result in violence, injuring workers. Voluntary arbitration of employment disputes was viewed as a more cooperative approach to resolving conflict than the use of economic pressure. Unfortunately, few employers perceived much incentive to engage in arbitration where an outside, third-party neutral would be granted the authority to determine the labor dispute's outcome rather than the employer.

The General Executive Board set up a complicated procedure that local assemblies had to follow before they could obtain strike funds.[16] Powderly believed that no employees should be able to enter a strike that would result in other employees losing their jobs; therefore, a procedure was needed to ensure that every employee possibly affected by a strike would have a voice in the strike decision.[17] Yet the red tape involved in obtaining strike funds caused great dissension between KOL leaders and members. In 1886, at least 538 local assemblies participated in either a strike or boycott against an uncooperative employer. Local assemblies were often left on their own to finance such actions, and the members bitterly resented the lack of support from the KOL's Executive Board because without adequate financial support most strikes were doomed to failure.[18]

The KOL's leadership preferred a fourth strategy as an alternative to the use of economic pressure tactics: namely, the education of KOL members and other citizens concerning the perceived evils of the existing industrial system, as well as the Knights' goals for societal improvement. Usually the leaders would meet with members of local assemblies in private sessions to inform them of the organization's goals and objectives. The emphasis on education rather than job action (strikes and boycotts) is further discussed in the next section.

Reasons for the KOL's Failure and Demise

Despite tremendous growth, the KOL experienced a sudden demise. From a high of 700,000 members in 1886, the KOL declined to 100,000 members by 1890 and ceased operations entirely as a labor organization in 1917. In general the KOL was unable to capitalize on its initial strike victory against Jay Gould's railroads in 1885, in which the Knights showed the public that an aggressive, well-disciplined

LABOR RELATIONS IN ACTION

The American Labor Movement: Yesterday and Today

"Unions are first and foremost, organizations seeking to improve the lives of those they represent by improving their conditions of work and by insuring respect for their dignity as workers. Organized labor believes that each worker is entitled to a fair day's pay for a fair day's work. That pay should include a share in the profits the worker helps to create and, thus, unions seek a larger share of those profits than 'market forces' might dictate. . . . those profits can only be created in a well-managed enterprise, where both capital and labor contribute to the result. Since its earliest days, the labor movement has sought to improve the quality of work-life, create workplace democracy and participate in joint employer-employee decision-making . . . we understand that confrontation and conflict are wasteful and that a cooperative approach to solving shared present and future problems is desirable."

SOURCE: AFL-CIO Committee on the Evolution of Work, *The Changing Situation of Workers and Their Unions* (Washington, D.C.: AFL-CIO, 1985), pp. 5–7.

"The industrial union organizing drive of the 1930s was a movement for democracy. Talk to the mass production workers who took part in it, and they will tell you that what they wanted more than anything else was dignity. They want freedom from the petty harassment of a foreman who could send a man home at will and regard those who curried his favor with steady work, preferred jobs, and promotion. They wanted unions of their own choosing which could stand up to the power of corporate employers and bargain on equal terms. Like democratic movements in America before and since, they believed that the human right to a job should take precedence over the property right to manage an enterprise as the employer sees fit."

SOURCE: *Rank and File*, ed. by Alice and Staughton Lynd (Boston: Beacon Press, 1973), p. 1.

" . . . the contemporary union may be viewed primarily as a response to modern industrialism. . . . Central to modern industrialism is the principle of rationality in the planning of enterprise decisions according to some cost-output standard. The application of this principle introduces tensions and strains in the management-worker relationship whenever it leads to decisions which in the eyes of the workers conflicts with their interest in job security, work satisfaction, and sense of equity."

SOURCE: Jack Barbash, *American Unions: Structure, Government, and Politics* (New York: Random House, 1967), p. 3.

"The present day union leader is likely to carry a briefcase, look like a business executive, and sport an undergraduate or professional degree."

SOURCE: Arthur R. Schwartz and Michele M. Hoyman, "The Changing Guard: The New American Labor Leader," *The ANNALS*, 473 (May 1984), p. 65.

"The problem with history is that it's written by college professors about great men. That's not what history is. History's a hell of a lot of little people getting together and deciding they want a better life for themselves and their kids."

SOURCE: Bill Talcott, organizer, as quoted in Studs Terkel, *Working* (New York: Avon Books, 1974), p. 468. ■

group could take on one of the most powerful capitalists of the day and win. Subsequent strike actions by local assemblies rarely resulted in attainment of the strikers' objectives. The KOL's identification with the drive to achieve the 8-hour workday as an industry standard initially encouraged membership growth.[19] However, as discussed in the next section, the KOL's endorsement of the 8-hour workday was not always matched by strong supportive actions.

The KOL's demise was in part caused by the faulty assumptions of the union's leadership. KOL leaders overestimated the extent to which employers and employees shared common interests. Although some common interests are shared, each group is motivated by self-interest. In a free-enterprise, capitalist economic system, employers are concerned about increasing a firm's efficiency and profitability, whereas employees are concerned about job security and improvements in their terms and conditions of employment (i.e., an increased cost from an employer's viewpoint). This inherent conflict of interests between employers and employees inevitably creates conflict within any employment relationship, which must be managed effectively.

KOL leaders also overestimated the extent to which all employees shared the same interests. The KOL was ahead of its time in its attempt to organize low-skilled employees—a goal eventually accomplished by unions within the Congress of Industrial Organizations beginning in the late 1930s. However, employees do not all share the same interests, particularly if they have different skills and working conditions. The one big union approach was further complicated by the many immigrant members whose differences in race, language, and religion presented communication and cooperation barriers.[20]

A lack of legislation protecting the rights of employees to join unions and engage in collective bargaining presented a significant barrier to union organizing and bargaining efforts. Employers were free to discriminate against employees who dared to engage in union activities or express dissatisfaction with current terms or conditions of employment without fear of any legal liability. Lack of a legal right to join unions and engage in collective bargaining was a significant problem for all early labor organizations, a point that will be discussed further in Chapter 3.

The inability of KOL leaders (particularly Powderly) to identify with members' goals was another cause of the union's demise. The KOL's leaders insisted on adopting a middle-class program of long-term social and economic reform, which had little to do with the immediate job-related problems confronted by many members. Many of the members showed little, if any, interest in the Knights after they joined. Almost all local assembly meetings required the members to dress up after a day's work to engage in intellectual discourse about developing a more moral and cooperative society. In essence, the members had nothing to do except "ceremonialize, play politics, and study."[21] Powderly felt intellectually superior to many of his members and instead of listening to members' needs, he imposed his goals, on his terms: "I will talk at no picnics. . . . When I speak on the labor question I want the individual attention of my hearers and I want the attention for at least 2 hours and in that 2 hours I can only epitomize. At a picnic where . . . the girls as well as the boys swill beer I cannot talk at all."[22] The preference for intellectual deliberation over immediate, job-related action is perhaps best illustrated by Powderly's approach to the 8-hour workday movement.

The 8-Hour Workday Movement and the Haymarket Riot

One of the more important reforms desired by many employees in the late 1800s was reducing the prevalent 10-hour workday to 8 hours. Samuel Gompers, who was a Knights member and would later become president of the rival American Federation of Labor (AFL), urged Powderly to support a nationwide general strike to begin on May 1, 1886, to demand employers adopt an 8-hour workday. Powderly was receptive to the 8-hour day, as it would give employees more leisure time to pursue intellectual activities. However, Powderly did not join with Gompers to support the planned strike because he did not believe the length of the workday was the major problem: "To talk of reducing the hours of labor without reducing the power of machinery is a waste of energy."[23]

Supporters of the 8-hour workday believed that, if instituted, it would result in more people working in order to produce the same amount of work in the shorter workday, thereby reducing the unemployment problem. On May 3, 1886, some workers striking over this issue in Chicago become involved in a skirmish with the police, and at least four strikers were killed. A leader of this dispute published an inflammatory circular urging "Revenge!" and "Workingmen to Arms!" The circular also indicated that a mass rally would be held the next day at Haymarket Square in Chicago. The stage was set for an event (known later as the Haymarket Riot) that virtually eliminated the KOL's effectiveness.

On May 4, 1886, approximately 3,000 people attended the scheduled meeting, which began peacefully. Police who monitored the meeting were ordered by their chief to return to the station. However, Police Captain Bonfield, whom the governor of Illinois later charged as being responsible for the incident, ordered them back to the meeting. During a speech a bomb was thrown into the gathering of police, killing 7 and wounding 60. What happened next is uncer-

A mass rally by strikers supporting the 8-hour workday movement began peacefully but ended in violence and death in Chicago's Haymarket Square.

Courtesy of the Library of Congress.

tain. The *Chicago Tribune* reported that "anarchists and rioters poured in a shower of bullets before the first action of the police was taken."[24] Yet another report in the same article stated that the police opened fire on the crowd immediately after the bomb exploded. Regardless of the order of events, the police did shoot into the crowd, killing several and wounding 200.

Eight individuals allegedly responsible for the incident were arrested. Four of the eight were hanged, one committed suicide in prison, and three were eventually pardoned by the governor of Illinois after serving some of their sentences. The workers' trial was at best shoddy: for example, the handpicked jury included a relative of one of the bombing victims.[25] The trial evidence never established who threw the bomb; however, the accused were judged guilty by the *Chicago Tribune* before the trial took place. More specifically, the paper stressed that the "mob" was led by "two wirey whiskered foreigners,"[26] who were "Nihilistic Agitators."[27]

The Knights were not directly labeled in the immediate press accounts of the strike or in the subsequent series of unsuccessful strikes over the 8-hour workday, which involved nearly 340,000 employees. However, the strikes contributed to the organization's demise for at least two paradoxical reasons. A substantial body of public opinion believed the Knights had been involved in the strikes. Yet many of the Knights' members criticized their leadership for not actively participating in the events during and after the Haymarket Riot.[28] Indeed, Powderly strongly discouraged protest strikes over the 8-hour workday, fearing they could result in violence and believing instead that members should write essays on the subject.

The American Federation of Labor (AFL)

An outgrowth of the Federation of Organized Trades and Labor Unions of the United States and Canada, the **American Federation of Labor** (AFL) was formed in 1886 after some of its member national unions (most notably the Cigar Makers) were expelled from the Knights.[29] **Samuel Gompers**, a major founder of the AFL, had become disenchanted with the KOL's long-range social reform philosophy and reluctance to endorse the use of economic pressure tactics when necessary to obtain labor's goals. Many skilled craft workers who were already members of an established local craft union prior to joining the KOL became increasingly frustrated with the KOL's one big union approach, which placed a lower priority on some narrowly tailored issues affecting only craft employees such as requirements to enter a recognized craft occupation. The KOL focused on broader issues of interest to less skilled workers who comprised the majority of the KOL's membership. Gompers was also upset about KOL activities involving his own craft union, the Cigar Makers Union, in particular, the KOL's practices of raiding the Cigar Makers' Union in search of new KOL members and supplying strikebreakers to employers being struck by the Cigar Makers' Union.

Gompers met with the KOL's leadership in December 1886 to discuss these problems, but the meeting did not resolve the situation. Indeed, Gompers became incensed when a pamphlet was circulated among KOL representatives that attacked Gompers personally by indicating "the General Executive Board has never had the pleasure of seeing Mr. Gompers sober."[30] Gompers and other like-minded craft union leaders decided it was time to form an organization exclusively dedicated to serving the interests of skilled craft workers, and the American Federation of Labor (AFL) was established. Unlike the KOL, the AFL was not established as a national union with a one big union membership philosophy. The AFL was a federation or organization to which other established national unions representing a skilled craft or occupation could belong. Through the AFL, established craft unions could share information and ideas and develop common approaches to issues of mutual interest.

To avoid the top-down control previously experienced under the KOL's structure, each AFL-affiliated national union retained independence to control its own internal affairs. The AFL relied upon the principle of **decentralized authority** to maintain the locus of control within each national union rather than the AFL's leadership. To reduce competition between member national unions for members, the AFL adopted the principle of **exclusive jurisdiction**, which specified that only one national union would be chartered as the representative of each recognized skilled trade (e.g., carpenters, painters, cigar makers). All of the members of each national union would be employed in the same craft and thus possess similar skills and training, and confront similar working conditions and problems. The homogeneous nature of the national union's membership made it easier to identify and reach consensus on bargaining priorities and tactics. Established craft unions, such as the Cigar Makers, dominated the early development of the AFL.

It is impossible to discuss the AFL apart from Gompers because "in the early years, the AFL existed only in the person of Gompers and in the annual conventions."[31] With the exception of 1895, Gompers was president of the AFL from its founding in 1886 until his death in 1924. Therefore, much of the discussion of the goals, strategies, and organization of the AFL is from the perspective of Gompers, a point of view that is clearly reflected when examining the goals, structure, and tactics of modern-era labor organizations as will be discussed in Chapter 4.

Gompers placed little emphasis on intellectual betterment, and he scorned other union leaders' pretensions to show labor union members the course of action they should pursue.[32] Gompers criticized the KOL as representing "a hodgepodge with no basis for solidarity with the exception of a comparatively few trade assemblies."[33] Gompers believed that the goals and organization of unions should flow directly and naturally from the members' needs, not from the pronouncements of top leaders who structured unions based on their own views of what society should be rather than the reality of what it was.

Gompers particularly scorned those union leaders who tried to change the existing social system through revolutionary means.[34] Although Gompers was a socialist in his early years, he grew to despise this philosophy, contending that it was economically unsound, socially wrong, and impossible to apply in an industrial setting.[35] Gompers believed that union members should work for equitable treatment within industrial society rather than revolt against it.[36]

Thus, the AFL's major goal was to improve the short-term, job-related economic interests of its members through the existing capitalistic system. This goal was attacked by the critics of the AFL as representing **pure and simple unionism**. Gompers embraced this intended insult; indeed, he seemed to devote most of his attention to ensuring that the AFL's "pure and simple" approach to collective bargaining successfully differentiated it from other labor organizations.

Pure and simple unionism had two major objectives. The primary objective was economic betterment of the organization's members. Gompers believed the "truth," or essence, of labor unions should be measured in terms of their economic accomplishments:

"Economic betterment—today, tomorrow, in home and shop, was the foundation upon which trade unions have been built. Economic power is the base upon which may be developed power in other fields. It is the foundation of organized society. Whoever or whatever controls economic power directs and shapes development for the group or the nation."[37] The AFL's notion of "employee dignity" equated with economic gains. This view differed from Powderly's contention that employee dignity was attained by participation as equals in meaningful work and in other societal concerns.[38]

Gompers also stressed a second objective of pure and simple unionism—the enhancement of the capitalist system, which could benefit both employees and employers. Gompers was aware of other competing economic systems in the world at the time but concluded that no other economic system was capable of producing greater wealth in which workers might gain their fair share. Without capitalism, neither employees nor employers would receive sufficient revenues. The AFL therefore believed labor and management shared some similar interests. However, Gompers did not agree with Powderly that this situation would eventually lead to complete employer-employee agreement on all issues. Gompers realized that major differences of opinion would occur over the distribution of revenues and that employees would probably have to pressure employers to receive their fair share.

Strategies and Tactics of the AFL   Unlike the KOL, AFL unions relied upon the strike and other economic pressure tactics to supplement organizing and collective bargaining efforts when necessary to achieve desired outcomes. Gompers believed that economic pressure was a viable collective bargaining tactic: "A workman must convince his employer that he is entitled to an advance in wages. . . . Why should the wage-earner work for less than living wages, which he would have to do if he could not strike? The worker is expected to continue to work at whatever wages his employer is willing to give in order to save the public from inconvenience."[39]

A second AFL tactic (particularly after its headquarters moved to Washington, D.C.) was that of involvement in the political arena. Gompers, an aggressive lobbyist, attempted to translate election votes of AFL members into "rewards" for political friends of labor and "punishments" for political enemies of labor. It was a politician's stand on labor issues, not party affiliation, that mattered most to the AFL. However, political efforts during Gompers's leadership were not widespread throughout the AFL's member unions.[40]

AFL political efforts were directed at influencing politicians within the existing two-party system instead of forming a third political party. Gompers felt that establishing a third "labor" party would divert too much time from fundamental collective bargaining efforts. Gompers was also concerned that any new political party could fall under the control of socialists.[41]

Another AFL goal was to improve the public image and status of organized labor and collective bargaining. Gompers devoted much attention to the National Civic Foundation (NCF), formed in 1899 to promote industrial peace through collective bargaining. The NCF, composed of prominent labor, management, and political officials, attempted to guide public opinion toward the positive aspects of collective bargaining. However, at least one observer of industrial relations has questioned the success of this tactic, believing that "its rhetoric surpassed its performance."[42]

Organization of the AFL The AFL's organizational structure was based on two related principles: exclusive jurisdiction and decentralized authority. The AFL avoided the "one big union" concept—which proved ineffective for the KOL—and insisted on the principle of exclusive jurisdiction. This principle rested on the twofold observation that (1) each craft or trade had unique working conditions and job interests and (2) combining members of different trades into one organization would jeopardize those interests and cause unnecessary dissension. The AFL believed in authorizing only one union to represent each defined craft (e.g., carpenters, painters, and cigar makers).

Gompers also strongly believed the AFL was a voluntary organization held together by the mutual self-interests of members. Unlike Powderly, who believed that centralized authority was necessary to achieve the Knights' objectives, Gompers viewed the central AFL as a "rope of sand," dependent entirely on the acceptance of its members. Thus, the real authority was decentralized within the AFL and rested with various national unions and their member locals. As is further discussed in Chapter 4, these principles continue to influence contemporary union organizations.

Although Gompers was an active organizer, claiming to have helped organize 28 different craft unions, the AFL's early growth was not spectacular.[43] Its original membership of 150,000 had increased to only 250,000 some six years later. The initial slow growth was due to aggressive employer opposition to organized labor, the lack of legal protection for engaging in organizing and collective bargaining activities, and the difficulties raised by the economic depression of 1893. Yet Gompers could view these modest membership gains as a tribute to the AFL's powers of "stability and permanency."[44]

From its formation until World War I, the AFL was directly or indirectly involved in three prominent events: the Homestead and Pullman incidents and the formation and demise of the Industrial Workers of the World.

The Homestead Incident

The Carnegie Steel Works, located in Homestead, Pennsylvania, was ironically the scene of one of the more violent episodes in labor history. The founder of the works, Andrew Carnegie, was a renowned philanthropist who gave every indication of being receptive to organized labor. In one article, written before the Homestead incident, Carnegie stated that a strike or a lockout was a "ridiculous affair" because it represented only a test of strength instead of determining what was "fair and just."[45] Carnegie also believed that labor-management problems would occur in large firms run by salaried managers instead of owners because the former group had no permanent interest in the desires of the workmen.

Carnegie's remarks proved prophetic in the **Homestead incident** of July 6, 1892. Although many have labeled the incident a strike, one labor historian has noted that no strike vote was ever taken by the membership[46] and that the employer prohibited the employees from working, thus constituting an employer lockout. During negotiation between the mill and the Amalgamated Association of Iron, Steel, and Tin Workers (an affiliate of the AFL), a 15-foot-high solid board fence, topped with barbed wire, was constructed around the building. Andrew Carnegie was vacationing in Scotland during negotiations and had delegated these duties to a management official named Henry Clay Frick. The union labeled the structure around the steel mill "Fort Frick." Members were also undoubtedly aware that Frick was negotiating with Pinkerton detectives while labor-management negotiations were being conducted. Frick intended to use Pinkerton detectives inside the facility to protect the company's property and as strikebreakers.

On June 30, 1892, the company made its last offer, which represented a substantial wage reduction from previous wages,[47] and locked out its 4,000 employees. Workmen then began an around-the-clock surveillance of the plant. One newspaper account indicated, "The line of pickets covers the river, roads,

The bloody confrontation between Pinkerton agents and employees of the Carnegie Steel Works in Homestead, Pennsylvania, in 1892 was one of the most violent in labor history and actually set back the cause of unions in the steel industry.

© AFL-CIO

and railways so tightly that no stranger can enter the town without being known to the strikers."[48] On the morning of July 5, 300 Pinkerton agents gathered at Ashtabula, Ohio, and proceeded by rail to Youngstown, Ohio. The Pinkerton agents then traveled up the Monongahela River by barge. On July 6, word reached the townspeople that the Pinkerton agents would be entering the plant from the river. Six thousand people lined the riverbanks at 2:00 A.M., and employees prepared two small cannons, one on each side of the river, to be used on the Pinkerton agents.[49]

The Pinkerton agents attempted to land on the company's beach at 5:00 A.M.; shots were exchanged, and three Pinkerton agents were killed. Shooting by both sides continued for 12 hours, with an additional 7 townspeople killed and 50 wounded. The Pinkerton agents surrendered to the townspeople and were forced to run a bloody gauntlet before being locked up for their protection. The townspeople took the Pinkerton agents' weapons, which resulted in 8,700 National

Guard militiamen being sent to secure the town. There were few further altercations between Pinkerton agents and strikebreakers.[50] What initially appeared as a victory for locked-out workers soon turned into a long struggle as the company maintained the lockout and waited for the employees' morale to decline as economic hardships due to lost wages mounted. The incident ended for all purposes some five months later (November 20, 1892) when the union lifted its prohibition against returning to work.

Homestead has been labeled the Waterloo of unions in the steel industry. Although the steelworkers' union was one of the strongest unions of its day, the Homestead Incident proved that a well-financed and determined employer opposed to bargaining could defeat union employees. National membership in the Amalgamated dropped from 24,000 in 1892 to 8,000 in 1894. On the local level, only 800 of the original Homestead employees were ever reinstated, and the steel industry operated on essentially an open-shop basis until the 1930s. Carnegie's mills showed a dramatic increase in profits when the union was eliminated,[51] a message that encouraged other employers to take an anti-union stance.

Although Homestead represented a victory for management, the AFL and organized labor did benefit to some extent from the situation. First, Gompers demonstrated to existing and potential union members his very real concern about the Homestead situation.[52] The funds contributed by the AFL to help defray the employees' legal expenses also demonstrated that the AFL was interested in helping its member unions in a material sense.[53] Finally, workers' concerns in the Homestead incident received more sympathetic newspaper coverage than had occurred during the Haymarket Riot. The press charged Carnegie with provoking the situation. For example, the *Chicago Tribune* strongly criticized the company's use of Pinkerton agents and contended that Carnegie's company, as well as any large industrial organization, "has duties and obligations toward society which it must not forget, and not the least of them is to do all in its power, and make all of the concessions it can, to preserve civil and industrial peace."[54]

The Pullman Strike

In the late 1800s, strikes were not uncommon in the railroad industry. For example, the Great Upheaval of 1877 involved independent railroad employee associations protesting wage cuts, resulting in a bitter and violent confrontation in which more than 100 employees were killed and several hundred badly wounded.[55]

Yet the **Pullman strike** of 1894 assumed particular significance because of the principal personalities involved (Eugene Debs and George Pullman) and the emergence of the American Railway Union as a rival labor organization to challenge the AFL's leadership of the American labor movement. The Pullman strike also approached being the only U.S. revolutionary strike involving a strike in one industry that nearly escalated into a labor dispute involving all industries nationwide.[56]

As a result of the 1893 depression, the Pullman Palace Car Company laid off 3,000 of its 5,800 employees and cut wages 25 to 40 percent. Both actions were important because they occurred in the context of a company town created by company owner George Pullman's social experiment to provide a paternalistic environment for company employees. The Pullman Palace Car Company owned all the houses, buildings, and services (e.g., water) in the town; employees were not allowed to own their own homes.[57] Although the Pullman company cut employees' wages, there was no corresponding reduction in the rent and other service charges employees were required to pay. Thus, the wage cuts resulted in some employees receiving a net two-week pay of $1 to $6 during the winter of 1893.

This situation generated much hostility among employees, many of whom were members of the American Railway Union (ARU), formed in 1893. The ARU was completely independent from the AFL; indeed, it competed for skilled craftsmen with the AFL-affiliated railway brotherhoods. The ARU accepted any white employee, regardless of specific job classification, so that railroad employees could present a unified front to the railroad companies.[58] Many railroad employees believed that permitting all types of railroad workers to join the same union would make it more difficult for employers in the industry to create dissension among the different craft unions by playing one against the other in wage negotiations.

The ARU's local unions had sole authority to call a strike, and the Pullman strike began on May 11, 1894. Eugene Debs, the ARU's president, informed the strikers that the strike should represent a protest against philosophical issues instead of mere material betterment: "The paternalism of Pullman is the same as the interest of a slave holder in his human chattels. You are striking to avert slavery and degradation."[59]

At first the strikers followed Debs's orders not to damage railroad property. The ARU instead adopted a strategy of not operating any train that included a Pullman sleeping car—the common practice was to cut these cars from the train and move them to the side tracks. If any employee was discharged for this action, then the entire crew would quit, leaving the train immobilized. This tactic, employed in 27 states and territories, was intended to make railroad carriers put pressure on Pullman to agree with the ARU's bargaining position.

Railroad employers rallied behind Pullman and countered the union's strategy by hiring strikebreakers. Railroad employers also decided to transport some federal mail on nearly every train, enabling them to obtain a labor injunction prohibiting the ARU from interfering with the operation of any train used to transport federal mail. The legality of the labor injunction issued was subsequently upheld by the U.S. Supreme Court.[60] Some 16,000 troops, dispatched by President Grover Cleveland to enforce the injunction, either delivered the mail and operated the trains or protected strikebreakers so that food and other perishable items could be delivered throughout the country.

The strike then took a particularly ugly turn; employees burned at least 700 railroad cars in Chicago on July 7, 1894. Interestingly, management was also criticized in this incident for failing to take minimum security measures such as guarding or locking the railroad cars. Some individuals speculated that management officials may have deliberately provoked the incident to receive additional support from the government. This possibility is suggested because all the burned cars were old (i.e., newer, more expensive Pullman cars had previously been removed from the property), and very few of the cars were loaded with any product.[61]

The resulting negative public opinion and increased action by the federal troops forced Debs to seek Gompers's cooperation. Debs wanted Gompers to call a national strike to enforce the ARU's last bargaining offer, which was simply management's reinstatement of the striking employees. Gompers refused to support Debs, contending that he did not have authority to order AFL-affiliated unions to engage in a general strike. Gompers also believed that the proposed settlement would, in effect, admit to the public that the ARU had failed to win any material benefits for its members. Much of Gompers's reluctance was based on his view of Debs as being "a leader of irregular movements and lost causes."[62] However, Gompers's inaction might also have been caused by his desire to eliminate a potential rival to the AFL and bolster his reputation in the business community.

Debs was eventually convicted and sentenced to six months in prison for violating the federal labor injunction issued in the Pullman strike.[63] The ARU, which had grown to 150,000 members in one year, quickly faded from existence. Organized labor did learn an important lesson from this strike: it would be difficult to alter the existing system against the wishes of a persistent, if not exceptionally stubborn, owner (Pullman), the federal government (troops, injunctions, legislation), the AFL (which supported this system), and negative public opinion (fueled by exaggerated and dramatic newspaper articles).

The Industrial Workers of the World (IWW)

The Industrial Workers of the World (IWW) was formed as an alternative to the AFL on June 27, 1905. William "Big Bill" Haywood, initial organizer of the IWW, originated the organization's goals in calling the convention of 209 delegates to order with the following remarks:

> Fellow Workers . . . We are here to confederate the workers of this country into a working class movement that shall have for its purpose the emancipation of the working class from the slave bondage of Capitalism. . . . The aims and objects of this organization should be to put the working class in possession of the economic power, the means of life, in control of the machinery of production and distribution without regard to capitalist masters.[64]

Delegates to the initial convention were a collection of traditional trade unionists such as Haywood; prominent socialists such as Eugene Debs and Daniel DeLeon; labor activists such as Mother Jones; and Syndicalists who essentially opposed all forms of government control over private citizens.[65] The initial goal of the IWW was to overthrow the existing capitalist system by any means necessary because it felt that employers and employees had nothing in common. The IWW and the Knights agreed on one point: the existing wage and profit system had to be changed. The Knights, however, stressed that employees and employers had common interests and appropriate reforms could create peaceful and gradual change. The IWW, on the other hand, had no reservations about using any method that would result in the quick destruction of capitalism.

The IWW also wanted to remove any societal aspect or group that supported capitalism. This approach placed the IWW in direct opposition to the AFL. The IWW regarded the AFL as an "extension of the capitalist class"[66] because it advocated pure and simple unionism, which was dependent on capitalism. Haywood believed that Gompers had sold out the ARU when he had not supported Debs in the Pullman strike, and he viewed Gompers as an arrogant, power-hungry leader.[67] Thus, the IWW appeared to have two general enemies: capitalism and the AFL, which did not recognize a working-class movement of hourly employees as being a class-conscious group apart from the rest of society. An analysis of the IWW reveals that establishing goals can be an easier task than accomplishing them.

The IWW never established an effective organization; in fact, its leaders never made up their minds about precisely what kind of organizational structure should be adopted.[68] Like the KOL, the IWW adopted a one big union approach to membership criteria. Most of the IWW officials agreed with Haywood's objective of organizing "every man that earns his livelihood either by his brain or his muscle."[69] However, major differences arose over how to organize one big union into an effective organization. Some members felt that the IWW should work slowly, for example, infiltrate the established AFL unions and gradually persuade members that the IWW cause was best. Others felt that this temporary acceptance of collective bargaining with the capitalists only made employees "better paid slaves" and would hinder the quick and necessary overthrow of the capitalist system.[70]

In addition to organizational differences, there were at least four reasons for the demise of the IWW, reasons that served as negative lessons for contemporary organized labor.

1. **Lack of permanent membership and financial base.** A large proportion of the IWW consisted of itinerants—individuals who either were unemployed or traveled from job to job, particularly in the agriculture, mining, and lumber industries. This contributed to an unstable financial base. Many IWW leaders thought members' dues should not be mandatory; instead, they should be paid out of a voluntary "inner conviction"; for example, in 1907 only 10,000 members out of the total 31,000 members paid any dues. The lack of revenues resulted in meager strike funds, and by 1909 the organization was deeply in debt.

2. **Inability of the IWW to satisfy members' interests.** The IWW was not very successful in achieving significant improvements in members' wages, hours, or other terms and conditions of employment.[71] The wide range of economic, social, and political ideas expressed by leaders within the IWW made it difficult for the organization to develop a consistent organizing or bargaining message that appealed to most workers. Like the KOL, the IWW focused too much on long-range political and economic change in society and not enough on the daily struggles workers confronted to achieve job security at fair wages. The average worker was less concerned with helping the exploited masses and more focused on just trying to look out for his or her own interests.[72]

3. **Identification of the IWW with sabotage and violence.** The relationship between the IWW and sabotage and violence was ambiguous. The IWW in 1914 became the only labor organization to ever officially endorse sabotage as a legitimate form of worker protest at its convention. Certainly IWW leaders' speeches to mass groups of workers often contained fiery rhetoric regarding the alleged abuses of the capitalist system and the need for workers to rise up to change the current economic and political system. Yet few prosecutions of alleged IWW-instigated violence resulted in convictions. IWW leaders often stated that sabotage does not necessarily equal destruction of equipment. For example, employees could "sabotage" the

company by "malicious obedience" (following the work rules to the letter, thereby creating a slowdown) and by informing customers that the company's product was of inferior quality.

Evidence suggests that the IWW's leaders denounced any type of physical violence.[73] Yet there are also some accounts of incidents in which the IWW members and leaders pledged a "life for a life" or "an eye for an eye."[74] At a minimum, it appears that the IWW did not actively discourage the media's efforts to portray the labor organization as being linked to violence.

4. **Alienation of the news media and government officials.** The newspapers enhanced the IWW's reputation for violence by labeling members as "desperate villains who set fire to wheat fields, drove spikes into sawmill-bound logs, derailed trains, destroyed industrial machinery, and killed policemen."[75] Part of this negative image was enhanced by leaders of IWW factions who would damn one another in the press. The IWW also engaged in several "free speech fights"—soapbox speeches in local communities. This strategy, which has since been copied by various protest groups, including students, relied on there being more participants than there were available jail spaces. City officials, faced with such a situation, typically allowed the "unlawful" demonstration to continue.[76]

The press, never enthusiastic about unions in general, reserved a special hatred for the IWW. One editorial against the IWW stated: "They would be much better dead, for they are absolutely useless in the human economy; they are the waste material of creation and should be drained off into the sewer of oblivion there to rot in cold obstruction like any other excrement."[77]

The IWW also remained alienated from the government. It did not actively use the existing political system because many of its transient members could not meet voter registration requirements. The IWW also incurred the wrath of the federal government when it refused to support U.S. involvement in World War I, proclaiming instead that the war represented a capitalistic plot to force the working class to fight the war while capitalists made huge profits from the sale of war materials. The government responded to the IWW's antiwar stance by arresting more than 100 leaders for stirring up discontent against the government (sedition) and sentencing most of them to prison terms ranging from 5 to 20 years. Big Bill Haywood, while out on bail and waiting to hear if the U.S. Supreme Court would hear an appeal of his conviction, decided to escape to Russia, which had just undergone its own worker revolution with the overthrow of the ruling czar.[78] Upon Haywood's arrival in Russia he was proclaimed a working-class hero by the new communist government. Until his death in 1928, Haywood served as a communist-government spokesperson, giving many speeches to Russian workers encouraging them to be productive and make a success of their worker-controlled society. With most IWW leaders in jail, the labor organization ceased to play any significant role in the U.S. labor movement in 1918, although the organization remains today with a handful of members.

The onset of World War I found the AFL under great stress. The AFL had been the first national labor organization to withstand a severe economic depression, a hostile press, reluctant or hostile employers, and three rival labor organizations (KOL, ARU, and IWW). Yet the AFL had internal pressures from at least three sources: (1) socialists and other related political groups that advocated independent political action and the organization of unskilled industrial employees; (2) pacifist members who wanted the AFL to remain neutral or take a stand against the war[79]; and (3) member unions that became involved in jurisdictional disputes over which union's members should be permitted to perform specific job tasks caused by increased specialization and technological change (for example, the plumber was no longer completely responsible for the installation of a water and heating system for a building). Perhaps the most lingering concern of the AFL was that the largest and growing proportion of the unorganized labor force, the low and semi-skilled industrial employees, remained barred from membership in the AFL's skilled, craft union structure.[80] This concern and its eventual resolution are discussed more in the following section.

WORLD WAR I TO WORLD WAR II

The period from World War I to World War II witnessed several important phenomena:

1. The inability of the AFL to make substantial membership gains in the 1920s.

2. The continued development of employer strategies to minimize union growth.

3. Increased union concern over the need to organize low and semi-skilled industrial employees, which led to a bitter rivalry between the AFL and the Congress of Industrial Organizations (CIO).

Some union organizing drives in various industries are cited briefly to give a further indication of the problems and prospects facing organized labor in this period.

Union Organizing after World War I: Problems and Prospects

The AFL overcame its initial reluctance toward participating in World War I and eventually pledged its cooperation when the United States became directly involved in the war. The government, aware of the necessity of uninterrupted production during wartime, attempted to respond by meeting some of labor's interests. Government agreements with the AFL provided for the enforcement of trade union standards in all government contracts; labor representatives were appointed to all government agencies, including the War Labor Board; and Gompers was made a member of the Advisory Commission of the National Council of Defense. In short, organized labor was elevated to a more prominent status than had heretofore been seen. Accordingly, the AFL had a sizable growth in membership during this period (an increase from 2,370,000 members in 1917 to 3,260,000 members in 1919). The AFL's legislative interests were also addressed when Congress imposed restrictions on the number of immigrants entering the country, thus reducing the supply of labor competing for available jobs in the economy.

The rather sharp increase in the cost of living that followed World War I, coupled with the newly recognized status of labor, resulted in an unprecedented number of strikes. For example, the Seattle General Strike occurred in 1919, along with other strikes by actors, New York waterfront employees, and coal miners. The most widespread strike in 1919 involved the steel industry, where some 367,000 employees walked off the job in 70 major cities. The outcome of the 1919 steel strike was a major setback to organized labor in the steel industry. Many possible factors contributed to the setback. Some were very similar to those previously described in the Homestead and Pullman incidents, whereas others reflected factors faced by unions in the 1920s and early 1930s. Internal union difficulties were a major factor contributing to the strike's outcome (i.e., an organizing campaign conducted by 24 unions instead of one common industrial union; improvised leadership rather than a consistent union approach to strike issues; and poor financial resources necessary to conduct an effective strike action). U.S. Steel was successful in withstanding the economic pressure of the strike by using strikebreakers and maintaining strong ties with other companies and social institutions such as the press and religious leaders. The strike was terminated by the participating unions without a labor agreement. Another 15 years would elapse before organized labor would again make membership gains in the steel industry.[81]

During this period many other unions appeared unable to organize companies that, like U.S. Steel, firmly believed that unions were not in the ownership's best interests. For example, another 1919 strike almost paralyzed the coal industry when no miners returned to work until President Woodrow Wilson persuaded them to accept a temporary wage increase and submit all other issues to a newly appointed Bituminous Coal Commission. In 1920 the commission awarded increases ranging from 20 to 30 percent, but this was the last victory for mine employees for several years.

Despite increased status and militancy, something went wrong for organized labor in the 1920s. Dubbed the "Golden Twenties" for many in the United States, it was a dreary decade for hourly laborers—both in terms of real income[82] and for labor unions in terms of membership. Between 1920 and 1924, total union membership declined from 5,110,000 to 3,600,000; membership in AFL unions dropped from 4,078,000 to 2,866,000. By 1930 total union membership dropped to 3,400,000, and AFL membership dropped to 2,700,000.[83] This decline was caused by at least two major factors: (1) aggressive employer opposition and (2) organized labor's inability to overcome anti-union sentiment among potential union members.[84]

Counteractions by Employers

Concerned with the increased status given labor during the war, employers actively engaged in efforts to roll back gains in union membership, beginning in the 1920s and continuing through the 1930s. These tactics ranged along a continuum from aggressive opposition to labor unions to formation of an acceptable alternative to unions. Many employers adopted a variety of tactics from both ends of the spectrum.

Employers actively opposed unions through the **open-shop movement.** The alleged purpose of this movement was to ensure that employees had the freedom to determine if they would choose to join a union. The employer-sponsored open-shop movement was in part a reaction to the efforts of some unions to have employers agree to contract language imposing a **closed-shop** rule that required an individual to belong to the union covered by the contract before the employer would agree to hire the individual. Rationale for the open-shop movement can also be found in its companion name, the **American Plan,** because employers believed that employees should adhere to the traditional American value of "rugged individualism" instead of the "foreign, subversive, and corrupt" principle of collective activity through labor unions.

Other employers took more aggressive steps to prevent employees from joining a union. For example, some employers would hire **spies** to pose as employees in order to determine which employees had pro-union sentiments.[85] Pro-union employees or those otherwise identified as troublemakers because they complained about wages or working conditions would be discharged and possibly **blacklisted,** meaning that their names would be given to other employers in the area who would then refuse to hire anyone whose name appeared on the list. Employer violence against participants in union organizing drives was also a potential strategy to counter unions during this period.[86] A variation of the open shop (American Plan) occurred in the 1930s with the development of the **Mohawk Valley Formula.** This systematic approach was used when a union attempted to organize or strike a company in the community. The Mohawk Valley Formula typically consisted of the following steps:

> Form a citizens' committee in the community [to rally support for the employer and against the union], label the union leaders as outside agitators, stir up violence or the fear of violence, have a "state of emergency" declared, organize a back-to-work movement, and finally have the back-to-work employees march into the plant protected by armed police.[87]

Some employers sought to counter employee desires for union representation by offering an alternative model to unionism. The 1920s saw widespread employer paternalism, which asserts that employees should trust their employer to know what is best for employees' interests and to always act in ways to enhance such employee interests. Employees are viewed as members of a family that the employer heads. Some employers during this period began to offer a number of employee benefits aimed at improving the social welfare of employees (e.g., improving living conditions in company housing, free lunches, baseball fields, vacations, pensions, and employee counseling).[88] Employers felt that employees receiving these benefits would be indebted to the employer and realize that unions were not necessary to obtain improvements that benefited employees.

Many employers created **company unions** to represent a substitute model for unions. Called an **Employee Representation Plan** (ERP), company unions included as many as 1.5 million employees and appeared superficially similar to unions in that selected employee representatives would discuss working conditions with management officials. ERPs differed from independent unions in two major respects. First, independent unions had more autonomy than ERPs. Employers often influenced the selection of ERP officers, financed the organization, could veto any decision made by the joint labor-management committee, and could disband the ERP anytime the employer was not pleased with its operation. Second, ERPs were usually limited to a single facility, and employees under ERPs could neither press for work rules that would remove unfair competition from other facilities nor push for legislation at the local, state, or federal level.[89]

Labor's Inability to Overcome Antiunion Sentiment

The lack of organizing gains during the 1920s also has to be attributed to the antiunion public sentiment and the activities and attitudes of organized labor. "While job insecurity may have deterred some employees from joining unions in the face of employer opposition, many of them apparently felt that unions were no longer as necessary as they had formerly believed them to be. What profit strikes or other agitation for collective bargaining when the pay envelope was automatically growing fatter and a more abundant life seemed to be assured with our rapid approach to the final triumph over poverty?"[90]

Many potential members also believed that much of organized labor was corrupt and subject to control by the socialists and communists. Racketeering had become a feature of some local union-employer relationships. For example, in one incident a union official signed a two-paragraph agreement with three major employers guaranteeing no wage increase for three years and requiring all employees to join the union or be discharged. None of the employees had ever solicited the union, nor did they ever see a union official during the life of the contract. This type of sweetheart contract was often coupled with financial kickbacks to the union official, meaning the employer paid the union official a portion of the wage savings.[91]

Some labor unions had also been accused of harboring communists and other political radicals. Many prominent union leaders would occasionally accept help from almost any group that would devote time and effort in organizing employees, believing that they could control these political elements once the local union had been established. However, union leaders overestimated their ability to control such political elements in some instances. One former president of the Steelworkers Union recalled how communists could dominate local union meetings by using the V technique, whereby the leader would find a seat in the center of the auditorium in about the second or third row. Then the following would ensue: "A few rows back, two of his associates would locate about ten seats apart, and this same pattern would be followed all the way to the rear of the hall. When the chief spokesman opened debate, his line would then be parroted all the way through the V behind him, giving an illusion of widespread strength. They would also wait until other union members, tired and bored, had gone home before trying to push through their own proposals."[92]

The AFL devoted much of its attention during the 1920s to overcoming its negative public image.[93] This effort detracted from active organizing efforts, particularly since Gompers, in declining health, had lost much of his former physical enthusiasm for organizing activity. In 1924 Gompers died, and his successor, William Green, did not revive any major organizing activities, choosing to focus primarily on maintaining the status quo.[94] The failure of the AFL's leadership to initiate organizing efforts among the rapidly expanding low and semi-skilled workers in mass-production industries such as auto, rubber, and steel eventually led to the formation of the Congress of Industrial Organizations (CIO).

Rise of the CIO and Industrial Unionism

Major disagreement occurred within the AFL over organizing the large ranks of unskilled and semi-skilled employees. Tremendous technological shifts occurring during and after World War I reduced the demand for highly skilled employees; hence, an increasing percentage of the labor force consisted of production workers. In 1926, for example, 85 percent of the hourly employees at Ford Motor Company required less than two weeks of training.[95] Because craft employees no longer dominated the industrial scene, some AFL leaders believed that to maintain its influence within the labor movement the AFL needed to organize low and semi-skilled production employees as well.

Many AFL unions did not want to enroll production employees. Some AFL leaders believed these employees were inferior to craft employees and possessed less bargaining power, whereas others thought their inclusion would confuse and distort the AFL's organization, fearing a return to the failed one big union model of the KOL and IWW. William Green himself did not view industrial employees as being compatible with the AFL's organizational principle of exclusive jurisdiction.

Some AFL leaders thought that a separate union would be needed for each company's or industry's products. Thus, if General Electric had fifty different products, then fifty different AFL unions (each having exclusive jurisdiction over its members' interests) would be needed for effective collective bargaining. In other words, at least fifty separate collective-bargaining agreements could be negotiated by GE and its unions. Other AFL leaders believed that industrial unionism would at least weaken the AFL's concept of organized labor. The president of one AFL union urged his members to stamp out "the awful serpent of industrial trade unionism that would destroy this International and weaken the entire structure of the Labor Movement."[96]

The issue came to a head in 1935 under the direction of John L. Lewis, president of the AFL's United Mine Workers Union. The AFL rejected the concept of industrial unionism through three separate votes at its 1935 convention.[97] On November 9, 1935, the **Committee for Industrial Organization** was formed. The Committee's purpose was allegedly "educational and advisory"; but in reality, it was intended to promote organizing among the unorganized workers in the mass-production industries.[98]

In January 1936, AFL leaders were shocked to find that the Committee for Industrial Organization had been formed by some AFL unions. Green and his supporters thought the industrial unionism issue had been buried once and for all at the 1935 convention. The Committee not only discussed the industrial union concept but also asked the AFL to immediately grant industrial union charters to a number of industries such as the rubber workers and the autoworkers. The Committee further insisted that an organizing campaign be started at once in the steel industry.

The AFL, confronted with the most serious challenge in its history, ordered the Committee to disband or get out. Personalities intensified the issue. **John L. Lewis,** a powerful man in voice and action, sought and obtained power and publicity through his union activities.[99] Lewis managed to provoke AFL leaders into a confrontation while at the same time whipping his United Mine Workers members into a "lather of rage" against the AFL.[100] The split over the industrial unionism issue resulted in seven unions with almost a million members being expelled from the AFL for practicing **dual unionism** (i.e., supporting a rival labor organization while a member of your present union). In 1938, the seven expelled unions along with other supporters of the Committee for Industrial Organization quickly held a convention in Pittsburgh, Pennsylvania, and created a rival and completely independent labor federation, the **Congress of Industrial Organizations (CIO),** electing John L. Lewis as president.[101]

The development of the CIO coincided with a significant upsurge in union membership aided greatly by passage of the **National Labor Relations Act**

(NLRA) in 1935 granting most private-sector employees the legal right to join unions and bargain collectively (discussed further in Chapter 3). By November 1937, the CIO's affiliated unions had organized 75 percent of the steel industry, 70 percent of the automobile industry, 65 percent of the rubber industry, and about one-third of the maritime and textile industries.[102] The AFL also saw rapid growth in membership during the late 1930s and 1940s. AFL unions organized the skilled-trade workers in each mass-production industry, often putting them in competition with the CIO union chartered to represent employees of all skill levels within a particular industry. The steady growth of the AFL during the late 1930s was also aided by employers' preference for dealing with the more conservative AFL organization instead of taking their chances with the new, unpredictable, and more politically radical CIO.[103]

The CIO was able to establish itself as a successful labor organization. At least five factors seem to account for the CIO's success: strong leadership, realistic goals, effective use of sit-down strikes, passage of the NLRA, and changes in employees' attitudes toward independent unions.

Strong CIO Leadership The aggressive and effective CIO leaders (John L. Lewis, Sidney Hillman, and David Dubinsky, among others) infused new life into a union movement previously content with resting on its laurels. Most of the CIO union leaders had extensive organizing experience and prided themselves on keeping in touch with their membership.[104] Union leaders' accomplishments should not be overstated, however, because organizing drives involved the tireless efforts of many individuals who typed up circulars, contacted prospective members, and provided routine services that ensured union election victories. In fact, one biographer of John L. Lewis indicated his lack of involvement in the many organizing chores by noting that he preferred "arriving only in time for the triumphant finale."[105]

Much organization effort in the steel, mining, automobile, and other industries was effectively directed toward second-generation immigrants. Some 30 percent of the CIO leadership came from a "new immigrant" background. One historian notes, "The success of the CIO was based on the mobilization of ethnic workers and on their willingness to join unions."[106]

Realistic Goals Coming from a background of former membership in the AFL, CIO leaders embraced the pure and simple (business) unionism philosophy, focusing on improvements in members' job-related economic interests as the highest priority and support for a free enterprise, capitalist economy. John L. Lewis remarked: "I think most people have come to realize, that we cannot progress industrially without real cooperation between workers and management, and that this can only be brought about by equality in strength and bargaining power of labor and management. Labor is sincere in its desire to help. It looks forward to an industrial procedure which will increase productive efficiency and lower prices to the consumer."[107]

The Effective Use of Sit-Down Strikes The CIO also used a most successful tactic for gaining employer recognition of its unions—the sit-down strike, in which employees stayed inside the plant rather than picketing outside the plant gates. This technique was very successful because employers were reluctant to physically remove the employees from the plant for fear that their equipment could be damaged in the confrontation.

The tactic was initially applied by the IWW at a General Electric facility in 1906, but the most famous sit-down strike occurred in December 1936 at a General Motors facility in Flint, Michigan. At one time, 26,000 General Motors employees had belonged to a union, but in early 1936, there were only 122 union members, many of whom were management spies.[108] A local grassroots organization led by the United Auto Workers (UAW) union was secretly established to build up the union at Flint. The sit-down strike was locally planned and carried out. Lewis and the CIO preferred to organize the steel industry before attempting major organizing drives in the automobile industry. The CIO, however, did lend its active support once the strike was under way.

The sit-down strike at Flint lasted 44 days and received widespread community support while hindering GM's efforts to reverse its negative profit situation of previous years.[109] The strike resulted in employer recognition of the union, a fact noticed by many employees in other trades. Between September 1936 and June 1937, some 500,000 employees in the rubber, glass, and textile industries put the technique to use. Although effective, the sit-down strike was short-lived because public opinion eventually frowned on this tactic, and a subsequent decision by the Supreme Court declared that such strikes illegally deprived an employer of control over the owner's property.

Passage of the NLRA Act Another (and perhaps the most significant) reason for the increased number of union members was the passage of the National Labor Relations (Wagner) Act in 1935. The federal government indicated through this law that collective bargaining was in the national interest. More important were the provisions establishing the National Labor Relations Board to administer union representation elections, define employer unfair labor practices, and enforce the legal rights of employees to join unions.

Changes in Employees' Attitudes Many employees' negative attitudes toward organized labor changed dramatically. The Great Depression of the 1930s caused many employees to realize that job security could not be achieved solely through hard work and loyalty to the employer. These employees now viewed unions as a mechanism to promote job security, secure economic gains, and provide some voice to the worker over job-related issues.

By the onset of World War II, organized labor had reversed its membership decline of the 1920s, rising to almost 9 million members in 1940. Yet the rivalry between the CIO and the AFL was intense and sometimes violent as AFL and CIO organizers clashed over the right to represent factory employees. James Hoffa, a former president of the International Brotherhood of Teamsters (then an AFL union), recalled organizing drives of 1941 and the violence between the CIO and his union: "Through it all the members wore two pins, putting on a Teamsters button when we were around and switching to a CIO button when those guys showed up. They were waiting to see which union was going to win the battle. You couldn't really blame them. They were scared out of their britches because they didn't want to get caught in the bloody middle."[110]

The AFL-CIO rivalry existed in almost every industry[111] and extended to the local level, where it was common for an employer to have both AFL and CIO unions representing the same employees. Even employers with the best intentions could not build an effective labor-management relationship in this environment.

WORLD WAR II TO THE PRESENT

The AFL at first did not want the United States to become involved in World War II; however, this attitude changed after the bombing of Pearl Harbor. Concern over the nation's defense prompted union–management cooperation. For example, both union and management officials participated on War Production Board subcommittees. Such panels weighed employee suggestions, which saved 31 million man-hours and $44 million during World War II.[112]

The cooperative spirit was not total, particularly from the standpoint of strikes taken during wartime. In February 1943, organized labor complained to President Franklin Roosevelt that consumer price increases granted during wartime had resulted in the cost of living workers faced rising far more than wage increases permitted by the government under the 1942 wage and price control "Little Steel Formula."[113] The United Mine Workers conducted a series of strikes to obtain wage increases of $2 a day in 1943. These actions resulted in President Roosevelt's seizing the mines before a compromise wage settlement was eventually obtained.

The public viewed these and other strikes with anger and alarm, considering them violations of the no-strike pledge announced by organized labor in 1941. Negative public sentiment increased when labor strikes continued and, after 1942, increased every year of the war. The number of employee days lost to strikes was estimated to be the equivalent of no more than one day per year per worker for the four war years.[114] Yet the mere act of participating in a strike was viewed by some as unpatriotic.

Labor's collective-bargaining focus shifted at the end of the war to the issues of full employment and further wage increases in order to sustain consumers' purchasing power and create an expanding market demand for industrial goods. Union members, remembering the economic reconversion period following the end of World War I, were also concerned about employer policies aimed at restricting union growth and wage gains.

Union members' expectation that the end of wartime wage and price controls would produce significant economic gains at the bargaining table coupled with employers' expectation that the return of millions of military personnel to the private-sector labor force would create an excess supply of labor and therefore reduce pressure to improve job terms or conditions charted a course for conflict. Unions backed their postwar bargaining demands with strikes. "During no period in the history of the United States did the scope and intensity of labor-management conflicts match those recorded in the year following VJ Day, August 14, 1945."[115] In this one-year period, more than 4,600 strikes, involving 5 million employees and resulting in almost 120 million man-days of idleness, affected almost every major industry. Strikes were basically nonviolent, representing essentially economic tests of strength and endurance between labor and management. Generally, both unions and employers wanted to be free to resolve their differences at the bargaining table without government interference or the imposition of wage and price controls that had been used during World War II.

Developments in Organized Labor Since World War II

Three major developments have occurred in organized labor since World War II: increased concern over new collective-bargaining issues, organizing drives aimed at white-collar and public-sector employees, and the merger of the AFL and CIO.

New Collective-Bargaining Issues The return to peacetime after World War II and, particularly, the Korean War saw increased efforts to extend the provisions of the labor agreement to include all aspects of the collective-bargaining relationship. In the late 1950s and early 1960s, the relative scarcity of jobs coincided with the need for price stability to ease the deficit in international payments.

Unions directed their collective-bargaining efforts toward guaranteeing members job security in the face of possible technological advances and wages that would compensate for inflation. Organized labor's response toward technological change (discussed in more detail in Chapter 8) brought notable results during this period, including the Automation Fund Agreement between Armour and Company and the Packinghouse Workers and Meat Cutters' unions (1959), the Mechanization and Modernization Agreement in the Pacific Coast longshore industry (1960), and the Long-Range Sharing Plan negotiated between Kaiser Steel and the United Steelworkers (1962).

Employee benefits represented a second new bargaining area. Before World War II, labor cost was overwhelmingly straight-time pay for time actually worked.[116] Subsequent bargaining efforts by labor unions (and personnel policies of nonunion firms) have resulted in a substantial increase in employee benefits (pensions, insurance plans, and so forth), which are currently around 35 percent of payroll costs for unionized employers and 27 percent of payroll costs for nonunion employers.[117]

The trend in multiyear labor agreements after World War II put pressure on union leaders to safeguard wage increases against the possibilities of inflation. In 1948 General Motors and the United Auto Workers negotiated a long-term agreement with a cost-of-living (COLA) provision that adjusted wages for inflationary changes during the life of the contract. This contract provision spread to other labor–management negotiations. In 1952 almost 3 million employees (approximately 20 percent of the employees covered by labor agreements) had cost-of-living provisions in their contracts.[118] Relatively low rates of annual inflation in recent years have reduced the importance of COLA clauses as a safeguard for the value of employee wages, and the number of employees covered under such contract clauses has declined.

Recent competition from foreign companies and nonunion organizations in the United States has resulted in **concession bargaining**, in which management seeks to obtain from the union more flexible work rules and reduced labor costs (e.g., wages, benefits). Work-rule modifications include scheduling changes, fewer rest breaks, and combining job classifications (i.e., broadening job descriptions) to give management more flexibility in employee work assignments.

Wage and benefit concessions represent a significant organized-labor development since World War II. Audrey Freedman of the Conference Board notes that in today's globally competitive business environment, "wages, even under union bargaining pressures, are far more responsive to economic conditions. . . ."[119] Examples of wage and benefit concessions intended to provide management with greater labor-cost flexibility include:

- **Two-tiered wage plans**, where employees hired after a labor agreement takes effect will receive a lower hourly pay rate than co-workers already on the payroll as of the date the contract took effect.

- **Lump-sum wage** payment usually paid as a flat dollar amount associated with a firm's economic performance for a given time period. This wage payment does not alter the employee's hourly wage rate and often occurs instead of granting a cents-per-hour or percentage increase in an employee's base hourly wage rate.

- **Health-care cost shifting**, which shifts a greater proportion of the costs of providing employee health-care coverage from the employer to the individual employee through a variety of methods such as higher deductibles, co-payments for services, or increasing the percentage of the monthly insurance premium charge paid by the employee.

Organization of Public-Sector Employees   A second major development in organized labor since World War II involves the organization of different types of employees. More specifically, public (government) employees (discussed in Chapter 13) have received increased attention from union organizers and are now the most heavily organized employee segment in the labor force.

Merger of the AFL and CIO   Perhaps the most dramatic postwar development in organized labor was the merger of the AFL and CIO. The intense rivalry between them did not end after World War II. However, the presence of three influences during the 1950s resulted in the eventual merger of these organizations in 1955.[120]

First was the change in the presidents of the AFL and CIO. Phillip Murray became president of the CIO when Lewis resigned in 1940 and continued the verbal feud against the AFL and its president, William Green. In November 1952, however, both Green and Murray died. George Meany succeeded Green as AFL president and Walter Reuther succeeded Murray as the CIO president. Meany and Reuther were not particularly fond of each other, but unlike Green and Murray, they had not previously gone on record criticizing each other. Therefore, the change in leadership at the AFL and CIO presented an historic opportunity to change the future for both labor organizations through merger without either labor leader losing face.

Another influence contributing to the AFL-CIO merger was the recognized ineffectiveness of union raiding. The two labor organizations investigated employee representation elections in which the AFL tried to organize employees affiliated with CIO unions, and vice versa. During a two-year period (1951–1952), 1,245 such elections involved some 366,740 employees, with only 62,000 employees changing union affiliation. This figure overestimates the number affected because it does not consider the offsetting nature of elections. An AFL union could organize a CIO-represented factory of 1,000 employees only to have a CIO union organize an AFL factory of 1,000 employees—the net change being zero. In fact, the extensive raiding during 1951 and 1952 resulted in a net gain for the AFL of only 8,000 members, or only 2 percent of the total number of employees involved.[121]

Both the AFL and the CIO finally realized that organized labor would benefit if the energies devoted to raiding each other were spent on organizing nonunion employees. Accordingly, many of the AFL and the CIO unions signed a no-raiding agreement in 1954. Instead of concentrating on differences emphasized in raiding activities, the two major federations could now look at similar goals that might be more easily attained by a merger.

One similar goal was the desire of both organizations to reward their political friends and punish political enemies.[122] In many instances, the separate AFL and CIO labor organizations had failed to achieve this goal. For example, the AFL and CIO working independently were unable to defeat Senator Taft in his reelection bid (one of the authors of the Taft-Hartley Act, who organized labor perceived as being anti-labor) and failed to elect Adlai Stevenson (a supporter of organized labor) in the presidential race over Dwight D. Eisenhower. Both AFL and CIO leaders believed that a merger might increase their effectiveness in the political arena.

The AFL-CIO merger on December 12, 1955, involved 15,550,000 members, making the new organization the largest trade union center in the world. In recognition of the longer history of the AFL, George Meany became the president of the merged AFL-CIO and Reuther was elected vice-president. Meany believed the merger would lead to more employees becoming unionized and to a greater political influence for labor within the American two-party system.[123]

The merger resulted in the continued reduction of union raiding. It also reduced the influence of union locals within the national unions because they could no longer threaten to affiliate with the rival national organization.[124] However, as discussed further in the next section, the AFL-CIO merger has not resulted in a tremendous increase in union membership or political influence. It did reduce the former divisiveness within organized labor, but it cannot be concluded that the merger was a significant impetus for growth and change.

Aspects of Organized Labor Unchanged Since World War II

Organized labor as it existed at the end of World War II compared with its present state appears to have more similarities than differences.[125] For example, exclusive representation, in which one union is granted the legal right to represent a specified group of jobs based upon the majority approval of the employees filling those jobs, continues to be an important part of U.S. labor relations policy. Collective-bargaining agreements that contain jointly negotiated work rules specifying wages, hours, and other terms or conditions of employment remain the primary focus of labor and management practitioners. Once a contract is negotiated, the no-strike/lockout clause and grievance-arbitration procedure clause in the contract ensure that rights disputes during the contract's term over the interpretation or application of the contract's language can be resolved without resort to a work stoppage or other job action. The government has also continued to maintain a basically noninterventionist role in private-sector labor relations, preferring union and management representatives to voluntarily resolve their own disputes whenever possible.

Since World War II, unions have continued to be involved in the political process at the federal, state, and local levels. Unions' support for political candidates and issues over the years has resulted in mixed success. Unions have historically been involved in politics to gain and protect basic legal rights to organize and bargain with employers on behalf of their members' interests. Unions act as an interest group on behalf of their members and as a leader of a broader social movement seeking to protect the interests of workers in general (e.g., support for the minimum wage, 40-hour work week, quality public education, antidiscrimination initiatives, and improved job safety and health conditions).[126] Organized labor has traditionally been linked more closely with the Democratic

LABOR RELATIONS IN ACTION

Organized Labor and Campaign Finance Reform

In the 2000 election cycle, four of the top five organizations providing political campaign funds were labor organizations [i.e., American Federation of State, County, and Municipal Employees (AFSCME), Service Employees International Union (SEIU), Communications Workers of America (CWA), and the International Brotherhood of Electrical Workers (IBEW)].[1] Traditionally, organized labor has targeted approximately 90 percent of its campaign donations to support Democratic candidates ($54 million in 2002), while many companies traditionally divided their donations among candidates of both parties. Over the past decade more industries (e.g., defense contractors, commercial banking, health-care professionals, accounting firms) have shifted the bulk of their campaign giving to support Republican candidates. Business political campaign contributions in total outpace contributions by labor organizations by a 12-to-1 margin.[2]

In 1996 the AFL-CIO began a concerted effort to increase political campaign support efforts to elect mostly Democratic Party candidates as well as target some Republican incumbents for defeat. In response, organized labor has been subjected to efforts by business and other conservative, Republican support groups to enact federal and state legislation to make it more difficult for unions to use their organizational funds for political purposes.[3] According to supporters, such so-called paycheck protection bills are intended to ensure that union dues cannot be spent to support political candidates or issues with which an individual union member might disagree.[4] Opponents who refer to such proposals as "paycheck deception" bills argue that union leaders are elected by the union's membership to advance their interests and many important issues affecting workers are related to the passage and enforcement of laws and administration policies (e.g., trade, jobs, taxes, education). Imposing complex and administratively costly burdens on unions without including other organizations that also spend members' funds for political purposes (e.g., companies, the Christian Coalition, National Rifle Association, Sierra Club) would be discriminatory and clearly a partisan political effort to limit union support for primarily Democratic candidates.[5]

Perhaps the best example of the paycheck protection debate occurred in California in the spring of 1998 when voters defeated Proposition 226, which would have prohibited unions from using employees' union dues for political purposes in California unless employees gave their written consent each year. Despite initial widespread support for the proposition in public opinion polls (71 percent in favor versus 22 percent against), four months later, 53 percent of the voters defeated this legislative proposal.[6]

What caused this dramatic turnaround in voter sentiment? The answer to this question reflects three general tactics used by unions. First, state labor organizations were able to persuade many California employers to remain neutral in the debate over Proposition 226. Labor groups made it clear that any effort to restrict union campaign contributions would result in their effort to secure similar restrictions on the political contributions of corporations or other interest groups.[7] Opposition to Proposition 226 was also aided by the support of many nonprofit organizations, including the American Cancer Society, American Lung Association, and American Heart Association, which were concerned that their revenues tied to paycheck deductions could be significantly reduced because of the broad language used in drafting the paycheck protection proposal.

Second, organized labor mounted a successful media campaign designed to persuade voters that the real intent behind those supporting Proposition 226 was to reduce the ability of unions to be an effective voice for workers in the political process. Organized labor also contended that passage of this legislation could result in the privatization of education, weaken patient protections against HMOs, "gut Medicare," and export American jobs. Best estimates suggest that backers of Proposition 226 spent $4–5 million, whereas unions and other opponents to the legislation spent between $20 and $30 million. Third, unions conducted an effective grassroots campaign targeting union members in the state. Each union member in California received a letter and brochure about Proposition 226. A videotape explaining the referendum was also sent to 300 local unions in California. Thousands of rank-and-file union members were mobilized to stuff envelopes, knock on doors, and make more than 1 million calls to voters.

Congress enacted the **Bipartisan Campaign Reform** (McCain-Feingold) **Act of 2002** in an effort to curb the growing influence of so called *soft money* in federal election campaigns. Some of the law's key provisions include:[8] (a) a ban on unlimited (soft money) contributions by unions, corporations, and individuals donated to national political parties for purposes other than to advocate for a candidate's election or defeat; (b) increases the amount an individual may contribute to a House or Senate candidate from $1,000 to $2,000 and grants permission for an individual to donate $95,000 over a two-year period to all candidates and political parties (so called *hard money*); and (c) within 60 days of a general election or 30 days of a primary election, unions, corporations, and some independent interest groups are prohibited from running so-called "issue ads," which don't endorse the election or defeat of a specific candidate but do indicate candidates' current positions or prior votes on specific issues of interest to the target audience.

In the 2002 election campaign concluded prior to the passage of the new campaign finance reform bill, the Democratic Party's soft money campaign contributions totaled $245.8 million compared to the Republican Party's $250 million.[9] The Republican Party's hard money donations of $332 million far exceeded similar contributions to the Democratic Party, which totaled $163 million. Unless the Democratic Party is able to significantly increase its individual donor base, the Republican Party should enjoy a significant hard money advantage under the new campaign finance law, which forces political parties to rely less on soft money contributions. Some experts suggest that soft money contributions, which used to go directly to the national or state political parties, will now be controlled by individual political action committees (PACs). Also referred to as 527 committees, these organizations can contribute unlimited amounts of soft money, which can be used to support issue-oriented voter education campaigns, get-out-the-vote efforts, or voter registration drives. This will permit both labor and business PACs to directly control both the political message and method of delivery during election campaigns rather than having to rely on a national or state political party to filter the contributor's preferences through the strategy of that political party. Unions are likely to remain an important interest group in American politics and a voice for American workers. Efforts to curb union political activity by other interest groups opposed to such activity will also likely continue. ■

SOURCES:
[1] The Center for Responsive Politics, "Top Donors to Political Candidates and Parties Revealed," *News Release,* October 18, 2000, at http://www.opensecrets.org/pressreleases/oct18_00_release.htm.
[2] AFL-CIO, "In 2002 Elections, Once Again, Big Business Far Outspends Unions," 2003 at http://www.aflcio.org/issuespolitics/politics/outspend.cfm; Thomas B. Edsall, "Big Business's Funding Shift Boosts GOP Trend May Put Squeeze on Democrats' Finances," *Washington Post,* November 27, 2002, p. A1.
[3] David Corn, "Union Dues, Political Don'ts: California's Initiative to Strip Union Political Power Is a Model of Things to Come," *The Nation* 266 (May 18, 1998), p. 16; Mark Melman, "Union Member Contribution Check-offs: A Democratic Perspective," *Campaigns & Elections* 19 (May 1998), p. 60.
[4] Reed Larson, "McCain-Feingold Would Gut Employee Rights," *Human Events,* February 12, 2001, p. 10; R. Bradley Adams, "Note: Union Dues and Politics: Workers Speak Out Against Unions Speaking for Them," *Florida Journal of Law and Public Policy* 10 (Fall, 1998), pp. 207–225.
[5] John Nichols, "Real Paycheck Protection," *The Nation* 272 (March 26, 2001), p. 8; Harold Meyerson, "Union Bust," *The New Republic,* April 13, 1998, pp. 11–14.
[6] Owen Ullmann, Aaron Bernstein, et al., "A Bazooka Aimed at Big Labor Backfires on the GOP," *Business Week,* June 15, 1998, p. 55; Grover G. Norquist, "Big Labor Buys Some Time," *American Spectator* 31 (August 1998), p. 60.
[7] John Gizzi, "Big Business was AWOL in Paycheck Protection Fight," *Human Events* 54 (June 6, 1998), p. 7.
[8] Craig Gilbert, "Campaign Reform Takes a Pounding; Lawyers Toss Book at McCain-Feingold," *Milwaukee Journal Sentinel,* December 8, 2002, p. A-1.
[9] Thomas B. Edsall and David VonDrehle, "Republicans Have Huge Edge in Campaign Cash," *Washington Post,* February 14, 2003, p. A1.

Party than the Republican Party because Democrats have traditionally been more supportive of union goals and legislative priorities. Union support for Democratic candidates and policies is not universal. For example, the AFL-CIO's Executive Council did not endorse Bill Clinton in the 1992 presidential election, although members of union households supported Clinton and Democratic senators and members of Congress in the 1992 and 1994 elections (67 percent and 63 percent, respectively). AFL-CIO-affiliated unions strongly opposed passage of the North American Free Trade Agreement yet President Clinton persuaded Congress to approve the legislation.[127]

A declining union density level in the private sector has led some to question whether organized labor's influence has also declined in American politics. Demonstrating the importance of organized labor as an interest group in politics, members of union households cast 23 percent of all votes in the 2000 presidential election, although unions represented only 13.5 percent of the total labor force.[128] When organized labor has been able to present a united front on issues, some legislative success has been achieved, as evidenced by passage of the Occupational Health and Safety Act (1970); Employee Retirement and Income Security Act (1974); the Worker Adjustment and Retraining Act (1988); the Civil Rights Act of 1991; the Americans with Disabilities Act (1990); and the Family and Medical Leave Act (1993). On the other hand, unions have failed to gain passage of an increase in the federal minimum wage and universal health-care coverage, or to prevent federal intervention by the Bush administration in 2002 labor disputes in the West Coast shipping industry and the airline industry where such intervention was viewed by labor as weakening the bargaining position of the unions involved in those disputes. Organized labor also failed to elect Democratic candidate Vice-President Al Gore to the presidency in 2000 and Republicans regained control over both the House of Representatives and Senate in the mid-term 2002 elections as public attention focused on national security and foreign policy issues in the wake of the September 11, 2001, terrorist attacks rather than domestic economic conditions.

AFL-CIO president John Sweeney has attempted to reenergize organized labor's political clout in several ways. First, Sweeney has increased union financial contributions targeted to support candidates who have demonstrated support for labor's goals. For example, in the 1996 congressional campaign the AFL-CIO announced plans to raise and spend $35 million to educate Americans on pro-union issues and help Democratic House candidates. Of the 44 first-term Republican congressmen targeted for defeat by the AFL-CIO, 27 percent were defeated.[129] Unions have also sought to build coalitions with other community-based groups (e.g., consumer, student, civil rights, environmental, senior citizens) to broaden the support base for many political issues (e.g., health-care reform).[130] The AFL-CIO has announced plans as part of the 2004 campaign to spend $20 million in a new campaign entitled "the Partnership for America's Families," which will target nonunion voters, particularly blacks, Latinos, and women.[131]

Since the end of World War II, the AFL-CIO has continued to experience some difficulty in achieving consensus among its member unions, as have national unions. Understandably, political consensus is difficult to achieve among the diverse national unions within the AFL-CIO and increasingly diverse membership within national and local unions. This problem occurs in any large organization, particularly one that grants a large amount of autonomy to its members. The AFL-CIO is always subject to the threat of national unions withdrawing from it. The federation also realizes that many large national unions could get along quite well without its support. For example, the expulsion of the Teamsters (IBT) in 1957 and the disaffiliation of the United Auto Workers (UAW) in 1968 from the federation did not hinder these organizations' ability to increase their membership, grow in influence, and engage in collective bargaining. (Both the IBT and the UAW have since reaffiliated with the AFL-CIO.)

Lack of consensus may also be found at the local union level, especially when younger employees become members. Most labor unions have a long tradition of struggle and sacrifice; their leaders have risked physical hardships merely to gain employer recognition of their union. However, many of the younger members are unaware of labor history and focus on asking union leaders, "What have you done for me lately?" An increasing number of mergers between national unions have also presented challenges to union leaders in how to organize the union's structure to meet the increasingly diverse needs of union members in different occupations or industries. This issue is discussed further in Chapter 4.

Since World War II, unions have continued to purse primarily short-term economic and job security goals rather than emphasizing long-range reform. The experience of the KOL and IWW taught organized labor an important lesson: union goals should relate to members' needs instead of being abstract, long-range efforts to change the existing social-economic system. The period since World War II has witnessed tremendous economic growth and technological change affecting union members' interests. Union leaders believe these job-related issues deserve a higher priority than other societal concerns. Even when unions make bargaining concessions, as they sometimes might, because of recessionary economic conditions, the concessions are typically viewed as short-term economic exchanges (e.g., lower wages in exchange for enhanced job security).

SUMMARY

In obtaining a contemporary perspective on organized labor, one must be aware of the evolution of labor–management relationships and of various labor organizations that have attempted to influence those relationships. Current labor organizations have learned important lessons from their historical counterparts. Criteria for comparing the effectiveness of various labor organizations are their structural and financial stability; their ability to work within established political and economic systems; and supportive or disruptive features of the social environment, such as mass media, legislation, and the ability of union leaders to identify and satisfy members' goals and interests. Organized labor did not exert much influence before 1869, although employees became increasingly concerned with working and market conditions associated with mass production. The active years of organized labor can be grouped into three time periods: 1869 to World War I, World War I to World War II, and World War II to the present.

continued on page 72

LABOR RELATIONS IN ACTION

Labor History Time Line—Selected Events

Year	Event
Late 1700s	Emergence of local craft unions in large East Coast cities (e.g., New York, Philadelphia)
1842	The Massachusetts Supreme Court in *Commonwealth v. Hunt* establishes a legal precedent that workers have a right to combine together for the purpose of pursuing lawful end (goals) using lawful means (tactics).
1850	U.S. economy begins to shift from an agricultural base to a manufacturing (industrial) base. Regional and national product markets emerge with larger firms able to use new technology and improved transportation modes (roads, rail) to mass produce goods.
1869	Noble Order of the Knights of Labor organized.
1880s	Use of the labor injunction to prohibit or restrict employee's concerted activities replaces reliance on criminal or civil conspiracy trials as a management legal strategy.
1886	8-hour day movement gains momentum; Haymarket Square Riot occurs in Chicago, IL; American Federation of Labor (AFL) is organized, electing Samuel Gompers as president.
1892	The Homestead strike involving the Amalgamated Association of Iron, Steel & Tin Workers and steel mills owned by Andrew Carnegie occurs.
1894	Eugene Debs leads the American Railway Union in a strike against the Pullman Company resulting in federal troop intervention in the labor dispute.
1898	Congress attempts to extend mediation and voluntary arbitration of labor disputes to the railroad industry by passing the Erdman Act. The law declared unconstitutional by the U.S. Supreme Court in 1908.
1905	The Industrial Workers of the World (IWW) organized.
1908	U.S. Supreme Court declares a national product boycott by the United Hatters' Union to be a violation of the Sherman Anti-trust Act.
1911	Triangle Waist Company fire in New York City leads to the death of 146 clothing workers. Focuses national attention on the poor working conditions facing many industrial employees.
1913	Congress creates the U.S. Department of Labor and the department's head (Secretary of Labor) designated a member of the president's cabinet.
1926	Railway Labor Act enacted granting employees in the private-sector railroad industry the right to form unions and bargain collectively.

Year	Event
1932	The Norris-LaGuardia Act enacted placing restrictions on the issuance of labor injunctions during labor disputes and making a "yellow-dog" contract unenforceable in federal court.
1933	U.S. Secretary of Labor Frances Perkins becomes of the first woman to serve as a member of the president's cabinet.
1935	National Labor Relations (Wagner) Act enacted granting most private-sector employees the right to form unions and bargain collectively. The Committee for Industrial Organization created by several AFL unions to encourage efforts to organize workers in the mass-production industries (auto, steel, rubber, etc.).
1936	Railway Labor Act amended to add coverage of the airline industry.
1938	The Committee for Industrial Organization is reorganized as the Congress of Industrial Organizations (CIO), electing John L. Lewis as its first president. Fair Labor Standards Act enacted establishing a federal minimum wage of 25 cents per hour and requiring time and one-half pay for hours worked in excess of 40 hours in a regular workweek.
1947	Labor Management Relations (Taft-Hartley) Act enacted over the veto of President Truman. Retains NLRA protections for employee collective activity but adds protection for the right of individual employees not to engage in collective activity and imposed restrictions on union conduct similar to restrictions imposed on management conduct by the NLRA.
1952	Presidents of both the AFL and CIO die of natural causes in the same month, setting the stage for new leadership by AFL president George Meany and CIO president Walter Reuther.
1955	AFL and CIO labor organizations merge to form the AFL-CIO, electing George Meany as president and Walter Reuther as vice-president.
1959	Labor Management Reporting and Disclosure (Landrum-Griffin) Act enacted to regulate the internal affairs of unions and their relationship with individual union members.
1962	President John F. Kennedy issues Executive Order 10988 permitting federal employees to organize and engage in collective bargaining. Encourages states to enact similar legislation granting state and local public employees bargaining rights.
1963	Equal Pay Act enacted prohibiting different wage rates based on sex for workers performing the same job who are subject to coverage under the Fair Labor Standards Act.
1964	Civil Rights Act enacted prohibiting discrimination based upon race, color, religion, sex, or national origin in hiring, apprenticeship, compensation, terms or conditions of employment, and union membership.

Continued

Year	Event
1968	Public-sector employee unrest leads to increased organizing, bargaining, and strikes involving public employees (e.g., police, firefighters, teachers, and sanitation workers). Martin Luther King is assassinated while helping to lead a sanitation workers strike in Memphis, TN. Age Discrimination in Employment Act enacted making it illegal to discriminate against individuals 40 years of age or older in regards to hiring, discharge, or other employment decisions on the basis of the individual's age.
1970	Occupational Health and Safety Act enacted to provide a safe and healthy work environment for American workers.
1974	Employee Retirement Income Security Act (ERISA) enacted to protect the assets of private-sector employees provided for under employer-established benefit plans (e.g., pension plan).
1975	Economy begins to transition from an industrial-based to a service-based economy.
1978	Civil Service Reform Act enacted converting previous presidential executive orders establishing bargaining right for federal employees into permanent legislation.
1980	Increasing global competition ushers in a decade in which many U.S. firms are forced to undergo dramatic change in order to remain competitive. Concession bargaining involving management demands for union cost concessions in exchange for promises of improved job security becomes common. Flexible work rules take on increased importance in efforts to improve productivity and product/service quality. Some bargaining relationships stress increased labor–management cooperation as a means to improved competitiveness that can benefit management's and labor's interests.

Three major labor organizations developed in the period from 1869 to World War I: the Knights of Labor (KOL), the American Federation of Labor (AFL) under Gompers, and the Industrial Workers of the World (IWW). These organizations had different goals, strategies, and organizational characteristics, which in part furnished reasons for the demise of the KOL and IWW. The Haymarket Riot, the Homestead incident, and the Pullman strike hurt organized labor, although Gompers managed to derive some benefit from each of these events.

The period immediately following World War I saw limited growth in union membership. Factors contributing to this situation included several strategies used by employers to counter union organizing campaigns. Internal differences occurred within the AFL regarding the advantages of organizing the heretofore nonunion low- and semi-skilled employees working in the emerging mass production industries like auto, rubber, and steel. This disagreement led to the formation of a rival union organization, the Congress of Industrial Organizations (CIO), whose major objective was to organize industrial employees. The CIO achieved substantial membership gains in the late 1930s and 1940s.

Year	Event
1981	Members of the Professional Air Traffic Controllers Union (PATCO) engage in an illegal strike to support bargaining demands and are discharged by the Reagan administration. This act widely interpreted by practitioners in the private and public sectors as evidence of a new employer "get tough" policy in labor relations. Organized labor is forced to expend its resources fighting to defend established legal rights and employment conditions rather than expanding or improving employment interests.
1988	Worker Adjustment and Retraining Notification Act enacted (made effective February 1989). Requires employers who employ 100 or more employees to provide 60 days advance notice of any plant closing or major layoff, but enforcement of the act requires an employee or their representative to sue the employer in court.
1991	Americans with Disabilities Act enacted to protect disabled persons from discrimination in regards to hiring, discharge, or other terms and conditions of employment. Civil Rights Act of 1991 enacted amending Title VII of the Civil Rights Act to permit suits for punitive damages for violations involving intentional discrimination and endorsing the use of alternative dispute resolution methods to resolve employment discrimination claims.
1992	North American Free Trade Agreement enacted (effective January 1, 1994) intended to promote trade between the United States, Canada, and Mexico.
1993	The Family and Medical Leave Act enacted permitting employees of employers who employ 50 or more employees to take up to 12 weeks of unpaid time off in the event of a birth, adoption, or foster care of a child; or to care for a child, parent, spouse, or themselves involving a serious health condition.
2001	9-11 terrorist attack on U.S. targets occurs. Organized labor and business interests join in efforts to rebuild and provide aid to victims of the attack. Negative impact on travel-related industries leads to layoffs and renegotiation of labor contract terms.

Three major developments have occurred in organized labor since World War II. Concern has increased over new collective-bargaining issues; organizing drives have been aimed at public employees; and the AFL and CIO have merged. Although several influences prompted the AFL-CIO merger, the impact of this event on contemporary union–management relationships is difficult to assess. More similarities than differences are apparent when the state of organized labor at the end of World War II is compared with its present state. Organized labor remains a minority, yet influential, interest group in our society. Organized labor has continued to have mixed success in the political process. The short-term, job-related economic and job security interests of employees have remained basically unchanged since World War II and continue to be the top bargaining priorities for unions in contract negotiations with employers.

KEY TERMS

Knights of Labor (KOL)	spies
Terrence V. Powderly	blacklisted
one big union	Mohawk Valley Formula
local assembly	company union
Haymarket Riot	Employee Representation Plan
American Federation of Labor (AFL)	sweetheart contract
Samuel Gompers	V technique
decentralized authority	Committee for Industrial Organization
exclusive jurisdiction	John L. Lewis
pure and simple unionism	dual unionism
Homestead strike	Congress of Industrial Organizations (CIO)
Pullman strike	National Labor Relations Act of 1935 (NLRA)
Industrial Workers of the World (IWW)	sit-down strike
William "Big Bill" Haywood	concession bargaining
jurisdictional disputes	AFL-CIO
open-shop movement (American Plan)	Bipartisan Campaign Reform Act of 2002
closed shop	

DISCUSSION QUESTIONS

1. Discuss the similarities and differences between the Knights of Labor (KOL) and the Industrial Workers of the World (IWW).

2. Considering the four criteria for evaluating the strength of a labor organization identified in the introduction to Chapter 2, why did the AFL survive and the IWW fade into obscurity?

3. Briefly explain how the Haymarket Riot, Homestead strike, and Pullman strike helped as well as hurt the AFL.

4. Discuss some employer tactics used to prevent or minimize union growth prior to passage of the National Labor Relations Act in 1935. Which, if any, of these tactics would be legal today?

5. Discuss the similarities and differences between the AFL and the CIO.

6. What were several reasons behind the merger of the AFL and the CIO? To what extent will these or other factors continue this merger into the near future—say, the next 10 years?

7. Discuss two similarities of organized labor as it existed at the end of World War II compared to organized labor today.

8. Are unions an important force in U.S. politics today? Why or why not?

EXPLORING THE WEB

History of the Labor Movement

Explore the following pages on the history of the labor movement in the United States.

1. General History Pages   A Short History of American Labor, adapted from the March 1981 AFL-CIO *American Federationist*

http://www.albany.edu/history/history316/LaborMovementHistory.html

An Eclectic List of Events in U.S. Labor History, compiled by Allen H. Lutins

http://www.lutins.org/labor.html

Unions Online. Labor History

http://www.teamster.org/about/history.htm

2. Labor Unions See the Preamble to the Knights of Labor Constitution (1878) linked from Michael Gordon's syllabus for his course on the History of the American Working Classes, which he teaches at the University of Wisconsin, Milwaukee. Examine other links of interest at this site.

http://www.uwm.edu/Course/448-440/preamble.htm

ABG Combines Legacies of Three Unions, from the United Steelworkers of America

http://www.uswa.org/uswa/program/content/272.php

A Brief History of the United Steelworkers of America

http://www.uswa.org/uswa/program/content/217.php

History of the United Auto Workers

http://www.ukans.edu/history/VL/USA/labor.html

3. The Haymarket Riots Chicago Public Library. 1886, May 4: Haymarket Tragedy

http://www.chipublib.org/004chicago/disasters/haymarket.html

Locate the Haymarket bibliography published on this site.
Chicago Historical Society. History Files. The Haymarket Affair

http://www.chicagohs.org/history/index.html

Mining Company Guide to American History. The Haymarket Riot

http://americanhistory.miningco.com/library/weekly/aa042998.htm

4. The Pinkertons What role did the Pinkerton Detective Agency play in labor relations in 1880s? Read an account published by the Public Broadcasting Service. The Hated Men in Blue. (The Pinkertons). The American Experience/Carnegie

http://www.pbs.org/wgbh/amex/carnegie/sfeature/mh_blue.html

5. The Pullman Strike Read the parable of Pullman. What events led up to the strike?

http://www.kentlaw.edu/ilhs/pullman.htm

REFERENCES

1. David A. Zonderman, "Surveying the Survey Texts: Recent Works in American Labor History," *Labor History* 43 (August 2002), pp. 335–343; Thomas Dublin, "Labor History on the World Wide Web: Thoughts on Jumping onto a Moving Express Train," *Labor History* 43 (August 2002), pp. 343–357; Robert Ozanne, "Trends in American Labor History," *Labor History* (Fall 1980), p. 521. See also Barry Goldberg, "A New Look at Labor History," *Social Policy* 12 (Winter 1982), pp. 54–63; and Robert H. Zieger, "Industrial Relations and Labor History in the Eighties," *Industrial Relations* 22 (Winter 1983), pp. 58–70.

2. Henry Pelling, *American Labor* (Chicago: University of Chicago Press, 1960), pp. 12–13.

3. Edward B. Mittelman, "Trade Unionism 1833–1839," in *History of Labor in the United States*, eds. John R. Commons et al. (1918; reprint ed. New York: Augustus M. Kelly, Publishers, 1966), vol. 1, p. 430.

4. Jack Barbash, *American Unions: Structure, Governance, and Politics* (New York: Random House, 1967), p. 3.

5. Norman J. Ware, *The Labor Movement in the United States 1860–1895* (New York: Vintage Books, 1929), pp. 139–140.

6. William C. Birdsall, "The Problems of Structure in the Knights of Labor," *Industrial and Labor Relations Review* 6 (July 1953), p. 546.

7. For a discussion of how the expansion of the markets affected unionization among the shoemakers, see John R. Commons, *Labor and Administration* (New York: Macmillan, 1913), pp. 210–264.

8. T. V. Powderly, Thirty Years of Labor: 1859–1889 (Columbus, Ohio: Excelsior, 1889), p. 21.

9. Ibid., p. 163.

10. Philip Taft, *Organized Labor in American History* (New York: Harper and Row, 1964), p. 90.

11. Gerald N. Grob, *Workers and Utopia* (Evanston, Ill.: Northwestern University Press, 1961), p. 35. Powderly was most concerned about the evils of drinking; for example, he spent almost 50 pages of his autobiography, *Thirty Years of Labor*, discussing this issue.

12. Birdsall, "The Problems of Structure," p. 533.

13. Melton Alonza McLaurin, *The Knights of Labor in the South* (Westport, Conn.: Greenwood Press, 1978), p. 39.

14. Joseph G. Rayback, *A History of American Labor* (New York: Macmillan, 1968), p. 174.

15. Joseph R. Buchanan, *The Story of a Labor Agitator* (1903; reprint ed. Westport, Conn.: Greenwood Press, 1970), pp. 318–323.

16. For details of these procedures, see Taft, *Organized Labor*, p. 91.

17. Powderly, *Thirty Years of Labor*, pp. 151–157.

18. It should be noted that local assemblies were somewhat responsible for this situation as they contributed only $600 to the General Assembly's strike funds in 1885–1886 (McLaurin, *The Knights of Labor*, p. 54). For more details of KOL strike activities, see Norman J. Ware, *The Labor Movement in the United States, 1860–1895* (1929), pp. 117–154. It should be further noted that the Knights made more effective use of boycotts than any previous union. However, as was true with strikes, the boycotts were instigated by the local assemblies and forced on the Knights' national leaders (Grob, *Workers and Utopia*, p. 61).

19. Donald L. Kemmerer and Edward D. Wickersham, "Reasons for the Growth of the Knights of Labor in 1885–1886," *Industrial and Labor Relations Review* 3 (January 1950), pp. 213–220.

20. Foster Rhea Dulles, *Labor in America: A History*, 3d ed. (New York: Thomas Y. Crowell, 1966), p. 127.

21. Ware, *The Labor Movement*, p. 96.

22. Dulles, *Labor in America*, p. 135.

23. Powderly, *Thirty Years of Labor*, p. 514. It should also be noted that Powderly believed Gompers misled employees by advocating the 8-hour workday without telling them that their wages would be proportionately reduced. Most workers thought they would receive 10 hours' payment for 8 hours of work.

24. "A Hellish Deed!" *Chicago Tribune*, May 5, 1886, p. 1.

25. For additional details of the rigged nature of the trial, see Samuel Yellen, *American Labor Struggles* (1936; reprint ed. New York: Arno Press, 1969), pp. 60–65.

26. "A Hellish Deed!"

27. "Their Records," *Chicago Tribune*, May 5, 1886, p. 1. See also Paul Avrich, *The Haymarket Tragedy* (Princeton, N.J.: Princeton University Press, 1984).

28. Sidney Lens, *The Labor Wars: From the Molly Maguires to the Sitdowns* (Garden City, N.Y.: Doubleday, 1973), p. 67.

29. The origination of the AFL was changed between 1881 and 1889 to include activities under the Federation of Organized Trade and Labor Unions. At least one historian has claimed that the revised date is regrettable since the parent organization (Federation of Organized Trades and Labor Unions) had little similarity to the AFL in terms of effective organization and broad-based support (Ware, *The Labor Movement*, p. 251). See also Glen A. Gildemeister, "The Founding of the American Federation of Labor," *Labor History* 22 (Spring 1981); and Harold C. Livesay, *Samuel Gompers and Organized Labor in America* (Boston: Little, Brown, 1978), pp. 75–86.

30. Samuel Gompers, *Seventy Years of Life and Labor* (New York: E. P. Dutton, 1925), p. 266.

31. Norman J. Ware, *Labor in Modern Industrial Society* (1935; reprint ed. New York: Russell and Russell, 1968), p. 262.

32. Dulles, *Labor in America*, p. 155.

33. Gompers, *Seventy Years of Life and Labor*, p. 245.

34. Samuel Gompers, *Labor and the Employer* (1920; reprint ed. New York: Arno Press, 1971), pp. 33–34.

35. Stuart Bruce Kaufman, *Samuel Gompers and the Origins of the American Federation of Labor: 1848–1896* (Westport, Conn.: Greenwood Press, 1973), p. 173. For details of this relationship, see Gompers, *Seventy Years of Life and Labor*, pp. 381–427.

36. Louis Reed, *The Labor Philosophy of Samuel Gompers* (1930; reprint ed. Port Washington, N.Y.: Kennikat Press, 1966), p. 20. See also an editorial by Gompers in the *American Federationist*, June 1924, p. 481; and Sarah Lyon Watts, *Order Against Chaos: Business Culture and Labor Ideology in America 1880–1915* (New York: Greenwood Press, 1991), pp. 9–10.

37. Gompers, *Seventy Years of Life and Labor*, pp. 286–287, 381–427.

38. Alice Kessler-Harris, "Trade Unions Mirror Society in Conflict between Collectivism and Individualism," *Monthly Labor Review* 110 (August 1987), p. 33.

39. Gompers, *Labor and the Employer*, p. 202.

40. Marc Karson, *American Labor Unions and Politics: 1900–1918* (Carbondale, Ill.: Southern Illinois University Press, 1968), p. 29; and Julia Green, "Strike at the Ballot Box: The American Federation of Labor's Entrance into Election Politics, 1906–1909," Labor History 32 (Spring 1991), pp. 165–192.

41. Reed, *The Labor Philosophy of Samuel Gompers*, pp. 106–110.

42. Milton Derber, *The American Idea of Industrial Democracy: 1865–1965* (Urbana, Ill.: University of Illinois Press, 1970), p. 117.

43. Gompers, *Seventy Years of Life and Labor*, p. 342. For additional details regarding early AFL organizing, see Philip Taft, *The AF of L in the Time of Gompers* (1957; reprint ed. New York: Octagon Books, 1970), pp. 95–122.

44. Dulles, *Labor in America*, pp. 163–164.

45. Andrew Carnegie, "An Employer's View of the Labor Question," in *Labor: Its Rights and Wrongs* (1886; reprint ed. Westport Conn.: Hyperion Press, 1975), pp. 91, 95. For a recent collection and analysis of material pertaining to the situation, see David P. Demarest Jr., ed., *The River Ran Red* (Pittsburgh: University of Pittsburgh Press, 1992).

46. Yellen, *American Labor Struggles*, p. 81.

47. For details of the wage package, see Ibid., pp. 77–80. See also E. W. Bemis, "The Homestead Strike," *Journal of Political Economy* 2 (1894), pp. 369–396; and Linda Schneider, "The Citizen

Striker: Workers' Ideology in the Homestead Strike of 1892," *Labor History* 23 (Winter 1982), pp. 47–66. For some additional insights into Frick's background, see Carol Aymowitz, "Frick's Homey Mansion," *The Wall Street Journal*, September 24, 1990, p. A-12.

48. "Surrounded by Pickets," *New York Times*, July 4, 1892, p. 1.

49. "Mob Law at Homestead," *New York Times*, July 7, 1892, p. 1.

50. "Leader O'Donnell Is Glad," *New York Times*, July 12, 1892, p. 2; and "Bayonet Rule in Force," *New York Times*, July 13, 1892, p. 1.

51. Lens, *The Labor Wars*, p. 77.

52. "A Talk with Gompers," *New York Times*, July 7, 1892, p. 2; and "Provoked by Carnegie," *New York Times*, July 7, 1892, pp. 2, 5.

53. Taft, *The AF of L in the Time of Gompers*, p. 136.

54. "Arbitrate the Homestead Strike," *Chicago Tribune*, July 8, 1892, p. 4. See also "The Origin of the Trouble," *New York Times*, July 8, 1892, p. 2.

55. Yellen, *American Labor Struggles*, p. 3.

56. Lens, *The Labor Wars*, p. 81. See also Susan Kay Morrison's unpublished paper, "Eugene V. Debs: His Ride on the Pullman," 1981.

57. For additional details about the town, see Almont Lindsay, *The Pullman Strike* (Chicago: University of Chicago Press, 1967), pp. 38–60.

58. For more details regarding ARU's organization, see Philip S. Foner, *History of the Labor Movement in the United States*, vol. II (New York: International Publishers, 1955), p. 256.

59. Lindsay, *The Pullman Strike*, p. 124.

60. *Debs, Petitioner, In re*, 158 U.S. 564 (1895).

61. Lindsay, *The Pullman Strike*, p. 215.

62. Gompers, *Seventy Years of Life and Labor*, p. 403.

63. J. Robert Constantine, "Eugene V. Debs: An American Paradox," *Monthly Labor Review* 114 (August 1991), pp. 30–33.

64. *Proceedings of the First Convention of the Industrial Workers of the World* (New York: Labor News Company, 1905), p. 1.

65. Melvyn Dubofsky, *'Big Bill' Haywood* (Manchester, U.K.: Manchester University Press, 1987), pp. 35–37.

66. *Proceedings of the First Convention of the Industrial Workers of the World*, 1905, p. 143.

67. Bill Haywood, *Bill Haywood's Book: The Autobiography of William D. Haywood* (New York: International Publishers, 1929), p. 73.

68. Melvyn Dubofsky, *We Shall Be All: A History of the Industrial Workers of the World* (Chicago: Quadrangle Books, 1969), p. 481.

69. Haywood, *Bill Haywood's Book*, p. 181.

70. For additional details pertaining to these differences, see Dubofsky, *We Shall Be All*, pp. 105–119; Joseph Robert Conlin, *Bread and Roses Too* (Westport, Conn.: Greenwood, 1969), pp. 97–117; and Lens, *The Labor Wars*, pp. 154–155.

71. David J. Saposs, *Left-Wing Unionism* (1926; reprint ed. New York: Russell and Russell, 1967), p. 148.

72. Louis Adamic, *Dynamite: The Story of Class Violence in America* (1934; reprint ed. Gloucester, Mass.: Peter Smith, 1963), p. 174.

73. Conlin, *Bread and Roses Too*, pp. 97–117. See also Fred Thompson, *The IWW: Its First Fifty Years* (Chicago: Industrial Workers of the World, 1955), pp. 80–87.

74. Adamic, *Dynamite*, pp. 163–164.

75. Conlin, *Bread and Roses Too*, p. 96.

76. Philip S. Foner, ed., *Fellow Workers and Friends: I. W. W. Free Speech Fights as Told by Participants* (Westport, Conn.: Greenwood Press, 1981), p. 15.

77. Conlin, *Bread and Roses Too*, p. 68.

78. Haywood, *Bill Haywood's Book: The Autobiography of William D. Haywood*, pp. 361–364.

79. For additional details, see Frank L. Grubbs, Jr., *The Struggle for Labor Loyalty: Gompers, the AFL, and the Pacifists, 1917–1920* (Durham, N.C.: Duke University Press, 1968).

80. James O. Morris, *Conflict within the AFL: A Study of Craft versus Industrial Unionism, 1901–1938* (1958; reprint ed. Westport, Conn.: Greenwood Press, 1974), pp. 9–10.

81. Taft, *Organized Labor,* pp. 355–358; and Francis Fox Piven and Richard A. Cloward, *Poor People's Movements* (New York: Pantheon Books, 1977), p. 104. For details of this strike, see Lens, The Labor Wars, pp. 196–219.

82. Frank Stricker, "Affluence for Whom? Another Look at Prosperity and the Working Classes in the 1920s," *Labor History* 24 (Winter 1983), pp. 5–34.

83. Lens, *The Labor Wars,* pp. 222, 296, 312.

84. Derber, *The American Idea,* p. 246. For an application of these reasons to a specific industrial situation during this time period, see Stephen L. Shapiro, "The Growth of the Cotton Textile Industry in South Carolina: 1919–1930" (Ph.D. diss., University of South Carolina, 1971), pp. 168–171.

85. For additional details regarding this tactic, see Clinch Calkins, *Spy Overhead: The Story of Industrial Espionage* (1937; reprint ed. New York: Arno Press, 1971).

86. Violence was limited neither to this time period nor to the employer. One of the more publicized episodes of employer violence was the Ludlow Massacre of 1914. The mining camps in Colorado were involved in a strike for union recognition when, on April 20, militiamen opened fire on a tent colony, killing two strikers and one boy. They then set fire to the tents, killing two women and 11 children. For more details of this event, see Leon Stein, ed., *Massacre at Ludlow: Four Reports* (reprint ed.; New York: Arno Press, 1971). Perhaps one of the more vivid examples of union violence occurred in Herrin, Illinois (1922), where miners tortured and killed at least 26 management officials and strikebreakers. For details of this episode, see Saul Alinsky, *John L. Lewis: An Unauthorized Biography* (New York: Vintage Books, 1970), pp. 43–50.

87. Richard C. Wilcock, "Industrial Management's Policies toward Unionism," in Milton Derber and Edwin Young, eds., *Labor and the New Deal* (Madison: University of Wisconsin Press, 1957), p. 293.

88. For a case study of paternalism, see "Welfare Work in Company Towns," *Monthly Labor Review* 25 (August 1927), pp. 314–321. For a more thorough discussion of employer counteractions during this time period, see Larry J. Griffin, Michael E. Wallace, and Beth A. Rubin, "Capitalist Resistance to the Organization of Labor before the New Deal: Why? How? Success?" *American Sociological Review* (April 1986), pp. 147–167.

89. Derber, *The American Idea,* pp. 220–221; and Morris, *Conflict within the AFL,* pp. 40–41. For more details on ERPs, see Ware, *Labor in Modern Industrial Society,* pp. 414–435. For a contemporary assessment of the problems and prospects facing the single-firm, independent union, see Arthur B. Shostak, *America's Forgotten Labor Organization* (Princeton, N.J.: Industrial Relations Section, Department of Economics, Princeton University, 1962).

90. Dulles, *Labor in America,* p. 245.

91. This example was drawn from a more detailed account of racketeering during this period found in Sidney Lens, *Left, Right, and Center: Conflicting Forces in American Labor* (Hinsdale, Ill.: Henry Regnery, 1949), pp. 86–108.

92. David J. McDonald, *Union Man* (New York: E. P. Dutton, 1969), p. 185. See also Max Gordan, "The Communists and the Drive to Organize Steel, 1936," *Labor History* 23 (Spring 1982), pp. 226–245. For further historical insights into the relationship between organized labor and communism, see Harvey A. Levenstein, *Communism, Anticommunism and the CIO* (Westport, Conn.: Greenwood Press, 1981).

93. James O. Morris, "The AFL in the 1920s: A Strategy of Defense," *Industrial and Labor Relations Review* 11 (July 1958), pp. 572–590.

94. See, for example, "William Green: Guardian of the Middle Years," *American Federationist* 88 (February 1981), pp. 24–25.

95. Bruce Minton and John Stuart, *Men Who Lead Labor* (New York: Modern Age Books, 1937), pp. 14–15.

96. Morris, *Conflict within the AFL,* p. 216.

97. For additional details pertaining to the background of this historic convention, see Herbert Harris, *Labor's Civil War* (1940; reprint ed. New York: Greenwood Press).

98. Lens, *The Labor Wars,* p. 284.

99. Cecil Carnes, John L. Lewis: *Leader of Labor* (New York: Robert Speller, 1936), p. 299.

100. David Dubinsky and A. H. Raskin, *David Dubinsky: A Life with Labor* (New York: Simon and Schuster, 1977), p. 226.

101. The seven unions were the United Mine Workers; the Amalgamated Clothing Workers; the International Ladies Garment Workers Union; United Hatters; Cap and Millinery Workers; Oil Field, Gas Well and Refinery Workers; and the International Union of Mine, Mill, and Smelter Workers.

102. Benjamin Stolberg, *The Story of the CIO* (1938; reprint ed. New York: Arno Press, 1971), p. 28.

103. Milton Derber, "Growth and Expansion," in Derber and Young, *Labor and the New Deal,* p. 13; and Steve Rosswurm, ed., *The CIO's Left-Led Unions* (New Brunswick, N.J.: Rutgers University Press, 1992).

104. See, for example, John Hutchinson, "John L. Lewis: To the Presidency of the UMWA," *Labor History* 19 (Spring 1978), pp. 185–203; and Steven Fraser, *Sidney Hillman and the Rise of American Labor* (New York: The Free Press, 1991).

105. James Arthur Wechsler, *Labor Baron: A Portrait of John L. Lewis* (New York: William Morrow, 1944), p. 71; and Robert H. Zieger, "Leadership and Bureaucracy in the Late CIO," *Labor History* 31, no. 3 (1990), pp. 253–270.

106. Thomas Gobel, "Becoming American: Ethnic Workers and the Rise of the CIO," *Labor History* 29 (Spring 1988), p. 174.

107. S. J. Woolf, "John L. Lewis and His Plan," in *American Labor Since the New Deal,* Melvyn Dubofsky, ed. (Chicago: Quadrangle Books, 1971), pp. 110–111.

108. Lens, *The Labor Wars,* p. 295.

109. Sidney Fine, *Sit-Down: The General Motors Strike of 1936–1937* (Ann Arbor: The University of Michigan Press, 1969), pp. 156–177. For another perspective of the sit-down strike, see Daniel Nelson, "Origins of the Sit-Down Era: Worker Militancy and Innovation in the Rubber Industry, 1934–1938," *Labor History* 23 (Winter 1982), pp. 198–225.

110. James R. Hoffa and Oscar Fraley, *Hoffa: The Real Story* (New York: Stein and Day, 1975), p. 65.

111. For a detailed account of the AFL-CIO rivalries in several industries, see Walter Galenson, *The CIO Challenge to the AFL* (Cambridge, Mass.: Harvard University Press, 1960).

112. Richard B. Morris, ed., *The U.S. Department of Labor Bicentennial History of the American Worker* (Washington, D.C.: U.S. Government Printing Office, 1976), p. 236.

113. For details of this formula and the extent that cost-of-living estimates exceeded this formula, see Taft, *Organized Labor in American History,* pp. 549–553 and 557–559.

114. Dulles, *Labor in America: A History,* p. 334.

115. Arthur F. McClure, *The Truman Administration and the Problems of Postwar Labor, 1945–1948* (Cranburry, N.J.: Associated University Press, 1969), p. 45.

116. George H. Hildebrand, *American Unionism: An Historical and Analytical Survey* (Reading: Addison-Wesley, 1979), pp. 36–37.

117. U.S. Bureau of Labor Statistics, "Employer Cost for Employee Compensation—March, 2002," *News Release,* June 19, 2002, p. 12.

118. Robert M. MacDonald, "Collective Bargaining in the Postwar Period," *Industrial and Labor Relations Review* 20 (July 1967), p. 568.

119. Audrey Freedman, "How the 1980's Have Changed Industrial Relations," *Monthly Labor Review* (May 1988), p. 37.

120. For a more detailed discussion of historical attempts at the merger of the AFL and CIO, see Joel Seidman, "Efforts toward Merger 1935–1955," *Industrial and Labor Relations Review* 9 (April 1956), pp. 353–370.

121. "Document: AFL-CIO No-Raiding Agreement," *Industrial and Labor Relations Review* 8 (October 1954), p. 103.

122. "A Short History of American Labor," *American Federationist* 88 (March 1981), p. 14.

123. George Meany, "Merger and the National Welfare," *Industrial and Labor Relations Review* 9 (April 1956), p. 349.

124. Richard A. Lester, *As Unions Mature* (Princeton, N.J.: Princeton University Press, 1958), p. 25.

125. John T. Dunlop, "Have the 1980s Changed Industrial Relations?" *Monthly Labor Review* 111 (May 1988), pp. 29–33.

126. Herbert B. Asher, Eric S. Heberlig, Randall B. Ripley, and Karen Snyder, *American Labor Unions in the Electoral Arena* (Lanham, MD: Rowman & Littlefield, 2001), pp. 3–8.

127. Ken Jennings and Jeffrey W. Steagall, "Unions and NAFTA's Legislative Passage: Confrontation and Cover," *Labor Studies Journal* (Spring 1996), pp. 61–80; and Jefferson Cowie, "National Struggles in a Transnational Economy: A Critical Analysis of U.S. Labor's Campaign against NAFTA, *Labor Studies Journal* 21 (Winter 1997), pp. 3–32.

128. Lorraine Woellert, "Business Vows to Get Out the Vote; A GOP-industry Push Is Taking a Page from Labor's Playbook," *Business Week*, October 7, 2002, p. 98. See also: Taylor E. Dark, *The Unions and the Democrats* (Ithaca, N.Y.: Cornell University Press, 1999); William Form, *Segmented Labor, Fractured Politics: Labor Politics in American Life* (New York: Plenum Press, 1995).

129. Gary C. Jacobson, "The Effect of the AFL-CIO's 'Voter Education' Campaign on the 1996 House Elections," *Journal of Politics* 66 (February 1999), pp. 185–194.

130. Marc Cooper, "Antiwar Labor Pains: Unions Are Edging Into the Peace Movement, but They Are Still Minor Players," *The Nation*, December 9, 2002, p. 18; *Building Bridges: The Emerging Grassroots Coalition of Labor and Community*, eds. Jeremy Brecher and Tim Costello (New York: Monthly Review Press, 1990).

131. Thomas B. Edsall, "Labor Targets Nonunion Voters: $20 million Turnout Effort Expands Effort to Regain Influence," *Washington Post*, February 27, 2003, p. A4.

CHAPTER 3

Labor Law: Background and Basic Principles

Labor relations law provides a framework defining the legal rights and responsibilities of the parties engaged in the labor relations process. This chapter introduces the basic legal foundation regulating the major phases of the labor relations process: organizing unions, negotiating labor agreements, and ensuring employee rights in contract administration. It is essential today not only to know the law but to understand and appreciate the interrelationships between the law and the labor relations process. Practitioners should recognize that having a legal right to act does not always mean it is in one's practical best interest to exercise that legal right.

This chapter logically follows the one on the historical development of unions in the United States because labor relations law and union development go hand in hand. Law as it pertains to labor is traced from the first major court case involving union activities, through the development of common law and the use of antitrust legislation that inhibited the growth of unions, to the laws that pertain to most private firms today: the Norris–La Guardia, Wagner, Taft-Hartley, and Landrum-Griffin Acts. Because these acts cover most U.S. industries and businesses, a substantial amount of space is devoted to their content. The Railway Labor Act, which principally covers railroads and airlines, is also explained and assessed. A final section briefly considers several other laws that can affect the labor relations process.

Origin of Labor Relations Law

Article I, Section 8 of the **U.S. Constitution** grants Congress the right to pass laws regulating interstate and international commerce. Labor relations activities can affect interstate commerce and therefore have been the focus of many statutory laws to regulate various aspects of the employment relationship since the late 1800s. The First Amendment of the U.S. Constitution, which ensures the rights of peaceful assembly, freedom of association, and free speech, usually has been interpreted as allowing employees to form and join unions and has provided the justification for union picketing (to communicate information to possible union members and union supporters). The Fifth Amendment contains due process provisions and the Fourteenth Amendment prohibiting state laws from depriving citizens of their constitutional rights provide equal protection under law and play an important role in defining the framework of American labor law.

Early U.S. history was governed by the application of **common law**. Common law is used to resolve a legal dispute when no constitutional or statutory law applies to that dispute. To resolve a dispute in such situations, judges develop legal principles or procedures that over time are adopted by other judges in similar disputes and come to represent the common law. Early U.S. common law was based upon English common law principles as modified by local custom and practice.

One notable example of a common law doctrine that has created much controversy in recent years is the **employment-at-will (EAW) doctrine.** The EAW doctrine states that employment relationships established for an indefinite duration may be terminated by either the employer or employee at any time for any or no stated reason. Employers have historically relied upon this common law doctrine as a basis for terminating employees for a wide variety of reasons without permitting the terminated individual to legally challenge whether management's decision or reasoning was correct. Although the doctrine has been modified by the passage of laws and court interpretations intended to prohibit employers from discharging individuals for certain protected reasons (e.g., joining a union; an individual's race, sex, religion), in many states the EAW doctrine remains to protect management's right to discharge employees. This doctrine is more thoroughly discussed in Chapter 12.

Modern U.S. labor relations law relies primarily on federal and state statutory laws or local government ordinances; judicial decisions interpreting and applying statutory laws and local ordinances; and decisions by administrative agencies (e.g., the **National Labor Relations Board** [NLRB], U.S. Department of Labor) responsible for administering specific labor laws. Congress has enacted numerous labor relations laws in the interest of employees and employers, public welfare, and interstate commerce. Three major ones—the **Norris–La Guardia Act,** the **Labor Management Relations Act,** as amended, and the **Railway Labor Act**—are discussed at length later in this chapter. Under the **preemption doctrine,** federal law takes precedent over state law or local ordinances whenever both seek to regulate the same conduct and there is a conflict between them.[1] The preemption doctrine underscores the importance of labor relations as an area that affects the national economy and therefore benefits from the uniformity and stability that federal regulation of issues can provide. State legislatures may pass laws and local municipalities may enact ordinances to fill voids in federal laws or to extend regulation to issues not regulated by federal laws, such as the right of state and local public employees to engage in collective bargaining.

The judicial branch of government, with its court system at the federal, state, and local levels, functions to determine a law's constitutionality and conformity to legal standards; to assess the accuracy of interpretations by administrative agencies; and to issue injunctions that restrict or require certain activities. In addition, the courts must decide issues not covered by existing laws and make rulings under the general guide of "equity." These decisions constitute case law, which has developed over the years establishing precedents and providing guidance for future legal decisions.

The executive branch includes various administrative agencies created by Congress to interpret and administer some labor laws. These government agencies establish policies and make rules to guide the administration of labor laws. Although administrative agency decisions may be appealed to federal courts, the courts are encouraged by Congress to give great deference to the expertise of agencies in interpreting and applying an applicable labor law. Some of the more important administrative agencies mentioned include:

- **National Labor Relations Board** (NLRB): Administers the National Labor Relations Act as amended by the Labor Management Relations (Taft-Hartley) and Landrum-Griffin Acts; conducts union representation elections and adjudicates unfair labor practice charges.

- **Federal Mediation and Conciliation Service** (FMCS): Provides mediation services to unions and management in collective bargaining and assists these parties in selecting arbitrators in grievance administration; provides training programs to encourage more cooperative labor management relations.

- **U.S. Department of Labor** (USDOL): Performs many employment-related services, such as research and data-collecting functions; administers federal wage and safety laws; and enforces federal contract compliance under equal employment opportunity requirements. In addition, the USDOL's head (Secretary of Labor) serves as a member of the president's cabinet responsible for employment-related matters.

- **National Mediation Board** (NMB): Handles union representation issues under the Railway Labor Act; provides mediation services to parties in negotiations; assists in resolving disputes over contract interpretation; and in cases involving emergency disputes, proposes arbitration and certifies the dispute to the president as an emergency.

- **National Railroad Adjustment Board** (NRAB): Hears and attempts to resolve railroad labor disputes growing out of grievances and interpretation or application of labor agreements.

- State and local administrative agencies: Are responsible for the enforcement and administration of state laws and local ordinances involving labor relations topics.

Early Legal Interpretations Involving Labor–Management Relationships (1806–1931)

As discussed in Chapter 2, early labor unions in the United States had to struggle for their existence. The legal system was primarily focused on protecting employer property rights to advance the economic growth of the nation with little importance placed on protecting the rights of employees within the emerging free-enterprise economic system. Employer property rights were defined in broad terms to include both the right to control tangible property (e.g., plant, equipment, employees) and intangible property (e.g., right to engage in normal business, right to make a profit). Due to the absence of statutory laws regulating labor relations, the judiciary exerted great control over conflicts of interests between employers and employees from the early 1800s to the 1930s.

Criminal Conspiracy Doctrine

Under English common law it was illegal for two or more workers to join together for the purpose of pressuring their employer to improve their wages or working conditions. In 1806, one of the first major labor law cases in the United States, known as the "Cordwainers case," occurred when a group of journeymen shoemakers in Philadelphia were indicted, convicted, and fined $8 each for forming an illegal criminal conspiracy. The shoemakers had joined together in an attempt to raise their wages and refused to work with nonmembers or at a wage rate less than they demanded. Twelve jurors (all businessmen) found the shoemakers guilty of forming an illegal combination for the purpose of raising their own wages while injuring those who did not join the coalition.[2]

The prosecutor in the trial stated: "Our position is that no man is at liberty to combine, conspire, confederate and unlawfully agree to regulate the whole body of workmen in the city. The defendants are not indicted for regulating their own individual wages but for undertaking by a combination, to regulate the price of labor of others as well as their own. It must be known to you, every society of people are affected by such confederacies; they are injurious to the public good and against the public interest."[3]

The application of the common law criminal conspiracy doctrine to attempts by employees to organize unions aroused much public protest, not only from employees but also from factory owners who feared the closing of their factories if their employees' dissatisfaction grew too strong. These concerns were undoubtedly considered in 1842 when the Supreme Judicial Court of Massachusetts in **Commonwealth v. Hunt** set aside the conviction for criminal conspiracy of seven members of the Journeymen Bootmakers' Society, who refused to work in shops where nonmembers were employed at less than their scheduled rate of $2 per pair of boots.[4] While not rejecting the criminal conspiracy doctrine, the court instituted an ends/means test to be applied on a case-by-case basis to determine if the ends (goals) sought by the combination of workers were legal and if the means (tactics) used by the workers were also lawful. The court concluded it was not illegal for workers to seek to protect their own economic interests in maintaining a desired wage rate, nor was it illegal to refuse to work as a means of encouraging an employer not to hire an individual at a lower wage rate thus undercutting the current established rate of pay for a particular type of labor. Of course, the employer was free to replace any employee who refused to work in order to continue normal business operations.

Civil Conspiracy Doctrine

The *Commonwealth v. Hunt* (1842) decision virtually ended the use of the criminal conspiracy doctrine in labor relations. However, the courts soon developed the civil conspiracy doctrine, which held that a group involved in concerted activities could inflict harm on other parties (e.g., customers or other employees) even though the workers were pursuing a valid objective in their own interest.[5] In *Vegelahn v. Guntner* (Mass. S.Ct. 1896), an injunction was issued against a union that was picketing their employer to obtain higher wages and shorter hours.[6] Although the court agreed that higher wages and shorter work hours were legitimate ends for workers to pursue, the court concluded that picketing accompanied by threats of violence could unlawfully intimidate individuals who desired to continue to work for the employer or customers who sought to do business with the employer and, therefore, was an unlawful means to accomplish an otherwise lawful end. Only where both the workers' ends and means were lawful would the concerted activity be permitted.

Breach of Contract (Contractual Interference) and Use of the Labor Injunction

Around 1880 many states began loosening restrictions on who could serve on juries (e.g., removing property ownership requirements), which permitted more hourly workers to perform jury duty service. As a consequence, juries became less willing to convict workers of criminal or civil conspiracy charges. Employers turned to the courts for a quicker and more reliable means of restricting employee concerted activities, which the legal system provided in the form of a **labor injunction**.[7] A labor injunction was a court order prohibiting or restricting certain activities in conjunction with a labor dispute. The advantage of a labor injunction over a jury trial was that a preliminary labor injunction could be issued by a judge without a formal jury hearing and was often based solely on statements or evidence provided by the employer intended to demonstrate the need for the labor injunction. It might be weeks or months before the labor organization might get a chance to challenge the credibility of the employer's evidence or offer alternative evidence at a hearing to show why a labor injunction was not appropriate. By that time the employer had often already prevailed in ending the labor dispute on terms favorable to the employer's interest aided by the labor injunction's restrictions on workers' ability to use effective economic pressure tactics against the employer.

The courts' long-standing interest in enforcing the terms of contracts led many employers to require their employees to sign a **yellow-dog contract**—an agreement stating that they would neither join a union nor assist in organizing one.[8] Because this contract would be a condition of continued employment, any violation would allow the company to discharge the employee. More importantly, if any outside union organizer attempted to solicit employees to join a union or engage in other concerted activity such as a strike to improve wages or working conditions, such activity could be enjoined by a judge on the grounds that it was an attempt to interfere with a legal contractual relationship between the employer and its employees. Union organizers who violated the court order could then be charged with contempt of court and possibly fined and imprisoned.

Application of Antitrust Legislation to Labor Unions

Another legal obstacle confronting labor organizations in the late 1800s was the application of antitrust law to restrict union organizing and bargaining activities. Congress passed the **Sherman Antitrust Act** in 1890 to regulate the increasing power of certain large corporations to engage in anticompetitive practices (e.g., cutthroat pricing; restricting competitor's access to necessary raw materials) that tended to drive smaller firms out of the marketplace.[9] The Sherman Antitrust Act neither explicitly included nor excluded labor unions from coverage as an illegal combination in restraint of interstate commerce. However, all of the congressional debate and testimony leading to passage of the bill focused on the business practices of employers, not labor organizations.

The U.S. Supreme Court decided to apply the Sherman Antitrust Act to labor organizations in the 1908 landmark decision *Loewe v. Lawlor* (better known as the *Danbury Hatters* case).[10] The United Hatters of North America (UHU), having organized 70 of 82 firms in the hat-manufacturing industry, wanted to organize Loewe & Co., one of the few remaining nonunion employers located in Danbury, Connecticut. As a part of the UHU's campaign to gain union recognition as the bargaining agent for employees at Loewe & Co., the union organized a nationwide boycott assisted by the American Federation of Labor (AFL) directed at persuading all retailers, wholesalers, and customers not to buy, sell, or handle the company's hats. The boycott was successful, prompting Loewe & Co. to sue alleging that the UHU's boycott interfered with the company's ability to engage in its normal interstate commerce of selling hats. The Supreme Court ruled that unions were covered under the Sherman Act and that the union's boycott did illegally obstruct Loewe & Co.'s ability to engage in its normal interstate commerce. The Court awarded the employer triple damages ($252,000), as provided for under the Sherman Act and ruled that individual union members could be held liable for paying the damage award if the labor organization itself did not have sufficient funds to pay the claim.

The *Loewe* v. *Lawlor* decision had several important impacts on labor relations. First, the decision essentially eliminated the use of the boycott, which had previously been considered a very effective union tactic for bringing economic pressure against an employer to persuade the employer to agree to union proposals. It also raised concerns in the minds of some union leaders as to whether the courts might extend the ruling on boycotts to include other union tactics (e.g., picketing, strikes, or handbilling) also intended to impose economic pressure on an employer's business operations. Second, the Court's decision to hold individual union members personally liable for damages resulting from the actions of their labor organization dealt a serious blow to union organizing efforts. Not only could an employee face discharge for participating in union organizing activity, but if the organizing activity was declared to be an antitrust violation, the employee might also risk loss of personal assets acquired over the individual's work career.

One positive aspect of the *Loewe* v. *Lawlor* decision was that it clearly demonstrated to AFL president Samuel Gompers and other labor leaders the need to expand state and local union political efforts to include Congress and other federal branches of government. An aggressive campaign led by the AFL to address labor concerns about the Court's interpretation of the Sherman Antitrust Act led to the enactment of the Clayton Act in 1914. Included among the Clayton Act's amendments to the Sherman Act were the following provisions:

[The] labor of a human being is not a commodity or article of commerce. Nothing contained in the antitrust laws shall be construed to forbid the existence and operations of labor [unions] . . . nor shall such organizations . . . be held or construed to be illegal combinations or conspiracies in restraint of trade.

No restraining order or injunction shall be granted . . . in any case between an employer and employees . . . growing out of a dispute concerning terms or conditions of employment, unless necessary to prevent irreparable injury to property. . . .

> No such restraining order . . . shall prohibit any person or persons . . . from ceasing to perform work . . . recommending, advising, or persuading others by peaceful means so to do . . . peacefully persuading any person to work or abstain from working . . . peacefully assembling in a lawful manner, and for lawful purposes.[11]

When AFL president Gompers read the provisions of the Clayton Act, he proclaimed it U.S. labor's Magna Carta because it would free organized labor from the restraints of antitrust prosecution. Gompers's joy, however, was short-lived, as a series of Supreme Court decisions in the 1920s left no doubt that the Clayton Act was not labor's Magna Carta.[12] Rather than viewing the Clayton Act as a repudiation of the Court's prior interpretation of the Sherman Act, the Supreme Court interpreted Congress's intent in passing the Clayton Act as only reaffirming a labor organization's right to exist so long as it sought to achieve lawful ends using lawful means. In fact, the Clayton Act hurt union growth and development more than it helped because under the act, employers could now seek labor injunctions for alleged antitrust violations on their own, whereas under the Sherman Act only a U.S. district attorney could seek such an injunction from a court.

Some states attempted to address perceived labor law deficiencies on their own by enacting state labor legislation to grant legal bargaining rights to employees or restrict the circumstances under which a state court judge could issue a labor injunction to ban employee activity during a labor dispute. For example, in 1921, the U.S. Supreme Court declared a law enacted by the Arizona legislature and upheld by the Arizona state supreme court unconstitutional in violation of the Fifth and Fourteenth Amendments.[13] The Arizona law sought to deny a judge the right to issue a labor injunction to halt otherwise peaceful picketing during a labor dispute. The Court majority declared that the Arizona law unlawfully denied the employer of a restaurant being picketed during a wage dispute his due process and equal protection right to obtain a labor injunction to prevent the picketing from damaging normal restaurant operations. The dissenting opinion argued that states such as Arizona ought to be free to determine for themselves whether some restrictions on employer property rights (e.g., limiting access to injunctive relief) might not be imposed if necessary to protect other legitimate rights of employees to participate in bargaining over work conditions.

The 1920s were a difficult period for organized labor. Although a period of general economic growth and prosperity, unions confronted an environment where labor injunctions were easier to obtain; the court system strongly supported employer property rights; favorable legislation protecting employees' right to organize and bargain collectively was absent; and employers commonly used antiunion tactics (such as "goon squads," yellow-dog contracts, and blacklisting). Although the Railway Labor Act (covered later in this chapter), passed in 1926, granted bargaining rights to railroad employees, this was primarily a time of regrouping, self-analysis, and trying to preserve the status quo for most unions.

The Norris–La Guardia Act

The 1929 stock market crash and ensuing economic depression forced a reassessment of the extent to which private-sector employers could manage the economic welfare of the country. As unemployment rose and individuals' savings declined, political pressure mounted on Congress to take a more active role in regulating the economy, including more protection for basic workers' rights. In 1932, Congress passed the Norris–La Guardia Act (also called the Federal Anti-Injunction Act) to accomplish three basic public policy goals.[14] First, to allow employees a greater voice in seeking to advance and protect their legitimate interests, Congress limited the power of federal courts to intervene in labor disputes through the issuance of a labor injunction. Activities that previously had been routinely enjoined to the benefit of employer interests were now lawful to engage in (e.g., peaceful picketing or publicity; encouraging employees to join a union; union economic or legal aid provided to employees during a labor dispute). A temporary restraining order obtained solely on the basis of an employer's statements could be effective only for five days to restrict some alleged unlawful employee conduct. To extend the ban through the issuance of a temporary or permanent labor injunction, an employer must prove in a hearing in which employees or their union representative can offer counterevidence that the following conditions exist:

1. Unlawful acts have been threatened or committed;
2. substantial and irreparable injury to the employer's property has or will likely occur as a result of such unlawful acts;
3. greater injury would be inflicted on the employer by denial of an injunction than on the union (employees) by granting an injunction;
4. the employer has no other adequate legal remedy;
5. public safety officers are either unable or unwilling to adequately protect the employer's property; and
6. the employer has satisfied any existing legal duty to bargain in good faith in an effort to settle the labor dispute (including the offer of mediation, voluntary arbitration, etc.) before going to court.

Injunctive orders issued by a court are required to describe the specific conduct being enjoined, eliminating the previous use of general or vaguely worded "blanket injunctions."[15]

The Norris–La Guardia Act also declared that a yellow-dog contract would be unenforceable in federal courts and thus no longer a basis for obtaining a labor injunction to prevent conduct that might breach such an employment contract.[16] However, many employers continued to discharge or otherwise discriminate against employees for engaging in union activities.

The Norris–La Guardia Act also encouraged the courts to adopt a more impartial or neutral role in seeking to protect and enforce the legitimate rights of employers and employees. Acts for which a labor injunction was not obtainable under the Norris–La Guardia Act were no longer considered to be antitrust violations under the Clayton Act.[16] Rejecting the Supreme Court's interpretation and application of the antitrust laws during the 1920s, Congress reinstated the use of the economic boycott as a legitimate means of worker protest so long as it was used to pursue a lawful purpose and applied in a lawful manner. The Norris–La Guardia Act also expressed congressional support for the process of collective bargaining as an appropriate means for employees to improve and protect their employment interests.

Although the passage of the Norris–La Guardia Act signaled a change in U.S. labor relations policy, the act did not establish an independent administrative agency to enforce the act's provisions. This meant that organized labor had to pursue enforcement through the judicial system, which historically had not been responsive to labor's needs and interests. Another deficiency of the Norris–La Guardia Act was that no specific employer unfair labor practices were identified and prohibited. These deficiencies were not resolved until three years later.

The National Labor Relations (Wagner) Act of 1935

Franklin D. Roosevelt, who was backed strongly by labor unions, was elected president in 1932 along with a new Congress receptive to labor legislation as a means of ending a long depression. President Roosevelt promised Americans a "New Deal" based upon a belief that market forces alone were incapable of putting the public's interests ahead of private ownership's interests, creating a need for government involvement in managing the economic welfare of the country. One of the first acts of this new administration was to encourage Congress to pass the **National Industrial Recovery Act** (NIRA), a law designed to stabilize economic activity by allowing businesses to form associations that would draw up codes of fair competition to standardize marketing, pricing, financial, and other practices.[17] Upon approval of the codes by the National Recovery Administration, firms could display the "Blue Eagle" symbol that supposedly signified compliance and identified firms from which customers should purchase their goods and services. Section 7 of the NIRA required the codes to guarantee employees the right to unionize without employer interference, and a National Labor Board (NLB) was later established to help settle disputes and to determine violations under Section 7.

Because the NIRA did not require employers to bargain with unions and the NLB could not enforce its orders effectively, the law was not very effective in protecting employees' rights to organize and bargain collectively. In 1934 Congress issued a joint resolution calling for the president to establish a National Labor Relations Board (NLRB) to investigate violations under Section 7 of NIRA and to conduct elections to determine whether employees wanted independent union representation.[18] The new board, created like its predecessor by executive order of the president, had trouble enforcing its orders and determining appropriate employee organizational units for conducting elections. In 1935, the Supreme Court ruled the NIRA unconstitutional when one of its codes of fair competition was applied to an employer engaged in intrastate commerce going beyond Congress's authority to regulate interstate commerce.[19]

One month later, Senator Robert Wagner, chairman of the NLRB and an active participant in labor law matters, steered through Congress a separate labor relations law—the **National Labor Relations** (Wagner) **Act** (NLRA).[20] The NLRA established a new national labor policy that sought to ensure the free flow of commerce; labor peace and stability; and protection of the public's interests by encouraging the process of collective bargaining and preventing employer interference with the exercise of employee rights defined in the act. The **National Labor Relations Board** (NLRB) was authorized to investigate and decide unfair labor practice charges and conduct representation elections (other provisions are covered later in the chapter).

Congress perceived that without legal protection for employee rights, the economic power of employers far exceeded that of individual employees and inevitably led to labor unrest, which had a detrimental effect on economic growth and the public's interests. "The Wagner Act is premised on an industrial relations model that there are two classes in the industrial world, labor and management, and that these two classes have very different, in fact opposing interests."[21]

Employee rights protected from employer discrimination in Section 7 of the NLRA included the right to form or join a union, bargain collectively, or engage in other concerted activity for mutual aid and protection (see Exhibit 3.1). Common employer tactics used previously to discourage union activity such as discharge or refusal to hire for union activity, company spies, blacklisting, employee representation plans (company unions), and yellow-dog contracts were declared to be unfair labor practices by the NLRA.

Many employers believed the NLRA would be ruled unconstitutional like the National Industry Recovery Act.[22] However, the Supreme Court declared the NLRA constitutional in 1937, recognizing the important impact labor relations can have on interstate commerce and thus endorsing Congress's right to regulate labor relations.[23] With Supreme Court approval of the NLRA and improved economic conditions in the United States, unions experienced tremendous growth, almost tripling in membership to 8.4 million members by 1941.[24]

Union activities in the decade following passage of the NLRA caused many to believe that the labor relations pendulum had swung too far in favor of unions and the exercise of collective employee rights. Examples of union actions that precipitated much public concern were strikes over union representation rights between competing AFL and CIO unions, union strikes or boycotts over bargaining issues, a union refusal in some cases to negotiate in good faith with an employer, and pressure on job applicants to become union members at companies with a negotiated **closed shop** union security clause under which an employer agreed to hire only job applicants who were members of a union representing the firm's workers.

As a reaction to employer criticisms of the NLRA and growing public concern over organized labor's actions, in 1947 Congress amended the NLRA by enacting the **Labor Management Relations** (Taft-Hartley) **Act** (LMRA).[25] Leaving the original language of the NLRA virtually unchanged, the LMRA added language intended to address certain identified deficiencies and direct more attention to the legitimate rights of individual employees and employers involved in

Exhibit 3.1

Rights of Employees

> **Sec. 7**—Employees shall have the right to self-organization, to form, join, or assist labor organizations, to bargain collectively through representatives of their own choosing, and to engage in other concerted activities for the purpose of collective bargaining or other mutual aid or protection, and shall also have the right to refrain from any or all such activities except to the extent that such right may be affected by an agreement requiring membership in a labor organization as a condition of employment as authorized in section 8(a)(3).
>
> SOURCE: Labor-Management Relations Act, 1947, as amended.

the labor relations process. Calling it a "slave labor act," labor groups immediately mounted a successful campaign to have President Truman veto the bill; however, Congress easily overrode Truman's veto.

Significant Changes under the LMRA

To emphasize Congress's intent to fairly balance labor relations policy, the National Labor Relations Act (NLRA) was renamed the *Labor Management Relations Act* (LMRA). Similar to employer prohibitions included in the NLRA, a section of union unfair labor practices was added to the LMRA, making it illegal for unions to engage in actions that discriminated against any employee's exercise of rights protected under Section 7 of the LMRA. Language was added to Section 7 granting individual employees the right to refrain from engaging in otherwise protected concerted activity (except as that right might be limited by a lawful union security clause requiring membership or support of a labor organization).

Congress agreed that membership in a particular labor organization should not be a precondition for employment and therefore made the closed shop union security clause illegal. However, Congress recognized that some level of union security was necessary to ensure that employees who desired union representation could achieve a reasonably effective voice in protecting and advancing their workplace interests. Employers and unions were permitted under the LMRA to negotiate voluntary agreements to either require an employee join a union (**union shop** clause) or pay a fee equivalent to regular union dues and initiation fees (**agency shop** clause) if the employee held a job in a bargaining unit represented by the union. Congress did agree to permit individual states to pass a more restrictive ban on union security agreements applicable to their state (a so-called **right-to-work law**). Union security issues will be discussed further in Chapter 4.

The LMRA addressed employer criticism of an NLRB policy that severely restricted an employer's right to speak out on the question of union representation during an organizing campaign and a Supreme Court decision finding that policy an unconstitutional prohibition of employers' First Amendment free speech right.[26] Section 8 (c) of the LMRA protects the expressing of any opinions or arguments about labor relations issues *so long as such expression contains no threat of reprisal or promise of benefit.*

To encourage unions and employers to live up to their negotiated contractual terms, Section 301 permitted the parties to a collective bargaining agreement to sue in court for breach of contract if necessary to obtain the other party's compliance with the terms of the agreement. Prior to this change an employer was forced to sue separately individual union members who participated in a work stoppage in violation of a contractual no-strike agreement, which was both time consuming and expensive. While permitting an employer to sue a union directly for economic damages under Section 301, Congress removed the right to sue individual union members to recover economic damages from a breach of a labor agreement's terms.

Since 1959, there have been two successful legislative attempts to enact major changes in the LMRA. The LMRA was first extended to cover the U.S. Postal Service in 1970 (see Chapter 13) and then to cover private-sector profit and nonprofit health-care institutions in 1974.

Labor Management Reporting and Disclosure (Landrum-Griffin) Act

In the late 1950s, a special Senate committee headed by John McClellan vigorously pursued the abuses of power and corruption by some union leaders, particularly those of the Teamsters and specifically of Dave Beck and James Hoffa.[27] Exposing shocking examples of union corruption and abuses of power, Congress reacted in 1959 by passing the **Labor-Management Reporting and Disclosure (Landrum-Griffin) Act (LMRDA).**[28] The LMRDA is primarily designed to protect the rights of individual union members in their relations with their own union and to ensure that labor organizations operate in a democratic and financially responsible manner. Unlike the LMRA, which applies to both union and nonunion employees, the LMRDA covers only individuals who are members of a labor organization.

For example, the LMRDA requires that all local union officers be elected by secret ballot vote of union members at least once every three years and national union officers at least once every five years. Union members must approve any increase or decrease in the amount charged for union membership dues, initiation fees, or other special assessments. A union's constitution and by-laws are considered to be a binding contract between the union and its members, enforceable in court. Unions are required to file annual reports with the U.S. Department of Labor containing information on union assets and liabilities, union officer salaries, and current union operating rules. These reports are available to the public. Labor organizations are among the most regulated organizations in U.S. society today.

Title VII of LMRDA did contain some amendments to the LMRA. Of most importance was the addition of Section 303 to the LMRA granting neutral, secondary employers harmed by an unlawful secondary strike, boycott, or picket a right to sue the guilty labor organization for economic damages.

National Labor Relations Board (NLRB)

The rights of employees provided by the LMRA are not self-enforcing, and a weakness of the previous NIRA had been the lack of any effective enforcement mechanism. Coupled with a court system that previously favored employer property rights over employee rights, Congress took the extraordinary step in 1935 of designating an independent federal administrative agency, the **National Labor Relations Board** (NLRB), to be the primary interpreter and administrator of the newly created NLRA. To ensure the constitutionality of the NLRA, Congress provided that unfair labor practice decisions of the NLRB could be appealed for review to an appropriate federal court. The courts were instructed by Congress to pay great deference to the policies of the NLRB in interpreting what Congress intended the law to accomplish.

The NLRB is headquartered in Washington, D.C., and headed by a five-member panel termed the Board.[29] Board members are nominated by the president to serve a five-year term and must be confirmed by the U.S. Senate. Terms of Board members are staggered to ensure that not all vacancies occur at the same time, although due to delays in the nomination and confirmation process there have been periods where several Board seats were vacant at the same time, affecting the ability of the NLRB to function effectively.

As political appointees, Board members generally reflect the basic labor relations philosophy of the president who nominated them. The nomination

LABOR RELATIONS IN ACTION

Selected Recent Labor Relations Cases Decided by the U.S. Supreme Court and the NLRB

Liability for Filing a Retaliatory Lawsuit

In a 5–4 decision, the Court concluded that the NLRB could not impose liability on an employer who filed an unsuccessful lawsuit against several unions alleging unlawful acts if the employer could prove there was a reasonable basis for filing the lawsuit. *BE & K Construction Company v. NLRB*, 122 S. Ct. 2390 (2002).

Back Pay Remedy

In a 5–4 decision, the Court ruled that the Immigration Reform and Control Act prevents the NLRB from awarding a back-pay remedy to an undocumented alien even though an employer can be found guilty of committing an unfair labor practice in violation of the undocumented alien's employee rights under the LMRA. The NLRB could impose other remedies for the employer's unfair labor practice such as a cease-and-desist order and an order to post notices admitting the unlawful conduct and informing company employees of their basic employee rights under the LMRA. *Hoffman Plastic Compounds, Inc. v. NLRB*, 122 S. Ct. 1275 (2002).

Definition of a Supervisor

The Court unanimously agreed that the party asserting that an employee is a supervisor and thus excluded from coverage under the LMRA has the burden of proving the employee's supervisory status. The Court split 5–4 in finding that the NLRB's application of the three-part test to determine supervisory status was incorrect in the case at issue. To be a supervisor under the LMRA, an individual must (1) perform at least one of the specified supervisory functions (e.g., hiring, performance evaluation); (2) using independent judgment not of a clerical or routine nature; and (3) in the interests of the employer. The Court refused to enforce the Board's determination that 12 registered nurses did not use independent judgment in carrying out supervisory functions because such decisions involved the exercise of ordinary professional or technical nursing judgment. The Court agreed that the NLRB had a right to inquire regarding the degree of independent judgment an individual employee exercised on a case-by-case basis but could not automatically exclude an employee merely on the grounds that the judgment exercised was professional or technical in nature. *NLRB v. Kentucky River Community Care, Inc.*, 121 S.Ct. 1861 (2001).

Union Recognition

The Court unanimously upheld the NLRB's decision that an employer may not refuse to bargain with an incumbent union on the grounds that the union had lost majority status shortly after the employer had previously entered into a contract with such union. *Auciello Iron Works, Inc. v. NLRB*, 116 S. Ct 1754 (1996).

Definition of "Employees" Under LMRA

Even though the majority of work duties performed by members of a "live chicken catching crew" were performed at the site of chicken farmers who subcontracted with the chicken-processing plant to raise the chickens to a marketable age (size), crew members were "employees" of the chicken processing plant and not excluded from coverage under the LMRA as agricultural laborers. *Holly Farms Corp. v. NLRB*, 116 S. Ct. 1396 (1996).

Union Organizers

The Court unanimously upheld the NLRB's decision that paid union organizers are "employees" within the meaning of the LMRA when applying for a job or after being hired by the employer. Therefore, individuals acting as "salts" are protected against employer retaliation in the form of discharge or discipline for participating in any protected activity under Section 7 of the act, such as attempting to organize a union among employees. *NLRB v. Town & Country*, 116 S. Ct. 450 (1995).

Successor Employer Bargaining

Overruling a 1999 Board policy, the Board returned to the previous policy, which holds that an incumbent union in a successor employer situation is entitled to a rebuttable presumption of continuing majority support. This would permit employees to file a valid decertification petition or another union to file a valid representation petition or the successor employer to file an employer election petition challenging the union's presumption of continuing majority support. A successor employer's duty to bargain with an incumbent union continues until the date on which a lack of majority employee support for the union can be established. *MV Transportation*, 337 NLRB No. 129 (2002).

Unilateral Employer Withdrawal of Union Recognition

Applying legal principles established by the U.S. Supreme Court in *Allentown Mack Sales & Service v. NLRB*, 522 U.S. 359 (1998), the Board held that an employer may unilaterally withdraw union recognition of the exclusive bargaining unit representative only if the employer can prove the union has lost majority employee support as of the date of the employer's unilateral withdrawal of recognition. Alternatively, an employer may obtain an NLRB supervised election to determine if the majority of bargaining unit employees support the incumbent union if the employer can demonstrate a good-faith reasonable uncertainty regarding the union's continued majority support. The Board would prefer employees directly express their desire for or against union representation through a secret ballot representation election rather than an employer acting unilaterally to withdraw union recognition. *Levitz Furniture Company of the Pacific, Inc.*, 333 NLRB No. 105 (2001).

Duty to Bargain

When an employer has been found guilty of bad faith bargaining and issued a remedial order to bargain in good faith, such bargaining must occur for a "reasonable time" before the union's majority status as bargaining representative can be challenged. "Reasonable time" refers to a period no less than six months nor longer than one year. The exact length of time good-faith bargaining would be required is determined on a case-by-case basis based on several factors, including: whether the negotiations are for an initial contract or seek to amend an existing agreement, the complexity of the issues being negotiated and the parties' bargaining procedures, the total amount of time elapsed since the start of bargaining and the number of bargaining meetings held, the amount of progress the parties have made and how close the parties appear to be to reaching a settlement, and whether the parties have reached a good faith bargaining impasse. *Lee Lumber and Building Material Corp.*, 334 NLRB No. 62 (2001).   *Continued*

Employer Use of Employees in Pro-company Union Representation Election Campaign Videos

While finding that the employer in the instant case unlawfully solicited employees to appear in a campaign election video, the Board established four clear conditions, which, if met, would permit employers to solicit employees to appear in a union election campaign video. To be lawful: (1) the solicitation to participate in the campaign video must be in the form of a general announcement that discloses the purpose of filming and assures employees that participation is voluntary; no retaliation will occur against employees who do not voluntarily choose to participate, and no rewards or benefits will be provided to those employees who do participate; (2) employees may not be pressured to make a decision regarding their participation in the presence of a supervisor; (3) there can be no unlawful conduct connected with the employer's solicitation for voluntary participants; and (4) the solicitation cannot occur in a coercive atmosphere created by the employer's commission of other unfair labor practices. *Allegheny Ludlum Corporation*, 333 NLRB No. 109 (2001).

Coverage of Teaching and Research Graduate Assistants

The Board ruled that graduate teaching and research assistants at a private university met the definition of "employee" and thus were entitled to exercise protected employee rights under the LMRA. *New York University*, 332 NLRB No. 111 (2000).

Coverage of Medical Interns, Residents, and Fellows (House Staff)

Reversing previous policy, the Board ruled that hospital interns and residents in a private hospital are employees covered by the NLRA even though they are students. Therefore, these employees have the right to organize and join a union and participate in other protected concerted activities. *Boston Medical Center Corp.*, 330 N.L.R.B. 152 (1999).

Weingarten Rights Applied to Nonunion Employees

By a 3–2 vote, the Board reinstated a previous policy granting nonunion (unrepresented) employees covered by the LMRA a right to have a co-worker present during an investigatory interview with management where the employee had reason to believe that he or she might be subject to disciplinary or discharge action as a result of the investigation. Exercise of such a right is viewed as a form of concerted activity for mutual aid or protection. A nonunion employee also has a right to know the general nature of the alleged violation and a reasonable opportunity to meet with his or her co-worker prior to any investigatory meeting with management. *Weingarten rights* also apply to union-represented employees. *Epilepsy Foundation of Northeast Ohio*, 331 NLRB 676 (2000) enforced in part, *Epilepsy Foundation of Northeast Ohio v. NLRB*, 268 F.3d 1095 (D.C. Cir. 2002). See also *NLRB v. Weingarten*, 420 U.S. 251 (1975). ■

process is subject to intense lobbying by employers, unions, and other outside interest groups (e.g., National Right to Work Committee), who recognize the important role the Board serves in determining the balance between protection for employer and employee interests, particularly on legal issues where such interests may conflict. "Interpretations of the facts and law governing union-management relations is . . . dependent in part on the makeup of the board."[30] One study reported finding an apparent pro-employer or pro-union bias in only 20 percent of Board case decisions.[31] Recent decisions shown in the "Labor Relations in Action" box demonstrate the importance of presidential appointments to the Board and to the courts.

The Board has two primary responsibilities. One responsibility is to prevent employer and union unfair labor practices as defined by the LMRA, as amended, which interfere with the exercise of employee rights protected by the act. This responsibility is carried out primarily through the investigation, prosecution, and remedy of unfair labor practices. The second responsibility is to determine if covered employees desire representation by an independent labor organization for purposes of collective bargaining under the act. The Board establishes and conducts certification procedures to determine if a majority of eligible employees desire a specific labor organization to represent them for purposes of collective bargaining. Approximately two-thirds of the Board's case load involves unfair labor practice cases and one-third involves representation determination cases. The Board exercises final administrative decision-making authority in all unfair labor practice and representation cases.

The Board delegates authority to the general counsel and staff attorneys to investigate and prosecute unfair labor practice charges. The general counsel is nominated by the president to serve a four-year term and must be confirmed by the U.S. Senate. As with Board members, the general counsel's nomination and confirmation process is subject to interest group politics.

A major responsibility of the general counsel's office is to conduct a preliminary investigation of each unfair labor practice charge to determine if sufficient (prima facie) evidence exists to conclude that an unfair labor practice may have occurred. If insufficient evidence of a violation is found, the general counsel has the authority to dismiss an unfair labor practice charge and there is no appeal of that decision. This gives the general counsel tremendous influence in helping to determine the policy-making agenda of the Board, since the Board announces new policies or alters existing policies through the issuance of unfair labor practice decisions. The only cases in which the Board will have an opportunity to render an unfair labor practice decision are those cases in which the General Counsel's investigation concluded that evidence of an unfair labor practice existed.

The general counsel is also responsible for representing the NLRB whenever a Board decision or order is appealed to a federal court or when the Board seeks a court order to enforce its decision. The general counsel also serves as a legal advisor to Board members on matters pertaining to the interpretation or application of the LMRA or how past Board policies and procedures have faired upon review by the federal courts. The general counsel relies upon staff attorneys located at the NLRB's headquarters in Washington, D.C., as well as each regional NLRB office to help carry out the responsibilities of the general counsel's office.

For employees, a union, or a management practitioner, contact with the NLRB typically occurs at the regional or resident office level. The NLRB maintains

32 regional, 3 subregional, and 17 resident offices located throughout the country to handle unfair labor practice and representation election cases.[32] Each regional office is headed by a regional director who also manages any subregional or resident offices located within the regional office's geographic jurisdiction. The regional director and staff work with the general counsel to investigate unfair labor practice charges and are delegated authority by the Board to administer all representation election procedures. More than 90 percent of unfair labor practice cases filed annually are resolved at the regional office level. NLRB regional and field office locations handle more than 150,000 annual requests for information from employers, unions, and employees regarding the LMRA, as amended and NLRB policies and procedures.

Employer and Employee Coverage under the LMRA, as Amended

To promote the public policy goals of the LMRA as amended, Congress sought to include as many employers and employees as possible under the statute's coverage. The U.S. Constitution restricts the right of Congress to regulation of private sector employers whose operations have *the potential to vitally affect interstate commerce.* If an employer is subject to coverage under the statute, the employer's employees are also covered (protected) by the statute unless they fall into a category of employee specifically excluded from coverage (e.g., agricultural workers). The term **NLRB jurisdiction** refers to those employers and employees to whom the NLRB can apply the language of the LMRA.

The NLRB may refuse to assert jurisdiction in cases where it believes the effect on interstate commerce is minor (de minimus)—for example, state-regulated industries such as real estate, horseracing, and dog racing. Individual states may assert jurisdiction over any case where the NLRB has declined to do so.[33]

From 1935 to 1950 the Board relied on the judgment of individual regional directors to determine an employer's ability to affect interstate commerce on a case-by-case basis. To reduce the inconsistencies inherent in this approach and improve the objectivity of decisions, the Board adopted a set of monetary standards (guidelines) applicable to different types of employer operations (see Exhibit 3.2). In 1959 as part of the LMRDA, Congress prohibited the Board from refusing to apply or altering the monetary standards then in effect without congressional approval. The standards measure the total dollar volume of an employer's operations, either gross revenue or the value of products or services sold (outflow) or purchased (inflow) over a 12-month period (e.g., the most recent calendar or business tax year or 12 months immediately preceding the filing of an unfair labor practice charge or representation election petition). Meeting the specified dollar threshold using any one of the available measurements is sufficient to permit the NLRB to assert jurisdiction over the case and apply the terms of the LMRA.

Congress excluded some individuals from the definition of an employee subject to coverage under the LMRA, as amended. Specifically excluded by statutory language are:

- Agricultural laborers—An employee whose primary duties involve ordinary farming operations performed prior to a product's readiness for initial sale.[34] Some individual states (e.g., Arizona, California, Hawaii, Idaho, Kansas, Massachusetts, Wisconsin) have enacted a collective bargaining law that covers agricultural laborers in their state.

Exhibit 3.2

NLRB Jurisdictional Standards Determining Employer Coverage under the LMRA

- **Nonretail Business**—Direct or indirect sales through others of goods to consumers in other states (called *outflow*), of at least $50,000 a year; or direct or indirect purchases through others of goods from suppliers in other States (called *inflow*), of at least $50,000 a year.
- **Retail Business**—At least $500,000 total annual volume of business.
- **Office Building**—Total annual revenue of $100,000, of which $25,000 or more is derived from organizations that meet any of the standards except the indirect outflow and indirect inflow standards for nonretail firms.
- **Public Utility**—At least $250,000 total annual volume of business, or $50,000 direct or indirect outflow or inflow.
- **Newspaper**—At least $200,000 total annual volume of business.
- **Radio, Telegraph, Television, and Telephone Firms**—At least $100,000 total annual volume of business.
- **Private Health-Care Institutions**—(e.g., hospital, HMO, clinic, nursing home)—At least $250,000 total annual volume of business for hospitals; at least $100,000 for nursing homes, visiting nurses associations, and related facilities; at least $250,000 for all other types of private health-care institutions.
- **Hotel, Motel, Residential Apartment Houses**—At least $500,000 total annual volume of business.
- **Transportation Enterprises, Links, and Channels of Interstate Commerce** (e.g., interstate bus, truck)—At least $50,000 total annual income from furnishing interstate passenger and freight transportation services *or* performing services valued at $50,000 or more for businesses which meet any of the jurisdictional standards except the indirect outflow and inflow standards established for nonretail firms. [*Note:* Airline and Railroad operations are covered under the Railway Labor Act (RLA), not the LMRA, and thus are not subject to NLRB jurisdiction].
- **Transit Systems**—At least $250,000 total annual volume of business.
- **Taxicab Companies**—At least $500,000 total annual volume of business.
- **Associations**—The annual business of each association member is totaled to determine whether any of the standards apply.
- **Private Universities and Colleges**—At least $1 million gross annual revenue from all sources (excluding contributions not available for operating expenses due to limitations imposed by the donor).
- **Any Firm with a Substantial Impact on National Defense.**
- **U.S. Postal Service** by enactment of the Postal Reorganization Act of 1970.
- **Symphony Orchestras**—At least $1 million gross annual revenue from all sources (excluding contributions not available for operating expenses due to limitations imposed by the donor).
- **Social Service Organizations Not Covered under Any Other Standard**—At least $250,000 gross annual revenue.

SOURCE: Office of the General Counsel, NLRB, *A Guide to Basic Law and Procedures under the National Labor Relations Act* (Washington, D.C.: U.S. Government Printing Office, 1997), pp. 35–37.

- Individuals employed by an employer covered under the Railway Labor Act (rail and airline industries).
- Individuals employed as a domestic by a private household (e.g., cook, nanny, butler, chauffeur, gardener, personal assistant).
- Individuals employed by a parent or spouse. On a case-by-case basis, other individuals may be excluded from a particular bargaining unit because evidence demonstrates their self-interest is more closely aligned with that of ownership rather than other employees in a bargaining unit.

- Individuals employed by a public-sector employer (federal, state, or local). Public-sector labor relations issues are discussed further in Chapter 13. U.S. Postal Service employees are the only exception to the public employee exclusion rule. As part of a settlement to end an illegal strike by postal workers, Congress enacted the **Postal Reorganization Act of 1970,** which placed postal workers under coverage of the LMRA, greatly expanding the number and types of issues over which workers could legally bargain. Unlike other private-sector employees covered by the LMRA, postal workers have no legal right to strike but may invoke final and binding arbitration as a means of resolving interest disputes that may occur during contract negotiations. Interest arbitration will be discussed further in Chapter 9.

- Independent contractors are considered self-employed and thus are treated as an employer, not an employee, under the LMRA. Merely calling someone an independent contractor is not sufficient evidence to establish their employment status. In general, an independent contractor is an individual who offers a service for a fixed fee to provide a specified result. The wages of an independent contractor are at risk in the sense that any profit is dependent upon the contractor's ability to deliver the agreed-upon work product at a cost below the fixed fee agreed upon in advance. Independent contractors control the manner in which work is performed and generally furnish their own training, tools, or other work materials.

- Supervisors were not originally excluded from coverage under the 1935 NLRA but Congress added the exclusion as part of the LMRA (Taft-Hartley) amendments in 1947. Section 2 (11) of the LMRA defines a supervisor as "any individual delegated management authority to perform or effectively recommend one or more of the following functions affecting employees: to hire, transfer, suspend, lay off, recall, promote, discipline, discharge, adjust grievances, assign work, or reward employees so long as the exercise of such authority requires the use of independent judgment which is not merely routine or clerical in nature."[35] To be a supervisor the evidence must show that (1) the individual performs at least one of the specified supervisory functions, (2) that the individual has been delegated authority to perform such supervisory functions in the interests of the employer (as opposed to performance as a routine part of the individual's professional responsibilities), and (3) that the individual exercises independent judgment when performing supervisory duties (as opposed to merely carrying out the decisions of some other manager). The mere fact that a professional employee (e.g., nurse, teacher, engineer) exercises independent judgment or discretion in performing job duties does not automatically exclude that individual from coverage under the LMRA.[36] The supervisory exclusion has since been extended to include any manager who participates in the formulation or execution of management policies and procedures so long as such activity involves the exercise of independent judgment or discretion.[37]

Concerted and Protected Employee Activity

Concerted activity implies some action taken by or on behalf of two or more employees to express a complaint or grievance relating to conditions of employment under the employer's control, for example, work procedures, staffing levels, pay or benefits, safety conditions, hours of work, discipline or other matters affecting wages, hours, or other terms and conditions of employment. The LMRA does not protect complaints or grievances of a purely personal nature (i.e., of concern to a single employee).

To be protected under the LMRA, the concerted activity must be for a protected purpose described in Section 7 of the act and engaged in using lawful means. For example, tactics used to form or join a union or engage in collective bargaining or other mutual aid or protection cannot involve violence, sabotage, or a disproportionate loss or disruption to the employer relative to the seriousness or importance of the employees' complaint or grievance. On a case-by-case basis, the National Labor Relations Board must decide whether the act is concerted and if so, whether the act is for a lawful purpose using lawful means.

Employees are not required to provide management with an opportunity to resolve a complaint or grievance prior to engaging in some form of concerted and protected activity to express a complaint or grievance.[38] Nor are employees required to accept any management proposal for resolving a complaint or grievance even though management believes the proposed settlement terms are fair and appropriate. Although unrepresented (nonunion) employees covered under the LMRA have a right to engage in concerted and protected activity, they do not have a right to require their employer to engage in collective bargaining with them over a solution to the grievance dispute. The duty to bargain cannot be lawfully imposed until a labor organization has been legally certified as the exclusive bargaining representative of an employee group. The union recognition (certification) step is discussed further in Chapter 5, and the duty to bargain in good faith is discussed in Chapter 6.

The **Interboro doctrine** represents an exception to the requirement that an employee be able to prove that he or she acted with or on the express authorization of one or more other employees in order to be considered engaged in concerted activity.[39] A single bargaining unit member can be implied to be acting in concert with other bargaining unit members covered under the same contract terms whenever the individual acts alone to enforce a term or condition of a collective bargaining agreement. Even if the employee has not previously discussed the issue (e.g., safety concern, denial of pay or promotion) with other employees or no other employee is present at the time the employee expresses the grievance complaint to a member of management, no adverse action could be taken against the individual merely for expressing the grievance so long as the complaint concerned a term or condition of the existing collective bargaining agreement.

The exercise of Section 7 rights through concerted activities is not unlimited. For example, reasonable restrictions on the right to strike can occur based upon a strike's objective, its timing, or the conduct of the strikers. If a strike's purpose is to achieve a closed shop contract provision forcing the hiring of only union members, its purpose would be illegal; therefore, the strike would be illegal. If a strike occurs in violation of a no-strike provision in the contract, the timing of the strike is inappropriate, and all striking employees may be disciplined. Further, strikers do not have the right to threaten or engage in acts of violence. Neither sit-down strikes nor refusals to leave a plant are protected strike activities. Strikers also exceed their rights when they physically block persons from entering a struck plant or when threats of violence are made against employees not on strike. Strike issues are further explained in Chapter 9.

NLRB Unfair Labor Practice Procedure

The procedure for an unfair labor practice (ULP) charge (Exhibit 3.3) starts when an employee, employer, labor union, or individual files a charge with an NLRB office within six months of the date the alleged violation occurred. The party filing the charge is termed the **charging party** and the party accused of committing the violation is termed the **respondent**. The general counsel's office, with the aid of the NLRB regional office staff, will investigate the ULP charge to determine if sufficient evidence exists to believe a ULP violation may have occurred. The investigation may involve interviews with potential witnesses, examination of documents, or other necessary steps. A ULP charge may be settled or withdrawn at any point in the ULP procedure prior to a final Board decision. If insufficient evidence to support the charge is found during the preliminary investigation, the ULP charge is dismissed and there is no further appeal of such a decision by the general counsel. In cases alleging an unlawful boycott or strike, the NLRB must request a federal district court to issue a temporary restraining order.

If the investigation confirms that the ULP charge has merit, a reasonable effort will be made to achieve a voluntary settlement of the charge from the respondent. If no voluntary settlement is reached, a formal ULP complaint and notice of a hearing date before an **administrative law judge** (ALJ) will be issued. The ALJ presides over the formal ULP hearing and makes a written report to the Board containing findings of fact based upon the hearing evidence and recommendations regarding an appropriate remedy for any ULP violations. In FY 2002 there were 30,161 ULP charges filed (up 7.2 percent from the previous year), which resulted in the issuance of 4,022 ULP complaints in a median time of 93 days.[40] The voluntary settlement rate for ULP charges with merit has ranged between 91.5 and 99.5 percent over the 10-year period prior to FY 2002. The percentage of ULP charges filed found to have merit has ranged from 32 to 40 percent of charges since 1980.

At the formal ULP hearing conducted by the ALJ, the general counsel will represent the charging party, acting as a prosecutor by attempting to prove by a preponderance of the evidence that the alleged unfair labor violations did occur. The respondent (most often an employer) will typically be represented by private counsel, who will attempt to defend the respondent against the ULP charges. The burden of proof always initially rests with the charging party and thus the general counsel will always go first in presenting opening statements, written and oral testimony, and closing statements. All witnesses are subject to cross-examination by the other party after being questioned under direct examination by the party who called them as a witness. The Board rarely hears oral arguments or testimony from any of the parties in a ULP case and therefore places a great deal of importance on the ALJ's findings regarding the credibility and demeanor of witnesses who testified during the hearing. The ALJ's written report is sent to all parties as well as the Board. All parties are authorized to appeal the ALJ's decision to the Board. The Board has final agency authority to decide all ULP charges.

Unfair labor practice cases can be classified into two broad categories or types: **routine** or **lead case**. Routine cases involve ULP charges that do not raise any new or novel issues of labor law and can be determined by application of existing relevant Board policies and legal principles. Such cases are typically decided by a three-member Board panel. Lead cases are ULP charges that either raise a new or novel labor law issue or present the Board with an opportunity to initiate a new policy or change a significant established policy interpreting the LMRA, as amended. Because of the precedent setting nature of lead cases, a decision requires the participation of all Board members. The Board adopts the recommended decision and order of the ALJ in approximately 85 percent of ULP cases but has the authority to reject or alter the ALJ's recommendations in every ULP case.

Section 10 (c) grants the Board broad authority to fashion an appropriate remedy for ULP violations.[41] At a minimum the Board will issue a **cease-and-desist order** instructing the respondent to stop committing the ULP violations immediately and in the future. It is common for the Board to order a respondent to **post written notices** at places where employees will see them to inform employees about the ULP violations that have occurred, the respondent's pledge not to commit such violations in the future, and the basic rights of employees protected by Section 7 of the LMRA. Such notices may remain on display for a period of time ranging from six weeks to six months. Additional remedies fall under the heading of **affirmative action** necessary to provide a make-whole-type remedy to individuals adversely affected by the occurrence of a ULP. Depending upon the specific type of ULP committed, affirmative action could include one or more of the following: reinstatement, back pay, promotion, restoration of seniority rights or other benefits to which the individual should have been entitled had the ULP not occurred, expunging any reference to the illegal action from an individual's personnel file, an order to bargain in good faith, an order to reopen an illegally closed plant or return illegally relocated work, decertification or disestablishment of a union as employees' exclusive bargaining representative, or union repayment of illegally withheld or overcharged dues or fines.

The Board has no authority to award punitive damages in any case no matter how many separate or intentional ULP violations were committed by a respondent. A charging party alleging unlawful discharge is under an affirmative duty to seek comparable employment to mitigate the respondent's potential back-pay liability while awaiting a final determination of the merit of the ULP charge. Although the Board can order a party to bargain in good faith, the Board has no authority to order either union or management representatives to accept any specific change in a term or condition of employment.[42] The Board could rule that a current employment policy or practice is unlawful and cannot continue to be enforced but could not order the guilty party to change the policy or practice in a way to make it lawful.

Parties may appeal a Board ULP decision to an appropriate federal appeals court, as shown in Exhibit 3.3. While the Board relies primarily on voluntary compliance by respondents with its ordered remedies, when necessary the Board may also petition an appropriate federal appeals court for an order enforcing the Board's decision. An unfair labor practice decision can be appealed to the District of Columbia Circuit Court of Appeals, which has jurisdiction over where the Board is located; an appeals court having jurisdiction over the location where the ULP occurred; or an appeals court having jurisdiction over the location of the appealing party's principal residence or business headquarters.

Upon review of the Board's decision, a court of appeals may enforce the order as written, modify the decision, remand the case back to the Board for fur-

Exhibit 3.3

Basic Procedures in Cases Involving Charges of Unfair Labor Practices

CHARGE

Filed with Regional Director; alleges unfair labor practice by employer of labor organization.

INJUNCTION

Regional Director must ask district court for temporary restraining order in unlawful boycott and certain picketing cases.

INVESTIGATION

Regional Director determines whether formal action should be taken.

WITHDRAWAL-REFUSAL TO ISSUE COMPLAINT-SETTLEMENT

Charge may with Agency approval be withdrawn before or after complaint is issued. Regional Director may refuse to issue a complaint; refusal (dismissal of charge) may be appealed to General Counsel. Settlement of case may occur before or after issuance of complaint (informal settlement agreement subject to approval of Regional Director; formal settlement agreement executed simultaneously with or after issuance of complaint, subject to approval of board). A formal settlement agreement will provide for entry of the board's order and may provide for a judgment from the court of appeals enforcing the board's order.

INJUNCTION

General Counsel may with board approval ask district court for temporary restraining order after complaint is issued in certain unfair labor practice cases.

COMPLAINT AND ANSWER

Regional Director issues complaint and notice of hearing. Respondent files answer in 10 days.

HEARING AND DECISION

Administrative Law Judge presides over a trial and files a decision recommending either (1) order to cease and desist from unfair labor practice and affirmative relief or (2) dismissal of complaint. If no timely exceptions are filed to Administrative Law Judge's decision, the findings of the Administrative Law Judge automatically become the decision and order of the board.

DISMISSAL

Board finds respondent did not commit unfair labor practice and dismisses complaint.

REMEDIAL ORDER

Board finds respondent committed unfair labor practice and orders respondent to cease and desist and to remedy such unfair labor practice.

OTHER DISPOSITION

Board remands case to Regional Director for further action.

COURT ENFORCEMENT AND REVIEW

Court of appeals can enforce, set aside, or remand all or part of the case. U.S. Supreme Court reviews appeals from courts of appeals.

SOURCE: National Labor Relations Board.

ther consideration, or refuse to enforce the Board's decision. Approximately 50 percent of final ULP Board decisions (or approximately 1 percent of all ULP charges filed) are appealed annually to federal courts, making the NLRB one of the most active federal agencies involved in federal court litigation. In FY 2002, 159 ULP cases were appealed to the federal courts, with private parties initiating the appeal in 86 cases and the NLRB seeking a court enforcement order in the other 73 cases.[43]

A federal court must enforce the Board's ULP decision if (1) the decision is a reasonable interpretation of congressional intent as expressed in the language of the LMRA, as amended, and (2) the decision is supported by substantial evidence (facts and reasoning) contained in the case record.[44] The lack of substantial evidence in the case record to support the Board's decision is cited most frequently by a court in refusing to enforce all or part of the Board's decision. The courts do pay great deference to the Board's interpretations of the LMRA and to witness credibility determinations by an administrative law judge during the ULP hearing. On balance, the NLRB has a very successful track record of having its decisions enforced by federal appeals courts. In FY 2002, U.S. Courts of Appeal decided 106 ULP cases, of which 64 Board decisions were enforced entirely; 11 cases were partially enforced; 8 cases were remanded to the Board for further consideration; and enforcement was denied in 23 cases.

A court of appeals decision in a ULP case can be appealed for possible review by the U.S. Supreme Court **(petition for certiorari)**. To be reviewed, four of the nine Supreme Court justices must agree to hear the case. Cases most likely to be accepted for review are those that raise a new or novel labor law question not previously addressed by the Court or that raise an issue on which lower courts of appeal have rendered different interpretations, thus creating a so-called legal split among the courts of appeal. Agreeing to hear such a case on appeal would allow the Supreme Court to resolve the legal question and establish a binding precedent that lower courts and administrative agencies (e.g., NLRB) would have to follow in deciding future similar cases. The Supreme Court agrees to review less than 1 percent of all petitions for certiorari it receives.

Assessment of the LMRA, as Amended, and NLRB Administration

The LMRA and its administration have critics in the academic community. Professor James Gross, an authority on the LMRA, has stated: "The current national labor policy favors and protects the powerful at the expense of the powerless. In the essential moral sense, therefore, the current national labor policy is a failure."[45] Professor Janice Bellace has suggested that most labor commentators find the current application of labor laws has actually discouraged unionism:

> Current labor law tolerates long delays in getting to an election and in having the election results certified. Labor supporters will also point out that even when there is a union at a work place, labor law permits the threatened and actual replacement of strikers from the first day of the strike. They will decry this, particularly because rules on the labor contract do not maintain the status quo when the contract expires, thus enabling employers demanding concessions to take back in a flash those contract items gained by the union over the years. Finally, labor supporters deride a statute with remedies so weak they do not deserve the label 'remedy'.[46]

The language of the LMRA has remained relatively unchanged by congressional action since 1959, even though the labor relations environment has undergone substantial change over the same time period. The labor force has become substantially more diverse, with increased labor force participation by women and racial and ethnic minorities. The economy has transformed from a manufacturing base to a service-information technology base, creating a truly global economy where products, information, and monetary resources are easily transported across national boundaries, expanding product/service markets and increasing competitive pressures on both employers and employees. Emphasis by Congress and the legal system on protecting individual employees' right to equal treatment and the establishment of minimum employment standards has also de-emphasized the role of collective bargaining as a means of providing employees a voice in determining employment interests.[47]

The lack of congressional action to address labor law reforms has been attributed to the fact that "for many decades, both organized labor and especially employers have had enough support in Congress to block any significant amendment that either group strongly opposes. Enough support does not mean a majority; it means a minority that is big enough, well organized enough, and committed enough to tie up a bill through the arcane supermajority requirements of the Senate—for example through filibuster—or to sustain a presidential veto."[48]

Labor union advocates would like to see several reforms of the LMRA enacted. Among desired reforms are greater access by union organizers to communicate with employees during organizing campaigns and stronger penalties for unfair labor practices committed by employers against union supporters (e.g., elimination of offsets for interim earnings in computing back pay awards for unlawful discharge). Union advocates have also sought unsuccessfully to eliminate management's right to permanently replace otherwise lawful economic strikers during a labor dispute. Union advocates have also opposed efforts to weaken the unfair labor practice provision in Section 8(a)(2) prohibiting employer domination or interference with the operation of a labor organization under the guise of promoting cooperative labor relations as a means of improving productivity and employee involvement in work decisions.[49]

Some employer advocates would clearly favor an expansion of an employer's right to create work teams and have those teams deal with a wide range of employment issues involving work processes, compensation, productivity, safety, and other work rules.[50] Many employers are interested in efforts to expand the application of so-called *Beck rights*, which reinforce the basic right of an employee not to become a full member of a union in order to meet the requirements of a negotiated union security clause and to pay a bargaining unit representative, where required by contract, only those regular charges associated with the duties of representing the bargaining unit.[51] *Beck rights* will be discussed further in Chapter 4.

The NLRB also has its critics among labor and management officials. One area of concern over the years has been the amount of time required to complete ULP case decisions by the Board. Both administrative law judges and Board members share the responsibility for administrative delays that have occurred.[52] The General Accounting Office (GAO) released a damaging report to Congress entitled "Action Needed to Improve Case-Processing Time at Headquarters." This report revealed that between 1984 and 1989 only about 67 percent of the 5,000 cases appealed to the Board in Washington were decided within one year. Ten percent of the cases took from three to more than seven years to decide. Such time delays existed even though the number of cases assigned was only 874, compared with 1,875 in 1980. Between 1984 and 1989, the medians for processing unfair labor practice cases ranged from a low of 273 days to a high of 395 days—two to three times higher than medians during the 1970s. For representation cases, the medians ranged from 190 to 256 days, higher than the medians during the 1970s. The GAO report identified several reasons for the excessive delays: (1) lack of standards and procedures for preventing excessive delays, (2) lack of timely decisions on leading cases, and (3) Board member turnover and vacancies (the highest in history during the 1980s).[53]

Beginning in 1994 under the leadership of NLRB Chairman William Gould, several initiatives were undertaken to make the NLRB more efficient. These included:

- Creating a "super panel" system for processing certain cases, whereby a panel of three board members meets each week to hear cases involving issues that lend themselves to quick resolution without written analysis by each Board member's staff.

- Creating "speed teams," which are used to reduce the amount of staff time devoted to cases in which the Board is adopting the recommended decision of an administrative law judge.

- Providing "settlement judges" who are assigned in select cases to conduct settlement discussions.

- Permitting "bench decisions" in certain cases in which oral arguments are heard in lieu of written briefs. After the oral arguments are presented, the administrative law judge reads the decision into the record and later certifies the transcript that contains the decision.

- Creating advisory panels composed of distinguished labor and management attorneys to provide the board and the office of the general counsel with practical input on a wide range of topics.

- Increasing the use of the injunction as a means of stopping certain violations quickly and providing an incentive for voluntary compliance.[54]

In processing 4,610 ULP cases in fiscal year 2001, NLRB regional offices required a median time of 101 days from the charge filing date to the issuance of a formal complaint.[55] Additional time is required for cases that require an administrative law judge hearing and a review and decision by the Board. Employers were the named respondent in 90.2 percent of cases that resulted in the issuance of a formal ULP complaint. The majority (51 percent) of ULP charges against employers involved alleged unlawful discharge or other discriminatory acts against employees, while 49 percent of employer ULP cases involved an alleged refusal to bargain in good faith. Of alleged ULP charges filed against unions, 75.4 percent alleged some general discriminatory act, 9.4 percent involved alleged unlawful secondary strike, boycott, or picket activity, and 5 percent alleged bad faith bargaining.

Transportation-Related Labor Relations Laws (Railway and Airlines)

Rail and air transportation labor relations are covered by the **Railway Labor Act** (RLA). Enacted in 1926 with bipartisan labor and management support to apply only to the railway industry, the RLA was actually the first comprehensive collective bargaining law. In 1936, the RLA was amended to extend coverage to a new and developing transportation industry—airlines—although airlines continued using their established local system boards for grievance dispute resolution. Like other labor laws, the RLA did not develop overnight; it resulted from years of union activity and attempts to pass laws accommodating railway labor relations.[56] The primary goal of the RLA is the avoidance of disruption in transportation services by encouraging collective bargaining.

Under the RLA, if a union and employer are unable to resolve their differences over negotiating terms of their labor agreement (a **major dispute**), the dispute is subject to mandatory mediation through the National Mediation Board (NMB). If mediation does not succeed, the parties have the option of proceeding to final and binding arbitration. If either party declines to submit the dispute to arbitration, a 30-day status quo period is invoked during which the president may appoint an emergency board to investigate the dispute and make recommendations regarding a settlement.

Since the enactment of the RLA, over 97 percent of the collective-bargaining disputes mediated by the NMB have been resolved without a strike or other form of interruptions of commerce. Historically, about 85 percent of presidentially appointed emergency boards (PEB) established have dealt with disputes in the railroad industry. In recent years, there has been a dramatic drop in the use of emergency boards.[57] In FY 2002, only one PEB was established involving a dispute over economic issues between United Airlines and the International Association of Machinists (IAM). The IAM's members voted to reject the settlement terms proposed by the PEB and voted in favor of a strike. Subsequent negotiations between United Airlines and the IAM produced a voluntary settlement, which was ratified by union members on March 5, 2002, thus avoiding the threatened work stoppage.[58]

The National Railroad Adjustment Board (NRAB), a bipartisan group of 18 union and 18 management representatives, was established to assist in resolving grievances arising during the term of a labor agreement over the interpretation or application of the contract's terms (**minor dispute**). Where the board could not agree to a settlement, the grievance may be settled by an arbitrator selected by the parties.[59]

Over the past five years, the NMB has closed an average of 5,537 arbitration cases and 79 representation cases annually.[60] The NMB is empowered to conduct representation elections and to help resolve interest disputes that develop during negotiations between union and management representatives over what the terms and conditions of employment will be as stated by contract language. Under the RLA, labor agreements never expire but do become amenable for negotiation of proposed changes as of a specified date. In 2002, the NMB began using a new method for conducting representation elections called Telephone Electronic Voting (TEV). Eligible voters are given two passwords to use in casting their representation election ballot by telephone rather than a mail-in paper ballot. The NMB believes the system is very secure and will save the agency substantial time and expense in conducting representation elections.

There are several differences between the RLA and the LMRA:

1. The RLA covers the railway and airline industries, whereas the LMRA covers most other private-sector employers engaged in interstate commerce.

2. Union representation under the RLA requires a showing of support from the majority of all employees in the particular craft or class who are eligible to vote. Union representation under the LMRA requires a showing of support from the majority of eligible voters who actually cast a valid written ballot on election day. If there were 50 eligible voters of whom 44 cast a valid ballot, under the RLA a union would need 26 "Yes union" votes to be certified as the exclusive bargaining representative for the 50 employees. Under the LMRA, a union would only require 23 "Yes union" votes to be certified as the exclusive bargaining representative for the same size (50 employees) unit.

3. A significantly higher percentage of employees in the railway and airline industries are organized by unions under the RLA compared to other private-sector employees covered under the LMRA.

4. Under the RLA, the union cannot strike and the employer cannot lock out until they have exhausted the impasse resolution procedures required by the NMB. Under the LMRA, the parties can engage in self-help actions if (a) the dispute involves a mandatory subject of bargaining, (b) there is no current contract language barring the action, and (c) good-faith bargaining responsibilities have been met.

5. Under the RLA, arbitration of minor disputes (grievances) in the railway industry is mandatory, and the government bears the expense of arbitration. Under the LMRA, grievance arbitration procedures are negotiated by the parties, and the parties pay for the arbitration (airline grievance arbitration is similar to arbitration under the LMRA).[61]

Assessment of the RLA

Faced with such problems as changing markets for freight transportation, severe competition, government regulation, and public interest in uninterrupted railroad service, labor relations in the railway industry are unique. Complicating the situation further are the chronic financial instability of the numerous independent railroads; the presence of strong, competing craft unions; and tradition-bound work rules. These factors affect labor relations in the following ways: (1) Because the public depends on railroad transportation for many essential goods, much effort has been made to avoid strikes (five interventions by Congress). (2) With the "fractionated" craft unions, the labor relations process takes much time and creates many opportunities for disputes. (3) The tradition-bound work rules of the operating crafts strictly control not only how a particular job will be performed but also which craft will be assigned the job. These work rules slow the introduction of new technology and magnify the problems of a declining industry.[62] Any assessment of the RLA must be kept in proper perspective. There are over 7,000 labor agreements in the railroad and airline industries, and about

1,000 railroad and 200 airline agreements (mostly local) are in negotiations during any given year.[63] Further, any measure of the act's effectiveness must be made with reference to its objectives—to promote free collective bargaining and protect the public from interrupted flows of commerce.[64]

Regarding negotiations, mediation has been the most important method of intervention under the RLA; however, few nationwide railroad wage cases have been settled by mediation since 1936. Its greatest success has been in settling minor controversies after the major issues have been resolved. This does not mean that mediation is unimportant—minor disputes left unresolved could easily lead to major strikes in future negotiations.

Deregulation Legislation

The Airline Deregulation Act of 1978 ended government controls of fares and routes, and the Motor Carrier Act of 1980 reduced the amount of economic regulation of the industry by the Interstate Commerce Commission. The Staggers Rail Act of 1980 gave railroads more flexibility in setting rates and service levels.[65] Initial concerns that deregulation might result in only a relatively few large carriers, reducing competition within the industry, have largely proved unfounded. Airline deregulation prompted the introduction of 128 nonunion carriers, but by 1987, only 37 had survived. There has been increased merger activity by the major airlines, ticketing agreements between major carriers and regional and commuter airlines, hub-and-spoke airports, and frequent-flier programs to promote airline customer loyalty.[66] Deregulation also encouraged price competition, with 90 percent of passengers traveling at discount prices averaging 60 percent below the coach price. During the same time accident rates have not increased, and service to small communities has not deteriorated; however, there have been increased congestion at airports and in the airways, delays in departures and arrivals, threats to safety, and a general decline in the quality of air service.[67] Profitability in both the railroad and airline industry has been reduced by the slow pace of economic recovery, although large (Class 1) railroad operators appear to be making a faster recovery than most major airlines.

Airlines were particularly hard hit by the terrorist attacks of September 11, 2001. Not only were air operations suspended or significantly reduced for several days following the attacks, but in subsequent months the public demonstrated an increased reluctance to fly and additional security costs have imposed a significant cost burden on airlines.[68] Congress created the Air Transport Stabilization Board (ATSB) and funded a $10 billion loan program to aid airlines' economic recovery. Most airlines have adopted a variety of cost-cutting strategies to cope with revenue declines, including significant employee layoffs, postponement or cancellation of equipment orders, reduced flight schedules, and negotiated economic concessions from employees.

Promising Developments Regarding the RLA

Despite problems, several events and developments provide the basis for some optimism:

- Recent negotiations have been characterized by greater union–management cooperation, which has resulted in fewer conflicts and outside interventions.

- Emergency board procedures have been drastically improved, and the ritualism and legalism so prevalent in the 1960s have been reduced.

- Encouraging progress has been made on some long-standing manning and work-rule issues, such as the fireman on diesel trains, combined road and yard service, and interdivisional runs.

- New leadership has had a positive influence on both management and unions, and neutrals and government officials have provided capable assistance in the bargaining and dispute resolution processes.

Critical issues remain to be resolved, including secondary picketing, bargaining stalemates, restrictive work rules in some agreements, intercraft wage structure problems, and crew size disputes.[69]

In 2003 an effort was made to reform the Railway Labor Act to require parties unable to reach a voluntary settlement during negotiations to submit their dispute to final-offer binding arbitration where a panel of arbitrators would have a limit (e.g., 30 days) in which to select either the employer's or union's final offer to settle all issues in dispute.[70] The proposal is supported by employer organizations such as the Air Transport Association, Regional Airline Association, and Communities for Economic Strength Through Aviation (CESTA) as well as Senator John McCain (R-AZ), chair of the Senate Commerce, Science, and Transportation Committee, who has scheduled hearings on the matter. Proponents of the proposed change believe it would help speed up the lengthy negotiation process provided under the RLA and reduce the threat of strikes, particularly important to the economically stressed airline industry. Mandatory arbitration of interest disputes would reduce airline unions' ability to use the strike threat as a means to attain better contract settlement terms, which represent higher labor costs to employers. There have been three major strikes in the airline industry since 1994, with the longest lasting three months involving pilots at regional carrier Comair owned by Delta Airlines. Shorter strikes involved flight attendants at American Airlines and pilots at Northwest Airlines.[71]

Airline labor unions oppose the proposed RLA reform, arguing it is unnecessary and would remove airline employees' fundamental right to engage in strike action, creating an imbalance in bargaining power favoring employers and undermining the viability of the collective-bargaining process in the airline industry.[72] A credible strike or lockout threat can be a powerful incentive to motivate bargaining parties to be realistic and seek a voluntary settlement in order to avoid the potential costs or risks associated with a work stoppage. Some employers, such as Southwest Airline, which historically has enjoyed good labor relations with its employee unions, have adopted a neutral stance regarding the proposed reform.[73]

On balance, the RLA appears to have accomplished its primary goal of facilitating cooperative labor relations in the airline and railroad industries and avoiding significant service disruptions. While both labor and management might create their own wish list of labor law reforms, as a joint airline labor-management committee concluded, "the potential for disruption far outweighs the marginal gain that any legislative refinements might provide."[74]

Other Laws That Affect Labor Relations

Other statutes and executive orders, more narrow in scope, influence labor relations either directly or indirectly. The following section highlights only their major provisions; however, practitioners find that detailed knowledge of them is essential to most business operations. (Related legislation is summarized here, but its specific implications for labor relations activities and unions are discussed in the appropriate chapters.)

The Americans with Disabilities Act of 1990

The Americans with Disabilities Act (ADA) of 1990, which covers an estimated 40 million disabled Americans, went into effect in January 1992. Considered a "Bill of Rights" for Americans with a wide variety of disabilities, the act applies to employment, public accommodations, transportation, and telecommunications. The employment provisions cover virtually every aspect of the employment process. The act prohibits discrimination in advancement, discharge, compensation, training, and other terms and conditions of employment that are usually included in collective bargaining agreements. The act requires employers to make reasonable accommodations for disabled employees, except when doing so would subject the employer to undue hardship. This subject will be addressed more fully in Chapter 8.

Bankruptcy Act

Bankruptcy legislation enacted in 1984 includes standards for the rejection of collective-bargaining agreements by companies for obtaining modifications in labor agreements. It requires companies to provide relevant information to unions and engage in good-faith efforts to reach an agreement that could avoid the necessity to declare bankruptcy. In cases where no agreement can be reached, the act specifies the requirements for terminating or altering provisions of an existing labor agreement. (See Chapter 6 for more details.)

Worker Adjustment and Retraining Notification Act

Triggered by major plant closings without notification, the Worker Adjustment and Retraining Notification Act (WARN) was passed in 1988. WARN requires employers with 100 or more employees to give 60 days' advance notice to employees (excluding those employed less than 20 hours per week) who will be affected by a plant closing or major layoff. Also, the union, the chief elected local government official, and the state government must be notified. The law permits a union and employer to negotiate language in their collective-bargaining agreement that could require more than 60 days of advance notice be provided.

Situations where WARN Act notice requirements would apply include the following:

- A "plant closing" resulting in an employment loss for 50 or more workers at one site within a 30-day period.

- A "mass layoff" of at least 33 percent of the workforce (minimum of 50 employees) within any 30-day period.

- A "mass layoff" involving at least 500 employees within any 30-day period.

Remedies available to affected employees for employer violations include back pay and benefits for up to 60 days and payments (maximum of $500 per day) to local communities for a period of up to 60 days. One criticism of the statute is that it requires the injured party to bear the economic cost of initiating enforcement action by filing a lawsuit in a federal district court rather than having the U.S. Department of Labor initiate such legal action.

WARN ties in closely with the Job Training Partnership Act (JTPA), which provides funds to state and local governments for training and retraining. In cases of plant closing and mass layoff, state "rapid response" teams are available to work with labor and management officials to set up retraining and reemployment programs for the affected workers.

Racketeer Influenced and Corrupt Organizations Act of 1970

The Racketeer Influenced and Corrupt Organizations Act (RICO), part of the Organized Crime Control Act of 1970, forbids anyone involved in racketeering from investing in or controlling through racketeering activity any enterprise (business or labor union) engaged in interstate commerce. The law provides for penalties of up to $25,000, 20 years of imprisonment, and forfeiture of all relevant property. A person found guilty of a RICO violation may be required to divest all interests in the organization and restricted from any future activities in that or a related organization. In addition, any persons who suffered damages from the prohibited activities are entitled to recover triple the amount of damages.

Employment Discrimination Laws and Executive Orders

The **Civil Rights Act of 1991** prohibits any form of employment discrimination by companies, labor unions, and employment agencies on the basis of race, color, religion, sex, or national origin. The Equal Employment Opportunity Commission is a federal administrative agency created to enforce the statute through investigating complaints, attempts at conciliation, and lawsuits filed on behalf of the complainant.

The **Age Discrimination in Employment Act of 1967**, as amended in 1978, 1984, and 1986, prohibits employment discrimination against those over the age of 40, permits compulsory retirement for executives who are entitled to pensions of $44,000 per year or more, and authorizes jury trials in covered cases.

Executive Order 11246, as amended by **Executive Order 11375**, prohibits employment discrimination in the federal government and by federal government contractors and subcontractors receiving $50,000 or more. Those having contracts of $50,000 or more and employing 50 people or more are required to establish affirmative action plans that prescribe specific goals and procedures for increasing the percentage of minority employees. Firms that fail to comply could lose part or all of their contracts.

The **Vocational Rehabilitation Act of 1973** (Section 503) requires holders of federal government contracts in excess of $2,500 to take affirmative action to employ and advance in employment qualified physically and mentally disabled individuals. Further, if any disabled individual believes that a federal contractor has failed or refused to comply with the act, he or she may file a complaint with the Department of Labor, which will investigate the complaint and take any warranted action. In addition, Section 504 extends coverage to organizations receiving federal financial assistance and is enforced by the Department of Health and Human Services.

Related Labor Relations Laws

The **Uniformed Services Employment and Reemployment Rights Act of 1994** (USERRA) clarifies and extends the Veterans' Reemployment Rights Act of 1940 to protect the job rights of individuals called to perform military service on behalf of the United States. Also, the Vietnam Era Veteran Readjustment Assistance Act requires employers with government contracts of $10,000 or more to take affirmative action to employ and advance disabled veterans and qualified veterans of the Vietnam War.

The **Social Security Act of 1935**, as amended, established two national systems of social security for protection against loss of income resulting from unemployment, old age, disability, and death: (1) retirement, survivors, and disability insurance, and health insurance for persons over age 65; and (2) unemployment insurance, which operates under a state-administered, federal-state plan whose operating costs are paid by the federal government. The **Fair Labor Standards Act of 1938** administered by the U.S. Department of Labor covers a variety of employment issues, including minimum wage and overtime pay requirements, child labor, and migrant and seasonal agricultural worker protections.

Other important laws include the wage laws and **Employee Retirement and Income Security Act of 1974** (covered in Chapter 7), the **Occupational Safety and Health Act of 1970** (covered in Chapter 8), the **Family and Medical Leave Act of 1993** (covered in Chapter 7), and federal and state laws and local ordinances that pertain to public sector labor relations and equal employment opportunity.

SUMMARY

This chapter has presented the major provisions of federal labor relations laws in the United States. These legal influences must be understood to fully appreciate the remaining chapters in this book because nearly all issues in labor relations are either directly or indirectly influenced by labor relations law. The legal question of whether one has a right to act is separate and distinct from the practical question of whether it is in one's best interest to exercise such a right under the prevailing circumstances. Union and management practitioners should give consideration to the legal and practical costs, benefits, and risks of actions in making operational decisions.

Although many think of law in terms of statutes passed by the U.S. Congress or state legislatures, labor relations and other types of law proceed not only from statutes but also from the U.S. Constitution, judicial decisions, and administrative decisions of government agencies. Similar case law and administrative law develop at the state and local government levels. Developing the legal influences historically, this chapter began with the early struggles of labor unions to exist as they faced an unsympathetic judiciary and lack of legislation intended to protect workers' rights. Several hurdles included the criminal conspiracy and civil conspiracy doctrines, as well as the breach-of-contract rulings. Then the Sherman Act, passed primarily to control business monopolies, was applied to restrict labor unions' activities also. With the support of labor, the Sherman Act was amended by the Clayton Act; however, this act in initial court decisions also proved unfavorable to unions.

The 1920s did bring passage of the Railway Labor Act (RLA), but little legislative action occurred in other sectors. However, the 1930s, with the country confronting a severe economic depression, brought about major changes. The enactment of the Norris–La Guardia Act removed many legal restrictions on the types of employee concerted activity that could be used to peacefully pressure employers to grant favorable employment improvements. Federal courts began to take a more neutral stance in labor disputes, attempting to balance the legitimate exercise of employee and employer rights.

Congress passed the National Labor Relations Act in 1935 covering most private sector employees to control employer unfair labor practices and established the National Labor Relations Board to enforce the rights of employees to form and join unions, bargain collectively, and engage in other concerted activities for mutual aid or protection. Then, in 1947 and again in 1959, Congress amended the National Labor Relations Act with passage of the Labor Management Relations (Taft-Hartley) Act and the Labor Management Reporting and Disclosure (Landrum-Griffin) Act, respectively. The LMRA's amendments added union unfair labor practices and restrictions on union security clauses. The LMRDA added regulations governing the internal operations of unions and restrictions on secondary strike, picketing, and boycott activities.

Starting in 1863, union activity in the railroad industry played a key role in the legislative arena. The Railway Labor Act of 1926, whose major purpose is to provide for stable and effective labor relations without major interruptions in commerce, established procedures for resolving labor disputes and created the National Mediation Board and National Railroad Adjustment Board to accomplish the act's purposes. The airline industry was added to coverage under the RLA in 1936.

While the legal rights of employers and employees to pursue their respective interests in a free-enterprise system will inevitably create certain conflicts and stress, on balance the legal environment has provided reasonable stability in U.S. labor relations, encouraging economic growth. The acceptance of collective bargaining, widespread use of no-strike or lockout clauses, final and binding arbitration of rights disputes, improved employer-union cooperation on important issues, and infrequent need to use national emergency dispute procedures provide support for progress in protecting the legitimate rights of both employers and employees.

Key Terms

U.S. Constitution
common law
employment-at-will doctrine
National Labor Relations Board
Norris–La Guardia Act (1932)
National Labor Relations Act (1935)
Labor Management Relations Act (1947)

Labor Management Reporting and Disclosure Act (1959)
Railway Labor Act (1926)
Clayton Antitrust Act (1914)
Loewe v. Lawlor (1908)
yellow-dog contract
closed shop

union shop
agency shop
right-to-work law
NLRB jurisdiction
Postal Reorganization Act (1970)
concerted and protected activity
interboro doctrine
respondent
charging party
administrative law judge
routine ULP case
lead ULP case
cease and desist order
posting of written notices
affirmative action
petition for certiorari
major dispute under the RLA
preemption doctrine
Federal Mediation and Conciliation Service
U.S. Department of Labor
National Mediation Board
National Railroad Adjustment Board
criminal conspiracy doctrine
Commonwealth v. Hunt (1842)

civil conspiracy doctrine
labor injunction
Sherman Antitrust Act (1890)
minor dispute under the RLA
Americans with Disabilities Act (1990)
Bankruptcy Act (1984)
Worker Adjustment and Retraining
    Notification Act (1988)
Racketeer Influenced and Corrupt
    Organizations Act (1970)
Civil Rights Act (1991)
Age Discrimination in Employment Act
    (1967)
Executive Orders 11246 and 11375
Vocational Rehabilitation Act (1973)
Uniformed Services Employment and
    Reemployment Rights Act (1994)
Social Security Act (1935)
Fair Labor Standards Act (1938)
Employee Retirement and Income
    Security Act (1974)
Occupational Safety and Health Act
    (1970)
Family and Medical Leave Act (1993)

DISCUSSION QUESTIONS

1. How have the major labor relations laws helped or hindered the development of unions?

2. How were yellow-dog contracts and labor injunctions used to limit the activities of union organizers or slow union growth?

3. Why did the 1914 Clayton Act, called U.S. labor's Magna Carta by AFL president Samuel Gompers, fail to live up to union leaders' expectations?

4. What was the intent or purpose of Congress in passing (a) the 1932 Norris–La Guardia Act, (b) the 1935 National Labor Relations (Wagner) Act, and (c) the 1947 Labor Management Relations (Taft-Hartley) Act?

5. Although the National Labor Relations Act gives employees certain rights, these rights are not unlimited. Discuss.

6. Should the NLRB's administration of the LMRA be termed a success? Why or why not?

7. Why is there still a separate labor relations law for the railway and airline industries?

8. Should the LMRA be amended to (a) cover agricultural laborers or (b) index the NLRB's jurisdictional standards (i.e., monetary threshold for affecting interstate commerce) to take into account the effects of inflation?

EXPLORING THE WEB

Labor Relations and Law

1. **Case Law**   Find a recent (1994) Supreme Court opinion involving the United Mine Workers of America in which the case *Lechmere* v. *NLRB* is cited. Use one of the following well-established sites.

Cornell University. One of the best sites for legal research.

http://supct.law.cornell.edu/supct/index.html

Findlaw Legal Information Center. A good commercial site.

http://www.findlaw.com/casecode/index.html

2. **National Labor Relations Board**   Go to the Web site for the National Labor Relations Board to see the NLRB's current organization, rules and regulations, decisions, and manuals. The URL for the National Labor Relations Board is:

http://www.nlrb.gov

Included also are press releases, public notices, and a weekly summary of current events. Find a recent decision on Caterpillar, Inc. Search the Press Releases to read former NLRB Chairman William Gould's speech delivered on June 18, 1998, in which he discussed enforcement of the NLRA and NLRB administrative reform. Gould was Chairman from 1994 through 1998.

You can use Internet search engines to find articles made available on the Web by law firms that distribute bulletins and newsletters to keep their clients informed on changes in labor law. Go to the Web site for Constangy, Brooks & Smith, click on Legal Updates and then look at the Executive Labor Summaries for November/December 2002. What was reported about the "frequency of NLRB injunctions for interim relief from the courts in pending unfair labor practice" under George Bush's administration?

http://www.constangy.com

Go to the Web site for the National Right to Work Legal Defense Foundation and search for articles on the NLRB.

http://www.nrtw.org

3. **U.S. Code**   When legislation becomes law, it is incorporated into the U.S. Code in the appropriate sections. Identify sections of the U.S. Code affected by these acts related to labor relations: Railway Labor Act, Americans with Disabilities Act, Worker Adjustment and Retraining Notification Act, and National Labor Relations Act. How does the Code define "unfair labor practices"?

Cornell University

http://www4.law.cornell.edu/uscode/

Hint: Search the names of the acts by using the Table of Popular Names.

GPO Access (Government Printing Office)

http://www.gpoaccess.gov/multidb.html

U.S. House of Representatives

http://uscode.house.gov/usc.htm

REFERENCES

1. Walter E. Oberer, Kurt L. Hanslowe, and Timothy J. Heinsz, *Labor Law: Collective Bargaining in a Free Society*, 4th ed. (St. Paul, Minn: West, 1994), pp. 358–359.

2. J. R. Commons and E. A. Gilmore, *A Documentary History of American Industrial Society* (Cleveland, Ohio: A. H. Clark, 1910), p. 68.

3. Quoted by John Fanning in "The Balance of Labor-Management Economic Power under Taft-Hartley," *Proceedings of the 40th Annual Meeting of the Industrial Relations Research Association*, ed. Barbara D. Dennis (Madison, Wis.: IRRA, 1988), p. 70.

4. *Commonwealth* v. *Hunt*, 45 Mass. 111 (1842).

5. E. E. Herman and G. S. Skinner, *Labor Law* (New York: Random House, 1972), p. 21.

6. *Vegelahn* v. *Guntner*, 44 N.E. 1077 (1896). See Herbert L. Sherman, Jr., and William P. Murphy, *Unionization and Collective Bargaining*, 3d ed. (Washington, D.C.: Bureau of National Affairs, 1975), p. 3.

7. John R. Commons, *History of Labour in the United States*, Vol. 2 (New York: Macmillan, 1946), p. 504. See also *Sherry* v. *Perkins*, 147 Mass. 212 (1888).

8. *Hitchman Coal & Coke Company* v. *Mitchell*, 245 U.S. 229 (1917).

9. *Sherman Anti-Trust Act*, 26 Stat. 209 (1890).

10. *Loewe* v. *Lawlor*, 208 U.S. 274 (1908).

11. 38 Stat. 731 (1914).

12. *Duplex Printing Press Co.* v. *Deering*, 254 U.S. 443 (1921).

13. *Truax* v. *Corrigan*, 257 U.S. 312 (1921).

14. 47 Stat. 70 (1932).

15. A labor dispute was defined as "any controversy concerning terms or conditions of employment, or concerning the association or representation of persons in negotiating, fixing, maintaining, changing, or seeking to arrange terms or conditions of employment regardless of whether the disputants stand in the proximate relation of employer and employee." 47 Stat. 70 (1932).

16. *United States* v. *Hutcheson*, 312 U.S. 219 (1941).

17. Irving Bernstein, *Turbulent Years: A History of the American Worker, 1933–1941* (Boston: Houghton Mifflin, 1971), pp. 1–36. See also Bruce Nelson, "Give Us Roosevelt: Workers and the New Deal Coalition," *History Today* 40 (1), January 1990, pp. 40–48.

18. Alvin L. Goldman, *The Supreme Court and Labor-Management Relations Law* (Lexington, Mass.: D.C. Heath, 1976), pp. 26–28; and Sherman and Murphy, *Unionization and Collective Bargaining*, pp. 7–9.

19. *Schecter Poultry Corporation* v. *United States*, 295 U.S. 495 (1935).

20. *National Labor Relations Act*, 49 Stat. 449 (1935).

21. Janice R. Bellace, "The Future of Employee Representation in America: Enabling Freedom of Association in the Workplace in Changing Times Through Statutory Reform," *University of Pennsylvania Journal of Labor & Employment Law* 5 (Fall 2002), p. 5, at http://web.lexis-nexis.com. See also Bruce E. Kaufman and David Lewin, "Is the NLRA Still Relevant to Today's Economy and Workplace?" *Labor Law Journal* 49 (September 1998), pp. 1113–1126.

22. Goldman, *The Supreme Court*, pp. 28–31.

23. *NLRB* v. *Jones & Laughlin Steel Corporation*, 301 U.S. 1 (1937).

24. Bernstein, *Turbulent Years*, pp. 769–771.

25. *Labor Management Relations Act*, 61 Stat. 136 (1947).

26. *NLRB* v. *Virginia Electric & Power Company*, 314 U.S. 469 (1941).

27. Goldman, *The Supreme Court*, pp. 31–39.

28. *Labor Management Reporting and Disclosure Act*, 73 Stat. 519 (1959).

29. *Fact Sheet on the National Labor Relations Board* (Washington, D.C.: NLRB Office of Information, 2003), pp. 1–2 at http://www.nlrb.gov/facts.html. Additional information regarding the NLRB's organizational structure, procedures, and decisions are available at the NLRB's home page at http://www.nlrb.gov.

30. William N. Cooke and Frederick H. Gautschi III, "Political Bias in NLRB Unfair Labor Practice Decisions," *Industrial*

and Labor Relations Review 35 (July 1982), p. 549.

31. William N. Cooke, Aneil K. Mishra, Gretchen M. Spreitzer, and Mary Tschirhart, "The Determinants of NLRB Decision-Making Revisited," *Industrial and Labor Relations Review* 48 (January 1995), pp. 254–256.

32. Arthur F. Rosenfeld, "NLRB General Counsel Issues Report on FY 2002 Operations," *NLRB Press Release,* (February 4, 2003), pp. 1–6.

33. Bruce S. Feldacker, *Labor Guide to Labor Law,* 4th ed. (Upper Saddle River, N.J.: Prentice-Hall, 2000), pp. 12–14.

34. *Holly Farms Corporation v. NLRB,* 116 S.Ct. 1396 (1996).

35. Sec. 2 (11), *LMRA* 61 Stat. 136 (1947). See also *NLRB v. Kentucky River Community Care, Inc.,* 532 U.S. 706 (2001).

36. *NLRB v. Yeshiva University,* 444 U.S. 672 (1980); *Boston Medical Center Corporation and House Officer's Association/Committee of Interns and Residents,* 330 NLRB 152 (1999).

37. *NLRB v. Bell Aerospace Company,* 416 U.S. 267 (1974).

38. *NLRB v. City Disposal Systems, Inc.,* 465 U.S. 822 (1984); *NLRB v. Washington Aluminum Company,* 370 U.S. 9 (1962).

39. *NLRB v. City Disposal Systems, Inc.,* 465 U.S. 822 (1984).

40. Office of the General Counsel, "NLRB General Counsel Issues Report on FY 2002 Operations," *NLRB News Release,* February 4, 2003, pp. 1–6.

41. Leonard R. Page, "NLRB Remedies: Where Are They Going," *Labor Law Journal* 51 (no. 2, Summer 2000), pp. 67–75.

42. *H.K. Porter Company v. NLRB,* 397 U.S. 99 (1970). See also *BE & K Construction Company v. NLRB,* 536 U.S. 516 (2002) and *Hoffman Plastic Compounds, Inc. v. NLRB,* 535 U.S. 137 (2002).

43. Office of the General Counsel, *NLRB News Release,* February 4, 2003, p. 4.

44. *Ford Motor Company v. NLRB,* 441 U.S. 488 (1979); *Charles D. Bonanno Linen Service v. NLRB,* 454 U.S. 404 (1982).

45. James A. Gross, "The Demise of the National Labor Policy: A Question of Social Justice," in *Restoring the Promise of American Labor Law,* Sheldon Friedman et al., eds. (Ithaca, N.Y.: ILR Press, 1994), pp. 57–58.

46. Janice R. Bellace, "Labor Law Reform for the Post Industrial Workplace," *Labor Law Journal* 45 (August 1994), p. 460.

47. James J. Brudney, "The Changing Workplace: Reflections on Group Action and the Law of the Workplace," *Texas Law Review* 74 (June 1996), pp. 1563–1599.

48. Cynthia L. Estlund, "The Ossification of American Labor Law," *Columbia Law Review* 102 (October 2002), p. 1540.

49. Estlund, "The Ossification of American Labor Law", pp. 1536–1158. See also William B. Gould, *Agenda For Reform: The Future of Employment Relationships and the Law* (Cambridge, Mass.: MIT Press, 1993) and Paul C. Weiler, *Governing the Workplace: The Future of Labor and Employment Law* (Cambridge, Mass.: Harvard University Press, 1990).

50. Michael C. Harper, "The Continuing Relevance of Section 8 (a)(2) to the Contemporary Workplace," *Michigan Law Review* 96 (no.8, August 1998), pp. 2322–2383.

51. Jeff Canfield, "Note: What a Shame: The Broken Beck Rights System in the Real World Workplace," *The Wayne Law Review* 47 (Fall 2001), 1049–1074; Peter Capelli, "Old Laws Hobble the New Economy Workplace," *Sloan Management Review* 42 (no. 2, Winter 2001), pp. 110–111.

52. Samuel Estreicher and Matthew T. Bodie, "Review Essay—Administrative Delay at the NLRB: Some Modest Proposals," *Journal of Labor Research* 23 (no. 1, Winter 2002), pp. 87–105. See also Edward B. Miller, *An Administrative Appraisal of the NLRB,* 4th ed. (Fairfax, Va.: John M. Olin Institute for Employment Practice and Policy at George Mason University, 1999).

53. United States General Accounting Office, *National Labor Relations Board: Action Needed to Improve Case-Processing Time at Headquarters* (Washington, D.C.: Superintendent of Documents, 1991), pp. 1–7.

54. *Three-Year Report by William B. Gould IV, Chairman, National Labor Relations Board* (Washington, D.C.: National Labor Relations Board, March 7, 1997), pp. 2–5; "Press Release" (Washington, D.C.: National Labor Relations Board, August 26, 1998).

55. *Sixty-Sixth Annual Report of the National Labor Relations Board for the Fiscal Year Ended September 30, 2001* (Washington, D.C.: U.S. Government Printing Office, 2003), pp. 5–11. See also Douglas S. McDowell and Kenneth Huhn, *NLRB Remedies for Unfair Labor Practices* (Philadelphia: Industrial Research Unit, University of Pennsylvania, 1976), pp. 245–246, and William N. Cooke, Aneil K. Mishra, Gretchen M. Spreitzer, and Mary Tschirhart, "The Determinants of NLRB Decision-Making Revisited," *Industrial and Labor Relations Review* 48 (January 1995), pp. 254–256.

56. Nancy Brown Johnson, "Airlines: Can Collective Bargaining Weather the Storm?" in *Collective Bargaining in the Private Sector,* Paul F. Clark, John T. Delaney, and Ann C. Frost, eds. (Champaign, Ill.: Industrial Relations Research Association, 2002), pp. 16–20; Charles M. Rehmus, "Evolution of Legislation Affecting Collective Bargaining in the Railroad and Airline Industries," in *The Railway Labor Act at Fifty,* Charles M. Rehmus, ed. (Washington, D.C.: U.S. Government Printing Office, 1977), p. 4.

57. *Sixty-First Annual Reports of the National Mediation Board* (Washington, D.C.: National Mediation Board, 1996), pp. 8–19.

58. *Annual Performance Report for the Fiscal Year Ending September 30, 2002* (Washington, D.C.: National Mediation Board, 2003), pp. 28–29.

59. Rehmus, "Collective Bargaining," in *The Railway Labor Act at Fifty,* pp. 14–15.

60. *Annual Performance Report for the Fiscal Year Ending September 30, 2002* (Washington, D.C.: National Mediation Board, 2003), pp. 11, 18, and 24.

61. *Fact Finding Report, Commission on the Future of Worker-Management Relations* (Washington, D.C.: U.S. Departments of Labor and Commerce, May 1994), pp. 99–100.

62. Douglas M. McCabe, "The Railroad Industry's Labor Relations Environment: Implications for Railroad Managers," *ICC Practitioners' Journal* 49 (September–October 1982), pp. 592–602.

63. Charles M. Rehmus, "The First Fifty Years—and Then," in *The Railway Labor Act at Fifty,* Rehmus, ed., p. 246.

64. Beatrice M. Burgoon, "Mediation under the Railway Labor Act," in *The Railway Labor Act at Fifty,* Rehmus, ed., p. 23.

65. "Deregulation in Three Transport Industries Has Produced Widely Diverse Labor Market Results," *Daily Labor Report,* May 13, 1986, p. A-13.

66. Mark Kahn, "Introduction," *Cleared for Takeoff: Airline Labor Relations Since Deregulation,* Jean T. McKelvey, ed. (Ithaca, N.Y.: ILR Press, 1988), p. 3.

67. Alfred Kahn, "In Defense of Deregulation," *Cleared for Takeoff: Airline Labor Relations Since Deregulation,* Jean T. McKelvey, ed. (Ithaca, N.Y.: ILR Press, 1988), pp. 344–345. For a legal analysis, see Beth Adler, "Comment: Deregulation in the Airline Industry: Toward a New Judicial Interpretation of the Railway Labor Act," *Northwestern University Law Journal 80* (Winter 1986), pp. 1003–1006.

68. *Annual Performance Report for the Fiscal Year Ending September 30, 2002* (Washington, D.C.: National Mediation Board, 2003), pp. 16–17.

69. Donald E. Cullen, "Emergency Boards Under the Railway Labor Act," in *The Railway Labor Act at Fifty,* Rehmus, ed., pp. 176–183. Also see "The Railroads Lose Their Bargaining Unity," *Business Week,* April 10, 1978, pp. 31–32, 55.

70. Sara K. Goo and Kristin Downey, "Airlines Aim to Make Strikes More Difficult; Industry Lobbies to Revise Labor Law," *Washington Post,* January 7, 2003, p. E-1; Cynthia Wilson, "Airlines Seek Changes in Labor Law," *St. Louis Post-Dispatch,* January 15, 2003, p. C-1.

71. Russell Grantham, "Airlines Push Labor Law Overhaul; Lengthy Negotiations Decried," *Atlanta Journal-Constitution,* February 9, 2003, p. 1Q.

72. "ALPA Protests Changes to Railway Labor Act," *Aviation Daily,* January 13, 2003, p. 4.

73. Trebor Banstetter, "Southwest Airlines Stays Clear of Labor Laws Fight," *Fort Worth Star-Telegram,* November 8, 2002, p. 2.

74. Nancy Brown Johnson, "Airlines: Can Collective Bargaining Weather the Storm?" in *Collective Bargaining in the Private Sector,* Clark, Delaney, and Frost, eds. 2002, p. 20.

The Great Temperature Debate

The employer is a small, nonunion furniture manufacturer with 15 employees engaged in interstate commerce. Both of the employees involved in this case worked in the machine shop building as band-saw operators. Because the band saws were located near the shop's large overhead door, to facilitate the disposal of sawdust, the band-saw operators were often subject to lower temperatures and drafts on cool or cold days, whereas other employees farther from the overhead door often felt too warm. To resolve this long-standing problem, the plant manager established a rule that stated: "The overhead door will remain open when the temperature in the shop exceeds 68 degrees and closed when the temperature is at or below 68 degrees."

On the day in question, employees Drake and Keeler, who were both band-saw operators, complained to the shop supervisor that they were too cold and requested that the overhead door be closed. When questioned by the shop supervisor, the majority of the other shop employees present responded that they thought the door should be left open. The thermometer on the wall of the shop supervisor's office, located in approximately the center of the machine shop building, read 72 degrees.

On this day, employee Drake was wearing a sleeveless shirt and shorts. Employee Keeler was dressed in blue jeans, a short-sleeved shirt, a flannel shirt, and a heavy sweater. Both Keeler and Drake claimed it was too cold and drafty at their workstation near the open overhead door. The shop supervisor refused to close the overhead door because the majority of employees wanted it left open. Drake and Keeler decided to walk off the job for the remainder of the day to protest the cold temperature at their workstation.

Upon returning to work the following morning, Drake and Keeler were informed by the plant manager that they had been fired for leaving work the previous day without management's permission. Drake and Keeler subsequently filed an unfair labor practice charge with the NLRB, alleging their discharge represented unlawful discrimination against their right to engage in concerted and protected activity under Section 7 of the LMRA. Drake and Keeler requested a remedy to include reinstatement with full back pay and restoration of any lost privileges.

QUESTIONS

1. Since Drake and Keeler's employer meets the standard for coverage under the LMRA by engaging in interstate commerce, which specific employee right protected by Section 7 of the LMRA could Drake and Keeler argue they were engaged in that at least partially motivated the employer's decision to discharge them?

2. On what grounds might the employer try to argue that the discharge of Drake and Keeler was an appropriate (legal) exercise of management's rights?

3. Was the employer's discharge of Drake and Keeler an unfair labor practice under the LMRA, as amended? If so, what should be the appropriate remedy?

Discharge for Consulting with an Attorney

Susan Clay was employed as an administrative assistant at a company that provided in-home care services to senior citizens in Maryland. After approximately 16 months on the job, Ms. Clay received a job performance evaluation on April 28 that rated her performance as "slightly below above average." On August 30, Ms. Clay received a written "Employee Warning Report" from her employer. The report stated that Ms. Clay would be discharged if her employer did not see "marked improvement in her job performance by the end of the next four week period." The report included several statements that Ms. Clay believed to be untrue. Among those statements was an allegation that Ms. Clay had refused the assistance of her supervisor during a meeting on August 4; that her supervisor had discussed performance problems with Ms. Clay in that August 4 meeting, which was attended by the company's owner; that Ms. Clay was told in the August 4 meeting that she was not being efficient or productive in most aspects of her job; and that Ms. Clay had received a previous warning regarding her job performance on June 23.

Ms. Clay's supervisor demanded that Ms. Clay sign the August 30 "Employee Warning Report," but Susan Clay declined to do so. Ms. Clay took the written warning report home in order to review it. The following day (August 31) on Ms. Clay's scheduled day off she telephoned her supervisor and stated, "due to the seriousness of the libel contained in the document, I have been advised to seek counsel before formally responding." The supervisor relayed Ms. Clay's message to the owner. Later on August 31, the company's owner telephoned Ms. Clay to say that having received Ms. Clay's earlier message, "I think it is time we part company. It will not be necessary [for you] to return to the office."

As an at-will employee not covered by the terms of an employment contract, Ms. Clay decided her only alternative was to sue the owner for wrongful discharge under state common law. Ms. Clay believed that Maryland public policy mandates that all individuals be given an opportunity to consult with an attorney concerning important matters affecting their lives, including their employment. Ms. Clay alleged she was fired by the owner because the owner knew the written warning report issued to Ms. Clay contained false statements and the owner must have feared that she would retain counsel and sue the owner for defamation. Alternatively, the owner simply didn't want to continue to employ an employee who had consulted an attorney about a work-related matter.

A court hearing was held, at which time the owner cited several Maryland court cases that stated that for a wrongful discharge to occur, the public policy in question must be a pre-existing, unambiguous, specific pronouncement contained in the state constitution, law, or prior court decision specifically prohibiting the employer's action or protecting the employee's conduct. While there may be a general right of free speech, the right to speak does not equate to the right to be employed. The owner acknowledged that Ms. Clay might have a general right to consult an attorney but such a general right does not equate to a public policy removing an employer's right to terminate an at-will employment relationship for any reason including the fact that an employee consulted or threatened to consult an attorney regarding an employment-related matter. Since Ms. Clay failed to establish a legitimate public policy cause of action, the employer requested the court to dismiss Ms. Clay's wrongful discharge claim and require her to pay all court costs associated with the lawsuit.

QUESTIONS

1. Should a state court have the legal authority to recognize the existence of a public policy based on inference or interpretations of general principles of equity or public opinion?

2. Should Ms. Clay's wrongful discharge claim be upheld or dismissed? Explain your reasoning.

Determination of Supervisory Status

The union sought to become the exclusive bargaining representative for a group of five harbor pilots employed by Pacific Coast Docking Pilots (the employer). The union won a National Labor Relations Board (NLRB)–supervised secret ballot election by a vote of five to zero. The employer refused to recognize and bargain with the union in an effort to force a federal court to determine if the five harbor pilots who composed the bargaining unit were supervisors or employees. The union filed an unfair labor practice against the employer for a refusal to bargain in good faith. The Board granted summary judgment in favor of the union, which the employer then appealed to a federal court of appeals for review.

The employer argued that the harbor pilots should be classified as "supervisors" and therefore excluded from the definition of "an employee" covered under the LMRA, as amended. The burden of proving the supervisory status of an employee is on the party asserting such a status. Under Section 2 (11), LMRA defines a supervisor as:

> any individual having authority, in the interests of the employer, to hire, transfer, suspend, lay off, recall, promote, discharge, assign, reward, or discipline other employees, or responsible to direct them, or to adjust their grievances, or effectively to recommend such action, if in conjunction with the foregoing the exercise of such authority is not of a merely routine or clerical nature, but requires the use of independent judgment.

The Supreme Court has established a three-part test for determining the supervisory status of an individual under the LMRA, as amended (*NLRB v. Health Care & Retirement Corp.*, 511 U.S. 571 [1994]). First, an employee must perform at least one of the 12 specific functions outlined in the statutory definition of a supervisor under Section 2 (11) of the LMRA. Second, in performing one of these functions, the individual must be required to exercise independent judgment. Third, the exercise of independent judgment must be "in the interest of the employer." The third test is typically the easiest to prove because virtually any action related to the attainment of a legitimate business goal or purpose of the firm will be considered an act "in the interest of the employer." Most cases involving the determination of supervisory status will rest on an analysis of the evidence related to parts one and two of the three-part supervisory status test.

The employer maintains that the docking pilots make recommendations on hiring and promotion decisions, assign work to employees, and are responsible for directing employees' work during the docking process. More specifically, the employer states that the advice of docking pilots is almost always followed in making decisions regarding whom to hire or promote into a docking pilot position or relief docking pilot position. U.S. Coast Guard regulations require that docking pilot trainees make trips with licensed docking pilots before becoming eligible to obtain a docking pilot's license. Docking pilots are required to evaluate the performance of trainees on such trips and provide a recommendation as to the suitability of each trainee for the job position of docking pilot. Docking pilots do not discipline other employees, adjust employee grievances, or evaluate the job performance of non-trainee pilots. The final authority for all hiring and promotion decisions rest with the president and vice president of the employer.

When a large ship enters a port, it requires the assistance of tugboats to maneuver into a position to dock or undock. The docking pilot receives from the employer a list of the ships scheduled to arrive or depart the port on a given day. The information provided by the employer includes such items as the current location and dimensions of each ship. The docking pilot uses this information together with current information on factors such as the wind and water current speed to determine the number of tugboats required to accomplish the docking procedure. Once a ship's captain has entered the port, a tugboat delivers the docking pilot to the ship. The docking pilot then assumes command of the ship from the ship's captain and directs the docking procedure. The docking pilot communicates directly with the captain of each tugboat involved to ensure that each tugboat will render the necessary assistance to ensure a safe and accurate docking experience. Essentially, the docking pilot communicates what must be accomplished to each tugboat captain, who then determines what actions his tugboat crew must take to accomplish the defined objective. Each tugboat captain is responsible for directing his or her own boat crew to carry out the instructions of the docking pilot. Tugboat captains have been previously determined by the NLRB to be supervisors under the LMRA. Once the docking procedure is completed, the docking pilot returns control of the ship to the ship's captain and reboards one of the tugboats to prepare for the arrival or departure of the next ship on the daily schedule.

The employer argues that the docking pilot's determination of how many tugboats will be required to perform a particular docking operation constitutes an assignment of work using independent judgment, which is a supervisory function under the LMRA's definition of a supervisor. The employer also notes that a docking pilot "responsibly directs" others during the docking procedure by giving orders to the tugboat captains regarding the number and placement of towing lines to ensure a safe and efficient docking procedure.

The union believes that the five docking pilots are professional employees covered by the LMRA, not supervisors. The docking pilots have no authority to hire anyone, although they may be asked to give a professional opinion regarding the qualifications of an applicant for a vacant docking pilot position. Compliance with Coast Guard regulations, which requires less experienced pilots to ride along with a more experienced pilot to learn information about a particular port before assuming responsibility for docking procedures in that port, represents a discharge of professional responsibility, which is a job duty of being a docking pilot. The docking pilots do not discipline other employees, handle grievances, or formally evaluate other employees' job performance.

The union further argued that instructions given by docking pilots to other tugboat captains (who are supervisors) during docking procedures are part of the job duties of a professional docking pilot. The docking pilot has no authority to order members of a tugboat captain's crew to perform any specific job duties. The determination of the number of tugboats required to perform docking procedures is a function of the size of the ship to be docked and prevailing sea and weather conditions. This determination does not require the exercise of significant independent judgment on the part of the docking pilot.

QUESTION

1. Should the docking pilots be classified as supervisors and thus excluded from participating in a bargaining unit for purposes of collective bargaining? Explain your reasoning.

Challenge of Employer Policy on "Inquiries by Government Representative"

Section 8 (a) (1) of the LMRA makes it an unfair labor practice for an employer to interfere with, restrain, or coerce employees in the exercise of rights guaranteed in Section 7 of the act. Sec. 8 (a) (4) makes it an unfair labor practice for an employer to discharge or otherwise discriminate against an employee for filing an unfair labor practice charge or giving testimony in any NLRB proceeding. The employer's employee handbook provided to every company employee contained the following written policy entitled "Inquiries by Government Representative":

> From time to time, management may be called, visited or sent written communication by a representative of a federal, state, or local government agency investigating a possible violation of law or seeking other information.

> It is our policy to cooperate with all authorized government agencies in the legitimate pursuit of their regulatory or enforcement functions. The following procedures must be followed for all such contact other than those regarding routine forms and other communications relating to sales taxes, business licenses and permits, and routine local health inspections.

> If you are the person contacted, immediately notify the person in charge of your Facility. If the visit is made after hours, contact the department vice president. If this fails, call the Emergency Phone number which is posted at all company facilities. Additionally, these guidelines should be followed:

> Be cordial to the person making the request. The visitor should be treated with the same courtesy as any guest at the Facility.

> Do not volunteer any information, or admit or deny the truthfulness of any allegation or statement the inspector may make, nor sign any written statements, such as reports or affidavits, without express approval from a company attorney.

During the course of an investigation into the alleged unlawful discharge of two employees at the company's nonunion facility for union activity, several employees expressed a reluctance to be interviewed by NLRB staff investigators or to testify at any unfair labor practice hearing out of concern that such action on their part could be viewed by management as a violation of the above-stated company policy, thus subjecting them to possible disciplinary action.

A separate unfair labor practice charge was filed alleging that the company's "Inquiries by Government Representative" policy was unlawful under the LMRA.

The employer presented three arguments why the current policy should be considered lawful under the LMRA. First, the policy states that it only applies to members of management, as indicated by the first sentence "From time to time, management may be called . . . " Second, the policy does not mention union activity or the NLRB. Third, no employee was disciplined for participating in the NLRB's ULP investigation regarding the alleged unlawful discharge of two employees for union activity.

QUESTIONS

1. Does the employer's policy "Inquiries by Government Representative" represent a violation of Section 8 (a) (1) of the LMRA? If so, what should be the appropriate remedy?

2. Does the employer's policy "Inquiries by Government Representative" represent a violation of Section 8 (a) (4) of the LMRA? If so, what should be the appropriate remedy?

CHAPTER 4

Unions and Management: Key Participants in the Labor Relations Process

As noted in Chapter 1, two key participants in the labor relations process are the union, which as the exclusive bargaining agent represents employees in the bargaining units, and management, which represents the owners or stockholders of the company. This chapter first provides a general explanation of the goals, strategies, and organizational structure of the company and the union for labor relations purposes. Because companies and unions are organized differently to meet different purposes, basic goals, strategies, and organizational structures will be presented that may be adjusted to meet respective differences. The second part of the chapter focuses on union governance and structure by describing the characteristics of unions, government at the various levels, organizational structure, and problems with corruption and misuse of power within a few unions. The final section covers union security, a subject vital to the union's role in gaining bargaining strength and meeting members' expectations.

Goals and Strategies: Management and Unions

Unions and management of companies have goals that are similar and those that may at times conflict. Their goals provide direction and serve as the basis for their organization's strategies, plans, and organizational structure. Exhibit 4.1 displays some major goals for both companies and unions, which in several cases are similar and consistent and in others have potential for conflict. The areas of potential conflict create possibilities for an adversarial relationship, and the areas of agreement create possibilities for cooperation and labor peace. As will be noted, most of the time unions and management are able to settle their differences without resorting to a work stoppage (0.0002 of total man-days are lost to

Exhibit 4.1

Goals of the Company and the Union

The Company Wants	The Union Wants
To survive and remain competitive	The company to survive and remain competitive as well as for the union to survive and remain secure
To grow and prosper	The company to grow and prosper as well as the union
To achieve a favorable return on its investment	The company to achieve a favorable return on its investment and return "fair" wages to employees
To effectively use human resources	The company to effectively use human resources within the rules and policies of the agreement and to achieve job security and employment opportunities for members
To attract, retain, and motivate employees	The company to attract, retain, and motivate employees within the rules and policies of the agreement
To protect management's rights to make decisions and retain flexibility	To protect union and employee rights that were negotiated and included in the labor agreement
To obtain a commitment from the union that there will be no strike for the duration of the agreement	To obtain a commitment from the company that there will be no lockout for the duration of the agreement

work stoppages). The collective bargaining process itself is a mechanism designed by the parties and confirmed by the U.S. Congress as the preferred method for resolving differences between unions and management.

Both the company and the union want the company to survive and remain competitive. Union agreement with this goal is logical because the employees would lose their jobs and the union would not survive without the company. Likewise, the union wants to survive as the representative of the employees of the company and will take steps to retain this designation. When a company wishes to remain nonunion or to have the union decertified, an inevitable conflict occurs.

The company wants to grow and prosper—a sign of success of its management. The union agrees with this goal and supports it because it creates more opportunities and benefits for employees, adds union members, allows more funds for union activities, and strengthens the union as an institution. Likewise, both company and union want the company to achieve a favorable return on its investment. Although they may disagree on what is meant by "favorable," both parties understand the mechanics of the financial side of the business. However, the union also wants to achieve a favorable or "fair" return for the employees' efforts, input, and contribution. Here, there may be a disagreement over what is a favorable return to the investors and a "fair" return to the employees.

Two related goals of the company are to achieve the effective use of its human resources and to attract, retain, and motivate employees. The union accepts these goals for the company as long as the company abides by the provisions that were negotiated and included in the collective bargaining agreement. For example, the company may wish to have the most productive employee work on an overtime assignment to be able to ship a rush order; however, the agreement may require that overtime assignments be made on a rotating basis. The presence of the union does not prevent making overtime assignments to the most productive employee; however, the overtime provision is a negotiable subject, and the parties must live by the provisions that they agree on.

The company wants to protect its rights to make decisions and retain the flexibility to operate the business. The union accepts the philosophy that some decisions are best made by management, including the type of products, the price of the products, financial policies, customer relations, advertising and promotion decisions, product design, and plant layout. At the same time, the union represents the interests of employees and attempts to provide protection and guarantee job opportunities for them by negotiating provisions in the labor agreement, such as contracting out work, use of seniority, and promotions and transfers to provide these rights.[1]

The company wants a union commitment to have no work stoppage for a specified period; this guarantees a stable workforce and allows the company to make production promises to customers. This commitment comes in the form of a "no-strike" clause in the labor agreement. The union may want a commitment from the company that employees have the right to have their grievances heard by management and may appeal them to a third-party neutral (arbitrator) when necessary to resolve differences.

Once the union and the company decide on their respective goals, they determine the appropriate strategies to reach these goals. Companies have been involved in strategic planning much longer than unions, and their strategic plans are usually more detailed and sophisticated. Only in recent times have unions started to think and operate in terms of strategic planning.

Company Strategic Planning

A company's strategy in labor relations is determined by its managerial philosophy, the ethics of its management, its economic condition, the composition of the workforce, competition in the industry, the time in the life of the company, and the capabilities of management. Management has choices about its strategy. It may believe that the company is better off remaining nonunion and devote much time and effort to ensuring positive human resources management. Some employers resist unions bitterly to ward off the large wage gap between union and nonunion employees (weekly earnings averaged $760 for union members versus $599 for nonunion workers in 2003, according to the Bureau of Labor Statistics). Management members who are in a highly competitive industry may be willing to do almost anything to keep unions out. Management at other companies may choose to change from a hard-bargaining approach to one of labor-management cooperation after it finally accepts the philosophy that both parties would gain more by cooperating than by conflicting. Exhibit 4.2 shows the range of company strategies in labor relations, from union suppression to labor–management cooperation.

Nonunion Companies' Strategies

Some authorities believe that profound changes in labor relations began in the 1980s and were brought on by forces external to union–management relationships. These forces include competition from abroad, deregulation, and competition from nonunion companies. More and more companies are finding that their

Exhibit 4.2

Company Strategies in Labor Relations

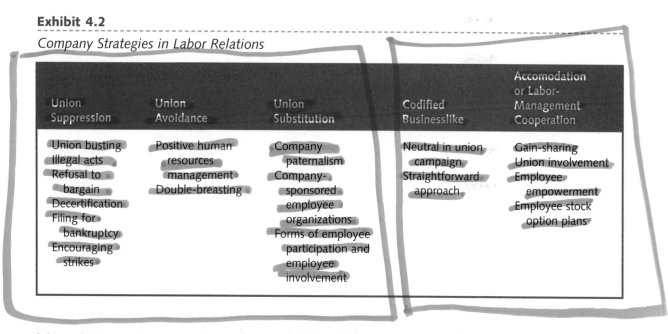

Union Suppression	Union Avoidance	Union Substitution	Codified Businesslike	Accomodation or Labor-Management Cooperation
Union busting Illegal acts Refusal to bargain Decertification Filing for bankruptcy Encouraging strikes	Positive human resources management Double-breasting	Company paternalism Company-sponsored employee organizations Forms of employee participation and employee involvement	Neutral in union campaign Straightforward approach	Gain-sharing Union involvement Employee empowerment Employee stock option plans

labor relations strategies are driven by economic choices and their need to adapt to new, more competitive business conditions. Because union suppression, union avoidance, and union substitution strategies have existed in different forms since the Industrial Revolution, a company may choose to attempt to maintain its nonunion status by preventing or supplanting unions. Another company may choose one of the nonunion strategies as a legitimate response that has been forced on it to cut costs, innovate, enter new markets, and devise flexible labor force strategies. This latter approach focuses on costs and productivity of human resources and the management of human resources.[2]

A company may use a more aggressive approach, called the *union suppression* strategy, to maintain its nonunion status or to destroy the union. The 1980s and 1990s have seen several highly visible examples of the union suppression strategy. One example is Greyhound, which was reorganized through a leveraged buyout, thereby incurring high debt. Although the company was profitable, the new owners went into contract negotiations determined to reduce their labor costs. No agreement was reached, and the union went on strike. The company announced that it was prepared to replace striking employees and had accumulated over $54 million in its strike preparation fund to defeat the union. The company had to borrow $25 million and suffered a first-quarter loss of $56 million. A few months later, Greyhound filed for reorganization in bankruptcy court. With numerous unfair labor practice charges against the company and with back pay claims in excess of $125 million, Greyhound began operating as a nonunion interstate bus line.[3] Then the parties reached an agreement after a three-year strike.

Other extreme and in some cases illegal tactics used by some companies to avoid unionization include the following:

- Developing a spy network (tattletales) to identify union supporters
- Refusing to hire former employees of unionized companies (but giving the applicant a reason other than prior union affiliation for employment denial)

- Establishing a case for discharge (including documentation) of known union advocates
- Seeking to determine prospective employees' attitudes toward unions from interviews, references, and so on, then refusing to hire them (again giving another reason) if they are pro-union
- Giving psychological tests (job-interest questionnaires) to determine the likelihood that an applicant will be interested in a union
- Locating new plants in areas where union membership is low and expanding the company's nonunion plants
- Using a standard application of a State Employment Service that asks applicants whether they have been a member of a union and using the application as part of the preemployment inquiry[4]

Some employers facing union-organizing campaigns have committed unfair labor practices deliberately, with the expectation of economic returns to them.[5] One study of employers led to this disappointing conclusion:

> [I]n the past, the compliance system [of the National Labor Relations Act] has been inadequate to the extent that some employers have found it profitable to commit unfair labor practices in order to forestall unionization. Those employers obeying the law because "it's the law" have faced a greater probability of incurring costs of unionization and may have been at a competitive disadvantage to employers who violated the law. Such inequities do not encourage compliance with the law and provide evidence of the need for labor law reform.[6]

When illegal practices yield economic returns to the violators, ethical questions are raised as to the fairness of the law and its application. Some companies that select the *union avoidance* strategy take a strong stance against union representation, even in facilities where unions already exist. They open nonunion facilities and attempt to keep them nonunion. They shift their capital investments away from the unionized facilities and make plant improvements in the nonunion plants. Where the union represents the employees, they attempt to reduce the labor costs by lowering wages and benefits, modifying traditional work practices, and encouraging decertification to the point of committing illegal actions. In these situations, the labor relations environment is highly adversarial, and union-management collaboration is not considered an option.[7]

One company, Ingersoll-Rand Company, was reported as initiating an antiunion corporate strategy. Its strategy included the following: (1) concentrate on building or buying new U.S. plants in open-shop states, and acquire other firms whose plants are partly or wholly nonunion, (2) relocate production from union plants to nonunion plants, and (3) use labor and community relations techniques that bypass local union officers, encourage union decertification, and oppose union-organizing efforts. Union representation had declined from 100 percent to 25 percent of Ingersoll-Rand's eligible workforce. Top company officials were reported as saying that the company wanted to remain "union-free," to listen to employees as individuals, not through a third-party union, and to stop unions from forcing the company to take actions with which it disagreed.[8]

Some companies adopting the union avoidance strategy practice *positive human resources management* or operate *double-breasted*. Company officials who adopt positive human resources management recognize the importance and necessity of maximizing "employee voice." Moreover, they implement the claim that people are the most important asset of the organization. Such organizations involve their employees in the decision-making processes of their organizations. These efforts are included under the general umbrella of "participative management," "total quality management," and "total quality control" programs.[9] In unionized organizations, the union is sometimes involved; those efforts are covered in Chapter 7.

Companies such as IBM, Texas Instruments, and Eastman Kodak have essentially adopted this strategy. Positive human resources management programs include the following elements:

- The absence of symbols of rank and status such as parking spaces, company cars, or country club memberships for managers

- Carefully considered surroundings—locating where high-quality schools and universities are near and keeping individual facilities small

- Overall corporate strength—high profits, fast growth, high technology, or dominant market position

- Programs to promote employment security, such as work sharing or overall reduction in pay to avoid layoffs in hard times

- Promotion from within—job posting, career development, and training and education programs

- Influential human resources management programs, for example, having the human resources manager report directly to top management

- Competitive pay and benefits, especially having compensation that is equitable externally and internally and comparable to the pay at unionized companies

- Management that listens—using systematic approaches such as attitude surveys, open-door policies, and appeal procedures

- Careful grooming of managers—focusing on long-term results, using assessment centers, and appraising in terms of competence and employee relationships[10]

Double-breasting exists when one company has two or more subsidiaries, one unionized and the others nonunion or open shop. These arrangements take several forms: (1) a holding company has financial control of one or more operating subsidiaries, (2) a unionized company buys a nonunion subsidiary and continues to operate it as nonunion, and (3) a nonunion company buys a unionized subsidiary and continues to operate it unionized. At present, the law requires the open-shop and unionized units of a holding company to be separately managed and operated as distinct entities. The National Labor Relations Board (NLRB) determines whether two seemingly separate companies should be treated as one by considering the following guidelines: interrelation of operations, centralization of control of labor relations, common management, and common ownership or financial control.[11] The Board stated:

> No one of these factors has been held to be controlling, but the Board opinions have stressed the first three factors, which go to show "operational integration," particularly centralized control of labor relations. The Board has declined in several cases to find integration merely upon the basis of common ownership or financial control.[12]

A third company strategy to maintain nonunion status is the *union substitution* strategy. This strategy originated in the company paternalism and company unions common in the 1920s but still exists today in the form of employee committees and other forms of employee participation. Although the National Labor Relations Act (NLRA) has outlawed company unions and unlawful assistance to unions affiliated with national organizations, some companies have organized and supported employee committees for the purpose of discussing and resolving grievances.[13] Even though these committees differ from traditional unions because they do not negotiate labor agreements, they could subsequently come under the provisions of the NLRA if their discussions over wages and employment conditions are interpreted as negotiations by the NLRB. Further, the employer could be directed to disband the committee or recognize and bargain with committee members as a labor union.[14]

Many nonunion companies have initiated employee involvement programs to restore the sense of working in a small business, to gain employee commitment to the enterprise, to dissuade union organizing, and to provide feedback to enhance motivation and productivity. Over 85 percent of companies in a Conference Board survey have a system for giving nonunion employees information about the competitive conditions or economic circumstances of their company. The majority have employee participation programs, such as quality circles and small-group discussions of production and quality of work, and have provided formal complaint and grievance systems.[15]

During recent years, nonunion companies have become more concerned about employee terminations, which are estimated to be about 3 million each year in the United States. At least half of these terminations occur without the employee being protected by either law or contract. In other words, the employee is terminated under the *employment-at-will doctrine* that states that either the employer or the employee is free to terminate the employment relationship "at will" (at any time, for any reason or no reason). Laws exist that prohibit discrimination on the basis of race, sex, color, religion, age, national origin, and union activities, and a collective bargaining agreement usually protects employees against termination without "just cause" (see Chapter 12).

Some nonunion companies provide arbitration as a fair method of resolving employee grievances, and some companies establish grievance procedures with arbitration as the last step. A pronounced increase in the number of employment arbitration cases in the nonunion sector is predicted because of the legislative encouragement of mediation and arbitration in the Americans with Disabilities Act and the U.S. Supreme Court's suggestion that predispute agreements to arbitrate will be upheld by the courts.[16] (More discussion on this topic is provided in Chapter 11.)

The most common system for resolving employee grievances is the open-door policy, wherein employees may present their grievances to management representatives. The success of this system depends on how conscientious managers at all levels are in fulfilling this policy and whether employees fear that presenting their grievances to managers above their immediate supervisor will have undesirable consequences.

Other forms of nonunion grievance procedures include grievance appeal boards, appeal steps up to top management, and peer review committees.[17] The grievance appeal board allows employees to present their grievances to a board for a final decision. In this system, three management members and two employees might hear the grievance and decide the outcome. Although the system is sometimes called a "jury of one's peers," management representation is usually greater than that of employees and can outvote employee board members if necessary.[18]

Unionized Companies' Strategies The labor relations function in unionized companies differs from that in nonunion companies in several ways. First, in the unionized setting, two parties, the union and management, are involved. Instead of decisions being made by management alone, many decisions, such as wages, hours, promotion, layoffs, and other terms and conditions of employment, are made bilaterally through negotiations. Second, the presence of the union formalizes the employee-representation activities because employees may file a grievance if they believe that the company has violated terms of the negotiated agreement. Third, the negotiated rules and policies that govern the employment relationship for those employees covered under the collective-bargaining agreement essentially become company policy because both parties have to abide by the terms that they have negotiated.[19]

One strategy adopted by unionized companies is the *businesslike, codified strategy*. These companies accept unions as the legitimate representative of the employees and conclude that if the employees want a union, they will deal with it. They do not attempt to have the union decertified, do not commit flagrant unfair labor practices, and do not try to substitute participative groups for unions. Company managers respect and trust their union counterparts and expect the same in return. For the relationship to last, both parties must realize that respect and trust are fundamental to both their futures. The approach of these companies is to deal directly and bargain with the union over wages, hours, and terms and conditions of employment at the appropriate times. When the labor agreement negotiations are complete, managers of these companies administer the agreement as they interpret it. In other words, they "go by the book." Although General Electric was known in the 1950s for its "take-it-or-leave-it" approach to labor negotiations, its strategy today can be categorized as a businesslike approach. The remaining chapters explain this approach to labor relations. Also, as noted previously, strategies of companies and unions change during their lifetimes and with economic conditions, changes in leadership, and personalities of participants.

The fifth strategy shown in Exhibit 4.2 is one of *accommodation and labor-management cooperation*. This strategy entails the union cooperating with management, rather than the parties having an adversarial relationship. Management and unions actively work together to create an organizational climate and a way of operating that will allow employees to participate directly in decisions in their work areas as members of task teams and as members of problem-solving groups. Unions represent their members in decision making and in collective bargaining.[20]

Unions can contribute to companies' strategic planning and implementation activities. For example, a union can provide input from a clearly defined group of employees, as well as transfer information about corporate plans and direction to those represented employees. The union leaders can help the rank-and-file employees better understand the business plan and lend credibility to the plan. Although these contributions are clearly positive, union involvement in strategic planning takes more time because the union leadership must meet with the membership to explain planned actions. Also, to retain a competitive edge, upper management often does not want to reveal new directions and planned actions. As a result, unions typically have a greater opportunity to have a role in strategy implementation than in strategy formulation. For example, if a company is facing increasing losses because of foreign competition, the company may enlist the assistance of the union in finding ways to reduce costs. Alternatives include cooperative approaches to job design or developing a new reward system, such as gain-sharing, to encourage labor-management cooperation. Another possibility is the introduction of new technology to improve productivity, which may include restructuring existing jobs.[21] (This topic is discussed further in Chapter 8.)

> For organizations and unions to achieve a more collaborative relationship, managers, unions, and employees must overcome their resistance to change. Managers must develop a more open, less authoritarian managerial style; unions must abolish their traditional "us versus them" approach and adopt the team concept; and employees must accept a greater worker commitment and more involvement in determining how to get the job done and how to get it done right.[22]

Employee empowerment is reflected in employee involvement and participation programs, which include quality circles, quality-of-work-life efforts, labor-management participation teams, and autonomous work units. These efforts address such issues as product quality, work-unit performance, new technology, safety and health, and supervision. Here, union leaders and members accept responsibility for success of the organization. Unions demonstrate their capacity to confer value to their members and create wealth for all of the organization's stakeholders.[23]

This relationship ensures that unions and management focus on common goals, which include the health of the business in a changing economic environment, and new issues, such as adopting new technology to ensure competitiveness and business survival. Management accepts unions as stakeholders in an ongoing complex, multistakeholder organization designed to ensure survival and provide an equitable return for all involved in the process. Several companies and unions have already proceeded in this direction. General Motors (GM) and the United Auto Workers (UAW) have included cooperation, gain-sharing, and teamwork in the GM Saturn plant. The Amalgamated Clothing and Textile Workers (now United Needle Trades, Industrial, and Textile Employees Union [UNITE]) and Xerox have organized Horizon Study Teams to investigate and make recommendations on a wide range of strategic business decisions. Harley Davidson and its two unions co-manage the Kansas City plant. (Other examples are discussed in Chapter 9.)

To achieve this new union role, management and union leaders must develop different skills. Union leaders need business decision-making skills; they must understand the business and the problem-solving process. At the same time, they must maintain contact with the membership to better represent members' interests. Management must take steps to reorient its views from seeing unions and labor agreements as constraints to recognizing a more cooperative union-management relationship. Management must provide the union and its leadership with a secure position as the legitimate, permanent representative of the bargaining unit employees. This means abandoning efforts to decertify the union or to reduce the union's importance at the workplace. It means developing a mutual trust between parties at every level of the organization.[24]

Companies may choose a mixed strategy, which can encompass union avoidance, union substitution, or labor–management cooperation, at various sites in a multiplant operation. For example, a company may operate double-breasted and strongly oppose the union at one of its nonunion plants while at the same time engaging in labor–management cooperation at another plant. Such strategic choices are made at the highest levels of the organization, and the advantages and disadvantages of each strategy are seriously debated and deliberated before any strategy is adopted by the company.

Upper management considers the market pressures, operational and financial factors, and collective bargaining relationships in its deliberations. If market pressures are intense as a result of import penetration, management may be inclined to choose union avoidance in the nonunion sector. However, if a high proportion of the plants are unionized, management may choose the labor-management cooperation strategy. Researchers continue to examine which factors lead to certain strategies.[25]

Union Strategic Planning

Labor unions, like other organizations, define their operational goals, determine their organizational strategies and plans, develop policies and procedures, and manage their resources to reach their goals and maximize their performance. Unions also are involved in long-range planning, establishing procedures for budgeting, attracting able staff members, communicating with members to provide information and to obtain reliable feedback, and establishing controls for financial accountability.[26]

Labor unions in the United States have been involved in strategic planning for only a short time. For years, unions as a rule reacted to managerial decisions with little concern for long-range implications. Today, more and more unions are finding it essential to become involved in strategic planning. Several unions, such as the Communications Workers, the Auto Workers, and the Steelworkers, have recognized the need for long-range strategic planning and created strategic planning committees. To survive, all unions must develop such plans. A typical union's strategic plan includes: (1) a mission statement, (2) analysis of the external environment, (3) internal analysis of the union's strengths and weaknesses, (4) long-term and short-term objectives, and (5) strategy development. A survey of American Federation of Labor–Congress of Industrial Organizations (AFL-CIO) unions found the following:

1. Typical mission statements are to organize workers for the purpose of collective bargaining; to foster legislation of interest to the working class; and to disseminate economic, social, and political information affecting workers' lives and welfare. As an example, see Exhibit 4.3 for the AFL-CIO's mission statement.

2. The analysis of the external environment includes an examination of the changing demographics of the workforce (toward more worker diversity), appraisal of current and future political and legislative concerns, consideration of labor's image, and analysis of employer practices and industry trends.

Exhibit 4.3

AFL-CIO's Mission Statement

What We Stand for: Mission and Goals of the AFL-CIO

The mission of the AFL-CIO is to improve the lives of working families—to bring economic justice to the workplace and social justice to our nation. To accomplish this mission we will *build* and *change* the American labor movement.

We will build a broad movement of American workers by organizing workers into unions.
We will recruit and train the next generation of organizers, mass the resources needed to organize and create the strategies to win organizing campaigns and union contracts. We will create a broad understanding of the need to organize among our members, our leadership and among unorganized workers. We will lead the labor movement in these efforts.

We will build a strong political voice for workers in our nation.
We will fight for an agenda for working families at all levels of government. We will empower state federations. We will build a broad progressive coalition that speaks out for social and economic justice. We will create a political force within the labor movement that will empower workers and speak forcefully on the public issues that affect our lives.

We will change our unions to provide a new voice to workers in a changing economy.
We will speak for working people in the global economy, in the industries in which we are employed, in the firms where we work, and on the job everyday. We will transform the role of the union from an organization that focuses on a member's contract to one that gives workers a say in all the decisions that affect our working lives—from capital investments, to the quality of our products and services, to how we organize our work.

We will change our labor movement by creating a new voice for workers in our communities.
We will make the voices of working families heard across our nation and in our neighborhoods. We will create vibrant community labor councils that reach out to workers at the local level. We will strengthen the ties of labor to our allies. We will speak out in effective and creative ways on behalf of all working Americans.

SOURCE: http://www.aflcio.org/aboutaflcio/about/mission/, April 3, 2004.

---

3. The internal analysis includes an examination of the union's internal functioning, such as union governance, openness for discussion of diverse opinions, and appraisal of the professional staff whose jobs are to provide service to the members.

4. Organizational objectives are set for short-term and long-term activities. Short-term objectives may include meeting membership needs through collective bargaining, reducing substance abuse, improving pensions, and enhancing job security. The most common long-term objective is simply the survival of the labor organization.

5. Further work is needed to define strategies for addressing labor unions' long-term concerns for continual survival and growth as institutions.[27]

Some unions, like the UAW, have established internal commissions to participate in strategy planning. The report of the Commission on the Future of the UAW, entitled "A Strong Union in a Changing World," addressed the union's major economic concern about the erosion of the nation's industrial base and related problems of corporate flight and disinvestment. It also urged more effective use of the media in presenting the union's public positions on tax policy and fairness, dislocated employees, the changing workforce, issues of sexism and racism, and rapid change in technology and methods of work.

The Communications Workers of America is one union that has effectively instituted strategic planning for its success. Over the last two decades, the CWA has faced serious challenges as a result of product market deregulation and technological change. In 1983, the court-ordered divestiture of AT&T broke up the Bell system. In 1983, AT&T and its affiliated telephone companies employed 650,000 CWA employees, and both parties enjoyed a regulated environment that had a centralized bargaining system and stable labor–management relations at the national level. Telephone companies had no serious competition, and cost increases could be passed on to consumers if the state regulatory commissions would approve the requested rate increases.

Union density in the telecommunications industry fell from 56 percent in 1983 to 24 percent in 2001 due to downsizing by the Bell companies, reclassifying jobs from technical and professional to managerial (not eligible for union membership), and creation and growth in mostly nonunion companies, such as MCI. In the 1990s, the CWA was faced with organizational uncertainty and complexities with a membership accustomed to easy contract victories and predictable, paternalistic labor relations. The CWA decided to transform itself from a telephone workers union to the "union of the information age," which would focus on information services. Instead of being a union predominantly of telephone employees, the CWA would expand to printing and publishing, radio broadcasting, journalists, computer programmers, software specialists, and others. The CWA made adjustments at the bargaining table; it began negotiating retraining provisions for its members, pension enhancements, and early retirement bonuses. To ward off health insurance concessions, it had to mobilize its members for contract fights. Mobilizations included one-on-one postcard messages, workrule (following rules and instructions in excessive detail) campaigns, wearing common colors or arm bands on certain days of the week to show solidarity, public rallies, and campaigns of letter writing to state and local politicians. The CWA negotiated company neutrality pledges, expedited elections, and card checks for union recognition, through which the CWA gained over 30,000 members by 2001. Through mergers with eight smaller national unions, the CWA has gained over 227,000 new members. The CWA agreed to support regulatory changes by use of its political influence in exchange for explicit benefits guarantees and job security. Thus, over the last 20 years, the CWA has taken strategic steps to transform itself from a telephone workers union to a "union of the information age" and has intertwined its collective bargaining, political, and organizing activities to make it one of America's most effective and successful unions.[28]

Several other international unions, such as the Air Line Pilots Association, Steelworkers, Service Employees International Union, American Federation of Teachers, and the Bakery, Confectionery, and Tobacco Workers have undertaken strategic planning efforts. These international unions have added new terms to their operational language, such as strategy development, organizational assessment and planning, and implementation. They have used surveys, interviews, and focus groups for building participation and consensus. The results have been mission statements, goals and priorities, assignment of responsibilities, funding activities and budget allocations, dues split between the local and international unions, and measures for evaluating success.[29]

Although strategic planning is still a rare event in local unions, it will become more common as international unions provide leadership and assistance to these efforts. Efforts to date include the rebuilding of the steward system, new budget and management information systems, new internal and external organizing programs, and restructuring of the board and staff organization.[30]

Unions have made labor concessions as a quid pro quo for debt restructuring. They have increased the frequency of union representation on corporate boards of directors, usually in exchange for wage concessions (in the automobile, airline, trucking, and food processing industries). Unions have obtained direct ownership in corporations through employee stock ownership plans and have attempted direct buyouts of several companies. These forms of union involvement have come about not by virtue of the union's statutory rights but by virtue of the union's accumulation of market and financial power.[31]

Company Organization for Labor Relations Activities

There are many organizational structures for labor relations activities in U.S. companies. The following discussion introduces some of the basic organizational considerations, although different company characteristics will alter these designs.[32]

In larger corporations, the labor relations function is usually highly centralized, with policy, strategic planning, and bargaining decisions made at the corporate level. In fact, the final economic decisions are usually made by the chief operating executive with the advice of corporate-level labor relations managers. In smaller companies with only one or a few facilities, these decisions are made at the plant level and shared by plant management with the plant labor relations manager, who offers advice.

In larger companies, at the operations or plant level, the plant manager and plant labor relations manager play the key roles in certain labor relations activities, such as contract administration, grievance handling, and monitoring labor relations activities. In smaller companies, activities at the plant level also include bargaining, strategic planning, and policy formulation.[33]

The duties and responsibilities of all labor relations managers and specialists are determined in large part by the organizational structure and its degree of centralization or decentralization of authority. The duties typically include corporatewide responsibility for policies, procedures, and programs ranging from union organizing drives at nonunion facilities to negotiations with the union at others.

Exhibit 4.4 shows the organizational chart for the labor relations function in a large, complex company. As shown in the organizational chart, the vice president of personnel and industrial relations reports directly to the president and has the director of labor relations reporting to him or her. Each of the company's six product lines has its own labor relations organization.

A large, diversified company having several divisions or product lines will typically have a vice president of industrial relations, which includes human resources and labor relations activities, who reports directly to the president and has the director of labor relations reporting to him or her.

Exhibit 4.4

Labor Relations Organization: Dotted-Line Relationships

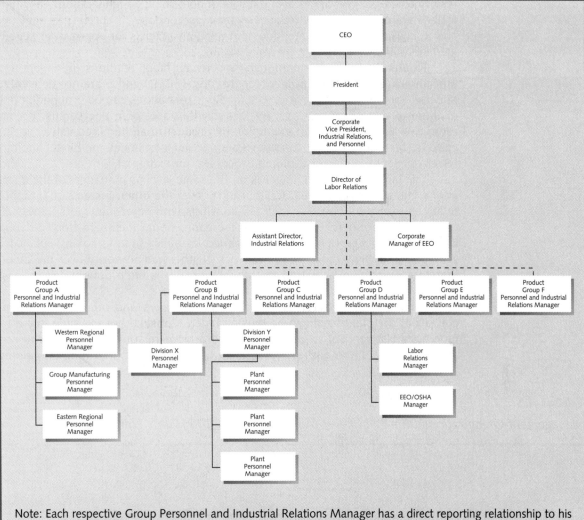

Note: Each respective Group Personnel and Industrial Relations Manager has a direct reporting relationship to his or her respective group management while maintaining a "dotted-line" relationship to the corporate staff, which has the responsibility for formulation of corporatewide labor relations policies and procedures.

As each group is dependent upon the corporate function as the formulator of this policy, the lines of communication and working relationships are strong, and the level of communication very high.

Their function is to administer corporate policies and procedures as formulated by the Vice President of Personnel and Industrial Relations and his or her staff.

SOURCE: Audrey Freedman, *Managing Labor Relations* (New York: The Conference Board, 1979), p. 28.

Labor relations managers at the plant level also typically have responsibilities for both human resources and labor relations activities. They help implement related corporate and divisional policies, participate in contract negotiations, and resolve employee grievances over daily labor agreement administration. They typically are accountable both to the plant manager for daily labor relations activities and to divisional or corporate industrial relations officials for approval of negotiated labor agreements.

Exhibit 4.5 suggests relationships between labor relations managers and other managers at the plant level (operations B, C, D, and E are not delineated in detail for the sake of brevity). The facility's operations can be grouped in one or more of the following ways: by location (furnace room one versus furnace room two at a steel mill, for example), by product (manufactured valves versus gaskets, for example), by function (such as maintenance), or by technology (electroplated and chemical plated processes, for example).

The labor relations manager is on the same level as managers of the operations, but neither individual has authority over the other. Instead, plant labor relations managers have *line-staff* relationships with other managers. Line-staff relationships occur when two or more organizational members from different lines of authority work together on a particular policy (a no-smoking policy, for example) or activity (such as grievances). Neither has authority over the other; therefore, resolution or output of this relationship is often determined by past perceived benefits each has derived from the other.

Relationships between labor relations managers and other management officials at the plant level can be tension laden. Consider, for example, the attitude a shift supervisor might have toward a labor relations manager who has awarded to the union a grievance against him or her for performing bargaining

Exhibit 4.5

Management Organization at the Plant Level (Approximately 1,100 Hourly Employees)

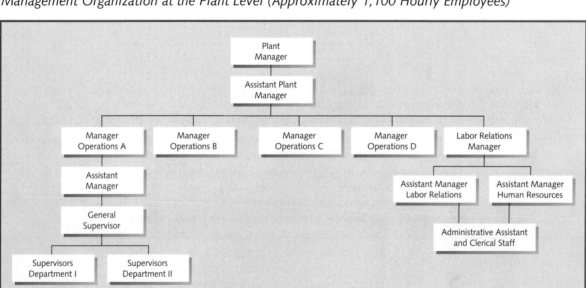

unit work (Chapter 10) or who has overturned a discharge decision made by the supervisor (Chapter 12).

Union Governance and Structure

Unions as organizations are fundamentally different from business organizations. Business organizations are built on the assumption that power, authority, and legitimacy flow downward from the owner or stockholders through management. Union organizations, on the other hand, have mechanisms such as a written constitution and bylaws that ensure an opportunity for members to participate in the governance of the organization—hold office, attend meetings, vote in elections, or express dissatisfaction with the leadership. Thus, in the democratic organization of a union, power, authority, and legitimacy ultimately flow upward from the consent of the governed. If the leadership of a union wishes to move in a new direction, such as toward greater union-management cooperation, the new direction ultimately depends on the approval of the membership. If elected leaders do not consider new initiatives in terms of the political realities, they will be rejected by the vote of the members. For example, in cases where the members do not trust management's actions in a joint cooperative effort, the leadership must put forth the appropriate effort to build a trusting relationship before developing the joint effort.[34]

Nearly a hundred different international (an international union has local unions outside the United States, such as Canada) and national unions and over 60,000 local unions exist in the United States; their governance is discussed in this chapter following a brief description of their organizational structure. As with companies, unions' organizational structures reflect their activities. Exhibit 4.6 shows the organizational chart of an international union, which includes the

Exhibit 4.6

Organizational Chart of an International Union

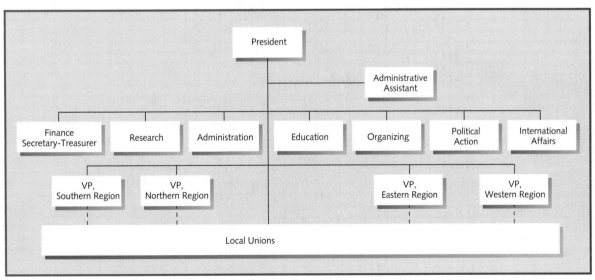

various officers, operational departments and staff, regions, and local unions. In this case, the basic functions include financial activities handled by the secretary-treasurer, research, administration, education, organizing, political action, and international affairs. These activities are usually carried out at the union's national headquarters, with some headquarters' staff members possibly working in the field. The regional offices are headed by a vice president, who has an advisory relationship with the local unions in the region. Regional offices are established to better serve the needs of the local unions and to represent the national office in the region.

At the local union level, the organizational structure is fairly simple. Exhibit 4.7 shows the officers and the shop stewards. In small unions, these are all part-time positions; only in the larger unions does the financial support allow full-time union leaders. Most local unions have at least one vice president, a secretary, and a treasurer. The addition of any other officer, such as the sergeant-at-arms in Exhibit 4.7, depends on the needs of the union. Shop stewards are usually elected to represent the membership in their respective departments. The following section explains how unions are governed at the different levels and presents some of the major problems in the governing process.

To understand union governance, one can compare the union with a unit of state or federal government. The executive, legislative, and judicial activities occur at various levels. The local union meetings and national conventions are the legislative bodies; the officers and executive boards comprise the executive bodies; and the various appeal procedures serve the judicial function. A union

Exhibit 4.7

Organizational Chart for a Local Union

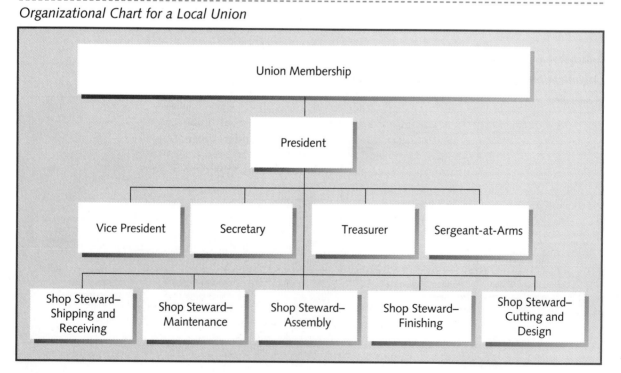

can also be compared with a private organization because it is a specialized institution having a primary purpose of improving the economic conditions and working lives of its members.

Unions claim the democratic ideal, but realistically they must rely on a representative form of government. On the whole they seem to be as democratic as local, state, and federal governments. In fact, the union membership has more of a say in the way the union operates than most citizens have in their governments or most stockholders have in their corporations.[35]

To appreciate unions as organizations, one must recognize their wide diversity, the organizational relationships of the various levels, the functions of the officers, and the varying degrees of control. The next section explores the characteristics of craft and industrial unions, the functions of local union officers, and the government and operations of local unions. The national or international union, which is composed of the local unions within a craft or industry, is explained in a similar framework. Not to be overlooked are the various intermediate levels of union organizations that provide specific functions for their affiliated unions. A fourth level for many union organizations is the federation, or the AFL-CIO, whose organizational structure, functions, and officer responsibilities are also discussed.

The Local Union

Although there are generally four levels of unions—local, national (or international), intermediate, and the federation of unions—the local union is the main point of contact for the individual employee. The typical union member often identifies more closely with the local union than with the other union levels. He or she attends and sees local officers at the local meetings and workplace. When the union member has a grievance, the local union officers are the first to assist. When a strike occurs, the local union officers are the ones who make continuous contact with the strikers on the picket line. Although the national union may negotiate the master labor agreement under which the local union member works and the AFL-CIO may deal with the president and Congress on certain issues facing the nation, the local union serves as the vital link between the individual union member and the national union, which in turn might link with the AFL-CIO.

Organizationally, the local union is a branch of the national union. It receives its charter from the national union and operates under the national union's constitution, bylaws, and rules. The constitution of the national union prescribes the number and types of officers, their duties and responsibilities, and the limits of their authority. Although union constitutions vary in length and content, they often mandate certain financial reports and require that a certain number of meetings be held, that the local labor agreement conform to the master labor agreement negotiated by the national union if there is companywide bargaining, and that approval to call a strike be obtained by the local union. With the trend toward greater centralization of authority by the national union, the local union over the years has lost much of its operational flexibility.

Differences between Local Craft and Industrial Unions The operation of the local union in large part depends on the type of employees making up its membership. Although there is not a clear-cut division between them, unions can be divided generally into two groups: craft and industrial.

Differing Union Organizations The **craft unions** are composed of members who have been organized in accordance with their craft or skill, for example, bricklayers, electricians, carpenters, or ironworkers. **Industrial unions** have been organized on an industry basis, for example the Steelworkers, Auto Workers, Chemical Workers, Mine Workers, and so on. This, of course, does not mean that there are no skilled employees in the steel, auto, or rubber industries; but it does mean the electricians in a steel plant would likely be members of the Steelworkers.

Differing Scope of the Labor Agreement The craft and industrial unions differ in other ways that have an effect on their operations. First, the craft unions, which frequently represent the building trades, usually negotiate short labor agreements (supplemented by detailed agreements on special topics, such as apprenticeship programs and safety) that cover a defined geographical region, and each has considerable independence from the national union compared with industrial unions. Because of the nature of their work, craft union members may work on several job sites for several employers in a given year under the same labor agreement. The labor agreement covers the construction companies and a number of building trades' unions in the particular geographical area.

The industrial union, on the other hand, may be covered by a national labor agreement negotiated between the company and the national union, which covers all of the company's unionized plants. For example, GM plants in Atlanta, Detroit, and Los Angeles are covered by the same master agreement. Well over 100 pages long, it explains in detail the wage plan, transfers, pensions, layoffs, and so on. A separate local agreement is negotiated to cover matters of concern to the specific local plant and its employees, which must be consistent with the master agreement. In plants having no national labor agreement, a plantwide agreement covering production and maintenance employees is typically negotiated.

Differing Skills Types of skills help demonstrate another difference in local union operations. The craft members are highly skilled artisans who have completed formal training, usually in a formal apprenticeship program. Many industrial employees, on the other hand, do not require much prior job training. Therefore, the craft union members often feel that they have higher status than their industrial counterparts. The training programs available for the industrial union members are usually offered by the company, whereas the training received by members of craft unions is jointly controlled and operated by the unions. So craft unions select those who will be offered the apprenticeship training, whereas companies alone select the trainees in the plants. Such an arrangement has allowed the craft unions to limit the numbers in the craft, sometimes to only their families and friends.

Differing Job Characteristics The nature of their work creates a unique opportunity for craft unions to operate under conditions that approximate a closed shop. Because many of the work assignments last only a short period, the craft members, such as electricians on a building project, return to the union hiring hall for their next assignment after their part of a project is completed. Upon receiving the assignment, the union members could report to another job site and work, possibly for another company. Usually, these arrangements are worked out in advance by the business agent of the craft union and the companies who agree to operate under the existing labor agreement. In other words, the union hiring hall serves as a clearinghouse or placement office for the construction companies as well as the union members. Because the hiring hall must be operated in a nondiscriminatory manner, nonunion employees may also use its services; however, use by nonunion employees is still quite rare. In comparison, the typical member of the industrial union is hired by the company and will work for the same employer—usually at the same facility—until retirement or employment is terminated.

Differing Leadership Roles Another difference between craft and industrial unions pertains to the roles of the business agent and shop stewards of the craft union and the local union officials of the industrial unions. The **business agent**, the full-time administrator of the local craft union, provides many of the same services as the local union president of a large industrial union. Both are considered the key administrative officials of their respective local union halls, and they lead the local union negotiations and play a key role in grievance administration. However, the business agent has additional duties, such as administering the union hiring hall, serving as the chief "watchdog" over the agreement at the various work sites, and appointing an employee on each job site to serve as the shop steward. The **shop steward**, who may be the first person on the job or a senior employee, handles employee grievances, represents the business agent on the job, and contacts the business agent if anything goes wrong.

The shop steward is the personification of the union to the members; the impressions of the steward greatly influence the members' perceptions of the union. Where impressions of the steward are positive, members also have positive views of grievance procedures and have greater union commitment. Stewards spend about 12 hours per week on labor relations matters; between 50 and 80 percent of this time is spent on grievance handling. Therefore, training of shop stewards in grievance handling is important because it results in less time required to process grievances, an increased likelihood that the shop steward will seek reelection, and the ability of the steward to devote more time to improving relations between the union and management.[36]

Most unions have ongoing steward training programs, which include such subjects as enforcing the contract, filing grievances, and monitoring health and safety violations. However, some unions have made arrangements with universities to offer college-credit courses specifically designed to provide a broader understanding of organized labor's role in achieving social justice and to increase the effectiveness of stewards as advocates in the workplace and the community. As one example, Queens College in New York City began offering the course "Labor at the Crossroads" in 1986 for stewards of Local 1180 of the Communications Workers of America. With its success, Queens College began offering an Urban Leadership Program, which is a special sequence of college-credit courses that could be applied to a bachelor's or master's degree. Today, over 150 Local 1180 members are enrolled in Urban Leadership courses every year.[37]

In local industrial unions, the president may or may not serve full-time. If the position is full-time, the salary comes from union dues. If the position is part-time, the president is compensated from the union treasury only for the time taken off the company job (at the regular rate of pay). Presidential duties include participating in local negotiations, maintaining the local union office, chairing local union meetings, assisting in grievance administration, and ensuring that management abides by the agreement. On many occasions, a staff member of the international union (usually the **international union representative**) assists local officers in negotiations and in administering the labor agreement and ensures that the local's activities conform to the national constitution and directives. The shop steward, the elected representative in each department in the plant or facility, represents the members at local union meetings, handles grievances at the shop level, and collects dues, if necessary.[38] Union officers may be granted preference in shift assignment and protected from layoffs; however, they must be involved in the day-to-day administration of the collective bargaining agreement.

Involvement in union leadership depends on individuals being convinced of the importance of the cause of the union. This is necessary because the union leadership, whether a shop steward or the local union president, will be devoting a certain number of hours each month without pay to provide services to coworkers. Employees who take on the role of union officer tend to do so because they are concerned about the well-being of their coworkers and have received encouragement from these peers. They are more likely to have been employed for a longer period and tend to have a lesser degree of job satisfaction.[39]

Many unions today are neither pure craft unions nor pure industrial unions in nature. They are likely still concentrated in their traditional sector (that is, the core of the UAW is the automobile industry and the United Steelworkers, the steel industry, for example). Many unions are more appropriately described as "general unions" because of their multijurisdictional organizations. As an example, both the UAW's and the steelworkers' organizing efforts occur in manufacturing, in the service industry, and in wholesale and retail trades.[40]

Government and Operation of the Local Union   There are several common ways for union members to participate in union activities: holding office, participating in meetings, attending conventions, voting (elections, ratification, and strike vote), and helping with the monthly newsletter.

Union members whose growth needs are not fulfilled on their job are usually more willing to become involved in union administration. Also, individuals are usually more willing to participate in union administration when their values are closely aligned with their role in the union.[41]

Participation in Meetings   Attendance at local union meetings often varies between 5 and 10 percent of the membership; attendance is higher, however, among union members who perceive a potential payoff for participation.[42] When the union is confronted with important business or a crisis, such as during union elections, taking a strike vote, negotiations, or ratifying the negotiated agreement, attendance also rises. Unions and their members have been criticized for their lack of attendance, but formal attendance cannot be taken as the real measure of membership participation. Much membership participation takes place on an informal basis at the plant level among employees, among friends during lunch, or between shop stewards and members during rest breaks. Concerns are channeled to the union leadership through these stewards, who regularly attend local meetings. The influence of these information channels over union policies and actions should not be underestimated. Local unions are learning to use survey methods and interviewing techniques to gather information about such issues as safety and health, contract provisions, promotional opportunities, job stress, perception of the union, recruitment of new members, and so on not only to prepare for negotiations but to improve the operations of the union and assess membership attitudes.[43]

Unions have much potential for increasing participation of local union members. For example, unions could allow members to provide volunteer services to the local union in lieu of paying local union dues; make full use of electronic information services, like the Internet, Web sites, and e-mail, to communicate and pursue union objectives; and find new ways to involve the rank-and-file members in organizing, bargaining, and political activities.[44]

Interestingly, union participation does not always lead to greater job dissatisfaction. In fact, active union membership in less adversarial climates will not be a source of increased job dissatisfaction. Therefore, if the labor relations climate is less adversarial, management should not fear or discourage employees to take an active role in their unions.[45]

The union leaders almost always attend local union meetings, as do departmental representatives, "hard-core" members, pressure groups, social groups, and aspirants to union leadership positions. Union stewards are expected to attend local union meetings and represent the interests of those in their unit. Although direct votes occur only on major issues, the union steward can usually reflect the membership views.[46]

Locals have tried numerous ways to increase attendance of regular members, such as providing beer, sandwiches, movies, and door prizes; fining members who miss a specified number of meetings; or refusing to let them seek an elected office. Although some gimmicks may increase the attendance in the short run, many members still feel the meetings are "long, boring, and frustrating affairs."[47]

Local meetings are held at a time that meets with the approval of the majority. Although they often start late and last too long, the average length is about two hours. The content inspires little attendance because much of the time is devoted to reading reports from the treasurer, project leaders, and committee chairpersons. Opportunities are provided for members to discuss these reports, but this procedure itself takes time, especially when a grievance involving someone in attendance is presented or when a controversial issue is raised before the meeting as a whole. Parliamentary procedure is used at times to excess by quasi-parliamentary experts who may want to tie up the meeting. Although the meeting may stray from the ideal, generally the business of the local is accomplished.

Functions of the Meeting The local union meeting may seem boring and not well attended; however, it serves several vital functions in the local union government. First, the meeting is the union's single most important governmental activity, and all authority at the local level is derived from it. Second, the meeting provides an opportunity for members to communicate with union leaders, express gripes directly, and call attention to their concerns. Likewise, it is an opportunity for leaders to give information to members, present results of activities, seek union support, and give direction to the membership. Last, the meeting is the supreme legislative body; this is where decisions are made on such items as disposition of grievances, approval of expenses and constitutional changes, election of officers, and ratification of the contract.[48]

Because elections are so important to the democratic process, the U.S. Department of Labor has been authorized by Congress to develop rules governing union elections. (These rules are shown in the Labor Relations in Action on page 151).

The National or International Union

The national or international (these terms are used interchangeably in this chapter) union in the United States occupies the "kingpin" position in organized labor "because of its influence in collective bargaining—the core function of American unions." Size alone (Exhibit 4.8) indicates the magnitude of the influence of national unions—millions of members work under labor agreements that are directly or indirectly the result of national union actions. The local union operates under its constitution and directives, and the federation (AFL-CIO) derives its influence, prestige, and power from the affiliated national unions.

The national union operates under <u>a constitution</u> adopted in a convention by representatives from locals. These constitutions have evolved over time through three stages: first, the locals were initially careful to restrict the power of the national union; second, as national unions became more active in collective bargaining, political action, and so on, the locals became subordinate bodies; and third and currently, the constitution includes provisions that not only authorize the major national union functions but also protect individual rights and rights of locals in relation to the national union.[49]

The Convention The supreme governing body of the national union is its convention, which is usually held annually or biennially.[50] It serves the national union in many ways: as the constitutional assembly, the legislature of the na-

Exhibit 4.8

Twelve Largest National and International Unions

Organization	Members (in thousands)
National Education Association*	2,700
Service Employees International Union	1,312
American Federation of State, County and Municipal Employees	1,292
International Brotherhood of Teamsters	1,238
United Food and Commercial Workers	1,101
American Federation of Teachers	737
United Auto Workers	666
International Brotherhood of Electrical Workers	665
Communication Workers of America	635
Carpenters and Joiners of America*	531
International Association of Machinists†	399
United Steelworkers	370

*Not in AFL-CIO
†Includes some Canadian members
SOURCE: Membership data based on self-reported data from each national union's Web site as of August 1, 2003; updated by "Special Report," *Daily Labor Report* (December 17, 2003), p. C-4.

LABOR RELATIONS IN ACTION

Rules Governing Union Elections (U.S. Department of Labor)

1. All local unions must elect officers at least once every three years; international unions every five years.
2. Local unions are required to have direct elections by manual or mail ballots; international unions are permitted to elect officers by delegates.
3. Proper safeguards must be prepared for mail balloting, for example, insurance that all members received a ballot and have sufficient time to vote and return the ballot. With manual balloting, procedures for voter secrecy (private voting booths, a private table where the view is blocked by cardboard or a private room), and voter identification (driver's license or company badge) must be established.
4. The location, date, and time of the election must be convenient for all of the members.
5. Notice of the election, which contains the date, time, place, etc., must be mailed to every member 15 days prior to the election.
6. There must be reasonable notice of the rules governing nominations mailed to or posted for the membership. Nominations may be done orally at a union meeting or by mail, but every member must have a reasonable opportunity to nominate.
7. Requirements for voter eligibility are the same as the requirements for membership. Voter eligibility must be verified.
8. After the ballot is marked, it should be placed in a nearby ballot box by the voter and the voter should leave the area by a door different from the entrance of members who have not voted.
9. Neutral persons should conduct the elections and count the ballots.
10. Observers are a necessary part of the election process, and each candidate is entitled to one or more observers (depending on the polling hours, polling sites, and size of the election).
11. Each candidate has a right to have campaign materials mailed. Some unions do the mailing at the candidate's expense; some unions provide computer printouts of the membership lists or mailing labels of membership addresses.
12. The use of union or employer funds is prohibited. This ban applies to copying machines, campaigning in a union publication, use of union or employer cars, any property of the union or an employer, assistance by any employer or a relative who owns a business and just wants to help a family member get elected, etc. ■

SOURCE: Helen Boetticher, "How to Hold a Union Election and Stay Out of Trouble," *Labor Law Journal* 51, no. 4 (Winter 2000), pp. 219–224. © 1994, 1997, & 2000, CCH Incorporated. All Rights Reserved. Reprinted with permission from *Labor Law Journal*.

tional union, the final court for union decisions, and the means for nominating officers (and the election in many cases). The convention provides the time and place for national officers to report to the members their accomplishments and failures. It provides the agenda for policy formulation, program planning, and rule making. It represents the time in which the voice of the membership holds leaders accountable for their actions. However, not all activities are official; the convention provides a reward for drudgery work at the local, an opportunity for politicking and public relations, and a time and place for the members to "let their hair down."

The convention makes use of the *delegate system,* in which the number of delegates allowed depends on the number of members in the local. Because even the smallest union is allowed one delegate, the number of delegates is not in direct proportion to the size of the local, although larger locals usually have more delegates. The convention conducts its business similarly to Congress and various state legislatures in that much committee work (including the possible holding of hearings) is performed before debate and vote on the convention floor. However, much discussion also takes place in the convention hotel bars and in meeting rooms.[51]

Although many subjects may go before the convention, several continue to emerge year after year, such as the following:

- Internal government: dues; financial matters; and authority of the president, executive board, and locals

- Collective bargaining: problems with current agreements, membership requests for future negotiations, establishment of bargaining priorities, determination of strategy for next negotiations

- Resolutions in support of or against domestic and international public policies: labor law reform, inflation, interest rates, unemployment, international balance of payments, loss of jobs to foreign countries[52]

Leadership and Democracy   Between conventions, the national union is led by its executive board, whose members are elected by the membership. In some cases, executive board members are elected on a regional basis, and they are responsible for regional intermediate organizations that maintain contact between the locals in the region and the national. The relationship between the executive board and the national union president is usually specified in the constitution. For example, some national union presidents primarily carry out the policies of the executive board; others direct the affairs of the national union, subject to the approval of the board. However, the largest group of presidents has virtually unrestricted authority to appoint staff, regulate locals, and direct the activities of the national union. The rationale for allowing such great authority to be vested in the chief executive is that the union often finds itself in struggles with employers or in other situations where it must act decisively and quickly. Thus, a strong executive is needed, and a single spokesperson for the union is required. However, the concentration of power creates opportunities for misuse of power, and an internal system of checks and balances must be devised to ensure democracy and adequate representation. Experiences that brought on the passage of Titles I to VI of the Landrum-Griffin Act (covered later in this chapter) have shown that internal control often does not work effectively, however, and that government regulation is essential. Members' rights to participate in union elections and governance include the right to nominate candidates in elections, vote in elections, attend membership meetings, participate in the deliberations, and vote on the business at these meetings such as setting dues and assessments.[53]

Democracy within the union can improve its overall efficiency and effectiveness. Union leaders will better represent the members because they will know what the members want. Democracy will make it easier to eliminate corrupt and ineffective officers who do not represent the members' interests. Furthermore, paid union officials cannot do all the tasks needed within a union and have to rely on the efforts of unpaid leaders. These volunteer leaders will have a greater commitment to the union if they are involved in it democratically.

The components of democracy should include (1) shared sovereignty in decision making; (2) opportunities to participate in decision making; (3) access to complete information necessary for decision making; (4) guaranteed equal rights for individuals and respect for individual dignity; (5) the right to minimum economic, health and safety, and environmental standards; and (6) the right to a fair share of the value created by one's work.[54]

One slight sign of democracy and active participation by members has been the turnover rates of national union presidents. Some former international union leaders maintained their positions for extended periods (Dan Tobin, Teamsters, 45 years; John L. Lewis, Mine Workers, 39 years). In the 1950s and 1960s, the turnover rate for union presidents was about 20 percent, rising to 25 percent in the 1970s. Then, in the late 1980s, the turnover rate reversed to 10 percent. Although turnover is not the necessary prerequisite for union democracy, the general rule is that the union leader must be responsive to the membership and satisfy the membership's objectives to remain in office.[55] The president's tenure in office tends to be longer in larger unions, with formalized communication networks, centralized bargaining, and heterogeneous rank-and-file members.[56]

Profile of Labor Leaders Most labor leaders come from working-class families; 62.1 percent of their fathers were hourly employees. They have an average of 14.1 years of formal education. Over 70 percent have some college experience; 17 percent have postgraduate education; and another 27 percent are college graduates. They first joined a union for the same reasons most union members do today: 40 percent joined because it was a condition of employment, 33 percent joined because they believed in the goals of organized labor, and 25 percent wanted better pay and working conditions. Their reasons for pursuing union leadership positions included the following (80 percent or more responded positively to these survey items): challenging work, interesting work, extended my range of abilities, opportunity to learn new things, achieve something I personally valued, believed in the goals of the union, and opportunity to improve working conditions of fellow employees.[57]

A recent survey of national union leaders revealed some new directions, which included the following:

- Centralizing some of the national union's functions while pushing other decisions closer to the membership, such as taking a case to arbitration

- Broadening the scope of bargaining to include a more holistic approach, such as negotiating child-care and elder-care issues and member education

- Studying and learning from business organizations on subjects like strategic planning, clear objectives, a clear chain of command, and established rules and procedures
- Improving union and member effectiveness through goal setting, team building, and member surveys
- Improving communication with members by use of information technology, such as video conferences, Web sites, and e-mail[58]

Administration The operational departments of international unions vary in kind and number, but the typical international union will have at least the following departments: (1) executive and administration; (2) financial and auditing; (3) organizing and servicing; and (4) technical staff, which includes research, education, economics, law, publications, and public relations.

Likewise, the international unions create operating departments to serve various special interests among their membership. For example, the UAW established the Transnational and Joint Ventures Department for the 8,000 UAW members who were employed by three Japanese-managed vehicle makers at U.S. sites: the Toyota-General Motors, Ford-Mazda, and Chrysler-Mitsubishi joint ventures (Nissan remains nonunion).

The executive and administrative group includes the president, vice president(s), secretary-treasurer, and their assistants. This group is chiefly responsible for the activities of the overall union. In some cases the vice president may concentrate on organizing or collective bargaining, whereas the secretary-treasurer will focus on financial matters.

Salaries of international union presidents vary widely. In fact, the range of the gross salaries of the 20 largest international unions was from $125,212 to $329,792 per year in 2002 (an average of $223,691 per year). In comparison, the average total compensation of the 500 chief executive officers in Standard & Poor list was $2,235,073 in 2002. There were some exceptions. The Secretary-Treasurer of Teamsters Local 710 in Chicago earned $588,491 in 2002; this figure included his base salary plus earnings from commissions received on union member dues that had been deferred from prior years. Also, the heads of two major sporting unions earned significantly more; the head of the National Football Players Association earned $2.7 million and the head of the Major League Baseball Players Association earned $1 million in 2002. At the other end, there are thousands of union members, union stewards, and local union officials who receive no compensation for their union work and are reimbursed only for time lost from their jobs when involved in union business.

Policies on union compensation vary as well, and there is no correlation between the size of a union in terms of the number of members or assets under its control and the salary of the highest elected officer. For example, the president of the United Auto Workers (UAW) earned $125,212 in 2002, and the UAW has $1.15 billion of assets. The salary of the president of the National Education Association (NEA) ranked tenth in 2002 even though NEA's membership was twice as many as the Service Employees International Union, the second highest in number of members. The subject of salaries is addressed in unions' constitutions or governing documents either directly by setting the level of pay or indirectly by granting authority to elected delegates or executive board members who then establish salaries. The Communications Workers of America vests authority for setting salaries in delegates to its annual convention; The Electrical Workers give significant weight to compensation levels of other organizations of similar type and size; the Auto Workers link salaries of officers and staff to compensation earned by UAW members. In addition, the annual salary increases in a majority of the unions are linked to the increase in average hourly earnings of members.[59]

Professional Staff Members Unions have two kinds of professional staffs. The first group is either appointed or elected and holds such titles as international union representative, staff representative, business agent, or organizer. These staff members work away from the international union headquarters and assist local unions in bargaining, contract administration, and organizing. The second group performs more technical, specialized functions at the union headquarters. This group includes such professionals as industrial hygienists, physicians, economists, attorneys, accountants, computer operators, and specialists in education, media, public relations, and so forth. Interestingly, the staff members have formed staff unions, mostly to promote their job security and equitable salary schedules. Most of these unions are independent, but 13 of the 40 bargaining units have affiliated with a national labor union, such as the Communications Workers of America, the Steelworkers, and the Newspaper Guild. In addition, an association of these unions, called the International Congress of Staff Unions (ICSU), was formed in 1988 to share information and provide mutual support and assistance.

National unions have traditionally selected their staff through political processes by rewarding demonstrated leadership and loyalty at the local level. Union officers traditionally have been suspicious of college-educated persons and have believed that the staff should work its way up the ranks. More recently, national unions are using personnel practices used by business and government. With the election of more college-educated persons to national offices, much of the resistance to college education has declined. For example, Richard Trumka, secretary-treasurer of the AFL-CIO, is an attorney.

In the past there has been no recognized sequence of professional training for union officials, and experience and performance have been stressed in appointments and elected office. However, training has increased significantly over the last several years. Most national unions provide in-house training for their professional staff. Numerous universities have labor education programs that offer professional development for union members. The George Meany Center for Labor Studies in Silver Springs, Maryland, has an annual enrollment of several thousand. The Center, in cooperation with Antioch College, sponsors a college degree program designed for union staff, and several hundred union officials have graduated from this program.[60]

Services to and Control of Locals As indicated earlier, the locals are constitutionally subordinated to the national union, but the degree of subordination varies with the union. The national union provides services to the local union in several ways while at the same time controlling local union leaders. For example, where a national product market exists, a **master labor agreement** with one firm might be negotiated to cover all its facilities (such agreements have been negotiated in the steel, auto, rubber, aircraft, and electrical appliance industries). Also, a union such as the UAW may negotiate an agreement with a company like GM at the national level, and this agreement may establish a pattern for negotiating with other auto companies such as Ford and Chrysler. Following the negotiations of the master agreement between the national union and each company, the local union will negotiate a local agreement with officials at each plant, covering local rules, policies, and benefits. Deviations from the master agreement must be okayed by the national union. (See Chapter 6 for further coverage.)

The national union assists locals in collective bargaining, grievance administration, strike activities, and internal financial administration. These services also provide an opportunity for national union staff members to ensure that the local unions are conforming to national policies.

The international union representative, in addition to organizing new unions, also helps the local unions in grievance administration and labor arbitration. The national supports the local in strike situations, but the local must get approval to qualify for strike benefits. The national union provides counseling and consultation for internal financial administration (bookkeeping, dues collection, purchases, financing union lodges, and so on), but trusteeship (receivership) procedures are available whereby the national union can suspend local union control for abuses such as malfeasance, corruption, and misuse of funds in favor of a trustee under national direction.

Dues, Fees, and Distribution of Funds   Although all union members pay dues or fees to their national unions, the amount and form vary considerably. Such dues are the chief source of revenue for unions. Typically, the monthly dues are about $20, and the initiation fee is about $40. Some unions set a single rate, but most allow the local some flexibility in making the final determination. Frequently, dues are collected via a dues checkoff system. The member agrees to a payroll deduction of union dues, which are collected by the employer and paid directly to the union.

Several specialized unions with small memberships, such as the Director's Guild, Football Players, Mine Workers, and Iron Workers, charge over $100 for an initiation fee, and the Radio Association charges $2,000. Usually when dues are higher than average, the payments include premiums for insurance, pension payments, and other benefits.

The local unions forward a portion of the monthly dues for each member to the national union. The nationals use these funds for various purposes beneficial to the membership. Although the largest percentage of funds goes to the general fund, which covers administrative and operational costs and salary expenses, allocations are also made to accounts such as a strike fund, a convention fund, union publications, educational activities, and a retirement fund.[61]

Use of union dues and fees for political purposes and non-collective-bargaining activities has come under fire in the last few years. Union members who disagree with the manner in which their unions contribute or use their funds have challenged their unions. Recent court decisions have caused several unions, such as the Machinists, Auto Workers, Communications Workers, and American Federation of State, County, and Municipal Employees, to adopt dues rebate plans. These plans allow a rebate of a portion of member dues spent on political activities if the member requests it in advance (usually annually).

The U.S. Supreme Court has ruled that if a union uses dues and fees of protesting employees for non-collective-bargaining activities and purposes, it breaches its fiduciary duty of fair representation. In addition, a district court judge listed 12 activities, including political ones, that were considered non-collective-bargaining activities.[62] Unions can continue to solicit volunteer contributions through such units as the AFL-CIO Committee on Political Education (COPE), the UAW's Community Action Program (CAP), and the United Mine Workers' (UMW's) Coal Miners' Political Committee (COMPAC), but collections may be more difficult.

Although union membership has not increased over the past two decades, unions have been prosperous financially, and their influence has increased in recent years. The level of unions' assets and income has enhanced their ability to finance strikes and other union activities. For example, in 1960, private-sector union membership was 14.6 million, and its receipts were $1.4 billion. By 1987, union membership was 10.9 million, and its receipts were $11.8 billion. This is a drop in membership of more than 25 percent and an increase in receipts of more than 700 percent. Taking inflation into account, receipts increased 220 percent. On a per-member basis, the receipts in real dollars were more than doubled.[63]

Finances of unions are considerably decentralized across union levels, with a few local unions having more wealth and income than their national unions. Likewise, union finances are highly concentrated with a few unions dominating the scene. For example, the National Education Association generates about $800 million in annual revenue, and the UAW has assets of $1.15 billion.[64]

The unions' financial performance has improved considerably in the last 15 years. In fact, unions have a collective capacity to fund nearly a full year of prior-year services without the infusion of any new income. Furthermore, unions' decline in bargaining power and strike activity over the past two decades has not been due to any diminished financial capacity of unions to withstand strikes.[65]

Mergers of National Unions   Encouraged by the AFL-CIO merger, but mostly spurred by rising costs, the need for stronger bargaining positions, expensive jurisdictional disputes, decline for some U.S. industries, economies of scale, avoidance of external controls, and the need for self-preservation, mergers of national unions have occurred at a quickening pace.

Mergers occur through amalgamation, absorptions, and affiliations. An **amalgamation** occurs when two or more unions of roughly equal size form a new union. An **absorption** occurs when a small union merges into a larger union and the smaller union loses its separate identity. An **affiliation** occurs when a single-plant, single-company, or regional union merges into a national union. Although unions do not report the number of affiliations, absorptions are far more common. Since the AFL and CIO merger in 1955, there have been 22 mergers through amalgamations and 149 absorptions. There has been an increase in the rate of mergers since the 1950s. In the four-year period between 1955 and 1959, there were nine mergers, or a 1.8 percent increase. During the 1990–1994 period, there were 21 mergers, or 4.2 percent, and during the 1995–1999 period, there were 17 mergers, or 3.4 percent.[66] In 1995, the Clothing and Textile Workers merged with the Garment Workers Union to form UNITE, and the Rubber Workers united with the Steelworkers.

Mergers appear to play an important role in some national unions' strategies for growth and diversification. However, the rising trends in mergers are best

LABOR RELATIONS IN ACTION

NEA-AFT Merger?

In January 1998, the leaders of the two largest teacher unions, the National Education Association (NEA) with 2.7 million members and the American Federation of Teachers (AFT) with 737,000 members, announced that "substantial progress" toward a merger had been made. A successful merger would constitute the largest union in U.S. history with membership of 3.4 million.
Key differences included the following:

- Decision regarding whether to affiliate with the AFL-CIO. The larger NEA was an independent union, and the AFT was an AFL-CIO affiliate.

- Decision regarding whether state affiliates would be required to join the merger.

- Of the AFT members, 400,000 were nonteachers, such as nurses and meat inspectors, and accounted for nearly 50 percent of the AFT's membership, whereas the NEA operated primarily in educational institutions.

- The NEA had a long-time commitment to racial and gender quotas in its executive jobs, and the AFT did not provide such quotas.

- A mesh of historical philosophies, wherein the NEA saw themselves as professionals and modeled their association after the American Medical Association, and the AFT adopted the trade union model and fought for the right to form unions and bargaining collectively since its founding in 1916.

- State organizations stated that they had supported both Republican and Democratic candidates. By joining a larger organization, such as the AFL-CIO, which tends to be more pro-Democratic, they would lose their political flexibility.

On July 5, 1998, delegates to the NEA convention voted 58 percent to 42 percent against the merger.

NEA President Bob Chase and AFT President Sandra Feldman both announced their disappointment with the rejection; however, they indicated that the four years of negotiating the merger led to positive outcomes, such as joint projects on school infrastructure, school safety, discipline, and teacher quality. The leaders revealed that negotiation toward a merger would continue and that more than $100 million had been unnecessarily spent in their competitive rivalry. Although the merger has not occurred, there are continuing discussions and many joint projects. ■

SOURCES: Glenn Burkins, June Kronholz, and Rochelle Sharpe, "NEA, AFT Make Progress on a Merger," *The Wall Street Journal*, January 21, 1998, p. A-2; Steven Greenhouse, "Teachers' Groups Plan to Merge Creating Nation's Largest Union," *New York Times*, January 27, 1998, p. A-4; Steven Greenhouse, "Teachers See Close Ballot on Big Merger," *New York Times*, July 5, 1998, p. 6.

understood within the context of escalating employer opposition to unionism during negotiations and organizing, growth of nonunion competition, declining political and economic influence of unions, declining industries where unions are strong, foreign competition, and propensity of workers not to join unions.[67]

Potentially, the largest merger in U.S. history was rejected in July 1998 at the National Education Association convention (see "Labor Relations in Action" box). Typically, mergers have not succeeded immediately in welding together functions, organizational units, and staff members. They have required the time, patience, and good will of all parties as officers and staff members who have different personalities and modes of operation are meshed. The local unions must be accommodated as well as the employers and the collective bargaining relationships. Mergers have been particularly difficult when one of the unions feels a loss of its autonomy and when the merger occurs between unions whose prior dealings have been characterized by intense rivalry. Often members' pride is hurt, and fear surfaces when they find out that their union may be submerged by another.

In a more positive vein, the resulting larger unions gain more clout with industrial giants and can negotiate more as equals. The greater size generates resources to provide better training in collective bargaining, grievance administration, and steward leadership; to offer greater strike benefits; to lobby more effectively for legislation; and to maintain a staff to combat unfair labor practices. Moreover, successful mergers reduce the risks to smaller unions from technological change, economic recessions, declines in membership, unemployment, and financial strains.

Most officers of unions with 50,000 or fewer members (includes more than half of AFL-CIO affiliates) believe that mergers have the best prospects of providing and maintaining member services. The benefits include more effective lobbying, increased bargaining power, expertise, economies of scale, and more effective strikes. The trade-offs are reduction in membership participation and less attention to needs of special interest groups. The potential advantages of a merger coupled with the risks of not merging suggest that mergers of national unions will be continued in the future.

Intermediate Organizational Units

Structurally, between national headquarters and the locals lie the intermediate organizational units—regional or district offices, trade conferences, conference boards, and joint councils. These units usually operate under the guidance of their various national units, but their activities are important to the union members and employers in their areas.

The regional, or district, offices house the regional or district officers, the staff, and the international union representatives for the geographical area served. For example, Michigan has a number of Auto Workers' district offices; the Steelworkers have district offices in Pittsburgh, Birmingham, and elsewhere. The offices are established for national unions to better serve their respective locals.

Trade conferences are set up within national unions to represent a variety of industrial groups. For example, the Teamsters has established eleven trade conferences for such groups as freight, laundry, airlines, and moving and storage. These groups meet to discuss various mutual problems and topics of interest.

Conference boards are organized within national unions in accordance with the company affiliation to discuss issues that pertain to the union and the particular company. For instance, each of the national unions within the steel, auto, rubber, and electric industries has established conference boards that meet to discuss negotiations and related problems. Delegates are chosen from the local unions to represent the interests of their constituents at meetings, to plan the next negotiations, and then to relay these plans to the local union members.

__Joint councils__ involve groupings of local unions that have common goals, employers, and interests. Examples are the building trades councils established in most metropolitan areas in the United States. They negotiate with the association of construction employers in the area, coordinate their activities, and assist in resolving jurisdictional disputes between unions.

Independent Unions   There are 41 independent unions (not affiliated with the AFL-CIO). These unions represent mostly service and health-care providers. The largest union in the United States, the National Education Association (2,700,000 members), is among these independent unions. Other independent unions include the American Nurses Association (149,000 members), American Physicians and Dentists (1,690 members), Life Insurance Agents (1,150 members), National Labor Relations Board Union (1,370 members), Professional Engineering Association (510 members), and United Plant Guard Workers of America (26,000 members).[68] There are also approximately 1,500 independent local unions that have nearly half a million members. Independent local unions are found in a few large organizations such as DuPont, Texaco, Exxon, AT&T, and Procter & Gamble; in several medium-sized firms such as Dow-Jones, Weirton Steel, and Zenith; and in numerous small companies in a variety of industries.[69]

Employee Associations   Unions are supporting new employee associations that provide a wide range of services to their members. In Cleveland, 9 to 5: The Association for Working Women, a 15,000-member affiliate of the Service Employees International Union, provides a toll-free hotline, offers courses on sexual harassment and VDT injuries, and lobbies on workplace issues. In New York, AIM (Associate ILGWU Members), a 2,500-member affiliate of the International Ladies Garment Workers Union (now part of UNITE), provides English classes for its members, graduate-equivalency diploma classes, skills training, and legal assistance with immigration, minimum wage, safety and health, sexual harassment, disability, and pensions laws. In Montana, the 1,400-member Montana Family Union, sponsored by the AFL-CIO and made up of government employees, small business owners, and even priests, offers its members major medical benefits at less than 50 percent of their individual rates. Although critics refer to these employee associations as "watered-down unions," they are serving important social functions, and their membership has grown to 500,000 nationally while total membership in unions has declined to approximately 13 percent of the labor force.[70]

The American Federation of Labor and Congress of Industrial Organizations (AFL-CIO)

The AFL-CIO, while not including all U.S. labor unions, is composed of 65 national and international unions that have 60,000 local unions and about 13 million members. Members represent a diversity of occupations, such as actors, construction workers, barbers and hairdressers, steelworkers, bus drivers, railroad workers, telephone operators, newspaper reporters, sales clerks, garment workers, engineers, schoolteachers, and police. These AFL-CIO affiliates maintain day-to-day relationships with several thousands of employers and administer about 160,000 labor agreements. Most (over 99 percent) of these agreements are negotiated without strikes or other forms of conflict and serve as the basis of employment conditions under which many work.

Established in 1955 when the American Federation of Labor and the Congress of Industrial Organizations merged, the AFL-CIO recognized the principle that both craft and industrial unions are appropriate, equal, and necessary parts of U.S. organized labor. The federation accepts the principle of *autonomy*—each affiliated union conducts its own affairs; has its own headquarters, offices, and staff; decides its own economic policies; sets its own dues; carries out its own contract negotiations; and provides its own services to members.

No national union is required to affiliate with the AFL-CIO. About 40 unions remain outside the AFL-CIO. Member unions are free to withdraw at any time; however, their voluntary participation plays an essential role that advances the interest of every union. National unions continue their membership because they believe that a federation of unions serves purposes their own individual unions cannot serve as well.

Examples of AFL-CIO services include the following:

- Speaking for organized labor before Congress and other branches of government
- Representing U.S. labor in world affairs and keeping in direct contact with labor unions throughout the free world
- Coordinating activities such as community services, political education, lobbying, and voter registration with greater effectiveness
- Helping to coordinate efforts to organize nonunion employees throughout the United States

Another vital service enhances the integrity and prestige of AFL-CIO unions—they must operate under established ethical practice codes covering union democracy and financial integrity. The federation also assists in minimizing conflicts that cause work interruptions by mediating and resolving disputes between national unions, such as organizing disputes and conflicts over work assignments.[71]

Organizational Structure The AFL-CIO organizational structure, shown in Exhibit 4.9, illustrates the importance of the convention. Meeting every 2 years and at times of particular need, delegates decide on policies, programs, and direction for AFL-CIO activities. Each national or international union is authorized to send delegates to the convention. Each union's representation of delegates at the convention is determined by the number of dues-paying members. In addition, other affiliated organizations, such as state labor councils, are represented by one delegate each.

Between conventions, the governing body is the Executive Council, composed of the president, secretary-treasurer, and 51 vice presidents (10 of which are established as "diversity set-asides" elected by majority vote at the convention). The AFL-CIO's first president, George Meany, was succeeded in 1979 by Lane Kirkland, whose unexpired term was concluded by Thomas R. Donahue. In 1995, the biennial convention elected President John J. Sweeney, Secretary-Treasurer Richard Trumka, and Executive Vice President Linda Chavez-Thompson. They have been reelected twice since then, most recently in 2001 for four-year terms.

Exhibit 4.9

Organization Chart of AFL-CIO

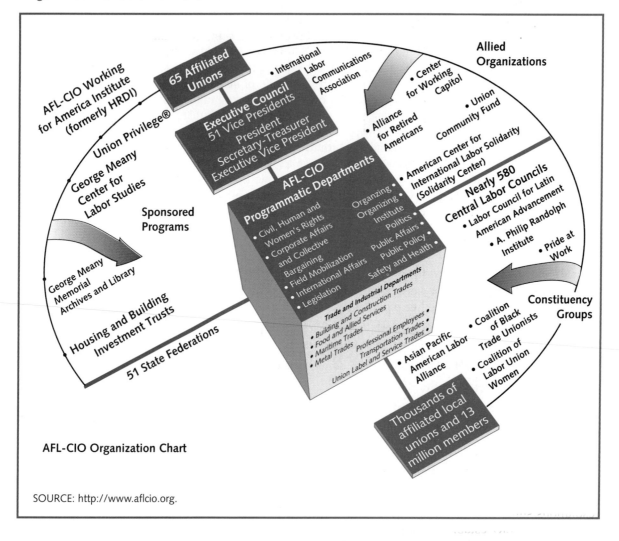

AFL-CIO Organization Chart

SOURCE: http://www.aflcio.org.

The other members of the Executive Council are likely to be current or previous presidents of international unions affiliated with the AFL-CIO. The Executive Council meets at least three times a year and handles operational duties involving legislative matters, union corruption, charters of new internationals, and judicial appeals from member unions.

The AFL-CIO has been criticized for the lack of minorities on its 54-member Executive Council. Although it now has three black members, it has only three female members, even though women make up 34 percent of the unionized members and 44 percent of the total civilian labor force.[72]

Between meetings of the Executive Council, the president, who is the chief executive officer, has authority to supervise the affairs of the federation and to direct its staff, and the secretary-treasurer handles all financial matters. To assist his administration, the president has appointed 15 standing committees on various subjects, which, with the assistance of the AFL-CIO staff, provide related services to member unions. The staff, located at headquarters in Washington, D.C., corresponds closely to these standing committees in order to better serve the member unions. (See Exhibit 4.9 for a listing of standing committees and staff divisions.) The General Board, composed of the Executive Council and one officer from each member union, is available to act on matters referred to it by the Executive Council.

The AFL-CIO has established 51 state central bodies (plus one in Puerto Rico) to advance the statewide interests of labor through political, lobbying, and organizing activities, which involve attempts to elect friends of labor, to have favorable legislation passed, and to organize nonunion workers, respectively. Each local union of the AFL-CIO–affiliated unions in a particular state may join the state organization and participate in and support its activities. In addition, 580 *local central bodies* have been formed by local unions of the national affiliates to deal with civic and community problems and other matters of local concern.

To accommodate and serve the interests and needs of various trade and industrial unions, the AFL-CIO has established eight *trade and industrial departments*. The Industrial Union Department represents the interests of industrial unions, mostly members of the former CIO. Another department, the Union Label Department, promotes the purchase and sale of union-made goods and services. The remaining departments represent the interests of such union groups as the building trades, food and beverage trades, maritime employees, metal trades, public employees, and professional employees. In addition, throughout the United States where there is sufficient interest and support, 976 *local department councils* have been organized.[73]

These local central bodies have become more active in recent years, particularly in the northeastern states. As an example, 60 percent of the councils in the northeast region have adopted the Union Cities program, which contains eight steps toward rebuilding the labor movement from the bottom up and helping to improve the lives of working families. These steps include mobilizing against anti-union employers, organizing grassroots lobbying/political action committees, creating strategies to create jobs and improve economic growth, sponsoring economic education, persuading city and county officials to pass resolutions supporting worker rights, and increasing union membership.[74]

The AFL-CIO established a no-raiding clause for its affiliated unions in 1962 to keep one affiliated union from attempting to draw members from another or seeking to represent a group of employees at a work site where a union already exists. Then, in 1962, the AFL-CIO set up an Internal Dispute Plan to adjudicate conflicts among its affiliated unions. Because the Teamsters had been an independent union from 1955 to 1987, when it rejoined the AFL-CIO, and because it is noted for its aggressive organizing activities, it was only natural that the Teamsters were involved in about half of the 23 decisions under the Internal Dispute Plan.[75]

The AFL-CIO's operations are financed through regular member dues, called *per capita taxes*, which are paid by affiliated unions on behalf of their members. Currently, the per capita tax is $.42 month, or $5.04 per year, for each member. Thus, the AFL-CIO's operating budget is over $60 million, of which nearly all covers regular operating expenses. A major portion of the budget goes to the salaries of the staff. The detailed financial report of the AFL-CIO is submitted to the delegates at each convention.[76]

The AFL-CIO recently recognized the potential of maintaining contact with employees who are not members of unions by establishing an **associate membership program.** They include those who voted for the union in elections where the union did not win, employees in nonunion companies who would vote for the union if given a choice, and employees who are represented by the union but have not joined it. There are over 300,000 associate union members, and the number continues to grow steadily. This program helps the AFL-CIO maintain contact with these employees.

The AFL-CIO offers Internet access to 17 million union members and retirees and offers computers at low cost. This new service is an extension of the Union Privilege Benefit Program (see Exhibit 4.10), which was offered in the 1980s. The benefits provide reduced attorney fees, lower-cost life and accident insurance, participation in a motor club, car repair discounts, travel club services, a Walt Disney discount, a parents' college advisor, reduced prices for educational books and software, mortgage and real estate advice, and a dental program. This program was also offered to nonunion members for a small fee. They would become "associate members," and the AFL-CIO hoped that the associate members would later become union members. In 1995, the AFL-CIO added a credit card with no annual fee and a low monthly interest for which the AFL-CIO received $75 million each year for five years.[77]

Other AFL-CIO activities are educational and informational, presenting the federation's stance on a variety of issues. For example, the AFL-CIO publishes a weekly *AFL-CIO News* that keeps members up to date on current events that pertain to them and presents various reports on problems and policies of organized labor. The AFL-CIO maintains the George Meany Center for Labor Studies, which offers short courses in union leadership development, and a Speaker's Bureau to provide labor speakers for high school and college classes. They also make educational films available to interested groups for a nominal fee.

In the political arena, the AFL-CIO receives much attention. As a representative of organized labor, it serves as the focal point of political activities. Not only does it lobby aggressively for favorable legislation, but it publishes the voting records of each senator and representative at both federal and state levels. It attempts to influence appointments, such as Supreme Court judges, the Secretary of Labor, and NLRB members, who are important to organized labor. Its policy of "reward your friends, punish your enemies" has not changed much since Samuel Gompers's day. The AFL-CIO's COPE has a network in each state and in most large communities. COPE seeks voluntary contributions to provide funds for its activities, which include voter registration, "get-out-the-vote" campaigns, preparation of leaflets and posters, and research on behalf of its candidates.

Although the Federal Election Campaign Act of 1971, amended in 1974, has restricted financial contributions to federal candidates, the AFL-CIO, COPE, and state and local bodies can still amass amazing support to help their candidates for office, especially when the candidate is clearly the choice of organized labor. Organized labor and corporations have become major players in the funding of political campaigns at the federal level, primarily through Political Action Committees.

Although organized labor has played a major role in U.S. politics, it remains independent of a national political party. Over the years it has been more

Exhibit 4.10

Union Plus Benefits from Union Privilege

Union Plus Benefits from Union Privilege

Benefits for Life

Union Plus benefits stand for quality and service - with prices working families can live with.

Best of all, Union Plus programs are designed specifically for working families. Our benefits have added features that are especially helpful in cases of disability or layoffs.

Who can use these benefits?

You don't have to join Union Plus or Union Privilege; as a member of an AFL-CIO union, you and your family are automatically eligible for our benefits. Most unions participate in most Union Plus benefits, but some international unions elect not to offer all the programs. Click here to find out which Union Plus benefits your union participates in.

Our Secret? Union Power.

Just as unions provide strength in the workplace, Union Privilege provides strength in the marketplace. We deliver the best benefits through the collective buying power of over 13 million AFL-CIO union members. And we do so without using union member dues.

Programs available outside the U.S.

Calculate your annual savings with Union Plus benefits

Money & Credit
- Credit Card
- Loans
- Mortgage & Real Estate
- Union-Made Checks
- Credit Education Information
- Your Credit Score

Insurance Deals
- Accident Insurance
- Life Insurance
- Auto Insurance
- Pet Insurance

Health & Well Being
- Health Savings
- Health Club Discounts

Education Services
- Union Plus Scholarship
- Union Plus National Labor College Scholarship
- Education Loan Program
- "Go to College" Process
- Powell's Bookstore
- Entertainment Discounts
- Theme park discounts
- Movie ticket discounts

Auto Advantages
- Car Rentals
- Auto Insurance
- Auto Buying Service
- Goodyear Tire & Service Discounts

Member Satisfaction & Advocacy

To guarantee the quality of our benefits, we only work with industry leading providers.

Our relationships don't stop after the initial program provider selection. We continuously update programs and monitor performance closely to ensure that they satisfy union members' needs time and time again.

Our member advocates also use the collective strength of union consumers to ensure members get prompt, courteous service and high-quality benefits -- as well as help in resolving any problems. With Union Plus programs, union members can rest assured their needs will be addressed and their voice will be heard.

CONSUMER CORNER

Sign up for updates

Save time and money with the tips and deals offered in the Union Plus emails. **Click here to sign up.**

For other benefits, visit the links below. Union Plus products and services help save money - and headaches.

House & Home
- Mortgage & Real Estate
- North American Van Lines

Legal Resources
- Immigration Legal Service

Pet Services
- Pet Insurance
- Pet Savings
- PETCO Discounts

Gift Shop
- Flower Discounts

Travel & Recreation
- Car Rentals
- Vacation Tours
- Bahamas Getaways
- Disney Hotel Savings

Computers & Tech
- Cingular Wireless Discount
- IBM Computer Discount
- Dell Computer Discount

Union-Made
- Auto Buying
- Cingular Wireless Discounts
- Goodyear Tire & Service Discounts
- Disney Hotel Savings
- Powell's unionized bookstore
- Union-Made Checks

Unique Union Benefits

PROVIDER EXCELLENCE

Union Privilege only works with top quality companies you can trust. Our program providers:

- Are respected specialists in their field
- Offer first-rate products and services nationwide
- Share our worker-friendly philosophy
- Demonstrate outstanding customer service
- Understand the importance of privacy and security

Ready for vacation? GO

SOURCE: http://www.unionplus.com/benefits/. Note: Visit www.unionplus.org for updated information.

closely aligned with the Democratic party, both philosophically and politically. It has become perhaps the single most important political force that has supported government programs to help the socially and economically disadvantaged. It has supported consumer and environmental protection and safety and health legislation that has benefited all employees, union and nonunion alike.

Organized labor has accumulated much power and influence through its own established network and has also been instrumental in organizing other politically active groups with socially oriented objectives, such as minorities and senior citizens. However, organized labor's overall political strength and effectiveness should not be exaggerated. In some states and municipalities, union membership is so negligible that its influence is inconsequential. In others, where union membership is high, its influence is significant, and political candidates must actively solicit its support.[78] The AFL-CIO does not control the membership's votes; however, members are an independent lot, and they have other reasons for voting for candidates.

AFL-CIO President John Sweeney has pledged his goal of increasing union membership 3 percent per year and to spend 30 percent of unions' budgets on recruiting new members (now it is about 2 percent). He has launched several programs to activate union organizing, including the following:

- Created the Union Summer Program, which enlisted 12,500 college volunteers to work for labor causes

- Staged rallies around the country to support the strawberry-field workers in California

- Conducted town hall meetings in thirty cities with rank-and-file union members

- Invested $35 million into election-year advertisements and political activities in the 2000 election[79]

Use of Information Technology by Unions

Virtually every international union in the United States uses the World Wide Web and other information technologies in the major areas of union activity:

1. Internal communications between union officers, staff, and members, particularly when they are geographically dispersed. Within every union, there are international representatives who are employed throughout the country and represent members in organizing and representational activities. E-mail communication serves as an immediate means of communication throughout the organization. Another union provides an e-mail alert system that gives weekly updates to union members and their representatives.

2. External communications, such as to inform the public about union issues potentially affecting the public, workers, and unions. The AFL-CIO Web site (www.aflcio.org/) gives members and nonmembers valuable information on matters dealing with worker rights, pensions, and benefits during layoffs, provides useful links to other resources, and provides a system allowing interested persons to receive e-mail updates about labor events from across the United States and the world. By the fall of 2002, the number of e-mail addresses in the AFL-CIO database was 600,000, and it is anticipated to reach several million in a few years.

3. Facilitation of bargaining activities, such as in negotiations, and informing members about employer practices. During the 2001 strike of Verizon by the Com-

munication Workers of America (CWA) and the 2003 negotiations, the CWA kept its members informed of the negotiations through a "members only" Web site.

4. Contract administration, such as communicating grievances and tracking decisions of arbitrators. Unions are better able to communicate with members in preparation for grievance meetings and arbitration hearing via e-mail communication. The American Postal Workers Union has a database of thousands of arbitrator decisions readily accessible to its arbitrator advocates.

5. Union organizing, such as making contact with potential union members and providing a means for interested employees to communicate with the union. The United Food and Commercial Workers (UFCW) is currently using the Internet in its attempt to organize employees at Wal-Mart. Its Web site (www.UFCW.com) keeps up-to-date information on the UFCW campaign activities.

6. Political action, such as informing potential voters about union views and those held by organized labor's friends and adversaries. Nearly every union Web site has political messages for the reader.

Union leaders see the Web as an important avenue for modernizing unionism and for bridging the gap between an increasingly heterogeneous work force and collective activity and solidarity. One Web site (www.labourstart.org/) collects daily labor news from newspapers from around the world and posts it. *LaborNet* (www.labornet.org/) promotes computer communications for strengthening and building organized labor. Some unions have created member-only "chat rooms" and forums; others have organized voting over particular issues in order to obtain membership input on issues facing the union. If the unions continue to adopt these technological innovations at their current pace, unions in advanced countries will be truly transformed organizations.[80]

The use of e-mail and the Internet has caused some concerns among organized labor. Among the concerns are the erosion of face-to-face contact, worry about "loudmouths" and "troublemakers" monopolizing the communications, the generation gap between older "pre-computer" leaders and the younger "computer techies," loss of confidentiality by "computer hackers" and "snoops," and worry that e-mail messages will overload the system and consume an extraordinary amount of time that could be used more effectively elsewhere.[81]

One of organized labor's greatest concerns is use of company intranets (computerized e-mail and Web site systems within a company). These add new communication possibilities to employer's union substitution strategies by linking workers to their supervisors and human resource specialists who are able to quickly disseminate company information and focus attention on resolving employee grievances. Employers' use of intranets is already widespread and has among its explicit objectives improved communication between workers and human resource departments and closer identification with the company.

Unions will also find themselves competing with alternative advocacy and worker rights organizations that are attempting to organize and represent workers. For example, the Professional Association of Contract Employees provides its members with group benefits and assistance with record keeping and contracting. Working Today is an organization that promotes the interests of freelancers, independent contractors, temporary and part-time workers, and people who work from their homes. It offers group health insurance, legal aid, financial services, and discounts on travel, computers, and office supplies.[82]

Union Corruption and the Landrum-Griffin Act

Like some business executives, a few union officials have encountered problems with law enforcement officials. Unethical and illegal practices, including corruption, racketeering, and embezzlement, have been discovered in some local and national unions. Union abuses of power were exposed by the McClellan hearings of the late 1950s. Large amounts from Teamsters pension funds had been misused. Union officials have been indicted for conspiracy to bribe a U.S. senator and for embezzlement. Indictments have been rendered where "ghost workers" were maintained on payrolls even though no services were performed. Although union corruption cannot be condoned, its magnitude is diminished by the savings and loan scandal in the United States in the late 1980s and early 1990s, in which 331 persons were convicted to serve an average sentence of $3\frac{1}{2}$ years and estimated cleanup costs were $500 billion, for an average cost of about $2,000 for each U.S. citizen.

In 1989, the Teamsters and the federal government settled charges that the union was under the influence of organized crime. The settlement occurred just before the scheduled opening of a trial for alleged violations under the Racketeer Influenced and Corrupt Organizations Act (RICO). The settlement barred persons allegedly involved in organized crime from participating in union activity and provided for three persons, jointly selected by the parties and acting separately from one another, to temporarily oversee union activities and supervise secret-ballot elections of union officers.

Although the Teamsters in 1995 represented one of the most democratic international unions because of the federal government's intervention, several recent incidents of union problems with the law have occurred:

- A fine of $52 million was charged against the Mine Workers during a 10-month strike against Pittston Coal Co. in 1989 for refusing to comply with a court injunction (in 1994, the U.S. Supreme Court unanimously vacated the fine because it was imposed without a jury).

- USX Corporation executives and two United Steelworkers officials were convicted of illegally entering into a kickback scheme (giving pensions to otherwise ineligible union officials who were former employees of USX) to secure union concessions for reopening of an Alabama steel mill.

- Two unions, the Carpenters and Paperworkers, were fined $110,000 for interfering with a $600,000 contract between a contractor and a pulp and paper plant after the unions held a meeting with the plant officials and threatened to set picket lines. In addition, the contractor was awarded $20 million in punitive damages.

An accurate assessment of union corruption is reflected by the following conclusion:

> Union corruption stories are front-page news. They create images that tend to linger and are reinforced each time new allegations are raised. Certainly, Jimmy Hoffa's lasting notoriety is evidence of this phenomenon.
>
> In fact, the level of corruption among unions and union leaders is negligible. The Labor-Management Reporting and Disclosure Act . . . insures

this. Very few institutions in American society are as closely regulated or as open to scrutiny as are American unions. . . . The evidence is clear that all but a minute fraction of American union leaders are honest and dedicated in the performance of their duties. Supporting this conclusion is an investigation by a former Attorney General that found serious problems of corruption in less than one-half of 1 percent of all local unions.

The AFL-CIO established the Ethical Practices Committee in its efforts to control corrupt practices and racketeering of its member unions, and its Executive Council was given the authority to suspend any affiliated union with corrupt practices. Then, in 1959, the U.S. Congress showed its concern with union abuse and the potential misuse of union power through passage of the Landrum-Griffin Act (the Labor-Management Reporting and Disclosure Act), which has several provisions governing union operations and government. For example, it governs the following:

- Disclosure by union officers and employees (and employers and their agents) about financial dealings, trusteeships, and any private arrangements made with any employees.

- Regulation of union trusteeships, including rules for their establishment and maintenance, and the protection of the rights of members of unions under trusteeship.

- Fiduciary responsibilities of union officers and representatives. It also disqualifies criminals and former communists from holding union offices, and it requires certain union officers to be bonded to ensure the faithful discharge of their duties and responsibilities.

- Rights to participate in union elections and governance, such as the right to nominate candidates in elections, to vote in elections, to attend membership meetings, to participate in the deliberations, and to vote on the business, such as setting dues and assessments.

The law was intended to promote union democracy and financial integrity. Success in the administration of the law requires initiative on the part of union members and availability of necessary information to union members.

In 1984, the Comprehensive Crime Control Act, containing the Labor Racketeering Amendments, was passed. These amendments, backed by the AFL-CIO, closed the loopholes in the existing laws against labor malfeasance. Convicted labor officials cannot hold any union position for up to 13 years; previous law allowed for elongated appeals during which the officials might remain in office. Any convicted management official must be transferred outside the labor relations function and cannot serve as a consultant or advisor in labor relations.

Union Security

A **union security clause** in the labor agreement makes it easier for the union to enroll and retain members. A reasonable level of union security is necessary for a labor organization to survive and effectively represent the interests of bargaining unit members. Upon National Labor Relations Board (NLRB) union certification under the LMRA, a union is granted an *irrebuttable presumption of ma-*

jority status support for one year. This provides the certified union a reasonable time in which to negotiate a first labor agreement with the employer without being concerned that it might be replaced by a rival union or by a decertification election. Any additional form of union security (e.g., union shop or dues check-off clause) must be obtained by a union through negotiation with the employer.

Union security provisions tend to strengthen the union's financial resources by increasing the number of dues-paying members. Unions seek to recoup their initial time and money investments spent on organizing employees at a facility by subsequently obtaining dues from the eligible members. Union leaders believe they are morally justified in asking bargaining unit members to help pay for services provided by the union because they are legally obligated to represent all bargaining unit employees.

Union security provisions can offer benefits to the employer and the union. Many might contend that employers prefer dealing with a weak rather than a strong union. A weak union can aid an employer's effort to terminate a union-management relationship, but it can frustrate an employer who earnestly tries to resolve working condition disputes through an established union–management relationship. It is commonly the union, not the employer, who sells the collective-bargaining agreement to the membership. A union has difficulty in accomplishing this objective when there are nonunion member factions within the bargaining unit that seek to undermine support for union policies.

Union officials contend that union security provisions also offer other advantages to the employer, such as less time spent in recruiting new members and collecting dues of existing members during the workday. However, management officials counter that this time saving will not result in more production because union officials might use the extra time to police the labor agreement and formulate additional grievances. Unions also maintain that morale can be improved if all employees are union members. Tensions arise when some employees do not pay for the services shared by all (the so-called *free rider* issue). However, a counterargument could be made that tensions are not reduced by union security, merely redirected. The possible anger of union members working with nonunion employees is replaced by the anger of nonunion bargaining unit members who feel forced to pay for unwanted union services.

Union Security Provisions

In view of their potential advantages and disadvantages, union security provisions have taken one or more of the following forms.

— **Closed Shop** For an employee to obtain a job in a **closed shop**, the employee must first become a member of a union. The closed shop was made unlawful by the LMRA in 1947.

— **Union Shop** The most common form of union security clause, the union shop clause is found in about 64 percent of private-sector labor agreements.[83] Under a **union shop** contract provision, the employee does not have to be a union member to be hired by the company. However, after being hired the employee must become a union member within a period of not more than 30 days (7 days in the construction industry) to remain employed by the company. The U.S. Supreme Court in *Communications Workers v. Beck* (487 U.S. 735 [1988]), held that a union shop clause only requires a bargaining unit member to become a **finan-**

cial core union member. This term refers to an individual who meets the minimum (core) union membership requirement of paying regular union dues and initiation fees. A union may impose additional lawful conditions for obtaining **full union membership** status (e.g., individual must be willing to comply with the union's constitution and bylaws). Under a union shop provision, an employer does not always have to honor a union request to discharge an employee who is not a union member if (1) the employer believes union membership was not offered to the employee on the same terms as other employees or (2) membership was denied for any reason other than the failure to tender dues.[84]

The *Beck* decision created a group of so-called "Beck rights" for bargaining unit employees. These "Beck rights" cover (1) notices to employees, (2) accounting of funds by unions and (3) procedure for implementation. Unions are required to notify current members annually of their Beck rights. For example, this notice requirement may be met with a notice in the December edition of the union's monthly magazine. Newly hired employees receive notice at the time the union seeks to have the employee pay dues. The employee may choose between being a nonmember agency fee payer (a financial core employee) or a "union member in good standing" who will become a full union member. The union is required to maintain an accounting system (subject to audit) that determines the percentage of employees' dues used for collective bargaining purposes (known as "chargeable fees") and those used for other activities not related to collective bargaining (known as "nonchargeable fees"). The union notifies employees that those who wish to exercise their Beck rights must do so annually, and the union then provides a "window period" (a certain time period each year) for application for a refund of a portion of dues (nonchargeable fees) for employees who exercise their Beck rights. In other words, employees who exercise their Beck rights must file once per year during a specific period designated by the union.[85]

On February 17, 2001, President George W. Bush issued Executive Order 13201 entitled "Notification of Employee Rights Concerning Payment of Union Dues or Fees." The Executive Order requires federal government contractors to post notices to employees. On January 2, 2002, the U.S. District Court for the District of Columbia held that the new rules would regulate in a core labor-management area that is regulated by the National Labor Relations Act and imposes a duty on employers the National Labor Relations Act does not impose. Therefore, the Court ruled that the new rules were preempted by the National Labor Relations Act and were unenforceable. This ruling was appealed and the Court of Appeals overturned the lower court's decision. Subsequently, the Labor Department began the regulatory process to implement Executive Order 13201, which should occur in 2004.

Agency Shop More commonly found in public-sector labor agreements, an **agency shop** clause does not require an employee to join the union but does require the employee to pay the union a sum equal to membership dues to remain employed. This provision assumes that employees should not be forced to join a union but nonetheless should help defray the bargaining and grievance costs. The U.S. Supreme Court has determined that the minimum legal requirements for union membership imposed by a union or agency shop clause are essentially the same.[86]

Before seeking to impose an agency shop provision on a bargaining unit member, the union must inform the employee of his or her right to become a financial core rather than full union member.[87] A union may not charge a financial core member for the cost of union expenditures unrelated to collective bargaining, contract administration, or grievance resolution activities if the financial core member objects to such use of dues money and if the financial core member notifies the union of his or her objection to such expenditures.[88] A union must notify all financial core members annually regarding the percentage of union dues assessments spent on nonchargeable activities, as well as the reasonable procedure by which the financial core member can object to such expenditures. If the financial core member objects, the union must reduce the amount of the financial core member's dues obligation by the percentage amount spent on nonchargeable activities. A financial core member who disagrees with the union's calculation of chargeable and nonchargeable expenditures may either appeal the dispute to final and binding arbitration or file an unfair labor practice charge with the NLRB. Some examples of chargeable union activities would be the costs of conducting contract negotiations, investigating and resolving grievances, conducting union business meetings, union publications such as newsletters intended to inform the union's membership about contract issues or grievance disputes, litigation costs incurred in the course of representational activities, social events or member benefits available to all bargaining unit members, and attendance at national or state union conventions. The NLRB recently ruled that the cost associated with union organizing is a chargeable expense as long as the employees being organized work for an employer in the same competitive markets as bargaining unit members already represented by the union.[89] Examples of nonchargeable union activities would be the cost of legislative lobbying, union benefits not available to financial core members, and charitable contributions such as a donation to the local United Way campaign.

The U.S. Supreme Court in another decision also applied *Beck* guidelines to similar expenses paid by public-sector employees' union dues.[90] The Court stated that public employees did not have to pay the portion of union dues that paid for any union activities that were not oriented toward the ratification or implementation of the dissenters' collective bargaining agreement. This decision was not clear cut, however, as it indicated, for example, that dues payments can properly go toward a teacher union's strike preparation activities even if a strike is illegal under state law. In essence, the Court agreed with the public-sector union that a strike threat represented a reasonable, albeit illegal, bargaining tactic in pursuit of legitimate bargaining unit objectives.

Contingency Union Shop Some labor agreements in right-to-work states (covered on page 174) have a contingency union shop provision stating that the union security provision currently in force will automatically convert to a union shop provision if the state's right-to-work laws are eliminated.

Union Hiring Hall According to a **union hiring hall** provision, employers hire employees referred by the union if the union can supply a sufficient number of qualified applicants. This provision is found in about 23 percent of all labor agreements but is much more common in certain industries such as construction (90 percent) and maritime (88 percent).[91] Unions are required to operate hiring halls in a nondiscriminatory manner, making them equally available to union members and nonunion employees. In reality, most nonunion individuals do not choose to seek employment through union-operated hiring halls. A hiring hall provision helps to strengthen union security by encouraging current union members to associate their union more closely with the provision of job opportunities.

Preferential Treatment Clause   A negotiated labor agreement provision that indicates current employees who may be union members will be given employment preference over nonemployees when a new facility is opened is called a **preferential treatment clause**. This arrangement was negotiated between the United Auto Workers and General Motors for the new Saturn manufacturing plant located in Spring Hill, Tennessee, and was upheld by the NLRB. Such an arrangement permitted General Motors to take advantage of the skilled labor pool represented by employees already on the payroll, some of whom were laid off for lack of work at the time the new plant was seeking to fill employment positions.

Dues Checkoff   A provision commonly used in conjunction with one of the previously cited union security provisions, **a dues checkoff** makes the collection of union dues more convenient for both the union and union members. It is not a union security clause in the strict sense of the word because it does not guarantee that some or all employees will become union members. However, a dues checkoff clause in the labor agreement allows a union member to have dues automatically taken out of his or her paycheck (similar to any other payroll deduction) and transferred to the union. In addition to the dues checkoff clause agreed to by the employer and union in the labor agreement, each individual union member must sign a separate document authorizing the deduction to be made before any union dues may be automatically deducted from the employee's paycheck. This provision is important to the union because it assures the union of an uninterrupted flow of income. Without a systematic dues deduction, union officers would have to spend a great deal of time contacting recalcitrant members who kept delaying their dues payments. In many cases, the employer automatically agrees to this provision in the first contract negotiation on the assumption that every other labor agreement contains it. The employer may charge a reasonable administrative fee to the union for the cost of dues collection and other paperwork associated with administering this contract provision. In negotiations, astute management officials usually bargain for something in return for this provision, such as flexibility in making work assignments, subcontracting, or writing job descriptions.

Right-to-Work Laws: Controversy and Effects

Employers, some employees, and the courts have long been concerned with union security provisions.[92] Efforts to have Congress impose a national ban on union security agreements as part of the LMRA (Taft-Hartley Act) in 1947 were unsuccessful. Congress believed that providing a reasonable opportunity to achieve union security aided in the effective representation of employees' interests in collective bargaining between their union representative and the employer. As a political compromise, Congress did enact Section 14(b) of the LMRA, which states:

> Nothing in this Act shall be construed as authorizing the execution or application of agreements requiring membership in a labor organization as a

Exhibit 4.11

Private Sector Average Annual Pay by State and Right-to-Work Status, 2001

Right-to-Work States	Average Annual Pay	Non–Right-to-Work States	Average Annual Pay
Alabama	$30,090	Alaska	$36,140
Arizona	$33,408	California	$41,358
Arkansas	$27,258	Colorado	$37,950
Florida	$31,551	Connecticut	$46,963
Georgia	$35,114	Delaware	$38,434
Idaho	$27,765	Hawaii	$31,250
Iowa	$28,840	Illinois	$39,058
Kansas	$30,153	Indiana	$31,778
Louisiana	$28,815	Kentucky	$30,017
Mississippi	$25,919	Maine	$28,815
Nebraska	$28,375	Maryland	$38,237
Nevada	$33,122	Massachusetts	$44,976
North Carolina	$32,026	Michigan	$37,387
North Dakota	$25,707	Minnesota	$36,585
Oklahoma	$28,020	Missouri	$32,422
South Carolina	$29,253	Montana	$25,194
South Dakota	$25,600	New Hampshire	$35,479
Tennessee	$31,491	New Jersey	$44,285
Texas	$36,039	New Mexico	$28,698
Utah	$30,074	New York	$46,664
Virginia	$36,716	Ohio	$33,280
Wyoming	$28,025	Oregon	$33,203
		Pennsylvania	$34,976
		Rhode Island	$33,592
		Vermont	$30,240
		Washington	$37,475
		West Virginia	$27,982
		Wisconsin	$31,556

SOURCE: Bureau of Labor Statistics, U.S. Department of Labor, "State and Industry Average Annual Pay for 2001 and Percent Change in Pay for All Covered Workers," November 15, 2003, at http://stats.bls.gov/news.release/annpay.t01.htm.

condition of employment in any State or Territory in which such execution of application is prohibited by State or Territorial law.

Under this provision, a state may initiate legislation prohibiting union membership as a condition of employment. Currently 22 states (44 percent) have a **right-to-work law** (Exhibit 4.11). In 2001, Oklahoma became the 22nd "right-to-work" state. During the political campaign, proponents of the change argued that Oklahoma would become more competitively positioned to create jobs if the state adopted the labor policies of neighboring states and argued for liberty, free choice, and individual initiative. Unions promoted the principle of majority rule as essential to workplace democracy and urged allowing parties to negotiate the union security issue without intervention from the state. Unions also claimed that the other Sunbelt states offered lower wages, tax relief, and other subsidies in order to attract jobs.[93]

Efforts to promote so-called state right-to-work laws are mainly conducted by the National Right to Work Committee, founded in 1955, whose stated purpose is to protect the employee's right to determine whether to join a union. Funded principally by employer contributions, the committee does not regard itself as being against unions but merely against union security provisions that compel employees to become members. However, allegedly, the committee's "pro-union, antiunion security" stance has been modified to a flat "antiunion" approach in recent years. A related but separate organization, the National Right to Work Legal Defense Foundation, provides legal representation in right-to-work cases.

There has been a long-running debate on the effects of right-to-work laws on wages and union membership. Because there is no single explanation for wage rates or union density rates and no cause-and-effect relationship has been identified, one cannot conclude that "right-to-work" laws cause lower wages or low union density rates. However, Exhibit 4.11, which compares the average pay of employees in right-to-work states with that of employees in "non–right-to-work" states, certainly shows a wage disparity in favor of employees in the latter.

Even more impressive is the comparison of union density rates between right-to-work states and non–right-to-work states (see Exhibit 4.12). Only 2 of the 22 (9 percent) right-to-work states have union density rates above 10 percent, whereas 24 (89 percent) non–right-to-work states (those states that allow the union and management to negotiate union security clauses) have union density rates of 10 percent or more.

Meaning and Morality of Right to Work Supporters of right-to-work laws contend the underlying definition affirms the right of every U.S. citizen to work for a living, despite whether he or she belongs to a union. In their view, compulsory unionism in any form (union shop, agency shop) contradicts a fundamental human right—freedom to join or not to join a union. Even Samuel Gompers, former president of the American Federation of Labor (AFL), occasionally stressed the necessity for "voluntarism" in labor unions:

> The workers of America adhere to voluntary institutions in preference to compulsory systems which are held to be not only impractical but a menace to their rights, welfare, and their liberty.[94]

Supporters further contend that nobody should be required to join a private organization, particularly if that organization uses the individual's dues to support causes that the individual believes are morally unjust or contrary to his or her religious beliefs. This attitude has been reinforced by Section 19 of the LMRA and actions by the U.S. Supreme Court, which, in effect, permit an employee to refuse to pay union dues because of a legitimate religious objection.[95]

Opponents of right-to-work laws contend the term *right-to-work* represents a gimmicky public relations slogan designed to restrict union security and related bargaining power. Opponents argue that unions do not deny anyone the fundamental freedom to seek work. Union security represents one of many negotiated employment conditions, such as work schedules, type of work performed, or wages, which a job applicant may choose to accept or reject if a job offer is made. If an employee does not like a particular working condition, that

Exhibit 4.12

Employees Who Are Union Members and Who Are Represented by Unions by State and Right-to-Work Status, 2002

Right-to-Work States	Employed Union Members (%)	Represented by Unions (%)	Non–Right-to-Work States	Employed Union Members (%)	Represented by Unions (%)
Alabama	8.9	10.5	Alaska	24.3	26.7
Arizona	5.5	6.6	California	17.5	18.9
Arkansas	5.9	6.8	Colorado	7.8	9.0
Florida	5.7	7.6	Connecticut	16.7	17.8
Georgia	6.0	7.0	Delaware	11.1	12.1
Idaho	7.1	8.9	Hawaii	24.4	25.4
Iowa	11.1	13.6	Illinois	19.6	20.6
Kansas	8.2	9.9	Indiana	13.3	14.5
Louisiana	8.1	10.3	Kentucky	10.0	11.2
Mississippi	6.6	8.0	Maine	12.9	15.1
Nebraska	7.9	11.1	Maryland	14.1	16.9
Nevada	15.2	16.7	Massachusetts	14.2	15.6
North Carolina	3.2	4.0	Michigan	21.1	22.0
North Dakota	8.1	9.8	Minnesota	17.6	18.3
Oklahoma	8.9	10.6	Missouri	13.2	14.5
South Carolina	4.9	6.1	Montana	14.1	15.5
South Dakota	5.6	6.9	New Hampshire	9.7	11.2
Tennessee	9.0	10.5	New Jersey	19.4	20.6
Texas	5.1	6.5	New Mexico	6.6	8.7
Utah	6.2	7.5	New York	25.3	26.6
Virginia	9.5	11.0	Ohio	16.7	17.9
Wyoming	7.8	9.8	Oregon	15.5	16.6
			Pennsylvania	15.5	16.6
			Rhode Island	17.2	17.9
			Vermont	9.5	11.0
			Washington	18.4	20.0
			West Virginia	13.3	14.0
			Wisconsin	15.6	16.4

SOURCE: Bureau of Labor Statistics, U.S. Department of Labor, "Union Affiliation of Employed Wage and Salary Workers by State," February 25, 2003, at http://stats.bls.gov/news.release/union.t05.htm.

employee is free to seek employment elsewhere. This argument can also be supported by a quotation from Samuel Gompers:

> [T]he union shop, in agreement with employers, mutually entered into for the advantage of both employees and unions and the maintenance of industrial peace . . . is to the economic, social, and moral advancement of all our people.[96]

Opponents further believe that union security provisions requiring some union attachment are moral because a person is a member of society with a responsibility to contribute to the common good. Because a union is legally required to represent all members of the bargaining unit in a fair and nondiscriminatory manner, it only seems fair that a bargaining unit member be required to help defray the costs of providing those services.

Impact of Right-to-Work Laws on the Union Organization and Employees

Research studies suggest that state right-to-work laws have a mixed effect on union membership levels and bargaining outcomes.[97] The presence of a right-to-work statute would appear to reduce union membership levels within a state 3 to 8 percent over the long term. Right-to-work laws appear to have no significant effect on employee wage rates but do appear to be positively associated with perceptions of a "better business climate," which in turn is positively correlated with greater industrial development activity over the long term. Of course, the presence of a right-to-work statue is typically one of several factors (e.g., tax structure, labor supply) used to measure the favorability of a state's business climate, making it difficult to determine the precise contribution of a right-to-work law to the overall perception of a favorable business climate and industrial development location decisions.

The bargaining unit members who choose not to join or financially support the union representing them for purposes of collective bargaining are referred to as **free riders.** Delaney (1998) notes that individuals with a college education are more likely to be a free rider than less-educated employees. This poses a challenge to unions seeking to expand union membership levels among workers in occupations requiring increasing levels of education and skills to effectively use available technologies.[98]

Right-to-work advocates claim that voluntary union membership increases union democracy by making leaders more responsive to members. With compulsory union membership, the members must remain "captive passengers" of the union if they wish to keep their jobs. Union leaders can become indifferent or even corrupt because members have no economic way of voicing their displeasure, such as by withdrawing their union membership dues support. Union leaders should have to earn their dues through their responsive, diligent actions. "Good unions don't need compulsory unionism—and bad unions don't deserve it."[99]

Opponents of right-to-work laws stress that under the LMRA, unions may be sued for lack of fair representation by bargaining unit employees who are nonmembers. The law also permits bargaining unit members to rectify ineffective or unresponsive union leadership problems by either electing new union leaders or electing to decertify the status of the current bargaining unit representative.

One research effort examined union members at a police organization in a right-to-work state. Dues-paying members were more likely to be male, married with more financial dependents, and have longer organizational tenure.[100] Another study also found that females as a group were more likely not to be union members, a finding possibly related to their lower wages, concentration in occupations with large proportions of nonunion members (e.g., professional specialties), and less employment in job categories having larger proportions of union members (e.g., precision production, craft, and repair).[101]

SUMMARY

This chapter discussed two of the major participants in the labor relations process: unions and management. First, the goals of unions and management were presented, with emphasis on where the goals are the same and where they have potential for conflict. Companies' labor relations strategies, ranging from union suppression to labor-management cooperation, were explained.

Union strategic plans, which are at the embryonic stage in most unions, were discussed, and examples from the AFL-CIO were presented. Companies and unions are structured according to their goals; typical examples of company labor relations organizations and organizations at various levels of unions were displayed.

The last part of the chapter focused on union governance. First, general characteristics of craft and industrial unions were explained. Then, the government and organizational activities of the local union, the national or international union, the intermediate bodies, and the federation (the AFL-CIO) were discussed. Because unions, like businesses and government, have experienced corruption and misuse of power and authority, examples of these problems and of steps that have been taken to seek a resolution were provided.

Unions show concern for the long-term survival and growth of their organizations when they attempt to negotiate a union security provision (such as union shop, union hiring hall, or agency shop) into the labor agreement. However, certain union security provisions cannot be negotiated in states having right-to-work laws, permitted under Section 14(b) of the LMRA. Controversy occurs over the meaning, morality, and impact on union organizations of a right-to-work law.

DISCUSSION QUESTIONS

1. Compare the steps companies may take to implement a positive human resources management program with principles of effective management.

2. What suggestions can you offer to emphasize common goals of companies and unions as opposed to conflicting goals?

3. Analyze the dilemma of nonunion companies in terms of employee termination under the employment-at-will doctrine.

4. Assess the strategic plans of the AFL-CIO and determine whether these plans provide direction for growth.

5. Locate a local union and a local plant and draw an organizational chart for each.

6. Select a craft union and an industrial union and point out differing characteristics of these two types of unions.

7. Compare the government of the local union with student governments and municipal governments, paying special attention to participation by members.

8. Explain why and how national unions' presidents have been able to accumulate so much authority and power.

9. Differentiate among the business agent of a local union, a shop steward, and an international union representative. How do their roles differ?

10. Because the AFL-CIO does not negotiate labor agreements on behalf of national unions, how can it claim to be the "spokesperson for organized labor" in the United States?

11. Compare the requirements for union democracy to any student organization with which you are familiar.

12. Formulate a one- or two-sentence argument for or against the right-to-work philosophy. Fully defend your statement from arguments that could be made against your position.

KEY TERMS

craft unions
industrial unions
business agent
shop steward
international union representative
constitution
convention
master labor agreement
amalgamation
absorption
affiliation
conference boards
joint councils

associate membership program
union security clause
closed shop
union shop
financial core union member
full union membership
agency shop
union hiring hall
preferential treatment clause
dues checkoff
right-to-work laws
free riders

EXPLORING THE WEB

Labor Unions, Mergers, and Union Security

1. UNITE and the History and Merger of Textile Unions   Explore links from the Web page for UNITE (Union of Needletrades, Industrial and Textile Employees), a labor union created in 1995 by the merger of two major unions, the International Ladies' Garment Workers' Union (ILGWU) and the Amalgamated Clothing and Textile Workers Union (ACTWU). Read articles on UNITE's "Stop Sweatshops" campaign.

http://www.uniteunion.org

The Kheel Center for Labor-Management Documentation and Archives at Cornell University provides reproductions of moving accounts of the Triangle Shirtwaist Factory Fire in 1911. From the Cornell site, you can read newspapers articles published in 1911 along with selections from the book by Leon Stein, *The Triangle Fire*, and view photographs and drawings depicting the fire.

http://www.ilr.cornell.edu/trianglefire/

2. Merger of the USWA and the AFGWU   In June of 2003, the United Steelworkers and the American Flint Glass Workers Union (AFGWU) signed an agreement to merge. The following two articles were published on the USWA Web site. The first one relates the story of the merger and a short history of Flint Glass Workers. The second one is a history of other USWA mergers with ten international unions.

http://www.uswa.org/uswa/program/content/230.php
http://www.uswa.org/uswa/program/content/543.php

3. Bureau of Labor Statistics and Current Union Membership   The Bureau of Labor Statistics publishes an annual report on union membership. Read the summary to discover more about the current status of labor unions. What percentage of the total people employed in protective services were members of unions in 2002?

http://www.bls.gov/news.release/union2.toc.htm

Read the article by David Denholm, "Unions Turn to Public Sector as Membership Declines." The article is available on the Web site of the Capital Research Center.

http://www.capitalresearch.org/pubs/pdf/x3770440101.pdf

4. Articles on Union Mergers   Read the article, "Falling Union Membership Prompting Mergers," excerpted from Laura M. Litvan's "Unions Have an Urge to Merge," published in *Investor's Business Daily,* August 8, 1997, and reproduced on the Web page for the National Center for Policy Analysis.

http://www.ncpa.org/pd/unions/pduni/pduni1.html

5. AFL-CIO Web Page   Provides current information about AFL-CIO speeches, news releases, activities, position papers, organization structure, and more.

http://www.aflcio.org

6. Right-to-Work Laws   Is your home state one of the 22 states that has right-to-work laws? See the map of right-to-work states on the site for The National Right to Work Legal Defense Foundation to find out if your state has right-to-work laws. Where in the Florida state statutes are the right-to-work laws? (Click on Florida on the map.)

http://www.nrtw.org/rtws.htm

7. Union Security Provisions in Labor Agreements   In the following example of labor agreements, which forms have been taken by the union security provision? (Closed shop, union hiring hall, union shop, agency shop, maintenance of membership, quasi-union shop, contingency union shop, preferential treatment clause, dues checkoff.) Examine the rights of the employer (management) and the employees (union) as set forth in the agreements.

2002–2005 Labor Agreement: United Transportation Union, Local 12 and Santa Cruz Metro Transit District

http://www.local23.org/bidspring04/contract/ccontents.html

Firefighter Labor Agreement
Labor Agreement entered into between King County Fire District 10 and International Association of Firefighters, Local 2878, January 1, 2001, through December 31, 2003

http://www.iafflocal2878.org/firefighter_labor_agreement.htm

REFERENCES

1. Audrey Freedman, "How the 1980's Have Changed Industrial Relations," *Monthly Labor Review* 111 (May 1988), pp. 35–39.

2. Martin M. Perline and David J. Poynter, "Union Orientation and Perception of Managerial Prerogatives," *Labor Law Journal* 40 (December 1989), p. 781.

3. Stephen R. Sleigh, Michael Kapsa, and Charis Hall, *The Costs of Aggression* (Washington, D.C.: Industrial Union Department [AFL-CIO], 1992), pp. 2–3.

4. Alan Balfour, "The Unenforceability of the UAW's 'Neutrality Pledge' from General Motors," paper presented at the Second Annual Meeting of the Southern Industrial Relations Association, 1981.

5. Charles R. Greer and Stanley A. Martin, "Calculative Strategy Decisions during Organization Campaigns," *Sloan Management Review* 19 (Winter 1978), p. 73.

6. Ibid.

7. William N. Cooke and David G. Meyer, "Structural and Market Predictors of Corporate Labor Relations Strategies," *Industrial and Labor Relations Review* 43 (January 1990), pp. 280–282.

8. Keith Knass and Michael Matuszak, "An Antiunion Corporate Culture and Quality Improvement Programs," *Labor Studies Journal* 19 (Fall 1994), pp. 21–39.

9. Douglas M. McCabe and David Lewin, "Employee Voice: A Human Resource Management Perspective," *California Management Review* 34 (Spring 1992), pp. 112–114.

10. Fred K. Foulkes, "How Top Nonunion Companies Manage Employees," *Harvard Business Review* 59 (September–October 1981), pp. 121–125.

11. Herbert R. Northrup, "Construction Double-breasted Operations and Pre-Hire Agreements: Assessing the Issues," *Journal of Labor Research* 10 (Spring 1989), pp. 219–227.

12. *Twenty-First Annual Report of the NLRB* (Washington, D.C.: U.S. Government Printing Office, 1956), pp. 14–15.

13. Herbert L. Sherman and William P. Murphy, *Unionization and Collective Bargaining* (Washington, D.C.: Bureau of National Affairs, 1975), p. 47.

14. *NLRB v. Cabot Carbon Co.*, 360 U.S. 203 (1959). The union challenged a General Foods job-enrichment program that divided employees into work groups for the purpose of working job assignments, scheduling overtime, and discussing job-related concerns with a consultant (with management representatives in attendance on occasion). While the NLRB ruled that no union existed, it could raise interesting issues in the future. *General Foods Corporation and American Federation of Grain Millers, AFL-CIO and Its Local 70*, 231 NLRB 122 (1977). Also see Donna Sockell, "The Legality of Employee-Participation Programs in Unionized Firms," *Industrial and Labor Relations Review* 37 (July 1984), pp. 541–556.

15. Audrey Freedman, *The New Look in Wage Policy and Employer Relations* (New York: The Conference Board, Inc., 1985), pp. 16–18.

16. Arthur Eliot Berkeley and E. Patrick McDermott, "The Second Golden Age of Employment Arbitration, *Labor Law Journal* 43 (December 1992), pp. 774–777.

17. Richard B. Peterson and Douglas M. McCabe, "The Nonunion Grievance System in High Performing Firms," *Proceedings of the 1994 Spring Meeting, Industrial Relations Research Association*, Paula B. Voos, ed. (Madison, Wis.: Industrial Relations Research Association, 1994), p. 529.

18. Douglas M. McCabe, "Corporate Nonunion Grievance Arbitration Systems: A Procedural Analysis," *Labor Law Journal* 40 (July 1989), pp. 432–438.

19. John E. Butler, Gerald Ferris, and Nancy K. Napier, *Strategy and Human Resources Management* (Cincinnati, Ohio: South-Western, 1991), pp. 147–158.

20. William N. Cooke and David G. Meyer, "Structural and Market Predictors," pp. 280–282.

21. Butler, Ferris, Napier, pp. 147–158.

22. Francis A. O'Connell, Jr., "The Changing Character of Industrial Relations: Comment," *Journal of Labor Research* 12 (Fall 1991), p. 323.

23. Robert T. Thompson, "The Changing Character of Employee Relations," *Journal of Labor Research* 12 (Fall 1991), pp. 316–317.

24. Edward E. Lawler III and Susan A. Mohrman, "Unions and the New Management," *The Academy of Management Executive* 1, no. 3 (1987), pp. 293–300.

25. William N. Cooke and David G. Meyer, "Structural and Market Predictors," pp. 292–294.

26. John T. Dunlop, *The Management of Labor Unions* (Lexington, Mass.: Lexington Books, 1989), pp. xii–7.

27. Christine L. Scheck and George W. Bohlander, "The Planning Practices of Labor Organizations: A National Study," *Labor Studies Journal* 15 (Winter 1990), pp. 69–84.

28. Harry C. Katz, Rosemary Batt, and Jeffrey H. Keefe, "The Revitalization of the CWA: Integrating Collective Bargaining, Political Action, and Organizing," *Industrial and Labor Relations Review* 56, no. 4 (July 2003), pp. 573–589.

29. Tracy Fitzpatrick and Weezy Waldsteing, "Challenges to Strategic Planning in International Unions," *Proceedings of the 46th Annual Meeting of the Industrial Relations Research Association*, Paula B. Voos, ed. (Madison, Wis.: IRRA, 1994), pp. 73–84.

30. Susan J. Schurman and Hal Stack, "From Strategic Planning to Organizational Change in Local Unions," *Proceedings of the 46th Annual Meeting of the Industrial Relations Research Association*, Paula B. Voos, ed. (Madison, Wis.: IRRA, 1994), pp. 85–94.

31. Katherine Van Wezel Stone, "Labor and the Corporate Structure: Challenging Conceptions and Emerging Possibilities," *The University of Chicago Law Review* 55 (Winter 1988), pp. 76–78.

32. John T. Dunlop, "Have the 1980's Changed U.S. Industrial Relations?" *Monthly Labor Review* 111 (May 1988), p. 33.

33. Audrey Freedman, Managing Labor Relations (New York: *The Conference Board, Inc.*, 1979), pp. 7–33.

34. Bert Spector, "Transformational Leadership: The New Challenge for U.S. Unions," *Human Resource Management* 26 (Spring 1987), pp. 3–11.

35. Alice H. Cook, *Union Democracy: Practice and Ideal* (Ithaca, N.Y.: Cornell University, 1963), pp. 19–26.

36. James E. Martin, John Christopher, and John M. Magenau, "A Longitudinal Examination of Union Steward Behaviors and Behavioral Intentions," *Proceedings of the 46th Annual Meeting of the Industrial Relations Research Association*, Paula B. Voos, ed. (Madison, Wis.: IRRA, 1994), pp. 422–431; Paul F. Clark, Daniel G. Gallagher, and Thomas J. Pavlak, "Member Commitment in an American Union: The Role of the Grievance Procedure," *Industrial Relations Journal* 21 (1990), pp. 147–157.

37. Gregory Mantsios, "Developing Rank-and-File Leaders: A Union/University Collaboration," *Labor Studies Journal* 26, no. 4 (Winter 2000), pp. 72–81.

38. Allan Nash, *The Union Steward: Duties, Rights, and Status* (Ithaca, N.Y.: New York State School of Industrial and Labor Relations, 1977), pp. 20–22.

39. Renaud Paquet and Isabelle Roy, "Why Do People Get Involved in Local Union Office? *Journal of Collective Negotiations in the Public Sector* 27, no. 1 (1998), pp. 73–75.

40. Victor G. Devinatz, "From Industrial Unionism to General Unionism: A Historical Transformation?" *Labor Law Journal* 44 (April 1993), pp. 252–256.

41. Steven L. McShane, "A Path Analysis of Participation in Union Administration," *Industrial Relations* 25 (Winter 1986), pp. 72–78.

42. John C. Anderson, "Local Union Participation: A Reexamination," *Industrial Relations* 18 (Winter 1979), p. 30.

43. John Lund, "Using Surveys to Learn More about Membership Attitudes," *Labor Studies Forum* 4, no. 4 (1991), pp. 1–4.

44. John T. Delaney, Paul Jarley, and Jack Fiorito, "Planning for Change: Determinants of Innovation in U.S. National Unions," *Industrial and Labor Relations Review* 49 (July 1996), p. 612.

45. J. Bryan Fuller and Kim Hester, "The Effect of Labor Relations Climate on the Union Participation Process," *Journal of Labor Research* 19 (Winter 1998), pp. 184–185.

46. James E. Martin and John M. Magenau, "An Analysis of Factors Related to the Accuracy of Steward Predictions of Membership Views," *Labor Law Journal* 35 (August 1985), pp. 490–494.

47. Leonard R. Sayles and George Strauss, *The Local Union*, rev. ed. (New York: Harcourt, Brace & World, 1967), pp. 96–100.

48. Ibid, pp. 93–105.

49. Jack Barbash, *American Unions* (New York: Random House, 1967), pp. 69–72.

50. The Landrum-Griffin Act requires a convention at least every 5 years, and some unions, such as the Teamsters, take the limit of 5 years.

51. George Strauss, "Union Government in the U.S.: Research Past and Future," *Industrial Relations* 16 (Winter 1977), p. 234.

52. Barbash, *American Unions*, pp. 76–80.

53. Marick F. Masters, Robert S. Atkin, and Gary W. Florkowski, "An Analysis of

Union Reporting Requirements Under Title II of the Landrum-Griffin Act," *Labor Law Journal* 40 (November 1989), pp. 713–722.

54. Susan J. Schurman and Adrienne E. Eaton, "Labor and Workplace Democracy: Past, Present and Future," *Labor Studies Journal* 21 (Summer 1996), p. 8.

55. Shulamit Kahn, Kevin Long, and Donna Kadev, "National Union Leader Performance and Turnover in Building Trades," *Industrial Relations* 25 (Fall 1986), pp. 276–289.

56. Lawrence French, David A. Gray, and Robert W. Brobst, *Political Structure and Presidential Tenure in International Unions: A Study of Union Democracy,* paper presented at the annual meeting of the Academy of Management, Detroit, 1980, 16.

57. Phillip L. Quaglieri, "The New People of Power: The Backgrounds and Careers of Top Labor Leaders," *Journal of Labor Research* 9 (Summer 1988), pp. 271–283.

58. Jack Fiorito, Lee P. Stepina, Paul Jarley, John Thomas Delaney, and Mike Knudstrup, "Visions of Success: National Leaders' Views on Union Effectiveness," *Labor Studies Journal* 22 (Spring 1997), pp. 14–16.

59. "How Much Pay Union Presidents Receive Varies Widely, Latest LM-2 Forms Show," *Daily Labor Report* (December 17, 2003), pp. C-1–C-8.

60. Paul F. Clark and Lois S. Gray, "Union Administration," in The State of Unions, eds. George Strauss, Daniel G. Gallagher, and Jack Fiorito (Madison, Wis.: *Industrial Relations Research Association,* 1992), pp. 179–193.

61. Charles W. Hickman, "Labor Organizations, Fees and Dues," *Monthly Labor Review* 100 (May 1977), pp. 19–24.

62. Ibid., pp. 117–118. Examples include recreation, social and entertainment activities, organization and recruitment of new members, convention attendance, general news publications, support of pending legislation, and contributions to charity.

63. James T. Bennett, "Private Sector Unions: The Myth of Decline," *Journal of Labor Research* 12 (Winter 1991), pp. 1–5.

64. Marick F. Masters and Robert S. Atkin, "The Finances of Major U.S. Unions," *Industrial Relations* 36 (October 1997), pp. 502–503.

65. Marick F. Masters, "Union Wealth: The Bargaining Power," *Journal of Labor Research* 18 (Winter 1997), pp. 106–107.

66. Gary Chaison, "Union Mergers and Union Revival," *Rekindling the Movement: Labor's Quest for Relevance in the 21st Century,* eds. Lowell Turner, Harry C. Katz, and Richard W. Hurd (Ithaca, N.Y.: ILR Press, 2001), pp. 238–240.

67. Gary N. Chaison, "The Form and Frequency of Union Mergers," *Labor Law Journal* 46 (August 1996), pp. 493–497.

68. James W. Robinson, "Structural Characteristics of the Independent Union in America Revisited," *Labor Law Journal* 43 (September 1992), pp. 567–575.

69. Sanford M. Jacoby and Anil Verma, "Enterprise Unions in the United States," *Industrial Relations* 31 (Winter 1992), p. 140.

70. Dana Milbank, "Labor Broadens Its Appeal by Setting Up Associations to Lobby and Offer Services," *The Wall Street Journal,* January 13, 1993, pp. B-1, B-5.

71. *This is the AFL-CIO* (Washington, D.C.: American Federation of Labor and Congress of Industrial Organizations, 1992), pp. 1–10.

72. Cathy Trost, "To the Union Chiefs, It's Still a Brotherhood," *The Wall Street Journal,* November 20, 1985, p. 30.

73. U.S. Department of Labor, Bureau of Labor Statistics, *Directory of National Unions and Employee Associations,* 1975 (Washington, D.C.: U.S. Government Printing Office, 1977), pp. 1–4.

74. Jill Kriesky, "Structural Change in the AFL-CIO: A Regional Study of Union Cities' Impact," *Rekindling the Movement: Labor's Quest for Relevance in the 21st Century,* eds. Lowell Turner, Harry C. Katz, and Richard W. Hurd (Ithaca, N.Y.: ILR Press, 2001), pp. 129–154.

75. Joseph Krislov, "The AFL-CIO Effort to Minimize Union Membership Conflicts: 1962– 1987," *Labor Studies Journal* 16 (Summer 1991), pp. 3–5.

76. *This is the AFL-CIO,* pp. 8–10.

77. Leo Troy, "Is the Future of Unionism in Cyberspace? *Journal of Labor Research* 24, no. 2 (Spring 2003), pp. 268–269.

78. David Greenstone, *Labor in American Politics* (Chicago: University of Chicago Press, 1977), pp. xiii–xxix.

79. Robert L. Rose, "New AFL-CIO President Seeks to Revitalize Old Federation," *The Wall Street Journal*, October 29, 1996, p. B-1; Steven Greenhouse, "Unions, Facing Decline, Increase Their Recruiting," *New York Times*, May 30, 1997, p. A-14.

80. Charles R. Greer, "E-Voice: How Information Technology is Shaping Life within Unions," *Journal of Labor Research* 23, no. 2 (Spring 2002), pp. 215–235; Richard Freeman, "Can the Internet Help Unions Rebound?" *Perspectives on Work* 7, no. 1 (2003), pp. 43–49.

81. Arthur B. Shostak, "Today's Unions as Tomorrow's CyberUnion: Labor Newest Hope," *Journal of Labor Research* 23, no. 2 (Spring 2001), pp. 242–243.

82. Gary Chaison, "Information Technology: The Threat to Unions," *Journal of Labor Research* 23, no. 2 (Spring 2002), pp. 251–256.

83. Bureau of National Affairs, Inc., *Basic Patterns in Union Contracts* (Washington, D.C.: Bureau of National Affairs Inc., 1995), p. 97.

84. Billie Ann Brotman and Thomas J. McDonagh, "Union Security Clauses as Viewed by the National Labor Relations Board," *Labor Law Journal* 37 (February 1986), pp. 104–115.

85. Jeff Canfield, "Note: What a Sham(e): The Broken Rights System in the Real World Workplace," *Wayne Law Review* 47 (Fall 2001), pp. 1049–1055.

86. *NLRB* v. *General Motors*, 373 U.S. 734 (1963); *Retail Clerks International Association Local 1625 AFL-CIO v. Schermerhorn et al.*, 373 U.S. 746 (1963); and *D. Louis Abood et al v. Detroit Board of Education*, 431 U.S. 209 (1977).

87. *California Saw and Knife Works*, 320 NLRB 224 (1995), enf'd. 133 F.3d 1012 (7th Cir. 1998). See also: "Guidelines Concerning Processing of Beck Cases," *Memorandum from the Office of the General Counsel*, August 17, 1998.

88. For further discussion of this issue, see Kenneth A. Kovach and Peter Millspaugh, "Implementing the *Beck* and *Lehnert* Union Security Agreement Decisions: A Study in Frustration," *Business Horizons* 39 (May/June 1995), pp. 57–65; Jan W. Henkel and Norman J. Wood, "Limitations on the Uses of Union Shop Funds after *Ellis:* What Activities Are Germane to Collective Bargaining?" *Labor Law Journal* 35 (December 1984), pp. 736–746; Peter Florey, "Fair Share Proceedings: A Case for Common Sense," *Arbitration Journal* 44 (March 1989), pp. 35–44; and David A. Lebowitz, "Limits on the Use of Agency Fees: The Revival of *Communications Workers of America v. Beck,*" *Employee Relations Law Journal* 18 (Winter 1992–1993), pp. 437–461.

89. *UFCW, Locals 951, 7, & 1036 (Meijer, Inc.) and Various Individuals*, 329 NLRB No. 69 (1999).

90. *Lehnert v. Ferris Faculty Association*, 500 U.S. 507 (1991).

91. Bureau of National Affairs, Inc., *Basic Patterns in Union Contracts*, p. 99.

92. For further historical insights into the right-to-work issue, see Gilbert J. Gall, *The Politics of Right to Work* (New York: Greenwood Press, 1988); and William Canak and Berkeley Miller, "Gumbo Politics: Unions, Business, and Louisiana Right-to-Work Legislation," *Industrial and Labor Relations Review* 43 (January 1990), pp. 258–271. For a classification system of right-to-work laws' various dimensions and related bibliography, see Thomas R. Haggard, "Union Security and the Right to Work: A Comprehensive Bibliography," *Journal of Labor Research* 11 (Winter 1990), pp. 81–106.

93. Raymond L. Hogler and Robert LaJeunesse, "Oklahoma's Right to Work Initiative: Labor Policy and Political Ideology," *Labor Law Journal* 53, no. 2 (2002), pp. 109–113. Also see Stan Greer and Charles W. Baird, "Reply to Hogler and LaJeunesse's 'Oklahoma's Right to Work Initiative: Labor Policy and Political Ideology,'" *Labor Law Journal* 54, no. 2 (2003), pp. 89–100.

94. National Right to Work Committee, "The Voluntarism of Samuel Gompers," (Fairfax, Va., n.d.), p. 1.

95. See, for example, "Supreme Court Reviews Objection to Agency Fee," Bureau of National Affairs Inc., *Daily Labor Report*, May 3, 1982, pp. 2, 3. Amendments to the NLRA put restrictions on religious reasons and can require a donation to a charity (other than the religion) equivalent to a fair share of union costs.

96. *The Truth about "Right-to-Work" Laws* (Washington, D.C.: American Federation of Labor and Congress of Industrial Organizations, January 1977), p. i.

97. For related complexities, see William J. Moore, "The Determinants and Effects of Right-to-Work Laws: A Review of the Recent Literature," *Journal of Labor Research* 19 (Summer 1998), pp. 445–469; William J. Moore and Robert J. Newman, "The Effects of Right-to-Work Laws: A Review of the Literature," *Industrial and Labor Relations Review* 38 (July 1985), pp. 571–575; Joe C. Davis and John H. Huston, "Right-to-Work Laws and Union Density: New Evidence from Micro Data," *Journal of Labor Research* 16 (Spring 1995),

pp. 223–230; and David T. Ellwood and Glenn Fine, "The Impact of Right-to-Work Laws on Union Organizing," *Journal of Political Economy* 95 (April 1987), pp. 250–274.

98. John T. Delaney, "Redefining the Right-to-Work Debate: Unions and the Dilemma of Free Choice," *Journal of Labor Research* 19 (Summer 1998), pp. 425–442.

99. Reed E. Larson, "Are Right-to-Work Laws Desirable? Yes," in *Contemporary Labor Issues,* eds. Walter Fogel and Archie Kleingartner (Belmont, Calif.: Wadsworth, 1968), p. 272.

100. John M. Jermier, Cynthia Fryer Cohen, Kathleen J. Powers, and Jeannie Gaines, "Paying Dues: Police Unionism in a Right-to-Work Environment," *Industrial Relations* 25 (Fall 1986), pp. 265–276.

101. Gary N. Chaison and Dileep G. Dhavale, "The Choice between Union Membership and Free-Rider Status," *Journal of Labor Research* 13 (Fall 1992), pp. 355–369.

Employee Rights under the Landrum-Griffin Act

Background

Paul Sanchez, a member of Local 1 of the Bartenders Union, speaks Spanish and is not sufficiently bilingual to understand the English language in either written or spoken form. Local 1 has 16,500 members, 48 percent of whom understand Spanish only.

For several years Local 1 has had its collective bargaining agreements, monthly newsletters, and various notices printed in Spanish to accommodate its Spanish-speaking members. At meetings held to nominate union officers and contract ratification meetings, which occur once every 3 years, English and Spanish translations are provided for the discussion that takes place. Monthly union meetings are conducted primarily in English and are attended by 50–75 members (less than 1 percent of the Union's total membership). Subjects debated during local union meetings include such topics as union expenditures, salaries of officers, general complaints with particular employers, and various other operational matters. Such debate is commonly referred to as "shop talk."

Spanish translation at monthly meetings is provided whenever union officer nominations take place or whenever Spanish-speaking members request their comments or those of others be translated for the benefit of other members attending the meeting. Such translation duties are typically performed by a bilingual local union officer, rather than hiring an outside, professional translator to be present at each monthly meeting.

Paul Sanchez, along with several other employees, petitioned Local 1's officers to provide a qualified translator who was not a member of the Union at all monthly membership meetings. This person would simultaneously translate all meetings proceedings and discussion into Spanish and English. The Union officers brought the petition request before the members at the next monthly meeting. With the union members in attendance acting as a legislative body in accordance with the Union's constitution and by-laws, Sanchez's proposal to hire a full-time outside translator for the monthly meetings was debated and defeated by a majority vote of those members in attendance. The majority of the members in attendance felt that the cost of hiring an outside translator for every monthly meeting was not justified based on the number of members who typically attended and the availability of bilingual union members who could perform the necessary translation duties upon request.

Union member Sanchez then filed a civil suit in federal court. He alleged the Union's failure to provide simultaneous translation at the regular monthly union meetings by an independent professional translator was a violation of his equal participation and freedom of speech rights under Title I of the Landrum-Griffin Act.

Relevant Statutory Language—Title I, Sec. 101 (a) Landrum-Griffin Act

(1) **Equal Rights**—Every member of a labor organization shall have equal rights and privileges within such organization to nominate candidates, to vote in elections or referendums of the labor organization, to attend membership meetings, and to participate in the deliberations and voting upon the business of such meetings, subject to reasonable rules and regulations in such organization's constitution and by-laws.

(2) **Freedom of Speech and Assembly**—Every member of any labor organization shall have the right to meet and assemble freely with other members; and to express any views, arguments, or opinions; and to express at meetings of the labor organizations his views, upon candidates in an election of the labor organization or upon any business properly before the meeting, subject to the organization's established and reasonable rules per-

taining to the conduct of meetings: Provided, that nothing herein shall be construed to impair the right of a labor organization to adopt and enforce reasonable rules as to the responsibility of every member toward the organization as an institution and to his refraining from conduct that would interfere with its performance of its legal or contractual obligations.

Title IV, Section 401 (e) Landrum-Griffin Act states in relevant part, "In any election . . . a reasonable opportunity shall be given for the nomination of candidates and every member in good standing shall be eligible to be a candidate and to hold office (. . . subject to reasonable qualifications uniformly imposed)."

QUESTIONS

1. Did the Union violate Title I, Section 101 (a) of the Landrum-Griffin Act in this case? If so, what should be the appropriate remedy?

2. Would it be legal under Title IV of the Landrum-Griffin Act for the union in this case to adopt a rule that required all candidates for union office to be proficient in both Spanish and English? Why or why not?

Financial Core Membership Rights under the *Beck* Decision

Background

The Company and Union are parties to a collective bargaining agreement that contains the following valid union security clause:

> It shall be a condition of employment that all employees of the company covered by this agreement who are members of the union in good standing on the date of this agreement shall remain members in good standing, and those who are not members on the effective date of this agreement shall, on the ninety-first (91st) day following the effective date of this agreement, become and remain members in good standing in the union.
>
> For purposes of this Agreement, an employee shall lose his good standing in the Union only for failure to tender periodic dues and initiation fees uniformly required of all members. The Business Manager of the Union shall notify the Company by certified mail of any employees the union deems to have lost "good standing" within the meaning of this Article.

On July 6, an employee named Budnik sent a letter to the Union informing the Union officers that he was resigning his union membership and claiming *financial core member* status. Budnik requested the Union to begin charging him the "new appropriate amount" of dues in compliance with *Beck* (1988). Budnik did not pay any dues money to the Union after he mailed the July 6 letter.

On July 28, the Company sent a letter to all bargaining unit members informing them that financial core membership status was available to them and that full union membership was not a legal requirement under the parties' current union security contract language. The Union sent a letter to Budnik on or about August 5 acknowledging receipt of Budnik's resignation letter. The Union informed Budnik that his insistence on financial core membership status would result in the loss of valuable membership privileges and benefits and that, as a financial core member, he would still be required "to pay the financial obligations of membership germane to the costs of collective bargaining, contract administration, and grievance adjustment." The Union encouraged Budnik to reconsider his decision to resign his union membership. The Union's letter closed with the disclosure that the Union was currently undergoing its annual financial audit and that, when that process was completed, all the expenses germane to collective bargaining duties would be identified.

The following February 23, the Union sent a letter to Budnik and advised him that, despite his resignation from the union, he was still required to comply with the terms of the current union security clause. The Union offered to let Budnik pay a sum equal to current monthly union dues to a "mutually agreed upon charity." The Union listed three charitable funds acceptable to it. Budnik did not agree to the Union's proposal and, instead, quit his job at the Company and filed an unfair labor practice against the Union alleging a violation of Sec. 8 (b)(1)(A) of the Labor-Management Relations Act (LMRA). Specifically, Budnik alleged that the Union failed to meet the requirements set forth in *Beck* regarding a union's duty to furnish information about the amount of dues money spent for legitimate collective bargaining purposes or to provide a procedure by which employees like himself could challenge the amount charged or the basis for calculating such charges.

In *Communications Workers v. Beck*, 487 U.S. 735 (1988), the Court upheld an interpretation that the LMRA does not permit a union, over the objection of a dues-paying nonmember, to expend funds collected from them under a union security agreement on activities not related to collective bargaining, contract administration, or grievance adjustment. In *California Saw & Knife Works*, 320 NLRB 222 (1995), the Board held that if a nonmember employee chooses to file a *Beck* objection to the payment of full union dues, the employee must be informed by the Union of the following information: the percentage of the reduction in fees for objecting nonmembers, the basis for the union's calculation, and the right to challenge these figures. Any Union-provided procedure for challenging the amount or method of dues calculation is appropriate so long as the procedure is not shown to be arbitrary, discriminatory, or in bad faith.

The Union cited the NLRB decision *Laborers Local 265 and Fred A. Newmann Co.*, in which the Board held that a union did not breach its duty of fair representation by failing to provide a *Beck* objector with *Beck*-related financial information, where the union expressly waived the objector's obligations under the union security clause and informed the objector that she would not be required to pay any dues or fees. The Union noted that Budnik is the only employee, out of the 300 bargaining unit members the Union represents, to request financial core membership status. The Union believed that the cost burden of gathering *Beck*-related financial information for use by a single employee would be prohibitive and detrimental to the Union's obligation to use resources wisely to represent the bargaining interest of all bargaining unit members. The Union believed that it had offered Budnik a reasonable accommodation that did not require him to pay any dues money to the union, thus ensuring that none of the objecting member's funds would be used for union expenditures. At the same time, the reasonable accommodation offered by the Union avoided the necessity of spending union funds to gather *Beck*-related financial information for only one employee. The Union requested that the unfair labor practice charge be dismissed.

QUESTIONS

1. What are the Union's legal obligations?
2. Did the Union commit an Unfair Labor Practice in this case? If so, what should be the appropriate remedy?

Labor Union Democracy

As a student, you are part of the student body that is represented by a Student Government Association. As a citizen, you are represented by elected officials at the local, county, state, and federal levels. As a student, you may be a member of a professional organization that is associated with your major.

How does the government of these organizations compare with the government of a labor union in terms of the following?

1. Constitution
2. Officers
3. Election of officials
4. Passage of proposals on policy and program activities
5. Meetings and governance
6. Affiliation with and obligations to a higher body

CHAPTER 5

Why and How Unions Are Organized

*T*his chapter focuses on the essential elements of unionization: why unions are formed, the procedures for organizing employees into unions, new union strategies for obtaining union recognition, and union decertification.

The chapter highlights employees' choices (1) whether to become involved in union formation where there is no union and (2) whether to vote for or against union representation if and when there is a representation election. Although an employee's choices to assist in the formation of a union, to vote for a union, and to join a union are highly interrelated, they are separate decisions. Employees may join unions voluntarily or be required to join. The circumstances in which an employee may be required to join a union were covered in Chapter 4. Employees who vote for union representation in an election in which the union loses are nevertheless left without union representation.

Why Unions Are Formed

Unions are not present in every organization; in many instances, employees have chosen to remain nonunion. This section provides explanations of employees' collective behavior that cut across many organizations; the following section attempts to explain what propels employees at a particular facility to vote for a union.

Work and Job Conditions Explanation

Alienation Theory The **alienation theory** is based on the belief that employees might seek collective action to relieve their feelings of alienation, which have resulted from the extensive use of machinery in manufacturing operations. Employees became alienated from their work because of the following reasons[1]:

- They lost contact with their own labor when the products they created were taken away from them, thereby reducing their spirit and status.

- They lost involvement in their work when the machine dominated, separating the work of the hand from the work of the brain.

- They became estranged from fellow employees when their work made them so tired and competitive that they were incapable of having authentic relationships.

As a result, employees might become aware of their common plight, and class consciousness could compel them to join together in a union or to engage in collective activities to improve their working situation. Unions can and do address a possible aspect of employee alienation, namely the employees' desire to speak their minds without fear of management reprisal. In other words, "intertwined with the motives for union membership is the almost universal desire to tell the boss to 'go to hell.'"[2] A union typically indicates to its potential members that the employees' rights to voice their opinions regarding a managerial action are protected by negotiated grievance procedures and disciplinary policies (see Chapters 10 and 12).

Employees might be dissatisfied with some aspect of their jobs while not being alienated from their work. Some research has shown that employees might join unions if they (1) are dissatisfied with physical characteristics of the workplace, low wages, or lack of benefits and (2) believe that a union will help them achieve the job-related conditions important to them.[3]

Scarcity Consciousness Theory—The Need for Job Security In his classic book, *A Theory of the Labor Movement,* Selig Perlman suggested that employees are attracted to unions on the assumption that unions will protect their jobs. Many employees, particularly manual workers, strongly believe they are living in a country of limited opportunity and become **scarcity conscious**—the employees collectively believe that jobs are difficult to obtain and retain. This belief is particularly true today for some industries, such as auto, steel, and coal. Thus, employees turn to unions for job protection.[4]

Unions therefore are attractive to the many employees concerned about job security, regardless of their skill or occupational level. Few employees, including white-collar employees and managers, are currently immune from the possibility of a layoff. Also, unions do offer several ways of strengthening employees' job security: They can negotiate work rules, which prescribe procedures for performing a job, thereby ensuring that a certain number of employees will be assigned work. They can negotiate apprenticeship programs, which ensure that qualified people are available for certain skilled jobs. They can negotiate seniority and layoff provisions, which require the company to lay off employees by their seniority and to recall the most senior ones first. They can negotiate grievance procedures, which include a final step of arbitration to protect them against unjust discharges, unfair treatment, and violations of the labor agreement. They can lobby for legislation protecting employees' job rights, in regard to such issues as plant closings and employment discrimination, which has been a viable alternative used by unions throughout the years. Here, unions attempt to strengthen job security by pressing for restrictions against cheap labor—foreign citizens, child labor, prison labor—quotas or restrictions against imported products such as steel, automobiles, and textiles, and adjustment assistance to employees who are displaced as a result of foreign competition.

Wheeler Model of Union Formation Hoyt Wheeler has provided a theoretical basis for union formation that entails a two-stage process. The first stage consists of the worker's readiness to take some form of aggressive action; the second stage represents that worker coming together with other workers as a group and deciding to take some form of collective action. A single employee usually begins to move toward unionization when he or she experiences feelings of deprivation about pay, security, and/or respect. The individual employee's thought process can be viewed as taking the individual along one or more possible paths toward readiness to take some form of aggressive action to demonstrate anger at the employer. The employee may take the path toward collective action and supporting the union under certain conditions.

Deprivation at work may occur when there is a gap between what employees expect from their work and what they receive in return. Three paths connect deprivation and readiness to take action. The first path is a "threat" or an "attack"; this results when the employer takes away or threatens to take away something the workers already have. The second path is "frustration"; this results when workers try to act in their own behalf. Their action is blocked or ignored and they have no voice and see no way of achieving effective voice as individuals. The third path is "rational calculation"; this path does not involve anger, but the workers become convinced that the benefits of unionization outweigh its costs.

Even though workers may mobilize along one of these paths, they may not choose unionization. Instead, they may choose some form of withdrawal, such as quitting their job, or revenge behavior, such as sabotaging the company's products. The conditions that promote collective action or unionization are love, hope, and saliency. Love is essentially the cohesion and solidarity wherein workers care enough for each other to act together and share good relationships. Hope prevails when workers believe that the union can do what is necessary to bring an end to their deprivation and frustrations. Saliency is recognition that problems exist and workers perceive that dramatic events and good leadership would contribute to facilitating action toward resolution.

Along with each of these conditions, which promote the union option, there are inhibiting conditions. One such condition is the fear of punishment for supporting the union, such as losing one's job or being laid off. Another is the general belief that "unions are wrong in principle." Either of these beliefs may dissuade a worker or a group of workers from taking action. The interaction of the workers' beliefs, their chosen paths, and the existing conditions may lead a group of workers toward collective action and unionization.[5]

Employees' Backgrounds and Needs

Employees' previous experiences with unions can strongly affect their attitudes toward unions and their decision to join one. Eighty-seven percent of those who have had experience with unions, usually as members, said they would vote for a union if given a choice; only 27 percent of those who have had no experience with unions would vote for the union if given the choice.[6]

Many might even be influenced by parental attitudes and family experiences regarding unions. One active union member stated, "I attended union meetings with my father before I was ever inside a church." Another commented, "My dad was a great union man and that's where I got it—if it wasn't union, it wasn't no good."[7] Of course, parental comments regarding unions may be unfavorable as well.

Unions, like all formal organizations, potentially satisfy the members' needs by providing a means of enhancing a sense of identity and maintaining self-esteem. Thus, unions can appeal to three interrelated social needs of members: the need for affiliation, or belonging; the need for status; and the need to belong to something purposeful, useful, and creative that is on a higher level than improved wages and working conditions.

The union's possible benefit of social affiliation is strengthened or weakened by the degree of prestige or self-esteem it offers its members. Some employees join a union for the same reason they would join any social organization, namely, to enjoy the responsibility and status associated with being a member of that organization. This feature can be particularly attractive to employees whose jobs are basically interchangeable and carry very few elements of prestige or room for advancement.

Employees who become union officers can often attain prestige or self-esteem in their dealings with management officials:

> As a shop steward or union officer or member of the grievance committee, a worker can become "a fellow your buddies look to." Such positions give him the opportunity to win other workers' approval by being "a fellow who stands up to the boss" with impunity. The role of "a fellow who stands up to the boss" is made more significant because the definition of the boss has been enlarged to include not merely the foreman but "the head office in Pittsburgh." He can win prestige as "a guy that gets results" in such matters as the distribution of work, assignment to jobs, seniority policy, and protection from discrimination.[8]

Chapter 10 discusses the notion that union officers and management officials are equals in their day-to-day administration of the labor agreement. However, as the preceding quotation suggests, the union steward can often emphatically disagree with a management official six levels above the steward on the organizational chart. This ability to challenge without fear of reprisal is not usually afforded nonunion employees or even management officials when they deal with their organizational superiors.

Studies of employee characteristics associated with employee votes have been mixed. Some have shown that employees' characteristics such as age, gender, and education are not closely associated with favorable union votes or attitudes.[9] Race appears to be the one exception—several studies have suggested that more black employees have positive attitudes toward potential union advantages than their white counterparts.[10] Other studies indicate that young people are more likely to support unions, and women are less likely to support unions.[11]

Procedures for Organizing Unions

In forming and joining a union, employees mainly consider whether the union will improve their personal situations in terms of wages and benefits, promotional opportunities, and job security. Can the employees expect to satisfy their job-related goals and needs by supporting a union? Will the union provide the means for achieving these goals? If employees perceive that a union will help them attain their goals, they will likely vote for it in an election and support its activities afterward. If they are not convinced, they will not vote for the union and will not support its activities.

The union's campaign to secure employee support may contribute to a union vote, especially among those who are familiar with the union's positions and who attend union campaign meetings. Employees who are satisfied with working conditions are less likely to attend union campaign meetings, but if they attend, they often become more favorable toward the union.

The company's campaign can affect the vote because it affects employees' belief in the anticipated influence of the union. If the company campaigns hard, some employees will believe that the employer has "seen the light" and will now improve conditions without the union. A strong antiunion campaign may convince some employees that the employer is so antiunion that the union cannot improve working conditions.[12]

Although there may be many reasons why a particular group of employees votes for or against the union in a specific election, several influences have been identified that affect union votes generally. Exhibit 5.1 shows the relationships among the general influences on employees.

Researchers have argued that social pressure influences employee votes. When employees know a number of union supporters within a work group, this knowledge helps to form group cohesion. When this group of employees is regularly blocked by employer actions, they respond as a group and their actions can lead to union formation. As union supporters, they are better able to convince others that the union has the power to bring about changes in the workplace and are more convincing in influencing other employees' votes.

Employees who are not satisfied with their pay, supervision, and/or work may view the union as the instrument to satisfy their job needs. Some researchers have argued that job dissatisfaction is the beginning of employees' efforts to start a union formation campaign. They argue that job dissatisfaction

Exhibit 5.1

Influences on Employees on Whether to Vote For or Against a Union

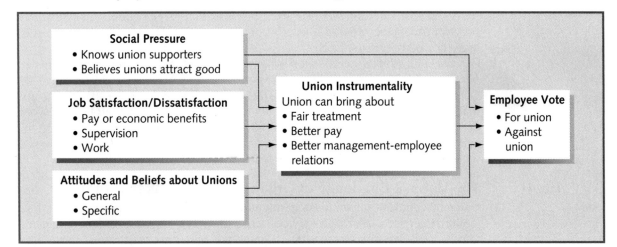

sets in motion a search to end the uncomfortable dissonance between what is desired (good pay, effective supervision, and so on) and what they are experiencing. Job dissatisfaction results in the formation of a coalition of employees designed to bring about changes in economic and working conditions.[13]

General beliefs about unions mean that an employee believes, for example, that a union will improve wages, benefits, and working conditions; provide a return to the employee for the dues paid; and secure pro-employee legislation. These general beliefs include whether an employee believes unions are autocratic, increase the risks of a plant closing, stifle individual initiatives, or ignore the members in strike decisions. To influence employees' general beliefs about unions, union organizers should place more effort on national campaigns, such as the "Union Yes" campaign of the American Federation of Labor–Congress of Industrial Organizations (AFL-CIO).

Specific beliefs about unions are more related to an individual's job and workplace. To influence employees' specific beliefs about unions, union organizers should focus attention on communicating the union's unique characteristics and its impact at the workplace. Specific beliefs that can be focused on include expectations about improvement in pay, benefits, and job security as a result of unionization.[14] Other beliefs include expected improvement in recognition, job advancement, worker participation, treatment by supervisors, and reduction in sexual and racial discrimination on the job.

In an organizing campaign, unions need to show employees that significant positive results will occur at their workplace if they vote and join a union. Unions must promote the union's ability not only to improve wages and benefits but to help make work more meaningful and increase employee participation. At the same time, the employer will attempt to show that it has acted reasonably toward employees and has been fair and sincere in dealings with employees.[15]

Social pressure, job dissatisfaction, and general and specific beliefs about unions interact with **union instrumentality**, which is the employees' perception of whether the union will be instrumental in attaining desired outcomes, such as higher wages, improved working conditions, job security, and protection from arbitrary treatment by management.[16] In general, if these interactions are positive, the employee will vote for the union; if not, the employee will vote against it.[17] For the individual employee, any one of the influences may cause the employee to vote a certain way. For example, if an employee believes his or her supervisor is considerate and supportive, this belief may be enough to cause a vote against union representation.[18]

An individual's decision on whether to vote for union representation depends on his or her subjective assessment of the benefits to be obtained as weighed against the subjective assessment of the cost. If the expected benefits are higher than the cost, the employee will vote for the union. Otherwise, the vote will be against representation. If employees have a good chance of promotion, can expect a higher wage based on their present level of effort, and are pleased with their supervisor, they probably will not vote for union representation.

The Union's Challenge of Organizing the Diverse Workforce

Unions recognize that some occupations, such as retail sales, registered nursing, janitorial services, and food services, are expected to expand. In addition, one-fourth of all workers in the United States are part-time employees; these employees are hired on a temporary basis (called by many "contingent workers"), are independent contractors, and are hired as subcontractors or leased workers. As noted earlier, minorities and skilled employees will also become a larger percentage of the workforce. In fact, in 2000, one-fourth of the workforce was minorities and the greatest increases came from the Hispanic and Asian populations. Unions must design organizing strategies to attract these employees.[19]

Organizing Professional Employees

Professional employees provide a challenge to unions and an opportunity to increase union membership. Although unions have made significant inroads in many professions, such as acting, professional sports, writing, music, nursing, and teaching, debate continues over the compatibility of unionism with professionalism. Excellent arguments have been conveyed on both ends of the continuum, and the unions must successfully address these concerns before they will increase the memberships of professional employee unions. On one side is the argument that the selection of a union entails the rejection of key professional values, such as collegial participation in organizational decision making, professional independence, and a merit-based performance and reward system. On the other side is the argument that collective bargaining is often the most effective method of achieving and maintaining these same professional values.

Evidence drawn from a study of collective bargaining agreements covering professional employees reveals that the overwhelming majority of contract provisions include subjects quite similar to those traditionally held in industrial sector agreements. These provisions include wages, fringe benefits, grievance-arbitration procedures, and so on. In addition to those traditional subjects, these agreements also address professional issues. These issues can be categorized into six groups: (1) professional standards, (2) mechanisms for professional participation in policy making, (3) regulation of professional work, (4) training and professional development, (5) commitment of organizational resources to professional goals, and (6) criteria for personnel decisions and the role of professionals in making these decisions. The conclusion was that, although there is variation in the collective bargaining agreements among professional employee unions, unionism and professionalism are not inherently incompatible. Moreover, professional values and interests can be incorporated into the bargaining process along with the economic and job security issues of professional employees. With concrete evidence of compatibility between professionalism and unionism, the opportunity is present for unions to promote their product and services.[20] A successful union organizing campaign of professional employees is presented in the Labor Relations in Action on page 198.

Activities of the Union in Organizing Employees

Employees' initial interest in unionization is usually based on their present dissatisfaction with some work-related situation coupled with a belief that each of them acting alone cannot change his or her current situation. The union does not create this dissatisfaction with working conditions among employees; instead, it is in the union's interest to improve job satisfaction among employees by negotiating to improve working conditions. Therefore, during an organizing

LABOR RELATIONS IN ACTION

A Union Organizing Success: A Story of the Organization of Home Care Professionals (OHCP)

The story of the OHCP is a compelling example of the potential for unionizing professional employees when they experience the restructuring of labor markets and reorganization of their work. The impetus for collective action was the desire for a voice in key decisions about the organization of work and the delivery of professional services.

The OHCP was formed by a group of 80 physical therapists, occupational therapists, and speech therapists who worked for a hospital-based home care company. These therapists spend most of their working hours alone in their cars or with their patients at their homes. They go to the office once a month for staff meetings and drop off paperwork every other day. Before the organizing campaign, only a few knew each other personally.

In the summer of 2000, the company announced changes in procedures and workload; these changes concerned the therapists because of their impact on their work and the quality of patient care. Then the company announced a 20 percent cut in pay. The therapists asked for a meeting with management, but the therapists were told that the pay cut would stand and there was nothing more to discuss.

The following month, about 60 therapists met in a borrowed church basement to consider forming a union. A labor lawyer attended and explained their legal rights and the procedures for establishing a collective bargaining unit. The therapists elected an executive committee and adopted a dues structure. A set of bylaws were adopted, and the executive committee composed a letter to the company CEO informing her of the OHCP's existence and asking for recognition of the OHCP.

After five days and no response from the company, the OHCP sent a petition to the NLRB. Then the CEO called and asked for a meeting with the executive committee. At the meeting, the HR manager asked, "What would it take for you to abandon this whole project?" Afterwards the OHCP filed an unfair labor practice charge. (The NLRB ruled that the company had committed an unfair labor practice.)

A representation election was scheduled by the NLRB. The company hired an out-of-state lawyer to advise its management during the campaign. During the campaign, therapists were called to the manager's office and questioned about loyalties, relationships, beliefs, and interests in the union. The CEO made frequent visits to team meetings. The company sent printed materials to the therapists' homes; one piece warned of what might happen in case of a strike. Managers telephoned individual therapists asking them to vote no and telling therapists how sad it would be to create a division between management and employees if a union came into play. The OHCP continued to hold meetings and formed needed committees, such as a fund-raising committee that held garage sales to pay for campaign literature and pay the attorney's fee.

On the weekend before the election, all bargaining unit members were called and reminded to vote. In October 2000, the NLRB held the election; the OHCP assembled at the company headquarters to observe the vote counting by the NLRB official. When the votes were counted, the OHCP won with 83 yes to 16 no.

After its victory, the OHCP set up a listserve for members for rapid communication. A college-aged child of one of the members set up and maintained the OHCP Web site, which contained a secure portion with a password for members only. During the negotiations, the negotiating team put out bargaining bulletins after each bargaining session. The OHCP was able to obtain addresses of 400 referring physicians; they were written a letter explaining the OHCP's goals and asking for their support. National and local professional organizations were informed of the OHCP, and one executive director wrote a personal letter to the CEO to express his concern about the pay cut and its impact on quality of care. An article was printed in a professional journal that was mailed to about 100,000 members. Members attended meetings of local professional groups to share information. A letter was written to all licensed therapists in the area asking them not to be replacement workers in case of a strike. Assistance from local established unions, such as picketers and the printing of handbills, was obtained. The OHCP handbilled the hospitals to inform staff members and patients of OHCP's goals.

By September 2001, there was still no collective bargaining agreement. The members of the OHCP decided to affiliate with the Communications Workers of America (CWA), and the CWA furnished two experienced bargainers, legal advice, printing resources, a toll-fee telephone number, mailings, and office space. After two more months of negotiations and no agreement, a strike authorization vote was taken.

Members of the executive committee met several times per week in each other's homes. There were daily e-mail and phone contacts. Bulletin board messages that responded to management messages were posted. There was a "thought of the day" posted to address a specific issue that may arise. The OHCP used its Web site and obtained e-mail addresses from most members in the unit.

After 12 months of negotiations, an agreement was reached and then ratified on January 3, 2002. The agreement restored the pay cut, established a formal grievance procedure, set up seniority rules, provided union access to internal mail service and voice-mail, allowed the union to meet with new hires during orientation, lifted productivity quotas, and set up a practice advisory committee to address quality issues.

During all of these events, the OHCP members gained strength through solidarity and developed friendships through these activities. At the monthly meetings the members were able to share opinions and ideas and maintained their focus on quality and professional development of their work as therapists. The members identified talent not known before. Some members were "good at writing or public speaking; others were great at photography, graphic design, public relations, and press contacts, and getting members involved and staying in touch. Some simply offered their help with mailings, and opened their homes when we needed meeting space. We have also had some good parties and events for supporting family members."

The president of the OHCP wrote the following in the November 2001 newsletter:

> We are not accustomed to making waves. We are accustomed to and prefer to work cooperatively and gently with people. Forming a union was certainly not something we had anticipated. We did it because we felt that we had no other way to maintain our personal and professional dignity and integrity. Our struggle for fairness at our workplace is something we can be proud of the rest of our lives, and it is a valuable lesson and example for our children. ■

SOURCE: Richard W. Hurd and Elisabeth Tenenholtz, "Charting Their Own Future: Independent Organizing by Professional Workers," *Proceedings of the 54th Annual Meeting of the Industrial Relations Research Association*, ed. Paula B. Voos (Urbana, Ill. Industrial Relations Research Association, 2003), pp. 172–179.

campaign, the union advertises the benefits that would flow from a negotiated collective bargaining agreement and successful handling of grievances.[21]

Most managers of nonunion companies incorrectly believe that labor unions initiate union organization drives; instead it is usually the employees themselves who begin the process by contacting the union. This contact with union organizers usually occurs after the employees believe that there is sufficient support for the union and that the union's expertise and representation will help them.[22]

Union organizers enter the campaign by playing three general roles that influence employees' decisions on whether to vote for unionization. First, organizers try to educate the workers on the benefits of the union, labor movement traditions, and protections afforded by union representation and the present laws. Next, union organizers attempt to persuade workers to vote for unionization and respond to statements and allegations made by management during the organizing campaign. Third, organizers try to support workers in their individual and collective actions.[23] To ensure that these roles are carried out capably, unions recruit and select union organizers with the appropriate education, competencies, and personality characteristics.

Unions, especially those in the service industries, are hiring union organizers who have different characteristics from the traditional union organizers in manufacturing. They are almost 15 years younger on average, ten times more likely to be female, average almost four more years of education, and have an average of about seven fewer years of union-organizing experience. They are six times less likely to have held elected positions in local unions and are less than half as likely to have served in appointed positions in local or national unions. Although nearly all of the union organizers in manufacturing were rank-and-file members early in their careers, only about half of the union organizers in the service industries were rank-and-file members.[24]

Union organizers must recognize that the workforce has changed sharply and has become more complex. Employees do not typically have a homogeneous set of problems; they are widely diverse. As well, the growth industry sectors and occupations are different from those that have been traditional strongholds for unions, such as manufacturing, mining, trucking, shipping, railroads, and construction. As a result, the selection of staff members to work as union organizers has changed. Instead of appointing staff members as political rewards, unions are selecting union organizers not only from the rank-and-file members but also from colleges, law schools, Volunteers in Service to America (VISTA), and other sources. Unions are then investing funds in training union organizers at the AFL-CIO's George Meany Center and improving their organizing capability through training at the newly created Organizing Institute (Exhibit 5.2).[25]

The union organizer does not create job dissatisfaction but rather assists in transforming this employee dissatisfaction into collective action. The union organizer tailors the organizing approach to employee concerns and problems and focuses on the special needs of various groups, such as older workers, female or minority workers, or white-collar workers. The organizer tries to sell the idea that group action via the union provides the instrument through which employee concerns and dissatisfaction can be most effectively addressed.[26]

The influence of union organizers should never be underestimated by a company. The union organizers may be first seen distributing handbills to employees as they leave the company parking lots. They dress like the employees

Exhibit 5.2

AFL-CIO Organizing Institute Informational Flier

Answers to Common Questions about the AFL-CIO Organizing Institute

What is the Organizing Institute?
The Organizing Institute was created in the fall of 1989 to promote and foster union organizing. In November of that year, we held the first weekend training session for people interested in a career as union organizers. Since then, we have developed a highly selective program to recruit and train a new generation of union organizers, to place them for training on the campaigns of designated unions, and to facilitate job matches for graduates into full-time, paid positions as union organizers with international unions affiliated with the AFL-CIO. In addition to this program, this Institute also has a variety of other programs designed to assist unions in the area of external organizing.

What does a union organizer do?
Union organizers assist workers in gaining union recognition at their work site. Where workers do not currently have a union, a union organizer will work with employees to build support and leadership to form their own local union, usually in the face of intense employer opposition. The union must prove it represents a majority and get recognition from the employer. This often, but not exclusively, happens through a secret ballot election held at the workplace. Ultimately, the goal is to win a binding agreement between the workers and their employer that includes real improvements in the living and working conditions of the employees.

What unions are participating in the Organizing Institute training program?
The following fifteen unions directly participate in the training program by providing internship and apprentice campaigns and hiring graduates: American Federation of State, County, and Municipal Employees (AFSCME), American Federation of Teachers (AFT), Communications Workers of America (CWA), Hotel Employees and Restaurant Employees (HERE), International Brotherhood of Teamsters (IBT), International Longshoremen's and Warehousemen's Union (ILWU), Service Employees International Union (SEIU), United Auto Workers (UAW), United Brotherhood of Carpenters and Joiners (UBC), United Food and Commercial Workers (UFCW), United Mine Workers of America (UMWA), United Steelworkers of America (USWA), Laborers International Union of North America (LIUNA), Oil, Chemical, Atomic Workers (OCAW), and Union of Needletrades, Industrial, and Textile Employees (UNITE).

How often are the 3-day training weekends held?
The 3-day trainings are held each month in various locations. They are held regularly in Washington, D.C., and in San Francisco. Other sites where we have held trainings include Chicago, Los Angeles, New York, and Atlanta.

What is the weekend session like? What are the costs?
The 3-day training is an intense and fascinating look at what it takes to be a union organizer. The sessions themselves are led by senior organizers from among the fifteen unions in the program. The talent and enthusiasm of the participants are a large part of the overall success of the weekend. Institute staff meet individually with participants on Sunday afternoon. The cost of the training, including housing and meals, are paid by the Organizing Institute. Travel to and from the training is the responsibility of the applicant.

How does job placement work?
The unions have told us that they are in need of talented and committed organizers to wage the battle for union recognition. Our track record on job matches for graduates bears out this claim. Over 95% of Institute graduates have been placed. The unions in the program are notified of all graduates. They then contact the apprentice to arrange interviews. You should notify the Institute if you have any preferences in selecting a position. This program works because it is directly linked to employment opportunities in union organizing. Unions and applicants alike are interested in the program because of the job-match component.

How much travel is involved? What is the pay?
The jobs vary by union and by location within a union. However, most jobs require the organizer to be available to work on the road at times, and in some jobs the organizer will work away from home most of the time. Even when working from home, long days, including regular evening and weekend work, is standard. Most unions look for flexibility in travel and relocation. The pay ranges from $18,000 to $30,000 per year plus benefits.

SOURCE: http://www.aflcio.org/orginst/qanda.html.

so that the employees will identify with them. Although their dress may be misleading, management should realize that union organizers are professionals at what they do. Like their counterparts in management, contemporary union organizers must understand the psychology of the workplace and the labor relations climate in which employees work. The union organizers must be able to (1) sort out these complex factors for the employees on a group or individual basis and (2) communicate in the employees' language how the union can assist in fulfilling their needs in the specific work environment.

As an example, Exhibit 5.3 lists a number of work-related concerns and problems. To the right of each is a possible course of action the union could take to satisfy the concern or to alleviate the problem. The union organizer would bring to the employees' attention outcomes that could result from such activities by the union on their behalf.

The union enters the organizing campaign knowing that it must convince the uncommitted employees that the union is composed not of outsiders but of concerned fellow employees, that the changes the union proposes are worth fighting for, that the union will be able to protect employees against reprisals, and that union officials can be trusted. The union realizes that its success depends on the development of a strong inside organizing committee to convey the message directly to employees who do not attend union meetings, and on the ability of the union organizer to convey his or her own personal commitment and concern, get to know the employees, listen to employees about their job concerns, and have employees themselves speak at public meetings to express their feelings and their commitment to the cause.

Exhibit 5.3

Union Strategy and Courses of Action to Achieve Employee Goals and Resolve Job-Related Concerns

Examples of Work-Related Problems and Employee Concerns	Actions by Unions to Encourage Employees to Join Union
Relations between employees and management are poor.	Union will represent the interests of employees to management.
Employees do not trust their employer's promises.	Union will negotiate a contract requiring management to abide by its agreements.
Employees prefer to deal with management as a group.	Union provides an opportunity for individual employees to deal as a group with the employer.
Employees want to have more influence in workplace decisions.	Union provides a mechanism for influence by collective bargaining and administering the agreement.
Employees feel that productivity improvement would be more effective if employees had more say in how programs are run.	Union provides a mechanism in which employees can provide input into those issues that affect the workplace.
Employees question the effectiveness of the company's system for resolving employee problems and grievances.	Unions typically negotiate a grievance procedure that provides representation of employees at each step and hearings before an outside, neutral arbitrator.

SOURCE: Richard B. Freeman and Joel Rogers, *Worker Representation and Participation Survey*, Princeton, N.J.: Princeton Survey Research Associates, 1994.

Researcher Kate Bronfenbrenner has identified union campaign tactics characterized as the "rank-and-file intensive strategy," which yields a higher union win rate than other tactics. This strategy focuses on representative leadership, personal contact, dignity and justice, and building an active union presence in the workplace. This strategy generates the worker participation and commitment necessary to withstand aggressive employer antiunion campaigns and to counteract any antiunion aspects of the economic, political, and legal climate. The components of the strategy are associated with union win rates, which are 12 to 26 percent higher than union win rates that do not employ this strategy (Exhibit 5.4).[27]

Activities of the Company in Union Organizing

The employer realizes that the keys to its success are whether it is able to sustain and increase employees' concern about how the union would perform if chosen and whether it can convince employees that the employer's past record shows that it deserves their support or at least a second chance. The employer enters the campaign with three advantages: (1) it has instant and prolonged access to the employees; (2) although it can make no promises during the election campaign, it informs employees of the possibility of improvement without cost and without the creation of a new bureaucracy; and (3) it can take advantage of the fact that most people find the thought of substantial change in their lives frightening.[28]

Employer campaign tactics attempt to avert an employee vote in favor of unionization. Usually more than one campaign activity must be used. The most commonly used employer tactics are hiring a labor lawyer, spreading rumors about loss of jobs, and spreading rumors about store or plant closings. In terms of making a difference in the outcome of the election, employees are more likely

Exhibit 5.4

Components of "Rank-and-File Intensive Strategy" That Are Associated with Higher Union Win Rates

1. Use of representative committees to be more in touch with concerns of the bargaining unit as a whole, to have better access to employees at the workplace, and to demonstrate to the employees that the union is a democratic and inclusive organization
2. Person-to-person contact, house calls, and small-group meetings
3. Conducting union bargaining surveys, selection of the bargaining committee, and working with rank and file to develop proposals before election
4. Focus on issues such as dignity, justice, discrimination, fairness, or service quality
5. Serious commitment of staff and financial resources to organizing, involvement of the international in union local campaigns, and training, recruitment, and effective utilization of rank-and-file volunteers from already organized bargaining units
6. Use of solidarity days (designated days to wear union buttons, hats, T-shirts, arm bands, etc.)

SOURCE: Kate Bronfenbrenner, "The Role of Union Strategies in NLRB Elections," *Industrial and Labor Relations Review* 50 (January 1997), pp. 195–211; Kate Bronfenbrenner and Tom Juravich, "It Takes More Than House Calls: Organizing to Win with a Comprehensive Union-Building Strategy," *Organizing to Win*, eds. Kate Bronfenbrenner, et al. (Ithaca, N.Y.: Cornell University Press, 1999), pp. 33–34.

not to choose the union when the employer spreads rumors about a store or plant closing. However, employees are more likely to choose the union when the employer intentionally delays the election and when the unions work closely with community leaders to facilitate community acceptance of the union. Two employer tactics that have backfired and are associated with employees' vote for the union are shifting work and jobs to other facilities and testing applicants to identify union sympathizers.[29]

Also, certain employer practices have their effect on the election. For example, the employer can influence the election outcome by changing the election unit composition and the date of the election but only modestly influence the election outcome by such activities as publicizing the disadvantages of the union, displaying posters, and making campaign speeches. Companies must be cautious in election campaigns because they may overdo their resistance and cause a negative reaction from employees, especially when both attorneys and management consultants are used.[30] Thus, if employers overreact to a union's campaign with suppressive tactics, such overreaction may create a more favorable climate for unionization.[31]

The use of consultants in organizational campaigns has increased dramatically. One study reported that most elections studied were directed by consultants. In these campaigns, employer unfair labor practices were committed in over half of the elections, and companies actively resisted the union by making captive audience speeches and writing letters to employees in nearly all of the cases.[32] Use of consultants to advise employers how to persuade employees not to vote for a union requires reports to be filed with the Secretary of Labor, even though the consultants have no direct contact with employees.[33]

Attorneys who specialize in union avoidance campaigns are often employed either to offer advice on questions of labor law or to devise strategy and conduct the union avoidance campaign. In addition, attorneys may offer legal advice; plan the week-to-week campaign strategy; interview supervisors to identify sources of employee discontent and to ameliorate the discontent that led to the organizing campaign; raise the perceived costs of union representation by such tactics as publicizing major layoffs and closings at unionized plants; train supervisors in how to effectively present the employer's position to the employees; prepare and edit campaign literature and speeches for company officials; and build support and sympathy for the employer in the local community. An inexpensive campaign in a small to medium-sized firm with one attorney could cost up to $30,000 in legal fees. An "all-out" campaign with several attorneys using all of the latest campaign tools, such as slick videotapes, visits by prominent politicians and civil rights leaders, and so on, could easily exceed $100,000. The cost of a campaign in a large, multiplant firm involving a dozen attorneys could exceed $1 million. These costs are incurred at the rate of $150 to $300 per hour for attorneys from specialized labor law firms ($400 per hour or more for "big name" attorneys).[34]

Illegal discharge and other forms of discrimination against union activists, used by employers to affect the outcome of the election, have increased dramatically in the past several years. Such discrimination reduces the probability of an organizing success by 17 percent and nearly cuts in half the likelihood of the first contracts being obtained. Nearly all these illegal activities occur during an organizing drive, just before an election, or during the first contract negotiations. Such violations generally occur when employers perceive the financial gains of keeping unions out are far greater than the cost of back-pay awards and reinstatement of union advocates, and such is often the case. One study reported that less than half of illegally discharged workers were offered reinstatement, and only 69 percent of those ever returned to work. Because it takes so long to settle a case, and reinstatement comes so long after the organizing drive, some employers have been able to frustrate the legal process and use it against the union and employees interested in the union.[35]

Some companies use as their guide the book *Winning Union Campaigns*, by Robert Pearlman, a former staff attorney with the National Labor Relations Board (NLRB). In the book, management is advised that the "consequences of illegal labor practices must be kept in perspective," and they must be "subordinated to the prime objective, which is remaining union free." Management is advised that the best bet is to "campaign aggressively" and avoid "playing the union's game" by allowing "fear of the NLRB to stifle communications." Pearlman advises that in the event the company loses the election after an aggressive campaign, the bargaining order won't be issued until 2 to 4 years after the election. By that time, employees will be too intimidated to support the union, and the union will not be in a position to take employees out on strike if negotiations reach an impasse.[36]

How do employers reconcile their personal ethics when either they or their representatives knowingly commit illegal practices by discharging an employee or a group of employees for exercising their legal right to support a union? Moreover, why does the U.S. Congress continue to tolerate such an imbalance in the legal procedures governing the exercise of statutory rights that have existed in the United States since 1935?

Methods for Organizing Unions

The three basic ways for organizing unions are through (1) voluntary recognition, (2) NLRB directives, and (3) secret-ballot elections (Exhibit 5.5).

By far the simplest and least confrontational path to union recognition is voluntary recognition. The most publicized example of voluntary recognition is General Motors' recognition of the United Auto Workers at its Spring Hill, Tennessee, Saturn plant (see Chapter 9).

Voluntary Recognition Within the voluntary recognition procedure, unions have increased the likelihood of organizing success by negotiating a pledge by the employer to remain neutral in the organizing process and/or through the establishment of card check (see Exhibit 5.6 for an example of a Union Authorization Card) procedures to avoid National Labor Relations Board elections. Although the number of these agreements has increased, two researchers located only 118 separate written agreements.[37] The neutrality agreements contain language stating that the employer would neither help nor hinder the union's organizing efforts, the employer would not communicate opposition to the union, the company would not refer to the union as a "third party," the company would not attack or demean the union or its representatives, and other similar provisions.

The language in the card check agreements typically calls for a third-party neutral to validate the cards to determine whether a majority of the bargaining

Exhibit 5.5

Basic Union Representation Procedures

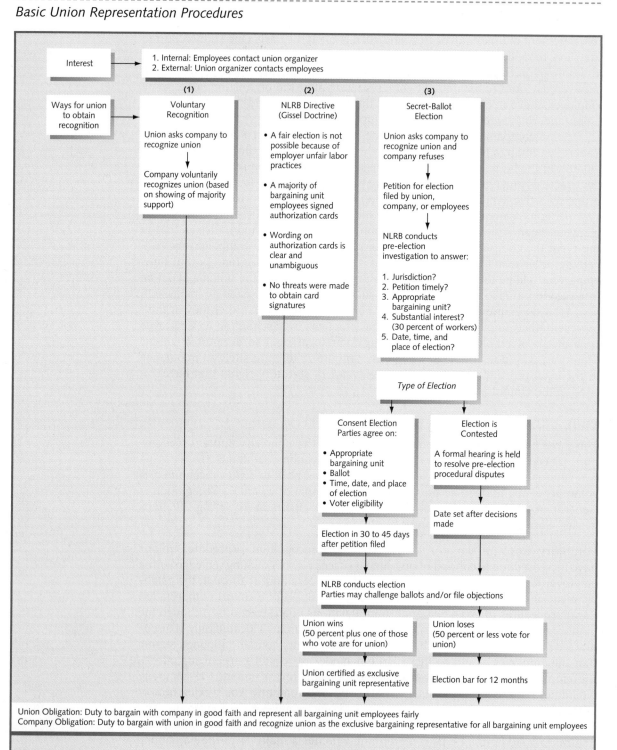

| Interest | → | 1. Internal: Employees contact union organizer
2. External: Union organizer contacts employees |

| | **(1)** | **(2)** | **(3)** |
| Ways for union to obtain recognition | → | Voluntary Recognition | NLRB Directive (Gissel Doctrine) | Secret-Ballot Election |

(1) Voluntary Recognition

Union asks company to recognize union

↓

Company voluntarily recognizes union (based on showing of majority support)

(2) NLRB Directive (Gissel Doctrine)

- A fair election is not possible because of employer unfair labor practices
- A majority of bargaining unit employees signed authorization cards
- Wording on authorization cards is clear and unambiguous
- No threats were made to obtain card signatures

(3) Secret-Ballot Election

Union asks company to recognize union and company refuses

↓

Petition for election filed by union, company, or employees

↓

NLRB conducts pre-election investigation to answer:

1. Jurisdiction?
2. Petition timely?
3. Appropriate bargaining unit?
4. Substantial interest? (30 percent of workers)
5. Date, time, and place of election?

Type of Election

Consent Election
Parties agree on:

- Appropriate bargaining unit
- Ballot
- Time, date, and place of election
- Voter eligibility

Election in 30 to 45 days after petition filed

Election is Contested

A formal hearing is held to resolve pre-election procedural disputes

↓

Date set after decisions made

NLRB conducts election
Parties may challenge ballots and/or file objections

Union wins (50 percent plus one of those who vote are for union)

Union loses (50 percent or less vote for union)

Union certified as exclusive bargaining unit representative

Election bar for 12 months

Union Obligation: Duty to bargain with company in good faith and represent all bargaining unit employees fairly
Company Obligation: Duty to bargain with union in good faith and recognize union as the exclusive bargaining representative for all bargaining unit employees

Exhibit 5.6

Example of a Union Authorization Card

United Food & Commercial Workers International Union
Affiliated with AFL-CIO-CLC

AUTHORIZATION FOR REPRESENTATION

I hereby authorize the United Food & Commercial Workers International Union, AFL-CIO-CLC, or its chartered Local Union(s) to represent me for the purpose of collective bargaining.

_____   _____
(Print Name)   (Date)

_____   _____
(Signature)   (Home Phone)

_____   _____   _____   _____
(Home Address)   (City)   (State)   (Zip)

_____   _____
(Employer's Name)   (Address)

_____   _____   _____
(Hire Date)   (Type Work Performed)   (Department)

                                    Day _____   Night _____   Full _____   Part _____
                                    Shift   Shift   Time   Time
_____   _____
(Hourly Rate)   (Day Off)

Would you participate in an organizing committee?   Yes _____   No _____

SOURCE: Courtesy of the United Food and Commercial Workers International Union.

---

unit employees want the union to represent them. Most of these agreements allow union access to the physical property of the employer and set limits on the union's behavior, most commonly not to attack management. In over 90 percent of the agreements, some form of dispute resolution, most frequently arbitration, is set up to resolve alleged violations or disputes that may occur during the term of the agreement. An example of a dispute is disagreement over the composition of the bargaining unit and eligibility of employees to sign the cards.

The union success rate with neutrality and card check agreements, as measured by the percentage of campaigns resulting in recognition, are high:

- Neutrality-agreements-only success rate was 45.6 percent.
- Card-check-procedure-only success rate was 62.5 percent.
- Card-check-procedure with neutrality agreements was 78.2 percent.

Two other types of language that appeared to increase the union's organizing success are (1) the requirement that employers provide the union with lists of employees and (2) an agreement that the parties place time limits on the campaigns. Problems in the administration of these agreements are most likely to occur in large, multiplant companies where the local managers fail to honor the language negotiated by their far-removed superiors at corporate headquarters.[37]

When employers sign neutrality agreements, the signing is likely to be negotiated within the context of a broader labor–management partnership. In addition to limitations on employer and union actions during the campaign, the union and its members agree to assist the company in meeting its performance goals and the union leadership spends more time communicating the positive contributions of the union, rather than responding to the employer's anti-union messages or attacking the employer. Typically the card check/neutrality agreements improve the relationship between the union and the company, and after the union is recognized, the union is more willing to accept flexible agreements to help companies in highly competitive environments.[38]

Most employers still refuse to voluntarily recognize the union even when union organizers present signed authorization cards (see Exhibit 5.6) from a majority of employees. Management might be concerned that these cards were obtained through inappropriate means (such as after drinking parties, under threats of violence, or through forgeries, for example). They also realize that authorization cards are not very accurate predictors of union success in representation elections. Unions win only a small percentage of elections when only a minimum number of employees sign authorization cards.

NLRB Directive In rare and very controversial cases, the NLRB may direct the employer to recognize and bargain with the union. Although the NLRB considers secret-ballot elections superior, it has discretionary authority to use alternative means to determine the majority interests of employees. In the landmark *Gissel* case, the NLRB decided (and the Supreme Court agreed) that a company may be ordered to recognize and bargain with a union under the following conditions:

1. Evidence reveals that a fair, impartial election would be impossible because of serious or numerous employer unfair labor practices.
2. Wording on the authorization cards is clear and unambiguous (Exhibit 5.6).
3. Employee signatures on the cards were obtained without threat or coercion.
4. A majority of employees in the bargaining unit had indicated their interest in having the union represent them by signing the authorization cards.[39]

In essence, the NLRB and the courts have concluded that holding another election in certain situations where the employer had made a fair and impartial election impossible would not be a realistic remedy because a rerun election would favor the party that had interfered with the first election.

NLRB *Gissell* bargaining orders do not occur very frequently. During a 10-year span from 1987 to 1996, the NLRB issued an average of 10 per year. Then, if appealed by the company to the U.S. Circuit Court of Appeals, only about 50 percent of the bargaining orders were enforced.[40]

An analysis of NLRB opinions issued since 1969 reveals a measure of predictability in deciding whether the NLRB will issue a *Gissel* bargaining order. The NLRB is more likely to issue a bargaining order:

- When it believes that an employer's illegal acts are deliberate or calculated.
- If the employer's conduct threatens the employees' economic interests.

LABOR RELATIONS IN ACTION

Objections to Joining the Union

"Why should I join the union when I get exactly the same wages and benefits without joining?"

"I can't afford to join. I've got a family to support, and my check just isn't big enough [to cover union dues]."

"I don't believe in unions. They are too strong and powerful now to suit me."

"I don't need a union. My employer is fair and will take care of me. What could the union get for me that I wouldn't have gotten anyway?"

"My husband (or other relative) doesn't like unions."

"The union does not do anything for you [grievances are not settled satisfactorily]. I don't like the people who are running things in the union."

"I can handle my own affairs. I can take care of myself. I'll make my own decisions. I do not intend to stay on this job forever; I'm looking for a promotion."

"My religion doesn't permit me to belong to any outside organizations."

"My boss doesn't believe in unions. I've seen what happens to union members."

"I don't want anything to do with unions. They are all corrupt."

"I don't know enough about the local or the union movement."

"I'm not interested. I just don't want to join."

"I'll think about it. Maybe I'll join someday."   ■

SOURCE: Organizing Committee, AFSCME Council 24, WSEU, 5 Odana Court, Madison, Wisconsin.

- If the employer's actions are characterized as vengeful and the NLRB does not believe the actions can be remedied without a bargaining order.

- When an employer promises to correct the grievances that led to union organizing and the NLRB finds that the only way to remedy the illegal promise is to issue a bargaining order.

- When the employer engages in a series of unfair labor practices rather than a single incident.

A NLRB-ordered bargaining order has little value without federal judicial enforcement (see Chapter 3) through the U.S. Circuit Courts of Appeal, which tend to rely on a case-by-case analysis. Before enforcing the NLRB's bargaining order, the courts require the NLRB to provide a "reasoned explanation" of why a rerun election would be futile. In general, if an employer's unfair labor practices seem reprehensible or egregious, the courts will be more likely to enforce the NLRB's bargaining order. For example, if a company takes unlawful actions such as terminating employees because of their union activities or make threats about the consequences of unionization, the courts will likely enforce the bargaining order.[41]

NLRB Secret Ballot Election

Pre–NLRB-Election Union Campaigns The union preelection campaign is not simply a process of exchanging letters and handbills and then holding an election. The campaign usually goes through several stages[42]:

1. Contacting employees as a result of either employee requests for help or distribution of union literature (handbilling) at the workplace by the union.

2. Determining interest by calling meetings, visiting homes, and counting responses to handbills. (See "Labor Relations in Action" box for an array of responses received by union organizers who were seeking support from employees.)

3. Setting up an organizing committee by identifying leaders and educating them about the benefits and procedures of the union, the law, and the issues likely to be raised by management.

4. Building interest by soliciting signatures on authorization cards (see Exhibit 5.6). (Most organizers will wait to announce that the union represents a majority until over 50 percent, and usually 60 to 80 percent, have signed cards.)

During this time the union discovers and highlights employees' problems, compares wages at their facility to wages at unionized facilities, and explains the role of the union in helping to satisfy their job-related needs. In other words, the union will attempt to convince the workers that they need a union and then that they should sign union authorization cards and should support the forthcoming organizing campaign by wearing union buttons, attending meetings, and signing up members. Although various means are available to gain support, research indicates that one-to-one contact, peer contact and persuasion, and high-quality, professionally designed written communications are most effective.[43] Other efforts used by unions include television and radio advertising, "hotline" telephone numbers, group meetings, and handbilling.

Organizing new locals is costly. Evidence shows that the cost of each additional union member is about $600.[44] These costs include direct, out-of-pocket expenditures for such items as the printing and mailing of leaflets and other literature, rent for office space, salaries for staff hired, and legal fees. These efforts take time from the union staff that could be devoted to providing services to present union members (handling grievances, arbitration, and negotiation).

The costs of organizing new members must be compared with the returns:

- Extra compensation made possible by increased bargaining power

- Additional dues and fees paid by new members

- Enhanced political influence

- Social benefits and satisfaction derived from extending membership to others[45]

Companies often learn of union-organizing attempts from supervisors or rank-and-file employees and through observing handbilling at the work site before they receive official notification (by letter or telegram) from the union demanding recognition. Some companies react vigorously, whereas others do little to acknowledge any union's attempt to organize the employees. Some employers tell their employees about their opposition and urge them not to sign union autho-

LABOR RELATIONS IN ACTION

Examples of Employer Messages during a Representation Election Campaign

- Tell employees that union contracts often contain wage cuts or givebacks.

- Mention that the union does not provide jobs and give examples of companies that have laid off employees who were union members.

- Explain that if the workers choose the union, the employer will be obligated to bargain with the union in good faith, but the employer cannot be forced to agree to contract provisions that are not in its best interests.

- Tell employees that a company must remain competitive and has a right to make a profit. If its labor costs are so high that it cannot sell its product at a profit, it cannot remain in business.

- Advise employees that they can revoke the authorization card and explain the procedure to do so.

- Indicate that the union dues vary but that typically dues are $50 per month or $600 per year.

- Tell employees that the employer has the legal right to hire permanent replacements for strikers. ■

SOURCE: Paul S. McDonough, "Maintain a Union-Free Status" *Personnel Journal* 69 (April 1990), pp. 108–114.

rization cards. Because the cards may specifically state that the signee favors union representation, any employee signature assists the union in establishing itself in the company. See "Labor Relations in Action" box for typical employer messages during a union campaign.

Filing a Petition for the Election Before 1935, to obtain recognition the union usually had to show its strength and employee interest in representation by such actions as strikes. The Wagner Act and the NLRB changed this situation by developing procedures and guidelines for peacefully determining the majority interest of employees through elections or some other comparable demonstration. The procedure is initiated when the potential bargaining representative for the employees files a petition for an election.

The NLRB is authorized to conduct an election only when a valid petition has been filed by an employee, group of employees, an individual or labor organization, or an employer. Usually the petition is filed by the union after it has requested union recognition from the employer and the request is denied. The petition must be supported by evidence (usually authorization cards) that a substantial interest in union representation (30 percent of the anticipated bargaining unit) exists. Further, it must show that the employer has declined a request by the union to be recognized as the exclusive bargaining agent. An employer cannot petition for an election until the union seeks recognition. If the employer could, it would petition at the time when the union's support was weakest. After receiving a petition, the NLRB will first determine whether it has jurisdiction and the petition is valid. If so, it will promptly notify the company and request a listing of employees. Companies are not required to submit this list but usually comply with the request as an act of good faith. Next, the NLRB will arrange a conference with the company and union to discuss the possibility of a consent election. Here, if both sides agree to the appropriate bargaining unit, voter eligibility, ballot, date, time, and place for the election, a consent election will be held. If either party refuses to agree on any of these items, a formal hearing to settle these matters will be conducted.

Election Investigation and Hearing If the union and management officials cannot agree to a consent election, the NLRB will investigate the petition, hold a hearing, and then direct an election if it finds that there is substantial interest in union representation. This investigation will secure answers to the following questions:

1. What is the anticipated appropriate bargaining unit?

2. Does substantial interest in representation (30 percent) exist among employees in the unit?

3. Are there any barriers to an election in the form of existing unions, prior elections, or present labor agreements?

Appropriate Bargaining Unit An appropriate bargaining unit is a grouping of jobs or positions in which two or more employees share common employment interests and conditions (community of interests) and which may reasonably be grouped together for collective bargaining purposes. Determination of an appropriate bargaining unit is left to the discretion of the NLRB, which decides in each representation case how employee rights can best be protected under the act. The Board's decision has, however, been limited by law in several ways. The statute includes the following:

- Professional employees cannot be included in a unit composed of both professional and nonprofessional employees unless a majority of the professional employees vote to be included in a mixed unit.

- A proposed craft unit cannot be ruled inappropriate simply because a different unit has been previously approved by the NLRB unless a majority of employees in the proposed craft union vote against being represented separately.

- Plant guards cannot be included in any bargaining unit that has nonguard employees in the unit because of the potential conflict of interest, such as searching a fellow union member's locker for stolen property.

- Supervisors and managers are not considered employees covered under the act and may not be in any bargaining unit. *Supervisors* are defined as "individuals who have authority in the interest of the employer, to hire, transfer, suspend, lay off, recall, promote, discharge, assign, reward, or discipline other employees, or responsibility to direct them, or to adust their grievances, or effectively to recommend such action, if in connection with the foregoing the exercise of such authority is not of a merely routine or clerical nature, but requires the use of independent judgment."

- Excluded are agricultural laborers, public employees (except postal employees), and independent contractors, although some of these may be covered in separate state statutes.

- Confidential employees and some family members (e.g., son, daughter, spouse) are excluded.

Thus, the NLRB's determination of the appropriate bargaining unit influences whether the union will win the election, who will vote in the election, whether one union will prevail in an interunion contest, whether craft employees will have their own union or be included in a plantwide unit, who the union must represent, who will be covered by the collective bargaining agreement, or whether the union will include key employees who could give direction and leadership for the bargaining unit employees.

Analysis of NLRB representation elections indicates that the success of a union campaign depends on the composition of the appropriate bargaining unit. When the appropriate bargaining unit is composed of similarly skilled groups, the union will likely succeed. This may be so because decisions within unions are made through a democratic process, and a degree of consensus is necessary to facilitate decision making and to win the support of the majority. However, when different skill groups comprise the bargaining unit, achieving consensus is more difficult, and majority support for the union likewise is harder to achieve and maintain. Thus, the NLRB's policy of including in a bargaining unit all "production and maintenance" employees within a plant (which would include a diversity of skills) may have contributed to the decline in union membership as a percentage of the total labor force. A more narrowly defined bargaining unit composed only of employees of similar skills (such as electricians) would favor the union winning the representation election and sustaining the continuation of the union.[46]

If the union wins, the appropriate bargaining unit may determine who will be required to join the union. Therefore, the composition of the bargaining unit is important to the employer, the union, and the public.

Some companies pay attention to these considerations and take preventive steps regarding management structure, employee interactions, and personnel policies and practices. For example, if the company prefers a large multiunit bargaining unit, it will retain centralized control on management practices and decisions. If it prefers smaller, independent units, it will decentralize decision making in these independent units. Because the union has no control over management structure and the authority-responsibility relationship, it can try to convince the NLRB that the bargaining unit should be composed only of those employees who are supporting the union.[47]

Should a plant have several small bargaining units, the employer may face different unions in negotiating several times throughout the year, which could cause continuous instability in labor relations. Separate units concerned with similar jobs may cause disputes over rights to jobs, leading to strikes or slowdowns. Should a small bargaining unit be merged with a nationwide bargaining unit, any confrontation that resulted in a strike could cause a nationwide shutdown and complications for customers in need of the companies' products. Chapter 6 covers the various bargaining structures and their implications.

The bargaining unit itself may cover employees in one plant or in two or more facilities of the same employer. The NLRB considers the "community of interests" in determining the composition of an appropriate bargaining unit. It evaluates the following factors:

- Interests of employees and employers
- Commonality of wages, working conditions, training, and skill
- History of collective bargaining either at the location in question or another facility owned by the company
- Transfers of employees among various facilities
- Geography and physical proximity of the workplaces
- Employer's administrative or territorial divisions
- Degree of separation (or distinctiveness) of work or integration (or interrelatedness) of work[48]

When the relevant factors do not give a clear indication for the composition of an appropriate bargaining unit, an election (commonly called a *Globe* election, from the original NLRB case) may be held to determine employee interests. For example, one group of electricians in a steel plant might wish to be represented by the International Brotherhood of Electrical Workers (IBEW) instead of the United Steelworkers of America (USWA). The USWA wants to include all electricians in a bargaining unit composed of all production and maintenance employees in the plant. Under such circumstances, the electricians' vote will determine whether they will be members of USWA, a separate electricians' union (IBEW), or no union.

The U.S. Supreme Court supported the NLRB's first rule-making effort to determine appropriate bargaining units for private acute-care hospitals. Eight standard bargaining units were established for approximately 4,000 acute-care hospitals: (1) all registered nurses, (2) all physicians, (3) all professionals except registered nurses and physicians, (4) all technical employees, (5) all skilled maintenance employees, (6) all business office clericals, (7) all guards, and (8) all other nonprofessional employees. Such rule-making practices reduce the number of cases in which employers are able to contest the number and composition of the appropriate bargaining unit. Employers sometimes intentionally use this tactic to delay the election and thereby increase the chances that the union will not win representational rights.[49]

In 2000, the Board ruled that, under the National Labor Relations Act a group of medical interns, residents, and fellows were employees and formed a proper bargaining unit, even though they were students. This ruling overruled a previous ruling that had excluded such individuals from bargaining units of employees. The Board reasoned that the interns, residents, and fellows were similar to apprentices, who had been considered statutory employees for a long time. Later in 2000, the Board extended its ruling and found that a group of graduate assistants (including teaching and research assistants) at New York University were employees. The Board rejected the university's contention that the graduate assistants were predominately students, not employees. The new Board composed of a majority appointed by President George W. Bush in 2003 may return to the rule that persons who are primarily students are not statutory employees and thus should not have collective-bargaining rights extended to them.[50]

Eligibility of Voters Before an election is conducted, voter eligibility must be determined. An employee is eligible to vote in a representational election if he or she is (1) employed in a bargaining unit job; (2) employed during the eligibility period, which is usually the payroll period immediately preceding the direction of the election; and (3) employed on the date of the election.

However, employees who are on sick leave, vacation, temporary layoff, or temporary leave, such as military duty, may vote in the election. In addition, the NLRB will occasionally consider irregularity of employment, such as in the construction, food processing, and longshoring industries. Economic strikers who have been replaced by permanent employees are allowed to vote in any election within 12 months after the strike begins. This policy ensures that management does not provoke a strike and hire replacements who could vote out the union. Employees hired after the union files its petition but before the election may be challenged for their eligibility by the union.

Untimely Petitions Several rules make a petition for a representation election untimely. The first is a legal requirement that prohibits any NLRB representation election where one has been held in the last 12 months or where a petition for election covers a group of employees who are already covered by an existing contract and already members of a legally certified union.

The second rule and potential barrier to elections is an administrative determination that was made in the interest of stable and effective labor relations. The NLRB rule, called the **contract bar doctrine,** specifies that a valid, signed agreement for a fixed period of 3 years or less will bar any representation election for the life of the agreement (a longer contract is still limited to 3 years). Thus, the contract bar doctrine could extend the 12-month statutory limitation on elections to 3 years. To do otherwise would be unfair to union and management officials who have negotiated a multiyear labor agreement in good faith.

"Names and Addresses" (Excelsior Rule) Within 7 days after the regional director of the NLRB has approved a consent election or after an election has been directed, the employer must file a list of names and addresses of all eligible voters with the regional director. This information is then made available to the union. Refusal to comply could be identified as a bad faith act on the part of the employer and cause the election to be set aside or the NLRB to seek the names and addresses by subpoena. The purpose of this disclosure rule is to give the unions access to employees that management already possesses.[51]

The Election The representation election, acclaimed as one of the great innovations of American labor law, is conducted by NLRB officials and is typically held within 48 days (median) of the initial request. NLRB data show that 90 percent of the eligible voters participate in NLRB elections, as compared with about 50 percent in major political elections.

The high voter turnout in union representation elections might be due to the convenient voting procedure (usually carried out on company property) and the belief of many employees that their vote more directly affects their lives (at least their working conditions) than do political elections. Finally, both unions and management realize that an employee could express union preference to a union representative and an opposite preference to the management representative to avoid a confrontation during the election campaign. Neither side is sure of employee voting preferences when faced with a secret ballot; therefore, union and management officials work to get out the vote.

Voter participation tends to decline the longer it takes for the NLRB to conduct the election. Thus, some employers are motivated to refuse to consent to an election in hopes of increasing the chances of the union losing the election. Also, because most single-unit elections are close, the number of nonparticipants affects the outcome of many elections.[52] Also, a small number of votes greatly influences the outcome of the election; research shows that a switch of eight votes would have changed the outcomes of half the elections.[53] Furthermore, small increases in the time to process cases are important; a delay of 10 days has proven to be a significant factor in differentiating employer wins from employer losses. The number of preelection days has also been linked to union losses. During the first 6 months of delay, there is an average drop-off in union victories of 2.5 percent per month. Consent elections have the highest victory rate.[54]

The size of the election unit has tended to be negatively related to union victories. The larger election unit is closely related to delay because it takes longer to process and is more likely to result in a hearing than in a voluntary settlement.[55] Recent research has also revealed that success in union organizing has been influenced positively by the size of the union and democracy within the union and negatively influenced by the union's propensity to strike and centralization of the union's decision making.[56]

A study of NLRB elections revealed that independent unions (those unions not affiliated with the AFL-CIO) have had a higher union win ratio than AFL-CIO affiliates. Thus, the AFL-CIO's "big labor" image may be a liability, and the AFL-CIO may need to encourage union autonomy, as did the AFL before the merger of the AFL and CIO in 1955, the year when union density reached 35 percent of the private workforce.[57]

Using a ballot with the appropriate company and union designations (Exhibit 5.7), a secret-ballot election is conducted under NLRB supervision, usually during working hours on payday at the employer's location. However, the NLRB has discretionary authority to conduct it by mail ballot. In 1998, the Board (the majority of members appointed by President Bill Clinton) approved a new procedure that encouraged the use of mail ballots in representation elections under any of the following conditions: (1) eligible voters were widely dispersed geographically, (2) eligible voters worked differing schedules and were not present at common locations at common times, or (3) where there was strike, lockout, or picketing. The Bush-majority Board may return to the previous policy, which allowed mail ballots *only* in situations where the circumstances indicated that a manual election was not feasible.[58]

The NLRB must determine whether the majority of the employees in an appropriate bargaining unit want to be represented by a union for collective bargaining purposes. It defines *majority* as the simple majority rule generally accepted in democratic elections, which means that those choosing not to vote in the election have decided to assent to the wishes of the majority who did vote. Therefore, a majority of the employees who vote (50 percent plus one of those voting) in the election must favor representation before a union will be certified by the NLRB.

Exhibit 5.7

Examples of Secret Ballots for Union Representation Elections

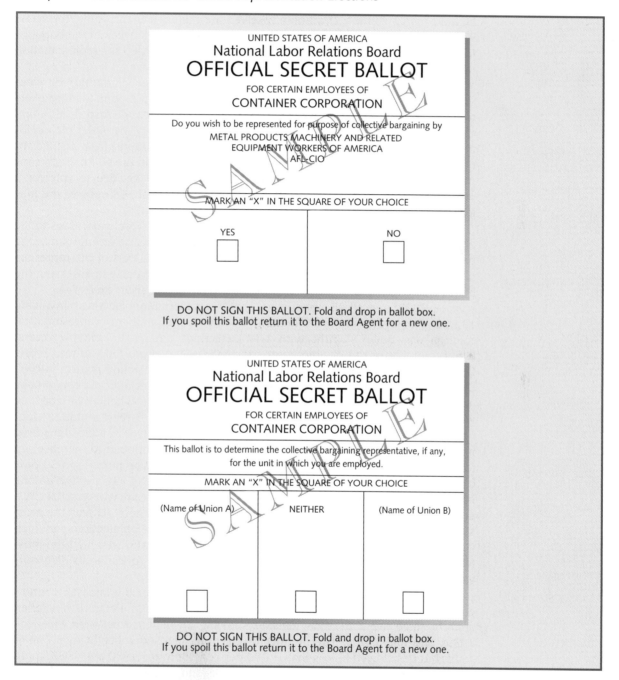

If two or more choices are placed on the ballot, a runoff election may be necessary between the choices receiving the two highest numbers of votes in the initial election. If the majority votes "no union," no representation election can be held for 12 months. If a union receives the majority of the votes, the NLRB will certify it as the exclusive bargaining agent of the employees in the bargaining unit. Interestingly, where more than one union has vied for representation rights in the same election, unions have fared extremely well.

Although only 4 percent of representation elections are multiunion elections (choice between two unions), one of the competing unions is more likely to win representation rights than in a single-union election. Also, multiunion elections bring out a substantially high number of voters.[59] The major reason for this positive vote is that two unions would have to gain support from a sufficient number of the bargaining unit's employees to be placed on the ballot. Such support usually indicates that the employees have already decided to vote for a union; the election is conducted to determine which union will receive the majority vote.

After the votes have been counted, either party has 7 calendar days to file objections alleging misconduct or to challenge the ballots of voters whom one party believes should not have voted in the election. This part of the representation process receives considerable criticism because the delay in assessing the ballot challenges and objections concerning misconduct seem excessive.

In 2002, the NLRB conducted 2,587 representation elections involving 182,221 employees; in the first 6 months of 2003, the number of representation election was down slightly, with 1,147 elections and 71,077 eligible voters. Ninety percent of the eligible votes cast ballots—far more than in any presidential election, or for any other political election. The election is usually conducted on the employer's premises during working hours and involves a subject about which most employees are vitally interested—whether or not they will be represented by a union. In 2002, unions won 1,445 representation elections, or 55.9 percent, compared with 54.1 percent of the 2,522 elections held in 2001. In the first half of 2003, the union win rate continued to increase, up to 57.3 percent. In every year since 1997, unions have won more than 50 percent of the NLRB-conducted representation elections. The most active unions have been the Teamsters, the United Food and Commercial Workers (UFCW), and the Service Employees International Union (SEIU). The SEIU was the most successful union, winning 68.9 percent of the representation elections in which it participated in 2002 and 80.2 percent in 2003. The states in which the most NLRB elections were held in 2002 were California, New York, Illinois, Pennsylvania, and Michigan.[60]

Several trends in union representation elections over the last half century can be identified. First, the number of union representation elections has fallen sharply since the mid-1970s, despite showing an increase between the mid-1950s and mid-1970s. The number of elections reached a height of 8,799 in 1973, but has slowed to less than 3,000 per year. Between 1980 and 1983, there was a precipitous drop of over 50 percent. Second, union success rates in representation elections have steadily declined since the 1940s, when union win rates averaged about 75 percent compared with the present win rate of just over 50 percent. Third, unions continue to be less likely to win NLRB-supervised representation elections involving bargaining units of over 100 employees.[61]

After the Election As noted in Chapter 1, the first step of the labor relations process, the recognition of legitimate rights and responsibilities of unions and management representatives, includes more than the representation election. After unions win bargaining rights in a representation election, they attempt to negotiate a labor agreement; however, they fail to secure the first contract 25 to 30 percent of the time. Several factors increase the likelihood of reaching agreement: existence of relatively high wages already at the company, presence of other bargaining units within the company, large election victories, and active participation of international union representatives. Factors that reduce the chances of attaining the first contract include location in a southern state with right-to-work laws, the national union having to approve the local union contracts, presence of outside labor-management consultants hired by the company,[62] NLRB delays in resolving employer objections and challenges to election results, employer refusal to bargain in good faith, and discrimination against employees after the election.[63]

Delays associated with filing objections to campaign conduct have increased threefold over the last 20 years, and the median amount of delay time is now about 210 days. Then, employers fail or refuse to bargain in good faith 13 percent of the time. This unfair labor practice adds approximately 140 days. Additional delay can occur if appeals are made to the full Board in Washington, D.C., or to the court of appeals or Supreme Court.

In addition to the delays, there has been a sixfold increase in the number of unfair labor practice charges for firing union supporters and an elevenfold increase in the number of back-pay awards. Research has discovered that employers discharge union activists or union supporters for two main reasons: (1) to get the key union organizers out of the facility, and (2) to send a chilling message to the rest of the workforce. With such trends in statistics, it does not appear that ethical considerations prevent all employers from breaking the law.

One researcher has found that unions are prompted to file unfair labor practices in 20 percent of the representation elections in which they participate. However, surprisingly, there appears to be no measurable differences in the outcome of the elections whether the unfair labor practices are filed or whether the unfair labor practices that were filed actually had merit.[64]

Duties of the Exclusive Bargaining Agent and Employer The exclusive bargaining representative (the union) chosen by the majority of the employees in the appropriate unit has the duty to represent equitably and fairly all employees in the unit regardless of their union membership and to bargain in good faith with the employer. The employer has a comparable obligation, that is, to bargain in good faith with the exclusive bargaining agent and to refuse to bargain with any other union seeking to represent the employees. Further, any negotiated labor agreement will cover the employees in the bargaining unit, regardless of their union membership status.

After Election Loss by Union After losing a representation election, typically the union reduces its activities because there can be only one election every 12 months. However, there are some creative ways in which the union can maintain contact with employees, particularly those who supported it during the campaign, and provide a representational service to those included in the bargaining unit. Exhibit 5.8 includes alternative activities that could increase the chances of success of any future unionization drive.

Exhibit 5.8

Possible Activities for Unions after Losing a Representation Election

1. Maintain in-plant committees, designate employees as union stewards, identify them with steward buttons, and through them, maintain contact with member and nonmember employees.
2. Distribute employment-related union literature in the plant during nonworking time and serve as the voice of employees on all matters of common employment-related matters of concern.
3. Union stewards can present employee grievances to management. If management refuses to meet with the union committee, employees may leave their work as a group to request a discussion of their employment-related problems directly with management. If the response is unsatisfactory, the union may engage in a work stoppage; however, striker replacement rules apply.
4. A nonmajority union can provide a shield of concerted activity for an individual employee who refuses to drive a faulty truck, reports Occupational Safety and Health Administration (OSHA) violations, refuses to act in violation of personal ethics or morality, or sues for unpaid overtime.
5. Help employees know and enforce their individual employment rights concerning workers' compensation, third-party tort claims, wage and hour violations, and so on.
6. In-plant committees help employees know and receive their entitlements, such as medical benefits, sick leave, severance pay, pensions, unemployment compensation, disability pay, and social security.
7. Inform employees of rights under common-law doctrines and exceptions to employment-at-will doctrine, including employee manuals, employment contracts, public policy exceptions, good faith exceptions, and tort suits involving outrageous conduct, defamation, and invasion of privacy.
8. Reinforcing OSHA statutory procedures: (1) establish in-plant safety committees; (2) file complaints through the union; (3) serve as representative of employees to accompany compliance officer on plant "walk-around," discuss claims, and participate in conferences; (4) act as representative of employees in the proceedings before the OSHA; (5) enforce the Hazard Communication Standard by filing complaints if employer fails to provide toxic training to employees and has not prepared a written communication program; and (6) petition for information contained on Material Safety Data Sheets.
9. Represent employees under plant closure laws, pregnancy leave acts, polygraph and privacy acts, and whistle-blowing statutes.
10. Represent employees under unjust discharge procedures modeled after labor arbitration.

SOURCE: Clyde W. Summers, "Unions without Majorities: The Potentials of the NLRA," *Proceedings of the 43rd Meeting of the Industrial Relations Research Association* (Madison, Wis.: IRRA, 1991), pp. 154–162.

Conduct of the Representation Election Campaign

All elections are conducted according to NLRB standards, which are designed to ensure that employees in the bargaining unit can indicate freely whether they want to be represented by a union for collective bargaining purposes. However, election campaigns differ substantially, and the strategies of individual unions and employers vary widely. For example, handbills similar to those in Exhibit 5.9 are often used in addition to speeches, informal talks, interviews, and films. Thus, the election campaign, one of the most interesting and controversial activities in labor relations, has led to a body of doctrines and rules. Because of changes in NLRB philosophy, those doctrines and rules are subject to change.

Campaign Doctrines and NLRB Policies

The **totality of conduct doctrine** guides the NLRB interpretations of unfair labor practice behavior. This doctrine essentially means that isolated incidents such

Exhibit 5.9

Examples of Handbills Distributed During Representation Election Campaigns

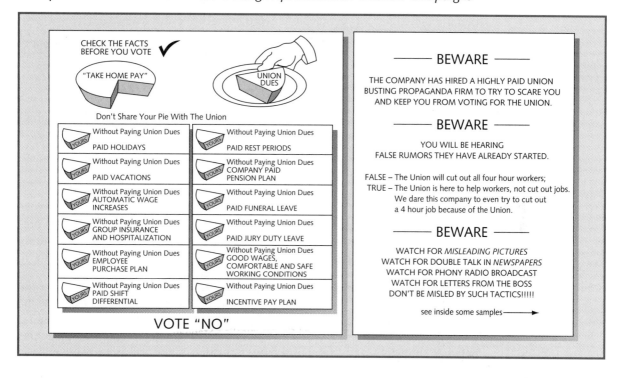

as campaign speeches must be considered within the whole of the general circumstances of the campaign and with the possibility that other specific violations have occurred.

Employer statements to employees may seem harmless on the surface, but under the circumstances that exist at the time of the statements, they may carry implied threats. For example, if an employer stated that a third-party intervention could make it economically impossible for it to continue in business, it would be making an illegal statement during a union election campaign. However, if the employer made the same statement during an attempted leveraged buyout, there would be no legal violation.

In 1982, the NLRB concluded that it would no longer probe into the truth or falsity of the parties' campaign statements but would intervene in cases where a party had used forged documents that render voters unable to recognize propaganda for what it is. The Board concluded that today's voters (employees) are more educated and sophisticated than their historical counterparts and can analyze materials more accurately. This assessment was influenced by a research study involving over 1,000 employees in thirty-one elections in five states. This study cast doubt on the previously held assumption that employees are unsophisticated about labor relations and are swayed easily by campaign propaganda. In fact, votes of 81 percent of the employees could have been predicted from their precampaign intent and their attitudes toward working conditions and unions in general. The study concluded that employees' votes appeared to be the product of attitudes that resulted from their everyday experiences in the industrial world and not from the campaign itself.[65]

The data used in the study were later reanalyzed, and the following additional (some different) conclusions were made[66]:

- Employer predisposition favoring the union is a very important determinant of voting behavior.

- Written communications distributed later in the campaign and meetings held early in the campaign most probably have an effect.

- Threats and actions taken against union supporters are effective in discouraging support for the union.

Thus far, these later analyses have not influenced the Board's position on election campaigns.

Captive Audience—24-Hour Rule

One legal approach used by employers to discourage union support includes presenting "captive audience" speeches, which are delivered to employees during working hours. The speeches, authorized by the Taft-Hartley amendments in 1947, must not be presented within 24 hours of an election, and the speech's content must not include threats of reprisal or promises of benefits. However, if the union has no acceptable means of communicating with the employees, as in the lumber and logging industry, where employees live on company property, and if the employer's unfair labor practices have created a serious election campaign imbalance, the NLRB and the courts may grant the union access to plant bulletin boards, parking lots, and entrances so that it may communicate with the employees. Still, it is extremely difficult for the union to respond effectively by using its traditional means of contacting employees, such as plant employee solicitations, distribution of literature before or after work, house calls, and union meetings.[67]

Polling or Questioning Employees

Polling employees or asking questions about their interest in unions was considered unlawful interference with employee rights in early days. In 1984, the NLRB announced that it would no longer automatically consider an employer interrogation about an employee's union sentiment an unlawful inquiry in violation of section 8(a)(1). It announced that it would examine the totality of the circumstances surrounding such interrogations in light of the following:

1. The background of the interrogation
2. The nature of the information sought
3. The identity of the questioner
4. The place and method of the interrogation

Therefore, an employer's questioning of open and active union supporters and other employees about their union sentiments in the absence of threats or promises does not necessarily violate the law. However, NLRB decisions since 1984 reveal that employers are still at risk in these interrogations because it is necessary only to establish that the questions asked may reasonably be said to have a tendency to interfere with the free exercise of an employee's rights under the act.[68]

Distribution of Union Literature and Solicitation by Employees on Company Property

The NLRB and the courts have long held that except in special circumstances employees may not be prohibited from distributing union-organizing materials or soliciting union support in nonworking areas during nonworking time[69] unless the employer can show that such activity would disrupt production, employee work, and plant discipline. For example, employees of restaurants and retail establishments cannot distribute union materials in customer areas, and employees of health-care institutions cannot distribute materials in areas designated strictly for patients.[70] However, distribution of materials by employees in such places as hospital cafeterias predominantly patronized by hospital employees cannot be prohibited.[71] In addition, the employer cannot prohibit distribution of union material if the basis for the prohibition is that part of its content includes political issues, such as right-to-work laws and minimum wages.[72] Nor can the employer prohibit employees from wearing buttons, hats, or T-shirts promoting the union.

Some employers publish *no solicitation rules* that prevent employees from discussing union organizing on working time. However, to be enforceable, these no solicitation rules must be posted in advance of the organizing drive, and these rules must prohibit all types of solicitation by employees except United Way.

The employer may limit the type of information distributed to employees by classifying company data as "confidential." The NLRB has upheld the discharge of five employees who distributed wage data comparing the company's wage scale with that of other plants in the area. The NLRB found that the company had declared this wage information to be confidential and that it had not been obtained in the normal course of employment.

For 35 years, the NLRB traditionally weighed the union's right to access employees in a unionizing campaign against the private property rights of an employer. In the 1992 *Lechmere* decision, the Supreme Court ruled (Justice Clarence Thomas wrote the court's opinion) that a company can ban a union organizer who is not an employee of the company from the property if the union has a reasonable alternative means of reaching individual employees with the union message, such as through newspaper advertising and home visits. The court would restrict exceptions to extraordinary situations in which the work site is isolated geographically and the union could not easily contact potential members except at the work site. Thus, the Supreme Court has made a distinction between employee and nonemployee access to individual employees during an organizing campaign and has made the union's efforts to communicate with employees more difficult, as well as more costly.[73]

The *Lechmere* decision applied to a store's parking lot designated for customer and employee use, and the store had strictly enforced a no solicitation rule to parties. Since the *Lechmere* decision, the NLRB has been faced with the application of the Supreme Court's decision in similar situations. The NLRB has ruled that nonemployee handbillers have access rights to a neutral third party's property, specifically from the entrance of the store and not merely the entrance to the parking lot. The union was able to show that handbilling at the entrance of the parking lot was dangerous and that the use of media was cost prohibitive.[74] Also, nonemployee union handbillers may be allowed on company property when and if the employer has allowed church and school groups, fundraisers, Boy Scouts, Little League teams, and so on, to solicit on company property.[75]

Showing Films during Election Campaigns

Films presented to discourage workers from joining unions have taken on new dimensions, especially since the 1950s, when the movie *And Women Must Weep* was produced by the National Right-to-Work Committee. This movie portrays union violence, strikes, vandalism, phone threats, a house bombing, and even the shooting of a baby of a dissident union member. Frequent use of the film by employers prompted the International Association of Machinists to produce a rebuttal film, entitled *Anatomy of a Lie*, which claims no evidence exists of a connection between the shootings and other misconduct and the union's activities. On-site interviews with persons involved in the strike are shown to reveal an opposite view of the employer film, and the president of the union is filmed stating that nearly 99 percent of the union members voted to strike. The NLRB's position regarding the showing of these films has varied; its current position is that their showing alone does not constitute an unfair labor practice and is not sufficient cause to have the results of an election set aside.[76]

Use of E-Mail

The use of e-mail by employees and employer e-mail policies has been an issue before the NLRB. In recent years, unions have been using e-mail in attempts to organize employees. Union supporters have used or attempted to use e-mail to transmit pro-union messages during organizing campaigns. The Board has found that employers violate the law when they discriminate in the enforcement of e-mail access policies based on pro-union content of employee messages. However, the Board has not decided a case where an employer has banned all nonbusiness use of company e-mails. The NLRB general counsel has issued an advisory memorandum and issued a complaint where the employer had a policy of not allowing any nonbusiness use of its e-mail system. The general counsel reasoned that at least some e-mails were more akin to oral solicitations than they were to the distribution of literature because e-mail messages were interactive in nature. The employer policy that barred use of its e-mail system to send all union-related messages even where both the sender and recipient were on nonworking time was too broad and unlawful. The new Board appointed by President Bush in 2003 will likely be asked to decide this issue.[77]

New Union Strategies

In response to employers' strategies to maintain nonunion status, unions have had to be creative in their actions. Some well-publicized strategies by unions include instituting cyberspace organization with the Internet, whereby employees can simply enter the search words "how to organize" and receive on-line information on union organizing; and hiring "union salts," whereby an union organizer applies for a job within a targeted company, goes to work, and solicits for union membership as an employee[78] (see "Labor Relations in Action" box).

The Auto Workers have been able to persuade Ford Motors to encourage its suppliers to allow UAW to organize two of Johnson Controls plants that supply car seats to Ford. Ford has been able to outsource (purchase from suppliers) these car seats and buy them as needed (just in time) for Ford car assembly. Because outsourcing has caused tension in the past, with the reduction in Ford employment resulting from it, the union is now able to represent employees of

Ford's suppliers, and Ford continues to use suppliers for car seats, which are available when needed. Therefore, Ford is able to minimize its inventories and continue to require suppliers to compete for the Ford business.[79]

However, the unions still have been met with some stiff resistance by automobile suppliers. In Cape Girardeau, Missouri, Dana Corporation hired outside consultants to tell employees that the UAW organizers cared nothing about the town and were strangers to the city. The consultant produced a 20-minute video, which was sent to each employee's home. Despite the UAW's long history of employee involvement, the company accused unions of thriving on conflict over cooperation. In addition, Dana hired 75 new employees during the organizing drive and noted that 24 of 37 of its own plants had closed since 1980 after they were unionized. The company explained that they were not closed because they were unionized; however, its point was that the union could not save any of the plants that were not competitive.[80]

The AFL-CIO has launched a $5 million advertising campaign that consists of the following four one-minute spots:

1. A bricklayer on a concrete ledge high above Chicago explaining how the union helps to make sure this job is safe

2. A nurse in Los Angeles pushing a child with a teddy bear explaining how hospitals are now run by dollars and cents, instead of doctors and nurses

3. A cook in Las Vegas hotel hugging her children in one scene and toiling in the hotel kitchen and praising the union for providing her family with health insurance

4. A machinist at a Harley-Davidson factory telling how the union's cooperation helped to rescue the motorcycle company and make it an economic success[77] (Exhibit 5.10)

The AFL-CIO has conducted public rallies in major cities to highlight the argument that rights of employees to join unions have been undercut by fierce employer hostility. In San Francisco, the target was the Marriott hotels; in North Carolina, the target was the Mount Olive Pickle Company; and in New York City, the rally involved limousine drivers and restaurant employees. The supporters were urged to seek support from community groups and clergy to help counter employer campaigns to keep unions out. The AFL-CIO cited a Cornell study, which reported that 75 percent of the private-sector employers aggressively opposed unions, 80 percent hired antiunion consultants, 32 percent dismissed employees involved in organizing drives, and 50 percent threatened to close plants if their employees chose a union.[81]

With President Sweeney's increased emphasis on recruiting new members, some unions have increased the portion of their budgets devoted to organizing. For example, the Service Employees International Union, which has grown from 625,000 to 1.1 million members since 1980, now spends 45 percent of its budget on organizing. Other unions spend as little as 2 percent on organizing efforts, and President Sweeney believes this low percentage must be increased for organized labor to regain its strength in the United States.[82]

On December 10, 2003 (International Human Rights Day), AFL-CIO unions held marches in 70 U.S. cities to begin a campaign to persuade Congress to pass a law making it easier for employees to unionize and to increase penalties on

LABOR RELATIONS IN ACTION

Union Salting: A New Union-Organizing Tactic

Town & Country Electric, a nonunion electrical contractor, needed to hire several licensed Minnesota electricians for construction work within Minnesota and advertised the positions through an employment agency. Eleven union applicants, including two professional union staff members, applied for jobs. Only one union applicant was interviewed; he was hired but was subsequently dismissed after only a few days on the job.

The IBEW filed a complaint with the NLRB against Town & Country. The complaint was that the company refused to interview applicants and refused to retain union members because of their union membership, which was in violation of the National Labor Relations Act (NLRA).

An administrative law judge and the board determined that all of the union applicants were "employees" under the language of the NLRA. Although the applicants had not been hired, applicants are covered under the prohibition of "discrimination in regard to hire" under the NLRA. The board found it immaterial that the union applicants intended to try to organize Town & Country employees upon securing employment, as well as the fact that the union would be paying these employees to organize a union.

The U.S. Court of Appeals for the Eighth Circuit reversed the NLRB and held that the board had incorrectly interpreted the definition of "employee" in the NLRA. The Court ruled that the NLRB did not protect employees who were working for a company while simultaneously being paid by the union to attempt to organize employees of the company.

The U.S. Supreme Court determined that the NLRA sought to improve labor-management relations by granting employees the right to organize, form unions, join unions, and assist in organizing unions. The high Court ruled that the meaning of the word "employee" was critical and that the language and definition of "employee" includes paid union organizers. The Court noted that the NLRB was created to administer the NLRA and will be upheld when its rulings are "reasonably defensible." The Court indicated that it relied on the NLRB's expertise and congressional intent in its ruling. Furthermore, the Court ruled that Congress had delegated the primary responsibility for developing and applying national labor policy and that the board's views are entitled to the greatest deference by the courts. The principal difference between **salting** and the traditional organizing is that salting is a "top-down" approach and traditional organizing is a bottom-up approach. Union salting may be called covert or overt. Covert salting is like a Trojan horse in that a full-time union organizer applies to a help-wanted ad placed by nonunion businesses. The union organizer does not reveal that he or she is employed by the union. The employer does not conduct a background or reference check, and the union organizer is hired by the employer. Once employed, the union organizer initiates an organizing campaign. Overt salting occurs when the union organizer reveals in the application process that he is employed by the union. If he is denied employment due to his union affiliation, he files a charge of an unfair labor practice against the employer for discriminating against him because of his union membership.

Since the Town and Country decision

Since the *Town and Country* decision, there has been a 53 percent increase in overt salting activities and a 47 percent increase in covert salting. By 2001, there were 55 union salting unfair labor practices cases before the NLRB. Of the 55 cases, 6 were dismissed and 3 were remanded to the administrative law judge. In 43 cases, the charges were upheld by the NLRB. These charges were associated with monetary penalties of back pay. These charges included unlawful discharge, unlawful layoff, refusal to consider for employment, refusal to recall from layoff, unlawful suspension, and refusal to reinstate strikers. Interestingly, nonunion contractors may join the Associated Builders and Contractors and take out salting insurance, which pays legal fees and up to 90 percent of back pay awards issued by the NLRB.

The appellate courts have cut back on some union salting activities by finding that an employer may fire a "union salt" if he falsified his employment application to obtain a job or the "union salt" violated a "moonlighting" policy that does not allow employees to hold two jobs at the same time. In other words, the court found that the dual employment rule was lawful if applied in a nondiscriminatory manner.

Legal proceedings

The NLRB has ruled that two factors must be present for a finding of guilt in a "refusal-to-consider" case. The general counsel must prove that the employer excluded "salts" from the hiring process and that an anti-union animus contributed to the employer's decision not to consider the salts. If these facts are established, then the burden of proof shifts to the employer to prove that it would not have considered the "salts" even in the absence of their union activity.

In "refusal-to-hire" cases, the general counsel must (1) show that the employer was hiring or had concrete plans to hire at the time the salting took place, (2) demonstrate that the "salts" had appropriate experience and training and were qualified for the position for which they applied, and (3) prove that anti-union animus was present and contributed to the decision not to hire the salts. If successful, the burden of proof shifts to the employer to prove that it would not have hired the salts even the absence of their union activity. Justification by the employer includes the hiring of other better qualified applicants or proof that the "salts" were not qualified for the vacant positions. ■

SOURCE: Jeffrey A. Mello, "The Enemy Within: When Paid Union Organizers Become Employees," *Labor Law Journal* 47 (October 1996), pp. 677–679; *NLRB v. Town & Country Electric, Inc.,* 116 S. Ct. 450 (1995); NLRB has developed guidelines in *FES (A Division of Thermo Power)* 331 N.L.R.B. No. 20, 5/11/00. See also Cory R. Fine, "Union Salting: Reactions and Rulings since *Town and Country,*" *Journal of Labor Research* 23 (Summer 2002), pp. 475–483.

employers who fire workers for supporting unions. President Sweeney pointed to a recent poll that 42 million Americans would join a union if they could.[83]

← Decertification Procedure —

Whenever employees believe that the union is not representing their interests, they may turn to a decertification procedure. In the last decade, decertification elections have nearly doubled, and researchers have identified a variety of reasons:

- Fair treatment of employees by employers
- Poor job by unions (especially smaller unions) of providing services to members

Exhibit 5.10

Union Advertising Flier

Today's Unions

Labor unions are made up of working people working together to solve problems, build stronger workplaces, and give working families a real voice. Unions stand for fair treatment of all working people—*on the job, in our communities,* and *in the economy.*

Unions give working people *a voice in government.* They represent working families before lawmakers and make sure politicians never forget that working families voted them into office.

Machinist Mike Gunarich, of York Pennsylvannia, is proud of his union and of his company. Working together, they pulled Harley Davidson through tough economic times and put the company back in the black.

Unions give workers *a voice on the job* about safety, security, pay, benefits—and about the best ways to get the work done. That helps working families, the companies that employ them, and the customers who use their products and services.

Unions work for equal treatment and fight discrimination. We marched with Dr. Martin Luther King Jr. in the 1960's, and we continue to fight for justice for women and minorities in collective bargaining as well as legislation.

For Erin McCarthy, a Las Vegas food services worker, being a union member means she has the job security, flexibility, and benefits she needs to raise her family.

When Chicago construction worker Michael Vukasovic is 30 stories up, he knows he can count on his trained union co-workers to be a solid, skilled, safety-minded team.

Unions help working families get a fair shake in today's economy. Union workers earn an average of $155 (or 33 percent) more each week than nonunion workers and are much more likely to have health and pension benefits. On the job and in national policy debates, we are committed to seeing that working families, not just rich CEO's, benefit from our labor.

Unions strengthen communities. We promote economic development, partner with community groups, and pitch in when disaster strikes.

Arthereane Brown, a Los Angeles nurse, says patients are well cared for because her union gives her a voice on the job about staffing levels and patient care.

SOURCE: http://www.aflcio.org/todays.htm.

- Inability of unions to negotiate an effective first contract after winning bargaining rights
- Striking employees having skills that can be readily replaced[84] so that when a strike occurs, the employer hires replacements

Any employee, group of employees, or employee representative may file a petition for a decertification election 12 months after the union has been certified or upon expiration of the labor agreement (see "contract bar doctrine" discussed earlier). This petition must be supported by at least 30 percent of the bargaining unit employees.

Exhibit 5.11
- -
Examples of Objective Evidence* of Union's Lack of Majority Status

1. Unsolicited communications from employees expressing a desire to become unrepresented
2. Any material change in the size or composition of the unit, such as a reduction in the number of employees
3. Date of union certification
4. Failure of the union to appoint a shop steward or committee
5. Failure of the union to process grievances
6. Failure of the union to actively represent employees on matters arising under the contract
7. Failure of the union to hold meetings that could be attended by the employees
8. Failure of the employees to attend union meetings
9. Failure of a majority of employees to authorize a dues checkoff if the contract provides for one
10. Whether the union has communicated a lack of interest regarding representation to either the company or the employees
11. Whether employees have filed or attempted to file a decertification petition of their own

*"Objective evidence" is defined as "reasonable grounds" to believe that an incumbent union no longer represents a majority of bargaining unit employees.
SOURCE: Clyde Scott, Kim Hester, and Edwin Arnold, "Employer-Initiated Elections, 1968–1992," *Journal of Labor Research* 18 (Spring 1997), p. 317.

Although employers cannot initiate the petition or assist in filing a petition for a decertification election, a company may raise a "good faith" doubt as to whether the union represents the majority of employees. The NLRB and the courts have developed presumptions and rules related to determining good faith doubt. First, there is a presumption of majority status for 1 year following certification by the Board. The second presumption is that majority status continues for up to 3 years if the collective bargaining agreement extends for 3 years. At the end of the certification year or the expiration of the 3-year collective bargaining agreement, the employer may rebut the presumption of the union's majority status by presenting objective evidence—that the union does not continue to represent the majority of bargaining unit employees.

Examples of this evidence include a reduction in dues-paying members, few employees crossed a union picket line during a strike, resignations from the union, or a petition by employees without company involvement.[85] (See Exhibit 5.11 for other examples of objective evidence.)

If the employees choose to decertify their union, another representation election cannot be held for 12 months. However, after a valid petition is filed with the NLRB, but before the election, the employer must still bargain with the union until the question of union representation is resolved.

Although employers must be careful of their role in the decertification process, they have exhibited growing interest in it. For example, a one-day seminar, "The Process of Decertification" by Executive Enterprises is designed to teach management representatives about the entire process of decertification. Many employers have concluded that they should become more involved, especially because they are becoming aware that they do not necessarily have to play a passive role in the decertification process.

Employers may become active participants in the decertification efforts after the petition is filed; however, they should do so only after analyzing the costs and benefits of such a strategy. For example, if the company actively campaigns against the present union and the union wins the election and continues to represent employees, the long-term relationship with the union may be irreparably damaged. Moreover, if the company's relationship with the present union is reasonable and productive, it might be wiser to retain it than chance a later replacement by a more militant union.

If the employer chooses to become engaged in the decertification campaign, similar representation election rules and policies apply. For instance, after the petition is filed with the NLRB, the employer may communicate with employees and forcefully state its opposition to the present union, lawfully respond to employee questions, and inform them about the decertification election process. The employer may conduct captive audience speeches, send letters to employees, and conduct small group discussions during the decertification election campaign. Management may tell employees about the employer's perception of the disadvantages of the union and that the employer prefers to deal directly with individual employees instead of through a third party and wants to build a "trusting, team-oriented" relationship with employees, not an adversarial one. At the same time, employers must be careful not to plant the idea of decertification in the minds of employees by offering unsolicited advice, distributing booklets that explain how to decertify the union, or circulating a decertification petition. During the union decertification campaign, union officials will attempt to convince employees of the benefits of continued union representation.[86]

Decertification campaigns are conducted by unions and management in a manner similar to certification campaigns. Decertification elections are usually initiated by a group of employees who are not satisfied with the working conditions and economic provisions achieved by the union through collective bargaining. During the campaign period, the union officials prefer to use handbills, conduct personal visits, and make special pleas with members to refuse signing any decertification petition. Management prefers to rely on legal counsel and small group meetings with employees. Researchers have found both management and the unions have been successful in their campaigns when they emphasize personal contacts with employees and listen genuinely to their concerns, instead of mailing letters and giving out handbills.[87]

Employers must be aware of related unlawful activities, such as the following:

- Obtaining NLRB forms for employees who may be interested in union decertification

- Providing services such as typing, assistance in phrasing the petition for decertification, and use of company stationery by employees who are interested in launching a decertification campaign

- Initiating discussions on how or whether to decertify the union

- Allowing supervisors or any other persons identified with management to promote the decertification process[88]

Unions respond to any challenge to their existence as the certified representative of the bargaining unit employees. They attempt to convince the employees that there are reasons to continue their union membership and representation and not to seek decertification. They do this by improving the level of services to the employees and by attempting to gain improvements in benefits through negotiation.[89]

The number of decertification elections, the number of employees in the bargaining units, and the percentage of elections lost by unions have remained steady over the last five years. The number of elections averaged just over 400 per year, the number of employees eligible to vote averaged 23,734 (less than .0018 of all union members), and about one-third of the elections were won by unions. The Teamsters were involved in 38 percent of the decertification elections and retained bargaining rights in about 30 percent of the elections.[90]

Research has identified several explanations for union decertification. First, the affiliation status of the local union involved in the union decertification election is important because affiliated unions have greater resources available to hold membership support and ultimately to retain union representation. In 440 of 492 decertification elections involving independent local unions, the union was decertified; whereas, in only 36 of 1,155 elections involving AFL-CIO affiliates was the union decertified.

A second factor affecting decertification is the availability of local employment and income opportunities. As employment opportunities increase, there is a decreased likelihood of support for the retention of the union. However, as income opportunities exceed the average, there is increased support to retain the union. Furthermore, where employees face income and employment opportunities that are limited to part-time, low-wage employment, support for union retention is significantly lower. For those employees whose income from part-time employment is relatively small, the expense of continuing to support the union is reduced. These reasons may help to explain such corporate strategies as moving to small southern towns where alternative employment is relatively sparse and increasing the number of part-time employees.[91]

The employees, like the employer, must be aware of possible consequences of their activities attempting to decertify the union. Decertification advocates must be prepared for pressure from union officials and isolation from fellow employees who are pleased with the union. The NLRB has upheld the union's right to discipline union members who actively participate in the campaign to decertify the union, as long as the disciplinary action does not affect the employee's employment status.[92]

In addition to decertification elections, there are the "raid" elections or multi-union elections. These elections occur when a different union (a challenger) attempts to replace an incumbent union. The bargaining unit employees are given a choice between (1) the incumbent union, (2) the challenger union, and (3) no union. Like other types of elections, the employer may campaign in an attempt to persuade employees to vote "no union," and the union in effect will be decertified. Between 1975 and 1989, there were 1,414 "raid" elections. The incumbent unions won 49.6 percent, the challenger unions won 40.9 percent, and 9.5 percent resulted in a no-union vote.

Companies have used several deunionization approaches in recent years. One is the withdrawal of recognition of the incumbent union on the grounds that it no longer holds majority status. In these cases, the employer must be able to show through objective evidence that a majority interest in the union no longer exists. Employers have been able to do this by showing that only a few employees are having their dues deducted through a "checkoff" system, a strike was called and few employees participated, and/or employees on their own signed a petition denouncing their union membership.[93]

From 1951 to 2001, an employer could lawfully withdraw recognition from an incumbent union if it could show that the union no longer had the support of a majority of the bargaining unit or had a good-faith doubt, based on objective evidence, of the union's majority status. The Board has indicated that it is "entirely appropriate" to place the burden of proof on the employer to show that there is an actual loss of majority support for the union. Another option was for an employer to petition for a Board-conducted representation election. In 2001, the NLRB changed its policy. Where there have been no unfair labor practices that tended to undermine the employees' support for the union, loss of majority now is the sole legal basis for withdrawing recognition from an incumbent union. The Board eliminated the "good-faith" requirement and now provides for the employer to seek a representation election if the employer can show a "reasonable uncertainty" that a majority of employees support the union. The logical conclusion is that employers should not be allowed to withdraw recognition of the union short of a representation election.[94]

SUMMARY

This chapter provides insights into reasons unions are formed. It discusses the most important theories and explanations ranging from alienation and class consciousness to the employees' backgrounds and personal desires. The role of a union is to fulfill employees' perceived needs and answer job-related concerns. Unionization efforts progress from first contacts with employees to signing the authorization cards, petition for election, hearings, determination of the appropriate bargaining unit, and the eventual representation election. Within this framework numerous rules, regulations, and legal requirements govern the union certification process. The procedures by which employees can be formed into unions through voluntary recognition, NLRB directives, and secret-ballot elections are explained.

Recently, unions have launched new strategies to organize nonunion employees. The AFL-CIO has taken the lead with the introduction of several programs under its auspices. Finally, in those cases where the union is judged by employees as not representing their interests, a decertification procedure is available through the election process. Generally, only a few employees and only small bargaining units have been involved in decertification elections.

KEY TERMS

alienation theory
scarcity consciousness theory
union instrumentality

contract bar doctrine
totality of conduct doctrine
union salting

Discussion Questions

1. Refer to the reasons why employees become members of unions to assess the means used by union organizers to meet these needs.

2. Select an organization with which you are familiar, and determine the number of bargaining units that would be appropriate for its structure.

3. Explain the contract bar doctrine. How would it influence the negotiation of the first labor agreement?

4. Discuss the shifting position of the NLRB regarding representation election campaigning. Appraise each position.

5. Prescribe a "do" and "don't" list for supervisors involved in unionization campaigns so that they will not commit any unfair labor practices.

6. Why do you believe employers are becoming more interested in decertification elections?

7. Explain the following statement: "It is not the union that organizes the employees; it is management."

8. What would be a good response from a union organizer for each statement in the "Labor Relations in Action" box on page 211?

9. What new strategies have unions used to counter employer efforts to maintain nonunion status? Appraise the effectiveness of these strategies.

Exploring the Web

Salting

1. Definition. What Is Salting?   Read the definition published by the Industrial Workers of the World from a union's point of view.

http://www.iww.org/organize/workplace/salt.shtml

The Associated Builders and Contractors, a national trade association, provides an overview of salting issues that discusses abuse, pros and cons, current legislation, and hiring practices.

http://www.abc.org/documents/saltingsolutions.pdf

2. Salting and the Courts   A major Supreme Court case from Cornell's law page. *National Labor Relations Board* v. *Town & Country Electric, Inc.,* and *Ameristaff Personnel Contractors, Ltd.,* 516 U.S. 85 (1995).

http://supct.law.cornell.edu/supct/html/94-947.ZS.html

Michael Ballot is a professor at the Eberhardt School of Business, University of the Pacific, Stockton, California.

http://law.wustl.edu/WULQ/81-1/p201%20Howlett.pdf

3. Salting and Congress   Locate the text of a bill, introduced in the U.S. House of Representatives in April 2003, that would "amend the National Labor Relations Act to protect employers rights." What does the bill say about "salting"? What is the current status of the bill? Locate references to this bill in the Congressional Record.

http://thomas.loc.gov

Go to the Web site for the House Committee on Education and the Workforce. Here you can search for testimony and statements from Committee hearings from the 106th Congress. Use the search block to search for "salting" and locate statements by witnesses who provided testimony for and against the practice of salting.

http://edworkforce.house.gov

4. Business and Trade Publications Online   Kelly Russell, "Salting the workplace: union organizers aiming to put contractors out of business? Companies see themselves as targets of lawsuits, unfair labor practices complaints," *Mississippi Business Journal*, June 24, 1996.

http://msbusiness.com/archives/18v26n/Cover/10508.php

Search the American City Business Journal's Web site for articles on salting. Change the date block to "All issues." Free registration is required to view articles.

http://www.bizjournals.com

Try to find other articles from business publications on the Web. Remember to be aware of the publishing reputation of the source and to investigate the authors' credentials before you cite the source in a paper or project.

5. Union Organizing Activities.   See the AFL-CIO site to learn about the Organizing Institute and Union Summer Program, which involves students and others.

http://www.aflcio.org/aboutunions/oi/

REFERENCES

1. Kai Erikson, "On Work and Alienation," *American Sociological Review* 51 (February 1986), p. 2. For examples of this situation, see Michael Hanagan and Charles Stephenson, *Confrontation, Class Consciousness, and the Labor Process* (New York: Greenwood Press, 1986).

2. Clinton S. Golden and Harold Ruttenberg, "Motives for Union Membership," in *Unions, Management, and the Public*, eds. E. Wight Bakke, Clark Kerr, and Charles W. Anrod (New York: Harcourt, Brace, 1948), p. 49.

3. M.D. Dunnette and W.K. Kirchner, *Psychology Applied to Industry* (New York: Appleton-Century-Crofts, 1965), pp. 199–200; and Henry S. Farber and Daniel H. Saks, "Why Workers Want Unions: The Role of Relative Wages and Job Characteristics" (Working Paper, Cambridge, Mass.: M.I.T., 1978), pp. 27–28. See also W. Clay Hamner and Frank J. Smith, "Work Attitudes as Predictors of Unionization Activity," *Journal of Applied Psychology* 63 (1978), p. 415; William J. Bigoness, "Correlates of Faculty Attitudes Toward Collective Bargaining," *Journal of Applied Psychology* 63 (1978), pp. 228–233; Chester A. Schreisheim, "Job Satisfaction, Attitudes toward Unions, and Voting in a Union Representation Election," *Journal of Applied Psychology* 63 (1978), pp. 548–552; J. G. Getman, S. B. Goldberg, and J. B. Herman, *Union Representation Elections: Law and Reality* (New York:

Russel Sage Foundation, 1976); Edward L. Harrison, "Employee Satisfaction and Voting Behavior in Union Representation Elections," In *Toward Renewal of Management Thought and Practices,* eds. Dennis F. Ray and Thad B. Green (State College, Miss.: Southern Management Association, Mississippi State University, 1978), p. 169.

4. Selig Perlman, *A Theory of the Labor Movement* (1928; reprinted New York: Augustus M. Kelley, 1968), p. 242.

5. Roger D. Weikle, Hoyt N. Wheeler, and John A. McClendon, "A Comprehensive Case Study of Union Organizing Success and Failure: Implications for Practical Strategy," *Organizing to Win,* ed. Kate Bronfenbrenner et al. (Ithaca, N.Y.: Cornell University Press, 1999), pp. 199–203.

6. Hoyt N. Wheeler and John A. McClendon, "The Individual Decision to Unionize," in *The State of the Unions,* ed. George Strauss, Daniel G. Gallagher, and Jack Fiorito (Madison, Wis.: IRRA, 1991), pp. 65–67.

7. Joel Seidman, Jack London, and Bernard Karsh, "Why Workers Join Unions," *Annals of the American Academy of Political and Social Sciences* 274 (March 1951), pp. 775–784.

8. E. Wight Bakke, "Why Workers Join Unions," *Personnel* 22 (July 1947), p. 3.

9. J.G. Getman, S.B. Goldberg, and J.B. Herman, *Union Representation Elections: Law and Reality* (New York: Russel Sage Foundation, 1976). See also Henry S. Farber and Daniel H. Saks, "Why Workers Want Unions: The Role of Relative Wages and Job Characteristics," *Journal of Political Economy* 88 (April 1980), pp. 349–369; and Jack Fiorito and Charles R. Greer, "Gender Differences in Union Membership, Preferences and Beliefs," *Journal of Labor Research* (Spring 1986), pp. 145–164.

10. Farber, *Why Workers;* and Stephen M. Hills, "The Attitudes of Union and Nonunion Male Workers toward Union Representation," *Industrial and Labor Relations Review* (January 1985), pp. 179–194.

11. Hoyt N. Wheeler and John A. McClendon, "The Individual Decision to Unionize," pp. 64–67.

12. J.M. Brett and T.J. Hammer, "Organizational Behavior and Industrial Relations," in *Industrial Relations Research in the 1970s: Review and Appraisal,* eds. T. A. Kochan, et al. (Madison, Wis.: Industrial Relations Research Association, 1982), pp. 245–251.

13. Jeanette A. Davy and Frank Shipper, "Voter Behavior in Union Certification Elections: A Longitudinal Study," *Academy of Management Journal* 36 (February 1993), pp. 187–199.

14. Satish P. Deshpande and Chockalingam Viswervaran, "Predictors of Unionization: The Role of Specific Beliefs, General Beliefs, and Normative Pressures," *Labor Studies Journal* 19 (Fall 1994), pp. 68–69.

15. Satish P. Deshpande and Jack Fiorito, "Specific and General Beliefs in Union Voting Models," *Academy of Management Journal* 32 (December 1989), pp. 883–895.

16. Thomas A. DeCottis and Jean-Yves Le Lovarn, "A Predictive Study of Voting Behavior in a Representation Election Using Union Instrumentality and Work Perceptions," *Organizational Behavior and Human Performance* 27 (February 1981), pp. 103–118. Also see Stuart A. Youngblood, Angelo S. DeNisi, Julie L. Molleston, and William H. Mobley, "The Impact of Work Environment, Instrumentality Beliefs, Perceived Labor Union Image, and Subjectivity Norms on Union Voting Intentions," *Academy of Management Journal* 27 (December 1984), pp. 576–590; Masoud Hemmasi and Lee A. Graf, "Determinants of Faculty Voting Behavior in Union Representation Elections: A Multivariate Model," *Journal of Management* 19 (November 1, 1995), pp. 13–32.

17. Stuart A. Youngblood, William H. Mobley, and Angelo S. DeNisi, "Attitudes, Perceptions, and Intentions to Vote in a Union Certification Election: An Empirical Investigation," in *Proceedings of the Thirty-Fourth Annual Meeting: Industrial Relations Research Association,* ed. B.D. Dennis (Madison, Wis.: Industrial Relations Research Association, 1982), pp. 244–253; Tom Langford, "Involvement with Unions, Union Belief Perspectives, and Desires for Union Membership," *Journal of La-*

bor Research 15 (Summer 1994), pp. 257–270.

18. Edward L. Harrison, Douglas Johnson, and Frank M. Rachel, "The Role of the Supervisor in Representation Elections," *Personnel Administration* 26 (September 1981), pp. 69–70.

19. Dorothy Sue Cobble, "Union Strategies for Organizing and Representing the New Service Workforce," in *Proceedings of the 43rd Annual Meeting of the Industrial Relations Research Association* (Madison, Wis.: IRRA, 1991), p. 76.

20. David M. Rabban, "Is Unionism Compatible with Professionalism?" *Industrial and Labor Relations Review* 45 (October 1991), pp. 97–112.

21. Michael E. Gordon and Angelo S. DeNisi, "A Re-examination of the Relationship between Union Membership and Job Satisfaction," *Industrial and Labor Relations Review* 48 (January 1995), p. 234.

22. John J. Hoover, "Union Organization Attempts: Management's Response," *Personnel Journal* 61 (March 1982), pp. 214–215.

23. Thomas F. Reed, "Do Union Organizers Matter? Individual Differences, Campaign Practices, and Representation Election Outcomes," *Industrial and Labor Relations Review* 43 (October 1989), pp. 102–117.

24. Thomas F. Reed, "Profiles of Union Organizers from Manufacturing and Service Unions," *Journal of Labor Research* 11 (Winter 1990), pp. 73–80.

25. Charles McDonald, "U.S. Union Membership in Future Decades: A Trade Unionist's Perspective," *Industrial Relations* 31 (Winter 1992), pp. 19–21.

26. James A. Craft and Marian M. Extejt, "New Strategies in Union Organizing," *Working Paper Series* (Pittsburgh, Penn.: University of Pittsburgh, 1982), p. 304.

27. Kate Bronfenbrenner, "The Role of Union Strategies in NLRB Elections," *Industrial and Labor Relations Review* 50 (January 1997), pp. 195–211.

28. Julius G. Getman, "Ruminations on Union Organizing in the Private Sector," *The University of Chicago Law Review* 53 (Winter 1986), p. 59.

29. Richard B. Peterson, Thomas W. Lee, and Barbara Finnegan, "Strategies and Tactics in Union Organizing Campaigns," *Industrial Relations* 31 (Spring 1992), pp. 370–374.

30. John J. Lawler and Robin West, "Impact of Union-Avoidance Strategy in Representation Elections," *Industrial Relations* 24 (Fall 1985), pp. 406–420.

31. Satish P. Deshpande and Chockalingam Viswervaran, "Predictors of Unionization: The Role of Specific Beliefs, General Beliefs, and Normative Pressures," *Labor Studies Journal* 19 (Fall 1994), pp. 68–69.

32. Donna Sockell, "Contemporary Challenges of Labor Law," in *Proceedings of the Fortieth Annual Meeting of the Industrial Relations Research Association*, ed. Barbara D. Dennis (Madison, Wis.: Industrial Relations Research Association, 1988), pp. 85–90.

33. *United Autoworkers v. Secretary of Labor*, 678 F. Supp. 4 (D.C., 1988).

34. Bruce Kaufman and Paula E. Stephan, "The Role of Management Attorneys in Union Organizing Campaigns," *Journal of Labor Research* 16 (Fall 1995), pp. 439–454.

35. William N. Cooke, "The Rising Toll of Discrimination against Union Activists," *Industrial Relations* 24 (Fall 1985), p. 437.

36. "Adherence to Labor Laws Not in Management's Interests, Says Ex-NLRB Staff Member," *Report on Union Busters, RUB Sheet* (Washington, D.C.: AFL-CIO, March/April, 1990), p. 1.

37. Adrienne E. Eaton and Jill Kriesky, "Union Organizing Under Neutrality and Card Check Agreements," *Industrial and Labor Relations Review* 55 (October 2001), pp. 42–57.

38. Adrienne E. Eaton and Jill Kriesky, "No More Stacked Deck: Evaluating the Case Against Card-Check Union Recognition, *Perspectives on Work* 7, no. 2 (2003), pp. 19–21.

39. *NLRB v. Gissel Packing Co.* 385 U.S. 575 (1969). An authorization card signifies that the employee desires to be represented by the union in collective bargaining. The employee thereby authorizes the union to represent him with his employer. The signed card may be

used later by the union as proof of majority representation, as support to demand recognition, and as evidence that there is "substantial interest" among the bargaining unit to support a petition to the NLRB for representation election. Schlossberg and Sherman, *Organizing and the Law*, p. 50.

40. Peter J. Leff, "Failing to Give the Board Its Due: The Lack of Deference Afforded by the Appellate Courts in *Gissel* Bargaining Order Cases," *The Labor Lawyer* 79 (2002), pp. 109–111.

41. Gil A. Abramson, "The Uncertain Fate of *Gissel* Bargaining Orders in the Circuit Courts of Appeal," *The Labor Lawyer* 18 (2002), pp. 121–136.

42. Harry E. Graham and Karen N. Neilsen, "Union Representation Elections: A View From the Heart of It All," *Labor Law Journal* 42 (July 1991), pp. 438–441; William E. Fulmer, "Step by Step through a Union Campaign," *Harvard Business Review* 59 (July–August 1981), pp. 94–95; Clyde Scott, Kim Hester, and Edwin Arnold, "Employer-Initiated Elections, 1968–1992," *Journal of Labor Research* 18 (Spring 1997), pp. 315–331.

43. David R. Stephens and Paul R. Timm. "A Comparison of Campaign Techniques in Contested Faculty Elections: An Analysis of the Florida Experience," *Journal of Collective Negotiations in the Public Sector* 7 (1978), pp. 167–177.

44. Paula B. Voos, "Does It Pay to Organize? The Cost to Unions," *Monthly Labor Review* 107 (June 1984), pp. 43–44.

45. Paula Voos, "Union Organizing: Costs and Benefits," *Industrial and Labor Relations Review* 36 (July 1983), pp. 576–580. Also see Paula Voos, "Trends in Union Organizing Expenditures, 1953–1977," *Industrial and Labor Relations Review* 38 (October 1984), pp. 52–66.

46. Rebecca S. Demsetz, "Voting Behavior in Union Representation Elections: The Influence of Skill Homogeneity and Skill," *Industrial and Labor Relations Review* 47 (October 1993), pp. 99–113.

47. Robert Sebris, Jr., and Robert D. McDonald, "Bargaining Unit Determination Case Trends of the NLRB," *Labor Law Journal* 37 (June 1986), pp. 378–382.

48. Robert J. Alberts, "The Appropriate Bargaining Unit, Geographic Proximity, and The 'Nearest Neighbor': An Alternative Analysis," *Labor Law Journal* 41 (July 1990), pp. 424–426.

49. Clyde Scott and Nicholas A. Beadles II, "Unit Placement Decisions in Acute-Care Hospitals," *Labor Law Journal* 44 (March 1993), pp. 143–152; Satish P. Deshpande and David J. Flanagan, "Union Certification Elections in Hospitals," *Labor Studies Journal* 21 (Fall 1996), pp. 56–71.

50. Kenneth R. Dolin and Ross H. Friedman, "Recent Developments and the Likely Effect of Changes at the National Labor Relations Board," *Labor Law Journal* 54, no. 1 (2003) p. 15.

51. *Excelsior Underwear, Inc.*, 156 NLRB 1236 (1966).

52. Richard N. Block and Myron Roomkin, "Determinants of Voter Participation in Union Certification Elections," *Monthly Labor Review* 105 (April 1982), pp. 45–47.

53. Myron Roomkin and Richard N. Block, "Case Processing Time and the Outcome of Representation Elections: Some Empirical Evidence," *University of Illinois Law Review* 1981, reprinted in *Oversight Hearings on the Subject "Has Labor Law Failed?"* (Washington, D.C.: Committee on Education and Labor, 1984), pp. 844–845.

54. Marcus H. Sandver and Herbert G. Heneman III, "Union Growth through the Election Process," *Industrial Relations* 20 (Winter 1981), pp. 109–115.

55. William N. Cooke, "Determinants of the Outcomes of Union Certification Elections," *Industrial and Labor Relations Review* 36 (April 1983), pp. 402–414.

56. Cheryl L. Maranto and Jack Fiorito, "The Effect of Union Characteristics on the Outcome of the NLRB Elections," *Industrial and Labor Relations Review* 40 (January 1987), pp. 225–238.

57. Victor G. Devinatz and Daniel P. Rich, "Representation Type and Union Success in Certification Elections," *Journal of Labor Research* 15 (Winter 1995), pp. 85–92.

58. Dolin and Friedman, "Recent Developments and the Likely Effect of Changes

at the National Labor Relations Board," p. 13.

59. Marcus Hart Sandver and Kathryn J. Ready, "Trends in and Determinants of Outcomes in Multi-Union Certification Elections," *Journal of Labor Research* 19 (Winter 1998), pp. 164–171.

60. "Number of Elections Up Slightly in 2002; Unions' Win Rate Continues to Edge Up," *Daily Labor Report*, (June 10, 2003), pp. C1–C5; updated by "Fewer Representation Elections Held in First Half of 2003 than in Prior Year," *Daily Labor Report* (December 24, 2003), p. C-1.

61. Henry S. Farber, "Union Success in Representation Election: Why Does Unit Size Matter?" *Industrial and Labor Relations Review* 54 (January 2001), pp. 329–345.

62. Study Calls for Labor Law Reform to Aid Unions Seeking First Contracts," *Daily Labor Report*, July 10, 1985, p. A-10.

63. William N. Cooke, "The Failure to Negotiate First Contracts: Determinants and Policy Implications," *Industrial and Labor Relations Review* 38 (January 1985), pp. 163–178.

64. Karen E. Boroff, "Unfair Labor Practice Filings in Organizing Elections: New Data and Analysis," *Labor Law Journal* 47 (November 1997), pp. 655–661.

65. *Shopping Kart Food Market*, 94 LRRM 1705 (1977); Julius G. Getman, Stephen B. Goldberg, and Jeanne B. Herman, *Union Representation Elections: Law and Reality* (New York: Russell Sage Foundation, 1976); and Neal Orkin and Mara Landberg, "Election Campaign Propaganda: Board Policy Then and Now," *Labor Law Journal* 46 (July 1995), pp. 440–446.

66. William T. Dickens, "The Effect of Company Campaigns on Certification Elections: Law and Reality Once Again," *Industrial and Labor Relations Review* 36 (July 1983), pp. 574–576.

67. Richard N. Block, Benjamin W. Wolkinson, and James W. Kuhn, "Some Are More Equal Than Others: The Relative Status of Employers, Unions and Employees in the Law of Union Organizing," *Industrial Relations Law Journal* 10, no. 2 (1989), p. 220.

68. David P. Brenskelle, "Questioning Employees Concerning Union Sentiment Remains a Risky Proposition," *Employee Relations Law Journal* 13 (Summer 1987), pp. 141–147.

69. *Republican Aviation Corp.* v. *NLRB*, 324 U.S. 793 (1945).

70. Justices Twice Back Right to Distribute Union Literature on Company Property," *The Wall Street Journal*, June 23, 1978, p. 6; Peter G. Kilgore, "No-Solicitation/No-Distribution Rules: The Word Battle of 'Time' Versus 'Hours' Continues." *Labor Law Journal* 35 (November 1984), pp. 671–672.

71. *Beth Israel* v. *NLRB*, 46 U.S.L.W. 4765 (June 22, 1978).

72. *Eastex, Inc.* v. *NLRB*, 46 U.S.L.W. 4783 (June 22, 1978).

73. NLRB Member Oviatt Says *Lechmere* Creates Presumption Against Union Access," *Daily Labor Report*, February 3, 1992, p. A-5; "Employers and Union Foresee More Costly Organizing Tactics," *Daily Labor Report*, January 29, 1992, p. A-15; and "*Lechmere* Decision Makes Organizing More Difficult for Unions, NLRB Attorney Says," *Daily Labor Report*, June 5, 1992, p. A-1.

74. Karen E. Boroff, "Shopping for Access after *Lechmere*," *Labor Law Journal* 46 (June 1995), pp. 366–370; Eileen P. Kelly, Owen Seaquest, Amy Oakes, and Lawrence S. Clark, "*NLRB* v. *Lechmere*: Union Quest for Access," *Journal of Labor Research* 15 (Spring 1994), pp. 155–167.

75. Kevin Conlon and Catherine Voight, "Distinguishing *Lechmere*: Union Organizers' Access to Employers' Property," *Labor Law Journal* 44 (August 1993), pp. 496–501.

76. Joseph A. Pichler and H. Gordon Fitch, "And Women Must Weep: The NLRB as Film Critic," *Industrial and Labor Relations Review* 28 (April 1975), pp. 395–410.

77. Dolin and Friedman, "Recent Developments and the Likely Effect of Changes at the National Labor Relations Board," p. 18.

78. Scott D. Rechtschaffen, "The New Strategy of Union Organizing," *HR Focus*, June 1998, p. 3.

79. Oscar Suris and Robert Rose, "UAW is Boosting Efforts to Organize Workers at Major Auto Parts Suppliers," *The Wall Street Journal*, June 28, 1996, p. A2.

80. Robert L. Rose, "UAW's Own Disorganization Hinders Drive to Organize," *The Wall Street Journal*, November 1, 1996, p. B4.

81. Steven Greenhouse, "Labor Campaign Highlights Workers' Right to Unionize," *New York Times*, June 25, 1998, p. A12.

82. Steven Greenhouse, "Labor Rallies in Support of Bill to Back the Right to Join Unions," *New York Times*, December 11, 2003, p. A25.

83. Steven Greenhouse, "AFL-CIO Puts Recruiting At Top of Its Agenda," *New York Times*, February 17, 1997, p. 8.

84. James B. Dworkin and Marian Extejt, "Why Workers Decertify Their Unions: A Preliminary Investigation," paper presented at the Annual Meeting of the Academy of Management, August 1979.

85. Robert W. Schupp, "When Is a Union Not a Union? Good Faith Doubt and Its Limitations in Collective Bargaining," *Labor Law Journal* 48 (June 1997), pp. 369–370.

86. Clyde Scott, Kim Hester, and Edwin Arnold, "Decertification Elections: An Analysis of Recent Activity," *Labor Law Journal* 46 (February 1995), pp. 67–74.

87. David M. Savino and Nealia S. Bruning, "Decertification Strategies and Tactics: Management and Union Perspectives," *Labor Law Journal* 43 (April 1992), pp. 201–208.

88. William A. Krupman and Gregory I. Rasin, "Decertification: Removing the Shroud," *Labor Law Journal* 30 (April 1979), pp. 234–235.

89. Trevor Bain, Clyde Scott, and Edwin Arnold, "Deauthorization Elections: An Early Warning Signal to Decertification?" *Labor Law Journal* 39 (July 1988), pp. 432–436.

90. "Number of Elections Up Slightly in 2002," pp. C-1–C-5.

91. David Meyer and Trevor Bain, "Union Decertification Election Outcomes: Bargaining-Unit Characteristics and Union Resources," *Journal of Labor Research* 15 (Spring 1994), pp. 117–136.

92. *Tawas Tube Production, Inc.* 151 NLRB 9 (1965).

93. Edwin Arnold, Clyde Scott, and John Rasp, "The Determinants of Incumbent Union Victory in Raid Elections," *Labor Law Journal* 43 (April 1992), pp. 221–228; Clyde Scott and Edwin Arnold, "Raid Elections: An Analysis of Employer Campaigns," *Labor Law Journal* 41 (September 1990), pp. 641–648. Also see Robert W. Schupp, "When Is a Union Not a Union? Good Faith Doubt by An Employer," *Labor Law Journal* 42 (June 1991), pp. 357–364.

94. Martha B. Perdrick, "Withdrawal of Recognition: NLRB Toughens, Loosens Standards," *Labor Law Journal* 52 (Fall 2001), pp. 166–169.

The T-Shirt Offer and Picnic Photographs

On the day before the Union election, the Union hosted a free picnic luncheon for employees during the first and second shifts' meal breaks in a parking lot adjacent to the Young Skin's plant. At the picnic, the Union took 88 snapshots. During the luncheon, union representatives distributed "Union Yes" T-shirts carrying the slogan, "The Best Things in Life Are Negotiable. Union Yes." Between "Union" and "Yes" was a square containing a check mark. To receive a T-shirt, employees were required to sign a pro-union petition that was to be used as a hand-bill on election day, headed "We Are Voting Yes on August 2nd!" and stating that the under-signed employees agreed to openly support the Union and asked their co-workers to join them.

The Company contended that the distribution of T-shirts costing $4 to $5 each repre-sented an unlawful grant of benefit that the Union used to induce employees to sign the pro-Union petition by requiring signing as a condition of receiving a T-shirt. The Company com-pared the T-shirt offer to a union's offer to waive union initiation fees contingent on an employee's signing a union authorization card. The Supreme Court found such a fee waiver unlawful in a previous case, because it "allow[ed] the Union to buy endorsements and paint a false portrait of employee support during its election campaign." The Company said the mone-tary value of the T-shirts was irrelevant, noting that the waived initiation fee in the Supreme Court case was a "nominal" $10.

The Union stated that it was clear to all concerned that the T-shirts were inexpensive and that their free distribution would not interfere with employee free choice. It is a considerable leap to conclude that the offer of these "Union Yes" T-shirts contingent on employees' signing a pro-union petition was an inducement tantamount to buying endorsements.

The Supreme Court in the previous case ruled that all employees, regardless of their views on unions, had an economic interest in obtaining the fee waiver that was offered as an induce-ment to sign union authorization cards. The inducement here—the "Union Yes" T-shirt—however, would reasonably be desirable only to employees who favored the Union and wanted to proclaim their pro-Union view. Thus, the Union's requiring employees to sign a pro-union petition to obtain a pro-union T-shirt would not reasonably induce nonsupporters to sign the petition and thereby allow the Union to paint a false portrait of employee support.

Even if the T-shirts might be desirable to nonsupporters, the Union in that event had a justifiable interest in trying to ensure that T-shirts were distributed only to employees who would wear them as campaign paraphernalia in support of the Union. Requiring employees de-siring T-shirts to sign a pro-Union petition was a reasonable means for the Union to try to ac-complish this objective.

The Company also contended that the Union created an atmosphere of fear and coercion by photographing employees at the picnic luncheon. In many of the photographs, employees posed for the camera, sometimes displaying their Union T-shirts. The photographs were taken for the purpose of memorializing the chicken meal and perhaps to publish in a Union newspa-per. Two employees later said they were "concerned" or "felt funny" about their pictures being taken.

The Company contended that the employees who were photographed might well have thought that their responses to the Union campaign activity were being recorded for the pur-pose of future retaliation. The Union responded that although photographing some activities might suggest retaliatory purpose, the Union photographed employees enjoying a picnic, which each employee voluntarily chose to attend. When a company security guard attending the picnic asked why a union representative was taking photographs, the Union representative stated, "You are all going to make the front page of *USA Today*," and "We want to remember this fun-filled memory." Union representatives stated that the photographs were taken for submission to the Union's newspaper. Copies of the photographs were later given to employees at a party celebrating the Union's victory in the election (217 in favor of the Union, 200 against it, and 16 challenged ballots). The Company seeks to overturn the election results based on its objections to the Union's T-shirt distribution and the photographing of employees at the Union picnic.

QUESTIONS

1. Must illegal conduct occur to overturn the results of a union representation election?
2. Compare the present case to the following ones:

   - *NLRB v. Savair Mfg. Co.*, 414 U.S. 270 (1973); 84 LRRM 2929 (1973)
   - *Pepsi Cola Bottling Co.*, 289 NLRB 736 (1988); 128 LRRM 1275 (1988)
   - *Mike Yurosek & Sons, Inc.*, 292 NLRB 1074 (1989); 130 LRRM 1308 (1989)

3. Did the Union interfere with the outcome of the election by offering the T-shirts? Why or why not?
4. Did the Union interfere with the outcome of the election by taking the photographs at the picnic? Why or why not?

The Loudspeaker Campaign Tactic

Acoustical Enterprises (the Employer) manufactures commercial acoustic soundproofing material at a plant in Echo, South Dakota. On December 20 the Union filed a petition with the NLRB seeking certification as the exclusive bargaining representative of Acoustical production and maintenance employees. An election was set for 2:00 P.M. on February 18.

As the election approached, the main issue became the wages and benefits received by the nonunion employees at the Echo plant versus those received by unionized employees at a Bronx, New York, plant owned by the Employer. Acoustical made divergent statements about the extent of any difference between the two plants, and the election rhetoric became quite heated. In particular, the Union repeatedly made disparaging remarks about Acoustical's main spokesperson, Fran Orange. On the day before and on election day, the Union parked a car mounted with a loudspeaker system 25 to 30 yards from the Acoustical plant's main entrance. On both days, the Union broadcast music and campaign messages focusing on wage and benefit issues and on Ms. Orange from approximately 6:50 A.M. to 7:05 A.M. and from just before 12:00 noon to 12:35 P.M. Also, on February 17 the Union broadcast from 3:25 P.M. to 3:40 P.M. and just before and after 5:30 P.M. These broadcasts were intentionally made to coincide with the beginning and ending of the day shift (7:00 A.M.–3:30 P.M.) and with lunch breaks (12:00–12:30 P.M.) at the plant. The February 17, 5:30 P.M. broadcast coincided with the end of an overtime day shift.

The loudspeaker system had a range of well over 100 yards, and the Union's messages were clearly heard on the plant grounds. Because of industrial noise, however, the broadcasts were inaudible inside plant buildings when machinery was in use. However, at the lunch break, when no machinery was in use and when employees were outside the plant buildings, the broadcasts were more easily heard. Employees were not free to leave the plant area during their lunch break.

The election was held as scheduled, and the Union won by an eighty-one to seventy-one vote. The Employer filed election objections, including one over the Union's sound car broadcasts. The Employer contended that the broadcasts violated the long-standing rule of *Peerless Plywood Co.*, 107 NLRB 427 (1953), which prohibits speeches by either the Union or the Employer to massed assemblies of employees, on company time, within 24 hours of an election.

On March 17 the Union requested Acoustical to bargain. The Employer refused. On April 11 the Union filed an unfair labor practice charge under Section 8(a)(1), (5) of the LMRA. The Employer admitted refusing to bargain but contended that the Union had been improperly certified and therefore no legal duty to bargain could be imposed.

QUESTIONS

1. Review the captive-audience, 24-hour rule. Should the rule apply in this case, although the Union was not on the Employer's property and had no legal authority to require employees who were on the employer's property to listen to the Union's broadcasts?

2. Why does the Employer typically have a significant advantage over a Union in conveying its message during a representation election campaign?

3. Did the Union's broadcast violate the captive-audience rule? If so, should the results of the election be overturned and a rerun election scheduled? Why or why not?

A Refusal to Work Overtime

This nonunion company manufactures transparent plastic sheets and has 100 employees with annual sales of $5 million. All employees were told when initially hired that overtime work would be expected to be performed whenever it was deemed necessary by management. None of the six employees making up the casting department had ever refused to perform a previous overtime work assignment.

During the 3 weeks before April 5, the employees in the casting department had been required to work overtime often. Such overtime work was necessary because of the volume of customer orders. Some employees had begun complaining about the increasing regularity of overtime work assignments, which they viewed as "excessive." Job duties in the casting department required employees to regularly lift heavy glass molds used in making plastic sheets. On some days during this 3-week period, one or two employees in the department had been absent from work, thereby forcing the other employees to pick up the slack.

On April 5 the department was short one experienced employee. Shortly after 1 P.M. the casting department employees were informed by Department Manager Susan Post that overtime would be required that day to finish the backlog of customer orders. On this particular day, the variety and size of molds being used required an extraordinary amount of heavy lifting by the employees in the department. Around 2 P.M. that day, the five employees met during their afternoon break and decided that they would not work overtime that evening.

At 3:45 P.M., employee Jones began preparing to shut down his casting machine by 4 P.M. (the end of the regularly scheduled work shift), as did the other four employees. Department Manager Post observed what was happening and approached employee Jones to ask him why he was shutting down his machine. Jones replied that he and the other employees had decided not to work overtime that day. Jones went on to explain that the employees felt physically tired from all of the overtime work performed during the past several weeks and the work performed that day and were concerned that an employee might drop a heavy casting mold, injuring themselves or a co-worker. Manager Post requested that the employees continue to run their machines until 4 P.M., and the employees agreed to do so.

Manager Post left the department and returned approximately 5 minutes later with the company president. Manager Post then interviewed each employee separately, asking if he intended to work overtime that night. Each employee responded that he did not intend to work overtime that night. Manager Post then informed each employee that if he did not work overtime that night, the employee would be suspended without pay for 2 days. The five employees left the plant at 4 P.M. and did not return to the job until April 8, following their 2-day suspension. Since returning, the employees have not refused any other overtime assignments. Employee Jones, acting on behalf of all five employees, filed an unfair labor practice charge with the NLRB. Jones charged that the employees' refusal to work overtime was a concerted action protected by the LMRA, and thus, the employer's 2-day suspension without pay was illegal.

QUESTIONS

1. What are some alternative actions management should have considered in deciding how to manage this incident? Discuss the pros and cons of these alternative actions.

2. Did the 2-day suspension without pay of the five casting department employees for refusing to work overtime violate the LMRA as amended? If so, what should be the appropriate remedy?

Bulletin Board Use

The company (Employer) operates a merchandise catalog distribution center in Wichita, Kansas, employing 1,000 workers. The Union began an organizing campaign among distribution center employees. For many years the Company has published an employee handbook, which contained the following bulletin board policy:

> Bulletin boards are located throughout the Center [distribution center], generally near time clocks. Company announcements such as policy changes, holiday schedules and Company news of general interest are posted on these boards. Personal postings are not permitted.

Employees who supported the Union placed printed material on the bulletin boards advertising upcoming union meetings and soliciting union support. On discovery, managers removed the union material from the bulletin boards. The Union subsequently filed an unfair labor practice charge alleging the Company's removal of the union materials from the bulletin board represented unlawful interference with employees' right to solicit for the purpose of organizing a union under the LMRA.

The Employer maintained that managers were simply enforcing a nondiscriminatory policy barring all solicitation materials from Company bulletin boards that were not approved by the Company. The Employer noted that management had given employees permission to post on bulletin boards a company-approved newsletter that did include a section advertising employee personal items for sale (e.g., car, television set, golf clubs). Certain other company-sponsored solicitations for the United Way and March of Dimes charities had also previously been approved for posting on company bulletin boards.

Several employees testified that other employee communications had also been posted on several company bulletin boards in the past, such as thank-you notes, party announcements, Christmas cards, a solicitation for maid service, and donation request when an employee was hospitalized or died. Such unapproved announcements were often posted for several weeks before being removed from bulletin boards. The employer responded that items such as those mentioned by the employees who testified were, for the most part, connected to company-sponsored events or charities.

QUESTIONS

1. Is an employer required to have bulletin boards at the workplace?
2. If an employer did not provide bulletin boards at the workplace, would employees have a right to provide and mount their own bulletin boards?
3. If there are company-provided bulletin boards at the workplace, does the employer have a right to restrict the purpose or type of material that can be posted on such boards?
4. In this case, did the Employer unlawfully deny union supporters access to use company bulletin boards for union solicitation purposes? Explain your reasoning.

Nonemployee Union Solicitation Activity

In October the Union began an organizing drive involving nursing personnel employed at the Medco Hospital (the Employer). In November, Medco's management revised a portion of the existing no-solicitation and distribution policy to read as follows: "Visitors, patients and other nonemployees may not solicit or distribute literature on any hospital property for any purpose at any time."

The hospital operates a cafeteria that is open to serve employees, patients, and the general public. On December 4, two (nonemployee) union organizers entered the hospital cafeteria accompanied by some off-duty nursing employees. The off-duty nursing employees proceeded to distribute union literature provided to them by the two union organizers. The two union organizers did not personally hand out any union literature or attempt to solicit any employees to sign a union authorization card. The two union organizers did remain seated in the cafeteria for approximately 5 hours and answered questions about the Union initiated by interested employees. Sitting on the table where the two (nonemployee) union organizers were seated was an open box containing union literature.

On December 10 the two union organizers accompanied by several off-duty nursing employees again entered the hospital cafeteria and engaged in the same actions as those previously described as occurring on December 4. After approximately 30 minutes, the human resources (HR) manager for the hospital entered the cafeteria and spoke to the two union organizers. The HR manager informed the two union organizers that they were in violation of the hospital's no-solicitation and distribution rule. The HR manager gave the two union organizers permission to stay for 15 minutes to have a drink or 30 minutes to eat a meal, after which time they would be arrested if they refused to leave. The two union organizers left the hospital cafeteria voluntarily and proceeded to file an unfair labor practice charge alleging the hospital unlawfully barred their access to the hospital cafeteria. There was no evidence to show that the Employer had ever allowed solicitation or distribution activity by nonemployees to occur on its premises in the past.

QUESTIONS

1. Did the Employer unlawfully deny the two nonemployee union organizers access to the hospital's cafeteria? If so, what should be the appropriate remedy?

2. Would the Employer's no-solicitation policy prohibit the two nonemployee union organizers from entering the hospital's property anywhere at anytime?

Atlas Towers: Composition of Bargaining Unit

The Atlas Towers is a 30-story hotel in Atlantic City, New Jersey. The hotel derives approximately 83 percent of its gross revenues from its convention business. It has 1,250 rooms and employs about 832 regular, full-time nonsupervisory employees. The hotel has four restaurants, three cocktail lounges, a nightclub, recreational facilities, 52 meeting rooms, and an exhibition hall.

Because it is mainly a convention hotel, its facilities and organizational structure have been designed specifically for the purpose of serving convention business, and its operations are closely coordinated and functionally integrated. The conventions require each department to cooperate with the others to provide the promised services. Thus, the front office, sales, catering, reservations, food and beverage, and communications employees are involved in selling conventions to prospective customers and in making an effort to ascertain customers' needs during their stay.

Atlas Towers has an extensive internal communications and record-keeping system. This consists of a MICOR computer system, a pneumatic tube system linking the front desk and other parts of the facility, communications (PBX) and food and beverage outlets, a beeper paging system, and a walkie-talkie system. The booking, planning, and execution of conventions require close coordination among all hotel areas. Preconvention meetings are held to review a convention resume that outlines the convention functions and roles of each area. The convention resume is circulated to approximately 40 different departments and contains instructions for each.

General Manager James Ussery sends numerous memoranda to the department heads, assistant department heads, and assistant area managers. These memoranda demonstrate Ussery's close involvement in minor details of the hotel's day-to-day operation and reflect management's highly centralized control. Individual department heads oversee routine operations in their areas but do not establish basic work policies or have final control over department functions.

The hotel's human resources (HR) department establishes uniform personnel policies, including wages and benefits, that apply to all hotel employees except property operations employees, whose terms and conditions of employment have been specified in a collective bargaining agreement. Human resources screens all applicants and refers qualified applicants to the department managers for interviews. The HR director must approve all personnel decisions, including any discipline that supervisors recommend. Hotel employees have an employee cafeteria, employee locker rooms, and a recreation program. Employee training programs have been established throughout the hotel in which employees of different departments participate. Some employees receive cross-training in other departments; for example, some communications employees received training to make them more aware of what goes on in the front office. There is also a "priority one" training program that covers any employee who has face-to-face contact with guests.

The hotel has a uniform transfer policy. The HR department posts openings, and employees from any area may apply. The employee's current supervisor must sign a form, and the HR department must approve the transfer. Numerous transfers have occurred among departments, including approximately 27 transfers in 2 years from housekeeping to other departments. There have also been transfers from the food and beverage and stewards area to housekeeping, and from communications to housekeeping, secretary, front office, and accounting. Other transfers have occurred from food and beverage to sales, front office, and accounting; from office to food and beverage; from housekeeping to the front desk; from greeter to catering; from bellhop stand to food and beverage; from communications to accounting; from room service to secretary; from personnel to catering; from public facilities to security; and from stewards area to bellhop stand.

Employees from different areas have frequent contact with each other. Contacts between accounting personnel and other employees include the following: front office cashiers issue keys to food and beverage employees, restaurant cashiers, housekeeping, engineering, and laundry employees; shipping and receiving employees deal with engineering, food and beverage, laundry, and housekeeping employees in handling goods to be picked up by other departments or delivered; night auditors have contact with restaurant employees when they pick up reports and read registers in the restaurant outlets; accounts payable clerks obtain approvals for payments of invoices from every department; and restaurant cashiers occasionally assist the hostesses or greeters in the dining rooms.

Laundry employees have contact with buspersons, banquet employees, kitchen employees, the storeroom clerk, shipping and receiving, communications, catering, room service, and the bellhop stand. Employees from other departments bring laundry to be cleaned and pick up clean laundry and uniforms.

Housekeeping employees maintain contact with the front desk cashiers through the MICOR system regarding all room status changes. The front desk provides house counts to housekeeping for budgeting and scheduling purposes. Housekeeping employees have contact with food and beverage employees when they clean restaurant outlets and work with public facilities employees in cleaning areas around the meeting rooms.

Food and beverage employees maintain contact with the front office or house count and the pay-in-advance guest list. They have contact with restaurant cashiers and night auditors and work closely with the inventory control office. The convention services department advises food and beverage as to the services each convention requires. Food and beverage employees work with housekeeping employees in setting up VIP rooms.

Communications employees assist cashiers regarding guest telephone charges (using the pneumatic tube system). Operators take restaurant reservations when food and beverage receptionists are not available. Restaurant cashiers call operators to verify guest room numbers, and operators call outlets to locate guests and give out information regarding the hours of the food and beverage outlets. Housekeeping employees call operators if a message light is left on in a vacant room or if a telephone is missing or damaged. Public facilities employees notify operators when a telephone needs to be removed from a meeting room. All departments notify communications when repairs are necessary.

Some interchange of employees between departments occurs, mainly in emergency situations. Accounting employees have worked as bartenders, and credit employees have worked as hostesses. During an ice storm, accounting employees assisted housekeeping. Catering, sales, and accounting employees have worked as bar cashiers. Housekeeping employees sometimes fill in at the laundry and uniform room and also fill in for the restroom attendants. Housekeeping employees have filled in as waitresses or buspersons. They help in shipping and receiving when a large order arrives, and occasionally they substitute for lobby porters (bellhop stand).

The Union had proposed that the appropriate bargaining unit should consist of all full-time and regular part-time housekeeping, laundry, public facility, and exhibit employees as follows:

All full-time and regular part-time housekeeping, laundry, public facility, and exhibit employees employed by the Employer at its Atlantic City facility, including aides, on-call aides,
Continued

247

turn-down aides, attendants, the payroll clerk, dispatchers, night cleaners, stock-room attendant, locker room attendant, drapery attendant, washman, chuteman, laundry attendant, linen runner, seamstress, uniform room attendant, meeting room attendant, banquet houseman and assistant team leaders, excluding office clerical employees, secretaries, property operations employees, front office employees, food and beverage employees, steward employees, room service employees, communication employees, the hostesses, guest greeters, purchasing employees, human resources employees, the tower clerk, marketing and sales employees, accounting employees, security employees, guards and supervisors as defined in the Act.

The Employer proposed a unit consisting of all employees employed at the facility, excluding only property operations department employees, confidential employees, security officers, guards/watchmen, and supervisors as defined in the NLRA.

The regional director of the NLRB had determined the bargaining unit to include the following:

All full-time and regular part-time food and beverage employees, steward employees, room service employees, guest services employees, bellmen, cashiers, and stockroom attendant; excluding office clerical employees, secretaries, property operations employees, communication employees, housekeeping, laundry and public facility and exhibit employees, human resources employees, purchasing employees, the Tower clerk, marketing and sales employees, accounting employees, security employees, guards and supervisors as defined by the Act.

The decision of the regional director has now been appealed to the board in Washington for a decision.

QUESTIONS

1. Explain the importance of the Union's and Employer's position regarding the composition of the appropriate bargaining unit.
2. What criteria does the Board use to determine an appropriate bargaining unit?
3. Considering the views of the Employer and the Union and the decision of the Regional Director, what should the Board decide represents the appropriate unit? Explain your reasoning.

REFERENCES

Arlington Hotel Co., 126 NLRB 400 (1960).

77 Operating Co., 160 NLRB 927 (1966).

Regency Hyatt Hotel, 171 NLRB 1347 (1968).

Holiday Inn, Alton, 270 NLRB 199 (1984).

Holiday Inn, Southwest, 202 NLRB 781 (1973).

Holiday Inn, 214 NLRB 651 (1974).

Days Inn of America, 210 NLRB 1035 (1974).

Ramada Inn v. NLRB, 487 F.2d 1334 (1973).

Westward-Ho Hotel, 437 F.2d 110 (1971).

Campaign Threats or Implied Promise of Benefit?

Do the oral or written statements made by employer representatives during a representation election campaign contain any unlawful threats or implied promises of benefit in violation of Section 8(a)(1) of the LMRA?

In early June, the Union filed a petition with the NLRB requesting a representation election be held in a bargaining unit comprising 880 employees of the Jackson Equipment Company (the Employer). The Employer had previously rejected the Union's request for voluntary recognition. The Union's election petition was supported by 426 (52 percent) valid union authorization card signatures. There were 880 employees declared eligible to vote in the election, which the Union lost by a vote of 391 for to 489 (55.5 percent) against union representation. The Union filed several objections to the Employer's conduct during the election.

The Union charged that the Employer's statements made during the election campaign threatened that if the Union won the election the employees' benefits would be reduced. Such a threat tends to discourage employees from freely exercising their Section 7 rights under the act. The Company contended that these statements were merely a factual response to union promises to increase employees' wages. The Company cited 22 out of 33 leaflets distributed by the Union that referred to improved employee benefits at some unionized plants. Here are the Employer's statements:

> Neither the Company nor the Union can predict what will be in the contract. Your wages and benefits could turn out to be higher, lower, or the same as they are. . . . I'm sure the Union will try to tell you there is some sort of law that will prevent the Company from negotiating for anything less than you now receive. That statement is simply not based on facts. I've given your supervisors copies of a decision in which the court upheld the Employer's right to inform his employees that he may not even have to agree to the continuance of existing wages and benefits. These facts may seem harsh, but I think it's important that you know the truth about the collective-bargaining process before you vote.
>
> Remember, bargaining means putting everything on the table, including the benefits you already have. Bargaining with a union can be a complicated and time-consuming process during which the Union and the Company negotiate to get an agreement that both sides are satisfied with. And bargaining starts from scratch, which means that everything is negotiable. As I have told you, we would bargain in good faith. But, I would not sign a contract that I did not believe was in this plant's best interest. Sometimes, when a company takes this position, the Union tries to force a settlement. This usually leads to a breakdown in bargaining and can result in a strike—which hurts everyone.
>
> You should know, however, that the benefit package given our plant employees from the time the plant opened was better than those at other unionized plants owned by the Company. You were given greater benefits voluntarily by the Company. Those in unions bargained repeatedly with the Employer for more than 20 years for their benefits. . . . Your pay increases are a result of the fair and responsible compensation policy we follow. There is no question in my mind that our wages are better than the Union wages I've seen in contracts of other companies in our area. A vote of "no union" is a vote to continue the pay practices we have been committed to at our plant since the day we began operations.

The Union also objected to other employer statements on the grounds that they implied a promise to do things differently or better if the employees voted against the Union. Such a promise, conditioned on whether an employee does or does not choose to exercise his or her lawful Section 7 right to select a bargaining representative, is in the Union's view a form of "positive coercion" and destructive of an atmosphere in which employees may freely decide the bargaining representation issue.

The Company contends it was only informing employees of how good conditions were at the plant. The conditions referred to were changes that had begun at the plant before the onset of the Union organizing campaign. The statements made by the plant manager were as follows:

> I admit, no employer is perfect. However, I am totally convinced that we can best resolve our differences without the Union and the adversarial relationship the organizers have tried to develop. In order to move ahead, we must work together, not fight each other.
>
> Unions are known chiefly for extracting dues from you, calling strikes, making promises, and causing confusion among employees. I am asking for a vote of confidence and a chance to prove what we can accomplish by working together, without interference by a union. I am asking for a chance to continue the improvements we have underway at our plant, without interference by the Union.
>
> I know that mistakes have been made. The fact that we are having a union election at this time indicates to me that some of you felt it was necessary, at one time, for an outsider to represent you, that management was unresponsive to your needs and concerns. It has been difficult to bring back to the plant the positive feelings that most of you had about the Company, but I sincerely feel we have turned the corner. I am aware of your frustrations with machine problems, material flow problems, overtime problems, inconsistent interpretation of company policies, pay inconsistencies, and management in general. Also, the personnel function has not been as sensitive to your needs as it should have been or could be. I admit that these things could have been diagnosed sooner and acted upon. However, we all know it is easy to quarterback Friday night's football game on Monday morning.
>
> I believe today we are building a management team that is willing to recognize its shortcomings and is actively working to correct them. It is not an easy job, but with your help it can be done. Programs have been developed to: (1) improve scheduling in the plant, (2) reduce scrap, (3) provide foremen training development, (4) improve the quality of our product, (5) purchase required machinery, and (6) improve our housekeeping.

Finally, the Union charged that a company supervisor unlawfully questioned and threatened two open and active union supporters. About 2 weeks before the election, supervisor Bates asked employee Culp what he thought the Union could do for him, and then told Culp, "If it came down to where you all went out on strike and they had people out, they could go out and hire because the Company had 100 to 200 people waiting for jobs. . . . They would use us as an example for the Company's other plants here in the South."

Approximately 1 week before the election, supervisor Lofton asked employee Rogers how he was going to vote. When Rogers replied, "For the Union," Lofton inquired whether Rogers was sure he was doing the right thing. Supervisor Lofton further asked Rogers if he knew that if the Union won he could lose his benefits and told him he should think twice about voting for the Union. *Continued*

251

Questions

1. Do these employer statements constitute an unlawful threat in violation of Section 8(a)(1) of the LMRA? Why or why not?

2. Do the employer statements constitute an unlawful promise of benefits in violation of Section 8(a)(1) of the act? Why or why not?

3. Did the questioning or statements by either supervisor Bates or supervisor Lofton constitute unlawful interrogation in violation of Section 8(a)(1) of the act? Why or why not?

4. Should the NLRB give consideration to its "Totality of Conduct" doctrine in reaching a conclusion about the alleged violations in this case? Explain your answer.

5. Develop some guidelines for managers who may be talking with employees about the Union during an organizing campaign.

Designing Union Election Campaign Literature

Purpose

The purpose of this exercise is to allow students to use creativity and gain experience in designing legal election campaign materials that effectively communicate common employer or union themes.

Instructions

This exercise may be completed on an individual or group basis. Using one or more of the common employer and union representation election campaign themes described in Exhibit 3.1, design a poster to encourage employees to vote either for or against union representation. Some students (groups) may be assigned to create a poster stressing employer campaign themes, while other students may design a union campaign poster. Students should be allowed to view the finished poster and choose a winner for "Best Company" and "Best Union" poster. The best poster is the one that the group majority judges would be most likely to *lawfully* influence (persuade) employees to vote in the intended direction.

Students may wish to develop a description of the type of company or bargaining unit employees that are the target of the union's organizing campaign as a focus for their poster design. A local firm's description may be used as a mock organizing target, or news items concerning a recent organizing campaign reported in newspapers, business periodicals (e.g., *Business Week,* BNA's *Daily Labor Report*), or other sources.

Note: The same type of exercise may be used to give students experience in preparing and presenting a brief five- to ten-minute oral presentation on the advantages or disadvantages of union representation.

PART 2

The Bargaining Process and Outcomes

Part 2 pertains to key activities and issues involved in the labor relations process of negotiating a labor agreement (contract) setting forth work rules pertaining to wages, hours, terms and conditions of employment, and the rights and responsibilities of the parties governed by the contract's terms. These topics are approached from the vantage point of legal and practical proscriptions on related behavior as well as with an eye to the realities forged out of the relationships between union and management officials.

CHAPTER 6

Negotiating the Labor Agreement

N*egotiation is a common feature of everyday life. Although this chapter covers negotiations between union and management officials over conditions of employment, many aspects of negotiations or collective bargaining have broader applications to other bargaining activities in society. This chapter first defines collective bargaining and explains initial influences affecting it. Subsequent sections consider negotiation preparation activities, such as bargaining team selection, proposal formulation, and cost estimates; bargaining strategies and tactics; and legal requirements. The chapter places these diverse collective-bargaining considerations in perspective by describing a "bargaining power model," a likely resolution framework.*

Collective Bargaining: Definition and Structure

Collective bargaining is an activity in which union and management officials attempt to resolve conflicts of interests by exchanging commitments in a manner intended to sustain and possibly enrich their continuing relationship. [Collective bargaining is a special form of interdependent social interaction, in which the attainment of desired outcomes by one party is dependent on the behavior of another party.] A dispute that arises between the union and management over what the terms and conditions of employment will be is termed an **interest dispute.** The basic objective of collective bargaining is to resolve such interest disputes by reaching an agreement acceptable to both parties (union and management).[1]

Attitudes of union and management officials toward collective bargaining and the negotiated settlement influence their relationship during the term or duration of the labor agreement. The fact that both parties generally understand that they will return to the bargaining table in future negotiations affects their strategic choices regarding acceptable tactics and outcomes in current negotiations. Defining success in collective bargaining often entails both objective and subjective criteria. Objectively measuring the economic value or cost of specific settle-

256

ment terms to each bargaining party is one way to measure success. Comparing settlement outcomes to industry or area averages is another way. Depending on the prevailing bargaining conditions, maintaining the status quo or even giving up less than one might have been expected to give up under the circumstances could be defined as a successful bargaining outcome. Yet another criterion for measuring successful negotiations is whether a bargaining settlement contributes to building a positive relationship between union and management representatives that is necessary for the effective implementation of contract terms on an everyday basis. It is not unusual for both union and management negotiators to claim success at the conclusion of contract negotiations. This may be due to the different priorities each party may place on achieving a desired outcome on specific bargaining subjects or a reflection of different criteria being applied by each party to measure success. A successful bargaining settlement reinforces a labor–management relationship in which the parties, although not always agreeing, nonetheless trust each other to be honest and straightforward in their positions without trying to unnecessarily damage the other party.[2]

Bargaining Structure

Bargaining structure has two general dimensions: (1) employee groupings that can affect the collective-bargaining outcome and (2) the employees and employers who are subject to the provisions of the negotiated labor agreement. Unions are responsive to several groups within and outside their organizations. Every organization has informal work groups (the night-shift crew or the company bowling team, for example) that have unique preferences and place pressures on union officers to achieve their preferences in collective bargaining. Other examples of groups within a bargaining unit who may seek to press special bargaining interests during negotiations include skilled craft employees, women, minorities, high- or low-seniority employees, and part-time employees.

In some cases, union and management officials are influenced by other collective-bargaining settlements. For example, a labor settlement between city government and the police might influence subsequent negotiations between the city and firefighters. The term **pattern bargaining** is used to describe a situation where union or management negotiators informally attempt to extend a negotiated settlement from one formal structure to another. Pattern bargaining may occur among similar companies in the same industry. For example, the United Auto Workers (UAW) has traditionally designated one auto manufacturer in each cycle of contract negotiations as the lead firm with whom the union will attempt to achieve a contract settlement. Terms of the "lead" contract would then be used as a pattern for negotiating labor agreements with other automakers during the same time frame. Pattern bargaining might also occur if union or management negotiators attempt to apply a settlement obtained for one segment of an industry (automobile manufacturing) to another company that produces related products such as tires or headlights.

Management and union negotiators might prefer pattern bargaining as a way to take wages out of competition from company to company. The objective of standardizing wages through pattern bargaining is beneficial for management because it will reduce concern about competitors receiving a labor cost advantage; it is also beneficial to union negotiators because it builds a perception among similar types of workers (represented by the same union under contracts at different firms) that they are receiving equal and fair treatment from their union in securing negotiated improvements desired by the union's membership.[3] Sometimes management negotiators actively resist pattern bargaining in order to try to negotiate contract settlement terms that will provide the firm with a labor cost competitive advantage over other firms with whom the same union bargains. Increased competition by firms not covered under union contracts (both domestic and international competitors) has also forced some firms to resist union pattern settlement proposals.

The Bargaining Unit

The second dimension of the bargaining structure, the **bargaining unit,** refers to the employees and employers who will be bound by the negotiated labor agreement. As discussed in Chapter 5, any appropriate bargaining unit (ABU) determined by the National Labor Relations Board (NLRB) for representation election purposes is, by definition, a unit appropriate for negotiating purposes (see the first example in Exhibit 6.1). Once a union has been certified as the representative of an ABU, two or more ABUs represented by the same union may be combined together for the purpose of negotiating a single labor agreement to cover all ABUs if such a combination is acceptable to both the union and the employer. Whether to combine ABUs together for negotiation purposes is a **nonmandatory** subject of bargaining.[4]

Choosing to combine ABUs for negotiation purposes is a form of **centralized bargaining** (see the remaining examples in Exhibit 6.1), of which there are two major types. *Single employer/multiplant bargaining* may be used when one company has several separate facilities, each having a separate ABU. A **multiemployer bargaining unit** involves more than one employer combining together to negotiate a single contract covering employees at each of the participating employer's firms who are represented by the same union. Multi-employer bargaining may be found in industries such as trucking, construction, longshore, newspaper, and professional sports. Some union–management bargaining relationships choose to combine ABUs under a master contract to negotiate certain issues (e.g., wages, pension plans) that are equally applied to employees throughout an industry or at different locations of the same employer. Working

Exhibit 6.1

Possible Structures for Collective Bargaining

Structure	Example
1. Single employer—single union	
Single location	ABC Manufacturing Co.—UNITE
Multiple locations	General Motors—UAW
2. Single employer—several unions	
Single location	Johnson Metal, Buffalo, New York—all crafts and industrial unions
Multiple locations	General Electric—IBEW and IUE
3. Multiple employers—single union	Trucking Management Incorporated—Teamsters
4. Multiple employers—several unions	Association of General Contractors of North Alabama—Birmingham Trade Council

conditions or terms specific to an individual ABU may then be bargained separately at the local facility and incorporated as a local addendum to the master contract.

One or both parties might prefer centralized bargaining because of product interdependence, market factors, or legal considerations. For example, a company may have three manufacturing facilities, each having a separate ABU. If the products at the facilities are *interdependent* (Facility A's product is needed for Facility B, whose product is in turn completed with products at Facility C), then management would probably prefer centralized bargaining producing a single contract expiration date and only one risk of a possible strike at all facilities—instead of three different contract expiration dates and possible separate strikes at each of the facilities if each ABU negotiates a separate contract. Separate bargaining at each bargaining unit would risk an interruption in firm operations three times compared to a single risk of shutdown under centralized bargaining. Of course, should a work stoppage actually occur the potential magnitude of the impact would be greater under centralized bargaining because all ABUs covered would be affected.

If the three facilities operate *independently* of each other—each facility producing a complete product or service by itself (e.g., three steel mills, each producing steel beams; or three facilities producing unrelated products such as baseball gloves, cereal, and marbles), management would probably prefer to negotiate a separate contract to cover the ABU at each independent facility. Separate negotiations would probably result in different contract expiration dates for the three facilities. Although each separate contract would involve the risk of a work stoppage when it expired, if one facility went out on strike the others could still continue production. In the case of facilities that produce similar products, management could transfer some of the orders from the struck facility to other nonstruck facilities where labor contracts had not expired.

Some believe that conglomerate companies with a wide range of products have too much bargaining power over unions. One sample of nine conglomerates revealed 846 different manufacturing products sold. A union threatening a strike to shut down one of these manufacturing facilities or even an entire product line might not be able to put sufficient pressure on a conglomerate to reach a bargaining settlement.[5] A union would prefer centralized bargaining in this situation, realizing that a strike could effectively shut down the company's entire operations, thereby increasing union bargaining strength. Market factors also influence the degree of centralization of the bargaining unit. In a highly competitive product/service market, a multiemployer (centralized) negotiating unit would be desirable to employers who fear being placed at a competitive disadvantage if other employers subsequently negotiate lower wage rates. This would be particularly true of an employer with fewer resources (less bargaining power) than the union with whom the employer must bargain and whose firm's operation also had a high **degree of labor intensiveness** (i.e., the proportion of an employer's total operating costs comprised of labor costs). Combining with other employers into a multi-employer bargaining unit strengthens the individual employer's bargaining power and also minimizes another potential problem—the loss of customers to competitors should a work stoppage occur.

Unions are also concerned about market problems in some industries (construction, coal, trucking, ladies' garments, longshore, and others) and attempt to extend the bargaining unit to include all unionized employers in a geographic area producing the same competitive product. This approach is taken to prevent a few employers with above-average bargaining power from separately negotiating lower wages, thus attaining lower production costs, thereby attracting customers from other unionized firms, which could result in layoffs for some union members. In essence, unions are attempting to standardize wages, hours, and other terms of employment to reduce the importance of labor costs as a competitive factor and force employers to compete on the basis of other nonlabor factors, such as product design, product quality, customer service, and so on.

Multi-employer bargaining also has other advantages and disadvantages. A union engaged in multi-employer bargaining has a powerful advantage over rival unions because the NLRB holds that while a multi-employer bargaining unit is intact, it is the only appropriate bargaining/election unit.[6] Thus, the NLRB will dismiss a rival union's petition for an election in a single firm as long as the incumbent union and the firm are participants in a multi-employer negotiating unit. Both labor and management can benefit from the cost savings that accrue from having to prepare for fewer contract negotiations when separate ABUs are combined to form a centralized negotiation unit. The costs of preparing for and conducting negotiations can also be shared among employers participating in a multi-employer bargaining unit.

Centralized bargaining tends to become more formal and less flexible in terms of meeting employee and employer concerns at the individual workplace. Because terms must be applied across different employee groups often at different locations, bargaining outcomes tend to reflect a broader regional, corporatewide, or industry perspective rather than local conditions prevailing at any particular plant location. For example, wage and benefit trend data used to identify an appropriate bargaining outcome are more likely to reflect prevailing industry or national averages rather than local labor market conditions.

Finally, multi-employer bargaining can create tensions among the member employers. An employer might consider pulling out of the multi-employer group if it feels it can get a better deal negotiating separately with the union. To legally withdraw from an existing multi-employer bargaining unit an employer must provide both the union and other unit employers with reasonable advance notice (e.g., prior to the expiration date of the current agreement and before negotiations have commenced on a new contract to replace the expiring agreement).[7] Where there is a clear disparity in the size of the participating firms, larger employers may attempt to control the decisions of the multi-employer group. This may become a problem for smaller employers within the group whose perceptions may differ from larger employers regarding the affordability or administrative burden of accepting certain union bargaining proposals.

The decision to engage in centralized bargaining can also be affected by legal guidelines. The size and makeup of each party's bargaining team are nonmandatory subjects of bargaining.[8] A union representing a particular bargaining unit could permit representatives from other unions who also bargain separately with the same employer to sit in on negotiations as part of the union's bargaining team. Although the employer cannot control who sits on the union bargaining team, the employer could legally require that only the legal union representative of the bargaining unit covered by the contract being negotiated be permitted to decide whether to accept or reject management bargaining proposals.[9] Union representatives from other bargaining units could function as observers in the negotiation process but could not exercise any authority over determining settlement terms.

The NLRB has also ruled unlawful a **lock-in agreement** between unions, which requires each union-represented bargaining unit covered by the agreement not to reach a final contract settlement until all unions covered by the agreement are willing to settle.[10] The intent of such a lock-in agreement is to prevent an employer with multiple bargaining units covered under separate contracts from using a **whip-saw bargaining strategy** to obtain concessions from one bargaining unit which could then be used as leverage to seek similar or additional changes in contract terms in subsequent negotiations with other bargaining units. The lock-in agreement forces the employer to address the concerns of all bargaining units at the same time rather than selectively choosing the order in which negotiations with particular bargaining units will proceed.

The U.S. Supreme Court ruled that it was unlawful for an employer to withdraw from an established multi-employer bargaining arrangement during a bargaining impasse without the union's consent.[11] The employer's withdrawal was not allowed, and the employer was bound to any subsequent agreement reached by the union and the multi-employer bargaining group. An employer may legally withdraw from a multi-employer negotiating unit before the onset of bargaining preparations by notifying the other employers and union(s) involved in the unit of the withdrawing employer's intention and the effective date of such withdrawal.

Negotiation Preparation Activities

Selection of the Negotiating Team and Related Bargaining Responsibilities

The selection of the number and type of individuals who will make up the bargaining team for each party is an important decision that can affect the outcome of negotiations. Exhibit 6.2 suggests some characteristics of an effective negotiator, although few individuals are likely to possess all of these characteristics to the ideal degree. Management generally selects negotiating team members based on the perceived need for each individual's skills and experience. Management generally wants at least one line manager who supervises bargaining unit employees on its team to either interpret or answer negotiating issues related to daily work operations.

In determining the size of each negotiating team, smaller teams are generally preferable, with a maximum suggested size of nine.[12] Teams larger than nine tend to experience increasing coordination problems (e.g., task assignment, delegation of authority, pressure to conform) and require additional time to reach consensus on bargaining issues. Sometimes bargaining team size is influenced by a desire to match the size of the other party's team. A bargaining structure that emphasizes centralized industry or corporate-level bargaining or multiple parties (on either the employer or union side) tends to expand the size of negotiating teams.

Unions apply selection criteria similar to those of management, but in addition, they must weigh certain political considerations. For example, an elected

Exhibit 6.2

Some Common Characteristics of an Effective Negotiator

- Able to say *no* effectively.
- Has integrity and the ability to inspire confidence in his or her judgement ability.
- Able to plan effectively and conduct research necessary to become thoroughly knowledgeable about bargaining issues and trends.
- Able to discern the *bottom line interests* of other parties.
- Even-tempered and able to tolerate conflict and ambiguity.
- An excellent communicator (i.e., able to speak, write, and listen effectively).
- Self-confident and pragmatic (able to establish realistic bargaining expectations and accurately assess the benefits, costs, and risks of insisting on specific settlement terms).
- Good physical and mental stamina.
- Able to understand the short- and long-term implications of specific bargaining proposals on the parties' interests.
- Understands the importance of *face saving* and is willing to provide opportunities to the other party to do so (or conversely, knows when to take advantage of such opportunities when offered by the other party).
- Willing to take calculated risks in order to achieve desired bargaining outcomes without seriously jeopardizing constituents' best interests.
- Knows how and when to ask relevant questions and interpret the other party's responses (even no response to a question or action may, in fact, represent a meaningful response).
- Has a sense of humor to relieve stress or establish rapport with the other party. Always laughs with the other party, never at the other party.

union leader may think it is important to appoint at least one or more representatives from key constituent groups within the bargaining unit (e.g., skilled trade, largest department or occupation, women, minorities) to serve on the union's negotiating team. This choice helps to ensure that the special interests of key constituent groups will be considered in negotiating settlement terms, which will enhance the probability that tentative contract settlement terms will be approved by a majority of the union's membership.

The union negotiating team may be elected by the membership or appointed by elected union officers depending on the wording of the union's constitution and bylaws. Where direct election of negotiating team members is permitted, there is always a risk to current leaders that one or more rivals for union leadership may be elected to serve on the team. This can create some problems in attempting to achieve consensus on bargaining priorities, strategies, tactics, and acceptable settlement terms.

Union and management negotiators seek bargaining team members who can keep their emotions and opinions in check. An indiscreet negotiating team member can unintentionally reveal confidential settlement points and strategies to the other team. In some cases, union and management negotiators may agree to release information in the form of a joint statement to outside third parties (e.g., news media) during negotiations. This tactic helps to reduce rumors or misleading claims that can damage progress being made toward a settlement at the bargaining table.

Proposal Determination and Assessment

Management relies on several sources to determine a union's likely bargaining goals in contract negotiations. A review of recent settlements negotiated by the company's competitors and by other local firms may help to identify likely bargaining subjects as well as possible settlement outcomes. The company and union may have negotiated settlements at other facilities that might also be used as a starting point in the current negotiations. Some management officials obtain bargaining insights by reviewing the proceedings of the national union's convention or visiting the union's Web site.

One study of local union officials reported that staff representatives/business agents and organizers were more likely to rely upon formal information sources (e.g., libraries, union research departments, databases) than informal sources (e.g., personal networks, telephone inquiries) to gather information for use in contract negotiations.[13] Formal training in research methods also increased the number of information sources used by a union official in preparing to perform role functions such as contract negotiations.

Attention should be given to the parties' previous negotiations, particularly to those issues that the union actively sought and reluctantly dropped. Compromise settlements on previous issues also generate valuable clues because compromise does not always mean permanent resolution of the issue. An analysis of previous grievances at the facility can also identify certain trouble spots. GM, for example, uses a computerized analysis of number, type, and resolution status of grievances in their negotiation preparations. However, caution must be taken not to overemphasize these grievances. Unions often step up grievance activity in the six months prior to negotiations to dramatize widespread concern over certain bargaining issues—concerns perhaps more tactical than real.

Formulating Proposals and the Bargaining Range

Management negotiators need to be proactive rather than reactive in preparing for contract negotiations. Traditionally, many management negotiators chose to wait for the union to present its bargaining proposals before determining management's bargaining response. Often, this approach permitted the union to control the bargaining agenda and left management negotiating over how many or to what extent to grant union demands for improvements in employment terms of interest to the union's membership. Increased competitive pressures caused many union employers to initiate work-rule changes to decrease labor costs and improve productivity and quality, requiring management negotiators to take a more proactive stance at the bargaining table. Rather than waiting for the union to raise every issue, management negotiators put forward their own proposals concerning issues, such as health-care cost containment, broadening job descriptions, and subcontracting or outsourcing of certain bargaining unit work. Management may well prefer to defer presenting proposals on any issues it expects the union to initially present (e.g., wage rates, pension benefits) so as not to "tip their hand" to the union.

In formulating bargaining proposals, managers often perform a close analysis of the current labor agreement to determine desirable changes in contract language that will reduce labor costs and give management more flexibility in making operating decisions. Assume, for example, that the current contract prohibits managers from performing any bargaining unit work. Management might propose allowing supervisors to perform bargaining unit work under at least three conditions: (1) when training new employees, (2) in emergency situations (usually interpreted to mean when employees' lives or production equipment are jeopardized), and (3) when experimental production efforts are involved.

Management and union officials may propose contract language intended to nullify the impact of prior adverse arbitration decisions. For example, an arbitrator's decision that the company will pay for an employee's safety shoes could be nullified by negotiating new contract language that reads, "The Company will provide the employees with safety shoes and deduct the cost of these shoes from the employee's paycheck." Both union and management will typically contact union stewards and first-line supervisors, respectively, to determine if any contract language has been difficult to administer during the term of the current labor agreement and thus, ought to be modified.

Efforts will also be made to research data from government reports, especially from the U.S. Departments of Commerce and Labor, and from various labor relations services such as the Bureau of National Affairs, Commerce Clearing House, and Prentice-Hall. Data pertaining to wages, benefits, safety and health, technological change, job security, productivity, legal developments, and so on, from these and other sources give both parties substantial information with which to prepare for negotiations. It is difficult to ever be over-prepared to conduct contract negotiations but there is real risk involved for any negotiator who enters bargaining underprepared.

The Bargaining Range

Union and management officials enter collective bargaining with their own ideas of an acceptable settlement, although both parties know the other will not agree entirely with their position. Therefore, both parties usually enter negotiations with a range of acceptable positions, which give them some room for maneuvering. These positions can be given priorities and grouped into a **bargaining range**, one for management and the other for the union. Exhibit 6.3 illustrates bargaining ranges for a few issues; however, it is common for the parties to negotiate a hundred or more bargaining issues.

Both management and union representatives have upper and lower limits on their respective ranges. Management's upper limit is usually determined by its objectives, such as profitability and growth. A settlement above this perceived upper limit would be incompatible with the company's objectives. The point beyond which a party would prefer no settlement to settlement on unacceptable terms represents that party's **resistance point** on a particular bargaining issue. For example, management might prefer to close, move its operations, or bring new employees into its existing facility rather than agree to a settlement that would make operations less profitable. On the other hand, management may not want to be known as the cheapest employer in the area, nor would it want to be unable to recruit, retain, and reward its employees. These concerns help place a lower limit on management's bargaining range—a minimum offer that management feels is necessary to maintain employee morale and output.

A union's upper limit is usually shaped by two factors: (1) desired employment levels and (2) the ability to promote and sustain a strike. A union realizes that there is often a trade-off between pressing for economic gains (higher wages and improved benefits) and the number of jobs that may be available at

Exhibit 6.3

Bargaining Ranges for Union and Management Negotiators

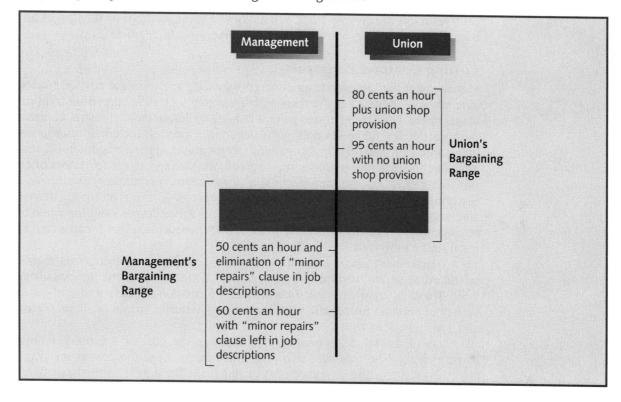

that higher labor cost. Higher labor costs increase management's incentive to look for ways to substitute capital for labor (e.g., technological innovation), use less labor (e.g., layoffs), or find a less costly labor supply (e.g., subcontracting bargaining unit work to nonunion employers or moving work operations to lower-cost domestic or international labor markets). Unrealistic union bargaining proposals are likely to be discounted by management and can serve as a hindrance to serious negotiation over meritorious issues. Also, a strike cannot be initiated, let alone successfully concluded, if union leaders call a strike over an unrealistic bargaining demand (e.g., $5-an-hour wage increase when union members recognize that management could realistically afford a raise of only $.80 an hour).

On the other hand, union leaders realize that there is a lower limit on the bargaining range and that a settlement below this limit would result in membership dissatisfaction. Because union leaders are strongly influenced by their desire to ensure the survival of the union and their continued election as union officers, they would seldom accept a settlement below this perceived resistance point. It is important for union leaders to solicit input from members regarding their bargaining interests and priorities and to inform members about current bargaining conditions and trends, thereby encouraging the members to form realistic bargaining expectations.

The bargaining range, although bounded by upper and lower limits, represents a multitude of issues. Assigning priorities to these issues and their possible combinations produces bargaining ranges of an almost infinite number of possibilities. Bargaining ranges can change during negotiations as bargaining issues get linked in package proposals (see Exhibit 6.3) covering several subjects or in response to new information, usually becoming finalized as the parties approach the contract expiration date or a strike/lockout deadline.

Costing Contract Proposals

Management has an overriding concern regarding the eventual cost of a labor agreement because it has the responsibility of paying for the agreed-on terms of employment. Management will generally need to determine the cost of contract proposals at several points during the negotiation process including prior to the first bargaining meeting (prebargaining preparation), during negotiations, and after final contract terms have been agreed on. Management negotiators often use two general costing approaches in negotiations: preparation of employee background data and calculation of a cents-per-hour wage increase. Unions also engage in costing efforts for the purpose of either determining the value of management proposals or helping to persuade management that it can afford to grant union proposals.

Management usually obtains statistical summaries of employees cross-tabulated by several variables (age, sex, marital status, seniority, job classification). These summaries provide immediate information necessary to cost out a variety of contract proposals, such as health insurance, vacations, funeral pay, and pensions.

One of the most important calculations is the cost of a cents-per-hour wage increase. The true cost of a wage increase includes the cost of the wage increase itself plus the increased cost of all benefit items paid on the basis of an employee's straight-time hourly wage rate (e.g., holiday and vacation pay, sick leave and jury duty pay, paid rest and lunch periods, overtime pay, call-in pay). The **roll-up factor** is an estimate of the total cents-per-hour costs of employer benefit items affected by a change in the straight-time hourly wage rate as a proportion (percentage) of the current average hourly bargaining unit wage rate. For example, if the total cents-per-hour costs for the employer benefit items affected by a wage rate change amounted to $3.60, and the current average hourly bargaining unit wage rate was $10, then the roll-up factor or cost would equal $3.60 ÷ $10 = $.36, or 36 percent. The actual cost of the wage increase calculated in the example presented below would be $20,800 plus the roll-up factor cost [$20,800 × .36 = $7,488] for a total annual wage cost of $28,288.

An illustrative calculation of a one-cent-per-hour wage increase for a bargaining unit of 1,000 employees is as follows:

$20,800	*Straight-time pay* (1,000 employees × 40 hours a week × 52 weeks × $.01).
7,488	*Roll-up cost* for benefit items directly affected by the wage increase (profit sharing, pensions, life insurance, employer contributions to social security, shift differential if paid on a percentage basis, unemployment insurance, workers' compensation, and so on), estimated for illustrative purposes at 36 percent of the straight-time wage rate.
$28,288	True cost of a one cent-per-hour wage increase.

A negotiator should be prepared to bargain over either a cents-per-hour wage increase or a percentage wage increase. Since the union will normally introduce the wage issue first when presenting its initial bargaining proposals, the union will initially determine whether the format for wage negotiations will be cents-per-hour or a percentage increase in the current hourly wage rate. Assuming the average hourly straight-time wage rate for the 1,000-member bargaining unit in the previous example was $10 per hour, the cost of a 1 percent wage increase for this bargaining unit would be calculated as follows: .01 $\times$ $10 = .10¢ per hour $\times$ 1,000 employees $\times$ 2,080 hours = $208,000 straight-time pay + roll-up cost of $74,880 ($208,000 $\times$ .36) = $282,880. Negotiators must be mindful of the magnitude dollar difference in cost when negotiating on a percentage versus cents-per-hour basis.

Union officials may submit proposals that are difficult to cost, thereby weakening management's related objections based on cost estimates during negotiations. Assume, for example, that a current contract provision provides a Sunday work premium of 75 cents an hour if the employees have no absences during their regularly scheduled work week. The union proposes that employees working on Sunday receive this premium pay regardless of their attendance record during the week. Management can examine past payroll records to estimate the added cost of this proposal, which is a difficult task if there are thousands of employees involved and an uncertain indicator of extra absences that might occur if this proposal is accepted. Other proposals, such as extending a previous labor agreement's three-day paid leave for the death of an immediate family member to include first cousins, are nearly impossible to precisely estimate cost because it is very difficult to gather accurate data needed to cost the item. In addition, many cost items, such as overtime hours and holidays worked, have to be estimated using past payroll records and anticipated future production and staffing requirements, which may not always be perfect predictors of future operating experience.

Union negotiators may formulate proposals that benefit members' interests while saving management money, a difficult task requiring much ingenuity. Examples include the following:

- Allowing police to keep a squad car for personal use, thereby reducing crime statistics and related expenses.

- Allowing sabbaticals for which professors receive one-half their salaries for nine months, and management keeps any surplus funds if a replacement teaches the professors' classes at a lower pay rate.

When presenting cost analyses information at the bargaining table it is important to clearly explain how cost estimates where obtained and any underlying assumptions on which estimates may rest.[14]

Collective Bargaining Behavior

Two Bargaining Approaches

Although each bargaining situation is unique and depends on the negotiators' personalities and the issues involved, collective bargaining behavior generally falls into one of two strategic approaches: **distributive bargaining** or **mutual**

LABOR RELATIONS IN ACTION

Bargaining in the Auto Industry

On July 16, 2003, the United Auto Workers (UAW) union opened negotiations with DaimlerChrysler AG's Chrysler unit (DC), marking the beginning of contract negotiations with the Big Three auto manufacturers (General Motors Corp. [GM] and Ford Motor Co. are the other two). The UAW sought to replace the current four-year labor agreements at each firm scheduled to expire on September 14.[a] Unlike the generally good economic and industry conditions surrounding the 1999 contract negotiations, both labor and management were aware that the Big Three faced a declining share of the domestic U.S. market while costs (particularly for health care and pension benefits) continued to rise. Neither the union or automakers appeared to consider a strike a very real possibility given the competitive pressures that confronted the Big Three automakers.

The Big Three auto manufacturers' market share fell to a record low 57.6 percent in August 2003 despite offering consumers economic incentives averaging $3,687 per vehicle.[b] Labor cost per vehicle for the Big Three auto manufacturers averaged $8,655 compared to $6,052 for primarily nonunion auto transplant firms such as Toyota, Nissan, Honda, BMW, and Mercedes.[c] GM was under particular cost pressure with 2.5 retirees for every active worker in 2002 and expenditures of $5 billion annually on health-care costs for current employees and retirees. Pension and health-care costs tend to be lower at many transplant competitor firms because such operations have begun in the United States more recently, employing a labor force whose average age is younger and with few current retirees eligible for current pension benefit payments.[d] Due to lower equity prices in the stock market and interest rate declines in recent years, the value of assets designated to fund pension benefit obligations have declined at many firms. GM's pension fund was underfunded by $19.3 billion dollars in 2002.

The 2003 negotiations were the first under the leadership of new UAW president Ron Gettelfinger, who served as a UAW vice president and head of the Ford department during the 1999 contract negotiations. Historically, the UAW has selected one of the auto companies as its primary negotiating target in an attempt to negotiate a favorable settlement whose terms could then form a pattern for settlement talks at remaining auto firms. Given the need to maintain stable operating environments at the Big Three unionized auto firms in 2003, the union adopted a different bargaining strategy. The UAW's 2003 strategy was to conduct separate but simultaneous negotiations with each of the Big Three automakers in an attempt to reach a new agreement at all three firms prior to the September 14 contract expiration date. By emphasizing settlement rather than confrontation, the UAW hoped to forge a working partnership with auto firms that would recognize the legitimate interests of both ownership and employees in determining final settlement terms. While the UAW certainly sought to coordinate its bargaining goals and strategy in conducting separate negotiations with each automaker, simultaneous negotiations still afforded the opportunity for each automaker to structure final contract language to best meet the needs of that firm's competitive position.

The auto companies' goals for the 2003 contract negotiations included gaining more flexibility to reduce labor costs and introduce plant rules intended to increase productivity. Reducing the rate of increase in pension and health-care costs were two important areas in which automakers hoped to achieve some cost savings. More permanent labor cost reductions achieved by reducing the total number of employees covered under the contract's terms was also an important goal. To accomplish such workforce downsizing would require gaining the union's cooperation in plans to close or merge certain company operations as well as continued outsourcing of various component parts of the automobile production process to outside suppliers who could perform the work at lower costs.

Parts produced by Big Three unionized employees included labor costs of approximately $22 per hour compared to a more modest $14 per hour at many outside, often nonunion parts suppliers.[e]

While current economic conditions served to moderate union members' expectation of compensation gains in 2003 bargaining, the UAW did focus on trying to maintain current compensation rates and particularly resisting any company efforts to shift a substantially larger share of health-care costs to union members and retirees covered under the contracts. Big Three automakers under the 1999 pattern bargaining agreement paid virtually 100 percent of employees' health-care insurance premium costs, highly unusual even for union contracts today. Health insurance premiums rose 13.9 percent in 2002, with future increases expected to continue during the term of the next labor agreement.[f] Like many union contracts, auto industry agreements typically contain a variety of features designed to help reduce health-care costs such as employee co-payments or deductibles, requiring generic drugs be used when available, delaying new-hire eligibility for health-care coverage, requiring outpatient surgery when medically possible, wellness program, utilization review, preadmission testing, or requiring a second opinion in certain cases.

One concern the UAW's leadership sought employer's help with was the declining trend in auto worker union membership within the auto industry. From a peak membership of 1.5 million members in 1979, the UAW's 2002 membership had declined to an estimated 675,898 members.[g] Even though the 1999 contract had contained a ban on plant closings, the number of employees at the Big Three automakers still declined by approximately 50,000 jobs over the four-year term of the agreement. Organizing more nonunion (transplant) auto manufacturing (e.g., Mercedes, Honda, Nissan, Hyundai, and Toyota) plants as well as ensuring that job cuts at the Big Three automakers are accomplished primarily through normal attrition (e.g., not replacing employees when the current job holder retires) are union objectives intended to enhance both members' job security and the union's security. Faced with the prospect that the number of employees at Big Three auto plants would continue to decline further during the term of the 2003 agreement, it became very important for the UAW to secure contract language that might facilitate future membership growth at nonunion plants as well as encourage the Big Three domestic automakers to direct more future business toward unionized parts suppliers. More specifically, the UAW sought to get Big Three automakers to agree to contract language such as a *neutrality pledge*, which obligates the employer to take a neutral stance during UAW efforts to organize any of the automaker's nonunion operations. The UAW also sought to obtain employer agreement to an *authorization card check recognition* procedure, which obligates the employer to grant voluntary recognition to the UAW as the bargaining agent for plant employees if the union can show it has obtained voluntary signatures from a majority of the affected employees authorizing the UAW to act as the employees' legal bargaining representative. The card check procedure avoids the time and expense of seeking certification through a National Labor Relations Board supervised secret-ballot election.

After two months of negotiations, the UAW and DaimlerChrysler AG were able to announce a tentative contract settlement just prior to the scheduled contract expiration date of midnight on September 14. The UAW and Ford Motor Company announced a similar tentative contract settlement on Monday, September 15, followed by a tentative UAW-GM agreement on Thursday, September 18. The parties declined to release any details of the tentative contract settlements pending a vote by the union's membership covered under each labor agreement to approve the proposed contract settlement terms.[h] Both company and union leaders spoke positively of the new labor agreements as rep-

Continued

resenting a good balance between the needs of employees, the union, and management, reflecting a desire to create a more competitive operation while fostering a stable labor relations environment. The UAW also reached new labor agreements covering workers at parts supplier Visteon Corporation (a Ford Company spin-off) and Delphi Corporation (a GM parts supplier spin-off) made possible by the terms of the 1999 labor agreements at Ford and GM. Combined, the new agreements at the Big Three and two independent parts suppliers (Visteon and Delphi) will cover 291,510 current employees, 369,810 retired workers, and 105,420 spouses of deceased autoworkers.[i]

Basic economic terms are similar in all three labor agreements. These terms include a $3,000 lump-sum signing bonus payable upon ratification of the 2003 agreement, a performance bonus in the 2nd year, a 2-percent base hourly wage increase in the 3rd year, and a 3-percent base hourly wage increase in the 4th year.[j] Pension benefits are improved for current employees and current retirees will receive an $800 lump sum payment each year of the four-year agreement. Health-care benefits remain essentially unchanged, with the employer continuing to pay the insurance premium cost of providing the benefits.

The new contracts will permit all three companies to move forward with plans to sell, merge, or close some facilities expected to affect as many as 50,000 current employees over the four-year term of the labor agreements. Impacted employees may be eligible for certain enhanced early retirement options and will retain transfer rights to fill any available job openings at other company facilities for which they are qualified. GM agreed to hire 2,250 employees to fill skilled trade apprentice slots over the term of the agreement. Both Ford and GM committed to ensuring that sufficient capital investment and new business will be directed toward parts supplier spin-offs Visteon and Delphi to ensure those operations remain viable during the contract's term. The companies will seek to work more closely with the UAW in making outsourcing decisions to ensure that unionized operations have an opportunity to fairly compete for the available business.

Contracts also maintain a commitment to the principle of *equality of sacrifice*, which in the auto industry means that top management at each company must take the lead in accepting reductions in compensation or benefit terms in an amount at least equal to (in percentage terms) the level of reductions required of covered employees. The UAW agreed to meet with management representatives at both Visteon and Delphi within 90 days of the contract's ratification date for the purpose of negotiating a possible supplemental agreement that could change compensation rates for new hires at each firm to make wages more competitive with those of other competitors in the auto parts industry. Such a two-tier wage agreement would only affect those individuals hired after the approval of the supplemental agreement. Some companies and unions who have tried two-tier wage plans have abandoned them because of dissatisfaction and increased turnover among lower tier hires over time. One way to address this problem is to include contract terms that permit lower tier pay rates to gradually rise over the term of the labor agreement to narrow or eliminate the wage difference for employees performing the same job but initially hired at the lower tier rate.

Union members at DaimlerChrysler, Ford, GM, Visteon, and Delphi Corporation voted to ratify the terms of the 2003 labor agreement, although the UAW did not release any vote totals indicating the margin by which the positive vote occurred. The 2003 labor agreements provide the unionized segment of the auto industry an opportunity to continue to work toward lower production costs and enhanced productivity and quality improvements. It is important that both labor and management continue to forge a partnership that recognizes and addresses the legitimate needs of all parties to encourage business growth and profitability capable of sustaining excellent compensation levels and job security. ■

SOURCES: [a] Catherine Hollingsworth, "Less Than Favorable Market Conditions Form Backdrop for UAW-Big Three Talks," *Daily Labor Report*, July 3, 2003, pp. C1–2.

[b] Steven Gray, "Big Three Lose Market Share," *Washington Post*, October 1, 2003, p. E03.

[c] David Kiley, "Foreign Companies Cast a Long Shadow on UAW Negotiations," *USA Today*, August 6, 2003, p. 1B; Jeffrey Ball, Lee Hawkins, Jr., and Sholnn Freeman, "The Economy: Big Three, UAW Show Rare Unity; Amid Foreign Pressure, Auto Makers, Union Look to Set Standardized Deals," *The Wall Street Journal*, September 8, 2003, p. A-2.

[d] Hollingsworth, "Less Than Favorable Market Conditions Form Backdrop for UAW-Big Three Talks," pp. C1–2.

[e] David Welch, "The UAW: Using Trade-Offs to Gain Traction," *Business Week*, September 8, 2003, p. 80; Jeffrey Ball, "The Economy: UAW, Big Three Push for Early Contract Pacts," *The Wall Street Journal*, September 12, 2003, p. A-2.

[f] Bill Brubaker, "Health Insurance Premiums Up 13.9%," *Washington Post*, September 10, 2003, p. E02.

[g] John Porretto, "UAW May Lose Up to 50,000 Jobs in 4 Years," *Associated Press News Release*, September 24, 2003, pp. 1–2; Jennifer Dixon, "UAW a Hard Sell in South," *Detroit Free Press*, September 13, 2003, pp. 1–7.

[h] Greg Schneider, "Chrysler, UAW Agree on New Labor Pact," *Washington Post*, September 15, 2003, p. A12; Tom Brown, "UAW Ends Contract Talks with Big Three," *Reuters News Release*, September 18, 2003, pp. 1–2; "UAW, Big Three Reach Tentative Agreements," *UAW News Release*, September 19, 2003, p. 1.

[i] Schneider, "Chrysler, UAW Agee on New Labor Pact."

[j] "UAW Members at Daimler-Chrysler Ratify New Pact," *UAW News Release*, September 26, 2003, pp. 1–3; Tom Brown, "UAW: Union Workers Ratify Chrysler Pact," *Reuters News Release*, September 26, 2003, pp. 1–2; "UAW Members at Ford and Visteon Rarify New Contracts," *UAW News Release*, September 30, 2003, pp. 1–2; John Porretto, "UAW Workers at Ford Ratify 4-Year Pact," *Associated Press News Release*, September 30, 2003, p. 1; "UAW Members at GM and Delphi Ratify New Contracts," *UAW News Release*, October 6, 2003, pp. 1–2; "UAW Ratifies GM, Delphi Contracts," *Reuters News Release*, October 6, 2003, p. 1.

gain bargaining.[15] Each of these approaches can lead to a voluntary settlement of bargaining issues, and in neither approach does either party typically get everything it wants.

A distributive bargaining approach tends to view the two parties' interests to be in conflict and the negotiation process as a win-lose (zero sum) exercise. Gains for one party's goals must come at the expense of the other party. Bargaining issues like wages, for which the economic gain or cost of proposed settlement terms can be estimated by the parties, lend themselves to a distributive bargaining approach. The primary focus of a distributive bargainer is to maximize his or her own party's interests, although to accomplish this may require some consideration and satisfaction of the other party's key interests.

A distributive bargainer seeks to achieve settlement at (or as close as possible to) the other party's resistance point (i.e., the point beyond which the other party would prefer no settlement to settlement on their opponent's proposed terms). Each negotiator tries to discover where the other party's resistance point lies on each issue and to modify the opponent's position and perceptions to achieve a settlement on preferred bargaining terms. An effort is made to restrict and structure communications for strategic advantage (e.g., control of the bargaining agenda). A distributive bargainer's persuasive efforts focus on convincing their opponent that the distributive bargainer's proposal is more acceptable than the opponent's or that settlement on the distributive bargainer's proposed terms is preferable to the costs or risks of nonsettlement. Distributive bargainers may respect each other's abilities more than they trust each other's intentions. Finally, there is a greater willingness to rely on bargaining power, if necessary, to force the other party's acceptance of proposed settlement terms.

Mutual gain bargaining is sometimes referred to as **win-win bargaining** or the more recent popular term **interest-based bargaining**.[16] Mutual gain bargaining differs from traditional distributive bargaining in a number of important ways. Negotiators approach the bargaining process as a mutual problem-solving exercise. Open and honest communication about each party's interests, intentions, and the merits of specific bargaining proposals is encouraged. Mutual gain bargaining lends itself particularly to bargaining issues in which both parties perceive a common threat or need and successfully resolving the problem can benefit the interests of both parties. For example, resolving problems such as maintaining competitiveness, adapting to technological change, and meeting employee health-care needs might lead negotiators to a mutual gain bargaining approach.

Mutual gain bargaining encourages and values mutual trust and respect between the parties. In addition to concern for the parties' respective substantive interests, there is concern about the effects of the negotiation process and outcomes on the quality of the parties' continuing bargaining relationship. Efforts are made to identify multiple alternatives to each negotiating problem that are capable of meeting both parties' key interests. Negotiators focus less on narrowing the gap between each party's position and more on expanding the number of mutually satisfactory solutions. Bargaining power is a less important determinant of bargaining outcomes because the parties agree in advance on some objective criteria or standards to use in evaluating the merits of specific bargaining proposals. For example, the industry or local area average might be agreed on to determine the number of paid holidays that employees should receive. This approach encourages mutual trust and an understanding of the other party's needs and objectives and emphasizes the commonalities between the parties instead of their differences.[17]

Strategies and Tactics

Some bargaining strategies and tactics may be appropriate for use in either a distributive or mutual gain approach to bargaining. *Using persuasive arguments and objective evidence* in support of bargaining proposals or *painting a picture of the loss or gain* to ensure that negotiators understand what is at stake for the parties' interests, as well as the relative costs/benefits of reaching agreement versus continued disagreement, are two examples. *Summarizing bargaining progress* to date often helps to clarify perceptions and direct future negotiations on specific subjects. *Presenting a bargaining proposal in writing*, as well as explaining it orally, helps to ensure the other party understands the proposal. *Listening carefully* for ideas and emotions, not just facts, and noting *nonverbal cues* (e.g., eye contact, tone of voice, facial or hand expressions, reaction of other team members) can often provide information about the importance and degree of commitment to statements being made at the bargaining table.

Use of a *bargaining caucus* provides time away from the bargaining table to discuss bargaining proposals or strategies, conduct costing, gather additional information, or simply avoid making a statement at the bargaining table that one is not prepared to make. *Use of positive reinforcement,* such as expressing appreciation for specific bargaining behavior or acknowledging the acceptable portions of the other party's proposal, can help to establish a positive environment in which to continue negotiations. *Linking issues (package proposal),* such as the example in Exhibit 6.3, is another strategy that can be used to resolve a large number of issues in a fairly short time or aid in resolving the few remaining unsettled issues late in the negotiation process. As different types of issues become linked, it may be more difficult to evaluate the relative value of different proposed packages.

Two final strategies or tactics that may be appropriate in either a distributive or mutual gain approach to bargaining are *matching concessions* and *splitting-the-difference.* Many negotiators operate under the assumption that concessions granted by one party will be reciprocated or matched by concessions of relatively equal value from the other party, although not necessarily involving the same bargaining issue. Most negotiators prefer to leave all settlements reached during the negotiation process as tentative settlements until all issues have been resolved. What a party finds acceptable in the later stages of bargaining may be determined in part by the prior pattern of concessions and whether the established concession pattern is perceived to be equitable or fair. The acceptability of simply splitting the difference as a means of resolving settlement terms, particularly near the end of negotiations where the prior concession pattern is known, may depend on a party's perceived equity in the tentative contract terms already reached and the priority of the unsettled bargaining issues to that party's key bargaining interests. In addition to the general strategies and tactics mentioned above, Exhibit 6.4 presents a list of bargaining strategies or tactics appropriate for use in distributive bargaining. Exhibit 6.5 presents a list of bargaining strategies and tactics appropriate for mutual gain (win-win or interest-based) bargaining.

The Bargaining Power Model

Bargaining power is an important concept that can affect the process and outcomes of negotiations, particularly when the parties adopt a distributive bargaining approach. Because negotiation is an interdependent activity, it is important to focus on the difference between the bargaining power of each bargaining party rather than simply assessing the amount of bargaining power possessed by a single party. Evidence of a party's greater bargaining power is the ability to obtain settlement on that party's preferred terms rather than less favorable terms proposed by another party.

Chamberlain and Kuhn present one of the better-known bargaining power models.[18] One party's bargaining power can be conceptualized as equal to the other party's cost of disagreeing with proposed settlement terms divided by their cost of agreeing to such terms. These union or management bargaining power equations can be applied to assess the parties' relative bargaining power regarding specific bargaining proposals or to a post hoc analysis of final settlement terms to assess which party possessed greater bargaining power. Although the bargaining power model is presented as an equation, it is an imprecise formula based on two major assumptions: (1) union and management negotiators cost issues in a similar manner and are rational individuals, and (2) if it costs more for a party to disagree than to agree with the other, then the party will agree to the other party's proposal. Each side can increase its bargaining power by either

Exhibit 6.4

Some Strategies and Tactics for Use in Distributive Bargaining

- Undermine the other party's position. Question the validity of assumptions, facts, or conclusions; focus on omissions, inconsistencies, or other perceived weaknesses in the other party's reasoning or information.

- Offer initial proposals well removed from your party's resistance point on each bargaining subject.

- Concede slowly from initial bargaining positions. The other party will value more highly (and thus reciprocate in kind) those concessions that it has to work hard to get.

- Attempt to appear firmly committed to bargaining proposals.

- Threaten the other party's key interests (e.g., job security, sales, public image) to impose pressure by increasing the other party's perceived costs of failing to settle on your party's proposed terms. For a threat to be perceived as credible, the party receiving the threat must believe that the party making the threat is both able and willing to perform the threatened act.

- Offer to reward key interests of the other party (e.g., increase job security, grant greater access to information, grant economic incentive) to persuade them to settle on your preferred terms. This approach is intended to lower the other party's costs of agreeing to your party's proposed terms.

- Seek opportunities to delay negotiations as a means of imposing time pressure on the other party before a settlement deadline (e.g., contract expiration date, strike/lockout date).

- Seek to maximize the perceived value of your party's concessions while minimizing the value of concessions granted by the other party.

- Threaten to withdraw a proposal if it is not accepted within a reasonable time. Alternatively, make the initial proposal contingent on acceptance by a specified deadline. This approach can also be used to counter another party's delay tactics when addressing proposals.

- Schedule marathon bargaining sessions in an effort to wear down the other party's resistance or concentration level. Time pressure during the late stage of bargaining may make such marathon bargaining sessions necessary if the parties seek to reach an agreement before a strike or lockout deadline is reached.

- Make a final offer. Whether a so called "final offer" is really final depends on the perceived credibility of the negotiator making the offer.

increasing the other party's costs of disagreement or reducing the other party's cost of agreement to proposed contract terms.

To illustrate this strategic framework, consider a union bargaining proposal for a 10-minute cleanup time before the end of the work shift. First, the union could reduce management's cost of agreeing with the cleanup time proposal by eliminating some of its other bargaining proposals in exchange. The union negotiator might also reduce management's perceived agreement costs by demonstrating that there are currently many different cleanup practices at the firm. Some departments do not have cleanup time, whereas other departments let their employees stop work a half-hour early to clean up. If the total cleanup time in the plant were calculated, it would probably amount to 15 minutes per employee. It would be difficult for management to discipline employees who are abusing cleanup time because no consistent policy regarding this issue is enforced in the plant. This contract provision would enable management to wipe the past practice slate clean and establish a consistent policy. Management could instruct supervisors to enforce a 10-minute cleanup time policy, which could actually save the company money.

Exhibit 6.5

Some Strategies and Tactics for Use in Win-Win (Mutual Gain) Bargaining

- Set realistic bargaining objectives.
- Clarify the interests underlying each party's proposals on specific issues. Avoid becoming fixated on another party's stated position. Focus instead on understanding a party's key interests at stake regarding the issue being negotiated.
- Use brainstorming to generate alternative proposals designed to meet the parties' respective interests on each subject.
- Identify the bargaining subject where the parties share mutual interests and those subjects where the parties interest may conflict. Begin negotiations on subjects of mutual interests, seeking to establish a bargaining pattern that can later be used as a model to address more difficult issues which involve conflicting interest.
- Exhibit empathy toward the other party's interests and concerns.
- Identify and mutually agree on objective standards for evaluating the merits of specific bargaining proposals.
- Open negotiations with a clear statement of your party's intent to negotiate cooperatively and invite the other party to participate in such an approach. For a win-win bargaining approach to succeed, both parties must be committed to the process.
- Ask questions to clarify the substantive content or intent behind specific bargaining proposals.
- Share objective information about specific bargaining subjects with the other party.
- Seek to incorporate as much of the other party's proposal as possible into your party's counterproposal on a bargaining subject. This helps to demonstrate a willingness to accommodate the other party's interests and helps to focus subsequent bargaining on those aspects of the proposal where a conflict of interests remains.
- Explain how or why your party's proposal meets an important need or interest of the other party.
- Openly discuss perceived obstacles or barriers to achieving a voluntary settlement (e.g., personalities, tactics, competitive environment, or status of the bargaining relationship).
- Minimize emotional outburst.
- Avoid strategies or tactics that might undermine your credibility as a negotiator or damage the level of mutual trust and respect between the bargaining parties.

If management does not accept this argument, the union could follow the second strategic approach—increasing management's cost of disagreeing with the union's proposal. A union might threaten to withhold approval of some management-proposed contract term or publicize the poor working or safety conditions at the plant that could harm employee recruitment efforts or customer relations. A strike threat might carry some credibility if management knew that widespread dissatisfaction existed over this issue and any disruption in current production would economically harm the firm.

Factors Potentially Affecting Both Bargaining Power Equations

Some factors that may affect union and management bargaining power are prevailing economic conditions (e.g., unemployment rate, labor supply, sales volume), goodwill, public image, and government intervention. For example, high unemployment in the area increases the union's cost of disagreeing with management because strikers could find it difficult to find employment at other firms while reducing management's disagreement costs by making striker replacements easier to hire. One factor that can influence the decision to strike, especially in small plants, is goodwill, which pertains mostly to internal relationships. Management and union negotiators do not want antagonistic attitudes that develop during negotiations or a strike to linger when operations are resumed. Negotiators also do not want their activities labeled irresponsible or insensitive to the public interest, thereby adversely impacting each party's public image. Possible government intervention for vital industries (e.g., airline, railroad) or in the case of a national emergency dispute (discussed in Chapter 9) must also be considered, especially if management or the union believes government intervention will weaken its bargaining position.

Factors Affecting a Union's Disagreement and Agreement Costs

Financial supplements given to union members can lower both a union's disagreement costs and management's bargaining power. Employees might be able to supplement their incomes during a strike through their spouses' employment, union strike benefits, personal savings, aid from other labor organizations, or public aid. Union strike benefits rarely are intended to cover all lost income resulting from strike participation and usually average $50 or less per week. Whether a union provides strike benefits may often determine whether union members will vote to strike, as well as how long they will stay out on strike. Although the amount that each union member receives during a strike is minimal, the total amount of annual strike payments can be large. Most unions pay strike benefits when funds are available and the strike has been sanctioned by the national union leadership, but often additional stipulations may require that the member be in good standing, complete a waiting period, or establish a need for the payments.

Public aid (e.g., welfare and unemployment compensation) can also reduce union members' disagreement costs by supplementing their incomes when they go on strike. These assistance programs might exist at the federal or state level and are subject to various qualifications, such as a waiting period for striking employees to qualify for unemployment compensation. Many arguments can be made for and against public aid being given to union members on strike. Proponents of public aid might claim the following:

- Strikers are taxpayers when they work, so when they do not work, they should receive aid.

- Tax dollars are used to feed hungry people in other countries and prisoners in this country, so strikers who are needy should receive the same consideration.

- Even though some persons may be against public aid for strikers, they should not be against public aid for the families of strikers who are directly affected.

- Eligibility for public support should be based on need as determined by law, not on whether a person is on strike.

Opponents of public support to strikers also make several arguments:

- Legislators never intended to provide public aid to strikers, particularly because strikers have refused bona fide employment by refusing to go back to work.

- Giving public aid to strikers violates a traditional policy of government neutrality in labor-management relations.

Factors Affecting Management's Agreement and Disagreement Costs

Management's costs of agreeing to union proposals can be reduced if it can pass on the cost of a negotiated settlement to customers. The increased globally competitive nature of many product markets makes it difficult for many employers today to simply pass cost on to consumers in the form of product or service price increases. Some regulated firms like electric utilities operate under pricing guidelines, which permit the company to raise prices to cover legitimate increases in business operating costs. Management's disagreement costs (and union bargaining power) can be increased if any of the following factors occur: low inventories combined with high customer demand; fear of permanent loss of customers during a strike; or high fixed costs, such as rent, interest on loans, payments for equipment, and salaries of nonunion personnel, that could continue to accrue even if production were reduced or eliminated.

Complexities Associated with the Bargaining Power Model

Bargaining power "costs" are often imprecise figures associated with calculation difficulties, large and sudden change, and other complexities. Some issues, such as inserting the job requirement "perform minor repairs" into employees' job descriptions, will undoubtedly save the company money because lower skill noncraft employees may perform these duties less expensively than more highly skilled maintenance employees, particularly those working at overtime or other premium wage rates. However, management cannot calculate the precise dollar-cost savings associated with this provision, particularly if the union negotiator fears that agreeing with a "minor repairs" clause would incur imprecise yet large political costs, such as skilled maintenance members rejecting the proposed labor contract or the union leader's reelection bid.

Perceived or estimated costs associated with use of the bargaining power model are subject to change during negotiations. The government may suddenly announce wage-price controls or guidelines, forcing unions to agree to wage settlements comparable to the limits set by the government. Or, management could receive a sudden influx of rush orders from a major customer near the contract expiration date. Management's disagreement costs may sharply increase, particularly if the customer indicates that he or she will take unfilled orders to a competitor.

The limitations of the bargaining power model do not eliminate its usefulness. Union and management officials do assign costs, however crudely, and direct their strategies toward increasing the other party's disagreement costs relative to agreement costs.

Intraorganizational Bargaining

Another important aspect of the bargaining process is **intraorganizational bargaining**, which refers to the negotiations that occur within each bargaining party as management and union negotiators attempt to achieve consensus within their respective organizations.[19] Sometimes the most difficult bargaining is that which occurs within each party rather than between union and management negotiators.

Management's chief negotiator sometimes takes a backseat to other management officials, particularly lawyers, at the bargaining table. Often the need to comply with corporate policy may complicate local plant negotiations by reducing a management negotiator's flexibility to deviate from a policy intended to cover a variety of different plant settings. When a settlement is reached, it is also subject to second-guessing by other managers, who usually contend that management negotiators could have obtained a better deal. The union is not exempt from internal disputes either, particularly because its chief negotiator is seldom given a free hand in selecting the negotiating committee. In many cases, at least one member of the union's negotiating team is a political rival of the chief negotiator. More prevalent are factions that attempt to obtain various bargaining demands regardless of the chief negotiator's preferences.

Management and union negotiators spend much time resolving differences within their respective organizations. One observer of labor–management negotiations noted the following: "[A] large share of collective bargaining is not conflict but a process by which the main terms of the agreement, already understood by the negotiators, are made acceptable, not to those in charge of the bargaining but to those who will have to live with its results."[20]

Ethical and Legal Considerations in Collective Bargaining

Union and management negotiators' bargaining behavior often involves at least two general ethical dimensions. The first ethical dimension, moral or ideal behavior, is subject to varying definitions instead of an either/or distinction. However, negotiator behaviors such as bribing the opponent to reach a settlement, stealing an opponent's confidential information, publicly demeaning or humiliating an opponent, or using electronic surveillance to "bug" an opponent's meeting areas are clearly at the unethical end of the continuum.

Some bargaining behaviors have more general and longer-range ethical implications. Consider, for example, the reflections of Lee Iacocca, former chief executive officer of Chrysler Corporation:

> As long as Detroit was making money, it was always easy for us to accept union demands and recoup them later in the form of price increases. The alternative was to take a strike and risk ruining the company.
>
> The executives at GM, Ford, and Chrysler have never been overly interested in long-range planning. They've been too concerned about expediency, improving the profits for the next quarter—and earning a good bonus.
>
> They? I should be saying "we." After all, I was one of the boys. I was part of that system. Gradually, little by little, we gave in to virtually every union demand. We were making so much money that we didn't think twice. We were rarely willing to take a strike, and so we never stood on principle. I sat there in the midst of it all and I said: "Discretion is the better part of valor. Give them what they want. Because if they strike, we'll lose hundreds of millions of dollars, we'll lose our bonuses, and I'll personally lose half a million dollars in cash."
>
> Our motivation was greed. The instinct was always to settle quickly, to go for the bottom line. In this regard, our critics were right—we were always thinking of the next quarter. "What's another dollar an hour?" we reasoned. "Let future generations worry about it. We won't be around then." But the future has arrived, and some of us are still around. Today we're all paying the price for our complacency.[21]

The second ethical dimension, conforming to professionals standards, is more complicated when applied to negotiators' behaviors. Top union and management bargaining team officials would likely agree on at least three professional commitments in their bargaining behaviors:

1. To obtain the best possible settlement benefiting their party's interests

2. To convince their respective bargaining team members and other constituents that they are effective negotiators

3. To communicate with the other negotiating team in an honest, respectful fashion to enhance the parties' continuing labor relations relationship after the collective bargaining agreement is reached

All three of these standards are attainable, although maximizing the first two may strain and alter the third. In other words, it is difficult to convince one's bargaining constituents that the best settlement possible was obtained after revealing the complete truth to the negotiating opponent. This perhaps helps explain why distributive bargaining is still more common than mutual gain bargaining in labor negotiations today. A completely honest and open negotiator may be exploited by his or her opponent, commit to a position that allows no further concessions, or sacrifice what might have been successfully gained through a less candid approach. Many successful negotiations feature ritualistic elements, such as describing elaborate but irrelevant statistics, using histrionics, or staging false fights or temper tantrums.

Successful negotiators realize that credibility is a necessary personal attribute, and lying or uttering a deliberate falsehood can destroy credibility and ruin a negotiator's effectiveness. However, a fine line exists between lying and withholding the complete truth. Negotiators are not going to volunteer items that could damage their bargaining positions. Negotiators may also exaggerate or bluff on occasion, although this is risky behavior if a negotiator is not prepared to have his or her bluff called by the other party:

> The principled negotiator doesn't resort to trickery, but that doesn't mean he naively gives away his position. Not all principled negotiators agree on just how principled you have to be. It's OK to mislead the other side as to your intentions, [one principled negotiator] argues. You can say I'm not going to give in, and then give in 5 minutes later. But never give the other side misinformation about the facts.[22]

The Legal Duty to Bargain in Good Faith

Union and management officials are not completely free to shape or ignore ethical considerations in collective bargaining. The government, through the Labor Management Relations Act, as amended, requires that both union and management organizations negotiate in good faith in an effort to voluntarily settle bargaining disputes. **Good-faith bargaining** essentially means each party must demonstrate a sincere and honest intent to reach a labor agreement and be reasonable in their bargaining positions, tactics, and activities.

In attempting to decide the merit of a bad-faith bargaining unfair labor practice charge, the NLRB must assess the totality of each party's conduct, which includes both overt behavior and underlying motivation or intent. However, good faith represents a state of mind difficult to define precisely. For example, the duty to bargain in good faith does not require a party to reach a settlement, agree to a specific proposal, or make a concession to the other party. Yet for settlement to occur, an underlying presumption in collective bargaining prevails that concessions will typically be made by both parties. Violations of good-faith bargaining can come from four sources: the nature of the bargaining issues, specific bargaining actions (called *per se* violations), totality of conduct, and successor employer bargaining obligations.

Nature of Bargaining Subjects

Over the years, the NLRB and the courts have categorized bargaining issues as illegal, mandatory, or voluntary. **Illegal bargaining subjects** involve a violation of law, and there is no legal duty to bargain over such an issue. If the parties were to include such an illegal term in their contract (e.g., permitting management to pay less than the federal minimum wage for covered employees), that portion of the parties' contract would be unenforceable. Other examples of illegal terms would include a closed-shop union security clause, a "whites only" employment clause, mandatory retirement at age 62, and compensation terms that violate the provisions of the Fair Labor Standards Act (e.g., not paying covered employees overtime pay for hours worked in excess of 40 hours per week).

There is a duty to bargain in good faith over **mandatory bargaining subjects**, which may have a direct affect on bargaining unit members' wages, hours, or other terms and conditions of employment. Exhibit 6.6 presents a list of some mandatory subjects of bargaining. Mandatory bargaining subjects compose the bulk of the bargaining agenda during labor contract negotiations.

Management may not legally change an existing employment term involving a mandatory bargaining subject unless the current contract clearly gives management the right to do so; the union has clearly waived its right to bargain over the subject; or both parties have bargained in good faith and reached a voluntary agreement. If no current contract is in effect covering the proposed change, management could institute a proposed change after bargaining in good faith to an impasse with the union over the subject. A **good-faith bargaining impasse** occurs at the point in negotiation where neither party is willing to modify its position on a bargaining subject further. Interest disputes involving a mandatory bargaining subject are also the only subjects over which a lawful strike or lockout may occur.

There is no duty to bargain over a business decision that involves a fundamental change in the nature, scope, or direction of the firm.[23] This would include decisions to sell the firm or buy another firm, major equipment purchases, the number or types of products or services to produce, financing sources or terms to meet operating needs, and marketing decisions. Even though not required to bargain about a business decision itself, an employer may be required to bargain over the *effects* of that business decision on bargaining unit employees' job security or economic interests (e.g., severance pay, transfer rights, seniority rights, layoff or recall rights).[24] An employer may be required to bargain over a decision to transfer or relocate bargaining unit work if the business decision does not involve a substantial change in the nature of the employer's operation (e.g., same work being performed under similar work conditions at the new location but using different [non-bargaining unit] employees).[25]

Union and management officials may also negotiate **voluntary bargaining subjects** (also termed *nonmandatory* or *permissive*) that do not directly affect bargaining unit members' terms or conditions of employment and are not illegal.

Exhibit 6.6

Some Mandatory Subjects of Bargaining*

Hourly wage or incentive (piece) rate of pay	Identity of the insurance carrier
Bonus pay	Health-care cost containment plan
Profit-sharing plan	Clothing or tool allowance
Employee stock ownership plan	Hours of work
Lump-sum pay	Mandatory overtime policy
Two-tier wage plan	Pension plan
Call-in pay	Tax deferred (e.g., 401k) savings plan
Shift differential pay	Job or income security guarantee
Jury duty pay	Job classification system
Overtime pay	Job duties and qualifications
Cost-of-living adjustment clause	Job transfer rights and procedure
Funeral leave pay	Job promotion criteria and procedure
Vacation pay	Layoff and recall procedure
Holiday pay	Seniority rights
Paid rest periods	Length of job probationary period
Paid lunch period	Grievance-arbitration procedure
Employee discounts on company products or services	Management rights
Child-care assistance plan	Subcontracting of bargaining unit work
Dental insurance	Joint union-management cooperation plan
Life insurance	Employee testing procedures (e.g., drug test)
Effective and expiration time and date of the contract	Performance evaluation methods and procedure
Waiver of right to bargain (e.g., "zipper clause")	Safety and health standards and procedures
Leave of absence	Successorship clause
Health and accident insurance	No strike or lockout clause

*The subjects listed are not intended to represent an all-inclusive list of possible mandatory bargaining subjects.

For example, a jointly funded industry marketing promotion plan, strike insurance, an interest arbitration clause, or improved pension benefits for retired employees (former bargaining unit members). Unlike mandatory subjects, voluntary bargaining subjects do not require either party to bargain. In fact, insisting on their bargaining and inclusion in the labor agreement to a point of impasse would be an unfair labor practice. For example, in a case involving Dupont Company managers' asking employees to participate in a promotional videotape, the NLRB determined this action was a voluntary bargaining subject that did not have to be negotiated with the union because it was not part of the employees' day-to-day responsibilities, employees were not compelled to participate, and the taping was not a matter of deep concern to the employees.[26]

Specific Bargaining Actions

In some cases a specific, single action by an employer constitutes an unfair labor practice in bargaining. For example, management commits a per se violation whenever it does the following:

- Refuses to meet with the union to negotiate its proposals.

- Implements a wage change without consulting the union.

- Insists to a point of impasse on a provision requiring that a secret-ballot election be held before a strike can be called.

- Refuses to furnish requested information to the union that is relevant and necessary for the union to perform its legal bargaining duty (e.g., supply cost and other data relating to a group insurance plan administered by the employer).

If an employer claims an **inability to pay** for a union's bargaining proposal, the union is entitled access to company financial information necessary to validate the employer's inability to pay claim. An inability to pay is legally distinct from expressing an *unwillingness to pay* the cost of a union bargaining proposal, and thus this obligation is sometimes complicated to apply.[27] In one case the NLRB found the employer did not commit a violation when it refused a union's request for information because the employer's stated desire to bring its labor costs in line with its competitors, which might be nonunion, was a legitimate bargaining goal and not a statement of the employer's inability to pay.[28] Yet in other cases although the employer tried to couch its refusal to furnish information requested by a union as a competitive issue rather than a claim of inability to pay, the NLRB found that the employer's intent was to claim an inability to pay.[29]

Any information requested by the union is subject to the following prerequisites:

1. The union must make a good-faith demand or request for the information.

2. The information sought must be *relevant and necessary* for negotiations. This typically means the information sought must pertain to a mandatory subject of bargaining and is not available from any other source reasonably accessible to the union.

3. The information must be supplied to the union promptly and in a form reasonably useful for negotiation purposes.

A union commits a per se violation when it engages in the following:

- Insists on a closed-shop or discriminatory hiring clause.

- Refuses to meet with a legal representative of the employer about negotiations.

- Refuses to negotiate a management proposal involving a mandatory subject.

Totality of Conduct

In evaluating the underlying intent behind specific bargaining actions, the NLRB and the courts often apply the **totality of conduct doctrine.** This legal doctrine states that even though individual acts when viewed separately do not constitute a bargaining violation, such acts may constitute an unfair labor practice when viewed as a pattern of conduct in the totality of the circumstances surrounding the negotiations. A prominent and controversial example of this legal consideration involved a bargaining strategy used by the General Electric Company (GE) called **Boulwarism** after the late vice president of General Electric, Lemuel Boulware.[30]

GE contended that it simply approached bargaining in a manner similar to its product marketing—by researching the employees' desires and the firm's competitive position and then presenting a fair bargaining proposal to the union. GE would refuse to modify its original proposal unless the union could present new and significant information bearing on the issues at the bargaining table, which the union, in the company's view, was rarely able to do. GE management contended that this approach was not capricious, but "fair and firm," because management's bargaining position was based on a careful examination of the "facts." This approach, the company maintained, represented a sincere bargaining effort aimed not at destroying the union but rather at eliminating a time-consuming and unnecessary ritual from collective bargaining (such as initial unrealistic offers that both parties know will not be accepted). GE coupled its bargaining table strategy with a separate communication campaign aimed at convincing bargaining unit employees that the company's offer was fair and reasonable and implying that any delay in reaching agreement would be the responsibility of union leaders, not management.

Unions representing General Electric employees termed the company's approach "hard bargaining" that was not flexible enough to reasonably consider alternative union views on bargaining subjects. GE unions believed that the company's communication campaign directed at bargaining unit members represented an effort by management to undermine the union's legal status as the employees' bargaining agent by attempting to bypass dealing with union negotiators at the bargaining table in favor of dealing directly with employees.

GE's Boulwarism strategy was found, based on the totality of conduct doctrine, to be a violation of good-faith bargaining primarily because it attempted to bypass the employees' exclusive bargaining agent (the union) with a direct campaign intended to persuade each employee to pressure their union representative to accept management's terms.[31] The U.S. Supreme court was careful to point out that "hard bargaining" without other condemning evidence was not, per se, an unfair labor practice itself. Other condemning evidence present in the GE case included a refusal to supply cost information on an insurance program, vague responses to the union's detailed proposals, a prepared lecture series instead of counteroffers, and a "stiff and unbending patriarchal posture" even after it was apparent that the union would have to concede to the employer's terms. Management can legally communicate to the employees its own bargaining proposals and the reasons for them, as well as explain why management opposes specific union bargaining proposals, as long as such communication is not intended to undermine the status of the union as the employees' bargaining agent.[32]

Other rulings involving employer or union conduct have provided the following examples of conduct that may constitute bad-faith bargaining:

- *Surface bargaining:* A party is willing to meet at length and confer but merely goes through the motions of bargaining without any evidence of a sincere desire to reach an agreement. Surface bargaining includes a party making proposals that it knows the other party cannot accept, taking an inflexible attitude on important issues, or offering no alternative proposals.

- *Dilatory tactics:* Unreasonable procrastination in executing an agreement, unreasonable delay in scheduling meetings, willful avoidance of meetings, evasive tactics, unreasonable delay in providing data for bargaining, and similar tactics are evidence of bad faith.

- *Imposing unreasonable conditions:* Attempts to specify conditions on bargaining or the administration of a labor contract will be scrutinized closely to determine whether such conditions are onerous or unreasonable (e.g., insisting that all grievances be resolved before collective bargaining can start). In addition, the requirement of agreement on a specific item as a prerequisite to negotiating other issues may reflect a bad-faith bargaining intent.

- *Unilateral changes in conditions:* Such actions as changing the compensation or fringe-benefit package unilaterally during bargaining without having reached a good-faith bargaining impasse is a strong indicator of bad-faith bargaining.

- *Commission of unfair labor practices:* Committing unfair labor practices (such as promoting withdrawal from the union, reducing work hours, and engaging in discriminatory layoffs) during negotiations is indicative of bad faith.

Managerial Rights

One very important mandatory subject of bargaining of interest to employers is the subject of **management's rights.** Before the passage of the National Labor Relations Act (NLRA) in 1935, management rights and discretion in operating facilities were seldom questioned, and managers were virtually free to run their operations as they saw fit. In many cases, unions were considered intruders into managerial prerogatives because there were few laws regulating managers' actions toward employees. Although unions have become more accepted today, managers remain concerned over the gradual erosion of their rights in the labor relations process.

Under common law, management officials were relatively free to manage their businesses and their employees. In unilaterally running the operation, the employer drew from the concepts of property rights and the laws of agency, as well as the legal and social acceptance of "private enterprise," "ingenuity," and the "profit motive." Hence, management assumed the right to manage as derived from the property rights of the owner. The authority of the owner is delegated to management, which in turn directs the employees in achieving the goals of the company. Following this line of reasoning, management contends it cannot share its prerogatives with employees or any other group because such an action would represent a dereliction of legal responsibility to the ownership.

There is no question that management can organize, arrange, and direct the machinery, materials, and money of the enterprise; however, at least one author contends that managers have no comparable right to direct the employees. Property rights carry no duty on the part of others to permit themselves to be managed. Employees can quit or be discharged without regard to the employer's property rights. Thus, management's property rights have never extended over the employees. "What has happened is that, through the union, the employee has acquired sufficient power to exercise the legal right that he has always possessed."[33]

Most unions in the United States, unlike their European counterparts (see Chapter 14), are typically reluctant to become "partners with management"—directly involved in managerial rights pertaining to layout of equipment, financial policies, sources of materials, and so forth. Union officers realize that often union members prefer to second-guess or challenge the wisdom of management decisions instead of supporting or echoing them. It is more difficult for union leaders to effectively criticize business policy decisions that they have jointly participated in deciding with management representatives.

Yet the unions' desire to avoid involvement in traditional areas of management decision making is not absolute. Management rights are exercised to achieve significant managerial goals of organizational flexibility and efficiency. Unions are concerned about managerial actions to achieve these goals, which may appear arbitrary or inconsistent or entail adverse consequences for union members' jobs or economic security.[34] Some research has found that craft and industrial unions have become more interested in joint determination of traditional management issues (e.g., products to be manufactured, services to be performed, and customer relations) over the past 20 years. This new emphasis is largely attributed to competitive pressures, which have influenced union officials to evaluate a broader range of managerial decisions that could reduce union members' job opportunities.[35]

Until 1960, management rights clauses contained in labor agreements tended to be based solely on the **reserved rights doctrine**, which essentially holds that all rights to manage the firm are reserved to management except to the extent management has voluntarily agreed to limit or restrict such rights through language found elsewhere in a labor agreement. For example, if the labor agreement is silent on overtime administration, then under the reserved rights doctrine, management can assign overtime to whomever it sees fit. A typical **short-form management's rights clause** prior to 1960 based on the reserved rights doctrine might state the following:

> *Employer retains all rights to manage, direct, and control its business in all particulars, except as such rights are expressly and specifically modified by the terms of this agreement or any subsequent agreement.*

Many managers assumed that the broad language of the short-form management's rights clause guaranteed management's complete discretion in those matters not specifically included in the labor agreement. Primary reliance by management on the reserved rights doctrine to protect its managerial prerogatives was dealt a setback by the U.S. Supreme Court's 1960 decision in the *United Steelworkers v. Warrior and Gulf Navigation Company* (as discussed in Chapter 11).[36] In this case, the employer refused the union's request to take a grievance dispute to final and binding arbitration because the employer argued that the issue involved was not covered under the parties' labor agreement and therefore the right to determine the outcome of that issue was reserved to management. The Court stated that where there isn't clear evidence regarding the parties' intention to cover a specific subject under a labor agreement's terms, the arbitrator could determine whether an issue was covered under the parties' agreement to arbitrate contract disputes, and any doubts about coverage should be resolved in favor of permitting the grievance dispute to be arbitrated.

In response to the U.S. Supreme Court's decision in *Warrior and Gulf Navigation Company*, many management representatives sought to negotiate a more specific, detailed list of specific subjects over which management intended to reserve the right to control. Such contract language became known as a **long-form management's rights clause** and is the most common form of management rights clause found in labor agreements today (see Exhibit 6.7). Presumably, arbitrators, upon seeing such a detailed list of management prerogatives clearly stated in the labor agreement, would rule in management's favor on whether the

Exhibit 6.7

Example of a Long-Form Management's Rights Clause

Article 2
Management Rights

The company has, retains and shall possess and exercise all management functions, rights, powers, privileges and authority inherent in the company as owner and operator of the business, excepting only such rights that are specifically and expressly relinquished or restricted by a specific Article or Section of this Agreement.

The company shall have the exclusive right to manage facilities; to direct the working forces; to fix or change the number, hours, and duration of work shifts; to establish or alter work schedules or standards; to control the use of scheduling of operations; to allocate and assign work to employess; to schedule overtime; to hire, classify, train, promote, transfer, suspend, demote, discipline; to discharge employees for just cause, . . . and to discipline or discharge employees for violation of such rules and regulations; to determine safety, health, and property protection measures for any and all employees, operations, and facilities; to select and to change tools, equipment, machinery, material, layout, and facilities with which it shall carry on its operations; to determine the products to be manufactured or sold or the services to be rendered; to determine at all times the number and composition of the work force as a whole or of any unit, shift, job classification, or work within such job classification; to create new organization groups deemed appropriate by the company and to determine the organization and structure of each; to determine, implement, modify, or eliminate techniques, methods, processes, means of manufacture, maintenance, and distribution, schedules, crew, or production team sizes, and line speeds; to control raw material; to shift types of work and production or maintenance in and out of any facility; to place production, service, maintenance, or distribution work with outside contractors or subcontractors; to use labor-saving devices; to determine and implement actions necessary to operate as economically and efficiently as possible when and where the company deems the same necessary or desirable, including layoff of employees; to determine the qualifications and duties of employees; to establish or modify reasonable quality and quantity standards; to judge the quantity and quality of workmanship required and discipline or discharge employees whose work does not meet such standards; to establish or revise pay grades for jobs; to change the method of compensation of employees, to establish or modify job classifications and related rates of pay, or revise or eliminate existing jobs; to transfer and assign work and duties to job classifications when the company deems the same necessary or desirable; to select, demote, promote, or transfer bargaining unit employees from one unit, section, department, division, plant, or other unit to another; to transfer work from one job to another; to determine the location of the business, including the establishment of new plants, departments, divisions, or subdivisions and the relocation, closing, selling, merging, or liquidating of any plant, department, division, or subdivisions thereof either permanently or temporarily; to determine financial policy, including accounting procedures, prices of goods or services rendered or supplied, and customer relations; to determine the size and character of inventories; to determine the policy affecting the selection and training of new employees; to determine the amound of supervision necessary; and generally to control and direct the company in all of its affairs and operations.

SOURCE: Excerpted from a labor agreement.

grievance is subject to arbitration. However, the long-form management's rights clause has its problems:

1. It is difficult to anticipate and clearly list every item over which management might seek to maintain unilateral discretion. Arbitrators tend to view a detailed long-form management's rights clause as expressing management's intent to define all its prerogatives. A detailed listing of management's rights in a labor agreement makes it more unlikely an arbitrator

would permit management to retain exclusive control over any otherwise mandatory subject of bargaining that management might claim it merely forgot to include in the negotiated management's rights clause.

2. Since the union must agree to all wording contained in the management's rights clause of the labor agreement, it may be necessary for management negotiators to give the union a concession on another issue to obtain a strongly worded management's rights clause. For example, management may have to allow the union a strong union security clause, such as a *union shop* clause, previously discussed in Chapter 4.

Both long and short forms of management rights clauses can cause additional problems. By insisting on including the management rights clause in the labor agreement, management runs the risk of stirring up ideological differences with the union. Rights included in the management's rights clause may also influence union bargaining goals in subsequent negotiations.

For managers, the advantages of a long-form management's rights clause outweigh the potential risks. Approximately 80 percent of labor agreements contain a management rights clause that helps remind arbitrators, union officials, and other managers (particularly first-line supervisors) that management retains its administrative initiative to establish the status quo.[37]

Successor Employer Bargaining Obligations

The increased level of merger and acquisition activity among firms in recent years has raised several concerns regarding the duty to bargain. Whether a change in ownership at a unionized firm results in a "new" versus "successor" employer depends on the degree of continuity in the business enterprise after the ownership change occurs.[38] Purchasers would generally prefer to be classified as a **new employer,** who has no legal duty to automatically recognize any former union as the bargaining representative of current employees and thus is under no duty to bargain over the establishment of employment terms or to abide by the terms of any prior labor agreement negotiated by the former owner.

Where there is *substantial continuity in business operations,* the purchaser is classified as a **successor employer,** whereas a lack of substantial continuity in business operations characterizes a new employer. Degree of business continuity can be evaluated by examining factors such as the percentage of former union-represented employees who continue to be employed after the ownership change; whether there is any substantial change in the location of the firm, type of customers served, or products produced; degree of change in equipment or other technological processes; and the percentage of managers under the former owner who continue to manage employees after the change in ownership.

A successor employer has a legal duty, on request, to recognize the union that represented bargaining unit members under the former owner as continuing to represent the same bargaining unit structure under the current ownership. A successor employer must also be willing, on request, to engage in good-faith bargaining over the terms of a new labor agreement covering bargaining unit employees. A successor employer is not generally obligated to continue to enforce the terms of a previously existing labor agreement unless the contract contained a **successorship clause** that the purchaser knew about at the time of the ownership transfer. A successorship clause represents a mandatory subject of bargaining and requires an employer not to sell or merge the firm unless the purchaser is willing to take on the terms of any existing labor contract. One 2003 survey reported a successorship clause was present in approximately 30 percent of labor agreements.[39] An earlier study reported successorship clauses were more common in nonmanufacturing industries and were present in more than 50 percent of labor contracts in some industries (e.g., utilities, apparel, retail, transportation, foods, insurance and finance).[40]

Collective Bargaining under Bankruptcy Proceedings: The *Bildisco* Decision

What happens to the existing bargaining agreement if management files for bankruptcy and contends that it can no longer honor the labor agreement? This question was addressed in the U.S. Supreme Court's 1984 *Bildisco* decision, which involved a building supply distributor who filed a petition for reorganization under Chapter 11 of the bankruptcy code.[41] After filing the bankruptcy petition, the company failed to pay the scheduled wage increases specified in the labor agreement and also failed to give collected union dues to the union. The company also moved to reject the collective bargaining agreement entirely.

The NLRB agreed with the union that this unilateral action violated the good-faith bargaining duty under the Labor Management Relations Act (LMRA). However, the Supreme Court disagreed with the NLRB and determined that management's behavior in this situation did not violate the good-faith provision. The Court's decision in *Bildisco* gave management more discretion in its collective-bargaining efforts with the union. Because many members of Congress did not fully agree with the *Bildisco* decision, the Bankruptcy Reform Act of 1978 was amended (P.L. 98-353) in June 1984 to make it more difficult for employers to abandon the terms of an existing labor agreement after filing a petition for bankruptcy. Under current law an employer cannot reject the terms of a valid labor agreement before obtaining approval of the employer's petition for bankruptcy from a federal bankruptcy court judge. To obtain the approval of the bankruptcy court judge, the following conditions must be proven:[42]

1. The debtor in possession must make a proposal to the union to modify the collective-bargaining agreement based on the most complete and reliable information available at the time.

2. The proposed modifications must be necessary to permit the reorganization of the firm and must ensure that all the creditors, the debtor, and all other affected parties are treated fairly and equitably.

3. The debtor must provide the union with the information it needs to evaluate the employer's proposed contract modifications. The union cannot demand information simply for the purpose of making a counterproposal.

4. The debtor must meet at reasonable times with the union and bargain in good faith in an effort to reach an agreement on proposed modifications to the collective bargaining agreement.

5. The union's refusal to accept the employer's proposed modifications must been without good cause.

6. In the bankruptcy court judge's view, the balance of equities in the case must clearly favor permitting the debtor (employer) to reject the collective bargaining agreement.

Legal Remedies Associated with Violations of the Duty to Bargain in Good Faith

NLRB remedies in unfair labor practice cases are designed to stop further violations and return any adversely affected parties to the position they would have been in had the unfair labor practice violation(s) not occurred. As discussed in Chapter 3, a typical Board remedial order might consist of one or more of the following:

1. A *cease-and-desist order* to halt any further unfair labor practice violations (e.g., cease enforcement of an illegally adopted change in contract language).

2. A requirement that the respondent (guilty party) *post written notices* for a reasonable period (e.g., four to six weeks) in the workplace informing employees of their basic rights under the LMRA, the specific unfair labor practices committed by the respondent, and the respondent's pledge not to commit such violations in the future.

3. Whatever affirmative actions might be necessary to remedy the adverse effects of any unfair labor practices, often referred to as a *make-whole remedy*. Examples include: reinstatement with back pay; restoration of lost seniority rights or other benefits denied an employee because of the unfair labor practice violation; requirement to furnish necessary and relevant bargaining information upon proper request by another bargaining party; discontinuance of any policy found to be a violation of employees' protected rights; removal from employee records of any reference to unlawful disciplinary action taken against an employee; return of unlawfully transferred work to its previous location; or an order to begin or resume bargaining in good faith.

The Board has no authority to award punitive damages, regardless of the respondent's willful intent, the number of specific violations committed, or the respondent's history of committing similar violations in prior cases.[43] The Board also lacks the authority to order an employer or union to agree to any specific term or condition of employment. Even where back pay is awarded, the amount owed by the respondent would be reduced by the amount of interim earnings the employee (charging party) may have received while the unfair labor practice charge was pending (e.g., income from another job, unemployment compensation).

Union officials have contended that present NLRB remedies are inadequate, particularly in cases of bad-faith bargaining. Because NLRB decisions can be appealed to the courts, it might take two or three years for a final determination to occur. During the interim period the employer's ability to delay labor costs increases by postponing negotiations results in lost economic benefits for bargaining unit members. Once the employer is found guilty of bad faith bargaining, the Board can only issue an order to stop bargaining in bad faith and begin good-faith negotiations. No remedy is available for the lost income opportunities or possible deterioration in union's bargaining power caused by the unlawful time delay in reaching a voluntary settlement of bargaining issues.

SUMMARY

Collective bargaining occurs when union and management attempt to resolve conflicting interests by mutually agreeing to acceptable terms or conditions of employment. Sometimes this activity is centralized and more than one appropriate bargaining unit can be combined to form the negotiation unit (the employees and employers who are subject to the provisions of the labor agreement). Most often the structure of bargaining in the private sector is decentralized, with a separate contract negotiated to cover employees in each separate bargaining unit of an individual employer at a specific location. Management and union negotiators are involved in three general prenegotiation activities: selecting the negotiating team, researching and formulating proposals and the bargaining range, and costing these proposals. Bargaining behavior during collective negotiations can be extremely varied, but choosing a distributive or mutual gain approach to bargaining will dictate which specific bargaining behaviors are likely to be effective. Intraorganizational bargaining is also an important and challenging part of achieving success in labor negotiations.

The relative distribution of bargaining power between the parties can be an important determinant of bargaining outcomes, especially in a distributive bargaining approach. Raising the other party's costs of disagreement or lowering the other party's costs of agreement with your proposals aids in attaining a bargaining settlement on your party's proposed terms and thus increases your party's bargaining power. Bargaining costs can and should be calculated in negotiations, albeit sometimes rather imprecisely.

Collective bargaining occurs within a legal framework, which regulates the parties' bargaining responsibilities and behavior. Both union and management negotiators have a legal duty to bargain in good faith, demonstrating both reasonableness and a sincere effort to reach a voluntary settlement of interest disputes affecting employees' wages, hours, and other terms or conditions of employment. Good-faith bargaining enhances the opportunity for labor peace and stability necessary for the production of goods and services. The need to remain competitive and to successfully attain the respective interests of employers and employees helps to ensure the parties have a common goal to promote realistic and ethical conduct during the negotiation process.

KEY TERMS

collective bargaining	whip-saw bargaining strategy
interest dispute	bargaining range
pattern bargaining	resistance point
bargaining unit	roll-up factor
mandatory/nonmandatory bargaining subjects	distributive bargaining
centralized bargaining	mutual gain (win-win or interest-based) bargaining
multi-employer bargaining unit	intraorganizational bargaining
degree of labor intensiveness	good-faith bargaining
lock-in agreement	illegal bargaining subjects

good-faith bargaining impasse
voluntary (permissive or
   nonmandatory) bargaining
   subjects
inability to pay
totality of conduct doctrine
management's rights

Boulwarism
reserved rights doctrine
short-form management's rights clause
long-form management's rights clause
new employer
successor employer
successorship clause

DISCUSSION QUESTIONS

1. What are some situations in which management or the union would pre-
    fer centralized bargaining? In what situations might both prefer centralized
    bargaining? Discussion should take into account specific legal considera-
    tions affecting centralized bargaining.

2. Take a recent labor negotiation example with which you are familiar and an-
    alyze the relative bargaining power of union and management in those ne-
    gotiations. What factors appear to increase each party's bargaining power or
    weaken their bargaining power and why?

3. Assume that you are a management negotiator and the union presents the
    following proposal: Any overtime assignment will be guaranteed a mini-
    mum of 2 hours at time-and-a-half the base hourly rate for the classifica-
    tion. Previously, employees working overtime received time-and-a-half pay
    for the hours they worked but no 2-hour guarantee. Indicate in some de-
    tail how you would cost out this proposal. Also discuss some arguments
    the union might use to make it easier for management to accept this pro-
    posal (i.e., to reduce management's agreement costs).

4. Good- and bad-faith regulations might be easier to define than implement.
    Discuss different types of evidence that might be used prove or disprove a
    charge of bad-faith bargaining.

5. Are current legal remedies for bad-faith bargaining adequate to promote
    compliance with the LMRA's goal of good-faith bargaining? Why or why
    not? What recommendations would you suggest for improving compliance
    with the goal of promoting good-faith bargaining?

6. Evaluate the validity of the following statement: "Communication of factual
    information plays a very small role in labor–management negotiations be-
    cause this activity is largely determined by established rituals."

EXPLORING THE WEB

Bankruptcy and Collective Bargaining

1. Definitions   How does the U.S. Department of Labor define "collective bargaining"?

> http://stats.bls.gov/bls/glossary.htm

2. Law and Legislation   The Bildisco Case is a landmark Supreme Court case dealing with bankruptcy and collective bargaining. Use the Findlaw site to read the case and discuss its significance. Search for other cases involving bankruptcy and collective bargaining that have been decided since 1984. Try a word search in Findlaw or look for cases that cite the Bildisco Case.

NLRB v. Bildisco & Bildisco. 465 U.S. 513 (1984)

http://laws.findlaw.com/US/465/513.html

Use Cornell's law pages to examine a section of the U.S. Code affected by the Bildisco case.

Bankruptcy   Rejection of collective bargaining agreements.   11 U.S.C. § 1113 (1996)

http://www.law.cornell.edu/uscode/11/1113.html

Go to Cornell's overview of labor law and in the case of conflict between the National Labor Relations Act and the Bankruptcy Code, find out which generally prevails.

http://www.law.cornell.edu/topics/labor.html

Using the House of Representatives' Web site, Thomas, search for Public Law 98-353, Bankruptcy Amendments of 1984. Why is the site named "Thomas"?

http://thomas.loc.gov

3. Articles about Bankruptcy and Collective Bargaining   Read an overview of bankruptcy law and how it has affected collective bargaining from the Web site of Paul K. Rainsberger, Director of University of Missouri's Labor Education Program. What was the Packwood-Rodino bill?

http://www.missouri.edu/~labored/1997-21.html

From the Web site of the law firm of Covington and Burling, here is an example of the information that law firms make available to their clients and to anyone searching the Web. This article was written by Michael St. Patrick Baxter and is reprinted from *Bankruptcy Developments Journal*. What was the intention of Congress in enacting section 1113 of the Bankruptcy Code?

http://www.cov.com/publications/download/oid6022/BAXTER_3.pdf

REFERENCES

1. For a more detailed conceptualization of various behavioral and situational aspects of negotiation behavior and a thorough bibliography, see Leonard Greenhalgh and Roy J. Lewicki, "New Directions in Teaching Negotiations: From Walton and McKersie to the New Millennium," in *Negotiations and Change*, eds. Thomas A. Kochan and David B. Lipsky (Ithaca, N.Y.: Cornell University Press, 2003), pp. 20–34 and James A. Wall and Michael W. Blum, "Negotiations," *Journal of Management* 17, no. 3 (June 1991), pp. 273–303.

2. "Interest-based Bargaining: Evidence from Quebec," *Worklife Report* 14, no. 4 (Winter 2003), p. 2; and Ira B. Lobel, "Realities of Interest-Based (Win-Win) Bargaining," *Labor Law Journal* 45 (December 1994), p. 771.

3. For related considerations, see Kathryn J. Ready, "Is Pattern Bargaining Dead?" *Industrial and Labor Relations Review* 43, no. 2 (January 1990), pp. 272–279; discussions of Ready's article by Peter Cappelli, Daniel J. B. Mitchell, and Kathryn J. Ready, *Industrial and Labor Relations Review* 44, no. 1 (October 1990), pp. 152–165; John W. Budd, "The Determinants and Extent of Pattern Bargaining," *Industrial and Labor Relations Review* 45, no. 3 (April 1992), pp. 523–539; and John W. Budd, "The Intrepid Union Political Imperative for UAW Pattern Bargaining," *Journal of Labor Research* 26 (Winter 1995), pp. 43–57.

4. *Don Lee Distributor, Inc., et al. v. NLRB,* 145 F.3d 834 (6th Cir. 1998).

5. For a discussion of several factors associated with centralized bargaining in the United States and other countries, see Harry C. Katz, "The Decentralization of Collective Bargaining: A Literature Review and Comparative Analysis," *Industrial and Labor Relations Review* 47 (October 1993), pp. 3–22.

6. Douglas L. Leslie, "Labor Bargaining Units," *Virginia Law Review* 70 (April 1984), p. 414; Douglas L. Leslie, "Multiemployer Bargaining Rules," *Virginia Law Review* 75 (1989), pp. 241–278.

7. Bruce Feldacker, *Labor Guide to Labor Law,* 4th ed. (Upper Saddle River, N.J.: Prentice-Hall, 2000), pp. 54–55.

8. *General Electric Company and International Union of Electrical, Radio and Machine Workers,* 173 NLRB 253 (1968).

9. *Utility Workers Union of America and Ohio Power Company et al.,* 203 NLRB 230 (1973).

10. *United Paperworkers International Union, Locals 620, 14, and 197 and International Paper Company,* 309 NLRB 44 (1992).

11. *Charles D. Bonanno Linen Supply v. NLRB,* 454 U.S. 404 (1982).

12. Leigh Thompson, *The Mind and Heart of the Negotiator* (Saddle River, N.J.: Prentice-Hall, 1998), pp. 160–161.

13. Margaret A. Chaplan and Edward J. Hertenstein, "The Information Needs of Local Union Officials," *Library Trends* 51 (Summer 2002), pp. 50–69.

14. Sam Ashbaugh, "The Art and Science of Costing Labor Contracts," *Government Finance Review* 18 (December 2002), pp. 33–34.

15. For a discussion of distributive bargaining, see Richard E. Walton and Robert B. McKersie, *A Behavioral Theory of Labor Negotiations* (New York: McGraw-Hill, 1965). For a discussion of mutual gain bargaining, see Roger Fisher and William Ury, *Getting to Yes* (Boston: Houghton Miflin, 1981) and William Ury, *Getting Past No: Negotiating with Difficult People* (New York: Bantam Books, 1991).

16. Joel Cutcher-Gershenfeld, "How Process Matters: A Five-Phase Model for Examining Interest-Based Bargaining," in *Negotiations and Change: From the Workplace to Society,* eds. T. Kochan and D. Lipsky (Ithaca, N.Y.: Cornell University Press, 2003), pp. 141–160.

17. Roy J. Lewicki and Joseph A. Litterer, *Negotiation* (Homewood, Ill.: Richard D. Irwin, 1985), p. 108.

18. Neil W. Chamberlain and James W. Kuhn, *Collective Bargaining,* 2d ed. (New York: McGraw-Hill, 1965), pp. 162–190.

19. Dudley B. Turner, "Intraorganizational Bargaining: The Effect of Goal Congruence and Trust on Negotiator Strategy Use," *Communication Studies* 41 (Spring 1990), pp. 54–75; Richard E. Walton and Robert B. McKersie, *A Behavioral Theory of Labor Negotiations* (New York: McGraw-Hill, 1965), pp. 281–351.

20. Albert Blum, "Collective Bargaining: Ritual or Reality?" *Harvard Business Review* 39 (November–December 1961), p. 65.

21. Lee Iacocca, *Iacocca: An Autobiography* (New York: Bantam Books, 1984), p. 304.

22. Jeremy Main, "How to Be a Better Negotiator," *Fortune* 108 (September 19, 1983), p. 143; see also, Roy J. Lewicki and Joseph A. Litterer, *Negotiation* (Homewood, Ill.: Richard D. Irwin, 1985), p. 8. See also Chris Provis, "Ethics, Deception, and Labor Negotiations," *Journal of Business Ethics* 28 (November 2000), pp. 145–158.

23. *First National Maintenance Corporation v. NLRB,* 452 U.S. 666 (1981).

24. *Fibreboard Paper Products Corporation* v. *NLRB*, 379 U.S. 203 (1964).

25. *Dubuque Packing Co and UFCE, Local 150-A*, 303 NLRB 386 (1991); enf. in *UFCW, Local 150-A* v. *NLRB*, 1 F.3d 24 (DC Cir. 1993); Roger Wolters and Stuart Langdon, "The Duty to Bargain over Business Decisions: The *Dubuque* Case," *Labor Law Journal* 43 (September 1992), pp. 579–587.

26. *E. I. Dupont de Nemours & Company and Chemical Workers Association Inc., a/w International Brotherhood of Dupont Workers*, 301 NLRB 155 (1991).

27. See, for example, Katrina L. Abel, "Current Developments in Labor-Management Relations," *Employee Relations Law Journal* 15, no. 2 (Autumn 1989), pp. 281–289; and Bureau of National Affairs Inc., "Union Attorney Sees NLRB as More Willing to Inquire Whether Bargaining Is Serious," *Daily Labor Report* no. 24 (February 5, 1991), pp. A-6, A-7.

28. *Graphic Communications International Union, Local 508* v. *NLRB*, 977 F.2d 1168 (7th Cir. 1992).

29. *ConAgra Inc. and Congreso de Uniones Industriales de Puerto Rico*, 321 NLRB 944 (1996); and *Stroehmann Bakeries Inc. and Bakery, Confectionery and Tobacco Workers Local Union No. 116*, 318 NLRB 1069 (1995).

30. Virgil B. Day, "Bad Faith Bargaining?" *Contemporary Labor Issues*, eds. Walter Fogel and Archie Kleingartner (Belmont, Calif.: Wadsworth, 1968), pp. 388–392; and Lemuel R. Boulware, *The Truth about Boulwarism* (Washington, D.C.: Bureau of National Affairs, 1969).

31. *NLRB* v. *General Electric Company*, 418 F.2d 736 (1969); *General Electric Company* v. *NLRB*, 397 U.S. 965 (1970). See also Thomas P. Brown IV, "Hard Bargaining: The Board Says No, the Courts Say Yes," *Employee Relations Law Journal* 8, no. 1 (Summer 1982), pp. 37–51.

32. Francisco Hernandez-Senter, Jr., "Closing the Communication Gap in Collective Bargaining," *Labor Law Journal* (July 1990), pp. 438–444.

33. Stanley Young, "The Question of Managerial Prerogatives," *Industrial and Labor Relations Review* 16 (January 1963), p. 243.

34. Marvin Hill, Jr., and Anthony V. Sinicropi, Management Rights (Washington, D.C.: Bureau of National Affairs, 1986), p. 6.

35. Martin M. Perline and David J. Poynter, "Union Orientation and the Perception of Managerial Prerogatives," *Labor Law Journal* 40 (December 1989), pp. 781–788.

36. *United Steelworkers of America* v. *Warrior & Gulf Navigation Company*, 363 U.S. 574 (1960).

37. Bureau of National Affairs, Inc., *Basic Patterns in Union Contracts* (Washington, D.C.: Bureau of National Affairs, 1995), p. 79.

38. *NLRB* v. *Burns Security Services*, 406 U.S. 272 (1972); *Fall River Dyeing & Finishing Corp.* v. *NLRB*, 107 S.Ct. 2225 (1987); *Golden State Bottling Co.* v. *NLRB*, 414 U.S. 108 (1974). See also Clyde Scott, Trevor Bain, and John Robb, "The Successorship Doctrine: Fall River Dyeing and Beyond," *Labor Law Journal* 45 (April 1994), pp. 230–239.

39. The Bureau of National Affairs, Inc., "2003 Employer Bargaining Objectives," *Collective Bargaining Bulletin* 8 (January 2003), p. s-27.

40. Editors of *Collective Bargaining Negotiations and Contracts, Basic Patterns in Union Contracts*, 14th ed. (Washington, D.C.: The Bureau of National Affairs, 1995), p. 5.

41. *NLRB* v. *Bildisco & Bildisco*, 104 S.Ct. 1188 (1984).

42. John Wren and Kent Murrmann, "Chapter 11 and Collective Bargaining Agreements," *Employee Relations Law Journal* 16, no. 1 (Summer 1990), pp. 17–27.

43. *H. K. Porter Co., Inc.* v. *NLRB*, 397 U.S. 99 (1970).

Classification of a Bargaining Subject

The company and union have had a bargaining relationship for more than 20 years. On July 11, bargaining unit member Allan Engle was performing his assigned work duties of cleaning the bathroom on the second floor of the company's administrative building when he glanced up and observed a camera approximately six to eight feet away located in an air vent and pointed directly at him. Engle reported his discovery to three other bargaining unit members, including union steward Luther Hall, who went to the second-floor bathroom in question and confirmed that the hidden camera was there. The following day the local union president was notified, but when she went to investigate, the hidden camera had been removed.

On July 15, local union president Wanda Jackson was asked to meet with the company's HR manager Susan Albright. Albright asked Jackson if she had heard about the camera that was discovered in the sanitation department's restroom. Albright went on to say that the camera had been installed by the company because of a reported theft problem in that area, and the company's legal counsel had advised her that it was lawful as long as the company had a legitimate business reason for doing so. Albright stated that once the camera had been discovered and union members appeared irate over the issue, the camera was immediately removed by management.

Local union president Jackson believed the company could have accomplished its theft investigation through less intrusive means, and the union did not approve of management's invasion of employees' privacy. The union sent a letter to the company, dated August 1, indicating that an internal investigation by union members had also uncovered hidden cameras being used in the employees' physical fitness room. On August 16, Jackson sent a hand-delivered letter to HR manager Albright demanding that the company bargain over the subject of video camera use in the workplace. The company refused to bargain over the subject, whereupon the union filed an unfair labor practice charge alleging that the company's action violated Section 8 (a)(5) and (1) of the LMRA, as amended.

Positions of the Parties

The union argues that the use of surveillance cameras in the workplace for providing evidence of work-rule violations by employees for which they could be subject to discipline or discharge is clearly an issue that is germane to the working environment and job security interests of union members. Therefore, the union believes management has a legal duty to bargain in good faith, on request, over issues such as the number and location of video cameras within the workplace. Other issues bargaining unit members might have an interest in bargaining include whether employees will be given prior notice that their conduct may be subject to filming; who will have access to the video recordings made; for what purposes the video recordings may be used; and the circumstances under which the cameras can be required to be removed.

The company essentially makes two arguments. First, the company believes it has an absolute right to engage in actions (like using cameras) to protect the legitimate business-related interests of the ownership. The company noted that it had for many years used 17 video cameras located both inside and outside company buildings to observe activity for protecting company property from theft or damage and to discourage other work-rule violations (e.g., drug use, sleeping on the job). These 17 cameras were in plain sight, and their existence had been known to the union's membership for many years without any prior objection from the union. In recent years, 11 additional hidden video cameras had been installed inside the company to

Continued

observe specific areas where employee misconduct was suspected. To require management to bargain in advance over the use or placement of such surveillance equipment would significantly reduce the effectiveness of this method of monitoring employee conduct on the employer's premises.

Second, management argues that even if the Board were to find that a duty to bargain existed, under the circumstances in this case, the union has waived its right to bargain over the subject of surveillance cameras. The company points to the length of time it has used video cameras without any objection by the union as evidence that the union has acquiesced in this practice and essentially acknowledged management's right to use surveillance cameras for legitimate business reasons. The company acknowledges that the union has a right to file a contractual grievance over any alleged misuse or abuse of surveillance methods leading to a lack of just cause for disciplinary or discharge action against a bargaining unit member. However, the right to grieve a management discipline or discharge decision is not equivalent to a right to require management to bargain, in advance, over the right to use camera surveillance as a legitimate investigatory technique.

QUESTIONS

1. What is a mandatory subject of bargaining?
2. Can a union waive its right to bargain over a mandatory subject of bargaining?
3. Was management's refusal to bargain over the subject of surveillance camera usage in the workplace a violation of the duty to bargain in good faith under the LMRA, as amended? If so, what should be the appropriate remedy? Discuss the merits of the parties' respective positions in this case.

Unilateral Work Rule Changes

Over the years the company had unilaterally implemented several plant rules (e.g., use of company telephones, excused absences from work), including the following two rules:

1. **Perfect attendance**—All employees who have a perfect attendance record in a 12-month calendar year will receive special recognition from the Company. (Note: There was no evidence introduced to show that any employee had ever received any special recognition under the announced rule before the implementation of the new attendance bonus rule.)

2. **Discharges**—The company has the right to discharge or discipline any employee for just cause. The term just cause shall include . . . drinking or possessing any alcoholic beverage on company property or company time or reporting for work while under the influence of alcohol or drugs.

During the term of the current labor agreement, the company announced the implementation of two new work rules:

1. As of March 1, any injuries requiring treatment will now be accompanied by a drug/alcohol test.

2. As of March 1, any employee who achieves perfect attendance for a week will receive a wage bonus of $1 per hour for that week. Any employee who achieves perfect attendance for an entire month will receive a total wage bonus of $1.50 per hour for the month.

Three days after the two new work rules were announced; the union contacted management and requested to bargain over each of the rule changes. The company representative refused the union's request to bargain on the grounds that the subjects at issue were not mandatory subjects of bargaining and even if they were, the current contract language gave management the right to act unilaterally regarding the two rule changes. Management cited the following portions of the parties' current labor agreement:

- **Section 3: Management's rights**—The management of the plant, direction of the working forces, and work affairs of the Company, including but not limited to the right . . . to discipline or discharge for just cause; to issue, enforce and change Company rules . . . is reserved to the Company.

- **Section 8: Wages**—The rates of pay and classifications set forth are agreed upon by the parties and are attached hereto and made a part of this Agreement. The wage rates set forth are the minimum rates under this Agreement and are not to be construed as preventing the employer from paying or the employee from accepting pay or benefits.

- **Zipper clause**—Except as provided herein, this Agreement resolves all the bargainable issues for the term thereof.

Continued

QUESTIONS

1. What is the purpose of a zipper clause?

2. Which, if any, of the two new rules involve a mandatory subject of bargaining? Explain your reasoning.

3. Did management's unilateral implementation of the two new work rules without providing the union with prior notice or an opportunity to bargain constitute a violation of the duty to bargain in good faith under the LMRA, as amended? If so, what should be the appropriate remedy?

Duty To Bargain over a Work Relocation Decision

The employer operates a meat-slaughtering, processing, and packing business at several U.S. plant locations including Hog Heaven, Nebraska, where this labor dispute occurred. The company and union have been engaged in a bargaining relationship for many years, with the most recent contract covering a 3-year period (subsequently extended 1 additional year). Before the Hog Heaven plant's closing, the union represented 1,900 to 2,000 employees at the plant.

Five years ago the Hog Heaven plant began experiencing economic difficulties. As profit losses mounted, the company began to receive pressure from its financial lenders and finally sought some labor cost concessions from the union. After voluntary midterm negotiations with the union, employees voted to accept productivity standards for use in determining incentive pay increases to aid the company's financial situation. Despite the work-rule changes, the company's financial problems continued to mount. In June, management notified the union of its decision to close the "beef kill" and related departments effective December 12. The company also notified the union that in order to remain competitive, high productivity levels would have to be maintained in the "hog-kill-and-cut" department. In August of that year, the parties agreed to eliminate all incentive pay options while continuing to require employees to meet the higher productivity standards previously jointly agreed to in midterm bargaining. In exchange, the company agreed that it would not seek any further cost concessions from the union for the remaining 2 years of the contract's term. The company's estimated cost savings from the August concession by the union was approximately $5 million annually.

In December, the company sought a $5 million loan from the firm's financial lenders to modernize the Hog Heaven plant. The loan application was rejected by the firm's financial lenders. In January of the new year, the company's primary bank called due a $10 million loan and indicated it intended to revoke the company's $45 million line of credit. The company immediately instituted several cost-saving measures and was able to raise the necessary funds to pay off the $10 million loan.

In March, management asked the union to agree to a speed up (i.e., an increase in the number of animals slaughtered per hour) on the hog-kill line to raise productivity. The union rejected this proposal citing safety concerns, prompting the company to announce on March 31 that it intended to close the hog-kill-and-cut department within 6 months. The union did not immediately request to bargain over management's announced intent to close the hog-kill-and-cut department.

In early June, the company proposed letting the hog-kill-and-cut department continue operating until the end of the contract's term (September 1), if the union would agree to grant a wage freeze by July 1. The company later expanded its proposal to include a profit-sharing plan in exchange for a wage freeze by July 1. The union's membership rejected the company's proposal in a vote on June 9.

On June 10, after learning of the union members' rejection, the company issued a press release confirming that the hog-kill-and-cut department would be closed. The press release also announced for the first time that the company planned to relocate the hog-kill-and-cut operation to an unspecified new location. On June 16, the company obtained a new $50 million line of credit from its lender with the stipulation that the bank could withdraw from the financial arrangement at any time. *Continued*

On June 23, the union requested extensive corporatewide information from management for verifying the company's need for labor cost concessions affecting the hog-kill-and-cut department employees. The company objected to the union's information request on the grounds of relevancy and confidentiality. In a letter to the union, the company stated: "Your request for this information appears to be related to a desire to negotiate with the Company as to its decision to close part of its operations." The company denied that it had any legal duty to bargain over a decision to close part of its business and thus was under no duty to provide information for facilitating such negotiations.

Another vote on the wage freeze/profit-sharing proposal was scheduled by the union for June 28. On June 24 the company advised the union's membership that a favorable vote on the wage freeze/profit-sharing proposal would save the hog-kill-and-cut department. Nevertheless, on June 28, union members voted once again to reject the wage freeze/profit-sharing proposal.

On July 1, the company notified the union that the decision to close the hog-kill-and-cut department was final. Ten days later the company announced the purchase of a plant in Bacon, Illinois, as a replacement for the plant in Hog Heaven, Nebraska. The Bacon, Illinois, plant opened on October 1. On October 3, the hog-kill-and-cut department at the Hog Heaven plant was closed, eliminating 530 jobs.

Negotiations between the union and company concerning the possible relocation of other Hog Heaven plant operations were conducted during the July–October period of that same year. The company sought labor cost concessions in exchange for a promise not to relocate remaining operations at the Hog Heaven plant. During these negotiations the union was rebuffed each time it tried to bring up the relocation of the hog-kill-and-cut department as a bargaining subject. The company's position was essentially that the hog-kill-and-cut department had already been closed, and there was no duty to bargain over the decision to close it. On October 19, an agreement on wage concessions was reached between the company and union affecting 900 remaining workers at the Hog Heaven plant. Early the next year the company lost its bank financing. On October 15, unable to obtain additional operating capital investment, all operations at the Hog Heaven, Nebraska, and Bacon, Illinois, plants ceased, and the assets at both plant locations were subsequently sold.

QUESTIONS

1. What is the difference between so called *decision* bargaining and *effects* bargaining?
2. Did the company's refusal to bargain over the decision to relocate the hog-kill-and-cut operation from the Nebraska plant to a new plant in Illinois violate the employer's duty to bargain in good faith? If so, what should be the appropriate remedy? Explain your reasoning.

Mini-Bargaining Simulation

Purpose

To provide each student practice in negotiating a term or condition of employment through the collective bargaining process. For a more in-depth bargaining experience refer to the bargaining simulation exercise in Appendix A.

Instructions

1. Each student will be assigned as a member of either a union or management bargaining team.

2. Each bargaining team will prepare an initial bargaining proposal concerning a *funeral leave policy*. Each team should be prepared to present their initial bargaining proposal to the other party's bargaining team at the first scheduled in-class bargaining meeting. The instructor will provide information regarding the scheduling of in-class bargaining meeting time. All negotiations between union and management bargaining teams will occur during class time. Teams are free to meet outside of class time for the purpose of conducting bargaining research on funeral leave policies or to plan team bargaining strategy and tactics.

3. The goal of each bargaining team is to reach agreement on a funeral leave policy that meets the interest of each party. Any final agreement reached between the parties should be placed in writing and signed by authorized representatives of each bargaining team. A written copy of any final agreement reached should be furnished to the instructor.

Background

The employer operates a large retail store in a popular shopping mall that serves a surrounding three-county area. There are 100 employees in the bargaining unit who currently earn an average hourly wage rate of $10.50. No current language in the parties' labor agreement addresses the issue of funeral leave. The union has requested management bargain over such a formal policy and the company has agreed to do so.

The past company practice regarding employee's request for funeral leave has been to handle each request on a case-by-case basis, with the employee's department head having the authority to authorize unpaid time off from work to allow an employee to attend a funeral. During the previous 12-month period there have been 20 request for funeral leave, of which 16 were granted. The average length of time off from work for the 16 funeral leave requests that were granted was 2.8 days. Employees' regular work schedule consist of 8 hours per day, 5 days per week although the store's regular hours of operation are seven days per week from 10 A.M. to 10 P.M. daily.   *Continued*

In preparing a bargaining proposal on the subject of funeral leave policy contract language should be drafted carefully in order to anticipate and avoid potential problems or issues that might arise in the actual application of the funeral leave policy during the term of the parties' labor agreement. Issues to consider include the following:

- How many days (hours) of funeral leave will be provided?

- Will time off from work for funeral leave be paid or unpaid? If paid, at what rate of pay?

- Will part-time employees qualify to receive the funeral leave benefit?

- What type of death occurrence would qualify an employee to take funeral leave? Be sure to be specific when defining terms such as what constitutes an "immediate family member."

- Should funeral leave be granted upon the death of a "domestic partner," "significant other," or "personal friend"?

- Should the same amount of time off from work be granted in every case or are there defined circumstances or reasons that would qualify an employee for variable amounts of time off?

- If paid leave is granted for a specified period of time, could an employee extend leave time upon request by using either other paid leave time (e.g., vacation days, holidays, sick leave days) or by using unpaid leave days?

- Must an employee actually attend the funeral in order to receive funeral leave? If so, what might constitute adequate proof of an employee's attendance at a funeral?

- Must an employee offer any proof to verify a death has occurred in order to receive funeral leave? If so, what type of evidence or proof would be acceptable?

- What is the procedure an employee must follow to request funeral leave?

- How far in advance must an employee request funeral leave to cover a period of absence from work?

- Who has authority on behalf of the employer to grant or deny an employee's funeral leave request?

CHAPTER 7

Economic Issues

The ability to achieve economic gains in the form of higher wages and improved benefits is one important criterion workers use to gauge the effectiveness of a union. From an employee's perspective, the economic rewards from work largely determine his or her standard of living. When management adopts a goal of minimizing operating costs as a means of optimizing profits, this creates an inevitable conflict of interest between employees' desire for economic gains and an employer's desire to minimize higher operating costs. This chapter discusses a number of factors that help to determine the economic terms of employment, as well as current wage and benefit trends and issues.

As the new century began, the U.S. economy appeared to be among the best in the world, experiencing strong growth, low inflation, and a steady creation of new jobs. Much of the increase in family net worth was attributed to gains in the stock market, as a record 48.8 percent of families owned stock directly or indirectly through mutual funds and retirement savings accounts in 1998.[1] From 1990 to 1999, productivity rose at an average annual rate of 1.96 percent, whereas real hourly compensation costs for nonfarm businesses rose only 1.14 percent.[2]

The 2001 economic recession was attributed to several factors, including structural changes in some industries accounting for almost 80 percent of job losses (e.g., manufacturing, information technology); the bursting of the dot-com bubble, causing investors to lower valuations on a wide range of U.S. firms; corporate scandals (e.g., Enron, WorldCom, Health South, Arthur Anderson); lower consumer confidence levels; cost-cutting strategies employed by firms to improve productivity and profitability, often resulting in permanent job losses; and heightened security concerns due to terrorist activity.[3] The 2001 economic recession was officially declared over in November, 2001 by the Business Cycle Dating Committee of the National Bureau of Economic Research.[4] The end of the economic recession was followed by a period dubbed the *jobless recovery* because, unlike previous economic recessions since World War II, job growth did not recover quickly even though productivity rates and company profits improved.[5] Increasing competition from global competitors, rising employment costs (e.g., health care, defined benefit pension obligations) coupled with an inability to simply raise product or service prices to cover such increased costs have made companies reluctant to add permanent workers and encouraged strategies to reduce labor requirements through technological innovation or outsourcing jobs to lower cost suppliers, often in other countries.

Wages and other economic benefits represent income necessary to attain a desired standard of living to an employee; a cost to be minimized to the employer; and a basis for creating tax revenue to the government. Wages also serve as a factor in the allocation of resources. For example, wages influence an individual's selection of an occupation and movement from one firm, industry, or location to another. Wages influence managers' decisions on plant location, investments in machinery and capital equipment, and employment levels. As wage and benefit costs rise, at some point it becomes more cost effective for an employer to invest in production or service delivery technologies that require less labor. Thus, employees may price themselves out of certain labor markets in which substitutes for labor are available to an employer at lower costs.

Wage and benefit issues represent mandatory subjects of bargaining, as discussed previously in Chapter 6. Under the Labor Management Relations Act (LMRA), union and management negotiators are required to bargain in good faith over subjects such as pensions, health care insurance, shift differential, overtime pay, job evaluation, and incentive pay systems if either party presents a bargaining proposal on such topics during negotiations. Union and management negotiators spend many hours annually bargaining over wages and wage-related issues. This chapter focuses on the methods of wage determination and factors used by negotiators in determining the wage package—wages and other economic benefits.

Union and management officials have to agree on what the term *wages* means before they can successfully bargain over this issue. For instance, wages may refer to an employee's base hourly wage rate, average gross hourly earnings, average weekly earnings, or incentive pay (payment per product completed). Basic wage rates for each job class are usually listed in the labor agreement; however, other wage payments (overtime, incentive pay, shift differentials, and other compensation earned in the regular work week) may have to be computed in accordance with provisions in the labor agreement.[6] After agreeing on the language for the basis of wage negotiations, the parties consider various factors in determining specific wage rates for different jobs or wage ranges covering different job classes.

Industrial Wage Differentials

The existence of wage differentials among individuals, jobs, industries, or geographic regions can be explained in a variety of ways. However, any explanation must consider the interrelationships between labor and capital as factors of production and as contributors to productivity. Jobs with varying duties and responsibilities are often assigned different wage rates. Besides these occupational wage differences within a firm, there are regional, industry, and shift differences that may affect an employee's wage rate. Retail employees in the South generally earn less than those in the North; electricians and laborers in the building trades generally have higher wage rates than electricians and laborers in manufacturing firms. Industrial wage differentials may be explained in terms of three interrelated factors: (1) the degree of competition or monopoly in the product market, (2) the value added by workers in a particular industry, and (3) the percentage of total costs that labor costs represent.

- **Competition in the product market.** First, if a firm has a monopoly or near monopoly (the product is essential, with no or few available substitutes), then increased labor cost can easily be passed on to the consumer by raising the product price. In such cases, the employer may resist higher wages less rigidly in negotiations because higher labor costs do not necessarily adversely impact the firm's competitiveness or profit margins. Conversely, many firms that are affected by global competition in their product markets find it increasingly difficult to simply pass along increased labor costs in the form of higher product or service prices unless other competitors are also absorbing similar labor costs increases. Nonunion or foreign competitors are unlikely to pay compensation terms equal to or greater than those terms required under union labor agreements. Under highly competitive market conditions, unionized employers must bargain harder to ensure that labor cost increases do not force higher product prices that might make the firm less price competitive. In industries where employers face fewer competitive threats, wages tend to be proportionately higher.

- **Value added by employees.** The term *value added* refers to the contribution of factors of production to the value of a final product. Comparing the value added by labor's contribution in different industries helps to explain industrial wage differentials. For example, the value added by labor in sawmills, cotton weaving, clothes manufacturing, and the mobile home industry is significantly lower than corresponding figures in the steel, petrochemical, and paper industries. However, because employees must use machines, which represent capital investments, and because such a close interrelationship exists between labor and capital investments in machinery and equipment, exact determination of labor's contributions has become a complicated process. It is sometimes difficult to accurately measure the value added by an individual employee when that person functions as part of a "team" or performs only one or a few tasks required to create the final product or service. In unionized settings, negotiations between union and management representatives ultimately determine the amount of value added attributed to labor.

- **Labor costs as percentage of total costs.** A firm's **degree of labor intensiveness,** which measures the proportion of total operating costs comprised of labor costs, must also be considered in determining employee wage rates. More labor-intensive organizations, such as health-care facilities, professional sports, and government, have high labor costs in relation to total costs. Any upward adjustment in labor costs will have a bigger impact on such a firm's competitiveness when compared with the effect on a less labor-intensive firm that may grant an equal-size increase to their employees. Less labor-intensive firms, such as petroleum refining, chemical, and electricity-generating firms, can afford to offer relatively high wage and benefit levels because fewer work-

ers are employed, and thus the impact of labor costs on the firm's total operating costs competitiveness is less.

Usually, firms with a high ratio of labor costs to total costs are more likely to resist wage increases in contact negotiations than less labor-intensive firms. For
example, if a hospital where labor costs are 60 percent of total costs grants a 10
percent wage increase, it must raise prices about 6 percent. A petroleum refining plant where labor cost is 5 percent of total costs would have to raise its price
about 0.5 percent to cover a similar 10 percent wage increase. If competitive
conditions preclude or limit an employer's ability to raise product prices, the
wage increase cost must be funded from firm profits; cost savings from other operating areas (e.g., finance, marketing) or higher labor productivity; finding a
cost-effective way to employ less labor (e.g., outsourcing, new technology); or
some combination of these strategies. Nonetheless, the relation of labor cost to
total cost can be an important factor in explaining differences in wages for similar jobs across different employers or industries.

Occupational Wage Differentials and the Role of Job Evaluation and Wage Surveys

Within a company or industry, maintaining rational and fair wage relationships
among various jobs is important. These relationships are often maintained using a **job evaluation** program, but in other cases, they are determined by individual or collective bargaining.[7] The process of determining the relative importance of each job to the organization helps in understanding occupational wage
differentials; therefore, the following steps in a job evaluation program are presented.[8]

Evaluating Jobs within the Organization

Before conducting a job evaluation program, an organizational analysis should
be conducted to evaluate the organization's objectives, structure, and authority
and responsibility relationships. The findings from this analysis help ensure that
the job content is up to date.

The organization then selects and measures the job factors that are found
at least to some extent in all of the organization's job classifications. Job factors
can vary substantially depending on the type of organization, but skill (education and training), effort, responsibility (for people and equipment), and working conditions (hazards, surroundings) are typically selected. Management must
consider the minimum amount of each job factor or qualification necessary to
adequately perform a particular job. For example, it may be nice to employ a
typist who can edit, interpret, and make complex economic subjects understandable, but few organizations can find or are willing to pay wages needed to
attract such a qualified person.

Next, an appropriate job evaluation system for appraising jobs according
to the established job factors is selected.[9] Three common job evaluation methods used are ranking, classification, or a point system. The ranking method
compares jobs nonquantitatively in terms of each job's relative value to a firm's
success, ranking jobs from most to least valued. The classification and point-
system methods compare jobs to predetermined numerical rating scales de-

signed to measure one or more job factors about each job. A firm's job evaluation systems may use 10 to 15 different job factors, with these factors often divided into subfactors. For example, effort may be divided into physical and mental effort.

The foundation of job evaluation is job analysis, which is a process of sys-
tematically securing information and facts about the jobs to be evaluated. The
job evaluation process focuses on the job, not the employee in the job, for analysis. A well-written job description can help management demonstrate that selection decisions regarding which individual will hold a particular job were
legally nondiscriminatory based on an assessment of the requirements of the job
and the candidate's qualifications.

The job classifications resulting from job analysis will receive the same rating whether the employee holding the job has a master's degree or high school
diploma, is lazy or ambitious, or is a high or low performer. Job analysts use observation, interviews, and questionnaires to gather data about the jobs that are
used to formulate job descriptions and job specifications. Job descriptions include written summaries of a job's duties and responsibilities. Job specifications
include the personal characteristics that an employee must possess to qualify
for the job. Both are used in the job evaluation process. As firms try to relate
wages to various degrees of duties and responsibilities, they must also pay more
to employ those who have higher qualifications in education, training, and skills.

Lawler has noted that as work structures continue to be altered and employees' job responsibilities become more varied and complex, it becomes increasingly difficult and perhaps less relevant to focus compensation systems on
an analysis of job titles as opposed to focusing on the contributions of individuals or teams who actually perform those jobs.[10] Some combination of job-based
evaluation and individual or group-based performance evaluation may provide
a more comprehensive compensation system designed to enhance the competitiveness of the firm and employees' perceived equity in the effort-reward exchange between the individual and the organization.[11]

Management often prefers to conduct its job evaluation independently of
the union. Management may prefer not to share its weightings of the job factors,
particularly when it believes certain factors (such as training, skill, and responsibility for equipment) should receive more compensation than others. Excluding union participation in the job evaluation process may reduce the time required to complete the process; however, subsequent application of job
evaluation results may generate grievances that then must be resolved on a
case-by-case basis. Some companies seek to encourage union participation in
the job-evaluation process both to benefit from the insight of workers who actually perform different jobs and to increase the acceptance of the results of job
evaluation by bargaining unit members.

Some union leaders view job evaluation with disfavor because it tends to
limit bargaining and freeze the wage structure.[12] Unions prefer to establish wage
scales through collective bargaining when both internal and external labor market factors can be considered in determining the value or worth of a job. Although unions reserve the right to file grievances to resist or express dissatisfaction with job evaluation, they seldom show strong opposition unless firms
attempt to use job evaluation as the sole criterion for wage determination or as
a substitute for collective bargaining.[13] In fact, some unions regard job evalua-

tion techniques not only as useful guides in negotiating wages but as a means to more effectively explain the negotiated wage settlements to their members.[14]

Regardless of the job-evaluation method used, the objective is to develop a wage structure that prices jobs with less skill, effort, and responsibility at lower wage rates than jobs with greater skill, effort, and responsibility. Exhibit 7.1 presents an example of a wage structure for a firm that includes job titles, labor grades, point ranges, and starting wage rates for each labor grade. Because a numerical score should indicate the relative value of the job, the greater the score, the higher the labor grade and the hourly wage rate.

Surveys to Compare Firms' Wage Structures

Wage surveys are conducted to ensure that external labor market considerations, such as comparable wages, are included in the wage structure. Although firms attempt to rationalize their wage structure internally through job evaluation, they must also maintain competitive wages externally to ensure that the firm can recruit and retain qualified employees. Usually a wage analyst either visits, sends questionnaires to, or conducts telephone interviews with the wage analysts of similar organizations or comparable firms.[15] Some trade or professional groups conduct annual wage surveys among their member firms and share the information with participating firms. Unions often conduct independent wage surveys as part of their preparation for collective bargaining.

The U.S. Department of Labor also periodically conducts area wage surveys and publishes the results.[16] Two of these publications are the National Compensation Survey (NCS) and the Occupation Employment Statistics (OES)

Exhibit 7.1

Typical Wage Structure for a Manufacturing Firm

Job Titles	Labor Grade	Points	Starting Hourly Wage Rate
Janitor	I	200–249	$6.55
Material handler	II	250–299	8.30
Shipper	III	300–349	9.45
Tool room keeper	IV	350–399	10.20
Machinist B	V	400–449	10.50
Maintenance worker	VI	450–499	11.80
Mechanic	VII	500–549	12.00
Painter	VIII	550–599	13.30
Carpenter	IX	600–649	14.10
Truck driver	X	650–699	14.68
Electrician	XI	700–749	17.19
Tool and die maker	XII	750–799	17.42
Machinist A	XIII	800–849	18.49

SOURCE: Adapted from *Collective Bargaining Negotiations and Contracts* (Washington, D.C.: Bureau of National Affairs Inc., 1992), p. 18:331.

survey, which provide wage data by occupation for different geographical areas. The OES survey covers a larger number of geographical areas, but the NCS survey provides more detailed information about specific occupations based on the duties and responsibilities of the job (e.g., knowledge, complexity, scope of responsibility).

The party conducting the survey provides the responding firms with titles, descriptions, and specifications of the jobs in the wage survey. Participating firms supply the starting wage rate and the economic benefits paid individuals in these job classifications (Exhibit 7.2). After the wage survey is complete, the firm must determine how the data will be used. For example, does it want to lead the industry, compete with a specific competitor, or pay the industry average? The final wage plan should contain a certain number of job classes; wages for each job class; wage ranges (from starting to top wages) for each class; policies and procedures for wage adjustments (seniority, merit, and so on); procedures for job changes to a different class, including temporary job changes; procedures for dealing with jobs that pay above or below their wage range; and a policy on union involvement.

Production Standards and Wage Incentives

Unions and management sometimes negotiate provisions in the labor agreement that cover wage-related issues such as production standards, time studies, and wage-incentive payments. Production standards refer to the expected employee output that is consistent with workmanship quality, operational efficiency, and reasonable working capacities of normal operators. These standards are often determined by time studies that involve analyses of time and motions of workers on the job, and the resulting standards are used to assess performance and determine the wage incentives for individual employees or groups of employees.

Performance standards that are not accepted as realistic by both labor and management can be demoralizing and adversarial when used to determine workers' pay.[16] Unrealistically high performance standards will ensure lower performance ratings for many workers, thereby reducing pay and motivation levels. Unrealistically low performance standards will ensure that many workers easily

Exhibit 7.2

Typical Results from a Wage Survey

Job Title	A	B	C	D	E	F	Average Wage
Janitor	$6.00	$6.25	$6.75	$6.80	$7.00	$6.20	$6.50
Assembler	10.00	10.60	10.30	10.70	9.90	10.30	10.30
Shop clerk	11.00	10.00	10.75	10.25	10.40	10.60	10.50
Welder	12.60	12.30	12.00	12.00	12.30	12.60	12.30
Electrician	16.50	17.00	17.50	17.00	16.75	17.25	17.00
Tool and die maker	18.00	17.00	17.75	17.25	17.50	17.50	17.50
Machinist	19.00	18.50	18.00	18.75	18.25	18.50	18.50

meet or exceed work requirements, encouraging some workers to slack off during remaining scheduled work hours and discouraging workers from seeking to improve performance beyond the established norm. Performance standards also should be periodically updated to reflect changes that occur in materials and methods used to perform job tasks.

When incentive wage plans are negotiated, the structure and design are included in the contract, although specific details may not be included. Contract language defining the role of the union in setting and challenging production standards and wage rate changes and its right to be consulted on related issues is also usually included. Some contracts include provisions about time studies and the involvement of unions. A small number permit a union observer during the time study, and a few provide special training for the union time study representative. Other provisions include procedures used for timing an employee, specification of the meaning of "typical employee," advance notice to the employee holding the job being studied, and specification for fatigue and personal allowances in setting production standards.[18]

Although wage-incentive plans such as gain-sharing, piece rates, and profit sharing vary in structure and specific content, their goals are essentially the same: (1) to increase employee productivity, (2) to attract prospective employees to the company, and (3) to reward employees monetarily for their increased productivity. A typical individual wage-incentive plan is one in which employees are paid for the number of pieces or jobs completed. Others pay bonuses or premiums to employees for production above the standard. Many varieties of incentive plans exist, but all are similar in concept.

The majority of production employees are paid an hourly wage rate. A major reason for an hourly-based compensation plan is that many production jobs are machine paced, so employees have limited control over the pace of work and thus the number of items produced during scheduled work hours. Many companies and unions have investigated the additional use of various incentive pay plans as a way to stimulate employee productivity. Increased interest in incentive plans has resulted from increased foreign and domestic competition, adoption of various employee involvement (EI) and total quality management (TQM) practices, heightened interest in labor-management cooperation, and employer efforts to obtain wage concessions from unions.

The majority of *Fortune* 1000 firms have adopted one or more reward incentive plans that seek to tie pay to organizational performance, but few firms cover the majority of their employees under any single incentive plan.[19] A sample of 141 employers involved in negotiating a labor agreement in 2003 reported the following incidence of incentive or variable pay plans in their current contracts: individual incentive plan (9 percent), group incentive plan (7 percent), profit-sharing plan (7 percent) and gain-sharing plan (4 percent).[20] Although companies tend to report that plans such as profit sharing, employee stock ownership, gain-sharing, skill-based pay, team incentives, and open pay information are successful, evidence is less clear over the ability of such plans to sustain initial productivity or pay satisfaction improvements over time.[21]

Employees may not be as enthusiastic about reward-incentive plans as employers. A survey of 1,500 employees reported that most workers preferred rewards based on individual performance rather than team, group, or company performance and preferred to receive rewards in the form of a base pay rate increase rather than a one-time bonus or incentive payment.[22] Lack of employee support along with previously mentioned employer concerns have led to a slow-down in the rate at which companies are adopting reward-incentive plans.

Profit-sharing plans cover between 6 to 27 percent of employees in most industrialized countries where government tax policies often encourage the adoption of such plans.[23] The U.S. Chamber of Commerce reports a survey of 301 organizations, which found that 26 percent of organizations offered a profit-sharing plan with an average payout of $481 per employee.[24] Plans typically provide an annual cash payment or some payment into a pension plan. Since the 1800s, neither the American Federation of Labor (AFL), the Congress of In-dustrial Organizations (CIO), nor the AFL-CIO have ever opposed profit-sharing and other incentive systems, and only a few individual unions have ever taken a position opposing such plans.[25]

Some companies have negotiated profit-sharing plans that provided cash bonuses based on the company's profit to partially or totally take the place of hourly base wage increases (e.g., American Airlines, Ford, General Motors (GM), and International Harvester). In 2003, U.S. union employees of DaimlerChrysler AG received profit-sharing checks averaging $460 compared to $160 for union-represented employees at Ford Motor Co. and $940 per union worker at General Motors.[26] Reflecting increased competition and lower market demand for autos, profit-sharing checks in 2003 were substantially lower than those received in 2000 when union workers at DaimlerChrysler AG received individual profit-sharing checks averaging a record $8,100; Ford employees' profit-sharing checks averaged $8,000; and GM employees' profit-sharing checks averaged $1,775.[27]

Profit sharing does have some critics. First, some are concerned that union participation in profit sharing could lead to more union influence on major man-agement decisions other than wages. Second, a costly profit-sharing plan could drain company funds that could otherwise be used for capital improvements or research and development.[28]

In a group incentive or **gain-sharing plan**, companies make monetary pay-ments to a specific group or groups of employees for producing more output or generating cost savings beyond some established goal. Incentives may include group bonuses, group piece rates, profit sharing, production sharing, and cost-reduction sharing. In some cases, plans may be limited to a few employees, to specific departments, to other organizational divisions or extended to cover the entire company workforce. Although group incentives aim to increase produc-tion and reduce costs, they are also designed to increase teamwork, provide greater job security, and achieve acceptance of new technology.

Many national unions adopt a neutral position toward gain-sharing plans, preferring to allow local unions to address such proposals on a case-by-case basis.[29] Union leaders may be wary of including gain-sharing plans as part of wage negotiations out of concern that management might tend to treat such plans as a substitute for traditional negotiated hourly wage improvements dur-ing a contract's term. It may be easier to adopt gain-sharing or other variable incentive plans if such plans are negotiated in addition to, rather than instead of, traditional straight-time hourly wage improvements.

There are a variety of group incentive plans. One of the most popular is the **Scanlon plan**, a group plan for sharing labor-cost savings that was developed by former union leader Joseph Scanlon in the late 1930s. A Scanlon plan provides bonus payments based on a computed ratio of total labor costs (TLC) to total production values (TPV), which typically equal monthly sales, plus or minus inventory adjustments. A reduction in the ratio would be a labor-cost savings. For example, if the employees were to reduce costs by working harder, producing more efficiently, and saving on wastes and the TLC/TPV ratio declined from 50 to 40 percent, the 10 percent labor cost savings would be shared with the employees.[30]

The **Rucker plan** is based on a change in the ratio between labor costs and dollar value added. The value added equals sales less purchased materials. Under this plan, if employees lower the ratio between labor costs and dollar value added, the productivity gains are shared. Under both the Scanlon and Rucker plans, employees receive between 25 and 75 percent of the available bonus pool, often distributed in the form of a percentage of each employee's hourly wages.[31]

The term **improshare plan** is derived from "improved productivity through sharing."[32] Improshare productivity measurements use traditional work measurement standards for a selected base period. A monetary reward is granted whenever the number of labor hours required to produce the output during a measured period (e.g., week or month) is less than the number of hours required during the base period. Both blue- and white-collar employees are typically included in an improshare plan, and all participants share equally in the bonus pool created. A study of improshare programs in 34 unionized companies showed an average productivity gain of 26.9 percent after the first year, whereas the average gain for 38 nonunion plants was 21.5 percent.[33] Another study of 112 firms that had introduced improshare found that the median increase in productivity in the first year was 8 percent and that cumulative productivity gains had risen to 17.5 percent by the third year, after which they leveled off.[34]

A review of several studies reports that gain-sharing and profit-sharing plans generally provide a sustainable 3 to 6 percent increase in productivity.[35] Keys to the successful implementation of alternative reward systems in a unionized firm include (1) developing a cooperative relationship between union and management, which is based on genuine mutual trust and respect for each party; (2) involvement of the union in the development and implementation of the reward system; (3) effective communication of the program to covered employees; (4) flexibility to adapt the reward system to operating conditions and changing business needs; and (5) establishment of realistic achievable goals, particularly with respect to group incentive plans.[36] Employees' ability to understand the goals of a reward system and how those goals were established, how the attainment of plan goals will be measured, and how payouts are determined have a strong effect on covered employees' perceptions of both procedural and distributive justice under a reward system.[37]

Group incentive programs are based on the assumption that by linking earnings to performance, employees will adjust their efforts to optimize income. Because bonuses are tied to group effort, employees should have more incentive to work cooperatively. Considerable evidence suggests that the combination of employee participation programs and group incentive programs can exceed the gains made by either program alone. Employees have little incentive to share their performance-enhancing ideas with management without corresponding rewards. In addition, employees with no participation in decisions cannot respond effectively to such incentive programs. A union can provide more direct and open channels of communication for a collective voice and enhance employee input; however, contract language with fixed wage classifications and confrontational negotiations may inhibit cooperation and employee response to reward incentives. Thus, in general, unionized firms may have an environment more conducive to employee participation because of their participation in the collective bargaining process, but nonunion firms may have an environment more conducive to implementing group incentive programs.[38]

One additional alternative reward plan that has received attention in recent years is **skill-based pay** (SBP).[39] Rather than setting base pay on the job an employee performs, SBP systems base compensation on the skills or knowledge an employee possesses that are valued by the employer. Sixty percent of *Fortune* 1000 firms report using SBP, although it typically applies to less than 20 percent of employees in a firm.[40] Changes in operating methods or the introduction of new technology requiring employees to acquire new skills or enhance existing skills may serve as an impetus for adopting a SBP plan. A proliferation of different job classifications may be reduced by grouping employees into a smaller number of skill blocks. Skill blocks can be defined based on natural work groups (e.g., assembly, painting), a set of existing job classifications, normal skill progression within a particular trade (e.g., welder), or team based. Each block has a defined set of skills, and employees can acquire skills through training and work experience both within a block and in preparation to qualify for a different skill block. An SBP plan encourages a more flexible labor force, enhances employee skills acquisition, and aids a company in adapting to a changing competitive environment.[41]

SBP plans can be successfully implemented in a unionized firm as demonstrated by such firms as GM, Ford Motor Company, AT&T, Corning, Maxwell House, and Harley-Davidson Motor Company.[42] Establishing the initial composition of skill blocks, determining individuals' access to training opportunities, and creating an appeals procedure for handling disputes over the administration of the plan are key issues affecting the success of SBP plans. Union representatives may initially prefer to handle the implementation of a SBP plan as a trial project governed by a negotiated memorandum of understanding separate from the parties' negotiated labor agreement. An SBP plan is typically one part of a broader effort to introduce work-practice changes to enhance a firm's competitiveness. As with the introduction of other alternative reward systems, union involvement in planning, implementing, and administering an SBP plan can help to ensure employees' acceptance of the plan and attainment of the plan's potential benefits.

Arguments Used by Management and Union Officials in Wage Determination

Union and management representatives recognize that no single causal influence affects wage determination; however, both parties will use any identifiable influence to support their arguments for or against a wage increase. Related factors often used to bolster wage claims include differential features of the work performed (usually determined by job evaluation), wage comparability, ability to pay (financial condition of the organization), productivity, cost of living, and legal requirements.[43] Union and management officials do not always accept the same criteria. Moreover, each may emphasize different criteria at different times, particularly if adopting a distributive bargaining strategy. During prosperous times, unions tend to emphasize the employer's ability to pay; during recessions, management may emphasize its poor financial position. Similarly, during periods of rapid inflation, unions emphasize cost-of-living adjustments; when prices are stable, management places much weight on the lack of necessity for cost-of-living adjustments.

Pressure from domestic and international competition has reduced management's ability to simply pass increased labor costs on to the customer in the form of higher prices for goods and services. This has caused employers to place more emphasis on operating efficiency, cost-cutting measures, and productivity improvement. During difficult economic times, employers tend to de-emphasize industry wage patterns and focus more attention in wage negotiations on their firm specific labor costs, expected profits, and labor market conditions.

Differential Features of the Work: Job Evaluation and the Wage Spread

The job evaluation process described in the preceding section can influence the wages assigned to various job classifications in an organization. The relative influence of job evaluation can be seen in the **wage spread**, which represents the internal distribution of the proposed or negotiated wage increase to the bargaining unit employees (Exhibit 7.3).

The six employee job classifications in Exhibit 7.3 range in skill and pay from Classification A (highest) to Classification F (lowest), which conform to the results of management's job evaluation procedure. Management would generally prefer the wage spread in example 2 because it gives more highly skilled employees a higher hourly wage increase that could maintain or increase their wage differential over less-skilled employees while utilizing fewer employee classifica-

Exhibit 7.3

Three Examples of Internal Wage Spreads

Example	Number of Employees	Employee Classification	Percentage of Plants Total Employees	Increase In Cents Per Hour
1	184	A	16%	57.0
	197	B	18	50.0
	165	C	15	48.0
	237	D	21	46.0
	149	E	13	44.0
	193	F	17	42.0
	1,125			
2	381	A and B	34	60.0
	402	C and D	36	44.0
	342	E and F	30	34.0
	1,125			
3	1,125	A through F	100	47.2

tions compared with example 1, simplifying administration of the pay system. Maintaining this wage differential is important to management for two reasons: (1) it helps ensure that current skilled employees do not leave because of higher wages offered by other firms, and (2) it offers some motivation to employees in lower paid classifications to train for higher skill-level classifications within the company.

Unions support the job evaluation principle that higher rated jobs should receive a higher rate of pay than lower rated jobs. However, job evaluation ratings are not the only factor unions believe should be considered in determining the size or amount of wage improvements. One concern of union negotiators (which should be shared by management) is to ensure that the negotiated wage spread will result in sufficient votes by bargaining unit members to ratify the proposed labor agreement. Satisfied union members will also enhance a union leader's reelection prospects. Assume, for example, that Classification C in Exhibit 7.3 represented a politically influential group of employees. To satisfy this important group of bargaining unit constituents, union negotiators might prefer the wage spread illustrated by example 1, which grants Classification C employees a 48-cents-per-hour wage increase, or example 3, which grants a 47.2-cents-per-hour increase, rather than management's preferred wage spread (example 2), which only grants classification C employees a 44-cents-per-hour increase. The union might even propose a different wage spread that would give the employees in Classification C a much higher wage increase.

To encourage employees to ratify a tentative contract agreement and foster employees' perception of equity in wage adjustment, management might agree to an across-the-board increase to all employees regardless of their job classification. Granting an equal cents-per-hour increase in wages to all bargaining unit employees has the effect, over several contract renegotiations, of narrowing the wage spread between different rated job classifications. If wage spreads narrow too much, management could experience increased dissatisfaction among employees holding higher rated jobs, thereby leading to problems of increased turnover and absenteeism or lower productivity among these workers. Union and management negotiators might attempt to address the potential problem of narrowing wage spreads over time by agreeing to an equal percentage increase in hourly base wage rates (rather than an equal cents per hour increase), which would maintain existing wage spreads. Another alternative to maintain a desired wage spread between higher and lower skilled employees would be to negotiate a special cents-per-hour increase only applicable to certain higher rated jobs (**skill pay differential**) in addition to an equal cents-per-hour wage improvement granted to all job classifications.

Within the same or similar job classifications, one of the principal goals of unions is to reduce wage dispersion among employees with satisfactory job performance. This goal can be summarized in the phrase "equal pay for equal work." Unions seek to achieve this goal by negotiating a single rate of pay for each job classification and a seniority-based progression of wage rates within a defined employee classification up to some defined maximum rate. This approach is commonly used in job classifications that have two or more steps or grades that an employee may advance to over time based on some established criteria (e.g., work experience, demonstration of advanced job skills, or successful completion of training). A single wage rate (one pay grade for all employees in a given classification) eliminates wage dispersion between employees in the same classification, and seniority rules help control overall wage rates by requiring similar treatment to workers who have the same plant or companywide seniority. Because of the "spillover" effect of union wage practices, even nonunion firms experience less wage dispersion over time than one might expect.[44]

Contract language that specifies a newly hired employee will be paid less than other employees performing a similar job is referred to as a **two-tier pay plan.** Approximately 28 percent of sampled union contracts expiring in 2003 featured a two-tier wage plan with manufacturing firms slightly more likely than nonmanufacturing firms to have one.[45] Approximately two-thirds of two-tier wage plans are temporary in nature, allowing a new hire over time (e.g., the term of the contract) to rise to the same pay level as other similarly classified workers. Some bargaining relationships extend the two-tier concept to include eligibility for some employee benefits. Exhibit 7.4 presents an example of a two-tier pay schedule.

A two-tier wage plan achieves immediate labor-cost savings as job openings are filled by lower-paid "new hires," and it may facilitate a favorable contract ratification vote, since the wages of current bargaining unit members would

Exhibit 7.4

Examples of Two-Tier Pay Scales

Job Classes and Hourly Rates for Employees on Payroll Prior to March 1, 2003	
Job Classes	Wage Rate
0	$9.40
1	9.60
2	9.80
3	10.00
4	10.20
5	10.40
6	10.60
7	10.80

All Employees hired after March 1, 2003, shall be considered new hires and . . . shall be paid according to the [following] bracket rate:

Job Classes and Hourly Rates for Employees on Hired After March 1, 2003	
Bracket	Wage Rate
0	$6.00
1	6.10
2	6.20
3	6.40
4	6.60
5	6.80
6	7.00
7	7.20

not be adversely affected by implementation of a two-tier plan. Because a union may legally negotiate a wage differential based on factors such as skill, type of work, or seniority, it appears to have ample latitude to negotiate two-tier wage levels if the union does so in a "good faith and honest" effort to meet an employer's demand for lower labor costs in a manner that best protects the economic interests of current bargaining unit members. Auto parts suppliers Visteon and Delphi recently agreed in their 2003 labor agreement with the United Auto Workers union to begin within 90 days negotiations on the adoption of a two-tier wage and benefit plan as a means of making the unionized auto suppliers more competitive with other lower costs auto parts suppliers. Wages at Visteon and Delphi are currently $9–11 higher than other unionized parts suppliers and $13–16 higher than nonunion parts suppliers.[46]

Some bargaining relationships have found that the costs of increased friction over time between lower- and upper-wage tier employees outweighs the initial labor-cost savings of a two-tier wage plan and in subsequent negotiations have eliminated such language from their labor agreement.[47] If lower-tier employees view the pay situation as inequitable, they may vote to remove union leaders responsible for negotiating the wage terms or support union decertification. Likewise, lower-tier employees may feel less commitment to their employer, thereby increasing turnover rates and lowering productivity, which results in higher relative labor costs to the company.[48]

Wage Comparability

A common argument in wage negotiations is that wage rates in one bargaining unit should be equal or related to the wage rates in comparable bargaining units. **Wage comparability** is given considerable weight in wage determination, although these comparisons can become quite complicated and may be based on biased information.[49] Wage surveys can be helpful, but they do not measure how the job content, method of payment, regularity of employment, supplemental unemployment benefits, vacations, pensions, and holidays vary from company to company. Fundamental considerations such as the size of the appropriate labor market and occupational and geographical differentials must be recognized. At first glance, it appears that bus drivers in Miami would have duties identical to those of bus drivers in Chicago. However, many differences in these similar jobs can exist, such as weather conditions, number of scheduled stops, location of scheduled stops, number of passengers, and so on. Furthermore, a major difference could arise in situations in which the bus drivers are required to make change for passengers. In such cases, a union could claim that this job responsibility creates a safety hazard by increasing the likelihood of robberies and would seek adequate compensation for this additional risk.

The relative importance of wages to total costs (**degree of labor intensiveness**) is also a significant factor in wage comparability. For example, if a modern, highly automated textile mill pays wages that account for 30 percent of total costs, a 10 percent increase in wages would equal a 3 percent change in the sales price. However, in an old textile mill with out-of-date machinery, where wages account for 65 percent of total costs, a 10 percent increase in wages would equal a 6.5 percent change in sales price. Even though wage data are often largely fragmented or deficient, negotiators still have to rely on wage comparability in arguing for or against certain levels of wages. Therefore, both parties continue to look for commonalities with other companies, local firms, or similar jobs that can provide a base from which to present their proposals.

Ability to Pay

The **ability to pay,** or the financial condition of the organization, is a commonly used standard for wage determination given much weight by unions during periods of high profitability.[50] Management rarely claims a true "inability to pay" except in extreme cases where the firm is losing money or is otherwise financially threatened, because to make such a claim triggers a union's legal right to independently examine the company's financial records under the duty to bargain in good faith for the purpose of verifying the employer's claim. Management more commonly responds to union wage demands by expressing an "unwillingness to pay" based on factors such as productivity rates, wage survey data, other capital needs, industry settlement patterns, or other relevant factors.

Ability to pay has limited usefulness as the sole criterion for wage determination for several reasons:[51]

1. Wages based solely on the ability to pay would create a chaotic wage structure and would cause a change in the wage-costs-price relationships that have evolved over time.

2. To be consistent, the ability to pay must work both ways, causing wage reductions when profits are nonexistent or inadequate. Such an approach would be generally unacceptable to unions.

3. It is extremely difficult to determine the share of profits that should be used for wage increases. If the profit is distributed to employees in the form of higher wages and an insufficient amount is shared with stockholders, there will be no incentive for investment, thereby limiting the firm's growth potential.

4. Wages supposedly are paid to employees in accordance with their relative value to the firm, their contribution to its goals, and the relative importance of their services. If ability to pay is the major factor, the relationship between actual pay and actual value could become distorted.

5. Wages are negotiated for future application. Basing wage changes on past profits is no guarantee that future profit levels will remain high enough to sustain the firm's profitability at the higher agreed-on wage levels.

Productivity

In 2002, the average annual productivity rate for U.S. workers in the nonfarm business sector rose 5.4 percent, compared to a decline in unit labor costs of 2.4 percent, helping to fuel a rebound in business profits.[52] Labor productivity represents a measure of the value of output created relative to the hourly costs of the labor necessary to produce that output (see Exhibit 7.5 for an international comparison of manufacturing productivity).

Although no argument has been advanced with more conviction or sophistication than that wages should vary with changes in productivity, union and management negotiators often experience difficulty in attempting to apply the principle to specific negotiations. For example, the rate of change in productivity varies widely from industry to industry, firm to firm, and even plant to plant.

Not only is productivity itself difficult to measure accurately, but any change in productivity (usually measured in output per employee-hour) results from many causes, only one of which is labor.[53]

Those who study productivity have generally agreed that new capital investment and mechanization have been the primary causes for greater productivity, but there are still important issues to reconcile. Who should share in the revenue resulting from increased productivity—the employees, stockholders, or consumers? What is the proper balance among the contributing factors of production—labor and capital investments? Any use of productivity data must be handled carefully because the available data are only approximate estimates. Output per employee-hour often overstates gains attributed to labor and understates the relative contributions of advanced technology, improved methods, better machines, product quality, and so on to the value created by an hour of paid labor.

To remain competitive, companies and employees must be more productive. Union negotiators often argue that productivity gains may be used to pay for higher wage or benefit costs. Conversely, rising labor costs without offsetting gains in productivity may act as an incentive for management to find lower cost substitutes for employing additional labor (e.g., outsourcing, mechanization, and plant relocation). In 1960, the Longshoremen's Union allowed mechanization of the waterfronts, increasing productivity by 140 percent.[54] Annual wages for top-rated longshoremen rose to over $50,000 plus benefits, but the number of jobs declined from 16,400 to 9,600. The same principle applies to other industries; high productivity is the only way to warrant high wages. However, as witnessed in many manufacturing industries over the past 15 years, steady productivity

Exhibit 7.5

Average Annual Rates of Change in Manufacturing Output per Hour for the United States and Selected Countries

Country	1979–2001	2001
United States	3.2%	−.4%
Canada	2.1	−2.0
France	4.2	2.8
Germany (unified)	2.4	1.4
Italy	2.2	1.7
Sweden	4.3	0.0
United Kingdom	3.6	1.3
Netherlands	3.2	0.4
Japan	3.5	−1.6
Korea	–	3.2
Taiwan	5.9	6.3

Productivity data is affected by factors such as the amount of output (product or service produced), number of hours worked, hourly compensation costs, value of goods/services produced, and the currency exchange rate. Productivity data represent the combined contributions of labor, management, new technology, capital investment, capacity utilization, and energy use.

SOURCE: U.S. Department of Labor, "International Comparisons of Manufacturing Productivity and Unit Labor Cost Trends Revised Data for 2001," *News Release* (February 26, 2003), Table 8.

growth has not led to a comparable increase in employment opportunities or significant real wage gains. One possible explanation for the inverse relationship between productivity growth and growth in real wages is that workers in the United States lack sufficient power to encourage or require employers to share a sufficient proportion of productivity gains with workers.[55]

A gain-sharing plan was previously discussed as one way to share productivity gains with employees who help create them. Over one-third of large companies have implemented some type of gain-sharing program.[56] In addition to providing an economic incentive for workers to improve the quantity and quality of outputs, productivity sharing plans may also serve to reduce grievances, absenteeism, and turnover, and to improve labor–management relations.[57]

Problems with productivity sharing Although productivity sharing offers an innovative approach for mutual gain-sharing and cooperative activity, it too has its problems. Foremost is the measurement of productivity, because many possible measures exist. Some jobs do not lend themselves to precise measurement of output. It is much easier to measure bricks laid per hour by a worker than the value of that same worker spending one hour in a meeting discussing safety issues affecting the job. In jobs that are not routine or repetitive, exact measures are impossible.

Another problem is locating and organizing productivity data in such a manner that it may be useful to a firm. Serious arguments over the contribution of specific factors to increased productivity can inhibit the success of any productivity bargaining. What is the chief contributor to productivity gains? Is it the skill, efforts, or attitudes of the employees? Or is it the advanced technology of the machinery and equipment, efficiency of the operations, or the scale of operations? Or is it the interaction between these sets of factors?[58]

Because productivity gains are shared by labor and management under the productivity bargaining concept, they will certainly give rise to rigorous and complicated negotiations. Evidence suggests that many unions do not consider gain-sharing plans as a substitute for traditional hourly wage gains but rather as an additional pay benefit, substitute for wage concessions, or a means of maintaining parity with an industry wage pattern.[59]

Examples of bargaining for productivity improvement have occurred in the construction industry. Negotiations there have resulted in agreements to reduce work stoppages and contract language covering jurisdictional disputes, inefficient work rules, illegal featherbedding, and the duties of nonworking union stewards. Interestingly, the stimulus for productivity bargaining in the construction industry was the loss of work that increasingly went to nonunion contractors, along with the desire of union members to protect or expand their employment opportunities, particularly during unfavorable economic conditions.[60]

Effect of unions on productivity and efficiency Recently, there has been considerable debate and research about the effect of unions on productivity and efficiency. Labor productivity appears to be higher in unionized firms, particularly in manufacturing and construction. Explanations vary but often cite the following reasons:

- Improved morale brought about by higher wages, benefits, and improved, working conditions.
- Less employee turnover at unionized firms.

- Higher levels of firm-specific skills, resulting in part from more training opportunities and greater employee longevity on the job.

- More pressure on management to invest in better methods, such as technological improvements, to reduce unit labor costs.

- More effective grievance procedures, which help to resolve employee problems more quickly and therefore improve productivity.

- The ability to negotiate subjects related to industrial accidents and diseases that can reduce lost work time and consequently increase productivity.[61]

A union can also promote efficiency when employees, through their union power, ensure that managers treat them fairly and gain a voice to influence decision making that leads to higher morale and greater productivity. Productivity is also enhanced by the fact that unionized workplaces attract and retain more highly skilled and experienced employees because of higher wages, the opportunity to be heard, and the assurance of fair treatment, which can also increase employees' loyalty to the firm.[62] Unionized firms are just as likely as nonunionized firms to adopt advanced manufacturing technologies as a means of enhancing productivity growth and competitiveness.[63]

On the other hand, it may be argued that unions can decrease productivity by reducing managerial flexibility, limiting the use of merit-based compensation, imposing work-rule restrictions such as limits on work loads or tasks performed, and increasing the size of work crews.[64] To what extent unions are shown to have a positive or negative effect on productivity is often determined by the methodology researchers use to measure productivity.[65]

On balance, unions generally have a positive effect on productivity. However, productivity gains are not generally sufficient to completely offset the higher labor costs (higher distribution of profits to meet employees interests) attributable to unionization. Therefore, unionization may lower the rate of return per dollar of capital invested (one measure of profitability). This effect is most likely to be noticeable in unionized firms operating in product or service markets with relatively little competition and high profit margins.[66]

Cost of Living

During periods of rising prices, unions support their wage demands in part by referring to the cost of living. Union negotiators advance the argument that a rise in the cost of living without a commensurate wage increase is equivalent to a cut in real wages or a drop in purchasing power. Thus, the proposition that wages should be raised at least in proportion to the rise in living costs may seem quite fair and reasonable.

Employers are often concerned that a firm has little control over how much inflation may increase over a specified time period, making the employer's liability for pay more unpredictable. Wage payments based solely on an increase in the cost of living are also not tied to the need for increased labor productivity or the actual operating experience (profit/loss) of the firm. Where contract negotiations cover two or more plants, the additional concern is that the cost of living may vary by geographical location, either overestimating or underestimating the true cost of living if regional or national inflation rates are used in computing cost-of-living wage adjustments.[67]

Cost of living usually refers to the **Consumer Price Index** (CPI) computed by the U.S. Labor Department's Bureau of Labor Statistics, which measures changes in the price of goods and services purchased by a typical American household on a monthly basis.[68] The index covers 207 categories of goods or services (e.g., food, housing, health care, entertainment), sampled from 44 urban geographical areas around the country. Approximately 21 percent of manufacturers and 11 percent of nonmanufacturing labor agreements contain a cost-of-living adjustment clause.[69]

Comparable Worth

Women earn an average of 76 cents for every dollar earned by men.[70] The AFL-CIO estimates that over a work career, a 25-year-old female employee will lose $523,000 in pay compared with a male worker of the same age. Some federal legislation has been enacted to protect workers against wage discrimination, such as the Equal Pay Act of 1963, the Civil Rights Acts of 1964 and 1991, and the Age Discrimination in Employment Act of 1967. These laws prohibit paying male employees more than female employees unless the wage difference is justified on the basis of skill, effort, responsibility, working conditions, seniority, or performance. **Comparable worth** may become an issue in wage setting as a means of extending the legal concept of equal pay for equal work to include equalizing pay rates between different jobs that make comparable contributions to the attainment of an organization's goals.

Proponents of the comparable worth issue state that women earn less pay because they are disproportionately represented in lower-evaluated and therefore lower-paying jobs and that the value placed on these jobs has been arbitrarily established by companies or negotiated with a union.[71] Implementation of a comparable worth plan is based upon the assumption that the worth of different jobs can be measured and compared with reasonable accuracy, but subjectivity by raters in the job evaluation process may challenge the validity of this key assumption.[72]

Unions are more likely to raise the comparable worth issue in bargaining units covering a mix of jobs that tend to be predominantly occupied by members of one sex, such as a telephone company where operators and office employees tend to be mostly female and line and installation jobs tend to be held primarily by higher-paid males. Regular audits of compensation practices, an effective job evaluation process, and basing wage adjustments on valid job performance appraisal and objective market wage data help to ensure gender-neutral pay equity.

Wage Adjustments during the Term or Duration of the Labor Agreement

Because most negotiated labor agreements have a term of more than one year, it is common to include contract language that allows the adjustment of wages during the term of the contract. The most common term or duration of a labor agreement is 3 years (52 percent of 315 contracts surveyed), followed by more than 3 years (29 percent), 2 years (14 percent), and 1 year or less (6 percent).[73] In recent years there has been a trend in basic goods manufacturing industries (e.g., auto, textiles, petroleum, paper) to negotiate longer term contracts (4 to 6 years).[74] Methods used to adjust employee base wage rates during the term of a labor agreement include a **cost-of-living adjustment (COLA)** clause, **deferred wage increase** (also called an *annual improvement adjustment*), and a **wage re-opener clause.**

A COLA clause imposes a contractual obligation on an employer to change rates of pay in accordance with a collectively bargained formula and appears in approximately 16 percent of labor contracts.[75] When negotiating COLA provisions, union and management representatives usually consider the following issues:

1. Selection of the particular price index and base point. Most labor agreements use the all-cities CPI-W (consumer price index for urban wage earners and clerical workers). The beginning date of the contract is usually specified as the base point. The CPI-W is used to measure the rate of inflation from the base point to the end of the period when the COLA adjustment is scheduled to be paid.

2. Frequency and timing of the wage adjustment. Quarterly adjustments are more common in manufacturing industries, whereas annual adjustments are most common in nonmanufacturing firms. Employers would generally prefer less frequent adjustment periods (e.g., annual rather than quarterly) to delay the time when the employer must expend the funds, thus permitting the firm to use that cash in the interim and delaying the imposition of roll-up costs (as discussed in Chapter 6) incurred whenever an employee's base wage rate is adjusted upward. Unions would generally prefer quarterly COLA payments because it puts the money into the hands of bargaining unit members sooner and increases the value of benefits affected by the roll-up factor.

3. The most common negotiated formula for COLA adjustments is a 1 cent-per-hour increase for each .3 point increase in the CPI-W during the specified base period. For example, if during the base period the CPI-W rose 1.3 points, then the employer on the specified adjustment date would increase a covered employee's base wage rate by 4 cents per hour ($1.3 \div .3 = 4.33 \times \$.01 = 4¢$ rounded off to nearest whole cent). Some contracts negotiate an alternative formula specifying a percentage change in wages in accordance with a specified percentage change in the CPI-W.

4. Effect of COLA on other elements of the compensation package. There is little uniformity found in labor contracts on this issue. Some agreements may include COLA adjustments only for the purpose of computing gross hourly earnings to avoid roll-up cost. Other labor contracts may use the COLA-adjusted base wage rate in computing all items related to wages and benefits (e.g., holiday pay, vacation pay, sick leave pay).

One means of reducing the uncertainty regarding the amount of upward adjustment in wages under a COLA clause is to negotiate a maximum and minimum cap for such payments. A cap would guarantee a specified minimum and maximum adjustment during the term of the labor agreement regardless of the actual rise in the rate of inflation during the period. A minimum guarantee would benefit bargaining unit members in that management generally insists on negotiating smaller base hourly wage increases when a COLA clause is included in the labor agreement because part of the employee's wage gain is expected to be provided by the COLA payment during the contract's term. A maximum cap would reduce management's wage liability risk should an unexpected rapid escalation in inflation occur during the contract's term. Despite the apparent advantage of a cap to both parties, only an estimated 25 percent of COLA clauses contain any form of caps, indicating the difficulty encountered in reaching a mutual agreement on what constitutes a reasonable minimum or maximum guaranteed COLA payment.

Deferred wage increases are negotiated in multiyear contracts to provide some adjustment in base wage rates beyond the first contract year. Contracts are sometimes referred to as being back-loaded, front-loaded, or even-loaded as a means of indicating in which years of the contract most of the wage improvement occurs. For example, a 3-year contract that averaged a 3 percent annual wage gain could provide annual wage adjustments of 5, 3, and 1 percent (front loaded); 1, 3, and 5 percent (back loaded); or 3, 3, and 3 percent (even loaded). As with the timing of COLA adjustments, unions generally favor transferring cash into the hands of bargaining unit members as quickly as possible, whereas management prefers delaying the transfer of money as long as possible. The loading of economic improvements in a labor agreement can be used as one measure of the relative bargaining power between the parties.

A wage re-opener clause is written to permit wages to be renegotiated at a specified point in time during the term of the contract or whenever some predetermined event occurs (e.g., profits exceed a certain level; the CPI has risen by a specified amount). A wage re-opener clause may enable a contract settlement to occur under conditions where the future operating environment of the firm is unclear. A wage re-opener clause can also reduce the risk of long-term contracts by permitting wages to be renegotiated in the later years of the contract's term. Some labor agreements may also contain re-opener contract language that permits certain non-wage items to be renegotiated during the term of the contract.

Lump sum pay adjustments

Lump sum pay adjustments appeared in approximately 10 percent of labor contracts in 2003, down from 13 percent in 2002.[76] The most common payment was a flat amount—an average of $869 in 2002. Only 14 percent of contracts provided a lump-sum bonus in the second year, and only 9 percent provided a third-year lump sum payment. Lump sum pay adjustments are popular with management because they do not change the employee's base hourly wage rate and thus have no impact on increasing roll-up costs.

Employee Benefits

In 2003, unionized U.S. employers paid benefit costs averaging $10.72 per hour worked (34.9 percent of each payroll dollar) compared with nonunion employers' benefits expenditure of $5.67 per hour worked (26.5 percent of each payroll dollar).[77] Exhibit 7.6 presents a complete breakdown of employer cost per hour worked by bargaining status. Benefits are an important part of an employee's compensation and include insurance costs, pension payments, payments for time not worked (such as vacations, sick leave, and holidays), legally required payments for unemployment and workers' compensation, paid rest and lunch breaks, and bonuses. Legally required payments (e.g., Social Security, workers'

Exhibit 7.6

Employer Costs per Hour Worked by Bargaining Status. March 2003

Type of Compensation	Union	Nonunion
Total Compensation (wages + benefits)	**$30.68 (100.0%)**	**$21.36 (100.0%)**
Wages and salaries	**19.95** (65.0%)	**15.69** (73.5%)
Total Benefits	**10.72** (34.9%)	**5.67** (26.5%)
Individual Benefit Categories		
Paid Leave (e.g., vacation, holiday, sick leave)	**2.19** (7.1%)	**1.38** (6.5%)
Supplemental Pay (e.g., overtime, shift differential, lump sum pay)	**1.11** (3.6%)	**.59** (2.8%)
Insurance (e.g., life, health, short and long term disability)	**2.99** (9.7%)	**1.34** (6.3%)
Retirement & Savings (e.g., defined benefit plan, defined contribution plan, cash balance plan)	**1.73** (5.6%)	**.54** (2.5%)
Legally required benefits (e.g., Social Security, unemployment compensation, workers' compensation)	**2.61** (8.5%)	**1.80** (8.4%)
Other Benefits (e.g., severance pay, supplemental unemployment benefits)	**.08** (0.3%)	**.02** (0.1%)

Source: U.S. Bureau of Labor Statistics, "Employer Cost for Employee Compensation—March 2003," News Release, June 11, 2003, p. 11.

and unemployment compensation) for many years constituted the single largest category of benefit expense incurred by both union and nonunion employers. In 2003, health insurance became the highest single benefit costs item for unionized employers, thus making it an important bargaining topic in labor negotiations. Unionized employers incur substantially higher cost than nonunion employers for health insurance because policies provided for under union contracts generally provide a wider range and higher dollar amount of health-care coverage to employees. The following sections present major areas of employee benefits, relying largely on an analysis of 141 collective bargaining agreements by the Bureau of National Affairs.[78]

Insurance

Of 141 union contracts surveyed, 89 percent provided life insurance, and 93 percent covered hospitalization and surgical expenses. Other common health-care benefits found in union contracts are doctor visits (94 percent), prescription drugs (93 percent), mental health (89 percent), dental care (84 percent), vision care (62 percent), and domestic partner coverage (27 percent). Approximately 36 percent of union employers participate in multiemployer health insurance plans that enable plan participants to negotiate lower insurance rates and fee schedules with health-care providers, as well as spread administrative costs over a large number of plan participants.

Tight labor market conditions in the late 1990s caused many employers to improve health insurance benefits as an incentive to attract and retain qualified workers. This was a change from the bargaining trend of the early and mid-1990s, when employers often sought to shift a greater proportion of health-care costs onto employees or reduce health-care benefits as a means of controlling rising health-care costs. During recent years generally weak demand for labor and increased pressure on company profit have once again focused employers' attention on managing health-care costs effectively. Health-care benefits have been the principal issue in several major strikes that have occurred in recent years at companies such as General Electric, Hershey Foods Corporation, and Lockheed Martin Corporation.[79]

Health-Care Cost Containment

Health-care insurance premium costs rose 13.9 percent in 2003, the largest annual increase since 1990, and followed an 11 percent increase in 2002[80] In 2003, the average annual health insurance premium cost for single coverage was $3,383 and family coverage averaged $9,068.[81] Employer efforts to either reduce the costs of health-care coverage or shift a greater portion of the cost burden to employees often conflicts with employees' pressure on their unions to maintain or expand health-care benefits while minimizing additional cost to bargaining unit members.

Unions and employers jointly recognize the importance employees place on the provision of health-care benefits and the need to cooperate in seeking cost-effective means of providing such benefit coverage. A number of contract provisions designed to lower health-care costs are found in most union contracts, including some provision for copayments, deductibles, and premium contributions by employees. Union employees typically pay a smaller proportion of such expenses compared to similar types of provisions applicable to nonunion employees. Raising copayments per doctor's office visit or deductible amounts paid by the employee before insurance coverage begins can impact employees differently depending on how frequently they use medical services. Increasing the proportion of insurance premium cost paid by the employee affects all employees covered under the same policy provision equally and therefore is sometimes preferred as a cost-sharing mechanism over raising employee co-pay or deductible amounts. Other cost-containment provisions found in union contracts include a generic drug requirement (74 percent), delayed new hire eligibility (50 percent), pretax spending account (50 percent), preadmission testing (45 percent), wellness program (43 percent), usage review (42 percent), outpatient surgery requirement (38 percent), and required second opinion (32 percent).[82]

Many union contracts provide more than one type of health-care plan. Traditional **fee-for-service** plans have declined in use over the past decade and currently are found in 39 percent of contracts. Most popular are **preferred provider organization** (PPO) plans (68 percent of contracts), which permit an employee to pay a lower rate for health-care services if the employee agrees to use health-care providers approved by the PPO plan. To become an approved health-care provider, a doctor must agree with the insurance provider in advance that he or she will accept a lower reimbursement rate than the traditional fee-for-service rate for most health-care services provided. **Health maintenance organization** (HMO) plans, which restrict an employee's choice of health-care provider to the HMO, are available in 48 percent of contracts. A few contracts permit the employee to choose under which one of the different health-care plans provided the individual will be covered.

Income Maintenance

Income maintenance provisions usually involve issues such as work or pay guarantees, **severance pay** (separation or termination pay), or a **supplemental unemployment benefit plan** (SUB). Severance pay plans provide a lump-sum payment on termination and are included in 42 percent of manufacturing contracts but only in 25 percent of nonmanufacturing labor agreements. More senior workers and those who earn higher wages are generally entitled to a proportionally larger severance payment.[83] In most cases, severance pay is extended only to employees whose jobs have been terminated as a result of permanent shutdown; who are laid off beyond an established minimum period; or who have no prospect for recall. If the current contract does not specifically provide for severance pay, this is a mandatory subject of bargaining that a union will generally request to bargain over should a significant lay off or plant closure occur.

A supplemental unemployment benefit (SUB) plan provides pay in addition to unemployment compensation to which the individual would be entitled and is found in 12 percent of labor contracts. A few SUB plans provide individual accounts in which the employee has a vested right and from which he or she may withdraw money for reasons other than lack of work. The most common method provides payment of an amount equal to a percentage of the employee's take-home pay with unemployment compensation deducted. Plans involving the UAW are the most beneficial for covered workers, ensuring that SUB payments combined with unemployment compensation payments will equal 95 percent of an employee's take-home pay minus $12.50 in work-related expenses. Other plans range from a $10 per week minimum to 90 percent of take-home pay. Other issues to be negotiated as part of a SUB plan include the duration of benefits, length of service requirements to qualify for coverage, and employer financial requirements to fund the plan.

Work sharing provisions are found in 6 percent of labor contracts. As a means of avoiding or minimizing layoffs among bargaining unit members, qualified employees agree to share the available work opportunities by having each employee work a reduced number of hours. An employer may benefit from such an arrangement by retaining quality workers who, if laid off, might accept employment elsewhere and not return to work when future work opportunities became available.

Premium Pay—Overtime and Other Supplements

Most labor agreements specify daily or weekly work schedules and provide premium pay for hours worked beyond regularly scheduled hours. Most agreements call for an 8-hour day and a work week of 40 hours—Monday through Friday. Overtime premiums are usually paid for work over 8 hours per day at a time-and-a-half rate, which is more beneficial to the worker than the Fair Labor Standards Act (FLSA) requirement of time-and-a-half payment for work in excess of 40 hours in a week. For example, employees on a 4-day, 40-hour work week would receive 8 hours of overtime pay under typical union contract language, whereas the FLSA would require no overtime pay. Payment of double-time for hours worked on certain days such as Sunday or holidays has declined in union contracts as employers have successfully bargained to eliminate such special pay incentives. Employers who operate on a continuous basis (e.g., retail stores open 24 hours per day, 7 days per week) typically negotiate work schedules that do not require the use of premium pay in order to meet normal operating schedules.

Many labor agreements also contain provisions for overtime administration. For example, overtime assignments may be restricted to qualified employees within a specific job classification, department, or work shift. Management may be required to offer overtime work assignments to more senior workers first, or a contract might specify that overtime opportunities be awarded on a rotating basis regardless of seniority. In some cases, when management has had difficulty getting employees to voluntarily work overtime, a provision making overtime work mandatory may be negotiated. Excessive use of overtime as a means of avoiding the additional employment costs associated with hiring more regular workers can lead to a labor dispute. Most employees (and union leaders) understand the necessity for overtime work periodically and usually value the additional income opportunity.

Some labor agreements that provide equalization of overtime hours count the hours whenever an overtime opportunity is offered even though the employee refuses the offer. For example, if an employee is offered 4 hours of Saturday morning overtime and he or she turns it down, those 4 hours for overtime-equalization purposes would still be noted as if the employee had worked them. Likewise, unions have sought provisions in a labor agreement that would enable their members to better plan their off-the-job activities, such as minimum advance notice of required overtime work or the right to refuse overtime work for certain specified reasons.

Various other forms of **premium pay** are also included in most labor contracts. For instance, **shift differentials** (e.g., premium payments for working the night shift) are provided in most of the agreements. Other forms, such as **reporting pay** (guarantees some minimum number of hours' pay for employees who report for scheduled work but find no work) and **call-in pay** (which typically guarantees four hours' pay for employees called in to work during an employee's nonscheduled work hours), are also usually included. Other pay supplements may include pay for temporary transfer, hazardous work, travel, work clothing or tool allowance, or bonus pay for certain specified purposes (e.g., Christmas bonus, good attendance or safety record).

Payment for Nonwork—Holidays, Vacations, and Rest Periods

Labor agreements often contain payments for various nonwork periods such as bereavement leave (84 percent), jury duty leave (87 percent), sick leave (65 percent), military leave (54 percent), personal leave (39 percent), and voting leave (12 percent). The two most expensive paid-leave benefit provisions deal with holiday and vacation pay. In 2003, 91 percent of union employees received paid holidays, compared to 78 percent of nonunion employees.[84] The median number of paid holidays provided under 400 union contracts sampled was 11 with a range from 5 to 19.[85] Nearly all union contracts provide holidays for Labor Day, Independence Day, Thanksgiving, Christmas, New Year's Day, and Memorial Day. Good Friday, Christmas Eve, and the day after Thanksgiving appeared in over half of the agreements sampled. Martin Luther King, Jr.'s birthday was granted as a paid holiday in 14 percent of labor agreements, although it was more common in nonmanufacturing than manufacturing labor agreements. Most contracts contain some eligibility requirements for holiday pay (e.g., specified length of service (usually 4 weeks) before being granted a paid holiday or a requirement the employee must perform any scheduled work the day before and after the holiday). Other issues that should be covered in contract language include holidays falling on Saturday, Sunday, a regularly scheduled day off, or during a paid vacation period, and premium pay for hours worked on a paid holiday.

In many industrialized countries, employees are guaranteed a paid vacation by law; however, in the United States there is no such legal guarantee.[86] For example, after 1 year of service, workers receive 25 paid vacation days in France; 24 days in Germany; 22 days in Spain; and 20 days in Belgium, Ireland, the Netherlands, Australia, and the United Kingdom. The U.S. Bureau of Labor Statistics reports that 90 percent of workers covered under a union contract receive a paid vacation compared to 78 percent of nonunion employees.[87] Only 40 percent of part-time employees were eligible to receive a paid vacation.

Employees covered under union contracts typically qualify for more paid vacation days after fewer years of service compared with nonunion employee benefits. Union contracts typically provide for one week of paid vacation after 1 year of service; two weeks of vacation after 2 years of service; three weeks of paid vacation after 8 years of service; four weeks of vacation after 15 years of service; five weeks after 21 years of service; and six weeks after 28 years of service. There has been a sharp increase in agreements allowing 5- and 6-week vacations over the past 20 years and a slight decrease in the years of service required to qualify for nearly all types of vacations. Vacation-scheduling provisions appear in almost all labor agreements, covering issues such as annual plant shutdowns and consideration of employee seniority and employee preference. Such provisions are essential in large organizations to reduce potential disputes between employees and to ensure that adequate personnel are available to meet planned operating schedules.

Pensions

As the life expectancy of U.S. workers has increased (77.2 years in 2001), pension benefits have taken on added importance as a source of income to sustain an individual's standard of living after leaving the labor force.[88] In 2003, only 49 percent of all private-sector employees participated in some type of employer- or union-sponsored pension plan (union employees = 83 percent; nonunion employees = 45 percent).[89] Only 35 percent of all employees earning less than $15 per hour were covered under a pension plan.

Nearly all labor agreements make some reference to pension plans, whether in the form of a general statement mentioning the plan or a fully detailed provision. Items usually mentioned include age for retirement (normal and early), disability retirement, benefits available and requirements for qualifying, vesting provisions, administration procedures, and financial arrangements. The presence of a union tends to greatly increase pension coverage and alter the provisions of pension plans in ways that benefit senior employees and equalize pensions among bargaining unit members.[90] Union members typically receive larger pension benefits than nonunion employees at the time they retire and also receive larger increases in such benefits in the years after their retirement. Union members also retire at an earlier age than nonunion employees.

In 1987, the *Age Discrimination in Employment Act* (ADEA) was amended to prohibit any mandatory retirement age (with limited exceptions for certain occupations such as airline pilots), ending the common pension plan use of 70 as a mandatory retirement age. Although this amendment helped extend the career of senior employees, the Supreme Court's controversial *Betts* decision in 1989 ruled that virtually all employee benefit programs are exempt from challenge under the ADEA unless the employee could prove "intentional discrimination" on the part of the employer.[91]

The majority (68 percent) of union contracts include a **defined benefit pension plan,** which guarantees a specified dollar benefit payment per month to a covered employee on retirement. Knowing the amount of pension benefit to be received in advance aids an employee in retirement planning, and having the pension benefit amount guaranteed reduces the investment risk incurred by the employee. Some younger employees who have grown up in an era of generally rising stock market values express a preference for a tax-deferred 401(k) plan as a retirement savings vehicle (a type of **defined contribution pension plan** discussed below). However, stock market declines in recent years have served to remind employees of the risk associated with investing for long-term security in a stock market which historically has periods of growth and decline.

Some unions negotiate 401(k) savings plans whereby the employee can invest his or her own dollars in a savings account and have the contribution matched by an employer contribution up to a specified limit (e.g., 50 cents per dollar invested by the employee up to an amount equal to 3 percent of the employee's salary).[92] During the recent recession, a number of employers suspended discretionary company matching contributions to employee 401(k) plans as a cost-savings measure, although employees were still eligible to contribute to their individual accounts.[93] Most union leaders prefer a 401(k)-type savings plan to be in addition to, rather than a replacement for, a traditional defined benefit pension plan.

Unions generally oppose efforts by an employer to use an **employee stock ownership plan** (ESOP) as a basic pension plan.[94] Investing pension savings in a single company greatly increases the risk to the employee's investment should the firm experience poor future performance (and thus a decline in the value of its stock price). Firms in some industries such as airlines, steel, and trucking have negotiated ESOPs as a management trade-off for union wage concessions.[95] Employee stock ownership plans under a union contract are more likely to permit union employees to vote their own shares of stock, have some direct representation on the governing board of the plan, and be more involved in the development and implementation of the plan.

Research on the effects of ESOPs on labor relations is tentative at this time because of the lack of widespread or long-term experience; however, a few preliminary conclusions may be reported:[96]

- Labor–management cooperation does not emerge automatically when publicly traded companies move into employee ownership.

- Employee ownership leads to greater identification of the employees with the company, and employees receive more information about the company;

supervisor–employee relations become more cooperative; and employees and managers express positive attitudes about employee ownership and the organizational climate.

- No evidence supports the concern that employees want to take over companies with ESOPs and restructure management roles and authority from top to bottom.

- Employee ownership does not have an automatic effect on employees' motivation, work effort, absenteeism, or job satisfaction; however, greater integration of the employee into the organization and more employee participation in decisions do have positive results.

- Generally, the role of the union does not change except when the union makes an early and ongoing effort to become involved in the change process, and unions initiate few changes in labor–management relations.

- Companies with an active employee ownership philosophy that try to translate it into concrete cooperative efforts have the strongest effect on positive employee attitudes.

- The presence of an ESOP does not make a firm more productive, efficient, or profitable; however, most studies show that employee-owned firms performed successfully on a number of financial variables, such as profits, stock appreciation, sales, and employment growth.

Most nonunion employees covered by a pension plan are enrolled in a defined contribution plan whereby the employer agrees to contribute a specific dollar amount to an account established in an employee's name. The employee may also contribute their own dollars to the account's balance. The ultimate value of the employee's retirement benefit depends on the amount of employer and employee contributions to the account, along with the investment gains or losses experienced by the account. Unlike defined benefit plans whose value is insured by the federal government through the Pension Benefit Guaranty Corporation should the employer default on pension obligations, the value of a defined contribution plan is not guaranteed. Allowing the employer to define the amount to be contributed rather than guarantee the value of the account at the time of retirement permits the employer to control the cost of providing a pension benefit and shift the investment risk to the employee to ensure that the account balance will be adequate to fund the employee's retirement security.

A survey of 171 company pension plans in 2002 found that 63 percent of plans surveyed were underfunded.[97] During periods when the value of pension fund's investments decline, an employer with a defined benefit plan must make additional contributions to the pension fund to ensure pension fund liabilities are met. This can create a financial burden on a firm that may also be faced with declining profits and lower sales revenues. An employer with a defined contribution pension plan does not have to make additional resource allocations to cover declines in the value of an individual's pension account and may even be able to reduce the amount of employer contribution to an individual's account under such plans citing current poor economic conditions facing the firm.

A **cash balance pension plan** represents a relatively new and controversial retirement savings approach that combines features of both defined benefit and defined contribution plans.[98] Under a cash balance plan, an employer typically agrees to make a specified contribution to an employee's retirement account, which is guaranteed to earn a specified rate of interest generally pegged to an index such as the 1-year Treasury bill rate. On reaching retirement age, a retiree may generally choose to accept an annuity payment (e.g., $10,000 per year for life) based on the value of the account balance or receive a lump-sum distribution equal to the value of the account balance. Because the amount of benefit earned each year of employment is steady under a cash balance plan, an employee who does not anticipate remaining with the employer for an extended period might earn a greater pension benefit during a shorter employment tenure compared with an employee covered under a traditional defined benefit plan, which typically computes the amount of pension benefit earned based on the average of an employee's three highest salary years, which typically would not occur until late in a worker's career. Conversely, a more senior employee covered under a defined benefit plan might actually experience a 30 to 50 percent reduction in pension benefits if the pension plan were converted to a cash balance plan.[99]

Over 300 firms, including AT&T, IBM, Citigroup Inc., Bell Atlantic, Sun Co., Hallmark Cards, and Eastman Kodak, have adopted cash balance plans; however, such plans are found in only 10 percent of union contracts.[100] A federal judge in Illinois recently ruled that IBM's cash balance plan represented a violation of the *Age Discrimination in Employment Act* (ADEA) because it provided more benefits to younger workers, raising questions about the legality of other employers' cash benefit plans.[101] While this ruling is likely to be appealed, it has slowed the momentum of employers contemplating converting their defined benefit plan to a cash balance plan. Some experts believe that some employers may simply choose to end their current defined benefit plan and establish a defined contribution plan instead.

Pension plans under union contracts often offer several early-retirement options to the employee. For example, agreements provide such options as retirement at age 60 after 10 years of service; retirement at age 55, but only when the combined age and service years equal 85; or retirement after 30 years of service, without regard to age. Although nearly all of the contracts contain vesting provisions stating that an employee whose service is terminated continues to be entitled to earned benefits, the **Employee Retirement Income Security Act (ERISA) of 1974** has very specific regulations governing vesting requirements of pension plans.[102] Although management and labor may negotiate provisions covering pensions that are more favorable than the law requires, most agreements for the time being will no doubt closely correspond to the legal minimum. Under a **cliff vesting schedule**, an employee is considered fully vested after completing three years of service. Under the alternative **graded vesting schedule**, an employee would be 20 percent vested after two years of service and then add an additional 20 percent per year for each additional year of service until becoming fully (100 percent) vested after six years of service.

The majority of basic pension plans found in union contracts are financed solely by employer contributions. Approximately two-thirds of union contracts also provide supplemental savings accounts (e.g., 401[k]plan) to which an employee may contribute additional retirement savings. When a basic pension plan requires a covered employee to contribute, labor agreements include very specific language about the amounts that the employer and the employee contributes.

Family and Child-Care Benefits

After an 8-year effort in the U.S. Congress, the **Family and Medical Leave** Act (FMLA) of 1993 was passed.[103] This act requires private employers of 50 or more employees to provide eligible employees up to 12 weeks of unpaid leave for their own serious illness; the birth or adoption of a child; or care of a seriously ill child, spouse, or parent. For eligibility, an employee must have been employed for at least 1 year and worked at least 1,250 hours within the previous 12 months. The Department of Labor (DOL) is assigned administrative responsibility for the act, and civil suits by employees are allowed.

Now more than 10 years after the FMLA's enactment, it is clear that the law has served to make employers more aware of family work/life issues without imposing any significant costs or administrative burdens on them.[104] The U.S. Department of Labor reports that 16.5 percent of eligible employees actually take leave time provided under the FMLA, with a median length of 10 days leave.[105] The most common reason for taking leave is for the employee's own health (52.4 percent) followed by care for a newborn, newly adopted, or newly placed foster child (18.5 percent). Among employees who needed to take leave but did not, the most common reason cited for not taking leave was they could not afford to do so (77.6 percent). This has prompted some advocates to encourage Congress to amend the FMLA to provide paid rather than unpaid leave, although employer opposition to such a change and federal budget deficits makes enactment unlikely at the federal level in the near future.[106] Beginning in 2004, California will be the first state to authorize partially paid family and medical leave benefits under the state's disability insurance fund, although legislation to provide paid family leave benefits has been introduced in 27 other states.[107]

Some employers are concerned about the broader definition of "serious medical condition" being applied by the U.S. Department of Labor and some courts in comparison to how that term has typically been defined in cases under the *Americans with Disabilities Act* (ADA).[108] Some employers also report administrative difficulty in managing FMLA intermittent leave requests where an employee is absent for a block of time (e.g., 4 hours each Friday for treatment) or works a reduced daily or weekly work schedule. Intermittent leaves comprise 27.8 percent of all employee leave requests. Approximately 23 percent of employers report providing additional leave time beyond the 12 weeks specified under the FMLA, and a majority of employers report granting leave time for one or more reasons beyond those covered by the FMLA (e.g., attending school functions—68 percent; routine medical care—73 percent).[109]

Unions are free to negotiate family and medical benefits that exceed those provided by the FMLA. Because family and medical leave is a mandatory subject of bargaining, the employer is legally obligated to bargain with the union over these subjects.[110] Negotiable issues might include the amount of leave provided and reasons for taking leave, paid or unpaid status of leave time granted, substitution of other paid leave (e.g., sick leave, vacation days) for unpaid FMLA leave, or the method used to determine what 12-month period is used to calculate the 12 weeks of unpaid FMLA leave available within a 12-month period (e.g., calendar year, 12-month period beginning with the employee's date of hire, 12-month period beginning when the employee's first FMLA leave starts). If the company and union have negotiated a general nondiscrimination clause, it is important to ensure that specific laws such as the FMLA to which the contract clause applies are included in the contract language. This would permit the resolution of FMLA disputes under the parties' contract grievance-arbitration procedure rather than requiring an employee to file a complaint with the U.S. Department of Labor or pay a private attorney to pursue a court claim.

Other Benefits

Companies and unions also bargain over a wide range of other benefits. The American Bar Association estimates that half of all U.S. citizens need the services of an attorney annually.[11] **Prepaid legal service plans** are a relatively inexpensive means of providing legal assistance to employees without imposing substantial administrative burdens on an employer. An estimated 19 million individuals were covered under such plans in 2002, a 20 percent increase during the previous 2-year period. Prepaid legal service plans operate in a manner similar to HMOs. In exchange for a monthly premium ($16–$26), subscribers are entitled to free legal advice, representation, and document reviews from a network of approved attorneys who provide the service for a fixed fee paid by the plan's provider. Some plans offer a full array of services, ranging from counsel for criminal offenses to routine matters such as a will, divorces, house closings, and landlord–tenant problems.

Approximately 60 percent of union contracts provide some type of **employee assistance plan** (EAP), which provides counseling services to employees, covering a wide range of problems such as personal finance, marital relationships, stress management, or substance abuse. The U.S. Labor Department estimates that employers save $14 in costs related to employees' problems for every $1 invested in an EAP program.[12] Many employers and unions view an EAP plan as another means of effectively managing employee health-care costs in a proactive manner by providing employees with timely assistance in identifying and resolving problems.

The need to improve employee job skills to match changing job requirements has led more firms to provide **education tuition aid**.[13] Found in 47 percent of labor agreements sampled, education tuition aid helps to cover expenses incurred by an employee who seeks additional education and training related to the employee's career. Larger bargaining units with more than 1,000 members are likely to have a wider variety of benefits than smaller bargaining units, and some benefits such as a **transportation subsidy** to offset travel expenses to and from work are more common in nonmanufacturing (29 percent) than manufacturing (5 percent) industries.

Union Effects on Wages and Benefits

The degree to which unions influence wage and benefit levels is a commonly debated subject among labor economists. In a 1963 classic book, *Unionism and Relative Wages in the United States,* Greg Lewis concluded that union wages ranged between 10 and 15 percent higher than nonunion wages.[14] By the 1970s, the union wage differential had climbed to 20–30 percent in most industries. Further analysis reveals a greater impact on wages of blue-collar employees, younger employees, and less educated employees. Since the 1980s an increasingly competitive global economy has served to narrow the union–nonunion wage differential.[15]

Exhibit 7.7

Union vs. Nonunion Employee Median Weekly Earnings, 2002

Industry	Union	Nonunion	Annual Union $ Advantage
Manufacturing	$654	$619	$1,820
Construction	845	559	14,872
Transportation	782	605	8,204
Communications and public utilities	857	785	3,744
Wholesale trade	664	623	2,132
Retail trade	505	430	3,900
Services	650	592	3,016
Government	770	640	6,760
Finance, insurance, and real estate	598	681	−4,316

Nonunion data include the earnings of managers and other salaried (non-bargaining unit) employees.

• Data for both union and nonunion groups exclude employer paid benefits although union members typically enjoy an even greater advantage in fringe benefit comparisons (see data in Exhibit 7.6).

SOURCE: U.S. Department of Labor, "Union Members in 2002," *News Release*, February 25, 2003.

The data in Exhibit 7.7 present the union-nonunion wage differential by industry. A positive union wage advantage is present in every industry listed except finance, insurance, and real estate. Unlike in Europe, where narrower union-nonunion wage differences appear to foster more cooperative labor relations, there does not appear to be any significant lessening of employer opposition to unions in the United States despite the narrowing wage gap. Perhaps this merely indicates that the gap has not narrowed sufficiently in the view of many employers to warrant a change in their labor relations philosophy. Unions also have a spillover effect on wages and benefits in nonunion companies. Union wage and benefit changes "spill over" into nonunion companies because nonunion employers who want to retain their nonunion status will respond to union wage increases by raising the wages of their employees.[16] Such increases are provided not only to reduce the threat of unions but to provide equity and maintain morale and productivity.

SUMMARY

Economic issues include wages and the variety of economic benefits that make up what is commonly called the economic package. The negotiation of economic issues consumes a substantial amount of time, and outcomes on such issues affect both parties' satisfaction with the negotiation process. Wage differentials between jobs result from several industrial, occupational, and regional factors. Job evaluation is one method used to determine the worth of a job to an organization and helps to ensure internal wage equity among jobs in an organization and to attract and retain qualified employees. To attract and retain qualified employees, an employer must also maintain external equity between similar jobs in the organization and other organizations competing to hire such labor.

In addition to a base wage, some firms also provide either individual or group wage incentives as a means of tying employee job performance more closely to the attainment of organizational objectives. Negotiators use a variety of criteria to determine an acceptable wage structure. Commonly accepted criteria include differential features of jobs, comparable wages, ability to pay, productivity, and cost of living.

Because labor agreements usually are negotiated for periods greater than 1 year, provisions are commonly negotiated to adjust wages during the life of the contract. A common form of wage adjustment is the cost-of-living adjustment (COLA), which adjusts wages in accordance with changes in the consumer price index. Another less common form of wage adjustment during the term of a contract is the wage reopener clause, which permits wages to be renegotiated at a predetermined time.

Employee benefits account for 34.9 percent of a unionized employer's payroll dollar. Numerous types of benefits exist. The major ones include insurance, income maintenance, premium pay, payment for no work, pensions, and legally required payments. Employee demands for benefits such as improved health-care insurance, tax-advantaged pensions, prepaid legal and child-care services, family leave, and tuition aid are likely to increase over the next 5 years.

KEY TERMS

- degree of labor intensiveness
- job evaluation
- profit-sharing plan
- gain-sharing plan
- Scanlon plan
- Rucker plan
- ability to pay
- Consumer Price Index (CPI)
- cost-of-living adjustment clause (COLA)
- improshare plan
- skill-based pay
- wage spread
- skill pay differential
- two-tier pay plan
- wage comparability
- call-in pay
- defined benefit pension plan
- defined contribution pension plan
- employee stock ownership plan (ESOP)
- comparable worth
- deferred wage increase
- wage re-opener

- lump sum pay
- fee-for-service plan
- preferred provider organization (PPO)
- health maintenance organization (HMO)
- severance pay
- supplemental unemployment benefit plan
- work sharing
- premium pay
- shift differentials
- reporting pay
- cash balance pension plan
- Employee Retirement Income Security Act (ERISA) of 1974
- cliff vesting schedule
- graded vesting schedule
- Family Medical Leave Act (FMLA) of 1993
- prepaid legal service plan
- employee assistance plan
- education tuition aid
- transportation subsidy
- spillover effect

DISCUSSION QUESTIONS

1. List the main factors that may help to explain the wage differentials for three jobs in an organization with which you are familiar.

2. Explain why job-evaluation plans must take into consideration external and internal factors if they are to be successful.

3. Assume that labor and management are negotiating a labor agreement and the wage spread becomes an issue of disagreement—management wants a wider wage spread, and the union wants a smaller wage spread. Why should management be cautious about the union's proposal, even though the total costs may be the same?

4. For each of the wage criteria given in the chapter, state the union's expected arguments and management's expected counter-arguments, given the following conditions:

   a. High profits, a growing firm, a healthy economy, and the cost of living rising at 4 percent per year.

   b. Low profit, sales growth is stagnant, uncertain economic conditions, and the rise in cost of living is fluctuating by 3 to 4 percent each month.

5. Assuming that a firm's costs for employee benefits are 35 percent of payroll, why doesn't the firm just let the union determine the manner in which the amounts are apportioned to various benefits, such as insurance, holidays, and vacations, without negotiating each specific clause?

6. Which type of pension plan would you prefer to be covered under (i.e., defined benefit, defined contribution, or cash balance) and why if you were an employee? An employer?

7. To what extent do child-care benefits and family leave become issues that a union can exploit in an effort to organize more union members? Explain your reasoning.

8. What type of control should an employee have over shares issued under an employee stock ownership plan?

EXPLORING THE WEB

Economic Issues

1. Sources of Economic Data   It is important to know how to find out about economic indicators that affect wages and benefits. Using the Web site for the Bureau of Labor Statistics, answer the following questions.

What was the annual inflation rate at the end of 2002? (Remember that the inflation rate is the percent change in the Consumer Price Index over a specific period of time.)

During the first quarter of 2002, what were the median weekly earnings for males aged 25 and over?

U.S. Department of Labor, Bureau of Labor Statistics

http://www.bls.gov

Use the Economic Report of the President to answer these questions. Use the link for statistical tables in spreadsheet format.

What was the civilian unemployment rate in 2002 for all civilian workers? What was the exchange rate, in U.S. dollars, for the euro in the fourth quarter of 2002?

http://w3.access.gpo.gov/eop/

2. Comparable Worth   Read the definition of comparable worth on Encyclopedia Britannica's Women in American History page.

http://www.britannica.com/women/articles/comparable_worth.html

Deborah Walker, a research fellow at the Center for the Study of Market Processes at George Mason University, presents an argument against comparable worth policies in an article published on the Cato Institute Web site. The Cato Institute is a nonpartisan public policy research foundation.

http://www.cato.org/pubs/pas/pa038.html

What is the American Federation of State, County, and Municipal Employees doing in the area of pay equity for women?

http://www.afscme.org

3. Employee Stock Ownership Plans What economic conditions between 1981 and 1993 created the existence of ESOP companies in the steel industry? According to the Worker Ownership Institute, sponsored by the United Steelworkers of America and management of companies partially or wholly employee owned, how far back in history can the concept of employee ownership be traced?

http://www.workerownership.org/ESOP.html

REFERENCES

1. Mary William Walsh, "Boom Time a Bad Time for Poorest, Study Finds; Economy: New Worth Rose for Middle-Income Families, but Lowest Earners Were Worse Off, a Federal Survey Says," *Los Angeles Times*, January 19, 2000, p. 1; Albert B. Crenshaw, "Net Worth of U.S. Families Up Sharply; Stock Surge Spurred 17.6% Gain for 'Typical' Household from '95 to '98," *Washington Post*, January 19, 2000, p. E-1.

2. Bureau of Labor Statistics, "Productivity and Costs," *News Release*, February 8, 2000, p. 4 at http://stats.bls.gov/prhome.htm; Elia Kacapyr and Berna Miller, "Taking What's Given—Working for a Living," *American Demographics* 19 (April 1997), pp. 16–17.

3. Mortimer B. Zuckerman, "So Where Are All the Jobs?" *U.S. News & World Report* 135 (September 22, 2003), p. 86.

4. Justin Fox and Anna Bernasek, "Things Are Looking Up—Unless You Want a Job: This Economic Recovery Is Different and That Has a Lot of People Worried. Should They Be?" *Fortune* 148 (September 29, 2003), p. 73.

5. James C. Cooper and Kathleen Madigan, "A Jobs Recovery, Yes. A Hiring Boom, No. Intense Cost Pressures and Weal Pricing Will Keep Payrolls from Surging," *Business Week*, October 20, 2003, p. 33; Jared Bernstein, "The Young and the Jobless: Why Those New to the Workforce Stand to Lose the Most," *American Prospect* 14 (October, 2003), pp. A17–19.

6. Susan Jackson and Randall S. Schuler, *Managing Human Resources Through Strategic Partnerships*, 8th ed. (Mason, Ohio: South-Western, 2003), pp. 416–445; John W. Budd, "Union Wage Determination in Canadian and U.S. Manufacturing," *Industrial and Labor Relations Review* 49 (July 1996), pp. 673–690; Jules Bachman, *Wage Determination: An Analysis of Wage Criteria* (Princeton, N.J.: D. Van Nostrand, 1959), pp. 1–21.

7. Bachman, *Wage Determination: An Analysis of Wage Criteria*, p. 58.

8. For further reference, see Thomas Bergmann and Vida Scarpello, *Compensation Decision Making*, 4th ed. (Mason, Ohio: South-Western, 2001); George T. Milkovich and Jerry M. Newman, *Compensation*, 6th ed. (Boston: Irwin McGraw-Hill, 1999).

9. Roger J. Plachy and Sandra J. Plachy, *Building A Fair Pay Program*, 2nd ed. (New York: American Management Association, 1998), pp. 124–210; David W. Belcher, "Wage and Salary Administration," in *Motivation and Commitment*, eds. Dale Yoder and H. G. Heneman, Jr. (Washington, D.C.: Bureau of National Affairs, 1975), pp. 6–95.

10. Edward E. Lawler III, *Rewarding Excellence: Pay Strategies for the New Economy* (San Francisco: Jossey-Bass, 2000), pp. 116–119.

11. For a review of alternative methods, see Robert L. Heneman, "Job and Work Evaluation: A Literature Review," in *Strategic Reward Management: Design, Implementation, and Evaluation* (Greenwich, Conn.: Information Age, 2002), pp. 275–301.

12. Harold D. Janes, "Issues in Job Evaluation: The Union View," *Personnel Journal* 51 (September 1972), p. 675. See also Research Department, International Association of Machinists, *What's Wrong with Job Evaluation?* (Washington, D.C.: International Association of Machinists, 1954).

13. Harold D. Janes, "Comparative Issues in Job Evaluation: The Union View, 1971–1978," *Personnel Journal* 58 (February 1979), pp. 80–85.

14. David Belcher and Thomas J. Atchison, *Compensation Administration*, 2d ed. (Englewood Cliffs, N.J.: Prentice-Hall, 1987), pp. 154–155.

15. Belcher and Atchison, *Compensation Administration*, pp. 107–124.

16. U.S. Bureau of Labor Statistics, *National Compensation Survey: Occupational Wages in the United States, July 2002*, Bulletin 2561, September 2003, at http://www.bls.gov/ncs/ocs/ncbl0552.pdf; U.S. Bureau of Labor Statistics, *Occupational Employment and Wages, 2001*, News Release, November 6, 2002, at http://www.bls.gov.news.release/ocwage.nr0.htm.

17. Royal J. Dossett, "Work-Measured Labor Standards—The State of the Art," *Industrial Engineering* 24 (April 1995), pp. 21–25.

18. "Return of the Stopwatch," *The Economist* 326 (January 1, 1993), p. 69; Herbert G. Zollitsch, "Productivity, Time Studies and Incentive-Pay Plans," in *Motivation and Commitment*, eds. Dale Yoder and H. G. Heneman, Jr. (Washington, D.C.: Bureau of National Affairs, 1975), pp. 6–61.

19. Gerald E. Ledford, Jr., and Edward E. Lawler III, "Reward Innovations in Fortune 1000 Companies," *Compensation and Benefits Review* 27 (July/August 1995), pp. 76–80.

20. Bureau of National Affairs, "2003 Employer Bargaining Objectives," *Collective Bargaining Bulletin* 8 (January 23, 2003), p. S-12.

21. Woodruff Imberman, "Gainsharing: A Lemon or Lemonade?" *Business Horizons* 39 (January–February 1996), pp. 36–40; Adrienne E. Eaton and Paula B. Voos, "Unions and Contemporary Innovation in Work Organization, Compensation, and Employee Participation," in *Unions and Economic Competitiveness* (Armonk, N.Y.: M. E. Sharpe, 1992), pp. 176–177.

22. Robert J. Paul, Brian P. Niehoff, and William H. Turnley, "Empowerment, Expectations, and the Psychological Contract—Managing the Dilemmas and Gaining the Advantages," *Journal of Social-Economics* 29 (2000), pp. 471–485; Peter V. LeBlanc and Paul W. Mulvey, "How American Workers See the Rewards of Work," *Compensation and Benefits Review* 30 (January/February 1998), pp. 24–28.

23. "Sharing the Spoils," *The Economist* 341 (November 30, 1996), p. 80; Edward M. Coates III, "Profit Sharing Today: Plans and Provisions," *Monthly Labor Review* 114 (April 1991), pp. 19–25.

24. "2002 Employee Benefits Study," *Pension Benefits* 12 (May 2003), p. 4.

25. John Zalusky, "Labor's Collective Bargaining Experience with Gainsharing and Profit Sharing," *Proceedings of the 39th Annual Meeting of the Industrial Relations Research Association* (Madison, Wis.: Industrial Relations Research Association, 1987), pp. 177–178.

26. Jamie Butters, "Chrysler Group to Pay Profit-Sharing Bonuses to Auto Workers This Year," *Detroit Free Press*, February 21, 2003, at EBSCOhost database: *Newspaper Source*, item #2W63041676780.

27. "Chrysler Gives Workers $8,100 Bonus," *Associated Press*, February 28, 2000, at http://www.washingtonpost.com/wp-srv/aponline/20000228/aponline121713_001.htm.

28. "Potential Dangers in Expansion of Current Auto Profit Sharing Plans Cited by Attorney," *Daily Labor Report*, March 24, 1982, p. C-1.

29. Timothy L. Ross and Ruth Ann Ross, "Gainsharing and Unions: Current Trends," in *Gainsharing and Employee Involvement*, eds. by Brian Graham-Moore and Timothy L. Ross (Washington, D.C.: Bureau of National Affairs, 1995), pp. 179–191.

30. Timothy L. Ross and Ruth Ann Ross, "Gain Sharing: Improved Performance," in *The Compensation Handbook*, eds. Lance A. Berger and Dorothy R. Berger (New York: McGraw-Hill, 2000), pp. 227–240; Theresa M. Welbourne and Luis R. Gomez Mejia, "Gainsharing: A Critical Review and a Future Research Agenda," *Journal of Management* 21, no. 3 (1995), pp. 562–564; J. Kenneth White, "The Scanlon Plan: Causes and Correlates of Success," *Academy of Management Journal* 22 (June 1979), pp. 292–312.

31. Welbourne and Gomez Mejia, "Gainsharing: A Critical Review," p. 563.

32. Mitchell Fein, "Improshare: Sharing Productivity Gains with Employees," in *The Compensation Handbook*, eds. by Lance A. Berger and Dorothy R. Berger (New York: McGraw-Hill, 2000), pp. 217–226.

33. Mitchell Fein, "Improved Productivity through Workers' Involvement," *Hearings before the Subcommittee on General Oversight of the Committee on Small Business* (Washington, D.C.: U.S. Government Printing Office, 1982), pp. 118–123.

34. Roger T. Kaufman, "The Effects of IMPROSHARE on Productivity," *Industrial and Labor Relations Review* 45 (January 1992), pp. 311–315.

35. Roger T. Kaufman and Raymond Russell, "Government Support for Profit Sharing, Gainsharing, ESOP's, and TQM," *Contemporary Economic Policy* 13 (April 1995), pp. 38–39.

36. Glenn Dalton, Jennifer Stevens, and Robert Heneman, "Alternative Rewards in Union Settings," in *Strategic Reward Management: Design, Implementation, and Evaluation* (Greenwich, Conn: Information Age, 2002), pp. 153–161; Glenn Dalton, "The Glass Wall: Shattering the Myth That Alternative Rewards Won't Work with Unions," *Compensation and Benefits Review* 30 (November/December 1998), pp. 38–45; Douglas P. O'Bannon and Craig L. Pearce, "An Exploratory Examination of Gainsharing in Service Organizations: Implications for Organizational Citizenship Behavior and Pay Satisfaction," *Journal of Managerial Issues* 11 (Fall 1999), pp. 363–378.

37. James H. Dulebohn and Joseph J. Martocchio, "Employee Perceptions of the Fairness of Work Group Incentive Pay Plans," *Journal of Management* 24 (July–August 1998), pp. 469–488.

38. William N. Cooke, "Employee Participation Programs, Group-Based Incentives, and Company Performance: A Union-Nonunion Comparison," *Industrial and Labor Relations Review* 47 (July 1994), pp. 594–608.

39. Gerald E. Ledford, Jr., and Robert L. Heneman, "Pay for Skills, Knowledge, and Competencies," in *Strategic Reward Management: Design, Implementation, and Evaluation* (Greenwich, Conn: Information Age, 2002), pp. 409–423.

40. Ledford and Lawler, "Reward Innovations in Fortune 1000 Companies," pp. 76–80.

41. Brian Muray and Barry Gerhart, "An Empirical Analysis of a Skill-Based Pay Program and Plant Performance Outcomes," *Academy of Management Journal* 41 (February 1998), pp. 68–78.

42. Kenneth Mericle and Dong-One Kim, "From Job-Based Pay to Skill-Based Pay in Unionized Establishments: A Three-Plant Comparative Analysis," *Relations Industrielles* 54 (Summer 1999), pp. 549–578.

43. Irving Bernstein, *Arbitration of Wages* (Berkeley: University of California, 1954), pp. 26–27; Craig Overton, "Criteria in Grievance and Interest Arbitration in the Public Sector," *Arbitration Journal* 28 (1973), pp. 159–166; Howard S. Block, "Criteria in Public Sector Interest Disputes," in *Arbitration and the Public Interest*, eds. G. G. Somers and B. D. Dennis (Washington, D.C.: Bureau of National Affairs, 1971), pp. 161–193.

44. Richard B. Freeman, "Union Wage Practices and Wage Dispersions within Establishments," *Industrial and Labor Relations Review* 36 (October 1982), pp. 3–21.

45. Bureau of National Affairs, "2003 Employer Bargaining Objectives," p. S-11.

46. Julie M. McKinnon, "Auto Union to Consider Two-Tiered Wage Structure," *The Blade*, September 25, 2003, pp. 1–2; Joann Muller, "You Sure I Agreed to That?" *Forbes* 172 (October 27, 2003), p. 66.

47. Carey W. English, "Two-Tier Pay Stirs Backlash among Workers," *U.S. News & World Report*, September 23, 1985, p. 61; "IRRA Panelists Address the Two-Tier Implications for Fair Representation and Equal Opportunity," *Daily Labor Report*, January 10, 1985, pp. A-5–A-7.

48. Daniel J. B. Mitchell, "Two-Tier Compensation Structures: Their Impact on Unions, Employers, and Employees," *Industrial and Labor Relations Review* 45 (July 1992), pp. 814–815; James E. Martin and Melanie M. Peterson, "Two-Tier Wage Structures and Attitude Differences" in *Proceedings of the Thirty-eighth Annual Meeting: Industrial Relations Research Association*, ed. B. D. Dennis (Madison, Wis.: Industrial Relations Research Association, 1986), pp. 78–79.

49. Frederick W. Cook, "Compensation Surveys Are Biased," *Compensation and Benefits Review* 26 (September–October 1994), pp. 19–22.

50. Sumner Slichter, *Basic Criteria Used in Wage Negotiation* (Chicago: Chicago Association of Commerce and Industry, January 30, 1947), p. 25.

51. Bachman, *Wage Determination: An Analysis of Wage Criteria*, pp. 251–258.

52. U.S. Bureau of Labor Statistics, "Productivity and Costs, Third Quarter 2003," *News Release*, November 6, 2003, p. 10.

53. See, for example, "The 'New Economy'—American Productivity," *The Economist* 368 (September 13, 2003), p. 62; Aaron E. Cobet and Gregory A. Wilson, "Comparing 50 Years of Labor Productivity in the U.S. and Foreign Manufacturing," *Monthly Labor Review* 125 (June 2002), pp. 51–65.

54. Aaron Bernstein, "Productivity—Not Pay Cuts—Will Keep Union Members Working," *Business Week*, August 25, 1986, p. 32.

55. Madeline Zavodny, "Unions and the Wage-Productivity Gap," *Economic Review—Federal Reserve Bank of Atlanta* 84 (Second Quarter 1999), pp. 44–53; Thomas J. Volgy, John E. Schwarz, and Lawrence E. Imwalle, "In Search of Economic Well-Being: Worker Power and the Effects of Productivity, Inflation, Unemployment and Global Trade on Wages in Ten Wealthy Countries," *American Journal of Political Science* 40 (November 1996), pp. 1233–1252.

56. Jeffrey B. Arthur and Linda Aiman-Smith, "Gainsharing and Organizational Learning: An Analysis of Employee Suggestions Over Time," *Academy of Management Journal* 44 (August 2001), p. 737.

57. Omar Azfar and Stephan Danninger, "Profit-sharing, Employment Stability, and Wage Growth," *Industrial & Labor Relations Review* 54 (April 2001), pp. 619–630; General Accounting Office, *Productivity Sharing Programs: Can They*

Contribute to Productivity Improvement? (Washington, D.C.: U.S. Government Printing Office, 1981).

58. Jerome Rosow, "Productivity and the Blue-Collar Blues," *Personnel* 48 (March–April 1971), pp. 8–10.

59. William N. Cooke, "Employee Participation Programs, Group-Based Incentives, and Company Performance: A Union-Nonunion Comparison," *Industrial and Labor Relations Review* 47 (July 1994), pp. 594–609.

60. William F. Maloney, "Productivity Bargaining in Contract Construction," *Proceedings of the 1977 Annual Spring Meeting: Industrial Relations Research Association* (Madison, Wis.: Industrial Relations Research Association, 1977), pp. 533–534.

61. Robert J. Flanagan, "The Economics of Unions and Collective Bargaining," *Industrial Relations* 29 (Spring 1990), pp. 300–304; William W. Winpisinger, "Output: Collective Bargaining and Productivity," in *Collective Bargaining: New Dimensions in Labor Relations*, ed. F. J. Havelich (Boulder, Colo.: Westview Press, 1979), pp. 25–28.

62. Maryellen R. Kelley and Bennett Harrison, "Unions, Technology and Labor-Management Cooperation," in *Unions and Economic Competitiveness*, eds. Lawrence Mishel and Paula B. Voos (Armonk, N.Y.: M. E. Sharp, 1992), pp. 247–250; Jacob Mincer, "Union Effects: Wages, Turnover, and Job Training," *Working Paper Series* (Cambridge, Mass.: National Bureau of Economic Research Inc., 1985), p. 42.

63. Michael H. Small and Mahmoud Yasin, "Human Factors in the Adoption and Performance of Advanced Manufacturing Technology in Unionized Firms," *Industrial Management + Data Systems* 100, no. 8 (2000), p. 389.

64. Susan McDowell and William Lesser, "The Effect of Unions on Productivity: An Analysis of the Cattle Kill Floor," *Agribusiness* 3 (Fall 1987), pp. 273–280; Ronald S. Warren, Jr., "The Effect of Unionization on Labor Productivity: Some Time-Series Evidence," *Journal of Labor Research* 6 (Spring 1985), p. 199; Charles Brown and James Medoff, "Trade Unions in the Production Process," *Journal of Po-*

litical Economy 86 (June 1980), pp. 355–359.

65. Brian Chezum and John E. Garen, "Are Union Productivity Effects Overestimated? Evidence from Coal Mining," *Applied Economics* 30 (July 1998), pp. 913–918; Merwin W. Mitchell and Joe A. Stone, "Union Effects on Productivity: Evidence from Western Saw Mills," *Industrial and Labor Relations Review* 46 (October 1992), pp. 135–145; J. T. Addison and A. H. Barnett, "The Impact of Unions on Productivity," *British Journal of Industrial Relations* 20 (July 1982), pp. 145–149; John T. Addison, "Are Unions Good for Productivity?" *Journal of Labor Research* 3 (Spring 1982), p. 137; Robert S. Kaufman and Roger T. Kaufman, "Union Effects on Productivity, Personnel Practices, and Survival in the Automotive Parts Industry," *Journal of Labor Research* 8 (Fall 1987), pp. 332–349.

66. "Union Productivity Effects" *Monthly Labor Review* 108 (January 1985), p. 60; Richard B. Freeman and James L. Medoff, What Do Unions Do? (New York: Basic Books, 1984), pp. 162–190.

67. David A. Dilts, "The Consumer Price Index as a Standard in Negotiations and Arbitration," *Journal of Collective Negotiations in the Public Sector* 23, no. 4 (1994), pp. 279–285.

68. Todd Wilson, "Consumer Prices Up Slightly More in 2002, Led by Energy and Hospital Services," *Monthly Labor Review* 126 (March 2003), pp. 3–8; John J. Greenlees and Charles C. Mason, "Overview of the 1998 Revision of the Consumer Price Index," *Monthly Labor Review* 119 (December 1996), pp. 3–9; Brent R. Moulton, "Basic Components of the CPI: Estimation of Price Changes," *Monthly Labor Review* 116 (December 1993), pp. 13–24; Alan B. Krueger and Aaron Siskind, "Using Survey Data to Assess Bias in the Consumer Price Index," *Monthly Labor Review* 121 (April 1998), pp. 24–33.

69. Bureau of National Affairs, "2003 Employer Bargaining Objectives," p. S-11.

70. AFL-CIO, "It's Time for Working Women to Earn Equal Pay," 2003, p. 1, at http://www.aflcio.org/yourjob economy/women/equalpay/index.cfm ?RenderForPrint = 1

71. Paula England, "The Case for Comparable Worth," *Quarterly Review of Economics and Finance* 39 (1999), pp. 743–755; Laura Pincus and Bill Shaw, "Comparable Worth: An Economic and Ethical Analysis," *Journal of Business Ethics* 17 (April 1998), pp. 455–470; "Comparable Worth in Industrialized Countries," *Monthly Labor Review* 115 (November 1992), pp. 40–42.

72. E. Jane Arnault, Louis Gordon, Douglas H. Joines, and G. Michael Phillips, "An Experimental Study of Job Evaluation and Comparable Worth," *Industrial and Labor Relations Review* 54 (July 2001), pp. 806–815.

73. Bureau of National Affairs, "First-Half 2003 Bargaining Produces Average Wage Increase of 3.4 Percent," *Daily Labor Report* 133 (July 11, 2003), pp. D4–D5.

74. Bureau of National Affairs, "2003 Employer Bargaining Objectives," p. S-6.

75. Bureau of National Affairs, "2003 Employer Bargaining Objectives," p. S-11; Editors of Collective Bargaining Negotiations and Contracts, *Basic Patterns in Union Contracts*, 14th ed. (Washington, D.C.: Bureau of National Affairs, 1995), pp. 111–113.

76. Bureau of National Affairs, "First-Half 2003 Bargaining Produces Average Wage Increase of 3.4 Percent," p. D-4; Bureau of National Affairs, "Frequency of Lump-Sum Payment Provisions Rose in 2002," *Collective Bargaining Bulletin* 4 (February 20, 2003), pp. 21–22.

77. U.S. Department of Labor, "Employer Cost for Employee Compensation—March 2003," *News Release*, June 11, 2003, p. 11.

78. Bureau of National Affairs, "2003 Employer Bargaining Objectives," pp. S-14–S-25.

79. Joshua Partlow, "Health Care a Growing Issue in Labor Talks," *Washington Post*, June 18, 2003, p. E2; "Rising Health Care Costs Posing Challenges for Unions at the Bargaining Table," *The Labor Relations Research Association Online*, December 19, 2002, pp. 1–3.

80. Bill Brubaker, "Health Insurance Premiums Up 13.9%," *Washington Post*, September 10, 2003, p. E2; Bill Brubaker, "Health Costs Up 11%, Survey Finds Yearly Rise Biggest Since '92, Some Area Insurers See Hikes Ahead," *Washington Post*, September 7, 2001, p. E1.

81. Gary Claxton et al., *Employer Health Benefits: 2003 Annual Survey* (Menlo Park, Calif.: The Kaiser Family Foundation, 2003), pp. 1–2.

82. Bureau of National Affairs, "2003 Employer Bargaining Objectives," p. S-17.

83. Cristina Pita, "Advance Notice and Severance Pay Provisions in Contracts," *Monthly Labor Review* 119 (July 1996), pp. 43–50.

84. U.S. Bureau of Labor Statistics, "Employee Benefits in Private Industry, 2003" *News Release*, September 17, 2003, p. 5.

85. Editors of Collective Bargaining Negotiations and Contracts, *Basic Patterns in Union Contracts*, 14th ed. (Washington, D.C.: Bureau of National Affairs, 1995), pp. 57–63.

86. Diane Stafford, "The Kansas City Star, Mo., Workplace Column," *Knight Ridder Tribune Business News*, August 21, 2003, p. 1; "U.S. Short on Vacation Time," *San Francisco Chronicle*, July 16, 1999, p. B4.

87. U.S. Bureau of Labor Statistics, "Employee Benefits in Private Industry, 2003," p. 5.

88. Michael Woods, "Life-Expectancy Formulas Overestimate Longevity, Researchers Find," *Knight Ridder Tribune Business News*, September 16, 2003, p. 1.

89. U.S. Bureau of Labor Statistics, "Employee Benefits in Private Industry, 2003," p. 3.

90. Richard B. Freeman, "Unions, Pensions, and Union Pension Funds," *Working Paper Series* (Cambridge, Mass.: National Bureau of Economic Research., 1983), p. 50.

91. *Ohio Public Employees Retirement System v. Betts*, 492 U.S. 158 (1989).

92. "Unions and Workers Often at Odds over Negotiation of 401(k)s," *Collective Bargaining Bulletin* 4 (December 30, 1999), p. 156.

93. Arleen Jacobius, "More Plan Sponsors Do Away with 401(k) Match," *Pensions & Investments* 31 (August 18, 2003), p. 4.

94. Patrick P. McHugh, Joel Cutcher-Gershenfeld, and Michael Polzin, "Employee Stock Ownership Plans: Whose Interests Do They Serve?" *Proceedings of the 49th Annual Meeting of the Industrial Relations Research Association* (Madison, Wis.: Industrial Relations Research Association, 1997), pp. 23–32; Roger G. McElrath and Richard L. Rowan, "The American Labor Movement and Employee Ownership: Objections to and Uses of Employee Stock Ownership Plans," *Journal of Labor Research* 13 (Winter 1992), pp. 99–103.

95. Joseph R. Blasi, *Employee Ownership through ESOPs: Implication for the Public Corporation* (New York: Pergamon Press, 1987), pp. 29–30.

96. Joseph Blasi, Michael Conte, and Douglas Kruse, "Employee Stock Ownership and Corporate Performance among Public Companies," *Industrial and Labor Relations Review* 50 (October 1996), pp. 60–79; Blasi, *Employee Ownership through ESOPs*, 1987, pp. 40–44.

97. "Nearly Two-thirds of Pension Plans Underfunded," *Employee Benefit Plan Review* 57 (May 2003), p. 22; Albert B. Crenshaw, "Business Pushing Pension Change," *Washington Post*, September 2, 2003, p. E1.

98. U.S. Department of Labor, "Types of Retirement Plans," Retirement Plans, Benefits & Savings, December 14, 2003, pp. 1–4, at http://www.dol.gov/topic/retirement/typesofplans.htm; U.S. Department of Labor, "Frequently Asked Questions about Cash Balance Pension Plans," December 14, 2003, pp. 1–2, at http://www.dol.gov.ebsa/FAQs/faq_compliance_cashbalanceplans.html; U.S. Department of Labor, "Fact Sheet: Cash Balance Pension Plans," May 2003, pp. 1–9.

99. Curt Anderson, "Congress, Feds Examine Pension Plan," *Associated Press*, September 22, 1999, pp. 1–3, at http://www.washingtonpost.com/wp-srv/aponline/19990922/aponline023454_000.htm.

100. Kathleen Day, "IBM Workers Continue to Fight Pension Changes," *Washington Post*, April 18, 2001, p. E1; Albert B. Crenshaw, "Cash Balance Pension Plans Fall under Scrutiny," *Washington Post*, September 21, 1999, p. E1; Mike Hudson, "Pension Plans Spark Outrage," *Detroit Free Press*, September 22, 1999, pp. 1–3 at http://www.freep.com/business/qretire22.htm.

101. Albert B. Crenshaw, "Judge Finds Age Bias in IBM Pensions," *Washington Post*, August 1, 2003, p. E3.

102. U.S. Department of Labor, *What You Should Know About Your Pension Rights*, January 2002, pp. 27–30.

103. U.S. Department of Labor, *Compliance Assistance: The Family Medical and Leave Act*, December 15, 2003, pp. 1–11, at http://www.dol.gov/esa/regs/compliance/whd/1421.htm; Jane Waldfogel, "Family Leave Coverage in the 1990s," *Monthly Labor Review* 122 (October 1999), pp. 13–21; Tim Barnett, Winston N. McVea, Jr., and Patricia A. Lanier, "An Overview of the Family and Medical Leave Act of 1993," *Labor Law Journal* 44 (July 1993), pp. 429–433.

104. Michael Prince, "FMLA Hasn't Been a Big Burden for Employers," *Business Insurance* 37 (September 29, 2003), pp. 1–4.

105. David Cantor, Jane Waldfogel, et al., *Balancing the Needs of Families and Employers: The Family Medical Leave Surveys*, 2000 Update (Rockville, Md.: Westat, 2000).

106. National Partnership for Women & Families, "America Celebrates Ten Year Anniversary of the Family & Medical Leave Act," *Press Release*, August 5, 2003, pp. 1–2.

107. "California Authorizes Partially Paid Family and Medical Leave," *HR Focus* 79 (November 2002), p. 8; Mary Ann Milbourn, "California Workers Can Receive Paid Family Leave Starting Next July," *Knight Ridder Tribune Business News*, September 24, 2002, p. 1.

108. Margaret M. Clark, "FMLA Anniversary Events Focus on Workplace Flexibility Options," *HRMagazine* 48 (March 2003), p. 30; David L. Hudson, Jr., "Changing Act," *ABA Journal* 89 (September 2003), p. 15; Sheng Hengst and Brian H. Kleiner, "Implications of the Family and Medical Leave

Act for Organizations," *Managerial Law* 44 (1/2) 2002, pp. 9–15.

109. David Cantor, Jane Waldfogel, et al., *Balancing the Needs of Families and Employers: The Family and Medical Leave Surveys, 2000 Update*, 2000, Chapter 5.

110. AFL-CIO Working Women's Department, *Bargaining Fact Sheet: Family Leave and Expanding the Family and Medical Leave Act* (Washington, D.C.: AFL-CIO, 2001), pp. 1–4; Frederick L. Douglas, "Collective Bargaining under the Family and Medical Leave Act," *Labor Law Journal* 45 (February 1994), pp. 102–105.

111. Ryan Mahoney, "Prepaid Legal Insurance Plans: Justice For All?" *Birmingham Business Journal* 20 (January 17, 2003), pp. 1–3; Charlotte Garvey, "Access to the Law," *HRMagazine* 47 (September 2002), pp. 82–92.

112. Fonda Phillips, "Employee Assistance Programs: A New Way to Control Health Care Costs," *Employee Benefit Plan Review* 58 (August 2003), pp. 22–24.

113. Cynthia J. Guffey, Judy F. West, and Charles S. White, "Employer Educational Assistance: An Assessment of the Impact on Organizational Commitment," *Management Research News* 20, no. 1, 1997, pp. 12–30.

114. Greg Lewis, *Unionism and Relative Wages in the United States* (Chicago: University of Chicago Press, 1963).

115. David Neumark and Michael L. Wachter, "Union Effects on Nonunion Wages: Evidence from Panel Data on Industries and Cities," *Industrial & Labor Relations Review* 49 (October 1995), pp. 20–38; Richard B. Freeman and James L. Medoff, "The Impact of Collective Bargaining: Illusion or Reality," in *U.S. Industrial Relations 1950–1980: A Critical Assessment*, eds. Jack Stieber et al. (Madison, Wis.: Industrial Relations Research Association, 1981), pp. 53–54.

116. Susan Vroman, "The Direction of Wage Spillovers in Manufacturing," *Industrial and Labor Relations Review* 36 (October 1982), pp. 102–103.

A Change in the Medical Insurance Plan

The employer designs, installs, and maintains private telephone systems for customers. Employees in the bargaining unit have been represented for many years by the Union. The parties' current collective bargaining agreement provided for the following medical insurance benefits: "basic medical benefits covering reasonable and customary charges; and major medical benefits with an unlimited maximum benefit; a dental benefit plan; and long term disability benefits. These benefits are described by the specific insurance contracts to be filed with the Union's district office."

The company had been experiencing declining profits for several months attributed to a general economic recession and the loss of a major client. In June the management team reviewed the current situation and forecast for the firm's near-term future and decided to adopt a strategy of cutting operating costs. As a part of this strategy, the three top managers of the firm, who were also its owners, agreed to eliminate their salaries, and two members of the administrative staff were laid off.

The company's principal source of capital funding was a loan arrangement with a local bank, which permitted the company to borrow up to 80 percent of the value of current accounts receivable. Whenever a customer paid a bill for which the receivables had been pledged to the bank as collateral for the loan, the payment had to be applied to reduce the amount of the outstanding loan. When new business was obtained providing additional accounts receivables, the company could pledge these receivables to the bank and obtain additional loan capital to continue operations. The company's current loan was due to expire on September 1, and because of the company's current financial problems, the bank informed the company managers that the current loan must be fully paid by the end of September and no new loan would be issued by the bank.

At about this same time the company was notified by its current insurance carrier that medical insurance premium cost for employee coverage would be increasing by 40 percent to $28,000 per month. The insurance carrier also requested an advance payment equivalent to two months' premium expense to continue the coverage because the company had been late in making premium payments in the past. The company president did not believe the company could afford to make the higher insurance premium payments and therefore found another insurance company who would provide medical insurance coverage for employees at a cost of $22,000 per month. A meeting was requested by management officials with union representatives to inform the union about the new medical insurance plan.

The meeting occurred on October 8, at which time management explained the new medical insurance plan to union officials. The only significant difference between the old and new plans concerned the prescription drug benefit. Under the old plan, employees were issued a prescription card that allowed the employee to fill any prescription for a cost of $4. The new plan would require the employee to first pay a deductible amount before the insurance plan would cover any prescription drug expenses. Covered prescription drug expenses under the new plan would be reimbursed to the employee at the rate of 80 percent of the employee's actual cost. The company believed the new plan would save the firm $26,000 annually in premium cost compared to the old medical insurance plan. Management further asserted that the new insurance plan complied with the parties' contractual language to provide medical insurance coverage. At this same meeting, the company president also informed union leaders that management would like to reduce current employee wage rates by 20 percent to enable the firm to submit more cost-effective bids to obtain new customer orders.

Union representatives asked several questions about the medical insurance plan described by management officials, not all of which managers could answer. Company officials provided the union with the name and address of the new insurance carrier and suggested the union contact the carrier directly for detailed information about the plan. Union officials subsequently held a meeting with bargaining unit members at which the company's proposals to cut wages 20 percent and change insurance carriers was discussed. Employees voted unanimously to reject both proposed changes. Employees were particularly concerned about the lack of a drug prescription card under the new medical insurance plan. Union officials reported the results of the employees' vote to management.

Upon learning of the employees' negative vote, the company president told union leaders that they must not have explained the new medical plan to employees in the right way. Management requested that the union hold another meeting with employees at which management representatives could explain the new medical insurance plan. Union officials agreed to the meeting provided union officials were also present.

On the date of the scheduled employee meeting, the local union president was tied up on union business and did not arrive at the meeting until 25 minutes after it had begun. The local union president stated that when he arrived, management officials were already in the process of explaining the new medical insurance plan to the assembled employees and had passed out enrollment cards for employees to fill out for the new plan. The local union president advised employees not to sign the enrollment cards because the union had not agreed to the new medical insurance plan. The company president replied that the change needed to be made quickly and he had already decided to change carriers and adopt the new insurance plan.

QUESTIONS

1. In your opinion, was management's request to change the insurance carrier (plan) reasonable? Explain your reasoning.

2. In your opinion, did union officials exhibit a cooperative and reasonable response to management's proposed change? Explain your reasoning.

3. Does the employer have a legal right to implement the change to a new insurance carrier (medical insurance plan) in this case? Why or why not?

Discontinuance of a Pay Practice

For a three-year period the employer granted no wage increases to employees due to the company's adverse financial situation. In July 1999, the employer implemented a new policy to provide an annual wage improvement for employees. Each employee's annual wage improvement was comprised two components: (a) a fixed percentage of the employee's base hourly wage rate that all employees received and (b) an additional merit based percentage increase, which varied depending upon management's evaluation of each employee's job performance. The employer considered factors such as the cost of living, the company's current and projected financial situation, and the amount granted by other employers in the industry to determine the amount of the across-the-board percentage increase.

On July 1, 1999 and 2000, employees received a 3 percent across-the-board increase and merit increases ranging from 0 to 2 percent. On July 1, 2001, the employer granted a 4 percent across-the-board increase and merit increases ranging from 0 to 2 percent.

In November 2001, employees voted to certify the union as their bargaining representative. The union and company representatives began negotiations on an initial contract in January 2002. During 2002, the parties held 16 bargaining meetings, eventually reaching a final contract settlement in June 2003. The owner of the firm testified that some discussion had occurred among management concerning whether to grant a wage increase on July 1, 2002. According to the owner, the company's attorney had advised against granting any wage increase, as it might be interpreted as an unfair labor practice by the union. When union officials became aware that management was conducting employee performance evaluations in 2002, the union negotiator asked management if it intended to grant employees a wage increase on July 1, 2002, consistent with the firm's established past practice. The management negotiator responded that the parties were currently in negotiations over wages and the negotiations would take care of the wage issue. When employees asked the plant manager whether or not wage improvements would be granted on July 1, 2002, they were told by the plant manager that wages were frozen because of the negotiations with the union.

After the company failed to grant any wage improvement in July 2002, the union filed an unfair labor practice charge alleging that the company's failure to grant the wage increase constituted a violation of the employer's duty to bargain in good faith. The union's position was that the employer had an established policy of granting a pay increase on July 1 of each year. According to the union, the failure to grant a wage increase on July 1, 2002, represented a unilateral change in an established term or condition of employment in violation of the employer's duty to bargain in good faith. The union had never agreed to suspend payment of the annual wage improvement plan, nor had the parties already bargained in good faith to an impasse over the bargaining subject.

The employer maintained that the Labor Management Relations Act prohibits an employer from making a unilateral change in a mandatory bargaining subject such as wages for union-represented employees. The company was concerned that, if management went ahead and granted a wage increase without having obtained the union's approval as to the amount and timing of such an increase, it would constitute a unilateral change in employees' wage rates. The company relied upon the advice of its legal counsel in making the decision not to grant any wage increase while negotiations were still under way with the union toward an initial labor contract.

QUESTIONS

1. Does the company's failure to make a wage adjustment consistent with past practice on July 1, 2002, constitute a violation of the employer's duty to bargain in good faith? Explain your reasoning.

2. If an employer were found guilty of bad-faith bargaining in a case like this, should employees be entitled to a back-pay remedy? If so, how could the NLRB determine the appropriate amount to be awarded?

Employee Benefits

Directions

1. From an *employee's* perspective, rank-order the importance of the following employee benefits as a part of a compensation plan where 1 = the most important benefit and 16 = the least important benefit.

___ Employee assistance plan
___ Defined benefit pension plan
___ Defined contribution pension plan
___ Cash balance pension plan
___ Major medical insurance plan
___ Life and accidental death benefit
___ Short- and long-term disability benefit
___ Prepaid legal service plan

___ Child care assistance plan
___ Education tuition aid
___ Transportation reimbursement
___ Supplemental unemployment benefit
___ Paid holidays
___ Paid vacation
___ Paid sick leave
___ Dental insurance plan

2. List the factors which were most important to you in determining your ranking priorities among the benefits listed above (e.g., age, sex, current job, prior work experience, marital status, number of dependents, and knowledge of employment conditions at other firms).

3. If asked to perform the same ranking task from an *employer's* perspective, would your rankings change and if so, how or why?

CHAPTER 8

Administrative Issues

Several important administrative issues can cost as much as or more than negotiated wage increases. This chapter focuses on six broad areas that impact both contract negotiation and administration issues: (1) technological change and its impact on labor relations, (2) job security and seniority, (3) employee training, (4) work restructuring, (5) safety and health, and (6) accommodating employees with disabilities.

Management seeks flexibility in arranging work content and schedules to maximize efficiency. Unions seek to protect employees' jobs and job rights when workplace changes occur. The attempts of management and labor to achieve their respective interests are discussed throughout this chapter.

Technological Change and Job Protection

Technological change refers to changes in the production process that result from the introduction of labor-saving machinery and changes in material handling and work flow. **Automation**, a type of technological change, goes one step further in that machines perform tasks formerly performed by humans, and the human operator is replaced by automatic controls.[1] Technological change may affect a job by altering the tasks or equipment used and thus the job skills required, the pace or scheduling of the work, or a job's characteristics (e.g., degree of exposure to health and safety hazards, frequency of interaction with co-workers, closeness of supervision, job stress level).

Use of new technology is a means by which firms and nations seek to gain a competitive advantage in the arena of international competition. Often the competitive advantage gained from the introduction of new technology is short lived. Such technology often becomes available to competitors fairly rapidly, lessening the competitive advantage of being the first to possess the technology. Longer-term competitive advantage derives from the ability of workers to apply technology in a highly efficient manner. This requires workers who are well trained and motivated.

Technological change generally occurs in three phases: (1) the development phase, in which key choices about the design and configuration of the new technology are made; (2) the resource allocation phase, in which claims for resources by different organizational units are presented and evaluated against performance criteria; and (3) the implementation phase, in which the new technology is constructed, put into service, and modified if necessary. The third phase, implementation, is typically when the union enters the picture because implementation of new technologies affects the work structure and consequently the employees performing the job tasks. The consequences of the implementation of new technologies naturally are the concern of the employees, as well as the union that represents their job-related interest.[2] Unions seek to protect the job interests of their members affected by technological change through (1) negotiating contract language (see later discussion of work scheduling, electronic monitoring, outsourcing, seniority rights); (2) lobbying for or against government legislation and assistance programs (see later discussion of Worker Adjustment Retraining and Notification Act); and (3) providing direct services to members (e.g., career counseling, job referral, short-term economic support, retraining, social-psychological support).

Unions and employers have a long history of bargaining over the effects of technological change. Approximately 26 percent of labor agreements contain some language that address in some manner the introduction of new technology. Only 17 percent provide for discussion with or notification to the union in advance of the introduction of new technology, and only 8 percent require an employer to retrain workers displaced by technological change.[3] One study reported the elements of creating a new work system (e.g., team-based work system, job rotation, worker participation, pay for knowledge, profit sharing, or gain-sharing) being discussed in one-third or fewer negotiations, with an agreement on these types of bargaining issues being reached in only 9 to 16 percent of contract settlements.[4]

These low percentages are partially due to the fact that current labor law classifies most decisions concerning the implementation of new technology as a nonmandatory bargaining subject.[5] This limits a union's bargaining role to issues regarding the *effects of technology* on members' interests after management decides what technology to use and when, where, and how to implement it. Essentially this forces a union to adopt a reactive rather than proactive stance in seeking to represent bargaining-unit members' interests on technology change decisions. Critics of the current legal designation of technology issues as nonmandatory bargaining subjects argue that permitting unions to bargain over the full range of issues that arise concerning technology would provide valuable information to management from employees who work most closely with the technology, likely speed the adoption of new technologies, and enhance employees' acceptance of technological change efforts benefiting the implementation goals of both management and employees.[6]

Some companies do see advantages in voluntarily involving employees and union representatives in the early stages of selecting new technology as a means of achieving a sustainable competitive advantage.[7] Employees and union representatives may accompany engineers on trips to vendors, provide input to assess the merits of available technologies, and render opinions on what types of equipment to purchase. Employees may contribute valuable insight into how to operate the equipment and how to organize the work process after the new technology is implemented. When a union is consulted early in the technology development process, it is more likely to become an advocate for the new technology and better able to assure its members that the technology will secure more jobs than it threatens.

The General Motors–United Auto Workers agreement provides for advance notice, special committees to deal with technology-related layoffs, and guaranteed employment with full pay as long as the displaced employee is willing to be retrained.[8] The International Association of Machinists (IAM) has adopted an integrated program with several employers with whom the union has a bargaining relationship to create a **high performance work organization (HPWO)**, which is capable of saving and creating jobs while remaining globally competitive and stimulating company growth.[9] The HPWO envisions a partnership in which both management and labor take responsibility for ensuring that the firm will adapt to competitive market and technological demands by sharing information, continuously training workers, and adapting work rules to meet each firm's needs (see Labor Relations in Action Box). General Electric and Westinghouse negotiated provisions with the International Brotherhood of Electrical Workers that require advance notification of technology, committees, retraining, and safety measures for people who work with robots.[10]

Although more firms are seeking to involve and empower employees in adapting to technological change (see Labor Relations in Action Box), many firms are not.[11] A bargaining relationship characterized by mistrust or leaders on either side not committed to developing a more cooperative relationship or insecure in their own position will inhibit technology change efforts. The need for consultation with the workforce may be viewed as a loss of authority by some supervisors and middle managers, who may resist transferring their power to employees. For innovative work practices to be effective, upper management and union leaders must communicate their commitment to cooperation with all employees within the organization.

Unions are often portrayed as being obstacles to technological change in the workplace because many Americans remember publicity given to railroad fireman who wanted to remain on diesel engines, the reluctance of plumbers to adapt to plastic pipes, airline crew members who resisted a reduction in the number of cockpit crew members needed to fly more modern aircraft, or the resistance of typographers to computerized typesetting in the newspaper industry. Unions are depicted as negotiating complex work rules that restrict management's ability to manage the workplace and management's right to introduce technological advancements. Yet some unions have clearly encouraged changes in job design, skills training, employee involvement in decision making, teamwork, gain-sharing, improved labor–management communications, and more cooperative labor relations.[12] In fact, unions have generally accepted the doctrine of "high wages, high productivity, and low labor costs" as the best approach to maintaining income growth and employment stability for union members.[13] As Joseph Hunt, president of the Iron Workers' union, has stated: "We have to make our contractors more competitive to gain market share. If they don't have a job, there's no job for us [our members] to work on."[14]

Technological change can have both positive and negative effects on employees, and a union must represent members affected by both types of change. In general, technological progress in the United States has resulted in higher productivity, the elimination of many menial and dangerous jobs, higher wages,

LABOR RELATIONS IN ACTION

High Performance Work Organization (HPWO) Partnership Principles

Union and management leaders responsible for their respective organizations are asked to write and sign a *Partnership Agreement* signifying a real commitment to partnership as a means of implementing meaningful change in the work environment. The following principles help define what components comprise a true partnership:

- **Shared decision making** concerning issues critical to the competitiveness of the business including costs and work processes.

- **Development of continuous learning and skill building** to meet the changing education needs of all employees.

- **Continuous integration of leading-edge technology** that utilizes the skills, knowledge, and insights of employees. Leading-edge technology includes equipment, new materials, work processes and labor relations intended to both stabilize and grow the business and the workforce.

- **A co-determined definition of quality and its continuous measurement and improvement.** Quality includes meeting customers' expectations and is critical to the ability of the firm to grow and its employees to prosper.

- **Shared technical and financial information.** Access to relevant and timely information is necessary for parties to make appropriate decisions. Open and honest communication between labor and management serves to build trust in a partner.

- **Ongoing co-determination of costs** such as design, prototype development, production, and administrative overhead. This requires a cost accounting system capable of assigning cost to various elements in the work process.

- **Acceptance of the union as an independently chosen representative of employees.** Through the collective bargaining process including the use of a contract grievance procedure, the parties can seek to resolve conflicts of interests that may arise while seeking to expand opportunities for cooperation.

- **Union and management leaders willing to advocate the partnership concept and motivate all employees to participate in bringing about positive workplace changes.**

- **A jointly developed Strategic Business Plan.** The plan should cover current products and services, development of new products and services, and the goals and direction to be taken by the partners to achieve future growth. ■

SOURCE: International Association of Machinists, *HPWO Partnership Key Components*, 1996–2000, pp. 1–3 at http://www.goiam.org/visit.asp?c = 507.

Describing HPWO

LABOR RELATIONS IN ACTION

Creating a Labor-Management Partnership at Work

The Collective Bargaining Forum was created in 1984 as a mechanism for union and management practitioners, government representatives, academics, and others interested in promoting a more co-operative approach to labor relations to exchange ideas and information. Cooperation between labor and management occurs along a continuum ranging from merely stating an intent to cooperate to actually sharing joint decision-making authority in managing a firm to effectively meet changing market, technological, and performance competitive challenges. Although a relatively small number of labor–management relationships would currently qualify as true partnerships, the work practices of some of the most successful firms appear to be moving in the direction of creating a true partnership with labor whereby competitiveness is perceived as a joint venture requiring the talent and dedication of both parties to achieve long-term success.

Following are 10 guidelines or benchmarks established by the Collective Bargaining Forum in its document *Compact for Change*, which can be used as goals toward which to strive or to evaluate the extent to which a labor–management relationship currently reflects a true partnership[a]:

1. The parties should jointly work to increase productivity and enhance the quality of products to assure employees of long-term security and a rising standard of living.
2. Management should reflect the continued improvements in productivity and the quality of products in its decisions regarding worker compensation, the organizational structure, pricing, and investment.
3. Unions and employers should jointly develop the leadership and technical skills of their workers.
4. Unions and employers should jointly develop ways to promote teamwork and employee involvement in developing and administering personnel policies and in strategic decision making to achieve organizational goals.
5. The employer and union must commit to open and early sharing of all information relevant to corporate strategies and the relationship between the parties.
6. The employer and unions should share their views and agree on how employee representation will be determined at new facilities.
7. Permanent separation of workers will be an action of last resort.
8. Both the union and the employer should be jointly committed to a work environment in which disputes are resolved in an amicable manner, without resort to strikes, lockouts, or hiring replacements.
9. Both parties should be committed to worker participation at all levels of decision making to provide continuous improvements in products, services, employment security, and productivity.
10. It is essential that employees have input in the design and application of new technology and in the planning and development of any new system for the allocation of tasks.

Full partnership provides a mechanism for accommodating both the mutual and competing interests of labor and management. This entails equal participation in formulating and implementing firm strategies regarding planning, investments, markets, production, and human resources from the boardroom to the shop floor. With participation in decision making comes acceptance of the responsibility for the results of such decisions. Partners share both the risks and rewards; therefore, mutual trust and respect between the parties for each other's legitimate interests must be the foundation on which any partnership is based. ■

George R. Gray, Donald W. Myers, and Phyllis S. Myers, "Cooperative Provisions in Labor Agreements: A New Paradigm?" *Monthly Labor Review* 122 (January 1999), pp. 40–42.

shorter hours, and a higher standard of living.[15] Technological advances have brought about numerous positive effects:

1. The ability to produce greater wealth with less effort.
2. Machinery performing tasks that humans cannot or performing tasks more reliably and efficiently, thereby lowering production costs and permitting products to be sold at lower prices.
3. Better working conditions.
4. Backbreaking or hazardous work assignments are minimized.
5. Skill levels of some workers will increase, with consequent increases in pay.

Although technological change has many positive effects, it may also produce some negative effects. Technology advances have permitted the elimination of some jobs or a reduction in the responsibility or skill level required to perform other jobs (deskilling), resulting in lower employee compensation and less job security for those employees holding such jobs. In some cases, machinery such as robotics may be less able to react and adjust to unforeseen circumstances or changes in the operating environment than would a well-trained human operator. Technology often carries higher capital costs, which must be paid for through a combination of labor cost savings and higher product output. To the extent that competitors adopt similar technology, increasing product supplies relative to the market demand for such products, the price of goods may decline, thereby extending the time required to recover a firm's capital investment in technology.

Technology has also increased the sophistication of methods used to monitor employees at the workplace. A 2003 survey of 1,100 respondents by the American Management Association reports that 52 percent of companies engage in some form of e-mail monitoring and 22 percent of firms have terminated an employee for an e-mail work rule violation.[16] This monitoring may include e-mail or other computer files, video camera recordings, electronic beepers to monitor employee location, supervisors listening to telephone conversations, computerized tracking systems of phone use, and computer monitoring in which video display terminals (VDTs) keep track of employee productivity and activity, including counting keystrokes, error rates, time taken to complete tasks, and time away from the terminal.[17] Data collected are provided to supervisors, who may use the information to determine production standards and pay rates, monitor speed and accuracy, evaluate performance, or discipline for failure to perform in a satisfactory manner.[18]

Employers argue that electronic monitoring of employees is a useful way to objectively evaluate their performance, increase productivity, prevent theft or other unlawful activity on company property, avoid potential legal liability arising from a failure to reasonably monitor employee workplace activity, monitor compliance with safety regulations, and plan for future business needs. Union officials often respond that electronic monitoring can be a source of stress on employees, measures only quantitative aspects of job performance, erodes employees' dignity, and invades employees' privacy. Few federal or state laws provide any significant protection for employee workplace privacy rights.[19] Unions are often under pressure from members to negotiate work rules to provide such protection in labor agreements.

A union might propose contract language covering one or more of the following requirements:

- An outright ban on one or more types of unreasonable or obtrusive electronic monitoring activities.
- Advance employee notification that their performance is subject to electronic monitoring.
- Imposing a "beep" provision requiring the employer to use a light or audible tone to inform employees when they are being monitored.
- Prohibiting management from collecting information not directly related to an employee's work performance.
- Prohibiting disclosure of employee information collected to other people or companies without prior employee approval or unless in connection with a criminal investigation.
- Availability of counseling or other health-related services necessary to manage job stress or related conditions arising from exposure to electronic monitoring activities.

Management negotiators would want to ensure that any agreed upon electronic monitoring work rule:

- Clearly inform employees that electronic communication equipment (e.g., computers, cell phone) cannot be misused for unprofessional or inappropriate communications (e.g., racial slurs, sexual harassment).
- Inform employees that electronic communication equipment necessary to perform assigned job duties will be provided by the company and represents company property.
- Inform employees that they have no reasonable expectation of privacy in the use of company property for electronic communications purposes.
- Require that employees sign a consent form or provide other evidence acknowledging they have read and understood all electronic monitoring work rules and the consequences for their violation.

Job Security and Personnel Changes

Most job growth over the next decade is expected to occur as the result of the need to replace employees who leave current job positions rather than the creation of additional (new) job positions. The shift in employment opportunities from goods-producing (manufacturing) to service-producing industries (e.g., retail trade; communications; services; transportation; finance, insurance, and real estate) will continue, with the services and retail trade industries accounting for almost 75 percent of the 22.0 million wage and salary jobs expected to be filled over the 2000–2010 period.[20] The 30 fastest percentage growth occupations through 2010 are concentrated in health care and computer-related jobs.[21] Twelve of the 30 (40 percent) fastest growing occupations (e.g., computer software engineer, database administrator, physician assistant, audiologist, special education, preschool, kindergarten, and elementary school teachers) require a bachelor's or higher education level. Nine (30 percent) of the fastest growing occupations (e.g., personal and home care aides, physical therapist aides, veterinary assistants, dental assistants, pharmacy technicians) require only a short or medium-length period of on-the-job training. One thing not likely to change for employees and the unions who represent them is a desire to obtain **job security**.

Job Security Work Rules

A primary union concern is to ensure that members' jobs are protected from elimination resulting from technological change or unreasonable managerial decision making. Unions have been able to protect jobs by negotiating contract language concerning subjects such as job security guarantees, subcontracting, outsourcing, work assignments and jurisdiction, work scheduling, and the weight accorded seniority in personnel decisions.

Job security work rules are provisions that attempt to make jobs more secure, such as spreading the workload by placing limits on the load that can be carried, restricting the duties of employees, limiting the number of machines one operator can tend, or requiring standby crews.[22] Such practices when carried to an extreme are known as **featherbedding**, which exhibits "unreasonable limits to the amount of work employees may do in a given period. . . . payment for unneeded employees, unnecessary tasks, work not performed, or jobs duplicating those already done."[23] This practice is viewed negatively by managers and the public as a waste of resources, and unions have been forced to abandon or severely limit the use of such work rules in an era of global competition.

Congress attempted to help reduce featherbedding practices when it amended the Labor Management Relations Act (LMRA) in 1947 and included Section 8(b)(6), which prohibits a labor union from causing or "attempting to cause an employer to pay or deliver or agree to pay or deliver any money or other thing of value, in the nature of an exaction, for services which are not performed or not to be performed."[24] Workload restrictions underlie many labor relations conflicts. From an overall (macro) viewpoint, union leaders agree that change is necessary for economic progress, but from an individual (micro) view, where significant adjustment would be necessary, change may be resisted by workers and their unions.[25]

A commitment to employment security has several advantages for both employers and employees. Such a commitment may motivate employees to support change, encourage employers to invest more in training employees, reduce costs associated with turnover, retain critical skills needed by the firm, and maintain employee morale. Building strategic partnerships with management based on a mutual recognition of the contributions that labor and management make to enhance a firm's competitiveness is one approach to improving job security.[26]

The collective-bargaining process is the means by which unions and management attempt to resolve conflicts between employees' desire for greater job security and employers' desire for greater flexibility and cost effectiveness in adjusting the size and duties of the labor force to the workload. Some examples of issues affecting job security covered by negotiated work rules include the following:

- *Job assignment:* Reducing crew size, adding duties, or eliminating unneeded jobs.

- *Job content:* Combining jobs such as millwright, welder, rigger, and boilermaker, or allowing journeymen to perform helpers' tasks.

- *Hours:* Providing clean-up time, flexible work schedules, mandatory overtime policy, advance notice of shutdown, or more working hours for the same pay.

- *Seniority:* Restricting the use of seniority in filling job vacancies, bumping, or determining work schedules.

- *Wages:* Permitting pay for knowledge, gain-sharing, severance pay.

- *Training:* amount and type provided, employee eligibility criteria to receive training.

Union and management representatives must determine which job security work rules are appropriate in each bargaining relationship. Not all restrictive work rules intended to maintain a specified staffing level are illegal. Work rules negotiated between the longshoremen and shipping companies that prevent truckers and warehousemen from unloading cargo from containers within 50 miles of a ship docking pier were upheld by the U.S. Supreme Court because they were the product of voluntary bargaining between two informed parties. These work rules were designed to preserve a portion of the traditional longshore work that is dwindling because of use of shipping containers.[27]

Plant Closures, Downsizing, and WARN

In 1988, congress enacted the **Worker Adjustment and Retraining Notification Act (WARN)** in response to data that showed large numbers of employers either shut down or initiated layoffs while giving employees or community leaders less than 14 days' advance notice or no notice at all. This law requires employers with 100 or more employees to give 60 days' advance notice of a plant closing or major layoff (i.e., termination of 50 or more workers at the same work location within a 30-day period or a major layoff affecting at least 50 employees who make up at least 33 percent of the workers at a work site), to employees (excluding those employed less than 20 hours per week), unions, and state and local governments.[28] WARN also allows negotiation of labor contract language requiring more than 60 days' advance notice.

Although providing workers with advance notice of shutdown has been shown to reduce the probability such notified workers will experience unemployment in transitioning to a new job opportunity, passage of the WARN has not had a substantial impact on increasing the number of employers providing or displaced workers receiving advance notice of layoffs or plant closures.[29] From 1995 to 1997, only 44.3 percent of the 3.6 million workers displaced because of plant shutdown, insufficient work, or jobs being abolished received any advance written notice.[30] In 2003, 68 percent of manufacturing and 28 percent of nonmanufacturing labor agreements surveyed provided for advance notice of shutdown.[31]

Several possible reasons exist for the failure of the WARN Act to provide more employees and community leaders with advance notice of significant job displacement events.[32] Some employers may be unaware or confused regarding their notification responsibilities under WARN despite the U.S. Department of Labor's efforts to provide guidance to encourage voluntary employer compliance. The language of the act itself serves to undermine its potential. Exempting firms with fewer than 100 employees eliminates a substantial portion of the labor force from receiving required advance notice. The WARN act also has many exemptions applicable to covered employers. For example, an estimated 50 percent of layoffs involving 50 or more workers are exempt from any advance notice requirement because the number of affected employees is less than one-third of the employer's active workforce (one-third rule).

WARN requires employers found liable for a violation to provide the affected employees up to 60 days' back pay and benefits.[33] Because the law designates no federal agency as responsible for enforcing the law, employees must take the expensive step of hiring an attorney to sue their employer in federal district court for any alleged violation of the WARN Act. A union may sue for damages on behalf of its members under the WARN Act, and state law determines the time limit imposed for filing such claims.[34]

On occasion, the rules under the WARN Act and the LMRA are intertwined. In 1991, the *Dallas Times Herald*, which had a long-standing bargaining relationship with the Dallas Typographical Union and Mailers Local, actively misled the unions about rumors of a closing during negotiations for a new contract. On the date the sale was finalized, the business was closed. The *Times Herald* then informed employees and the union. The National Labor Relations Board (NLRB) ruled that remedies (back pay) owed to employees under the LMRA were separate from payments required under the WARN Act. Therefore, an employer's payment for back pay and benefits arising from a violation of the WARN Act would not offset any back-pay liability arising from an unfair labor practice finding involving the same affected workers under the LMRA.[35]

Subcontracting, Outsourcing, and Work Transfer

Subcontracting (also called "contracting work out") usually occurs when a firm determines that it cannot perform all the tasks that are necessary to operate its business successfully or that another firm can perform the needed tasks (janitorial and cafeteria services, equipment repair, parts production, and so on) better or at a lower cost. **Outsourcing**, a similar process, is a cost-cutting strategy of shifting work away from one's own plant to lower-cost, sometimes nonunion producers or purchasing parts needed in production from these producers.[36] For example, outsourcing of electronic equipment needs by auto manufacturers over the 1998–2004 period increased at an average annual rate of 43 percent while similar outsourcing in the consumer electronics industry rose at an average annual rate of 61 percent.[37] Various flexible staffing arrangements have emerged in response to increased competitive demands in a wide range of domestic and international industries (e.g., banking, information technology, telecommunications, engineering functions, cleaning services, food services).

Advantages of subcontracting and outsourcing have been cited as lower costs (particularly labor costs), increased profitability, productivity and quality improvements, increased operating flexibility, speed, and faster access to innovative technology with less capital risk.[38] While most companies that outsource report achieving positive benefits, the magnitude of gains are often less than expected. Employee concerns over possible job loss, poor selection or monitoring of outsourcing suppliers, insufficient training provided to individuals responsible for managing outsourcing activities, and failure to develop a clear plan detailing outsourcing objectives, expected benefits, and performance measures are all factors that can contribute to unsuccessful outsourcing efforts.

In recent years, GM and other auto manufacturers have been seeking to expand outsourcing of certain parts production and introducing less labor-intensive production methods such as modular manufacturing, which permits various modules (e.g., dashboards, headliners, exhaust system) to be assembled by outside suppliers, requiring an auto manufacturer's workers to engage in only the final assembly of such preassembled modules.[39] The United Auto Workers (UAW) union has adopted a dual strategy of attempting to delay job cuts or limit such cuts to normal attrition rates at Big Three auto plants while at the same time becoming more aggressive in seeking to organize nonunion auto supply plants to reduce the labor costs differential between primary auto manufacturers and auto suppliers.[40] DaimlerChrysler recently announced plans to build a new truck manufacturing plant in Canada financed in large part by outside suppliers whose employees would independently operate various areas within the plant itself (e.g., truck body welding shop, paint shop).[41]

Use of the just-in-time inventory control method to minimize inventory carrying costs has left firms particularly susceptible to disruptions in the flow of parts caused by selective strike actions at key supplier's plants or their own plant. This increases the importance to management of developing stable and cooperative labor relations with workers and their union representatives. A strike by machinists at Boeing in 1995, the first since 1989, was caused in large part by outsourcing. Between 1989 and 1995, Boeing's worldwide workforce had shrunk by 62,000, and forecasts for plane production were the lowest in 11 years. To help win orders in Asia, the aircraft industry's fastest growing market, Boeing agreed to farm out parts production to manufacturers in those countries (sometimes a requirement imposed by home countries in order for foreign firms to do business there). As an example, one supplier selected was Shanghai Aviation in China, with 2,000 employees who earned $120 per month compared to $3,530 per month earned by Boeing employees in Seattle, Washington, for producing 1,500 tail assemblies for Boeing. Although Boeing's aircraft are still assembled in Seattle, many of their fuselages and components, such as landing gear, are now produced in and imported from Asia.[42]

In some cases, the parties attempt to reverse outsourcing activities. For example, at the GM plant in Doraville, Georgia, the UAW and GM organized a joint union–management team to study the feasibility of keeping outsourced work. The committee found a way to produce seat cushions for one of GM's midsize models in-plant for less than the vendor charged. The team bid on the work and won the contract; now the cushions are produced at the Doraville plant. Since then, the corporate office has decided to assign the assembly of GM-10 cars to that plant rather than shutting it down.[43]

The subcontracting process, seemingly a normal economic practice, can be a volatile and complicated collective-bargaining issue. Unions often attempt to influence management's decisions to subcontract by restricting management's freedom to subcontract bargaining-unit members' work in order to protect and maximize members' work and economic opportunities. For example, a union might seek to have management agree not to subcontract or outsource work as long as necessary personnel and equipment were available to perform the work in a timely manner. Alternatively, a union might propose no subcontracting or outsourcing of work without providing the union an opportunity to demonstrate how the work could be performed in-plant by bargaining-unit members as cost effectively as it could if the work were outsourced to another supplier. A union may also request information from management to document the type and amount of bargaining-unit work being subcontracted by the employer.

Negotiation practices regarding subcontracting clauses may vary across industries because unions in the construction and apparel industries do not usually attempt to limit subcontracting. Instead, unions in these two industries often attempt to extend the provisions of the collective-bargaining agreement to the subcontractors that are commonly used in those industries. Under the LMRA, subcontracting of bargaining-unit work is considered a mandatory subject of bargaining. However, a company would not be required to bargain if all of the following conditions were met: (1) subcontracting was motivated solely by economic conditions, (2) subcontracting was a common method of doing business in the industry, (3) the current subcontracting decision did not differ much from similar decisions made by the company in the past, (4) there was no adverse impact on bargaining-unit employees, and (5) the union had previously been given an opportunity to bargain over changes in established subcontracting practices.[44]

Arbitration likewise has played an increasingly important role in the subcontracting issue. In determining whether management had a contractual right to subcontract certain bargaining-unit work, an arbitrator might consider several factors, such as the presence and clarity of contract language granting management a right to subcontract, any evidence of an established past practice regarding subcontracting, the history of the parties' prior negotiations over the issue of subcontracting, the intended duration of the subcontracting decision, the employer's business justification for contracting out, and any evidence of antiunion animus (i.e., a desire or intent to weaken the bargaining unit or union representative by subcontracting work).[45]

Work relocation is similar to subcontracting and outsourcing. An employer who unilaterally transfers bargaining unit work to another location has a duty to bargain over the decision to relocate the work if the relocation decision does not involve a basic change in the nature of the employer's operation.[46] To avoid the duty to bargain, the employer must prove that (1) the work performed at the new location differs significantly from the bargaining unit work performed at the previous location, (2) labor costs were not a factor affecting the decision to relocate the work, or (3) the union representative of bargaining unit employees could not have offered sufficient labor cost concessions to reasonably justify any change in the employer's decision to relocate the work. Even where there is no duty to bargain over the decision to relocate bargaining unit work, an employer would still have a duty to bargain over the effects of the relocation decision on bargaining unit members (e.g., transfer rights, severance pay, pension rights).[47]

Even when a duty to bargain over the work relocation decision exists, an employer satisfies its bargaining duty by negotiating in good faith with the union to a voluntary settlement or reaching a bargaining impasse, at which point the employer could legally implement the work relocation decision. This puts pressure on a union to adopt a reasonable approach in proposing alternative actions that might alter the employer's perceived need to relocate some or all of the planned work affected.

Arbitrators as well have limited management's right to relocate bargaining-unit work when they conclude that the parties have already placed limits on work relocation by including in their labor agreements the following standard contract provisions: (1) a recognition clause that acknowledges the union's status as representative of employees within the established scope of the bargaining unit, (2) clauses that establish job classifications and wage rates, (3) seniority clauses that include layoff and recall procedures, and (4) job security clauses that limit the circumstances in which employees can be terminated or jobs eliminated.[48] Practically speaking, there is usually good reason for an employer to bargain about a work relocation decision, as well as its effects. A union may offer helpful suggestions or concessions that make the relocation less necessary. More importantly, if the company acts unilaterally and its acts are later determined to be unlawful, it risks large back-pay awards and in isolated cases a costly order to reopen a closed operation.[49]

Work Assignments and Jurisdiction

When changes in technology, job descriptions, work materials, or processes occur, sometimes labor disputes develop over which workers will be assigned to perform particular jobs or job duties. Such disputes may occur if: (1) two or more unions representing different bargaining units within the firm claim jurisdiction for their members to perform the available work assignment; (2) bargaining unit employees believe their work is being assigned to other employees outside the bargaining unit, such as supervisors; or (3) a disagreement occurs within a union over which members should perform particular work assignments. These disputes over work assignments are called **jurisdictional disputes** (see Exhibit 8.1 for an example of a work jurisdiction clause in a labor agreement).

The LMRA, as amended, makes it unlawful for a union to engage in or encourage a work stoppage to force an employer to assign work to a particular union or craft. The LMRA provides a special NLRB procedure for resolving jurisdictional disputes within 10 days after an unfair labor practice charge is filed. Factors considered by the NLRB in resolving these types of disputes are skills and work expe-

Exhibit 8.1

Example of a Work Jurisdiction Clause

It is the intent of the parties to this agreement to protect the work performed by employees in the bargaining unit.

The employer recognizes that it is important and desirable to use its own equipment and drivers to the greatest extent possible before using subhaulers and/or noncompany trucks.

The union recognizes that under certain conditions, such as those dictated by customer demands, equipment requirements, daily dispatch determinations, materials to be hauled and similar factors, that subhaulers and/or noncompany trucks are necessary and have been so used throughout the industry for many years.

The employer, in accordance with the above, must however, determine the number, type and location of its working equipment in conformity with its business requirements. The employer further must be able to determine, in keeping with sound business practices, the extent to which it will replace equipment that is too costly to operate, obsolete, or damaged.

Under these conditions, the employer agrees the subhaulers and/or noncompany trucks will not be used as a subterfuge to defeat the protection of the bargaining unit work.

In keeping with the above, the union recognizes that the employer will use such subhaulers and/or noncompany trucks as required by location and classification only after all the available company trucks at such locations and in similar classifications have been initially dispatched.

rience required to perform the work; any union certifications already awarded by the NLRB, industry, and local practice; prior arbitration decisions; the employer's desires; and cost effectiveness and operating efficiency of assigning the work to a particular bargaining unit or craft.[50] The AFL-CIO's Building and Construction Trades Department representing 15 affiliated national unions, and several national contractors' associations have generally sought to avoid using the NLRB jurisdictional dispute procedure by voluntarily establishing a national joint board to consider and decide cases of jurisdictional disputes in the building and construction industry.[51] Management of the Philadelphia Convention Center recently announced the signing of a 10-year agreement with six unions representing convention center employees aimed at specifying how the six unions will work together to reduce jurisdictional disputes and labor costs.[52] The agreement is expected to help pave the way for a $500 million expansion of the Convention Center.

Some labor agreements require that bargaining unit work be performed only by bargaining unit employees except in instructional, experimental, or emergency situations. In instructional situations, there must be a clear, direct, and immediate connection between work done by members of management and instructions given to bargaining unit employees. Experimental work includes the introduction of a new technique, method, or procedure. Emergency conditions might occur as the result of unforeseen circumstances, such as a tornado, fire, or power outage, that call for immediate action.[53] However, it is generally recognized that bargaining unit work may be performed by supervisors in situations requiring only a few minutes of time.

Intra-union work assignment problems, although not as critical and dramatic as other issues, are often very sensitive political matters for local union leaders. Conflicts between members of the same union over work assignments can cause problems, especially in industrial unions having both craft and semi-skilled employees as members. Whenever production processes are automated, reassignment of work from skilled employees to semi-skilled production employees can cause emotional conflicts within the union. For example, having pipe fitters do welding tasks when welding is not included in their job description gives rise to disputes.

To resolve these conflicts, unions favor specific, written job descriptions and would like to assert a right to refuse to perform work outside their jurisdictions. However, management typically prefers the increased flexibility in making work assignments provided by more general job descriptions that include phrases such as "perform related duties" and "make minor repairs."[54] Implementation of a team-based production system encourages cross-functional training and broader multiskill job descriptions that provide greater flexibility in assigning job duties to team members.

Work Scheduling

Collective bargaining agreements often deal with work scheduling, such as determining the timing or duration of a work shift, day, or week. Management has a right to determine work schedules unless restricted by negotiated language in the labor agreement. For example, management has a right to suspend operations temporarily, reduce the number of shifts, or change the number of days to be worked. Even when the labor agreement contains some restrictions on work scheduling, management can usually make unscheduled emergency changes in the work schedule if such changes are made in good faith and for reasonable cause, such as extreme weather conditions, bomb threats, or civil disturbances. The 5-day, 40-hour work week has been accepted as a standard work schedule in most U.S. industries since passage of the Fair Labor Standards Act (1938) requiring employers to pay a covered employee time and one-half for hours worked in excess of 40 during the same work week.

Unions in the United States and elsewhere have shown increasing interest in **flextime** work schedules, which allow an employee to start and finish work at his or her discretion, as long as the specified total number of hours per week or per day are worked and the employee is present at work during a core-hour period (e.g., 9:00 A.M. to 11:00 A.M. and 1:30 to 3:30 P.M.). Some employers use flexible work schedules as a hiring incentive to attract applicants in occupations with a current labor shortage. These programs are designed to better match job requirements with the personal needs of individual employees. Although flextime has much potential for meeting employee needs, some work operations require all workers to be present at the same time, and in these cases, work schedules cannot be altered unless the entire group accepts the alternative schedule.[55]

The Role of Seniority in Personnel Changes

Employers usually have a free hand in selecting initial hires that best fit the prescribed job requirements and needs of the firm. However, once any employee has been selected and placed on a job within a bargaining unit, the employer must abide by provisions of the labor agreement regarding personnel decisions such as promotions, transfers, and layoffs. The concept of **seniority** is often a factor used to determine personnel decisions that affect bargaining unit employees. Seniority has played a key role in labor relations since the 1920s, when foremen's discretion (often abused) in personnel decisions was replaced by seniority-based decisions affecting compensation or reward structures, promotion, transfer, layoff, and recall decisions.[56]

Seniority is usually measured by the length of an employee's continuous service in a company (plant) or in a specific department or job line-of-progression (e.g., welder 1, welder 2, etc.). Seniority may be used to determine **benefit rights** (e.g., vacation entitlement or scheduling) or **competitive job rights** (e.g., promotion, layoff or recall, work assignments, transfers, shift preference). When used to determine benefit rights, every employee's seniority should be measured on the same basis from the date of initial employment in the company or specific plant location. This approach ensures equitable treatment of employees for entitlement to certain benefits that have no meaningful connection to the type of job the employee performs for the firm.

Determining who among competing employees will be entitled to a job promotion or transfer presents a different issue, because in determining competitive job rights the ability to perform the job is an important consideration. Management would generally prefer to measure seniority for determining competitive job rights on a department or job line-of-progression basis. This measurement approach gives more assurance that the most senior applicant will be qualified to perform the job and eliminates the risk of grievance claims filed by employees from other departments who might claim an ability to perform a job in another department and possess greater seniority than other applicants based on their length of service with the firm.

Seniority provisions are found in 91 percent of all labor agreements and cover issues such as how seniority accrues, in what types of decisions it will be used, and in some cases, how it can be lost for a variety of reasons (e.g., layoff, failure to respond to recall, unauthorized absences, or taking a job elsewhere during a leave of absence).[57] Seniority is considered very important by most union members, and management seldom objects to providing some sense of job security or benefit priority to long-service employees. Seniority serves as one of the few objective measures that can be used to distinguish between two or more employees and is also used by nonunion employers in making some personnel decisions.[58] Arbitrators may also consider a grievant's seniority as a possible mitigating circumstance in deciding the appropriateness of a discipline or discharge decision.

Some authors argue that the increasing level of organizational instability resulting from rightsizing, outsourcing, mergers, increased global competition, and declining union density have weakened employers' commitment to seniority and in turn, weakened employees' loyalty and commitment to their current employer.[59] Individuals entering the labor force today must expect to work for multiple employers over the course of their work career, making seniority difficult to attain with any single employer. Other authors criticize seniority as a discriminatory concept because some groups with a higher proportion of more recent entrants to the labor force (e.g., women, minorities) are often among the first to be laid off when applying the "last-in-first-out" principle on which seniority preference is based.[60]

In some cases, union and management agree to include a seniority provision in the labor agreement called **superseniority**, which provides that highly skilled technical employees or union officials directly involved in contract negotiations or grievance handling will be the last ones laid off. This provision allows a company to retain essential skills and at the same time promote stable labor relations by ensuring individuals skilled in contract negotiation and grievance-handling techniques will remain available to resolve any labor disputes that might arise.

Seniority also plays a role in determining job promotion and transfer decisions. Personnel changes within an organization that advance an employee to a position of more responsibility, usually accompanied by a wage increase, are promotions. Promotion provisions usually rely on both ability and seniority as factors used to determine the personnel decision, although the weight accorded each factor can vary in different labor agreements. Although seniority can be easily and objectively determined, the measurement of ability is more complex. Job transfer provisions cover personnel changes from one job to another with relatively equal authority, responsibility, and compensation. Seniority and ability are also usually the determining factors in making a job transfer decision.

Four basic types of seniority clauses used in promotion and transfer decisions are presented here, with the approximate percentage of contracts using each:

1. Seniority as the only determining factor (5 percent).

2. Among all employees who meet the minimum job requirements, seniority will be the determining factor (49 percent).

3. Where the best qualified candidates are relatively equal in ability, seniority will be the determining factor (40 percent).

4. Ability and seniority will be given equal consideration (2 percent).[61]

Management would generally prefer to give ability to perform the job more weight than seniority in making promotion and transfer decisions to enhance potential productivity. Unions often argue that because the exact determination of ability is so complex, the emphasis should be on ensuring that each candidate is qualified to perform the job effectively, and among such qualified candidates, seniority is an objective means of determining the candidate selected. The use of only seniority to determine eligibility for promotions and transfers is objective and administratively easy, but it does not ensure that the more senior employee will always be qualified to perform the job. In the small percentage of contracts that weigh seniority and ability equally, arbitrators have concluded that when seniority is relatively close, it is reasonable to use relative ability as the determining factor. If candidates' seniority differs extensively, ability must be substantially greater to justify selection of a less senior candidate.[62]

Ability to perform a job includes measuring factors such as relevant job skills, knowledge, attitude, behavior, performance, pace, and production. Techniques most commonly used to measure these criteria include tests, work experience, education, production records, performance ratings, personality traits, and absence, tardiness, and discipline records.[63] Each of these criteria may be limited in its specific relationship to the needs of particular jobs and thus, the determination of employee qualifications is usually based on several criteria.

Although the employer has the right to establish any valid criteria for assessing ability, promotion criteria and performance standards are mandatory bargaining subjects, and thus an employer must comply with any standards expressed in the parties' labor agreement. Selection and performance appraisal criteria and methods must also comply with the "Uniform Guidelines on Employment Selection Procedures" covering race, sex, national origin, and religious discrimination for covered employers.[64] Moreover, the provisions of the labor agreement itself must not be discriminatory or perpetuate past discriminatory practices.

Even though promotion and transfer procedures differ, most labor agreements require that job vacancies be posted for a specified period. Interested employees are then permitted to bid for available job vacancies within a reasonably specified time period. Other related labor agreement provisions may be included to prevent possible administrative problems. For example, agreements should prescribe whether an employee carries his or her seniority to a new position or whether seniority will be retained only after a predetermined period. Other provisions should specify whether an employee who transfers out of the bargaining unit or is promoted to a management position will be allowed to retain his or her seniority or lose it.

Seniority provisions pertaining to layoff and recall decisions are included in 94 percent of contracts, and nearly half consider seniority first in retaining employees during layoffs.[65] Most agreements also provide for recall of employees after layoffs in reverse order of layoff, but only if they are qualified for the open position. Increasingly, seniority has become the sole factor in layoff determination; however, some contracts still consider seniority as the determining factor only if employees are qualified for available jobs. In others, seniority is given consideration only when ability is equal.

Advance notice of impending layoffs to the employees and the union, such as 1 to 4 days' notice, is required in 45 percent of labor agreements but is much more common in manufacturing agreements (68 percent).[66] Often, employees scheduled for layoff are permitted to displace or "bump" a less senior employee if the senior employee is qualified to perform the job. Such **bumping rights** are confined to the employee's own job classification or work group in a majority of cases. Unionized firms experience only slightly higher layoff rates than nonunion firms in both manufacturing and nonmanufacturing industries.[67]

Alternatives to layoffs as a means of cutting labor costs include pay freezes, pay cuts, productivity improvement through work rule changes, new products, normal attrition and hiring freezes, voluntary leave, early retirement, hours reduction, rotating layoffs, work relocation, and **work sharing.** Work sharing, where two or more employees share a job, each working fewer hours, is provided in 6 percent of labor agreements.[68] Work-sharing agreements generally specify they will be implemented for a limited time or that the company must consult with the union before work sharing may be implemented. Work sharing enables the employer to retain the skill mix of a full workforce and consequently to retain its investment in employee training, keeps the employer's unemployment compensation tax contribution rates from increasing, and is considered by many employers as more equitable than retaining some employees and laying off others. Employers have no right to institute work sharing arrangements without first bargaining to an impasse unless such action is permitted in the labor agreement, such as in the management rights clause.[69]

Legal Issues Involving Seniority in Administrative Determinations

Job rights guaranteed by the labor agreement may conflict with employees' legal rights. Use of seniority in administrative determinations such as promotions and layoffs has been the focus of much legal attention. In some cases it has been shown that minorities have been locked in departments or jobs with unfavorable lines of progression, and these practices tend to perpetuate past employment discrimination.[70] Congress specifically granted legal protection to bona fide seniority systems that were not enacted for the intentional purpose of discriminating on the basis of race, sex, and so forth even though the operation of such a seniority system might tend to perpetuate different treatment of some employees.[71] Appropriate remedies for an unlawful seniority plan can include the award of retroactive seniority to employees who were discriminated against.

Although the Supreme Court encourages voluntary affirmative action plans, it upheld the right of white employees to challenge promotions made under a court-approved affirmative action consent decree when the white employees did not participate in the negotiation of the plan.[72] The white employees sued their employer, claiming reverse racial discrimination, alleging that they had been denied promotions that had been awarded to less-qualified black employees under an affirmative action consent decree entered into by the employer and minority employees to settle the black employees' discrimination claim.

Merely because an affirmative action plan grants a preference to a certain class of employees (e.g., minorities) for the purpose of addressing past discrimination practices does not mean the plan is unlawful. The Supreme Court upheld a voluntary affirmative action plan negotiated between an employer and union intended to increase minority participation in a skilled-trade apprenticeship training program because the parties' intent in establishing the plan was lawful, the plan was designed to be of a limited duration, and it did not unnecessarily harm the interests of nonminority employees (i.e., no nonminority workers lost employment because of the plan and 50 percent of available training slots were filled by nonminority applicants).[73]

The Supreme Court has tended to view permissible affirmative action in employee layoffs somewhat differently because layoffs represent the loss of something an employee already has and a potentially permanent loss of income, thereby representing greater potential harm to adversely affected employees' interests. In one decision the Supreme Court indicated that in fashioning a remedy for past discriminatory practices a court can only award "competitive" seniority (more days of service than they have actually worked) to individuals who were the actual victims of a discriminatory practice.[74] The Supreme Court has also limited the use of racial preferences in layoff procedures intended to protect minority employees, even though the procedure is part of a negotiated labor agreement.[75] To ensure minority teachers' availability to serve as role models for minority students, a board of education and a teachers union agreed that the order in which employees were laid off would be determined based on seniority, except that at no time would the percentage of minority personnel fall below the current percentage of minority students enrolled. In practice, the layoff procedure resulted in more senior nonminority personnel being laid off while less senior minority personnel were retained. The Court recognized that the labor agreement provision represented an affirmative action effort. However, the provision could not be enforced because the presence of generalized societal discrimination is not a sufficiently compelling reason, absent evidence of specific discriminatory practices by the board of education or union, to warrant a special remedy such as racial preferences in layoffs. The Court noted that the same affirmative action goal could be accomplished without adversely impacting current employees' interests by establishing future minority hiring goals and time tables.

Accommodating seniority and affirmative action interests presents difficult dilemmas for both employers and unions. Assuming that employers have increased the hiring of women and minorities in recent years, the firm's seniority list would consist of more nonminority and male employees toward the top and a greater proportion of minorities and women toward the bottom. If an employer was forced to lay off employees, it would impact minority and female employees more severely under a typical "last-hired, first-fired" seniority provision. In those cases where plant, department, or job line-of-progression seniority is used, a layoff could erase much of the employer's progress in its minority- and female-hiring affirmative action plan. An employer who fails to explain to an individual the reason for his or her layoff may increase the probability that the employee may challenge the layoff decision, alleging some form of discrimination as its basis.[76] This issue represents an area of labor relations that afford both labor and management opportunities for a cooperative, mutual gain approach to resolving related issues in a fair and nondiscriminatory manner.

Employee Training

America's continued competitiveness in a global economy depends on how well our human resources are developed and managed. Many jobs in the future will require workers with higher levels of verbal, mathematical, organizational, and interpersonal skills. In 1964 less than 58 percent of U.S. workers had completed a high school education and less than 12 percent possessed a college degree.[77] By the year 2000, over 90 percent of U.S. workers had obtained a high school degree and 28 percent possessed a college degree, although the rate of increase in the percentage of workers attaining higher education levels has slowed in recent years.

Despite an increase in the education and training level of American workers, an estimated 20 percent of the U.S. population still reads at or below a fifth-grade level.[78] The American Management Association reported that 36 percent of job applicants lacked the basic math and reading skills to perform the jobs for which they applied.[79] This places critical importance on the issue of employee training and retraining to ensure future competitiveness.

Training can occur in formal, structured programs, such as apprenticeship training, new employee orientation, safety and health, basic skills (e.g., reading, math, and computer) or job-specific skills training. Training can also occur on a more informal basis, such as on-the-job training or mentoring by a more experienced employee. The availability of formal training programs has been shown to be positively correlated with larger-size firms, the use of so-called high-performance work practices (e.g., total quality management, work teams), use of more capital-intensive technologies, and workers' possessing higher levels of education.[80] Employees working in firms with a high turnover rate are less likely to receive training than those employed at firms with medium or low employee turnover.[81] Because union members tend to remain with the same employer for longer time periods than nonunion employees, over time union members have the ability to acquire more training related to firm-specific job tasks and technologies, which can enhance productivity.

Most firms offer one or more types of formal training; however, the specific types of training and amount of training provided vary by industry.[82] The most common types of formal programs provided focus training on employee orientation, safety and health, job skills, and workplace practices. The most common job skills taught are sales and customer relations, management skills, and computer skills. Although there is little difference in the total hours of formal training provided per employee between union and nonunion firms, unionized firms provide a greater percentage of training hours through formal, structured programs (36 percent) compared with nonunion firms (28 percent).[83] Greater employer willingness to invest in formal training programs in unionized firms may reflect the longer tenure of unionized employees with the same firm (43 percent have 10 or more years compared with 23 percent of nonunion employees with the same length of tenure), making the training investment more cost effective.

U.S. employers now recognize that they are facing a training dilemma because advances in technology and global competition require a more highly skilled workforce. With the exception of the building trade unions that have long been providers of apprenticeship training, U.S. unions have traditionally left training activities to management. Recently, unions have begun to take a more active role in response to increased interest from management in implementing new work practices such as continuous improvement in quality, productivity, and customer service. A survey of labor agreements scheduled to expire between 1997 and 2007 reported 154 (15 percent) contracts covering 854,803 workers contained language concerning high-performance work practices.[84] Ensuring that workers receive adequate training to meet current skills requirements and develop necessary future skills is important to unions seeking future economic gains and job security based on productivity enhancement.

For example, the UAW has joined Ford, GM, and DaimlerChrysler in developing an impressive set of programs for employees to upgrade their skills and further their education in personal and work-related matters. One program is the Paid Education Leave Program, which provides leadership training to both production and managerial employees to equip them to take an active role in the economic transformation occurring in the automobile industry.[85] Four unions— UAW, United Steelworkers of America, Communications Workers of America (CWA), and UNITE—in conjunction with the AFL-CIO's George Meany Center for Labor Studies and the U.S. Department of Labor, have organized the Labor Leadership Institute designed to develop skills for co-management within these respective industries. In San Francisco, the Hotel Employees and Restaurant Employees Union negotiated an agreement with 12 hotels to create a $3 million training program directed toward employee empowerment, consensus decision making, and skill development in new technologies.

Another effort to connect training with labor–management cooperation is the Bell South–CWA PARTNERSHIP program. In 1984, Bell South made a strategic corporate decision to cooperate with the CWA to have a more competitive and flexible workforce. It was determined that employees would need to take responsibility for developing and maintaining their skills to keep pace with changing job requirements, and they would have to master new jobs if their former jobs were eliminated. The mission of the PARTNERSHIP program is to prepare employees to take responsibility for their own career development and to provide them with the essential tools to accomplish their goals.[86]

Work Restructuring

Unions and companies are changing the nature of the work performed by employees.[87] **Work restructuring** programs have many different labels, such as employee involvement, worker participation, cross-training, multiskilling, or self-managed work teams; they all involve major departures from the traditional way of assigning specific tasks to each employee. For example, a work team may include 5 to 12 multiskilled workers who rotate jobs and produce an entire product with a minimal amount of supervision. The team approach wipes out tiers of managers and tears down bureaucratic barriers between departments. It requires employees to improve their technical and behavioral skills. Some work teams not only gain a more direct voice in shop floor operations but also take over some managerial duties, such as scheduling work and vacations, hiring new members, and ordering materials. These programs have unleashed enormous energy and creativity in employees and increased their feelings of dignity and self-worth and have enjoyed successes in such companies as General Electric, Champion International, Lucent Technologies, and Harley Davidson Motor Company.

A study by the U.S. Department of Labor and Ernst & Young found that American companies have discovered that investing in employees and innovative workplace strategies pays off in profits.[88] Innovative work practices are most effective when implemented in conjunction with employee training and empowerment programs. The study found that those companies that adopted aggressive employee development and involvement practices, such as skill training and team-based management, made significantly larger productivity gains than those that did not.

Despite the advantages of adopting innovative workplace strategies, one survey reports that 35 percent of responding plant-level managers indicated employee empowerment or self-directed work teams had not been implemented at their firms and two-thirds of respondents who did confirm the use of such practices indicated they affected 25 percent or less of the firm's employees.[89] While innovative work practices may have a positive affect on firm performance, the exact magnitude of that effect and the ability to sustain performance gains over time have yet to be clearly demonstrated.[90] One recent study reported that the adoption of many high-performance work practices actually resulted in greater wage inequality among employees within the firm over time.[91] There appears to be a gap between what some firms say about the importance of training and employee involvement and the commitment to expend scarce corporate resources and time to implement such practices.

One of the major efforts in work restructuring, particularly in the metals industry, has been the development of cell manufacturing. The need to improve product quality has driven companies to realize that using traditional functional layouts of similar machinery for batch manufacturing is costly and obsolete. Cell manufacturing involves placing groups of dissimilar machinery in a small, cell-like configuration dedicated to machining a particular part or family of parts. Cell manufacturing requires highly skilled employees who are generally more satisfied with their jobs because their tasks are varied and their authority is enhanced. Cell manufacturing is usually introduced with just-in-time (JIT) inventory control and employee involvement (EI) programs. In cell manufacturing, employees are trained to perform new tasks, assume more responsibility, relinquish old habits and ideas, and become more involved in decision making through participation in work teams. Cell manufacturing is not an antiunion device, and unions around the United States are actively involved in these innovative efforts to make their companies more competitive. A union's involvement and cooperation in these efforts serve to reduce employee resistance to changing to cell manufacturing.[92]

Safety and Health

Occupational safety and health clauses were found in 58 percent of labor agreements covering 1,000 or more employees scheduled to expire between August 1997 and July 2007.[93] The topics covered range from a pledge of cooperation on safety and health issues (64 percent) to the establishment of a joint local labor–management safety and health committee (50 percent), provision for protective clothing (41 percent), safety rules (36 percent), reporting of safety and health needs (31 percent), first aid and medical facilities (24 percent), the use of a separate grievance procedure for safety and health disputes (23 percent), joint labor–management involvement in conducting ergonomic evaluations and studies (23 percent), procedures for refusing to perform hazardous work (22 percent), and joint labor–management committee review of hazardous communication programs (22 percent). Many of these provisions have resulted from safety and health standards formulated under the **Occupational Safety and Health Act**

(OSHA) passed in 1970; the emergence of new biological, ergonomic, and chemical hazards in the workplace (e.g., AIDS, cumulative trauma); rising health-care treatment costs and greater awareness of the benefits of preventive health care; and an increase in legal claims filed by employees and attorneys related to occupational injury and disease.

The employer's overriding duty under OSHA is to furnish each employee with a work environment free from recognized hazards that may cause illness, injury, or death and to comply with all occupational safety and health standards adopted by the Department of Labor. In 2003, the Occupational Safety and Health Administration (an agency within the U.S. Department of Labor responsible for administering the OSH Act) had an operating budget of approximately $450 million and 1,123 inspectors to cover 111 million employees at 7 million work sites.[94] In 2002, OSH administration conducted 37,942 work site inspections finding 78,433 violations and resulting in penalties totaling $72.8 million. In addition, 26 states delegated authority by the federal OSH administration to operate their own safety and health programs in lieu of direct federal agency oversight conducted an additional 58,402 inspections finding 144,075 violations resulting in penalties of $75.9 million. Two-thirds of federal and state safety and health inspections are targeted at the construction and manufacturing industries, which historically experience a higher rate of job-related injuries and illnesses. The OSH administration works with both employers and labor organizations to improve awareness of and compliance with guidelines and work practices designed to improve the safety and health of employees.

In 2002, 4.7 million private-sector nonfatal injuries and illnesses were reported, or 5.3 cases per 100 full-time employees.[95] Due to revised reporting requirements effective January 1, 2002, the current data gathered from the *Survey of Occupational Injuries and Illnesses* is no longer comparable to data gathered during prior survey years. Approximately 2.5 million cases (2.8 cases per 100 full-time employees) required an employee to miss work days, transfer to a different job, or have restrictions placed on the work duties he or she could perform. Mid-sized firms (50–249 employees) recorded more cases than small or large firms, and the services, wholesale, and retail trade industries accounted for 54.3 percent of all injuries and illnesses reported due in part to the large total number of individuals employed in these two industries.

In 2002, 5,524 private sector fatal work injuries were reported, a decline of 6.6 percent from 2001.[96] Transportation incidents (e.g., vehicle collisions) accounted for 43 percent of fatalities. The number of incidents recorded in each event category (e.g., transportation incidents, assaults and violent acts, falls) declined in 2002 with the exception of fatalities associated with exposure to harmful substances or environments, which increased 8 percent from the prior year but accounted for only 10 percent of total fatalities.

A study by the Congressional Office of Technology Assessment (OTA) revealed that OSHA has generally performed its regulatory tasks with "workable accuracy" and that actual employer costs of compliance with OSHA standards were often less than the agency's initial estimates.[97] One reason for the lower than expected costs was employers' retooling and modernization efforts to meet OSHA standards. OTA reported, for example, that the costs of complying with OSHA's vinyl chloride standard was 25 percent less than initially estimated, and compliance with the cotton dust standard was 33 percent less than OSHA's estimate.

Employers must permit inspectors to enter their establishments and conduct inspections (although the employer may require the inspector to obtain a search warrant) and must post notices, provide equipment, and maintain records in accordance with OSH administration's rules and regulations.[98] Employees have a right to refuse to perform work that they believe represents a serious threat to their safety or health.[99]

OSHA applies some safety and health standards across all industries, while additional standards may be required for specific industries.[100] For example, employers are required to grant employees (or their designated union representative) access to the employee's medical records maintained by the employer or any records concerning the employee's exposure to toxic substances. As a general rule, OSHA does not require employers to measure employees' exposure to toxic substances or to conduct medical surveillance of employees to detect the effects of such exposure, but only to grant employees access to such information if such records are kept by the employer.

A second standard requires an employer to provide necessary personal protective equipment at no cost to the employee. This might include items such as protective helmets, eye and hearing protection, hard-toed shoes, or special goggles for welders. The hazard communications standard requires employers who manufacture or use materials to label all hazardous material containers, include a material safety sheet to inform customers about the nature and proper use of the hazardous materials, and train their employees to recognize and properly handle or avoid hazardous materials in the workplace. A fourth standard requires employers (except in certain low-hazard industries such as retail, insurance, and finance) to maintain an injury/illness log to record the occurrence of other than minor job-related injuries or illnesses and their causes—for example, injuries or illnesses that require more medical treatment than simple first aid or involve loss of consciousness, lost work time, or transfer to another job.

Another controversial safety and health-related issue was decided by the Supreme Court when it ruled that companies could not bar women from jobs that may be hazardous to unborn children.[101] The Court explained that decisions about the welfare of future children must be left to the parents. Unions and women's groups had challenged the policy of Johnson Controls, Inc., an automobile battery manufacturer, which banned women who could not prove they were infertile from working in areas of the plant where they were exposed to lead, the principal material used in making batteries. The challengers successfully argued that the company policy discriminated against female employees because they were blocked from being considered for higher-paying jobs. To reduce the possibility of potential employer liability, employers were advised to fully inform employees of any potential health or safety risks involved in the performance of a particular job.

The Johnson Controls (1991) decision, which permits the employee to decide if she is willing to risk exposure to potential hazards on the job, appears to be at odds with the recent Supreme Court decision in *Chevron U.S.A. Inc. v. Echazabal* (2002), in which the Court ruled that an employer cannot be required to make a reasonable accommodation to enable the hiring of a disabled person under the Americans with Disabilities Act if the job tasks could be hazardous to the disabled person.[102] The job applicant had a liver condition that the employer argued would pose a direct health threat to the job applicant because of chemicals present in its oil refinery, even though the applicant had been employed by an independent contractor at the oil refinery previously. The Court stated that were an employer to hire a disabled person who knowingly consented to the particular hazards of the job, the employer might run afoul of the OSHA mandate to ensure the safety of every worker.

Cumulative trauma disorders such as repetitive motion injuries, carpal tunnel syndrome, or noise-induced hearing loss accounted for 65 percent of the 392,000 new occupational illness cases reported in 1998.[103] The Bush administration has implemented changes in the reporting of job-related illness data so that it is no longer possible to track the occurrence of specific types of illness cases such as cumulative trauma disorders.[104] The OSH administration has issued voluntary guidelines to provide a flexible means to help employers identify and control ergonomic hazards in the workplace.[105] The OSH administration also decided it would not hold employers liable for OSHA standards regarding the estimated 20 million telecommuters who currently perform their jobs at home. However, OSHA does intend to enforce standards regarding manufacturing tasks that are performed in the home (e.g., manufacturing electronic components, lead fishing lures, clothing).[106]

Americans with Disabilities Act

The **Americans with Disabilities Act (ADA)** of 1990, which covers an estimated 43 million Americans, went into effect in January 1992. Considered a "Bill of Rights" for Americans with a wide variety of disabilities, the act applies to employment, public accommodations, transportation, and telecommunications. In the United States, approximately 17 percent of the population has a disability and two-thirds of disabled persons are unemployed, even though most indicate that they would prefer to be employed.[107] Labor force participation rates have increased for the moderately disabled (81.6 percent) but remain low (29.5 percent) for persons with severe disabilities.[108] In 2002, 22,768 discrimination claims were filed under the ADA, representing 18.9 percent of all types of discrimination claims filed with the Equal Employment Opportunity Commission.[109]

Passage of ADA has made job restructuring to meet the "reasonable accommodation" requirements a challenge to companies, as well as to the unions. A **person with disabilities** is broadly defined as (1) a person with a physical or mental impairment that substantially limits that person in some major life activity, (2) a person with a record of such a physical or mental impairment, or (3) a person who is regarded as having such impairment. Considerable controversy has occurred over the meaning and application of the term *disabled person*.[110] The U.S. Supreme Court has clarified this controversy to some extent by ruling that persons with impairments that are correctable are not disabled within the meaning of the Act.[111] For example, a vision impairment correctable through wearing eyeglasses or high blood pressure correctable through medication is not considered disabling.

Because most labor agreements do not include provisions on the initial selection of employees, ADA compliance in the hiring process is essentially the employer's obligation. However, employment decisions after initial hire, such as promotions, transfers, layoffs, and recalls, are addressed in most labor agreements and come under the employment provisions of ADA. Under ADA provisions, an employer must make **reasonable accommodation** for a person with a disability if that accommodation will allow the person to perform the "essential functions of the job." Thus, if an employer can make a modification in a job's requirements or structure that will not cause the employer "undue hardship" and that will allow a disabled employee to do the job, then that modification or change in the job must be made.

The Supreme Court has ruled that an accommodation requested by a disabled individual (e.g., assignment to a particular job) will not ordinarily be considered a "reasonable accommodation" under the ADA if such an assignment would conflict with the seniority rights of other employees.[112] A union has a legal duty to fairly represent both disabled and nondisabled members of a bargaining unit. Some national unions have prepared training manuals to aid local union representatives in anticipating and addressing ADA issues arising under a collective bargaining agreement.[113]

Job performance and other disciplinary problems relating to employee alcoholism or substance abuse are treated in a straightforward manner under ADA; that is, employers are not required to tolerate performance and disciplinary problems. Individuals who are currently using illegal drugs are excluded from coverage under ADA, although the following individuals would be protected under the act: (1) a person who has successfully completed a drug rehabilitation program or who has otherwise been rehabilitated and is no longer illegally using drugs, (2) a person who is currently participating in a rehabilitation program and is no longer illegally using drugs, and (3) a person who is erroneously regarded as illegally using drugs.[114]

An employer's responsibility toward employees impaired by alcohol or drugs primarily extends to accommodating treatment and recovery but not to accommodating diminished job performance or employee misconduct. The initiative for accommodation must come from the employee, not the employer. The employer's obligation in a unionized setting is significantly greater than in a nonunionized setting as a result of an established body of arbitration decisions going back many years. Not only must the employer comply with ADA, but labor arbitrators will consider mitigating circumstances in the case of long-term employees or when performance and disciplinary problems may have been caused by alcoholism or drug addiction.[115]

Although the ADA encourages the use of alternative dispute resolution procedures, such as mediation and arbitration, to resolve ADA claims without resort to court action, employees covered under both ADA and a collective bargaining agreement containing a broad nondiscrimination clause may have the opportunity to file a contractual grievance, as well as pursue a discrimination claim under the ADA. A denial of an employee's grievance claim arising under a collective bargaining agreement does not preclude the employee from subsequently pursuing a similar discrimination claim under the ADA.[116] The Supreme Court has applied a similar principle in a nonunion context, finding that the Equal Employment Opportunity Commission (EEOC) has a right to file a disability discrimination suit against a nonunion employer seeking employee-specific remedies (e.g., reinstatement and backpay) for proven violations of the ADA even though all employees were required to sign an agreement to submit all employment related disputes to final and binding arbitration.[117]

SUMMARY

This chapter has explored six general categories of administrative issues—technological changes, job security and personnel changes, employee training, work restructuring, safety and health, and accommodating employees with disabilities. Each of these areas has many important facets that may be negotiated and become part of a labor agreement.

Technological change, an essential ingredient of a dynamic economic system, is broadly defined to include such activities as introduction of labor-saving machines, power-driven tools, and automatic loading equipment. Although unions generally accept technological change as inevitable with both positive and negative impacts on bargaining unit members' interests, they attempt to negotiate contract language that will protect members' present jobs, ensure appropriate compensation for work performed, and establish the means for ensuring future protection of members' interests.

Job security and personnel changes are two interrelated issues that raise challenges for both labor and management. Unions often seek to protect their members by negotiating workload restrictions, limiting management's right to subcontract or outsource bargaining-unit work, demanding specific work assignments and jurisdiction, or structuring jobs and work schedules to benefit employees. When personnel changes occur, seniority may become a key decision criterion. Likewise, where firms are growing and opportunities for advancement are present, seniority and merit are key considerations. Employers and unions must consider EEOC regulations and court rulings in addition to the contractual language contained in a labor agreement when deciding personnel changes.

Employee training has taken on increasing importance in maintaining competitiveness in today's global economy. Unions and employers alike expend much effort in providing training programs to match employees' skills with the requirements of work restructuring. Work restructuring efforts are often initiated by management, but union cooperation is essential to the complete success of such programs. Although some unions are reluctant to become involved with them, major breakthroughs have been identified in some unions, such as the United Auto Workers and Machinists.

Safety and health issues have become more important since the passage of the Occupational Safety and Health Act of 1970. Recent improvement in decreasing the frequency of workplace accidents and illnesses can be attributed in part to a greater awareness of the economic benefits of hazard prevention; better cooperation between government, employers, and unions regarding approaches to improve workers' safety and health; and the presence of safety standards provided by federal and state laws.

The chapter concludes with a section on accommodating the Americans with Disabilities Act. The significance of the problems faced by disabled Americans and the potential benefits of addressing their problems by making reasonable work accommodations are addressed.

KEY TERMS

- technological change
- automation
- high performance work
  - organization (HPWO)
- deskilling
- job security
- featherbedding
- Worker Adjustment and Retraining
  - Notification Act (WARN)
- subcontracting
- outsourcing
- work relocation
- jurisdictional dispute

- flextime
- seniority
- benefit rights
- competitive job rights
- superseniority
- bumping rights
- work sharing
- work restructuring
- Occupational and Safety Health Act (OSHA)
- Americans with Disabilities Act (ADA)
- person with disabilities
- reasonable accommodation

DISCUSSION QUESTIONS

1. Why do unions' reactions to technological change vary in accordance with their industry affiliation?

2. Think of an industry or company with which you are familiar, and assume that you are the local union president. What types of clauses regarding technological issues would you attempt to negotiate with your employer?

3. Discuss some of the advantages or disadvantages in using seniority as a factor to determine shift preference or overtime assignments?

4. Explain why unions often place a priority on seniority in personnel decisions, whereas employers tend to emphasize ability to perform the job.

5. Who has the responsibility of ensuring a safe and healthy work environment? Should it be the employer, union, employees, or government?

6. To what extent are labor laws, such as those discussed in this chapter, still necessary today? What changes might occur if such laws were repealed?

7. Consider an organization with which you are familiar. What are some actions that could be taken on various jobs to reasonably accommodate an employee with a disability without causing undue hardship to the employer or unreasonably infringing on the collective bargaining rights of other bargaining-unit members?

EXPLORING THE WEB

Administrative Issues

1. WARN   What is the WARN Act and when was it enacted? Under what circumstances is an employer not required to give notice of a plant closing? Where in the Code of Regulations may the regulations resulting from the Act be found? Use the Web site of the U.S. Department of Labor to answer these questions.

http://www.dol.gov

2. Safety and Health   Summarize the opinion from the Supreme Court case in 1991 involving Johnson Controls, Inc., United Automobile Workers, and other unions (499 U.S. 187). What was the effect of the opinion on women in the workplace?

http://www.findlaw.com

Use the pull-down menu to search for Supreme Court cases and use *Johnson Controls* as a Party Name Search.

3. Electronic Monitoring   Following is a sampling of Web pages that offer publications on videotaping and use of electronic e-mail and communications as a way to monitor employees' activity in the workplace.

Go to the Web site of Morgan Lewis Counselors at Law and search for the following two articles:

Bovino, Scott C. (December 14, 2001). *Privacy: Protecting Your Clients and Their Customers, Workplace Monitoring and Security.*

Dichter, Mark S., and Michael S. Burkhardt (June 1999). *Electronic Interaction in the Workplace: Monitoring, Retrieving and Storing Employee Communications in the Internet Age.*

http://www.morganlewis.com

American Civil Liberties Union Freedom Network. Introduction to Electronic Monitoring in the Workplace.

http://www.aclu.org/issues/worker/legkit2.html

American Management Association Survey on Electronic Monitoring and Surveillance Based on the AMA survey of 2001. What percentage of companies surveyed used some type of workspace monitoring to prevent theft, violence, or sabotage?

http://www.amanet.org/research/pdfs/emsfu_short.pdf

4. Collective Bargaining, Labor Relations, Unions, and the ADA   See a list of publications provided by the Program on Employment and Disability at Cornell's School of Industrial and Labor Relations.

http://www.ilr.cornell.edu/ped

REFERENCES

1. Julius Rezler, *Automation and Industrial Labor* (New York: Random House, 1969), pp. 5–6.

2. Daniel B. Cornfield, "Labor Union Responses to Technological Change: Past, Present, and Future," *Perspectives on Work* 1 (April 1997), pp. 35–38; and Robert J. Thomas, "Technological Choice and Union-Management Cooperation," *Industrial Relations* 30 (Spring 1991), pp. 189–190.

3. Editors of Collective Bargaining Negotiations and Contracts, *Basic Patterns in Union Contracts,* 14th ed. (Washington, D.C.: Bureau of National Affairs, 1995), p. 81.

4. Joel Cutcher-Gershenfeld, Thomas A. Kochan, and John C. Wells, "How Do Labor and Management View Collective Bargaining," *Monthly Labor Review* 121 (October 1998), pp. 26–27.

5. Steven E. Abraham and Bart D. Finzel, "New Technology in Unionized Firms: Advantages of Mandatory Bargaining," *Employee Responsibilities and Rights Journal* 10 (March 1997), pp. 37–48.

6. Bart D. Finzel and Steven E. Abraham, "Bargaining over New Technology: Possible Effects of Removing Legal Constraints," *Journal of Economic Issues* 30 (September 1996), pp. 777–795.

7. John T. Delaney, "Workplace Cooperation: Current Problems, New Approaches," *Journal of Labor Research* 17 (Winter 1996), pp. 45–61.

8. John Lund, "Computerized Work Performance Monitoring and Production Standards: A Review of Labor Law Issues," *Labor Law Journal* (April 1991), pp. 195–203.

9. Miriam Szapiro, "National Union Supports for New Work Systems and Technological Change," *Labor Studies Journal* 21 (Summer 1996), pp. 73–95.

10. Richard M. Cyert and David C. Mowery, eds., *Technology and Employment: Innovations and Growth in the U.S. Economy* (Washington, D.C.: National Academy Press, 1987), pp. 129–133.

11. Maury Gittleman, Michael Horrigan, and Mary Joyce, "Flexible Workplace Practices: Evidence from a Nationally Representative Survey," *Industrial and Labor Relations Review* 52 (October 1998), pp. 99–115.

12. Mark Kizilos and Yonatan Reshef, "The Effects of Workplace Unionization on Worker Responses to HRM Innovation," *Journal of Labor Research* 18 (Fall 1997), pp. 641–656; Jeffrey H. Keefe, "Do Unions Hinder Technological Change?" in *Unions and Economic Competitiveness*, eds. Lawrence Mishel and Paula B. Voss (Armonk, N.Y.: M. E. Sharpe, 1992), pp. 109–110.

13. *Collective Bargaining Negotiations and Contracts* (Washington, D.C.: Bureau of National Affairs, 1992), p. 65:3.

14. Sherie Winston, "Ironworkers and Their President Are Polishing Up Performance," *ENR*, September 1, 2003, p. 1, at http://enr.construction.com/features/bizlabor/archives/030901.asp.

15. Richard M. Cyert and David C. Mowery, eds., *Technology and Employment: Innovation and Growth in the U.S. Economy* (Washington, D.C.: National Academy Press, 1987), p. 133.

16. American Management Association, *2003 E-Mail Rules, Policies and Practices Survey* (New York: AMA, 2003), pp. 1–8.

17. Robert H. Moorman and Deborah Wells, "Can Electronic Performance Monitoring Be Fair? Exploring Relationships Among Monitoring Characteristics, Perceived Fairness, and Job Performance," *Journal of Leadership & Organizational Studies* 10 (Fall 2003), p. 2

18. Keefe, "Do Unions Hinder Technological Change?" pp. 109–111.

19. Elise M. Bloom, Madeleine Schachter, and Elliot H. Steelman, "Justice in a Changed World: Competing Interests in the Post 9-11 Workplace: The New Line Between Privacy and Safety," 29 *William Mitchell Law Review* 897 (2003); Jitendra M. Mishra and Suzanne M. Crampton, "Employee Monitoring: Privacy in the Workplace?" *S.A.M. Advanced Management Journal* 63 (1998), pp. 4–14; Gary Anton and Joseph J. Ward, "Every Breath You Take: Employee Privacy Rights in the Workplace—An Orwellian Prophecy Come True?" *Labor Law Journal* 49 (March 1998), pp. 897–911.

20. U.S. Department of Labor, Bureau of Labor Statistics, "Tomorrow's Jobs," *Occupational Outlook Handbook, 2002–03 edition*, Bulletin 2540, 2003, pp. 1–7, at http://stats.bls.gov/oco/print/oco2003.htm.

21. Daniel E. Hecker, "Occupational Employment Projections to 2010," *Monthly Labor Review* 124 (November 2001), pp. 62–80.

22. Summer H. Slichter, James J. Healy, and E. Robert Livernash, *The Impact of Collective Bargaining on Management* (Washington, D.C.: Brookings Institute, 1960), pp. 317–335.

23. Robert D. Leiter, *Featherbedding and Job Security* (New York: Twayne Publishers, 1964), pp. 32–33.

24. Benjamin Aaron, "Government Restraint on Featherbedding," *Stanford Law Review* 5 (July 1953), pp. 687–721.

25. William Gomberg, "The Work Rules and Work Practices," *Labor Law Journal* 12 (July 1961), pp. 643–653.

26. Peter Lazes and Jane Savage, "A Union Strategy for Saving Jobs and Enhancing Workplace Democracy," *Labor Studies Journal* 21 (Summer 1996), pp. 96–121.

27. *NLRB* v. *International Longshoremen's Association*, 473 U.S. 61 (1985).

28. *The Worker Adjustment and Retraining Notification Act*, 29 U.S.C. 2101, et seq. (1988).

29. Parisis G. Gilippatos and Sean Farhang, "The Rights of Employees Subjected to Reductions in Force: A Critical Evaluation," *Employee Rights and Employment Policy Journal* 6 (2002), pp. 324–326; John T. Addison and McKinley L. Blackburn, "A Puzzling Aspect of the Effect of Advance Notice on Unemployment," *Industrial and Labor Relations Review* 50 (January 1997), pp. 268–288; John T. Addison and Jean-Luc Grosso, "Job Security Provisions and Employment Revised Estimates," *Industrial Relations* 35 (October 1996), pp. 585–603.

30. Bureau of Labor Statistics, "Table 3: Displaced Workers by Whether They Received Written Advance Notice, Reason for Job Loss, and Employment," *News Release*, August 19, 1998.

31. "2003 Employer Bargaining Objectives," *Collective Bargaining Bulletin* 8 (January 23, 2003), p. s-6.

32. John T. Addison and McKinley L. Blackburn, "The Worker Adjustment and Retraining Notification Act: Effects on Notice Provisions," *Industrial & Labor Relations Review* 47 (July 1994), pp. 660–661.

33. U.S. Department of Labor, *Fact Sheet: The Worker Adjustment and Retraining Notification Act*, 2004, pp. 1–5 at http://www.doleta.gov/programs/factsht/warn.htm.

34. *United Food and Commercial Workers Union, Local 751 v. Brown Group, Inc.*, 517 U.S. 544 (1996); *North Star Steel Co. v. Thomas*, 515 U.S. 29 (1995).

35. *Times Herald Printing Company d/b/a Dallas Times Herald and Dallas Mailers Union, No. 20 affiliated with Communications Workers of America and Dallas Typographical Union, No. 173 affiliated with the Communications Workers of America*, 315 NLRB 700 (1994).

36. Christian Zlolniski, "Labor Control and Resistance of Mexican Immigrant Janitors in Silicon Valley," *Human Organizations* 62 (Spring 2003), pp. 39–49; Kenneth L. Deavers, "Outsourcing: A Corporate Competitiveness Strategy, Not a Search for Low Wages," *Journal of Labor Research* 18 (Fall 1997), 503–519; and Murem Sharpe, "Outsourcing, Organizational Competitiveness, and Work," *Journal of Labor Research* 18 (Fall 1997), pp. 535–549.

37. Pamela Gordon, "Consumer, Auto Industries Surf Outsourcing Wave," *Circuits Asseblmy* 12 (March 2001), p. S2.

38. Dean Elmuti, "The Perceived Impact of Outsourcing on Organizational Performance," *Mid-American Journal of Business* 18 (Fall 2003), p. 33.

39. Daniel Howes, "GM Sees Leaner Plants: Tough UAW Choice: Fight Automakers on Job Cuts or Work with Them to Organize Suppliers," *Detroit News*, January 8, 1999, p. B-1; Dave Phillips, "Workplace Change: New Approaches Threaten Big Labor; Assembly, Supply Strategies Reinvent Workforce," *Detroit News*, December 21, 1998, p. F-12.

40. Charles R. Perry, "Outsourcing and Union Power," *Journal of Labor Research* 18 (Fall 1997), pp. 521–533; Justin Hyde, "GM Applies Lessons to New Factory," *Associated Press*, January 31, 2000, pp. 1–3; Daniel Howes, "Leaner, Diversified Carmaker Likely to Emerge after Strikes: Wall Street Analysts Say Walkouts Increase the Pressure to Restructure," *Detroit News*, July 26, 1998, p. A-3; David L. Littmann and William T. Wilson, "Neither GM nor UAW Can Afford to Mark Time," *Detroit News*, June 17, 1998, p. A-13.

41. "Makers, Unions Must Prepare for New Workplace," *Automotive News*, January 20, 2003, p. 12; and Joann Muller, "Other People's Money," *Forbes* 170 (December 23, 2002), p. 66.

42. "Widgetless in Wichita," *The Economist*, October 14, 1995, p. 77.

43. Donald P. Crane and Michael Jay Jedel, "Mature Collective Bargaining Relationships," in *Arbitration 1988: Emerging Issues for the 1990s*, ed. Gladys W. Gruenberg (Washington, D.C.: Bureau of National Affairs, 1989), p. 358.

44. Marvin J. Levine, "Subcontracting and 'Privatization' of Work: Private and Public Sector Developments," *Journal of Collective Negotiations in the Public Sector* 19, no. 4 (1990), pp. 275–277.

45. Marlise McCammon and John L. Cotton, "Arbitration Decisions in Subcontracting Disputes," *Industrial Relations* 29 (Winter 1990), p. 142.

46. *Dubuque Packing Company, Inc., and UFCW, Local 150A (Dubuque IL)*, 303 NLRB 386 (1991); enforced, 1 F.3d 24 (DC Cir. 1993).

47. Roger S. Wolters and Stewart D. Langdon, "The Duty to Bargain over Business Decisions," *Labor Law Journal* 43 (September 1992), pp. 583–587.

48. Kenneth A. Jenero and Patrick W. Kocian, "The Relocation of Work Between Plants: A Planning Checklist of Statutory and Contractual Obligations," *Employee Relations Law Journal* 20 (Spring 1995), p. 622.

49. Leonard E. Cohen, "The Duty to Bargain over Plant Relocations and Other Corporate Changes: *Otis Elevator* v. *NLRB*," *The Labor Lawyer* 1 (Summer 1985), pp. 525–532.

50. James K. McCollum and Edward A. Schoreder IV, "NLRB Decisions in Jurisdictional Disputes: The Success of the 10(k) Process," *Employee Relations Law Journal* 13 (Spring 1988), pp. 649–652.

51. The Construction Users RoundTable & The Building & Construction Trades Department, AFL-CIO, "Construction Industry Leaders Form Tripartite Initiative: Owners, Contractors, Unions Establish Collaboration to Improve Industry," *Joint News Release*, January 18, 2003, p. 1; NLRB, *42nd Annual Report*, p. 113. This board uses two procedural rules that are worthy of note: (1) A request for a decision in a specific case does not have to wait until the dispute occurs. Once the contractor makes the initial work assignments, a request for a decision can be made. Thus, time is saved by facilitating the dispute-resolution process. (2) Decisions of the board are not precedent setting. This does not mean that similar decisions within an area are not based on patterns; it means that conditions vary from region to region, union to union, and even agreement to agreement. Therefore, the board is not bound completely by precedent, but past practice is a factor. Custom in the industry and skills, training, and job content are important elements that are considered.

53. Elvis C. Stephens, "A Supervisor Performs Bargaining-Unit Work: Is the Contract Violated?" *Labor Law Journal* 31 (November 1980), pp. 683–688.

54. Slichter, Healy, and Livernash, *The Impact of Collective Bargaining*, pp. 266–276.

55. Hal Walls, "Flex and the Married Worker," *Industrial Engineer* 35 (September 2003), p. 24; Gillian Flynn, "The Legalities of Flextime," *Workforce* 80 (October 2001), pp. 62–66; and Jeffrey M. Miller, *Innovations in Working Patterns* (Washington, D.C.: Communications Workers of America and German Marshall Fund of the United States, 1978).

56. Frederic H. Harbison, *The Seniority Principle in Union-Management Relations* (Princeton, N.J.: Princeton University Industrial Relations Section, 1939), pp. 21–23.

57. Editors of Collective Bargaining Negotiations and Contracts, *Basic Patterns in Union Contracts*, p. 85.

58. Slichter, Healy, and Livernash, *Collective Bargaining*, pp. 104–105; D. Quinn Mills, "Seniority versus Ability in Promotion Decisions," *Industrial and Labor Relations Review* 38 (April 1985), pp. 424–425.

59. Andrew Sikula Sr., "The Five Biggest HRM Lies," *Public Personnel Management* 30 (Fall 2001), pp. 424–425.

60. Gangaram Singh and Frank Reid, "Are Seniority-Based Layoffs Discriminatory? The Adverse Impact of Layoffs on Designated Groups," *Relations Industrielles* 53 (Fall 1998), pp. 730–746.

61. Editors of Collective Bargaining Negotiations and Contracts, *Basic Patterns in Union Contracts*, pp. 85–87.

62. Roger I. Abrams and Dennis R. Nolan, "Seniority Rights Under the Collective Agreement," *The Labor Lawyer* 2 (Winter 1986), pp. 99–110.

63. William H. Holley, Jr., "Performance Ratings in Arbitration," *Arbitration Journal* 32 (March 1977), pp. 8–25.

64. Robert D. Gatewood and Hubert S. Field, *Human Resource Selection*, 5th ed. (Ft. Worth, Tex.: Harcourt, 2001), pp. 65–69.

65. Editors of Collective Bargaining Negotiations and Contracts, *Basic Patterns in Unions Contracts*, pp. 67–70.

66. "2003 Employer Bargaining Objectives," *Collective Bargaining Bulletin* 8 (January 23, 2003), p. S-26.

67. Mark Montgomery, "New Evidence on Unions and Layoff Rates," *Industrial and Labor Relations Review* 44 (July 1991), pp. 708–712.

68. "2003 Employer Bargaining Objectives," *Collective Bargaining Bulletin* 8 (January 23, 2003), p. S-26; and Mohamed Branine, "The Logic of Job-Sharing in the Provision of and Delivery of Health Care," *Health Manpower Management* 24 (1), 1998, p. 20.

69. Steven Briggs, "Allocating Available Work in a Union Environment: Layoffs vs. Work Sharing," *Labor Law Journal* 38 (October 1987), pp. 650–657.

70. *Franks v. Bowman Transportation Co.,* 424 U.S. 747 (1976).

71. *Teamsters v. United States,* 431 U.S. 324 (1977); *American Tobacco Co. v. Patterson,* 456 U.S. 63 (1982).

72. *Martin v. Wilks,* 490 U.S. 755 (1989).

73. *United Steelworkers of America v. Weber,* 443 U.S. 193 (1979).

74. *Firefighters, Local 1784 v. Stotts,* 467 U.S. 561 (1984).

75. *Wygant v. Jackson Board of Education,* 476 U.S. 267 (1986).

76. Scott David Williams, William M. Slonaker, and Ann C. Wendt, "An Analysis of Employment Discrimination Claims Associated with Layoffs," *S.A.M. Advanced Management Journal* 68 (Winter 2003), pp. 49–55.

77. Daniel Aaronson and Daniel Sullivan, "Growth in Workers Quality," *Chicago Fed Letter,* February 2002, p. 1.

78. U.S. Department of Labor, "Implications of Workplace Change," in *Futurework: Trends and Challenges in the 21st Century,* September 16, 1999, p. 3, at http://www.dol.gov.

79. Kirstin D. Grimsley, "Applicants Not Making the Grade," *Washington Post,* April 13, 1999, p. E1.

80. Lisa M. Lynch and Sandra E. Black, "Beyond the Incidence of Employer Provided Training," *Industrial and Labor Relations Review* 52 (October 1998), 64–81.

81. Harley Frazis, Maury Gittleman, Michael Horrigan, and Mary Joyce, "Results from the 1995 Survey of Employer Provided Training," Monthly Labor Review 121 (June 1998), p. 8.

82. Harley J. Frazis, Diane E. Herz, and Michael W. Horrigan, "Employer Provided Training: Results from a New Survey," *Monthly Labor Review* 118 (May 1995), pp. 3–17.

83. Frazis, Gittleman, Horrigan, and Joyce, "Results from the 1995 Survey of Employer Provided Training," p. 8.

84. George R. Gray, Donald W. Myers, and Phyllis S. Myers, "Cooperative Provisions in Labor Agreements: A New Paradigm?" *Monthly Labor Review* 122 (January 1999), pp. 29–45; Pat Costine and Thomas N. Garavan, "Trade Union Attitudes to Training and Development: The Road to a More Positive and Proactive Approach?" *Journal of European Industrial Training* 19, no. 10

(1995), p. 38; and John Hoerr, "What Should Unions Do?" Harvard Business Review 69 (May–June 1991), p. 42.

85. Henry P. Guzda, "Unions Active in Joint Training Programs," *American Workplace* (January 1995), pp. 1–4.

86. Dennis K. Allen, "Bell South–CWA Partnership: Teaming up to Meet the Challenges of a Changing Industry," *Employee Relations Today* (Summer 1994), p. 163.

87. Paul S. Adler, "Work Organization: From Taylorism to Teamwork," *Perspectives on Work* 1 (April 1997), pp. 61–65.

88. "News Release: U.S. Department of Labor and Ernst & Young LLP Study Finds Competitive Gains from Innovative Workplace Practices," May 31, 1995 (study conducted by Sarah C. Mavrinac, Neil R. Jones, and Marshall W. Mayer).

89. Patrick Herman, "The Untrained, Unempowered Masses," *Industry Week* 248 (December 6, 1999), pp. 94–96.

90. John Godard and John T. Delaney, "Reflections on the 'High Performance' Paradigm's Implications for Industrial Relations as a Field," *Industrial and Labor Relations Review* 53 (April 2000), pp. 491–493.

91. "Innovative Workplaces and Their Workers," *Monthly Labor Review* 126 (May 2003), p. 32.

92. Noel Harvey, "How Unions Should Respond to Cells," *Labor Studies Journal* 18 (Winter 1994), pp. 21–31.

93. George R. Gray, Donald W. Myers, and Phyllis S. Myers, "Collective Bargaining Agreements: Safety and Health Provisions," *Monthly Labor Review* 121 (May 1998), pp. 13–35.

94. U.S. Department of Labor, Occupational Safety & Health Administration, *OSHA Facts,* 2004, pp. 1–4, at http://www.osha.gov/as/opa/oshafacts.html.

95. Bureau of Labor Statistics, "Workplace Injuries and Illnesses in 2002," *News Release,* December 18, 2003, pp. 1–16.

96. Bureau of Labor Statistics, "National Census of Fatal Occupational Injuries in 2002," *News Release,* September 17, 2003, pp. 1–15.

97. "OSHA Rulemaking Process Credible but May Overstate Costs, OTA Says," *Daily Labor Report,* October 25, 1995, p. A-9.

98. *Marshall v. Barlow's Inc., 436 U.S. 307 (1978).*

99. *Whirlpool Corporation* v. *Marshall, 445 U.S. 1 (1980)*; Gateway Coal Co. v. United Mine Workers, *414 U.S. 368 (1974)*.

100. U.S. Department of Labor, Occupational Safety & Health Administration, "OSHA Requirements That Apply to Most General Industry," *OSHA Compliance Assistance Industry Quick Start,* 2004, pp. 1–2, at http://www.osha.gov/dcsp/compliance_assistance/quickstart/general_industry/gi_step2.html; and U.S. Department of Labor, Occupational Safety & Health Administration, "Job Safety and Health," *OSHA Fact Sheet,* 2002, pp. 1–2.

101. *United Automobile Workers Union (UAW)* v. *Johnson Controls,* Inc., 499 U.S. 187 (1991).

102. *Chevron U.S.A. Inc.* v. *Echazabal,* 536 U.S. 73 (2002). See also: Ronald Bayer, "Workers' Liberty, Workers' Welfare: The Supreme Court Speaks on the Rights of Disabled Employees," *American Journal of Public Health* 93 (April 2003), pp. 540–544; and Norman Daniels, "*Chevron v. Echazabal:* Protection, Opportunity, and Paternalism," *American Journal of Public Health* 93 (April 2003), pp. 545–548.

103. Bureau of Labor Statistics, "Workplace Injuries and Illnesses in 1998," *News Release,* December 16, 1999, p. 4.

104. Bureau of Labor Statistics, "Workplace Injuries and Illnesses in 2002," p. 3.

105. U.S. Department of Labor, Office of the 21st Century Workforce, "Target Ergonomics: Workplace Guidelines for Repetitive Motion Injuries," *XXI Magazine* (Fall 2002), pp. 8–13; and U.S. Department of Labor, Occupational Safety & Health Administration, "A Four-Pronged, Comprehensive Approach," *OSHA Effective Ergonomics: Strategy for Success,* July 9, 2003, pp. 1–2.

106. Frank Swoboda, "OSHA Exempts White-Collar Telecommuters," *Washington Post,* January 27, 2000, p. A1.

107. Gary F. Coulton and Roger Wolters, "Employee and Management Rights and Responsibilities under the Americans with Disabilities Act (ADA): An Overview," *Employee Responsibilities and Rights Journal* 6 (March 1993), pp. 55–56.

108. Thomas W. Hale, Howard V. Hayghe, and John M. McNeil, "Persons with Disabilities Labor Market Activity,

1994," *Monthly Labor Review* 121 (September 1998), pp. 3–12.

109. U.S. Equal Employment Opportunity Commission, *Charge Statistics FY 1992 Through FY 2002,* February 6, 2003, p. 1, at http://www.eeoc.gov/stats/charges.html.

110. Suzanne M. Crampton and John W. Hodge, "The ADA and Disability Accommodation," *Public Personnel Management* 32 (Spring 2003), pp. 143–154; Jeffrey A. Mello, "The Rights of Employees With Disabilities: Supreme Court Interpretations of the American With Disabilities Act and Their Implications for Human Resource Management," *Employee Responsibilities and Rights Journal* 13 (December 2001), pp. 175–189; and Lisa A. Schur, "But Is It Still a Disability? Judicial Views of Mitigating Measures Under the ADA," *Labor Law Journal* 50 (Summer 1999), pp. 146–155.

111. *Toyota Motor Manufacturing, Kentucky, Inc.* v. *Williams,* 534 U.S. 184 (2002); *Sutton et al.* v. *United Airlines Inc.,* 527 U.S. 471 (1999); *Murphy* v. *United Parcel Service, Inc.,* 527 U.S. 516 (1999); and *Albertson's Inc.* v. *Kirkingburg,* 527 U.S. 555 (1999).

112. *US Airways, Inc.* v. *Barnett,* 535 U.S. 391 (2002).

113. Paper, Allied Industrial, Chemical, and Energy Workers Union (PACE), *The Americans with Disabilities Act: Collective Bargaining and Other Issues,* 1998, pp. 1–12. See also: AFL-CIO, *Discrimination: Disability,* 2004, pp. 1–2, at http://www.aflcio.org/yourjobeconomy/rights/rightsatwork/disc_disability.cfm.

114. Jeffrey A. Mello, "Employing and Accommodating Workers with Disabilities: Mandates and Guidelines for Labor Relations," *Labor Law Journal* 44 (March 1993), pp. 162–170.

115. James W. Bucking, "Beyond the ADA: Protection of Employees with Drug and Alcohol Problems in Arbitration," *The Labor Lawyer* 11 (Winter–Spring 1995), pp. 1–5.

116. Coulton and Wolters, "Employee and Management Rights and Responsibilities," pp. 58–59.

117. *Equal Employment Opportunity Commission* v. *Waffle House, Inc.,* 534 U.S. 279 (2002).

ADA Claim for Reasonable Accommodation

Jack Hand was employed as a pipefitter's helper when he injured his back on the job. According to testimony from the neurosurgeon who treated Hand's injury, Hand was unable to lift over 10 pounds frequently or 20 pounds occasionally, could not sit or stand more than one hour without a break, and could not stoop, crawl, climb ladders, or perform overhead work. These work restrictions were considered permanent due to the degenerative condition of Hand's lumbar spine. Hand recognized that he could not perform the job he formally held at the time of his injury but did pursue other light-duty jobs (e.g., fire watch position or a job monitoring and checking for leaky pipes) at his employer's firm. After being repeatedly told that no light-duty jobs were currently vacant at the company, Hand quit and sued his employer for allegedly failing to provide him a reasonable accommodation under the ADA by refusing to assign him a "light-duty" job after his injury.

QUESTIONS

1. Does Hand meet the legal definition of a qualified individual with a disability who with a reasonable accommodation could perform the essential job functions of the light-duty position he seeks with the firm?

2. If an employer has some light-duty jobs in which individuals with injuries similar to Hand's have been previously or are currently employed, could the employer be required to create such a job vacancy for Hand to fill in order to provide him with a reasonable accommodation under the ADA?

The Outsourced Work

Rocket Motor Corporation (RMC) entered into a project labor agreement with 17 local building trades unions concerning a building remodeling project at one of the company's manufacturing plants. As part of the project labor agreement, the unions agreed not engage in any strikes, slowdowns, or other work stoppages and not to honor the picket lines established by any other labor organization at the job site. RMC agreed as part of the project labor agreement to hire contractors and subcontractors who would employ individuals to perform construction work for each specified type of trade represented by the 17 unions at terms and conditions of employment equal to the terms specified in any applicable union contract covering the type of construction work to be performed. The project labor agreement called for final and binding arbitration to resolve any disputes arising from the interpretation or application of the terms of the project labor agreement.

Bolton Engineering (BE) was one contractor hired by Rocket Motor Corporation to help remodel the company's paint facilities at the work site. As part of the contract entered into between RMC and BE, a pledge to adhere to the project labor agreement previously signed by RMC and the 17 unions was included. BE employed only a few supervisory employees of its own at the work site and relied upon unionized subcontractors to complete most of the assigned job site tasks. However, a significant portion of the metal fabrication work was subcontracted to two nonunion subcontractors whose employees performed the work off site. All of the metal fabricated parts built off site were eventually to be installed on the job site by union labor.

Local 82 of the Steel Fabricators Union (SFU) learned that BE was using nonunion labor at off-site facilities to perform metal fabrication work that could have been performed on-site by union members represented by the SFU. The prevailing wage for a steel fabricator under current area labor agreements covering SFU members was $20.73 per hour, whereas the off-site nonunion workers were paid $9.00 per hour to perform the steel fabrication work. Local 82 leaders believed that BE was in violation of the project labor agreement by subcontracting steel fabrication work to nonunion subcontractors who were paying their employees substantially less than the prevailing wage rate called for under Local 82's current contract. Failing to resolve the issue voluntarily with BE, Local 82, SFU filed a grievance that eventually went to final and binding arbitration. The union sought damages from BE in the amount of $1.6 million, the amount of the difference between the wages paid non-union employees who performed the steel fabrication work off site and what Local 82 members would have received had the work been performed by them on the work site.

QUESTIONS

1. Is BE bound by the terms of the project labor agreement, which it did not directly sign, including the duty to submit this labor dispute to final and binding arbitration for resolution?

2. Was the project labor agreement meant to apply only to work performed on the job site as BE contends, or could the terms of the project labor agreement also be applied to off-site work as well, as the union contends?

3. Is it legitimate for a labor organization to negotiate a work preservation clause that seeks to encourage contractors to perform work on the job site using union labor by imposing an economic incentive not to outsource the work elsewhere to lower paid employees?

4. What, if any, legitimate business interest of an employer is served by agreeing to a so-called work preservation agreement with one or more unions?

The Disputed Safety Bonus

Bob Dale and Sam Brady were employed as truck drivers by Jackson Transportation Inc. (JTI), a nonunion firm engaged in interstate commerce. JTI provided transportation services for Acme Steel Corporation (ASC) hauling steel coils between ASC's various plants and directly to various ASC customers. Dale and Brady performed all of their work assignments transporting steel coils on the property of ASC, which was also a non-union employer engaged in interstate commerce.

To encourage safe trucking operations, ASC implemented a safety bonus program that paid trucking firms employed by ASC $1 for each safe hour of work performed by each firm's employees. ASC strongly encouraged the transportation firms with whom it contracted for services to pass the $1 per safe hour of operation bonus on to their employees.

JTI decided to pass half of the safety bonus payment (50 cents) on to its truck drivers and keep the remaining 50 cents to fund certain safety equipment purchases and the company's annual Christmas party. Bob Dale learned from talking to drivers at other firms employed by ASC that they were receiving the full $1 bonus from their employers. This upset Dale, who thought his employer (JTI) should also be giving drivers the full bonus payment. Dale discussed his complaint with several other employees, including Sam Brady.

On December 9, Brady encountered Dale, who informed him that he was on his way to see Phil Cook, ASC's transportation manager at the plant where both Brady and Dale were assigned. Brady said he would accompany Dale to the meeting, as he didn't want to miss any of the fireworks. At the meeting, Dale explained to Cook his complaint about JTI not paying its drivers the full $1 bonus amount. Cook replied that essentially this was not a decision over which he had any control and any complaints should be delivered directly to JTI managers, not ASC. The meeting ended after about 15 minutes, and Dale and Brady exited Cook's office. Cook then telephoned R. C. Ridley, the JTI terminal manager who supervised Dale and Brady, and explained to him the nature of the conversation Cook had engaged in with Dale in Brady's presence.

On December 19, Ridley, accompanied by a security guard, escorted Dale from the ASC property, explaining that he was being removed because "they believed that he was trying get a union started because he had talked to Cook." Ridley told Dale that ASC had barred Dale from its property. Dale responded that he was not trying to start a union and had never even spoken to anyone about doing so. Ridley stated the company would have to investigate the matter further.

On that same date (December 19), Ridley, accompanied by a security guard, also escorted Brady from the ASC property. Ridley told Brady he was being removed from the property because he had been present when Dale met with Cook about the safety bonus issue. Brady indicated that he had not known in advance the specific nature of the statements that Dale planned to make that day in Cook's office.

On December 27, Ridley informed Dale that he was being terminated in the best interest of the company. Dale's written termination notice stated that he was terminated because he was "not able to function on ASC property." Ridley also informed Brady on the same date that he too was terminated because ASC did not want him back on their property. Brady's written termination notice stated the reason for termination was "not able to function on ASC property." Brady and Dale subsequently filed an unfair labor practice with the NLRB alleging that JTI's discharge action represented unlawful discrimination against them under the LMRA, as amended. *Continued*

QUESTIONS

1. Was the discharge of Dale and Brady a violation of Sec. 8 (a) (1) and (3) of the LMRA? If so, what should be the appropriate remedy?

2. Was the decision by JTI to award only half of the safety bonus money available to its truck drivers a lawful employer decision?

3. If you had been advising JTI on the safety bonus issue, would you have recommended the company retain half the bonus money for the purposes described by the company (i.e., buy safety equipment and pay for the annual Christmas party)? Why or why not?

CHAPTER 9

Resolving Negotiation (Interest) Disputes

L*abor–management negotiations do not lead to strikes very often. Major work stoppages were at a historic low level in 2002, accounting for lost work time totaling less than .005 of the total hours worked.[1] Media coverage of the strikes that do occur tends to overemphasize the connection between labor relations and the occurrence of work stoppages.*

This chapter begins with a discussion of the ratification of the negotiated labor agreement, the typical conclusion to most contract negotiations. Alternative interest dispute resolution procedures involving third parties, such as mediation, fact-finding, and interest arbitration, are also discussed. The chapter also examines the use of economic pressure (e.g., strike, lockout, boycott, picketing) as a means of encouraging the voluntary resolution of interest disputes.

Contract Ratification

Unlike management negotiators, union negotiators are typically only authorized to reach tentative agreement on contract terms at the bargaining table. The union's constitution and by-laws typically require that union members be given an opportunity to approve or disapprove proposed tentative settlement terms before a final contract agreement can be achieved. For example, the Steelworkers, Auto Workers, and United Mine Workers use a direct referendum. Some unions may require a simple majority approval from union members voting, whereas other unions might require a higher percentage of votes for approval (e.g., 60 percent). In recent years, union members have shown increasing interest in participating in the **contract ratification process,** and more ratification elections have been held.

The ratification process provides union leaders with an indication as to whether union members can live with the proposed agreement, even though they may not be completely satisfied with all of its provisions. Acceptance of the proposed contract's terms by a majority of the union's membership also provides management some assurance that the employees will comply with the letter and spirit of the agreement during its term. A vote to accept, therefore, is considered a commitment or willingness to be bound by the agreement.[2] When and if union members find the agreement unacceptable, they may vote to reject it, which they do about 10 percent of the time.[3]

Explanation of Voting Behavior

It is overly simplistic to say that union members vote for the contract when they like it and against it when they don't like it. Researchers have attempted to explain why and when union members will vote to accept or reject a tentative agreement. When employees perceive alternative employment opportunities are limited, members are more likely to approve proposed settlement terms. Satisfaction with the economic terms of the proposed settlement and a perception that their union has represented members' interest effectively also increase the probability a union member will vote to approve proposed contract settlement terms.[4] For example, when employees with the most seniority are to become eligible for a guaranteed income security plan, those employees could be counted on to favor ratification.

A "no" vote in a ratification election confronts employees with the potential costs of lost income and the uncertainty of when they will begin work again. Although the potential for contract rejection may create incentives for the union negotiators to try to get a little extra for the members, such extras come with increased anxiety as the strike deadline approaches.[5]

Reasons for Rejection of Tentative Contract Agreements

The most common reason why union members reject proposed settlement terms is genuine dissatisfaction with one or more of those terms. Union members may feel shortchanged in comparison with other agreements in their geographic area or industry. Internal union politics is another reason contract rejection may occur. Sometimes union leaders are elected by slight majorities, and their rivals will campaign against any labor agreement negotiated by the incumbent leaders. This problem can be exacerbated if the union permits members to choose members of the union's negotiating team and current leaders find rivals for union leadership elected to serve as part of the negotiating committee.

Communication problems between union leaders and members can sometimes play a role in contract rejection, although good communication can also facilitate contract approval. Upward communication flows are important because union leaders must understand what issues are most important to the majority of the union's membership if bargaining proposals and tentative agreements reached are to reflect those interests. For example, in industrial unions individuals holding skilled trade positions (electrician, carpenter, painter, machinists) usually represent a minority of the total membership. Such skilled trade members might vote to reject a contract if their wages did not compare favorably with those of similar skilled trades individuals employed in the same geographic area.

Downward communication flows are particular important in keeping members informed of progress toward achieving a settlement during negotiations and in explaining how members will be affected by contract language changes contained in the tentative contract settlement proposed for ratification. Particular care must be given to explaining changes in contract terms of high importance to members, such as the adoption of new wage payment methods or alterations in pension benefits or health care benefit plans.

Some groups (women, racial minorities, and younger employees) within the bargaining unit may base their contract ratification vote on the outcome of one or more very specific issues directly impacting them. Although equal employment opportunity laws have been passed, wage differentials continue to exist for racial minorities and women, and eliminating perceived intraplant inequities may be the primary determinant of how an affected employee votes on the contract ratification question. Moreover, young employees with low seniority often view pension and layoff issues, which are usually based on seniority or retirement age, differently from older employees, causing additional internal friction within a bargaining unit. Unless members in these subgroups believe that the agreement reflects their own personal needs, they may vote to reject it.[6]

Contract rejection can sometimes be used as a bargaining strategy by a union, although the effectiveness of such a strategy would tend to diminish over time as management negotiators adapted by being less willing to propose their best offer during initial negotiations in case they had to go back to the bargaining table after the initial tentative agreement was rejected. One research study reported that subsequent contract settlement obtained after an initial contract settlement was rejected by the union's membership did contain additional economic gains for union members in 65 percent of cases.[7] It is important that union leaders and managers attempt to keep members' expectations of bargaining success as realistic as possible during the negotiation process in order to avoid a negative reaction to proposed contract settlement terms that fall below unrealistically high expectations.

Obtaining the union negotiating team's strong endorsement of a proposed contract settlement can usually ensure that the majority of union members will support the negotiation team's recommendation.[8] Some contract concessions may be necessary in some cases to obtain the endorsement of the union bargaining team. Management negotiators must carefully weigh the costs of any required concessions against the probability contract rejection will occur without such an endorsement and the additional costs such a rejection might entail before any final contract settlement could be achieved (e.g., probability contract rejection could trigger a strike).

Impasse-Resolution Procedures Involving a Third-Party Neutral

Usually both parties attempt to resolve impasses, which can occur either before or after the contract's expiration date. In some cases, union and management officials need third parties either to facilitate the negotiation process or to render a final and binding decision to resolve the bargaining dispute. Mediation, fact-finding, and interest arbitration are three important impasse resolution procedures involving neutral, third parties to resolve interest (bargaining) disputes.

Mediation

Most union–management interest disputes are resolved voluntarily by the parities themselves without the need for assistance from an outside, third-party neutral. However, the **Federal Mediation and Conciliation Service (FMCS)** does provide assistance on average in more than 5,000 negotiations per year that conclude in a voluntary settlement by the parties without any interruption in the production of goods or services in over 90 percent of cases.[9] Mediation is the most commonly used third-party interest dispute resolution procedure, and the FMCS, along with some 18 state mediation agencies, helps to achieve Congress's goal of fostering stable labor–management relations in order to facilitate the free flow of commerce.

As part of the legal duty to bargain in good faith under the LMRA, bargaining parties are required to provide 30 days' advance notice to the FMCS or any other applicable state mediation agency that bargaining is occurring but no settlement has yet been reached. This notice can be filed electronically using a form available from the FMCS' Web site at www.fmcs.gov. A mediator will contact the bargaining parties and offer his or her services in aiding the parties to reach a voluntary settlement. Deciding to use the services of a third-party mediator is voluntary on the part of the bargaining parties except in the rare case where the dispute involves a "national emergency," discussed more fully later in this chapter.

A mediator has no legal authority to impose a settlement on the parties and thus functions more as an invited guest who can be required to leave if one or both bargaining parties no longer desire the mediator's continued involvement in the bargaining process. Mediators must rely on persuasion and their credibility as a facilitator in helping the bargaining parties reach agreement on their own. Mediators can perform a number of functions to assist the bargaining process, including: assist in scheduling meetings; keeping the parties talking; carrying messages back and forth; helping each party realistically assess its current bargaining position and alternatives; and suggest possible new approaches or terms to facilitate settlement.[10] The mediation process is much more an art than a science. Mediation has been described as a process that "has been helpful in a haphazard way largely because of the talents of certain individuals who themselves would find it difficult to say why they had been successful."[11]

Several characteristics and practices of labor mediators have been associated with mediator effectiveness. Effective mediators have tenacity—they do not give up without exhausting themselves, the parties, and all reasonable avenues of settlement. A second characteristic is experience, which simply means that the more times a mediator is involved in mediating labor disputes, the more effective he or she is likely to be in settling one. Finally, mediators who are active, who pressure the parties to reach a settlement, who generate their own settlement terms, and who play an independent role in the mediation process are more likely to be effective mediators.[12]

Carl Stevens's study of mediation focusing on the mediator's functions and tactics has identified several causal factors that lead to a negotiated settlement.[13] Timing of the mediator's involvement is one of the most important considerations. A mediator should enter the bargaining dispute before the parties become too fixed in their positions but not so early as to upset the power balance between the parties, causing them to harden their bargaining positions. In some instances, the mere entrance of the mediator may be sufficient for dispute settlement to occur. For example, assume that one of the chief negotiators leaves an active negotiation in a temper tantrum, vowing never again to return to the bargaining table. On subsequent reflection, the negotiator realizes a mistake was made but feels that calling the opposing negotiator would be embarrassing and perhaps indicate weakness. A common tactic used in such situations would be to call the mediator, who could schedule another meeting. Thus, mediation can represent a very important face-saving device for a bargaining party. In other cases, the parties do not desire any specific help from the mediator, but the availability of that mediator and the very existence of the mediation forum facilitate the bargaining process.[14]

Mediators are expected to possess a high level of knowledge concerning labor relations practices, economic and industry trends, labor and employment law, problem-solving techniques (e.g., interest-based bargaining), and best practices for building ongoing cooperative labor–management relations (e.g., labor–management committees; partnership training).[15] Mediators vary in their roles, behaviors, and styles. Some have been characterized as "deal makers" entering the negotiations at an early stage and actively attempting to persuade the parties to accept the mediator's proposed settlement terms. Others seem to prefer the role of "orchestrator," attempting to structure the negotiations to facilitate communication between the parties to provide greater insight into the issues in dispute. A mediator may become much more active in encouraging the parties to settle where a work stoppage appears immenient.[16]

A successful mediator is often an interpreter, who clarifies perceptions of the bargaining climate and possible costs of failing to reach an agreement. For example, if the parties disagree on data about the cost of living, comparative wage rates, and productivity, the mediator could assist in reaching agreement on what relevant source to use to obtain statistical data. If a negotiator underestimates the cost of a strike or lockout or overestimates the cost of an agreeing to the other parties' proposed settlement terms, the mediator may be able to provide insights enabling the negotiator to evaluate his or her positions more realistically. Often a mediator will hold separate meetings with each bargaining party before attempting to schedule a joint meeting between the parties. This provides the mediator a chance to better understand each party's rationale for current bargaining positions and the depth of commitment each party has for those positions. Developing trust between the mediator and each bargaining party is necessary before the mediator is likely to have much success helping the parties better understand and trust each other in the bargaining process.

Helping each party to understand the tactics or intentions of the other can also aid the bargaining process. If management bluffs about its willingness to accept a strike or to allow an ongoing strike to continue indefinitely, the mediator may attempt to diagnose management's true intentions and then advise the union. On the other hand, if the union threatens a strike to obtain an excessive bargaining demand, the mediator could attempt to diagnose what the union is "really trying to say" and so inform the company negotiator. By holding private caucuses with each party, the mediator becomes privy to much confidential information. Although no mediator would reveal confidential information to the other party, he or she can provide insight to the parties regarding the magnitude of the differences between them and encourage the parties that a settlement may be near if they continue bargaining. Mediators can apply pressure for settlement on one or both parties by using delays and deadlines in the mediation process, placing responsibility for settlement on the parties, engaging in marathon (around-the-clock) bargaining, emphasizing the costs of a strike or lockout, and making settlement recommendations in a joint conference.[17]

The parties, however, play the dominant role in shaping the mediation process. Where experienced negotiators have a clear understanding of their bargaining objectives and strategies, the mediator is primarily the servant of the parties. However, where less sophisticated negotiators have not clearly defined their bargaining objectives, the personal qualities and actions of an competent mediator may be able to gain the trust of the parties and create the type of negotiating atmosphere that achieves a settlement.[18]

Because there is no widely adopted code of professional conduct for mediators, and because potentially great danger exists from inept and unscrupulous practitioners, national organizations led by the Society of Professionals in Dispute Resolution (SPIDR) have developed a code of professional conduct to promote ethical behaviors by mediators. This code articulates qualifications for mediators, standards of practice, and ethical behavior. It proscribes impermissible actions of mediators, such as holding meetings with one of the parties without prior consent of the other party and revealing to one party what would be considered an acceptable settlement to the other. The code is patterned after the widely accepted Code of Professional Responsibility for Arbitrators of Labor-Management Disputes, adopted by the National Academy of Arbitrators, American Arbitration Association, and FMCS, which has existed since 1951 (revised most recently in 1995).[19]

Fact-Finding

Fact-finding is a semi-judicial process used primarily in the public sector to gather facts about a labor dispute for the purpose of publishing a public report containing the fact-finder's conclusions and often recommended terms of settlement. Like a mediator, a fact-finder has no legal authority to impose a final and binding settlement on the parties involved in the labor dispute. The fact-finder's purpose is to assess the facts and to organize and display them publicly in the hopes that the public will find the fact-finder's conclusions and recommendations to have merit and bring pressure on the parties in dispute to settle their differences.[20] Typically, both public employers and public employee unions recognize the need to be responsive to taxpayers or consumers of public services and seek to use support from such groups to bolster their respective bargaining positions.

Fact-finding may be used in major disputes under the Labor Management Relations Act (LMRA) and Railway Labor Act and under the 1974 health-care amendments of the LMRA. In major disputes, fact-finding reports are useful to presidents in determining what actions to take in national emergencies, such as when to seek an injunction or recommend legislation to resolve the dispute. Because fact-finding lacks the ability to ensure a final end to the labor dispute, this process does not have a good record in resolving disputes.

Interest Arbitration

Traditional interest arbitration involves the selection of a neutral person or panel to hear the bargaining positions of the parties and make a final and binding decision on what should be included in the negotiated agreement. This process differs from grievance arbitration (see Chapter 11), which is concerned mostly with resolving rights-type disputes over the interpretation or application of existing contract terms.

Interest arbitration in the United States dates back to the 18th century in the copper mines of Connecticut. It is not used very often in the private sector (approximately 2 percent of negotiations) to resolve contract negotiation disputes, with some notable exceptions such as the Amalgamated Transit Union, which has arbitrated over 700 cases and the legal provision for interest arbitration of postal worker interest disputes.[21]

Management and union representatives in the private sector prefer to control the outcome of interest disputes establishing the terms or conditions of employment and are reluctant to grant such authority to an outside arbitrator. Both parties have concerns about possible delay created in trying to schedule an arbitration hearing and the extra cost involved. In addition, management becomes particularly concerned if the arbitrator fails to take into account the economic effect of the arbitration decision on the employer's operations or if the award is above the industry average. Interest arbitration in the public sector is discussed more fully in Chapter 13.

Interest arbitration has been criticized on the assumption that arbitrators may tend to "split the difference" in resolving disputes, thereby causing the parties to take more extreme positions on issues in dispute. Whether an arbitrator has the flexibility to merely split the difference between the parties' offers is determined in part by the type of arbitration procedure used. Arbitrators have a number of criteria that can be used to determine what constitutes appropriate settlement terms of an interest dispute (See Exhibit 9.1). Most arbitrators will weigh the parties' positions and relevant supporting evidence in relation to specific criteria

Exhibit 9.1

Some Relevant Criteria an Arbitrator May Use to Decide an Interest Bargaining Dispute

- Comparability of relevant employee wage, hours, or other working conditions with similar private or public sector employees within the same geographic area or industry.
- Current economic conditions (e.g., inflation, unemployment, product/service demand, productivity).
- Occupational or job requirements (e.g., physical or mental abilities, degree and variety of skills required, prior work experience or relevant training, hazardous or unpleasant working conditions, degree of responsibility, creativity, stress).
- The financial ability of the employer to pay for the costs of any proposed settlement terms (including an assessment of current and future projected revenues during the term of the labor agreement).
- Whether a bargaining proposal involves a new bargaining subject (i.e., a subject not previously agreed upon in a prior contract between the parties' or not common in other labor agreements in the industry or geographic area).
- The potential effect of the arbitrator's decision on the encouragement of effective and stable labor relations within the parties' bargaining relationship.
- The availability of recommended settlement terms from a mediator, fact-finder, or other similar board of inquiry concerning the interest dispute.
- The general welfare and interest of the public.

to determine the dispute outcome rather than mechanically "splitting the difference" to determine the dispute's outcome.[22] Because neutrals may vary in the norms of their decision making, the parties can exert some degree of control over the dispute outcome by defining the decision criteria to be used by an arbitrator in advance.[23]

Another criticism of interest arbitration is it reduces the costs of not reaching agreement during face-to-face negotiations between the parties and thus exerts a so-called "chilling effect" on the parties' incentive to reach an agreement. Research does support a finding that fewer voluntary settlements are reached under negotiation systems permitting interest arbitration than under systems permitting a right to strike or lockout in the absence of a negotiated settlement.[24] If either party believes that it can gain a better settlement from an arbitrator than through negotiation, there may be an incentive to maintain unrealistic demands in the hope that an arbitrator might make a more favorable award than the other party is willing to offer at the bargaining table.

A third concern about interest arbitration is that the existence of the interest arbitration procedure may create a so-called "narcotic effect" on the bargaining parties. As the parties gain more knowledge of arbitrator decision outcomes or experience gains through arbitration beyond what a party might have expected in the absence of the interest arbitration option, the parties become increasingly reliant on interest arbitration to resolve bargaining disputes.[25] One study reported that knowledge gained by parties regarding arbitral preferences and decision criteria tends to make subsequent negotiations between the parties more realistic producing settlements closer to the norms established by the arbitrator during prior contract negotiation disputes.[26]

In fact, studies of the existence of the "narcotic effect" have produced mixed results. A study of the use of arbitration over an eight-year period under the Minnesota Public Labor Relations Act did not reveal its existence. However, earlier studies in New York and British Columbia had identified such an effect although the effect seems to fade after several years.[27]

Three Interest Arbitration Procedures

The interest arbitration procedure affording the arbitrator the greatest degree of flexibility to determine an appropriate settlement outcome is **conventional interest arbitration.**[28] Using this procedure, each party would present their proposed settlement terms and supporting evidence to the arbitrator, who would have the authority to decide what final terms of settlement were most reasonable on a case-by-case basis. The arbitrator could select either party's proposal or some compromise settlement terms between or beyond those proposed by the parties themselves. Exhibit 9.1 illustrates some relevant criteria an arbitrator might consider in determining what settlement terms are most reasonable or appropriate under the circumstances of each case.

Final-offer Total Package (FOTP) selection is a form of interest arbitration that restricts the arbitrator's authority by requiring the selection of either the employer's or union's final bargaining proposal on all issues in dispute. This is in effect a "winner take all" proposition where one party's position will prevail on all issues in dispute. FOTP selection carries the highest risk of loss to both parties, since neither party can guarantee that the arbitrator will select their proposals as the most appropriate or reasonable. FOTP selection does eliminate any chance for the arbitrator to simply "split the difference" between the union's and management's final proposed settlement terms. Theoretically, if both parties genuinely attempt to present acceptable proposals to the arbitrator, their positions will converge, enhancing the opportunity for them to settle their differences without third-party intervention.

A somewhat less risky alternative to FOTP is **final-offer issue-by-issue** (FOIBI) selection, where the arbitrator is restricted to selecting either the union's or employer's final proposal on each specific issue. The FOIBI procedure permits the arbitrator to assess each bargaining issue in dispute separately on its own merits to determine which party has the most reasonable proposal. While in theory one party could still be determined to have the most reasonable proposal on every issue in dispute, more likely one party's proposal would be judged more appropriate on some issues in dispute while the other party's position might prevail on other issues.

FOTP selection arbitration has been used in determining baseball salaries for several years. Similar to a strike threat, the threat of arbitration imposes a cost risk on the player and team owner for continuing to disagree on settlement terms. Because the arbitrator may select only one of the two offers submitted by the opposing sides, the parties are motivated to reach a negotiated voluntary settlement.

Research on FOTP arbitration in baseball has revealed that typically only the high-quality baseball players file for arbitration and seek to have their salaries decided in arbitration. Because the salaries of baseball players who qualify for arbitration are 80 to 90 percent higher than those of comparable ineligible players, baseball clubs have an incentive to substitute players with cheaper salaries for players whose salaries are raised through arbitration beyond management's own valuation of a player's worth.[29]

Interest dispute arbitration procedures do have some shortcomings, particularly if relevant criteria on which to base arbitration decisions are not supplied. More importantly, because labor negotiations usually involve multiple issues that may be in dispute between the parties, interest arbitration can become a very complex process. If the parties do not compromise on significant differences between their bargaining positions to reach agreement prior to arbitration, then using one of the final offer arbitration procedures would require the arbitrator to select one of the party's extreme proposals. This could heighten union–management tensions during the life of the contract and causing future difficulties in negotiating subsequent contracts.[30]

Mediation-Arbitration (Med-Arb)

Mediation-arbitration (or med-arb) is a variation on traditional mediation and interest arbitration procedures chosen by some bargaining relationships. It seeks to combine the two separate processes into one. Under the procedure, a third-party neutral selected by the bargaining parties will first function in the role of a mediator attempting to encourage the parties to reach a voluntary settlement. If no settlement occurs, the third-party neutral then switches hats to become an arbitrator empowered by the parties to make a final and binding decision to resolve the parties' interest dispute. Since the arbitrator would already be familiar with the parties' positions and supporting evidence on issues in dispute, less time would be required in the arbitration hearing to present those positions and have the arbitrator render a decision. By the same token, because the arbitrator has already functioned as a mediator in the dispute, one or both parties may be concerned that opinions formed during the mediation phase could influence the outcome of the arbitration phase, since the same individual would be functioning as both mediator and arbitrator. In theory under a med-arb procedure, most issues will be resolved voluntarily by the parties because in addition to the traditional pressures of bargaining there is the pressure of knowing that the mediator-arbitrator will make a final and binding decision if the parties fail to reach a voluntary agreement.

The Use of Economic Pressure to Resolve Interest Disputes

The ability to raise a party's costs of continuing to disagree with current proposed terms of settlement is an important factor that can encourage that party to compromise in order to avoid such costs. In most cases a credible threat of the costs associated with a work stoppage, whether initiated as a strike by employees or a lockout by the employer, is sufficient to motivate both union and management negotiators to seek a reasonable alternative. For such a threat to be perceived as credible, the party receiving the threat must believe that the party making the threat has both the ability and willingness to carry out the threat successfully. In commenting on the use of economic pressure tactics during good-faith bargaining, the Supreme Court stated:

> The policy of Congress is to impose a mutual duty upon the parties to confer in good faith with a desire to reach an agreement, in the belief that such an approach from both sides of the table promotes the over-all design of achieving industrial peace. . . . The presence of economic weapons in reserve and their actual exercise on occasion by the parties, is part and parcel of the system that the Wagner and Taft-Hartley Acts have recognized. . . . In one aspect collective bargaining is a brute contest of economic power somewhat masked by polite manners and voluminous statistics. Initially it may be only fear of the economic consequences of disagreement that turns the parties to facts, reason, a sense of responsibility, a responsiveness to government and public opinion, and moral principle; but in time these forces generate their own compulsions, and negotiating a contract approaches the ideal of informed persuasion.[31]

A **strike** is a temporary work stoppage by a group of employees for the purpose of expressing a grievance or enforcing a demand. Tactics often used to support a strike include picketing activity or a boycott of the primary employer's goods or services. The **primary employer** in a labor dispute is the employer with whom the striking employees (union) have a dispute and the employer who has the ability to end the dispute by agreeing to the employees' proposed settlement terms. The LMRA (Sec. 7 and 13) protects employees' right to strike so long as the strike is for a lawful purpose and is carried out using lawful means.

A lockout is a temporary work stoppage caused by an employer's withdrawal of employees' opportunity to work for the purpose of enforcing a bargaining demand or minimizing the employer's potential loss should employees control the timing of a work stoppage by initiating a strike. Another reason an employer might initiate a lockout is to protect the integrity of a multi-employer bargaining group. To counter a union's ability to selectively strike only certain competitors who may bargain together as a multi-employer group, if one group member is struck the other employers agree to lock out their employees, thus making the union extend the scope of the bargaining dispute to a larger number of its members and forcing the union to expend resources at a faster rate to support members affected by the strike or lockout actions. An example of this occurred in the 2003–2004 interest dispute between some 70,000 Southern California grocery workers represented by the United Food and Commercial Workers Union and three employers.[32] After union employees initiated a strike on October 11, 2003, against two grocery store chains owned by Safeway, Inc., other grocery store chains owned by Kroger Co. and Albertsons Inc. responded by locking out their employees. The longest supermarket work stoppage in U.S. history, the dispute principally over wage and health care benefit issues featured mediation; a rejection by employers of a union proposal to submit disputed issues to final and binding interest arbitration; and ultimately after four and a half months and millions of dollars in costs, a negotiated contract settlement by the parties.

During a lockout an employer can attempt to continue normal business operations by using nonbargaining unit personnel or hiring temporary replacements for locked-out employees.[33] Since the employer initiated the work stoppage, permanent replacement of locked out workers is not permitted. Otherwise, some employers might initiate lockouts as a means of replacing workers who had exercised their lawful right to join a union and engage in collective bargaining. A locked-out employee always has the right to return to work at any time during the lockout by notifying management of the employee's voluntary acceptance of the employer's proposed terms and conditions of employment (termed an **unconditional request for reinstatement**).

It is useful to think about strikes along two dimensions. The first dimension is whether the strike is legal or illegal, which essentially involves examining the ends (purpose) of the strike action and the means (tactics) used to carry it out. A strike called for a lawful purpose does not become unlawful merely because one or more individuals engage in unlawful conduct during the strike. Unlawful acts by individuals can be remedied without denying all participants their lawful right to strike. However, any employee who participates in an unlawful strike or engages in unlawful strike activity during an otherwise lawful strike loses the rights an employee engaged in a lawful strike would normally retain (discussed further later in the chapter).

A second dimension used to classify strikes is whether the work stoppage involves an economic dispute or is caused by the commission of an employer's unfair labor practice (e.g., a refusal to bargain in good faith). Whether a work stoppage is classified as an **economic strike** or an **unfair labor strike** has important implications for the rights of both employers and employees participating in the strike. It is possible that a strike that began over a wage dispute (an economic strike) to be converted into an unfair labor practice strike if the occurrence of an employer's unfair labor practice prolongs the work stoppage by becoming a reason for the strike's continuation.

Most work stoppages are classified as lawful economic strikes involving a dispute over subjects such as wages, benefits, hours of work, or management's rights. Sometimes employees are asked to support a strike to gain additional increases in desired terms or conditions of employment or to avoid (minimize) proposed management reductions in such terms or conditions. Additionally union members sometimes strike to achieve some institutional goal of their union such as a union security clause.[34]

Some types of economic strikes have been given their own special name. For example, the term **wildcat strike** generally refers to a strike that occurs in violation of an existing no-strike clause in a labor agreement and often without the approval or prior knowledge of union officials. Such a spontaneous work stoppage by one or more employees, if in violation of current contract terms, would be illegal and could result in the participating employees being subject to discipline or discharge by their employer. Some employees' refusal to work when confronted with perceived extremely dangerous and unsafe working conditions do not fit the definition of a wildcat strike because Section 502, LMRA specifically authorizes such concerted activity, which cannot be barred by the language of a contractual no-strike clause.[35]

A **sympathy strike** is a work stoppage by employees who have no dispute with their own employer but are striking to support another bargaining unit of their employer or a union representing employees at another employer. An employer may attempt to get a union to agree to add specific language to the parties' no-strike clause that prohibits employees from engaging in a sympathy strike during the term of the labor agreement.

A **jurisdictional strike** involves a dispute between two or more unions over the assignment of work (see discussion in Chapter 8). It is an unfair labor practice under the LMRA for a union to strike or threaten such action to force an employer to assign work to that union's members rather than another work group.

Reasons for Strikes

Work stoppages from 1982 to 2002 have been at or near historic low levels in terms of numbers of strikes, employees involved and days idled (Exhibit 9.2). The lockout involving the Pacific Maritime Association and the International Longshore and Warehouse Union involved 10,500 workers and accounted for 20 percent of all workers idled in 2002. Despite a few well-publicized strikes such as disputes between Lockheed Martin Company and the International Association of Machinists and the Hershey Foods Corporation and the Bakery, Confectionary, Tobacco Workers and Grain Millers union, the average length of work stoppages in 2002 was 21 days with only one dispute lasting more than 50 days.

Some researches have attributed the decline in the frequency of union strikes to their declining effectiveness as a means of placing economic pressure on an employer. An excess supply of labor in relation to the demand for labor in many occupations and geographic areas in recent years have made strike replacements both easier and less costly to obtain, dampening many union members desire to engage in a work stoppage.[36]

Work stoppages are not caused by one factor alone, although the most common issue over which strikes occur is wages, followed by plant administrative issues, such as safety, promotion policies, and job assignments. In recent years several work stoppages have involved the issue of health-care benefits, as union members have sought to resist employer health-care bargaining proposals aimed at reducing the employer's benefit cost for this item (see Chapter 7). The decision to strike depends on the total environment in which bargaining

Exhibit 9.2

Work Stoppages Involving 1,000 or More Employees in the United States, 1947 to 2002

	Employees Involved		Days Idled	
Years	Number/ Year	Number (Thousands)	Number of Days	Percentage of Working Time
1947–1950	300.3	1824.8	31,414	.29
1951–1960	331.5	1508.2	24,902	.19
1961–1970	298.8	1390.9	22,833	.14
1971–1980	269.4	1320.5	22,818	.11
1981–1990	64.2	427.1	9,673	.04
1991	40	392	4,584	.02
1992	35	388	3,987	.01
1993	36	18	3,981	.01
1994	45	322	5,020	.02
1995	31	192	5,771	.02
1996	37	273	4,889	.02
1997	29	339	4,497	.01
1998	34	387	5,116	.02
1999	17	73	1,996	.01
2000	39	394	20,419	.06
2001	29	99	1,151	<.005
2002	19	45.9	659.6	<.005

SOURCE: U.S. Department of Labor, Bureau of Labor Statistics, "Major Work Stoppages in 2002," *News Release,* March 11, 2003, pp. 3–4.

takes place. Interrelated factors that can influence the decision to strike include the economic positions of the union and company, characteristics of the production or service delivery process, the firm's market structure, business location, and occupational and demographic characteristics of the workforce.[37]

Researchers have shown that before 1980, strikes and economic activity were highly correlated, with strike activity rising during periods of economic growth and declining during economic recessions. During the 1980s this pattern did not occur, with low levels of strike activity recorded despite eight straight years of economic expansion after 1982. Between 1982 and 1990, employees involved in work stoppages in communications, government, transportation equipment, transportation, and construction made up 63 percent of all employees involved in work stoppages.[38] Exhibit 9.3 presents several conclusions researchers have reached concerning the causes of work stoppages.

Although strikes have traditionally been viewed as economic or legal conflicts, the psychological aspects are important. Psychologically, strikes can be categorized as a protest or as a group process for organizational change. Protest strikes include actions by the membership such as walking off their jobs. Partial strikes occur in the form of work slowdowns where employees "work to rule" following every detail of proscribed work processes, which often slows the normal pace of work flow. These protests may be in reaction to a unilateral change by management, such as introducing production quotas or working conditions or even in lowering thermostats in winter months.

As a group process, strikes require an important issue around which to mobilize the union's membership and adequate strike resources. Effective union leadership is critical to the success of any strike. Union leaders must instill unity among the membership, control courses of action, respond to the feelings of the group, and maintain communication with management. An individual union member's participation in a strike is often determined by perceived costs and benefits. If the perceived benefits are small and the costs are high, willingness to participate will be low. However, if the benefits are perceived to be high and the costs are low, willingness to participate will be high.[39] Employees who believe that their pay is inequitable are not very willing to strike for a small wage increase. On the other hand, they may be willing to strike to support the union for a large increase. The degree of commitment (loyalty) of an employee toward his or her union also has an important impact on an employee's willingness to strike, even more so than employees' perceived commitment to their employer. A union must help employees reduce the potential hardships of a strike (e.g., by providing strike benefits), to increase strike support.[40]

Strikes can have traumatic effects on the parties' attitudes; they can temper the militants with realism and radicalize the conservatives. Strikes may cause some members to question the credibility of their leaders or management. Most strikes end in some type of negotiated settlement. However, once a strike is over, much rebuilding must occur to restore good labor–management relations and co-worker relations between strikers and nonstrikers.[41]

Exhibit 9.3

Conclusions from Research on Work Stoppages Regarding the Likelihood of a Strike

Strikes are more likely when:

- The duration of the preceding contract is longer.
- Negotiations serve as a pattern setter for other firms/union pairs.
- The bargaining units are larger.
- There is a large variance (sharp drops and increases in earnings) in the firm's financial performance.
- Firms and industries have risk of injury or fatalities.
- Firms can inventory or stockpile goods.

Strikes are less likely when:

- Fewer issues are being negotiated (such as in a contract reopener over wages).
- Firms and industries employ a large proportion of women.
- Firms and industries pay a higher wage rate than other firms or industries.

SOURCE: Bruce E. Kaufman, "Research on Strike Models and Outcomes in the 1980s. Accomplishments and Shortcomings," in *Research Frontiers in Industrial and Human Resources*, eds. David Lewin, Olivia S. Mitchell, and Peter D. Sherer (Madison, Wis.: Industrial Relations Research Association, 1992), pp. 110–111.

Strategic Purposes of a Strike

Although the main purpose of the strike is to secure a contract, it may also serve other purposes. For example, a strike may be part of an overall union strategy to help resolve internal problems. A strike may have a cathartic effect on the union members, removing accumulated tensions and releasing frustrations resulting from monotonous work. In fact, strikes under these conditions might improve productivity when the strikers return to work. A strike might also help to unify members, serving to rally diverse prestrike membership factions to work toward a common goal winning the strike.

In some cases, a union may call a strike to show management it can unify the membership over a collective bargaining issue. Over time, frequent strike threats may lose their effectiveness. If such threats are never carried out, management may perceive that the union leader's strike threat lacks credibility. Sometimes union members may view participation in a strike as an investment in the credibility of future strike threats intended to reduce the need for future strikes to occur.

Union leaders may also believe that their members might be more willing to accept a slightly modified company offer if employees have experienced the loss of wages during a brief strike. In this sense, strikes are used to "roll the steam" out of employees and force them to adopt a more realistic perspective on the possibility of attaining stated bargaining objectives.[42]

Unions also have to consider the effects of a strike on their institutional security. During a strike, some union members may accept jobs elsewhere and decide not to return after the strike. Sometimes employers hire permanent replacements for union strikers, and the negotiations never result in a collective-bargaining agreement. Rival unions are sometimes waiting on the sideline for the legally recognized union to falter, hoping to get enough employees to shift their support to the rival union to win a union decertification election. With these considerations, a union must be aware that a decision to strike may be a risk to its own union security.

A strike may serve a strategic purpose for management as well. Although management cannot call a strike, it can take actions that it knows are likely to result in a strike. For example, management can demand that the union collect dues rather than have management deduct them from employee paychecks (the union dues check-off procedure is discussed in Chapter 4). Unions view this demand as a threat to their security and will often strike in response to it. Management's demand to subcontract bargaining unit work at will or to substantially change the wage system to the perceived detriment of covered employees will almost certainly lead to a strike. Thus, management may attempt to cause a strike when a strike is to its advantage, such as when inventories are high and customer demand is low. If nonunion employees can produce at a sufficient level to maintain acceptable production, if the union is weak, or if management knows that all employees will not support the strike, management may force a bargaining impasse as a strategy to secure more favorable contract terms.

Strike Experiences and Preparation

Strikes can range from very peaceful conflicts of short duration to protracted conflicts involving unlawful acts on both sides lasting months or even years. Strikes have no uniform sequence of events, although strikers' enthusiasm is generally highest during the early days of a strike. Indeed, the first few days on a picket line often draw a large portion of union members in an almost carnival-like atmosphere. After several weeks, it may be more difficult for a union to recruit members to walk the picket line.

Frustrations, antagonisms, and anxieties usually increase as the strike continues, with increased membership pressure being placed on union leaders to resolve the impasse.[43] The relative peacefulness of a strike is influenced by the attitudes of community citizens, particularly merchants and creditors, toward the dispute. A striker's spouse is perhaps the most influential individual in shaping a striker's behavior and attitudes. It is of course much easier for a striker to sustain a long strike if her or his spouse lends moral and financial support to the cause. On the other hand, tensions created by the strike can create permanent divisions among family members, friends, and other groups in the community as the strike endures and as individuals are asked to demonstrate their support.[44] Tensions can be especially heightened if the company continues to operate the business with either supervisory employees or striker replacements.

Parties must prepare for a possible strike before the contract expiration date, whether a strike is called or a settlement is reached. Exhibit 9.4 presents some of the potential costs faced by employers, unions, or individual employees during a work stoppage as well as possible actions to minimize or limit the adverse effects of such costs.

Union leaders must be certain of the extent to which members will actively participate during a strike and present a unified front against the employer. Usually a strike vote will occur either days or weeks before the contract deadline to indicate the strength of the membership's willingness to strike and bolster the credibility of any union strike threat. Strike votes are typically supported by the overwhelming majority of union members voting, although management negotiators may place less credibility on the validity of such votes the earlier the vote is taken in advance of the contract expiration date.

As the strike date approaches, union leaders must schedule pickets, ensure appropriate support for those on the line, and properly prepare the pickets for various situations, such as what to do when striker replacements cross the picket line. The union also has to determine qualified recipients of strike benefits, as well as any available public aid. Communication channels (telephone hotlines, Internet Web sites) must be established and maintained to keep union members informed about the progress of negotiations. Local 400, United Food and Commercial Workers, in preparation for a potential strike against Safeway Inc. and Giant Food LLC in the Washington, D.C., area, reported "selecting strike captains, handing out instructions for setting up picket lines, distributing the names of bail bondsmen and establishing a local strike fund."[45] In coordination with other local unions, the AFL-CIO Metropolitan Washington Council, and community groups, Local 400 distributed leaflets inside and outside of Giant and Safeway stores as well as appealed for support from local political leaders in an effort to achieve a fair contract settlement.

Management often spends much time in its strike preparations, particularly if it is essential that the employer continue to operate during a strike, as public utilities or health-care facilities must do. Management in manufacturing facilities must determine the feasibility of building inventories in advance of a possible strike or using a strategy of hiring striker replacements if the strike occurs.

Exhibit 9.4

Some Potential Strike or Lockout Costs and Mitigating Actions

---

Some Potential Employer Strike or Lockout Costs

- Lost sales revenue
- Loss of customers/market share (temporary or permanent)
- Continued fixed operating costs (e.g., utilities, taxes, rent, maintenance, debt service)
- Nonbargaining unit employee payroll costs
- Recruitment, selection, and training costs for temporary or permanent replacement workers
- Shutdown and start-up costs
- Negative publicity
- Legal fees
- Damage to bargaining relationship or co-worker relations (temporary or permanent)
- Increased stress level on managers, employees, and their families

Potential Employer Actions to Minimize or Limit Such Costs

- Build inventory in advance of an anticipated strike.
- Notify customers and suppliers in advance of strike potential and help arrange alternative sources to meet customer needs.
- Engage in a publicity campaign to inform the public (customers, civic leaders, and employees) about company efforts to resolve the labor dispute.
- Shift the struck work to other primary employer owned plants or outsource such work to other secondary employers.
- Continue business operations using some combination of non-B.U. employees; B.U. employees willing to cross the union's picket line; and temporary or permanent strike replacements.
- Existence of poor product market demand serves to decrease risk of market share loss and sales revenue.
- Purchase strike insurance or enter mutual aid pact with other employers.

Some Potential Union or Individual Employee Strike or Lockout Costs

- Loss of union members due to voluntary union membership resignation or permanent striker replacement.
- Loss of wage income or employee benefits coverage.
- Loss of union dues revenue.
- Cost of strike benefits provided, if any.
- Costs of operating a strike (e.g., printing costs, legal fees, picket line supplies such as coffee, food, or medical aid).
- Political cost to union's leadership if strike isn't won or won "big enough."
- Damage to co-worker (peer) relationships between strike supporters and nonsupporters.
- Continuing personal debt payments (e.g., auto, home, credit card, insurance, and telephone).
- Increased level of stress on work stoppage participants, their families, and communities.

Continued

Exhibit 9.4—cont'd

Some Potential Strike or Lockout Costs and Mitigating Actions

---

Potential Union or Union Member Actions to Minimize or Limit Costs

- Ensure adequate membership support prior to initiating any strike action.
- Solicit moral and financial support from outside organizations (e.g., other unions, community groups, general public).
- Increase individual savings rate in anticipation of income loss during work stoppage.
- Work with creditors to delay or reduce monthly debt payments.
- Ensure adequate funding of union strike benefit fund.
- Engage in publicity to demonstrate the merits of union members bargaining positions at issue in the work stoppage and the effectiveness of strike efforts to impose added costs on the employer's ability to operate.
- Product market conditions (e.g., high product demand increases an employer's cost of lost sales; a high level of market competition increases an employer's risk of market share loss in the event operations are curtailed).
- Labor market conditions (e.g., a relatively low supply of qualified labor reduces the risk of striker replacement).
- Establish support groups for strikers and their families to help maintain striker solidarity.
- Keep strikers informed about the progress of efforts to resolve the labor dispute.
- Encourage a consumer boycott of the primary employer's goods or services.

Continuing to operate during a strike may be a viable management alternative where the following conditions are met:[46]

- There is a high risk of loss of market share if the firm ceases operation.
- An adequate supply of labor is available to operate the firm at reasonable costs.
- The union's anticipated response to management's decision to continue to operate will be limited or manageable.

The use of strike replacements (particularly permanent replacements) during an economic strike escalates the tensions between the parties and often prolongs the length of a strike's duration.

Many organizations have an emergency strike manual that provide specific and detailed plans in the event of a strike. The manual typically has two major components: (1) specific job assignments for nonstriking employees, professional employees, and managers and (2) checklists of appropriate strike activities, such as notifying customers and suppliers, contacting law enforcement officials, and providing food and housing for those staying on the job. In cases where the work is highly automated, such as in the telephone industry, employees' strikes may be less effective because companies find it easier to continue to operate, at least during short strikes. Management might also seek professional assistance from employer colleagues, trade associations, or members of the Society for Human Resource Management.[47]

Although union and management officials carefully consider the advantages and disadvantages of work stoppage strategies and tactics, they are not entirely free to implement these activities as they please. While condoned as a viable part of the collective-bargaining process, the use of economic pressure tactics are extensively regulated by federal, state, and local laws.[48] Knowledge of labor law principles is essential to developing and implementing effective strike strategies and tactics.

Reinstatement Rights of Unfair Labor Practice and Economic Strikers

Employees engaged in an unfair labor practice (ULP) strike cannot be permanently replaced but may be temporarily replaced by an employer for the purpose of continuing normal business operations. An unfair labor practice strike can occur at any time to protest the commission of an employer unfair labor practice and cannot be barred by language contained in a negotiated no strike agreement. Participating in an unfair labor practice strike entails less risk for an employee in the sense that a striker knows he or she will eventually return to work when the dispute ends. Since the decision to participate in an unfair labor practice strike is voluntary, ULP strikers are not entitled to back pay for wages lost during their withdrawal of labor. An exception to this rule would occur if an employee's loss in pay was the direct result of an employer's unfair labor practice. For example, an illegally discharged employee would be entitled to back pay as part of a ULP remedy, but employees who subsequently engaged in a ULP strike to protest that illegal discharge would not be entitled to a back pay remedy.

Economic strikers may be either temporarily or permanently replaced by an employer for the purpose of continuing normal business operations.[49] The threat of hiring permanent striker replacements can significantly increase employees' perceived risk of engaging in or continuing a work stoppage. The United States is one of the few industrialized countries in the world that permits the permanent replacement of lawful economic strikers during a labor dispute.[50]

Employers hire replacement workers in approximately 14 percent of strikes.[51] Temporary replacements are more likely to be hired than permanent replacements during a strike, which may help to reduce some of the risks associated with hiring strike replacements. The use of strike replacements both lengthens the duration of strikes and increases the chance that violent acts will occur compared to strikes not involving the hiring of replacement workers.

If not permanently replaced, an economic striker has a right to be reinstated to the job at any time during a labor dispute after making an unconditional request for reinstatement to the employer. An economic striker's job is not considered to be filled on a permanent basis unless the employer indicates such an intent by hiring a replacement and the replacement is actually performing the job duties of the striker's position (as opposed to being in engaged in training in order to qualify to perform the normal job duties of the striking employee). If temporary replacement workers are hired during a strike, lawful strikers will go back to work after a settlement is reached and the temporary replacements will be dismissed.

An employer must be careful when hiring permanent strike replacements to ensure that no promise of continued or permanent employment is extended to replacements hired. Employees hired during a strike who receive a promise of permanent employment may sue an employer for breach of contract if subsequently laid off due to a negotiated strike settlement or NLRB-ordered unfair labor prac- tice remedy requiring striking employees be reinstated.[52] Offering "regular" em- ployment or "full-time" employment would not generally be considered equivalent to an offer of permanent employment. Other practical considerations may also discourage an employer from exercising the legal right to replace strikers. It is usu- ally not easy to replace all of the striking employees, especially if work operations are complicated and employees cannot be adequately trained in a short time.

Efforts to enact a legislative ban on the use of permanent strike replace- ments such as proposed in the Workplace Fairness Act in the early 1990s have not been successful. Employers have argued that a legislative ban against hiring permanent striker replacements would drastically shift the balance of relative bargaining power to unions and would result in higher labor costs. However, in a Canadian study where the hiring of permanent striker replacements is banned by provincial law, no evidence was reported supporting the contention that striker replacement legislation alters the existing balance of power between management and labor.[53] Despite support from President Clinton and a national poll of 1,000 Americans that showed that 65 percent of the respondents believed that companies should not be allowed to permanently replace striking workers, Congress refused to pass the Workplace Fairness Act, primarily because the ma- jority of Congress who supported the legislation could not obtain the 60 votes needed to end a Republican filibuster.[54]

Even in cases where an economic striker is permanently replaced, the striker retains a right to be placed on a **preferential recall list.** The employer must fill any permanent vacancy occurring in a bargaining unit position there- after by first offering the job vacancy to a qualified individual on the preferential recall list before the job vacancy could be filled by a job applicant not on the preferential recall list **(Laidlaw-Fleetwood doctrine).**[55] An employer and union may negotiate a reasonable time limit following a strike during which perma- nently replaced economic strikers would be entitled to exercise their preferential recall rights.[56] Factors that might affect what constitutes a "reasonable time pe- riod" could include:

- Historical data on normal employee attrition rates (e.g., voluntary turnover, discharge for cause, retirement, permanent disability).

- Future probability that new job openings may occur over some extended time period (e.g., new product development, plant expansion, industry economic forecast).

- The percentage of total employees eligible for recall who were actually recalled during the negotiated time limit.

An employer is not permitted to grant **superseniority** or retroactive seniority rights to permanent strike replacements in an effort to protect their recall rights in any future layoff situation where the labor contract calls for reinstatement to be accomplished according to seniority.[57] A grant of superseniority essentially exempts that individual from the normal application of seniority rights in mak- ing employment decisions. Since former economic strikers on a preferential re- call list were hired before the permanent strike replacements, former strikers on a preferential recall list almost always have more seniority than replacement workers hired during a strike.

Unlawful Strike Misconduct

Employees who engage in an unlawful strike or serious strike misconduct during an otherwise lawful strike forfeit their normal rights to reinstatement. In addition to forfeiture of job reinstatement rights, some strike misconduct may also represent a violation of criminal or civil statutes, subjecting an employee to legal penalties such as a monetary fine or imprisonment. Serious strike misconduct would include:

- Acts of violence directed at managers, co-workers, customers, suppliers, or the general public.

- Intentional destruction of private property (e.g., acts of vandalism or sabotage).

- Verbal threats intended to intimidate or coerce an individual in the exercise of his or her lawful rights.

All strike misconduct is examined in light of the surrounding circumstances, and the courts recognize the heightened emotions that exist and may affect the conduct of parties involved in a work stoppage. The use of derogatory language by picketers directed at individuals crossing an established picket line, although unpleasant or embarrassing for the target of such verbal abuse to endure, will not generally be classified as serious strike misconduct.[58]

Unions typically try to deter union members from crossing authorized union picket lines by adopting a rule permitting the union to impose a reasonable monetary fine on any union member who engages in such conduct.[59] A union may not prevent a union member from resigning his or her union membership at any time.[60] To avoid the imposition of a monetary fine for crossing an authorized union picket line, an employee would simply need to resign from union membership prior to crossing the picket line. Resigning one's union membership would not affect an employee's status as an employee of the company or as a member of the bargaining unit.

Employee Picketing Rights

Employees have a right to publicize a labor dispute involving a primary employer in a peaceful manner to encourage public support for the striking employees' (union's) position.[61] Such publicity often takes the form of picket activity, which is primarily regulated by state and local laws. Efforts by state and local authorities to restrict employee picket activity requires a careful balancing of employee First Amendment free speech rights, employer property rights, and the government's interests in maintaining labor peace, the free flow of commerce, and protecting the public's interests.

Some reasonable restrictions on the right to picket during a labor dispute include:[62]

- Banning picket activity conducted for an unlawful purpose or involving violence.

- Reasonable limits on the times when picketing may occur; noise level; number of picketers present at one time; or mandatory spacing between picketers to ensure entry or exit from the employer's property.

- Requiring that the content of picket signs be truthful and clearly identify the employer with whom the picketers have a labor dispute.

An employer generally has a right to establish reasonable rules to govern the exercise of free speech on private property. Union picket activity on the employer's private property may generally be banned if (1) the ban is applied in a consistent, nondiscriminatory manner and (2) the union has other reasonable means of communicating its message to the intended audience.[63]

Secondary Strike, Boycott, and Picket Activity

Up to this point the discussion has focused on labor disputes between a primary employer and his or her employees. A **secondary employer** (i.e., one with no direct authority to resolve the labor dispute) may become involved in a labor dispute either voluntarily or involuntarily. A secondary employer who knows or reasonably should have known that engaging in certain conduct would aid a primary employer during a labor dispute is presumed to have voluntarily joined the labor dispute as an **business ally** of the primary employer and therefore can be subjected to the same lawful economic pressure tactics that employees could engage in regarding the primary employer. A secondary employer who agrees to perform work normally done by striking employees (**struck work**) is the most common means of establishing ally status. A primary employer with several plants or ownership of separate firms may find nonstruck entities enmeshed in the labor dispute as a business ally of the primary employer if a high degree of interdependence or comingling of assets is established between the various operations sharing common ownership. Where different operations function independent of each other, common ownership by itself would not be sufficient to establish business ally status of the nonstruck operations. Nor does carrying on an established business relationship with a struck employer by itself establish that a secondary employer has waived its neutral status in the labor dispute. Business ally status is determined case-by-case based on an analysis of the totality of relevant circumstances.

Section 8 (b)(4) of the LMRA makes it an unfair labor practice for a union to engage in tactics for the purpose of pressuring a neutral, secondary employer into becoming involved in a labor dispute. This includes prohibiting a union from discouraging employees of a neutral, secondary employer from performing their normal job duties. However, lawful picketing to publicize a labor dispute that has the effect of causing secondary employees to honor a picket line is not unlawful so long as the intended purpose or object of such picketing was not to induce secondary employees to cease performing their regular job duties.[64]

In balancing the legitimate right of neutral, secondary employers not to be forced to participate in a labor dispute with striking employees' right to use economic pressure tactics against the primary employer and publicize the existence of a labor dispute, Congress did not intend to guarantee neutral, secondary employers complete freedom from economic loss as the result of the lawful exercise of strike rights. For example, a neutral secondary employer's driver scheduled to make a delivery to a struck employer's property who fails to make the delivery after encountering a union picket line at the struck employer's business is presumed to be acting in sympathy with the striking employees. The driver's voluntary decision not to cross the picket line represents a sympathy strike and as a **sympathy striker** the driver's strike rights are equivalent to those of the picketers whose picket line the driver refused to cross.[65] If the picket line was part of a lawful economic strike, the neutral, secondary employer could temporarily or permanently replace the driver if no other reasonable alternative action exists (e.g., reassignment of the driver to another delivery route that would not require him or her to encounter a picket line or rescheduling the delivery to another date where a driver willing to cross the picket line could be assigned to make the delivery). Even though the secondary employer may suffer some costs in the form of lost productivity, time delay, or even the loss of a sale, neither the primary employees' picket activity nor the secondary employer's driver's refusal to cross the picket line would become unlawful merely because the effect of their exercise of lawful strike rights caused an adverse economic impact on the neutral, secondary employer.

Common situs picketing **Common situs picketing** occurs at a location where a primary employer and one or more neutral, secondary employers are engaged in normal business operations at the same time. Common examples of such sites would be a construction worksite where several independent contractors are engaged in business or a shipping dock where several shipping companies may be engaged in business at the same time. The challenge becomes how to permit employees involved in a labor dispute with a primary employer at the site to engage in lawful picket activity without unnecessarily disrupting the ability of neutral, secondary employers to continue to operate at the worksite without becoming enmeshed in the primary employer's labor dispute. The **Moore Dry Dock doctrine** establishes guidelines for lawful picketing at a common situs of a labor dispute.[66] Picketing at a common situs is lawful if:

1. The primary employer is present and engaged in normal business operations at the common situs. Presence can be indicated by the primary employer continuing to schedule deliveries to the site, maintaining equipment at the site, or having setup or maintenance work continue to be performed at the site.

2. Picket signs must clearly identify the primary employer with whom the union has a labor dispute.

3. Picketing must occur at locations reasonably close to the primary employer's operations at the common situs.

Sometimes a primary employer will provide a schedule to the union listing dates and times when the primary employer will be present at the site and thus union picket activity would be permitted. Of course, the primary employer would be required to adhere to the published schedule. If the primary employer maintains an intermittent presence at a worksite so it is impossible for a union to know when the primary employer is or is not going to be present, the union is entitled to presume that the primary employer is present when conducting picket activity at the worksite.

Unions have argued that the employers who occupy a common worksite are so intertwined that a labor dispute with one employer is a labor dispute with all; therefore, unions allege that there are no neutral employers on the site. The Supreme Court rejected this union argument, ruling that general contractors and subcontractors on a building site were separate business entities and should be treated separately with respect to each other's labor controversies.[67] Therefore, picket activity at a common situs of a labor dispute must meet the *Moore Dry Dock* standard to be lawful.

A union may lawfully picket under the Moore Dry Dock standards at the location of a neutral, secondary employer so long as a primary employer is present and engaged in normal business operations at the neutral, secondary employer's site (so-called "picketing between the headlights"). This might occur where a struck primary employer is engaged in providing some service to its customers at the neutral, secondary employer's worksite (e.g., computer repair service is struck by its employees but continues to service accounts at various neutral, secondary employers' business locations during the strike). The union representing the primary employer's repair technicians might follow the repair truck from the primary employer's business and picket at the entrance used by the technician at the neutral, secondary employer's business while the repair person is inside the business. When the primary employer's technician leaves the customer's location, the union's picket activity would also have to cease and the union's picketers would have to follow the repair truck to the next customer's location.

During a labor dispute, the **reserve gate doctrine** permits entrances to a worksite to be clearly marked for the exclusive use of either a primary employer or a neutral, secondary employer and its employees, customers, and suppliers.[68] Picketing by a union during a primary economic labor dispute at a gate reserved for the exclusive use of a neutral, secondary employer would generally be illegal so long as the gate was properly marked, reasonably established, and used only by the neutral, secondary employer. A gate marked for the exclusive use of the primary employer involved in a labor dispute would not be reasonably established if the gate was located so as to unreasonably deny a union an opportunity to convey its intended picket message to the public (e.g., down a dead-end alley seldom used to gain entrance to the worksite). Proper use of reserved gates helps to minimize the disruption in neutral, secondary employers' ability to continue normal business operations at a common situs of a labor dispute while still permitting striking employees to picket the operation of the primary employer.

A situational application of the reserve gate doctrine occurs when a primary employer involved in an economic dispute turns his or her property into a common situs by hiring a neutral, secondary employer to perform work on the primary employer's property during a labor dispute. Such work might involve construction of new buildings, installation of new equipment, major maintenance projects, or other tasks that could be accomplished even though the employer's normal business operations have been curtailed due to the ongoing strike.

Striking employees of a primary employer normally have a right to picket at every entrance to the primary employer's property during a labor dispute. The **General Electric doctrine** establishes the conditions under which a primary employer could lawfully establish a gate on the primary employer's property reserved for the exclusive use of a neutral, secondary employer hired to perform some work for the primary employer during the labor dispute.[69] During a labor dispute, picketing may be prohibited at an entrance to the primary employer's property if the following conditions are met:

1. The gate must be reserved for the exclusive use of a neutral, secondary employer and only used by such employers, their employees, or suppliers. Once the neutrality of a reserved gate has been breached, the gate loses its neutrality and the union could lawfully picket the gate.

2. The work performed by the neutral, secondary employer on the primary employer's property cannot be struck work (i.e., work that except for the work stoppage would have been performed by bargaining unit members).

3. The work performed by the neutral, secondary employer cannot be work that would require a work stoppage to occur in order for the task to be completed. New construction projects, repairs on nonfunctional equipment, or installation of new equipment in a location not already occupied by existing equipment would generally meet this requirement. Major maintenance on equipment currently in use requiring such equipment to be taken out of service in order for the maintenance to be accomplished would not meet this third requirement. The purpose of this third requirement is to reduce management's incentive to force a strike as a means of avoiding payments due workers who were laid off as the result of equipment being taken out of service for maintenance.

Product Picketing Rights Unions sometimes choose to picket the products or services of the primary employer involved in a labor dispute by picketing at the site of neutral, secondary employers who sell the primary employer's product or service. **Product picketing** at a neutral, secondary employers business is lawful for the purpose of encouraging consumers to boycott the products or services of the primary employer involved in a labor dispute.[70] Picket signs must clearly identify the primary employer as the target of the picket activity and only urge a boycott of the primary employer's products or services, not a total boycott of all products or services sold by the neutral, secondary employer. To the extent consumers heed the union's boycott request; the effect will be to impose economic pressure on the primary employer to resolve the labor dispute. Before initiating any product picket activity the union may request a neutral, secondary employer to cease selling the primary employer's products or services for the duration of the labor dispute, which would eliminate the need for the union to engage in any picketing activity at the neutral, secondary employer's business. While the secondary employer is not required to grant the union's request, a prudent employer will weigh the likely effectiveness or duration of such product picket activity against the potential costs (e.g., lost sales, customer dissatisfaction, or negative publicity) it might entail for the neutral, secondary employer were it to occur.

There are two exceptions to a union's right to engage in product picketing at the business of a neutral, secondary employer. First, product picketing can be restricted or prohibited where evidence proves that the effect of such picket activity would cause a *near total boycott* (e.g., 90 percent loss of business) of the neutral, secondary employer.[71] This might occur in the case where the only products or services sold by the neutral, secondary employer consisted of the primary employer's products or services and the union's boycott appeal was very effective in causing customers not to purchase the primary employer's products or services. It may not be clear from the evidence how effective such a union product picket action might be prior to the onset of actual picketing activity. Therefore, a neutral, secondary employer may have to bear some period of picket activity during which evidence as to the effectiveness of the union's picket action can be gathered and presented to a court to obtain a labor injunction or presented to the NLRB to support an unfair labor practice charge against the union.

A second exception to a union's right to engage in product picketing occurs if the product of the primary employer being struck and a neutral, secondary employer are so intertwined (**merged product doctrine**) that it would be impossible for a consumer to boycott the primary employer's product without inducing a near total boycott of the neutral, secondary employer.[72] For example, if the employees of a car battery manufacturer initiated a product picket at a new car dealer who used the primary employer's batteries in all of the vehicles on the sales lot, it would be impossible for a customer to refuse to buy the primary employer's battery without also refusing to buy the neutral, secondary employer's car in which the battery is located.

Handbilling Rights Even where picket activity may be illegal, the LMRA permits other forms of publicity such as **handbilling** to communicate the existence of a labor dispute and seek public support. Attempting to hand a written notice to an individual is typically viewed as a less intrusive (and maybe less effective) means of communicating one's desired message than confronting that individual with picket signs carried by several individuals patrolling back and forth in front of an entrance. Shopping malls that include a multitude of separate employers give rise to some interesting questions about lawful union picket and handbilling activities. The Supreme Court has upheld the right of unions to peacefully distribute handbills urging customers not to shop at stores located in a mall (the handbill used is shown in Exhibit 9.5) until all construction under way at the mall was performed by contractors paying "fair" wages. The Court ruled that the handbill used by the union truthfully revealed the existence of a labor dispute and urged potential customers of the mall to follow a wholly legal course of action, namely, not to patronize the retailers doing business in the mall. The handbilling was peaceful. No picketing or patrolling was involved. The union was within its members' right of free speech to encourage consumers to protest substandard wages by refusing to shop at a mall where such wages were paid.[73]

National Emergency Dispute Resolution Procedures

When labor disputes develop to a stage where they are regarded as having an adverse effect on the national interest, they assume a special significance. Strikes that have a substantial adverse impact on national economic or defense interests are classified as **national emergency strikes** and the federal government has used three methods to deal with such strikes: (1) presidential seizure or other intervention, (2) procedures under the Railway Labor Act, and (3) procedures under the Labor Management Relations Act.

Presidential seizures or attempts at seizure where the government takes control of a company's assets and proceeds to operate the firm have occurred 71 times under four presidents—Lincoln, Wilson, Franklin D. Roosevelt, and Truman—in the interests of maintaining production when actual strikes or threatened strikes caused national emergencies. Most of these presidential seizure actions have occurred at a time when the United States was at war.

The Railway Labor Act provides a procedure for resolving national emergency work stoppages in the railroads and airlines that includes the following:

- The National Mediation Board (NMB) attempts to mediate the dispute, and if unsuccessful, recommends voluntary interest arbitration.

Exhibit 9.5

Handbill Used at Shopping Mall to Influence Shoppers

PLEASE DON'T SHOP AT EAST LAKE SQUARE.

The FLORIDA GULF COAST BUILDING TRADES COUNCIL, AFL-CIO is requesting that you do not shop at the stores in the East Lake Square Mall because of the Mall ownership's contribution to substandard wages.

The Wilson's Department Store under construction on these premises is being built by contractors who pay substandard wages and fringe benefits. In the past, the Mall's owner, The Edward J. DeBartolo Corporation, has supported labor and our local economy by ensuring that the Mall and its stores be built by contractors who pay fair wages and fringe benefits. Now, however, and for no apparent reason, the Mall owners have taken a giant step backwards by permitting our standards to be torn down. The payment of substandard wages not only diminishes the working person's ability to purchase with earned, rather than borrowed, dollars, but it also undercuts the wage standard of the entire company. Since low construction wages at this time of inflation means decreased purchasing power, do the owners of East Lake Mall intend to compensate for the decreased purchasing power of workers of the community by encouraging the stores in East Lake Mall to cut their prices and lower their profits?

CUT-RATE WAGES ARE NOT FAIR UNLESS MERCAHNDSIE PRICES ARE ALSO CUT-RATE.

We ask your support in our protest against substandard wages. Please do not patronize the stores in East Lake Square Mall until the Mall's owner publicly promises that all construction at the Mall will be done using contractors who pay their employees fair wage and fringe benefits.

IF YOU MUST ENTER The MALL TO DO BUSINESS, please express to the store managers your concern over substandard wage and your support of our efforts. We are appealing only to the public—the consumer. We are not seeking to induce any person to cease work or to refuse to make deliveries.

SOURCE: Supreme Court decision in *DeBartolo* v. *Florida Gulf Coast Building & Construction Trades Council*, 485 U.S. 568 (1988).

- If arbitration is rejected by one or both parties, a 30-day period is established during which wage rates, working rules, working conditions, and so forth would remain the same.

- If the dispute threatens to substantially interrupt essential transportation service to any section of the country, the president is notified by the NMB and can choose to appoint a Presidential Emergency Board (PEB). If the president chose not to appoint a PEB, either union or management would be free after the conclusion of the 30-day cooling off period described in the previous step to pursue a strike or lockout action.

- Within 30 days, the PEB appointed to investigate the dispute must issue a written report containing findings of fact regarding the dispute and recommending settlement terms to the parties. Union and management then have an additional 30 days to try and reach a voluntary settlement before either party could resort to any strike or lockout action. During this time, the status quo regarding terms and conditions of employment is maintained. If no voluntary settlement is reached, the president could request Congress to enact legislation mandating settlement terms to resolve the bargaining dispute.

Since the RLA's passage in 1926, its emergency provisions have been invoked about 200 times, an average rate of four times per year, and work stoppages have occurred at the end of the 60-day period at a rate of one per year since 1947. However, government interventions in railroad disputes have averaged about one per year since 1980 but only three PEB's have occurred in the airline industry since 1978.[74] Sixteen federal laws have been passed to deal with specific railroad labor disputes, usually by extending the strike date and involving a third-party mediator or arbitrator. The last time a federal law was passed to intervene was 1992, when Congress stopped a national rail strike and mandated mediation and arbitration of the disputes.

Sections 206-210 of the LMRA establish a procedure for managing a threatened or actual strike or lockout affecting an entire or substantial portion of a private sector industry that, if allowed to occur or continue in the opinion of the president of the United States, would threaten the national health or safety. These provisions include a step-by-step procedure to halt the strike or lockout for 80 days and provide the parties assistance in resolving their disputes. Exhibit 9.6 displays the steps in the national emergency procedure of the LMRA. Prior to engaging in any lawful strike or lockout, the party initiating the work stoppage must have bargained in good faith for 60 days; provided the FMCS at least 30 days' advance notice prior to the current contract's expiration that the parties' voluntary bargaining effort had not yet produced a settlement; and ensured that no contractual bar (e.g., a no strike or lockout clause) was still in effect.

The first step in the national emergency dispute resolution procedure is for the president to appoint a board of inquiry when the actual or threatened strike is believed to be of sufficient severity to imperil the national health or safety. Because of the urgency of the matter, the board will investigate the mandatory bargaining subjects in dispute, gather relevant facts, and make a report to the president in a very short time—usually one to three days.

After the president receives and studies the report, he or she may direct the attorney general to secure an 80-day labor injunction from an appropriate federal district court to prevent or end the strike. Once the injunction is issued, the board of inquiry is reconvened, and after the first 60 days of the injunction period, it will be asked to report to the president on the employer's last offer and any other relevant factors. During those 60 days, the FMCS will attempt to mediate a voluntary settlement between the parties in the dispute. Assuming no voluntary settlement is reached, the board reports the final employer bargaining proposal to the president, who will then instruct the NLRB to conduct and certify a secret ballot vote (between the 60th and 80th days of the injunction period), to determine if employees will accept management's final offer. If employees reject the offer, the attorney general must request the federal district court that issued the 80-day labor injunction to dissolve the injunction. After the 80th day when the labor injunction has expired, the union could legally strike or the employer could initiate a lockout. The final step in the procedure calls for the president to submit a full and comprehensive report to Congress, accompanied by any recommendations that he or she may have (e.g. propose legislation to mandate a settlement or require the parties to submit the dispute to final and binding interest arbitration).

In the first 22 years following the enactment of the LMRA, the national emergency dispute resolution procedure was used 29 times. However, since

Exhibit 9.6

National Emergency Procedure under LMRA
The date on which contract expires (zero point in the diagram) may or may not be the first day of the planned strike.

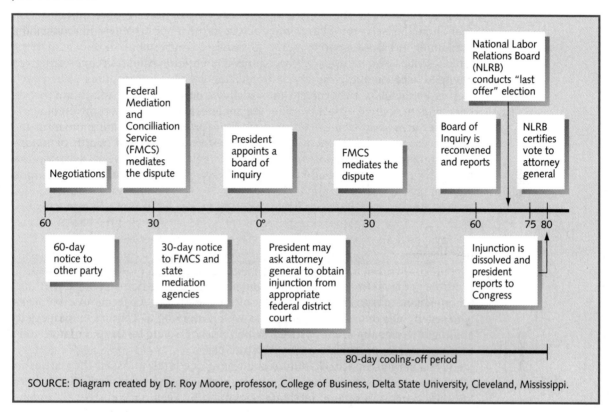

SOURCE: Diagram created by Dr. Roy Moore, professor, College of Business, Delta State University, Cleveland, Mississippi.

1960, it has been used only seven times (five times in 1971 with stevedoring and grain elevator operations). During a strike by eastern coal miners President Carter invoked the procedure in 1978, but a federal judge refused to grant the requested 80-day labor injunction because the attorney general failed to prove that the work stoppage actually represented a national emergency.[75] More recently, President Bush invoked the procedure to halt a lockout of West Coast dockworkers in 2002 where the key issue in dispute was shippers' plans to introduce new technology into port operations and union member concerns over the effect of such action on job security.[76] The Pacific Maritime Association representing shipping and cargo companies at 29 West Coast ports and the International Longshore and Warehouse Union representing some 10,500 dockworkers were able to reach a voluntary contract settlement prior to scheduled expiration of the 80-day labor injunction.

Several reasons have been identified to explain the infrequent need to invoke these national emergency procedures. Such reasons include the internationalization of some product markets, breakup of many centralized, industrywide bargaining arrangements, decline in the percentage of the workforce represented by unions, increase in nonunion operations, increase in the tendency of employers to break strikes by hiring replacement employees, and employer willingness to operate during a work stoppage.[77]

Other critics argue that the use of national emergency dispute resolution procedures subverts the bargaining process by interjecting government action that alters the balance of bargaining power in the labor dispute and reduces the bargaining pressure on one party to reach an agreement at the bargaining table.[78] Critics also believe the procedures do not work as effectively as Congress intended because of the rigidity and predictability of the procedures. When each step is predictable, either party may include the issuance of the injunction as part of its bargaining strategy. Also, the secret-ballot election on the employer's last offer often solidifies the union position rather than facilitating the bargaining process toward settlement. Lastly, because the presidential boards of inquiry are prohibited from proposing settlements, their effectiveness in securing the necessary public support and pressure to move the parties toward settlement is limited.

SUMMARY

Contract ratification plays an important role in helping both management and union leaders gauge the acceptability of tentative contract terms to employees who will be affected by those terms as well as serving to commit employees to abiding by terms that are approved. Union members vote to ratify tentative contract terms in approximately 90 percent of cases.

Various third-party dispute resolution procedures to assist the parties in resolving negotiation disputes were presented, ranging from mediation (where the third party attempts to facilitate resolution by keeping the parties bargaining, acting as a go-between, and offering alternatives) to arbitration, a quasi-judicial procedure in which the bargaining positions are presented to an arbitrator who makes a final and binding decision. Within the range of dispute resolution procedures are the med-arb procedure (which attempts mediation first and then arbitration if mediation fails) and fact-finding (in which the parties present their positions to the fact-finder, other facts are collected, and a report, which includes a recommended resolution of the impasse, is written and presented).

Although voluntary agreements are reached by the parties in the vast majority of negotiation disputes, sometimes one or both parties will resort to the use of economic pressure tactics (e.g., strike, boycott, picketing, lockout) to encourage a party to agree to proposed settlement terms. Work stoppages involve significant costs and risks for all participants and require careful consideration and preparation before embarking on such a course of action.

The right to strike or lockout for lawful reasons using lawful means is an intrinsic part of the labor relations process protected by law. It is a wise union or management representative who understands the difference between possessing a legal right and determining whether it makes practical sense to exercise such a right under the prevailing circumstances of a particular labor dispute. While data indicate that strike activity is less common in labor relations today, the potential threat of such action can still be a credible force encouraging the parties to carefully weigh the cost of agreement against the cost of continued disagreement. It is unfortunate that peaceful bargaining settlements do not attract the media or public attention that work stoppages engender.

Most strikes and related activities involve primary employers, but often secondary employers (not directly involved in the employer–employee relationship) are affected. A complex body of law and judicial decisions covers such activities as consumer and product boycotts and picketing, common situs picketing, and handbilling rights.

Strikes and related activities that have an adverse effect on the national interest may be declared national emergency strikes. Procedures are available in the Railway Labor Act and the Labor Management Relations Act to facilitate their resolutions. Although such impasses occur infrequently, they are significant when they do.

KEY TERMS

- contract ratification process
- mediation
- fact-finding
- interest arbitration
- Federal Mediation and Conciliation Service
- conventional interest arbitration
- final-offer total package
- final-offer issue-by-issue
- mediation-arbitration (med-arb)
- strike
- primary employer
- unconditional request for reinstatement
- economic strike
- unfair labor practice strike
- wildcat strike
- sympathy strike

- jurisdictional strike
- preferential recall list
- Laidlaw-Fleetwood doctrine
- superseniority
- serious strike misconduct
- secondary employer
- struck work
- business ally
- common situs picketing
- Moore Dry Dock doctrine
- reserve gate doctrine
- General Electric doctrine
- product picketing
- merged product doctrine
- handbilling
- national emergency strike

DISCUSSION QUESTIONS

1. What are the chief reasons union members reject tentative agreements?
2. What problems may result from contract rejection?
3. Define the major types of third-party interest dispute resolution procedures. How do they differ, and how do they appear similar?
4. What specific qualities should a mediator possess? Why do these qualities facilitate impasse resolution?
5. Why is interest arbitration used so infrequently in the private sector?

6. To what extent would you agree or disagree with the following statement: "Strikes are an intrinsic and essential element of the collective-bargaining process." Explain your reasoning.

7. What types of preparation do management or union leaders need to engage in prior to a work stoppage?

8. What are some potential costs or risks parties face during a work stoppage and how may such costs or risks be reduced or minimized?

9. Define and discuss the various types of economic pressure tactics union members may use during a primary labor dispute that could affect a secondary employer.

EXPLORING THE WEB

Strikes, Lockouts, and Collective Bargaining

1. **Bureau of Labor Statistics Reports on Collective Bargaining**   Go to the Collective Bargaining Agreements page on the BLS site and read the summary of the most recent annual Major Work Stoppages. Which strike created the most time lost for the year?

http://www.bls.gov/cba

2. **Collective Bargaining and the U.S. Code**   Title 29 is the section of the U.S. Code that contains Federal law on labor. Go to Cornell's Legal Information Institute and search Title 29 for the following terms: picketing, strikes, advanced workplace practices. What is included in the list of unfair labor practices in Section 158?

http://www4.law.cornell.edu/uscode/

3. **Labor Terms** Find the definition of several terms used in labor relations.

Boycott
What is the story behind the first use of this term?

http://www.worldwidewords.org/qa/qa-boy1.htm
http://www.sentex.net/~ajy/facts/words.html

Yellow-dog contract
What legislation outlawed these contracts? These sites provide a good labor history timeline and definition.

http://members.tripod.com/Norrit1/afl-cio/1930.htm
http://www.labor-studies.org/glossary_3.htm

Wildcat strike

http://www.uhwo.hawaii.edu/~clear/Glossary.html#W

4. **Michael Jordan and the NBA Lockout**   Following are examples of media reporting of the National Basketball Association Lockout of 1998. What were the reasons for the lockout? What is the difference between a strike and a lockout?

Chronology of NBA Labor Talks from CBS Sportsline, 1998.

http://cbs.sportsline.com/u/basketball/nba/locktimeline.htm

NBA Lockout Central. (1998). CBS SportsLine

http://cbs.sportsline.com/u/page/covers/basketball/nov98/lockoutcentral.htm

5. Mediation   The Federal Mediation and Conciliation Service regulations and those of other Federal agencies are provided in the Code of Federal Regulations. Read the Code of professional Conduct for Labor Mediators. Check Annual Report for descriptions of FMCS involvement in major labor disputes.

http://www.fmcs.gov/

REFERENCES

1. "Major Work Stoppages in 2002" *News Release* (Washington, D.C.: Bureau of Labor Statistics, U.S. Department of Labor), pp. 1–8.

2. Clyde W. Summers, "Ratification of Agreements," in *Frontiers of Collective Bargaining*, eds. J. T. Dunlop and N. W. Chamberlain (New York: Harper & Row, 1967), pp. 82–83.

3. Herbert J. Lahne, "Union Contract Ratification Procedures," *Monthly Labor Review* 91 (May 1968), pp. 7–10; and Federal Mediation and Conciliation Service, *Thirty-Fourth Annual Report* (Washington, D.C.: Government Printing Office, 1982), p. 21. (The FMCS no longer collects data on contract ratification outcomes.)

4. James E. Martin and Ruth D. Berthiaume, "Predicting the Outcome of a Contract Ratification Vote," *Academy of Management Journal* 38 (June 1995), pp. 916–928.

5. Peter Cappelli and W. P. Sterling, "Union Bargaining Decisions and Contract Ratifications: The 1982 and 1984 Auto Agreements," *Industrial and Labor Relations Review* 41 (January 1988), pp. 195–209.

6. William E. Simkin, "Refusal to Ratify Contracts," *Industrial and Labor Relations Review* 21 (July 1968), pp. 528–529.

7. Charles Odewahn and Joseph Krislov, "Contract Rejections: Testing the Explanatory Hypothesis," *Industrial Relations* 12 (October 1973), pp. 289–296.

8. D. R. Burke and Lester Rubin, "Is Contract Rejection a Major Collective Bargaining Problem?" *Industrial and Labor Relations Review* 26 (January 1973), pp. 832–833.

9. Carolyn Brommer, George Buckingham, and Steven Loeffler, "Cooperative Bargaining Styles at FMCS: A Movement Toward Choices," 2 *Pepperdine Dispute Resolution Law Journal* 465 (2002).

10. William E. Simkin, *Mediation and the Dynamics of Collective Bargaining* (Washington, D.C.: Bureau of National Affairs, 1971), pp. 25–28.

11. Carl Stevens, "Mediation and the Role of the Neutral," in *Frontiers of Collective Bargaining*, eds. Dunlop and Chamberlain, p. 271.

12. Steven Briggs and Daniel J. Koys, "What Makes Labor Mediators Effective?" *Labor Law Journal* 40 (August 1988), pp. 517–520.

13. Stevens, "Mediation and the Role of the Neutral," pp. 280–284.

14. Joseph Krislov and Amira Ealin, "Comparative Analysis of Attitudes Towards Mediation," *Labor Law Journal* 30 (March 1979), p. 173.

15. Patrice M. Mareschal, "Providing High Quality Mediation: Insights from the Federal Mediation and Conciliation Service," *Review of Public Personnel Administration* 18 (Fall 1998), pp. 55–67.

16. Richard B. Peterson and Mark R. Peterson, "Toward a Systematic Understanding of the Labor Mediation Process," in *Advances in Industrial and Labor Relations*, vol. 4, eds. David Lewin, David B. Kipsky, and Donna Sockell (Greenwich, Conn.: JAI Press, 1987), p. 145.

17. Richard B. Peterson and Mark R. Peterson, "Toward a Systematic Understanding," pp. 152–153.

18. Thomas A. Kochan and Todd Jick, "The Public Sector Mediation Process," *Journal of Conflict Resolution* 22 (June 1978), p. 236.

19. Robert A. Baruch Bush, "Efficiency and Protection or Empowerment and Recognition: The Mediator's Role and Ethical Standards in Mediation," *Florida Law Review* 41 (Spring 1989), pp. 253–286.

20. Michael Marmo, "The Role of Fact-Finding and Interest Arbitration in 'Selling' a Settlement," *Journal of Collective Negotiation in the Public Sector* 24, no. 1 (1995), pp. 78–82.

21. William H. Ross, Jr. "Situational Factors and Alternative Dispute Resolution," *Journal of Applied Behavioral Science* 24, no. 3 (1988), pp. 251–260.

22. Max H. Bazerman and Henry S. Farber, "Arbitrator Decision Making: When Are Final Offers Important?" *Industrial and Labor Relations Review* 39 (October 1985), pp. 76–89.

23. Max H. Bazerman, "Norms of Distributive Justice in Interest Arbitration," *Industrial and Labor Relations Review* 38 (July 1985), pp. 558–570.

24. Joseph B. Rose and Michael Piczak, "Settlement Rates and Settlement Stages in Compulsory Interest Arbitration," *Relations Industrielles* 51 (Fall 1996), pp. 643–645.

25. David E. Bloom and Christopher L. Cavanagh, "Negotiator Behavior under Arbitration," *American Economic Review* 77 (May 1987), pp. 353–355.

26. Craig A. Olson and Barbara L. Rau, "Learning from Interest Arbitration: The Next Round," *Industrial and Labor Relations Review* 50 (January 1997), pp. 237–251.

27. Frederic Champlin, Mario Bognanno, and Paul Schumann, "Is Arbitration Habit Forming? The Narcotic Effect of Arbitration Use," *Labour* 11, no. 1 (1997), pp. 23–42; and James R. Chelius and Marian M. Extejt, "The Narcotic Effect of Impasse-Resolution Procedures," *Industrial and Labor Relations Review* 38 (July 1985), pp. 629–638.

28. Robert Herndon, "Public Sector Dispute Resolution in Transition," *Public Sector Employment in a Time of Transition*, eds. Dale Belman, Morley Gunderson, and Douglas Hyatt, (Madison, Wis.: Industrial Relations Research Association), pp. 104–112.

29. Daniel R. Marburger and John F. Scoggins, "Risk and Final Offer Arbitration Usage Rates: Evidence from Major League Baseball," *Journal of Labor Research* 17 (Fall 1996), pp. 735–741.

30. David E. Feller, "The Impetus to Contract Arbitration in the Private Area," *Twenty-Fourth Annual NYU Conference on Labor* (New York: Matthew Bender, 1972), pp. 95–98.

31. Excerpts from NLRB v. *Insurance Agents' International Union*, 361 U.S. 477 (1960).

32. Alex Veiga, "California Grocery Workers Voting on Contract," *Associated Press*, February 28, 2004, pp. 1–2; Alex Veiga, "California Grocers Reject Binding Arbitration," *Associated Press*, February 4, 2004, pp. 1–2; "Secret Talks in California Grocery Strike Fail," *Associated Press*, January 11, 2004; and Alex Veiga, "Labor Leaders to Assist Grocery Strikers," *Associated Press*, January 21, 2004, pp. 1–2.

33. *Harter Equipment, Inc. and Local 825, International Union of Operating Engineers*, 280 NLRB 71 (1986; upheld, 829 F.2d 458 (3rd Cir. 1987); NLRB v. Brown, 380 U.S. 278 (1965); and *American Shipbuilding Company* v. NLRB, 380 U.S. 300 (1965).

34. James E. Martin and Robert R. Sinclair, "A Multiple Motive Perspective on Strike Propensities," *Journal of Organizational Behavior* 22 (June 2001), pp. 387–407.

35. *Gateway Coal Company v. United Mine Workers*, 414 U.S. 368 (1974) and B. A. Brotman, "A Comparative Analysis of Arbitration and National Labor Relations Board Decisions Involving Wildcat Strikes," *Labor Law Journal* 36 (July 1985), p. 440.

36. Michael H. LeRoy, "The Changing Character of Strikes Involving Permanent Striker Replacements, 1935–1990," *Journal of Labor Research* 16 (Fall 1995), p. 437.

37. Bruce E. Kaufman, "The Determinants of Strikes over Time and across Industries," *Journal of Labor Research* 4 (Spring 1983), pp. 173–174.

38. Bruce E. Kaufman, "Research on Strike Models and Outcomes in the 1980s: Accomplishments and Shortcomings,"

in *Research Frontiers in Industrial and Human Resources,* eds. David Lewin, Olivia S. Mitchell, and Peter D. Sherer (Madison, Wis.: Industrial Relations Research Association, 1992), pp. 78–79.

39. Marc Dixon and Vincent J. Roscigno, "Status, Networks, and Social Movement Participation: The Case of Striking Workers," *The American Journal of Sociology* 108 (May 2003), pp. 1292–1327; and Bert Klandermans, "Perceived Costs and Benefits of Participation in Union Action," *Personnel Psychology* 39 (Summer 1986), pp. 380–381.

40. James E. Martin and Robert R. Sinclair, "A Multiple Motive Perspective on Strike Propensities," pp. 402–403; Aaron Cohen, "Attitudinal Militancy and Propensity to Strike Among Unionized Engineers and X-Ray Technicians," *Human Relations* 45 (December 1992), pp. 1333–1366; and James E. Martin, "Predictors of Individual Propensity to Strike," *Industrial and Labor Relations Review* 39 (January 1986), pp. 224–225.

41. N. Nicholson and J. Kelly, "The Psychology of Strikes," *Journal of Occupational Behavior* (October 1981), pp. 275–284.

42. William Serrin, *The Company and the Union* (New York: Knopf, 1973), p. 4.

43. Alex Veiga, "Strike, Lockout Hurting Grocery Workers," *Associated Press,* January 26, 2004, pp. 1–2, and George Getschow, "Strike Woes Pile Up for Leader of Local That Started It All," *The Wall Street Journal,* August 8, 1977, pp. 1, 17.

44. Ashly McCall, "Metal Workers Picket Home of Plant Manager in Nappane, Ind.," *South Bend Tribune,* January 16, 2003, pp. 1–2, and John R. Emshwiller, "Strike Is Traumatic for a Quiet Village in Michigan Woods," *The Wall Street Journal,* July 30, 1977, pp. 1, 24.

45. Michael Barbaro, "Sides Prepare for a Grocery Strike," *Washington Post,* March 17, 2004, p. E01.

46. Charles R. Perry, Andrew M. Kramer, and Thomas J. Schneider, *Operating During Strikes: Company Experiences, NLRB Policies, and Government Regula-*

tions (Philadelphia: University of Pennsylvania, 1982), p. 38.

47. William R. Crandall and Michael L. Menefee, "Crisis Management in the Midst of Labor Strife: Preparing for the Worst," *S.A.M. Advanced Management Journal* 61 (Winter 1996), pp. 11–15; L. C. Scott, "Running a Struck Plant: Some Do's and Don'ts," *S.A.M. Advanced Management Journal* 38 (October 1973), pp. 58–62 and John G. Hutchinson, *Management under Strike Conditions* (New York: Holt, Rinehart and Winston, 1966).

48. Julius G. Getman and F. Ray Marshall, "The Continuing Assault on the Right to Strike," *Texas Law Review* 79 (February 2001), pp. 703–735.

49. *NLRB v. Mackay Radio & Telegraph Co.,* 304 U.S. 333 (1938).

50. George S. Roukis and Mamdouh I. Farid, "An Alternative Approach to the Permanent Striker Replacement Strategy," *Labor Law Journal* 44 (February 1993), pp. 81–88.

51. Peter Crampton and Joseph Tracy, "The Use of Replacement Workers in Union Contract Negotiations: The U.S. Experience, 1980–1989," *Journal of Labor Economics* 16 (October 1998), pp. 674–676.

52. *Belknap, Inc. v. Hale,* 463 U.S. 491 (1983); and David B. Stephen and John P. Kohl, "The Replacement Worker Phenomenon in the Southwest: Two Years after *Belknap, Inc. v. Hale,*" *Labor Law Journal* 37 (January 1986), pp. 48–49.

53. John W. Budd and Wendell E. Pritchett, "Does the Banning of Permanent Strike Replacements Affect Bargaining Power?" *Proceedings of the 46th Annual Meeting of the Industrial Relations Research Association* (Madison, Wis.: IRRA, 1994), pp. 370–376.

54. "Poll Shows Two-Thirds of Americans Oppose Replacing Workers Who Strike," *Daily Labor Report,* June 15, 1994, p. AA-1.

55. *Laidlaw Corporation v. NLRB,* 414 F.2d 99 (7th Cir. 1969); *NLRB v. Fleetwood Trailer Company,* 389 U.S. 375 (1967).

56. *United Aircraft Corporation,* 191 NLRB 62 (1971).

57. *NLRB* v. *Erie Resistor Corporation*, 373 U.S. 221 (1963); and William T. Krizner, "The Mackay Doctrine: Much More Than Mere Dicta," *Labor Law Journal* 49 (May 1998), pp. 997–999.

58. *North Cambria Fuel Co.* v. *NLRB*, 645 F.2d 177 (3rd Cir. 1981); see also: John R. Erickson, "Forfeiture of Reinstatement Rights through Strike Misconduct," *Labor Law Journal* 31 (October 1980), pp. 602–616.

59. *NLRB* v. *Allis-Chalmers Manufacturing Company*, 388 U.S. 175 (1967).

60. *Pattern Makers' League of North America* v. *NLRB*, 473 U.S. 95 (1985).

61. *Thornhill* v. *Alabama*, 310 U.S. 88 (1940).

62. *Lowe Excavating Company* v. *International Union of Operating Engineers, Local 150*, 327 Ill. App. 711 (2002) and Mary Swerczek, "Judge: Picketers Get 25 Seconds; Running Kaiser Strike Means Jail Time for 3," *The Times-Picayune*, May 13, 2000, p. B01.

63. *Lechmere Inc.* v. *NLRB*, 502 U.S. 527 (1992).

64. *NLRB* v. *International Rice Milling Company*, 341 U.S. 665 (1951) and *United Steelworkers of America* v. *NLRB*, 376 U.S. 492 (1964).

65. Bruce Feldacker, *Labor Guide To Labor Law*, 4th ed. (Upper Saddle River, N.J.: Prentice-Hall, 2000), pp. 276–278, 281–283.

66. *Moore Dry Dock Company and Sailors' Union of the Pacific*, 92 NLR 547 (1950); and *Sailors' Union of the Pacific* v. *NLRB*, 366 U.S. 667 (1950).

67. *NLRB* v. *Denver Building Trade & Construction Council*, 341 U.S. 675 (1951).

68. *Local 501, International Brotherhood of Electrical Workers* v. *NLRB*, 756 F.2d 888 (DC Cir. 1985).

69. *Local 761, International Union of Electrical, Radio & Machine Workers* v. *NLRB*, 366 U.S. 667 (1961).

70. *NLRB* v. *Fruit and Vegetable Packers & Warehousmen, Local 760*, 377 U.S. 58 (1964) and *NLRB* v. *Servette, Inc.*, 377 U.S. 46 (1964).

71. *NLRB* v. *Retail Store Employees Union, Local 1001, Retail Clerks International Association (Safeco Insurance Co.)*, 444 U.S. 1011 (1980).

72. *The Kroger Company* v. *NLRB*, 647 F.2d 634 (6th Cir. 1980).

73. *Edward J. DeBartolo Corporation* v. *Florida Gulf Coast Building & Construction Trades Council ET AL.*, 485 U.S. 568 (1988).

74. General Accounting Office, *Airline Labor Relations: Information on Trends and Impact of Labor Actions* (Washington, D.C.: U.S. General Accounting Office, 2003), pp. 15–16 at http://www.gao/gov/cgi-bin/getrpt?GAO-03-652.

75. C. Howard Davis, William M. Eisenberg, and Ronald E. Kutscher, "Quick Special Purpose Surveys Passed Test During Coal Strike," *Monthly Labor Review* 102 (February 1979), pp. 62–64.

76. Jim Puzzanghera, Jennifer Bjorhus, and Matt Marshall, "West Coast Ports to Reopen Today; Bush Uses Authority to Intervene in Dispute," *Knight Ridder Tribune Business News*, October 9, 2002, pp. 1–3; and J. Martin McOmber, "Six-Year Deal Ends West Coast Dockworker Dispute," *Knight Ridder Tribune Business News*, January 23, 2003, pp. 1–2.

77. Charles M. Rehmus, "Emergency Strikes Revisited," *Industrial and Labor Relations Review* 43 (January 1990), pp. 176–180.

78. Michael H. LeRoy and John H. Johnson IV, "Death by Lethal Injunction: National Emergency Strikes Under the Taft-Hartley Act and the Moribund Right to Strike," 43 *Arizona Law Review* 63 (Spring 2001).

The Aftermath of a Strike

On August 6, the collective-bargaining agreement between the company and the union expired. Two days later, the union called a strike at the company's facilities, including those at 3303 Express Lane, St. Louis, Missouri. The strike ended on August 28 with the signing of a new 3-year agreement. The following day, employees began returning to work. During the strike, a substantial number of bargaining unit employees at the plant crossed the union's picket line and continued to work.

On September 2, the union distributed materials to its union stewards for posting on bulletin boards maintained by the union at the company's facilities. One of the items posted was a commentary by author Jack London, entitled "Definition of a Scab":

> After God had finished the rattlesnake, the toad, and the vampire, he had some awful substance left with which he made a SCAB. A SCAB is a two-legged animal with a corkscrew soul, a water-logged brain, and a combination backbone of jelly and glue. Where others have hearts, he carries a tumor of rotten principles.
>
> When a SCAB comes down the street men turn their backs and angels weep in Heaven, and the devil shuts the gates of Hell to keep him out. No man has the right to SCAB, so long as there is a pool of water deep enough to drown his body in or a rope long enough to hang his carcass with. Judas Iscariot was a gentleman . . . compared with a SCAB; for betraying his master, he had the character to hang himself—a SCAB hasn't. Esau sold his birthright for a mess of pottage. Judas Iscariot sold his Savior for thirty pieces of silver. Benedict Arnold sold his country for a promise of a commission in the British Army. The modern strikebreaker sells his birthright, his country, his wife, his children, and his fellow man for an unfulfilled promise from his employer, trust or corporation.
>
> Esau was a traitor to himself. Judas Iscariot was a traitor to his God. Benedict Arnold was a traitor to his country. A strikebreaker is a traitor to himself, a traitor to his God, a traitor to his country, a traitor to his family, and a traitor to his class. THERE IS NOTHING LOWER THAN A SCAB. . . .

Union steward Cora Able immediately posted the "Definition of a Scab" along with another article, entitled "From Cora's Desk," praising the strikers and criticizing those who remained on the job, on a union bulletin board in the computer terminal room, adjacent to Room 102 at the company's plant. Able posted the items in response to a memo from chief union steward, employee Anita Cain, requesting that she do so.

Able has been responsible for posting material on the union bulletin board in the computer terminal room since she became the union job steward 3 years ago. Able had previously posted campaign literature regarding candidates for union office, notices of union meetings, and articles from union newsletters on this bulletin board. Able had also removed comic strips from the bulletin board. Before September 2, no company supervisor had ever told Able what she could or could not post on the union's bulletin board, nor had any company supervisor ever removed anything from this board before this date.

The company had no written rules concerning the posting of literature on the union's bulletin boards on the company's premises. Neither the current nor previous collective-bargaining agreements covering bargaining unit employees contained any provision regarding the union's bulletin boards at the company's facilities.

Continued

During the afternoon of September 2, company supervisor Joe Bay saw several employees near the bulletin board, apparently reading the posted articles. Supervisor Bay removed the "Definition of a Scab" and deposited it in a garbage can. Union steward Able noticed that the article had been removed and asked Bay where it was. Supervisor Bay told her he had removed it, balled it up, and thrown it into the garbage can.

Union steward Able took the sheet from the can, then got another copy from her desk, and hung it on the union bulletin board. In the presence of several other employees, supervisor Bay promptly snatched this copy down, telling Able, "this mess [isn't] going to hang up here." Bay then specifically prohibited Able from posting another copy and warned her of disciplinary action if she did so. Able called the chief union steward who spoke to supervisor Bay requesting that he leave the literature on the bulletin board. Bay then told the chief union steward that the "Definition of a Scab" had no business on the board and was causing animosity among the clerks.

A half-hour later, supervisor Linda Trevino informed union steward Able that another supervisor, Ralph Coe, wanted to see her. Coe had a copy of the "Definition of a Scab" in his hand, and he told Able, "We're not going to have this mess hanging in this office." In the presence of supervisors Trevino and Bay, Coe also warned Able that she could be disciplined "for insubordination." Union steward Able asked to be excused and on returning to her desk called chief union steward Miller again.

Fifteen minutes later, supervisor Trevino told Able, "We would like to see you for 5 minutes." Able told Trevino that she did not want to go back to supervisor Coe's office. However, Able complied on Trevino's assurance that the return to Coe's office would take only 5 minutes, long enough to receive an apology. In Coe's office, Able was asked to tell her side of the incident. Supervisor Coe apologized, as did supervisor Bay, for the way they had treated Able in front of the other employees. Coe did not retract his support for supervisor Bay's action in removing the article and preventing its reposting.

On September 1, union job steward Milton Musk posted a copy of the "Definition of a Scab" on a union bulletin board located in a break room next to Rooms 208 and 209, the Switching Control Center, at the company's plant. Musk had been responsible for posting material on this bulletin board for the past 3 years. As a matter of practice, Musk had posted on the board notices of union meetings, listings of job vacancies provided to the union, lists of union officers' names, announcements for an employee charitable organization, and the campaign material of candidates for union office. Occasionally, Musk removed cartoons from the board that had been posted by employees. Before September 1, no supervisor had ever told Musk what he could or could not post on the union bulletin board.

The "Definition of a Scab" remained on the union bulletin board in the Switching Control Center break room until about 4 P.M., September 1. About that time, supervisor Wesley Vie directed Musk to remove "Definition of a Scab." Union steward Musk said he did not wish to do so. Supervisor Vie removed the printed copy of the "Definition of a Scab" as Musk watched.

The following day, before 7 A.M., the "Definition of a Scab" again appeared on the bulletin board. Supervisor Tom Davis summoned union steward Musk to his office at approximately 8 A.M. and told him to take down the "Definition of a Scab" from the union's bulletin board. Musk protested that he did not put it up, and he should not have to take it down. Supervisor Davis then warned Musk that he would suspend him if he continued to refuse to obey the order to take it down. Supervisor Davis asked for Musk's building pass and key, whereupon Musk requested permission to make a telephone call. After consulting a union district steward, Musk removed the "Definition of a Scab." Musk again told Davis that it was unfair that he had to remove the article when he had not posted it. Supervisor Davis told Musk that he "didn't want trash like that posted."

The union filed an unfair labor practice charge contending that the company violated Section 8(a)(1) of the LMRA by removing the "Definition of a Scab" from union bulletin boards and by threatening employees with punishment if they posted or reposted the item on those bulletin boards. The company denied that it violated the LMRA on the grounds that the posting of Jack London's pejorative appraisal of nonstriking employees had disrupted the discipline of its employees and thus was beyond the protection of Sections 7 and 8(a)(1) of the act.

Questions

1. How does a union gain the right to use bulletin boards on a company's premises?
2. Why was the union so insistent on having the "Definition of a Scab" posted on the bulletin board?
3. Since the union is already recognized as the exclusive bargaining unit representative and the new contract terms have been settled, how or why does Section (8)(a)(1) apply to this case?
4. Did the supervisors' removal of the posted union material and threats to discipline union members for reposting the "Definition of a Scab" constitute an unfair labor practice under the LMRA? Explain your reasoning.

The Right to Strike

Seven of the Employer's 11 concrete truck drivers met several times during the week of September 16 to discuss their current wage rates; the lack of a medical insurance plan; and whether they should consider joining a union. After meeting with a representative of the national truck drivers' union, four of the seven drivers signed union authorization cards. Employee Santos, one of the card signers, wrote a letter that the seven employees presented to the company's plant manager on Friday, September 20. The letter stated, in part, "Today all employees wish to express a silent strike in pursuance of the right that our salaries be increased to $8.75 per hour. We will not work today . . . until an accord is reached."

Later that Friday morning, the company president met with seven employees and told them that the company was in no position to give any wage increase; however, steps were already under way to establish a medical insurance plan by the end of the year. The seven employees met outside the plant and decided the company's position was unacceptable. The company president stated that the board of directors would be meeting the following day (Saturday) to consider the matter. The seven employees continued their walkout during the rest of Friday.

The board of directors met on Saturday and calculated the annual cost of the employees' wage demand to be $108,000. The board found this unacceptable and decided to replace the seven drivers rather than agree to increase wages. Later on Saturday, the plant manager offered driver positions to three individuals who already had job applications on file with the company. All three applicants accepted the job offer and were scheduled to begin work the following week. On Monday, the seven drivers who had walked out on Friday returned to the company but remained outside the plant entrance. Upon learning that the seven drivers had not reported for work at 8 A.M. on Monday morning but were instead congregating in front of the plant, the company president prepared a letter that was given to each of the seven drivers outside the company's entrance at 9:30 on Monday morning. The letter referred to the walkout on the previous Friday and stated in relevant part: "The circumstances of having abandoned your work without first holding a dialogue, then bringing later on some demands which we cannot face economically at this time, in addition to your refusal to work if your conditions are not met exactly the way [you] stated them, we have to interpret it as a resignation from your job, leaving us without alternatives and unfortunately we have to accept your decision effective today Monday, September 23." The letter went on to state that the Friday work stoppage forced the company to fill some vacancies and curtail its operations in order to recover in part from the losses it had suffered.

After receiving the letters, the seven employees left the plant to attend a meeting with a union representative. Sometime later on that Monday, three of the employees returned to plant and requested reinstatement. The company reinstated the three drivers to their former job. The Union filed an unfair labor practice on behalf of the remaining four truck drivers alleging that each had been unlawfully discharged in violation of the LMRA, as amended.

QUESTIONS

1. Does the work stoppage by the truck drivers in this case represent an economic strike or an unfair labor practice strike?

2. What is the difference between the reinstatement rights of an unfair labor practice striker and an economic striker?

3. Did the employer unlawfully discharge the four truck drivers who never returned to work? Explain your reasoning.

The Reinstatement Offer

On September 13 two employees went on strike to protest their employer's refusal to bargain in good faith. The two employees were approached on the picket line by the company's manager on September 13 and told they were fired for going on strike. On September 16, the company circulated a letter to building tenants stating: "Management has made it clear that any employee who decides to strike, his employment will be terminated immediately with no chance of reinstatement. The building superintendent has assured us he will continue to work. However, two porters have chosen their own demise. Their employment is hereby terminated!"

On September 23, 10 days after the strike had begun, the company's manager sent a reinstatement offer to the two discharged employees by certified mail. The letter stated: "In view of your actions, management had no choice but to replace you. However, due to your fine performance at the position you held, management would be agreeable to reinstating you if you return to work immediately. Should you decide that you would like to return to work, please notify me within five (5) business days. If I do not hear from you I will have no choice but to search for permanent replacements." The two employees did receive the letter but made no response within the specified 5-business-day period or at any time thereafter.

The union filed an unfair labor practice charge on behalf of the two employees, alleging that they had been engaged in an unfair labor practice strike and therefore the employer's discharge was illegal. Approximately 2 years and 2 months later, the NLRB upheld the union's unfair labor practice charge, finding the employer's discharge of the two employees was illegal.

At the unfair labor practice hearing, the employer argued that if it were found guilty of unlawfully discharging the two employees, any back pay remedy should be limited to the first 15 days of the strike. The 15-day period covered the 10 days prior to the date on which management sent the two employees the offer of reinstatement and the 5 business days in which the employees had the opportunity to accept the offer but chose not to do so.

QUESTIONS

1. Did the strike on September 13 by the two employees represent an economic or unfair labor practice strike?

2. Did the company make a lawful reinstatement offer to the two employees, thus terminating the employer's back pay liability after 15 days from their original termination date? Explain your reasoning.

Product Picket Activity

The union engaged in an lawful economic strike against the Brown Bag Company (the primary employer) and decided to establish a product picket line at the site of the Stop & Shop grocery store, a secondary employer who used grocery bags produced by the Brown Bag Company. Although the Stop & Shop grocery store does provide boxes instead of bags to a few customers who specifically request a box, the vast majority of grocery items are carried from the store in bags produced by the Brown Bag Company.

The union's picket signs were carefully worded to identify the Brown Bag Company as the target of the picket action and to request customers of the Stop & Shop grocery store to only boycott bags produced by the Brown Bag Company. During the two days that picketing occurred, 150 of 4,300 customers who shopped at the Stop & Shop grocery store specifically requested a box to transport their groceries rather than a bag. Managers were able to provide enough boxes for about two-thirds of the customers who requested a box rather than use a grocery bag produced by the Brown Bag Company. A few customers brought their own containers from home (e.g., pillow case, bag, or box) to transport their grocery purchases. One customer, upon being told by a Stop & Shop manager that there were no more boxes available, left the store without purchasing or taking any of the grocery items she had brought to the checkout line.

The Brown Bag Company filed an unfair labor practice charge against the union, alleging that the union's product picket action was a violation of Sec. 8 (b)(4), LMRA. The employer sought an order to prevent the union from engaging in further product picket activity at the Stop & Shop grocery store. The employer argued that it is impossible for a customer to comply with the union's boycott of Brown Bag Company grocery bags without also refusing to purchase grocery items sold by the Stop & Shop grocery store, since the grocery store exclusively used grocery bags produced by the Brown Bag Company. As evidence the employer pointed to the fact that there were only enough boxes available for approximately 2.3 percent of the total customers who shopped at the grocery store during the two days of product picket activity. The employer argued it was not reasonable to expect that customers would bring their own containers with them to transport grocery items when shopping at the Stop & Shop grocery store.

QUESTIONS

1. Would the Stop & Shop grocery store in this case be classified as a neutral, secondary employer or a "business ally" of the Brown Bag Company? Explain your reasoning.
2. Should the merged product doctrine be applied in this case to declare that the union's product picket action was unlawful? Explain your reasoning.

PART 3

Administering the Labor Agreement

After the collective bargaining agreement has been negotiated and accepted by both union members and management, the day-to-day tasks of administering the agreement begins. Although not the most publicized nor the most dramatic part of labor relations, this process involves more union and management officials than contract negotiations and provides meaning and common law principles to the ageement. These chapters present the fundamentals of contract administration and labor and employment arbitration followed by a subject that relates to every workplace—employee discipline.

CHAPTER 10

Contract Administration

L*abor agreement negotiation is usually the most publicized and dramatic aspect of labor relations. Strike deadlines, negotiators in shirtsleeves working around the clock to avert a possible strike, and the economic settlement of the labor agreement receive attention from the news media. The day-to-day administration of the labor agreement, on the other hand, receives little, if any, recognition beyond that given by the involved parties. Contract administration, however, involves more labor and management officials than does negotiations, and it applies meaning and common-law principles to negotiated labor provisions. In contract negotiations, the union is typically the initiator, but in contract administration, management assumes this role. In other words, management exercises its administrative initiative to make decisions and to direct the business operations. Management makes many decisions such as who to promote, who to lay off, whether just cause exists for discipline, and so on. The union monitors these decisions and files a grievance when the union believes management's decision is inconsistent with the provisions of the labor agreement.*

This chapter first defines employee grievances and explores their sources and significance. The next section examines the grievance procedure: its typical steps, the relationships among grievance participants, and theoretical as well as practical concerns involved in contract administration. Alternative dispute resolution (ADR), a process to resolve grievances with the assistance of a neutral third party, is discussed. The chapter concludes with a discussion of the union's duty of fair representation.

Grievances: Definition, Sources, and Significance

An employee **grievance** represents the core of contract administration and is defined as an employee's alleged violation of the labor agreement that is submitted to the grievance procedure for resolution. A grievance is therefore distinguished from an employee's concern that is unrelated to labor agreement provisions and is not submitted to the grievance procedure. Grievances are usually written out at the first or second steps (Exhibit 10.1). This has several advantages for management and union officials:

1. Both union and management representatives need a written record of their daily problem resolutions. This record generates precedents that can guide future actions and save time in deciding similar grievances.

2. Written grievances tend to reduce the emotionalism present in many employee concerns. Verbal confrontation on an emotional issue can produce exaggerated accusations that may irreparably harm the relationship between the parties. Consequently, writing the grievance may be necessary for its rational discussion.

Exhibit 10.1

Examples of Incorrect and Correct Grievance Forms

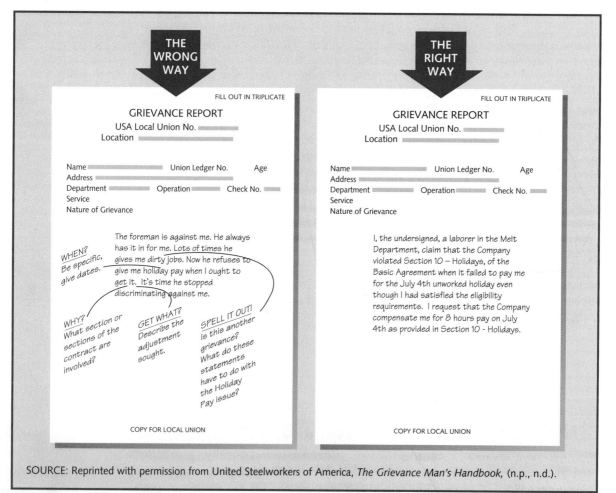

SOURCE: Reprinted with permission from United Steelworkers of America, *The Grievance Man's Handbook*, (n.p., n.d.).

3. A written statement allows management and union representatives to focus on the employee's original grievance. As will be discussed further, a grievance can proceed through several steps that involve many more individuals than the aggrieved employee. Union officials may expand one employee's initial allegation into a broader philosophical issue. For example, a complaint over the company's unilateral increase in prices of candy bars for the vending machine could conceivably be magnified in subsequent steps to protest the company's arbitrary and capricious actions in other working conditions.

4. Written grievances can benefit management in cases where the employee is apprehensive about signing a written protest. One research effort found that supervisors react negatively in subsequent performance ratings of employees who file grievances against them that are decided in the employees' favor.[1]

5. Even though most labor agreements permit a union officer to file a grievance on behalf of the grievant, requiring grievances to be written probably reduces the total number that management representatives must administer.

One definition of a grievance is extremely broad and hinges on the employee's perception that he or she has a grievance. Assume, for example, that Employee A protests Employee B's "immoral" behavior. This protest could be an oral complaint without reference to the grievance procedure, or the employee could insist the complaint represents a violation of the terms of the labor agreement. The supervisor can attempt to convince the employee that the complaint is unrelated to the terms of the labor agreement.

Suppose the employee cites a contractual provision in the argument, such as an article stressing the "company's obligation to maintain a work environment in as safe a condition as possible." After unsuccessfully discussing the issue with Employee A, the supervisor has two options: (1) to refuse to accept the employee's grievance or (2) to accept the employee's grievance and deny it in the written grievance answer on the basis that there is no contractual violation. Not wishing to risk a time-consuming unfair labor practice charge, the supervisor will probably take the second alternative.

The broad definition of a grievance realizes, then, that there is a difference between accepting an employee's grievance and deciding the merits of an employee's grievance. The broader definition safeguards against unfair labor practice charges and at the same time preserves management's right to deny the grievance in its written answer.

Reasons for Employee Grievances

Some research has focused on differences between employees who do not file grievances and employees who do. One such study found that employees who file grievances are younger; more active in their unions; and less satisfied with their job, supervisor, and union.[2]

To better understand the reasons behind employee grievances, the following example is given. A first-line supervisor administers a labor agreement that has the following provisions pertaining to management's rights and the scheduling of work to be performed on a holiday:

Article III: Management Rights
Section 1.   The Company's right to hire, fire, and direct the working force, transfer or promote is unqualified as long as this right is not used in any conflict with any provision of this contract.

Article IX: Holiday Scheduling
Section 1.   When less than a normal crew is required to work on a holiday, the following procedure will apply:
(a) The senior employee working in the classification desired will be given the opportunity to work.
(b) Employees assigned holiday work will be paid a minimum of 8 hours at time and one-half the contract rate of pay.
(c) If an employee works out of classification on the holiday, the senior employee in the appropriate classification will also be paid a minimum of 8 hours at time and one-half his or her contract rate of pay.

Article XII: Bargaining Unit Work
Section 1.   Supervisors may perform bargaining unit work only during emergencies.

With these provisions in mind, consider the following chain of events. A crane operator is needed to work the July 4th holiday. The senior employee in this classification starts work on his shift; however, after he has worked a half-hour, the crane breaks down and can no longer be operated. Management believes the maintenance department will be able to repair the crane within 2 hours. All job classifications typically perform some minor housekeeping and cleanup work, such as dusting and picking up debris around the workstation; however, there is also a janitor's classification in the labor agreement.

The first-line supervisor has at least four options. He can send the employee home, although Section 1(b) of the labor agreement compels management to pay that employee 8 hours at one and one-half times the employee's hourly pay rate. Consequently, the first option is not attractive to management.

The second option would have the employee remain at work and do nothing until the crane is repaired. Because management is already obligated to pay the employee for the entire shift, it does not cost any additional money to have the employee sit in the work shed until crane operations can be renewed. The first-line supervisor is not likely to take this option, particularly if higher-level management officials and other hourly employees see this individual being paid while not performing work.

The third option, having the crane operator perform minor housekeeping chores until the crane is repaired, appears most beneficial to management. Yet there is a good possibility that this action will result in a grievance from the senior employee in the janitorial classification, asking payment for 8 hours at time and one-half because Section 1(c) would apparently have been violated. Another option for the supervisor is to proceed on repairing the crane to minimize the lost time. Because the agreement allows supervisors to perform bargaining unit work only during emergencies, the supervisor must be prepared to convince the union that an emergency has occurred.

The employee could file a grievance for one or more of the following reasons.

1. To Protest a Contractual Violation   When labor and management officials negotiate a labor agreement, they are mainly concerned with agreement over the major issues. The negotiators are not concerned with determining the precise meaning of every word in the labor agreement, particularly if few or no previous problems have arisen from the contract language. Similarly, these officials cannot possibly anticipate all of the unique situations that could potentially destroy or add to the negotiated terms of the labor agreement. Consequently, union and management negotiators often gloss over the "unimportant" provisions, leaving potential interpretational problems to those who must live with and administer the labor agreement on a daily basis.

In the crane operator example, local union officials could contend that the crane operator did "work out of classification"—a clear violation of Section 1(c). Management, on the other hand, could contend that the needed holiday work was within the scope of a crane operator's job and point out the impracticality of paying an employee an amount equal to 12 hours' pay simply to dust or straighten up the workplace. Another management contention could be that minor housekeeping chores are performed by all employees; therefore, the crane operator did not work out of classification on the day in question. Hence, Article III, "Management Rights," would prevail in this situation. Even further, management could claim that an emergency has been created.

2. To Draw Attention to a Problem in the Plant   Some grievances do not protest violation of the labor agreement; instead, they stress that management has obligations beyond the scope of the labor agreement. Most grievances over alleged safety hazards fall into this category because labor agreements may not specify management's obligation in this area. The employee might realize that there is no contractual violation but still file the grievance to communicate concern to management over a safety issue. In our example, the grievance over holiday scheduling might have been filed, not over receiving payment for the senior janitor in the classification but to give union officers the forum in which to stress the inadequate number of maintenance employees for equipment repair.

Unions quite often draw attention to a problem in the hopes of setting the stage for future labor agreement negotiations. A common union tactic is to file several grievances over a particular issue to buttress and document union demands during negotiation of the subsequent labor agreement.

For example, labor unions adhering to a job-protection philosophy do not want supervisory personnel performing their members' work because these activities could reduce overtime opportunities or even result in employees being laid off. In the course of the workday, supervisors may perform several chores that could be classified as bargaining unit work. Employees file grievances whenever the supervisor engages in this practice no matter how minor that physical activity may be (e.g., changing a light bulb). Armed with several grievances, in formal contract negotiations the union can dramatize its concern that

(1) supervisors performing bargaining unit work is a widespread problem and (2) a contractual provision restricting supervisors from performing bargaining unit work would save the company time and money by eliminating related grievances.

3. To Make the Grievant and Union Feel Important

In nonunion settings, the authority of managerial policies and actions often goes unchallenged. However, the grievance procedure permits and encourages an employee to protest an alleged wrong committed by management officials. Some employees raise their perceived organizational status by calling their organizational superiors on the carpet to explain their actions. Such grievances are often filed against a supervisor who flaunts authority unnecessarily, to protest the supervisor's personality as well as actions.

Similarly, some union officials wish to emphasize their importance through grievance involvement. Those falling into this category use grievances and contract administration problems to advance to high political office in the union. One research study found a positive relationship between encouragement of grievances and union rivalry as measured by closeness of vote in the most recent union election. "As incumbent union leaders contend with challengers for member support, they may seek to use the grievance process to extend support for themselves."[3] Grievances in these cases provide a forum where the union steward can demonstrate his or her verbal and intellectual capabilities to other management and union officials. Other union officials might wish to strengthen the union as an institution through the grievance procedure. Here, the importance of the union (not of the union official) is stressed—the union is safeguarding its members from management's arbitrary and capricious actions.

On some occasions, employees have a genuine belief that their supervisor is mistreating them in work assignments and pay raises. These employees want an opportunity to explain their feelings and vent their frustrations. If they are not allowed to be heard, the beliefs of mistreatment will escalate.

4. To Get Something for Nothing

Some managers believe that a few employees file grievances to receive pay related to their skill in formulating and writing grievances instead of their work efforts. The janitor in our crane operator example might not have been inclined to file a grievance at the time the work was denied. Indeed, he may have had previously scheduled holiday plans and refused to work if management had made the initial offer. However, assuming the janitor's classification paid $8 an hour, the janitor might have felt that time and one-half for 8 hours ($96) was worth the effort to file a grievance. The payment could be particularly attractive to an individual who did not have to alter holiday plans to obtain it.

Employees filing grievances for this reason find opportunities in the area of overtime administration. A common labor agreement provision requires management to equalize overtime opportunity among qualified bargaining unit employees desiring overtime. In addition, management is often contractually required to pay the employee for the overtime worked by another employee if an administrative error was made. For example, assume the following list represents the names of employees in the electrician's classification who signed the daily overtime list, thereby volunteering to work overtime if the assignment occurs after the completion of their normal work shift.

Name of Employee	Number of Overtime Hours Worked and/or Refused Since January 1
A. Jones	89 hours
T. Grant	76 hours
B. Simms	43 hours

The figure to the right of the employee's name represents the number of overtime hours worked by the employee to date and also includes any overtime assignments refused by the employee—if Jones refused to work an 8-hour overtime assignment eventually worked by Grant, both employees are charged the 8 hours. If an overtime assignment for electricians is needed on the day in question, the supervisor checks the overtime list and determines that Simms is lowest in overtime hours. Consequently, the supervisor would give Simms the first opportunity to accept or refuse the overtime assignment.

Suppose, however, that Simms desires to receive the overtime payment without having to work the overtime assignment. Simms could accomplish this by actively avoiding or hiding from the supervisor at the end of his or her shift when overtime assignments are determined. Confronted with an overtime emergency, the supervisor has to offer the assignment to Grant, the employee next lowest in overtime. The next day, Simms could file a grievance on the "administrative error" and be paid the equivalent of Grant's overtime assignment for no corresponding work effort. Needless to say, this reason for filing a grievance draws management's ire, particularly because some employees appear to make a contest out of acquiring grievance "freebies," or payment for time not worked.

There are other reasons employees file grievances. Motives are as varied and complex as the employees' personalities and life experiences. For example, an argument with the employee's family, friends, or work associates might provoke a grievance. Other motives, such as poor employee/job match or a generally poor managerial climate, are perhaps more easily rectified by managerial action. Uncovering the motive behind a grievance may be helpful to management. However, it must be stressed that management must process the grievance even if it feels the employee's motives are illegitimate or improper.

Significance of Employee Grievances

Unresolved employee grievances can significantly affect both nonunion and union firms. In some cases, unsettled employee grievances have prompted successful union-organizing drives. Managers in nonunion firms might adopt some sort of grievance procedure to minimize discrimination suits, enhance employee input into organizational decision making, and minimize or eliminate the employee's desire to join a union. However, most nonunion grievance procedures do not enable the employee to have representation or to have his or her grievance decided by a third-party neutral, elements that are found in most grievance procedures in unionized firms.[4]

In unionized firms, employees often have unique concerns that are neither addressed in collective bargaining nor explicitly covered in the labor agreement.

Union officials therefore demonstrate their intent to represent members' particular job interests against perceived arbitrary managerial actions through the use of the grievance procedure. A union not demonstrating its interest in union members through an effective grievance procedure runs the risk of lawsuits (discussed later in this chapter under "fair representation") or membership dissatisfaction with union leaders, which, in turn, can result in members voting leaders out of office or decertifying the union.

Employee grievances and the grievance procedure can offer an organization two advantages, namely, *conflict institutionalization* and *open upward communication*. Employees who attempt to resolve grievances at an organization having no grievance procedure might participate in various job actions, such as sabotage, wildcat strikes, and job slowdowns, to solve the problem; or they might quit their jobs. Indeed, one study of New York state public school teachers under the age of 55 found that individuals with strong grievance procedures[5] in their labor agreements were less likely to quit than those working under weaker grievance procedures. All of these outcomes are costly to management, particularly when recruiting and training costs of employee replacements are considered.[6]

A grievance procedure, however, institutionalizes conflict. It recognizes that disagreements between employees, management, and the union are inevitable and provides an orderly, consistent approach for resolving differences. Grievances and related procedures represent a major upward communication forum for **employee voice**, whereby an individual has an opportunity to offer input into management's decision making and to discuss, even appeal, adverse employment actions.

Some think that grievances might assume even more significance because other employee-voice mechanisms are eroding as management, facing increased foreign and domestic competition, has become preoccupied with plant closings and large layoffs. Furthermore, many employees, while theoretically able to do so, are unwilling to pursue adverse job actions because of excessive costs and time delays.[7]

In one study, nearly half of the employees believed that the grievance procedure protected them against management high-handedness; however, these employees did not express a favorable opinion of the grievance procedure itself. They indicated that they did not believe their grievances were settled in a timely fashion; that if they filed a grievance, they would be exposed to management's reprisals; that the outcome of the grievance procedure was not fair and equitable; that the grievance procedure was not the best way to win one's case; and that once management makes up its mind, it wasn't open to change. Surprisingly, 57.3 percent of employees chose not to file a grievance, even when they were in a position where they would have been able to do so.[8]

Grievance filings affect not only the individual filing the grievance but also the supervisor against whom the grievance is filed. In a study of four organizations over 10 years, researchers found that grievance filers had slightly higher performance ratings, substantially higher work attendance rates, and markedly higher promotion rates than nonfilers. However, following the grievance filings, the grievance filers had significantly lower promotion rates in all four organizations, significantly higher turnover rates in three organizations, and significantly lower performance ratings in two organizations. Differences in work attendance were not significant.

The research also shows that the step in the grievance procedure where there is a settlement and a decision in favor of the employer makes a difference. The performance ratings, promotion rates, and work attendance were higher for grievants whose cases were settled at the first step of the grievance procedure than at subsequent steps. As well, performance ratings were significantly higher for grievants whose cases were decided in favor of the employer rather than for grievants. Thus, the conclusion is that relatively more negative outcomes result for grievants whose cases are resolved at higher steps rather than lower steps of the grievance procedure, especially if the grievant wins the grievance.

Analysis of grievance filings appears to reflect the performance of first-line supervisors. During the 10-year period, supervisors against whom grievances were filed or settled had higher turnover rates (mostly involuntary), better work attendance rates, and lower job performance ratings and promotion rates than supervisors against whom grievance were not filed.[9]

Grievances have also assumed research significance. Many studies have examined how grievances relate to organizational characteristics and to outcomes.[10]

Preparation for Grievance Processing

During the grievance procedure, the grieving party, typically the union, must persuade management that one or more of the provisions of the collective-bargaining agreement has been breached. If management disagrees, management will attempt to persuade the union that management has complied with the provisions of the collective-bargaining agreement. For example, if the agreement states that overtime will be assigned to the most senior employee who is available, the union will file a grievance when a more junior employee is assigned overtime first. In response, management may claim that the more senior employees were not available. On the other hand, if management is convinced that the union's grievance has merit, then management will probably attempt to reach a settlement of the grievance. As an example, the collective-bargaining agreement provides that call-back assignments be offered first to the most senior employee. When a call-back assignment occurs, the supervisor calls the most senior employee at home, receives no answer, and then leaves a message on the answering machine. The supervisor then calls the second most senior employee and offers an early call-back assignment at double pay. When the most senior employee reports to work at the regular time, he observes that the second most senior employee is already working. The most senior employee files a grievance and claims that he was home and the phone did not ring. An examination of the telephone records shows that the supervisor had called an incorrect number and left the message on another person's answering machine. Under this discovery, management indicates its willingness to pay the grievant for the hours worked at the double time rate.

In processing a grievance, each party should approach the grievance just as if the grievance would be proceeding to arbitration. There are several steps in building a persuasive case during the various meetings during the grievance procedure and in preparation for arbitration in the event the grievance is appealed to arbitration.[11] Exhibit 10.2 provides guidance in preparing for grievance meetings and for arbitration in the event the grievance is appealed to arbitration.

Exhibit 10.2

Preparation for Grievance Procedure Meetings (and for Arbitration Hearing)

Step 1: Gather Evidence
Since testimony of witnesses is the principal type of evidence, the investigator should identify persons on both sides of the grievance and interview all persons whose statements are relevant to the grievance. Often, the collective-bargaining agreement contains a provision requiring cooperation in developing the facts and contentions in order to increase the possibility that a resolution can be achieved at the initial steps of the grievance procedure. If relevant documents and other forms of physical evidence are not voluntarily offered, a written request with an explanation of why the documents are relevant should be mailed by registered mail. If the request is not honored, the arbitrator may draw adverse inferences about the withheld evidence in the event the grievance proceeds to arbitration.

Step 2: Determine the Facts and Substantiate Them
From the statements taken and evidence gathered, you should determine what facts the evidence establishes. Because the statements from witnesses will overlap, you should collate the statements in the following manner: (1) create a separate cover page for each fact established; (2) separate your witnesses' statements into the facts they address, noting the name of the witness on each; and (3) append the statement portions to the related fact cover pages.

Step 3: *Assess the Facts for Credibility, Accuracy, Reliability, and Consistency*
As you add factual claims, add your observation and conclusions about credibility, accuracy, and reliability furnished by each witness. Then compare each statement for consistency.

Step 4: Frame Your Arguments
The facts are obtained from the evidence and are what is objectively proven. Arguments are the way in which the facts show that the collective-bargaining agreement has or has not been breached and are reasons why those facts should affect the outcome of the grievance. For example, it is a fact that an employee had a satisfactory work record with the employer for 25 years; it is an argument that the employee's long-term record of satisfactory performance should mitigate the severity of any discipline imposed by the employer. Create a separate cover sheet for each argument and support each argument with a factual basis.

Steps 5 and 6: Seek Coherence, Consistency, and Credibility
Organize your arguments into a logical sequence. Then, make sure these arguments are coherent, consistent, and credible. For example, there is a contradiction when the union argues that the employee was defending himself if the union had earlier argued that the employee had been provoked.

Step 7: Prepare Witnesses Scripts
After a grievance meeting has been set up, outline the questions you will ask each witness. These questions will serve two purposes. (1) Establish the facts—you will ask unambiguous questions to which you already know the answer. If the answer is evasive, you should restate the question. If the answer is different from previous answers, you should remind the witness of an earlier statement. For example, "Mr. Jones, didn't you tell me when I previously asked you this very question . . . ." (2) Impeach the credibility of the witness by showing inconsistencies with previous statements, indicating prior acts of dishonesty or untruthfulness, and asking detail questions about testimony you believe to be perjurious. Witnesses have difficulty lying extemporaneously; liars are forced to remember details about previous lies instead of the truth that actually happened.

Step 8: Prepare Admissibility Challenges and Defenses
The fundamental rule is that evidence that is not reliable and not relevant should not be considered. Be prepared to argue that hearsay evidence should not prove the truth of the matter asserted. For example, hearsay would be what one witness heard another person say. The other person would not be available to be cross-examined, and cross-examination is an important due process right.

SOURCE: Mark I. Lurie, "The 8 Essential Steps in Grievance Processing," *Dispute Resolution Journal* 54 (November 1999), pp. 81–86.

Steps in the Grievance Procedure

The process for resolving employee grievances is specified in approximately 97 percent of existing labor agreements. However, the procedures are as varied as the labor agreements themselves. Some consist of only one step, whereas others contain as many as nine. Although no one grievance procedure is applicable to all labor-management relationships (21 percent of surveyed grievance procedures have two steps, and 51 percent have three steps), a four-step procedure illustrated in Exhibit 10.3 and discussed here is found in 19 percent of these procedures.

First Step of Grievance Procedure

The first step of the typical grievance procedure consists of two phases. First, the employee (with or without the union steward) discusses the alleged grievance with his or her first-line supervisor. Actually, the employee can file a grievance without any union endorsement. If agreement is not reached, then a written grievance is filed by the grievant or the union steward acting on the grievant's behalf. The supervisor then answers the employee's grievance in writing. Time limits for filing a grievance and managerial response exist in 69 percent and 63 percent, respectively, of the grievance procedures. If management or the union does not follow the time limits, the grievance might be challenged by either party as not meeting the procedural requirements in the labor agreement.[12]

The purpose of the discussion is to resolve the grievance as early and as informally as possible. The union does not want to delay any remedy, particularly back pay owed its members and reinstatement. Management does not wish to incur any unnecessary continuing liability if back pay is owed an employee who is suspended or discharged and remains unemployed until the grievance is eventually resolved.

In some cases, the oral discussion is *pro forma*—the employee initiates this step with a written grievance on the assumption that no amount of discussion will change his or her mind. Also, the supervisor may have made the decision that led to the grievance and has no plans to change the decision. As is true with the next two steps of the grievance procedure, if the employee accepts management's answer to the written grievance, then the grievance is considered resolved and subsequent steps are unnecessary.

Second Step of Grievance Procedure

In addition to the individuals in the first-step grievance meeting, the union grievance committee members and management's labor relations representative are brought in to discuss the supervisor's first-step grievance answer. Both of these individuals are aware of administrative precedent throughout the entire facility; their main role is to determine whether the grievance should be resolved at this stage on the basis of this precedent.

For example, Employee A files a grievance protesting management's unilateral action in reducing wash-up time in her work area. The union grievance committee might be aware, however, that (1) the contract does not have a provision pertaining to wash-up time, and (2) employees in other departments do not receive any time before the end of the shift to clean their hands. Therefore, he or she would probably encourage the grievant to accept the reduction in wash-up time rather than risk losing the privilege entirely in subsequent steps of the grievance procedure.

Exhibit 10.3

Example of a Typical Grievance Procedure

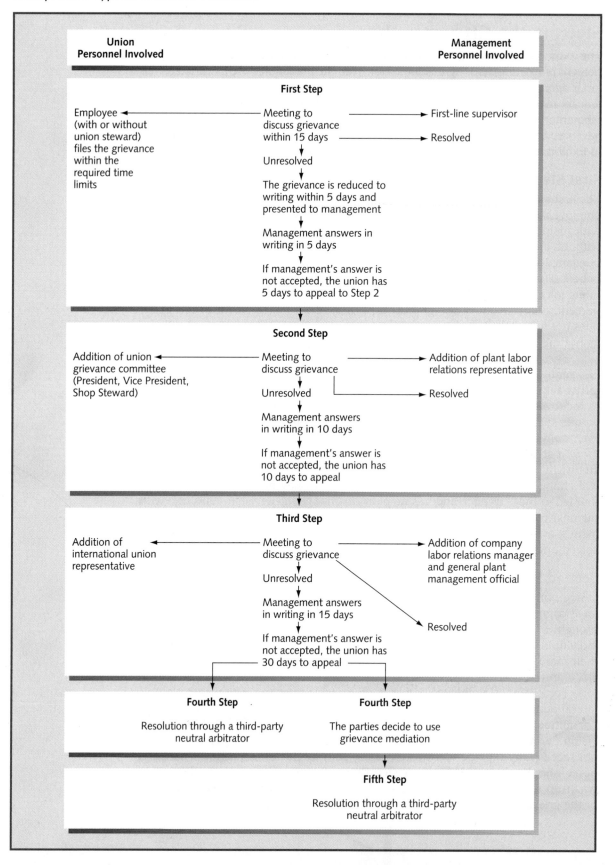

Union Personnel Involved		Management Personnel Involved

First Step

Employee (with or without union steward) files the grievance within the required time limits ← Meeting to discuss grievance within 15 days → First-line supervisor → Resolved

Unresolved

The grievance is reduced to writing within 5 days and presented to management

Management answers in writing in 5 days

If management's answer is not accepted, the union has 5 days to appeal to Step 2

Second Step

Addition of union grievance committee (President, Vice President, Shop Steward) ← Meeting to discuss grievance → Addition of plant labor relations representative

Unresolved → Resolved

Management answers in writing in 10 days

If management's answer is not accepted, the union has 10 days to appeal

Third Step

Addition of international union representative ← Meeting to discuss grievance → Addition of company labor relations manager and general plant management official

Unresolved → Resolved

Management answers in writing in 15 days

If management's answer is not accepted, the union has 30 days to appeal

Fourth Step — Resolution through a third-party neutral arbitrator

Fourth Step — The parties decide to use grievance mediation

Fifth Step

Resolution through a third-party neutral arbitrator

On another issue—for example, an employee working out of his or her normal work classification and demanding an upgrade in pay for the time worked—the labor relations representative might reverse the supervisor's first-step answer to avoid sending the grievance to the third step, where it might affect employees with similar work experiences in other departments. The second-step written grievance answer is furnished by the labor relations representative, and any precedent resulting from this answer usually applies only to the particular work department instead of the entire facility.

Third Step of Grievance Procedure

The third-step meeting involves the same individuals as the second step but also includes the labor relations manager and other management officials (such as a general foreman, superintendent, or assistant plant manager), members of the union's grievance committee (see Chapter 4), and the union's international union representative. These individuals are added because the grievance answer at this level could affect companywide operations, and both management and union representatives wish to obtain as much input as possible before making the decision.

One study found that during the third step the union discusses the grievance and its related rationale, and management mostly listens and does not attempt to resolve the grievance in this meeting. This step offers union officials several advantages:

- It provides new union stewards who sit in on the meeting with free training—many labor agreements require paid time off for grievance meetings.

- It impresses the grievant that many union officials back his or her interests.

- It may serve as a buck-passing device for the grievant's shop steward who claims that the union grievance committee, not he or she, decided not to pursue the grievance.

This step can also serve a therapeutic function for the grievant, who simply wishes to express concern to many levels of management officials. Perhaps the most important function of the third-step meeting is the inclusion of additional union and management officials who are not personally involved in the grievance outcome and can assess its merits with relative objectivity. The third-step grievance answer is usually written by the labor relations manager because the decision probably will have plantwide, even companywide, implications and applications.

Fourth Step of Grievance Procedure—Alternative Dispute Resolution (ADR)

In the fourth step, a third-party neutral may furnish either a final, binding **arbitration** decision or help the parties to resolve the issue themselves through **mediation**. (Arbitration is discussed in more detail in Chapter 11.)

Grievance Mediation   Grievance mediation is a formal step in the grievance procedure (before arbitration) designed to resolve grievances without the use of arbitration. Grievance mediation has several advantages over arbitration in the resolution of grievances. First, the parties have control over the outcome because any resolution is their decision, not that of an outside neutral. Second, grievance mediation is quicker because a resolution is reached at the mediation session. When the parties choose arbitration, it takes time to select the arbitrator (often a difficult task), schedule the hearing, make preparation for presentations at the hearing, and then wait for the arbitrator's written decision. Third, grievance mediation is more cost efficient. Although the cost of mediation may vary with different parties, the cost per grievance should be less than $500, whereas the cost of arbitration to each party is about $2,000 per grievance. In grievance mediation, there is no need for attorneys and advocates, no record of the discussion, no filing of written briefs, and no bills from the arbitrator for preparing the written decision. Fourth, grievance mediation promotes a continuing collaborative, problem-solving relationship, whereas the arbitrator must decide which side is right and which side is wrong, with one side being the loser. In addition, participants in the grievance mediation process develop skills that can be applied in future grievances. Last, even though arbitration is more informal than a court proceeding, grievance mediation is more informal than arbitration, and the parties may address multiple grievances in a single session.[13]

Exhibit 10.4 demonstrates the difference between a grievance arbitration hearing and a grievance mediation session, both designed to involve a third-party neutral in reaching resolution of a grievance.

Exhibit 10.5 highlights the best cases for mediation of employee grievances. First, there are cost and time savings. With a skilled mediator, the parties are able to address and potentially resolve several employee grievances at one setting, thereby providing for effective use of company and union resources. In arbitration, only one grievance is usually addressed during one hearing. Second, in mediation, the parties work together toward an acceptable resolution of the grievance, thereby building conflict resolution skills and developing a relationship to the parties' mutual advantages. Third, mediation provides a low-key, informal approach in an environment of civility that creates the potential for give and take with the end result an acceptable settlement to both parties. In arbitration, the environment is more informal than that of a courtroom; however, there is an adversarial relationship where one party will prevail over the other and the arbitrator must accept one party's position and reject the other's. Fourth, in mediation, more options are available to the parties, whereas the arbitrator is usually limited to upholding management's decision or sustaining the grievance. As an example, when a long-term employee with an excellent job performance record is terminated for excessive absenteeism, the employer wants to uphold its rules governing attendance, but would like to retain a highly skilled employee who has been an effective employee until recently. The union obviously wants to get the employee's job back. If the grievance goes to arbitration, the arbitrator is generally limited to upholding the termination, reinstating the employee with full back pay, or reinstating the employee without back pay (reducing the penalty from termination to a suspension). The parties have the potential to resolve the grievance on a win-win basis. The parties could agree to reinstate the grievant under a last-chance agreement, which prescribes certain attendance requirements. The union and the grievant are pleased because the grievant gets his job back; the company is pleased because it retains a highly skilled long-term employee; is protected by the last-chance agreement, which contains specific attendance requirements; and protects the integrity of its company rules.[14]

Exhibit 10.4

Grievance Arbitration vs. Grievance Mediation Scenarios

Grievance Arbitration: A hearing is scheduled eight months after the grievance was filed. The participants in the hearing are the grievant, the arbitrator, a court reporter, the union team (attorney, staff representative, local union officials, and witnesses to be called by the union), and the company team (attorney, human resource manager, line supervisor involved, and witnesses to be called by the company). During the hearing, witnesses are sworn, examined, and cross-examined and documents are submitted as evidence. Both attorneys make frequent objections, which are usually denied by the arbitrator. The hearing lasts from four to six hours; the court reporter will take two weeks to prepare a transcript; the two attorneys will take 30 days to prepare and submit written posthearing briefs; the arbitrator will prepare a written decision in 30 days. The time period from the filing of the grievance is 10 months; the combined out-of-pocket costs will be $7,000 to $10,000 (about $2,800 to pay the arbitrator's fee and expenses, $500 to pay the court reporter's fee, the remainder to pay attorney fees and expenses), not to include company and union participant time and costs.

Grievance Mediation: A grievance mediation conference is set up about three months after the grievance was filed. In attendance are the mediator, representatives of the union and the company (no attorneys and no court reporter). Each side provides a narrative description of the grievance, which summarizes its views of the facts and arguments supporting its position. Each group goes to separate rooms and the mediator visits both rooms to discuss the strengths and weaknesses of their respective positions. In three hours, the parties agree on how the grievance should be resolved. After a break for lunch, the process is repeated with another grievance and another set of representatives. The mediator does not write up any decision. The parties pay the mediator fee and expenses, which are about $1,000. The average costs, not counting union and company time and costs, are $500 for each grievance. If no settlement is reached, the mediator advises the parties of the possible outcome of the grievance if it should proceed to arbitration. Then, the parties attempt once again to resolve the grievance.

SOURCE: Peter Feuille, "Grievance Mediation," *Employment Dispute Resolution and Worker Rights in the Changing Workplace,* ed. Adrienne E. Eaton and Jeffrey H. Keene (Champaign, Ill.: IRRA, 1999), pp. 187–188.

Exhibit 10.5

A Case for Expanding the Role of Mediation in Resolving Grievances

1. Cost and time savings
2. Parties work together and build conflict resolution skills
3. Informal approach with an environment of civility and the potential for reaching an acceptable resolution
4. More options available to the parties than are available to an arbitrator

SOURCE: Judith P. Meyer, "The Pros and Cons of Mediation," *Dispute Resolution Journal* (Summer 1997), pp. 9–14.

Mediators take different approaches in assisting the parties in reaching a settlement of their differences. There are three categories of approaches; however, their distinctions are not "watertight," and the same mediator may shift from one type of approach to another during the same proceedings. Each of these approaches may be successful in different environments because the specific approach used by the mediator is highly dependent on the attitudes of the opposing parties.

The first approach is *transformation or collaborative mediation*. Here, the mediator tries to get the parties to discover their own separate and mutual resources and to understand the other party's point of view. This approach serves as a good starting point from which to move on, if necessary, to the other approaches to mediation. In the second approach, *evaluative mediation,* the mediator does not attempt to come up with a specific solution but concentrates on showing the respective strengths and weaknesses of each party's position. The mediator usually holds separate meetings with the parties in order to fully understand their positions. Then, effort is devoted to keeping the parties together, talking and listening, and moving toward a resolution.

The third approach is *directive or result-oriented mediation.* Here, the goal is to bring the parties to a certain agreement that the mediator believes is appropriate and achievable. The mediator first sits down with both parties and lets them talk to the mediator directly, not to each other, with the agitated party going first. The ground rules require that no personal attacks be made and no interruptions are allowed from the listener. Caucuses are allowed from time to time to cool tempers, to permit confidential communications with the mediator, and to move the negotiations toward closure. In addition, the mediator will probably spend time meeting separately with the opposing parties in an effort of helping each party understand the other position.[15]

With the success record of grievance mediation but with only 4 percent of the collective-bargaining agreements containing mediation as a step in the grievance procedure,[16] the question is: Why isn't mediation more widespread? One reason is that only a small fraction of all grievances filed are ever taken to arbitration (usually fewer than 20 percent and often as few as 2 percent). In addition, the majority of grievances that are appealed to arbitration are not arbitrated but are resolved without an arbitrator's decision. Therefore, most parties have inadequate motivation to change their grievance resolution practice to incorporate mediation. A second reason is that mediation is a quite fragile process because mediation cannot guarantee resolved grievances and the parties may still have to proceed to arbitration. In fact, the success of mediation depends on the continued existence of arbitration as the next step in the grievance procedure. A third reason that grievance mediation is not more widespread is that management is reluctant to accept it. Management appears to be the giving party and the union has an opportunity to "get something" from the employer in return for resolving the grievance and avoiding arbitration. Nearly always, the union is the party that files the grievance and is the party seeking a change in management's decision. For example, the union files a grievance when an employee is discharged, is not promoted, or does not receive a merit pay increase. Any compromise by the company to seek a settlement would be a change from management's previous decision. A final reason may be the self-interests of the arbitration advocates and arbitrators. Resolution of grievances through mediation infringes on the livelihoods of everyone who earns part or all of their professional income and status by arbitrating grievances. The vast bulk of the cost of arbitration is income to the arbitration professionals, and this income is lost if grievances are successfully mediated and not arbitrated.[17]

Successful grievance mediation depends on two key features. The first is the ability of the mediator. The experienced mediator will be able to point out the strengths and weaknesses of each party's position. Usually, there will be "sidebar" or "caucus" discussions with each party separately. If the parties do not reach a settlement, the mediator then provides an advisory opinion of the outcome if the grievance is appealed to arbitration. In other words, the mediator provides a "peek-a-boo" look at the likely outcome of an arbitration decision. The act itself creates substantial pressure on the party with the weaker position to reach a settlement in order to avoid the costs of losing in arbitration.

A second key feature for success is the motivation of the parties who have adopted the process. In cases where the parties are sufficiently motivated to try to improve their grievance resolution record, they tend to succeed because they have already decided to resolve differences on their own. Thus, "it may be more accurate to view mediation as a proxy for the positive grievance resolution attitudes held by the adopters than as a procedure which possesses some intricate ability to resolve grievances in a more cooperative manner than arbitration."[18]

The success of mediators has stimulated interest in adopting workplace ADR policies in other employment settings. Certainly the high number of employee complaints to government enforcement agencies, such as the Equal Employment Opportunity Commission (EEOC), has motivated many employers. The EEOC has jurisdiction over complaints of employment discrimination under the Civil Rights Act of 1991, the American with Disabilities Act, and the Age Discrimination in Employment Act. The number of employment discrimination charges filed with the EEOC averages over 70,000 each year. In addition, tens of thousands of charges over workplace disputes are filed with other federal, state, and local agencies each year. ADR has been introduced as a way of diverting these disputes from the courts and regulatory systems to an internal dispute resolution procedure. Additional stimulus has been provided by U.S. Supreme Court decisions that have upheld the validity of employment contracts that require employees to submit their discrimination claims to arbitration[19] (to be covered in Chapter 11).

During a one-year period, the EEOC conducted 11,700 mediations and more than 7,500 charges were resolved through the program. A comprehensive study of assessment of the participants in the program revealed that the participants had a positive experience with the procedure, the information provided, and the mediators. An overwhelming majority believed that mediation was fair, and they felt that they had a full opportunity to present their views. In addition, an overwhelming majority indicated that they would be willing to participate in the mediation program again if they were a party to an EEOC charge.[20]

As an example, the Americans with Disabilities Act encourages alternative dispute resolution (ADR) for resolving ADA claims. The mediator may help the parties reconcile their differences in making reasonable accommodation for the disabled employee. Types of reasonable accommodation may include one or more the following: acquiring equipment, modifying equipment, making architectural changes, modifying the work environment, providing services, introducing flexible hours, restructuring jobs by assigning marginal functions to another employee, or reassignment to a vacant position.

In reaching a reasonable accommodation, the employer is excused if its action would result in an undue hardship or if placement of a disabled person may put that employee or other employees at risk of his or her health and safety. The mediator may help the parties in resolving their differences regarding the employer's financial capabilities, disruption to its business, nature and duration of the risks involved, the potential severity of harm to the employee and others, or the likelihood that harm will occur. Likewise, mediation has potential for resolving equal employment opportunity, age discrimination, and other employee claims.

All grievance procedures—even though they may vary in terms of steps, time limits for the processing of each step, and participants—represent a progression of the initial grievance to higher-level management and union officials for consideration. These procedures can raise several administrative complexities (see "Labor Relations in Action" box) and often appear inflexible. However, they also serve as the arena for the dynamic social relationships and interactions among management and union officials.

Other Forms of ADR

While arbitration and mediation are the most common forms of ADR, the parties have the flexibility to design ADR approaches to meet their needs. Other forms include (1) open-door policies, (2) ombudsperson, (3) peer review systems, (4) early neutral evaluation, and (5) multistep approaches.

The _open-door policy_ means that supervisors and managers understand that part of their jobs is to solve workplace problems through open-door options and the company prohibits retaliation against any employee who is trying to resolve a workplace problem through the open-door procedure. The first step encourages employees to resolve any workplace problems with their immediate supervisor because the supervisor is the person who is closest to the situation and may be aware of the problems and may be in a position to offer a new perspective or new facts that may be helpful. If the employee is not satisfied with the supervisor's response or the employee needs to talk to someone other than the immediate supervisor (who may be responsible for the problem), the employee may take the problem to the next higher level supervisor. At any time, the employee may choose to talk with someone in the Human Resources Department or the Employee Relations Department and seek advice or assistance or to conduct an investigation. Possible limitations to this approach are reluctance of employees to bypass their supervisors in fear of retaliation, problems with upper management overturning a supervisor's decision, and fears by employees that the anti-retaliation policy will not hold up.

An _ombudsperson_ is a person employed by a company to help resolve personnel disputes. The ombudsperson functions as "go-between" between the aggrieved employee and the company manager. The ombudsperson does not have independent authority to impose a resolution of the dispute but attempts to find a "common ground" on which all parties can agree. Some concerns about the ombudsperson approach to employees is whether the ombudsperson will be neutral in disputes with managers and whether the ombudsperson, who is on the company payroll, will keep information in confidence.

Peer review systems shift the personnel decisions from management to the peers of the aggrieved employee. The peer review panel of employees conducts a hearing in which the aggrieved employee tells his or her side of the story and presents witnesses. The company presents its version of the story and presents witnesses. Then, the peer review panel functions as a judge or jury and renders a decision. Employees tend to believe that the peer review system is fair, and employers like it because employees usually don't blame the employer for final discharge decisions. Panel members may be chosen randomly or be selected from a specially trained group of employees. Also, the subjects may be limited and the decisions may be binding or advisory.

Early neutral evaluation is a process in which a neutral party is chosen jointly by the employee and the company to conduct an informal hearing at which the parties present their evidence and arguments. The purpose of the hearing is to narrow the issues and help the parties better understand the strengths and weaknesses of their positions. The neutral evaluator then renders a nonbinding, advisory opinion on the merits of the case. Assessment of early neutral evaluations show no discernible effect on the amount of time needed to dispose of the case, litigation costs, and the parties' views of fairness or satisfaction with case management. In addition, the parties may be hesitant to reveal their "real" positions because either one or both may believe the case will end up in trial.[21]

Grievance Resolution: Relationships and Flexibility

A wide variety of activities, tactics, and relationships occur between the most frequently involved union and management participants: the union steward and the first-line supervisor.[22]

Codified Relationships

Codified relationships stress the rights and privileges of union stewards and first-line supervisors established through the labor agreement and various union and management publications. These publications urge the steward and first-line supervisor to treat each other as "organizational equals" in grievance resolution, and to realize that both benefit from resolving grievances at their level instead of involving higher-level and possibly disinterested officials.[23]

Foremen and union stewards may be aware of normative philosophies and codes but often do not take them into account when interacting. For example, the *AFL-CIO Manual for Shop Stewards* strongly urges union stewards to present their grievances directly to the first-line supervisor in the first step of the grievance procedure.

> It is important to observe the steps in the grievance procedure even if the foreman has limited authority. Leapfrogging to a higher step may have undesirable effects. The lower level of management will resent this and will be more difficult to deal with the next time, or the company may seek to get the grievance thrown out because the proper steps were not followed.[24]

Yet many first-line supervisors maintain that they are often completely bypassed by the union steward in the grievance process. Indeed, the steward can also bypass the employee involved by filing a grievance in the name of the union. This "bypass capability" given to the union steward is not given to management or to the employee.[25]

Many first-line supervisors do not implement another codified relationship aspect: treating the union stewards as "organizational equals" in the grievance process. It is often difficult for a first-line supervisor, accustomed to giving daily

LABOR RELATIONS IN ACTION

Tough Contract Administration Questions

The grievance procedure involves more than a number of steps and related participants and time limits for filing, answering, and appealing grievances. Union and management officials, and sometimes arbitrators, often have to resolve complex administrative issues during the process; these are reflected in the following questions:

1. Can management interrupt and order back to work employees who are also union officials investigating a grievance?
2. Does an employer have the right to charge the union a fee for processing requested information pertaining to a grievance?
3. Can employees be discharged for secretly taping a grievance meeting?
4. Do outside union representatives have the right to visit the facility to investigate a grievance?
5. Is a grievance "legitimate" if it is filed or appealed by someone not affected by the grievance? by a group of employees? by a union official over the original grievant's objections? by someone who states the grievance orally but not in writing?
6. Do clear time limits between grievance steps mean that a grievance cannot be processed if the union exceeds these limits? Must the employer agree to the grievance if it exceeds these limits?
7. Does the initial time limit in which a grievance may be filed start from the day of the incident or the date of the grievant's knowledge/discovery?
8. Does management have to pay union officials for all of the time spent investigating and processing grievances during company work hours?
9. Can the effective date of management's grievance adjustment (paying for an overtime administrative error, for example) precede the date the grievance was filed?
10. Can an employer file a grievance against the union even if the labor agreement does not specifically refer to this action?

The answer to all of these questions is "it depends." A specific "yes" or "no" answer at a particular facility depends on the formal (labor agreement language and/or memorandums or understanding) and informal (past practices) arrangements between union and management officials. ■

work orders to the union steward, to turn around in a grievance meeting and consider the union steward as a peer. Some first-line supervisors can accept this situation; others have problems:

> This guy, Walker (union steward) here, doesn't realize that the gang is kidding him. They haven't got anything to kick about. All the stuff he is bringing up is old stuff. We've gone over it before with the other representatives. The other representative was sick of the job and gave it up. So the gang decided to elect this squirt because nobody else wanted the job. This fellow

doesn't know anything about the department. He's only been there 3 months. He's only a kid and doesn't know what it's all about. I haven't got time to rehash this all over again. . . . He's not qualified to talk about anything that happens in my department, and I haven't got time to waste with him. He brings up all this stuff and nonsense just so he can be a big shot.[26]

Codified relationships also suggest that first-line supervisors should have authority for resolving grievances at the first step of the procedure to give the employee a prompt response. Resolution of grievance at the first step can also help prevent the plantwide precedents that are established in the third step. However, other management officials, who prefer to be kept informed on employee grievances, often instruct the supervisors to inform the labor relations representative of the situation before taking any action. Indeed, one study found that 27 percent of 800 first-line supervisors believed that higher-level managers sharply limited their authority to settle grievances informally or at the first step.[27]

Power Relationships

Conflicting **power relationships** develop in situations where the foremen and union stewards pursue differing interests or goals. This situation has recently characterized shop-floor relationships in the steel industry:

The local unions became highly politicized; any leader who made peaceful overtures to the company was promptly denounced as a "sell-out artist." Union officials and supervisors conducted daily warfare over such matters as discipline, job assignment, and the handling of worker grievances. It was as though each side had to prove itself, day after day, that it had the capacity to hurt the other.[28]

Power relationships typically begin when both steward and supervisor are encouraged by their superiors to be attentive to problems in the department. The supervisor is encouraged to discover problems before they become grievances, whereas the steward is encouraged to talk to the potential grievant before that employee talks to the foreman. Competition for the employee's attention might become particularly intense, as one research study found that stewards and supervisors are equally successful in communicating with employees.[29]

Another type of power relationship results from the union steward's knowing the labor agreement better than the foreman does. Many union stewards are long-term employees who have been involved in numerous grievance meetings. The new supervisor may be a recent college graduate who is having his or her first taste of an industrial setting. In addition, union stewards can concentrate on particular provisions of the labor agreement and their application to the shop. The foreman, on the other hand, has major responsibilities for production scheduling, meeting departmental quality and quantity standards, participating in cost-reduction programs, and so on, which reduce the amount of time available for grievance and labor agreement analyses.

Intimidation is another power relationship strategy that can be employed by both the union steward and the supervisor. In some situations the union steward anticipates that the supervisor is vulnerable when he or she receives an excessive number of grievances—the supervisor will be concerned with how management officials will react to this apparent inability to resolve labor relations problems.

Even though the grievances might not be valid, some management officials might hold the following opinion:

> A supervisor who is the subject of grievances creates red flags for us. We expect supervisors to be able to handle most employee relations issues, and if they can't then we question whether or not they have a future with us. I know that grievances are sometimes filed with no justification whatsoever, but on the whole a supervisor who avoids formal grievances looks a lot better to management than a supervisor who's tying up his and our time in grievance hearings.[30]

Consequently, a union steward can use the threat of additional grievances (bogus or real) to persuade the foreman to concede to the grievance in question or to alter the foreman's overall approach to labor relations. The practice is explained by a union official:

> A short time ago we had a lot of trouble with a certain foreman. . . . He was making them toe the line . . . no quitting early, work from whistle to whistle, no sitting down, no horseplay, this and that. I told the committeeman there, "You do the same thing. Every time he does any work, even if he picks up a box, write a grievance. . . ." The first thing you know grievances started mounting—finally had a pile like that.
>
> Things got so bad . . . this foreman was removed from the department. He was moved to our department and it's his last chance. If he doesn't do good in this department, out he goes. So I went to the guy and told him, "It's your last chance here and you know it. You cooperate with us and we'll cooperate with you. If you don't we'll put the screws on you and out you go." Things are working out pretty good so far.[31]

Intimidation tactics are not always one-sided; a clever foreman can make industrial life very difficult for the union steward, probably without incurring an unfair labor practice charge. For example, many job classifications have a wide variety of work assignments, with some of these assignments being less desirable than others. A foreman could assign undesirable work assignments to the union steward, who would have little recourse as long as they were within his or her job classification. The foreman could also undermine the steward's formal position in the union by (1) restricting the amount of freedom and time for the steward to investigate the grievance and (2) refusing to resolve any grievance in the first step when the union steward is present with the grievant. These tactics are usually successful only if the union steward is inexperienced.

Regardless of the "success" of such actions, a grievance relationship governed by power and intimidation tactics distorts the primary purpose of contract administration: rational decision making.

Empathetic Relationships

Empathetic relationships occur between individuals when each is aware of the other's situation and is guided by an understanding appreciation. An example of this appreciation comes from a union steward's comment:

> You can't have industrial relations without giving and taking on both sides. You'll always win more cases by getting along with supervision than by be-

ing tough. You've got to swap and make trades. . . . Sometimes I have to talk like hell to explain some of the deals I make with them and sometimes I keep what I'm doing to myself if I see a chance to get something good later on. The thing some grievers never get through their heads is that a lot of bosses are on the spot themselves. If you go a little easy on them when they're on the pan, by God—you make friends—they'll stand by you some-time when you're back of the eight ball. Sometimes when I have a rotten grievance, I'll take the case up to the supe [superintendent] and let him know I won't push it hard.[32]

Empathetic relationships are aided when the first-line supervisor and the union steward realize that they both occupy marginal positions within their own orga-nizations. For example, one study found that first-line supervisors can have a rather loose identification with upper management. This might be due to several factors, including transient upper and middle management and reconsideration of the supervisor's original decision by other management officials.[33]

Union stewards have also experienced this situation in contract adminis-tration. On one hand, constituents expect their union steward to actively press every grievance because they think that the union should be attentive to their needs. Consequently, it is difficult for the steward to accept the foreman's first-step rejection of the grievance, even if he or she thinks the foreman is correct. On the other hand, union officials receiving the grievance in subsequent steps of the grievance procedure may tend to view the union steward as either ignorant of the labor agreement or gutless.

Flexible Consideration of Employee Grievances

The preceding varieties of interpersonal relationships reveal how individual objectives, strategies, and personalities force the contractual procedure to be more flexible in practice. This real-world consideration negates the theoretical principle that each grievance be considered on its individual merits. The griev-ant wishes to receive an answer uncolored by any political or tactical con-cerns, but the union must consider political influence and overall strategy in its determination of which grievances will be filed and pursued. Not all griev-ances are clear-cut issues; in fact, many involve confusing or opposing inter-pretations of the labor agreement. In these cases, management has two op-tions—decide the grievance in the employee's favor or appeal the grievance to arbitration. The latter alternative is not always attractive, particularly if man-agement realizes there is little contractual guidance in the issue (as in the ex-ample of the holiday scheduling of a crane operator) and insufficient past practice or precedent to support the decision. Contract administration has many gray areas that are open to interpretation. This uncertainty is com-pounded when the parties solicit a neutral party to resolve the issue in bind-ing arbitration. Also, the arbitrator's decision might refute management's ac-tion in terms that further erode management's discretion in future matters. Unions also tend to use arbitration only as a last resort because such cases can drain the union's treasury.

In these instances, flexibility may be possible with the addition of an infor-mal third-and-one-half step in the grievance procedure. This may not be spec-ified in the labor agreement but occurs after management's "final" third-step decision and before the third-party neutral hears the grievance. During the third-and-one-half step meetings, management and union representatives meet to discuss and trade grievances, dispatching several cases originally scheduled for arbitration. For example, they might trade a grievance requesting one-day pay upgrades for five employees who allegedly worked in a higher job classification for a grievance on management performing bargaining unit work filed against a very unpopular first-line supervisor, which would give one union member a two-hour overtime payment as a remedy. Usually the grievances involved in the negotiated package are settled "without prejudice" or without precedent to either party's position in future related issues. These settlements will not be binding in any future deliberations between the parties. However, settlement of the grievances preserves management's discretion on these issues and the union's right to file future related grievances.

Opponents of this practice contend that valid employee grievances are bargained away for an expedient settlement. Grievance trading in the third-and-one-half step can also discourage first-line supervisors from actively trying to resolve grievances if they believe their efforts will be overturned in a mass grievance settlement. For example, the following remarks were made by a foreman who had sent an employee home for repeated tardiness. The employee filed a grievance with the foreman's supervisor, who sent the employee back on the job.

> I went over to O'Brien's [the superintendent's office] to find out why he had overruled me. He handed me a line of salve about "having to do it." Said, "It was a small item after all" and that he "might want a big favor from the union sometime in the future." He said, "We have to trade back and forth. Sometimes we give in; sometimes they give in. That's why we never have any big trouble!" Then he said he might have to reverse some of my decisions again sometime, but if he did, not to get sore about it, because he wouldn't mean no offense by it. Well damn that noise! If O'Brien wants to make me look like a fool every time I make a decision, why by God, he can make all the decisions. You know two can play that game. I can give the boys [workers] every damn thing he can give them. Then when they come up with a big one that I know well he can't give them, I'll tell 'em to take it up to him.[34]

As a result of management using the third-and-one-half step in the grievance procedure, unions might be encouraged to file more grievances in the belief that they can obtain more from a trade involving fifty fabricated grievances than they can from five legitimate ones. Furthermore, settlements "without prejudice" can result in more grievances of the same sort because the issues are not considered jointly resolved by management or union officials.

Advocates of settlements short of arbitration believe that this process merely represents another legitimate cooperative effort between labor and management officials in efficiently dealing with day-to-day administrative problems. These individuals indicate that the union's and management's organizational self-interests require considerations and possible use of the third-and-one-half step grievance trading session. Opponents state that the third-and-one-half step hinders the union's **fair representation obligation** discussed in the next section.

The Union's Duty of Fair Representation ✗

Thus far, grievance procedures have been discussed from the perspectives of the union, management, and employee participants. As is true with most labor relations activities, grievance resolution can be strongly influenced by the fourth participant, the government. As noted in Chapter 5, the union has the right to be the exclusive bargaining agent for all employees in the appropriate bargaining unit. This right has a corresponding legal duty to fairly represent all of the bargaining unit employees, union members and nonunion members alike, in both contract negotiation and administration. This section focuses on the extent of the union's obligation, particularly when some of the bargaining unit employees believe the union has acted in an unsatisfactory manner.[35]

The fair representation issue is very difficult to resolve. On the one hand, some individual freedom must be sacrificed if the union wishes to effectively represent its members. However, the individual member's right to dissent must also be protected, and all employees represented must be safe from negligent or corrupt representatives. The National Labor Relations Act adds to this issue's complexity because it does not contain any explicit provisions obligating the union to represent fairly all bargaining unit employees. Therefore, jurisdictional disputes over the fair representation issue have occurred among the governmental participants, more specifically the National Labor Relations Board (NLRB) and the courts.

The NLRB had for many years claimed that it alone had jurisdiction to determine fair representation issues because related unfair labor practices came under its statutory jurisdiction. However, the Supreme Court countered the NLRB in a 1987 decision (*Breininger v. Sheet Metal Workers Local 6*) and indicated that district courts do have jurisdiction over such claims because the fair representation obligation is a fundamental part of federal labor relations policy and precedes the NLRB's statutory role in such cases.[36] A subsequent Supreme Court decision indicated that employees claiming breach of fair representation are also entitled to a jury trial.[37]

Related court decisions have addressed the following question: How far must the union go in representing employees whose interests or claims could potentially disrupt union goals and policies? The importance of this question is magnified when we consider that many decisions help some members while hurting others.

Under the agreement, there are competitive rights involving subjects like promotions, transfers, and layoffs. If there is one vacancy, only one employee can be promoted. Those not promoted may believe that they have grievances.

Union actions pertaining to seniority (such as merging seniority rosters and calculating seniority credits for employees returning from the leave) will hurt some bargaining unit members while helping others. Not surprisingly, two Supreme Court cases involving fair representation concerned the seniority issue.[38] These decisions indicated that the union satisfies its fair representation obligation in collective bargaining and grievance processing if it *considers the interests of all members* and *takes its ultimate position honestly, in good faith, and without hostility or arbitrary discrimination.*[39]

These rather broad guidelines were also applied in a landmark Supreme Court decision, *Vaca v. Sipes*, which considered the union's fair representation obligation in the grievance procedure. A bargaining unit employee claimed that the union "arbitrarily, capriciously, and without just or reasonable reason or cause" refused to take his grievance to arbitration. The employee, a long-term high-blood-pressure patient, returned to work after a sick leave and was judged by the company's doctor as being unfit for reemployment. The employee's personal physician, as well as a second doctor, indicated that the employee was fit for work; therefore, the employee asked the union to seek his reinstatement through the grievance procedure. The grievance was processed; however, the union, in attempting to strengthen its case before going to arbitration, sent the employee to a third doctor. The third doctor did not support the employee's position; therefore, the union refused to take the employee's case to arbitration.

The Supreme Court decided that the union, in this case, acted in good faith and was neither arbitrary nor discriminatory. It also indicated (in this and in another case) the following[40]:

- The employee has the burden of proof in establishing that the union breached its fair representation obligation.

- Fair representation does not require the union to take every grievance to arbitration because this would create an intolerable expense for the union and management and would destroy the effectiveness of the lower steps in the grievance procedure.

- Courts should only examine the union's fair representation obligation, not the merits of the case.

In the event that a union is found guilty of breaching its duty of fair representation (actions are arbitrary, discriminatory, and/or in bad faith), the costs to the union may become quite expensive. In one case, the remedy assessed against the union was payment of the grievant's attorney fees, the costs of litigation, and back pay to the grievant from the date the grievant was dismissed to the date the grievant was either able to find employment or should have been employed in a substantially comparable job.[41] In a 2002 case, the U. S. Court of Appeals in the District of Columbia upheld a ruling of the National Labor Relations Board that allowed an employee to proceed with his grievance and directed the union to pay the grievant for his own lawyer to represent him.[42]

The U. S. Supreme Court decision has indicated that any judicial examination of a union's performance must be "highly deferential," giving "wide latitude" to union officials in the performance of their duties. A breach of fair representation has to be so far outside a "wide range of reasonableness" that it is wholly "irrational" or "arbitrary." Moreover, a union's decision is not irrational simply because it turns out in retrospect to have been a bad settlement.[43]

Currently, fair representation poses two difficult questions to the union and the employer. First, what specific types of conduct constitute violation of the fair representation duty? As previously noted, the Supreme Court has given only broad guidelines ("arbitrary," "bad faith," "dishonest," and so on). Sometimes these guidelines can be rather easily applied; for example, a union refusing to process grievances of any black, female, or nonunion employees is clearly guilty of a violation.[44] Other cases can become more complicated. The union, while not needing to take every grievance to arbitration, has an obligation to consider the merits of the grievance and effectively use the grievance procedure. In some cases the courts have determined that union *"perfunctory conduct"* (simply going through the motions) makes the union liable for breach of fair representation. Related actions include:

- Providing inadequate defense of the grievant at an arbitration hearing
- Delaying grievance processing until the time limits in the grievance procedure have expired
- Failing to inform the grievant that the union accepted a different remedy than that asked for by the grievant
- Failing to keep members informed about an arbitration award that affects members' seniority rights[45]

Yet some courts have suggested that negligence or "honest mistakes" alone will not constitute a fair representation violation because union members always have the option of voting in new officers or even a new union to better represent them.

A second question concerns employer and union liability if the union fails to fairly represent a bargaining unit employee who has been discharged. Employees currently can sue the union and the employer for breach of the labor agreement including fair representation under Section 301 of the LMRA.

Assume, for example, that an employee is discharged, then later establishes that the union breached its duty of fair representation and the employee was unjustly discharged. Both employer and the union can be liable according to the Supreme Court in its *Bowen* v. *United States Postal Service* decision. Bowen, an employee for the Postal Service, was discharged for an altercation with another employee. Bowen sued both the union and the employer in the district court. His evidence at trial indicated that the responsible union officer, at each step of the grievance procedure, had recommended pursuing the grievance but that the national office, for no apparent reason, had refused to take the matter to arbitration. The jury found that the Postal Service had discharged Bowen wrongfully and that the union had breached its fair representation obligation.

The Supreme Court eventually found that both the employer and the union contributed to this wrongful discharge. The employer, of course, made the initially wrong termination decision and therefore owed Bowen reinstatement with some of his back wages. However, the Court also agreed that the union also owed Bowen a portion of his lost wages because he could not have proceeded independently of the union—if the union had arbitrated his grievance, he would have been reinstated. Thus, the employer was responsible for the back wages from the termination to the approximate date of his reinstatement if the union had fairly represented the grievant and the case had been submitted to an arbitrator who would have reinstated the grievant. The union was responsible for losses beyond that date. (See Exhibit 10.6 for determining the union's and the company's proportional liability.) It also contended that joint employer-union liability might be in the interest of national labor relations policy.

> In the absence of damages apportionment where the fault of both parties contributes to the employee's injury, incentives to comply with the grievance procedure will be diminished. Indeed, imposing total liability solely on the employer could well affect the willingness of employers to agree to arbitration clauses as they are customarily written.[46]

EXHIBIT 10.6

Determination of the Union's and Company's Proportional Liability

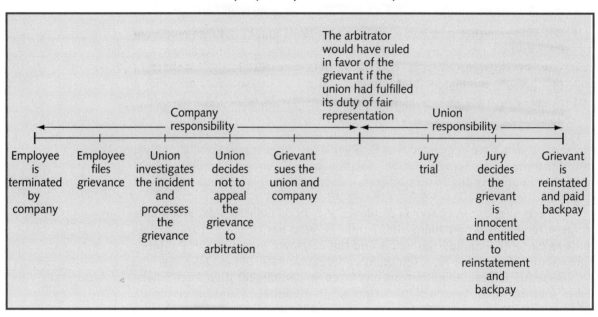

Bowen has controversial implications for the labor–management relationship. Managers believe that they should not be held accountable for the union's errors, particularly because management is legally prohibited from dealing in the internal affairs of the union. However, it can easily be argued that the union would not have violated the law in the first place if the company had not wrongly discharged the employee. There is also the possibility that this decision would encourage the union to take many marginal grievances to arbitration to avoid any possible breach of fair representation and related financial liability. In other words, it may be less expensive to take the case to arbitration than to defend against a breach of contract suit. Research has yet to verify that this situation could be detrimental to the labor–management relationship.

SUMMARY

Employee grievances and grievance administration extend collective bargaining by giving dynamic meaning to the negotiated terms of the labor agreement. A grievance is broadly defined as any employee's concern over a perceived violation of the labor agreement that is submitted to the grievance procedure for resolution.

An employee might file a grievance for any of various reasons, such as to protest a contract violation, to draw attention to a problem in the plant, to get something for nothing, or to feel more important. Regardless of motives for fil-

ing grievances, management must process them through the grievance procedure specified in the labor agreement.

Although no one grievance procedure applies to all labor-management relationships, two important aspects of a typical grievance procedure are inclusion
of higher-level management and union personnel and, particularly in the private
sector, binding arbitration by a third-party neutral. Grievance procedures typically offer an organization two major advantages: conflict institutionalization
and open upward communication. However, the grievance procedure as actually
carried out involves a variety of behavioral dimensions, including social relationships (codified, power, and sympathetic) enacted among the grievance participants in resolving the grievance according to appropriate contractual provisions. The variety of personalities and motives of the participants suggests a
flexible approach in grievance resolution instead of considering each grievance
on its individual merits.

Grievance mediation, a form of Alternative Dispute Resolution (ADR) procedure, was discussed and compared to grievance arbitration, another ADR
procedure. The advantages of grievance mediation, such as costs, informality,
skills development, and others, were explained. However, despite these advantages, grievance mediation remains less frequently used than arbitration. The
reasons for its less frequent use and the various approaches used were explained. As a result of its success, mediation is being used successfully by the
EEOC to resolve employment discrimination disputes. Other forms of ADR—
open-door policies, ombudsperson, peer review systems, and early neutral
evaluation—were presented.

Unions have a legal obligation to fairly represent bargaining unit employees in the grievance procedure. Although unions are not legally required
to take each grievance to arbitration, they must consider and process grievances in an effective, good faith manner. Legal and financial consequences to
the union and the employer can arise when the union violates its duty of fair
representation.

Key Terms

- grievance
- employee voice
- arbitration
- mediation
- codified relationships
- power relationships
- empathetic relationships
- third-and-one-half step
- fair representation obligation

Discussion Questions

1. A thin line differentiates employee grievances and employee complaints.
   Discuss the problems involved in defining a grievance, indicating why a
   broad definition of employee grievances is both confusing and necessary.

2. Discuss two reasons grievances might be filed, furnishing examples of these reasons other than those found in the text.

3. Why does a typical grievance procedure have so many steps when the employee is either right or wrong and a one- or two-step procedure would save time and money? In your answer, discuss the various functions, opportunities, and problems each of the grievance steps can offer.

4. Why is it difficult for union and management officials to resolve each grievance on its own merits?

5. Briefly discuss the broad judicial guidelines concerning unions' fair representation obligations to members. Also discuss the reasoning behind these obligations, furnishing some appropriate examples.

Exploring The Web

Grievance Procedures

1. Examples of Union Grievance Procedures   PACE Union

The Oil, Chemical and Atomic Workers International Union (OCAW) and the United Paperworkers International Union (UPIU) merged in 1999 to form PACE, the Paper Allied-Industrial, Chemical and Energy Workers International Union. Read an article on writing good grievances published in PACE's "Steward Review."

http://www.paceunion.org/docs/stewards/review3-3.pdf

Industrial, Technical, Professional Employees

http://www.itpeu.org/grievance.html

United Federation of Teachers

http:www.uft.org/?fid=83&tf=298

National Writers Union
See example grievances by clicking on Grievances in the left frame.

http:www.nwu.org

2. Shop Stewards   The International Brotherhood of Electrical Workers (IBEW) has a page that describes the responsibilities and rights of shop stewards.

http://www.ibew.org/resources.htm

3. Willamette University College of Law   Another good source for recent decisions and court cases related to collective bargaining and dispute resolution is the Dispute Resolution page produced by the Willamette University College of Law. Search Willamette Law Online.

http://www.willamette.edu/law

REFERENCES

1. Brian S. Klass and Angelo S. DeNisi, "Management Reactions to Employee Dissent: The Impact of Grievance Activity on Performance Ratings," *Academy of Management Journal* 32, no. 4 (1989), pp. 705–717.

2. Robert E. Allen and Timothy J. Keaveny, "Factors Differentiating Grievants and Nongrievants," *Human Relations* 38 (November 1985), p. 529.

3. Chalmer E. Labig, Jr., and I. B. Helburn, "Union and Management Policy Influences in Grievance Initiation," *Journal of Labor Research* (Summer 1986), pp. 269–284.

4. Douglas M. McCabe, "Corporate Nonunion Grievance Procedures: Open Door Policies—A Procedural Analysis," *Labor Law Journal* 41 (August 1990), pp. 551–557. See also Mark J. Keppler, "Nonunion Grievance Procedures: Union Avoidance Technique or Union Organizing Opportunity?" *Labor Law Journal* 41 (August 1990), pp. 557–563; George W. Bohlander and Ken Behringer, "Public Sector Nonunion Complaint Procedures: Current Research," *Labor Law Journal* 41 (August 1990), pp. 563–568; Richard B. Peterson and David Lewin, "The Nonunion Grievance Procedure: A Viable System of Due Process," *Employee Responsibilities and Rights Journal* 3, no. 1 (1990), pp. 1–18; and Richard B. Peterson and Douglas M. McCabe, "The Nonunion Grievance System in High Performing Firms," *Labor Law Journal* 45 (August 1994), pp. 529–534.

5. "Strong grievance procedures" define a grievance as a dispute over any condition of employment that affects employee welfare and ends in arbitration no matter what the subject of the grievance. Daniel I. Reese, "Grievance Procedure Strength and Teacher Quits," *Industrial and Labor Relations Review* 45 (October 1991), p. 35.

6. Richard B. Freeman and James L. Medoff, *What Do Unions Do?* (New York: Basic Books, 1984), p. 10.

7. Richard B. Peterson, "Organizational Governance and the Grievance Process: In Need of a New Model for Resolving Workplace Issues," *Employee Responsibilities and Rights Journal* 7 (March 1994), p. 13.

8. Renaud Paquet and Sylvain Dufour, "Toward A Better Understanding of Grievance Procedure in the Public Service—A Canadian Example," *Journal of Collective Negotiations in the Public Sector* 28, no. 2 (1999), pp. 103–107.

9. David Lewin and Richard B. Peterson, "Behavioral Outcomes of Grievance Activity," *Industrial Relations* 38 (October 1999), pp. 554–566.

10. For a fine research framework for grievances, see Michael E. Gordon and Sandra J. Miller, "Grievances: A Review of Research and Practice," *Personnel Psychology* 37 (Spring 1984), pp. 117–146. See also David Lewin, "Empirical Measures of Grievance Procedure Effectiveness," *Labor Law Journal* 35 (September 1984), pp. 491–496; Thomas R. Knight, "Feedback and Grievance Resolution," *The Industrial and Labor Relations Review* 39 (July 1986), pp. 487–501; Casey Ichiowski, "The Effects of Grievance Activity on Productivity," *Industrial and Labor Relations Review* 39 (October 1986), pp. 75–89; Thomas R. Knight, "Correlates of Informal Grievance Resolution Among First-Line Supervisors," *Relations Industrial* 41, no. 2 (1986), pp. 281–291; Brian Bemmels, Yonatan Reshef, and Kay Stratton-Devine, "The Roles of Supervisors, Employees and Stewards in Grievance Initiation," *Industrial and Labor Relations Review* 45 (October 1991), pp. 15–30; Jeanette A. Davy, Greg Steward, and Joe Anderson, "Formalization of Grievance Procedures: A Multi-Firm and Industry Study," *Journal of Labor Research* 13 (Summer 1992), pp. 307–316; Richard P. Chaykowski, George A. Slotsve, J. S. Butler, "Simultaneous Analysis of Grievance Activity and Outcome Decisions," *Industrial and Labor Relations Review* 45 (July 1992), pp. 724–737; Peter Capelli and Keith Chauvin, "A Test of an Efficiency Model of Grievance Activity," *Industrial and Labor Relations Review* 45 (October 1991), pp. 3–14; and Morris M. Kleiner, Gerald Nickelsburg, and Adam Pilarski, "Monitoring, Grievances, and Plant

Performance," *Industrial Relations* 34 (April 1995), pp. 169–190.

11. Mark I. Lurie, "The 8 Essential Steps in Grievance Processing," *Dispute Resolution Journal* 54 (November 1999), pp. 81–86.

12. *Basic Patterns in Union Contracts* (Washington, D.C.: Bureau of National Affairs, 1995), pp. 33–39.

13. Helen Elkiss, "Alternatives to Arbitration: Are Unions Ready for Change?" *Labor Law Journal* 48 (November 1997), pp. 675–690.

14. Judith P. Meyer, "The Pros and Cons of Mediation," *Dispute Resolution Journal* (Summer 1997), pp. 9–14.

15. Theodore J. St. Antoine, "Introduction: What ADR Means Today," *How ADR Works* (Washington, D.C.: Bureau of National Affairs, 2002), pp. 4–5.

16. Nels Nelson and A. Meshquat Uddin, "Arbitrators As Mediators," *Labor Law Journal* 46 (April 1995), p. 205.

17. Peter Feuille, "Grievance Mediation," *Employment Dispute Resolution and Worker Rights in the Changing Workplace*, eds. Adrienne E. Eaton and Jeffrey H. Keene (Champaign, Ill.: IRRA, 1999), pp. 197–205.

18. Fueille, "Grievance Mediation, pp. 197–198.

19. Richard E. Dibble, "Alternative Dispute Resolution in Employment: Recent Developments," *Journal of Collective Negotiations in the Public Sector* 29, no. 3 (2000), pp. 247–248.

20. E. Patrick McDermott, Anita Jose, Ruth Obar, Mollie Bowers, and Brain Polkinghorn, "Has the EEOC Hit A Home Run? An Evaluation of the Equal Employment Opportunity Commission Mediation Program from the Participants' Perspective," *Advances in Industrial and Labor Relations*, eds. David Lewin and Bruce Kaufman (Amsterdam: JAI, 2002), pp. 2–34.

21. Laura J. Cooper, Dennis R. Nolan, and Richard A. Bales, *ADR in the Workplace* (St. Paul, Minn.: West Group, 2000), pp. 659–672.

22. Judith L. Catlett and Edwin L. Brown, "Union Leaders' Perceptions of the Grievance Process," *Labor Studies Journal* 15 (Spring 1990), p. 61.

23. See, for example, Ralph Arthur Johnson, "Grievance Negotiation: An Analysis of Factors Popularly Associated with Success," *Labor Studies Journal* 9 (Winter 1985), pp. 271–279.

24. *AFL-CIO Manual for Shop Stewards* (n.p., n.d.), p. 37.

25. William D. Todor and Dan R. Dalton, "Union Steward: A Little Known Actor with a Very Big Part," *Industrial Management* 25 (September–October 1983), pp. 7–11.

26. Paul Pigors, "The Old Line Foreman," in *Organizational Behavior*, eds. Austin Grimshaw and John Hennessey, Jr. (New York: McGraw-Hill, 1960), p. 98.

27. Michael E. Gordon and Roger L. Bowlby, "Propositions about Grievance Settlements: Finally, Consultation with Grievants," *Personnel Psychology* 41 (Spring 1988), p. 120. Another study also found that a high proportion of local union leaders believe that first-line supervisors have no authority to resolve grievances. See Catlett and Brown, p. 59.

28. John P. Hoerr, *And the Wolf Finally Came* (Pittsburgh: The University of Pittsburgh Press, 1988), p. 22.

29. P. Christopher Earley, "Supervisors and Stewards and Sources of Contextual Information in Goal Setting: A Comparison of the United States with England," *Journal of Applied Psychology* 71 (February 1986), pp. 111–117. See also Mick Marchington and Roger Armstrong, "Typologies of Union Stewards," *Industrial Relations Journal* (Autumn 1983), p. 44.

30. David Lewin and Richard B. Peterson, *The Modern Grievance Procedure in the Unites States* (New York: Quorum Books, 1988), p. 195.

31. Delbert C. Miller and William Forum, *Industrial Sociology*, 2d ed. (New York: Harper & Row, 1964), pp. 401–402.

32. Melville Dalton, "Unofficial Union-Management Relations," *American Sociological Review* 15 (October 1950), p. 613.

33. Marc G. Singer and Peter A. Veglahn, "Correlates of Supervisor-Steward Relations," *Labor Studies Journal* 10 (Spring 1985), pp. 46–55. For a study and related methodology revealing a

sympathetic relationship, see Brian Bemmels, "The Determinants of Grievance Initiation," *Industrial and Labor Relations Review* 47 (January 1994), pp. 293, 300.

34. Melville Dalton, "The Role of Supervision," in *Industrial Conflict*, eds. Arthur Kornhauser, Robert Dubin, and Arthur Ross (New York: McGraw-Hill, 1958), pp. 183–184.

35. For related legal violations (unfair labor practices), see Paul A. Brinker, "Labor Union Coercion: The Misuse of the Grievance Procedure," *Journal of Labor Research* 5 (Winter 1984), pp. 93–102.

36. Arthur Hamilton and Peter A. Veglahn, "Jurisdiction in Duty of Fair Representation Cases," *Labor Law Journal* 41 (September 1990), p. 668. See also Martin H. Malin, "The Supreme Court and the Duty of Fair Representation," *Harvard Civil Rights—Civil Liberties Law Review* 27.

37. "Decision of Supreme Court in *Teamsters Local 391 v. Terry*," Bureau of National Affairs Inc., *Daily Labor Report*, no. 55 (March 21, 1990), pp. D-1–D-11. An appeals court decision interpreting a subsequent Supreme Court decision indicates the employee has a 6-month period to sue starting from when he should have reasonably known about the union's alleged breach of duty. "Court Affirms That Fair Representation Claim over Abandoned Grievance Was Untimely Filed," Bureau of National Affairs Inc., *Daily Labor Report*, no. 151 (August 6, 1990), p. A-1.

38. *Ford Motor Co. v. Huffman et al.*, 345 U.S. 320 (1953); and *Humphrey v. Moore*, 375 U.S. 335 (1964).

39. For examples of judicial decisions that have upheld and rejected unions' fair representation actions along these lines, see "Court Immunizes Union Failure to Pursue Grievance," Bureau of National Affairs Inc., *Daily Labor Report*, no. 48 (March 9, 1994), p. A-1; and "Court Finds UFCW Breached Duty, but Vacates Fee Award," Bureau of National Affairs Inc., *Daily Labor Report*, no. 101 (May 27, 1993), p. A-4.

40. *Vaca Sipes*, 386 U.S. 191 (1967); and *Amalgamated Association of Street, Electric, Railway and Motor Coach Employees of America v. Wilson P. Lockridge*, 403 U.S. 294 (1971).

41. "Union Must Pay Damages for Its Arbitrary Mishandling of Grievances," *National Public Employment Reporter*, July 5, 2001, p. 1.

42. "Unions under Scrutiny," *California Employment Law Letter*, May 13, 2002, p. 1.

43. "*Air Line Pilots Association, International v. Joseph E. O'Neill et al.*," Bureau of National Affairs Inc., *The United States Law Week*, March 19, 1991, pp. 4175–4180.

44. For an example of a relatively straightforward breach of fair representation, see *Hines v. Anchor Motor Freight Inc.*, 424 U.S. 554 (1976).

45. "Union Failure to Publicize Award Held Fair Representation Breach," Bureau of National Affairs, *Daily Labor Report*, no. 112 (August 13, 1984), p. 1.

46. *Daily Labor Report*, June 11, 1983, p. D-5. See also T. Charles McKinney, "Fair Representation of Employees in Unionized Firms: A Newer Directive from the Supreme Court," *Labor Law Journal* (November 1984), pp. 693–700.

Was This Grievance Arbitrable?

Issue

Was the grievance filed by Clinton Rowlett on May 7, 1997 processed in a timely manner in accordance with Section II of the labor agreement?

Background

On May 2, 1996, drivers of Delta Timberlands Corporation (the Company) were informed that they were being laid off because the paper mill located in Pine Bluff, Arkansas, was on strike. On the following Monday, May 5, the vice president of the Paperworkers Union, Local No. 544, filed a Grievance on behalf of the drivers. His statement of the grievance was:

> We, the drivers, feel that we are being discriminated against because we were laid off on May 2, 1996. The reason given by the supervisor was that the mill was blocked; however, on May 2, 1996, the independent contractors hauled 196 truckloads to the mill.

A Step 2 meeting was held on May 30, and the Company's answer was provided on June 12. The final sentence of the letter essentially gives the Company's position regarding the grievance.

> The Company has not violated the contract and retains the right, power, and authority to schedule the sourcing and receipts of fiber into converting facilities.

The Union made a verbal appeal of the Grievance to Step 3 on July 9; however, no meeting was held and no written request for a grievance meeting was made until November 11. The Company responded to the Union's request for a meeting with a letter dated November 15, in which Mr. Jack Hopeful stated:

> The request for a third step meeting was untimely. The grievance was referred to the third step on July 9, 1996, after which the Company was not contacted again until November 11. However, the Company agrees to a meeting to be held on the afternoon of November 18.

At the November 18 meeting, the Grievance was restated and the answer that followed the Step 2 meeting was reviewed. In summary, the Company stated that it had not violated Sections 6 and 12 of the contract and retained the right, power, and authority to schedule the sourcing and receipts of fiber into converting facilities.

The Grievance was then appealed to arbitration on February 2, 1997. A hearing was held on Thursday, April 23, 1997, and the parties agreed first to proceed with the issue of whether the case was arbitrable.

PERTINENT CONTRACT PROVISIONS

Section II   Grievance and Arbitration Procedures

> The Union agrees to maintain during the term of this Agreement a Grievance Committee that shall meet with representatives of the Company to settle grievances. The committee shall be duly authorized and empowered at all times to represent employees and the Union in handling grievances with the Company. When meeting with the Company to settle grievances, the committee shall not exceed four members in number. The Company is agreeable to holding grievance meetings at mutually convenient times, normally during working hours.

The settlement of such complaints or grievances shall be made in the following order and manner.

Step 1 The employee and/or his steward shall discuss his complaint with his immediate supervisor within five days following the date the incident occurred. If the employee was on an excused absence and he had no knowledge of it until his return to work, the five day period shall begin on his first scheduled workday following the return from the absence. The supervisor shall reply to the employee within five days of the date the complaint was brought to his attention.

Step 2 An appeal of the supervisor's verbal answer may be made by reducing the grievance to writing on the form provided, signed by the employee, and transmitting it to the supervisor for referral to the department manager within 10 days of the date the verbal answer was given. The department manager and/or his designated representative shall meet with the Grievance Committee within 10 days of the date the written grievance was received. He shall give his written answer within 10 days of the date of the meeting.

Step 3 An appeal of the department manager's answer must be made in writing to Step 3 within 10 days of the date of the department's answer at Step 2. Within 30 days of the date the appeal notice was received, discussion of the appealed grievance shall take place at a meeting attended by the applicable manager and/or his designated representative together with the international union representative and the Union Grievance Committee. The manager shall give his answer within 10 days of the date of the meeting.

Step 4 If no satisfactory settlement is reached on the matter within 15 days following the meeting, the Union may refer the matter to arbitration by notifying the Company in writing of such desire. The Union and the Company shall attempt to agree on an arbitrator within 14 days of receipt of a request to refer a dispute to arbitration. If the parties are unable to mutually agree on an arbitrator, the aggrieved party may request the Federal Mediation and Conciliation Service to submit the names of seven arbitrators to both parties. These parties agree to promptly select an arbitrator from the list to hear and decide the case, following the procedure of alternately striking names from the list. The arbitrator's decision shall be final and binding on all parties. A grievance must be filed and taken up in accordance with the time limits and procedures set forth in Steps 2 and 3 before it may be appealed to arbitration. The arbitrator shall hear the case as promptly as possible, affording each side reasonable opportunity to present witnesses and evidence in support of its case, and shall render an award in writing to both parties within 30 days following the last day of hearing on the matter. The fees of the arbitrator, including expenses, shall be paid equally by the Union and the Company. The award shall specify if reimbursement is intended and if so, to what extent, and shall otherwise provide a clear and concise decision on the matter. No more than one grievance shall be heard in any one arbitration hearing except by mutual consent of the parties. The arbitrator shall have no power to add to, subtract from, or change any of the provisions of this Agreement or any supplemental agreement hereto. Any of the time limits provided in the second, third, and fourth steps of the foregoing grievance and arbitration procedures may be extended by mutual agreement of the Company and appropriate union before the expiration of the time limit. "Days" in the Grievance and Arbitration provision shall mean calendar days, excluding Saturdays, Sundays, and holidays. The time limits on the various steps of the grievance and arbitration procedures will be suspended during economic shutdowns and repair shutdowns. *Continued*

The Company's Position

The Company argued that the maximum allowable number of days for processing a grievance in accordance with the labor agreement had been exceeded. This Grievance had taken 195 days to process. The Company provided data showing that the maximum number of days allowed to process a grievance under the contract is 95 days.

The Company contended that the Grievance was untimely processed between Step 2 and Step 3. The Step 2 meeting was held on May 30 and the Company response was given on June 12. However, only a verbal appeal was made by the Union on July 9. The verbal appeal did not comply with Step 3 of the labor agreement, which requires that an appeal to the Company's answer must be in writing and within 10 days of the date of the Company's answer to the Step 2 meeting. Further, a meeting regarding the Grievance was not held until November 18, which was far beyond the 30 days required by Step 3 of the labor agreement. At the Step 2 meeting, the Company had challenged the timeliness of the Grievance and did not hear from the Union about this Grievance until November 11, during a contract negotiating session. Further, it was not until three months later, on February 2, 1997, that the Company was notified of the Union's request for an arbitration hearing.

The Company had granted a grievance extension to the Union in the middle of the summer during the strike at the mill. However, the Grievance had not been appealed further and no request for a meeting had been made. When the request for a grievance meeting was made in November, the Company challenged the timeliness of the Grievance.

In its opening statement at the arbitration meeting, the Company informed the arbitrator that both parties have a mutual obligation to abide by the contract. The Company spokesperson stated:

> You negotiate a contract in good faith. I believe that the Company is certainly obligated to abide by the contract. But there are just a couple of clauses in the whole contract by which the Union has to abide. When it comes to their turn to abide by it, they don't want to. They want to hold the Company up to abide by everything in the contract; but they want to make exceptions.

The Company requested that its position be accepted because the maximum allowable days for processing grievances had been exceeded by 100 days. The Union had not complied with the labor agreement and the Grievance should be denied.

The Union's Position

The Union argued that the Grievance was timely filed after the May 2, 1996, notification of the layoff. A Step 2 grievance meeting was held on May 30, and the Company's response was given to the Union in a letter dated June 12, 1996.

Upon receipt of the Company's letter, the Union discussed appealing the Grievance further. The local union president testified that:

> I believe at this time that Sam (the union vice president) informed me that he had an agreement with the Company to extend the grievance because there was a strike out at the mill. Negotiations were continuing and they didn't have time to handle the grievance.

Further, the Union president was the person authorized to obtain an extension of the time limits and had stated at the hearing: "I was tied up in strike negotiations and got an extension on the time limit for the Grievance." It was not until around November 11 that the Union became aware of any problem concerning the timeliness of the Grievance.

The Union argued that there had been unusual circumstances surrounding this Grievance, and these circumstances should be considered by the arbitrator. These unusual circumstances included a 9-week strike at the mill, which required heavy involvement by the Union president. On several occasions during this strike, he assured the other union representatives that he had obtained an extension on processing this Grievance. Another set of unusual circumstances regarding this Grievance occurred on December 4, 1996, during the time when the Union could have processed the Grievance to Step 4 of the labor agreement. The local union president lost his bid for re-election and one day later suffered a heart attack that required an operation. Because the president was unable to process this Grievance during his recuperation and, although he was a lame-duck president, the Union contends that such unusual circumstances warrant an extension of time limits. (The former union president did not testify at the hearings).

Thus, based on the unusual circumstances surrounding this Grievance and the mutual agreement to extend the Grievance, the Union requested that the challenge on the lack of timeliness be rejected.

QUESTIONS

1. To what degree does the Grievance procedure in this case meet the requirements for an effective grievance procedure?
2. Assess the meaning of the last sentence in the Grievance procedure that states:

    The time limits on the various steps of the grievance and arbitration procedures will be suspended during economic shutdowns and repair shutdowns.

3. Would the issue of whether the case was arbitrable be considered procedural or substantive? Why?
4. Assess the relative strengths of each party's position.

Must a Union Process a Grievance of a Nonunion Employee?

On August 15, employees Billie Green, Mary Swallows, Betty Jones, and Edie Barnett lunched together in the company's parking lot. The discussion centered on Barnett's pending grievance concerning her recently completed layoff. Green, a nonunion employee, asked Barnett if she had said that Green had not been laid off also because she was providing sexual favors to a supervisor. When Barnett admitted that she had made the comment, Green asserted that Barnett's husband engaged in sexual conduct with Swallows, a union member. Swallows then slapped Green, and Green proposed that they leave the company property to settle the matter. Swallows slapped Green again, and then turned and walked away. Green became infuriated, followed Swallows, and kicked her in the back. The two fought for about four minutes.

Later that day, personnel manager Joe Rogalski called Green and Swallows for separate meetings to talk about the incident. Rogalski had talked with witnesses to the incident and their accounts gave conflicting reports as to who had struck the first blow. Because he could not determine who had started the incident, he had no recourse but to fire both of them. He advised them that they could file a grievance if they chose. At the end of the day, Green and Swallows met at the time clock. Green accused Swallows of lying and told her "Sooner or later I'll beat the hell out of you."

The next day, Green telephoned the plant and told the personnel department's secretary that she was going to file a grievance. The Union Grievance Committee was meeting that morning at the plant cafeteria. Green went to the meeting and spoke with grievance committee members Jack Nolan and Joe Caldwell about filing a grievance. Nolan told her to see union secretary Sue Cogdill. She spoke to Cogdill who told her, "We'll take care of it . . . just go up to the cafeteria and wait for me."

Earlier that same day, Swallows had met with the Union Grievance Committee in the cafeteria and had given her version of the incident. Green was later asked to give her version to the same group. Green believed that by meeting with the Grievance Committee she had officially filed a grievance. She then left the plant.

A week later, Swallows returned to work and Green was told by friends about Swallows' reinstatement. Green went to the plant to inquire about her grievance and was informed that no grievance had been filed on her behalf. She then confronted Cogdill and asked why her grievance had not been filed. Cogdill replied, "That's not normally my duty." Green then spoke to Rogalski, who explained that he could not rehire her because he had no written grievance from her. When she reminded him that she had told him earlier that she wanted to file a grievance, he responded that even if she had filed one, it would not have mattered because he and Cogdill had discussed the situation and decided to rehire Swallows. Green believed that her rights under the LMRA had been violated and filed a charge of an unfair labor practice with the NLRB alleging lack of fair representation by the Union.

QUESTIONS   *Rint group evals! ♡ Dave*

1. What are nonunion employee rights under the LMRA?
2. What is meant by fair representation?
3. When has the Union met its obligation of fair representation?
4. Has the Union in this case met its fair representation obligation? Explain.

CHAPTER 11

Labor and Employment Arbitration

Fake concerns is whats a matter, man and you think I ought to shake your motherfucking hand

This chapter covers (1) *traditional grievance labor arbitration*, which involves the dispute-resolution procedures stemming from the last step in the grievance procedure, and (2) *employment arbitration*, which is initiated by the employer. The traditional labor arbitration procedures are negotiated between the employer and the union, the representative of bargaining unit employees. Employment arbitration is promulgated by the employer to resolve statutory claims, including employment discrimination and disputes over application of company personnel policies, such as promotion under an employer handbook or policy manual. These two arbitration procedures are covered separately because, although they have some commonalities, they are distinctly different.

The *first difference is the presence of the union in the traditional labor arbitration procedure.* The union's role is to represent all bargaining unit employees, and the union and the company bilaterally negotiate an arbitration procedure that will best reflect both the interests of the employees covered under the collective bargaining agreement and the interests of the employer. Under employment arbitration, the employer unilaterally determines that disputes over employment subjects will be resolved in arbitration.

A second difference is the qualifications and selection of the arbitrators who hear the disputes. Arbitrators used in negotiated grievance arbitration have considerable experience and expertise in labor and employment matters and are selected mutually by the parties, who research their backgrounds, education, experience, and so on before making the selection. In employer-promulgated employment arbitration, arbitrators may be selected only by the employer from commercial arbitration lists or lists developed by the employer. In fact, some employers refuse to use arbitrators who have experience in the labor relations arena because employers believe that these arbitrators are likely to use the same standards as used in labor–management arbitration, such as an employer having the burden of proof in a discharge case.

A third difference lies in the framework for decision making. Under a collective-bargaining agreement, arbitration involves issues that arise over the interpretation and application of the agreement. Therefore, the agreement negotiated by the union and company establishes the framework ("four corners of the agreement") for the arbitrator's decision. Under employment arbitration, the decision of the arbitrator involves interpretation and application of company personnel policy or a statute.[1]

Development of Labor Arbitration

1865 through World War II

Arbitration first occurred in the United States in 1865, but it was used rarely before World War II, when it was used by the War Labor Board. In many cases employee grievances were resolved through sheer economic strength. For instance, a union desiring resolution of a particular grievance often needed to mobilize the entire workforce in a strike against the employer—a difficult task—before the company would attempt to resolve the grievance. Union and management officials were legally free to ignore the arbitrator's decision if they did not agree with it.

Other factors limiting the early growth of arbitration were the relatively few unionized facilities and the vague language found in labor agreements, which gave little contractual guidance for the arbitrator's decision. Consequently, the early arbitration process combined elements of mediation and humanitarianism in an effort to reach a *consensus decision,* one that would be accepted by both parties to a grievance. The arbitrator under these circumstances had to draw on diplomatic and persuasive abilities to convince the parties that the decision should be accepted.

Arbitration's popularity increased during World War II, when President Franklin Roosevelt's Executive Order 9017 provided for final resolution of disputes interrupting work that contributed to the war effort. Essential features of this order included a no-strike, no-lockout agreement and a **National War Labor Board** (NWLB) composed of four management representatives, four union representatives, and four representatives of the public—all presidential appointees. The Board was to encourage collective bargaining and, if necessary, resolve disputes over the terms of the agreements.

The advent of World War II encouraged the role of arbitration in several ways. Many union and management officials realized that uninterrupted wartime production was essential and that grievance resolution was more effectively accomplished through arbitration than through strikes.

The NWLB urged labor and management officials to resolve their own disputes and encouraged the parties to carefully define the arbitrator's jurisdiction in the labor agreements. Thus, the Board gave any negotiated restrictions full force when deciding cases and denied arbitration where it was reasonably clear that the arbitration clauses meant to exclude a subject from arbitral review. It further defined grievance arbitration as a quasi-judicial process, thereby limiting a decision solely to the evidence presented at the hearing.

Results of the NWLB's activities further popularized and enriched the arbitration process, as the Board resolved some 20,000 disputes during its tenure. In addition, these efforts served as a training ground for many arbitrators who were able to apply their newly acquired skills to the arbitration process after the war.

The Postwar Years and the Steelworkers' Trilogy

Although the use of arbitration increased during World War II, the role and authority of arbitrators were far from resolved.[2] Both parties in a labor dispute still remained legally free to ignore the arbitrator's award. In 1957, however, the Supreme Court declared in its *Lincoln Mills* decision that an aggrieved party could legally bring suit against a party that refused to arbitrate a labor dispute for violation of the labor agreement, under Section 301 of the Labor Management Relations Act. Thus, grievance procedures including arbitration could be subjected to judicial review, although much confusion remained over the court's role in these activities.

Either party could refuse to submit the grievance to arbitration if the labor agreement did not cover the issue in question. Some state statutes that made the agreement to arbitrate enforceable resulted in attempts to persuade the court to compel arbitration of various issues. Some courts then became involved in assessing the merits of a particular grievance and whether it should be arbitrated. These actions, of course, contradicted arbitral belief that arbitrators alone should rule on the merits of the grievance. Confusion resulted when labor and management representatives played the courts against the arbitrators in their attempts to obtain favorable decisions.

In 1960 the Supreme Court clarified and strengthened the arbitrator's role with three decisions commonly referred to as the **Steelworkers' Trilogy.** These decisions can be summarized as follows:

- Unless certain subjects are restricted from arbitration, the arbitrator, not the courts, determines whether the grievance is arbitrable. In addition, the courts have no business weighing the merits of the grievance.[3]

- Arbitrators have far more expertise than judges in interpreting the *common law of the shop* (experiences and past practices at a particular facility), which is fundamental to resolving existing grievances in a manner consistent with the continuing labor–management relationship.[4]

- Arbitrators have no obligation to the court to give their reasons for an award. Therefore, they have great latitude in fashioning a decision and its remedy.[5]

In summary, the Steelworkers' Trilogy greatly enhanced the authority and prestige of the arbitrator in interpreting the terms of the labor agreement and deciding the merits of a particular grievance. It also endorsed the arbitrator as most qualified to fashion a resolution of a grievance if it is based on the essence of the labor agreement. However, the Supreme Court has reaffirmed that the courts should determine whether a grievance should be submitted to arbitration when one party refuses, on the basis of its contention that the labor agreement excludes this particular subject from the arbitration procedure.[6] Other related decisions are presented in the next section.

Legal Obligations to Arbitrate and Enforce Arbitration Decisions

The Supreme Court has determined that the obligation to arbitrate a grievance cannot be nullified by a successor employer[7] or by the termination of a labor agreement. Management representatives in this latter situation argued that arbitration is a feature of the contract that ceases to exist when a contract terminates; therefore, a grievance cannot be processed to arbitration if the labor agreement is no longer in effect. Consequently, management representatives thought that the issue of severance pay was not subject to arbitration because the labor agreement had expired and management had decided to permanently close its operations. However, the Supreme Court indicated that arbitration was still appropriate because the labor agreement furnishes continuing rights, and the parties continued to express confidence in the arbitrator's expertise and in arbitration as a prompt, inexpensive alternative to lawsuits.[8] A Supreme Court decision indicated that management's obligation to honor a union's request for arbitration after the labor contract has expired occurs only if the dispute either arose before the contract expired or concerned "a right that accrued or vested under the agreement."[9]

Another issue resolved by the Supreme Court concerns how far the courts are willing to go in enforcing the role of the arbitrator. More specifically, what happens when one party is willing to arbitrate a grievance while the other party prefers to use the strike or lockout to resolve a dispute? As previously mentioned, a strike was a plausible alternative in resolving a grievance in the early years of arbitration. Also, the Trilogy did not specifically consider this alternative in its conclusions.

The award enforceability issue was brought before the courts in 1969 when a union protested a work assignment given to nonbargaining unit personnel. The union expressed its concern by striking even though the labor agreement contained a provision for arbitrating disputes over the terms of the agreement. In federal district court, management officials stressed that the union should use the contractually specified arbitration procedure and be enjoined or prevented from striking the employer. The Supreme Court agreed in its *Boys Market* decision.[10]

Elements of a Typical Arbitration Proceeding

Selection and Characteristics of Arbitrators

When the union and management need assistance in the selection of their arbitrator(s), the process usually begins with a request from the parties to an agency for a list of potential arbitrators. Annually, the parties will make approximately 40,000 requests for lists of arbitrators from which they make their selection. Unions and management rely primarily on three sources for lists of arbitrators. One source is the Federal Mediation and Conciliation Service (FMCS), an independent federal agency, that provides computer-generated lists of arbitrators through its Office of Arbitration Services in Washington. About 43 percent of the requests for arbitrator lists are made to the FMCS. Its activity is limited to providing lists of arbitrators and biographical data on each arbitrator, informing arbitrators of their selection, and following up to assure that the selected arbitrator renders a timely decision. For these services, the FMCS charges each party $30 per case and charges each arbitrator $100 per year to remain on the FMCS roster. Periodically, the FMCS will review its roster of arbitrators and exclude those who have been infrequently selected.

The parties will negotiate the specific procedure for selecting arbitrators and include the procedure in the collective-bargaining agreement. A common selection procedure is the *striking method*. For example, from a list of five potential arbitrators, one party will strike (mark through the name of the arbitrator so as to exclude) one arbitrator (usually the least desirable arbitrator) and then the other party will strike one arbitrator (usually the least desirable arbitrator from those remaining). The parties will continue to strike until there is one arbitrator remaining; the remaining arbitrator will be the one selected (unless the parties agree to request another list) and the arbitrator will be informed of the selection. Of course, if this procedure does not yield a selection, the parties may request another list or may ask the FMCS to make a direct appointment.

The second major source is the American Arbitration Association (AAA), a private, nonprofit organization that supplies hand-selected lists of arbitrators from three regional centers in Atlanta, Dallas, and Fresno. About 38 percent of the requests for arbitrator lists are made to the AAA. After selection, the AAA provides additional services, including establishing the location of the hearings, exchanging posthearing briefs, and forwarding the decision to the parties. The AAA offers a different range of services for which it charges from $50 to $350; the AAA charges each arbitrator $300 per year to remain on its list. Like the FMCS, it conducts a periodic review of its list to make sure that the arbitrators are considered acceptable to the parties.

The selection procedure used in AAA cases is called the *striking and ranking* procedure. Here, each party will strike the names of arbitrators who are not wanted and then will rank (1 = most preferred, 2 = second most preferred, and so on) the remaining arbitrators. The arbitrator selected will be the one who receives the highest rank among those remaining. As under the FMCS procedure, if this procedure does not yield an arbitrator acceptable to both parties, then the parties may request another list or ask the AAA to make a direct appointment.

The third major source is the 26 state and local agencies located primarily in the northern and western states. The number of arbitrators on the agency lists range from 270 with the New York Employment Relations Board to 15 with the North Carolina Department of Labor. About 18 percent of the requests for arbitrator lists are made to these agencies. The number of requests ranges from fewer than 50 to more than 300 per year, with 54 percent of the requests occurring in New York and New Jersey. The operational arrangements vary widely also. Some agencies provide lists of arbitrators to unions and management in both the private and public sector; some only to the public sector. Half of the agencies send out arbitrator lists on a random selection basis; half use a modified random, rotational, or discretionary system. Most agencies restrict membership on their arbitrator roster to state residents and residents of contiguous states. The Massachusetts Board of Conciliation and Arbitration, the New York State Employment Relations Board, the Washington Employment Relations Commission, and the Wisconsin Employment Relations Commission provide staff members to serve as grievance arbitrators at no cost to the parties, and the New York State Employment Relations Board has a roster of pro bono arbitrators who are seeking to gain experience as labor arbitrators. Under the state agencies, there are numerous and varied selection procedures.[11]

The Supreme Court by encouraging the use of arbitration contended that this essentially private, self-governing process is best suited to labor relations issues and to the unique needs of the parties at a particular facility. This means the particular arbitration procedures are essentially determined by the parties themselves, and there are no universally applicable rules concerning arbitration hearings. For example, the number of participants (even arbitrators) can vary; also, the location of the hearing might be at the plant conference room, a hotel room, or a courtroom. However, some considerations and procedures are acceptable for most, if not all, arbitration hearings. According to one study, only 16 percent of the grievances filed in the first step of the grievance procedure are eventually resolved in the arbitration hearing.[12]

First, the parties must decide the number of arbitrators needed to resolve a grievance. The most common method (approximately 82 percent of related provisions) is for a single impartial arbitrator selected by management and union officials to be solely responsible for the decision, with no help from other individuals in formulating the written decision. In about 11 percent of cases, the labor agreement specifies a three-member arbitration board or panel, with management and the union each selecting a member and these two individuals selecting the third member. Most decisions are made by this impartial arbitrator because the other two members of the panel are influenced by their respective management and union constituents, although the impartial arbitrator does consult with the other members. In either case, the arbitrator's decision is final and binding unless, in extremely rare circumstances, both management and the union agree to disregard or set aside the arbitrator's award or the courts overturn the decision.

Five percent of the labor agreements in the United States provide for a **permanent arbitrator** or umpire to resolve all disputes during the life of the labor agreement, and in 5 percent, there is a list of arbitrators who serve on a rotating basis.[13] Usually, the use of permanent arbitrators applies to large companies or industries in which a large number of arbitration hearings are anticipated. Presumably, the permanent arbitrator can better allocate and schedule time to meet the grievance load of the union and employer so that settlements can be reached more promptly. This type of selection arrangement also allows the permanent arbitrator to become more knowledgeable of the complex and unique terms of the parties' labor agreement and industrial operations.

Assume, for example, that an arbitrator is hearing a grievance in the railroad industry for the first time. How long would it take for the arbitrator to accurately interpret the meaning of the following witness's testimony?

> At 3 P.M. Mott Haven Yard was a busy place. A crew of gandy dancers tamped methodically on a frong near the switching lead. L.S. 3 was all made up and ready to be doubled over. She had forty-six hog racks on the head end and sixty-five empty reefers on the hind end. Her crew were all new men on the run. Mike Madigan, the hog head, had just been set up. Bill Blanchard, the fire-boy, was a boomer who had recently hired out. Jack Lewis, the brains of the outfit, had been a no bill since he was fired out of the Snakes for violating Rule "G." Brady Holms, the flagman, used to work the high iron in a monkey suit, and J.B. Wells was a "stu" brakeman, right off the street. Over the hump lead, the yard rats were riding 'em in the clear and typing 'em down. The east side switcher was kicking loaded hoppers around, despite the violent washouts of the yardmixer who had discovered a hot box. Two Malleys were on the plug and three more were at the coal pocket. Our train, Number B.D. 5, was all ready to pull out.[14]

A permanent arbitrator saves time and expense because the parties do not have to repeatedly explain the meaning of these terms in the arbitration hearing or show the work location. Greater consistency can be attained where one individual applies the same decision-making criteria to all of the arbitrated grievances. Consistent decisions aid union and management officials in the day-to-day administration of the labor agreement. They also should enable the parties to better predict the arbitrator's subsequent decisions on similar issues, perhaps decreasing the number of frivolous grievances referred to arbitration as the parties become more certain of the arbitrator's reasoning.

Seventy-four percent of the labor agreements specify an **ad hoc arbitrator,** meaning that the arbitrator will be selected on an *ad hoc,* or case-by-case, basis; union and management representatives choose an arbitrator for a specific grievance, then select other arbitrators for subsequent grievances arising during the life of the labor agreement. Particularly in the case of an established collective bargaining relationship, management and the union often reach an informal agreement regarding the appropriate arbitrator for a particular grievance. However, if they cannot agree, they usually obtain a list of arbitrators' names (a panel) from either the FMCS or the AAA. In some cases when the parties cannot agree on an arbitrator from the list provided, they might request that these organizations select an arbitrator.

Clearly, for unions and companies having few arbitration hearings, ad hoc arbitrators are less expensive than permanent arbitrators. Regardless of the grievance load, ad hoc arbitration offers the advantage of flexibility. Although permanent arbitrators usually are appointed by the parties for a specified period, either side can discontinue the appointment if it views the permanent arbitrator's decisions with disfavor. There is no obligation to retain the ad hoc arbitrator in future grievances if either side is displeased with the arbitrator's decisions.

Because some ad hoc arbitrators specialize in particular categories of grievances, such as job classification or wage incentives, they could be better informed than the permanent arbitrator on such issues. Permanent arbitrators may be more familiar with the parties but may have seldom encountered a particular issue in their arbitration experience. Because both types of arbitrators have comparative advantages and disadvantages, management and union officials should design the selection method that best meets their needs.

According to one survey, arbitrators are likely to be males over 50 years of age with more than 14 years of experience in arbitration and a law degree or a graduate degree in another discipline.[15] (See Exhibit 11.1 for a profile of members of the National Academy of Arbitrators.) Arbitrators' characteristics can be significant for at least two reasons. First, union and management officials select an arbitrator possessing certain characteristics that might, according to one study, include name recognition, reputation for integrity, and a specific geographical location. Other studies found that employers tend to prefer arbitrators with training in economics, whereas union and management officials who have law degrees prefer arbitrators who also have law degrees.[16]

Second, there is at least the possibility that certain background characteristics might influence arbitrator's decisions. However, research studies have not established a strong relationship between arbitrators' age, experience, and education and decision outcomes[17] (e.g., upholding or denying the grievance).

Although grievance arbitration is typically considered a wholly objective proceeding in which an impartial neutral hears testimony, receives evidence from the employer and union representatives, and then makes a decision based solely on the facts, questions of acceptability often intrude on the process. Because arbitrators are selected by the parties, some believe that the arbitrators' decisions are occasionally influenced by their concern over being selected to arbitrate future cases. If and when one of the parties believes that the arbitrator is

Exhibit 11.1

Profile of Members of the National Academy of Arbitration and Arbitration Data (462 responses from 600 members)

Age (average)	63
Years of arbitration	26
Percent of income earned by arbitration	76
Years as member at NAA	16
Education: Masters	12.6%
Law Degree	61.4%
Doctorate	22.6%
Number of arbitration cases per year	55
Number of cases mediated per year (50.8% mediated no cases)	5
Daily fee for arbitration	Range $400 to $2,000 (average $720)
Total arbitrator fee per case	$2,884
Daily fee for mediation	Range $650 to $1608
Accepted and completed cases in nonunion employment arbitration	45.9%

SOURCE: Michel Picher, Ronald Seeber, and David B. Lipsky, *The Arbitration Profession in Transition*, Ithaca, NY: Cornell/PERC Institute of Conflict Resolution, 2000, pp. 11–28; updated from http://www.fmcs.gov (accessed January 9, 2004).

concerned about continued acceptability, that party may select the arbitrator because of the belief that the arbitrator may owe them a favorable decision, thereby contaminating the process. This concern is the reason that the National Academy of Arbitrators inserted into the *Code of Professional Responsibility for Arbitrators of Labor-Management Disputes* the following passage: "An arbitrator must be as ready to rule for one party as for the other on each issue, either in a single case or in a group of cases. Compromise by an arbitrator for the sake of attempting to achieve personal acceptability is unprofessional."[18]

Prehearing Activities

On occasion, the parties may decide to write a prehearing brief, which highlights the issues and positions of the parties before the arbitrator arrives at the hearing. The briefs alert the arbitrator to the matters he or she will face at the hearing. These optional briefs, which are uncommon, vary in length from a one-page letter to an extensively footnoted document. Most of the time, the parties prefer to introduce the matter of arbitration at the beginning of the hearing.

The prehearing brief might backfire for the presenting party, who is subject to challenges on the assumed facts and inconsistencies that may surface in the witnesses' testimonies. On the other hand, prehearing briefs can be viewed as keeping the parties honest—they tend to approach their contentions thoroughly and are forced to adhere to them during the arbitration proceedings.

Perhaps most arbitrators would agree to the value of *prehearing stipulations*—joint union-management statements as to the issues involved and certain applicable grievance "facts." This saves time in the arbitration hearing, for neither party feels obligated to repeat what the other has either previously said or agreed to in principle. In addition, through the process of working together to stipulate the issues and facts, the parties may be able to resolve the dispute without arbitration. If briefs or stipulations are not agreed to before the hearing, the parties will have to educate the arbitrator on the background of the case.

The Arbitration Hearing

Held on a date convenient to the arbitrator and parties, the **arbitration hearing** varies in length from half an hour to several days, with an average length of one day. Union and management officials from the grievance site (e.g., the local union president and the labor relations manager) will likely be at the hearing and might present their versions of the arbitration case. However, either party might defer to another presenter, such as an international union representative or corporate manager of labor relations, at the hearing. Sometimes one or both parties employ an attorney; according to recent research, attorneys generally discourage prearbitration settlements between union and management and increase the use of prehearing and posthearing briefs.[19]

Variations also occur in the extent to which courtroom procedures and behaviors are used or required during the hearing. There are two perspectives on the arbitration process: (1) informal quasi-litigation (legalistic approach) designed to resolve a dispute between parties and (2) part of the ongoing collective bargaining process designed to facilitate conflict resolution (problem-solving approach). Those adopting the legalist approach argue that a more formal and orderly proceeding improves the process. Frequently, however, the advocates view arbitration as an adversarial procedure and adopt tactics to win the decision without considering that the parties have to live with each other after the decision. From the second perspective, arbitration is viewed as serving more purposes than simply resolving disputes. For example, arbitration has "cathartic value" by allowing a grievant to openly air a complaint against a management decision. The belief is that complaints, if left unresolved, will become more serious and possibly counterproductive. In addition, the negotiators of the collective-bargaining agreement are not able to anticipate and address every possible future scenario in the relationship between the employer and the union. To do so would unnecessarily lengthen the negotiations and add significantly to the length of the collective bargaining agreement. Such actions would make the negotiations more complex and even jeopardize the possibility of reaching an agreement.[20] A comparison of example behaviors of the legalistic v. the problem solving approaches is shown in Exhibit 11.2.

At the typical arbitration hearing, the first order of business is the introduction of joint exhibits. These exhibits usually include a copy of the relevant collective-bargaining agreement, which contains the provisions(s) one of the parties (usually the union) alleges has been violated, a copy of the grievance and the written responses to the grievance, and stipulated facts that are not in contention.

Then, the arbitrator will ask the parties whether they have agreed to the wording of the issue to be addressed. If the parties cannot agree on the wording of the issue, they may request the arbitrator to frame the issue after hearing the evidence presented at the hearing. The issue can become very complex, al-

Exhibit 11.2

Behavioral Examples of Legalistic versus Problem-Solving Approaches

Legalistic Approach

Drafting the statement of the issue in such a way that there is a definite winner and a definite loser

Looking for restrictions on the arbitrator's authority to hear issues not expressly stated in the written grievance

Insisting on a specific burden of proof at the beginning of the hearing (preponderance of evidence, clear and convincing evidence, or beyond a reasonable doubt)

Harsh and aggressive (eat 'em alive) cross examination in an attempt to destroy witness credibility

Objections to any form of hearsay evidence

Note for the record objections to certain types of evidence, even though the arbitrator has allowed the evidence to be introduced.

Problem-Solving Approach

Acknowledge that the parties have a mutual obligation to bring out all relevant facts.

Citing custom and/or practice of the parties.

Argue that the arbitrator should interpret provisions of the collective bargaining agreement in such a way that it will be reasonable and equitable to both parties.

Stipulate to certain facts where the parties have no dispute.

Ask questions which call for a narrative answer, e.g., ask the witness to tell the story about what happened in her own words.

Asking only a few nonthreatening questions on cross-examination

Using friendly and dignified behavior toward the opposite party

SOURCE: Adapted from Richard A. Posthuma and Maris Stella Swift, "Legalistic vs. Facilitative Approaches to Arbitration: Strengths and Weaknesses," *Labor Law Journal*, 52 (Fall 2001), pp. 181–182.

though it may be stated with deceptive simplicity. It is usually a one-sentence question to be answered by the arbitrator's award. Typical examples include the following:

- Did the company violate Section VI, Part 3, of the labor agreement when it transferred Sally Smith from the position of leadman to Welder III?

- Was Betty Brooks discharged for just cause? If not, what shall be the remedy?

- Did the duties of Machinist A's job undergo a significant change, thereby allowing the company to change the wage scale?

- Did Joe Jones's off-the-job activities have a sufficiently adverse effect on the company to justify dismissal?

The holiday scheduling grievance example in Chapter 8 illustrates the problems surrounding issue information. Assume, for example, that the labor agreement has *two* provisions pertaining to arbitration:

Article XX: Arbitration Procedures
Section 1.   The arbitrator's authority is solely derived from the clear and unequivolcal terms of the labor agreement.
Section 2.   The arbitrator may not add to, subtract from, or otherwise modify the express terms of the labor agreement.

In this situation, the union would claim that the issue pertains to the senior janitor's entitlement to holiday pay for the time involved because of the violation of Section 1 on the day in question. Management would contend that the issue of arbitrability is at stake, questioning whether the arbitrator has the authority to hear the case.[21] The determination of the specific grievance issue could take a lot of time, but it is important, for the nature of the issue often determines whether the grievance is upheld or denied.

The major part of the hearing is devoted to the presentation of (1) union exhibits, management exhibits, and jointly agreed-on exhibits (such as the collective-bargaining agreement and the employee's written grievance); (2) the opening statements in which each party's spokesperson states what he or she plans to prove and highlights the major issues and background of the case; (3) union and management witnesses for testimony and cross-examination and related evidence to support union and management contentions (such as pictures of a job site, warning letters, performance ratings, and so on); and (4) summaries and closing statements by the union and management representatives or submission of posthearing briefs that stress why their respective positions should be accepted by the arbitrator.

In 35 percent of cases, the parties agree to have a transcript of the hearing in order to have a written record of it. This written record may be desired for the convenience of the parties, for use in an appeal, and in the event the grievant may attempt to file an EEO charge afterwards. One or both parties may file a written posthearing brief after the hearing. The posthearing brief is actually a written summation of (1) the facts of the case, (2) the relevant contract language, (3) the arguments to support a position, (4) counterarguments to the opposing party's position, and (5) the requested decision from the arbitrator. The FMCS reports that in 81 percent of cases posthearing briefs are filed.[22]

A written _posthearing brief_ can be helpful when the arbitration case is very technical or complicated or includes statistical data that are difficult to explain in an oral argument.[23] In many cases, however, a posthearing brief is unnecessary if the parties have prepared and presented their cases well during the hearing.

This summary of arbitration proceedings does not do justice to the considerable effort and drama shown in preparing and presenting an arbitration case. The "Labor Relations in Action" box gives some techniques for preparing for an arbitration hearing.

Mental effort, skill, and tensions are not eliminated once the hearing begins. Assume, for example, that you are a labor relations manager charged with proving an employee deserved discharge for smoking marijuana on company premises. Consider the following:

- How do you prove the employee actually smoked the marijuana when the evidence was destroyed and it is the employee's word against supervisory observations?

- Can the supervisor convince the arbitrator that he or she had sufficient training to recognize the shape and smell of the object in a dimly lit location?

- Will the grievant's testimony be strengthened or broken under cross-examination?

- How long can the supervisor remain calm under cross-examination without becoming upset?

LABOR RELATIONS IN ACTION

Preparation Techniques for the Arbitration Hearing

1. Study the original statement of the grievance and review its history through every step of the grievance machinery.
2. Review the collective-bargaining agreement. Often, clauses that at first glance seem to be unrelated to the grievance will be found to have some bearing.
3. Assemble all documents and papers you will need at the hearing. Make copies for the arbitrator and for the other party. If some of the documents you need are in the possession of the other party, ask that they be brought to the arbitration. The arbitrator [might have] authority to subpoena documents and witnesses if they cannot be made available in any other way.
4. Interview all of your witnesses. Make certain they understand the theory of your case, as well as the importance of their own testimony. Run through the testimony several times. Rehearse the probable cross-examination.
5. Make a written summary of the testimony of each witness. This can be useful as a checklist at the hearing to ensure that nothing is overlooked.
6. Study the case from the other side's point of view. Be prepared to deal with opposing evidence and arguments.
7. Discuss your outline of the case with others in your organization. A fresh viewpoint will often disclose weak spots that you may have overlooked.
8. Read published awards on the issues that seem to be involved in your case. Although awards by other arbitrators on cases between other parties are not decisive as to your own case, they may be persuasive. The American Arbitration Association has published summaries of thousands of labor arbitration awards in its monthly publications. Use these summaries and their cumulative indexes as a research tool. ■

SOURCE: Robert Coulson, *Labor Arbitration—What You Need to Know*, 3d ed. (New York: American Arbitration Association, 1981), pp. 51, 52.

- What if the arbitrator gives little weight to the circumstantial evidence presented by the company and a great deal of weight to the grievant's previous long and exemplary work record with the company?
- Will the union introduce a surprise contention or witness not previously discussed in the grievance proceedings (e.g., that the grievant's discharge was due to the racial bias of the supervisor or because of a long-running dispute between the employee and supervisor)?

Management and union officials often enter arbitration hearings emotionally charged and uncertain. They are usually skillful in establishing their respective positions to the arbitrator's satisfaction and damaging their opponents' case by exploiting the opponents' weaknesses and uncertainties. The arbitrator must also display many skills in keeping an orderly hearing while at the same time objectively understanding and recording all of the facts presented.

One arbitrator has noted the following paradox: the union and management officials own the arbitration hearing, but the arbitrator is in charge of it. Union and management officials wrote the labor agreement and hired the arbitrator. Therefore, arbitrators should not treat the process as theirs, act like judges, be arrogant, or talk too much.

> Let the parties do the talking, work out the problems. You will be surprised how many knotty issues will be resolved during the hearing if you just ask the other side to respond, and then ask the original side to add something, and so on. By the time they have killed off each other's contrariness, the problem has disappeared.
>
> Do not try to take their procedure away from them. Give it back whenever they try to abdicate or place the burden of procedure on you. For example, it is an old ploy for one party or the other to say, Mr. or Ms. Arbitrator, do you want us to put in some evidence on this subject? This can put you into a trap. If your answer is no, then it is your fault when they lose the case because you excluded crucial evidence. If you say yes, then you are implying that the subject is important. Tell them it is up to them. Remind them that this is an adversary proceeding to elicit information and that it is their obligation to select whatever information they think is important.[24]

For example, many arbitrators have suggested that eliminating posthearing briefs represents a major way to reduce arbitration costs.[25] Yet, they also indicate that post-hearing briefs are significant in analyzing the case or writing the decision, and it is up to the union and management officials to determine if and when they are used.

Comparison of Arbitration and Judicial Proceedings

The arbitration proceedings share some similarities with judicial proceedings, but their differences are profound. Many arbitration hearings differ from courtroom proceedings in that testimony of witnesses is not always taken under oath and transcripts of the proceedings are not always taken. Arbitrators may subpoena witnesses at the request of one of the parties. This is particularly true if management requests the subpoena to protect bargaining unit employee witnesses whose testimony is used to support management's position. This way other employees realize the employee had to testify because he or she was under subpoena. However, arbitrators have the legal authority to subpoena witnesses in only a few states.

For over half a century, the fact remains that unions and companies have universally agreed that arbitration in the labor-management settings has advantages over litigation. These advantages are highlighted in Exhibit 11.3.

Common Law of the Shop

The most significant difference between arbitration and judicial proceedings is the arbitrator's reliance on **common law of the shop** principles in the resolution of disputes. Arbitrators, unlike judges, are selected by the parties to the dispute,

Exhibit 11.3

Advantages of Labor Arbitration over Litigation

1. The parties themselves can potentially save money and time because there are fewer legal procedures, less discovery, and fewer appeals. Also, the parties are able to select the arbitrator and set up the hearing instead of waiting for the court to schedule a hearing. They can also require a decision by the arbitrator in 30 to 60 days.
2. Parties select an arbitrator who has expertise in labor–management relations as opposed to a judge who may or may not have any experience in labor–management relations being assigned to the case.
3. Arbitration is a system of **self-government** in which the parties design the rules and procedures: how the arbitrator is selected, how many arbitrators, the authority of the arbitrator, and the like.
4. The parties negotiate and agree to the terms of their collective-bargaining agreement as opposed to a law enacted by a legislative body.
5. Labor arbitration is private process between the union and the company as opposed to a public tribunal with a public record; the arbitrator's decision may be published only with the consent of both parties.

SOURCE: Adapted from *Elkouri & Elkouri How Arbitration Works*, 5th ed., eds. Marlin M. Volz and Edward P. Goggin (Washington, D.C. Bureau of National Affairs, 1985), pp. 10–15.

and they are responsible for interpreting contract provisions that were negotiated and written by the parties to cover the specific location. Each of the over 150,000 separate labor agreements is different even though the subjects are similar. Judges are responsible for interpreting laws that are enacted by state and federal legislatures.

Thus, the arbitrator's major responsibility is to resolve a dispute in a manner that the parties can live with. Unlike judicial decisions in lower courts, the arbitrator's decision is usually final and not subject to further appeals. Consequently, arbitrators must be concerned with the subsequent effects of their decisions on union–management relationships. A judge has no such allegiance to the particular parties, the major responsibility being adhering to the statute in question, to established courtroom and legal procedures, and to precedent resulting from other applicable cases.

The common law of the shop often narrows the scope of arbitral decision making to the labor agreement language, intent of the parties, and past practices of the union and management officials at a particular industrial facility. The arbitrator uses these elements to convey to the union and management participants that their grievance is being resolved in terms of shop floor realities.

The distinction between judicial reasoning and common law of the shop principles can be shown through the following example. Assume that an employee has been discharged at Company A for drinking alcohol on the job. After an arbitral decision upholding the discharge has been reached, an employee at Company B is also discharged for drinking alcohol on the job. Strict adherence to judicial principles would uphold the second employee's discharge for drinking on the job. More specifically, the judicial principle of *stare decisis* (letting the decision at Company A stand in Company B's situation) would probably disregard the differences in work environments of the two companies.

However, the common law of the shop principles governing arbitration could lead the arbitrator to render an opposite decision at Company B than that reached at Company A. For example, supervisors at Company B may have been condoning this behavior, and other employees at this company may have been caught drinking on the job without being discharged for the infraction. Consequently, the arbitrator recognizes the two companies are independent with potentially unique circumstances and therefore deserve mutually exclusive decisions.

Evidence in Arbitration versus in Judicial Proceedings

It is also important to note that arbitrators are much more liberal than the courts in the types of evidence permitted at the hearing. For example, lie detector tests (polygraphs) have been allowed by some arbitrators under certain conditions (having the administrator of the polygraph present for cross-examination), although their use and weight in the arbitrator's decision remains controversial.[26] Usually, arbitrators give this evidence little weight unless the obtained information is corroborated by supporting evidence. The rationale for liberal admission of evidence is that the parties are seeking a solution to their perceived unique problem. In addition, some arbitrators maintain that arbitration performs a therapeutic function, that the parties are entitled to air their grievances regardless of the eventual decision. Arbitrators may allow aggrieved employees to digress from the pertinent subject or "tell it like it is" in front of higher-level union and management officials to serve this function.

Occasionally, new evidence is introduced by one or both parties in the arbitration hearing. The arbitrator may accept or reject this new evidence, depending on the weight attached to the following sometimes conflicting considerations: (1) the arbitrator's desire to learn all of the pertinent facts surrounding the grievance, (2) the need to protect the integrity of the prearbitral grievance machinery, and (3) general concepts of fairness.[27] Because union and management officials and their designated arbitration panels are entitled to receive all evidence presented at the hearing, the arbitrator will offer the opposing party additional time to review and respond to new evidence.

Offers of compromise settlements before the hearing are given no weight by the arbitrator. For example, management officials with no major weakness in their original position might compromise their third-step discharge decision before arbitration by offering the grievant reinstatement with no back pay. A union could potentially use this evidence to indicate to the arbitrator that management admitted being wrong by revising its original decision. However, arbitrators maintain that the parties should make every effort to resolve their disputes internally instead of going to arbitration. Thus, an offer of settlement between the parties is viewed by the arbitrator as a genuine attempt to accommodate differences and save costs of going to arbitration, not an admission of guilt.

Other types of evidence are subject to varying arbitral consideration. Hearsay (second-hand) testimony might be allowed[28]; however, it is typically given little or no weight unless it is corroborated by other testimony.

Arbitrators also vary in the weight they give to medical evidence presented in a grievance. Consider, for example, an employee who has her doctor testify that her previous back injury does not disqualify her from her present job. Management uses its doctor to counter the testimony, and the arbitrator now has to decide which doctor's testimony, if either, should be given the most weight. Exhibit 11.4 provides the results of two studies of arbitrators' use of medical evidence. Arbitrators are now more likely to rely on specialists' opinions, possibly

EXHIBIT 11.4

Survey of Arbitrators' Consideration of Conflicting Medical Opinions

	1975 Study	1987 Study
1. Use specialist over nonspecialist	0	77 (26%)
2. Use report that indicates most intensive examination	90 (51%)	133 (45%)
3. Use report that indicates most intimate knowledge of work performed	34 (19%)	79 (27%)
4. No response	53 (30%)	7 (2%)

SOURCE: Daniel F. Jennings and A. Dale Allen, Jr., "Arbitrators and Medical Evidence: A Longitudinal Analysis," *Labor Law Journal* (June 1994), p. 382. © 1994, 1997, 2000, CCH Incorporated. All Rights Reserved. Reprinted with permission from *Labor Law Journal.*

because of the increase in the number of specialists over the past 20 years. However, these and other statistical changes might be more attributable to the arbitrators who answered the survey and the unique cases they were considering. Arbitrators' considerations of conflicting medical opinions can be further complicated by offsetting response categories. For example, how would an arbitrator who responded positively to the first two situations in Exhibit 11.3 handle the testimony of a nonspecialist who gave the most extensive examination?

The Arbitrator's Decision

Characteristics and Scope

The *arbitrator's decision* is a written document submitted to the management and union officials. Its components are as follows:

1. Names of union and management representatives involved in the case, along with others who gave testimony (e.g., employees or expert witnesses)

2. A statement of the issue(s)

3. A statement of the facts surrounding the grievance

4. Pertinent provisions of the labor agreement

5. A summary of the union and management contentions

6. An analysis of the evidence and arguments in relation to the contract language

7. The arbitrator's decision (grievance upheld, grievance denied, or a compromise between union and management contentions)

Few prospective guidelines govern the form and content of the arbitrator's decision. However, the arbitrator should demonstrate through the decision a thorough understanding of all the facts and contentions raised in the arbitration hearing. Although arbitrators should address each argument and the evidence presented by both parties, some arbitrators address their decisions to the losing party because the winners do not have to be convinced they are right.

The necessity of the arbitrator's opinion has been the subject of considerable controversy. Some union and management officials basically look only at the arbitrator's award to see who "won" or "lost." Others read the decision to obtain principles and guidelines for future labor–management relationships and to assess the arbitrator's interpretative abilities.

Controversy notwithstanding, the decision should tell the parties how the dispute was resolved and why. "Ideally, an opinion convinces the losing party that its arguments were heard, that the system used to decide the case is a fair one, and that the result makes sense."[29] An arbitrator's decision should explain the relative weight given to the parties' evidence and contentions and should indicate in clear language the benefits to which the parties are entitled and the obligations that are imposed on them. Thus, the arbitrator's decision should *educate* the parties (including other union and management officials, who often select an arbitrator after researching his or her published decisions) within the context of the common law of the shop and established arbitration principles.

In some cases, the arbitrator's opinion can be even more important than the award. Assume, for example, the union grieves management's assignment of work normally performed in Job Classification A, loading trucks on Saturday, to an employee in Job Classification B, a laborer. Furthermore, the union seeks a remedy of eight hours at overtime rate of pay for the appropriate employee in Job Classification A, the senior employee in the shipping department, on the reasoning that the company's violation of the contract had deprived a Classification A employee of the overtime opportunity. However, the arbitrator denies the grievance and stresses the following in his opinion: "The various job classifications are for pay purposes only and do not restrict management's prerogative to assign work across different job classifications." This statement significantly harms the union in related matters, particularly if the language was not expressly stated in the labor agreement. Now the union will have a difficult time in grieving any work assignment controversy, even though the above decision pertained to one specific situation.

In other situations the arbitrator's gratuitous advice in the opinion may harm one or both of the parties. There is often a thin line between advising management and union practitioners on more effective and humane ways to run the operation and arbitrating the grievance solely on the merits of the case. The latter approach does not advise but merely determines whether management's action was justified under the terms of the labor agreement and applicable *past practice* (which will be discussed later in this chapter).

Decision-Making Criteria Used by Arbitrators

The arbitration decision is a deliberative process that requires on average about 2.5 days of the arbitrator's time to study the evidence and prepare a written decision.[30]

The arbitrator's decision is particularly important to the parties because nearly all labor arbitration decisions issued in the private sector are final and binding. In fact, less than 1 percent of the arbitration decisions are appealed to the courts. Of those decisions that are appealed, less than one-third are overturned by the courts. Thus, it appears that the lower courts are complying with the U.S. Supreme Court's guidance that the lower courts should refrain from reviewing the merits of arbitrators' rulings and should overturn an arbitrator's decision only when the arbitrator's decision is not based on the "essence" of the collective-bargaining agreement.[31]

Although arbitrators do not follow precise or identical methods in making decisions, one study indicated that individual arbitrators have been consistent in the importance they assign to various decision-making criteria over the years.[32] The following generally accepted guidelines have been developed and serve as focal points subject to interpretation, consideration, and application by arbitrators in resolving grievances.

Burden of Proof, Witness Credibility, and Cross-Examination The union files a grievance claiming that management violated the spirit or letter of the labor agreement. In such cases the union is the charging party and has the burden of proof in convincing the arbitrator that management acted incorrectly. A major exception occurs in employee discipline and discharge cases, in which management is the charging party and has the burden of proof in establishing that its actions were correct.

The burden of proof is typically approached through evidence (discussed earlier in this chapter) and testimony from credible witnesses. Witness credibility is often assessed through rather subjective behaviors such as talking softly or hesitantly, looking downward, or giving long, evasive answers to questions. The testimony is also subjected to cross-examination by the other party, who attempts to establish that the witness is inconsistent or unfamiliar with the facts or has bias or some other self-serving motive behind his or her testimony. A cross-examiner must avoid a major potential problem; namely, reinforcing the witness's testimony. This avoidance is easier said than done, as evidenced in Exhibit 11.5, which illustrates incorrect cross-examination after two direct questions.

As noted earlier, participants' general characteristic categories (e.g., age and gender of the grievant or arbitrator) do not have a strong correlation to the arbitrator's decision. Arbitrators are, however, influenced by witnesses' credibility, which includes perceived mental attitudes of the grievance participants. A rambling, disjointed presentation by a witness, a union or management representative, or a grievant who comes across as insolent or sneaky will likely receive a strong, negative arbitral evaluation that might not be offset by other decision-making criteria.[33]

Provisions of the Labor Agreement Obviously, an important decision-making criterion will be the provisions of the labor agreement, which reflect the collectively bargained rights of union and management officials. Adherence to common law of the shop principles stresses that the major function of the arbitrator is the interpretation of the labor agreement's provisions. Indeed, many arbitrators adhere at least in part to the **parole evidence rule**, which in its classic form holds that evidence, oral or otherwise, cannot be admitted for the purpose of varying or contradicting written language recorded in the labor agreement. Consider, for example, the following labor agreement provision: "Notice of a promotional opening shall be posted for 5 working days." Even though "5 working days" is clearer than "5 days," a dispute could arise if the contract specified "working days" and the Saturday in question was a regularly unscheduled day on which certain employees were called in for emergency overtime. One of the parties might successfully argue before the arbitrator that the term "working day" is clear and applies to days on which work is performed and that this precludes any evidence that Saturday was unscheduled and never contemplated as a working day. Rationale for this rule is that the parties have spent many hours in negotiating standardized employment conditions; thus, disregarding negoti-

EXHIBIT 11.5

Transcript from an Arbitration Hearing Reflecting Poor Cross-Examination

(Direct questions of employee witness by a union spokesperson)

Q: How did your supervisor sexually harass you?

A: He mooned me.

Q: Describe the circumstances to the Arbitrator.

A: I was working overtime and as far as I knew we were the only ones left in the laundry. As I was counting the inventory, the door to a broom closet opened, and there was this man's bare butt sticking out at me with his pants down around his ankles.

(Subsequent cross-examination of employee witness by a management spokesperson)

Q: Was the area near the broom closet well lighted?

A: No, it was rather dim.

Q: Was the broom closet well lit?

A: No, the light in the closet wasn't even lit.

Q: Was there a mirror that you could clearly see the face of the man?

A: No, I never saw his face when it happened. He stepped back into the closet, and I went and punched out right away.

Q: (Triumphantly) How then can you be sure that the bare fanny belonged to your supervisor?

A: Because of the tattoo.

Q: I've come this far so I might as well ask what is the significance of the tattoo.

A: Well he was always bragging to us women about his tattoo, describing it and offering to show it to us. Of course, none of us ever took him up on it but there it was—just as he had pictured it. (Whereupon the grievant proceeded to describe in some detail the tattoo that had been so prominently displayed.)

SOURCE: John J. Flagler, "A Few Modest Proposals for Improving Conduct of the Hearing," in Gladys W. Gruenberg, ed., *Arbitration 1990: New Perspectives on Old Issues,* Proceedings of the Forty-third Annual Meeting, National Academy of Arbitrators (Washington, D.C.: Bureau of National Affairs, Inc., 1991), p. 55.

ated terms would damage stable labor-management relationships and communicate to the parties that there is little or no point in reducing contract terms to writing.

A problem remains when the labor agreement language is ambiguous, because it normally cannot prescribe all essential rules or guidelines for day-to-day administration of labor relations. Also, many labor agreement terms, such as "reasonable," "make every effort," "minor repairs," and "maintain the work environment as safely as possible" might have resolved negotiation impasses but still pose interpretive problems for the arbitrator.

Some contract provisions that appear clear on the surface can cause differences of opinion among union and management officials as well as arbitrators. Consider the following three examples and related questions.[34]

Example 1: **"The company will provide required safety clothing."** Does the company have to pay for safety clothing or merely make it available for employees to purchase?

Example 2: **"An employee must work on the scheduled day before and after the holiday to receive holiday pay."** What happens when the employee works 3 hours the day before the holiday, goes home because of sickness, and works the full 8 hours the day after the holiday?

Example 3: "Management will distribute overtime as equally as possible." Does a supervisor making overtime request calls to employees' homes stop making such calls until contact is made with an employee whose telephone is busy or goes unanswered? Has the company met its obligation if the supervisor calls, leaves a message on the senior employee's answering machine, then offers overtime to the next senior employee?

Arbitrators prefer to approach the ambiguity problem initially in terms of the labor agreement and to construe ambiguous language or provisions of the labor agreement so as to be compatible with the language in other provisions of the agreement. Thus, the contract should be viewed as a whole, not in isolated parts, and any interpretation that would nullify another provision of the contract should be avoided. When ambiguity remains, the arbitrator must seek guidance from sources outside the labor agreement.

Intent of the Parties   Another guideline, the **intent of the parties,** refers to what union and management officials had in mind when they (1) negotiated the labor agreement or (2) engaged in an action that resulted in a particular grievance. Intent is entirely subjective; however, arbitrators consider observable behavioral manifestations of the intent to determine what a reasonable person would conclude from that behavior. For an example of labor agreement intent, consider the previously cited holiday pay situation. To demonstrate that it intended for holiday pay to be given only to those individuals who worked a full 8 hours the day before and the day after the holiday, management might supply the arbitrator with notes on various proposals and counterproposals made during labor agreement negotiations to prove what they intended the contract language to mean. Arbitrators are strongly influenced by this evidence of intent because they are reluctant to award a benefit that could not be obtained at the bargaining table.

An example of an action's intent considered in a grievance might occur when a supervisor believes an employee has stolen some company property. The supervisor approaches the employee stating the following:

> You and I both know you were caught stealing. Therefore, you have two options. You can file a grievance which will be denied in arbitration and the discharge on your record will make it difficult for you to find a job elsewhere. Or you can sign this resignation slip, quit, and we won't tell any other companies about the stealing incident.

The employee hastily signs the slip and leaves the company premises. However, the next day she returns, informing management that she wants to work because she never really quit. If the company refuses the employee's request and a grievance is filed, the arbitrator would have to determine the grievant's and management's intent. Observable behaviors of an employee intending to quit are cleaning out the locker, saying good-bye to colleagues, and asking management for the wages earned for that week. An employee usually resigns only after giving the decision careful thought and consideration. Because none of these behaviors were operative in this case, the arbitrator might attempt to determine management's intent in this action. Possibly, the supervisor was simply trying to do the employee a favor by letting her off the hook. However, management may have given the employee the alternative of quitting to avoid subsequent arbitration of the discharge and the risk of the discharge decision being overturned. The latter intent is viewed by arbitrators as being *constructive discharge.*

Under this principle, the arbitrator would view the termination of employment as being subject to the employee discipline provisions of the labor agreement. These provisions usually call for union representation and written explanation at the time of the employee's discharge. Because these procedures were not followed, many arbitrators would reinstate the grievant with full back pay. Sometimes, union and management officials attempt to convince the arbitrator of their specific intent by producing written notes of previous discussions so that there will be documentation of their related past behaviors.

Past Practice   The principle of **past practice** refers to a specific and identical action that has been continually employed over a number of years to the recognition and acceptance of both parties.[35] This decision-making criterion demonstrates to the arbitrator how the parties have carried out the labor agreement and has been used by both management and the union. Management is usually more concerned about past practice because it administers the labor agreement through various supervisory directives to the hourly employees. Because established contractual provisions place restrictions on managerial discretion, management attempts to avoid further reductions on supervisory decision making by pressing for a "zipper" clause to be included in the labor agreement, similar to the following:

Article XXVIII: Other Agreements
Section 2.   The parties do hereby terminate all prior agreements heretofore entered into between representatives of the company and the unions (including all past understandings, practices, and arbitration rulings) pertaining to rates of pay, hours of work, and conditions of employment other than those stipulated in this agreement between the parties.[36]

This clause does not guarantee that management does not add to its contractual restrictions by repeatedly handling a situation in a similar manner. A continued managerial practice of unilaterally giving employees a Thanksgiving turkey might become a binding, implied term of the labor agreement. Furthermore, management will likely have to negotiate a labor agreement provision to the contrary (even if the current labor agreement is silent on the subject) if it wishes to discontinue the gift in subsequent years.

In addition to interpreting ambiguous language or resolving problems not covered in the agreement, past practices may even alter clear and convincing contractual provisions. At one company, it had been a practice for many years to require clerks to perform cleanup operations at the end of their workday and to pay them no money for up to 10 minutes' work, 15 minutes straight time for 11 to 15 minutes' work, and time and one-half for work of more than 15 minutes in duration. There was clear contractual language specifying that work in excess of 8 hours per day would be computed at time and one-half overtime premium. The union eventually filed a grievance stating that clear contractual language compelled overtime payment for any amount of daily work exceeding 8 hours. However, the arbitrator maintained that past practice was more significant than the express terms of the labor agreement in this case.

> The written contract is, of course, the strongest kind of evidence of what the parties willed, intended or agreed upon. An arbitrator will not ordinarily look beyond its *unambiguous* language. Where, *however,* as here, the parties have unmistakably demonstrated *how they themselves* have read and regarded the meaning and force of the language, and *where the meaning varies* from its normal intendment, the arbitrator *should not,* indeed, *cannot* close his eyes to this demonstration.[37]

Past practice, although influential, is not interpreted the same by all arbitrators. For example, it is very difficult to determine in a consistent fashion how long or how frequently an action must be continued before it becomes a binding past practice.

Sometimes the nature of the issue further complicates the past practice criterion. Consider a situation in which management wants to unilaterally change a "clear" past practice of employee smoking at work. Some arbitrators indicated that management could not unilaterally change this past practice, particularly if no specified evidence was presented to show that smoking adversely affected efficiency or productivity. However, some arbitrators have let management establish a no-smoking rule, thereby disregarding past practice, for the following reasons[38]:

- Past practice pertains to employee benefits, not management's direction of the workforce, and smoking is not an employee benefit.

- The past practice of permitting employee smoking can be broken because this activity has now proven to be detrimental to employees' health.

Previous Labor Arbitration Awards   Also used as guidelines are previous arbitration awards when they could bolster either party's position in the arbitration case. Similarly, the arbitrator may cite these awards to refute the parties' contentions or to illustrate the arbitral opinion. Arbitrators accord some weight to prior arbitration awards issued at the same facility, particularly if the situation and contractual language are similar. Of course, few prior arbitration awards meet these requirements because the parties would be extremely reluctant to arbitrate the same issue a second time, given the first arbitrator's decision.

Arbitrators are far less likely to be influenced by awards concerning different labor agreements at other facilities because as arbitrators they recognize the common law uniqueness and autonomy of a particular operation. In fact, arbitrators might negatively regard the introduction of prior arbitration awards into a current arbitration hearing.

> Unwillingness to present a case solely on its own merits may come to be interpreted as a sign of weakness. Also it may be considered that citation of prior arbitration awards indicates either a lack of confidence in the judgment of an arbitrator or a belief that he may be swayed by irrelevant considerations. An attempt to induce an arbitrator to follow some alleged precedent may come to be recognized as at least bad etiquette.[39]

Numerous factors influence the success of the parties in arbitration cases, including the burden of proof, the types of issues, and legal representation. The evidence suggests that management prevails more often in contract interpretation cases, and unions win more often in disciplinary cases. Because the employer has the burden of proof in disciplinary and discharge cases and the union has the burden of proof in contract interpretation and application cases, apparently the party having the burden of proof does not prevail in most of the arbitration decisions. In addition, evidence indicates that legal representation influences the outcome of the arbitrator's decision. Furthermore, research has discovered that certain unions prevail more often than other unions. These unions include the Ladies Garment Workers; the Retail and Wholesale Clerks; the American Federation of State, County, and Municipal Employees; and the Operating Engineers. Possible explanations include that the union's duty to fairly represent all bargaining unit employees and the democratic nature of unions in determining which cases to take to arbitration may cause some unions to take some grievances to arbitration when they have little chance of prevailing in the decision.[40]

Current Issues Affecting Arbitration

Legal Jurisdiction

As previously noted, the Steelworkers' Trilogy and other judicial decisions clarified and enhanced arbitrators' roles in resolving employee grievances. Yet arbitration decisions can sometimes involve various government agencies and the courts, which might be concerned with specific aspects of a grievance. Consider, for example, a case in which a black union steward is discharged for insubordination. A grievance is filed and proceeds to arbitration under the terms of the labor agreement. However, the employee claims that the discharge was prompted by racial bias and the fact that he was a union steward as well. Conceivably, the discharge grievance could claim the attention of a number of persons—the arbitrator and officials from the Equal Employment Opportunity Commission (EEOC) and the National Labor Relations Board (NLRB). The problem involves untangling the various jurisdictional squabbles that could arise over this one grievance.

Labor Arbitration and the Equal Employment Opportunity Commission
The passage of the 1964 Civil Rights Act (amended by the Equal Employment Opportunity Act of 1972), subsequent judicial decisions, and the passage of the 1991 Civil Rights Act have emphasized that management's well-meant intentions are not sufficient to preclude a charge of racial discrimination. Indeed, in administering this aspect of public law, the EEOC holds that employers must actively devise and implement employment procedures that remove present and possible residual effects of past discrimination. Hiring, promotion, and discipline procedures may be carefully scrutinized by the EEOC to protect employees from arbitrary and discriminatory practices. In a unionized facility, arbitrators also often assume a related decision-making role, particularly in grievances protesting discipline of an employee. This situation poses at least two questions:

1. Should management, the union, and the employee turn to the arbitrator, the EEOC, or both in resolving a minority employee's grievance?

2. How do the courts and the EEOC view the arbitrator's decision in terms of Title VII of the 1964 Civil Rights Act?

The first question was answered by the Supreme Court in its 1974 *Alexander* v. *Gardner-Denver Company* decision. The Court contended that the arbitrator's expertise pertains to labor agreement interpretation and not to resolving federal civil rights laws. Moreover,

> The fact-finding process in arbitration usually is not equivalent to judicial fact-finding. The record of the arbitration proceedings is not as complete; the usual rules of evidence do not apply; and rights and procedures common to civil trials, such as discovery, compulsory process, cross-examination, and testimony under oath, are often severely limited or unavailable.[41]

Consequently, a minority employee is almost encouraged to pursue both the arbitration process and appropriate judicial procedures.

Some predicted that the *Gardner-Denver* decision would create havoc as every discrimination grievance lost in arbitration would be overturned by the appropriate government agency or the courts. Yet research does not support this prediction. One study found that a grievance reviewed by the EEOC or related agencies only stood a one-in-six chance of being reversed. Also, the chances of a trial court overturning a discrimination grievance heard by an arbitrator are slim, 6.8 percent according to one study and 10 percent according to another.[42] Apparently, the courts believe that arbitrators are adequately covering the legal considerations of discrimination in their decisions.

The Supreme Court's *Gilmer* decision, discussed later in this chapter, might enable arbitrators instead of the EEOC and the courts to resolve a discrimination grievance filed under the terms of the collective bargaining agreement. However, this has not yet happened. The EEOC, while encouraging use of alternative dispute-resolution techniques, including arbitration, to resolve discrimination claims, has not yet waived its involvement on the issue. Moreover, Congress, in the passage of the 1991 Civil Rights Act, reinforced *Gardner-Denver*'s rationale for judicial oversight in unionized settings.[43]

Labor Arbitration and the National Labor Relations Board Perhaps the most frequent supplements to arbitral decisions have come from the NLRB because the grievant could have been discharged for reasons pertaining to provisions of the labor agreement that are similar to laws, such as engaging in union activities on the job or acting overly aggressive in the capacity of a union official. Section 10(a) of the National Labor Relations Act provides that the NLRB "is empowered . . . to prevent any person from engaging in any unfair labor practice (listed in Section 8) affecting commerce. This power shall not be affected by any other means of adjustment or prevention that has been or may be established by agreement, law, or otherwise."

Although it has the power, the NLRB does not ignore arbitration awards covering unfair labor practice issues. In fact, it often withholds its jurisdictional determination and investigation pending the arbitrator's decision. In 1955 the NLRB's deferral to arbitration policy was formulated in the *Spielberg Manufacturing Company* case. In that case, the Board honored an arbitration award that denied reinstatement to certain employees guilty of strike misconduct. Resulting deferral guidelines stressed that the arbitration proceedings must be fair and regular, there must be adequate notice and representation, the arbitrator must address the issue of the alleged unfair labor practice, and all parties must agree to be bound by the arbitration awards.[49] However, the Board will disregard the arbitrator's award if it is ambiguous or if the Board obtains pertinent evidence not presented in the arbitration proceeding.

The NLRB's deferral to arbitration policy was enhanced in the *Collyer* case, in which the NLRB administrative law judge had found that the company had committed an unfair labor practice when it made certain unilateral changes in wages and working conditions.[45] The company maintained that the issues should be resolved through existing arbitration proceedings instead of the NLRB. The Board in essence agreed with the company's position. While reserving the right to investigate the merits of the issue, the Board maintained the following:

1. Related disputes can be better resolved through the special skills and experiences of the arbitrators.

2. The objectives of the National Labor Relations Act, industrial peace and stability, can be significantly realized through adherence to arbitration procedures established in the labor agreement.

Under *Collyer*, the employee was obligated to use the arbitration procedure before the NLRB would review the merits of the case.[46]

The NLRB's subsequent *Olin Corporation* and *United Technologies* decisions established new guidelines that make it even more likely that the NLRB will defer to arbitration decisions. Under *Olin*, the unfair labor practice does not have to be considered in the arbitration hearing. The NLRB will still defer to an arbitrator's award "if the contractual and unfair labor practice issues were factually parallel and the facts relevant to resolving the unfair labor practice were presented generally to the arbitrator."[47]

Under this deferral policy, there is potential for abuse by either the union or the company. The arbitrator makes his or her decision based on the facts that the parties voluntarily chose to present at the arbitration hearing. Either of the parties could purposely withhold evidence and deny the arbitrator the full record for the purposes of undermining the NLRB's deferral to the arbitrator's decision. Such an incomplete record would preserve for one of the parties a "second bite at the apple," and the arbitrator would be hard pressed to produce a decision based on the record equivalent to the kind of record developed at an NLRB trial.[48]

One research effort found that only about half of the arbitrators cited related external law in their decisions when at least one of the parties had filed an unfair labor practice charge with the NLRB. It also found that most of these arbitrators engaged in only cursory or conclusory consideration of relevant external law. The study urged that, at a minimum, arbitrators and union and management officials should be aware that they may provide the grievant his or her only opportunity to litigate a statutory claim; therefore, an explicit, informed choice should be made on "whether to vote, argue, discuss, and explore statutory issues in the arbitration forum, or to reject the discussion of such issues as inappropriate to the arbitration process."[49]

In summary, the Supreme Court has recognized the ability of arbitrators to interpret the labor agreement provisions and has even encouraged parties to arbitrate the issue before proceeding to the NLRB. However, this encouragement is not given to the same extent in Title VII Civil Rights Act disputes.

Labor Arbitration, the Courts, and Public Policy: The *Misco* Decision Federal courts can occasionally become involved when union or management officials request consideration of arbitration matters, particularly when a case heard by an arbitrator involves public policy considerations. The Supreme Court approached this situation in its *Misco* decision. Misco fired an employee who operated a "slitter-rewinder," which cuts rolling coils of paper, for allegedly smoking marijuana on company property. The grievant was arrested in his car in the company's parking lot. Police found a lit marijuana cigarette in the front ashtray of the car, and a subsequent police search of the car revealed marijuana residue.

The arbitrator reinstated the grievant because the evidence did not establish that the grievant smoked or even possessed marijuana on the company's premises. He noted the grievant had been in the backseat of the car. The arbitrator also refused to consider the police report as evidence and ruled that the case must be limited to what the employer knew at the time of the firing. Management appealed the arbitrator's decision to the courts, claiming that bringing the employee back would violate public policy—operating dangerous equipment under the influence of drugs.

In *Misco* the Court restated a principle established in an earlier decision (*W.R. Grace*). It said that a "court may not enforce a collective bargaining agreement that is contrary to public policy." However, the Court noted that the public policy must be *"explicit," "well defined* and *dominant,"* and *"ascertained by reference to the laws and legal precedents and not from general considerations of supposed public interests."* The Supreme Court upheld the arbitrator because none of these prerequisites were examined by the lower courts and would unlikely be found in this situation.[50]

Misco therefore reinforces the wide latitude given to arbitrators' decision-making authority by the Steelworkers' Trilogy. It will probably reduce the number of instances in which the courts "second-guess" the arbitrator's award on public policy grounds. However, the public policy exception, although made narrow by *Misco*, still exists. An employer does not have to honor an arbitration award that would require a violation of law (e.g., reinstating a bus driver who lacks a driver's license).[51]

Sexual harassment represents a controversial public policy issue that has been subsequently interpreted by arbitrators and judicial officials. The courts can have very different interpretations of this situation. For example, one federal district court vacated an arbitrator's award that reinstated an employee who allegedly harassed a female customer. The judge found that the arbitrator's decision contained some "disturbing comments" that evidenced bias in favor of the employee and insensitivity toward the customer-accuser. For example, the arbitrator noted that the employee was married and had children, whereas the customer weighed 225 pounds, "was unattractive and frustrated," and possibly fabricated the incident to attract her mother's caring attention. The judge ordered the case to be heard by a new arbitrator.[52]

However, another federal court refused to set aside an arbitration award reinstating an employee who, during a phone conversation, put down the receiver, approached a co-worker from behind, and grabbed her breasts. He then picked up the phone and said, "Yup, they're real." The court commented, "While we do not condone (the employee's) behavior, it was within the purview of the collective bargaining agreement and public policy for the arbitrator to order his reinstatement."[53]

LABOR RELATIONS IN ACTION

Things They Never Told Me Before I Became an Arbitrator

- The difficulty of setting up a hearing date when union and company representatives have such busy schedules.

- The ease of reading finished cases and the difficulty of writing one from scratch.

- The need to know about admission of evidence and reasons for sustaining and overruling objections at a hearing and making quick decisions about them.

- How physically tiring it is to fly or drive to some of the hearing sites.

- How unglamorous travel and hotels can be when all airports look alike and you are not even sure where you are.

- How mature and conscientious some parties can be in trying to do "what is right," while some parties enter the hearing armed for combat and confrontation.

- How much money, time, and effort could be saved if the parties prepared better and attempted to resolve their differences before arbitration.

- The role of the cancellation fee in making sure the parties are going forth to arbitration. (If there is no cost of canceling, one of the parties can abuse the arbitration process by canceling at a late date.)

- How one party will hold out for a compromise settlement until right before the hearing. When no settlement is forthcoming and their case is weak, the party will drop the grievance.

- How important the fee is to the parties—it cannot be too low because the parties think you are not good enough; it cannot be too high because you price yourself out of a job. ■

SOURCE: From an experienced, somewhat weary arbitrator who enjoys relaxing in anonymity.

Similar judicial rationale was used in the case of a trading-room secretary at a California brokerage firm. The secretary's boss admitted to calling her a "hooker" and a "bitch" and placing at least one condom on her desk. She filed a sexual harassment suit and was then told to submit her charge to an arbitration panel, which was mandated by the industry. The panel dismissed her charge agreeing with the defendant that "[i]t's just the way that it is in every trading room."[54]

Appraising Labor Arbitration's Effectiveness

Although the courts have praised the effectiveness of arbitration, some critical assessments have come from participants—union and management officials and even some arbitrators (see "Labor Relations in Action" box for some related insights).

Arbitrators seldom, if ever, know why they were not chosen for a subsequent grievance. Little information is available concerning why the parties continually return to some arbitrators but not to others. Exhibit 11.6 approaches this void by grouping criticisms that several union and management practitioners have leveled at arbitrators. These criticisms apply to two general areas: arbitrators' capabilities and ethics, and the potential procedural problems in the arbitration process.

Arbitrators' Capabilities and Ethics   Some contend arbitrators might compromise their decisions to minimize or avoid displeasure from one or both of the parties or even to ensure reemployment in future arbitration cases. The following are examples of compromise decisions that might be used to appease both sides.[55]

- Reinstating a discharged grievant without any back pay awarded
- Changing the 50–50 outcome assessment of one case to 51–49 in favor of the party who had lost the other three cases heard at the hearing

In some instances, union and management representatives believe that the arbitrator "owes them one" because of their support (financial and otherwise). One arbitrator, who expressed surprise to officials at being selected to replace another prominent arbitrator, was given the following reason why the previous arbitrator was fired:

> I'll tell you why we fired him. The last case he had ended here at about 4:00. Mr. _____ expressed considerable concern since he had to make a plane for New York and was running late. I assured him that he would have no problem. I carried his bags to his car, drove in excess of all the speed

Exhibit 11.6

Summary of Criticisms Union and Management Practitioners Have toward Arbitrators

1. Fails to treat all parties with respect (e.g., has offensive personal traits; tends to apply his or her feelings of "fairness" or "justice" as opposed to applying the parties' intent; regularly exceeds his or her authority).
2. Cannot control the hearing properly (e.g., cannot rule on objections, is too legalistic or not legalistic enough, cannot stop gratuitous hostile exchanges or rambling or redundant testimony).
3. Awards are either too brief or too long, unclear, take a long time, emphasize compromise, evidence poor reasoning or writing skills, or fail to give parties direction on language issues.
4. Either too much experience with management or the union or insufficient experience with labor relations as a neutral or with the jobs and industry in question.
5. Decides cases on grounds other than those argued (e.g., fails to consider precedents; is too academic; fails to pay sufficient attention at hearing; reviews evidence not presented in hearing; discusses cases with uninvolved parties before decision being issued; does not address all facts or issues).
6. Too expensive (e.g., generally unavailable in a reasonable time frame, thereby increasing potential back-pay liability; cancellation policy is unreasonable).

SOURCE: Adapted from Thomas L. Watkins, "Assessing Arbitrator Competence: A Preliminary Regional Survey," *Arbitration Journal* 47 (June 1992), p. 43.

limits, went through back roads, even proceeded through changing traffic lights. After a hectic ride and at considerable risk, I got him to the airport just in time to make the plane. I parked my car in a no parking zone. I even carried his bags to the gate. After all this, you know, that [deleted] ruled against me.[56]

Yet other participants or students of arbitration maintain that the arbitrator's indebtedness to the parties is a necessary ingredient of dispute resolution. They maintain that the arbitrator owes allegiance to both union and management, thereby providing a well-formulated decision. The ethics issue has been directly approached by three organizations: the National Academy of Arbitrators, the FMCS, and the AAA. These organizations have come up with the following guidelines:

- An arbitrator, deciding that he or she does not have the technical competence to deal with the issue under consideration, is expected to withdraw from the case. Issues commonly included in this category are incentive systems, job evaluation plans, and pension and insurance programs.

- An arbitrator is not to make an award public without the consent of the parties.

- Before an arbitrator's appointment the parties should be made aware of the arbitrator's fees for the hearing, study time, travel time, postponement or cancellation, office overhead expenses, and any work of paid assistants.

- If either party requests the arbitrator to visit the workplace, the arbitrator should comply.

- An arbitrator should not consider a posthearing brief that has not been given to the other party.

- If the arbitrator knows any of the parties or has any private issue in the organization, he or she must make disclosure of any potential conflict of interest before the hearing.

Other criticisms of arbitration have focused on the quality of the arbitrator's decision. The arbitrator's written opinion and award dissatisfy the parties if they do not reflect the original expectations and understandings of one or both regarding the nature or scope of the grievance. However, some arbitral decisions reflect legal considerations as much or more than union and management concerns expressed at the hearing. This potential "overlawyering" problem of arbitration decisions might be due to the large amount of legislation at the local, state, and federal levels that might pertain to the grievance, or the preferences of union and management officials and possibly the arbitrator[57] to minimize subsequent judicial reviews by considering related laws at the hearing and in the decision.

Management and union representatives might also obtain poor arbitration awards under the *garbage in, garbage out* theory. Because the arbitrator's decision is based on the merits of the grievance, a sloppy grievance formulation and presentation might result in a relatively lackluster arbitral decision. Sometimes union and management officials present an arbitrator with poorly conceived grievances that should have been resolved before going to arbitration. Such grievances are often prompted by political considerations—the union or management officials take the grievance to arbitration to show support for their union stewards or first-line supervisors even though they know them to be wrong. Arbitration in this sense serves as a buck-passing device; the errant union steward or supervisor is apparently given support but in reality is provided an education through the arbitrator's decision.

One almost inescapable concern arises from the finality of the arbitrator's award. Although the Supreme Court has encouraged single-person resolution of an industrial dispute, opponents of this practice suggest that an arbitrator has more authority than a judge, whose decisions may be overturned through judicial appeal. Unfortunately, many problems would result if arbitration awards were subjected to an appeals procedure. Any such procedure would be time consuming and expensive. If the arbitrator's award were reversed by a second arbitrator in the appeals procedure it would be impossible to determine which arbitrator wrote the "correct" decision. Also, the "arbitrator as judge of last resort" situation might beneficially place pressure on the arbitrator to produce high-quality opinions.

Procedural Problems The two general categories of procedural problems are time lag and expense of the arbitration proceedings. The FMCS reports that the average length of time between the filing of a grievance and an arbitrator's award was 326 days.[58]

Delay in arbitration is a concern of union and company advocates, especially in discharge cases. The discharged employee is likely to be unemployed after the discharge and faces an uncertain future. The employer probably has to fill the vacant position and faces the possibility of back-pay liabilities. Because it is an universally accepted principle that discharge decisions should be based on the facts known at the time of the decision and the passage of time does not alter the facts of the case, the length of time between the discharge should not affect the arbitrator's decision. However, research of arbitrators' decisions in discharge cases reveal that the longer the delay between an employer's discharge and the arbitrator's decision, the less likely the grievant will be reinstated.[59]

Although delay is harmful to employees, to the arbitration process, and to union–management relationships, a numbers of reasons have been identified as causes for this delay:

- Shortage of acceptable arbitrators coupled with the reluctance of the parties to take a risk on a new or inexperienced arbitrator

- Prearbitration activities, such as the steps in the grievance procedure and accommodating the schedules of busy advocates and arbitrators for the hearing

- Time after the hearing, which includes awaiting the transcript of the hearing and any posthearing submissions by the parties, such as posthearing briefs and any relevant precedent decisions of other arbitrators; time taken by the arbitrator to review the evidence and arguments; and posthearing submissions by the parties

Although discharge cases are handled more expeditiously than nondischarge cases at every stage of the process, except for arbitrator selection, the parties have the power to address the causes of delay and are capable of moving more quickly because it is in their mutual interests to do so.[60]

Another criticism directed at arbitrators is that they split their decisions in discharge cases, that is, they reinstate the grievant but without back pay. Split decisions are not uncommon in discipline and discharge cases because arbitrators generally exercise the right to modify a penalty when the penalty is found to be too severe based on the facts of the case. The arbitrator may conclude that the employee's misconduct warranted some penalty, but short of removal from the job. The parties themselves have the power to avoid penalty modification by the arbitrator simply by negotiating language that directs the arbitrator either to uphold the penalty imposed by management or to sustain the grievance and return the grievant to the job with back pay—no split decision. One study of such contract language in the telecommunication industry showed that the grievant was more often reinstated with full back pay than under the traditional contract language when the arbitrator is allowed to modify the penalty. Thus, if the arbitrator has no authority to modify the penalty, the arbitrator must be convinced that the penalty of removal is the appropriate penalty.[61]

Time delay is only one of several expenses associated with arbitration. The FMCS reports that arbitrators' average per diem rate of $720, when applied to the arbitrator's average hearing time (1.10 days), travel time (.45 days), and study time (2.44 days), plus average expenses ($318), resulted in an average charge of about $3,202 for an arbitrated grievance.[62] Although most labor agreements provide for the sharing of arbitration expenses between union and management organizations, each party can incur additional expenses such as the fees for the parties' attorneys, which usually exceed the arbitrator's fee; wage payments to plant personnel who take part in the proceedings; and stenographic transcription costs, if a record of the hearing is desired.

Arbitral fees have increased over the years, which is understandable in view of inflation. In many cases, however, management and union officials bring added expenses on themselves when they insist that the arbitrator review unnecessary materials, such as transcripts, prior arbitration awards, superfluous witnesses, and prehearing and posthearing briefs. They may also insist on expensive frills, such as renting a hotel suite for a neutral arbitration site, that do not materially affect the quality of a decision.

Expedited Arbitration Procedures   Some union and management officials have reduced expenses by expediting the arbitration procedures before, during, or after arbitration hearings. Prehearing suggestions include (1) appointing a panel of arbitrators for the length of the contract rather than working through a new list of arbitrators each time an arbitration is scheduled, and (2) appointing a permanent umpire for a specific amount of time (e.g., 1 year or the life of the agreement). Hearings may be expedited by substituting tape recordings for transcripts. Posthearing expedition includes (1) setting a deadline for the award to be returned to the parties, (2) reducing or eliminating the number of citings for the arbitrator to research, and (3) setting a maximum on the length of the award statement or establishing the maximum amount to be paid for the decision ahead of time.[63]

Other possibilities also exist for streamlining the arbitration process. For example, some grievances solely concern interpretations of the labor agreement. Unlike discipline cases, these grievances do not personally involve employee grievants and thus do not entail related therapeutic or political considerations.

Perhaps these grievances could be argued on paper without the necessity of a hearing and related expenses.[64]

The use of expedited or experimental approaches illustrates two fundamental issues concerning arbitration:

1. This process, although not perfect, appears to offer great advantages over alternative methods of grievance resolution, such as sudden strike activity.

2. Union and management officials created the arbitration process and are charged with controlling it in accordance with their jointly determined needs. They must monitor the process as well as their related actions and attitudes, to ensure a relatively inexpensive, efficient, and objective means of dispute resolution.

Employment Arbitration

Recently, employers have initiated and used **employment arbitration** in situations such as the following:

- Employment discrimination claims in union or nonunion firms (instead of using the courts)

- Employee grievances in nonunion firms (instead of using unilateral management decision making)

See the "Labor Relations in Action" box for a summary of how employment arbitration differs from arbitration found in labor agreements.

The use of arbitration to resolve employment discrimination suits was enhanced by the Supreme Court in *Gilmer* v. *Interstate Johnson Lane Corp.* A securities representative signed an employment application (Form U-4, which is common in the securities industry) in part agreeing to arbitrate any dispute, claim, or controversy with his employer that was required to be arbitrated under the employer's rules. After being terminated at age 62, Gilmer filed an age discrimination complaint with the EEOC and subsequently in federal court. The Supreme Court agreed with Gilmer's employer that arbitration, not the courts, was both the agreed-on and proper dispute resolution forum that did not counter the legislative history of the Age Discrimination in Employment Act.[65] A subsequent Supreme Court decision seemed to recognize arbitration as a proper resolution of other employment discrimination claims in the securities industry and possibly other industries as well.[66]

The Supreme Court's *Gilmer* decision appeared to be inconsistent with its previous decision in *Alexander* v. *Gardner-Denver Company.* Questions arose as to whether mandatory arbitration of civil rights claims could be required under a collective bargaining agreement and whether a union through the collective bargaining agreement could waive an employee's right to a jury trial under the civil rights statutes. The *Gilmer* decision did not involve union–management relations, and the employee (Gilmer) had signed a Form U-4 agreement (known as the Uniform Application for Securities Industry Registration or Transfer).

In the *Wright* decision in 1998, Ceasar Wright injured his right heel and back, sought permanent disability, and ultimately settled for $250,000. Three years later, he asked to be returned to work through the union hiring hall, and presented his doctor's approval. Wright worked for 9 days for four different companies, and none complained about this performance. However, when the em-

LABOR RELATIONS IN ACTION

How Employment Arbitration Differs from Arbitration Found in Labor Agreements

1. What are the conditions under which the arbitration system is devised?

If the arbitration system is established to avoid a union, then many acceptable, well-qualified arbitrators will refuse to serve. If the employer designs a system for the purpose of providing a mechanism for employees to resolve their grievance by an independent neutral party, qualified arbitrators will be willing to serve. Under a collective-bargaining agreement, the union and company have negotiated and designed the arbitration procedure that best fits their purposes. In other words, the parties design a system of self-governance for resolving conflicts.

2. What subjects will be covered under the employment arbitration system, and will employees be required to waive their statutory rights, such as employment discrimination on the basis of race, gender, age, national origin, disability, and so on?

If the employees are required to waive their statutory rights as a condition of employment, the arbitration decision may not stand a court review. Under a collective-bargaining agreement, arbitration involves contract interpretation and application of provisions negotiated and agreed to by the parties. Various federal agencies have different policies regarding deferral to arbitration.

3. How are the arbitrators selected? How long are they retained?

If the arbitrators are selected only by the employer and serve at the pleasure of the employer, then a perception may persist that the arbitrator is loyal to the employer and can be terminated if a decision unfavorable toward the employer is rendered. Under a collective-bargaining agreement, the arbitrators are selected and retained by a procedure negotiated and agreed on by the union and company. To avoid problems and misperceptions, selections may be made through independent agencies such as the American Arbitration Association and the Federal Mediation and Conciliation Service.

4. What are the employee's due process rights, if any?

Employment arbitration systems contain no guarantees of due process; however, under collective bargaining agreements, arbitrators recognize these important employee rights that include:

- Right to counsel by a union representative
- Right to face one's accusers
- Right to information to prepare for the arbitration hearing
- Right to notice of hearing
- Right to a copy of written charges against employee

5. Who pays the arbitrator?

Under employment arbitration procedures, the employer typically pays the arbitrator. The concern is that the arbitrator might show loyalty to the party who pays the fee. Under most collective-bargaining agreements, the union and the company jointly decide the method by which the arbitrator will be paid. Usually, the two parties share the costs; however, on a few occasions, the union and company

Continued

negotiate the method whereby the loser pays. To avoid the perception of bias toward the payer of the fee, one organization designed a system whereby each employee pays a monthly fee to support an arbitration system; the arbitrator, then, is paid jointly by the employer and from employee fees.

6. How final is the arbitrator's decision?

Under employment arbitration, the arbitrator's decision is final if the employer wants the decision to be final. Although overturning the arbitrator's decision would be bad policy unless fully justified, no legal basis exists for prohibiting the employer from taking such action. Under collective-bargaining agreements, the arbitrator's decision will stand in nearly all cases, except in those limited cases where the arbitrator's decision is inconsistent with public policy, the arbitrator is incompetent, or the arbitrator has personal ties with one of the parties.

7. How are employees who file grievances protected?

Under the employment arbitration system, employee protection survives as long as the employer allows the system to survive. Under the collective-bargaining agreement, employees who file grievances are protected under the grievance and arbitration procedure, which lasts as long as the collective-bargaining agreement lasts.

8. What issues are arbitrated under the arbitration systems?

Under the employment arbitration system, the employer decides the issues that may be grieved and arbitrated. Under the collective-bargaining agreement, the union and company jointly decide; this usually includes conflicts over interpretation and application of provisions of the collective-bargaining agreement.

9. What authority do arbitrators have to grant remedies?

Under employment arbitration, the employer determines the extent of the arbitrator's authority. However, when there are statutory issues involved, such as gender discrimination, sexual harassment charges, and so on, remedial authority may include awarding attorney fees, punitive and compensatory damages, interest on back pay, and so on—in other words, issues normally decided by a jury. Under a collective-bargaining agreement, back pay, reinstatement, and "make whole" remedies are common. Interest may be paid where the parties have agreed to such payments. In the federal sector, arbitrators have authority to award attorney fees and interest on back-pay awards. ∎

ployers realized that Wright had already settled a claim for permanent disability, they informed the union that they would no longer accept Wright for employment because a person certified as permanently disabled was not qualified to perform longshore work under the collective bargaining agreement. The union asserted that the employers had misapplied the collective-bargaining agreement and suggested that the American with Disabilities Act (ADA) entitled Wright to return to

Exhibit 11.7

An Employment Application Form under Mandatory Employment Arbitration

> I agree that I will settle any and all previously unasserted claims, disputes or controversies arising out of or relating to my application or candidacy for employment, employment and or cessation of employment with XYZ Company, exclusively by final and binding arbitration before a neutral arbitrator. By way of example only, such claims include claims under federal, state, and local statutory or common law, such as the Age Discrimination in Employment Act, Title VII of the Civil Rights Act of 1964, as amended, including the amendments of the Civil Rights Act of 1991, the American With Disabilities Act, the law of contracts and the law of tort.
>
> SOURCE: *Circuit City Stores, Inc. v. Adams,* 532 U.S. 105 (2001).

work if he could perform the duties of the job. The union contended that refusal of employment to Wright by the companies violated the collective bargaining agreement. When Wright contacted the union, the union advised him to file a civil suit under ADA, and Wright did so.

As their defense, the companies asserted that Wright had not exhausted his remedies under the collective-bargaining agreement. The Fourth Circuit Court of Appeals concluded that the language of the general arbitration clause in the collective-bargaining agreement was sufficiently broad to encompass a statutory claim arising under ADA.[67] However, the U.S. Supreme Court disagreed and decided that the contract language did not "contain a clear and unmistakable waiver of the covered employees' rights to a judicial forum for federal claims of employment discrimination."[68] Therefore, Wright was allowed to proceed with his civil suit under ADA.

In a 2001 case, *Circuit City Store* v. *Adams,* the U.S. Supreme Court reconfirmed its position that there was a strong federal policy that supported arbitration and ruled that the Federal Arbitration Act applied to all contracts of employment except those applicable to employees working in transportation. The Court stated that arbitration was a desirable and workable forum for resolving employment disputes, including those under federal discrimination laws. In this case, Adams had signed an employment application form to "settle any and all previously unasserted claims, disputes or controversies arising out of or relating to my application or candidacy for employment . . ." (see Exhibit 11.7). Then, in 2002, the Court clarified the role of the Equal Employment Opportunity Commission (EEOC) in cases where an employee had been required as a condition of employment to sign an agreement to arbitrate all employment discrimination claims. The Court ruled that the EEOC was not bound by an arbitration agreement because the EEOC had not been a party to such agreement. Therefore, the EEOC may go to court on a worker's behalf even though the employee had previously been required to sign an agreement to arbitrate all employment discrimination claims.[69]

Arbitral Dilemma The EEOC's policy is that mandatory arbitration systems imposed as a condition of employment were fundamentally inconsistent with U.S. civil rights laws. However, the EEOC is on record in support of alternative dispute resolution (ADR) which includes arbitration and mediation that resolves employment discrimination in a fair and credible manner if entered into voluntarily or *after* the dispute arises. In other words, the EEOC's position is that claimants have a legal right to decide whether to pursue a judicial forum or voluntarily choose to resolve their claim through arbitration.[70]

Where a union exists and when there is an overlap between the language in a collective bargaining agreement and provisions in a law, the question arises as to what the parties and the neutral arbitrator should do. The conclusions drawn after analyzing court cases are as follows:

1. When the contract language and provisions of the Labor Mangement Relations Act apply (covered in Chapter 3), the statutory and contractual issues should be addressed, the arbitrator must write the award to confirm that the statutory provisions were addressed, and the arbitrator's decision must not be repugnant to provisions of the statute.

2. When the collective-bargaining agreement does not address any statute, arbitrators should decide the case based on the merits of the case and the contract language, not the law.

3. When the collective-bargaining agreement contains principles found in the statute without any specific reference to the statute (e.g., there shall be no discrimination against employees), the principles incorporated in the statute may enter into the arbitrator's award.

4. When the statute is explicitly included in the collective-bargaining agreement (e.g., this agreement must comply with provisions of the ADA) and instructs the arbitrator to apply the statute, the arbitrator should render his or her decision consistent with the statute.[71]

Several studies have shown that the typical rank-and-file employee with only a job and a small amount of money at stake finds it difficult to obtain an attorney to accept a discrimination claim and take it to court. The time and effort for the attorney is not worth it to an expert practitioner who is probably operating on a contingency fee arrangement. The attorney prefers a professional or managerial employee who has the potential for a large payoff. As a result, only one in twenty discrimination claimants actually secure an attorney as counsel.

These studies also reveal rather startling results in the event the employee plaintiffs with job discrimination claims are actually able to reach court. These employees do not fare as well in court as do employees who take their cases to arbitration. In fact, claimants who take their cases to arbitration have won 55 to 63 percent of the time while less than 20 percent of the claimants have prevailed in court. While claimants may obtain larger recoveries from a jury in court than in arbitration, for the mass of employees without large financial claims, arbitration may be the superior option. As one legal expert concluded:

> It gets them back to work sooner, more often, with less cost, and without the psychological pain of court litigation.

In cases where the union represents the employees, unions have not been convinced that they should agree with the employers in making arbitration of discrimination claims the exclusive means of resolving such discrimination claims. Because unions have political characteristics wherein officers must stand for elections and many claimants are not yet aware (or satisfied) that, despite the statistics, they may fare better in arbitration than in court, there has not been a movement toward unions showing an interst in representing the bargaining unit employees with employment discrimination claims in arbitration. Employers who prefer arbitration have a selling task to perform to the skeptical employees as well as the union representatives. The employers must convince employees and union representatives that they are pressing for arbitration, not because they believe they will win more often, but that, win or lose, arbitration is less costly, less time consuming, and less disruptive than court litigation.[72]

Criticisms of Mandatory Employment Arbitration Mandatory employment arbitration procedures have given rise to major criticisms. Exhibit 11.8 highlights some reasons that courts have concluded that these procedures are not fair.

The Court's Observation of Arbitral Deficiencies Even the U.S. Supreme Court has observed possible deficiencies in the arbitration process:

- The lack of legal expertise of arbitrators to analyze complex statutes
- Due process limitations with respect to discovery, examination of witnesses, remedies, compiling an office record of the hearing, and so on
- Ineffective communication of the reasoning behind the arbitrator's decision

One critic of mandatory employment arbitration has said:

> The Supreme Court encourages the use of arbitration in employment disputes, through use of adhesive contracts (contracts of adhesion are standard form contracts, where in one party crafts the terms of the contract and the other parties lack the power to change the terms of the contract). These are hiring contracts to refer all employment disputes to arbitration, including statutory issues. These are contracts where one party has all the power to shape the terms of the agreement and the other parties little to none. The weaker party in the employer promulgated arbitration agreement is clearly the employee. These agreements have been instruments of grave injustice.

Exhibit 11.8
- -

Deficiencies Found in Mandatory Employment Arbitration

1. The company has control over the choice of arbitrators.
2. The company is allowed to change the arbitration rules and procedures at its discretion.
3. The employee is not provided basic due process rights, such as representation, discovery of information, knowledge of charges, facing the accusers, and so on.
4. The arbitrator does not have the same remedial authority as the court.
5. The arbitrator's decision is not written with a full explanation for his or her reasoning of the decision.
6. The employee is required to sign the arbitration agreement as a condition of employment. In other words, an applicant will not be hired or a current employee's employment will not be continued.
7. The employer pays the entire arbitrator's fee, and the arbitrator knows the source of the payment in advance of the hearing.

SOURCE: Alexandra Varney McDonald, "Escape from Arbitration," *ABA Journal* (August 1999), pp. 32–33.

... The Rehnquist court, in finding for these adhesive employment contracts, compelling enforcement of arbitration of statutory disputes before the dispute, sets the nation down the road of tyranny by the powerful.[73]

As a result of criticism, court decisions, and the Due Process Protocol for arbitration and mediation of statutory claims designed by the Task Force on Alternative Dispute Resolution (representatives of the most influential employment law and arbitration organizations),[74] several principles that provide a guide to procedural fairness have emerged (see Exhibit 11.9).

Payment to Arbitrators   One circuit court judge has already addressed one of the controversial issues under mandatory employment arbitration procedures, that being the payment of the arbitrator's fee. Chief Judge Harry T. Edwards, a distinguished scholar and a former labor arbitrator, addressed this issue in one of his decisions. He wrote that the judicial system is supported by government through taxes paid by citizens. Litigants do not pay judges who hear their cases, but private arbitrators do not work for free. Judge Edwards required the em-

Exhibit 11.9

Guidelines to Procedural Fairness in Arbitrating Statutory Discrimination Claims

Parties knowingly and voluntarily agree to submit their claim to arbitration.

Arbitration agreement which contains specific language with sufficient notice that signing the agreement represents an agreement to arbitrate all statutory employment discrimination claims (with inclusion of a representative list of employment discrimination statutes for illustrative purposes.

Pre-hearing consultation to address formulation of issues, production of evidence, witnesses lists, discovery, and application of rules of evidence.

Due process procedures which provide that the employee has a right of representation of his/her choosing, adequate discovery of access to all information relevant to the employee claim, arbitrator authority to subpoena relevant information upon a specific request by one of the parties, and a reasonably timely hearing.

Impartial and competent arbitrator who possesses personal qualities of honesty and integrity, discloses any prior association which might represent a potential conflict.

Joint selection of the arbitrator with each party having adequate information about the potential arbitrators' organizational associations, biographical data, published case decisions, copies of recent decisions, etc. to avoid the advantage to the "repeat player" in the arbitration process.

Written opinions and awards which would include the issues decided, the findings of facts, conclusion of law, materials supplied by the parties and information, such as relevant decisions of courts and administrative agencies, presented by the parties, arbitrator reasoning in reaching the decisions, the remedy sought and the remedy decided.

Publication of the decisions with the consent of the prevailing party to serve as a deterrent to future similar discriminatory acts.

Payment of the costs of arbitration shared by the parties to insure impartiality and based on the employee's ability to pay and the relevant necessity of incurred expenses for adequate presentation of the employee's case.

SOURCE: Roger Wolters and William H. Holley, Jr., "Arbitration of Statutory Employment Discrimination Claims in a Nonunion Environment: A Guide to Procedural Fairness," *Employee Responsibilities and Rights Journal* 12, no. 3 (2000), pp. 174–175.

ployer to pay the arbitrator's fee based on the fact that the employee had been forced by a condition of employment to give up his or her right to pursue his or her statutory claims in court. Therefore, Judge Edwards reasoned, a beneficiary of a federal statute (the claimant) would not have been required to pay a judge in a judicial forum and therefore should not be required to pay an arbitrator to decide the merits of his or her claim.[75]

Repeat Players In the absence of a union, the employment arbitration process is usually skewed against employees, particularly those who are not represented. When an employer is a repeat participant in the arbitration process, the employer has a distinct advantage over employees who are not likely to be involved in arbitration more than once or twice in their lifetimes. First, if the employer selects the arbitrator and pays the arbitrator for his or her services, the arbitrator may feel the pressure to rule in favor of the employer to be selected in future cases. For all practical purposes, the employer and the arbitrator are the "repeat players." Second, in the selection of the arbitrator even when both parties participate in the selection, unrepresented employees have little information on which to base their selection. Even when an employee has legal counsel, the attorney may or may not have access to the useful information about the arbitrators. In comparison, nearly all international unions and

EXHIBIT 11.10

Arguments for and against Mandatory Employment Arbitration (MEA)

Supporters of MEA argue:
1. MEA provides prompt resolution of the employment dispute without the costs of litigation.
2. MEA reduces legal expenses to the individuals who lack the resources to litigate a claim against an employer.
3. MEA provides for more expert and experienced decision makers (arbitrators) to decide disputes, instead of unpredictable juries.
4. MEA reduces public exposure of a jury award, which may include emotional distress and punitive damages.
5. MEA permits disputes and their resolutions to remain private.

Critics of MEA argue:
1. MEA requires employees to sign a predispute arbitration agreement as a condition of employment and therefore relinquishes the employees' statutory right to a jury trial in a judicial forum.
2. MEA does not guarantee either competence or impartiality of the arbitrator. The individual employee typically has less information about the arbitrator even when the employee is allowed to be involved in the selection.
3. MEA allows arbitrators who commonly award a make-whole remedy such as reinstatement with back pay (no punitive damages) to reduce the remedy when there has been a wrongdoing, and there is no deterrent effect on the employer.
4. MEA may have an intended or unintended effect of discouraging employees from exercising their rights to join a union, wherein they will be provided representation.
5. MEA does not develop a consistent pattern of interpretation of the law, which may provide guidance for the employer or the employees.

SOURCE: Mei L. Bickner, Christine Ver Ploeg, and Charles Feigenbaum, "Developments in Employment Arbitration," *Dispute Resolutions Journal* 52 (January 1997), pp. 10–12.

the American Federation of Labor–Congress of Industrial Organizations (AFL-CIO) have research staffs who can obtain evaluative information about arbitrators that would be useful in selection. Third, "repeat player" employers have certain strategic advantages because they have an institutional memory. Employers can keep records about the disposition of prior cases of the arbitrator; the unrepresented employee has no comparable resource. Because the union has a continuous relationship with the employer through the collective bargaining agreement, the union gains an institutional memory and becomes a "repeat player" in the arbitration process.[76]

Public Policy Implications for the Future Because there is much controversy about mandatory employment arbitration procedures and public policy issues will be dealt with in the coming years, arguments for and against mandatory employment arbitration procedures are summarized in Exhibit 11.10.

SUMMARY

The arbitration process was little used during the period from 1865 to World War II; however, during World War II, the National War Labor Board encouraged its widespread use. Although the increased reliance on arbitration continued after World War II, a major problem of enforcing the arbitrator's decision remained. Either party could refuse to abide by the arbitrator's decision, with uncertain consequences from the courts. This problem was initially approached in the *Lincoln Mills* decision, which provided a judicial avenue for enforcement, and the Steelworkers' Trilogy, three cases that established the superiority of the arbitration process over the courts in resolving industrial grievances. Subsequent Supreme Court decisions have indicated that termination of the labor agreement does not eliminate the possibility of arbitration, and injunctive relief might be granted when one party refuses to arbitrate according to grievance procedures established in the labor agreement.

Before the arbitration hearing, arbitrators must be selected on either an ad hoc or permanent basis. Each of these selection techniques has unique advantages depending on the particular circumstances. The same can be said of prehearing and posthearing briefs. Other elements of an arbitration hearing include the grievance issue, presentation of witnesses for testimony and cross-examination, and presentation of separate and joint exhibits.

The hearing scene is a dramatic one; union and management officials display their skills in attempting to convince the arbitrator that their positions are correct. The arbitration hearing shares many similarities with a judicial trial but differs in several ways. Perhaps the most significant difference is the arbitrator's reliance on the common law of the shop.

In determining the common law of the shop, the arbitrators give particular weight to the provisions of the labor agreement, the intent of the parties, past practice, and, to a much lesser extent, prior arbitration awards in arriving at their decisions. Because arbitration procedures differ in some respects from those used in a courtroom, various jurisdictional disputes can occur regarding interpretations of contract provisions by arbitrators and the legal interpretation of federal policy. For example, a discharge case decided by the arbitrator could be subsequently considered by the Equal Employment Opportunity Commission or the National Labor Relations Board.

Some criticisms directed toward arbitration pertain to the arbitrator's capability and ethics and potential procedural problems in the arbitration process. Certain arbitral problems, such as expense, time lag, and excessive formality, may be due to labor and management preferences rather than any characteristics inherent in the arbitration process. Management and union officials could reduce some of these problems by using expedited arbitration, new arbitrators, and grievance mediation.

Employment arbitration, which is used primarily with employees not represented by unions, was discussed. With favorable rulings from the U.S. Supreme Court, a growing number of employers have implemented mandatory employment arbitration for new hires as well as current employees. This type of arbitration requires an employee as a condition of employment to sign an agreement that requires all future employment disputes be resolved in arbitration. The deficiencies of mandatory employment arbitration were identified and attempts to rectify these deficiencies, such as guides to procedural fairness, were presented. Anticipated problems for the future of mandatory employment arbitration were also addressed.

KEY TERMS

- National War Labor Board
- Steelworkers' Trilogy
- permanent arbitrator
- ad hoc arbitrator
- arbitration hearing
- common law of the shop
- self-government
- parole evidence rule
- intent of the parties
- past practice
  employment arbitration

DISCUSSION QUESTIONS

1. How did World War II and the National War Labor Board greatly expand the use of arbitration?

2. "The Steelworkers' Trilogy greatly enhanced the arbitrator's authority when compared with previous years, yet it did not give the arbitrator final jurisdiction over certain issues." Thoroughly discuss the preceding statement in terms of the specific features of these judicial decisions; also consider current jurisdictional issues arbitrators face in terms of government agencies.

3. Discuss the similarities and differences between arbitration and judicial hearings with particular emphasis on the common law of the shop, admission of evidence, and the role of the arbitrator versus that of the judge.

4. Why are arbitrators' decisions usually lengthy when one sentence could indicate who was right and wrong? Your discussion of this question should include the purposes of arbitration and advantages, as well as disadvantages of an extensive arbitral decision.

5. Discuss two decision-making criteria used by arbitrators, furnishing specific examples (not mentioned in the text) of how these criteria can come into play.

6. Cite and defend three specific methods you would use to make the typical arbitration procedure more effective. Also indicate the advantages and disadvantages of your suggestions.

7. Discuss the following: "The refusal to use grievance mediation as a step prior to arbitration illustrates the stubbornness of many union and management officials."

 ## EXPLORING THE WEB

Labor and Employment Arbitration

1. Federal Mediation and Conciliation Service   The Federal Mediation and Conciliation Service (FMCS) was created by Congress in 1947 as an independent agency to "promote sound and stable labor-management relations," according to the description of the agency on the FMCS Web site. What services does the Service provide?

Use the site to define the following terms: *mediation, dispute mediation, preventive mediation,* and *alternative dispute resolution.*

http://www.fmcs.gov

2. Steelworkers' Trilogy   Using Findlaw, locate the three Supreme Court cases that are commonly referred to as the Steelworkers' Trilogy. Why are the cases important to labor arbitration?

United Steelworkers v. *American Manufacturing* (363 US 564)
United Steelworkers v. *Warrior and Gulf Navigation* (363 US 574)
United Steelworkers v. *Enterprise Wheel and Car* (363 US 593)

http://www.findlaw.com

3. National Academy of Arbitrators (NAA)   The NAA is a honorary and professional organization of 624 arbitrators in the United States and Canada. This Web site contains officers, members, membership qualifications, information on meetings, links to other ADR sites, and useful information for arbitrators.

http://www.naarb.org

4. Arbitration and Title VII of the Civil Rights Act   The U.S. Court of Appeals for the Ninth Circuit recently ruled, in 1998, that employees cannot be required, as a condition of employment, to arbitrate claims brought under Title VII of the Civil Rights Act. See a discussion of the case in *Loyola of Los Angeles Law Review.* "Arbitrary Civil Rights?: The Case of Duffield v. Robertson Stephens" was written by Robert S. McArthur.

http://llr.lls.edu/volumes/v32-issue3/mcarthur.pdf

5. American Arbitration Association   This Internet site provides good information on labor arbitration procedures and techniques as well as law and regulations. Find the statute on dispute resolution in the code for your state. Go to:

http://www.adr.org

Click on "ADR Law" and "State Statutes." Choose your state to see the Arbitration Code. You may also use Findlaw at http://www.findlaw.com to search for the statutes for your state. For example, the Florida Arbitration Code is under Section 682. In Findlaw, select U.S. State Resources, Florida, Primary Materials, Code, and search by the code number.

Just for fun, use the site search engine to look for information on the Association's role in settling sports disputes. What are the three major classes of disputes involving the Olympics that are resolved through arbitration?

References

1. Cynthia F. Cohen and Theresa Domagalski, "The Effects of Mandatory Arbitration of Employment Discrimination Claims: Perceptions of Justice and Suggestions for Change," *Employee Responsibilities and Rights Journal* 11, no. 1 (1998), pp. 27–40.

2. For a detailed historical perspective of labor arbitration, see Dennis R. Nolan and Roger I. Abrams, "American Labor Arbitration: The Early Years," *University of Florida Law Review* (Summer 1983), pp. 373–421.

3. *United Steelworkers of America v. American Manufacturing Company;* 363 U.S. 566–567 (1960).

4. *United Steelworkers of America v. Warrior and Gulf Navigation Company,* 363 U.S. 582 (1960).

5. *United Steelworkers of America v. Enterprise Wheel and Car Corporation,* 363 U.S. 598 (1960).

6. "*AT&T Technologies Inc. v. Communications Workers of America,*" *The United States Law Week,* April 8, 1986, p. 4341.

7. The case is *John Wiley and Sons v. Livingston* (1964), discussed in Ralph S. Berger, "The Collective Bargaining Agreement in Bankruptcy: Does the Duty to Arbitrate Survive?" *Labor Law Journal* 35 (November 1984), pp. 385–393.

8. *Nolde Brothers Inc. v. Local No. 358, Bakery and Confectionary Workers Union AFL-CIO,* 430 U.S. 254 (1977). See also Irving M. Geslewitz, "Case Law Development Since Nolde Brothers: When Must Post-Contract Disputes Be Arbitrated?" *Labor Law Journal* 35 (April 1984), pp. 225–238.

9. Paul F. Hodapp, "The U.S. Supreme Court Rules on Duty to Arbitrate Post-Contract Grievances," *Labor Law Journal* 42 (December 1991), pp. 827–829.

10. *The Boys Market Inc. v. Retail Clerk's Union, Local 770,* 398 U.S. 249, 250, 252–253 (1970). It should be noted that injunctive relief applies only when one party refuses to arbitrate issues that are subject to grievance procedures specified in the labor agreement. For additional details, see *Buffalo Forge Company v. United Steelworkers of America,* 428 U.S. 397 (1970).

11. Nels E. Nelson and Walter J. Gershenfeld, "The Appointment of Grievance Arbitrators by State and Local Agencies," *Labor Law Journal* 52 (Winter 2001), pp. 258–267.

12. Jeanette A. Davy and George W. Bohlander, "Recent Findings and Practices in Grievance Arbitration Procedures," *Labor Law Journal* 43 (March 1992), p. 187.

13. Bureau of National Affairs Inc., *Basic Patterns in Union Contracts* (Washington, D.C.: Bureau of National Affairs, 1995), p. 38.

14. Delbert C. Miller and William Form, *Industrial Sociology*, 2d ed. (New York: Harper & Row, 1964), p. 264.

15. Daniel F. Jennings and A. Dale Allen, Jr., "Labor Arbitration Costs and Case Loads: A Longitudinal Analysis," *Labor Law Journal* (February 1990), pp. 80–88.

16. David E. Bloom and Christopher L. Cavanagh, "An Analysis of the Selection of Arbitrators," *American Economic Review* (June 1986), pp. 408–422; and Arthur Eliot Berkeley and Susan Rawson Zacur, "So You Want to Be an Arbitrator: Update of a Guide to the Perplexed," *Labor Law Journal* 41 (March 1990), pp. 170–174. For a thorough analysis of arbitrator's backgrounds, experiences, and preferences, see Mario F. Bognanno and Charles J. Coleman, *Labor Arbitration in America* (New York: Praeger, 1992).

17. Clarence R. Deitsch and David A. Dilts, "An Analysis of Arbitrator Characteristics and Their Effects on Decision Making in Discharge Cases," *Labor Law Journal* 40 (February 1989), pp. 112–116; Brian Bemmels, "Gender Effects in Grievance Arbitration," *Industrial Relations* 29 (Fall 1990), pp. 513–525; Stephen M. Crow and James W. Logan, "Arbitrators' Characteristics and Decision-Making Records, Gender of Arbitrators and Grievants, and the Presence of Legal Counsel as Predictors of Arbitral Outcomes," *Employee Responsibilities and Rights Journal* 7 (1994), pp. 169–185; and Kenneth W. Thornicroft, "Gender Effects in Grievance Arbitration . . . Revisited," *Labor Studies Journal* 19 (Winter 1995), pp. 35–44.

18. Michael Marmo, "Acceptability As a Factor in Grievance Arbitration," *Labor Law Journal* 50 (Summer 1999), pp. 97–102.

19. Clarence R. Deitsch and David A. Dilts, "Factors Affecting Pre-Arbitral Settlement of Rights Disputes: Predicting the Method of Rights Dispute Resolution," *Journal of Labor Research* 12 (Winter 1986), p. 76.

20. Richard A. Posthuma and Maris Stella Swift, "Legalistic vs. Facilitative Approaches to Arbitration: Strengths and Weaknesses," *Labor Law Journal* 52 (Fall 2001), pp. 173–184.

21. For a fine conceptionalization of arbitrability's dimensions and implications, see Mark M. Grossman, *The Question of Arbitrability* (Ithaca, N.Y.: ILR Press, 1984).

22. http://www.fmcs.gov.

23. For guidelines pertaining to an effective management or union post-hearing brief, see Douglas E. Ray, "On Writing the Post-Hearing Arbitration Brief," *Arbitration Journal* (December 1992), pp. 58–60.

24. Ronald W. Haughton, "Running the Hearing," in *Arbitration in Practice*, ed. Arnold M. Zack (Ithaca, N.Y.: ILR Press, 1984), p. 37.

25. Jennings and Allen, "Labor Arbitration Costs."

26. See, for example, James B. Dworkin and Michael M. Harris, "Polygraph Tests: What Labor Arbitrators Need to Know," *Arbitration Journal* 41 (March 1986), pp. 23–33; Kimberly Janisch-Ramsey, "Polygraphs: The Search for Truth in Arbitration Proceedings," *Arbitration Journal* 41 (March 1986), pp. 34–41; Herman A. Theeke and Tina M. Theeke, "The Truth About Arbitrators' Treatment of Polygraph Tests," *Arbitration Journal* 42 (December 1987), pp. 23–32; and Marvin F. Hill, Jr. and Anthony Sinicropi, *Evidence in Arbitration*, 2d ed. (Washington, D.C.: Bureau of National Affairs, 1987).

27. Frank Elkouri and Edna Asper Elkouri, *How Arbitration Works*, 4th ed. (Washington, D.C.: Bureau of National Affairs., 1985), p. 302.

28. See, for example, Cynthia L. Gramm and Patricia A. Greenfield, "Arbitral Standards in Medical Screening Grievances," *Employee Responsibilities and Rights Journal* 3, no. 3 (1990), pp. 169–184.

29. Steven Starck, "Arbitration Decision Writing: Why Arbitrators Err," *Arbitration Journal* 38 (June 1983), pp. 30–33. See also David Elliot, "When the Hearing Is Over: Writing Arbitral Awards in Plain Language," *Arbitration Journal* 46 (December 1991), p. 53.

30. http://www.fmcs.gov.

31. Michael H. LeRoy and Peter Feuille, "Private Justice and Public Policy: Whose Voice Prevails in Arbitration?"

Proceedings of the 54th Annual Meeting of the Industrial Relations Research Association (Champaign, Ill.: IRRA, 2002), pp. 219–221.

32. Daniel F. Jennings and A. Dale Allen, Jr., "How Arbitrators View the Process of Labor Arbitration: A Longitudinal Analysis," *Labor Law Journal* (Winter 1993), p. 44.

33. Stephen M. Crow and James Logan, "A Tentative Decision-Making Model of the Strong and Weak Forces at Labor Arbitration," *Journal of Collective Negotiations in the Public Sector* 24, no. 2 (1995), pp. 111–120.

34. The first two examples are from Allan J. Harrison, *Preparing and Presenting Your Arbitration Case: A Manual for Union and Management Representatives* (Washington, D.C.: Bureau of National Affairs, 1979), pp. 23–24. The third example is suggested by Thomas R. Knight, "Arbitration and Contract Interpretation: *Common Law v. Strict Construction*," *Labor Law Journal* 34 (November 1983), pp. 714–726.

35. For arbitration examples of these dimensions of past practice, see Arthur Dobbelaere, Williams H. Leahy, and Jack Reardon, "The Effect of Past Practice on the Arbitration of Labor Disputes," *Arbitration Journal* 40 (December 1985), pp. 27–43.

36. This provision on past practice was taken from Walter E. Baer, *Practice and Precedent in Labor Relations* (Lexington, Mass.: Lexington Books, 1972), p. 8.

37. Ibid., p. 38.

38. Donald J. Petersen, "No Smoking! The Arbitration of Smoking Restricting Policies," *Dispute Resolution Journal* (January 1995), pp. 45–50.

39. William H. McPherson, "Should Labor Arbitrators Play Follow the Leader?" *Arbitration Journal* 4 (1949), p. 170.

40. David Dilts, Mark Crouch, and Mashaalah Rahnama-Moghadam, "Effectiveness in Grievance Arbitration: Are There Differences in Unions?" *Journal of Collective Negotiations in the Public Sector* 26, no. 4 (1997), pp. 333–338.

41. *Harrell Alexander, Sr v. Gardner-Denver Company,* 415 U.S. 60 (1974).

42. Michelle Hoyman and Lamont E. Stallworth, "The Arbitration of Discrimination Grievances in the Aftermath of Gardner-Denver," *Arbitration Journal* 39 (September 1984), p. 55; Karen Elwell and Peter Feuille, "Arbitration Awards and Gardner-Denver Lawsuits: One Bite or Two?" *Industrial Relations* 23 (Spring 1984), p. 295; Aubrey R. Fowler, Jr., "Arbitration, the Trilogy, and Industrial Rights: Developments Since *Alexander v. Gardner-Denver,*" *Labor Law Journal* 36 (March 1985), pp. 173–182. See also Elaine Gale Wrong, "Arbitrators' Awards in Cases Involving Discrimination," *Labor Law Journal* 39 (July 1988), pp. 411–417.

43. Stephen L. Hayford, "The Coming Third Era of Labor Arbitration," *Arbitration Journal* 48 (September 1993), p. 17. See also Martha S. Weisel, "The Tension Between Statutory Rights and Binding Arbitration," *Labor Law Journal* 42 (July 1991), pp. 766–772.

44. *Spielberg Manufacturing Company,* 112 NLRB 1080 (1955). See: John C. Truesdale, "NLRB Deferral to Arbitration: Still Alive and Kicking," http://www.NLRB.gov/press/

45. *Collyer Insulated Wire and Local Union 1098, International Brotherhood of Electrical Workers,* 192 NLRB 150 (August 20, 1977).

46. Curtis L. Mack and Ira P. Bernstein, "NLRB Deferral to the Arbitration Process: The Arbitrator's Demanding Role," *Arbitration Journal* 40 (September 1985), pp. 33–43. For a related research effort, see Benjamin W. Wolkinson, "The Impact of the Collyer Policy on Deferral: An Empirical Study," *Industrial and Labor Relations Review* 38 (April 1985), pp. 377–391.

47. Pat Greenfield, "The NLRB's Deferral to Arbitration before and after Olin: An Empirical Analysis," *Industrial and Labor Relations Review* 42, no. 1 (1988), pp. 34–49. See also "Remarks of NLRB Chairman Gould on Deferral to Arbitration," Bureau of National Affairs Inc., *Daily Labor Report,* no. 114 (June 16, 1994), pp. E-1–E-3.

48. James L. Ferree, "National Labor Relations Board Deferral to Arbitration," *Dispute Resolution Journal* 52 (Summer 1997), pp. 31–35.

49. Patricia A. Greenfield, "How Do Arbitrators Treat External Law?" *Industrial and Labor Relations Review* 45 (July 1992), p. 695.

50. "Decision of Supreme Court in *Paperworkers v. Misco, Inc.*," Bureau of National Affairs, *Daily Labor Report*, no. 230 (December 1, 1987), pp. D-1-D-5. See also Bernard F. Ashe, "Arbitration Finality and the Public-Policy Exception," *Dispute Resolution Journal* (September 1994), pp. 22–28, 87–89.

51. "Practitioners Assess Impact of Court Decisions Bolstering Finality of Labor Arbitration Awards," Bureau of National Affairs, *Daily Labor Report*, no. 238 (December 14, 1987), p. A-1. For additional consideration of public policy intertwined with arbitration decisions in drug testing, see Lorynn A. Cone, "Public Policies against Drug Use: *Paperworkers v. Misco Inc.*," *Labor Law Journal* 40 (April 1989), pp. 243–247. See also Bernard D. Meltzer, "After the Labor Arbitration Award: The Public Policy Defense," *Industrial Relations Law Journal* 10, no. 2 (1988), pp. 241–251; Robert F. Wayland, Elvis C. Stephens, and Geralyn McClure, "*Misco*: Its Impact on Arbitration Awards," *Labor Law Journal* (December 1988), pp. 813–819; and Arthur Hamilton and Peter A. Veglahn, "Public Policy Exceptions to Arbitration Awards," *Labor Law Journal* 42 (June 1991), pp. 366–370.

52. "Court Vacates Reinstatement of Employee Charged with Sexual Abuse of Customer," Bureau of National Affairs, *Daily Labor Report*, no. 61 (March 29, 1991), pp. A-4–A-5. See also "Reinstatement of Sexual Harasser Overturned as Public Policy Violation," Bureau of National Affairs, Inc., *Daily Labor Report*, no. 204 (October 22, 1990), pp. A-8–A-9.

53. "Accused Sex Harasser Gains Reinstatement," Bureau of National Affairs, *Daily Labor Report*, no. 70 (April 10, 1992), pp. A-1, A-2. See also Thomas J. Piskorski, "Reinstatement of the Sexual Harasser: The Conflict between Federal Labor Law and Title VII," *Employee Relations Law Journal* 18 (Spring 1993), pp. 617–623; and Christie L. Roszkowski and Robert F. Wayland, "Arbitration Review: Is the Public Policy against Sexual Harassment Sufficient Cause for Vacating an Arbitration Award?" *Labor Law Journal* 44 (November 1993), pp. 707–717.

54. Margaret A. Jacobs, "Men's Club: Riding Crop and Slurs: How Wall Street Dealt with a Sex Bias Case," *The Wall Street Journal*, June 9, 1994, pp. A-4, A-6; Barbara Presley Noble, "Attacking Compulsory Arbitration," *New York Times*, January 15, 1995, p. F-21; and "Reinstatement of Alleged Sexual Harassers Does Not Violate Public Policy, Forum Told," Bureau of National Affairs, *Daily Labor Report*, no. 6 (January 10, 1994), pp. A-10, A-11.

55. Richard Mittenthal, "Self-Interest: Arbitration's 'Unmentionable' Consideration," *Dispute Resolution Journal* (March 1994), pp. 70–72.

56. Harry J. Dworkin, "How Arbitrators Decide Cases," *Labor Law Journal* 25 (April 1974) p. 203.

57. "Arbitrator Traces Growing Legalism as Proceedings Are Modeled on Courts," Bureau of National Affairs, *Daily Labor Report*, no. 106 (June 3, 1991), p. A-6 and James Oldham, "Arbitration and Relentless Legalization in the Workplace," in *Arbitration 1990: New Perspectives on Old Issues*, ed. Gladys W. Gruenberg, Proceedings at the Forty-Third Annual Meeting, National Academy of Arbitrators (Washington, D.C.: Bureau of National Affairs, 1991), pp. 23–40.

58. Myers, "Arbitration Update."

59. Nels E. Nelson and A.N.M. Meshquat Uddin, "The Impact of Delay on Arbitrators' Decisions in Discharge Cases," *Labor Studies Journal* 23 (Summer 1998), pp. 3–19.

60. Allen Ponak, Wifred Zerbe, Sarah Rose, and Corliss Olson, "Using Even History Analysis to Model Delaying Grievance Arbitration," *Industrial and Labor Relations Review* 50 (October 1996), pp. 105–110.

61. Linda S. Byars, Limiting an Arbitrator's Remedial Power," *Labor Law Journal* 48 (January 1997), pp. 29–33.

62. http://www.fmcs.gov.

63. Nancy Kauffman, "The Idea of Expedited Arbitration Two Decades Later," *Arbitration Journal* (September 1991), p. 35.

64. Dennis R. Nolan and Roger I. Abrams, "The Future of Labor Arbitration," *Labor Law Journal* 37 (July 1986), pp. 441–442.

65. Thomas J. Piskorski and David B. Ross, "Private Arbitration as the Exclusive Means of Resolving Employment-Related Disputes," *Employee Relations Law Journal* 19 (Autumn 1993), p. 206; and Loren K. Allison and Eric H. J. Stahlhut, "Arbitration and the ADA: A Budding Partnership," *Arbitration Journal* (September 1993), pp. 53–60.

66. Helen LeVan, "Decisional Model for Predicting Outcomes of Arbitrated Sexual Harassment Disputes," *Labor Law Journal* (April 1993), p. 231. See also Robert A. Shearer, "The Impact of Employment Arbitration Agreements in Sex Discrimination Claims: The Trend Toward Nonjudicial Resolution," *Employee Relations Law Journal* 18 (Winter 1992–1993), pp. 479–488; Stuart L. Bass, "Recent Court Decisions Expand Role of Arbitration in Harassment and Other Title VII Cases," *Labor Law Journal* (December 1992), pp. 772–779; Stuart H. Bompey and Michael P. Pappas, "Is There a Better Way? Compulsory Arbitration of Employment Discrimination Claims after Gilmer," *Employee Relations Law Journal* 19 (Winter 1993–1994), pp. 197–216; and Evan J. Spelfogel, "New Trends in the Arbitration of Employment Disputes," *Arbitration Journal* 48 (March 1993), pp. 6–15.

67. George M. Sullivan, "*Alexander* v. *Gardner-Denver*: Staggered but Still Standing," *Labor Law Journal* 50 (March 1999), pp. 43–45. For a comprehensive analysis, see Donald J. Petersen and Harvey R. Boller, "Arbitral Responses to the Changing External Law of Discrimination," *Labor Law Journal* 49 (December 1998), pp. 1241–1253 and Harvey R. Boller and Donald J. Petersen, "Mandatory Arbitration Clauses," *Dispute Resolution Journal* 54 (February 1999), pp. 56–58.

68. *Wright* v. *Universal Maritime Service Corp.*, 119 S. Ct. 391 (1998).

69. Patricia Thomas Bittel, "Arbitration: Is This Where We Were Headed?" *Labor Law Journal* 53 (Fall 2002), pp. 130–131. Also see: *Circuit City Stores, Inc.* v. *Adams*, 532 U.S. 143 (2001);

EEOC v. *Waffle House, Inc.*, 534 U.S. 279 (2002).

70. Ellen J. Vargyas, "Verdict on Mandatory Binding Arbitration in Employment," *Dispute Resolution Journal* 52 (Fall 1997), pp. 10–14.

71. Charles J. Coleman and Jose A. Vazquez, "Mandatory Arbitration of Statutory Issues under Collective Bargaining: *Austin* and Its Progeny," *Labor Law Journal* 48 (December 1998), pp. 703–723. Also see Charles J. Coleman, "Invited Paper: Mandatory Arbitration of Statutory Issues: *Austin, Wright,* and the Future, in *Arbitration 1998: The Changing World of Dispute Resolution; Proceedings of the 51st Annual Meeting of the National Academy of Arbitrators*, eds. Steven Briggs and Jay E. Grenig (Washington, D.C.: Bureau of National Affairs, Inc., 1999), pp. 134–159.

72. Theodore J. St. Antoine, "Mandatory Arbitration: Something Old, Something New," *Perspectives on Work* 7, no. 2 (Winter 2004), pp. 21–22.

73. John L. Zalusky, "Circuit City Is to Workplace Justice as Voting in Florida Is to Democracy," ed. Paul B. Voos, *Proceedings of the 54th Annual Meeting of the Industrial Relations Research Association* (Champaign, Ill.: IRRA, 2002), pp. 260–261.

74. Lisa B. Bingham, "Emerging Due Process Concerns in Employment Arbitration: A Look at Actual Cases," *Labor Law Journal* 46 (February 1996), pp. 108–120; Marjorie L. Icenogle and Robert A. Shearer, "Emerging Due Process Standards in Arbitration of Employment Discrimination Disputes: New Challenges for Employers," *Labor Law Journal* 48 (February 1998), p. 84.

75. Morton H. Orenstein, "Mandatory Arbitration: Alive and Well or Withering on the Vine?" *Dispute Resolution Journal* 54 (August 1999), p. 86.

76. Lisa B. Bingham, "Employment Arbitration: Differences between Repeat Player and Nonrepeat Payer Outcomes," *Proceedings of the 49th Annual Meeting of the Industrial Relations Research Association* (Madison, Wis.: IRRA, 1997), pp. 201–207.

May Supervisors Perform Bargaining Unit Work?

Issue

Is the Company violating Section 18-A of the labor agreement when nonbargaining unit employees perform unit work? If so, what should be the appropriate remedy?

Background

The Company manufactures heating and cooling products. During the manufacturing process, a number of sheet metal parts have certain operations performed on them by use of punch presses, spot welding, machines, and so on. For final assembly of the products, conveyor lines are set up to assemble the product on a repetitive, progressive basis (like an automobile assembly line). Each assembly line employee performs a specific task. Time study engineers have determined the duties and time required for each position on the line, and the duties of each worker have been balanced to equalize the workload.

The supervisor on the assembly line is responsible for meeting certain production schedules. Also, he or she has to instruct and train new assemblers in their respective job duties. Although use of assembly line concepts results in an efficient method of production, there have been problems with their use. These include:

- In 1994, the turnover rate among assembly line employees ranged from 1.2 percent to 27 percent per month, and the absent rate ranged from 7.1 percent to 11 percent.

- In 1995, the figures were 7.3 percent to 18.7 percent of turnover and 5.8 percent to 14 percent for absences.

- In 1996, turnover became more severe, ranging from 9.4 percent to 28 percent, and absences ranged from 9 percent to 14.4 percent.

The Grievance in question was filed by the department's shop steward because a supervisor was observed working on the assembly line, thereby taking work away from bargaining unit employees. It was reported that the supervisor said that she would continue to work on the line until she got all the help that she needed. The adjustment requested by the Union was for the Company to pay the most senior employee for 4 hours at time and one half his regular rate of pay.

The Company denied the Grievance by informing the Union that employees on the line were new and were not familiar with the operations. The supervisor was helping them to keep the assembly line moving.

At the third step of the grievance procedure, the personnel manager denied the Grievance for the following reason:

A total of 43 assemblers were placed on the payroll during the month before the grievance, and 26 employees were absent on the day of the grievance. It was a matter of necessity that the supervisor help the new people and replacement people to keep the production schedule.

At the hearing, the parties agreed that in addition to deciding on the immediate Grievance, the arbitrator should set forth some guidelines that would spell out clearly when and under what conditions the supervisor could perform bargaining unit work. Also, the arbitrator was asked to decide the appropriate remedy when and if a supervisor was found to be performing bargaining unit work in violation of the agreement.

In the Company's post-hearing brief, the following questions were asked:

1. When does a supervisor's work qualify as instructional, experimental, or in response to an emergency per Section 18-A?

2. If the supervisor is working contrary to section 18-A, what should be the redress? Who is the injured party? Is the Company obligated to pay someone?

3. What if there has been no adverse effect upon any employee, and thus no grievant?

4. Who should be paid when no one was harmed?

PERTINENT CLAUSE OF THE CONTRACT
Section 18-A

Supervisors shall not be permitted to perform work usually performed by employees within the bargaining unit except where the work is for instructional or experimental purposes or in the case of an emergency.

Section 7-A (1)

The word *grievance* as used in this Agreement means a complaint filed by an employee or by the Union against the Company alleging failure of the Company to comply with some provision of this Agreement.

In addition, Section 7-A(4) refers to the policy on unresolved safety and health grievances that allows a grievance to be filed by a grievance committeeperson, acting on behalf of the union, alleging that the Company has failed to comply with Section 18-A. This grievance can be filed even though there is no injured party, in the sense that no employee was displaced.

The Union's Position

The Union agreed that absenteeism has been a problem, but that it had attempted to work with the Company on this problem. However, the Union cannot ignore the language of the agreement and allow non–bargaining unit members to perform bargaining unit work. It is management's responsibility to resolve the absenteeism problems.

The Union claimed that many of the instances where supervisors performed bargaining unit work were actually efforts by the company to institute a speedup on the assembly line. Further, it contended that there was a long-standing past practice of paying an employee on a time and one-half basis whenever work is performed by a supervisor.

The Union argued that the Company could recall laid-off employees to serve as assemblers or use utility employees on a temporary basis instead of having supervisors perform bargaining unit work.

The arbitrator was asked to instruct the Company to cease its attempts to institute speedups by having supervisors perform bargaining unit work.

The Company's Position

The Company explained that at the beginning of a shift, when assemblers are absent or tardy, the supervisor must ask for assemblers from other positions on the line. He or she may even have to borrow assemblers from other departments to serve as temporary replacements on the assembly line. Such actions require the supervisors to instruct the replacements in their new duties. Also, the supervisor may be required to perform bargaining unit work while waiting for an employee to fill a vacant position on the line. Such actions by a supervisor on these occasions

Continued

are an absolute necessity to keep the line moving and are considered emergency measures by the Company. Also, when new parts do not fit right, the supervisor helps the assemblers, which is considered experimental work.

The company contended that it was not its intent to have supervisors perform bargaining unit work. Supervisors have their own work to perform. The Company admitted that supervisors have worked for short periods of time to instruct new employees and to fill in during emergencies when employees were absent, tardy, or had to be relieved for restroom needs. However, with excessive turnover and absenteeism, supervisors had no other alternatives.

QUESTIONS

1. What is meant by "instructional" work?
2. What is meant by "experimental" work?
3. When does an "emergency" exist?
4. How would you rule if you were the arbitrator? Justify your decision. (You must address the Company's question in your decision.)

Demotion with a Pay Increase?

Background

ABC Company is engaged in the pickup, transportation, and delivery of packages within the United States and many foreign countries. The bargaining unit employees are represented by Truckers Union, Local 300. ABC maintains among its sorting and distribution facilities varying numbers of operating centers, where package delivery drivers report each morning to pick up their vehicles, which are loaded with packages, to commence their established delivery routes, and where they return each evening at the conclusion of the day with packages received from ABC customers for shipment to other destinations. The Company maintains and operates a fleet of tractor-trailer vehicles, commonly referred to as "feeders," which transport packages among the Company's various package handling facilities.

The Company is divided into approximately twenty-seven operational units called "districts" and is headquartered in Philadelphia, Pennsylvania. The principal distribution units within each district are the operating centers, which vary in size depending on the package volume in the areas where they are located. To facilitate the movement of packages throughout the system, the Company has "hubs," which are the large packaging sorting facilities, the largest being the Philadelphia hub, which employs more than a thousand employees.

The Company maintains several classifications for its bargaining unit employees within its hubs and centers. These include full-time package delivery drivers, also known as package drivers, and full-time tractor-trailer "feeder" drivers, such as Mr. James Simpson, the Grievant. The Company employs a large number of part-time package loaders, unloaders, sorters, and car washers. These part-time employees work in 4- to 5-hour shifts inside the hub building. These positions require only unskilled labor and are filled primarily by students. Package drivers are skilled employees who are responsible for driving the package cars and picking up and delivering the packages. Feeder drivers are considered more skilled than package drivers and transport packages over longer distances to the hubs for sorting and delivering locally. Both the package drivers and the feeder drivers typically work shifts of 8 hours or longer.

Although much of the Company's feeder operations are planned from day to day or week to week, there is a significant fluctuation in the volume of packages handled and processed at the Philadelphia hub. Together with other variables, the Company's operations necessitate adjustments in the work performed by the feeder drivers. When the volume drops, such as around the July 4th holiday, the least senior feeder drivers at the hub may be laid off. When this happens, the feeder drivers have the option of bumping into the building and replacing part-time employees for the duration of the time that they are on layoff.

In the present matter. Mr. Simpson, a tractor-trailer driver since April 22, 1998, exercised his option to replace a part-time employee 1 week during July 1998 and another week in December 1998. The Company paid Mr. Simpson at the rate of $12.11 per hour. At this time, the red-circled rate for part-time employees was $16.19 in July 1998 and $16.79 in December 1998. On August 12, 1998, Mr. Simpson filed the following Grievance:

> Nature of Complaint: Violation of Article 50 and any other Article that may apply.
> Violation of Article 50 Section 4 and any other articles that may apply.
> On the week ending 7/10/1998, I was not paid the appropriate rate of pay for work performed during this week. I was told I was laid off on that particular week but was able to work

Continued

in the hub. I worked 5 days in the hub. I should have been compensated at the rate applicable to the rates agreed to by the Company and the Union, for the work performed on those days.

I am also requesting a payroll correction as soon as possible.

Basis for Settlement or Withdrawal: Rates are "Red Circle."

The Grievance was appealed to Arbitration. The issue submitted was:

Did the Company violate the Agreement when it paid Jim Simpson $12.11 per hour during July 1998 and December 1998? If so, what is the remedy?

Relevant Provisions of the Agreement
Article 45—Seniority
Secion 2—Layoff and Recall

When it becomes necessary to reduce the working force, the last employee on the hub seniority list shall be laid off first and when the force is again increased, the employee shall be returned to work in the reverse order in which they were laid off, providing they still maintain seniority as described herein, and further providing the employees retained at the time of layoff or the employees recalled at the time of recall from layoff must be qualified to perform the work required. In a building where there are two or more package hubs, the affected driver may displace the least senior driver in the building.

After following the Philadelphia hub reduction of force procedure, the following shall apply:

After a one (1) day layoff, full-time seniority employees who may be subject to layoff will be assigned to displace one (1) or more part-time employees in the building if any part-time employees are working in that building. This will not apply to the two (2) most junior employees in each hub hired after ratification.

In such cases, the employee will be provided with eight (8) continuous hours of work (unless otherwise mutually agreed to by the Company and the Union) at the appropriate rate for the classification of work performed, except that:

A. If the laid-off employee displaces a part-time employee and continues to perform the same work as his full-time assignment, he will continue to receive his regular wage rate.
B. If in the hub there is an employee receiving a higher wage rate than the rate of the displaced part-time employee(s), the full-time employee will receive such higher rate.

Article 60—Section 8—Wages

Part-time seniority employees on the payroll as of 7/31/90 will receive the contractual increases of fifty cents (50¢) per hour on August 1, 1995, August 1, 1996, and August 1, 1997. Part-time employees presently in progression on July 31, 1995 shall receive on the anniversary of their seniority no less than is listed on the chart below:

Rate Paid to Part-time Employees Hired
Prior to July 2, 1987 ("Red-Circle Rate")

Aug. 1, 1994–July 31, 1995	$14.53
Aug. 1, 1995–July 31, 1996	$15.03
Aug. 1, 1996–July 31, 1997	$15.64
Aug. 1, 1997–July 31, 1998	$16.19
Aug. 1, 1998–July 31, 1999	$16.79
Aug. 1, 1999–July 31, 2000	$17.34

Position of the Union

The Union explained that the Company lays off full-time employees from time to time. These laid-off employees have several options under the Agreement. Laid-off feeder drivers who are full-time may (1) accept the layoff, (2) drop to the superqualified list where they work "on call" at their regular wage rate, (3) bump into the delivery classification if they have prior delivery experience and work at the delivery rate, or (4) bump into a part-time classification doing inside hub work with an 8-hour guarantee. Full-time employees who choose the fourth option must be paid "at the appropriate rate for the classification of work performed, except that. . . . if in the building there is a part-time employee receiving higher wage rate than the rate of the displaced part-time employee, the full-time employee will receive such higher rate."

Mr. Simpson was hired on April 22, 1998, and acquired seniority and became a regular full-time feeder driver on June 18, 1998. During July 1998, he was laid off for 1 week, and in December 1998, he was laid off for 1 week. On each occasion, he chose option 4 and bumped into the Philadelphia hub. While he was in the hub, he was paid at the rate of $12.11 per hour. He believed he was entitled to the highest rate in the hub, which was a "red-circle" rate of $16.19 in July 1998. In December 1998, the highest wage rate in the building for a part-time employee was $16.79. On both occasions, the red-circle rates for a part-time employee were the highest rates in the hub. The highest rate for part-time employees within the Philadelphia hub other than the red-circle rate in July 1998 was $13.44 per hour.

The Union stated that before 1992, part-time employees had a regular rate of pay, and there was only $1.51 difference in rates of pay between part-time employees and feeder drivers. During the 1992 negotiations, the Company proposed and the Union ultimately agreed to a two-tier wage system and a progression system. Under the Agreement, newly hired part-time employees began at an $8 or $9 wage rate and progressed over a 2- to 4-year period to a top rate, which was lower than the existing journeyman rate. Part-time employees at the journeyman rate had their wage rates "red-circled"; they were entitled to continue receiving their then current wage rate, which was not reduced to the new rates agreed to in the 1992 Agreement. These employees would continue to receive annual wage increases. Thus, the employees with red-circle rates received a higher wage than other employees in similar jobs. If employees with red-circle rates transferred to full-time employment, they would lose their red-circle status. Thus, over time, the number of red-circle employees would decline, and some facilities would eventually have no red-circle employees. However, the Philadelphia hub still had employees with red-circle rates in July 1998 and December 1998.

In the 1992 contract negotiations, the Company proposed and the Union agreed to a two-year progression under which drivers would progress from their beginning wage rate to the full wage rate. Before 1992 there had been a 6-month progression.

In 1995, Mr. Keith Smith, a driver, filed an earlier Grievance wherein he stated that he should be paid the highest rate, including the "red-circle" rate when he was laid off and bumped a part-time employee within the Philadelphia hub. The Company claimed that he was only entitled to the highest non–red-circle rate. The parties settled the grievance, and the Company agreed that the Grievant would "be paid the difference in the rate they paid for the period in question and the highest part-time rate (including the red-circle rate) in effect during the period in question." The Company agreed that it would "pay the highest rate (including the red-circle rate) in the future to any and all full-time employees who chose to work by displacing part-time employees during the time of layoff."

Following the settlement agreement, Mr. Lim Reed, business agent, local 300, posted a notice notifying the members of the bargaining unit. In January 1997, Grievances were filed because

Continued

525

the Company did not pay the red-circle rate to full-time employees who bumped part-time employees within the Philadelphia hub. When the Company refused to pay the red-circle rate to which it had earlier agreed, the Union sent the Company a strike notice, which referred the Company to the settlement agreement. Following that notice, the Company agreed to comply with the settlement agreement by paying the affected employees the red-circle rate.

Throughout 1995, 1996, and 1997, this issue had occasionally surfaced. On each occasion, the Company ultimately agreed to pay the red-circle rate as agreed in the Keith Smith grievance settlement. In other areas of the country, the Company began to take the position that it did not owe the red-circle rate and could pay a lesser rate to full-time employees who bumped part-time employees in the hubs. As a result, other Grievances were filed. One Grievance resulted in an arbitration decision by Arbitrator William Matt on February 9, 1997. Arbitrator Matt concluded that the term "higher wage rate" in Article 45 and in Article 60 included the red-circle rate. Then, at the next negotiations in 1998, the Company made a proposal that would have removed its obligation to pay the red-circle rate, but the Union refused to agree to the Company's proposal. The Company's proposal was withdrawn.

The Union presented as a witness, Mr. John Candle, a business agent with Truckers Union, Local 509, who testified that he had been present when this issue had been grieved on several occasions. He testified that the Company had stated that if the Union position was upheld, some employees would get more money when they bumped a part-time employee than they had been receiving in their regular job. He discussed this issue with Company officials, Mr. Lew Brooks and Mr. George Dikes. Mr. Candle stated that if the Company would agree to pay the red-circle rate to all grievants and others in their situation, he would agree on behalf of the Union not to claim that an employee could get more than the red-circle rate of pay. The Company caucused and returned the proposal. The Company officials' response was that they would not accept that offer; they were going for all or nothing. Mr. Candle told the Company that it should know that in the future, the Union was not going to settle and that if the Company lost the grievance, the decision might result in the Company paying employees more than their regular rate of pay.

The Company admitted that it had agreed to pay the higher rate in the hub, which included the red-circle rate. It admitted that there had been grievances arbitrated about the issue and that those arbitrations had resulted in decisions finding that the red-circle rate was the higher rate to be paid to laid-off employees who bumped part-time employees in the hub.

The Company claimed that it had never paid a laid-off employee more than the laid-off employee would have received on his regular job. Mr. Hershel Fite, the Philadelphia District Manager, testified that when he settled the grievances and agreed to pay the red-circle rate, he did not tell the Union that he would not pay the red-circle rate if it resulted in an increase in pay. He agreed that the settlement agreement was to cover all future instances when a full-time employee was laid off and displaced a part-time employee. However, he admitted he had never discussed with the Union whether employees would get a pay increase. He did admit, however, that Mr. Reed had told him that he believed the language in the settlement required the Company to pay the red-circle rate even if that wage rate was more than the truck driver's regular rate of pay.

Mr. Fite identified the letter sent by George Dikes, the corporate LR manager, in which Mr. Dikes stated that the settlement agreement signed by Mr. Fite would result in a laid-off employee receiving more than he or she would have made at his or her regular classification. Even after that letter of August 23, 1996, Mr. Fite settled grievances with Mr. Reed in 1997 by agreeing to do the same as he had in the original settlement agreement. Mr. Bob Kay, a retired district manager for the Company and a member of various contract negotiations, admitted that the "red-circle" rate is a wage rate and that it would be higher than the displaced part-time employee's wage rate.

The Union argued that the Company violated the Agreement by paying less than the red-circle rate to Mr. Simpson. The Agreement is clear and unequivocal. Article 60 and Article 45 provide that full-time employees who bump into inside hub classifications must be paid "at the appropriate rate for the classification of work performed, except that . . . if in the building there is a part-time employee receiving a higher wage rate than the rate of the displaced part-time employee(s), the full-time employee will receive such higher rate." Thus, it is undisputed that the highest wage rate paid to a part-time employee in the Philadelphia hub during the period in question was the red-circle rate.

Not only does the contract require the Grievant to be paid at the red-circle rate, but prior settlements between Truckers Union and ABC demonstrate that the Union's interpretation of the contract was accepted by the Company. The settlement agreement accepted by the Company is binding precedent. Thus, the Arbitrator must give binding precedential weight to this settlement.

The Union claimed that the Company may argue that Mr. Simpson should not get any amount more than what he was paid in his regular job, even if both the "all other" rate and the "red-circle" rate are greater than his regular rate of pay. However, the Company has no support for that claim in either the contract or the settlement agreement. There is no limitation that precludes a laid-off driver from receiving more than his or her regular rate of pay. Without such a limitation, the Company's argument must fail.

Other arbitrators have discussed this exact issue and have reached this same conclusion. After considering this same issue under the same contract, Arbitrator Matt concluded as follows:

> The Union invokes the "plain meaning" rule and urges that the phrase is clear and unequivocal. The argument is properly confined to the term "wage rate" since the parties agreed that the word "higher" means "highest."
>
> Literally, the Union is correct. The red-circle rate is undeniably a wage-rate even though it is paid to some but not all holders of the same job. The Company seeks to distinguish a red-circle rate from what it calls the "contract" rate, i.e., the negotiated rate for the job classification. This verbal distinction ignores the fact that a red-circle rate is also a contract rate, since it was at one time negotiated by the parties and thereafter maintained by contractual agreement.
>
> Thus, the "plain meaning" rule requires a decision for the Union, unless there is a persuasive reason for excluding red-circle rates from the phrase "higher rate."
>
> In sum, I conclude that red-circle rates are included in the phrase "wage rate" in Article 45, Section 2, B, and the corresponding provision in Article 60.

Arbitrator Ira Jacks reached the same result under the same contract language in another decision.

The thrust of the Company's argument is that it is unfair for laid-off full-time employees to receive a pay raise when they bump into part-time jobs and receive the red-circle rate. The Company contends that it violates the principles of "seniority" to allow a junior truck driver who is laid off and displaces an inside hub worker to be paid more than a more senior driver who is not laid off. The problem with this argument is that the provisions relied on by the Union and found operative by previous arbitrators are contained in Article 45, which deals with seniority. The Company is reduced to arguing that somehow the contract provision violates the principles of "seniority" when the specific and exact language of the seniority provisions of the contract are followed. The Company's argument "simply does not hold water," and the contract language simply must prevail. The language has remained the same even after the 1996 settlement agreement and Arbitrator Matt's decision. The Company did attempt to change the contract language, the Union would not agree to that change, and the language has remained the same. *Continued*

The Union contended that the Company is asking the Arbitrator to add a restriction that a bumping employee cannot receive a rate of pay higher than the bumping employee's regular rate of pay. That language is neither in the contract nor in the settlement agreement. The Company was offered but rejected that deal to settle a prior grievance. The prior grievance decisions have held that the red-circle rate is included in the higher wage category, and the Union has rejected the Company's attempt to renegotiate the contract language to exclude the red-circle rate from being paid under these circumstances. Thus, the Company is attempting to "get through arbitration what it could not get through negotiation."

The Union concluded:

> For the foregoing reasons, the Union respectfully contends that under the Collective Bargaining Agreement and the later settlement agreement entered into between the Union and the Company, the Grievant in this case is entitled to receive the red-circle rate in July 1998 of $16.19 per hour and in December 1998 of $16.79 per hour. The Company should therefore be ordered to pay the Grievant the difference in what it has paid him $12.11 per hour when he was working inside the Philadelphia hub and the rates it should have paid him, $16.19 per hour in July 1998 and $16.79 per hour in December 1998.

Position of the Company

The Company stated that in 1992, the Company and the Truckers Union agreed that part-time employees could be hired at a lesser rate than their existing pay rate, but the part-time employees presently employed would be "grandfathered" in at their existing rates of pay. Those employees hired before July 1987 would continue to be paid at their higher rate of pay, which was subsequently referred to as the "red-circle rate."

When a full-time employee bumped a part-time employee, Mr. Reed interpreted the contract to mean that the full-time feeder driver was to be paid the red-circle rate because that was the highest part-time rate in the Philadelphia hub. He addressed the resolution of certain grievances pertaining to this issue. In 1995 a feeder driver named Smith complained that the Company had failed to pay him the red-circle rate. Furthermore, two similar grievances were filed by feeder employees Horton and Gardner in early 1996 after a layoff following the Christmas season. Mr. Reed stated that he and District Labor Manager Fite resolved all of the grievances before arbitration on July 30, 1996. Mr. Reed interpreted the agreement that resolved these grievances to mean that laid-off feeder drivers who displaced part-timers would receive the red-circle rate and notified Union members about the resolution. Reed testified that when the Company did not pay the red-circle rate in February, 1997, he received grievances from other employees—Forehand, Kincer, Capel and Myers—about his failure. Reed sent a letter to Fite and gave him 72 hours to pay the red-circle rate or the Union would strike. Mr. Fite then agreed to pay the grievance.

Mr. Reed testified that the Union's position is that, unlike the prior grievants, Simpson should have received an increase in pay to the red-circle rate when he bumped into a lesser skilled part-time job. Mr. Reed maintained that this was the Union's position, even though the feeder drivers with greater seniority than Simpson would be earning less than Mr. Simpson. These more senior employees who continued work at their regular feeder jobs would then receive a lesser rate of pay than Simpson, who was laid off from the tractor-trailer classification.

Mr. John Candle testified that he had been a business agent at other locations. From 1985 to 1998, he was involved in negotiating and administering the Agreement and testified that it was his understanding that everyone at Local 300 would be getting the red-circle rate when they bumped into the hub. He stated that in 1998 there had been some negotiations about the rates of pay that laid-off feeder drivers would receive when they displaced part-time inside employees, but the Company's proposal addressing this issue eventually was withdrawn.

Mr. Cornelius Lambuth, a feeder manager who has been directly involved with Philadelphia feeder operations for nearly 20 years as a driver, supervisor, and manager, addressed the Company's records. The records show that employees Caruso, Bryant, and Linville were Philadelphia feeder drivers and that all had obtained their seniority ahead of Simpson. They were working at their regular feeder jobs on the same week as Simpson. During the week that these more senior employees were working, they were earning $12.11 per hour, but the red-circle rate at that time was $16.19 per hour.

Mr. Bob McCain, recently retired district manager, had been with the Company for more than 30 years. Mr. McCain testified that the red-circle rates were not rates of pay for positions but were only rates of pay for individuals who were hired before 1987. If those individuals left ABC's employment and then were reemployed, they would not receive their higher rates of pay.

Mr. Fite has been in charge of administering the Agreement with the Union. Fite testified about several grievances that were filed by the Union and settled before arbitration. These grievances involved the rate of pay full-time employees should receive when they bumped into lower-paying part-time jobs. In each instance, the red-circle rate claimed by the Grievants was less than their regular feeder rate of pay. The Union had never contended that these employees should receive a pay increase when they were laid off. Fite testified that when he settled these grievances, none of the employees received a higher part-time rate than their normal feeder pay rate, and the Union did not contend otherwise. Mr. Fite testified that paying the employees a higher rate of pay was never contemplated by him nor was it ever discussed with Mr. Reed. It was not until after Mr. Simpson filed his grievance that Mr. Reed for the first time claimed that a laid-off feeder driver was eligible for a pay increase when bumping into a part-time position in the Philadelphia hub.

The Company argued that the Union bears the burden of proving that the Company is contractually obligated to pay the Grievant a red-circle rate that was higher than his regular feeder rate. The Union bears the burden of proving the existence of a binding past practice to pay the red-circle rate that it claims existed. The evidence is clear that the Union has failed to meet these burdens.

The Company stated that the disputed language in the Agreement does not require the payment of the red-circle rate. The Union's argument is that the provision in the contract referring to the "higher rate" includes the red-circle rate, but this contention must fail for two reasons. First, red-circle rates are individual rates and have been paid only to employees who were working as part-time employees before July 1987 and who continued to be employed in that capacity. Second, the red-circle rate was not in existence at the time the parties originally agreed to the contractual provision paying employees who bumped down at the highest part-time rate. The parties could not have contemplated that the displaced employee would be making a rate higher than his or her regular full-time rate of pay.

The Company argued that the disputed language does not mention red-circle rates. An individual who was receiving the red-circle rate and who later leaves the employment of ABC will not receive the red-circle rate again upon returning to ABC. An individual hired as a part-time employee after July 1987 does not receive the red-circle rate. The individual nature of red-circle rates was recognized by Arbitrator Fishgood when he stated:

> It is clear that red-circle rates, which are used throughout the American industrial complex, are individual rates, they are not job rates. They are individual specific and normally when an employee leaves a job on which he was red-circled, his red-circle rate is lost.

Continued

A red-circle rate is a personalized rate that an employee is permitted to retain notwithstanding that it is above the agreed-on rate for the job he is performing. The rate that the Union is contending that the Grievant is entitled to is one that is paid to individuals, not to employees performing a specific job. The red-circle rate is generally accepted as a personal rate assigned to an individual employee, and that rate cannot be assigned to another employee by the Arbitrator.

The Company claimed that at the time, the language in the contract setting the rate of pay was agreed to, there were no red-circle rates. Therefore, at the time the parties agreed to pay the highest rate in the hub, they could not have contemplated paying the red-circle rate. The language that was agreed to in the contract has not changed since it was originally agreed to by the parties. Because the red-circle rate was not in existence at the time of the insertion of the disputed contractual language and because the parties could not have contemplated paying the red-circle rate, the contract language should not be construed to mean that the red-circle rate is included within the meaning of the "higher rate."

The Company complained that it has never given pay increases to bumping feeder drivers when they moved into less-skilled part-time work. The most these employees may have received was the same rate of pay they were earning in their regular job; however, they did not receive a rate of pay higher than they were making as a full-time employee. There has been no past practice on behalf of the Company to pay the red-circle rate. The Union has never taken the position that an employee should get a pay raise when the employee is laid off and works in a lesser-skilled position.

The Company argued that the Union's interpretation of the disputed language would produce a result that is inconsistent with seniority principles that underlie the Agreement. Article 45, Section 1, page 90, sets out the basic principle controlling all seniority issues arising under the Agreement. It provides very simply: "Seniority, as measured by length of continuous service with the Company, shall prevail at all times." There is no question that the Union's interpretation of the contract would violate this principle.

The Company further argued that the construction given by the Union would defeat the concept of rate progression embedded in the contract. The basic concept of paying more for higher-skilled jobs would be nullified. The Agreement is clear that employees progress from the unskilled inside positions to the skilled positions of package car driver and feeder driver. The Union's interpretation would allow employees to make more money by moving into lesser-skilled entry level jobs.

The Company argued that the interpretation advanced by the Union would produce a fundamental inequity. Mr. Simpson who was demoted would make more money than his fellow employees, Caruso, Bryant, and Linville, who continued to work in their regular feeder jobs. Rewarding the most junior employee at the expense of his more senior counterparts is contrary to the entire structure of the contract and its seniority system.

To the extent that these previous arbitrator opinions construe the contract to require a pay increase to a laid-off employee, the Company submits that these decisions are simply wrong. Reading the contract literally, as these opinions purport to do, yields an absurd result of junior employees making more than senior employees performing more skilled work. The Company argued that the underlying purpose of the contract between the Company and the Union is to recognize and reward length of service by providing enhanced pay and benefits as employees stay with the Company and move into more skilled, demanding jobs. This objective is frustrated if junior employees can take a demotion and receive a higher rate than their more senior peers. Because Arbitrators Matt and Jacks read the contract authorizing such an unequitable result, their reasoning is fatally flawed and must be rejected.

The Company concluded:

The Grievance is without merit and should be denied because the red-circle rate is not an individual rate that can be assigned by an arbitrator to any individual performing a job. Moreover, the evidence is clear that the parties did not intend that the "higher rate" as used in the contract include the later negotiated red-circle rate. The parties did not agree to pay displaced feeder drivers the red-circle rate when this would result in a pay increase for them. Finally, awarding the higher rate of pay to an employee who is laid off and who bumps into a lower skilled position would lead to inequitable results that completely undercut the seniority system and were never contemplated as agreed to by the parties.

QUESTIONS

1. What is the most persuasive argument for the Union?
2. What is the most persuasive argument for the Company?
3. How do the facts and arguments fit with the criteria used by arbitrators in making their decisions?
4. Of what value and use is the settlement agreement? Explain.
5. Of what relevance are the previous arbitrator's decisions?
6. Are settlements by the parties to avoid arbitration binding on the parties in future cases?
7. Based on the evidence and the wording of the Agreement, you be the arbitrator. Make your decision and give your reasoning.

No-Smoking Policy for Employees' Health and Safety

Background

This matter of arbitration stems from a letter to all Moreland Container employees from General Manager Jim Livings, dated January 24, 1999. This letter stated:

> As each of you are aware Moreland Container is initiating a Tobacco Free Environment on March 1, 1999. This decision is based on improving the health and safety of all our employees.
>
> It has been proven that tobacco products are carcinogenic and directly and indirectly related to lung cancer, oral cancer, heart disease, and stomach disorders. Moreland hopes, through this policy, to abate the spiraling cost of health insurance and to ensure a safer and healthier environment in which to work.
>
> For some of you, this transition will be difficult. In an effort to help our employees curtail or quit using tobacco products on the premises, we will be offering classes (to be announced) and support. The company is also preparing to assist those who want to quit with financial assistance. You will be receiving more on this in the next couple weeks.
>
> Thank you for your support.

Then, on March 3, 1999, Mr. Livings wrote another letter to "All Team Members" on the subject "Tobacco Free Environment Policy Violation." This letter stated:

> The Moreland Tobacco Free Policy began this month, and I want to clarify some issues surrounding it. First, I'm sure that each of you will do your utmost to adhere to this policy. However, in the event that a Moreland team member uses tobacco on the Moreland Container property, you need to be aware of the ramifications:
>
> Violation of the tobacco free policy is considered a willful violation of rules that affect the health and safety of Moreland Container team members. That is different from making a mistake. A willful violation means that you knew the rules, but planned and knowingly took actions to violate the policy. Accordingly, the consequences of willful violation are more severe. Violation of the Tobacco Free policy will result in the following:
>
> First Violation: One-Day, paid decision-making leave. You will be asked to consider whether you desire to continue your employment with Moreland Container.
>
> Second Violation: Termination of employment from Moreland Container

> I cannot emphasize enough the importance of this policy. The Tobacco Free Policy applies to all Moreland Container Team Members and any other persons entering the Moreland Container property. The policy is designed to protect the health and safety of Moreland Container team members. Moreland Container offers support if you desire to stop smoking. If you have any questions about the policy or how Moreland Container can help you stop smoking, please don't hesitate to ask.
>
> Again, thank you for your support of this important policy.

On March 10, 1999, the Union filed the following Grievance:

> Nature of Grievance:
> Unfair labor practices. The Company has allowed the use of tobacco products for many years and for no reason they stopped the use on company property.

> Settlement Desired:
> Allow the employees who want to use tobacco to continue to use in designated areas as has been allowed for so long.

On March 11, 1999, Management denied the Grievance. The Grievance was appealed, and on March 15, 1999, Management answered as follows:

> No violation of any article in the labor agreement. Local Union has failed to show what was violated.

The Grievance was appealed to arbitration.

Issue
Did the Company violate the Agreement on March 1, 1999, when it established a Tobacco Free Environment Policy at the Moreland Container property?

  If so, how, and if so, what shall be the remedy?

Relevant Provisions of the Agreement
Article I—Recognition
Section 1. The Company recognizes the Union as the sole collective bargaining agent on rates of pay, hours of work, and other working conditions for all of its production workers, and maintenance workers, at Moreland Container, exclusive of office and factory clerical employees, and all supervisory employees with authority to hire, promote, discipline, or otherwise effect such changes in the status of employees, or effectively recommend such action.

Article VIII—Grievance and Arbitration
The function and jurisdiction of the arbitrator shall be limited to a determination of the merits of the grievance, as reduced to writing under the grievance procedure, in accordance with the express language of this agreement. The arbitrator shall have no power to change, add to, or delete from the terms of this agreement.

Article X—Regulations
Section 2. The Union agrees that the management of the factory, including the following, is vested exclusively in the Company and that all functions not specifically granted to the Union by this contract likewise are vested exclusively in the Company, provided that this will not be used for the purpose of discrimination because of Union membership.

  (1) The direction of the working forces.

  (2) The right to hire, suspend, or discharge for just cause, including violations of this agreement.

  (3) The right to establish factory rules not in conflict with this contract.

Article XII—Agreement Complete
This agreement is complete. It may be amended by mutual agreement in writing. Such amendment may be effective during the term of this agreement and may extend the term of this agreement. This agreement does not operate to include, nor does it obligate the Company to continue in effect, any working condition, benefit or past practice which is not covered or contained in the agreement.

Continued

Position of the Union

The Union stated that it has represented the Moreland Container employees for many years, and its current agreement, which began on September 15, 1998, continues until September 15, 2003. The employees have been allowed to smoke and use other forms of tobacco in the plant for many years. In the late 1980s the Company put restrictions on the location in the plant where employees could smoke. In 1997 the Company decided not to allow the employees to smoke in the plant. The employees were allowed to smoke in certain areas outside the plant as designated by the Company. In March 1999, the Company changed the tobacco-use policy again. This change no longer allowed employees to smoke or use other forms of tobacco on Company property. The Union did not agree with this change in policy, subsequently filed a grievance, and processed it through the grievance procedure to arbitration.

The Union contended that it is very unreasonable for the Company not to allow its employees to smoke or use other forms of tobacco on Company property. The Union presented evidence that showed thirty-two of the employees smoke or use other forms of tobacco. Most of these employees are long-time employees of the Company. The Company changed its tobacco policy several times before the employees and Union were able to take a position. When the Company decided not to allow the employees to smoke in the plant, the employees went along with it. The Company designated the areas outside the plant for the employees to smoke. The employees were not happy with the change but went along with it. When the Company decided to disallow the use of tobacco on Company property, employees and the Union decided to challenge this action.

Mr. Charles Haywood, local union president, testified that several employees had been disciplined, and some had received a day off for smoking on Company property. Mr. Haywood testified that fifty-eight of the seventy-four employees had signed a petition, which stated that the Moreland Container employees should be allowed to smoke on Company property. Mr. Haywood testified that he was a smoker and that it was "real hard" to work a shift of 8 to 10 hours without smoking. Mr. Haywood testified that supervisors were allowed to leave company property and smoke. The Union asked, "Is it fair to allow supervision to leave the plant and smoke and require the employees to stay on the job for 8 to 10 hours without smoking?" The Union believes not.

Mr. Keith Dormey, chief steward, testified that he participated in the 1998 negotiations, and the Company never presented to the Union a proposal to negotiate the smoking policy. Mr. Dormey testified that the smoking policy was only mentioned once during the negotiations. He stated that Committeeman Hicks brought up the issue about having to go outside and smoke. Mr. Green, the labor relations manager, said to Mr. Hicks that he should feel lucky because the Company was thinking about having a no-smoking policy on company property. Mr. Dormey stated that he informed Mr. Green that if that was the Company's position, he should let the Union know now. Mr. Green did not respond. Mr. Dormey stated that a majority of the employees thought that they should be allowed to smoke on Company property, although many of them don't use tobacco.

Mr. Green stated that much was said during the course of the negotiations. Most of what was said should not have any influence on this Grievance whatsoever. Most of what Mr. Green said about smoking was already known. We all know that smoking is not good for your health. We also know that it is not a violation of the law to smoke. The Union claimed that it was very strange that Mr. Green would present the Union with the Company proposals without a smoking proposal when it was so important to them. The fact is that Mr. Green never made a proposal to the Union on smoking. If Mr. Green had presented the Union with a smoking proposal, it would have taken much longer to have reached an agreement because this is a very important issue to bargaining unit employees.

Mr. Jim Livings testified at the hearing to one item of importance, that is, he stated that the no-smoking policy was his policy and that Mr. Green had nothing to do with it.

The Union challenged the reasons the Company gave for the policy of no smoking on Company property. Mr. Green stated that when the employees were allowed to smoke outside, the nonsmokers had to walk through the area where the smokers were. Because the Company is the party that designated the smoking areas, the Company could have changed the location anytime. The Union was told during the grievance meeting that the Company would be able to save thousands of dollars on insurance premiums. However, neither Mr. Green nor Mr. Livings provided any data about savings on the costs of insurance. Furthermore, thus far, the employees have not had savings on their costs for insurance premiums.

The Union concluded:

> . . . the Union believes the Company went too far when it unilaterally put into place the tobacco free policy in question. We believe this question should have been settled at the bargaining table between the parties. As we have already stated, this policy is very unreasonable. We believe the Union presented the evidence to show the tobacco free policy is unreasonable, and that the employees should be allowed to smoke on Company property. We believe this is a negotiable item, and the Company should be required to negotiate with the Union.
>
> We ask that the employees be allowed to smoke, on Company property, in areas decided on by the Union and Company.

Position of the Company

The Company stated that during September and October of 1998, the Company and Union negotiated a new labor agreement. During these negotiations on September 9 and 10, 1998, the Company advised the Union of its intention to make the property smoke- and tobacco-free. The Union was invited to discuss the matter. If the Union had any objections or issues, that was the time to raise them. Both Company and Union witnesses to the bargaining agree that no objection to the smoke- and tobacco-free policy was raised by the Union. The only comment was that "employees won't like that," which was offered by one of the Union bargaining committee representatives. The Union witness present during negotiations admitted that the Union offered no objection, only a comment by Randy Hooks, a Union committee member.

In addition to the Company's notification of its smoke- and tobacco-free policy, the parties agreed to new contract language concerning a new "Article XII—Agreement Complete," on page 31 of *Joint Exhibit No. 2*. This language states in part:

> This agreement does not operate to include, nor does it obligate the company to continue in effect any working condition, benefit, or past practice which is not covered or contained in the agreement.

The Union was told to bring forth any past practices it felt needed to be part of the new agreement. The Union brought forth several items that it felt should be included, but none of the items presented concerned the right of employees to smoke or use tobacco on Company property. None of the items presented by the Union as past practices to be continued were agreed to by the Company. All were rejected by the Company for inclusion in the new labor agreement.

The Company claimed that the Grievance should be denied and dismissed for several reasons. First, there is no contract violation. The Company has not violated any article or section

Continued

of the Agreement. The Union is not able to cite any article or section violated. Article VIII, Grievances and Arbitration, of the current agreement describes a difference that "arises out of the terms, application, or interpretation of the agreement...may be referred to arbitration." There has been no violation of any term, application, or interpretation of any stated portion of this agreement.

The Company stated that smoking/tobacco use had been subject to redesignation at least since 1995, when Gwinn County passed an ordinance that amended the Clean Indoor Air Ordinance of November 1995, which regulated smoking in places of employment in the county. Even after the Company redesignated smoking areas, an argument can be made that the Company was still not in compliance with the law. The three areas designated were the patio picnic table awning areas, the employee entrance, and the railroad track end of the shipping dock.

All nonsmoking employees were being exposed to secondhand smoke, and as such, the Company was violating the Gwinn County ordinance section 9-8004 (#2) a.b.c. and Section 9-8005 (#7). The changes in smoking to a tobacco-free property actually put Moreland Container in compliance with the Gwinn County ordinance.

The Company claimed that during negotiations for a new labor agreement in September and October of 1998, the Company specifically brought up the fact that the Company intended to make the Moreland Container property smoke and tobacco free. That intent could not have been made more clear by Mr. Green's bargaining notes. Testimony of both Company and Union witnesses about the 1998 negotiations reveals that the Union clearly did not object to the Company's plans or intentions. The Union was given the very real opportunity to object to the Company's stated intention. In fact, the Union could have bargained to impasse over this issue alone to try and force a revision in the Company's smoke- and tobacco-free property plans, but the Union did not do this. The Union did not offer a single objection, protest, or statement in opposition. The only statement from one Union committee person was that employees "will not like that." The Company had every right to infer from this failure to object that the Union did not oppose the actual implementation of a tobacco-free policy later. The Company was legitimately surprised when the Union did object in March 1999. The Union clearly had waived its opportunity to bargain on this issue in 1998, and the Union waived any legitimate protest later in 1999.

The Company stated that the Union agreed to "Article XII—Agreement Complete" in the 1998 negotiations. This language specifically and clearly limits any requirement to abide by any past practice not contained in the Agreement. The Union was specifically asked to bring forth any past practice issues that it wanted to consider included in the new agreement. The Union did not bring forth any issues about smoking or tobacco use despite the fact that the Union had been put on notice by the Company that it was planning to make the Moreland Container property smoke and tobacco free. The Union waived its right, if indeed one actually existed, to bargain on the smoking/tobacco issue. The Union knew that the Company was planning on a smoke- and tobacco-free property. The Union could have bargained or attempted to bargain something different. The fact is that the Union waived this opportunity a second time during the 1998 negotiations when it agreed to the new "Article XII—Agreement Complete" language.

The Company claimed that the Union never said at any time before the filing of the Grievance that the Company did not have the right to make the property tobacco free. The Union had received continuous notice—formal and informal in meetings and one-on-one discussion—that the Company was implementing its stated intention to have a tobacco-free property. At no time did the Union offer any caution or protest that the Company would be in violation of the Agreement.

The Company argued that the contract does provide that the Company can establish work rules. No tobacco on company property is a work rule. Article X, Section 2, of the Agreement enumerates Management's rights, and that the following are vested exclusively in the Company, and included in this list is no. 5:

The right to establish factory rules not in conflict with this contract.

The Company argued that there was never any charge of not having bargained over this issue made by the Union either formally or informally. No unfair labor practices have been filed with the Board; there were no protest or Grievances that the Company failed to bargain over this matter. Bargaining took place in 1998 and given this opportunity, the Union waived any further right to negotiate on the subject.

The Company claimed that a business cost/necessity point was made. Company managers testified how unmanageable designated smoking areas are. Most (65%) of the bargaining unit people are not smokers. However, smokers are always trying for that extra smoke break. Production Manager Moot and other managers have difficulty keeping track of the smokers. Supervisors could not determine when a smoke break was a legitimate break or not. The nonsmoking employees were constantly complaining about improper smoke breaks, and this had an obvious effect on morale, productivity, efficiency, quality, and cost.

The Company argued that it used a reasonable implementation process. Employees received advance notification in December 1998; a memo of notification was sent out and posted on January 24, 1999. A memo that described the administrative details of the Tobacco Free Property Policy was posted on March 3, 1999. Employees were given the opportunity to sign up for smoking cessation programs and stop-smoking patch reimbursement. Current Union President Charles Haywood received a $300 reimbursement for patches.

The Company stated that no one has been terminated in the year and 7 months since the Tobacco Free Property Policy has been in effect. Approximately five or six employees have been given a 1-day paid decision-making leave because they were in violation, and the last such leave was in July 1999. This indicates a very high level of employee acceptance and compliance and provides proof of a fair and valid policy. This policy has proven itself because it does work. As a practical matter, the policy stands up to any test of reasonableness based on actual experience.

The Company noted that the Gwinn County ordinance dealing with smoking forced the Moreland Container Plant in 1995 to make changes in its smoking policy. After reading this ordinance, the plant officials believed that it was probably not in compliance until March 1, 1999, when the plant property was made tobacco free. The Company cannot return to the old designated areas if it wanted to. Each of those areas subjected nonsmoking employees involuntarily to secondhand smoke—the patio and umbrella area outside the break room, the shipping dock, and the employee entrance. None of these former designated areas are acceptable as smoking areas under the county's ordinance because nonsmokers were exposed to secondhand smoke in every case. Therefore, allowing smoking in these areas is not only a violation of the ordinance, but it is also unhealthy and unfair to the nonsmokers.

The Company claimed that bargaining unit employees had taken their breaks in one of two permissible places, the break room vending area and the bathroom as needed. The Union has never opposed or objected to this arrangement since its inception more than a year ago. If the Company were to be required to designate some other area of the property for smoking and tobacco use, where would it be? The general break area and the bathroom would not be appropriate. These locations would violate the Gwinn County ordinance, so the Company would be forced to redesignate the break areas. This seems to be both unreasonable to the

Continued

employees and to the Company. It would seem to violate the Company's prerogative of "directing the workforce" and its "right to establish factory rules" as stipulated in Article X. Therefore, if the Arbitrator changes a work rule or approves designated smoking areas on Company property, such decision would be in conflict with Article VIII of the Agreement:

> The function and jurisdiction of the arbitrator shall be limited to a determination of the merits of the grievance as reduced to writing under the grievance procedure, in accordance with the express language of this agreement. The arbitrator shall have no power to change, add to, or delete from the terms of this agreement.

The Company argued that other arbitrators have held that the Company has the absolute right to prohibit smoking inside, out of doors, and in those areas it controls either through ownership or through lease, because not only is smoking detrimental to one's health, but secondary smoke is detrimental to those who are around it. A smoker is a greater health risk than a non-smoker, and the owner of the property has the right to control its property (104 LA 174 [Fredric N. Richman, 1995]). Arbitrator Robert G. Howlett in a very similar case found that the Union had waived any right it might have had to bargain over a nonsmoking ban (90 LA 1186 [1988]).

In another case, *Koch Refining* v. *O.C.A.W.* (99 LA 733 [1992]), Arbitrator Gerald Cohen denied the Union's Grievance on a total ban on smoking. He stated:

> It is my belief that the subject of smoking in a refinery is not a matter of a working condition, but is a matter of rule-making authority possessed by the company. Other arbitrators have ruled similarly. *Wyandot, Inc.* 92 LA 457 (1989).

The Company concluded:

> The Company has shown that the Union had every chance to negotiate on the matter of a tobacco-free policy during the 1998 negotiation but did not, thus waiving any right to bargain on the matter or to mount a valid protest of the policy later on.
>
> Further, the Union also agreed to contract language in 1998 cutting off all claims to past practice that were not included in the collective bargaining agreement. They did this with full knowledge that the Company intended to make the Moreland Container operation a smoke- and tobacco-free property thus eliminating designated smoking areas.
>
> The Company has shown that it has the contractual right to establish factory rules, the Company retains all rights not granted to the Union by the contract, and there is clearly no contractual right to smoke on company property.
>
> The implementation of the tobacco ban on company property was fair and reasonable. In the nineteen months since implementation, only a small number of employees have been found to have violated the policy; none were terminated because of a second violation. The last person to have been found in violation was in July 1999. There has been acceptance of the policy by the general plant population. On property, smoking is not efficient, it creates a multitude of other issues, most dealing with keeping people on the job and from taking unauthorized smoke breaks.
>
> The health related reasons for a tobacco-free property speak for themselves. Presently, we are all very familiar with the health hazards smoking and tobacco use presents to tobacco users and non-tobacco users alike.
>
> For these reasons the company respectfully requests that the union grievance protesting the Tobacco Free Property Policy of the Moreland Container Plant be denied and dismissed.

QUESTIONS

1. Under which contractual provisions may a Company invoke workplace rules and regulations?

2. Under what circumstances may a Company implement safety and health rules and regulations for employees?

3. Are smoking privileges considered a past practice under the collective bargaining agreement? Did Article XII eliminate all past practices except those included in the new labor agreement?

4. Is the Company obligated to protect employees from conditions that are not healthy?

5. Of what value were Mr. Green's bargaining notes in support of the Company's position?

6. Of what value is the Gwinn County ordinance in support of the Company's position?

7. Did the Company have authority to take action against employees who violated their smoking privileges? What were the alternatives?

8. You be the Arbitrator: What is your ruling? What are your reasons for the ruling?

Reimbursement for Purchase of Boots?

Background

This matter of arbitration has as its origin the purchase of a pair of boots from Western Boot Co. for $204.25 on December 28, 2003, by Mr. Pat Acey, the Grievant. On December 12, 2003, Mr. Carl Brasil, District Manager, approved reimbursement. On February 25, 2004, Mr. Howard Weebles, President and CEO of Martin Electric Cooperative (MEC) (hereinafter also referred to as the Company) sent the following memo to Mr. Acey:

> Upon a recent audit of the uniform reimbursement accounts, it was found that you had purchased a pair of line worker boots. Because your classification at MEC is Line Truck Driver, you are not in the line worker classification and you are not eligible for this reimbursement.
>
> Please return to MEC $240.25. You may make payment by check or we can withhold it from your pay over the next three pay cycles. If this is the preferred method, please sign the authorization below.
>
> If you prefer to pay by check, please send the check to MEC by Friday, March 7, 2004.

On March 5, 2004, Mr. Acey authorized payment to the Company of $204.25. Mr. Acey signed this payment statement "under protest."

On March 5, 2005, the Union filed the following Grievance at Step 1:

> Statement of the Grievance:
>
> Member Pat Acey was refused reimbursement for boots purchased in violation of Article 21 Section 4.
>
> Settlement Requested:
>
> Member requests to be made whole.

On March 6, 2004, Mr. John Overton denied the Grievance and stated:

> Not considered a violation of Article 21, Section 4.

The Union appealed the Grievance to Step 2 on March 6, 2004. Mr. John Blanton wrote:

> The Union still feels this is a violation of Article 21, Section 4 of the contract.

On the same day, Mr. Brasil denied the Grievance and provided the following Company response:

> Article 21, Section 4 of the agreement has not been violated.

Mr. Blanton appealed the Grievance to Step 3 and wrote:

> The Union still feels this is a violation of Article 21, Section 4 of the contract.

In a letter dated April 14, 2004, Mr. Weebles provided the Company Step 3 response:

> This letter reaffirms MEC's decision of April 1, 2004. As you are aware, when we negotiated the contract last spring, the addition of lineworker boots to the uniform policy was specifically for the climbing classifications only.
>
> Therefore, Martin Electric does not feel this is a grievable offense as MEC did not violate the labor agreement.

In a letter dated April 23, 2004, Mr. Charles Snowden, Assistant Business Manager, and Mr. Paul Gaston, Business Manager, sent the following letter to Mr. Weebles and appealed the Grievance to arbitration:

> I have received your follow-up letter dated April 14, 2004, on the grievance meeting held on April 1, 2004. I am sorry that there has been some misunderstanding during negotiations, which you discussed in your letter. However, your response to this grievance is unacceptable to the Union and thus we wish to arbitrate. Enclosed please find the FMCS forms to be signed and returned to me.

On October 29, 2004, an arbitration hearing was held.

Issue

Is Pat Acey entitled to receive a pair of line worker boots, and, if so, should the Company be directed to reimburse Pat for the $204.25? In addition, should the Company be directed to comply with the CBA language and provide any and all members of the bargaining unit reimbursement, provided the $852.40 has not been exhausted in the employee's annual account?

Relevant Provisions of the Agreement

> Article 21—Tools, Equipment, and Other Protective Items

> Section 4. The Company agrees to pay up to $852.40 for each Union member per year for the purchase of Flame Retardant clothes, lineworker boots and leather work gloves.

Positions of the Parties

The Union

The Union stated that the action taken by Mr. Weebles, CEO/President, on February 25, 2004, to require Union member and Truck Driver Pat Acey to reimburse the Company for a pair of boots he had preapproval for purchase in the amount of $204.25 was grieved. It is the Union's position that Article 21, Section 4, "The Company agrees to pay up to $852.40 for each Union member per year for the purchase of Flame Retardant clothes, lineworker boots and leather work gloves," has been violated.

The facts presented show that Mr. Acey had received preapproval to purchase the boots. Documents support the fact that his supervisor, Mr. Bobby Macy, provided Mr. Acey with approval to purchase the boots at the same time Union witness Calvin Favor received approval to purchase his boots. Mr. Macy was not only Mr. Acey's supervisor, but he was also a member of the Company's negotiating team. The fact that Mr. Macy authorized Mr. Acey's boots and was on the Company's negotiating committee supports the Union's position that no classification was exempt from receiving this benefit. Mr. Macy did not attend the arbitration hearing to answer questions about his understanding on this issue, but Mr. Macy's agreement with the Union on this matter was confirmed through testimony of Mr. Weebles, who testified that he was disappointed that Mr. Macy had signed his approval for the purchase.

The Union argued that all Union witnesses present during the negotiations on the lineworker boots issue supported the joint understanding that all classifications, not just linemen or climbing classifications, were entitled to reimbursement for the purchase of lineworker boots. On the other hand, the Company's witnesses did not concur with each other on what classifications represented by the Union, if any, were exempt from the reimbursement for lineworker boots. Company witness Lawrence Stinger, Vice President of Support Services and Company negotiation committee member, stated clearly that he did not recall any dialogue that

Continued

would exclude any classification from the right of reimbursement. Mr. Macy, Company negotiation committee member, did not believe Mr. Acey was exempt from the reimbursement for lineworker boot provision because he authorized Acey to purchase a pair of boots and to receive reimbursement. The only witnesses who testified that they recalled the matter being discussed were Company witnesses, Mr. Weebles and Ms. Mary Miranda, Vice President of Employee and Member Services. Union witnesses and Union negotiation committee members, Favor, Snowden, and Randal Aldy, all testified that the intent of the language was to cover all the bargaining unit employees with no exclusion. The Union witnesses testified that the request for reimbursement for boots and gloves to be added to the Agreement came from the Union, and the Union agreed the final details of the lineworker boot language were negotiated between the parties.

The Union and all Union witnesses present on the negotiation committee claimed that the term "lineworker boots" in Article 21, Section 4 was merely a descriptive term for the type of boot, just as "leather work gloves" is a descriptive term for the type of gloves for which the Company will reimburse employees up to $852.40 annually. All Union witnesses supported this position. The Union's position is that the term *lineworker* as used in Article 21, Section 4 could not be interpreted in any other way than described by the Union. This Union did find it amusing that Ms. Miranda testified that, if the term hunting boots had been used as an adjective before boots, only hunters would be entitled to a pair of boots.

The Union agreed that the Company attempted to confuse the issue by trying to suggest a second theory for its refusal to reimburse Mr. Acey. It appeared to the Union that the Company's intent was to prove the type of boots purchased by Mr. Acey was not within the criteria negotiated, and linemen would not use them to climb. However, all witnesses questioned by the Company advocate as to whether they would climb in this type of boots stated they would. As a matter of fact, Lead Lineworker Calvin Favor stated he had used this type of boot to climb since working at the Company and currently has a pair in his closet at home.

Pat Acey, Line Truck Driver, testified that his filing of the Grievance was predicated on the belief that the Company has not complied with the appropriate provisions of the Agreement to effectuate his contractual right to be fully reimbursed as outlined in the existing Agreement. Mr. Acey did not file this Grievance for any reason other than his belief, and the Union concurred with that belief by agreeing to arbitrate the matter. All witnesses who were asked the question about whether Pat Acey could receive money beyond the $852.40 through his purchasing the boots responded in the negative.

The Union stated that it stands by this Grievance and believes that the only solution to this issue is that Pat Acey is entitled to the $204.25 and the Company should be directed to reimburse him for his lineworker boot purchase. In addition, the Company should be directed to comply with Article 21, Section 4 and provide this benefit to all Union members.

The Union argued that this case is the culmination of the Company's attempt to gain and enforce contractual changes that were not achieved through the negotiating process. Evidence submitted leaves no doubt as to the nature of the negotiations and the attempt by the Company to gain through the grievance process that which it forgot to ask for or inadvertently overlooked during negotiations. The language is clear and unambiguous. As such, the language must be supported in total by the arbitrator. The Union's first indication that all members of the bargaining unit were not entitled to reimbursement for lineworker boots occurred when Pat Acey was required to repay the Company for his purchase of lineworker boots.

Each Union witness who was involved in the latest negotiations testified about what was discussed. None of them recalled that the Company stated in any form that there was any intent to exclude any classification from the lineworker boot reimbursement provision of Article 21,

Section 4. Two Company witnesses testified that they had discussed that the lineworker boots were limited solely to climbing classifications. One of the Company's witnesses, Stinger, Vice President of Support Services and a Company negotiation committee member, stated that he did not recall any dialogue that would exclude any classification from the right to receive reimbursement for boots. In addition, another member of the Company's negotiation committee who did not share this exclusion understanding was Mr. Macy. Mr. Weebles clearly stated his disappointment of Mr. Macy's misunderstanding and signing of the approval for Mr. Acey's reimbursement.

The Union claimed that, after a review of the position descriptions for both Journeyman Lineworker and Line Truck Driver (Winch) jobs, one can only conclude that both classifications require a good pair of boots. These workers are exposed to weather, and the work is hard on an employee's feet and ankles. Specifically, the job responsibilities, environmental conditions, and physical requirements illustrate that the "riggers" of both jobs are similar, with the exception of climbing the poles. However, the Union pointed out that under Physical Requirements of the "Line Truck Driver (Winch)," the language specifically requires that job holder be able to sit, "climbs, kneels, pushes and pulls poles and wire."

All Union witnesses confirmed that the Union negotiation committee explained to the Union membership during the ratification vote on the contract that boots and gloves had been added to the new contract and that all classifications were now included in Article 21, Section 4.

The Union stated that, if the contract words are plain and clear, conveying a distinct idea, there is no occasion to resort to technical rules of interpretation, and the clear meaning will ordinarily be applied by the arbitrator. The Union claimed that an arbitrator cannot ignore clearcut contract language and may not legislate new language. The Union argued that to do so, the arbitrator would usurp the role of the Union and the Company.

While the Union continues to contend this language is not ambiguous, the Union believes any reasonable person would interpret the language of Article 21, Section 4 as Mr. Acey and the rest of the Union's negotiation committee have interpreted it. The Union concluded that, based on the evidence, arguments, and authorities, the grievance should be sustained in all respects.

The Company

The Company stated that, as a retail distributor of electricity, it employs a labor workforce of skilled and semiskilled employees classified into various jobs, or classifications, to construct, maintain, and operate an overhead distribution system of wires, poles, and attachments that delivers central station–generated electricity to its member-consumer homes, businesses, industries, and service establishments,. The labor classifications include working foremen, linemen, groundmen, truck drivers, mechanics, materialmen, equipment operators, and meter readers. The classified employees are represented by the Union on the terms and conditions of their employment.

For a number of years, the Company and the Union have periodically entered into formal written agreements memorializing the terms on which they have agreed. Historically, the parties in advance of the expiration of their agreements have notified one another in writing of issues they wished to negotiate and have then proceeded to negotiate in one or more face-to-face meetings between Management and Union committees. Such was the procedure that led to the parties entering into the current Collective Bargaining Agreement. The Company stated that the basic issue is the meaning and intent of Section 4, Article 21 dated July 1, 2002.

Mr. Acey is classified as a Line Truck Driver whose duties are prescribed by a Position Description dated October 1, 1995. As a Line Truck Driver, Mr. Acey is not considered a "climbing"

Continued

employee and is not authorized to climb poles using climbing devices attached to the climber's boots. Mr. Acey has never had training as a climber and is not certified as such either by formal training or by on-the-job training.

The Union's position is that every Union member of the bargaining unit, regardless of job classification, is entitled to reimbursement within the total dollar limitation allowed for purchase of specialty lineworkers boots. The Company's position is that the inclusion of lineworker's boots as a covered reimbursement item was negotiated in the Lineworker Climbing Classifications.

The Company explained that in 1994 OSHA issued new standards of work practices for the electricity industry that contained a revision of protective equipment requirements relating to flame-retardant clothing for workers exposed to hazards of flames and electric arcs. In response to this new standard and for the safety of Company employees who would be at risk, the Company instituted a requirement that all of its at-risk employees would wear flame-retardant clothing. The Union at the time requested that the Company participate in the cost of such clothing, but that request was denied. The Union proceeded to grieve such decision and asserted that, under the then-existing Collective Bargaining Agreement, such OSHA-required clothing should be deemed "safety equipment" and, therefore, provided to the bargaining unit at Company expense. The Grievance was denied. The Union did not proceed to arbitration.

In the following months, the Company entered into a voluntary program of renting at its own expense for the classified labor employees pants and shirts in order to meet the OSHA standards, but left it to the employees to furnish their own outerwear such as coveralls, coats, and jackets. In next labor agreement, this safety clothing program was negotiated into the Collective Bargaining Agreement for the renewed period 1996–1999 and simply provided that the Company would pay all the cost of the Company's approved "uniforms." The employees were still required to furnish at their own expense approved flame-retardant outerwear that they might wear over the flame-retardant uniforms.

Uniforms/safety-retardant outerwear continued to evolve as a benefits issue during the 1996–1999 contract term. In the Collective Bargaining Agreement effective for the subsequent period July 1, 1999, through June 20, 2002, the provision at Article 20, Section 4 became a dollar amount for "work clothes" and was thus recited:

> The Company agrees to pay up to $852.40 for each Union member per year for the purchase of work clothes.

In implementing such agreement, the Company in the same time frame adopted a revised Policy Number 3.13, "Uniforms," dated October 28, 1999, which continued to require a flame-retardant "uniform" and flame retardant outerwear to be worn by working foremen, linemen, meter readers, truck drivers, materialmen, and groundmen who were at risk and thus required to comply with the OSHA Safety Standards for flame retardant clothing. The revised Policy reflected the collectively bargained provision that the Company pay 100 percent of the cost of uniforms within a negotiated and agreed reimbursement amount. Thus, "uniforms" and "work clothes" became interchangeable terms denoting the flame-retardant shirts, pants, and outerwear being furnished by the Company. This was the state of the arrangements and agreements between the Union and the Company relative to "work clothes" when negotiations commenced in the Spring of 2002 for the contract renewal term to be effective July 1, 2002. It is in that historical context that negotiations reaching the present contractual provision occurred.

The Company claimed that, in accordance with the provision of Section 1, Article 1 of the 1999–2002 agreement, Mr. Snowden, Assistant Business Manager of the Union, wrote to Mr.

Weebles, CEO/President, on April 26, 2002, giving notice of those provisions that the Union desired to modify or amend in a new agreement to become effective for a new period beginning July 1, 2002. In an attachment to the notice letter, Mr. Snowden listed eight proposals or issues that he desired to add or change and to be the subject of negotiations. By Item 8, the Union sought to expand the annual reimbursement allowance for uniforms, or work clothes, to include "boots and leather gloves." The dollar amount was not sought to be enlarged but only the scope of the items that would be subject to reimbursement.

Over the course of the next several days, Ms. Miranda, in consultation with Mr. Weebles and other senior management, considered the Union's proposals and began to formulate formal responses to those proposals. On May 2, 2002, Ms. Miranda prepared a Company response to Item No. 8 concerning the boots and gloves initiative. Management by that response was willing to add boots and gloves to the annual uniform, or work clothes allowance, but not as the Union wanted. It is apparent that the generic term "work clothes" as contained in the 1999–2002 Agreement was being replaced with items specific, both in keeping with what had been the subject of the allowance in the past and as well what were to be additions. Thus, "flame-retardant uniforms" was to be a specified item for all classifications as before, but as far as boots were concerned, Management was limiting them to linemen or the climbing classifications. The adjective "linemen" was added before boots to limit their application. These contemporaneously recorded documents credibly support and demonstrate the Company's steadfast position on the meaning and intent flowing from the negotiations that took place and the meaning and intent of the parties in the language finally reached in the current Collective Bargaining Agreement. As reflected in a letter written by Ms. Miranda to Mr. Snowden, two days following the May 15, 2002, negotiating session, she summarized the items dropped or agreed at that point. In fact, the clause that is now the subject of this dispute is identical to the Company's counterproposal, with the exception that the word *uniforms* was changed to *clothes* in identifying the continued flame-retardant items of shirts, pants, and outerwear defined in Operating Bulletin 8.12, as had been the historical subject of the reimbursement benefit, and the adjective "lineman" as applied to the new boots was converted to the more politically and Title IV–correct gender-neutral "lineworker" terminology, in keeping with the other gender-neutral terminology being used throughout the agreement.

The Company argued that the first determination to be made is whether or not the clause concerning "linemen's boots" is clear and unambiguous in its meaning. In every contract— labor or otherwise—an essential element of the agreement between the parties is that there be a "meeting of the minds." Arbitrators look to the language of the contract itself to initially determine if the provision is clear and unambiguous, and thus an accurate and understandable expression of where and how the minds of the parties met on the particular subject or provision. However, if there is ambiguity, and thus a plain and reasonable difference of interpretation that can be placed on the words themselves, arbitrators turn to extrinsic evidence to glean an understanding of what the true meaning and interpretation ought to be of the language in dispute. Arbitrators do not formulate a new contract for the parties, but strive to arrive at what the parties intended and the meaning placed on the words they used in an effort to reconcile differences and preserve the subject, if at all possible, from being cast aside because of irreconcilable doubt. Thus, where an ambiguity is found to exist in a Collective Bargaining Agreement, evidence of the bargaining history between the parties can be received to aid in finding the meaning and intent of the particular provision. Basic contract law mandates that contractual provisions be interpreted in the context of the total agreement gleaned from looking at the language of the contract clause, the structure of the contract, the bargaining history, and other

Continued

relevant conduct of the parties. Surrounding circumstances may be considered in determining the meaning of the contract and the intention of the parties, as of the time of entering into the contract, in cases made necessary by reason of ambiguity and uncertainty of the contract language.

The Company concluded that purpose of reducing a labor agreement to writing is to express in understandable terms that the parties have reached and established by their negotiations leading to their settlement. When the words that are put on paper, however, later take on a character of ambiguity whereby one party seeks to take advantage and thwart the meaning of what has been solemnly agreed, then the arbitrator can look to the past history and what was done and said in reaching the agreement in order to understand what was intended and then enforce that intention.

Lineworker boots are the specific subject of this grievance, and there is no doubt that they are not ordinary boots or shoes and footwear for a nonclimbing classification worker. An employee would find little or no incentive to pay the extra money to purchase them out of his own pocket for his everyday common work wear. These boots are specially built and configured to accommodate climbing equipment, and they have a more pronounced heel construction to accommodate the metal cleat. Quite clearly, specialized lineworker boots are not required for a materialman, a meter reader, a mechanic, or a truck driver. The Union's post-contract insistence on an interpretation of the contract clause will mean a materialman in the storehouse or a meter reader will be just as entitled to Company reimbursement for his everyday, non–safety required footwear as the higher-classified, top journeyman lineman, for whom they are designed for rugged work and personal safety. By this grievance, the Union is simply trying to write into the current labor agreement a benefit not agreed to in the negotiations. Essentially to do so will be to rewrite that portion of the contract.

Mr. Acey is classified as a truck driver. He operates a truck and performs groundman duties when working with a line crew and assists a lineman from a ground position. Mr. Acey is not a climbing employee and has no requirement for lineworker boots. It was not contemplated by the parties at the time of entering into the current labor agreement that Mr. Acey would be eligible for reimbursement for his choice of footwear on the job and certainly not those specialized boots used by climbing lineman on the poles, who he would be assisting.

Accordingly, the Company asked that Article 21, Section 4 be interpreted as was intended and that the arbitrator deny this Grievance.

QUESTIONS

1. Is the contract language clear?
2. Of what relevance is the bargaining history in this arbitration?
3. Both parties addressed the role of the arbitrator. Why did each party do so? What is the arbitrator's role?
4. Using the principles used by arbitrators in interpreting contract language, how should you, as the arbitrator, decide? Give your reasoning.

Labor Arbitration Simulation

Basic Objectives

To provide each participant with an opportunity to experience the application of labor arbitration principles and procedures to the resolution of a contract administration (rights) dispute. Such experience will provide participants with greater insight into the labor arbitration process by having them prepare and present the case to an arbitrator (where applicable) who will decide the case.

Specific Objectives

1. To gain an understanding of labor arbitration case preparation, presentation, and the assessment of arbitration outcomes.
2. To develop an appreciation for labor arbitration principles, past practice, contract language, and presentation skills as factors influencing the outcome of arbitration decisions.
3. To gain an understanding of factors affecting the credibility and importance of evidence presented in a labor arbitration case.
4. To develop the ability to critically analyze case facts and to apply appropriate standards as criteria for determining arbitration decisions.
5. To gain an appreciation for the importance of preparation activities in improving the presentation of evidence and the development of reasonable arguments in support of one's position on any issue in dispute.

General Rules and Instructions

1. Divide the participants into teams of 3 to 5 members each and designate each team as either union or management.
2. The individual(s) selected to serve as the neutral, third party arbitrator may be either (a) an outsider (e.g., attorney, professor, arbitrator), (b) the instructor, or (c) a panel of 1 to 5 participants.
3. The role of the arbitrator is to: (1) determine (clarify or seek agreement to) the specific grievance issue to be decided; (2) conduct the arbitration hearing, including ruling on any procedural challenges concerning evidence, order or time limits for each party's presentation, etc.; and (3) issue a final decision (award) accompanied by an explanation of the reasoning behind the decision.
4. The formal arbitration hearing should take between 35 and 50 minutes.
5. After all of the evidence has been presented and the parties have completed their respective closing statements, two options exist for rendering the arbitrator's decision.

   Option 1: The arbitrator will issue an immediate oral decision and discuss the relevant underlying reasons.

   Option 2: The arbitrator will be given 5 to 7 days to provide the parties with a copy of his or her written decision stating the relevant underlying reasons and any supporting evidence, case citations, etc., deemed appropriate by the arbitrator. The arbitrator should be informed prior to the hearing date which option will be used to issue the arbitration award. *Continued*

6. A 15- to 30-minute feedback session should follow the conclusion of the labor arbitration simulation exercise. The purpose of the feedback session is to give participants and observers an opportunity to comment on procedural or substantive aspects of the parties' case preparations and presentations as well as the arbitrator's decision. Relevant arbitration principles and concepts should be emphasized in reviewing the participant's arbitration case experience.

Background Information About the Grievance Dispute

The following information is based on statements and evidence presented by union and management representatives during meetings held to discuss the grievance as provided for under the terms of the parties' agreement. The parties, unable to reach a settlement, have appealed the grievance to arbitration and are currently preparing to present the grievance issue to an arbitrator.

Mr. Jack House, age 44, was employed by the company for 15 years as a lead person in the maintenance department. Other positions within the maintenance department included those of dispatcher, maintenance mechanic, and pipefitter. The maintenance department was responsible for maintaining approximately 100 miles of pipeline used to transport water from the company's mountain reservoir to large commercial farms located in the valley below. The lead person's job was to provide leadership to a four-person crew which maintained different sections of the pipeline system and perform preventive maintenance or repairs if any water leaks were discovered. Maintenance crews spent most of their work hours outdoors exposed to the weather elements such as snow, rain, wind, heat, or cold.

The industrial relations manager for the firm received a letter from Mr. House requesting that he be reassigned to the position of dispatcher within the department for medical reasons. Mr. House stated that he suffered from a form of arthritis that was aggravated by repeated exposure to the elements. The dispatcher job was the only one within the maintenance department that did not require the employee to spend most of the work day outdoors.

The industrial relations manager wrote Mr. House informing him that no current vacancies existed in the dispatcher position and therefore the company could not accommodate his request at that time. The company did agree to allow Mr. House to reduce his daily work hours from 10 hours to 8 hours and no longer required him to perform emergency weekend assignments. Mr. House was requested to provide the company with some verification of his medical handicap.

Several weeks later the company received a letter from Mr. House's personal physician stating that within the past year Mr. House had been diagnosed as suffering from ankylosing spondylitis, a form of arthritis. The doctor suggested that the company accommodate Mr. House's medical condition by placing him in a position that required less outdoor activity.

The company asked Mr. House to undergo a physical examination by a company doctor in order to confirm the diagnosis of his condition. The results of the examination confirmed that Mr. House was suffering from the form of arthritis diagnosed previously by his own doctor. The company doctor agreed that Mr. House should be placed in a job that required less exposure to the weather than his current job assignment.

Approximately 1 year later, a vacancy in the dispatcher job position occurred due to the retirement of Frank Roberts. The company assigned Mr. House to fill the vacant dispatcher position and notified the union of the assignment. The union filed a grievance protesting the company's decision.

Six employees in the maintenance department including Mr. House, were qualified to perform the dispatcher position. Among those six employees, Mr. House had greater seniority within the maintenance department than all but one of the other employees. Randy Garnet, age 52, had been a lead person in the maintenance department 3 years longer than Mr. House and therefore possessed greater seniority. There is no substantial pay difference between the jobs of dispatcher and that of lead person. However, there is a substantial difference in the amount of physical effort required to perform the job duties of the respective positions as well as substantially better working conditions for the dispatcher job because these duties are performed inside whereas the lead person's job duties are performed primarily outside.

The union contends that past practice has been to assign the most senior person in the lead person classification to the position of dispatcher. Accordingly, the company should have offered the position to Mr. Garnet instead of Mr. House.

The company has federal government contracts and is a recipient of federal funds, subjecting it to coverage under the Rehabilitation Act of 1973. This statute prohibits discrimination because of an individual's handicap and requires covered employers to implement an affirmative action plan regarding employment opportunities for handicapped persons. A handicapped individual is one who has a physical or mental disability that constitutes or results in a substantial handicap to employment.

In 1995, the company adopted an affirmative action plan that essentially states that the company will not engage in any discrimination regarding the employment of handicapped persons and will take necessary steps to ensure that handicapped persons are provided with a reasonable opportunity to perform work for which the individual is qualified. The affirmative action plan was adopted unilaterally by the company without negotiation with the union. A notice was placed on the company bulletin board notifying employees of their right to declare themselves as handicapped under the plan and the availability of a copy of the affirmative action plan for inspection by employees or union officials in the Human Resources Management department.

The company considered its assignment of Mr. House to the dispatcher position to be an appropriate action in light of the affirmative action plan for handicapped employees. The local union president stated that she was unaware that the company had an affirmative action plan for handicapped employees. She also stated that in previous contract negotiations the company and union had agreed that the job positions of pipe tester and utility person could be used as work assignments for employees injured on the job and unable to perform their normal job duties. The position of pipe tester had not been filled over the past three years and was vacant at the time Mr. House was assigned to the dispatcher position. Both the job of pipe tester and utility person require job duties to be performed primarily outdoors under varying weather conditions; however, the physical requirements to perform both jobs are considered minimal.

The company has employment records showing that Mr. Goff, a handicapped employee, had worked as a dispatcher with the company for a period of 4 years. Mr. Goff ranked sixth on the seniority list amongst lead persons within the maintenance department. A former employee, Mr. Elton, had held the dispatcher job for 10 years prior to his retirement after suffering a serious on-the-job accident that left him confined to a wheelchair.

Relevant Contract Language

Article 2.

Each employee shall perform work assigned him or her by a supervisor.

Article 5.

Plant seniority is the total length of service accumulated by the employee at the company. Classification seniority is the total length of service accumulated by the employee within each department within the company. *Continued*

Article 6.

Classification seniority shall be used for progression from one job classification to the next or higher job classification. Plant seniority will be used to determine progressions in the Yardperson classification only.

Article 9.

Neither the company nor the union shall discriminate against any employee because of such employee's race, color, religion, age, sex, national origin, because he or she is a disabled veteran, veteran of the Vietnam Era, or qualified handicapped individual to the extent that those classes of persons are protected from discrimination by applicable law, nor against any employee because of membership or non-membership in a labor union.

Instructions for Union and Management Presenters

Each union or management team will be responsible for the following:

1. Reviewing the case background facts provided and performing all activities deemed necessary to prepare an effective arbitration case presentation (e.g., researching prior arbitration awards on the subject, selecting witnesses, rehearsing witnesses' testimony, preparing written evidence, etc.).
2. Presenting its case at the arbitration hearing to include: (a) an opening statement, (b) a presentation of written evidence and oral testimony, and (c) a closing statement (summation).
3. Determining its own intraorganizational structure, including selection of its chief spokesperson at the arbitration hearing, witness roles, assignment of specific tasks (e.g., research, writing a case presentation outline), and ensuring that all assigned tasks are performed satisfactorily.
4. Assume that the arbitrator knows nothing about the grievance dispute prior to the hearing date other than the general subject matter of the dispute. The arbitrator will rely on the parties to present at the hearing any evidence necessary to understand the grievance dispute and draw conclusions about its appropriate resolution. The labor arbitration hearing should take place within the context of the grievance information provided.
5. Carefully consider how to effectively present the information supplied in the case background section to the arbitrator. Creativity should be used in determining what type of information might be useful to support each party's arguments as well as whether to use the direct testimony of witnesses or prepared documents or exhibits to communicate such information. Neither team should attempt to "create" evidence or testimony that is not consistent (plausible) with the fact situation and circumstances provided in the case background. Arbitrators will generally accept as true any statement that is not contradicted by other testimony or evidence and is not inherently unbelievable (i.e., too unlikely or inconsistent with known reality).
6. Deciding prior to the hearing if any limits will be placed on the arbitrator's scope of authority to decide the case or order an appropriate remedy. Any such limitations jointly stipulated by the parties should be communicated to the arbitrator in writing prior to the arbitration hearing date.

Mandatory Employment Arbitration

After graduation and after weeks of pursuing a job, you finally have been offered an opportunity for employment with an excellent company, unlimited opportunity for advancement, and competitive benefits. On your first day of employment, you have been asked to attend an orientation program for all new employees. Along with 15 other new employees, you have observed a 30-minute video of the company, its product line, and prospectus for the future. You have also completed a multitude of employment forms, (e.g., insurance, tax forms, retirement, stock participation, etc.). Among the forms that you have been asked to sign is a copy of the Company Mandatory Employment Arbitration Agreement (similar to the one in Exhibit 11.7). The instructions indicate that this Agreement is a condition of employment with the company and that you must sign the Agreement if you want to work for the company.

Questions

1. Will you sign the Agreement?
2. Are you still excited about your employment opportunities with the company?
3. What are your alternatives?
4. What are the possible consequences?
5. What are the likely possibilities?
6. Have you waived your right to take the company to court in the event that in the future you believe the company has violated your employment rights?

CHAPTER 12

Employee Discipline

W*e devote an entire chapter to employee discipline, an important union–management issue, for the following reasons:*

- *It is the most commonly heard grievance in arbitration, making up approximately 50 percent of the decided cases.*
- *It is approached consistently by arbitrators, who typically rely on established principles to make their determinations.*[1]
- *It is the most likely to involve readers of this book, who are likely to discipline employees in their careers in unionized or nonunionized settings and have that action challenged by the union, government agencies such as the Equal Employment Opportunity Commission (EEOC), and/or the courts.*

Employee discipline is approached in this chapter by discussing its changing significance over time and its various elements, thereby enabling the reader to apply considerations discussed in Chapter 11 to this issue.

The Changing Significance of Industrial Discipline

Employee discipline represents both organizational conditions and actions. Organizational conditions can lead employees to form a disciplined work group that is largely self-regulated and willingly accepts management's directions and behavioral standards. Managerial actions are taken against an employee who has violated organizational rules.[2] This dimension has changed over time.

Historical Overview of Employer Disciplinary Policies

During the 18th and 19th centuries, the employer exercised "uncontrolled discretion" in directing the work crew. Discipline during this time was sometimes harsh. Employees who were verbally insolent to employers could have their tongues burned with a hot iron or be subjected to public humiliation (e.g., a public whipping in the town square).

By 1935, management's total discretion to discipline employees was challenged on pragmatic and legal grounds. Frederick Taylor's theory of *scientific management,* popular by 1920, stressed the financial waste that occurred when employees were discharged in an arbitrary or capricious manner. According to Taylor, management had an obligation to determine and obtain desired employee work behavior and to correct, rather than discharge, the employee who deviated from managerial standards.

The Wagner Act of 1935 legally shaped management's disciplinary policies. A primary feature of this legislation was the prohibition of discriminatory discipline of employees because of their union activities or membership. An independent agency, the National Labor Relations Board (NLRB), was created, in part, for enforcement purposes. Management often had to defend disciplinary actions against charges filed with this agency, with a potential remedy being reinstatement with back pay. This was the first time that management could be legally held accountable for employee discipline, a situation that encouraged further development of corrective disciplinary principles and policies.[3] The NLRB also affected organizational discipline procedures indirectly when it ruled that discipline and grievance procedures were mandatory issues subject to collective bargaining. As a result of this NLRB decision, nearly all existing collective bargaining agreements now have both a provision regulating discipline and a grievance procedure that makes possible the submission of discipline issues to arbitration.

From the 1940s to the present, managerial policies regarding employee discipline were greatly influenced by the growth and development of labor arbitration. Currently, arbitrators have the following three broad powers regarding discipline:

1. To determine what constitutes "just cause" for discipline
2. To establish "standards of proof and evidence"
3. To review and modify or eliminate the penalty imposed by management when warranted

Employment-at-Will Doctrine and Wrongful Discharge Consideration in Nonunion Employees

As indicated in Chapter 1, the number of union members in the workforce is 16.5 million, or 13.9 percent of the workforce, and unions represent another 1.7 million workers who are not members. In other words, nearly 85 percent of the U.S. workforce is not afforded the protection of a union contract or a collectively bargained grievance-arbitration procedure. Most of these nonrepresented employees are "employment-at-will" employees and may be discharged at will.[4]

Under the *public policy exception* to the employment-at-will doctrine, an employee is wrongfully discharged if and when the discharge is inconsistent with an explicit, well-established public policy of the state. As an example, an employer cannot discharge an employee for filing a workers' compensation claim after being injured on the job or refusing to break a law at the direction of the employer. (Forty-four states have made one or more public policy exceptions to the employment-at-will doctrine.)

Exhibit 12.1

Recognition of Employment-at-Will Exceptions, by State

State	Public-policy exception	Implied-contract exception	Covenant of good faith and fair dealing
Total	44	38	10
Alabama	yes	yes	no
Alaska	yes	yes	yes
Arizona	yes	yes	yes
Arkansas	yes	yes	no
California	yes	yes	yes
Colorado	yes	yes	no
Connecticut	yes	yes	no
Delaware	yes	no	yes
District of Columbia	yes	yes	no
Florida	no	no	no
Georgia	no	no	no
Hawaii	yes	yes	no
Idaho	yes	yes	yes
Illinois	yes	yes	no
Indiana	yes	no	no
Iowa	yes	yes	no
Kansas	yes	yes	no
Kentucky	yes	yes	no
Louisiana	no	no	no
Maine	no	yes	no
Maryland	yes	yes	no
Massachusetts	yes	no	yes
Michigan	yes	yes	no
Minnesota	yes	yes	no
Mississippi	yes	yes	no
Missouri	yes	no	no
Montana	yes	no	yes

The *implied contract exception* to the employment-at-will doctrine occurs when an employer and employee form an implied contract even though there is no express, written instrument regarding the employment relationship. For example, an employer may make oral or written representations to employees about job security or procedures that will be followed when adverse actions (discharges) are taken. These representations may create an employment contract. (Thirty-eight states have recognized the implied contract exception to the employment-at-will doctrine.)

The *covenant-of-good faith and fair dealing* exception to the employment-at-will doctrine means that employer personnel decisions are subject to the "just cause" standard, prohibiting terminations made in bad faith or motivated by malice. (Ten states have recognized the covenant-of good faith and fair dealing

Exhibit 12.1

Recognition of Employment-at-Will Exceptions, by State—Cont'd

State	Public-policy exception	Implied-contract exception	Covenant of good faith and fair dealing
Nebraska	no	yes	no
Nevada	yes	yes	yes
New Hampshire	yes	yes	no
New Jersey	yes	yes	no
New Mexico	yes	yes	no
New York	no	yes	no
North Carolina	yes	no	no
North Dakota	yes	yes	no
Ohio	yes	yes	no
Oklahoma	yes	yes	no
Oregon	yes	yes	no
Pennsylvania	yes	no	no
Rhode Island	no	no	no
South Carolina	yes	yes	no
South Dakota	yes	yes	no
Tennessee	yes	yes	no
Texas	yes	no	no
Utah	yes	yes	yes
Vermont	yes	yes	no
Virginia	yes	no	no
Washington	yes	yes	no
West Virginia	yes	yes	no
Wisconsin	yes	yes	no
Wyoming	yes	yes	yes

SOURCE: Charles J. Muhl, "The Employment-at-Will Doctrine: Three Major Exceptions," *Monthly Labor Review* 124 (January 2001), pp. 3–11.

exception to the employment-at-will doctrine.)[7] See Exhibit 12.1 for the listing of states that have exceptions to the employment-at-will doctrine.

A RAND Corp. study has found that employers overestimate potential costs of a wrongful discharge suit and incur indirect costs that are 100 times higher when they attempt to avoid these suits. These indirect costs occur when employers do not terminate employees who perform poorly, establish complex and more costly hiring and decision-making processes, or use severance payments to deter wrongful termination claims.[8]

Present-Day Significance of Discipline

Disciplinary systems are designed to discourage problematic behavior and to quickly correct problems when they are observed. The first-line supervisor is usually the first person to become involved in disciplinary action. The first-line manager usually conducts the initial investigation of the facts surrounding the employee's misconduct. Furthermore, it is usually the first-line supervisor who recommends disciplinary action and has the authority to take disciplinary action. Because certain employee rights must be protected, employers may decide to have an oversight of the supervisor's decisions to discipline and require higher-level approval before disciplinary action is taken. Therefore, it is possible to introduce some level of restriction on managers to protect employee rights without adversely affecting managers' belief in the effectiveness of the disciplinary system.[9]

Management, union officials, and employees at unionized firms are strongly affected by disciplinary actions and arbitrators' decisions concerning disciplinary actions. (See the "Labor Relations in Action" box for potential disciplinary situations that have occurred on an automobile assembly line.) An arbitrator has two typical options in a case involving a discharged employee. The arbitrator can (1) uphold management's discharge decision or (2) reinstate the employee with some or all back pay for wages lost as a result of the employee's forced absence.

Management loses more discipline cases than it wins, as arbitrators follow the second alternative in a majority of their decisions.[10] This loss is advertised when the reinstated employee is brought back to the shop floor. Reinstatement of the employee with back pay represents a financial loss to management, and supervisory authority may also be lost, for it is a rare supervisor who, on experiencing the return of one disciplined employee to his work group with a large back-pay check, will pursue subsequent disciplinary action with as much vigor and initiative.[11]

There is also no guarantee that the reinstated employee will perform well when returned to the job. Two studies have found that 51 to 62 percent of the reinstated employees performed their work in a "below average" capacity, with a majority having subsequent disciplinary problems.[12] Moreover, the seniority of the discharged employee (often considered an influential mitigating circumstance by arbitrators) was insignificant in predicting the employee's performance after reinstatement.[13]

Arbitral reversal of management decisions can also create tensions between different levels of management officials. As noted in Chapter 1, management participants in the labor relations process do not constitute a unified group. The first-line supervisor is often most involved in employee discipline: he or she has typically trained the employee; created past practices in the department that might influence the arbitrator's decision; and witnessed, reported, and in some cases, participated in the events resulting in discipline. The supervisor also directly administers discipline to employees.

Other management officials, such as labor relations representatives, monitor these activities to make sure that supervisory actions are consistent with company policy, reversing them if they are not, to avoid adverse arbitration. This reversal can cause tensions, as indicated in the following remarks of a first-line supervisor:

> I had this one troublemaker. He was a solid goldbricker. He couldn't cut the buck on any job. I tried everything, but he was lazy and he was a loudmouth. I caught him in the toilet after being away from his machine for over an hour. I told him he was through and to go upstairs and pick up his check. And [deleted]. Do you know what those college boys in personnel

LABOR RELATIONS IN ACTION

Disciplinary Possibilities on the Assembly Line

The following excerpts are taken from *Rivethead* (New York: Warner Books, 1992), written by Ben Hamper concerning his work experiences on an automobile manufacturing line. These situations reflect vivid, real-world employees' behaviors that management attempts to correct through disciplinary actions. Unions could claim management's response to each of these actions was inappropriate by filing a grievance that might, in time, be resolved by an arbitrator. The first five considerations involve employees Hamper knew on the line; the remainder of the events were perpetrated by Hamper and co-workers.

- Roy captured a tiny mouse at work and built a home for the rodent. He took care of the mouse until one lunch break when he claimed it was mocking his job performance. He then grabbed the mouse by the tail, took a brazing torch, and "incinerated his little buddy at arm's length."

- Lightnin' had no known job assignment but would spend each workday in the men's washroom leaning up against the last urinal wall, asleep.

- Jack hated the company and thought management was out to get him. One night he claimed that the company purposefully robbed him by not returning cigarettes for cash he placed into a vending machine. He then took a sledgehammer (which he labeled "the Better Business Bureau") and beat the vending machine to a glass and metallic pulp.

- Franklin was a man who took real pleasure in beating up other employees. He snuck up on one employee who refused to give him an extra pair of safety gloves and "smashed him over the head with a door latch." The employee received a dozen stitches in his head, and Franklin received a 30-day suspension.

- Louie peddled half pints of Canadian Club and Black Velvet at the workplace, delivering the alcohol to the customer's work station.

Mr. Hamper also admitted to drinking rather substantially at work. His regular intake included "a forty ouncer at first break, another one at lunch, then . . . a pint or two of whiskey for the last part of the shift."

He and another employee also doubled up on the job, where one employee would perform both jobs, allowing the other employee to sleep in a hiding place. This practice basically gave each employee a 4-hour nap during the work shift. ■

did? He gives them some bull about being sick and weakly and the next day he is sitting on a bench in the department next to mine. He says to me, "Well wise guy you don't count for nothin' around here. Every time I see you, I'm going to call you 'Mr. Nothin'."[14]

What management loses in arbitration hearings appears to be the union's gain. Most if not all union members believe the union should be responsive to problems arising from their day-to-day working conditions that remain after the formal labor agreement has been negotiated. There is no more dramatic example of union concern for its members than "saving" an employee's job. Almost every union newspaper contains at least one article per issue that describes (along with appropriate pictures of union representatives, the grievant, and the back-pay check) how the union successfully defended an employee against an unjust act of management. A representative article from one union newspaper proclaimed in bold headlines, "Worker Wins $5,895 in Back Pay When Fired for Opening Beer Can."[15]

Perhaps a disciplinary action carries the most significance for the affected employee. Discharge has been viewed by many arbitrators as *economic capital punishment*, for it deprives the employee of currently earning a livelihood and at the same time (with the discharge on his or her work record) makes it difficult to find future employment elsewhere. Any form of discipline represents an embarrassment to individuals who do not like being told they are wrong and, in some instances, have to explain their unpaid removal from work to their friends and family.

Elements of the Just Cause Principle in Employee Discipline

Discipline for Just Cause and Discipline's Legitimate Purpose

Arbitrators and government agencies such as the EEOC and the NLRB indicate that employee discipline must be for **just cause, which must meet all of the following criteria**[16]:

1. There is clear and convincing evidence that a disciplinary offense was committed by the grievant.

2. The disciplinary action taken by management was appropriate for the offense committed.

3. The discipline cannot be arbitrary or discriminatory; instead, it must be applied equally to employees given similar circumstances.

Although there is no legal or standard definition of "just cause," arbitrator Harry Platt might have said it best when he wrote:

> It is ordinarily the function of an Arbitrator in interpreting a contract provision which requires "sufficient cause" as a condition precedent to discharge not only to determine whether the employee involved is guilty of wrongdoing . . . but also to safeguard the interests of the discharged employee by making reasonably sure that the causes for discharge were just and equitable and such as would appeal to reasonable and fair-minded persons as warranting discharge. To be sure, no standards exist to aid an Arbitrator in finding a conclusive answer to such a question and, therefore, perhaps the best he can do is to decide what a reasonable man, mindful of the habits and customs of industrial life and of the standards of justice and fair dealing prevalent in the community, ought to have done under similar circumstances and in that light to decide whether the conduct of the discharged employee was defensible and the disciplinary penalty just.[17]

Arbitrators have long held that management has the right to direct the workforce and manage its operations efficiently. Indeed, inefficient operations harm both the employer and employees because subsequent reduced profits can result in employee layoffs. Discipline can improve efficiency by accomplishing the following interrelated purposes:

- *To set an example of appropriate behavior.* For example, management impresses on its employees the seriousness of being tardy by giving one tardy employee a five-day suspension.

- *To transmit rules of the organization.* As illustrated in the preceding purpose, management has transmitted a rule of the organization—lateness will not be accepted.

- *To promote efficient production.* Discipline those employees who either cannot or will not meet production standards.

- *To maintain respect for the supervisor.* In a sense, discipline shows the employee who is the boss. A supervisor who does not discipline poor employees weakens managerial authority.

- *To correct an employee's behavior.* Indicate what is expected, how the employee can improve, and what negative consequences might result in the future if the behavior does not change. The assumption here is that most employees have good intentions and will improve if management will simply show them the error of their ways.

Discipline can accomplish all these purposes, but arbitrators must be convinced that management based its action on "correction," which is discipline's only legitimate purpose. Because discharge is a terminal rather than a corrective action, it is appropriate only when all other attempts at correction have failed or the nature of the offense is so heinous as to make lesser forms of discipline inappropriate. Correction permeates the elements of the just cause principle of employee discipline as shown in Exhibit 12.2,[18] which is a guide for management in employee disciplinary cases.

Degree of Proof in Disciplinary Cases: Nature of the Evidence and Witness Credibility

An overriding consideration in discipline and discharge cases is management's burden of proof to establish that the employee committed an infraction. Such proof is easier to establish in situations having objectively measured indicators (e.g., absenteeism and related attendance records) than those that do not (e.g., insubordination).[19]

Subjective standards can also apply to other employee infractions. For example, one arbitrator contends that a major difference exists between "nodding off" (eyes closed, head nodding lower and lower, jerking up, and then nodding again) and "sleeping on the job," because the former condition, if successfully fought by the person, "would lead to completely restored wakefulness."[20]

Arbitrators use three levels of proof. The most often used level of proof by arbitrators is **preponderance of evidence,** wherein testimony and evidence must be adequate to overcome opposing presumptions and evidence. The second, **clear and convincing evidence,** is shown where the truth of the facts asserted is

Exhibit 12.2

Seven Tests for "Just Cause" Employee Terminations

(If the answer is "no" to one or more of the following questions, just cause for termination is not present or is seriously weakened.

1. *Notice.* Did the employer give to the employee forewarning or foreknowledge of the possible or probable consequences of the employee's disciplinary conduct?

   If no, the grievance is sustained.

2. *Reasonable rule or order.* Was the employer's rule or managerial order reasonably related to (a) orderly, efficient, and safe operation of the employer's business, and (b) performance that the employer might properly expect of the employee?

   If no, the grievance is sustained.

3. *Investigation.* Did the employer, before administering the discipline to an employee, make an effort to discover whether the employee did in fact violate or disobey a rule or order of management?

   If no, the grievance is sustained.

4. *Fair investigation.* Was the employer's investigation conducted in a fair and objective manner?

   If no, the grievance is sustained.

5. *Proof.* At the investigation, did the decision maker posses substantial evidence or proof that the employee was guilty as charged?

   If no, the grievance is sustained.

6. *Equal treatment.* Has the employer applied its rules, orders, and penalties even-handedly and without discrimination to all employees?

   If no, the grievance is sustained.

7. *Penalty.* Was the degree of discipline administered by the employer in a particular case reasonably related to the seriousness of the employee's proven offense?

   If no, the grievance is sustained.

If the answers to the questions above are YES, then additional questions are considered in determining the degree of penalty:

1. Are there any due process procedural violations of the employee's rights, such as failure to give notice of charges, not allowing the employee to face his/her accusers, or lack of counsel.

2. Are there any mitigating circumstances, such as a record of long-term service with the employer or fault on the part of management which may result in a penalty less than termination, such as reinstatement without back pay?

Source: Adapted from *Enterprise Wire Co. and Enterprise Independent Union*, 46 LA 359, 1996 (Carroll R. Daugherty). Also see: Adolph M. Koven and Susan L. Smith, *Just Cause The Seven Tests*, revised by Donald F. Farwell (Washington, D. C.: Bureau of National Affairs, 1992); Jack Dunsford, "Arbitral Discretion: The Tests for Just Cause," *Proceedings of the 42nd Annual Meeting of the National Academy of Arbitrators* (Washington, D. C.: Bureau of National Affairs).

highly probable. The third, **beyond a reasonable doubt,** represents a higher degree of proof, which some arbitrators use in "criminal" cases, such as selling illegal drugs on company property (e.g., selling illegal drugs on company property, or stealing) that can more adversely affect the grievant's chances of finding subsequent employment. Some believe that this level of proof is extraordinarily high and should not be used in arbitration because the level of proof used in NLRB and unemployment insurance cases do not require this level in theft cases.[21]

Another problem can occur when management uncovers the evidence while using search-and-seizure techniques. Few arbitrators deny the employer's right to impose, as a condition of employment, an inspection of the employee's clothes and packages on entering and leaving the plant; however, a problem arises when company officials search an employee's locker or, in some cases, home, with or without the employee's permission. Many arbitrators (and the Supreme Court in *Dennis M. O'Conner* v. *Mango Ortega*) permit evidence obtained without the employee's knowledge if it is from company property, even if the property (such as a locker or tool chest) is momentarily under the control of the employee. On the other hand, few, if any, arbitrators believe evidence should be accepted if management obtained the evidence by forcibly breaking into the employee's personal property, even if the property is located on company premises.

Arbitrators often have to assess witnesses' testimony in a discipline case. These individuals are deemed "credible" if they had neither motive for an incorrect version (e.g., personal bias against the grievant) nor physical infirmity (e.g., poor hearing).[22] Yet one arbitrator notes:

> It is simply impossible to tell by observation if someone is lying under oath. You cannot tell by looking at and listening to the person. A trial judge in Chicago once compiled a list of tests to see if a witness is telling the truth: does he perspire; lick his lips; fidget in his seat; is he shifty-eyed? From my experience as an arbitrator, I can tell you that shifty-eyed people often tell the truth, while most honest-looking people will lead you by the nose right down the primrose path.[23]

Documented and credible evidence is a necessary but not sufficient disciplinary element because other elements (as shown in Exhibit 12.2) have to be established to the arbitrator's satisfaction.

Effect of Work Rules on Discipline

Management's right to establish (even without initially advising the union) and administer work rules is generally acknowledged as fundamental to efficient plant operations. Yet managerial administration of work rules also assumes some fundamental responsibilities and obligations that, if not followed, may affect management's disciplinary efforts.

A first question that arises is, what happens if management has no rule governing the alleged offense committed by the employee? Such an event is not uncommon because employers cannot possibly anticipate the endless variety of employee misbehaviors. Arbitrators, for example, have upheld the discharges of employees who have done the following:

- Watched a fire develop and destroy a portion of a company over a lengthy period without notifying the company[24]

- Called management officials in the early morning hours to belch over the telephone[25]

- Urinated on the floor of a delivery truck even though there were restroom facilities nearby

- "Streaked" (ran naked) through a portion of an airport[26]

Needless to say, management had no previously established work rules covering these behaviors. Arbitrators have also upheld management's right to discipline employees for those offenses that are commonly regarded as unwritten laws—prohibitions against stealing or striking a supervisor, for example.

However, in most disciplinary situations, particularly those cases that are somewhat common in industry (poor performance, absenteeism, insubordination, and so forth), management is on weak ground with the arbitrator when it does not have established work rules. Furthermore, written work rules must be *reasonable* and *clear* and *state the consequences of their violation.* Reasonable rules are related to the orderly, efficient, and safe operation of the employer's business and the performance that the employer might properly expect of the employee. Unions will contend a rule is unreasonable if it is unrelated to business operations or outweighed by the employee's personal rights on and off the job.

Determining a rule's reasonableness can be complicated. For example, some arbitrators view a unilateral rule prohibiting smoking as "reasonable," particularly if management presents evidence that nonsmoking employees can be harmed by being exposed to secondhand smoke. However, other arbitrators regard a no-smoking rule to be unreasonable, particularly if a clear past practice has permitted this activity.[27] The reasonableness of an industrial work rule can vary according to industrial or company differences. A unilateral ban on moonlighting (working a second shift with another employer) is regarded as reasonable in the utility industry, which often needs emergency work performed during off shifts. Other industries not having emergency-related concerns might have a difficult time establishing the appropriateness of this rule.[28] Rule reasonableness can also vary within an industrial production facility. For example, an employer might reasonably require a longhaired employee working in the cafeteria to wear a hair net (for sanitary reasons); it would be unreasonable to request the same compliance if the employee worked in the shipping department. Further complications regarding rule reasonableness can occur when an employee is disciplined for off-the-job conduct. At first glance, this infraction would not appear to be job related; however, discipline would be appropriate if management establishes that it adversely affected the employer (e.g., damaged its reputation or standing in the community).[29]

The clarity of a work rule is also an important issue in corrective discipline because employees cannot adequately perform or correct behavior if they do not know what is expected. Management officials can create a problem when they discipline employees for infractions of a vague or confusing work rule, such as discharge for "gambling on company premises," or "falsifying an employment application." These rules may, at first glance, appear clear and conclusive; however, their vagueness becomes apparent to the first-time supervisor who tries to enforce them. "Gambling" poses a managerial problem, particularly if employees are disciplined for participating in a card game on company premises while a management representative is sponsoring a World Series pool with hourly employee participants. Also, does gambling occur when employees are playing cards during their lunch break for matches or a numerical score that management (perhaps correctly) assumes will be converted into cash payments once the employees are off the company premises?

In another example of a vague work rule, does omitting application information constitute "falsification?" Some arbitrators would say yes, particularly if the omissions are numerous and job related. Other arbitrators maintain that "falsification" involves a definite response and might not accept discharge, much less discipline, of the employee if management did not promptly seek an explanation for any blank application items.[30]

The existence of work rules carries the implicit if not explicit obligation for management to inform its employees of the rules and the consequences of their violation. Sometimes an employee disciplined for violating a rule contends that he or she was unaware of the directive. Management then usually has the difficult task of proving otherwise. Some arbitrators have even suggested that a card signed by an employee indicating he or she had read the rules is insufficient because it is signed in haste as part of the employee's orientation, and the signed card does not indicate that management has explained each rule to the employee, allowing time for questions. Many times management indicates in rules or warnings that an employee's continued misconduct could be "subject to dismissal." However, arbitrators regard this term as carrying the potential for lesser penalties such as written warnings or suspensions.

Finally, management must administer the rules consistently for those employees violating the rules under similar circumstances. Management will likely have its disciplinary action reduced or eliminated by the arbitrator if the union establishes that the employer was inconsistent or lax in enforcing the rule for the same misconduct on previous occasions or gave different penalties to employees who were involved in the misconduct.[31] Problems can also occur if management did not take different circumstances into account. In one case management stressed its consistent anti-horseplay approach by indicating that it had discharged not only the grievant in the current situation but also another employee who engaged in horseplay in the past. The arbitrator overturned management's action, however, noting that the horseplay committed in this case was far less serious than in the previous situation, where another employee placed razor blades in a doughnut.[32]

In assessing the degree of consistency, arbitrators place particular emphasis on past practice, which refers to the customary way similar disciplinary offenses are handled and penalized. Some organizations seek to impose consistent discipline by including a **price list** in the labor agreement; it cites specific rules and furnishes uniform penalties for single or repeated violations (Exhibit 12.3). This form of rule making has advantages: (1) the employee is clearly informed of the specific rules and consequences of violations, (2) the standardized penalties suggest consistent disciplinary action is implemented, and (3) if agreed to by the union, the price list assumes more legitimacy than a unilateral work rule posted by management. However, some individuals contend that the price list represents a mechanical imposition of discipline that runs counter to the corrective philosophy because it does not consider each case on its own. Say, for example, management finds two employees fighting—one a short-term employee, the other a long-term employee with a fine work record. According to the price-list approach, management is obligated to discharge both employees; yet it is likely that the arbitrator will reinstate the senior employee who has an excellent performance record and who would typically respond to corrective measures to retain job seniority investments.

Progressive Discipline

Progressive discipline refers to increasingly severe penalties corresponding to repeated identical offenses committed by an employee. It relates to correction in at least two ways: (1) by impressing on the employee the seriousness of repeated

EXHIBIT 12.3

Example of a Disciplinary Price List

Type of Offense	First Offense	Second Offense	Third Offense	Fourth Offense	Fifth Offense
1. Abusive language toward a supervisor	3-day suspension	Discharge			
2. Failure to punch in and out on time clock	Oral warning	Written suspension	3-day suspension	5-day suspension	Discharge
3. Failure to report an absence	Oral warning	Written suspension	3-day suspension	5-day suspension	Discharge
4. Stealing company property	Discharge				
5. Sleeping on the job	Written warning	3-day suspension	5-day suspension	Discharge	
6. Damage of company equipment	Written warning	3-day suspension	5-day suspension	Discharge	
7. Gambling or engaging in a lottery on company premises	5-day suspension	Discharge			
8. Striking a supervisor	Discharge				

rule infractions and (2) by furnishing the employee additional chances to correct his or her behavior before applying the ultimate penalty of discharge. Management might have to give an oral warning, a written warning, and at least one suspension before it can discharge an employee for repeatedly committing a similar offense, such as failure to wear safety equipment, poor attendance, or ineffective performance.

An oral warning represents an informal effort to correct and improve the employee's work performance. The informality of this reprimand is for corrective training purposes; however, the oral warning can be prejudicial to the employee if it is entered as evidence in arbitration hearings. This disciplinary action, however, is subject to the following employee defenses: (1) the employee might have thought the supervisor's remarks were instructional and been unaware of the disciplinary aspects or consequences of the warning, and (2) an oral warning given in private can lead to conflicting testimony—the employee can state that the supervisor never gave an oral warning. However, because of its relative harmlessness, the union seldom contests this form of discipline.

A **written warning** is a more serious matter because it summarizes previous oral attempts to correct the employee's behavior and is entered in the employee's work record file. More official than an oral reprimand, it brings disciplinary actions into focus by warning the employee of future consequences of rule violation.

A **suspension** is a disciplinary layoff without pay given by management to impress on the employee the seriousness of the offense. Oral and written reprimands might also achieve this purpose, but they do not involve a financial sacrifice by the employee. A suspension serves as an example of the economic consequences associated with discharge and at the same time indicates that management is willing to retain the employee if he or she will comply with directives and change errant ways. Management initially imposes a mild suspension (1 to 3 days) and will seldom impose a suspension greater than 10 days for a repeated offense. Under these circumstances, arbitrators are reluctant to reduce the suspensions unless it can be shown that other employees were given lesser penalties for identical offenses under similar circumstances.

Discharge, unlike suspension or warnings, is not a corrective measure because it means the employee is permanently removed from the company. As mentioned earlier, arbitrators have attached tremendous significance to the effects of discharge on the employee, regarding it as a last resort to be used when all other corrective attempts have failed and the employee totally lacks usefulness to the firm. An exception to this procedure occurs when the nature of the offense is so heinous (stealing, striking a supervisor, setting fire to company property) as to make other forms of corrective discipline inappropriate.

Progressive discipline also implies a *statute of limitations.* For example, it would be difficult to discharge an employee who has previously received two suspensions for failing to report an absence to management if the worker has worked for a fairly long time (say, three to five years) before committing a similar present offense. Management is usually not obligated to return to the first step, that is, an oral warning; however, discharge is not warranted—the employee's offense-free period indicates that corrective measures did have some effect and should be tried again before separating the employee from the firm. Some unions have been able to negotiate clauses which erase earlier disciplinary actions after a certain period of time (e.g., first action is erased if no other incident in two years).

A discipline price list does not take the statute of limitations into account—its penalties are for repeated infractions regardless of the intervening period. In these circumstances, should management negate its own price list by returning to a suspension even though discharge is the next step in the procedure? Or should it proceed with the discharge, knowing that many arbitrators, employing a statute of limitations, would reinstate the employee because of the period between his or her previous and recent offenses? Both courses of action have risks: In the first case, management might establish precedent that can adversely affect other cases; in the second, management might appear arbitrary in its discipline administration.

Last Chance Agreements   After the company gathers sufficient evidence to justify a "just cause" discharge and before issuing the removal notice, the union and the company may agree on a last chance agreement (Exhibit 12.4).

A **last chance agreement** is a negotiated written agreement signed by an employer, union, and employee whose conduct has been determined to be unacceptable. Its purpose is to settle a grievance over an employee's termination and to hold the removal in abeyance. It sets strict conditions for continued employment in return for the employer's agreement not to discharge the employee immediately. Because these types of cases are usually performance related (such as poor performance, excessive absences, being under the influence of illegal drugs), one goal of the last chance agreement is to rehabilitate the employee and

Exhibit 12.4

Last Chance Agreement

1. I understand and voluntarily agree that my continued employment by the company is based upon and constrained by the following terms:
2. I accept admission to the Employee Assistance Program and/or an accredited rehabilitation program as approved or recommended by the EAP.
3. As a condition of my continued employment, I will comply with all of the rehabilitation program's requirements to their successful conclusion. This includes but is not limited to attendance at all required meetings.
4. I recognize that my reinstatement may require participation of my spouse and adult children in my recovery program if so directed by the EAP.
5. I understand that my previous conduct/job performance warrants close supervision upon my return to work and will accept such supervision as a constructive part of my recovery and also give my consent to searches of my person or any property under my control or in my possession.
6. I understand that upon return to the workplace I must meet all established standards of conduct and job performance and that I will be subject to the Company's disciplinary procedures for any failure to meet the standards. If discharge is determined to be the appropriate penalty for any failure to meet the standards of conduct and job performance by the Company, I specifically acknowledge and agree that the Company need not satisfy the "cause" standard set forth in the collective bargaining agreement between the Company and the Union (if applicable to me) as applicable to other bargaining unit employees of the Company.
7. I agree to submit to alcohol/drug tests at any time the Company requests during the life of this Agreement.
8. I agree to waive my right to work overtime should I have a rehabilitation meeting scheduled that would be in conflict with the overtime assignment. Also, I understand that I may have to waive all overtime if my EAP counselor determines that in order to accomplish rehabilitation goals my hours of work should be limited, and I agree to comply with any request by the EAP counselor to do so.
9. I understand that I will be subject to the terms of this rehabilitation agreement until I have completed at least twenty-four (24) months of work following my return without further incidents of the conduct that led to this agreement (drug and/or alcohol use or job performance).
10. I agree that this constitutes my final opportunity for treatment and rehabilitation while employed by the Company. I further agree that any future alcohol or drug problem, positive drug and/or alcohol test (an alcohol test is positive if the level is equal to or greater than 0.02G/210L), refusal to be tested, or sample alteration will result in my immediate termination even though such may occur after the expiration of this agreement. I do understand what constitutes a positive alcohol/drug test.
11. I authorize and direct the Employee Assistance Provider, Substance Abuse Rehabilitation Provider and all other Health Care and Insurance Providers to release to my Employer all information concerning my assessment, participation, attendance, progress and any other information or records that may relate to my evaluation and rehabilitation, and I release and hold harmless such providers and the Company for any employment actions resulting from the release of such information.
12. I understand and agree that my reinstatement and continued employment are contingent upon my meeting satisfactorily all of the above, and that my failure to fulfill each and every provision of the Agreement relinquishes all defense on my part and subjects me, without recourse, to the immediate termination of my employment with the Company. If pursued through the grievance procedure established under the collective bargaining agreement (if applicable) to arbitration, the Arbitrator can only decide if this Agreement was violated. If this Agreement was violated, then the discharge must stand. If I am not subject to the terms of the collective bargaining agreement, I acknowledge and agree that I have no right to appeal a termination decision.

_____

Employee Signature

_____

Company Representative Signature

_____

Union Representative Signature

provide an opportunity for the company to keep an employee who has skills and training that cannot be easily replaced and for the union to save the job of one of its members. A successful last chance agreement tends to use shock value to motivate an errant employee to rehabilitate himself or herself. If the employee violates the last chance agreement, progressive discipline is not used. If the discharge is appealed to arbitration, the arbitrator is generally limited to determining whether the last chance agreement was valid and also whether the terms of the agreement were violated.[33]

One study in one plant over a 15-year period revealed that use of last chance agreements were effective in a majority of cases. Most employees who signed last chance agreements and were returned to work became effective, rule-abiding employees, at least in the short term. Because the discharged employee would have been costly to replace and there is no guarantee that the replacement will be equal in performance to the rescued employee, the last chance agreement strategy appears to be justifiable to the employee, the employer, and the union.[34]

Disciplinary Penalty and Mitigating Circumstances

Arbitrators will determine whether management was correct in assigning a particular disciplinary penalty for an employee found guilty of an infraction. In making this determination, arbitrators use several arbitral principles that have been developed over the years for considering management's discharge decisions (see "Labor Relations in Action" box for examples of typical cases). Arbitrators often consider **mitigating circumstances, which might reduce management's assigned penalty** (e.g., from a discharge to a suspension), based on one of three assumptions:

1. Management contributed to a problem and must therefore assume part of the responsibility for the wrongdoing.

2. The circumstances of the case were so unusual as to give great doubt that it will occur again, particularly if management uses corrective techniques instead of discharge.

3. Personal factors (such as marital, financial, or substance abuse problems) caused a stressed or troubled employee to perform the disciplinary incident (e.g., absenteeism, poor work performance, or insubordination). Therefore, the employee will not continue these infractions once his or her personal problems are identified and resolved.

An example of mitigating circumstances under the first arbitral assumption occurs when management has provided the employee with faulty tools and equipment and subsequently disciplines the employee for low production output. A more common example of mitigating circumstances occurs when a management representative provokes the employee into committing physical or verbal abuse. In a representative discharge grievance, an arbitrator reinstated an employee who was discharged for striking his supervisor after he found out that the supervisor was asking other employees questions regarding his wife's fidelity.[35]

Management might also contribute to a disciplinary infraction by condoning, either openly or tacitly, offenses committed in the shop. Related examples include supervisors observing employees engaged in horseplay without attempting

LABOR RELATIONS IN ACTION

Examples of Employee Misconduct and Mitigating Factors to Consider in Employee Discipline

Abusive behavior (a form of insubordination) occurs when an employee directs profanity, epithets, or verbal abuse toward a supervisor. Employee's defense has included (1) no intent of hostility or anger, (2) provocation from the supervisor, and (3) words used were "shop talk" which were frequently used in the department.[a]

Aggression toward supervisors includes verbal and physical abuse by subordinates that demean supervisors, undermine their authority, induce fear, and cause injuries. Reasons for setting aside employer-imposed discipline are severity of the infraction; provocation by the supervisor; the grievant's status, such as mental condition; employee's work history and seniority; lack of convincing evidence that the disciplinable offense occurred; and breach of contractual or due process requirements.[b]

Alcohol-related discipline occurs when an employee consumes alcohol on the job, possesses alcohol on the job, or reports to work under the influence of alcohol. Issues may involve whether there exists a "reasonable suspicion" that the employee was under the influence of alcohol, the employee refused to submit to an alcohol test, the employee failed the alcohol test, the employee was found drinking on the job or possessed alcohol on the job, or consumed alcohol off the job then reported to work under the influence of alcohol. Another consideration may be the existence of a last chance agreement that contains conditions with which the employee must comply in order to continue employment, such as testing without warning, participation in rehabilitation program, etc.[c]

Falsification of employment application occurs when an applicant writes incorrect information on an application for employment. Arbitrators consider a four-part test: was the misrepresentation willful?; was it material to the decision to hire?; was it material to the employer at the time of discharge?; did the employer act promptly and in good faith when it discovered the misrepresentation? Mitigating circumstances include the following: the employee did not understand the question or made an honest mistake; lack of connection (nexus) between the answer given and the employee's ability to perform the job; the employee had worked successfully over a year, and the employer did not act promptly when the misrepresentation was discovered.[d]

Fighting on the job occurs when one employee physically attacks another employee on the job. Although prohibitions against fighting in the workplace are considered a legitimate employer interest because employers are obligated to provide employees with a safe working environment, reasons for modification of penalties include the following: employee was provoked by another employee, employee was a victim of another employee's violent act, penalty was too severe given the nature of the fight, management in some way contributed to the problem that caused the fight, or the grievant had a long-term service record without discipline.[e]

Insubordination is the refusal of an employee to work or follow an order given by a supervisor. The employee is to obey now and grieve later. There are several qualifications: the employee's act must be knowing, willing, and deliberate; the order must be explicit and clearly given so that the employee understands its meaning and intent; the order must be work related and reasonable; the order must be given by someone with appropriate authority; the employee must be made aware of the consequences of failure to follow the supervisor's directive. Exceptions include: an employee is not obligated to follow an order that threatens the employee's health or safety or to engage in illegal or immoral behavior; employee refusal to participate in an investigative interview in the absence of a union representative after the employee has exercised his or her *Weingarten* rights.[f]

Refusal to work overtime occurs when an employee is scheduled to work overtime or the employee is required to work overtime because of skill requirements, emergencies, short-term labor demands, or interdependencies of operations and then the employee refuses to work. Penalties may be reduced or overturned when there is no warning of the consequences of the overtime refusal, order to work overtime was not clearly given, lack of proper notice, failure to apply progressive discipline, no previous discipline, or employee offered reasonable excuse for not working overtime.[g]

Sexual harassment misconduct occurs when one employee creates a hostile work environment for another employee or other employees. Arbitrators evaluate the degree to which the alleged misconduct is severe and/or pervasive, and the degree of discipline follows the Seven Tests of Just Cause[h] in Exhibit 12.2 on page 560.

Striker misconduct occurs when violence is directed toward strikebreakers or when strikers cause damage to nonstrikers' property or the employer's property. Factors that may modify the penalty include the following: the employee actions were not exceptionally vicious or willfully malicious; the grievant engaged in a single incident, not multiple incidents of physical violence; no damage was done to the employer-employee relationship; there was provocation to cause the misconduct; disparate or discriminatory treatment had occurred; and the employee has a long service or good work record.[i]

Tardiness occurs when an employee is late for work, is not ready for work at the starting time, or is not at his or her work station at the scheduled starting time. Factors considered in determining the degree of discipline are the definition of tardiness, the number of tardies and the period of time over which the tardies occurred, and the appropriateness of the penalty under the circumstances.[j] ■

SOURCES:
[a]Stanley J. Schwartz, "Insubordination: A Cardinal Sin in the Workplace," *Labor Law Journal* 48 (December 1993), pp. 756–770.
[b]Margaret A. Lucero and Robert E. Allen, "Aggression against Supervisors," *Dispute Resolution Journal* 53 (February 1998), pp. 57–63.
[c]Donald J. Petersen, "Arbitration of Alcohol Cases," *Journal of Collective Negotiations in the Public Sector,* 29, no. 3 (2000), pp. 175–193.
[d]Donald J. Petersen, "Trends in Arbitrating Falsification of Employment Application Forms," *Arbitration Journal* 47 (September 1992), pp. 36–37.
[e]Margaret A. Lucero and Robert E. Allen, "Fighting on the Job: Analysis of Recent Arbitration Decisions," *Dispute Resolution Journal* 5 (August 1998), pp. 51–57.
[f]*Discipline and Discharge in Arbitration,* ed., Norman Brand (Washington, D.C.: Bureau of National Affairs, 1998), pp. 156–161.
[g]Donald J. Petersen, "Arbitration of Employee Refusal to Work Overtime," *Dispute Resolution Journal* 52 (January 1997), pp. 21–27.
[h]Mollie H. Bowers, W. Sue Reddick, and E. Patrick McDermott, "Just Cause in the Arbitration of Sexual Harassment Cases," *Dispute Resolution Journal* 55 (November 2000/January 2001), pp. 40–85.
[i]Donald J. Petersen, "Arbitrating Cases of Employee Misconduct in Work Stoppages." *Dispute Resolution Journal* 5 (February 1998), pp. 44–52.
[j]Donald J. Petersen, "The Arbitration of Tardiness Cases," *Journal of Collective Negotiations in the Public Sector* 29, no. 2 (2000), pp. 167–174.

to stop the situation and subsequently disciplining employees for the action, and supervisors encouraging employees to violate quality standards in the name of production efficiency.

A thorough discussion of the numerous mitigating circumstances suggested by the second arbitral assumption regarding unusual circumstances is beyond the scope of this chapter, but the following example is illustrative: An employee has been repeatedly warned and suspended for failure to report his absence to management when he is unable to work a production shift; at the last suspension the grievant was informed that another infraction would result in discharge. One month after suspension the employee again failed to report his absence to management and was discharged when he reported to work the following morning. The employee contended (and added evidence in the form of a doctor's slip) that his wife became suddenly and seriously ill and that his concern for his wife, coupled with no telephone in the apartment, resulted in his failure to report his absence to management. Here, management has followed all the principles of progressive discipline; however, the employee's discharge might be set aside if the arbitrator concludes that the circumstances were so unusual as to give management no reason to think it will happen again in the future.

Arbitrators often consider the mitigating effects of the grievant's role as a union officer. Compared with other employees, union officials usually have special rights and privileges, particularly when conducting union business. Many arbitrators regard the union steward and foreman as organizational equals in discussion of union matters. Arbitrators therefore give the union steward leeway if harsh words are exchanged in these meetings, whereas other employees might be successfully charged with insubordination for identical actions.

Union officers can also have greater responsibilities that correspond to their rights. For example, arbitrators and the NLRB have upheld more serious disciplinary action for union officers who failed to prevent a wildcat strike than for employees who actually participated in the strike. This differential penalty implies that union stewards should be more knowledgeable about contractual prohibition against a wildcat strike and thus should uphold their contractual obligation to maintain uninterrupted production during the term of the labor agreement.

Perhaps the most commonly considered mitigating circumstance in discharge cases is the employee's work record. An arbitrator will likely consider reinstating a discharged employee who violated a work rule (e.g., one that prohibits insubordination) if that employee has a long and good work record with the company. The arbitrator in this situation realizes the potential of the employee returning to previous work habits, so he or she might reinstate the employee with no back pay, which would represent a suspension. One study has shown that discharges of grievants with little seniority (less than 2 years' service with the organization) are more likely to be upheld than discharges of grievants having more than 11 years of service.[36]

The most complicated and controversial mitigating circumstances are found in the troubled employee assumption. Many management officials contend that arbitrators exceed their authority to interpret the labor agreement in these discipline cases and instead assume the roles of clergymen, psychiatrists, and medical doctors in indicating that management has an obligation to nurture these employees even though this is not required by the contract language. One arbitrator acknowledged that he and some of his peers have addressed one troubled employee issue, alcohol abuse, with little medical or scientific foundation:

> Curiously, published arbitral decisions involving alcohol abuse rarely distinguish between social drinking, heavy drinking, and alcoholism—distinctions that are crucial in the mental health field. Moreover, although hundreds of arbitration decisions have adopted the popular view that alcoholism is a "disease" that involves "loss of control" over drinking, I am unaware of any decisions (including my own) that express an understanding of what arbitrators actually mean when they call alcoholism a "disease." Even in the literature of arbitration, there is little recognition of whether alcoholism is a medical disease, a social disorder, or some complex combination, and whether it has a natural progression and a unitary etiology.[37]

Application of the Just Cause Standard   In general, the arbitrator has the responsibility in discipline cases to determine whether an employer has applied the just cause standard. Just cause is generally considered a universal standard by which to evaluate an employer's disciplinary action. In almost 50 percent of all discipline and discharge arbitration cases, arbitrators have reversed or modified the employer's disciplinary action for failing to meet four just cause standards. Of those, the reasons were:

- 20 percent for failure to conduct a full and fair investigation of the employee's misconduct that yielded supporting evidence of the misconduct charge

- 20 percent for mitigating circumstances, such as the grievant had a lengthy and unblemished past disciplinary record

- 16 percent for arbitrary, capricious, discriminatory, or disparate treatment, which means the employer did not act evenhandedly and uniformly in determining the discipline

- 14 percent for improper administration of the employer's rules and requirements, which includes failure to inform an employee of applicable standards, lack of reasonableness in rules and job requirements, and lax enforcement of standards

Arbitrators have reversed the employer's disciplinary action because of failure to provide due process standards in 15 percent of disciplinary cases. Due process and procedural errors committed by employers include failure to follow progressive disciplinary procedures, failure to adhere to contractual notice requirements, denial of representation rights, excessive delay in imposing penalty, and failure to provide a formal charge of wrongdoing.[38]

Possible Collision between Discharge Decisions and Public Policy   As a general rule in arbitration of disciplinary cases, the parties depend on the finality of the arbitrator's decision. If the employer proves just cause for its disciplinary action, the arbitrator upholds the employer's disciplinary action. If the employer fails to prove just cause, the employee is returned to the workplace with an appropriate make-whole remedy. In disciplinary cases involving just cause determinations on sexual harassment charges, the finality of the arbitrator's decision becomes more complicated. After an alleged sexual harasser is disciplined and files a grievance, he is subject to the traditional application of the just cause principles whereby the grievant would be entitled to a due process hearing with the presumption of innocence. Furthermore, the arbitrator may consider the severity of the conduct, the employee's work and discipline record, length of service, potential for rehabilitation, proper investigation of the matter, and mitigating circumstances. However, courts may vacate an arbitrator's decision if the decision contravenes a significant public policy. Therefore, a court may vacate an arbitrator's decision if the court finds that an employee had engaged in illegal sexual harassment activities on the job.[39]

Due Process and the Weingarten Decision

Due process has both substantive and procedural aspects. Substantive due process focuses on the purpose or rationale of the work rules to ensure that an employee has not been arbitrarily disciplined or discharged. This aspect is reflected in the previously discussed purposes and elements of discipline. Procedural aspects of due process are usually covered in labor agreements and include the following:

1. The discipline process will follow certain time limits specified in the labor agreement.
2. The employee will be entitled to union representation when discipline is being administered and be given an opportunity to respond (defend himself or herself).
3. The employee will be notified of the specific offense in writing.

The due process procedure of union representation has been influenced by NLRB decisions and by the Supreme Court in its *Weingarten* decision. This decision will be discussed in detail because it illustrates the model of the labor relations process presented in Chapter 1 (see Exhibit 1.2) and because it illustrates the impact of the fourth participant, the government, on labor–management relations.

The *Weingarten* decision pertained to an employee who was believed to have paid only a fraction of the price of food she took out of the store. During the interview with management representatives she repeatedly asked for a union representative to be present but was denied. Management subsequently found her version of the incident to be supported, but in her emotional state, she admitted that over a period of time she had taken free lunches (totaling approximately $160) from the store, something a management official and other employees had also done. She was not disciplined for her actions; however, she informed her union representatives of the events and an unfair labor practice was filed. The NLRB decided that management did commit an unfair labor practice, violating Section 8(a)(1) of the National Labor Relations Act (mentioned in Chapter 3), by denying the employee union representation.

Union representation must be given to the employee at the employee's request when the employee reasonably believes an investigation could result in disciplinary action. Employees, however, have no legal requirement to bargain with any union representative who attends the interview.

The NLRB's *Weingarten* decision was appealed through the courts, and eventually upheld by the Supreme Court. Rationale for this decision was in part based on the union official's potential contribution to the disciplinary investigation:

A single employee confronted by an employer investigating whether certain conduct deserves discipline may be too fearful or inarticulate to relate accurately the incident being investigated, or too ignorant to raise extenuating factors. A knowledgeable union representative could assist the employer by eliciting favorable facts, and save the employer production time by getting to the bottom of the incident occasioning the interview. Certainly [the union representative's] presence need not transform the interview into an adversary contest.[40]

Earlier arbitrator decisions formed the foundation for the Supreme Court's opinions regarding an employee's right to union representation. Justice Brennan observed that "even where such a right is not explicitly provided in the agreement a 'well-established current of arbitral authority' sustains the right of union representation at investigatory interviews which the employee reasonably believes may result in disciplinary action against him."[41]

The Supreme Court ruled that an employee has the legal right to have a union representative present during an investigatory interview if the employee has reason to believe that the investigation will result in disciplinary action. The Court and NLRB adopted the several principles highlighted in Exhibit 12.5.

The *Weingarten* decision also refuted the company's contention that union representation is necessary only after the company has made its discipline decision. The Supreme Court contended that this practice would diminish the value of union representation, thereby making it increasingly difficult for the employee to vindicate himself or herself in the subsequent grievance proceedings. NLRB cases indicate that an employee who is discharged for just cause will not be reinstated

EXHIBIT 12.5
Application of Weingarten Rights

1. The employee's right stems from Section 7 of the National Labor Relations Act, which allows the employee to engage in concerted activities for mutual aid and protection.
2. The right can be exercised only if the employee chooses to request representation; the employer is not obligated to inform the employee of his or her legal right to union representation.
3. The employee must reasonably believe that disciplinary action could follow before requesting the presence of a union representative.
4. If the employee refuses to go through the interview, the request for representation having been denied, the employer may continue the investigation without the input of the employee.
5. The employer is not obligated to bargain with the employee's union representative during the interview.
6. If the employer denies the employee his or her right to union representation after the employee makes a legitimate request and continues the investigatory interview, the interview is considered an illegal interview and any information gained by the employer, even a confession to a misdeed such as theft, will not be allowed in a subsequent procedure, such as arbitration. Not to be confused, such rulings do not prove that the employee is innocent of the alleged crime; simply, the employer must prove the employee's guilt by some other means. For example, another employee may be willing to come forward as a witness to the employee's theft.
7. *Weingarten* rights do not apply if management had already decided to impose discipline and the purpose of the meeting is to communicate the disciplinary decision.

SOURCE: Neal Orkin and Miriam Heise, "*Weingarten* through the Looking Glass," *Labor Law Journal* 48 (March 1997), pp. 157–159. (c) 1994, 1997, & 2000, CCH Incorporated. All Rights Reserved. Reprinted with permission from *Labor Law Journal*.

solely because the employer violated his or her *Weingarten* rights. This means that if the employer has obtained evidence from sources other than from the illegal interview, the employee's discharge will stand. On July 10, 2000, the NLRB decided that *Weingarten* rights should be extended to employees in nonunion workplaces to afford them the right to have a co-worker present at an investigatory interview that the employee reasonably believes could result in disciplinary action.[42]

Exhibit 12.6 shows how the National Labor Relations Board has changed its position on employee *Weingarten* rights since 1982. With a majority of the Board members appointed by President George W. Bush, the Board's position may change again. On the other hand, if the Board's decision in 2000 is allowed to stand, application to nonunion employees raises several interesting issues for employers. First, there is a question of whether the rules developed by decisions of the National Labor Relations Board since the Supreme Court's 1975 *Weingarten* decision will be applied to nonunion settings. For example, an employee in a unionized setting does not have the right to union representation when the sole purpose of a meeting called by a management official is to communicate a previously determined disciplinary action.

Second, there is a question of who will serve as a witness. Although the decision that extended *Weingarten* rights to nonunion employees refers to a co-worker as a witness, questions that may be raised are: May an employee bring in his or her attorney as a witness? May the employee call in another supervisor? What if the employee wants to bring in a co-worker who is under investigation for the same wrongdoing? What happens if the employee calls for a co-

Exhibit 12.6

Evolving NLRB Policy on Employee Weingarten *Rights*

> 1975—The U.S. Supreme Court held that a unionized employee has the right to union representation at an investigatory interview when the employee reasonably believes that the investigatory interview could lead to disciplinary action. *NLRB* v. *J. Weingarten, Inc.*, 420 U.S. 251.
>
> 1982—The Board held that nonunion employees had *Weingarten* rights because Section 7 of the National Labor Relations Act gives employees the right to engage in protected concerted activities for mutual aid and protection. *Materials Research Corp.*, 262 NLRB 1010.
>
> 1985—The Board reversed itself and held that nonunion employees did not have *Weingarten* rights because such rights stem from the union's right to represent employees and *Weingarten* rights extend to employees only when there is an exclusive bargaining representative (union). *Sears Roebuck & Co.*, 274 NLRB 230.
>
> 1985—*Weingarten* rights are not applicable to nonunion settings. *E. I. DuPont De Neumours & Co.*, 289 NLRB 627 (*DuPont III*).
>
> 2000–2001—The Board reversed itself again and held that nonunion employees had *Weingarten* rights. Employees are afforded the right to have a co-worker present at an investigatory interview when the employee reasonably believes the investigatory interview could lead to disciplinary action. *Epilepsy Foundation of Northeast Ohio* v. *NLRB*, 331 NLRB 92, upheld by the U.S. Circuit Court of Appeals, No. 00-1332 (November 2, 2001) 2001 U.S. App. LEXIS 23722 (D.C. Cir. 2001).

SOURCE: Michael J. Soltis and Alexandra M. Gross, "Weingarten Redux: An Employer's Manual," *Labor Law Journal* 51 (Winter 2000), pp. 179–180; James F. Morgan, James M. Owens, and Glenn M. Gomes, "Union Rules Intrude Upon the Nonunion Domain: Workplace Investigations and the NLRB," *Employee Responsibilities and Rights Journal* 14 (March 2002), p. 36.

worker who is not readily available, for example, is on layoff, is on vacation, or has been suspended pending a more thorough investigation?

Third, there is a question of the role of the witness in a nonunion setting. In a unionized setting, a union representative may ask questions for clarification and consult with the employee. If there is an emotional confrontation, the union representative will try to defuse it. In a unionized setting, the union representative possesses knowledge of the grievance procedure and past practices of the parties and will be able to articulate the "common law of the shop" with the employer. A co-worker witness no doubt will not have such knowledge and expertise. In fact, a co-worker may be reluctant to serve as a witness because there may be fear of retribution from the employer and the co-worker is left unprotected because there is no collective-bargaining agreement that provides protection.

Fourth, there is a question concerning the employer's actions when an employer asserts *Weingarten* rights and requests a co-worker as a witness. One choice for the employer is simply to grant the request; this may be appropriate when the co-worker's presence may be beneficial to the investigation. A second choice is to discontinue the interview and continue the investigation without an interview with the suspected employee. If the employer rejects the employee's request for a co-worker representative and continues the interview, the interview would be considered an illegal interview and no information learned in the interview could be used to support the disciplinary action. However, the employer may discipline the employee on facts found through means other than the interviews. Moreover, if the employee is considered an at-will employee, the employee may be disciplined for "any reason or no reason" and probably will not have access to a grievance procedure or other forms of protection.[43]

A fifth dilemma for the employer is the pay for the co-worker representative. In a unionized setting, the collective-bargaining agreement usually addresses whether union officials will be paid for time spent on union representational activities and at what rate. In a nonunion setting, there is no collective-bargaining agreement. The employer may attempt to avoid the issue by scheduling interviews after hours. Then, the employer may contend that the co-worker is not entitled to any pay because the employer did not ask the co-worker to attend the interview. The co-worker representative's appearance at the interview was at the request of the employee being investigated.[44]

Another element of due process, written notice, has caused some problems for management and is a major reason for the involvement of labor relations representatives in the discipline process. For example, an employee gets into a heated argument with a supervisor, refuses to work an assignment, and shouts an obscenity at the supervisor. The foreman could discipline the employee for "directing obscene and profane language toward a management representative." Once the charges are in writing, management must convince the arbitrator that this charge warrants discipline, a task that is not easy given the usual arbitral recognition that obscene language is regarded as common shop talk in an industrial facility. In this instance, management would have been wiser to have disciplined the employee for a more serious offense: "Insubordination: refusal to follow supervisory orders." However, management can seldom change the offense once it is in writing and handed to the grievant. Consequently, a member of the industrial relations department is usually present for consultation or direction before the charges are reduced to writing.

Another related element of due process is *double jeopardy*—assigning an employee a more severe penalty than the one originally given. The rationale against double jeopardy is that management is held to any decision that purports to be final; therefore, it is important that it act only after ascertaining all relevant facts and determining the magnitude of the offense. Management can avoid the problem of double jeopardy if it makes clear to the grievant that the action taken in the first instance is tentative, pending further investigation by higher company officials. Usually, this takes the form of an indefinite suspension that, pending a subsequent investigation, can be converted to discharge without arbitral disapproval. A final element of due process is the keeping of secret records on the employee, which most arbitrators maintain is worse than keeping no records at all.

One arbitrator notes three alternative positions that the arbitrator can take regarding procedural or due process irregularities:

> (1) [T]hat unless there is strict compliance with the procedural requirements, the whole action will be nullified; (2) that the requirements are of significance only where the employee can show that he has been prejudiced by failure to comply therewith; or (3) that the requirements are important, and that any failure to comply will be penalized, but that the action taken is not thereby rendered null and void.[45]

Arbitrators tend to favor the third alternative, reasoning that management should suffer the consequences of its errors, but not to the point of exonerating an employee who is guilty of a serious offense (particularly if it has not prejudiced the employee's case).

SUMMARY

In many respects, employee discipline represents the most significant day-to-day issue in administering the labor agreement. For the union and management organizations, administration of discipline is a key factor related to control and production; the supervisor and the affected employee are even more directly and personally affected.

Management had a unilateral right to discharge or discipline employees until the 1930s, although psychological reform and efficiency movements in the early 1900s urged management to critically examine its disciplinary policies. Some managers realized that an employee represented an investment that could be unnecessarily lost because of whimsical disciplinary actions. These individuals realized that they had an obligation to provide employees with clear work rules and proper training that would minimize the number of discipline problems and lead to increased productivity. The establishment of the NLRB further refined employers' disciplinary policies, as employees discharged for their union activities could be reinstated to their jobs with back pay.

Discipline in unionized settings must be for just cause, a concept consisting of several dimensions. Management has the burden of proof to establish that an employee committed an infraction. Although discipline can accomplish several purposes for the organization, management may have to prove that its actions were taken to correct an employee's behavior. Correction suggests that an employee must be aware of work rules that are clear in their content, as well as consequences for their infraction. The work rules must also be reasonable—that is, related to the job—and consistently applied to all employees under similar circumstances.

Discipline's corrective emphasis also suggests progressive or more serious penalties be given to an employee for repeating a similar offense. Progressive discipline impresses on the employee the seriousness of repeated rule infractions while giving the employee additional chances to correct work behavior. Usually, management has to give an employee an oral warning for the first offense, then a written warning and suspension for subsequent, similar offenses. Discharge is a last resort, used only when all other attempts at correction have failed or the nature of the offense is so unacceptable as to make corrective efforts inappropriate.

Management must also establish that the penalty fits the crime and that it considered all possible mitigating circumstances before imposing discipline.

Management must also provide the employee with due process in the disciplinary procedure; that is, it must ensure that the appropriate contractual provisions are upheld. The employee usually has the right to union representation and the right to be notified of the offense in writing.

The U.S. Supreme Court has ruled that an employee has the legal right, a *Weingarten* right, to have a union representative present during an investigatory interview if the employee reasonably believes that the investigation could result in disciplinary action. Since this decision, the NLRB has provided guidance to the parties through case decisions and has extended *Weingarten* right to nonunion employees. The policy of the NLRB has changed over the years and has resulted in several questions of application.

KEY TERMS

wrongful discharge
just cause
preponderance of evidence
clear and convincing evidence
beyond a reasonable doubt
price list
progressive discipline

oral warning
written warning
suspension
discharge
last chance agreement
mitigating circumstances
due process

DISCUSSION QUESTIONS

1. Why is discipline the most significant issue for the union and management organizations? Describe how this significance has shifted over time.

2. One union newspaper indicated how it saved an employee's job. The employee was in the mechanic's classification and was discharged for refusing to comply with management's sudden, unilateral rule that mechanics must

perform janitorial duties. Given this sketchy situation, discuss the many possible reasons for the disciplinary action, indicating why the arbitrator might not have been convinced that management's discipline was for a legitimate purpose. (You are free to make and state assumptions in your answer.)

3. Explain in some detail the difficulties management would have in administering the following work rule in accordance with the disciplinary principles established in the chapter: "Any employee reporting to work under the influence of alcohol will be subject to discharge."

4. Indicate the comparative advantages and disadvantages of a disciplinary price list (see Exhibit 12.4) of disciplinary prerogatives in the labor agreement and a one-sentence contractual provision indicating "management has the right to discipline or discharge an employee for cause."

5. Although not subject to judicial scrutiny, evidence in an arbitration hearing still has its complexities. Discuss related considerations that could be involved in an arbitration hearing involving an employee who was discharged for smoking marijuana on the job.

6. Assume you are in charge of establishing a training program for supervisors in administering discipline. Based on the supervisor's potential role in the disciplinary process, formulate and discuss three major principles you would stress in this session.

EXPLORING THE WEB

Employee Discipline

1. Wrongful Discharge   A reference is made to a RAND study on the economic consequences of wrongful termination. Find an abstract of the study on RAND's Web site. Who are the authors of the study? Go to "About RAND" from the home page to find the meaning of the acronym. What other studies have been done by RAND on labor relations?

http://www.rand.org/Abstracts/index.html

2. Evidence in Disciplinary Cases   Use the Findlaw site on the Web to locate a case in which Magno Ortega is the plaintiff against the executive director of the hospital where Ortega was employed. The case involved management's methods used in an investigation on Ortega's acquisition of a computer and sexual harassment and is an illustration of one of the problems that can occur when management seeks evidence for disciplinary action. Find other cases that were cited in the opinion.

http://www.findlaw.com

3. Employment Discrimination   The Legal Information Institute at Cornell has an excellent Web site that allows for searching federal and state statutes and case law and provides additional Web links by subject searched. Search on "employment discrimination" and examine the discussion and related links. How do the acts discussed relate to employee discipline?

http://www.law.cornell.edu

4. Progressive Discipline   What is "progressive discipline"? Law firms often publish articles with free access on their Web pages for the use of their clients. Read an article on "progressive discipline" by Brent T. Johnson published on the Web page of the law firm of Fairfield and Woods, P.C. in Colorado.

http://www.fwlaw.com/progressive.html

5. Seven Tests for Just Cause   A common test for determining whether just cause existed for imposing disciplinary action was developed by arbitrator Carroll Daugherty in 1966. The standard is known as "The Seven Tests for Just Cause." What are the seven tests? Go to the following site provided by the American Federation of State, County, and Municipal Employees (AFSCME).

http://www.afscme.org/about/shb05.pdf

6. Work Rules   Work rules established by management must be clear and understandable and communicated effectively to employees. Comment on the reasonableness and clarity of sample work rules from the following site.

http://www.toolkit.cch.com/tools/wrkrul_m.asp

7. *Weingarten* Rights   For additional reading on due process and Weingarten rights, go to a site published by the Center for Labor Education and Research at the University of Hawaii

http://homepages.uhwo.hawaii.edu/clear/wein.html

References

1. Ahmad R. Karim, "Why Arbitrators Sustain Discharge Penalties," *Labor Law Journal* 45 (June 1994), pp. 374–378; and Stephen M. Crow, Elvis C. Stephens, and Walton H. Sharp, "A New Approach to Decision-Making Research in Labor Arbitration Using Alcohol and Drug Disciplinary Cases," *Labor Studies Journal* 17 (Fall 1992), pp. 3–18.

2. For consideration of other, more informal disciplinary actions taken by management, see Bruce Fortado, "Informal Supervisory Social Control Strategies," *Journal of Management Studies* 31 (March 1994), pp. 251–275.

3. For an example of how the NLRB can alter an organization's decision policies, see Marcia A. Graham, "Obscenity and Profanity at Work," *Employee Relations Law Journal* 11 (Spring 1986), pp. 662–677.

4. Richard E. Dibble, "Alternative Dispute Resolution in Employment: Recent Developments," *Journal of Collective Negotiations in the Public Sector* 29, no. 3 (2000), pp. 245–257.

5. Marvin J. Levine, "The Erosion of the Employment-At-Will Doctrine: Recent Developments," *Labor Law Journal* 45 (February 1994), pp. 79–89.

6. Milo Geyelin, "Fired Managers Winning More Lawsuits," *The Wall Street Journal*, September 7, 1989, B-1. See also William H. Holley, Jr., and Roger S. Wolters, "An Employment-At-Will Vulnerability Audit," *Personnel Journal* 66 (April 1987), pp. 130–138; and William H. Holley, Jr., and Roger S. Wolters, *Labor Relations: An Experiential and Case Approach* (Hinsdale, Ill.: The Dryden Press, 1988), pp. 33–35. See also Giles Trudeau, "Is Reinstatement a Remedy Suitable to At-Will Employees?" *Industrial Relations* 30, no. 2 (Spring 1991), pp. 302–315; P. S. Partee, "Reversing the Presumption of Employment-At-Will," *Vanderbilt Law Review* 44, no. 3 (April 1991), pp. 698–712; Jay E. Grenig, "Dismissal of Employees in the United States," *International Labor Review* 130, no. 5–6 (1991), pp. 569–581; Marcia P. Miceli, Janet P. Near, and Charles R. Schwenk,

"Who Blows the Whistle and Why?" *Industrial and Labor Relations Review* 45 (October 1991), pp. 113–130; Jeffrey M. Hahn and Kevin M. Smith, "Wrongful Discharge: The Search for a Legislative Compromise," *Employee Relations Law Journal* 15 (Spring 1990), pp. 515–539; "Employer Opportunism and the Need for a Just Cause Standard," *Howard Law Review* 103, pp. 510–529; A. D. Hill, *"Wrongful Discharge" and the Derogation of the At-Will Employment Doctrine* (Philadelphia: The Wharton School, 1987); Alan B. Drueger, "The Evolution of Unjust-Dismissal Legislation in the United States," *Industrial and Labor Relations Review* 44 (July 1991), pp. 644–660; Roger L. Anderson and James W. Robinson, "Is Arbitration the Answer in Wrongful Termination Cases?" *Labor Law Journal* 42 (February 1991), pp. 121–124; Daniel P. Westman, *Whistleblowing: The Law of Retaliatory Discharge,* (Washington, D.C.: Bureau of National Affairs, 1991); Paul F. Gerhart and Donald P. Crane, "Wrongful Dismissal: Arbitration and the Law," *Arbitration Journal* 48 (June 1993), pp. 56–70; Lisa B. Bingham, "Employee Free Speech and Wrongful Discharge," *Labor Law Journal* 45 (July 1994), pp. 387–400; and Melissa S. Baucus and Terry Morehead Dworkin, "Wrongful Firing in Violation of Public Policy: Who Gets Fired and Why," *Employee Responsibilities and Rights Journal* 7, no. 3 (1994), pp. 191–206.

7. Charles J. Muhl, "The Employment-at-will Doctrine: Three Major Exceptions," *Monthly Labor Review* 124 (January 2001), pp. 3–11.

8. "RAND Corp. Study Links Job Losses to States' Wrongful Termination Rules," Bureau of National Affairs, *Daily Labor Report,* no. 142 (July 23, 1992), p. A-2. For somewhat similar conclusions reached by another survey, see "Wrongful-Discharge Claims Increasing, Management Association Survey Finds," Bureau of National Affairs, *Daily Labor Report* no. 25 (February 6, 1990), pp. A-8, A-9.

9. Brian S. Klaas, Thomas W. Gainey, and Gregory G. Dell'Omo, "The Determinants of Disciplinary System Effectiveness: A Line-Management Per-

spective," *Industrial Relations* 8 (October 1999), pp. 542–550.

10. See Kenneth M. Jennings, Barbara Sheffield, and Roger S. Wolters, "The Arbitration of Discharge Cases: A Forty Year Perspective," *Labor Law Journal* 38 (January 1987), p. 35. See also Ahmad Karim and Thomas H. Stone, "An Empirical Examination of Arbitrator Decisions in Reversal and Reduction Discharge Hearings," *Labor Studies Journal* 13, no. 2 (Spring 1988), p. 47.

11. See, for example, Thomas R. Knight, "The Impact of Arbitration on the Administration of Disciplinary Policies," *Arbitration Journal* 39 (March 1984), pp. 43–56.

12. Arthur Anthony Malinowski, "An Empirical Analysis of Discharge Cases and the Work History of Employees Reinstated by Labor Arbitrators," *Arbitration Journal* 36 (March 1981), p. 39; and William E. Simkin, "Some Results of Reinstatement by Arbitration," *Arbitration Journal* 41 (September 1986), p. 56.

13. Chalmer E. Labig, Jr., I. B. Helburn, and Robert C. Rodgers, "Discipline, History, Seniority, and Reason for Discharge as Predictors of Post-Reinstatement Job Performance," *The Arbitration Journal* 40 (September 1985), p. 49. For additional considerations of this relationship, see Robert C. Rodgers, I. B. Helburn, and John E. Hunter, "The Relationship of Seniority to Job Performance Following Reinstatement," *Academy of Management Journal* 29 (March 1986), pp. 101–114; and I. B. Helburn, "Seniority and Postreinstatement Performance," in *Proceedings of the Forty-Third Annual Meeting, National Academy of Arbitrators,* ed. Gladys W. Gruenberg, (Washington, D.C.: Bureau of National Affairs, 1991), pp. 141–149.

14. D. C. Miller, "Supervisor: Evolution of a Forgotten Role," in *Supervisory Leadership and Productivity,* eds. Floyd Mann, George Homans, and Delbert Miller (San Francisco: Chandler, 1965), p. 113.

15. "Oil, Chemical, and Atomic," *Union News,* July 1970, p. 9.

16. *Hoosier Panel Co., Inc.,* 61 LA 983 (M. Volz, 1973). Marvin Hill, Jr. and Diana Beck, "Some Thoughts on Just Cause

and Group Discipline," *Arbitration Journal* 41 (June 1986), pp. 60–62.

17. *Riley Stoker Corp.*, 7 LA 767 (Platt, 1947).

18. For more thorough explanations of this exhibit, see Donald S. McPherson, "The Evolving Concept of Just Cause: Carroll R. Daugherty and the Requirement of Disciplinary Due Process," *Labor Law Journal* (July 1987), pp. 387–403; and Adolph M. Koven and Susan L. Smith, *Just Cause: The Seven Tests* (San Francisco: Kendall/Hunt, 1985).

19. David A. Dilts, Ahmad Karim, and Mashalah Kahnama Moghadam, "The Arbitration of Disciplinary Matters: Do Objective Standards Make a Difference in Proof?" *Labor Law Journal* 42 (October 1991), pp. 708–712.

20. Arthur Eliot Berkeley, "Asleep at the Wheel: How Arbitrators View Sleeping on the Job," *Arbitration Journal* 46 (June 1991), p. 48.

21. Randall M. Kelly, "The Burden of Proof in Criminal Offenses of 'Moral Turpitude' Cases," *Arbitration Journal* 46 (December 1991), pp. 45–48.

22. Laura Davis, "Discipline and Decisions: A Study of Arbitration Cases Dealing with Employee Discourtesy," *Labor Law Journal* 46 (February 1995), p. 84.

23. Edgar A. Jones, Jr., "Selected Problems of Procedure and Evidence," in *Arbitration in Practice*, ed. Arnold M. Zack (Ithaca, N.Y.: ILR Press, 1984), p. 62.

24. *Buick Youngstown Company*, 41 LA 570–753 (H. Dworkin, 1963).

25. *A. B. Chance Company*, 57 LA 725–731 (P. Florey, 1971).

26. Terry L. Leap and Michael D. Crino, "How to Deal with Bizarre Behavior," *Harvard Business Review* (May–June 1986), pp. 18–25. This article also furnishes eight criteria for management in determining whether discharge for previously unconsidered disciplinary infractions is justified.

27. Donald J. Petersen, "No Smoking!" *Dispute Resolution Journal* 50 (January 1995), p. 48.

28. For additional consideration of the "moonlighting" employee, see Muhammad Jamal, "Moonlighting Myths," *The Personnel Journal* 67 (May 1988), pp. 48–53.

29. Robert A. Kearney, "Arbitral Practice and Purpose in Employee Off-Duty Misconduct Cases," *Notre Dame Law Review* 69, no. 1 (1993), pp. 135–156; and Janie L. Miller, David B. Balkin, and Robert Allen, "Employer Restrictions on Employees' Legal Off-Duty Conduct," *Labor Law Journal* 44 (April 1993), pp. 209–219.

30. Donald J. Petersen, "Trends in Arbitrating Falsification of Employment Application Forms," *Arbitration Journal* 47 (September 1992), pp. 32–33.

31. Gregory G. Dell'Omo and James E. Jones, Jr., "Disparate Treatment in Labor Arbitration: An Empirical Analysis," *Labor Law Journal* 41 (November 1990), pp. 739–750.

32. Lisa Davis and Ken Jennings, "Employee Horseplay and Likely Managerial Overreaction," *Labor Law Journal* 40 (April 1989), pp. 248–256.

33. Kenneth Grinstead, "The Arbitration of Last Chance Agreements," *Arbitration Journal* 48 (March 1993), p. 71; Norman Brand, ed., *Discipline and Discharge in Arbitration* (Washington, D.C.: Bureau of National Affairs, 1998), pp. 303–315.

34. Peter A. Bamberger and Linda H. Donahue, "Employee Discharge and Reinstatement: Moral Hazards and the Mixed Consequences of Last Chance Agreements," *Industrial and Labor Relations Review* 53 (October 1999), pp. 3–19.

35. *Gindy Manufacturing Company*, 58 LA 1038–1040 (M. Handsaker, 1972).

36. Jennings, Sheffield, and Wolters, "The Arbitration of Discharge Cases," p. 43.

37. Tim Bornstein, "Getting to the Bottom of the Issue: How Arbitrators View Alcohol Abuse," *Arbitration Journal* 44 (December 1989), p. 47.

38. George W. Bohlander and Donna Blancero, "A Study of Reverse Determinants in Discipline and Discharge Arbitration Awards: The Impact of Just Cause Standards," *Labor Studies Journal* 21 (February 1996), pp. 3–10.

39. John B. LaRocco, "Just Cause Collides with Public Policy in Sexual Harassment Arbitrations," *Proceedings of the 49th Annual Meeting of the Industrial Relations Research Association* (Madison, Wis: IRRA, 1997), pp. 211–216.

40. *NLRB* v. *J. Weingarten, Inc.,* 420 U.S. 262, 1974. See also M. J. Fox, Louis V. Baldovin, Jr., and Thomas R. Fox, "The *Weingarten* Doctrine," *The Arbitration Journal* 40 (June 1985), pp. 45–54. The Weingarten decision has also been held by an appeals court to be applicable in at least some federal sector situations. See "Court Permits Union Representation at Meetings with DOD Investigators," Bureau of National Affairs, *Daily Labor Report,* no. 173 (September 7, 1988), A-1.

41. Ibid.

42. *Epilepsy Foundation of NE Ohio and Borgs and Hassan,* 331 NCRB No. 92 (July 10, 2000).

43. Ann C. Hodges, Courtney Mueller Coke, and Robert R. Trumble, "Weingarten in the Nonunion Workplace: Looking in the Funhouse Mirror," *Labor Law Journal* 54 (Summer 2002), pp. 94–95.

44. James F. Morgan, James M. Owens, and Glenn M. Gomes, "Union Rules Intrude Upon the Nonunion Domain: Workplace Investigations and the NLRB," *Employee Responsibilities and Rights Journal* 14 (March 2000), pp. 36–39.

45. R. W. Fleming, *The Labor Arbitration Process* (Champaign: University of Illinois Press, 1965), p. 139.

May an Employee Circulate a Group Grievance during Working Hours?

Issue

Did the company violate the agreement when it suspended Ms. Manley for signing and then circulating a group grievance during working hours?

Background

The grievant, Ms. Manley, is a 13-year employee who has worked mostly in the Shipping Department. On January 22, 1996, she was having lunch with her usual group when someone circulated a grievance form around her lunch table. The Grievance form, No. 81–05, was a group grievance that stated:

> We, the employees of Solar Energy, want the company to abide by the contract and to treat employees fairly and use seniority in its decisions.

Ms. Manley signed the form, as did a few others at the lunch table. At the table was Ms. Hartgrave, secretary-treasurer of the local union, who asked the grievant to take the form to her department and have employees in the Shipping Department sign it.

Ms. Manley then took the Grievance form to the Shipping Department and approached Mr. C. W. Outlaw, a bargaining unit employee but not a union member, and asked him to sign the form. She read the Grievance to him and he signed the form. Mr. Randolph Traxler, the plant manager, observed the signing when Mr. Outlaw handed the form back to the Grievant. Mr. Outlaw returned to work as did the Grievant; however, she also continued to ask other employees to sign the form (five others signed it after Mr. Outlaw).

Later, Mr. Traxler called Ms. Manley and Mr. Outlaw to his office and gave Ms. Manley the following Notice of Reprimand:

> Reason for Reprimand—Violation of Company Rules of Conduct, Category D (8): Prohibiting posting or distribution of any form of literature without express authorization of the Personnel Department or the plant manager. On January 22, 1996, you distributed to C. W. Outlaw a form that he had to take time to read and sign. This resulted in a slowdown of work production and interference with work. This will become a part of your work record. Further violation of this nature will result in discharge.

Ms. Manley later returned the Grievance form to Ms. Hartgrave, and returned to her job, and finished the day at work. Her suspension was from January 23 to 29, 1996 (five working days). Ms. Manley filed a grievance that was not settled by the parties in the grievance procedure. The Grievance was appealed to arbitration, wherein both parties were given full opportunity to present evidence, witnesses, and arguments on their behalf.

PERTINENT CONTRACT PROVISIONS

Article 11   Union Representative

A representative of the Union shall be granted reasonable access to the working areas of the plant, during working hours, for the purpose of investigation of grievances arising under the terms of this Agreement. Such access may be made upon reasonable prior notice to

Continued

the plant manager, or his designated representative, and it is mutually agreed that the Union representative may be accompanied by the plant manager, or his designated representative, during such access.

Article 14   Rules

Section 1.   For the purpose of plant discipline and safety, the Company has and retains the exclusive right to promulgate reasonable rules and regulations, from time to time, not otherwise inconsistent with the terms of this Agreement. However, any future new or changed rules or regulations will be discussed with the Union before the implementation of such change of rules.

Article 15   Discipline and Discharge

There will be no discipline or discharge imposed on any employee covered by this Agreement, except for just cause.

In the event of discharge or other disciplinary action, the Company will promptly furnish the affected employee with a written statement specifying the reason for the discharge or other disciplinary action. Such action on the part of the Company shall be subject to the grievance procedure specified herein, provided that a grievance is filed with the Company within five working days of receipt by the employee of the written statement specifying the reason for the discharge or other disciplinary action. Failure to file such grievance within five working days shall bar its consideration under any provisions of this Agreement.

Article 16   Nondiscrimination

Section 1.   The Company agrees not to discriminate against, interfere with, restrain, or coerce employees because of membership or lawful activity in the Union. The Union agrees not to intimidate or otherwise coerce any employee because of nonmembership in the Union or for the purpose of inducing such employee to become a member of the Union.

Article 19   Management Rights

Section 1.   It is understood and agreed that the Company has all customary and usual rights, powers, functions, and authority of management.

Section 2.   Subject to the terms and conditions of this Agreement, the management, direction, supervision, and control of the Company's business operations, working force, and plant are exclusively vested in the Company. Without limiting the generality of the foregoing, the Union recognizes that, subject to the express provisions of this Agreement, the right to plan, direct, and control the Company's business operations and working force; to hire, suspend, transfer, lay off, and, for just cause, to discipline or discharge employees; to determine the means and methods by which work is to be performed; to determine job classifications and standards of performance; to introduce or discontinue any production methods or facilities, including the right to subcontract work performed by employees covered by this Agreement, are all vested exclusively in the Company.

Section 3.   It is further understood and agreed that all rights heretofore exercised by, or inherent in, the Company, not expressly contracted away by the term of this Agreement, are retained solely by the Company, and that should the Company fail to exercise any of said rights, or exercise them in a particular manner, it shall not be deemed to have waived said rights to be precluded thereafter from exercising them in some way or manner.

Rules of Conduct

Purpose: These Rules of Conduct have been established for the purpose of ensuring the safety and health of all employees, to serve as a guide for self-discipline, to ensure fair and equal discipline, to maintain good housekeeping, and to operate the factory efficiently and safely.

Category D (8). Prohibits posting or distribution of any form of literature without express authorization of the Personnel Department or the plant manager. Disciplinary procedures for handling offenses in Category D are:

1. First offense—Five working day suspension.
2. Second offense—Discharge.

The Company's Position

The Company argued that the labor agreement clearly gives management the right to discipline employees for just cause. Also, the rules of conduct, which are part of the labor agreement, must be administered by management. Category D (8) states that an employee cannot post or distribute any form of literature without express authorization. Ms. Manley did not deny that she was seen securing C. W. Outlaw's signature. Because the Grievant testified that she did pass the form to another employee, the rules of conduct were appropriately administered, and she was suspended for 5 days.

The Company countered the Union's allegation of inconsistent administration of discipline by explaining that company conditions were different from a previous case. In an earlier case of insubordination, the Company was in the midst of its busiest time of the year. Although the employee was insubordinate, management decided that a 5-day suspension was not feasible because of the heavy work load. In the present case, the business conditions were different, and a 5-day suspension was justified.

The Company's response to the Union's allegation that other forms and products are distributed in the plant and employees are not disciplined for their actions was a statement that employees have to be caught breaking the rules. The Company readily acknowledged that the witnesses who testified that the rules (particularly those regarding distribution of literature) had been broken had their own self-serving views. It contended that employees seeing infractions of rules and supervisors catching employees breaking rules are completely different subjects.

Finally, the Company maintained that it had treated the Grievant fairly and equitably in its administration of the rules. In fact, the Company officials had explained to the Grievant that she could have been discharged. Thus, the Company concluded that the suspension should stand.

The Union's Position

The Union argued that the grievant, a job steward, has been a good employee for 13 years and the Company had issued no previous reprimands to her. Further, the Grievant and Ms. Hartgrave testified that employees have signed grievances on work time as a past practice and that the grievant, as a job steward, was not concealing her efforts to have employees sign the Grievant during working hours.

A union witness testified that "It is common knowledge to the employees and supervisors that employees sell Avon and Mary Kay products, raffle tickets, cookies, etc., openly in the plant during working hours. In fact, some supervisors have participated, and these activities are still taking place in the plant." Ms. Hartgrave, a tow-motor operator, testified that she picked up Avon orders in the Shipping Department and delivered them to the Assembly Department on her usual "runs" between departments. She would set the bag of Avon orders down in various departments, and those employees who had ordered Avon products would then pick them up during working hours.

Continued

The Union witnesses testified that it was a practice to have a union representative present when reprimands were given to employees. In this case, the Grievant was not allowed representation because Mr. Outlaw was not a union member or official. Although the grievant is a steward, she should have been afforded representation by her union.

The Union argued that the Company had discriminated against Ms. Manley by treating her unfairly and differently from another employee who had previously committed the more serious offense of insubordination. Thus, the Company was inconsistent in its administration of employee discipline.

The Union contended that the grievant did not distribute anything. Quoting Webster's Dictionary, which defines the work *distribute* as "to divide among several or many," the Union concluded that no distribution took place and therefore no rule could have been violated. It contended that the Company did not prove its case and concluded that the Company did not have just cause to suspend the Grievant. The Union requested that the grievant's record be cleared and that she be compensated for all lost wages and benefits caused by this suspension.

QUESTIONS

1. To what extent do current business conditions justify the Company in taking disciplinary action?

2. Has the Company been too lax in enforcing the work rules?

3. Should progressive discipline be applied in this case? Was the Company correct when it stated that it could have discharged Ms. Manley?

4. If employees have previously signed grievances during working hours and sold Avon and Mary Kay products, raffled tickets, how may the Company stop these actions?

5. Were Ms. Manley and Mr. Outlaw entitled to union representation? Should this omission affect the decision?

6. How should the arbitrator rule? Why?

Last Chance Agreement versus Just Cause– Progressive Discipline

Background

On March 27, 1998, the Company, the Union, and Mr. Danny Webb, the Grievant, entered into and signed the following Agreement:

Without precedent, the Company, the Union, and Mr. Danny Webb agree to the following:

1. Mr. Webb has reached the discharge step for progressive discipline under Category "B" rules. He is, hereby, given a final opportunity to save his job by compliance with conditions set forth in this agreement.

2. There will be a suspension from 3/27/98 to 4/20/98. Mr. Webb will return to work the week of 4/20/98.

3. There will be a probationary period of 18 months, which will expire September 27, 1999.

4. The violation of any plant rule during the probationary period will result in immediate discharge.

5. Any absence of scheduled work time, including tardiness, during the probationary period will result in immediate discharge, unless determined by supervision to be beyond Mr. Webb's control.

6. Mr. Webb understands that overtime is a part of his job.

7. Mr. Webb has been made aware of the Employee Assistance Program, for help with the problem with anger he says he has.

On April 27, 1999, Warehouse Supervisor Mr. Ted Holt wrote the following Notice:

Reason for Warning or Reprimand:
Violation of plant rules including negligent act resulting in damage to company property. Category B (12) Danny flipped over (2) crates of $1/_8$" × 48" × 60" heavy case (HC) glass in zone #326 on the top row and then took (1) crate of HC from the bottom and placed it in front of the damaged crate. This hid the flipped over crate. He went home without reporting the incident. Other employees observed the incident and reported to Tommy Biggers.

Supervisor's Comments:
Danny did not report the incident to any supervisor. He placed a crate in front of the two crates that he caused to flip over to hide the damage and presented a hidden danger to other employees. This is in violation of his Last Chance Agreement dated March 27, 1998, and therefore results in discharge.

On the same day, Mr. Joe Broadway, first vice president, Local Union no. 911, filed the following Grievance:

Statement of Grievance:
The Union ask that Mr. Webb be put back to work, and made whole for any lost wages.
Continued

The Company denied the Grievance in a letter dated June 11, 1999, to Mr. Thomas Rowe, president, Local Union no. 911. The reason given was:

> The facts of the case indicate that Mr. Webb did indeed tip two crates of glass, knowingly concealed the damage, and failed to report the incident to his supervisor. The disciplinary action taken was appropriate given the facts. Grievance denied.

The Grievance was appealed in a letter dated June 16, 1999. The appeal stated:

> L-26-9—The Union is in dispute with the Company's position pertaining to the discipline of this grievant; therefore this grievance is appealed to arbitration.

Issue
Was the Grievant's discharge for just cause?
If not, what is the remedy?

Relevant Provisions of the Agreement
Article 2—Management

2.01　The Union agrees that the Company is vested exclusively with the management of the business, including the direction of the working force, the right to plan, direct, and control all plant operations; the right to relieve employees from duty because of lack of work or for any other legitimate reason; the right to establish, change, or introduce new or improved production methods or facilities; and, except as expressly limited by the provisions of this Agreement, the right to hire, promote, suspend, demote, discipline or discharge employees for just cause.

2.02　All authority normally exercised by Management is and shall remain the exclusive prerogative of the Company, except where such authority is expressly limited by the terms of this Agreement.

2.03　Any alleged discrimination or violation of the terms of this Agreement deemed to exist as a result of the exercise of these prerogatives by the Company shall be subject to the Grievance Procedure of this Agreement.

Article 5—Settlement of Grievances
(e) Step 5: Arbitration

> . . . The arbitrator shall have jurisdiction and authority only to interpret, apply or determine compliance with the provisions of this Agreement insofar as shall be necessary to the determination of the grievance submitted to him, but he shall not have jurisdiction or authority to add to, subtract from or alter in any way, the provisions of this Agreement. . . .

Article 8—Complaint against Discharge or Suspension

8.01　In the event an employee who has been suspended or discharged by the Company believes he has been unjustly dealt with, such complaint may be processed under Step 3 of the grievance procedure. Any regular employee so affected will be given the reason for such discipline in writing and the Union shall be furnished a copy of same. The Company shall provide the Local President a copy of the disciplinary action by placing a copy in his mailbox.

8.02　It is understood, however, that any complaint arising under this Section must be presented by the Company in writing within three (3) calendar days after such suspension or discharge, or the particular case will be considered closed. The time limits set forth herein shall not include Saturdays, Sundays, or Holidays.

Article 32—Rules

32.01 For the purpose of plant discipline, the Company shall have the right to make and, after publication thereof, to enforce reasonable factory rules, not otherwise inconsistent with the terms of this Agreement.

32.02 The purpose of disciplinary action is not to punish, but to discourage repetition of misbehavior by the offender.

32.03 If the Company should post a new rule that the Union should consider unreasonable, it shall be subject to the grievance procedure.

32.04 The reasonableness of the following factory rules are agreed to by the parties and shall be subject to the following outlined disciplinary action.

Category B—This covers the disciplinary procedure for handling those types of offenses that require more severe penalty:
First Offense—Five-day suspension (working days)
Second Offense—Discharge
(12) Negligent acts resulting in loss of production or damage to Company property.

Position of the Company

The Company stated that on April 27, 1999, Mr. Webb, a forklift operator in the Shipping Department, was working the day shift pulling orders for glass crates from the warehouse. The order list from which the Grievant was working called for one crate of $1/16$" $\times$ 48" $\times$ 84", heavy case (HC) gray glass located in Zone no. 326. The Grievant proceeded to this location and was removing a two-crate pack (banded together) of the required glass when he accidentally tipped over a second two-crate pack, which was located immediately behind the first one. The tipped over pack made a loud noise when it fell, and the noise was heard by both the Grievant and two employees who were working in the "repair" area some 25 to 30 feet away. Instead of stopping to check to see what had happened, the Grievant proceeded to lower the two-crate pack he had on his forks, cut the band holding them together, set one single crate back on top of a three-tier stack, and drive off to the dock staging area with the single crate. His actions were observed by two other hourly employees who were working in the "repair" area and who subsequently reported the incident to supervision. Mr. Webb never reported the incident to any member of supervision. In fact, the Grievant created a safety hazard for his fellow employees by setting a single unbanded crate on a three-tier stack.

On investigation of the incident by area supervision, the Company determined that Mr. Webb had acted negligently in the performance of his duties. His failure to report the accident and making the situation a dangerous one by stacking a single unbanded crate on the three-tier stack reflected a total disregard for his job responsibilities and the safety of his fellow employees.

The Company argued that the Grievance is without merit. At the time of his discharge, Mr. Webb was working in a probationary status under the terms of a last chance agreement dated March 27, 1998. The terms of this agreement specifically state that "the violation of any plant rule during the probationary period will result in immediate discharge." The probationary period extended from March 27, 1998, through September 27, 1999. The present incident occurred on April 27, 1999, well within the probationary period. The last chance agreement was a final opportunity for the Grievant to preserve his job. Mr. Webb, the president of Local 911,

Continued

and the vice president of Local 911 all signed the agreement. The agreement has both a starting and ending time frame, and its probationary period does not exceed any of the probationary time frames outlined under Article 32—Rules of the Labor Agreement.

The Company argued that Mr. Webb had been given an opportunity to retain his job. The Company went beyond what the Labor Agreement demands in the way of "second chances." This is evidenced by the fact that a last chance agreement was entered into with the Grievant. Although the Company was well within its rights and the provisions of the Labor Agreement to discharge the Grievant in March 1998, it gave the Grievant a final opportunity to save his job. The last chance agreement was above and beyond the requirements of the Labor Agreement and demonstrates that the Company was not "out to get" the Grievant.

Eyewitness testimony from fellow employee Donnie Ossie indicated that he saw the Grievant tip over the two crates of glass in question. Although fellow employee James Staples did not see it, he testified that he heard a loud noise where Mr. Webb was working and asked Donnie Ossie if "Danny had turned over some glass." Even Mr. Webb himself admitted that he heard a loud noise when he attempted to lift two crates of glass (banded together) from the third tier, but he did not check to see if there was any damage. This action goes to the very heart of why the Grievant was charged for performing his job in a negligent manner. Basic common sense would dictate that a person would check to see if he had caused an accident and, if so, to report it to the proper authority.

The Company claimed that Mr. Webb is not an inexperienced novice in the workplace who can claim he did not know what he was supposed to do in such a situation. He confirmed that he had worked at the Company since 1973, that he was aware of the fact that he was supposed to report all accidents to supervision, and if cleanup was involved, that the person causing the damage was the one who was supposed to clean it up. Yet, despite his understanding of the rules, he failed to report the accident and clean up his mess. Furthermore, he exacerbated the situation by creating a safety hazard by placing a single crate of glass (unbanded) on the third tier.

The Company claimed that Mr. Webb did not admit to nor deny that he "could have" tipped over the two crates of glass. His lone defense was that he just did not know whether he had tipped the glass over. He did admit to hearing a loud noise as he was removing two other crates of glass. Again, the fact that the Grievant was experienced on the job and the fact that basic common sense would prompt any prudent person to check to see what had caused the noise call into question the credibility of the Grievant. The Grievant confirmed that the lone eyewitness was positioned at a location where he could have observed if any crates had been turned over. The noise created by the falling glass was of sufficient volume that another employee in the "repair" area heard and reacted to it. All these facts paint an undeniable picture that Mr. Webb acted negligently.

The Company stated that the Union alleged that forklift operators had been told by supervisors to stack single crates on the third tier. The Grievant testified that supervisors had instructed them to "pack the crates tight" against one another. When Mr. Webb was asked if any supervisor had ever told him to stack single crates on the third tier, Mr. Webb said that he had been told to pack them tight. When pressed further, Mr. Webb admitted that he had never been told directly by any member of supervision to stack single crates on the third tier. In fact, Mr. Webb confirmed that the standard method of operation was to stack two-crate packs of glass, which are banded together, when stacking three tiers high.

The Grievant was asked if he thought that stacking single crates, three tiers high presented a safety hazard to himself or to others. The Grievant said, "no." He further stated that on April 27, 1999, he broke the band on a two-crate pack, took one crate out, and returned the single crate to its former position on top of the third tier. Mr. Webb stated that the total width of a single crate was 12 to 13 inches wide and that the weight of a single crate would exceed 4,000 pounds. It is clear that such a crate would be less stable than a two-crate banded pack, yet Mr. Webb maintained that he did not believe this to be a safety hazard. In fact, he admitted to setting a single crate on the third tier as a freestanding object with no other standing crate behind it. This action violates even the Grievant's own version of the stacking instructions, which was to pack single crates tight against other crates. There were no standing crates behind the single crate that the Grievant placed on the third tier. This illustrates that Mr. Webb was negligent in the performance of his job and that he did indeed create a real safety hazard for himself and other employees.

Supervisor Brian Waters testified that the two crates of glass that were tipped over by the Grievant were valued at $2,320. This figure did not include the cost associated with removal and disposal of the broken glass. Mr. Waters testified that both of the crates of glass were total losses. Supervisor Waters pointed out that the proper way to handle crates of glass would have been to insert the forks of the forklift under the two-crate pack to be loaded but not to the point that the forks would extend beyond the two-crate pack being lifted. If the forks were fully inserted, they would extend below the next two-crate packs behind the two-crate pack being lifted. When the driver raised the forks to lift the front two-crate pack, the tips of the protruding forks will act as a lever on the second two-crate pack and cause it to topple. The Company's position is that this is exactly what Mr. Webb did when he toppled the crates of glass.

The Company concluded that it had presented unrefuted evidence that:

- The Grievant was given one more chance to save his job than was required by the labor contract.

- The Grievant had previously reached the discharge step for progressive discipline under Category B rules.

- The Grievant was working under a last chance agreement in which any violation would subject him to immediate discharge.

- The last chance agreement was agreed to by the Company, the Grievant, and the Union as evidenced by their signatures on the document.

- The last chance agreement specified a beginning and ending date, set a probationary period that was in line with the probationary periods used elsewhere in the labor contract, and specified that violation of any plant rules during the probationary period would result in immediate discharge.

- The incident that occurred on April 27, 1999, was within the probationary period of the last chance agreement (March 27, 1998, to September 27, 1999).

- The incident was witnessed by bargaining unit employee Donnie Ossie and heard by bargaining unit employee James Staples, as well as the Grievant himself.

- The Grievant removed a two-crate pack from the third tier, broke the band, removed a single crate, and set a single crate back on the third tier, thus creating a safety hazard.

- The grievant was never instructed by any member of supervision to stack a single crate on the third tier of any stack.

- The Grievant acted negligently in the performance of his job

Therefore, the Company respectfully requests that the Arbitrator deny this grievance.

Continued

Position of the Union

The Union stated that Mr. Webb was hired by the Company into the Flat Glass Department on April 23, 1973. He worked packing glass for 3 years and drove a forklift approximately 8 years. He had been working in this shipping department since 1991 and has worked all the jobs in the department. At the time of his discharge, he was a forklift driver, pulling stock.

On April 28, 1999, the Grievant worked the day shift (7:00 A.M. to 3:00 A.M.). Near the end of the shift, he was told by his supervisor that he was required to work overtime on the next shift. He was not the lowest in used overtime and went looking for Mr. Bob Crain, the Union Steward for the department on that shift. While he was looking for Mr. Crain, he saw Mr. Joe Broadway, the Local Union vice president. Mr. Broadway told the Grievant that Mr. Crain was in the personnel office to represent the Grievant. Mr. Broadway told the Grievant that the Company was going to fire him for turning over some glass the day before. Mr. Webb told Mr. Broadway he did not know anything about it. The Grievant went back to his department, and his supervisor told him that he was wanted in Mr. Don Grey's office. The Grievant and his supervisor went to Mr. Grey's office, where the Grievant was discharged for "violation of plant rules including negligent act resulting in damage to Company property. Category B (12)" and "violation of last chance agreement dated March 27, 1998."

The Union stated that Mr. Donnie Ossie testified that he and Mr. James Staples were working in the "repair" area of the shipping department approximately 30 to 40 feet from where the Grievant removed two crates of HC glass from the third stack with a forklift. The two crates were banded together. He stated that when the Grievant was getting the two crates down, the fork on the forklift tipped over two other crates of glass and that he heard glass breaking. He stated that the Grievant cut the bands of the two crates, put one crate back up where the two crates had been, and carried the other crate of glass with him. He testified that the Grievant said something to him, but he could not hear what he said because of the noise. He testified that there was space behind the two crates that were tipped and that, if they had been stacked properly, the two crates could not have fallen. He indicated that the two-crate pack that was tipped over was next to and behind the two-crate pack that the Grievant removed from the stack.

Mr. Ossie testified that the glass in question had been shipped from Mexico, that the crates were not very steady, and that the crates of glass from Mexico would sometimes fall if you looked directly at them. He testified that everyone who worked in shipping had broken some glass and that employees had to do the best they could. Mr. Ossie admitted that he did not see any broken glass in the area.

Mr. James Staples testified that he and Mr. Ossie were in the "repair" area and that he heard a noise and determined that it came from the area where Mr. Webb was loading crates of glass. He did not see any crates of glass fall and could not see the two crates that were laying flat. He admitted that it was common for people to break glass and that it was a noisy work area.

The Company had stated that the Grievant said that he had an order for one crate of $1/_{16}$" × 48" × 84" glass. He went into the area and pulled a two-crate pack of $1/_{16}$" × 48" × 84" glass from the third tier, cut the bands, and put one crate back on the third tier as he had been instructed to do by his supervisor. He then carried one crate with him and put it in the dock area. He testified that, when he was loading the two-crate pack of $1/_{16}$" × 48" × 84" glass, he heard a noise but could not see what had caused the noise and that he did not know whether or not he had turned over the two-crate pack of glass. He stated that he had to drive down the aisle before he could see the two crates laying flat on the top of the other crates. He did not know if they were laying flat before he got the two crates or not. He testified that he asked Mr. Ossie and Mr. Staples if they had heard the noise, but they could not hear him because of the noise in the plant, and he did not pursue it. He stated that he saw an empty space behind the two-crate pack of glass that he loaded but could not see any other crates behind on the third tier. The Grievant testified that he had broken glass before and that everyone who drove a forklift had broken glass. To his knowledge, no one had ever been disciplined for breaking glass. He stated that no one from Management ever talked to him about the alleged incident until the meeting near the end of the shift on April 28, 1998, and he knew nothing about the alleged incident until that meeting. Each employee testified that if the two crates of glass in question had been stacked properly, they would have been against the wall and could not have fallen.

The Union argued that the Company did not afford the Grievant anything that even slightly resembled due process. Mr. Crain testified that he made up his mind to discharge the Grievant at about 6:00 P.M. on April 27, 1999. At that time, he had talked only to his supervisors, none of whom had any direct knowledge of what had or had not happened. Until the meeting on April 28, 1999, the only supervisor who possibly had any direct knowledge of what happened was the supervisor to whom Mr. Ossie reported that the glass had been tipped over by Mr. Webb. There was no evidence that any Company official ever talked to Mr. James Staples until the day of the arbitration hearing. In other words, Mr. Crain made the decision to discharge Mr. Webb at 6:00 P.M. on the April 27, 1999, without talking to anyone other than Mr. Ossie, who could not have possibly seen the forks on the Grievant's forklift tip over the two-crate pack of glass in question. There was no evidence that any member of Management checked the wood on the crates to see whether there were marks other than those made by the forks on the lift truck. The Union argued that Mr. Crain made the decision to discharge Mr. Webb on April 27, 1999, at 6:00 P.M. and was not going to change his mind.

The Union stated that it is clear that the Company did not conduct a fair investigation and did not afford the Grievant due process by any stretch of the imagination. As such, that is grounds alone to sustain the Grievance. The majority of arbitrators have reversed discipline and discharge of employees when the employer has violated the basic notion of fairness and due process.

The Union stated that Mr. Webb testified that when he was getting the two-crate pack of $1/_{16}$" × 48" × 84" glass, he could see empty space behind them, that he could not see any other crates behind them, and that during the time he was removing the two-crate pack he heard a noise but could not tell what had caused it. Mr. Staples testified that he heard a noise but that it did not sound like glass was breaking. Mr. Webb testified that he broke the bands on the two-crate pack of glass, cut the band, set one crate back on top, and took the one crate he needed with him to the dock area. He stated that as he was backing up with the two-crate pack of glass, at some point he could see the two crates laying flat on top of the stack. The Grievant stated without reservation that he did not know if the two crates of glass were laying flat when he came to the row or if he had accidentally tipped them over.

The Union argued that the evidence clearly shows that the glass fell over on its own as a result of the Grievant possibly bumping the front of the stack or that the movement of the glass being lifted caused the row to move, causing it to tip over. Mr. Ossie testified that the glass that is packed at the Mexico plant would fall over if you looked at it. It is clear that the fork of the forklift could not have possibly tipped over the glass.

The crate extended 8 to 10 inches beyond the end of the forks. According to the order list, the glass was 48 inches wide. Allowing two inches on each side for the crate, the total width of the crates would be 52 inches. The forks were approximately 46 inches long. If two of the crates are 24 to 26 inches across, the forks would not go all the way through the four crates. If

Continued

the Grievant had attempted to raise the four crates up as described by Mr. Ossie, they would have had to have been stacked close together. If the two crates were set up from where they are shown to be laying, there is no possible way the forklift could have touched them. If the forks had gone under all four of the crates as described by Mr. Ossie, the forklift could not have lifted them, and they surely could not have fallen off the forks.

The Union stated that there were no marks of any kind anywhere on the wooden crates that could have been made by the forks on the forklift. If they had been tipped over by the forks, there would have had to be some type of marks on the wood. Thus, the crates could not possibly have been turned over or tipped over by the forklift driven by Mr. Webb.

The Union stated that the Company position that Mr. Webb set the single crate of glass back on top was destroyed by the testimony of the Grievant that just a few days before the alleged incident his supervisor had told him to do exactly as he did in this case. Therefore, the Company presented no evidence whatsoever that the Grievant was negligent or that he tried to hide anything.

The Union closed by stating:

> For all of the above, the Union requests that the arbitrator sustain the grievance, order the Company to reinstate the Grievant to his job without loss of seniority and make him whole for all wages and benefits lost.

QUESTIONS

1. What is a last chance agreement?
2. Does a last chance agreement limit the arbitrator's authority? If so, how? If not, why not?
3. Is the length of the probationary period in the last chance agreement reasonable? If not, does this period make the last chance agreement unreasonable?
4. What proof does the Company have that the Grievant did what he was accused of?
5. What are the mitigating factors? Should the arbitrator consider these mitigating factors in reviewing the penalty assessed by the Company?
6. You be the arbitrator. You decide and give your reasoning.

Racing Cars on Leave of Absence

Background

The Electronic Workers Union (EWU) is the bargaining representative for the production and maintenance employees of Hooper, Inc. in Beauregard, Alabama. During the term of their collective bargaining agreement dated May 5, 1989, the parties were unable to resolve a grievance involving the termination of Bubba Jones, a member of the bargaining unit. Under the provisions of the agreement's grievance procedure, the matter was appealed to arbitration.

The grievance was filed by Bubba Jones and his union representative, Jimmy Short, on August 15, 1990. It states:

> I, Bubba Jones, was terminated on August 5, 1990 from Hooper for engaging in employment while on a leave of absence. I race stock cars Class C at Beauregard Motor Speedway in my spare time for a hobby. I was hurt pretty bad in a car wreck one weekend racing. I then had to go on a leave of absence. While on leave of absence, my name was put in the newspaper for taking a first one time, first and second the second time, weeks later. The Company then found out about the articles and terminated me for engaging in employment while on a leave of absence. Now none of these races pays any money at all, just trophies. Also, most of the time I have had someone in my pit crew driving the car for me till I had recovered from injuries back on June 22, 1990. Larry Tate, Jim Grimes, and Billy Jack Jones have alternated driving the car most of the time. If this is employment, where is my paycheck? I wish to be reinstated with all seniority, back pay, and all benefits.

The parties stipulated that Bubba Jones's winnings while he was on leave totaled $65, including $10 won on July 2, $40 on July 9, $5 on July 16, and $10 on July 23. They agreed that he was on a leave of absence at the time he received these prizes and that the injury sustained by the Grievant in his June 22 accident was a lumbar strain—injuries to his neck and back.

Bubba Jones testified that he was 29 years old and had been hired by Hooper in June 1978. His last day of work was June 21, 1990. He reported off on personal leave on June 22. That night he was injured in a car wreck at the Beauregard Motor Speedway when he was hit from behind, and his car went into the wall. He sustained injuries to his neck and back. He reported off on sick leave for 6 or 7 days and then applied for a leave of absence. It was approved. His doctor indicated he would be able to return to work on September 12. During the period following his injury he went to a physician for treatment three or four times per week.

Mr. Jones testified that at no time during his leave did anyone from the Company contact him to tell him he should return to work because he was driving a race car. He said he was not employed by anyone at any time during his leave of absence. He denied receiving any compensation for working while on leave.

Mr. Jones stated that 1990 was his first year of racing. Before his injury he had won some prize money but had not won any races. He said there were three classes of racing at the Speedway. Class A is professional or semiprofessional, and the drivers receive compensation, but he was not aware whether the Speedway owners paid them. They receive prize money for all races. Class B is one step up from amateur, and they also receive prize money for all races. Class C is amateur, and only the "feature race" in Class C pays prize money: $50 for first, $40 for second, $30 for third, and $20 for fourth and fifth place. In the feature race, anyone who starts and finishes gets $10; anyone who starts and does not finish gets $5. In addition to the feature race, there are three other Class C races for which only trophies are awarded to winners.

Continued

Bubba Jones stated that the owner of the Speedway is Bill Gates. Gates paid him nothing other than the prize money for driving in the races. The Grievant's brother introduced him to racing, but before the 5 weeks prior to his accident, he had never raced. He never considered racing as a possible occupation but only as a hobby.

Mr. Jones stated that while he was on leave, he received sick leave pay of $198 per week. He said he was injured on a Wednesday. He did not race until about 2 weeks after that. At that time, because his car had been demolished in his accident, he drove one of his brother's cars. He said there are four or five people in the pit crew, who receive no compensation.

After August 5, the date of his termination, Mr. Jones said he continued to race and won additional prize money. He said that all the prize money he received was given to his brother to pay for repairs to the car he drove. Mr. Jones did not pay his brother anything in addition to that. His brother did not pay him, and Mr. Gates did not consider Bubba Jones to be his brother's employee. Mr. Jones said he finished out the summer and fall races using his brother's car. He said he had not been employed by his brother at any time after his termination.

After his termination, Mr. Jones got a job at Briarwood in landscaping. After he was laid off from Briarwood at the end of the season, he received unemployment compensation and has been unemployed since then.

Mr. Jones said he was never told by anyone at the Hooper Company that racing his car violated the agreement. No one from the Company ever called him to say that what he was doing was wrong and that he should stop. He said there was no withholding for taxes or social security from his winnings. His understanding with his brother was that he could keep the trophies, but his brother got the prize money.

Mr. Jones explained that the newspaper articles upon which the Company based its decision to fire him reported only "trophy" races in which he had won no money. He explained that that was the reason why his grievance stated there was no money associated with his racing. He said his name was not listed in any newspaper reports of feature races in which he actually did win money, although there was one "championship" race at the end of the year that paid more than $50 in Class C.

Mr. Jones said that when he wrote his grievance he had the newspaper articles about his races and knew they referred only to the trophy races he had won. When he filed the grievance he based what he said on what he knew was in the news articles. No one specifically had told him the Company had terminated him for the articles in the newspaper; he figured that was the reason.

Mr. Jones testified that there was a midseason race in addition to the championship race at the end of the season that paid more than $50 for first place. He did not win that race but did win $50 in it. That was on June 18, before his injury.

Billy Jack Jones, brother of the Grievant, testified that he was employed by Faust Auto Parts, Inc., as a mechanic and that he races stock cars as a hobby in Class C. He also testified that his brother had raced one of his cars in 1990. He said he had not paid his brother anything for driving the car and that he did not consider him his employee. They did have an understanding that any winnings would be put back into the car to keep it going. His brother was entitled to keep any trophies he won. Billy Jack testified that his pit crew members were also not paid; they performed their services as a hobby.

Jim Grimes, president and business manager for the local union, testified he had held that position since 1981 and before that had been chief steward. He said in his experience, he was unaware that the Company had any practice of monitoring amateur sports activities of employees who were on leave. He stated that there had never been a company directive that employees could not receive prize money while competing in amateur sports. It was the Union's understanding that amateur sport activities are not considered employment. If the Company had any question about an employee's ability to perform his or her job based on outside activities, the Company would have the right to cancel the employee's leave of absence and tell him or her to report to work.

Mr. Grimes recalled only one employee who had been terminated for working while on leave of absence. That employee owned a body shop and was receiving direct compensation for working on cars while on leave. He was self-employed.

The Issue

Did Bubba Jones violate Section XII, Leave of Absence, (G) Working While on Leave of Absence? If not, what is the appropriate remedy?

Relevant contractural provisions are as follows:

Section XII
Leave of Absence
(G) Working While on Leave of Absence
No employee may engage in other employment while on an approved leave of absence unless he first secures written permission from the Manager of Labor Relations. Failure to obtain such permission will result in termination.

Position of the Company

In 1983, the Company stated that it had terminated under the same language an employee on a medical leave of absence who worked for himself at a body shop and garage during the time he was on leave. This grievant had no intention of deceiving the Company and was in fact ignorant of the provisions of the agreement. The provisions of the agreement were clear and unambiguous, and the parties have agreed on the penalty for engaging in employment while on leave—termination.

In that case as in this, the Grievant was earning money from an activity that he had engaged in before his leave of absence and continued to be engaged in during the leave. In both cases, the Grievant did not ask permission from the company to continue to engage in such employment.

The Company argued that the applicable language in the case mandates that all other employment must cease while on a medical leave of absence, regardless of whether carried on before the leave, unless written permission is obtained from the Company. This mandate is particularly significant where the Grievant is unable to perform his duties at the Company but continues to engage in the same activity for profit that he was engaged in when he suffered his injury, thereby depriving the employer of his services.

The Company contended that the fact that the Grievant earned only $65 while on leave is not at all relevant to this case. If he had advanced to Class A or B, he might have earned as much as a fully employed person in many industries. It is also irrelevant that the Grievant gave his brother his earnings. Once the Grievant won the prizes, he could do whatever he wished with his prize money. The principle is not the amount earned or the time during which he was employed as a race driver. The principle is that the Grievant violated the contractual rule; the penalty is termination.

The Company responded to the Union contention that this is a recreation or hobby; not employment, by asking, "What is the result of that argument had the Grievant been so proficient as a driver that during the period of his leave he had raced at tracks all around the Southeast?" The point is that he was engaged in this employment for profit while on medical leave without asking permission and that it was the same employment in which he initially injured himself.

Continued

597

The Company pointed out that the *American Heritage Dictionary* defines *employment* as follows:

1.a. The act of employing, b. The state of being employed. 2. The work in which one is engaged; business. 3. An activity to which one devotes time.

Under these definitions, the Grievant was clearly engaged in an activity to which he devoted time, and moreover, from which he received financial renumeration, irrespective of the amount.

The Company claimed that if the arbitrator were to allow this grievance, it would be a change in the words of provisions of the agreement, an action prohibited by the agreement.

Position of the Union

The Union stated that Bubba Jones's activity was not employment. The majority of cases in which an employer attempts to enforce a provision similar to the one in the instant case involves an employee who is "moonlighting" by holding a second job during off hours. It is usually clear in these cases that the employee has engaged in other employment. Arbitrator Volz, in *Alcan Aluminum Corp*, 90 L.A. 16 (1987), held that the Company must meet its burden of proof by showing that the Grievant engaged in other employment within the meaning of the applicable provisions. He cited *Ballentine's Law Dictionary*:

Work. Noun: Employment. Any form of physical or mental exertion, or both combined, for the attainment of some object other than recreation or amusement....Physical or mental exertion, whether burdensome or not, controlled or required by an employer.

In *Standard Brands, Inc.*, 52 L.A. 918, 919 (1969), the Grievant, while on a leave, frequently waited on customers and closed a friend's tavern at night but was not paid. Arbitrator Trotta determined that this was not employment.

The Company discharged Jones for engaging in employment while on leave of absence. Clearly amateur stock car racing does not fall under the definition of the word "work." Jones raced stock cars purely for recreational purposes. He did not consider himself an employee, and no taxes were withheld for maintenance of his brother's car. Therefore, Jones was not self-employed, nor did he work for another employer. Jones himself stated this best in his grievance, "If this is employment, where is my paycheck?" The fact that Jones won a little money and two trophies does not turn a recreation into a job or employment.

The Union claimed that the Company had not published a rule that certain recreation would be considered employment. For discharge to be just, the employee must reasonably know his actions might lead to discharge. An employee could not have known stock car racing would result in discharge. To give such an interpretation to Section XII (G) would be unfair to Jones. While stock car racing may not have been the wisest thing to do while on leave of absence, It certainly is not employment and no different from any other form of recreation.

Jones considered a later job to be employment. After his separation and after he was released for work in September, Jones worked for a landscaping business. This was a job: It was work considered by him to be employment.

The previous arbitration's matter is distinguishable. The employee had established an auto repair and body shop business in 1976. While on a leave in 1982, he was working in his repair shop. The Company discharged him for working while on leave. The arbitrator upheld the discharge, because he concluded the employee was engaged in self-employment that was supported by a stipulation of the parties that he was "working" during his leave. Unlike that case, Jones was not working while on a leave of absence but was only engaged in recreation.

The Union concluded that the Company has failed to meet its burden of proof by showing that Jones was engaged in other employment within the meaning of the provision. Therefore, the grievance of Bubba Jones should be sustained and he should be reinstated to his employment with full back pay and without loss of seniority and benefits, less any interim earnings from employment.

SOURCE: The authors express their appreciation to Dr. Paul Gerhart, Case Western Reserve University, for providing this case.

QUESTIONS

1. Evaluate the use of dictionary definitions in terms of their value in the arbitration proceedings.
2. Of what value is the use of previous arbitration cases and decisions of other arbitrators?
3. Does the arbitrator have any leeway in making a decision based on the language of Section XII?
4. After reviewing the elements of employee discipline, did the Company violate the agreement? Explain. If so, what would be the remedy?

Is an Employee Entitled to Have a Witness at a Disciplinary Interview?

Terry Williams, an employee at a Memphis, Tennessee, plant, clocked out on Friday afternoon at 3:30 P.M., half an hour before his regular workday ended. He was later seen distributing union leaflets on the sidewalk near the main plant by plant manager Otto Payonzeck. Payonzeck confronted Williams and asked him what he was doing at the Southhaven, Mississippi, plant 8 miles south of Memphis. Payonzeck then called the personnel office at the Memphis plant to see if Williams had permission to be at Southhaven.

When Williams reported to work the next day, he was called to a meeting with supervisors Fisher and Gray and personnel administrator Harless. As soon as Williams entered the room, he recognized the people and asked to be permitted to call another employee into the room as a witness. Harless responded that it was not necessary because they were only going to ask him some questions and therefore he did not need a witness. Williams then asked to make a phone call, and this request was likewise rejected.

The supervisors and Harless proceeded to ask Williams questions about what he did after he left work early on the previous workday. The meeting lasted 15 minutes, and Williams refused to answer any questions. In fact, Williams' response to most questions was that it was none of their business. He was permitted to leave the meeting and was told to return at 10 A.M. During the break, he called the NLRB's regional office. At 10 A.M., he returned to the meeting and was told that he was being suspended for 3 days.

Supervisor Fisher said that on the morning of the day that Williams was suspended, he met with Harless to determine disciplinary action. Gray had suggested discharge; however, it was decided to suspend Williams for 3 days. Fisher said that Williams was refused a witness and the telephone call because they were not going to fire him, they were just going to suspend him. In fact, Williams refused to answer any questions about the rule infraction of leaving early to distribute union literature.

Supervisor Gray's version of the incident varied slightly from Fisher's. She recalled that Harless told Williams, after denying his request to use the telephone, that he was being suspended for 3 days, but Harless would continue to investigate the matter.

QUESTIONS

1. Was Williams entitled to have a witness at the meeting with Harless, Gray, and Fisher? Explain.
2. To what remedy is an employee entitled if his or her rights have been violated?
3. What would happen if the Company had a union, and Williams was a member? What if the Company had no union? Explain.
4. Should this suspension be upheld? Explain.

PART 4

Applying the Labor Relations Process to Different Labor Relations Systems

Part 4 presents the opportunity to apply the previous chapters' discussions of the labor relations process to various labor relations situations. Collective bargaining in the public sector at all governmental levels is discussed, and a discussion of foreign labor relations processes is presented for comparative purposes.

CHAPTER 13

Labor Relations in the Public Sector

T*he public sector has become an important factor in the U.S. labor scene. As the number of public employees has increased, so has the number of these employees joining unions. This chapter presents an overview of labor relations in the public sector and provides a brief summary of the similarities and differences in public- and private-sector labor relations. It also examines public-sector bargaining at the local, state, and federal levels and concludes with a discussion of labor relations affecting some groups of public-sector employees.*

Significance of Public-Sector Labor Relations

The field of public-sector labor relations has developed from a time when public employees were required to lobby their respective legislators for favorable employment terms to one in which bona fide collective bargaining occurs. Public-sector labor relations has moved from an earlier period characterized by rapid union growth, management's inability to react to collective bargaining, and a fear of strikes to a period characterized by slower union growth, most states providing public employee bargaining rights, and a willingness on the part of public employers to take strikes.[1] With many state legislatures and the U.S. Congress interested in reducing government costs, management strategies, such as downsizing and privatization of public services, have caused many public employees to become more concerned about their job security and welfare.[2] Therefore, union leaders are showing increased attention to public employees' concerns in these areas (see "Labor Relations in Action" box).

In 2002, 7.4 million union members made up 37.9 percent of total public-sector (federal, state, and local) employment.[3] About 33 percent of federal employees, 31 percent of state employees, and 43 percent of local government employees are union members. This union density level is much higher than the 9.3 percent of private-sector employees represented for purposes of collective bargaining.

In terms of government function, unions represent a majority of postal employees, teachers, firefighters, police, and bus and urban transit employees. There are also major differences in public-sector union membership based on geography. Public-sector union membership is much greater in the Northeast, North, and West than in the South and Midwest. For example, public-sector union membership is 74.4 percent in New York, 70.3 percent in Rhode Island, 69.0 percent in Hawaii, and 60.7 percent in New Jersey as compared with 5.1 percent in Mississippi, 8.6 percent in North Carolina, 10.2 percent in South Carolina, and 11.0 percent in Virginia.[4]

Exhibit 13.1 presents a listing of some national unions representing public-sector employees. Some national unions (e.g., United Auto Workers, International Association of Machinists), which predominantly represent private-sector employees, have also diversified their organizing efforts in recent years to attract public-sector employees. The Service Employees International Union (SEIU) now represents over 600,000 public-sector employees in the United States, Canada, and Puerto Rico.[5]

The so-called "free rider" issue mentioned in the discussion of private-sector union security issues in Chapter 4 is an important factor affecting union membership among federal employees.[6] Under the Civil Service Reform Act (CSRA) of 1978 and the Postal Reorganization Act, union security clauses, such as a union agency shop, are prohibited. Therefore, unions are required to represent all employees in recognized bargaining units but receive no fees or dues from those who choose not

EXHIBIT 13.1

Some Unions Representing Public Employees

Union	Number of Public Employee Members Represented
American Federation of Government Employees (AFGE)	600,000
American Federation of State, County, and Municipal Employees (AFSCME)	1,400,000
American Federation of Teachers (AFT)	1,000,000
American Postal Workers Union (APWU)	330,000
Fraternal Order of Police (FOP)	240,000
International Association of Firefighters (IAFF)	310,000
National Air Traffic Controllers Association (NATCA)	15,000
National Association of Letter Carriers (NALC)	300,000
National Education Association (NEA)	2,700,000
National Federation of Federal Employees (NFFE, IAM)	7,500
National Rural Letter Carriers Association (NRLCA)	100,000
National Treasury Employees Union (NTEU)	150,000

SOURCE: *Directory of U.S. Labor Organizations, 1997 edition*, ed. C. D. Gifford (Washington, D.C.: The Bureau of National Affairs, 1997), pp. 47–78; updated from each union's Web page.

to be union members. Because the so-called free riders receive benefits at no cost to them, there is not a significant incentive to join and pay dues. The American Federation of Government Employees (AFGE) is the largest union representing federal government employees. Although its membership is 199,000, the AFGE is legally required to represent nearly 600,000 federal government employees and negotiates over 300 collective bargaining agreements. In other words, 66 percent of the federal government employees who are represented the AFGE do not pay dues; therefore, 34 percent of those who are members pay dues to provide representational services (bargaining, grievance handling, arbitration, etc.) for the other 66 percent (see Chapter 4 for discussion of union security issues). As a result, the U.S. federal government is the nation's largest "open shop" employer.[7]

Labor Legislation in the Public Sector

The presence of a strong public-sector bargaining law may be influenced by the general public's attitude toward collective bargaining, the degree of private-sector employers' opposition to unions, and the degree to which state legislators are viewed as being more "liberal," among other factors.[8] Favorable legislation protecting employees' right to bargain, regulating unfair labor practices, and establishing impasse procedures to resolve both interests and rights-type labor disputes is a significant factor encouraging the growth of public-sector bargaining within a state.[9]

As shown in Exhibit 13.2, 23 states have passed legislation allowing collective bargaining, which covers police and fire, state, education, and municipal employees. Twelve states (Alabama, Arizona, Arkansas, Colorado, Louisiana, Maryland, Mississippi, Missouri, North Carolina, South Carolina, Virginia, and West Virginia) have no legislation that allows these types of public employees to participate in collective bargaining. The remaining states have legislation that allows collective bargaining for one or more of the police and fire, state, education, and municipal employee groups. Thirty-two states provide bargaining rights to police and

EXHIBIT 13.2

Public Sector Collective Bargaining Laws Covering Police & Fire, State, Education and Municipal Employees

Alaska	Massachusetts	New York
Connecticut	Michigan	Ohio
Delaware	Minnesota	Oregon
Florida	Montana	Pennsylvania
Hawaii	Nebraska	Rhode Island
Illinois	New Hampshire	Vermont
Iowa	New Jersey	Wisconsin
Maine	New Mexico	

SOURCE: Bureau of National Affairs, "Public Sector Bargaining—State Comparison Chart," in *Collective Bargaining Negotiating and Contracts,* May 18, 2000, pp. 8:2901–2952; updated by "State Labor Laws," *BNA Labor Relations Reporter,* Washington, D.C., 2003.

firefighters, 35 states provide bargaining rights to public education employees, 26 states provide bargaining rights to municipal employees, and 23 states provide bargaining rights to state employees.[10]

Forty-one states have enacted statutes permitting public school employees to bargain collectively with boards of education, and over 80 percent of the teachers are covered by collective-bargaining agreements.[11] Although the content of these agreements may vary, the typical agreement would include provisions such as those found in Exhibit 13.3.

The scope of bargaining subjects covered under most state bargaining laws include wages, hours, and other terms or conditions of employment similar to the scope of bargaining under the private-sector LMRA. However, a majority of the states have some statutory limitations on the scope of collective bargaining, such as limitations guaranteeing management rights. Another important element of labor legislation is unfair labor practices. Although these vary somewhat from state to state, most states have legislation defining unfair labor practices for some or all public employees that are similar to the types of discrimination banned under the private-sector LMRA (e.g., bad-faith bargaining, threats or reprisals for engaging in concerted and protected activity).

Thirteen states permit public-sector strikes by some groups of public employees either by statutory law or judicial decision.[12] These states are Arkansas,

Exhibit 13.3

Provisions in a Collective-Bargaining Agreement between Teachers and Boards of Education

A *management rights clause* is designed to clarify and protect the rights of the employer and to limit the authority of an arbitrator. Such a clause would include the right to supervise all operations; determine the size of the workforce; introduce new methods, programs, or procedures; hire and discharge employees for just cause; and maintain an orderly, effective, and efficient operation.

A *grievance procedure* is a step-by-step sequence of steps for resolving allegations of violations of the provisions of the collective-bargaining agreement.

A *no-strike and no lockout provision* is included to guarantee continued operation for the life of the agreement. Some agreements provide for discipline of employees who participate in a work stoppage in violation of the no-strike clause and penalties to the union that encourages a work stoppage.

A *zipper clause* stipulates that the written agreement is the complete and full contract between the parties and that neither party is required to bargain over other items during the term of the agreement.

Maintenance of standards incorporates a school district's current and past practices, such as teaching hours, relief periods, leaves of absence, extra compensation for work outside regular teaching hours, etc.

A *reduction-in-force* provision provides the criteria used in layoffs. Usually seniority in a certified field is used in layoff and recall, and some agreements provide for bumping rights.

A *wages and benefits* provision addresses wage increases, such as across-the-board increases, step increases, cost-of-living increases based on the Consumer Price Index, and merit increases. Benefits would include insurance (life, health, and dental), pensions, sick leave, personal days, funeral leave, holidays, etc.

Other issues include grievance arbitration, teacher evaluation, class size, school calendar, etc.

SOURCE: Fred C. Lunenburg, "Collective Bargaining in the Public Schools: Issues, Tactics, and New Strategies," *Journal of Collective Negotiations in the Public Sector* 29, no. 4 (2000), p. 259.

LABOR RELATIONS IN ACTION

Privatization of the Public Sector

Privatization of public-sector services or transfer of governmental services to the private sector has received much attention over the last two decades. This focus is due largely to perceived cost differences between public- and private-sector service delivery. However, an important consideration is the role of public employee unions in the privatization process as an interest group and as political actors in blocking the privatization efforts.

A hallmark of the conservative agenda begun in the Reagan administration in the 1980s was the initiative to reduce the scope and size of government. This initiative was manifested in the call for privatization of services formerly provided exclusively by government agencies. Privatization has come in many forms: contracting out or outsourcing of support services, such as janitorial or maintenance services; vouchers for use in education; management contracts to operate an agency such as an airport. Needless to say, public-sector unions have strongly opposed privatization and feel threatened with the loss of jobs to public employees. In addition, privatization has already caused reduction in the percentage of union membership in hospitals, bus and urban transit, sanitary services, and education. Privatization will likely remain a contentious issue in the public sector, particularly because of the charter school movement in elementary and secondary education and the two-front assault from the Bush administration: (1) an announcement that the administration would place as many as 850,000 jobs, half of the federal workforce, up for bids to private contractors and (2) limitations on collective-bargaining rights for employees of the Department of Homeland Security.[a]

One consideration in the decision whether to privatize is the differing labor laws that cover private- and public-sector employees. Collective bargaining rights for employees in the private sector are covered primarily under the Labor Management Relations Act (LMRA); employees of interstate carriers in the railroad and airline industries are covered under the Railway Labor Act (RLA). Collective bargaining rights for state and local public employees are covered under various state laws; and federal government employees are covered under the Civil Service Reform Act. When government services are contracted to private firms, employees performing such services are covered under different statutes. This means that in some states in which no laws are in place to protect public employees' right to bargain, employees of the private contractor will be covered. Also, in some states where a public-sector labor law provides bargaining rights to public employees, the employees of firms contracting government services now have to seek union representation through the procedures of the LMRA or the Railway Labor Act (RLA), whichever is applicable.

Another issue in privatization is that a different employer takes over the responsibilities for the contracted public service, and this employer is responsible to the contracting agency for the performance of the public service, not directly to the citizens. The private employer takes over the publicly owned buildings and equipment either by renting or purchasing them or, in regard to small contracts, provides equipment and building space already owned but charges overhead costs to the public employer.[b] Although the advantages of privatization should be similar for the same type of public service whether currently provided by a unionized or unrepresented (nonunion) public workforce, the type of relationship between the union and city management is a significant factor. If the union-management relationship is very cooperative, the probability of the city contracting out services currently performed by union represented employees is lower than in a nonunion city. On the other hand, the probability of a city considering privatizing when a bargaining relationship is very adversarial is higher than in a nonunion city.[c]

Another interesting dilemma is the difference in employees' rights to strike. In most public-sector jurisdictions, the right to strike has been eliminated or limited. If services performed by public employees were contracted to a private employer covered by the LMRA or the RLA, employees now performing such services would have a legal right to strike under those statutes.[d]

In recent years, more public employee unions have been accepting the challenge of demonstrating that they can compete successfully with private-sector employers who offer similar services.[e] Phoenix, Arizona; Indianapolis, Indiana; Charlotte, North Carolina; and Philadelphia, Pennsylvania are examples of communities in which public employee unions have demonstrated their ability to deliver more cost-effective, higher-quality, and more effective public services than competing private-sector firms.[f] ■

SOURCES:

[a]Terry Thomason and John F. Burton, Jr., "Unionization Trends and Labor-Management Cooperation in the Public Sector," *Going Public: The Role of Labor-Management Relations in Delivering Quality Government Services*, eds. Jonathan Brock and David B. Lipsky (Champaign, Ill.: Industrial Relations Research Association, 2003), pp. 94–100.

[b]Timothy D. Chandler and Peter Feuille, "Municipal Unions and Privatization," *Public Administration Review* 51 (January/February 1991), pp. 15–22.

[c]David A. Dilts, "Privatization of the Public Sector: De Facto Standardization of Labor Law," *Journal of Collective Negotiations in the Public Sector* 24, no. 1 (1995), pp. 37–47.

[d]Chandler and Feuille, 1994.

[e]Robert Hebdon, "Contracting Out in New York State: The Story the Lauder Report Chose Not to Tell!" *Labor Studies Journal* 20 (Spring 1995), pp. 3–10.

[f]Lawrence L. Martin, "Public-Private Competition: A Public Employee Alternative to Privatization," *Review of Public Personnel Administration* 19 (Winter 1999), pp. 59–70.

California, Colorado, Hawaii, Idaho, Illinois, Louisiana, Minnesota, New Jersey, Ohio, Oregon, Pennsylvania, and Vermont. For example, in California, the state supreme court ruled that strikes by public employees other than police or firefighters were not illegal as long as they did not represent a substantial or imminent threat to the public's health or safety.[13]

Most states prohibit public employee strikes and may authorize a variety of potential sanctions for illegal strike activity varying from injunctions to dismissals, jail sentences, substantial fines, and loss of union recognition. Decreasing use of the strike as a bargaining tactic has occurred in recent years in the public sector, similar to the trend in the private sector. Unionized public-sector employees in states that grant a legal right to strike are only slightly more likely to be involved in strikes compared with states that ban public employee strikes. Educators are the employee group most likely to participate in strikes, and strikes in education are more likely to occur in five states (California, Illinois, Michigan, Ohio, and Pennsylvania).[14]

In states that allow some public employee groups to strike, certain employees, such as police, firefighters, hospital employees, and correctional employees, are usually prohibited from striking under any circumstances. Services of these employees are often deemed to be critical to the health and safety of the citizens. Police, firefighters, and teachers are the public employee groups most likely to be offered an alternative dispute resolution procedure to the strike, such as mediation, fact-finding, or interest arbitration (discussed later in this chapter).

Most federal employees' bargaining rights are governed by Title VII of the CSRA. One group of federal workers, U.S. Postal Service employees, are the only public employees covered under the private-sector Labor Management Relations Act (LMRA) as specified in the Postal Reorganization Act of 1970.[15] Unlike other private-sector employees covered under the LMRA, postal workers are not permitted to legally strike but are granted access to final and binding interest arbitration as a means of resolving bargaining disputes.

Federal-Sector Labor Relations Legislation

Federal-sector labor relations are governed by the CSRA, which was passed in 1978. Although the CSRA retained many provisions of previous executive orders, the following discussion centers on the provisions of Title VII, "Federal Service Labor-Management Relations." Also important to remember is that the CSRA is applied within a framework of federal personnel rules and policies affecting merit system principles, civil service functions, performance appraisal, staffing, merit pay, senior executive service, and adverse employment actions such as discipline or discharge.

The CSRA established the **Federal Labor Relations Authority (FLRA)**, an independent, neutral agency that administers the federal labor relations program and investigates unfair labor practices. The FLRA oversees the creation of bargaining units, supervises elections, prescribes criteria for determining national consultation rights, conducts hearings and resolves complaints of unfair labor practices, resolves exceptions to arbitrator awards, and assists federal agencies in dealing with labor relations issues. It is headed by a chairperson and two members, appointed on a bipartisan basis for 5-year terms.

The FLRA's structure provides for a General Counsel whose office prosecutes unfair labor practice charges and incorporates the existing **Federal Service Impasse Panel (FSIP)**, which provides assistance in resolving negotiation impasses. The General Counsel investigates any alleged unfair labor practices, prosecutes complaints under the act, and exercises such powers as the FLRA may prescribe.[16]

The role of the FSIP is to resolve bargaining impasses between federal agencies and unions in the federal government that arise over the negotiation of terms and conditions of employment. The FSIP is composed of a chairperson and at least six other members who are appointed by the president for 5-year terms, are familiar with federal government operations, and are knowledgeable about labor-management relations. The FSIP has jurisdiction over seventy-one federal departments and agencies representing 1.8 million federal employees. The FSIP appoints an executive director, who is responsible for the day-to-day operations.[17]

Although the Federal Mediation and Conciliation Service (FMCS), the federal agency established in 1947 by the LMRA, is required to assist the parties in resolving negotiation impasses, either party may request that the FSIP consider the matter or pursue binding arbitration. The panel must investigate the impasse and recommend a procedure for resolution or assist the parties through whatever means necessary, including fact-finding and recommendations. If these actions fail, the FSIP may conduct a formal hearing and take legal action to settle the dispute.

Appropriate Bargaining Units and Union Recognition in the Federal Sector

An appropriate bargaining unit for exclusive union representation purposes may be established on an agency, plant, installation, function, or other basis to ensure a clear and identifiable community of interests among employees and to promote effective federal agency operations. The criteria used for determining the extent to which employees in different federal jobs share a sufficient community of interests are similar to those used by the National Labor Relations Board (NLRB) in the private sector. These include comparing jobs to identify common duties and skills, similar working conditions, common supervision, degree of work interdependence, and physical proximity of the jobs. No single factor determines the decision, but rather an evaluation is made based on a preponderance of the evidence. Similarly, certain positions are generally excluded from the bargaining unit, such as confidential employees, management and supervisory personnel, human resource management employees, and professionals, unless they vote in favor of inclusion. About 60 percent of all eligible employees are represented by various labor organizations in 2,218 bargaining units, and 58 percent are covered by labor agreements.[18] A federal agency accords **exclusive recognition** to a labor union if the union has been selected as the employee representative in a secret-ballot election by a majority of the employees in the appropriate unit who cast valid ballots.

Negotiable Subjects in the Federal Sector

In the federal sector, the agency and the exclusively recognized union have a duty to meet at reasonable times and confer in good faith with respect to *mandatory* subjects of collective bargaining, such as certain personnel policies and practices and working conditions, to the extent that appropriate laws and regulations allow such negotiations. The parties may voluntarily agree to bargain over certain *permissible* subjects, but the CSRA does not require negotiation over such subjects—one party can legally refuse to negotiate these issues. Permissible subjects include numbers, types, and grades of positions assigned to any organizational unit, work project, or tour of duty; technology of the workplace; and methods and means of performing the work. Subjects *prohibited* from negotiations include wages (except for certain blue-collar employees) and the following management rights:

- To determine the mission, budget, organization, number of employees, and internal security practices

- To hire, assign, direct, lay off, and retain employees in accordance with applicable law

- To suspend, remove, reduce in grade or pay, or take other disciplinary action

- To assign work, subcontract, and select employees for promotion from properly ranked and certified candidates and other appropriate sources

- To take whatever actions may be necessary to carry out the agency's mission during emergencies

Although the CSRA limits the scope of negotiable subjects, the parties have ample opportunity to negotiate many issues, as illustrated in Exhibit 13.4. The fact that management and the union are required to bargain in good faith does not mean that the parties must reach an agreement on these issues but only evidence a good-faith intent to do so.

Under the CSRA, the FSIP is responsible for resolving interest disputes that result in an impasse during negotiations. If mediation or fact-finding fails to resolve the dispute, the FSIP may use arbitration to render a final and binding decision to resolve the interest dispute. Management's position tends to prevail in 58 percent of disputes resolved through arbitration conducted by the FSIP, a higher management win rate than typically prevails under state and local interest arbitration procedures (see discussion later in this chapter).[19]

Exhibit 13.4

Subjects That Could Be Included in a Master Labor Agreement in the Federal Sector

Union recognition	Sick leave
Official time	Health and safety
Discipline and counseling	Contracting out
Grievance procedure and arbitration	Child care services
Dues withholding	Call-back, standby, and on-call duty
Employee performance	Workers' compensation
Merit promotion	Performance appraisal
Training	Hazard and environmental pay
Equal employment opportunity	Reduction-in-force
Travel	Position classifications
Annual leave	

Unfair Labor Practices in the Federal Sector

The CSRA specifies unfair labor practices to protect the rights of individual employees, labor organizations, and federal agencies. Employee grievances over matters concerning adverse action, position classification, and equal employment opportunity are covered by other laws, statutes, or agency rules and cannot be filed as an unfair labor practice charge under the CSRA.

The CSRA prohibits unfair labor practices very similar to those prohibited under previous executive orders and the LMRA. For example, prohibited management activities include restraining and coercing employees in the exercise of their rights; encouraging or discouraging union membership; sponsoring, controlling, or assisting a labor organization; disciplining union members who file complaints; and refusing to recognize or negotiate with a designated labor organization. The CSRA prohibits unions from interfering with, restraining, or coercing employees in the exercise of their rights; attempting to induce agency management to coerce employees; impeding or hindering an employee's work performance; calling for or engaging in job actions (e.g., work slowdown or strike); and discriminating against employees or refusing to consult, confer, or negotiate with the appropriate federal agency. Unfair labor practice remedies available to the FLRA include the issuance of a cease and desist order and/or an appropriate make-whole type of remedy, such as requiring that an employee be reinstated with back pay.

The CSRA makes it an unfair labor practice to refuse or fail to cooperate in impasse procedures and decisions. The FLRA has authority to revoke recognition of a union that commits an unfair labor practice or encourages a strike or slowdown. The FLRA can also require the parties to renegotiate a labor agreement in accordance with an FLRA decision and seek a temporary restraining order to halt suspected unlawful conduct while an unfair labor practice case is pending.

The CSRA requires that all negotiated agreements in the federal sector include a grievance procedure with binding arbitration as its final step. A grievance is broadly defined to include any complaint by an employee, labor organization, or agency relating to employment with an agency and any claimed violation, misinterpretation, or misapplication of any law, rule, or regulation affecting conditions of employment. Certain issues are exempt from the grievance procedure, such as employee appointment, certification, job classification, removal for national security reasons or political activities, issues concerning retirement, and life and health insurance. However, the scope of grievance procedure coverage has been extended considerably. In fact, all matters within the allowable limits of the CSRA are within the scope of any grievance procedure negotiated by the parties, unless the parties have specifically agreed to exclude certain matters from coverage. Thus, unlike private-sector negotiations, which often focus on union efforts to expand the scope of grievance subjects, federal-sector negotiators often focus on management proposals to remove specific items from the scope of grievable subjects. Negotiated grievance procedures serve as the exclusive forum for bargaining unit employees in most cases; however, in cases of adverse employment action (e.g., suspension, reduction in grade, or discharge for poor performance), the employee may choose either the negotiated grievance procedure or an applicable statutory procedure, but not both. Depending on the nature of the employee's grievance claim, the employee might receive a hearing before the FLRA, the Equal Employment Opportunity Commission (EEOC), Merit Systems Protection Board (an independent agency established to hear federal employee grievances under CSRA), or a federal court.[20]

Labor-Management Partnerships in the Federal Government

In 1993, President Clinton directed Vice President Gore to conduct a 6-month National Performance Review of the federal government. The results of this review led President Clinton to issue Executive Order 12871, which established the National Partnership Council (NPC) composed of federal agency and union officials, with the purpose of recommending reforms to empower federal employees as full partners with management to promote labor-management cooperation and improve the delivery of government services.[21] Federal negotiators were to be guided by a legislatively mandated "good government" standard, the pursuit of increased quality and productivity, customer service, employee empowerment, mission accomplishment, efficiency, organizational performance, and, in the case of the Department of Defense, military readiness. Specific examples of successes of labor-management partnerships included:

- Partnership between the Internal Revenue Service (IRS) and the National Treasury Employees Union (NTEU) modernized and restructured the IRS and resulted in measurable improvements in customer service and job satisfaction.

- Partnership between the American Federation of Government Employees (AFGE) and Defense Contract Management Command resulted in overwhelming improvement in customer service ratings as the workload increased 100 percent and the workforce downsized, with $900,000 saved from a reduction in labor-management litigation.

- Partnership between the James A. Haley Veterans' Hospital and AFGE Local 547, the Florida Nurses Association, and the Tampa Professional Nurses Unit reduced delivery time for critical medication from 92 minutes to 20 minutes, cut turnaround time for X-ray reports from 8 days to 1 day, and reduced processing time for pension and compensation exams from 31 days to 18 days.

- A NTEU–Customs Service partnership yielded a seven-step strategy to increase seizures of illegal drugs. During the first six months, narcotics seizures increased by 12 percent and drug currency seizures increased by 74 percent.

- Partnership between the Defense Distribution Depot in San Joaquin and AFGE 1546 saved $950,000 per year by reducing workplace accidents by 20 percent and ergonomic injuries by 40 percent, reduced overtime expenses from $9.8 million to $1.4 million, and reduced production costs from $25.42 per unit to $23.48 per unit.[22]

Within a month after taking office, on February 17, 2001, President Bush signed Executive Order 13203, which immediately dissolved the National Partnership

Council and revoked any "orders, rules, regulations, guidelines, or policies implementing or enforcing Executive Order 12871." The current director of the Office of Personnel Management informed the federal government department heads that President Bush was motivated by his conviction that a partnership was not something that should be mandated for every agency in every situation. However, while agencies were no longer mandated to form partnerships with their unions, they were strongly encouraged to establish cooperative labor-management relations.

In a study of 60 labor-management partnership councils in eight federal agencies employing more than 310,000 bargaining unit employees, researchers found:

> First, partnership can improve labor-management communications.
> Second, it can also contribute to the enhancement of the labor relations climate.
> Third, partnership has the potential to improve agency performance.
> Fourth, management commitment and commensurate union strength are essential to realizing the potential of collaboration.[23]

Homeland Security Act

In November 2002, Congress passed and President Bush signed the Homeland Security Act (HSA). This act transferred several existing agencies into the Department of Homeland Security (DHS), which would operate along four functional lines: Border and Transportation Security, Emergency Preparedness and Response; Chemical, Biological, Radiological and Nuclear Counter-Measures; and Information Analysis and Infrastructure Protection. The total workforce of the DHS will be over 170,000 federal government employees. From a labor-management relations standpoint, over 40,000 of these employees were members of preexisting bargaining units. These included 24,324 employees within the Immigration and Naturalization Service (Justice Department); 11,731 in the Customs Service (Treasury Department); 3,486 in the Coast Guard (Department of Transportation); and 2,498 in Animal and Plant Health Service (Department of Agriculture). The provision that makes labor unions nervous is Section 730, which states:

> Notwithstanding any other provision of this title, the Secretary of Homeland Security may, in regulations prescribed jointly with the Director of the Office of Personnel Management, establish, and from time to time adjust, a human resources management system for some or all of the organizational units of the Department of Homeland Security, which shall be flexible, contemporary, and grounded in the public employment principles of merit and fitness.

Under the Civil Service Reform Act, the president has authority to exempt from coverage any group of federal employees for national security purposes. Under the Homeland Security Act, the president may waive employee and union rights granted under the Civil Service Reform Act if such application would have a substantial adverse impact on the ability of the department to protect homeland security and/or the agency, subdivision, or unit's mission and responsibilities are materially changed and a majority of the affected employees are assigned intelligence, counterintelligence, or investigative work directly related to terrorism investigation as their primary duty.[24]

Postal Reorganization Act of 1970

The Postal Reorganization Act (PRA) signed by President Nixon on August 12, 1970, fulfilled the desires of the postal unions to have their labor-management relations programs established by statute. Under previous presidential executive orders authorizing bargaining by federal workers, the Post Office Department never fully accepted collective bargaining, even though it was the largest single employer in the United States and had the largest proportion of employees belonging to unions. Another interesting note is that the legislation placing postal employees under the private-sector LMRA was proposed by President Nixon and adopted by Congress to resolve an illegal strike by postal workers—a far different approach than that used by the federal government to resolve a similar illegal strike by air traffic controllers in 1981.[25]

The PRA created the U.S. Postal Service (USPS) as an independent entity within the executive branch of the federal government. The office of postmaster general, previously a position in the cabinet, was made independent of Congress and the president. The postmaster general was selected by an 11-member board of governors. Under the PRA, wages, hours, benefits, and other terms and conditions of employment are mandatory bargaining subjects to be determined through collective bargaining. Grievance and arbitration procedures are also subject to negotiation. The NLRB supervises representation elections and prosecutes unfair labor practices. Although the right to strike was denied postal employees, a fact-finding and binding interest arbitration procedure was made available if a bargaining impasse persisted longer than 180 days after bargaining began. Since the PRA was passed, contracts have been negotiated without any major disruption in the delivery of postal services.

The parties have often relied on the arbitration provision of the PRA to resolve one or more bargaining issues. For example, in 1984 an arbitration panel agreed with the management position that postal service wages were higher than comparable private jobs, but decided that this discrepancy should be corrected over time rather than all at once.

In 1991 the USPS in separate negotiations with four unions representing postal employees reached an impasse over wages, cost-of-living allowances, health insurance, safety and health, subcontracting, and automation. The unresolved issues from all four negotiations were submitted to interest arbitration; however, the Mail Handlers broke ranks, resumed negotiations, and signed a 3-year agreement in February 1991. The agreement included provisions for lump-sum payments in lieu of wage increases, cost-of-living adjustments, and a two-tiered wage schedule with new hires being paid at 20 percent less than regular employees for their first 96 weeks of employment. A five-member arbitration panel issued its award for a 4-year contract covering the American Postal Workers Union (APWU) and the National Association of Letter Carriers (NALC), who combined represent approximately 87 percent of postal employees. This award included wage increases for each year of the contract, a lump-sum payment, cost-of-living adjustments, a new starting rate for new hires, an increase in the number of part-time employees, and provisions involving the transition to automation. Ten days later, the Postal Service and the Rural Letter Carriers Association reached an agreement that included similar economic provisions but included eligibility for cash bonuses based on customer satisfaction and financial performance of the Postal Service.[26]

In the fall of 1995, arbitration panels resolved interest disputes between the Postal Service and two of its unions, the APWU and the NALC, by rendering a decision for a 4-year agreement that provided a pay increase of just over 5 percent, a one-time cash payment of $400, and cost-of-living adjustments beginning with the second year.[27] The 1998–2000 USPS-APWU contract represented the parties' first negotiated agreement in 11 years that did not involve the use of interest arbitration.[28] The 2-year contract provided wage improvements, a reduction in employees' portion of health-care premium cost from 18 to 16 percent, and protection from layoffs. The 1998 USPS-NALC negotiations did result in an interest arbitration award that established a 3-year contract term and granted letter carriers a pay classification upgrade from level 5 to level 6 to compensate for the increased physical and mental demands of a letter carrier's job caused by automation.[28] In 2002, the U.S. Postal Service and each of its major unions (the American Postal Employees Union, the National Association of Letter Carriers, and the Postal Mail Handlers Union) reached agreement to extend their respective collective-bargaining agreements to 2004.

Similarities Between Private- and Public-Sector Bargaining

Although differences are found between private- and public-sector labor relations, similarities also exist. First, many of the participants in public-sector bargaining are trained and gain their experience in the private sector. Labor relations practitioners in the public sector tend to rely on the private-sector approach to labor relations with appropriate modification as needed. State and local bargaining statutes often use NLRB criteria for appropriate bargaining units, subjects for collective bargaining, use of labor injunctions, and standards for arbitration. Some unions that represent a significant number of public employees, such as the SEIU and the Teamsters Union, have much experience in private-sector labor relations. Other unions (such as the National Education Association; the American Federation of Teachers; the American Federation of State, County, and Municipal Employees; and civil service employee groups) often hire professional staff members with private-sector labor relations experience.[30]

A second similarity is the reason why employees form and join unions. Public employees, like their private-sector counterparts, form and join unions when they are dissatisfied with some term or condition of employment, which includes their work, supervision, and promotional opportunities; have a favorable attitude toward unions as institutions; and believe that unionization will be instrumental in yielding positive outcomes.[31] In fact, public employees tend to hold more favorable attitudes toward a desire for union representation than do private-sector workers and perceive public managers to be less hostile toward unionization compared with their private-sector counterparts.[32]

A third similarity is that the collective-bargaining settlement will often be influenced by the personalities of the negotiators and their abilities to increase their bargaining power relative to the other party (the bargaining power model has been discussed in Chapter 6). To reiterate briefly, each party increases bargaining power over the opponent by either increasing the cost to the opponent of disagreeing or reducing the cost to the opponent of agreeing. Public opinion represents a most significant cost item in public-sector labor relations—both union and government officials often structure their tactics in a manner intended to gain public support for their position, which places pressure on the other party to concede negotiation items.

However, public opinion and political support can be a double-edged sword in the bargaining process. Public unions can use at least three general strategies to increase management's cost of disagreeing with the union's position.[33] The first technique is a union threat to "blow the whistle" on a questionable practice unless the government agency agrees with the desired settlement. Examples include threatening to release information on the unpublicized practice of dumping raw sewage in a river or on the dollar amount of government officials' liquor bills, which are paid by the taxpayers. Of course, the union is hoping that government officials will capitulate rather than risk vote loss in subsequent elections as a result of the public revelation of such information. Management's cost of disagreeing can be more directly increased by a union's threat of withdrawing political support.[34] Public employees tend to vote at a higher rate than other individuals. A threat to withhold candidate endorsements or campaign support, both manpower and financial, may also be used to increase pressure on elected officials in a position to influence bargaining outcomes. The success of this tactic depends on the number of union members and the ability of the union to mobilize a cohesive voting bloc.

The union can also use various job action techniques to raise management's cost of disagreeing. Strikes by public employees have occurred often despite legal sanctions. Perhaps these actions are taken under the assumption that most public-sector strikes have eventually been resolved without fines or other sanctions, even though they are illegal. Some other job actions that have been used are also outside the law or proscribed by the job requirements (for example, government employees in New York raising the toll bridges at rush hour when walking off the job), whereas others are marginally outside the law or job requirements (for example, all public employees calling in to say they are too sick to work).[35]

From the union standpoint, a most promising job action is working within the law while placing pressure on management to resolve the dispute. Job slowdowns fall marginally into this category because most public-sector labor agreements give management the right to discipline employees for poor performance. Yet there is a thin line between a job slowdown and malicious obedience (also called **work-to-rule**) by which the employees follow the agency's rules to the letter. For example, a fingerprint technician is charged with verifying an individual's address during his criminal booking. This could be done by simply telephoning the individual's purported residence. However, a more time-consuming but accurate verification method would be for the fingerprint technician to personally visit the individual's residence. Needless to say, the home-visit approach would create an assignment backlog. Other public employees can also use bureaucratic rules to their advantage. For example, tollbooth employees could check paper currency serial numbers against a list of counterfeit bills, or postal workers could check each item to ensure a proper ZIP code. Malicious obedience has the tactical advantage of cutting back on the delivery of public services. More importantly, employees continue to receive wages under this tactic while being relatively immune from disciplinary actions.

Public-sector unions can also reduce management's cost of agreeing with the union by campaigning for referendums to fund the negotiated labor settlement or eliminating some of their initial proposals.[36] Public employee unions can also push for certain issues that contribute significantly to their economic well-being at little cost to the political incumbents. Employee pensions usually fall into this category because they can be increased without immediate cost implications; the bulk of pension costs would be incurred under some future politician's budget.

Management can reduce its political cost of agreeing on wages by publicizing a rather low across-the-board settlement along with general improvements in the pay step plan. This plan usually gives progressive salary increases to each job classification. For example, an employee in a particular classification might receive a 5 percent wage increase after 3 years' service in that classification. Management can improve the employee's situation by either raising the percentage increase or reducing the number of service years needed to qualify for a step wage increase. However, it is difficult to determine and report the precise cost of these changes. Most news media presentations are limited to specific reports on the average wage gain of public employees and ignore the more detailed cost implications of a modified pay step plan.

Another similar issue is the continuing controversy over nonunion employees' obligation to pay for their representational rights. Public-sector employees not joining unions may be required to pay for representational services provided by the union (collective bargaining, grievance handling, arbitration, and so on) but not for non–collective bargaining activities (such as political action committees, lobbying, or public relations activities).[37] The nonmember has the burden of objecting to inappropriate expenditures of his or her agency or fair-share fee, but the union must provide written notice to nonmembers of their right to raise objections and provide sufficiently detailed information about the nature of dues expenditures to permit the nonmember to make a reasonable determination whether to challenge a particular expenditure as chargeable.

In summary, public-sector collective bargaining has some similarities to the process found in the private sector. In both situations, the parties are trying to increase their bargaining power relative to the other party's by increasing the other party's cost of disagreeing with their party's position or by reducing the other party's cost of agreeing with their party's position. There are several differences between public- and private-sector bargaining processes; however, once these differences are acknowledged and understood, one can better appreciate the public sector as it fits into the overall framework of labor-management relations in the United States. Moreover, skills learned in private-sector labor relations are easily transferred to the public sector.

Differences Between Private-Sector and Public-Sector Bargaining

An understanding of public-sector labor relations requires recognition of some of the differences and similarities between the public and private sectors.

Market Economy Does Not Operate in Public Sector

One difference between the public and private sectors can be explained in terms of the economic system and the market economy. Unlike the private sector, many public services (such as public education, welfare services, police and fire protection) are supplied to the citizens at little or no additional cost (beyond taxes). The cost of such services is spread across many individuals rather than expecting each customer to pay the entire cost of the services used or available for use. The market economy therefore does not operate in the public sector and cannot act as a constraint on union and management negotiators.

Moreover, monopolistic conditions often exist in the public sector, and public organizations often control the services rendered or the products offered. For example, the police and fire departments are the primary organizations that provide certain types of security protection. Public education has very little real competition from the private sector, and even that is usually among only more affluent families. Thus, products and services provided by the government cannot be readily substituted if they become more costly.

The lack of substitute goods or services distinguishes public-sector collective bargaining from related activities in the private sector and adds to the critical nature of public services. For example, citizens usually take sanitation services for granted; yet a strike by city garbage collectors would be regarded as a public crisis because there is no immediate alternative means for garbage disposal. The lack of substitute services also eliminates one of management's strike costs: loss of business to a competitor. In fact, some union leaders contend that municipal leaders use a strike to their advantage by transferring payroll savings resulting from a strike to other government budgetary accounts.

Finally, the relatively vague aspects of particular public service institutions may make productivity bargaining difficult. Clear and precise productivity measures are a necessary first step in productivity bargaining (although many private-sector companies have these figures and do not engage in productivity bargaining). Most public-sector bargaining parties do not have specific productivity measures at their disposal and could not engage in productivity bargaining even if they desired this approach. Many public services are provided regardless of customer use. Police officers and bus drivers can legitimately contend that they should not be financially punished for nonuse of their services; their salaries should not be a direct function of the number of crimes detected or riders served, respectively, if the service is available for all. Hence, much of the public-sector wage determination process is based on a comparison of similar jobs in the public and private sectors rather than on employee performance records. Because the market does not act as a significant moderator in the public sector, budgetary limitations, public attitudes, and administrative discretion must operate to successfully maintain order, equity, and balance in collective bargaining relationships.[38]

Relationship between the Budget and Public-Sector Bargaining Processes

The budget usually tends to play a more conspicuous role in public-sector collective bargaining than in private-sector bargaining. In recent years, public employers have been under severe budget constraints, necessitating an increased emphasis on costs reduction. To the extent taxpayers are unwilling to approve revenue increases through the political process, cost reductions must come from curtailing public services or finding more cost-efficient ways of providing public services at current levels. Public employers have experienced increased pressure to emulate changes in labor relations practices occurring in the private sector by privatizing (i.e., outsourcing or subcontracting) some public services, broadening job classifications and multiskill job descriptions, using more part-time or contingent employees, paying for performance, adopting flexible and alternative work schedules, reducing supervision and encouraging employee involvement and empowerment, decentralizing and streamlining bureaucratic operating structures and methods, and increasing labor-management cooperation.[39]

Most municipal budgets are published in advance before public hearings and subsequent adoption. Although many citizens ignore public hearings, key taxpayers, such as local companies, give close attention to the budget in terms of its implication for increased property or business taxes. The anticipated salaries for public employees are recorded as separate line items on the budget, something not done in the private sector. Thus, the opportunity exists for concerned taxpayers to pressure city officials in the hopes of keeping the budget and subsequent taxes at a minimum.

The specific influence of the budget on the public-sector bargaining process remains uncertain. Some suggest that a great deal of flexibility exists in the budget bargaining relationship in terms of budget padding, transfer of funds among line items, and supplemental or amended budgets that can often be filed after the final approval date.[40] In these cases, the government officer in charge of labor relations may have little concern with the agency's financial activities. The following related comments were expressed by a former director of the budget for New York City:

> The director of the budget is less a part of a unified management team than a part of the problem, an adversary not unlike the union leaders themselves. . . . Underlying the situation is the belief held by most labor negotiators that they know "what it takes" to effect a settlement and that, in the large complex public body, alleged or actual limits on available resources have no effect upon the ultimate settlement. And they are, in fact, largely correct.[41]

Similarly, as illustrated by one union official's comment, public-sector unions seldom allow the budget to influence their collective bargaining strategies and settlements:

> The budget does not mean too much to me—if we based our bargaining demands on the budget, we would never get any money. The union is never cognizant as to the amount [in the budget] because there never is enough money. We are aware of the dire need for money and campaign politically [to obtain additional funds], but when we go into negotiations we don't discuss the budgetary problems.[42]

Union negotiators' major concerns pertain to securing benefits for their members; it is up to management to find sufficient funds for an equitably negotiated settlement. Thus, there is little union-management agreement over the budget's significance in contract negotiations; few if any public-sector collective bargaining agreements have provisions specifying the role the budget will assume in the collective bargaining process.

The amount of funds available certainly is an important consideration, which is why trade legislation such as the North American Free Trade Agreement (NAFTA) bears close scrutiny. If reducing tariff barriers encourages the flow of capital to move toward countries with low taxes and few regulations limiting business practices, less investment in the United States could reduce or alter the number and types of jobs available and thus the demand for and ability to pay for public services. This result could have a negative spillover effect on public employees. For example, two of the wage standards commonly used to determine wages through negotiation or arbitration are (1) wage comparability and (2) an employer's ability to pay. If tax revenues decline or if wage rates for private sector jobs grow less rapidly or even decline, public-sector management negotiators would certainly use these arguments to defend more modest wage proposals in negotiating with public-sector unions.[43]

Employee Rights and Obligations

Another way that public employment differs from private employment is that public employees have some legal rights and obligations that private employees do not. Numerous laws and executive orders pertain only to public employees. Public employees' political activities, personal appearance, place of residence, and off-the-job behavior are regulated more closely than most private-sector workers. For example, public employees in particularly sensitive jobs and those whose misdeeds are most susceptible to adverse publicity, such as teachers, police officers, and firefighters, are held to a higher conduct standard than most other employees.[44] Because citizens pay the taxes that pay public employees' salaries, employers have to be careful of the image employees project.

Although freedom of speech and association are constitutional rights, there are limits to their exercise by public employees. The Supreme Court has identified several reasons for which these rights may be limited, including the need to maintain discipline and harmony in the workforce, the need for confidentiality, and the need to ensure that the proper performance of duties is not impeded.[45] However, public employers cannot give priority to efficient work operation over an employee's First Amendment right to expression about a matter of public concern.

Generally, the courts have not attempted to substitute their judgment for that of executive branch officials regarding whether an individual public employee should be dismissed. Rather, they have sought to establish guidelines for the constitutional treatment of public employees in adverse action cases, such as a discharge. Procedural due process requires the right of notice of the proposed government action; the reasons for the action; the opportunity to respond; the right to a hearing before an impartial official; and the rights to counsel, to confront accusers, and to cross-examine and subpoena witnesses.

In *Board of Regents v. Roth* (1972) the Supreme Court delineated the following grounds on which a public employee whose employment has been terminated could assert the right to procedural due process[46]:

- Where an employee had a property right to the job

- Where the termination harmed the individual's reputation and/or adversely affected his or her future employability

- Where termination was in retaliation for an exercise of a protected constitutional activity, such as the freedom of speech or freedom of assembly

In the case of *Cleveland Board of Education* v. *Loudermill* (1985), the Supreme Court held that before tenured public employees can be fired, they must be informed of the charges against them and be given an opportunity to respond.[47] Tenured employees' due process rights under the U.S. Constitution include written or oral notice of the charges against them, an explanation of the employer's evidence, and an opportunity to rebut the evidence.

Collective Bargaining Structures and Decision-Making Processes

The bargaining structure within municipal governments is very decentralized, and with few exceptions, negotiations are conducted on a single-employer basis. The bargaining unit coverage extends only as far as the municipal jurisdiction, and municipal officials are reluctant to relinquish their political autonomy and decision-making authority. The city manager or chief administrative officer of the municipality will most often serve as chief negotiator, followed by the personnel director or an attorney retained by the city.[48] An increased level of political activity by public employees, increased level of strike activity, and occurrence of prior job actions by organized public employees are factors that increase the likelihood that a labor relations specialist will be included on the negotiations team. However, if the negotiation activities become complex, the city is more likely to employ a labor relations professional as the chief negotiator.[49]

Defining the appropriate bargaining unit in the public sector is more difficult than in the private sector. In the private sector, legislation and related enforcement agencies provide direction for determining an appropriate bargaining unit. For example, plant guards in the private sector are required to be in separate bargaining units, and supervisors are not eligible for membership in a bargaining unit. The public sector, especially at the state and local levels, experiences many different combinations of appropriate bargaining units. Depending on the particular applicable state law or administrative determination, public-sector supervisors can be prohibited from joining unions, they can be in the same bargaining units as other employees, or they can join unions in separate bargaining units.[50]

Of the differences between public- and private-sector labor relations, one of the potentially most important, but often ignored, is the unionization of supervisors and other managers. While private-sector supervisors and managers lack representational rights under the Labor Management Relations Act, public-sector supervisors and other lower- to middle-level managers have the right to engage in collective bargaining in more than a dozen states, including the most highly populated states. There have been questions about the loyalty, identity, and organizational commitment of public-sector supervisory unions, and the logic for exclusion is rooted in the need of the employer to have the undivided loyalty of supervisors and other managerial employees. However, research has identified little negative effect from the unionization of supervisors. Potential problems seem to arise with the highest-level supervisors on issues concerning strikes and discipline, especially when supervisors are in the same bargaining units as employees. Based on research in New Jersey, supervisors could both receive representation in their role as employees and act on the job in a managerial capacity. In other words, supervisors can "wear two hats"; they are loyal to the mission of the agency and act as supervisors to further the mission of the agency while they are also union members.[51]

Another organizational difference applies to the chief negotiator in the public sector, who often lacks authority to reach a final and binding agreement with the union on behalf of the public organization. The **sovereignty doctrine** makes it difficult to delegate decision-making authority to specific administrative officials. Many elected officials still refuse to give up their legislative authority to make final decisions on matters that they believe are important to effective government operations because they feel responsible directly to the electorate. Elected officials do not want appointed negotiators to bind them to wage settlements and other provisions of collective bargaining agreements that they believe are unworkable.[52] For example, unionized schoolteachers might encounter a variety of managers in collective negotiations—the school principal, the superintendent of schools, the school board, and possibly state education officials. The problem of determining "who speaks for management" can negatively affect the negotiation process in two ways:

1. Management negotiators at the bargaining table can defer to other management officials in the bargaining process. Union officers are often shuffled off to a variety of government officials in collective bargaining on the premise that another individual has specific authority for a particular issue or a portion of available funds. Often, political rivalries prompt certain government officials to either intervene or pass the buck in the hopes of looking good at another official's expense. This situation can result in a more confusing collective bargaining relationship than is typically found in the private sector. In some cases, it can almost entirely prevent serious collective-bargaining efforts between management and the union.

2. The unwillingness of some government agencies to delegate sufficient authority to a labor relations representative can result in a lack of labor relations understanding on management's side of the negotiation table. In some cases, taxpayers are affected if unions take advantage of the inexperienced management negotiators. Perhaps in other cases a public strike could have been avoided if the parties had had a more realistic understanding of the collective-bargaining process.[53]

Research has shown that when the chief negotiator is a higher-level position in the organizational structure, the parties are less likely to reach an impasse. This is because the chief negotiator from a higher-level position has greater authority to make crucial decisions during the negotiations, thereby simplifying the process. Where outside consultants serve as the chief negotiator, public-sector unions are more likely to make "end runs" to higher-level government officials whom the union negotiators perceive as having greater authority to make binding decisions in the negotiations. Such activity occurs away from the bargaining table and makes the negotiations between the parties at the bargaining table more difficult. In reference to bargaining strategies covered in Chapter 6, chief negotiators who use the "mutual gain bargaining strategy" decrease the likelihood of an impasse, and the negotiators who use a "distributive strategy" increase the likelihood of a bargaining impasse. In reference to impasse procedures covered in Chapter 9, prior use of arbitration increases the likelihood of a bargaining impasse.[54]

Negotiable Issues and Bargaining Tactics

Exemption by statute of many traditional collective bargaining subjects (particularly at the federal level) limits the ability of both unions and managers to resolve some disputes through the bargaining process. Under the CSRA, most compensation issues affecting federal budgets are excluded from the scope of mandatory bargaining subjects (except for postal workers covered under the private-sector statute, the LMRA). In many states operating under merit system rules and regulations, related subjects such as promotion, pension plans, and layoff procedures cannot be negotiated.[55] Merit or civil service systems establishing rules for governing terms and conditions of employment existed before the passage of state laws authorizing collective bargaining as a procedure for determining work rules affecting public employees. This situation sometimes can lead to conflict regarding which system should take precedent in determining the outcome of disputes over the determination or application of particular work rules. Legislators should clearly address this potential dilemma when drafting public-sector bargaining laws to minimize conflicts over whether collective bargaining or civil service procedures should take precedent.[56]

Some public-sector bargaining relationships attempt to get around statutory limitations on bargaining subjects by removing such discussions from the formal bargaining process. One study found that some public-sector labor agreement provisions are not actually negotiated between the parties, whereas other decisions are jointly determined but not included in the formal labor agreement.[57] Thus, relatively few generalizations can be made regarding the scope of collectively bargained items in the public sector.

Public-sector bargaining tactics also differ from those in the private sector. Negotiations in the private sector stem from a bilateral relationship—management and union representatives negotiate the terms of the labor agreement with little involvement from outside groups. **Multilateral bargaining** is a term used, particularly at the state and local levels, to describe the involvement of multiple parties in the collective bargaining process.[58] For example, elected (e.g., mayor, city council member) and administrative (e.g., city manager, police chief) officials may share decision-making responsibility over some issues on the employer side. Various community interest groups (e.g., taxpayer, minority, environmentalist, business) perceive themselves as stakeholders potentially affected by the outcomes of negotiations and may also seek to actively influence the bargaining process by bringing pressure on either the employer or union(s) to approve acceptable bargaining terms. The outcomes of the negotiating process may affect the need for additional revenues (e.g., taxes) to fund improved employment terms or the quantity or quality of public services provided citizens.

The ability to impose political costs or rewards on a bargaining party often becomes as important in determining public-sector bargaining outcomes as the ability to impose or minimize economic costs affects bargaining power in the private sector. Thus, public-sector negotiations often become an exercise in politics—who one knows and what one can do to help or hurt a government official's political career. Public unions have demonstrated an ability to use multilateral bargaining and political pressure to increase economic gains and job security for their members.[59]

Public-sector unions often have opportunities to engage in **end-run bargaining** before, during, or after negotiations, which involves a union making a direct appeal to a legislative body or government official who has the final decision-making authority rather than dealing exclusively with the designated management negotiator present at the bargaining table. For example, one mayor made concessions to a police association in return for its endorsement in the gubernatorial primary. The mayor changed the regular police work schedule from 5 days on and 2 off to 4 days on and 2 off (increasing the annual days off by 17), guaranteed two patrol officers in every car, and agreed that 50 percent plus one of the patrol cars in each police district would be on the street during night hours.[60] Because public-sector unions are often politically potent, elected officials are generally more receptive to this end-run tactic than a private-sector corporation president or majority stockholders of a corporation might be. In fact, such attempts by a union to bypass the designated management negotiators of a private-sector organization would probably result in an NLRB unfair labor practice finding of refusal to bargain in good faith.

Occasionally, the media aids a party's use of the end-run tactic by allowing management and union negotiators to present their positions through the press rather than to the other party at the bargaining table. Public-sector bargaining usually receives more press coverage than similar activities in the private sector because more information is typically furnished to the media by the bargaining parties and the eventual settlement has a more direct impact on the government's constituents. Use of the end-run tactic can harm the collective bargaining process, as evidenced by a union leader's account of one contract negotiation between New York City and its uniformed forces:

> All of this [bargaining issues] should have been brought to the bargaining table. It would have given both labor and management a chance to work out of these very difficult trouble spots. . . . But, almost nothing was done at the table; instead both sides took to the television, advertising, and the loud and dramatic press releases. . . .
>
> Experts . . . know the best way to insure trouble is to bring collective bargaining into the public arena. Instead of labor and management representatives talking to each other, they will talk to the public and to their principals only. Invariably, the wrong things will be said.
>
> Management will talk of the "irresponsibly high demands" of the workers, and about how services will have to be cut back or taxes raised. . . . The labor leader now has to talk tough. The strike threat becomes almost obligatory, because he is now put in an impossible squeeze. When the union leader goes public he first must talk to the people he represents, and retain their confidence. Understandably, the public responds not to the facts of the situation but to the militant rhetoric. Everybody loses in the process, a process that has little or nothing to do with collective bargaining.[61]

The media play an important role in determining the priority issues, providing information about bargaining issues, and helping the public formulate its attitudes toward the negotiating parties. The local media is highly influential because many times it is the primary source of information for the general public. Because voters cannot directly observe union and management interactions, they rely on the media, which itself has biases. These biases include personal beliefs, ideologies and prejudices, budgetary and technological constraints, and a tendency to deal with problems stereotypically.

During negotiations, both parties try to manipulate the media because often the negotiation outcomes are shaped as much by people's perceptions of what is reasonable or necessary as they are by the factual merits of a bargaining position. In fact, sometimes the parties jointly manipulate the media to their own advantage. The union may blame city officials for its members receiving less than the wage increase they demanded; city officials in turn blame the union for a tax increase needed to pay for a wage increase that was given.[62]

Accompanying the growth of collective bargaining in the public sector have been efforts to open up the bargaining process to citizen observation and participation through the enactment of so-called **sunshine laws**. The rationale for this approach is that citizens can provide more input into how tax dollars are spent by their involvement, and openness reduces public distrust of the bargaining process. Although every state has some form of sunshine law, 25 states require labor negotiations to be conducted in the open, and 12 states even require that the strategy sessions in preparation for labor negotiations be open.[63] The open approach to public-sector bargaining differs widely from the private sector in that a private enterprise's owners (stockholders) are excluded from collective bargaining sessions.

Negotiators often seek to avoid "bargaining in the sunshine" because it becomes more difficult to make necessary trade-offs amongst bargaining priorities and terms when every constituent affected by those trade-offs can observe the deliberations. Negotiators may spend too much time posturing for the benefit of key constituents in the public audience, thereby prolonging the amount of time required to get down to the parties' "bottom-line" bargaining interests and positions. One study found the presence of a sunshine law to have no significant effect on bargaining outcomes in a national cross-sample of police and firefighter negotiations.[64]

Grievance Administration

The public sector has widely accepted the grievance procedure with binding arbitration as the mechanism for resolving conflicts over the interpretation and application of the collective bargaining agreement. Although most grievance procedures are multistep, unlike in the private sector, most grievances are not settled at the first step. Instead, grievance disputes tend to be settled at the second or third step. Some evidence indicates that where there are fewer steps in public-sector grievance procedures, grievances are resolved more quickly. Once a grievance is appealed to arbitration, the parties make a significant effort to resolve the grievances before the formal arbitration hearing. At an arbitration hearing, labor and management representatives are most likely to present their own case rather than rely upon an outside attorney to represent their party as is common in the private sector.[65]

Similar to the private sector, legalism is creeping into the arbitration process in the public sector. Increased legalism means greater use of attorneys, posthearing briefs, written transcripts, and over adherence to formal rules of order. Although grievance arbitration (as well as conciliation, mediation, and fact-finding) initially was intended to avoid legalism, the process of arbitration appears to be evolving as part of the problem rather than part of the solution. In addition, labor and management initially viewed the informality of the arbitration process as the primary reason for its effectiveness; however, the increase in formality has caused a decline in the willingness of the parties to use arbitration as an alternative dispute resolution process.[66]

The types of grievance subjects arbitrated in the public sector do not vary significantly from the private-sector experience, and in both sectors, discipline and discharge cases constitute the largest single category of grievance disputes.[67] Public-sector union stewards may be less likely to file a written grievance if a cooperative bargaining relationship exists, which provides and encourages informal methods of resolving employment disputes.[68] A number of alternative dispute-resolution methods are being encouraged on the federal, state, and local levels to ensure fair and cost-effective resolution of employee grievances. Among techniques being used are mediation, peer review panels comprised of employees or employees and managers, and arbitration.[69] Mediation programs typically report dispute settlement rates in the 75 to 90 percent range, and arbitration may reduce attorney fees and settlement costs by 20 percent.[70]

The Right-to-Strike Controversy

The right to strike, considered by many a vital instrument for successful collective bargaining, is usually prohibited by statute in the public sector.[71] Even though public employee strikes are illegal in most states, there appears to be no research evidence to support the proposition that the presence of a statutory strike ban significantly reduces the occurrence of public employee strike activity.[72]

The basic argument given for legislative prohibition of strikes is that the services provided by public organizations are essential to the general welfare of the citizens. Work stoppages or refusals to work would adversely affect the delivery of such vital services and create disorder in the community. As is true with many industrial relations concepts, the words *essential services* are subject to many diverse interpretations. Some maintain that all public services are essential, whereas others suggest that many public employee classifications (such as clerks, mechanics, and librarians) are no more essential than their counterparts in the private sector who are granted a right to strike. Police and firefighters are almost always viewed as crucial for public safety; however, at least one police strike saw no increase in the area's crime rate. One political official, believing that criminals fear irate citizens more than they fear the police, commented, "Hoods have no rights without police protection. Shop owners will use their shotguns."[73]

The right to strike in the public sector has other debatable dimensions. Some would prohibit public-sector strikes because they would place too much power in the hands of a union relative to taxpayers. Also, unions would unnecessarily benefit at the expense of other groups that are dependent on government revenues but do not have a right to strike or participate in power ploys with public officials.[74]

One research study found that successful bargaining gains in the public sector occur when unions either use the threat of a strike despite its illegality or intertwine themselves closely with their employers by exchanging patronage for political support.[75] Some contend that the right to strike in the public sector is not essential to collective bargaining because public-sector unions are already influential interest groups and effectively use their lobbying and political support techniques to obtain collective bargaining goals.

Regardless of the arguments for or against the right to strike or statutory penalties imposed for illegal strike activity, significant strikes have occurred in the public sector. When illegal strike activity occurs or management permanently replaces lawful strikers, strike settlements may be delayed as union representatives seek to negotiate terms granting all strikers or discharged employees amnesty or reinstatement to their former jobs. Although there would generally be no legal obligation for a public employer to bargain over or grant such a union proposal, public or political pressure to end the strike may cause a public employer to voluntarily agree to such a proposal.[76]

Interest Dispute Impasse-Resolution Procedures in the Public Sector

Because legislation usually prohibits public employees from striking or requires participation in impasse-resolution procedures before striking, these procedures play an important role in resolving interest disputes over what the terms and conditions of employment will be in the public sector. Because multiple laws exist that govern labor relations in different governmental jurisdictions, many different impasse-resolution procedures may be mandated or encouraged. These procedures normally involve a third party, who assists the parties in reaching an agreement without interrupting services or endangering the public interest (see discussion of **mediation, fact-finding,** and **interest arbitration** in Chapter 9).

Public-sector impasse-resolution procedures are controversial and have received considerable attention. Impasse-resolution procedures may combine mediation, fact-finding and conventional or final-offer arbitration.[77] For example, Connecticut has mediation, fact-finding, and arbitration for state employees; fact-finding and arbitration for municipal employees; and mediation and fact-finding for teachers. Mediation is a legislatively mandated mechanism in public-sector bargaining in 35 states, followed by fact-finding which is required in 31 states.[78] Some form of interest arbitration is provided for firefighters in 21 states and the District of Columbia, for police in 20 states, for educators in 8 states, for municipal employees in 6 states, and for state employees in 5 states.[79]

Mediation Mediation involves a third-party neutral who has no binding authority to decide a dispute but assists the parties' efforts to reach a voluntary agreement. Of the impasse-resolution procedures used in the public sector, mediation is the least intrusive and is little more than an adjunct to the negotiations process.[80] "Mediation is probably the most used and least studied dispute resolution procedure. This is because the mediation process is relatively informal and unstructured reflecting the personal style of the mediator, the preferences of the union and employer representatives, and the intensity of the dispute."[81] The key ingredient for mediator effectiveness is experience, with related mediator training and knowledge. Effective mediators need tenacity—for example, not taking "no" for an answer—and they need to take an active role in the process by such actions as pressuring the parties with successive proposals for compromise rather than simply relaying messages back and forth to the parties.[82]

Mediation tends to be more successful when the parties are unsure of themselves or have personality conflicts. Mediation is generally less effective when followed by another impasse-resolution procedure but more effective when followed immediately by arbitration rather than fact-finding.[83]

Fact-Finding and Arbitration Fact-finding and arbitration are separate impasse-resolution procedures; however, they are discussed and assessed jointly because of their many similarities. Both involve a third-party neutral who conducts a quasi-judicial hearing to assess union's and management's collective bargaining positions on issues in dispute. Those neutrals who are generally accepted to serve as fact-finders or arbitrators are likely to have much labor relations experience, as evidenced by their membership in the National Academy of Arbitrators, and are more likely than not to be attorneys trained in the evidentiary process.[84] (see "Labor Relations in Action" box).

Fact-finders have multiple roles in the impasse-resolution process. A fact-finder must interpret data and information presented and recommend settlement positions to the parties.[85] Fact-finding is intended to encourage a voluntary settlement by the parties by providing an objective assessment of the dispute from a credible and neutral third party. However, the fact-finder's recommendation is not binding on the bargaining parties.

Unlike mediation or fact-finding, arbitration entails a binding decision by a third-party neutral who settles the negotiation impasse. The degree of flexibility an arbitrator has in resolving the bargaining dispute depends on the procedure adopted by the parties or mandated by applicable law. Conventional arbitration permits the arbitrator to decide the most appropriate outcome based on the evidence presented. The arbitrator's discretion is more restricted under a final-offer arbitration (FOA) procedure, which typically has two variations. Total package selection FOA requires the arbitrator to choose either the union's or employer's final offer covering all disputed issues. Issue-by-issue FOA still requires the arbitrator to select either the union's or employer's final offer, but it does permit the arbitrator to make that decision on an issue-by-issue basis. In both cases, FOA means the arbitrator can select only one party's final offer; there is no compromise or splitting the difference, which increases the potential risk to the parties of submitting a dispute to an arbitrator rather than controlling the decision outcome themselves through reaching a voluntary settlement.[86]

Fact-finding and arbitration can be successful in resolving impasses because these techniques provide deadlines for the parties to resolve their differences, fresh knowledgeable perspectives, and political advantages because negotiators can blame the neutral for the eventual settlement. Politicians sometimes criticize fact-finder or arbitrators, calling them "outsiders" or "limousine liberals" who have no accountability to taxpayers—they make the decisions and then leave town. The mere possibility that these procedures might be used to determine negotiation outcomes is intended to pressure the negotiators to resolve their differences voluntarily for fear that the third-party neutral might not understand or agree with their bargaining proposals.

These techniques can also carry some disadvantages. For example, the fact-finder's recommendation and arbitrator's decision may lead to settlement terms but may not resolve the genuine union-management differences underlying the interest dispute. These techniques might cause the parties to cement

LABOR RELATIONS IN ACTION

The Facts about Fact-Finding

There is virtually no consensus about fact-finding. How it is spelled is not even clear. "Fact-finding," "factfinding," or "fact finding" have found their way into statute or state agency documents. Most dictionaries spell it with a hyphen.

Just what facts is a fact-finder to find? Naturally the parties have their preferences, and most of the time they are at odds. In one notable case involving the firefighters of Iowa City, perhaps the clearest analogy ever of the fact-finder's role was presented. There were five hours of testimony with respect to the city's ability to pay. The city, of course, noted how various budget lines had been reduced for lack of funds. The firefighters followed, pointing out the growth of other lines, some of which were labeled "miscellaneous" and all of which, the firefighters asserted, were the new "hiding places" for money in the city's "overflowing coffers."

Finally, the time for closing arguments came. The firefighter spokesman reached under the table for a used brown lunch bag and hauled out three walnut shells and a pea. After refreshing the fact-finder's memory about "the old shell game," he proceeded to demonstrate how, at least in an honest shell game, the pea was always present. It was only a matter of finding it. The fact-finder was left with the clear inference that unless he could find a "pea" in Iowa City of sufficient size to fund the firefighters' request, the "game" could not possibly be honest. In the spokesman's opinion, the "facts" the fact-finder was supposed to find were green, but they weren't peas!

Another unsettled question about fact-finding is exactly what role fact-finding should play. One pundit even raised the question, "Should a fact-finder be concerned with whether his report will be rejected?" Given that fact-finding is part of a dispute-resolution process, it seems obvious to most of us that he should. In one well-known teacher dispute, the fact-finder was convinced that the teachers' position was correct, and moreover, he was told by the board's negotiator that the superintendent "wants a strike." Foolishly, he recommended the full 8 percent increase sought by the teachers even though he believed the teachers would settle for less. The strike lasted 10 weeks.

Most state statutes contain a list of criteria that fact-finders shall consider in making their recommendations. Among them is always one that opens Pandora's box, for example, ". . . and such other factors that are customarily considered in making recommendations in labor disputes." One consideration must be what recommendation will most likely be accepted by the parties. Especially when fact-finding is followed by the right to strike, a failure to recognize the relative power of parties is foolhardy. Some might argue that the role of the fact-finder is to persuade the union membership and public body's constituency of the righteousness of the fact-finder's recommendations. However, most fact-finders are not even second-rate prophets, let alone God (though some pretense along these lines does appear to be a prerequisite for the profession). Their recommendations are no closer to what is "right" than are the positions of either party. Besides, it is doubtful whether a union member or voter ever read a fact-finding report. The bottom-line recommendation is what gets read, and if it is close enough to what constituents will tolerate, it will be accepted.

A better analogy for a fact-finder is a general, all-purpose maintenance worker with a rusty station wagon filled with tools and spare parts. No two calls are alike—the parties, the issues, the propensity to want a settlement, and many other factors all differ. Moreover, the fact-finder won't know what is needed until after the process is well along. Even then, it is often difficult to diagnose. With experience and good fortune, maybe the "maintenance worker" will keep things running smoothly. If the maintenance worker guesses wrong, the boiler may blow up. However, the question of who was "right" is irrelevant! ■

SOURCE: A neutral who wishes to remain anonymous.

their respective positions during negotiations because negotiators believe they can get a better deal from the arbitrator or more favorable recommendations from the fact-finder. Instead of earnestly attempting to resolve differences during negotiations, negotiators focus their time and thoughts on preparing for the fact-finder or arbitrator, thus producing a so-called **chilling effect** on the bargaining process. Rather than being viewed as a risk to be avoided, fact-finding or arbitration simply becomes another bargaining strategy. If either party believes that it could get a better settlement from an arbitrator than from negotiation, an incentive exists to maintain excessive demands in hopes that the arbitrator may "split the difference" and make a favorable award. When one side acts in such a manner, the other side has no realistic choice but to respond similarly, widening the gap between the parties and chilling the prospects for reaching a voluntary settlement.[87]

Research into this aspect of arbitration has produced mixed results. Analysis of arbitral decisions regarding police impasses revealed that some management officials are reluctant to reveal their final offer before arbitration because the arbitrators will use management's final offer as a starting point in their decisions.[88] Yet this concern appears less relevant in a study of several arbitration awards in firefighters' interest disputes, for which the majority of arbitrators took an intermediate or compromise stance on negotiation issues, such as wages and clothing allowances, but did not compromise on other issues, selecting either management's or the union's final position.[89]

Another concern about public-sector interest arbitration is that the mere existence of impasse-resolution procedures could create a so-called **narcotic effect.** Once the parties start using fact-finding or interest arbitration procedures, they may become increasingly reliant on them in subsequent negotiations. Research studies find that this frequently expressed concern is not warranted, and the so-called narcotic effect tends to dissipate over time in subsequent contract negotiations.[90]

Effectiveness of Fact-Finding and Arbitration Many variables influence the bargaining process and outcomes. One general measure of effectiveness is the "cost to at least one of the parties of continuing to disagree while lowering the cost to the other party of agreeing voluntarily."[91] Union and management officials are likely to push disputes to the last step of an impasse-resolution procedure when one or both parties:

- Are uncertain of future costs or continued collective bargaining (a situation that particularly applies to inexperienced negotiators)[92]

- Expect to receive a better settlement through the impasse procedure

- Need to pass the blame for an "unfavorable" settlement to a third-party neutral instead of accepting personal responsibility for the results[93]

Assessing fact-finding is particularly difficult. Its effectiveness does not hinge on the fact-finder's ability; this individual is presented facts by the parties in hopes that he or she will agree with their respective positions. The success of such a procedure is based on the assumption that the fact-finder's report will structure public opinion, which will in turn place pressure on the parties to resolve their differences in accord with published recommendations. Thus far, no concrete evidence shows that public pressure has noticeably affected public-sector management and union officials. The views of the participants themselves appear to be divided, with time delays and disagreement over the weight attached by the fact-finder to factors such as wage comparability being among the criticisms voiced.[94]

In general, participants, as well as analysts, appear to be satisfied with interest arbitration procedures used in the public sector. Compulsory arbitration of interest disputes does reduce the occurrence of public-sector strikes.[95] Voluntary settlement rates of interest disputes tend to be highest when the parties have a legal right to strike (94.7 percent of cases), followed by the availability of FOA issue-by-issue selection (87 percent), FOA total package selection (84.1 percent), and conventional arbitration (75.7 percent).[96] Compulsory interest arbitration also appears to have a small positive effect on wage and benefit improvements for affected employees.

Arbitrators in interest disputes tend to rely, at least initially, on internal wage comparisons and to consider the unique and historical circumstances of the particular community and the desirability of maintaining such circumstances. The criterion of ability to pay plays a secondary role behind comparable wages and cost of living unless well-supported arguments against this are presented. In addition, interest arbitrators view their role in the arbitral process as continuing the existing nature of the parties' relationship that has stemmed from the bilateral process of negotiations. Arbitrators believe that any major deviations from this relationship must come from the parties, not the arbitrator.[97] In wage disputes using FOA, evidence suggests that arbitrators are heavily influenced by wage settlements in comparable units of government. As a result, national unions discourage their local union affiliates from settling for a wage less than the targeted statewide settlement terms.[98]

Even though some management officials may fear arbitration, arbitrators have not stripped them of their rights and authority. Interest arbitration settlements have not proven to be significantly different from outcomes reached through voluntary negotiations under similar circumstances. The public, in general, has accepted the use of alternative dispute-resolution procedures to avoid public-sector strikes, and most significantly, arbitration has been increasingly adopted as an impasse-resolution procedure in the public sector.[99]

Referendum

One final impasse-resolution procedure that is sometimes used to resolve public-sector interest disputes is to submit unresolved issues to a taxpayer referendum or vote. The following item, for example, might be placed on a ballot: "Do you approve of granting a wage increase of X cents per hour to our police officers at an estimated additional annual cost to property taxpayers of Y million dollars?"[100]

One advantage of the referendum procedure is that it avoids having an outsider (fact-finder or arbitrator) determine the cost of a negotiated settlement. Citizens should complain less if the union's settlement was achieved in a democratic manner. Similarly, a union's integrity would be at stake if it refused to abide by the "will of the public." Yet, this procedure could turn collective bargaining into a public relations campaign directed at a body of individuals (citizens) largely unfamiliar with labor relations' complexities. Furthermore, the procedure has no precedent in private-sector labor relations because no company submits labor agreement proposals to stockholders or consumers for approval.

Referendum, or direct submission to the electorate for final and binding settlement of interest disputes, has been used in several Texas cities. Employees have won over two-thirds of the elections involving civil service and bonus issues but lost 56.6 percent when the issue was pay parity.[101] Use of a referendum has two potential advantages[102]:

1. It ensures that the negotiations will be conducted in a pragmatic, realistic environment where the parties have an incentive to reach an agreement and costs are too high to fail to reach an agreement.

2. It motivates citizens to take an active interest in the matter of public employment.

In cities where the referendum method has been used, the assessment of this approach has not been favorable. First, the electorate has little understanding of the law and the issues, and it is highly susceptible to propaganda campaigns by both parties. Second, the referendum appears to help make the strong stronger and the weak weaker without regard for what is equitable or reasonable for all the parties involved.[103] There are many varieties and combinations of public impasse-resolution procedures, yet the objectives remain the same: to avoid strikes, to minimize dependence on outsiders, to maximize good faith bargaining between parties, to protect the public interest, and to build labor-management commitment to accountability and mutual problem solving.

Prospects for Future Public-Sector Labor Relations

Labor relations expert James Craft has projected 20 years into the future of public-sector labor relations. He forecasts the following.

- There will be intense emphasis at all levels of government on reducing costs and improving efficiency. The private sector will continue to serve as a model to reshape government with goals of improving cost efficiencies, reducing size of government, stimulating an entrepreneurial spirit, and creating a customer orientation. Governments at all levels will continue to contract out services to the private sector and use competitive bidding to control costs. These actions will have direct implications on government labor relations.

- The number and percentage of public-sector employees who will be union members will increase. Among the reasons are (1) a more favorable general image of unions, (2) public-sector employees perceive unions as having greater influence in providing job security and greater protection of their general benefits and welfare, (3) the attitudes and behavior of public-sector managers, unlike the private-sector managers, are less resistant to employees being represented by unions, and (4) there are many opportunities in the public sector for unions to organize those who are not presently well represented, such as public-sector nurses and doctors, college professors, home-care workers, and increased numbers of security employees.

- There will be increased rivalry among unions who react to the changing operations of governments. For example, when a government contracts out services to a private employee, it creates employment in the private sector, which creates opportunities for private-sector unions to represent the new employees.

Such actions may create tensions between the American Federation of State, County, and Municipal Employees, which represents primarily public-sector employees, and other unions, such as the Communications Workers of America and the United Food and Commercial Workers, which represent primarily private-sector employees.

- There will be few, if any, totally new union tactics and actions. The unions will rely less on the use of formal strikes, and more emphasis will be placed on political actions for several reasons: (1) there is greater maturity in the relationships between the parties and understanding of the collective-bargaining process, (2) there is concern among employees in the nonessential services that they may create interest in contracting out their jobs, and (3) there is less tolerance among the public for strikes by employees in the public sector.

- There will be increased interest in merit-, market- and performance-based compensation models, which include group-based incentive pay that potentially can reduce costs and reward employees for savings.

- There will a growing emphasis on the development of labor management cooperation and collaboration at all levels of governments. Both unions and employers will recognize the mutual benefits of a more cooperative relationship and move toward constructive processes such as interest-based bargaining, as described in Chapter 6.[104]

SUMMARY

Public employee unions over the past 40 years have grown to represent a majority of employees in education, police, and fire protection in state and local governments and a significant proportion of workers in the federal sector. Public employers and employees are under pressure to deliver an increasing variety of public services in the most cost-efficient and timely manner possible. Concepts familiar to private-sector labor relations over the past 20 years, such as downsizing, cost reduction, outsourcing, and productivity improvement, have made their way into the bargaining reality of public-sector labor relations as well.

Most states have one or more comprehensive laws regulating state and local public-sector labor relations. Such legislation typically specifies the administrative setup, union recognition procedure, bargaining rights, impasse procedures, unfair labor practices, and strike provisions applicable to covered employees. The Civil Service Reform Act (CSRA) of 1978 regulates federal employee labor relations. The administrative agencies under the CSRA include the Federal Labor Relations Authority, the General Counsel, and the Federal Service Impasse Panel. Within this framework, the parties attempt to negotiate and administer labor agreements covering permissible subjects. Also available for assistance are the Federal Mediation and Conciliation Service, labor arbitrators, and fact-finders, who provide important dispute resolution services for the parties.

Public- and private-sector labor relations differ in several ways: (1) by its very nature, public service differs from private-sector services economically and in its demand characteristics; (2) the effect of the budget on bargaining processes differs; (3) the bargaining structure differs, affecting decision-making processes;

(4) negotiable issues and bargaining tactics may be less predictable; (5) the right to strike is usually prohibited by law; and (6) effects on and approaches to labor relations differ. Public- and private-sector similarities include the role of personalities and skills of negotiators and the interplay of bargaining power model variables, such as public opinion, political support, and various forms of job actions.

Impasse-resolution procedures often established as a substitute for public employees' lack of a legal right to strike include mediation, fact-finding, arbitration, and various combinations of these. Such terms as *chilling effect* and *narcotic effect* have become common in assessing the effectiveness of these procedures. Public employee unions do appear to have had a positive impact on raising wage and benefit levels for public employees and in garnering a larger proportion of public-sector budgets to address employee interests. Although public-sector union membership growth rates are likely to moderate in future years, public employee unions will continue to play an important role in determining labor relations policy and outcomes in the public sector.

KEY TERMS

Federal Labor Relations
  Authority (FLRA)
Federal Service Impasse
  Panel (FSIP)
exclusive recognition
work-to-rule
sovereignty doctrine
multilateral bargaining

end-run bargaining
sunshine law
mediation
fact-finding
interest arbitration
chilling effect
narcotic effect

DISCUSSION QUESTIONS

1. Think of a public organization with which you are familiar. Explain how it differs from a private company in terms of the following:

   a. Nature of its service

   b. Relationship between its budget and collective bargaining processes

   c. Bargaining structure and decision-making processes

   d. Negotiable issues and bargaining tactics

   e. Its right to strike

2. Using the same public organization as in Question 1, discuss the similarities between collective bargaining in this organization and a typical negotiation between a private company and its union.

3. Explain why some states do and other states don't have a public-sector bargaining law or laws that cover some public employees but not others.

4. Describe the different types of impasse-resolution procedures used in the public sector and discuss the relative effectiveness of each.

5. What are some possible advantages or disadvantages of expanding the scope of bargaining in the federal sector to include issues like wages and benefits?

6. Should public employees have the same right to strike as private-sector employees are granted under the Labor Management Relations Act? Why or why not?

7. Should all public employees have a right to submit interest disputes to final and binding arbitration in exchange for giving up the right to engage in legal strike activity? Why or why not?

Exploring the Web

Labor Relations in the Public Sector

1. Federal-Sector Labor Relations Legislation   The Federal Labor Relations Authority is an independent agency responsible for administering the labor-management relations program for Federal employees worldwide. What is the mission of the Federal Service Impasses Panel?

http://www.flra.gov

How did the Postal Reorganization Act of 1970 affect labor-management relations in the Postal Service?

http://www.usps.gov/history/

2. Articles on Public-Sector Unionism   The Public Service Research Foundation, a private nonprofit organization, makes available papers and pamphlets that "address a variety of issues related to public sector unionism and union influence on public policy."

In "Beyond Public Sector Unionism," Foundation president David Denholm discusses the differences between public- and private-sector unionism. How does he argue that public-sector collective bargaining goes against the public interest?

http://www.psrf.org/issues/beyond.jsp

3. Labor Relations and Teachers   From the previous site, read also David Denholm's "The Impact of Unionism on the Quality of Education."

The Education Policy Institute in Washington, D.C., provides links to information on teacher unions. What are some of the differences between the National Education Association (NEA) and the American Federation of Teachers (AFT)?

http://www.educationpolicy.org/files/neaftbk/httoc.htm

4. Bureau of Labor Statistics on Major Work Stoppages in the Public Sector
The BLS reports "major work stoppages," which include worker-initiated strikes and lockouts by their employers involving 1,000 workers or more. What percentage of the total major work stoppages in 2002 occurred in the public sector?

http://www.bls.gov/news.release/wkstp.nr0.htm

REFERENCES

1. David Lewin, Peter Feuille, and Thomas Kochan, *Public Sector Labor Relations: An Analysis and Readings*, 2d ed. (Glen Ridge, N.J.: Thomas Horton & Daughters, 1988), pp. 1–5.

2. Dale Belman, Morley Gunderson, and Douglas Hyatt, "Public Sector Employment Relations in Transition," in *Public Sector Employment*, eds. D. Belman, M. Gunderson, and D. Hyatt (Madison, Wis.: Industrial Relations Research Association, 1996), pp. 1–9.

3. Bureau of Labor Statistics, "Union Members in 2002," *News Release*, February 25, 2003,

4. Terry Thomason and John F. Burton, Jr., "Unionization Trends and Labor-Management Cooperation in the Public Sector," *Going Public: The Role of Labor-Management Relations in Delivering Quality Government Services*, eds. Jonathan Brock and David B. Lipsky (Champaign, Ill.: Industrial Relations Research Association, 2003), p. 69–83.

5. Service Employees International Union, "SEIU's Public Service Employees," 2002, pp. 1–2 at http://www.sein.org/public_employee/abtpubemp.html.

6. James L. Stern, "Unionism in the Public Sector," in *Public Sector Bargaining*, 2d ed., eds. Benjamin Aaron, Joyce M. Najita, and James L. Stern (Washington, D.C.: The Bureau of National Affairs, 1988), pp. 66–67; Marick F. Masters and Robert S. Atkin, "Reforming Federal Sector Labor Relations: Recommendations of President Clinton's National Partnership Council," *Labor Law Journal* 45 (June 1994), pp. 353–354; updated by Courtney D. Gifford, *Directory of U.S. Labor Organizations*, 1997 edition (Washington, D.C.: Bureau of National Affairs, 1997), p. 81.

7. James T. Bennett and Marick F. Masters, "The Future of Public Sector Labor-Management Relations," *Journal of Labor Research* 24, no. 4 (Fall 2003), pp. 537–538.

8. Heejoon Park, "State Legislation of Public Sector Collective Bargaining: An Event History Analysis," in *Proceedings of the Fiftieth Annual Meeting, Industrial Relations Research Association* (Madison, Wis.: Industrial Relations Research Association, 1998), pp. 23–32; Susan Schwochau, "Interest Group Tactics and Public Sector Labor Relations Policy," *Journal of Labor Research* 15 (Fall 1994), pp. 331–354.

9. Jeffrey S. Zax and Casey Ichniowski, "Bargaining Laws and Unionization in the Local Public Sector," *Industrial and Labor Relations Review* 43 (April 1990), pp. 447–463; Greg Hundley, "Who Joins Unions in the Public Sector? The Effect of Individual Characteristics and the Law," *Journal of Labor Research* 9 (Fall 1988), pp. 301–306; Richard B. Freeman and Casey Ichniowski, "Introduction: The Public Sector Look of American Unionism," in *When Public Sector Workers Unionize*, eds. Richard B. Freeman and Casey Ichniowski (Chicago: The University of Chicago Press, 1988), p. 3.

10. Bennett and Masters, "The Future of Public Sector Labor-Management Relations," pp. 534–536.

11. Fred C. Lunenburg, "Collective Bargaining in the Public Schools: Issues, Tactics, and New Strategies," *Journal of Collective Negotiations in the Public Sector* 29, no. 4 (2000), p. 259.

12. John Lund and Cheryl L. Maranto, "Public Sector Labor Law: An Update," in *Public Sector Employment in a Time of Transition*, eds. Dale Belman, Morley Gunderson, and Douglas Hyatt (Madison, Wis.: Industrial Relations Research Association, 1996), p. 48.

13. *County Sanitation District No. 2 of L.A. County v. L.A. County Employees Association*, 699 P.2d 835 (1985); Raymond L. Hogler, *Public Sector Strikes: Employee Rights, Union Responsibilities, and Employer Prerogatives* (Alexandria, Va.: International Personnel Management Association, 1988), pp. 5–6.

14. Robert Hebdon, "Public Sector Dispute Resolution in Transition," in *Public Sector Employment in a Time of Transition*, eds. Dale Belman, Morley Gunderson, and Douglas Hyatt (Madison, Wis.: Industrial Relations Research Association, 1996), pp. 87–92.

15. Charles J. Coleman, "Federal Sector Labor Relations: A Reevaluation of Policies," *Journal of Collective Negotiations in the Public Sector* 16, no. 1 (1987), pp. 37–52.

16. Ibid.

17. George W. Bohlander, "The Federal Service Impasse Panel: A Ten-Year Review and Analysis," *Journal of Collective Negotiations in the Public Sector* 24, no. 3, (1995), pp. 194–195.

18. Bohlander, "The Federal Service Impasse Panel: A Ten-Year Review and Analysis."

19. Charles G. Smith, "Winning and Losing in Federal Sector Dispute Resolution," *Public Personnel Management* 23 (Summer 1994), pp. 301–319.

20. Peter Feuille, "Unionism in the Public Sector: The Joy of Protected Markets," *Journal of Labor Research* 12 (Fall 1991), pp. 351–353 and Jill Kriesky, "Trends in Dispute Resolution in the Public Sector," in *Employment Dispute Resolution and Worker Rights in a Changing Workplace*, eds. Adrienne E. Eaton and Jeffrey H. Keefe (Champaign, Ill.: Industrial Relations Research Association, 1999), pp. 249–250.

21. William J. Clinton, *Presidential Executive Order No. 12871: Labor-Management Partnerships*, October 1, 1993 at http://www.opm.gov/npc/html/eo12871.htm; William J. Clinton, "Memorandum for the Heads of Executive Departments and Agencies," *News Release*, October 28, 1999, pp. 1–2 at http://www.opm.gov/pressrel/1999/pres_statement.htm.

22. Martin H. Malin, "Public Sector Labor Law Doctrine and Labor-Management Cooperation," *Going Public: The Role of Labor-Management Relations in Delivering Quality Government Services*, eds. Jonathan Brock and David B. Lipsky (Champaign, Ill.: Industrial Relations Research Association, 2003), pp. 278–279.

23. Marick F. Masters and Robert B. Albright, "Federal Labor-Management Partnerships, Perspectives, Performance, and Possibilities," and Terry Thomason and John F. Burton, Jr., "Unionization Trends and Labor-Management Cooperation in the Public Sector," *Going Public: The Role of Labor-Management Relations in Delivering Quality Government Services*, eds. Jonathan Brock and David B. Lipsky (Champaign, Ill.: Industrial Relations Research Association, 2003), pp. 177–207.

24. Marick F. Masters and Robert R. Albright, "Labor Relations in the Department of Homeland Security: Competing and Perspectives and Future Possibilities," *Labor Law Journal* 54, no. 1 (2003), pp. 66–83.

25. Richard W. Hurd and Jill K. Kriesky with reply by Herbert R. Northrup, "The Rise and Demise of PATCO," *Industrial and Labor Relations Review* 40 (October 1986), pp. 115–127; Herbert R. Northrup, "The Rise and Demise of PATCO," *Industrial and Labor Relations Review* 37 (January 1984), pp. 167–184.

26. Michael H. Cimini and Susan L. Behrmann, "Collective Bargaining, 1991: Recession Colors Talks," *Monthly Labor Review* 115 (January 1992), pp. 26–27.

27. "Arbitration Panel Awards Postal Union Four-Year Contract with Raises, Colas," *Daily Labor Report*, October 3, 1995, pp. A1–A2.

28. American Postal Workers Union, "President Biller, National Executive Board, Rank and File Bargaining Advisory Committee Urge Ratification," *News Release*, December 17, 1998, pp. 1–5 at http://apwu.org/Bulletins/ns32121798.htm.

29. National Association of Letter Carriers, "Over 240,000 City Letter Carriers Win Pay Upgrade Due to Automation," *News Release*, October 11, 1999, pp. 1–2 at http://www.nalc.org/pm1995.html.

30. Tim Bornstein, "Legacies of Local Government Collective Bargaining in the 1970s," *Labor Law Journal* 31 (March 1980), pp. 165–173.

31. Jack Fiorito and Lee P. Stepina, "Explaining the Unionism Gap: Public-Private Sector Differences in Preferences for Unionization," *Journal of Labor Research* 17 (Summer 1996), pp. 463–478; Kate Bronfenbrenner and Tom Juravich, *Union Organizing in the Public Sector* (Ithaca, N.Y.: Cornell University Press, 1995); Lee A. Graf, Masoud Hemmasi, Kenneth E. Newgreen,

and Warren R. Nielsen, "Profiles of Those Who Support Collective Bargaining in Institutions of Higher Learning and Why: An Empirical Examination," *Journal of Collective Negotiations in the Public Sector* 23, no. 2 (1994), p. 155.

32. Richard Freeman, "Through Public Sector Eyes: Employee Attitudes toward Public Sector Labor Relations in the U.S.," in *Public Sector Employment in a Time of Transition*, eds. Dale Belman, Morley Gunderson, and Douglas Hyatt (Madison, Wis.: Industrial Relations Research Association, 1996), pp. 71–73.

33. These techniques were formulated in various discussions with Paul Gerhart of Case Western Reserve University.

34. Kevin M. O'Brien, "Compensation, Employment, and the Political Activity of Public Employee Unions," *Journal of Labor Research* 13 (Spring 1992), pp. 189–203; Michael Marmo, "Public Employee Unions: The Political Imperative," *Journal of Collective Negotiations in the Public Sector* 4, no. 4 (1975), p. 371.

35. Paul D. Staudohar, "Quasi-Strikes by Public Employees," *Journal of Collective Negotiations in the Public Sector* 3 (Fall 1974), pp. 363–371.

36. Richard B. Freeman and Casey Ichniowski, "Introduction: The Public Sector Look of American Unionism," in *When Public Sector Workers Unionize*, eds. Richard B. Freeman and Casey Ichniowski (Chicago: The University of Chicago Press, 1988), pp. 1–13.

37. John Lund and Cheryl L Maranto, "Public Sector Law: An Update," pp. 39–47.

38. Michael Moskow, J. J. Loewenberg, and E. C. Koziara, *Collective Bargaining in Public Employment* (New York: Random House, 1970), pp. 14–18; H. H. Wellington and R. K. Winter, Jr., "Structuring Collective Bargaining in Public Employment," *Yale Law Journal* 79 (April 1970), pp. 806-822.

39. Dale Belman, Morley Gunderson, and Douglas Hyatt, "Public Sector Employment Relations in Transition," in *Public Sector Employment in a Time of Transition*, eds. D. Belman, M. Gunderson,

and D. Hyatt (Madison, Wis.: Industrial Relations Research Association, 1996), pp. 4–5.

40. Milton Derber, Ken Jennings, Ian McAndrew and Martin Wagner, "Bargaining and Budget-Making in Illinois Public Institutions," *Industrial and Labor Relations Review* 27 (October 1973), pp. 49–62; Kenneth M. Jennings, J. A. Smith, and Earle C. Traynham, Jr., "Budgetary Influences on Bargaining in Mass Transit," *Journal of Collective Negotiations in the Public Sector* 6, no. 4 (1977), pp. 333–339.

41. Frederick O. R. Hayes, "Collective Bargaining and the Budget Director," in *Public Workers and Public Unions*, ed. Sam Zagoria (Englewood Cliffs, N.J.: Prentice-Hall, 1972), p. 91.

42. Derber et al., "Bargaining and Budget-Making," p. 58.

43. David D. Dilts, William H. Walker, and Constanza Hagman, "The Impact of the North America Free Trade Agreement on Public Sector Collective Bargaining," *Journal of Collective Negotiations in the Public Sector* 23, no. 1 (1994), pp. 92–94.

44. Michael Marmo, "Public Employees: On-the-Job Discipline for Off-the-Job Behavior," *The Arbitration Journal* 40 (June 1985), p. 23; Marvin Hill, Jr., and Donald Dawson, "Discharge for Off-Duty Misconduct in the Private and Public Sectors," *The Arbitration Journal* 40 (June 1985), pp. 24–33.

45. Kevin A. Banasik, "Government Regulation of Federal Employee Speech: *United States* v. *National Treasury Employees Union*, 115 S.Ct. 1003 (1993)," *Harvard Journal of Law & Public Policy* 19 (Fall 1995), pp. 200–209; David H. Rosenbloom, "Public Personnel Administration and the Constitution: An Emergent Approach," *Public Administration Review* 35 (February 1975), pp. 52–59.

46. *Board of Regents* v. *Roth*, 408 U.S. 564 (1972); *Perry* v. *Sindermann*, 408 U.S. 593 (1972).

47. *Cleveland Board of Education* v. *Loudermill*, 470 U.S. 532 (1985).

48. Timothy D. Chandler and Timothy A. Judge, "Management Chief Negotiators, Bargaining Strategies, and the

Likelihood of Impasse in Public Sector Collective Bargaining," *American Review of Public Administration* 28 (June 1998), pp. 146–166.

49. Rafael Gely and Timothy D. Chandler, "Determinants of Management's Organizational Structure in the Public Sector," *Journal of Labor Research* 14 (Fall 1993), pp. 381–397.

50. Stephen L. Hayford, "An Empirical Investigation of the Public Sector Supervisory Bargaining Rights Issue," *Labor Law Journal* 26 (October 1975), pp. 641–652; Alan Balfour, "Rights of Collective Representation for Public Sector Supervisors," *Journal of Collective Negotiations in the Public Sector* 4, no. 3 (1975), pp. 257–265; and William H. Holley, Jr., J. Boyd Scebra, and William Rector, "Perceptions of the Role of the Principal in Professional Negotiations," *Journal of Collective Negotiations in the Public Sector* 5, no. 4 (1976), pp. 361–369.

51. Adrienne E. Eaton and Paula B. Voos, "Wearing Two Hats: The Unionization of Public Sector Supervisors," *Going Public: The Role of Labor-Management Relations in Delivering Quality Government Services*, eds. Jonathan Brock and David B. Lipsky (Champaign, Ill.: Industrial Relations Research Association, 2003), pp. 295–309.

52. Louis V. Imundo, Jr., "The Federal Government Sovereignty and Its Effect on Labor-Management Relations," *Labor Law Journal* 26 (March 1975), pp. 145–152.

53. Milton Derber, "Management Organization for Collective Bargaining in the Public Sector," in *Public Sector Bargaining*, eds. Benjamin Aaron, Joseph Grodin, and James Stern (Washington, D.C.: Bureau of National Affairs, 1978), pp. 80–117.

54. Timothy D. Chandler and Timothy A. Judge, "Management Chief Negotiators, Bargaining Strategies, and the Likelihood of Impasse in Public Sector Collective Bargaining," *Annual Review of Public Administration* 28 (June 1998), pp. 160–161.

55. I. B. Helburn and N. B. Bennett, "Public Employee Bargaining and the Merit Principle," *Labor Law Journal* 23 (October 1972), p. 619; I. B. Helburn, "The Scope

of Bargaining in Public Sector Negotiations: Sovereignty Reviewed," *Journal of Collective Negotiations in the Public Sector* 3 (Spring 1974), pp. 147–166.

56. Richard C. Williams, "Resolution of the Civil Service–Collective Bargaining Dilemma," *American Review of Public Administration* 24 (June 1994), pp. 149–160.

57. Paul F. Gerhart, "The Scope of Bargaining in Local Government Negotiations," *Labor Law Journal* 20 (August 1969), pp. 545–552.

58. Margorie Sarbaugh-Thompson, "Bargaining Over Education Policy: Who Represents the Community?" *Journal of Collective Negotiations in the Public Sector* 26, no. 3 (1997), pp. 223–245; Thomas A. Kochan, "A Theory of Multilateral Collective Bargaining in City Governments," *Industrial and Labor Relations Review* 27 (July 1974), pp. 525–542.

59. Marick F. Masters, "AFSCME as a Political Union," *Journal of Labor Research* 19 (Spring 1998), pp. 313–349; Marick F. Masters and Robert S. Atkin, "Financial and Political Resources of Nine Major Public Sector Unions in the 1980s," *Journal of Labor Research* 17 (Winter 1996), pp. 183–198; Rafael Gely and Timothy D. Chandler, "Protective Service Unions' Political Activities and Departmental Expenditures," *Journal of Labor Research* 16 (Spring 1995), pp. 171–185; Robert G. Valletta, "The Impact of Unionism On Municipal Expenditures and Revenues," *Industrial and Labor Relations Review* 42 (April 1989), pp. 430–442.

60. Peter Feuille, "Police Labor Relations and Multilateralism," *Journal of Collective Negotiations in the Public Sector* 3 (Summer 1974), p. 216.

61. Victor Gotbaum, "Collective Bargaining and the Union Leader," in *Public Workers and Public Unions*, ed. Zagoria, pp. 83–84.

62. Michael Marmo, "Public Employee Collective Bargaining: A Mass-Mediated Process," *Journal of Collective Negotiations in the Public Sector* 13, no. 4 (1984), pp. 291–307.

63. "Characteristics of 'Sunshine' Laws in the 50 States," *The Chronicle of Higher Education*, October 10, 1984, p. 18.

64. Kevin M. O'Brien, "The Impact of Sunshine Laws on Police and Firefighter Bargaining Outcomes," *Applied Financial Economics* 5 (December 1995), pp. 425–432.

65. George W. Bohlander, "Public Sector Grievance Arbitration: Structure and Administration," *Journal of Collective Negotiations in the Public Sector* 21, no. 4 (1992), pp. 282–283; Greg Stewart and Jeanette A. Davy, "An Empirical Examination of Grievance Resolution and Filing Rates in the Public and Private Sectors," *Journal of Collective Negotiations in the Public Sector* 21, no. 4 (1992), pp. 331–334.

66. Barry M. Rubin and Richard S. Rubin, "Creeping Legalism in Public Sector Grievance Arbitration: A National Perspective," *Journal of Collective Negotiation in the Public Sector* 30, no. 1 (2003), pp. 3–12.

67. Debra J. Mesch and Olga Shamayeva, "Arbitration In Practice: A Profile of Public Sector Arbitration Cases," *Public Personnel Management* 25 (Spring 1996), pp. 119–132.

68. Michael J. Duane, "To Grieve or Not to Grieve: Why Reduce It To Writing?" *Public Personnel Management* 20 (Spring 1991), pp. 83–88.

69. Jill Kriesky, "Trends in Dispute Resolution in the Public Sector," in *Employment Dispute Resolution and Worker Rights in the Changing Workplace*, pp. 251–254.

70. Joseph I. Goldstein and Martin F. Payson, "Alternate Dispute Resolution of Employment Matters in the Public Sector," *Spectrum: The Journal of State Government* 68 (Fall 1995), pp. 36–42.

71. Michael H. Cimini, "1982–97 State and Local Government Work Stoppages and Their Legal Background," *Compensation and Working Conditions* 3 (Fall 1998), pp. 32–34; John Lund and Cheryl L. Maranto, "Public Sector Labor Law: An Update," in *Public Sector Employment in a Time of Transition*, p. 30.

72. Dane M. Partridge, "The Effect of Public Policy on Strike Activity in the Public Sector," *Journal of Collective Negotiations in the Public Sector* 19, no. 2 (1990), pp. 87–94; Robert E. Doherty, "Trends in Strikes and Interest Arbitration in the Public Sector," *Labor Law Journal* 37 (August 1986), pp. 473–475; Craig Olson, "Strikes, Strike Penalties, and Arbitration in Six States," *Industrial and Labor Relations Review* 39 (July 1986), p. 539.

73. "Crime Rate Is Same Despite Police Strike," *Miami Herald,* July 20, 1975, p. 15-A.

74. Paul D. Staudohar, "Reappraisal of the Right to Strike in California," *Journal of Collective Negotiations in the Public Sector* 15, no. 2 (1986), p. 91.

75. Theodore Kheel, "Resolving Deadlocks without Banning Strikes," *Monthly Labor Review* 91 (July 1969), pp. 62–63.

76. Michael H. Cimini, "1982–97 State and Local Government Work Stoppages and Their Legal Background," 1998, p. 34.

77. U.S. Department of Labor, Labor-Management Services Administration, *Summary of Public Sector Labor Relations Policies, 1976* (Washington, D.C.: Government Printing Office, 1976), pp. 1–126.

78. Mark D. Karper, "Fact Finding in Public Employment: Promise or Illusion, Revisited," *Journal of Collective Negotiations in the Public Sector* 23, no. 4 (1994), pp. 288–296.

79. John Lund and Cheryl L. Marnto, "Public Sector Labor Law: An Update," in *Public Sector Employment in a Time of Transition*, pp. 31, 48, 50–54.

80. David A. Dilts, Ahmad Karm, and Ali Rassuli, "Mediation in the Public Sector: Toward a Paradigm of Negotiations and Dispute Resolution," *Journal of Collective Negotiations in the Public Sector* 19, no. 1 (1990), pp. 49–50.

81. David Lewin, Peter Feuille, Thomas A. Kochan, and John T. Delaney, *Public Sector Labor Relations: Analysis and Readings* (Lexington, Mass.: D.C. Heath, 1988), pp. 334–335.

82. Steven Briggs and Daniel J. Koys, "An Empirical Investigation of Public Sector Mediator Effectiveness," *Journal of Collective Negotiations in the Public Sector* 19, no. 2 (1990), pp. 121–126.

83. Thomas A. Kochan, "Dynamics of Dispute Resolution in the Public Sector," in *Public Sector Bargaining*, eds. B. Aaron, J. R. Grodin, and J. L. Stern

(Washington, D.C.: Bureau of National Affairs, 1979), pp. 150–190; Thomas P. Gilroy and Anthony Sinicropi, "Impasse Resolution in Public Employment: A Current Assessment," *Industrial and Labor Relations Review* 25 (July 1972), pp. 500–501.

84. Stanley W. Elsea, David Dilts, and Lawrence J. Haber, "Factfinders and Arbitrators in Iowa: Are They the Same Neutrals?" *Journal of Collective Negotiations in the Public Sector* 19, no. 1 (1990), pp. 61–81.

85. Debra J. Mesch, "A Union-Management Cooperative Program Gone Wrong: Some Unintended Consequences of a Fact-Finding Program," *Journal of Applied Behavioral Science* 30 (March 1994), pp. 43–62; Kenneth M. Jennings, Steve K. Paulson, and Steven A. Williamson, "Fact-Finding in Perspective," *Government Union Review* 8 (Summer 1987), pp. 54–70; Nels Nelson, "Fact-Finders View the Factfinding Process," *The Journal of Collective Negotiations in the Public Sector* 19, no. 2 (1990), pp. 141–149.

86. For an excellent review of the distinctive nature of arbitration in the public sector, see Helen LaVan, "Arbitration in the Public Sector: A Current Perspective," *Journal of Collective Negotiations in the Public Sector* 19, no. 2 (1990), pp. 153–163.

87. Lewin, Feuille, and Kochan, *Public Sector Labor Relations,* p. 229; Frederic C. Champlin and Mario F. Bognanno, "Time Spent Processing Interest Arbitration Cases: The Minnesota Experience," *Journal of Collective Negotiations in the Public Sector* 14, no. 1 (1985), pp. 53–64; Charles M. Rehmus, "Public Employees: A Survey of Some Critical Problems on the Frontier of Collective Bargaining," *Labor Law Journal* 27 (September 1976), pp. 588–599.

88. Craig E. Overton and Max S. Wortman, "Compulsory Arbitration: A Strike Alternative for Police?" *Arbitration Journal* 28 (March 1974), p. 40.

89. Hoyt N. Wheeler, "Is Compromise the Rule in Fire Fighter Arbitration?" *Arbitration Journal* 29 (September 1974), pp. 176–185.

90. James R. Chelius and Marian M. Extejt, "The Narcotic Effect of Impasse Resolution Procedures," *Industrial and Labor Relations Review* 38 (July 1985), pp. 629–637; Marian M. Extejt and James R. Chelius, "The Behavioral Impact of Impasse Resolution Procedures," *Review of Public Personnel Administration* 5 (Spring 1985), pp. 46–47.

91. Paul F. Gerhart and John E. Drotning, "Do Uncertain Cost/Benefit Estimates Prolong Public-Sector Disputes?" *Monthly Labor Review* 103 (September 1980), pp. 26–30; Frederic Champlin and Mario F. Bognanno, "Chilling' under Arbitration and Mixed Strike-Arbitration Regimes," *Journal of Labor Research* 6 (Fall 1985), pp. 375–386.

92. David E. Bloom, "Is Arbitration Really Compatible with Bargaining?" *Industrial Relations* 20 (Fall 1980), pp. 233–244.

93. Henry S. Farber, "Role of Arbitration in Dispute Settlement," *Monthly Labor Review* 104 (May 1981), p. 34.

94. Hebdon, "Public Sector Dispute Resolution in Transition," pp. 102–103.

95. Morley Gunderson, Robert Hebdon, and Douglas Hyatt, "Collective Bargaining in the Public Sector: Comment," *American Economic Review* 86 (March 1996), pp. 315–326.

96. Hebdon, "Public Sector Dispute Resolution in Transition," pp. 110–112; Michael A. Zigarelli, "Dispute Resolution Mechanisms and Teacher Bargaining Outcomes," *Journal of Labor Research* 17 (Winter 1996), pp. 135–148.

97. Richard A. Turpin, "An Analysis of Public Sector Interest Arbitrators' Assessments of Wage Comparability," *Journal of Collective Negotiations in the Public Sector* 27, no. 1 (1998), pp. 45–51; Richard A. Turpin, "Factors Considered by Public Sector Interest Arbitrators in Assessing Ability to Pay," *Journal of Collective Negotiations in thePublic Sector* 26, no. 1 (1997), pp. 1–7; Gregory G. Dell'omo, "Wage Disputes in Interest Arbitration: Arbitrators Weigh the Criteria," *The Arbitration Journal* 44 (June 1989), pp. 4–8; Susan Schwochau and Peter Feuille, "Interest Arbitrators and Their Decision Behavior," *Industrial Relations* 27 (Winter 1988), pp. 37–55.

98. Craig A. Olson and Paul Jarley, "Arbitration Decisions in Wisconsin Teacher Wage Disputes," *Industrial and Labor Relations Review* 44 (April 1991), p. 546.

99. Karl O. Magnusen and Patricia A. Renovitch, "Dispute Resolution in Florida's Public Sector: Insight into Impasse," *Journal of Collective Negotiations in the Public Sector* 18, no. 3 (1989), pp. 241–252; J. Joseph Loewenberg, "Compulsory Arbitration in the United States," in *Compulsory Arbitration*, ed J. J. Loewenberg et al. (Lexington, Mass.: D.C. Heath, 1976), p. 166; Hoyt N. Wheeler, "An Analysis of Fire Fighter Strikes," *Labor Law Journal* 26 (January 1975), pp. 17–20.

100. J. H. Foegen, "Public Sector Strike-Prevention: Let the Taxpayer Decide," *Journal of Collective Negotiations in the Public Sector* 3 (Summer 1974), p. 223.

101. I. B. Helburn and J. L. Matthews, "The Referendum as an Alternative to Bargaining," *Journal of Collectible Negotiations in the Public Sector* 9, no. 2 (1980), pp. 93–105.

102. Raymond L. Hogler and Curt Kriksciun, "Impasse Resolution in Public Sector Collective Negotiations: A Proposed Procedure," *Industrial Relations Law Journal* 6, no. 4 (1984), pp. 481–510.

103. Donald T. Barnum and I. B. Helburn, "Influence the Electorate Experience with Referenda on Public Employee Bargaining," *Industrial and Labor Relations Review* 35 (April 1982), pp. 330–342.

104. James A. Craft, "Future Directions in Public Sector Labor Relations: A 2020 Perspective," *Journal of Labor Research* 24, no. 4 (Fall 2003), pp. 543–558.

Removal of an Employee from a Federal Government Contract

Background

Excell, the Company, provides contract security services to a federal governmental facility (several buildings) in Martin, Tennessee; the bargaining unit employees are represented by the United Plant Guard Union. At this site, federal research projects are being done, where many employees are required to have a secret security clearance.

This matter of arbitration stems from an incident that occurred on December 3, 1999. Charlie Shaw was scheduled to work the 3:00 P.M. to 11:00 P.M. shift as the roving guard. When he arrived at work, his on-site supervisor, Al Phillips, assigned him to write a report concerning a U.S. Government employee who claimed that she had been accosted in the parking lot. Shaw stated that he interviewed the woman and wrote a report at that time; however, this report was never found by the Company. Ms. Joyce Snow, the Government's Contract Officer's Technical Representative (COTR), located in Nashville, Tennessee, claimed that she did not receive the report and that Shaw failed to note on the 1103 officer's log for December 3, 1999, as required, that he had taken this report.

At approximately 5:15 P.M., on December 3, 1999, the Martin Police Department responded to a call from Uncle Gerald's Day Care Center, located on federal government property for use by federal employees. The incident at Uncle Gerald's involved the alleged sexual assault of a child by one of her teachers. Shaw claimed that he was called at 5:10 P.M. to report to the day care center, but he did not note on the 1103 officer's log the time that he was notified of the incident. Shaw claimed that he responded immediately and met the Martin police officers at Uncle Gerald's. Because of questions concerning the Martin police officers' authority to investigate an incident on federal property, Shaw contacted COTR Snow to clarify the issue. Shaw informed Ms. Snow that the Martin police were on the premises investigating the alleged sexual assault incident, but there was a question concerning whether they had jurisdiction to investigate the matter.

Ms. Snow instructed Shaw to inform the police that they had jurisdiction to investigate and also instructed Shaw to get a copy of the Martin police officers' report and attach it to Shaw's report. Snow instructed Shaw to inform Atlanta Control Center that the alleged sexual assault incident had occurred and to direct Atlanta Control Center to send a federal investigator to Martin, Tennessee. Shaw claimed that Snow told him to include with his report two blank report forms that he was to sign, so that, if there were mistakes in his written report, it could be changed.

The Martin police officers left the property at approximately 5:55 P.M., and Shaw remained at Uncle Gerald's to complete his report until 6:30 P.M. Thereafter, Shaw failed to carry out Ms. Snow's instructions to call Atlanta Control Center about sending a federal investigator to Martin.

On Shaw's Incident Report Form 3155 filed on the alleged sexual assault incident, he entered the code number as 2010, which refers to assisting a law enforcement officer, whereas code 1120 refers to other sexual offenses. Because of this labeling and Shaw's failure to follow through with Ms. Snow's instructions, the Atlanta Control Center was unaware of the seriousness of the incident at Uncle Gerald's.

Shaw made a notation on Form 3155 about the attachments to the report with a reference to the Form 3155 continuation sheet. There was no reference to a police report being attached

Continued

nor any signed blank report forms. Entries numbered 25 and 26 on the report, which dealt with the identity of the suspect and what happened to the suspect, were not completed.

On December 7, 1999, the Company suspended Shaw for 5 working days. On December 11, 1999, Ms. Snow orally notified Mr. Phillips that Shaw was denied from working on the government service contract. Mr. Billy Woods, Excell's Contract Officer, telephoned Ms. Snow to inquire into the basis for her determination. Mr. Woods requested documentation from her concerning that determination. Soon thereafter, Mr. Woods visited Martin to investigate the circumstances underlying Ms. Snow's denial of Shaw's work determination. When he arrived at the site, Shaw was with Phillips in the Company's office located in the Federal Building. Woods discussed with Shaw the allegations underlying Snow's demand for his removal from the contract. Shaw admitted to Woods that he failed to notify Atlanta Control Center to send an investigator as Snow had instructed and admitted that the report he submitted failed to have the correct notation of offense listed in the report; however, he felt he had timely responded to the call from Uncle Gerald's. Then, Woods personally discussed the issues with Snow at her Nashville office, and Snow indicated to Woods that she was unwilling to rescind Shaw's denial of work and that he was not permitted on the property.

On December 15, 1999, Snow formally issued Shaw's denial of work letter and set forth several reasons for the denial. These include Shaw's failure to report correct information to the Atlanta Control Center, failure to make an accurate report on the woman who alleged she was accosted, and failure to make the same on the 1103 officer's log. Because Excell had no other work site in the Martin area, it terminated Shaw's employment on receiving the denial of work notice from Ms. Snow.

On December 18, 1999, the Union grieved Shaw's removal from work. The Grievance stated:

We are protesting Charlie Shaw's removal from duty since General Services Administration has given no justifiable cause for his removal. Charlie has a good work record on this and past contracts.

Remedy: That Charlie be reinstated to full time duty with all back pay.

On February 11, 2000, a meeting was held to examine whether Shaw's denial of work determination could be altered. Mr. Robert Richards, the Company's president, stated that the Company's position was bound by the service contract with the federal government to adhere to Ms. Snow's request for Shaw's removal from the site. Ms. Snow gave reasons for the denial of work determination in her December 15, 1999, letter. She questioned the quality of Shaw's writing skills in his incident report. She stated that she had given Shaw specific instructions on report writing on prior occasions, but, from an examination of Shaw's report on December 3, her efforts obviously had not helped Shaw to become a better officer.

Shaw and the Union were given an opportunity to address Snow. However, the Union did not present any additional factual information concerning the issues. Shaw addressed the factual basis for Ms. Snow's determination, and he disputed the response time to Uncle Gerald's. He acknowledged that he had mislabeled the 3155 incident report on Uncle Gerald's; instead of listing other sexual offenses, he listed assisting other officers. Shaw admitted that he forgot to inform Atlanta Control Center to send an investigator to Martin, Tennessee, as Snow had instructed.

Ms. Snow's position was not changed by the Union and Shaw, and Snow decided to adhere to her determination that Shaw could not return to the federal property. Excell likewise decided to adhere to its decision concerning Shaw.

Mr. Woods wrote his version of the meeting in his letter of February 12, 2000:

Mr. Shaw presented his version of the details of the incident in question and asked for reconsideration for his position with Excell.

Mr. Richards presented the position of the Company on the issue. He related that in accordance with the contract between Excell and GSA, the Contracting Officer's Technical Representative (COTR), can deny an individual from working on this contract. On 15 December 1999, Ms. Snow, the COTR, presented a letter requesting that Shaw be denied from working on this contract. Because Excell only has the one federal government contract in Martin, TN, Shaw was terminated.

Ms. Snow presented the position of GSA concerning her consideration of withdrawing the letter removing Shaw from the property. Ms. Snow related that her decision was final and would not withdraw her letter.

Further discussion was not necessary and the meeting was adjourned.

The Grievance was then appealed to arbitration.

Issue

Did the Company have just cause for the discharge of Charlie Shaw? If not, what shall be the remedy?

Relevant Collective Bargaining Agreement Provisions

Article I

Recognition and Effective Date

This agreement, signed June 3, 1999, made effective June 3, 1999, is entered into between the United Plant Guard Union, certified as the collective bargaining representative by the National Labor Relations Board decision dated October 24, 1989. "All full time and regular part time security officers performing guard duties as defined in section 9(b)(3) of the National Labor Relations Act, as amended, employed by Excell at the Federal Office Building, Martin, TN, excluding all office clerical employees, and supervisors as defined in the Act, as amended, and all other employees," and as the said unit may hereafter be amended by the National Labor Relations Board.

Article III

Work of Employees

1. The work of employees shall be the work presently performed by employees within the bargaining unit and new or additional bargaining unit work assigned to the unit by the Company. Employees covered by this Agreement shall perform all duties and assignments outlined by the Employer and the Company's client, the General Services Administration.

Article V

Management Rights

1. The Union recognizes that any and all rights concerned with the management of the business and the direction of the work force are exclusively those of the Company. The Company retains all of its normal, inherent common law rights to manage the business, whether or not exercised, as such rights existed prior to the time any Union became the bargaining representative of the employees covered by this Agreement, except as limited by, and consistent with the rights of the Union and its represented employees as set forth in this Agreement or as established by law, statutes and governmental regulations. The sole and exclusive rights of Management shall include, as so limited, the right to: . . . suspend, discharge, or other-

Continued

wise discipline employees for just cause; determine, establish and implement terms and conditions of employment; establish or continue policies, practices, or procedures for the conduct of the business and, from time to time, to change or abolish such policies, practices or procedures in order to prevent any redundancy or duplication of work or for any other reason provided such rights and policies are not in conflict with any benefits of employees as conferred by this Agreement or otherwise; . . . take any other measures which are reasonable and necessary for the orderly efficient and profitable operation of its business.

Article XI

Procedure on Open Jobs

1. When a vacancy occurs, the vacancy will be offered to the present employees in accordance with their Bargaining Unit Seniority before assigning a new employee to the post.

   However, the present employee candidates must meet the requirements for the job vacancy, be acceptable to the Contracting Officers Technical Representative (the General Services Administration Federal Officer in charge of security), and the final selection will be at Company discretion which will be based on applicable selection criteria.

Article XII

Grievance and Arbitration
It is understood that no arbitrator shall have any authority to add to, detract from, or in any way alter or modify the provisions of this Agreement.

Position of the Company

The Company stated that it had just cause to discharge Charlie Shaw and acted in accordance with Article V of the Collective Bargaining Agreement. The Company discharged Shaw, a security guard who is responsible for the security of federal government facilities, after the federal government denied him further work on the service contract that the Company has with the U.S. Government. The government's right to demand removal of guards from performing work on the service contract is affirmed in the parties' Collective Bargaining Agreement, the Company's rules and regulations, the client's rules and regulations, and the nature of the business. The Grievant admitted deficiencies in his performance, which conformed with the reasons Ms. Snow stated were the basis for her demand for removal. Snow's determination that Shaw had breached government rules and requirements was not arbitrary or capricious.

The Company claimed that the Grievant's conduct constituted a dischargeable offense under the Company's policy and just cause for discipline under the Agreement. The Company's rules and regulations contained in its Standard Operation Procedures (SOP) are reasonable and just. The Company conducted a full and thorough investigation of Shaw's conduct and provided him with ample opportunity to address the basis for his removal. Because the Company had no work to which Shaw could be assigned after he was denied access to the work at the federal facility, the Company was left with no other option but to treat this circumstance similar to a prior circumstance in which the Company terminated the employment of the Union's chairman. The Union failed to present any evidence that Shaw's discharge was motivated by anything other than his own conduct. Therefore, discharge is the appropriate action.

The Company argued that the Grievant committed misconduct warranting discharge. He was aware of or should have been aware of the scope of the rules and regulations that governed his employment. There was no evidence that the Union or Shaw was unaware of the rules and regulations that governed his employment, including those found in the General Services Administration (GSA) service contract with Excell. The Union and Shaw were on notice that unacceptability to the client would subject Shaw to discharge.

The Company contended that Article V of the Agreement grants the Company ". . . the right to . . . determine, establish, and implement terms and conditions of employment . . . " Article V grants the Company the "sole and exclusive rights . . . [to] . . . take any other measures which are reasonable and necessary for the orderly, efficient and profitable operation of its business." Article III of the contract specifically recognizes the Company's SOP. The Company's SOP has been placed at the various guard posts at the Martin facility since May 1991. The SOP provides on page 1 that guards are subject to scrutiny from the Company's client, and therefore, guards should be familiar with all the requirements of the client where the services are rendered. The SOP's table of offenses provides for discharge for the first offense for: "e.g., violation of Company or Client rules." The SOP put Shaw on notice that he could be discharged for any act that violates Client rules, requirements, and regulations.

Article XI, Procedures on Open Jobs, in the Agreement, specifically recognizes the U.S. Government's right to determine the acceptability of guards for open jobs. This provision recognizes the COTR's role in reviewing and accepting personnel.

The Company claimed that the Grievant was aware that the client's rules and regulations included suitability. The U.S. Government provides guards with required post orders to be followed by each guard. All employees have been instructed to read post orders daily. In FY99, the U.S. Government indicated that it had the right to find Company personnel ineligible and enumerated reasons for ineligibility. These post orders are work rules to which the guards must adhere when performing services under the service contract and Article III of the Agreement.

There is no evidence that the Union was unaware of the service contract's requirements on eligibility. The Union's chairman had been discharged under similar circumstances on a date preceding Shaw's dismissal. The Company told the Union at that time that the Company was bound to the service contract's removal from duty provisions. The Union did not appeal this issue to arbitration even though its grievance on this issue was denied by the Company.

Other provisions of the Collective Bargaining Agreement give further evidence that the Union was aware, before the Union's chairman was discharged, that the U.S. Government can make suitability determinations of bargaining unit employees and could promulgate rules and regulations that affected the employment status of the guards. The Union recognized in Article XI that present employees must be acceptable to the COTR for job vacancies and left final selection for open jobs to the discretion of the Company.

The evidence shows that the Union and Shaw were aware of, or should have been aware of, the full scope of rules and requirements that govern Shaw's employment, including the suitability requirement in the service contract. Even if the Union and Shaw did not read the service contract, the SOP, the parties' contract, and the post orders, it must be assumed that they knew that a security officer working at a secret-clearance government facility is subject to acceptability by the U.S. Government.

The Company stated that the Grievant violated provision "a.g." in the SOP's table of offenses, which provides for discharge on the first offense for violation of Company or Client rules. Discharge is an appropriate penalty when a violation of Client rules occurs.

The Company stated that the U.S. Government has clear work rules applicable to this case, that is, that the employee be suitable or otherwise not objectionable to the COTR. The U.S. Government has even enumerated in the service contract the work rules, a breach of which will result in an unsuitable or objectionable declaration. Two of these provisions are applicable to Grievant's performance. The Grievant breached provision 7B in the service contract when he neglected his duty by failing to carry out Ms. Snow's instructions to inform the Atlanta Control Center to send an investigator, and he failed to give Atlanta Control Center cor-

Continued

rect information when he mislabeled the code identifying the incident. Shaw breached provisions 7B and 7C in the service contract when he failed to completely fill out the incident report and the 1103 officer's log concerning the alleged report of the accosted victim.

Shaw attempted to justify his omission of a reference to the accosted victim incident in the 1103 officer's log by claiming that the parking lot incident was a "stale" incident. However, there is no evidence that Shaw previously ever made this claim. His explanation is an obviously convenient, after-thought attempt to justify his deficient performance. Despite his claims that he filed the report on the accosted victim, the alleged report was never found. Shaw claimed that he interviewed the woman and wrote a report, but this appears highly suspect for several reasons. First, Shaw could not remember "when" he made his report. He testified that "I believe it was before" the Uncle Gerald's incident. However, he had not done the report before the Uncle Gerald's incident. The report was never found, whereas the Uncle Gerald's report completed on the same day was located on the morning of December 4. Shaw had entered on the 1103 officer's log the day care incident and a notation that contractors were working, but he did not note that he had taken a report from an alleged accosted victim in the parking lot incident.

Shaw readily admitted most of the deficiencies cited by Ms. Snow. There is little question that Snow's determination on removal was based on the breach of client's rules. The breach of the government's rules constitute a breach of provision "a.g." in the Company's SOP. The Union and Shaw are subject to the dictates of the GSA service contract. The Union attempts to avoid the guard suitability requirement found in the service contract by asking the Arbitrator to address only the Collective Bargaining Agreement. The Union makes ". . . a distinction between the right to work on the Martin, TN, account and the right to work for the Company." The Union claims that it is not a party to the service contract, and therefore, the service contract does not affect rights of the parties under the Collective Bargaining Agreement. These arguments are specious and ignore the parties' Collective Bargaining Agreement.

The Company argued that the service contract and Collective Bargaining Agreement are inseparable. The terms and conditions of employment governed in the Collective Bargaining Agreement are dependent on the service contract. The relevant contract provisions include a few terms and conditions of employment for bargaining unit employees in the Collective Bargaining Agreement that do not rely on or that are not contingent on provisions of the service contract. The work of employees, notice of layoff, the hours of work, and the eligibility for job vacancies provisions of the Agreement are all subject to the dictates of the Company's client. Articles III and V of the Agreement address rules, requirements, and regulations governing employee conduct.

Article I, Recognition Clause, provides that the contract rights only apply to employees employed by the Company at the Federal Office Building. Article III grants the bargaining unit described in the Recognition Clause certain work only at the Martin federal site. Seniority rights are based on bargaining unit status. The contract's coverage does not extend to other locations where the Company provides protective services, and there is no contractual right on behalf of the employees to work at these other locations.

The Company argued that the client's dissatisfaction constitutes just cause. This principle is well established in the context of a contractor's provision of plant security to a client. The only condition placed on the client dissatisfaction necessary to justify discharge is that the dissatisfaction be grounded in good faith opinion about the employee. It is well established that where the employee is performing work in relation to the government that bears on national security, the government's dissatisfaction should be given great weight in considering a discharge.

An Employer has a right to protect its business and business reputation from employees who would hurt those interests by drawing a rebuke from the client. The Company was justified in considering the effect that Shaw's conduct and a possible default by the client might have on other bargaining unit employees, particularly where a default would result in the termination or nonrenewal of the Company's contract with the client.

The Company claimed that it is well recognized that security guards, by virtue of the very nature of their work, are held to a high standard of conduct. The Arbitrator should view the Grievant's conduct in light of this higher standard expected of security guards, the secret nature of the site he guarded, and the consequences a default on the service contract would have on the Company as a security contractor.

The Company claimed that it fully investigated Shaw's conduct before discharging him. Mr. Phillips determined that a 5-working-day suspension was appropriate after Shaw's admission that he forgot to perform the critical assignment of requesting Atlanta Control Center to send an investigator to Martin. Then, Ms. Snow orally notified Mr. Phillips of her determination that Shaw be removed from the work. Mr. Woods investigated Snow's claims through a telephone call and a personal visit to Martin. Shaw acknowledged the code entry error in his incident report and his failure to follow through with Snow's instructions. The investigation confirmed that Shaw had failed to make an entry into the daily log concerning the accosting incident, and the Company was unable to find the alleged report of the incident. The Company found that he was deficient in the report about the incident at Uncle Gerald's. These findings support Snow's justifications for removal, which followed the issuance of Shaw's suspension.

The Company claimed that the Union incorrectly argued that principles of double jeopardy apply. The deficiencies in Shaw's job performance were related to Snow's reasons for removal. They were over-and-above Shaw's conduct, which resulted in his suspension from employment. The fact that the Company considered Shaw's suspension when assessing the discharge penalty does not constitute double jeopardy.

There is no evidence that Shaw was treated disparately. He was treated in the same manner as the Union's former chairman. There was no evidence that any employee who the government found unsuitable and requested to be removed was not terminated. The Company's SOP provides for discharge on the first offense for any act that violates the Client's rules. The Company acted in conformance with the table of offenses in the SOP, and discharge was the appropriate penalty for Shaw's conduct.

Termination was not unreasonable. The Company was left with no choice but to discharge Shaw when it had no place to put him to work. This action certainly comports with Article V for the Company to take any measures necessary for the orderly and efficient operations of the business. The determination of proper discipline is a prerogative of Management and should not be easily disturbed. When Management acts in good faith on a fair investigation and fixes a penalty not inconsistent with that imposed in other cases, an Arbitrator should not disturb it. An arbitrator should modify a disciplinary decision only if the punishment has no reasonable relation to the offense committed and shows an abuse of discretion.

The Company challenged the appropriateness of the Union's requested remedies should the Arbitrator sustain the Grievance. The Union seeks Shaw's reinstatement to the federal facility with full back pay. Should the government not allow Shaw to return to the site, the Union requests that the Arbitrator order the Company to put Shaw on another site in close proximity to Martin under the wage and benefits of the parties' Collective Bargaining Agreement. If either of the above options fail, the Union requests that the Arbitrator direct the Company to find Shaw a job with another employer at a wage that is substantially equivalent to those at the

Continued

Company. In the last circumstance and until another employer is found, the Company must pay Shaw the wages and benefits found in the Collective Bargaining Agreement, although Shaw does not work under the contract.

The Company argued that the Union seeks the Arbitrator to add to and modify the parties' Collective Bargaining Agreement by requiring remedial measures that are not encompassed within the Agreement. Such action would violate the provisions found in Article XII and Article I, which makes clear that the contractual provisions only apply to the Martin site.

The Company concluded:

> The Company had just cause to discharge Shaw. The Company acted in accordance with the Agreement and properly discharged Shaw on the basis that he was no longer suitable to perform services which he was hired to perform. The Company's actions were justified under the circumstances.
>
> The Company fully investigated the events of December 3. There is no evidence of disparate treatment.
>
> More importantly, Shaw's termination was reasonably related to the Government's unsuitability determination. The Company is a protective service which undisputedly cannot tolerate inadequate job performance. This position is reasonable and not an abuse of discretion. This conclusion is particularly true where the denial of work determination was made by the Company's client, the U.S. Government. In the absence of any evidence of abuse of discretion between the Client and the Company, the Company's decision to discharge the Grievant should not be disturbed or modified.
>
> Accordingly, the Grievance should be denied.

Position of the Union

The Union contended that this is a unique case and "not your run of the mill" discharge case because of the intimate involvement of the GSA. Although the Company has a contract with the GSA, which permits it to determine whether an employee is suitable for work on a contract, an unsuitability determination by the GSA is not, in and of itself, just cause for discharge.

The Union argued that Excell did not present any witness to the incidents that occurred on December 3, 1999. The only evidence on those incidents were presented through Mr. Shaw and through the Martin police officer, Ms. Joy McPhail.

On December 3, 1999, Shaw reported for work and was instructed by Mr. Phillips, his on-site supervisor, to take a report from an employee of the United States Department of Agriculture (USDA) who had claimed that she had been accosted on a previous day by an unidentified male in the parking lot outside the building. Shaw did as he was instructed; he interviewed the woman and gathered the information necessary to complete a report. Shaw prepared the report and telephoned Atlanta Control Center to notify them of the report code, the type of incident, and the case control number. He placed the report in the report tray for later pickup and review by Mr. Phillips.

About 5:00 P.M. the Martin Police Department was notified of a case of alleged child sexual abuse. A uniformed officer in a marked car responded to Uncle Gerald's behind the Federal Building. A uniformed officer summoned detectives from the Crimes Against Children Unit (CACU), which is the specialized unit for investigating allegations of sexual abuse involving children for further investigation.

Officer Joy McPhail and her partner, Detective Mike Moore, arrived at the Federal Building at approximately 5:10 or 5:15 P.M. Shaw responded to the location about 5:15 or 5:20 P.M. By that time, the uniformed police officer had left the scene. Mr. Shaw responded to a radio/telephone call from Pam Berry, the Child Care Manager. Shaw was to meet an officer at Uncle Gerald's. When he arrived at Uncle Gerald's, he looked for an officer, but there were no uniformed officers. It took a very brief period to determine that there were two plainclothes detectives of the Martin Police Department.

Detective Moore approached Shaw and identified himself as a member of the CACU and gave Shaw a very brief overview of the situation. Shaw stood by to assist as needed. Shaw observed that the two detectives were doubtful as to their jurisdiction to investigate and take a report on the allegation of child sexual abuse arising in a building operated by the Federal Government. Even though Shaw told them that they did have jurisdiction, they were still doubtful. So Shaw called Ms. Snow, the GSA security specialist, to confirm this.

Ms. Snow confirmed that the CACU had jurisdiction and told him to tell them that they should take a report. She also told Shaw to make out a report himself and to attach the CACU report to his report. She told him to call Atlanta Control Center to advise them of the report and to "tell them that they may wish to send a Federal investigator up to Martin to investigate this incident." Shaw told Detective Moore that the CACU had jurisdiction, and they should make a report. Shaw told Detective Moore that he would like a copy of the report so it could be attached to his.

Mr. Shaw remained at the scene until about 6:30 P.M. to gather evidence for his report. He walked back to the office and called Atlanta Control Center. He gave Atlanta Control Center the code number of his report, the type of offense or incident, and the other data that Atlanta Control Center needed for its records. He also received the case control number.

The Union stated that Ms. Snow requested that Shaw be removed from work on the site in her December 15, 1999, letter because Shaw had failed to report correct information to Atlanta Control Center. However, every bit of information that Shaw gave to Atlanta Control Center about the incident at Uncle Gerald's was correct. He was assigned to assist another law enforcement agency, and he chose that designation because he received the radio call and was told to meet another officer. When he got there, he found out that the other officers were from the specialized unit in the Martin area for investigating allegations of criminal sexual misconduct involving children. As a security guard, he had no training to take over that investigation; the best step for him was to defer to the experts in the field, the detectives from CACU. He assisted and helped them. He chose the incident code from the code books entitled "assist another law enforcement agency," and he wrote the code that corresponded to that incident type on his report.

The Union stated that, although the Company can argue that Shaw should have put down other sexual misconduct or something of that designation as a more accurate description of what occurred, there is a difference in judgment here. Shaw responded to meet another officer and to assist another law enforcement agency. No one can conclude from that designation that Shaw put down incorrect information and reported incorrect information to Atlanta Control Center.

The Union admitted that Shaw neglected to suggest to Atlanta Control Center that they may wish to send a federal investigator. For that omission, the Company disciplined him by issuing him a 5-day suspension. In addition, the Company alleged that Shaw gave false information to Ms. Snow. Ms. Snow was present at the third step Grievance meeting in February 1993, but she was not present at the arbitration hearing. The Union suggested that she was not at the hearing because she wasn't asked to be present.

The Company alleged that Shaw neglected to make a report of an alleged confrontation that a woman had suffered at the hands of an unidentified male in the parking lot outside the

Continued

Federal Building. Shaw received his assignment from his supervisor, who said "Go take this report," and Shaw took the report. The report was on an incident that had occurred a day before December 3, 1999, so this report was a report of stale information that probably should have been documented by a security officer at an earlier time. However, it may have just come up, if the woman had not reported it before December 3, 1999. Neither party knows the facts because the Company did not produce that woman to testify, it did not produce the supervisor to testify, and it did not produce the report itself. Shaw testified that he took the information, completed the report, notified Atlanta Control Center, and placed the report in the tray for his supervisor's review.

The Union addressed the issue of Shaw's alleged failure to document the report of the USDA employee on the log that guards are required to keep. Shaw explained that the purpose of the log was to document incidents that occurred during his watch. The incident about which the report was written did not occur on that day, so it would have been inappropriate to mark on the log the USDA woman's allegations. The Union contrasted the situation presented by the USDA employee with the situation presented at Uncle Gerald's. The Uncle Gerald's incident does include a notation because it actually occurred on his shift, whereas the incident involving the USDA woman did not occur on his shift.

The Union stated that Shaw was given a 5-day suspension for failing to notify Atlanta Control Center that they may wish to send a federal investigator to Martin, and he was discharged because GSA asked that he be removed from the contract. The Union requested that the Arbitrator consider the seriousness of this misconduct because the CACU was already on the scene investigating the incident and had jurisdiction. The CACU personnel investigated the incident and took a report. They had the ability under local law to prosecute. The Union admitted that Shaw failed to notify Atlanta Control Center, which was an oversight on his part. However, this failure was not intentional, and he was not insubordinate. The situation was chaotic with a lot of emotional outcries on that day at Uncle Gerald's, and Shaw's oversight was understandable.

The Company took all of those factors into consideration and concluded that his failure to notify the Atlanta Control Center to send a federal investigator was not a dischargeable offense. In fact, the Company concluded that the appropriate penalty was a 5-day suspension. The Company considered the 5-day suspension when it decided to fire him. There is a double jeopardy problem here. Double jeopardy principles prevent the Company from discharging an individual for an incident for which he has already been disciplined. The only allegation proven is that Mr. Shaw failed to notify Atlanta Control Center of the need of having a federal investigator. He was discharged within a week of suspending him for 5 days for that same reason. That is not just cause for discharge.

The Union stated that there are two contracts in this case; however, the Arbitrator has authority under only one of them. When Excell signed a contract with GSA to provide security at the Federal Building complex, Excell ceded authority to GSA to make determinations as to whether employees of Excell are "acceptable." In other words, GSA can decide and can enforce its decision that a certain employee will not be permitted to work on the contract. The Company also signed a contract with the Union, which Excell promised that it would discharge employees only for just cause. The Union contended that the two promises made by Excell cannot be reconciled. The Company's position to permit GSA veto authority over employees on the contract does not excuse it from the contractual provision requiring it to have just cause for discharge.

The Union stated that another factor to consider is that the Company offered Shaw a job in August 2000. There is nothing to suggest that the offer was an offer of settlement. However, this offer was not communicated to the Union and was not conditioned on withdrawing or settling the Grievance. It was just an offer to Shaw to have him come and work at the General Appliance Park (a new contract gained after Shaw's termination) between 25 and 40 hours a week at a wage of $10.75. In this regard, Mr. Woods testified that in his 17 years at Excell, he could not recall a time when his company had offered a job to somebody who had been previously fired. Thus the Company's position was undermined because it indicated that the Company itself recognized that it did not have cause to fire Shaw.

The Union argued that there is nothing in the Collective Bargaining Agreement that states that withdrawal of access is grounds for discharge. The seniority provision does not state that seniority terminates if the person is removed from work on the contract. The Grievance and Arbitration procedure does not state that Grievances protesting a removal from the contract are nonarbitrable.

The Management Rights article states that discharge may only be for just cause, and Shaw's discharge was not supported by the just cause standard. The Union position is supported by the 5-day suspension, not discharge, and the offer of employment at General Appliance Park.

As remedy, the Union requested that Shaw be reinstated to employment and that the Arbitrator direct the Company to make good faith effort to have Shaw reinstated to his job at the federal complex in Martin. Then, if that is not possible, the Union requested that the Arbitrator direct the Company to employ Mr. Shaw at the wage and at the benefits contained in the Collective Bargaining Agreement in a job within a reasonable proximity of the greater Martin area, but not at the $10.75 per hour that the Company offered.

If all that fails, the Union requested the Arbitrator to direct the Company to attempt to find a job for him, even if it's with another employer, at a wage that is substantially equivalent and at benefits that are substantially equivalent to the wages and benefits provided at Excell. Finally, the Union stated that its requested remedy includes full back pay from the date that Shaw last received full wages through the date on which he is reinstated to the payroll.

QUESTIONS

1. Assess the arbitrator's authority under the Collective Bargaining Agreement where there is a federal government contractor.

2. Under the elements of discipline (tests for just cause), has Excell met all of these requirements?

3. What is double jeopardy? Does it apply here?

4. If Shaw worked for a private employer without a federal government contract, should his treatment have been different? If so, why? If not, why not?

5. Evaluate the Union's proposed remedies.

6. You be the arbitrator. Was Shaw's employment terminated for just cause? If not, what is the appropriate remedy?

Discharge of Postal Letter Carrier for Off-duty Conduct

Background

This matter of arbitration stems from an indictment of Thomas Allen for one count of arson–first degree and ten counts of burglary in Quitman County, Mississippi, on March 28, 1999. In a letter dated March 30, 1999, Postmaster Billy Como wrote:

> This is written notice that you have been removed from employment with the Postal Service. This action is being taken in accordance with Article 16 of the Agreement.
>
> There is reasonable cause to believe you have committed a crime for which a sentence of imprisonment may be imposed.
>
> Specifically, by the indictment dated March 28, 1999, you were indicted in the Superior Court of Quitman County for one count Arson–First Degree and ten counts of Burglary.
>
> These aforementioned charges are so egregious in nature that retaining you in postal employment would not be in the best interest of the Service.

In a letter dated April 9, 1999, Mr. Jesse G. Bolton, Attorney for Mr. Allen, wrote to Human Resources Manager Walter E. Flatten:

> I have been asked to assist Mr. Allen in regard to his removal from the Postal Service.
>
> Although there has been an indictment of Mr. Allen by the Superior Court of Quitman County, MS, it is probable that the indictment has overstated the underlying facts and it is also possible that some or all of the charges could be changed or minimized.
>
> The arraignment date in the case was set for March 28th, 1999, and this was suspended or continued on an indefinite basis.
>
> Mr. Allen is 47 years old and has never been charged with any criminal offense involving moral turpitude. He has only had one speeding ticket, in the year 1968, while in the service of the United States Air Force.
>
> His character and reputation in the community in which he lives are exceptional, and there is a reasonable possibility that a sentence of imprisonment will not be imposed. From the earliest days of the charges, restitution was made by the subjects and accepted by the affected party or parties. The house for which the one count of arson was made, according to my information, was unoccupied at the time, and restitution for damage to that house has largely been accomplished by and through the replacement of the house and acceptance of the same by the owner. The only reason that has been delayed is because the accused parties have been doing all the physical labor themselves.

On April 13, 1999, Mr. Allen filed the following Grievance:

1. Nature of Grievance: (Be specific: what, where, when, etc.)
   This is a Step 2 Appeal filed in behalf of Thomas Allen, a reg. Carrier at the Marks, MS post office, from an adverse decision rendered at Step 1. Mr. Allen was issued a Notice of Removal on March 30, 1999 in accordance with Article 16 of the National Agreement. Mr. Allen received the letter on April 4, 1999.

2. Contract Violation: this action is a violation of Article 16 of the National Agreement.

3. Corrective Action Requested:

The Union respectfully requests that the Notice of Removal be rescinded and the Grievant be made whole for all lost wages and benefits. The facts do not reveal reasonable cause to believe the Grievant is guilty.

On April 21, 1999, Mr. Flatten wrote the following letter to Mr. Bolton. This letter stated:

In accordance with Article 1, Section 1 of the National Agreement, the Rural Carriers' Union is the exclusive bargaining representative of Mr. Allen. As such, I cannot grant your request for a summary outline of the evidence the Postal Service has obtained.

In accordance with Article 15, Section 3, Step 1 of the National Agreement, Mr. Allen has a contractual right to file a grievance on any action taken by the Postal Service. In the event Mr. Allen exercises this right, he would be represented by the Rural Carriers' Union.

On the same date, Mr. Flatten wrote a letter to Mr. Allen. This letter stated:

On April 4, 1999, you received a Notice of Removal from the Postal Service based on charges listed in indictment bill dated March 28, 1999. These charges included one count of Arson–First Degree and ten counts of Burglary.

You have not presented any rebuttal evidence on your behalf and the Postal Service has reason to believe that you are guilty of a crime for which a sentence of imprisonment may be imposed. Therefore, I find no basis to alter your removal.

You have the right to appeal this action in accordance with Article 15, Section 3 of the National Agreement within 14 days of your receipt of this decision.

In a letter dated May 22, 1999, State Steward Robert Thorne of the Rural Carriers' Union appealed the Grievance. In a letter dated May 13, 1999, Mr. Statten, Labor Relations, gave Management's Step 2 answer. He stated:

In the instant case management contends that the employee was given the benefit of the doubt. Since we have a copy of the indictment, we have reason to believe that the grievant may be guilty of a crime for which a sentence of imprisonment may be imposed. Arbitrators have consistently ruled that by having an indictment we have met the burden of having reasonable cause to believe that the grievant is guilty of a crime for which a sentence of imprisonment may be imposed. The grievance is therefore denied.

On September 26, 1999, the Union appealed the Grievance to Arbitration.

Issue

Did the Postal Service violate Article 16 of the Agreement when it suspended Mr. Thomas Allen indefinitely? If so, what shall be the remedy?

Relevant Articles of the Agreement

Article 16—Discipline Procedure

Section 1. Statement of Principle

In the administration of this Article, a basic principle shall be that discipline should be corrective in nature, rather than punitive. No employee may be disciplined or discharged except for just cause such as, but not limited to, insubordination, pilferage, intoxication (drugs or alcohol), incompetence, failure to perform work as requested, violation of the terms of this Agreement, or failure to observe safety rules and regulations. Any such discipline or discharge shall be subject to the grievance-arbitration procedure provided for in this Agreement, which could result in reinstatement and restitution, including back pay. *Continued*

When there is reasonable cause to believe an employee is guilty of a crime for which a sentence of imprisonment can be imposed, the advance notice requirement shall not apply and such an employee may be immediately removed from a pay status.

Position of Management

Management stated that Mr. Allen was indicted on one count of arson in the first degree and ten counts of burglary by a Grand Jury of Quitman County, Mississippi, on March 28, 1999. Each of the eleven counts carries a maximum sentence of 20 years' imprisonment as provided by Mississippi State Law. The total would equate to 220 years' imprisonment for the alleged crimes if he were convicted and given the maximum sentence.

The Postal Service obtained a copy of this indictment and questioned him. Mr. Allen was then removed from employment. A letter from Mr. Jesse G. Bolton, Attorney at Law, on Allen's behalf was forwarded to Mr. Flatten. This letter advised Mr. Flatten of arguments he thought were pertinent to Allen's case and requested information relative to the case at hand. Mr. Flatten advised Mr. Bolton that the Union was the authorized bargaining agent recognized to represent Allen and that no documents would be forthcoming.

Management argued that arbitral precedent had established that the burden of proof does not encompass the normal "doctrine of just cause" in these types of cases. Arbitral precedent has established that the proof required in similar cases requires that Management has only to establish that it had reason to believe that Mr. Allen was guilty of a crime for which a sentence of imprisonment may be imposed. Arbitral precedent has established that the proof required comes in the form of an indictment by a grand jury composed of the defendant's peers. Management removed Allen based on an indictment for which the charges have not been denied.

Management stated that Postmaster Billy Como had obtained a copy of the indictment on the advice of Labor Relations. Allen was given an opportunity to respond to the indictment and did not deny any of the charges. Mr. Como testified that he had copies of two newspaper articles from adjoining counties that pertained to Allen's situation before issuing him his removal notice. At no time did Allen ever profess his innocence of the charges.

Management explained that Mr. Allen and an accomplice burglarized a hunting cabin, took items, which according to a newspaper article, included a shotgun, and then burned down the cabin. The charge of first-degree arson indicates that the cabin was completely burned. The charges have yet to be dropped and are still pending.

The Grievant had his chance to convince Management that the charges were ill-founded, and he did not. Management argued that it has more than met its required burden of proof. Management proved that it had reason to believe that Allen was guilty of a crime for which a sentence of imprisonment may be imposed. Thus, removing the Grievant was done to protect the integrity of the Postal Service.

Management argued that it has been well established through arbitral precedent that a party cannot make its case at arbitration. The Union has attempted to do so by bringing in character witnesses who testified on the Grievant's behalf. The Union presented the testimony of Postmaster Como about his reluctance to remove Allen; this should not be considered in the ninth hour. These had not been contentions during the processing of the Grievance. If these had, Management may have provided rebuttal testimony. Other members of the community who may not have known Allen as intimately as the witnesses could have offered their opinions about suspending someone who had been indicted on ten counts of burglary, stealing a shotgun, and burning someone's property down. Management could have provided Mr. Jim Smith, a Labor Relations Specialist, to testify as to what advice he gave Mr. Como and whether he had the authority to make or instruct Mr. Como in either of these official capacities.

Management claimed that the only argument raised in Allen's defense during the processing of this Grievance was that Allen had made restitution and that the charges levied against Allen would be dropped; however, the charges have not been dropped. Mr. Robert Thorne testified that at Step 2 of the Grievance Procedure, the Union did not mention anything about the community wanting Allen returned to work. Nothing pertaining to these arguments was raised before arbitration.

Management argued that Allen's character and standing in the community are irrelevant and have nothing to do with the action that Management took. Management's action was based on an indictment that was instituted by a jury of his peers, based on evidence examined pertaining to his alleged involvement of a crime for which a sentence of imprisonment may be imposed. Management gave Allen ample time to offer a rebuttal to the charges or time to have the charges dropped. Management did not profess the guilt or innocence of the Grievant. The Mississippi Bureau of Investigators evidently still believes that other matters have yet to be resolved because Allen still faces possible charges for the indictment.

Management stated that the overwhelming majority of Arbitrators have consistently ruled that the standard of proof required to be sustained by Management in cases where the issue in dispute had criminal connotations is "reasonable cause." Where Arbitrators sometimes use the words "just cause," the burden of proof still does not rise to the level of the traditional doctrine of just cause.

Management addressed the principle of "nexus." Pertinent considerations on the disposition of this case are as follows:

1. Whether there in fact was a reasonable basis to believe Allen guilty of the alleged crime.

2. Whether there was a sufficient relationship between the alleged crime and Allen's job as a carrier or such other jobs to which he might be assigned in accordance with his seniority that would warrant removal.

Management has stated consistently that, if the charges had been dropped and evidence furnished stating the same, Allen would be returned to work. In regard to establishing a nexus, Allen is a rural letter carrier and meets the public each day. His job requires constant contact with the public.

Management stated that Marks is a small rural community with about 2200 to 2300 residents who know of the charges brought against Allen. Allen was indicted by a grand jury of his peers. Evidently, they were not persuaded that his former image should cloud their duty; others may not also. The Postal Service has a responsibility to maintain the public's confidence. The drafters of the National Agreement recognize this responsibility and provided language in the form of Article 16.

Management admitted that Mr. Como initially testified that he had been directed by Management to take this action and would not have done so if he had not been directed. On cross-examination, he was asked who he worked for. Under oath, he said his boss was Mr. Jimmy Whitestone, Manager of Post Office Operations. Whitestone directed Como in the performance of his duties to do what was expected of him. Labor Relations has a responsibility to advise Management officials of the proper procedures to take in disciplinary matters that are consistent with Postal policies and contractual procedures. Mr. Como stated that Labor Relations advised him on how this type of situation is normally handled. Postmaster Como read Article 16 in the National Agreement, and he was satisfied that he complied with Article 16.

Mr. Como testified that he felt like Allen and other employees of the Marks Post Office were family. This explained his reluctance to remove Allen. Como stated that he had no problem

Continued

upholding Postal Service's policies once it was explained to him that the action taken was consistent with the Postal policy on how to handle situations wherein an employee had been indicted for a crime for which a sentence of imprisonment may be imposed. Como issued the removal based on the indictment after he gave Allen an opportunity to respond.

Mr. E. L. Elton, the Mayor of Marks, testified that he was surprised when he learned that Allen was the accused; however, he did not condone these types of actions. Mr. Willie Andrews, a postal customer on Allen's route, testified that he was shocked when he learned that Allen was the accused. He also did not condone these types of actions. These individuals knew Allen on an individual, personal basis. They stated that they were speaking on his behalf for personal reasons. Management asked: "What about those who do not know the Grievant on a personal basis? I wonder what they might say?"

Management stated that this Grievance should still be denied if this higher form of just cause is applied. Arbitrators have ruled consistently that the "reasonable cause" standard is the only proof required before removing an employee for criminal considerations. Arbitral jurisprudence has established the reason for the position taken by Management.

Management closed by stating:

Management has stated consistently that management based its decision to remove the grievant on an indictment. Proof of the grievant's guilt, innocence, former standing in the community or whether restitution has been made is irrelevant to this proceeding. What is relevant is, whether Management had substantive information in hand, prior to removing the grievant. Based on arbitral precedent, an indictment has been deemed to be the proper information on which one should base a decision of this nature.

The Union offered, in the grievant's defense, that the charges either would be dropped or are in the process of being so. However, they have not. If they had been dropped the grievant will be put back to work. If not, our final decision will be predicated on the outcome of his arbitration. The grievant still faces the possibility of criminal conviction with possible sentencing ranging from 1 to 220 years imprisonment.

Whether the Arbitrator applies the reasonable cause or the just cause standard, Management has proven that the action taken was proper in accordance with Article 16 of the National Agreement. Management asks that the Arbitrator find the same and deny this grievance in its entirety.

Position of the Union

The Union claimed that Postmaster Billy Como, Allen's immediate supervisor, testified that it was not his decision to remove Allen. Como testified that he did not notify the Labor Relations office in Jackson, MS, after Allen was indicted. The Labor Relations office was informed about the indictment by a relative of Mr. Flatten, who attended a church service in Marks. When the Labor Relations office learned of Mr. Allen's indictment, it directed Como to obtain a copy of the indictment and forward it to Jackson. Como dutifully obtained a copy of the indictment, which is a public record.

Como testified that, if it had been up to him, he would not have removed Allen, and Allen would still be working. Como testified that he did not draft the notice of removal; he was told by the Labor Relations office to sign and deliver it to Allen. Como clearly indicted that this entire matter was handled by the Labor Relations office in Jackson.

The Union stated that where the imposition of discipline is not recommended or initiated by the employee's first-line supervisor, the discipline cannot stand. When higher-level authority does more than advise: when it takes over the decision-making role and eliminates the contractual responsibility of local supervision—and then concurs in its own decision—a substantive due process violation occurs. Such violation cannot be overlooked as a mere technicality. The bi-level disciplinary procedure provides a unique protection for employees. It cannot legitimately be disregarded, and the employer's neglect to follow it creates a breach of contractually established due-process requirements of such importance as to require that the resulting discipline be overturned.

The Union argued that the Postal Service did not have just cause to remove Thomas Allen. The record reflects that the Postal Service did not carry its burden in showing that just cause existed for Allen's removal. Throughout the Grievance Procedure and at the hearing, the Postal Service took the untenable position that because Allen had been indicted, the Postal Service was privileged to remove him pursuant to Article 16 of the National Agreement. Article 16 only allows the Postal Service to immediately remove an employee from pay status when there is "reasonable cause to believe an employee is guilty of a crime for which a sentence of imprisonment can be imposed."

The Postal Service has taken the position that standards of just cause did not apply to this case, and the Postal Service made no serious efforts to show that just cause existed. The Postal Service is mistaken that "reasonable cause to believe" eliminates the overriding principle of Article 16 that all discipline must be for just cause.

The Union argued that the relationship between the "reasonable cause to believe" language and the "just cause" principles that underlie the party's discipline procedure was the subject of a previous arbitration decision. The Arbitrator stated that the parties appeared to recognize that in a criminal case, disciplinary action must be for "just cause."

The Union claimed that the Postal Service cannot carry its burden and show either that it had "reasonable cause to believe" or that it had just cause to remove Mr. Allen. The Postal Service essentially admitted that it did nothing but rely on the indictment in removing Mr. Allen. The Postal Service offered no evidence that an independent investigation of any kind was ever considered or carried out. Thus, it is difficult to see how the Postal Service could have had "reasonable cause to believe."

The Union contended that the charges contained in the indictment remain allegations and in no way prove that Mr. Allen is guilty of them. The Postal Service was provided with information from Mr. Allen's criminal attorney, who represented that "it is probable that the indictment has overstated the underlying facts, and it is also possible that some or all of the charges could be changed or minimized." This information was obviously discounted by the Postal Service; no reasonable explanation has even been offered as to why. Any suggestion that this information was less valuable or could not be considered because it did not come from Mr. Allen's collective bargaining representative is ridiculous. This information goes directly to the question of "reasonable cause to believe." It is noteworthy that the Labor Relations office in Jackson had caused the removal letter to be issued to Mr. Allen within 48 hours of the issuance of the indictment, thus making it difficult, if not impossible, to engage in a meaningful investigation. The sequence of events is clear. The Labor Relations office in Jackson fortuitously learned of Mr. Allen's indictment and then required Postmaster Como to issue a notice of removal.

The Union stated that the Postal Service is required to demonstrate that Allen's alleged criminal conduct had a significant bearing on his ability to perform his job as a rural letter carrier. It is well established that the Postal Service may discipline an employee for off-duty misconduct only when it affects the employer-employee relationship. In this case, the Postal Service made little effort and was unable to show that Mr. Allen's indictment had any negative effect on the efficiency of the Postal Service's operations or its image.

Postmaster Como testified that Mr. Allen was a very good employee with no disciplinary history. There was no evidence that any of Allen's co-workers did not want to work with him

Continued

661

or that any customers would object to his return to the route. Postmaster Como testified that there was overwhelming community support for Allen. When the Postal Service attempted to remind Postmaster Como of a conversation the day before the hearing at the Marks Post Office, where a female customer apparently had something negative to say about Allen, Postmaster Como explained that the customer was not upset with Allen because of the indictment but because Allen was an outspoken supporter of the construction of a nearby medical waste incinerator. The female customer was one of the incinerator project's most vocal opponents. Thus, the Postal Service has been unable to produce a shred of evidence indicating any opposition to Allen's continued employment with the Postal Service. The Postal Service's own witness, Postmaster Como, suggested that there was overwhelming support for Allen.

The Postal Service introduced three newspaper articles to show that the Postal Service's image had been tarnished by the indictment. One article with the headline, "Ming: No arrests yet in arson case," made no mention of Allen. The other two articles indicated only that Allen had been indicted. Neither article made any mention that Allen was a Postal employee. Marginal newspaper coverage, especially with no reference to the Postal Service, is meaningless. The newspaper clippings clearly were not considered when the Labor Relations office in Jackson issued the notice of removal. Postmaster Como indicated that he had not sent the articles to the Labor Relations office and that he had only shown them to the Management Advocate the day before the arbitration hearing.

The Postal Service was unable to show that Allen's indictment posed a threat to himself, his co-workers, or his customers or that the image of the Postal Service would have been tarnished by his employment. Mr. Allen was well liked, the community wanted him back on his route, and the image of the Postal Service would not have suffered if he had remained on the job.

The Union presented three witnesses on behalf of Mr. Allen. Mr. Willie Andrews, a psychiatric social worker and Quitman County Board of Education member, testified that Allen was an excellent carrier who often went beyond the call of duty. He stated that he was happier with his mail service when Allen was carrying the route. Mr. Andrews had known Allen for 10 or 15 years and stated that he was shocked when he learned of Allen's arrest and indictment. He indicated that the Postal Service's image would be improved if Allen were returned to work.

Mayor E.L. Elton testified that he has known Allen all of his life and was in disbelief when told that Allen had been indicted. Mr. Elton was a very satisfied customer and would like to see Allen return to his duties. As mayor, Mr. Elton was in a unique position to gauge community sentiment and testified credibly that there was "very strong support" for Allen's return to work. He believed that the image of the Postal Service would not be tarnished if Allen were returned to work.

Ms. Hortense Balk, a lifelong Marks resident, owned the property that was destroyed in the fire that Allen is accused of intentionally setting. The destroyed property was a hunting cabin that Ms. Balk rented to hunters. Ms. Balk was shocked when she learned that Allen had been indicted because she had known Allen all of his life. Ms. Balk testified that she did not press charges against Allen and noted that Allen had already rebuilt the hunting cabin. Ms. Balk testified that he did such a great job that she thought about moving into it. The Union noted that the fact that Allen made restitution to Ms. Balk should not be construed as an admission that he is guilty of a crime for which a sentence of imprisonment can be imposed. If anything, Allen's gesture reflects favorably on his character. Despite the personal loss felt by Ms. Balk, she does not believe that Allen should lose his job.

The Postal Service did concede that if the indictment was dropped or Allen was acquitted in a trial, he would be immediately returned to work. The Postal Service must do its part in managing its employees and imposing discipline where appropriate. The Postal Service has ceded all judgment to the criminal process and to a District Attorney who has sat on an indictment for almost 10 months with no specific date set for trial.

The Union stated that the Postal Service had an affirmative duty to investigate on learning of the indictment but did not. The Postal Service is required in cases of alleged off-duty misconduct to determine whether that alleged misconduct would affect the integrity of the operations of the Postal Service. If the Postal Service had been able to offer credible testimony in this regard, it may have met its burden under just cause. However, the Postal Service made no efforts to address these issues.

The Union concluded:

> The removal of Thomas Allen was not properly initiated by Mr. Allen's supervisor, Postmaster Como. Instead, the removal was forced on Postmaster Como by Labor Relations in Jackson. This is a clear violation of Article 16 of the National Agreement. There is no exception which allows the Postal Service to ignore the judgments and desires of its front line supervisors, even in cases where employees have been indicted for off-duty misconduct.
>
> The record reveals that the Postal Service failed to meet its burden to show that it had "reasonable cause to believe that Mr. Allen was guilty of a crime for which the sentence of imprisonment could be imposed." The Postal Service also failed to show that removal was for just cause.
>
> The record reflects that Thomas Allen is an Air Force veteran and an exemplary 18 year Postal employee. He does not pose a threat to his Postmaster, his co-workers or his customers. Indeed, these people want him back on the route. The Postal Service never had and does not now have a valid reason for removing Allen.
>
> The Union requested that the Arbitrator hold the Postal Service to its contractual promise that all removals be supported by just cause. As none exists here, it is requested that the grievance be granted and that Mr. Allen be reinstated with full back pay with interest and benefits to the date of his removal.

QUESTIONS

1. Explain the principle of "nexus" as it applies to off-duty misconduct. How does it apply in this case?

2. Distinguish between arrests, indictments, and convictions.

3. How much weight should be given to the following:

   a. Postmaster Como's testimony that he did not make the decision to remove Allen

   b. Ms. Balk's testimony that Mr. Allen has restored the burned cabin

   c. The District Attorney had not taken the case to trial

   d. The support from Allen's customers and community support

4. Does it make any difference that Mr. Allen is employed in the public sector, instead of the private sector? Give your reasoning.

5. Did the Postal Service act appropriately when it did not grant Attorney Bolton's request for information relevant to Mr. Allen's Grievance? If so, explain. If not, explain.

6. Should the Union be allowed to provide "character" witnesses on behalf of Mr. Allen? If so, why? If not, why not?

7. What level of proof should be used in this matter? Why?

8. Weigh the evidence and consider the burden of proof and the levels of proof. Be the arbitrator and support your decision.

CHAPTER 14

Labor Relations in Multinational Corporations and in Other Countries

W*ith the development of a global economy, movement in eastern Europe and China toward greater political democracy and market-oriented economies, and the reduction of trade and travel restrictions within the western European and North American countries, the study of labor relations within multinational corporations (MNCs) and foreign countries becomes imperative to today's student. This chapter begins with a general discussion of the operations of MNCs in a global economy and unions' approaches and problems in dealing with MNCs. Then concerns about globalization and free trade are addressed and principal characteristics of the labor relations systems of the major trading partners of the United States are presented.*

Multinational Corporations and Transnational Collective Bargaining

The growing interdependency among nations and the activities of **multinational corporations (MNCs)** have become important facets of economic life. Although multinational corporations have existed for more than 150 years, their numbers and share of world output have expanded their importance and visibility in recent years.

MNCs are now producing and marketing their products in several countries, instead of producing only at the home base and selling abroad, and they are doing so with increasing impact. Many of the largest MNCs have been labeled "stateless corporations" because a high percentage of their assets are outside their home country.

U.S. multinational corporations (MNCs) are enormous in size. As examples, the annual revenues of Wal-Mart Stores ($246 billion in 2002) are about the same as the gross national product of the country of Austria. The annual revenues of

General Motors ($187 billion) and Exxon Mobil ($182 billion) are about the same or greater than the countries of Poland, Indonesia, or Thailand.[1]

To indicate the enormousness of MNCs, the following are facts to consider:

- Of the largest 100 largest economies in the world, 53 are MNCs and 43 are countries.

- ExxonMobil, the world's largest company in terms of sales, has annual revenues greater than the gross national product (GNP) of all but 20 of the 220 nations in the world.

- The 1,000 largest MNCs account for 80 percent of the world's industrial production.

- In 1962, almost 60 percent of the largest MNCs were U.S. based; in 2004, of the largest 500 MNCs, only 185 were headquartered in the United States, 126 were headquartered in the European Union, and 108 in Japan.

- MNCs and their subsidiaries employ 90 million workers, 20 million in developing countries; they pay more than $1.5 trillion in wages, pay more than $1.2 trillion in taxes, and contribute 25 percent to the gross world product.[2]

The enormousness of international trade and investment activities may be measured by gross product, employment, exports and imports, and direct foreign investments. In 2001, the dollar gross product of U.S. affiliates of foreign companies was $486 billion; seven countries—Canada, France, Germany, Japan, the Netherlands, Switzerland, and the United Kingdom—accounted for more than three-fourths of the gross product. Manufacturing accounted for nearly half of this gross product and the employment by the U.S. affiliates of foreign companies was 6.4 million employees. Exports of goods by U.S. affiliates were $163.6 billion and imports were $369.5 billion.[3] The amount of outlays by foreign direct investors to acquire or establish U.S. businesses was $52.6 billion in 2002 (down from $147.1 billion in 2001); the total outlays in 2000 were a record $335.6 billion.[4]

Because of their size, MNCs appear intimidating to smaller countries. For example, foreign firms account for almost half of Ireland's employment and two-thirds of its output. In some larger countries, MNCs have raised concern about their economic influence. In Australia, the ten largest industrial MNCs each has annual sales larger than the government's tax revenue. Still, on average, MNCs employ two-thirds of the workforce in their home country and produce two-thirds of their output at home. In addition, MNCs usually pay better wages than their domestic counterparts and create jobs faster. For example, in poorer countries such as Turkey, wages paid by foreign firms are 124 percent above average, and their workforces have expanded by 11.5 percent per year, compared with 0.6 percent by local firms.[5]

Exchange rates have a great deal to do with the trade between countries and production within a specific country. The importance of fluctuating exchange rates is reflected in Exhibit 14.1, which shows the indexes of hourly compensation costs for production workers in manufacturing for 30 countries during periods from 1980 to 2002. In 2002, hourly compensation costs for manufacturing production workers in Belgium, Germany, Denmark, Norway, and Switzerland were 7 to 28 percent higher than those in the United States. Compensation costs were 82 percent of the U.S. figure in the United Kingdom, 73 percent in Australia, 56 percent in Spain, 25 to 43 percent in Hong Kong, Korea, and Taiwan, and 11 percent in Mexico.

EXHIBIT14.1

Indexes of Hourly Compensation Costs for Production Workers in Manufacturing for 30 Countries or Areas, 1980–2002

Country Or Area	Percentage of Workforce In Unions	Index (United States = 100)					Compensation Costs in 2002 U.S. Dollars
		1980	1990	1994	1998	2002	
United States	13.2	100	100	100	100	100	$21.33
Canada	29.2	92	107	92	85	75	16.02
Brazil	16.2	14	17	—	—	12	2.57
Mexico	20.0	30	12	15	10	11	2.38
Australia	25.0	82	88	80	80	73	15.55
Hong Kong	18.0	15	22	28	29	27	5.83
Israel	56.0	39	57	53	65	57	12.14
Japan	24.1	57	87	125	97	88	18.83
Korea	11.6	0	28	37	27	43	9.16
New Zealand	34.3	54	56	52	50	42	8.89
Singapore	14.5	15	22	37	42	34	7.27
Sri Lanka	30.0	2	2	—	03	2	.42
Taiwan	34.9	10	27	32	28	25	5.41
Austria	53.0	87	114	127	119	99	21.07
Belgium	76.6	134	127	134	125	107	22.79
Denmark	75.2	111	126	120	122	114	24.23
Finland	85.0	84	139	110	116	101	21.56
France	10.0	91	103	100	98	82	17.42
Germany	32.1	125	144	160	151	118	25.08
Greece	30.0	38	45	—	48	—	—
Ireland	55.0	60	79	—	72	71	15.09
Italy	40.0	81	119	95	92	70	14.93
Luxembourg		122	110	—	—	89	18.91
Netherlands	28.0	123	125	122	111	102	21.74
Norway	65.8	119	147	122	128	128	27.40
Portugal	42.0	21	24	27	30	—	—
Spain	11.0	61	78	67	65	56	12.04
Sweden	84.0	127	141	110	119	95	20.18
Switzerland	32.4	113	139	145	131	113	24.11
United Kingdom	32.0	76	84	80	89	82	17.47

Note: Dash indicates data not available.

SOURCE: "International Labor Comparisons of Hourly Compensation Costs for Production Workers in Manufacturing," 2002, U.S. Department of Labor, *Foreign Labor Trends* (Washington, D.C.: U.S. Department of Labor, Bureau of International Labor Affairs, 1999–2003); http://stats.bls.gov/news.release/ichcc.t02,htmx.10/6/2003.

In 1980 Japan's hourly cost was 57 percent of that of the United States; however, it had increased to 125 percent by 1994 and then dropped to 88 percent by 2002. In Germany, in 1980 the cost was 25 percent higher than the United States; but it had risen to 160 percent of U.S. compensation costs by 1994 and then fell to 118 percent by 2002.

Operating in different countries creates opportunities for MNCs to bypass protective tariffs by making parts in one country and assembling the final product in another. For example, the European Union accused Ricoh, a maker of photocopiers, of making 90 percent of its parts in Japan, doing the assembly work in the United States, and shipping products from the United States as U.S. exports. Such situations create other possibilities in the auto industry because England, France, and Italy limit the Japanese share of its auto market. With Japanese automakers locating in the United States, such issues provide challenges in trade between countries.[6]

U.S. MNCs prefer to locate production facilities in foreign countries that have a decentralized bargaining structure. Labor relations features like union density and strike intensity do not appear to be nearly as important. The most important reason for locating production facilities are the national endowments of the particular country.[7]

MNCs have the capacity to force concessions from unions by threatening to shift production to another country and essentially pit one group of employees against another. One automaker that operates a plant in Ohio sought to introduce new technology; the union resisted because the membership would lose jobs. The company then took a number of the union leaders to a new plant in Juarez, Mexico—just across the border from El Paso—showed them the technologies used in the plant, and said: "It is your choice. Either you concede what we are asking in terms of bargaining or the work that you do in Ohio will be transferred to Juarez. If you think this is an idle threat, this is the plant. This is the production process."[8]

Organized labor has been critical of the effect of U.S. MNCs on employment and labor relations for the following reasons:

- U.S. MNC's foreign investments deplete capital resources needed for domestic investment and undermine economic growth and new job creation at home.

- U.S. MNCs export U.S. technology to exploit low-cost foreign labor, depriving American employees of their rightful share of the rewards of technology.

- U.S. MNCs substitute imports from their affiliates in low-wage countries for American-made goods, thereby undermining the American wage standard, depressing economic conditions at home, and decreasing employment and payrolls.

- U.S. MNCs displace U.S. exports with foreign-produced goods from their foreign affiliates, thereby adversely affecting the U.S. trade balance.[9]

Foreign MNCs have grown rapidly and installed facilities in the United States. Unions have often viewed these MNCs with suspicion, but the management and employment practices tend to be more similar to those of home-based firms than dissimilar. The labor relations activities and decisions tend to be locally determined and highly decentralized. American unions have found that organizing foreign-based MNCs has been just as difficult as organizing a home-based company. In addition, the management of the various plants of foreign-based MNCs uses essentially the same tactics to keep unions out of the plant. These tactics include use of lawyers and management consultants, positive human resources management, consultation with employees on decisions, delays allowed under National Labor Relations Board procedures, and local politicians making statements to support the company. Unions essentially use the same organizing tactics, with the addition of negative publicity directed toward the foreign owners and appeals to American patriotism. With these counteractive tactics, the results of elections have not been significantly different—approximately 50 percent wins for the unions. Whenever American unions have contact with foreign-based unions, these contacts are generally of the information-sharing nature.[10]

In some cases, MNCs transplant their management practices into their foreign affiliates. In recent years, Japanese MNCs have been successful in making this transfer in unionized plants. In Fremont, California, New United Motor Manufacturing, Inc., the joint venture between General Motors and Toyota, was successful. The Fremont plant had one of the worst labor relations records in the United States but its performance has become one of the best in the industry. Successes have also been noted by the Japanese-owned MNC Sumitomo Rubber, which purchased the Dunlop tire plant in Birmingham, England.

Japanese practices that have been introduced include elimination of executive perks, such as reserved parking places and separate cafeterias, work teams of six to eight members who rotate jobs, emphasis placed on trust between managers and employees, managers spending more time on the shop floor with the employees, regular meetings to inform employees about production and financial results of the company, wearing of "team" jackets by managers and employees, flexibility in job assignments, and holding each employee responsible for the quality of products produced.

Not all results of management transfer are positive, however, especially when sales decline, the foreign manager may not speak the local language, or employees resist imposition of a new way of doing things. In Forrest City, Arkansas, for example, the Sanyo Company, maker of televisions and microwave ovens, had only one Japanese manager who spoke English, so every meeting required an interpreter. When sales lagged, the company demanded medical insurance cuts, changes in the seniority system, and the right to shift employees from job to job. The union reacted by striking for three weeks, and there were incidents of stone throwing, tire slashing, and charges of an attempted fire-bombing, resulting in 39 persons arrested.[11] The plant has since closed.

Unions particularly have difficulty dealing with MNCs for the following reasons:

1. *If a strike occurs* in the parent company country, the union does not shut down the flow of financial resources to the corporation. Operations in other countries continue to function and generate profits, which may relieve management of much pressure in negotiations and reduce the costs of the strike.

2. *MNCs have an internal source of products* from facilities in several countries and use this position as leverage to bargain down wages, benefits, and other conditions of employment (called **whipsawing** the union). If a strike occurs at one facility, the MNCs increase production at other units, destroying the

potency of the strike.[12] Many specific examples of whipsawing can be identified. General Motors (GM) was able to expand the work week from 37.5
hours to 40 hours by convincing the union in Germany that it must increase
hours to retain competitiveness. GM has considered increasing its auto production in Brazil and Mexico as part of its wage concession demands, and
when Canadian unions resisted wage concessions, GM considered shifting
production back to the United States.

3. *MNCs with complex tiers of management* do not delegate authority to local
   management to make labor relations decisions, thereby complicating the
   negotiation process because unions do not know who is in charge.[13] Empirical evidence indicates that most unions have not encountered different
   behavior between domestic and foreign-owned MNCs, but there seems to
   be a wider variation in behavior among the MNCs than among single-
   nation corporations in terms of grievance settlement before arbitration,
   amount of local autonomy in negotiations, and difficulty in negotiating the
   first agreement.[14] However, because budget and investment decisions are
   made at the home office, local negotiations are certainly affected.

4. *MNCs shift profits to different facilities*, manipulate prices on internal trans-
   actions, and change marketing emphasis, confusing the unions in negotiations when they seek the facts necessary to address and resolve collective
   bargaining issues.

Because U.S. unions are accustomed to bargaining on ability to pay and are entitled to wage and financial information that allows them to conduct informed
negotiations, they are frustrated when MNCs furnish only information that is required by law. Such information about MNCs' locating plants in foreign facilities
and operating data on these plants may be refused by the MNCs with the approval of the NLRB.[15]

Union Approaches to Multinational Bargaining and Employer Reactions

A primary motivator for American and foreign-based unions to seek transnational bargaining and to standardize labor conditions among the MNCs is to
lessen competition from lower-wage areas and to protect their own standards—
in other words, to take wages out of competition. To combat the power of the
MNCs and to seek objectives that are mutually beneficial to the unions and their
members, union leaders have tried two main approaches: (1) collective bargaining and (2) legislative enactment. Through collective bargaining, unions have either attempted to bargain directly with the MNCs or coordinate their bargaining
activities with unions in other countries by sharing information and supporting
one another's activities.

The unions have become frustrated with attempts to achieve any degree of
transnational bargaining, so they have concentrated on the adoption of codes of
conduct to regulate MNC behavior. The International Labor Organization, a tripartite organization with governments, employers, and unions from 150 countries
represented, established labor codes that state the MNCs should give priority to
human rights, employment, safety, occupational development, social justice, and

promotion and advancement of local nationals, and should provide stable employment and pay comparable wages.

The Organization for Economic Cooperation and Development, an international organization headquartered in Paris, has also established "Guidelines for MNCs" concerning conduct in labor–management relations. These guidelines include certain rights: the rights to organize and bargain collectively, to have access to data for negotiations, to be trained as a member of the workforce, and to be given advance notice of changes in operations. Further, subsidiaries of MNCs are expected to observe employment standards comparable to those in the host countries; MNCs are expected not to threaten to shift production to other countries to influence negotiations or to prevent unionization, and local management representatives should be authorized to negotiate on behalf of the MNCs.[16]

Unions, as well as some governments, have asserted that collective bargaining on a national basis has considerable limitations in facing MNCs. This assertion is based on the belief that MNCs have adopted global strategies, so a union acting alone within one nation cannot effectively respond. Likewise, some governments are uneasy about the fact that MNCs cannot easily be made accountable to any one country's economic and social policies. Moreover, there has been persistent fear that if a union or government in one country acted without the support of unions or governments in other countries, it would risk transfer of operations by the MNC to a more hospitable nation.[17]

The creation of the European Union has led to a resurgence of interests in prospects of transnational collective bargaining. However, recent initiatives have taken the form of joint consultation and adherence to labor rights principles at a transnational level rather than true collective bargaining.

The aim of European trade unions is to achieve European-level collective bargaining. Despite the long recognized hurdles, there have been positive steps toward this end. First, the European Trade Union Confederation (ETUC) has become an effective voice for trade unions in the political arena and has the potential to become the spokesperson for European trade unions in collective bargaining. Second, new agreements between trade unions in two countries have been signed. These agreements grant reciprocal memberships to members in both unions and provide for cooperation between these unions in exchanging information, developing closer coordination with respect to European works councils, harmonization of pay demands, and training. Third, cross-national coordination of collective-bargaining strategies is taking place. Trade unions are agreeing on a common bargaining strategy and exchange of information. In 1998, trade unions in Germany, Netherlands, Belgium, and Luxembourg agreed to make pay demands reflect inflation and productivity gains and agreed to bargain on reducing the hours of work. The ETCU has established bargaining committees comprising officials from European-level federations who are responsible for collective bargaining. The intent is to achieve some consistency in collective bargaining across national boundaries.[18]

In the past few years, the number of global agreements signed by MNCs has increased. These agreements between MNCs and international trade union organizations commit the companies to observing standards and principles in their operation worldwide. These principles generally relate to various aspects of worker rights, employment, and other areas of corporate social responsibility. As of the beginning of 2004, there were 30 global agreements in place. Although the number is small, the companies involved include some of the world's largest, most high-profile and "internationalized" MNCs. For example, DaimlerChrysler employs 370,000 worldwide, Volkswagen employs 320,000, French retailer Carrefour employs 300,000, and Danish business services organization ISS employs 250,000. In total, the 30 companies that have signed the global agreements employ around 2.5 million. Nearly all of the companies involved are headquartered in western Europe. General Motors Europe signed a global agreement in 2002.[19]

Most MNCs generally consider transnational labor relations a distant prospect and one that will not be lightly entertained by management. Part of management's opposition stems from the unions' potential for shutting down production internationally. Furthermore, transnational bargaining would introduce a tri-level structure of bargaining that would include multinational negotiations, followed by national ones, then local. This additional level would increase the complexity of negotiations, as well as companies' vulnerability to strikes at the international level without a comparable reduction in vulnerability at the national and local levels.

In some cases, countries themselves are not encouraging investments by MNCs; taxation policies, building limitations, requirements for local partners, the possibility of nationalization and expropriation of facilities, and the risks of political uncertainties are factors deterring MNC investment. Less-developed countries seek additional investments by MNCs for economic stimulus to the countries' development, income, employment programs, and so on, and MNCs find these countries attractive because of the low wage structure, tax incentives, and political guarantees. Such advantages are particularly appealing to the MNC that must operate in a very competitive product market. However, when unions press via transnational bargaining for improved wages, benefits, and working conditions—all socially desirable goals for the populace—they become a force running counter to the short-run national economic goals of the country. The economic boost MNCs can give a developing nation will not occur if firms fail to locate there; MNCs might well decide to avoid countries with the high wages and benefits that transnational bargaining has instituted.

Obstacles for Unions in Bargaining with Multinational Corporations

American and foreign unions face formidable tasks in their efforts to arrange transnational bargaining because they must be successful in mediating and balancing the conflicting interests of different groups encompassed by the MNCs' employees, labor leaders, companies, and governments.[20] In fact, unions themselves provide some of the more important obstacles to transnational bargaining; however, these obstacles are not insurmountable. Only when these obstacles are overcome can attention be turned to external factors.

Differences in Labor Relations Laws Legal systems for labor relations vary widely among countries. There are different methods for determining union representation, different union jurisdictions and structure, and differences in the scope of bargaining.[21]

Absence of a Central Authority Unions lack strong, centralized decision-making authority regarding transnational affairs, and most national union leaders are reluctant to allow a transnational body to make decisions that affect their unions and members.

Cultural Differences Among complicating factors are the differences in ideological and religious beliefs among, for example, free trade unions and socialist- or communist-linked unions. Such differences have made joint undertakings between unions in the free world and elsewhere almost impossible.

Lack of Coordination of Activities Unions have not been very successful in coordinating their transnational bargaining, boycott, and strike activities. An excellent example occurred in the last major rubber strike of Goodyear, Uniroyal, B.F. Goodrich, and Firestone. Each had extensive overseas operations. Support for the U.S. strikes came from the International Federation of Chemical, Energy, Mining, and General Workers Unions (ICEM), which has affiliates in Europe, North America, and Japan. The ICEM Rubber Division approved a ban on overtime by employees of nonstruck companies and a system of monitoring and preventing shipments to the United States. At the end of the strike—the longest rubber strike in U.S. history—the ICEM claimed that its efforts had had a significant effect on the bargaining outcome; however, the facts seemed to contradict this claim. A study by Northrup and Rowan of the U.S. rubber workers' strike did not reveal a single instance of interference with tire shipments from Europe, Japan, or North America; in fact, they found that imports jumped substantially in anticipation of the strike and never fell below the prestrike level. Furthermore, even Canadian imports were significantly increased during the strike, reversing what had occurred several years before, when U.S. rubber workers refused to support a strike by Canadian rubber workers.[22]

Differing National Priorities The economic, social, legal, and political differences among countries serve as yet another obstacle to transnational bargaining. Few if any countries would subvert their national needs in the interest of developing an international system of labor relations.

Employer Resistance Employer resistance is less obvious than other obstacles at this time, mostly because of the inability of the unions to overcome the other hurdles that they face. Once the initial hurdles are overcome, employers' opinions and attitudes concerning transnational collective bargaining will no doubt emerge, but in the meantime, MNCs may sit idly by until the initial hurdles are eliminated.

Effects of Unions on Multinational Corporations

Research conducted mostly in European countries has indicated that unions have had little direct effect on investment and production allocation policies of MNCs. However, they have had considerable indirect effect because union relations with employers help shape the investment climate of a country.

Thus far, MNCs rarely have been able to afford to switch production to other countries as a bargaining or union intimidation tactic because of the costs involved. They no doubt would shift production to another country in cases where a labor dispute stops production and the move is economically and practically possible. However, such decisions are considerably limited because companies must have the necessary excess production capacity available and management must expect the labor dispute to last sufficiently long to justify a shift in production before it would be feasible.

Overall, little evidence exists of substantial negative effects of MNCs on labor relations in countries in which they operate. MNCs usually offer prevailing or superior wage standards and provide comparable working conditions for several reasons. The strengths of unions in the respective countries, the highly integrated and institutionalized nature of labor relations systems, and the socioeconomic and political climates of the countries have clearly constrained the potential for direct adverse effect.[23]

Conclusions and Predictions on Transnational Bargaining

Systematic investigations of transnational collective bargaining reveal that it does not yet exist in any realistic form and is not likely to occur in the immediate future. MNCs are generally opposed to it, and trade unions are not of a single mind regarding its desirability. Although there have been several cases of information exchange between multinational unions and a few instances of union–management consultation, only one trade union secretariat—the International Transport Workers Federation (ITF)—has actually negotiated an agreement (with shipping companies). Furthermore, only in the unique U.S.-Canadian and the European Union environments do much transnational activities occur.

There has been no identifiable trend toward transnational collective bargaining by companies and unions in the United States, Europe, or Japan. Some believe that no effective transnational collective bargaining will occur in the near future. However, others believe that such collective bargaining is inevitable. It will probably develop first in either the European Community, North America, or Central America and deal initially with general topics, such as employment protection, investment policies, and codes of fair practices, before broadening into other bargaining topics.

Globalization and Concerns about Free Trade: The Case of the North American Free Trade Agreement (NAFTA)

The net effect of free trade—globalization—has been gains to consumers in lower prices, greater efficiency in the overall economy, and reducing poverty in developing nations. However, the distribution of the net benefits of free trade and globalization has been uneven. American jobs have been lost in major industries, such as the automobile, steel, textile, footwear, and consumer electronics, whereas jobs in the aircraft, computers, entertainment, and finance industries have increased. One estimate reveals that 6.4 million manufacturing workers were displaced from 1979–1999 due to imports and a total of about 17 million workers were displaced during this time period. While most of these workers found new employment, the new jobs were with lower pay.[24] A study by the Institute of International Economics found that 69 percent of the people who lost their jobs between 1979 and 1999 as result of cheap imports in sectors other than manufacturing found new jobs. However, 55 percent found jobs at lower pay and 25 percent took jobs with pay cuts of 30 percent or more.[25]

Over the 1979–1999 period, manufacturing accounted for about 37 percent of the total nonagricultural jobs lost while manufacturing represented about 18 percent of all nonagricultural employment. More startling, nearly as many workers lost manufacturing jobs (16.8 million) during the 1979–1999 period as were employed in manufacturing in 1999 (18.5 million). Then, in October 2003, manufacturing employment showed its highest monthly increase in over three years. This increase was due to a recovering economy and a weakened dollar in the international markets.[26]

There is concern in the United States, the European Union, and Australia that Ireland, South Africa, Russia, and India (where there are 2 million college graduates per year and 80 percent speak English) may do for the service sector what China has already done for manufacturing. (Japan has similar concerns in regard to northern China, where Japanese is spoken.) In the near future, competition will come from the Philippines, where there are 300,000 college graduates each year who speak English and Malaysia. Any product can be manufactured in China less expensively than in the richer, high-wage countries. Now, it is just a matter of time before any service that can be electronically transmitted will be produced in India more cheaply. Currently, an IT professional with five years' experience earns $96,000 per year in the United States, $75,000 in Britain, and $26,000 in India. In fact, over the next three years, a New York securities firm plans to replace 800 American software engineers, who earn $150,000, with an equally competent team in India, who earn an average of $20,00 per year. Cheaper communications allow companies to move back-office tasks such as data entry, call centers, and payroll processing to poorer countries, such as India, which has three huge advantages for companies: a large pool of well-educated young workers, low wages, and the use of the English language. It is predicted that as many as 3.3 million jobs (500,000 industrial technology jobs) will move abroad by the year 2015.[27]

Organized labor has taken a stand against expansion of free trade pacts with other countries. At the World Trade Organization meeting in December 1999, the AFL-CIO sent more than 30,000 representatives to protest removal of trade barriers with China and its entry into the World Trade Organization. Unions feared the continued exodus of good-paying jobs by companies now in the United States relocating to China and other countries in southeast Asia. As an example, in 1994, China exported $39 billion worth of goods to the United States; in 2003, China exported $137 billion worth of goods to the United States, a trade imbalance of over $100 billion. Concerned about the deterioration of high-paying jobs lost to other countries, in November 2003 the AFL-CIO sent over 20,000 representatives to participate in a march to protest a closed-door meeting of trade ministers from North, Central, and South America who were discussing the next steps in creating a free trade zone for all countries in North, Central, and South America.[28]

North American Free Trade Agreement (NAFTA)

One of the free trade agreements signed by the United States is the **North American Free Trade Agreement (NAFTA)**, an agreement between Canada, Mexico, and the United States that removed most barriers to trade between and investments in these three countries. Many of the tariffs were eliminated immediately, and the others were to be phased out over 5 to 15 years. NAFTA was approved by Congress in 1993, signed by President Clinton in 1993, and took effect on January 1, 1994. Under NAFTA, three countries became a single, giant, integrated market of almost 400 million people with $6.5 trillion worth of goods and services traded annually. Then, in 2003, the Bush administration began negotiation of a Central American Free Trade Agreement that would include the countries of

Costa Rica, El Salvador, Guatemala, Honduras, and Nicaragua and completed a free-trade agreement with Australia. These agreements would be similar to NAFTA whereby tariffs would be eliminated on trade with the United States. In addition, discussions began on a Free Trade Area of the Americas that would cover 34 North, Central, and South America countries, extend trade agreements similar to those under NAFTA, and cover a population of 800 million.[29]

The promises of NAFTA included creation of new and better jobs, rising incomes, and economic growth acceleration to underdeveloped countries in Central America, and while there would be environmental challenges, extra resources would be available. Economists have attempted to identify the effects of NAFTA on the economies of the United States, Canada, and Mexico. After 10 years, there has been expansion in trade and foreign investment; in fact, U.S. exports to and imports from Canada and Mexico now account for about one-third of its trade (up from one-fourth in 1990). However, there has been a contraction in manufacturing employment in the United States, economic stagnation in Mexico (Mexico's grew about 1 percent in the past 10 years, Korea's grew 4.3 percent, and China's grew 7 percent), and significant environmental problems, especially along the U.S.-Mexico border. A survey by the Woodrow Wilson Center in Washington revealed that 29 percent of Mexicans believed that Mexico had benefited, 33 percent believed that Mexico had been hurt, and 33 percent said it made no difference. In Mexico, productivity rates have improved; however, real wages have risen only slightly. In several areas of the agricultural sector, there has been a near disaster for most farmers, who have to compete with America's government-subsidized products, such as corn. Up to 90 percent of the heads of families in some communities now spend at least 6 months per year working in the United States and Canada; they earn in 4 months the amount they would earn in Mexico in an entire year. Mexican producers of horticultural products, fresh vegetables, and fresh fruits have nearly doubled their exports to the United States. Sadly, successive governments have failed to deal with structural problems of corruption, poor education, red tape, crumbling infrastructure, lack of credit, and an inadequate tax base.[30]

Since the early 1990s, about 600,000 Mexican farm jobs have been lost due to lower import barriers for beans, apples, grapes, and other crops. In 2010, tariffs on imported corn will be eliminated, and loss of jobs will increase. These job losses in agriculture have fueled migration into urban areas, where 80 percent of the population now resides. Migration to the cities is much faster than the rate of new jobs. Investments encouraged by NAFTA have produced 300,00 jobs, mostly in the northern cities; however, a million people enter the labor force each year. As a result, 40 percent of the labor force, about 12 million workers, do not have stable employment. Most of them work in the informal sector as street vendors, maids, and short-term workers—jobs that provide no social security protections. The rural jobs losses have swelled the ranks of undocumented Mexican workers in the United States.

Minimum wages are set each year by a commission of government, business, and labor representatives. The 2002 minimum wage was equal to $120 a month, which is the same in real terms as wages were in 1980. While the value of exports was 10 times greater than in 1990, the total compensation of these workers is still roughly one-sixth of what similar workers in the United States earn. Factories continue to use outdated equipment and inefficient work systems, and technological improvements have been concentrated in the export-oriented plants owned by global corporations, particularly in the electronics and automobile industries. Managers realize that they must adapt to new work arrangements and raise the skills of their employees; however, only a few companies, usually foreign owned, have introduced quality control methods and workplace systems that promote efficiency or provide formal training for employees. Until changes are implemented, Mexican workers will see few gains from free trade.[31]

Along the border with the United States, the number of *maquiladoras* plants (assembly plants for export using imported parts and components) rose 67 percent to 3,655 during the first 7 years after NAFTA was enacted in 1993. However since 2000, more than 850 have shut down and employment is down more than 20 percent from its peak of 1.3 million. Companies like Delphi are courted by China with tax incentives, low wages (assembly workers earn $0.57 per hour), worker training, and access to the latest technology.[32]

One disputed study estimated that 110,000 jobs per year have been lost in the United States due to NAFTA; however, the United States generates an average of more than 2 million jobs per year, and a great majority of these new jobs pay above the median wage. In Canada, there were initial concerns about the flight of low-skilled manufacturing jobs to Mexico and a depressing effect on the Canadian tax base; however, unemployment rates were 11 percent in 1990 and were 7 percent in 2000, and Canada has actually experienced a budget surplus. The end result is that NAFTA did not achieve as much as the politicians promised, but neither was there the "giant sucking sound" of work moving south that presidential candidate Ross Perot predicted.[33]

North American Agreement on Labor Cooperation (NAALC)

The North American Free Trade Agreement (NAFTA) provided several side agreements, which were designed to protect employees and the environment. The North American Agreement on Labor Cooperation (NAALC), one of the two side agreements, went into effect on January 1, 1994. The NAALC commits the United States, Canada, and Mexico to implement, enforce, and improve labor principles through national legislation and institutions. Its objectives are to be furthered by intergovernmental cooperation and by a procedure established to resolve complaints based on a monitoring system and a series of steps to resolve unsettled disputes (up to arbitration). More than two dozen complaints (seven against the United States; two against Canada; 15 against Mexico) have been submitted. These complaints included infringements on the right to freedom of association, charges of discrimination, and occupational health and safety violations. Thus far, the NAALC has failed because the three countries disagree on its aims. Canada and Mexico consider the NAALC a way to achieve greater intergovernmental cooperation; the United States focuses on the dispute-resolution mechanisms. As a result, limited success has been achieved on either front because the parties seldom engage in active cooperation and are reluctant to use the conflict resolution mechanisms.[34]

Thus far, the NAALC has fallen far short of the expectations of Canadian and U.S. labor organizations. First, it does not offer remedies to workers whose legal rights have been violated. Second, it is procedurally difficult to sanction NAFTA governments that fail to enforce their own labor laws and violate the NAALC's 11 labor principles (see Exhibit 14.2). While arbitration offers sanctions, the procedures are cumbersome, and only occupational safety and health, child labor, and

Exhibit 14.2

Eleven Principles of the North American Agreement on Labor Cooperation

1. Freedom of association and protection of the right to organize
2. Right to bargain collectively
3. Right to strike
4. Prohibition of forced labor
5. Labor protection for children and young persons
6. Minimum employment standards, such as minimum wages and overtime pay
7. Elimination of employment discrimination
8. Equal pay for women and men
9. Prevention of occupational injuries and illnesses
10. Compensation in cases of occupational injuries and illnesses
11. Protection of migrant workers

SOURCE: http://www.mac.doc.gov/nafta/3006.htm (December 15, 2003).

minimum wage issues may be arbitrated. Core labor rights of freedom of association, bargaining collectively, and strikes are not subjects for arbitration. So far, no arbitration panel has been called into service. Although the NAALC has not met expectations, it has provided an important education and research role. Trade unions have publicized abuses for all to see and have brought together cross-border coalitions among unions that have otherwise been formed. Of the 24 union submissions of alleged violations (7 against the United States, 15 against Mexico, and 2 against Canada), four were brought to an equitable resolution after widespread negative publicity or threat of negative publicity. The conclusion of one study is:

> The labor law side agreement is withering as an effective labor law enforcement and MNC compliant strategy. To sustain as an institution designed in part to motivate labor law enforcement and business compliance with labor policy, the remedy and penalty aspects of the NAALC will need to be revisited.[35]

Jon Hiatt of the AFL-CIO concluded that the case history of NAALC has indicated that, even "when workers win, they still lose." He concluded that no workers have been reinstated in any NAALC cases, there have been no concrete remedies ordered, and no financial sanctions imposed. In fact, he concluded that corporate or government behavior has changed very little as a result of any cases brought under the NAALC. Hiatt recommends several specific actions:

- The NAALC should be made a part of NAFTA, which does not address worker rights, instead of being a side agreement

- All 11 principles of worker rights covered by NAALC (see Exhibit 14.2) should be subject to final and binding dispute resolution and subject to possible sanctions.

- The NAALC should address the need to raise a country's labor standards where inadequate, not just the obligation to adhere to a country's existing laws.

- The time frame for dispute resolution should be shortened.

- Where a dispute involves an allegation that a company has violated the law, that company should be required to participate in the hearing.[36]

Another assessment of the NAALC found five general trends. First, most of the alleged violations of the NAALC side agreements have involved lack of or improper enforcement of labor laws in Mexico. Second, labor unions and human rights groups in one of the NAFTA countries are more likely to file the complaint in their own country against another country. Third, most of the complaints allege violations of workers' rights to organize labor unions in Mexico, where independent unions have tried to organize workers. Fourth, the submission process has resulted in conferences, seminars, and public reports. While these are not effective remedies, employers' desire to avoid public attention has facilitated resolution in those cases where the submissions were voluntarily withdrawn. Fifth, the dispute resolution procedure has provided a platform for those parties who want to raise concerns about the enforcement procedures in the NAFTA member countries[37]

Unions in Other Countries

With the growing interdependency among nations, major improvements in communication and travel between countries, and the increasing role of MNCs, the need to learn more about labor relations systems in other parts of the world is imperative. Books have been written about many of the specific topics in this chapter, so no attempt is made to present detailed descriptions or analyses of labor relations systems in the countries mentioned. This section presents unique and interesting features of a variety of countries with the hope of encouraging readers to pursue more thorough investigations. Its coverage ranges from the developing countries of Central and South America to the countries nearest our borders—Mexico and Canada—to the major trading partners of the United States such as Japan and the western European countries. The extent of discussion of each country's labor relations system is determined by its proximity to the United States; its trade, economic, and political relationships with the United States; and its uniqueness among the world's labor relations systems.

Many U.S. residents tend to view the rest of the world in terms of their own patterns of living. The fact is that virtually no country has a labor relations system like ours. One example of the differences between countries is the degree of employee protection against termination without cause. In the United States, only 20 percent of employees have such protection. In other words, the majority of American employees can be terminated from their employment without any justification unless termination is a violation of a contractual agreement, such as a collective bargaining agreement, or a law. As shown in Exhibit 14.3, 50 percent of Canadian employees are protected, and 90 percent in Australia and the United Kingdom are protected. In Belgium, France, Germany, Italy, and Spain, 100 percent of employees are protected against termination without cause. As discussed in Chapter 12, there are basic principles for terminating employees for cause.[38]

Canada has several major departures from typical U.S. labor relations practices. Unions of Europe have much closer ties to political parties; Japanese unions

EXHIBIT 14.3

Percentage of the Labor Force That is Protected against Termination without Cause

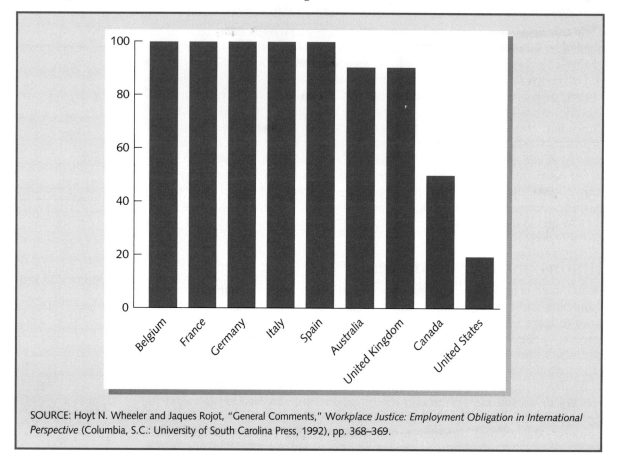

SOURCE: Hoyt N. Wheeler and Jaques Rojot, "General Comments," *Workplace Justice: Employment Obligation in International Perspective* (Columbia, S.C.: University of South Carolina Press, 1992), pp. 368–369.

are organized on the enterprise level; and Central American unions are split along ideological lines. By contrast, the U.S. labor relations system is based on majority rule, exclusive representation for bargaining agents, and political independence. Exhibit 14.4 presents an overview of distinguishing features of foreign labor relations systems; the following discussion briefly explains these systems.

Another distinguishing feature between labor relations in the United States and that of other countries of the world is the percentage of employees who are union members. Exhibit 14.5 shows that the United States is classified among the least unionized countries, such as Columbia, Egypt, France, Mexico, Portugal, and Spain. Denmark, Finland, and Sweden are the most unionized countries, with 80 percent or more of the workforce being unionized.

Canada

Canada's labor relations system is affected by a number of variables: foreign influences, climate, natural resources, and two major linguistic and cultural groups. Its economy is subject to cyclical fluctuations resulting from harsh winters, sea-

EXHIBIT 14.4

Overview of Distinguishing Features of U.S. and Foreign Labor Relations Systems

United States
Exclusive bargaining representation
Majority rule
Political independence
	Western Europe
	Exclusive bargaining representation nonexistent
	Much negotiation between employer association
	  and union confederation with individual bargain-
	  ing under the resulting agreement
	Many fringe benefits established by law
	Worker participation mandated in many countries

Canada Influence by unions and companies from United States Two major linguistic and cultural groups Decentralized and fragmented collective bargaining Legal influence within provinces	
	Japan Labor–management consultation/teamwork Lifetime employment in large firms Enterprise unions Wage system with much weight on seniority

Central and South America
Wide variation in the degree of sophistication in
  labor relations systems
Close connection between trade unions and
  political parties
Voluminous labor codes and government regulations
  that cover wages and terms of employment
Predominantly negotiations at plant level only
	Australia
	Decentralized bargaining
	Nonunion bargaining
	Unfair dismissal law
	
	Eastern Europe
	Little collective bargaining
	No labor agreements

sonality of its industries, and foreign influences (mostly the United States). In addition, Canada's geographical spread and regional concentration of resources and production have led to decentralized and fragmented collective bargaining. The penetration of U.S. corporations into Canada has had a significant effect on Canadian labor relations because many major decisions still are made in the United States. The French- and English-speaking division of Canada has produced two distinct labor movements; furthermore, relationships between management, which is primarily unilingually English-speaking, and the predominantly French-speaking workforce have not been ideal.[39] In 1995 the citizens of Quebec, Canada's predominantly French-speaking province, voted by a slight margin to remain in Canada. Of the four largest labor unions in Canada, three are in the public sector. Half of the largest 16 unions have their headquarters in the United States. The Canadian Autoworkers and the Canadian Paperworkers are two of the largest unions and were formerly affiliated with U.S.-based unions.

Although the public-sector unions continue to represent 75 percent of public employees, private-sector unions have begun to recruit members outside their traditional jurisdictions to offset their decline in membership. The Steelworkers now represent many hotel and restaurant employees, and the Canadian Autoworkers represent fishermen on the East Coast of Canada. In addition, some significant mergers have taken place, such as the Canadian Retail, Wholesale Union (formerly part of a U.S. union) with the Canadian Autoworkers.[40]

In 1956, union membership in Canada and the United States was about one-third of the labor force. Union membership in Canada has remained at

EXHIBIT 14.5

Comparison of Worldwide Union Density: 2000–2003

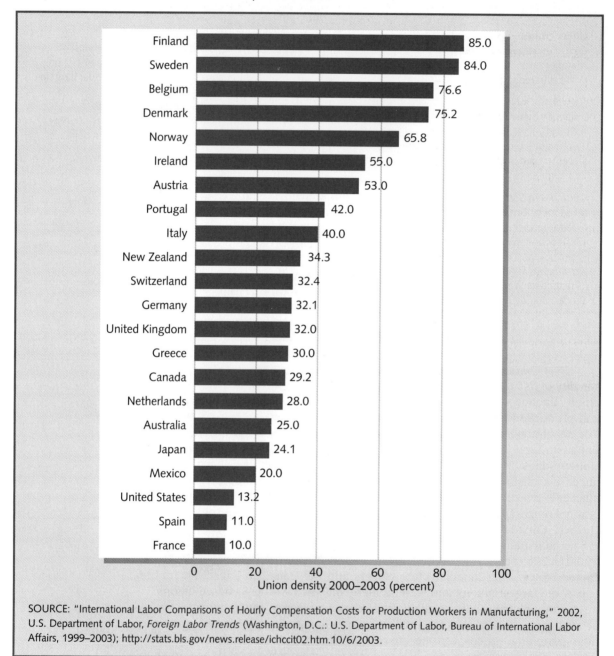

SOURCE: "International Labor Comparisons of Hourly Compensation Costs for Production Workers in Manufacturing," 2002, U.S. Department of Labor, *Foreign Labor Trends* (Washington, D.C.: U.S. Department of Labor, Bureau of International Labor Affairs, 1999–2003); http://stats.bls.gov/news.release/ichccit02.htm.10/6/2003.

about the same strength, whereas the United States has faced serious membership erosion.

Despite the fact that surveys in both the United States and Canada show that 40 percent of the workforce desire union representation, 90 percent of those desiring union representation in Canada are actually represented whereas only 39 percent of those desiring union representation in the United States are represented.[41]

The differences between the success of Canadian unions and U.S. unions can be attributed to several interrelated factors: favorable labor laws, more aggressive union organizing, less employer opposition, and supportive public policy. Favorable labor laws contribute to union organizing activity and success (about 70 percent in Canada, compared with around 50 percent in the United States, restrict employer opposition to unions, and therefore lead to increases in union membership—29.2 percent in Canada versus 13.2 percent in the United States). As a result of greater union membership, unions are able to mobilize greater resources (such as financial resources, union staff, member participation and voting) to achieve greater effectiveness in terms of organizing and bargaining successes and to have greater political influence.

Since 1980, unions in the United States have been unable to recruit sufficient members to offset job losses, and union membership has fallen to 13.2 percent of the total labor force. At the same time, Canadian unions have gained 700,000 members, an increase of 20 percent.[42] Unions in Canada have used their strength to achieve major bargaining gains and have wielded significant political influence, while the U.S. unions have been placed in a defensive bargaining and political position.

There are numerous explanations for the fact that union density in Canada (30 percent) is more than twice that of the United States (13 percent).

- Major Canadian employers have a greater likelihood of accepting unions.

- Canadian employers are less likely to engage in anti-union practices.

- Canadian unions have exhibited greater activity in recruiting new members and have assigned a higher priority to organizing than in the United States.

- Canadian unions have greater political influence than in the United States.

- There are faster certification procedures and fewer delays than in the United States.

- There is greater job protection for striking workers, and use of replacement workers during strikes and lockouts is restricted in some provinces.

- There is widespread use of card-based certification rather than secret-ballot votes in some of the largest jurisdictions.

- Some labor boards have greater remedial powers, for example, to certify the union without a vote or to order a first collective bargaining agreement.

- In some provinces, there is arbitration available for the first contract.

- Employer campaigning activities are more restrictive.

- There is no such thing as a right-to-work law in Canada; in fact, 7 of 11 provinces in Canada have made the agency shop (see Chapter 4) the statutory minimum.[43]

- The distinction between mandatory and voluntary subjects for collective bargaining has never been adopted in Canada.

In 1991 the Supreme Court of Canada rendered a ruling opposite to the *Beck* decision in the United States (see Chapter 4). Unions can use membership dues for activities not directly related to collective bargaining, including political contributions. If the decision had gone the other way, unions would have seen their political activities thwarted by lack of funds and a restriction on their support for the New Democratic Party (NDP).[44]

The two major federations, the Canadian Labour Council (CLC) and the Canadian Federation of Labor (CFL), continue their long-standing opposition to NAFTA. They maintain that Canada has been ill served by the U.S.-Canada FTA and that expanding free trade to Mexico would cause numerous manufacturing jobs to be lost to Mexico without improving conditions for the Mexican workers.[45]

Mexico, Central America, and South America

Collective bargaining in Central and South America is less extensive and sophisticated than corresponding activities in the United States; however, the number of agreements has been increasing. About one-fourth of the employees are covered by labor agreements in Mexico, Venezuela, and Argentina—much more than in the United States. This amount reflects more of a government extension of contract terms than actual industrywide bargaining patterns. The extent of development of collective bargaining may be illustrated in three categories:

1. The advanced group, as exemplified in parts of Mexico and Argentina.
2. A much larger middle group in which bargaining ranges from advanced collective bargaining with larger firms to very simple or no bargaining in smaller firms, as in Chile and Brazil.
3. A large third group in which collective bargaining is not widespread, as in Costa Rica, Ecuador, and Nicaragua.

Mexico is highly unionized, representing about 30 percent of the economically active population and nearly 50 percent of the formal sector workforce. Most, but not all, unions are in labor centrals allied with Mexico's Institutional Revolutionary Party (PRI). By far the largest central is the Confederation of Mexican Workers (CTM), which has been recognized as the spokesperson for the labor sector.

The traditional centrals have long sacrificed freedom of action to gain political influence and position. However, the importance of political influence to workers has declined as the economy has decentralized and privatized. Unions must obtain more for workers through enterprise collective bargaining and less through influence with the government. With NAFTA and facing international competition, unions and employers are finding it increasingly necessary to work together to improve productivity, competitiveness, and quality, if companies and jobs are to survive and profits and wages are to increase.

Mexico has undergone profound changes over the last 20 years. It has changed from a closed, import-substitution economy to become part of the open, market economy. It has joined the Organization for Economic Cooperation and Development (OECD) and entered into the North American Free Trade

Agreement (NAFTA) in 1994. Mexico is experiencing a dramatic political change from a system dominated by the Institutional Revolutionary Party (PRI) for more than 70 years with strong worker and peasant sectors and featuring leftist, nationalist, and often anti-American rhetoric to a more multiparty, democratic system, with a closer relationship with the United States.

Of the over 40 million in the economically active population, about 39 percent are employed in the formal sector. These jobs are covered by social security and related programs funded through employer and smaller worker contributions (medical care, small pension, and IRA-like compulsory retirement savings plan, and a housing loan fund). The formal sector workers also receive profit sharing. Another 20 percent of the economically active population works in tiny enterprises in the semiformal sector, where few are covered by social security. The remaining 40 plus percent are marginally underemployed or self-employed in the informal sector.

Mexico has comprehensive, progressive labor laws. Its constitution and laws provide extensive rights and protections for labor and favor union organization. Mexico has ratified 78 International Labor Organization (ILO) Conventions, and 68 are currently in force. However, there are many enforcement problems; the legal protections for union organization also can unintentionally protect and facilitate racketeering, sweetheart protection contracts, and undemocratic practices in many unions. These practices have been fairly widespread, but not universal. The CTM has recognized the need to address corrupt practices and has agreed to promote changes that would lead to the elimination of protection contracts. Nevertheless, such contracts are with respected businesses and more than 50 percent of all labor contracts contain sweetheart protection clauses.[46]

In theory, Mexican workers have the freedom to form independent unions. This freedom is derived from the Mexican constitution, Mexican federal labor laws, and Convention 87 of the International labor Organization. In practice, there are significant restrictions on the exercise of this freedom. Restrictions include barriers to union recognition and registration, excessive reporting requirements, and the requirement that the government recognize union officers.

Understanding the Mexican labor relations system in practice requires an understanding of the interaction of the government, unions, and employers involving the existence of (1) the exclusion clause, (2) the protection clause, and (3) the ownership of the contract. An *exclusion clause* is essentially a closed shop clause because it requires a worker to be a union member before he or she is hired or can continue to be employed. Existing unions are protected because the union may require the employer to dismiss an employee for such reasons as disagreements with union leadership and membership in another union. *A protection clause* is a contract between an employer and a passive union that protects the employer from a more demanding union. Protection clauses appear in 80 to 90 percent of all collective bargaining agreements in Mexico and allow the employer to choose the union with which they want to negotiate. Once chosen, the union is recognized and a contract signed almost before an organization begins operations—only one or two workers are needed. In fact, there is no requirement for workers to be notified that there is a union or a contract. Any organizing drive by another union will be blocked by the existence of the employer-recognized union and its contract. *Ownership of the contract* means that only one collective bargaining agreement may be in effect at a single workplace even though there may be multiple unions. A newly organized union may go to court to prove that it represents the majority of the workers and should have the right to the collective-bargaining agreement with the employer. However, in practice, it is usually difficult for a new union to gain ownership of the contract and achieve recognition by the labor department and the local conciliation and arbitration boards.[47]

The Mexican Constitution and the Federal Labor Law guarantee the right to strike; however, a 6 to 10 days' notice is required, followed by government mediation. If a strike is ruled nonexistent or illicit, employees must remain at work, return to work within 24 hours, or face dismissal. If the strike is ruled legal, the company must shut down totally, management may not enter the premises until the strike is over, and striker replacements may not be hired. In the administration of these laws, unions have accused government authorities of stretching the legal requirements to rule that strikes are nonexistent or illicit so that they can prevent potentially damaging strikes.

Under Mexican law, closed shops are allowed in collective bargaining agreements, as are exclusion clauses, which allow union leaders to veto new hires and force the firing of anyone the union expels. Under Mexican law, several mandatory benefits and protections are provided. Work shifts are 8 hours for the day shift, 7 hours for the night shift, and 71/2 hours for a mixed shift. The work week is 48 hours with a full day of rest. Workers are paid double for overtime and triple for more than nine hours. Overtime is voluntary and often refused. A Christmas bonus equal to at least two weeks' wages must be paid to employees in December of each year. Mexican workers are guaranteed seven holidays per year and are paid double time for work on holidays. Employees are entitled to six working days of paid vacation after one year of service, with more days added as the years of service increase. Employees are entitled to a vacation bonus equal to 25 percent of the weekly salary. Employees are also entitled to severance pay when termination is without "just cause"; however, this money is usually paid anyway rather than having to prove "just cause" to the labor board.[48]

Under Mexico's constitution, workers are entitled to participate in the profits of the enterprise. Employees shall participate in the profits at a percentage rate fixed by the National Committee for Workers' Profit-Sharing in Enterprises. This committee is required to consider the general condition of the Mexican economy, the promotion of industrial development, the right of capital to obtain reasonable interest, and the necessity of reinvestment of capital. Fifty percent of the profit shared is distributed equally among employees in accordance with the number of days worked during the year. The remaining 50 percent is distributed among eligible workers in proportion to the earnings for the year.[49]

The opening of the Mexican markets to NAFTA and international trade, the devaluation of the peso, plant closings, and corporate downsizing to become more competitive have created an economic challenge to the entire country. Free collective bargaining in the last few years has been limited voluntarily and replaced by annual national pacts negotiated by the government, the major trade unions, and employers with the major goal of controlling inflation. Many efforts have been made by employers, unions, and the government to create greater flexibility and labor–management cooperation to improve productivity, quality, and employee renumeration.[50]

In Central and South America, negotiations between unions and employers take place primarily at the plant level. Only Argentina, Venezuela, and Mexico have widespread industrywide bargaining. The principal reason for this arrangement is that legislation in the various countries typically does not require employers to bargain except at the plant level.

An interesting departure from most of the rest of the world is the important role of collective bargaining between employers and nonunion employees. In fact, over 25 percent of the labor agreements in Columbia and Venezuela are negotiated without trade unions. Obviously, the unions look with disfavor on this arrangement because employers use the nonunion groups as a means to bypass trade unions.

In the more industrialized countries of the world, people interpret labor–management relations to mean the wide range of relationships between employers and employees. However, people of Latin American countries tend to define labor relations in terms of the voluminous labor codes and government regulations.

Labor relations vary widely among the countries in Central America, but they have one common feature: a close connection between trade unions and political parties. For example, in Mexico, unions constitute a large section of the ruling political party and therefore are assigned a quota of candidates on the party's ticket for office. Thus, unions have some assurance of having a voice in the party's program and on its council. Some unions have been very effective in gaining relatively high wages for members. For example, the electrical workers in Mexico earn two to three times more than the urban working class.[51] Likewise, unions have been criticized because they have made gains for their own members while neglecting the interests of the great mass of people, including the peasants, who are terribly poor.

Labor agreements vary in content both within countries and among countries. In Argentina, labor agreements include provisions that set forth in some detail the employment conditions and establish a highly developed shop steward system to administer grievances and ensure that employers abide by the agreements. In Chile, labor agreements are more general, but they do establish certain minimum rules and include a grievance mechanism to enforce the agreement. In Brazil, where unions have struggled since 1945 to have a greater say in determining employment rules and conditions for their members, they have achieved more through labor legislation than by engaging in collective bargaining.

In Central American countries, political parties maintain close ties with unions for their support, votes, and influence. Likewise, trade unions depend on the politicians for laws to protect their members, to legalize their organizations, and to regulate their relations with employers. On the other hand, political parties have appealed to organized labor to favor their own policies, and in some cases, they have accommodated organized labor in hopes that it will remain satisfied and continue to support the existing economic and political system.[52]

Cuba

Although not a major trading partner of the United States, Cuba, the largest island nation in the Caribbean sea, is on the brink of social, economic, and political change. With the Helms-Burton Law designed to discourage foreign investments and the demise of the Soviet Union (Cuba's major source of economic subsidies), Cuba has been struggling to survive, and its future direction is not entirely clear. As with the former Soviet bloc countries in eastern Europe, an option for change is toward economic privatization and political democracy. If this occurs, the developing relationships between government, business, and labor will need to be examined.

Before the 1959 revolution, Cuba had more organized workers than any other Central American country, except Mexico, Brazil, and Argentina. In the 1960s, labor unions were replaced by the Advanced Workers' Movement, which comprised between 10 and 15 percent of the workforce. The role of labor unions was curtailed, and unions were not deeply involved in defending workers' rights and had little input on employment-related matters. As labor became dormant, Cuba attempted transition to a "planned" market economy, which had limited success. With failures in agriculture in the 1970s, Cuba began to reactivate the role of labor unions by encouraging worker input into decision making, defending workers' rights, and informing managers of current and impending problems in the production process.

Despite the "union reactivation," Cuba has retained a fundamentally Stalinist approach to labor well into the 1990s. Nonpaid voluntary work is encouraged, strikes are prohibited, free collective bargaining does not exist, and workers remain militarized to sustain the "heroic" tempo of the revolution. Only a small semifree market in the tourism industry exists. However, tourist dollars are paid to the government, and employees are paid in devalued pesos (in 1958 the peso and the U.S. dollar were equivalent; today the peso is less than one-quarter the value of the dollar).

As countries in eastern Europe have moved toward more democratic and pluralistic economies, so shall Cuba in time. The future choices will then be the various forms of labor participation programs, such as work councils, employee collectives, and greater reliance on collective bargaining at the enterprise level. Unions have become the primary means by which workers are represented. Unions represent a broader segment than their membership; they represent retired pensioners, the unemployed, and so on. Unions in eastern Europe have become political partners within the framework of tripartite arrangements (government, labor, and management). Whether these approaches are suitable for Cuba after the transition from Fidel Castro will be open for debate. What is certain is the continuing economic globalization; the question will be whether Cuba will participate in that process.[53]

Western Europe

Unionization in Western Europe is significantly greater than in the United States, with the exception of France and Spain. Of the largest countries, the range is from 10 percent in France to over 80 percent in Finland and Sweden. Unions have been able to use this membership strength to accumulate political influence at the national level. Furthermore, they have been able to coordinate their efforts with large, well-established labor parties in government to achieve their goals.

As in the United States, union membership in western Europe is declining. Nationwide and industrywide bargaining is less frequent, and employers are winning more concessions for efficient work rules and wages. Also, as in the United States, unions are trying to sign up new members in growing industries, such as leisure and finance, where technological change has fueled worries about job security.[54] Unions have achieved significantly greater worker participation in the operation of the firm—many times through legislative mandate and sometimes through management reaction to wildcat strikes and worker dissatisfaction. In addition, public opinion in these countries strongly supports the idea that worker participation enhances production, fosters harmony, and enriches the workers personally.

The labor relations system in western Europe can be contrasted with that of the United States in a number of ways.[55]

1. In the United States, unions are selected by the majority of the appropriate bargaining unit and certified as the exclusive bargaining representative, whereas in western Europe, exclusive representation is not a common concept.

2. In the United States, the exclusive bargaining representative has a monopoly over all employee bargaining, and the employer is required to bargain only with the legally certified union. In western Europe, the employer often bargains with a number of unions in addition to worker councils elected by the employees.

3. In western Europe, negotiations take place between representatives of employer associations and those representing a confederation of unions; in the United States, this bargaining arrangement is adopted in only a few industries, primarily construction.

4. In North America, the focus of union–management interaction is the shop floor, whereas in Europe, bargaining at national levels is more important to the unions.[56]

5. The number of fringe benefits established by law is greater in Europe; therefore, trade unions have found that they can obtain benefits more quickly through the political arena and have tied themselves more closely to political parties.

6. Western European countries have a greater commitment to employee training. For example, German firms spend twice as much on this activity as U.S. firms, or nearly 17 times as much per apprentice. About 65 percent of each class of middle school graduates in Germany enter apprenticeship training. In contrast, 57 percent of high school graduates in the United States enroll in postsecondary education, and the majority drop out before graduation.

One major reason for the disparity in support for employee training between Germany and the United States is the role of unions and employer associations. German companies band together in employer associations to negotiate with unions over wages and other personnel matters, such as training. Because unions represent over 30 percent of the labor force and unions are stronger in Germany, the labor agreements require investments in training, and collective bargaining provides the mechanism for collecting fees. This approach is similar to the high-quality apprenticeship programs financed by contracts between craft unions and employer associations in the U.S. construction industry.[57]

European Union (EU)

By 1992 the economies of 12 countries in western Europe were joined together as the European Union (EU) (Exhibit 14.6). The EU consisted of 12 nations in western Europe: Belgium, Denmark, Germany, Greece, France, Ireland, Italy, Luxembourg, the Netherlands, Portugal, Spain, and the United Kingdom. In 1995, Austria, Finland, and Sweden joined the EU. The EU's goal is to gradually eliminate economic barriers among member countries. The original target date of December 31, 1992, called for the elimination of restrictions on the movement of goods, capital, and labor across national borders.[58] On May 1, 2004, the European Union added 10 countries (Czech Republic, Cyprus, Estonia, Hungary, Latvia, Lithuania, Malta, Poland, Slovakia, and Slovenia) to its membership, making a total of 25 countries. The European Union has grown to 450 million people. In 2004, the 25 countries of the European Union will attempt to adopt a constitution, which will include employment and social issues (see Exhibit 14.7 for the draft of employment-related issues).[59]

The Charter of Fundamental Social Rights (called the "Social Charter") was approved by all EU countries except Great Britain. This arrangement establishes certain standards for working conditions throughout the EU so that some countries cannot attract industry merely because their pay and working conditions are below those of other countries. The charter stipulates statements of principles on fundamental rights that include freedom of association and encourages collective bargaining, vocational training, equal treatment for men and women, health and safety, child protection, and rights of information, consultation, and participation for workers.[59]

Critics of the Social Charter have argued that the EU has returned western Europe to a re-regulation phase that will raise labor costs, inhibit employment growth, and disproportionately affect the poorer employees. Critics contend the end result of mandated benefits in the Social Charter will lead to higher costs and an erosion of their external competitive position.[60]

Companies are already considering the effects of the EU, which could include increased mobility of employees between operations in the various countries, more recruiting from overseas, more active monitoring of pay and benefits developments in other countries, and increased language training, as well as a premium placed on language skills. These areas and others will provide much opportunity for trade unions to be involved at the bargaining table.

The European Works Council (EWC) Directive was adopted in 1995 to provide a legal right for workers and their representatives to be consulted and informed about MNCs operating in more than one country in the EU. Any MNC employing more than 1,000 workers in the European Economic Area (EEA includes the EU countries plus Norway, Iceland, and Liechtenstein) and with 150 workers in at least two member states had to establish a procedure for informing and consulting employees when the workers asked for it. Estimates of the number of MNCs covered by the directive range from 860 to 1,500. By 1996, it was estimated that close to 500 MNCs had negotiated voluntary agreements. Although

EXHIBIT 14.6

The European Union

these agreements are indeed transnational, their effect on worker representation, unions, economic performance, and labor markets has yet to be determined.[61]

Each of these EWCs meets at least once a year to discuss the firm's changes, its business environment, employment issues, and future plans. Senior managers present information to employee representatives who are asked to respond, and consultation takes place over corporate decisions that affect workers in more

Exhibit 14.7

Employment-Related Elements of the Charter of Fundamental Rights

Prohibition of slavery and forced labor
Protection of personal data
Freedom of assembly and association, including trade union matters
Freedom to choose an occupation and the right to engage in work
Equality in employment matters including prohibition against employment discrimination based on sex, race, color, ethnic or social origin, nationality, genetic features, language, religion, disability, age, sexual orientation
Information and consultation
Right of collective bargaining and action
Right of access to placement services
Unjustified dismissal
Fair and just working condition including health, safety, and dignity
Child labor and protection
Family and professional life including protection against dismissal connected to maternity and the right to paid maternity leave and parental leave following birth or adoption of a child
Social security and assistance in cases such as maternity, illness, industrial accidents, dependency or old age and loss of employment.

Source: *European Union 2003*, Washington, D.C.: U.S. Printing Office, 2003, pp. 17–19.

than one country. Most EWCs allow employee representatives to hold their own meetings before and after the main sessions, and some EWCs are developing new forms of communication between the annual events. Although EWC activities are separate from trade union activities and European trade unions are not actively involved, the EWC provides a mechanism for promulgating industrial relations policy initiatives across national boundaries and implementing new regulatory measures in industrial relations within the European Union.[62]

In 2002 the euro, the new common currency of the EU, replaced the national currencies, and identical notes and coins are used within the EU countries. The single EU currency will encourage the formation of a single European economy as the corollary of a single European market. A single currency is expected to make European markets for goods and services more integrated and more efficient. Therefore, European firms will need to become more integrated and efficient to compete against each other and foreign competitors, who will be attracted to the EU as the internal barriers disappear. A wave of consolidations is expected among businesses, which has already begun in banking, retailing, and manufacturing. As in the United States during the 1990s, the mergers and consolidations have evoked cost-cutting and major layoffs. Unions and governments will have to be attentive to the problems that coincide with the events.[63]

Great Britain

The traditional system in Great Britain is characterized by voluntary collective bargaining, implemented without legal compulsion through unenforceable labor agreements that have been negotiated by a large number of multiunion-multiemployer negotiating committees. The United Kingdom has nearly 600 labor unions, over three times the number in the United States, and a manufacturing firm typically negotiates with about seven unions. One of the most important negotiations involve the Engineering Employers' Federation, representing 5,000 companies, and the Confederation of Shipbuilding and Engineering Unions, representing 34 unions and over 2 million employees. This agreement sets forth general guidelines that establish the floor for additional bargaining at the plants. Labor agreements are administered at the plant level; however, they are not enforceable by law, and grievances are not subject to private arbitration.

Shop stewards are volunteers serving without pay. Unlike their U.S. counterparts, they cannot be removed by union executives. Often they accumulate much authority and influence at the plant and have more control over local union affairs than any national union official. Steward councils composed of union stewards from various unions and work councils representing members of the various departments are important in the labor relations system.

Labor agreements at the plant level are often negotiated by representatives of the national union, steward councils, and work councils. These agreements usually have no fixed term and include letters of understanding, minutes of meetings, and oral understandings. Although there is no legal obligation to negotiate, unions have gained extensive power and control over jobs, refusing to work with any employer whom they find in bad standing and maintaining strict membership discipline.

From 1979 to 1999, under the British conservative party's leadership, union membership in Great Britain was nearly halved (to 32 percent). In 1979, 90 percent of workers had their pay determined by collective bargaining; now, under 40 percent are covered by such agreements. An explosion of contingent pay plans has occurred, such as profit sharing, employee stock ownership, and merit pay. This era of deregulation included new industrial relations legislation being passed every 2 years, with changes affecting these areas. The responsibility for industrial relations was placed at the company level, and any collective bargaining agreement would cover only a single firm. Before, there had been multiemployer bargaining.

Today, management is free to decide whether to recognize the union. Disputes must be confined to specific locations, and secondary activities are prohibited. Employees must vote by ballot before union officials can call a strike. Compulsory union membership was outlawed, and workers can disregard a democratic vote to strike and continue to work.

In 1998 the New Labor Party introduced its industrial relations program, which differs from the conservative majority in three crucial areas. First, the first ever minimum wage was introduced in April 1999. Second, the belief was that the pendulum had swung too far in favor of unfettered management; therefore, laws supporting greater fairness at work, union recognition, and individual rights have been passed. Third, the New Labor party has embraced the European Union Social Charter, which supports maximum weekly hours of work and establishment of work councils in consultative and information-providing roles.

The New Labor Party's industrial relations program boosts both collective and individual rights. The new collective element is the statutory procedures for union recognition, and the individual rights include unfair dismissal, maternity pay, and representation rights. The government's objective is to promote labor–management cooperation over a statutory recognition procedure. The Central Arbitration Committee (CAC), similar to the National Labor Relations Board, has been established. If the union can demonstrate that a majority of the employees in the workplace are union members, then recognition will be automatic. If sufficient interest in the union exists, the CAC has authority to arrange an election.[64]

For the first time in 20 years large numbers of nonunion British employers are now seriously considering the issue of granting union recognition. After a prolonged period of "managerial Thatcherism," named after British's anti-union prime minister, trade unions are finding an improved industrial-political environment, especially with the passage of the Employment Relations Act of 1999, which established a statutory mechanism for gaining union representation.[65]

Under the New Labor Party, individual employees qualify under the unfair dismissal law after one year of service. Employees have the right to have their cases heard before an industrial tribunal. If the tribunal finds that an employee has been unfairly dismissed, the employee may receive back pay of up to 50,000 English pounds. Maternity benefits are available for up to 18 weeks, and family-parental leave (unpaid) is available for up to three months. Also, employees (both union and nonunion) are allowed to be accompanied by a fellow employee or union representative of their choice during the grievance or a disciplinary procedure.

The Tony Blair government signed the EU's Social Chapter. This signing included the Working Time Directive and the European Works Council Directive. The Working Time Directive includes a 48-hour weekly limit, night workers limited to 8 hours every 24 hours, one day off each week, and four weeks' paid annual vacation. The European Works Council Directive requires a large multinational company to set up a works council to provide greater information about the organization and to consult with employees on various matters that affect employees and their companies.[66]

Germany

Unlike the collective bargaining-oriented system of labor relations in the United States, the German system features two distinct levels and mechanisms for employee representation, one of which is directly concerned with collective bargaining. The 16 major unions reach highly general bargaining agreements with employer associations, usually annually. These agreements provide a general framework for implementation at the local level with emphasis on the specific circumstances of the company and the work councils at the work site.

In Germany the most important formal focus of wage bargaining is at the regional industry level, followed by the company or plant level. Because unions in Germany are organized on an industry basis, they generally do not have to compete for members. The largest union is the engineering union, I.G. Metall, which covers about 35 percent of employees. The I.G. Metall's main objective is to increase employment in engineering industries, such as autos and steel. Therefore, I.G. Metall needs to ensure that wage developments do not erode the competitiveness of engineering in the world economy. Much time in negotiations is spent discussing world engineering prices, export prospects, evolution of world prices and costs, prospective growth in labor productivity, and exchange rates.[67]

The general bargaining agreements are then tailored to specific circumstances within each company and operate within the work council system. Thus, bargaining between the industrial unions and the employer associations covers issues such as the costs of labor and human resource management practices, taking them out of competition among the individual firms.[68]

Wage Determination—Collective Bargaining With the unification of Germany, efforts have been made to harmonize pay rates for employees in the former republic of East Germany and those in western Germany. By 2004 in the public sector, the pay rates in eastern Germany were 92.5 percent of those in western Germany, 97 percent in the postal service, and 90 percent in the rail services. It must also be noted that employees in western Germany receive a range of payments, such as holiday pay, 13th month payment, and capital formation payments, not available to employees in eastern Germany. In addition, the working time in eastern Germany is 1.64 hours per week longer than that in the west.[69]

Wages and salaries in Germany are determined either by collective bargaining agreements or individual contracts. Although maximum hours per week are 48, actual working time is determined by collective bargaining. Vacations are legally fixed at a minimum of three weeks per year but may be extended through collective bargaining to up to six weeks.

Ninety percent of western German wage and salary earners are covered by collective bargaining agreements. Nearly all employers are members of an employer association and generally negotiate as members of the association. If an agreement is reached, it is legally binding on all members of the association. If the Ministry of Labor declares the collective bargaining agreement as "generally binding" (covers more than 50 percent of the workers in an area and is in the public interest), all employers in the same industry must abide by the agreement regardless of whether they are members.[70]

In 2000, Chancellor Gerhard Schroder helped to broker a new deal between employers and I.G. Metall, Germany's largest union of 3.4 million members. The deal limits wage increases to productivity increases and follows a labor agreement that would last several years instead of one. Under the 2000–2002 labor agreement, workers would receive a 3 percent increase in May 1, 2000, and a 2.1 percent increase in May 2001. Also, the new agreement keeps the work week at 35 hours, which is more than the union's demand of 32 hours. Chancellor Schroder hailed the agreement as a boost for the government's effort to create jobs (unemployment has been around 10 percent) while controlling for inflation.[71]

Co-determination After World War II, union and employer groups wanted to reshape their social, economic, and political institutions, including collective bargaining. A broad consensus emerged that economic concentration was not desirable, even considered dangerous, and that the only way the market economy could function safely was to temper the power of private enterprise by allowing free collective bargaining and worker participation or **co-determination** (*Mitbestimmung*) in management. In May 1951, the coal-steel co-determination law was passed to provide full-parity representation of labor and management on the supervisory boards of big mining and steel enterprises. In 1952 a Works Constitution Act was passed to establish works councils based on the idea of partnership and a traditional works council system. The law granted far-reaching consultation and partnership rights in personnel, economic, and social matters. In 1972 the law was amended to expand unions' rights. Union leaders were given virtually unlimited access to plants, were allowed to participate in plant meetings in an advisory capacity, and were given advance notice of the agendas of such meetings.

In 1976, the Codetermination Act of 1976 was passed; this act extended co-determination rights to large enterprises outside of the iron and steel industries. After six months of employment, employees are eligible to participate in the election of works councils. Because 80 to 90 percent of the elected work council members are union members, union have far-reaching control over this instrument of worker participation. The works council at each facility has the right to be informed, to be consulted, and to participate in company decisions. For example, if the company is planning employment changes, the workers have the right to be informed and consulted about personnel planning, vocational training, and new work methods.[72]

These consultation rights cover planned structural changes and prospective changes in equipment and working methods that affect job requirements, all decisions concerning manpower planning, and individual dismissals. If management fails to consult the works council on an employee dismissal, the dismissal will be rendered null and void. The works council has full co-determination rights with the employer on a set of issues as prescribed by law. These rights include commencement and termination of working hours, regulation of overtime, introduction and use of technical devices to monitor employee performance, bonus rates, and health and safety measures. Failure to reach an agreement on any of these issues leads to their adjudication through a conciliation panel.[73]

Regarding employee dismissals, the works council cannot prevent dismissals; however, it can suspend management's decision, and the dismissed employee must be able to remain on the job until a final court decision has been made. Thus, the German industrial relations system consists of a series of statutory mechanisms to share power over certain activities within the enterprise, as well as an overlapping private collective bargaining system.

At the plant level, labor representation and participation are implemented by worker members on the supervisory board, which appoints and in turn oversees the executive board, which controls the day-to-day management activities. In the coal, iron, and steel industries, the supervisory board is composed of an equal number of workers' and owners' representatives plus a neutral outsider. Three of the five labor representatives are nominated by the union, and two must be company employees. One member of the board is the labor director, who is in charge of personnel and social matters. By law, this director cannot be appointed or removed without the approval of the labor representatives on the supervisory board; therefore, in practice, the labor director is usually a union nominee.

In the small and medium-sized companies (up to 2,000 employees), the law provides for one-third worker representation on the supervisory board. As a result, the influence of unions on management decisions is not as strong as in the coal, iron, and steel industries. In larger companies (with more than 2,000 employees), labor has equal representation with stockholder representatives on the supervisory board. The members of the board elect a chair, and the labor representatives elect the vice chair. The labor members must include representatives of both blue and white collar workers and at least one managerial employee. Unions are also represented among the labor members and may have full-time union officials who are outside the company. The law provides for an industrial relations director who is a full member of the executive board and is responsible for personnel and social affairs of the enterprise. Unlike the iron and steel industries, this director may be appointed over the objections of the labor representatives on the supervisory board.

Employers have opposed parity co-determination and challenged the constitutionality of the 1976 law, but the Federal Constitutional Court rejected the suit and ruled that the act was compatible with the basic law. Unions have long desired to extend their rights beyond the coal, iron, and steel industries and have been successful. Although unions and management have their differences, both parties agree that worker participation has yielded a stabilizing element in the German industrial relations system.[74]

Central and Eastern Europe—Former Soviet Bloc Countries

Trade unions represent workers all over the region; however, their major role in many countries has been to exert political pressure. For instance, Solidarity in Poland, the original independent union in eastern Europe, has 2.5 million members and played a major role in the breakup of the Soviet bloc. Trade unions in Czechoslovakia led the revolution, and then members voted out the old leadership and democratized the union movement; however, the unions wanted the country to be divided along Czech and Slovak ethnic lines. In the former Soviet Union, the trade union movement has been in a state of rapid flux; however, coal miners have maintained their relative strength throughout the developments.[75]

Some countries in the former Soviet bloc are enjoying success in attracting new industries. Offering lower wages and lower manufacturing costs, businesses primarily from western Europe are investing in central Europe particularly. The transition to a market economy in Russia has been slow and judged not successful thus far. With 60 million workers, many have not been paid on time or are paid in rubles, which have continually lost their value. Factories do not have the funds to upgrade their plants, buy products from one another, or make payrolls. Faced with massive restructuring and operational inefficiencies that have been allowed to develop over the years, unemployment remains high.[76]

In the new Russia, employee shareholders appear to have little formal power, and trade unions also seem to lack power. Under communist control, trade unions were state organizations that were appendages to state-owned firms. Trade unions mainly served as social service organizations that helped to distribute social benefits. In other words, trade unions were company unions and had little independent power.[77]

The transformation of the labor relations system in Russia is proceeding slowly. Both unions and employers are basically independent of the state. At the national level, unions are independent of employers. At the enterprise level, collective bargaining is not being implemented.[78] Unions are only just beginning to learn the fundamentals of confronting management, negotiating contracts, and mapping out effective strike strategies.

The transfer of labor institutions from western Europe to central and eastern Europe has been slowly progressing. Although central and eastern Europe represent only 5.7 percent of Germany's foreign investments, the Czech Republic (10th) and Poland (5th) are among the 10 most attractive locations for Germany's direct investors. Germany has become the leading direct investor in Hungary and the Czech Republic, where it competes with the United States and France for the leading position. However, there is no evidence that these German companies are exporting the "German model" to eastern European countries. Instead, the German companies have adapted to the host country's institutions and environment and transferred only those labor relations practices, such as heavy emphasis on vocational training, long-term employment commitment, and consensual work organizations, which would be acceptable in the host country.[79]

The cultures, traditions, and beliefs of West Germans have been slowly introduced in East Germany. For example, Work Councils have been introduced in Hungary, and German labor legislation has been introduced in Slovenia. The nature of collective bargaining varies widely from merely endorsing legislation for consultation only to regulation of conflict. Collective agreements on pay appear to be widespread in the unionized sectors; however, employers refuse to negotiate on any other issues. Hungary and the Czech Republic have had the most employment deregulation and workplace change, but unions exercise fewer controls over employment contracts and working hours than elsewhere.

For numerous reasons, the countries in central and eastern Europe have not rapidly adopted western Europe's labor institutions. First, unions in the Soviet bloc functioned primarily as a department of the state; today, unions operate as truly voluntary organizations that gain their power through the support of their members. Union members are not prepared for "solidaristic" actions of open conflicts, legal rights, and duties of union members. Second, under communistic socialism, there was a paternalistic mentality, "cradle to the grave," whereas now, unions must rely on "voluntary" collective action to become effective. Third, unions in western Europe focus mostly on high-profile wage agreements; whereas in the past, unions focused on providing social and insurance services and had greater visibility on the plant floor. As a result, union members are disappointed in the western European–style unions, which have less frequent contact with its current members. Most experts believe that the adjustments will be steady and progressive; however, these will not be achieved overnight.[80]

Japan

Japan's labor relations system has four distinguishing characteristics: labor–management consultation and teamwork, lifetime employment, a wage system based on seniority, and the enterprise or company union. Management and employees communicate considerably more in Japan than in most other countries. Ninety percent of all Japanese companies have some sort of labor–management consultation. The flow of information is extensive. As examples, management reports to employees on the company's financial status, its problems, its expectations and plans, and on contemplated technological innovations before they occur. All aspects of employment, training, discipline, working conditions, and employee benefits are open for examination. Joint consultation includes subjects that a U.S. manager would classify as management prerogatives.[81]

Research has shown that when Japanese firms increase their information sharing with employee unions, the negotiations are shorter and easier, unions tend to demand and accept lower wage increases,[82] and profitability and productivity are improved.[83]

Teamwork and consensus building are a cultural heritage in Japan. Japanese employees feel comfortable with this approach, and both sides stress sharing of goals, responsibilities, and rewards. The communication links are through the normal channels at work, such as meetings, newsletters and bulletins, labor unions, and labor-management councils.[84]

Lifetime employment, a standard in Japan since the 1950s when employers agreed to this arrangement to quell labor unrest, has been applied to regular employees of large employers (500 or more employees), which make up about one-third of the nonagricultural workforce. These "regular employees" are hired after completing high school or college, with the expectation that they will be retained by the company until they reach the mandatory retirement age of 60. Legal, written contracts are nonexistent; however, unacceptable behavior may lead to a suggested voluntary resignation or a "hidden discharge." The result of this lifetime employment has been eagerness of employers to invest in training these long-term employees and responsiveness of employees not only to participate in training but to willingly accept innovation and technological advancement, knowing that they will not be adversely affected by a layoff.[85]

Although lifetime employment and seniority-based wages have been a long-term tradition within the Japanese labor relations system, the economic recession of the 1990s caused many Japanese businesses to consider changes in this tradition. While companies have generally made efforts to avoid layoffs, other measures have been taken, such as reduced hiring of new graduates, relocation of employees to subsidiaries, and restrictions on wage increases. Some of the major corporations are in the process of modifying the lifetime employment system, and many companies are more inclined to dismiss employees earlier than the usual retirement age of 60. As a result, there are indications that the degree of employee loyalty to their company has declined.[86]

When Japanese companies locate a plant in the United States, they most likely do not adopt the lifetime employment concept. Although over half of the Japanese plants have explicit "no-layoff" policies, only 5 percent of their plants located in the United States have a similar policy. The Japanese plants use temporary workers as a buffer to enhance employment security for their core workforce, whereas the U.S. counterparts use layoffs to adjust to a shortfall in demand for workers. For example, auto parts plants typically lay off employees for one month when retooling is required to meet new customer specifications. In Japan, companies tolerate periods of substantial underemployment to avoid layoffs. In fact, some Japanese companies donate their employees to perform community service during temporary slowdowns.[87]

The **wage system** in Japan has several distinguishing characteristics:

1. Salaries are paid monthly, even if the employee has been absent (with justification) from work.

2. Wage differentials are small between regular line employees and staff personnel, all of whom are members of the same union.

3. Wage distinctions exist between amounts earned for one's work (for example, efficiency output) and amounts earned for just being an employee (such as allowances for housing, transportation, and dependents).

4. Wages are accepted as permanent and lasting for the employee's entire career, including a minimum annual increase and a lump sum at retirement.[88]

Length of service and age are more highly correlated with wages in Japan than in other industrially developed countries. For example, between the ages of 40 and

50 the Japanese workers' wages are 67 percent greater than those of 21- to 24-year-old employees, whereas in the United States, the older employees' wages average only 23 percent more than those of younger workers. The smaller difference in income levels between managers and workers than in other countries contributes to the sense of unity among employees. Wage increases and promotions are primarily governed by the employee's age and the length of service in the company. The seniority-based wage system serves as a means of guaranteeing stability of employment throughout employees' careers within the company and is closely connected to the lifetime employment concept. In addition to wages, employees are provided fringe benefits that enable them to enjoy recreation and leisure activities, such as athletic competition, employee excursions, and so on. Employees have access to facilities for hobbies, including sports, reading, and board games. Companies offer special allowances for company-owned housing, dormitories for single workers, and various health and welfare benefits. Workers in smaller companies (which make up 60 percent of the total workforce) do not receive the same benefits or job security as those who are employed in the larger companies.[89]

The **enterprise union** is composed of employees working for a single employer at a single location. These unions comprise nearly 90 percent of all union organizations in Japan and include all categories of skills among employees of a company. The development of the enterprise union has been aided substantially by the system of lifetime employment and a heavy reliance on seniority. Thus, the individual employee identifies more closely with the company than does the typical employee in many western countries.

The enterprise unions are affiliated at the national level and have national organizations in the textile, electricity, shipbuilding, automobile, steel, appliance, and chemical industries. They hold conferences to discuss industrial policies; however, they do not discuss such topics as wages, working conditions, and other employment policies. These topics are discussed within the enterprise union. At the national level, industrial problems are discussed in a more general context, and issues such as economic growth, employment forecasts, retirement ages, and improved communications are addressed.[90]

Japan has over 70,000 unions; however, only about 25 percent of the workforce belongs to a union (far less than the 35 percent in 1975). The decline in union density is due in part to the reduction in the percentage of workers employed in manufacturing and other industries that tend to be highly unionized.[91]

Unions have received low wage increases in the last several years and are becoming more adversarial. Although the workdays lost because of strikes in Japan average less than in Canada, Australia, and the United States, workday losses are greater than those of Sweden, Norway, Germany, Austria, and the Netherlands, where work council systems prevail.

In the private sector, collective bargaining covers almost every conceivable aspect of labor–management relations. The results are formalized into a "comprehensive labor agreement." Issues that affect management and production, such as new plants and equipment and subcontracting, are normally handled in the process of the regular close consultations between the union and management. The comprehensive labor agreements normally do not cover wages because wages are determined in separate annual negotiations held during the *Shunto* (spring labor offensive). Wage negotiations are conducted by individual enterprises and their respective unions with coordination within an industrial group. In the public sector, both wages and employment conditions are determined by law. The National Personnel Authority makes annual recommendations (based on salary surveys) for salary increases for public employees to the Cabinet and national legislature, which makes the final determination.[92]

With Japan's strong trade balance (exports exceeding imports) and the subsequent appreciation of the yen, products made in Japan and shipped elsewhere have become more expensive, and pressures have mounted to reduce production and labor costs or to shift more production to countries where wages are lower, such as China, Korea, Taiwan, Singapore, or Hong Kong.

In the final analysis, Japanese employers and unions eventually will have to face many critical issues that may cause a break with the traditional system: early retirement, higher unemployment, elimination of automatic pay increases and promotions, introduction of labor-saving devices, union emphasis on job security rather than wage hikes, decline of employee loyalty to the firm, and declining competitiveness with rapidly developing countries such as Brazil, China, South Korea, Singapore, and Taiwan.[93]

Korea[94]

Korea has a tripartite labor relations system in which the Ministry of Labor serves as the governmental agency that formulates labor relations policy and implements and enforces labor relations laws, including child labor, forced labor, employment equality, wages, hours of work, and safety and health. The government continues to receive criticism of its policies concerning freedom of association and right to organize because the government refuses to register new trade unions in the public sector and arrests and imprisons trade unionists who participate in strikes.

The other parties, trade union federations and employer organizations, represent their constituents concerning labor relations matters by giving advice and guidance and serving on government advisory commissions. The Korean Employers' Federation (KEF) serves as an umbrella organization representing 13 regional employers' association, 30 trade associations, and about 4,000 enterprises. The KEF claims industrial peace and national economic development as its primary objectives and advocates its members' interests to the government and legislative bodies. In addition, the KEF provides advice to its members on labor law and industrial relations matters.

The 6,150 unions in Korea, with a membership of 1.6 million, may be organized by company, by occupation, by region, or by industry. While the majority of unions in Korea are enterprise-based unions, there are 44 industrial federations and 2 national federations: the Federation of Korean Trade Unions (FKTA) and the Korea Confederation of Trade Unions (KCTU). The FKTU is the largest labor organization in Korea and represents nearly 1 million workers in 3,408 unions. The KCTU grew out of an illegal "dissident" union movement and did not gain legal status until November 1999. The KCTU now represents about 600,000 workers in 16 industrial federations.

In the early 1990s, Korea was one of the fast-growing Asian "tiger economies," averaging 9 percent annual economic growth per year. However, in 1996, the Korea economy was slowed by the Asian financial and economic crisis, and in 1998, its economy actually declined by 6.7 percent. Then in 1999–2000, the economy grew at a rate of about 10 percent, only to decline again in 2001 with the worldwide economic slowdown. By 2002 and 2003, the Korea economy had regained its strength and returned to a growth status of around 7 percent. Production of semiconductors and radio, television, and communication equipment grew at a rate of over 20 percent, and motor vehicle production grew at 8.1 percent. However, textile production declined 6 percent as employers found lower cost producers in Southeast Asian countries.

Korea is governed by numerous labor laws. The Korean constitution guarantees freedom of association, the right to bargain collectively, and the right to collective action. However, strikes are prohibited in government agencies, state-owned enterprises, and defense industry companies. A majority of union members must vote in favor of striking by direct, secret, and unsigned balloting, and the union must report the planned strike in advance and in writing to the appropriate administrative agencies. There were 322 strikes and 16 lockouts in 2002 involving a total of 93,859 workers and a loss of 1.5 million working days.

Labor relations is governed by five separate laws; the most comprehensive is the Trade Union and Labor Relations Adjustment Act (TULRAA), which among other provisions protects workers from dismissal for organizing and joining unions and for participating in union activities. A worker may seek relief for any such unfair labor practice by filing a complaint with the Labor Relations Commission (LRC) or by bringing a civil suit against the employer. Employers who are found guilty of an unfair labor practice can be required to reinstate the worker and provide back pay.

Individual and collective labor disputes are adjudicated and mediated or arbitrated by the LRC, which operates at the regional and national levels. In 2002, a total of 9,121 cases were filed with the LRC; 8,024 cases were adjudicated and 1,097 were mediated or arbitrated. As a general rule, collective bargaining takes place at the enterprise level, but a union may delegate negotiation responsibility to the trade union federation with which it is affiliated. Collective bargaining usually covers wages, hours of work, workers' welfare, and other employment conditions. The collective bargaining agreements are valid for up to two years; however, if a new agreement is not concluded by the expiration date of a current agreement even though the parties are engaged in negotiations, the existing agreement will remain in effect for another three months. Negotiations may extend to trade union activities during working hours and issues concerning full-time union officers. By 15 days after completion of negotiations, the collective bargaining agreement must be submitted to the appropriate administrative agencies. If any provision of the agreement is determined to be unlawful, the parties may be ordered to amend the unlawful provision(s).[95]

Australia

Australian unions are organized more on a craft or occupational basis than on an industrial or enterprise basis. Unions have organized 25 percent of the workforce, but this average underestimates their pivotal influence in key sectors, such as mining (88 percent), transport, construction, and manufacturing (81 percent), and the public sector (50 percent). The Australian Council of Trade Unions (ACTU) is the only umbrella organization for all Australian unions. It has 46 registered unions representing about 1.8 million workers and has a branch in each state.

Australia has a highly centralized labor relations system that differs markedly from its American counterpart, although significant movement toward enterprise bargaining has been made in the last five years. The Australian system is characterized by industrywide or companywide "Awards," which are negotiated by company, union and sometimes government officials and then submitted to the federal Australia Industrial Relations Commission (AIRC) for ratification or resolution of differences. Such "Awards" establish minimum wages and working conditions for specific categories of workers and are the approximate equivalent of an American collective bargaining agreement. As an example, if a union claims a wage for one class of worker, such as a metal machinist, an "Award" for a wage increase would apply to all machinists in the same class throughout Australia. This mechanism has led to rampant wage-push inflation in the 1970s as unions fought to protect the value of workers' real wages. In the 1980s, the government restricted wage claims and price increases by companies. In the 1990s, an increasing number of agreements were based on productivity in the form of enterprise agreements, but most workers remained solely under the awards system.

In addition, individual companies and their employees or unions may negotiate supplemented "over award" wage benefits based on market conditions. These benefits when registered are known as "certified agreements" (achieved through enterprise bargaining) if they cover most or all of company's workforce or "Australian Workplace Agreements" if they cover an individual employee. Although 80 percent of all wage and salary earners are covered by the "Awards" system, the greatest portion of employees receive over-award payments through some form of enterprise agreement.

The Australian constitution restricts the federal government's role in industrial relations to "conciliation and arbitration for the prevention of industrial disputes extending beyond the limits of one state." However, state governments are not restricted from enacting legislation concerning wages or other benefits, and most states have established State Industrial Relations Commissions that fulfill similar functions to the federal AIRC. There is no legal provision per se for the right to strike in Australia, and unions and workers are prohibited from striking in companies engaged in interstate commerce, except when they are negotiating a new employment agreement. Any strike must concern a matter specifically related to the negotiations. The strike is known as a "protected action" during a "bargaining period," and industrial disputes are then intended to be settled via conciliation and, if necessary, compulsory arbitration by the AIRC. In the past five years, the number of workdays lost to industrial actions has been steadily declining. For disputes within a state, each state government has its own varying restrictions on unions and workers' right to strike. When unions strike outside of a bargaining period or engage in secondary boycotts, they can be sued by employers for damages under common law. Moreover, union officials and individual strikers can be held personally liable.[96]

In Australia, unions are allowed to negotiate provisions in collective bargaining agreements that require employees who are not union members to pay a bargaining fee (similar to the agency shop arrangement in the United States covered in Chapter 4). Unions have been successful in the inclusion of these provisions in 236 agreements by 2002; however, employers have launched a campaign to pass legislation that would prohibit the bargaining fees.[97]

An unusual part of the Australian labor relations system is the allowance of a nonunion bargaining provision. Companies may negotiate agreements with their nonunion employees without the union. Although unions vehemently oppose this provision and practice, 11 nonunion agreements have been negotiated, but only one of which covers a large number of employees. Unions fought against the inclusion of this provision in the act because they believed that it would lead to deunionization, reduced wages, and poorer working conditions.[98]

Also, Australian law contains a stringent provision that forbids the "unfair dismissal" of employees, thereby making it more difficult for employers to terminate employees.[99] With the unfair dismissal legislation, some may infer that the legislation would raise the costs and reduce the willingness of employers to dismiss employees. Under the administration of the unfair dismissal law, employers who have dismissed employees without just cause have been encouraged to develop a rule-based disciplinary system. When and if this is done, the disciplinary rules will not inhibit the use of dismissal.[100]

China

Before China opened to the rest of the world and engaged in reform, labor relations in China were unusual. Labor relations were in fact relations between the employee and the government, instead of between work units and laborers. The Premier of the State Council was the only boss; the only authoritative labor relationship was formed between the central government and the workers. This abnormal arrangement came to an end in the last two decades. However, the Chinese employment system is more complex now than it was in the late 1970s. There are 730 million employees in China; 240 million in urban areas and 490 million in rural areas. Within the urban areas, there are many types of employers: state-owned enterprises, state units, collective units, private and individually owned enterprises, and foreign-owned enterprises. The government is not involved in hiring among the collective units and private enterprises, and the state-owned enterprises now have more autonomy in employment decisions. Although employment remains rather stable, employers now treat staffing levels more flexibly than in the past. In 2001, employers terminated their relationship with 1.4 million workers, and these workers had no right to appeal the employment decisions.[101]

The leading trade union organization is the All-China Congress of Trade Unions (AFCTU), which was founded in 1921, one year after the founding of the Communist Party of China (CPC). When the CPC took over, trade unions were one the three Leninist Mass Party organizations, but they were not given any bargaining status at the national or enterprise level. In the 1950s, the trade union movement helped the CPC bring industry under state control. In the early 1960s, the AFCTU sought and achieved a short-lived institutional upgrade; however, the Cultural Revolution in 1965 brought about a purge of the AFCTU and its disbandment. In 1978, with the removal of the Maoist regime and the launching of modernization of China with a goal of quadrupling China's GNP by 2000 coupled with ownership, enterprise management, and distribution of wealth, trade unions were once again reconstituted to play a more appropriate role.

Trade unions in China had been dominated by "welfarism" and played a role in surveillance and control of the workers rather than serving as a political representative of the working class. Trade unions were viewed more as a "caretaker" of workers that channel their grievance to higher authorities. In China, the CPC controlled the unions and dictated the unions' programs. The CPC held absolute control of the union, and the union leaders remained answerable only to the heads of state, not the working population. In 1992, the National People's Congress passed amendments to the Trade Union Law in which unions were given consultative status rather than collective bargaining power. The fact of the matter was the trade unions were given the task of supporting the state's economic program.[102]

The Chinese system has evolved from a centrally planned economy to a guided market economy open to foreign investments. Under the centrally planned economy, employees were assigned to state-owned enterprises that guaranteed lifetime employment and a wide range of benefits, including housing and education. Wage levels were set centrally, and the Communist Party served in a supervisory capacity in the factory. In the 1980s, changes in employment relations began to align with an emerging market economy; that is, enterprises attempted to become more competitive, and firms with foreign investments were allowed to operate without undue state interference. Centralized job allocation and state guarantees of lifetime employment were relaxed, and firms no longer were required to provide social welfare benefits. In the mid-1980s, employment laws required that new workers be hired on fixed-term contracts, but the terms could not exceed four years. In addition, employers were authorized to dismiss employees under certain circumstances. The authority of factory managers was increased, and pay linked to performance was introduced. In the early 1990s, new regulations allowed factory managers to lay off surplus workers through voluntary resignations but required the firms to try to find work for these employees and/or train them for new jobs. Meanwhile, the government did not allow independent unions or any form of collective action in industrial disputes. State-controlled trade unions continued to exist at the enterprise, industry, and regional levels. A dispute settlement law that applied to a broad range of issues was passed, and arbitration tribunals were also established. However, individual disputes accounted for 93 percent of the disputes, and work stoppages were likely to come in the form of spontaneous actions in the outlying provinces, which are less subject to control from Beijing and foreign-owned enterprises. In recent years, there have been rising protests against unemployment and job insecurity, thereby suggesting a role for dispute-resolution procedures designed to secure and maintain industrial peace.

In 1990s, China industrialized rapidly and became the largest recipient of foreign direct investment of all developing countries and increasingly engaged in international trade. In 1994, China consolidated its labor laws and applied them to domestic and foreign-invested enterprises. The 1994 act gave the state-controlled unions the right to enter into collective bargaining with employers on a prescribed range of matters, including wages and working conditions. Technical assistance on collective bargaining dispute-settling procedures was provided by the International Labor Organization (ILO). Minimum standards on wages, hours of work, health and safety, and discrimination against women and young workers were established. By 1995 there were fewer than 11,000 collective bargaining agreements, but it is unclear to what extent bargaining actually took place. In fact, the Chinese workers have little faith in their unions, which perform primarily a social welfare function.

In China, there still existed a gap between the formal rules and actual practice. The formal system of laws and regulations, which is supplemented by local interpretation, is unevenly enforced. For example, firms were able to extend working hours beyond the 60 hour a week maximum by seeking permission from the local government authority, and permission was rarely denied. Local officials sacrificed enforcing labor standards in the interests of attracting investments and generating additional jobs. In order to be competitive, firms followed a formal strategy of cost reduction and productivity; young female workers were employed in low-skilled light manufacturing jobs, and violations of working conditions and dismissal regulations were common. There remained numerous surplus workers (about one-third of the workforce) and this surplus has contributed to significant problems.[103]

In recent years, the state-owned enterprises have tried to modernize their practices. When this occurred, the gap between the status of manager and workers in enterprises widened. Managers of the enterprises assume increased powers in employment, personnel adjustment, and wage distribution, while workers observed that their status fell due to job cuts and rising unemployment. Therefore, the dominant role in enterprise employment relations was passed from the state to managers. The economic reforms have given autonomy to enterprises and their managers on issues like employment and wages. The reforms have also given workers the right to select their jobs. Regulations and control by the market have replaced regulation and control by the state. In some state-owned enterprises, arbitration, mediation, and litigation were being used in labor disputes.

The penetration rate of labor unions in private businesses has been far below that of state-owned enterprises. Labor unions, used to long-term workplace relationships and stable labor contracts, find it challenging to adapt to the characteristics of Chinese private businesses. Foreign-owned enterprises have occurred through joint ventures and cooperative relationships. From the beginning, these firms have managed to attract high-quality workers and have offered higher wages than those in the state-owned enterprises. In the state-owned enterprises, the tradition is low wages and high benefits; in the foreign-owned enterprises, workers are rewarded on the basis of productivity.

By October 2002, the Ministry of Labor and Social Security issued the "Trial Regulation over Collective Bargaining on Wages," which allows the parties to bargain collectively. Over time, this regulation will establish a mechanism that involves employers, worker representatives, and government in the resolution of labor disputes; however, much work is still to be done.[104]

Reform in the employment system must be viewed within its full context because China has moved from a controlled economic system to a socialist market system aimed at opening China to the world. The guiding ideas of the employment reforms are to reduce government management, strengthen government's ability to offer services to workers, and maintain workers' rights and benefits. As a result the following changes have been adopted:

- Moving the central government from controlling all administrative details of work to focusing on a few basic factors, such as minimum wages.

- Shifting from "approval ahead" to "supervise behind." Before economic reform, enterprises needed to ask government for instructions and approval before solving a problem. Now, government has established laws and regulations that explain the government's requirements for enterprises and the government needs only to "supervise from behind."

- Changing from unilateral decision making to bilateral consulting. In a centralized planned economy, the government decided whom to hire. With reform, the interests of three parties, the government, the enterprise, and the employee, are considered. Today, the enterprise can select the employees, and a worker can select their work unit and position.

- Adopting minimum standards. In the past, Chinese managers relied on detailed regulations and labor conditions. In 1994, legislation set minimum standards for wages and established the age at which young people can be employed.

- Adopting new kinds of enterprises. In a controlled economy, all enterprises were publicly owned. Now, consistent with international rules, there are all kinds of public and private enterprises that have the same rights and are treated equally under the law.

- Sticking to a market orientation. With economic reform, there have been challenges and resistance. For example, the bilateral labor contract system was strongly opposed, but it is now one of the basic elements of the employment system.[105]

In the Western world, labor and management enter negotiations, which typically lead to collective bargaining agreements. In China, autocratic management, nepotism, and unprofessional, undisciplined management techniques have dominated the workplace. Managers have viewed their firm as their personal kingdom, and paternalism has led workers to expect a certain level of economic and noneconomic support from their employers. Unity of labor–management interests has usually been more important than personal disagreements. While there has been significant change in China since 1988, China is a long way from embracing Western-style employment relations, strong unions, and collective bargaining. China remains constrained by its cultural and political history and by a large supply of low-wage workers. Moreover, its labor relations system does not appear likely to demonstrate major changes for many years.[106]

SUMMARY

Multinational corporations and transnational collective bargaining are becoming increasingly important topics of labor relations. Although multinational corporations continue to grow in sales volume, capital investments, and economic influence, they have also aroused trade unions in various countries to combine their energies, skills, and power in an effort to negotiate on an equal footing. Thus far, little success has been achieved because of legal, political, social, economic, and organizational obstacles. However, it is obvious that transnational collective bargaining could have a tremendous impact on the world's economy if the obstacles can be eliminated. Time will tell whether unions will be able to overcome the obstacles.

With the growing interdependency among nations, it is imperative that students who study labor relations learn more about labor relations systems throughout the world. This chapter highlights the major features of the major trading partners of the United States. The labor relations system of Canada has expressed concern over the United States' economically dominant role in North America and its influence in the internal affairs of that country. Its system features two major linguistic and cultural groups and highly decentralized collective bargaining activities that are governed by provincial law. Mexico, the other partner with Canada and the United States in the North American Free Trade Agreement (NAFTA), has fairly well-developed labor laws but has deficiencies in their administration. The effects of NAFTA on jobs and trade unions are discussed.

Cuba, the largest Caribbean island, has a labor relations system which has suffered under the Castro regime, but is showing signs of change. Labor relations vary widely among the countries in Central and South America, but they have one common feature: a close connection between trade unions and political parties.

Unionization in most of western Europe is significantly greater than in the United States, and there is wide implementation of co-determination and employee participation policies. In 1992, 12 countries in western Europe joined together to form the European Union (EU), which provided for greater deregulation and a decrease in trade and travel barriers between member countries. In 2004, the European Community (EU) added 10 countries and the EU market grew to 450 million. The formation of the EU increased the need to learn more about the labor relations system in each of these countries and will probably bring these countries closer together. In the past, the labor movements in many eastern European countries were dominated by the Soviet Union. The countries of the former Soviet bloc are now trying to adjust to a market economy.

Unique features of the Japanese system include labor–management consultations, teamwork, a lifetime employment policy, a wage system primarily based on seniority, and the enterprise union. However, international money exchange rate fluctuations and recession could quickly alter these special union-management relationships of the Japanese system.

South Korean labor relations have developed rapidly from a strike-ridden system in 1987 to more successful collective bargaining. With high growth rates, South Korea still has problems of discrimination against women and employment of child labor. The Australian system involves the right to strike, decentralized bargaining, nonunion bargaining, and an unfair dismissal law.

The chapter ends with a description of the Chinese labor relations system, which has experienced rapid change in recent years; however, the system has far to go before becoming similar to Western labor relations systems.

KEY TERMS

- multinational corporation (MNC)
- whipsawing
- co-determination
- North American Free Trade Agreement (NAFTA)
- wage system
- enterprise union

DISCUSSION QUESTIONS

1. Although we share a common border with Canada, its labor relations system is affected by a number of variables that do not greatly affect the United States. Enumerate and explain these variables.

2. Explain why labor unions in many Latin American countries have developed more slowly than those in the United States.

3. Western Europe seems to be uniquely involved with various forms of worker participation. What are some reasons that these worker participation systems have developed so fully there instead of elsewhere?

4. What are the four special features of the Japanese system? Why haven't they been adopted in the United States?

5. Although multinational corporations seem to be growing in size and influence, what must occur before transnational collective bargaining can be effectively carried out?

6. Which features of Canada's labor relations system would you transfer to the United States?

7. Assess the transformation of the Australian labor relations system.

8. Give your assessment of the requirements for Cuba to develop a free, independent trade union. Is it essential for a free society?

EXPLORING THE WEB

Labor Relations in Multinational Corporations and in Other Countries

1. The International Labour Organization   The International Labour Organization (ILO) has established labor standards for 150 countries represented by the Organization. How does the ILO say that these standards are enforced? What is the Declaration of Philadelphia? (Click on About the ILO.)

http://www.ilo.org

2. Foreign Labor Trends   Search the Foreign Labor Statistics Home Page of the Bureau of Labor Statistics to find the following information:

Hourly compensation costs in U.S. dollars for production workers in manufacturing in 2002 for the United States, France, Canada, Mexico, and Ireland.

How did the unemployment rate in Canada compare with the rate in the United States in 2003?

http://stats.bls.gov/fls

3. Guidelines for Multinational Corporations   Under the Guidelines for Multinational Corporations established by the Organization for Economic Cooperation and Development, summarize the content of the section under Employment and Industrial Relations. Under Competition, what actions may adversely affect competition? Use the search block to search for Guidelines.

www.oecd.org

4. Multinational Labor Organizations   Search for membership information and mission statements for the following labor organizations:

International Federation of Airline Pilots Association

http://www.ifalpa.org

International Metalworkers Federation

http://www.imfmetal.org

International Federation of Chemical, Energy,
Mine and General Workers (ICEM)

http://www.icem.org

REFERENCES

1. "Fortune Global 500," *Fortune*, July 21, 2003, p. 106.

2. George Melloan, "Feeling the Muscles of the Multinationals," *The Wall Street Journal*, January 6, 2004, p. A19.

3. William J. Zeile, "U.S. Affilitates of Foreign Companies," *Survey of Current Business* 83, no. 8 (August 2003), p. 38–45.

4. Thomas W. Anderson, "Foreign Direct Investment in the United States," *Survey of Current Business* 83, no. 6 (June, 2003), pp. 55–56.

5. "The World's View of Multinationals," *The Economist*, January 29, 2000, p. 21.

6. Thane Peterson, "Is Japan Using the U.S. as a Back Door to Europe?" *Business Week*, November 14, 1988, p. 57.

7. Mario F. Bognanno, Michael P. Keane, and Donghoon Yang, "The Influence of Wages and Industrial Relations Environments on the Production Location Decisions of U.S. Multinational Corporations," *Working Paper*, January 1998, p. 23.

8. Harry Shaiken, "Globalization and the Worldwide Division of Labor," *Monthly Labor Review* 110 (August 1987), p. 47.

9. Marvin J. Levine, "Labor Movements and the Multinational Corporation: A Future for Collective Bargaining?" *Employee Relations Law Journal* 13 (Winter 1987–88), pp. 382–398.

10. Rajib N. Sanyal, "Unionizing Foreign-Owned Firms: Perceptions of American Union Officials," *Labor Studies Journal* 14 (Winter 1989), p. 66.

11. "Hands Across the Workplace," *Time*, December 26, 1988, pp. 15–18; "Working for the Japanese," *Time*, September 14, 1987; Paul Hemp, "Britain's 'Intransigent' Rubber Workers Bow to Japanese Management Practices," *The Wall Street Journal*, March 29, 1988, p. 26.

12. "Canada's UAW Thumbs Its Nose at Concessions," *Business Week*, July 26, 1982, p. 23.

13. Charles R. Greer and John Shearer, "Do Foreign-Owned U.S. Firms Practice Unconventional Labor Relations?" *Monthly Labor Review* 104 (January 1981), pp. 45–47.

14. Duane Kujawa, "Collective Bargaining and Labor Relations in Multinational Enterprise: A U.S. Public Policy Perspective," in *Research in International Business and Finance*, ed. Robert G. Hawkins (Greenwich, Conn.: JAI Press, Inc., 1979), p. 37.

15. Robert F. Banks and Jack Stieber, "Introduction," in *Multinationals, Unions, and Labor Relations in Industrial Countries* (Ithaca, N.Y.: New York State School of Industrial and Labor Relations, 1977), p. 1.

16. See Richard L. Rowan, Herbert R. Northrup, and Rae Ann O'Brien, *Multi-*

national Union Organizations in the Manufacturing Industries (Philadelphia, Penn.: University of Pennsylvania, 1980).

17. Geoffrey W. Latta and Janice R. Bellace, "Making the Corporation Transparent: Prelude to Multinational Bargaining," *Columbia Journal of World Business* 18 (Summer 1983), p. 73.

18. Hoyt N. Wheeler, *The Future of the American Labor Movement* (Cambridge, Mass.: Cambridge University Press, 2002), pp. 160–162.

19. "Update on Global Agreements," *European Industrial Relations Review,* June 2003, pp. 26–29.

20. Banks and Stieber, *Multinationals, Unions, and Labor Relations,* pp. 11–12.

21. Levine, "Labor Movements and the Multinational Corporation," pp. 392–398.

22. G. B. J. Bomers, *Multinational Corporations and Industrial Relations* (Amsterdam, The Netherlands: Van Gorcum, Assen, 1976) p. 179.

23. Herbert R. Northrup, "Why Multinationals Bargaining Neither Exists Nor Is Desirable," *Labor Law Journal* 29 (June 1978), pp. 330–331.

24. Lori G. Kletzer, "Globalization and American Job Loss: Public Policy to Help Workers," *Perspectives on Work* 6, no. 1 (2002), pp. 28–30.

25. "Stolen Jobs?" *The Economist,* December 13, 2003, pp. 13–15; "Relocating the Back Office," *The Economist,* December 13, 2003, pp. 67–68.

26. Michael Schroeder, "U.S. Manufacturing Activity Surges," *The Wall Street Journal,* December 2, 2003, p. A-2.

27. "Stolen Jobs?" *The Economist,* December 13, 2003, pp. 13–15; "Relocating the Back Office," *The Economist,* December 13, 2003, pp. 67–68; Charles Schumer and Paul Craig Roberts, "Second Thoughts on Free Trade," *New York Times,* January 6, 2004, p. A27.

28. http://www.aflcio.org/issuespolitics/globaleconomy.

29. http://www.fas.usda.gov/info/factsheets/nafta.

30. "Free Trade on Trial" *The Economist,* January 3, 2004, pp. 13–16; Joseph E. Stiglitz, "The Broken Promise of NAFTA, *New York Times,* January 6, 2004, p. A27.

31. Francisco Zapata, NAFTA: Few Gains for Mexico's Workers," *Perspectives on Work* 6, no. 1 (2002), pp. 22–24.

32. "Mexico: Was NAFTA Worth It?" *Business Week,* December 22, 2003, pp. 66–72.

33. "Free Trade on Trial" *The Economist,* January 3, 2004, pp. 13–16; Joseph E. Stiglitz, "The Broken Promsie of NAFTA, *New York Times,* January 6, 2004, p. A27.

34. Rainer Dombois, "The North American Agreement on Labor Cooperation: Designed to Fail?" *Perspectives on Work* 6, no. 1 (2002), pp. 19–21.

35. Mario F. Bognanno and Jiangfeng Lu, "NAFTA's Labor Side Agreement: Withering as an Effective Labor Law Enforcement and MNC Compliance Strategy?" *Multinational Companies and Global Human Resource Strategies,* ed. William N. Cooke (Westport, Conn.: Quorum Books, 2003), pp. 391–393.

36. Jon Hiatt, "Discussion," *Proceedings of the 52nd Annual Meeting of the Industrial Relations Research Association,* ed. Paula B. Voos (Champaign, Ill.: IRRA, 2000), pp. 278–280.

37. Diana Chew and Richard A. Posthuma, "International Employment Dispute Resolution Under NAFTA's Side Agreement on Labor," *Labor Law Journal* 53 (2002), p. 45.

38. Hoyt N. Wheeler and Jaques Rojot, "General Comments," in *Workplace Justice: Employment Obligations in International Perspective* (Columbia, S.C.: University of South Carolina Press, 1992), pp. 368–369.

39. Joseph B. Rose and Gary N. Chaison, "Union Density and Union Effectiveness: The North American Experience," *Proceedings of the 9th World Congress of the International Industrial Relations* Association (Sydney, Australia: International Industrial Relations Association, 1992), p. 528.

40. Jean Boivin, "The Transformation of Canadian Employment Relations," *Perspectives on Work* 1, no. 2 (1997), pp. 40–44.

41. Rafael Gomez and Seymour Martin Lipset, and Noah Meltz, "Frustrated

Demand for Unionization: The Case of the United States and Canada Revisited," *Proceedings of the 53rd Annual Meeting of the Industrial Relations Research Association,* ed. Paula B. Voos (Champaign, Ill.: IRRA, 2001), pp. 163–171.

42. Joseph B. Rose and Gary N. Chaison, "Canadian Labor Policy as a Model for Legislative Reform in the United States," *Labor Law Journal* 46 (May 1995), p. 259. See Richard N. Block and Karen Roberts, "An Overview of Labor Standards in the United States and Canada" *Labor Law Journal* 49 (September 1998), pp. 1127–1133.

43. Daphne G. Taras, "Explaining Canadian-American Differences in Union Density," *Proceedings of the 53rd Annual Meeting of the Industrial Relations Research Association,* ed. Paula B. Voos (Champaign, Ill.: IRRA, 2001), pp. 153–159.

44. Joseph B. Rose and Gary N. Chaison, "Linking Union Density and Union Effectiveness: The North American Experience," *Industrial Relations* 35 (January 1996), pp. 78–105.

45. *Canada* (Washington, D.C.: U.S. Department of Labor, Bureau of International Labor Affairs, 1992), pp. 5–11.

46. *Mexico* (Washington, D.C.: U.S. Department of Labor, Bureau of International Labor Affairs, 2002), pp. 4–6. For more information about Mexican legislation involving employment security and employment discrimination, see: Charles Hollon, "Discrimination in Employment Provisions in the Mexican Federal Labor Law," *Employee Responsibilities and Rights Journal,* 11, no. 1 (1998), pp. 65–70; Charles Hollon, "Individual Employee Employment Security under Mexican Federal Labor Law," *Labor Law Journal* 47 (October 1996), pp. 648–656.

47. Russell E. Smith, "NAFTA and Industrial Relations in Mexico: What's Important Now?" *Perspectives on Work* 6, no. 1 (2002), pp. 25–27.

48. *Mexico,* Washington, D.C.: U.S. Printing Office, 2002, pp. 4–6.

49. Charles J. Hollon, "Employee Profit Sharing under the Mexican Labor Law," *Labor Law Journal* 47 (May 1996), pp. 323–326.

50. Craig Torres, "Mexico Reaches Wage and Price Accord," *The Wall Street Journal,* October 30, 1995, p. A14.

51. Everett M. Kassalow, *Trade Unions and Industrial Relations: An International Comparison* (New York: Random House, 1969), pp. 302–303.

52. "Europe's Unions Are Losing Their Grip," *Business Week,* November 26, 1986, pp. 80–84.

53. Karl O. Magnusen and Leonardo Rodriguez, "Cuba, Labor, and Change," *Labor Studies Journal* 23 (Summer 1998), pp. 22–39.

54. Everett M. Kassalow, "Conflict and Cooperation in Europe's Industrial Relations," *Industrial Relations* 13 (May 1974), pp. 156–163.

55. "Eleven European Leaders Endorse EC Worker Rights Code, Thatcher Objects," *Daily Labor Report,* December 12, 1989, p. A-3; "Social Charter: Action Programme Released," *European Industrial Relations Report* no. 112 (January 1990), pp. 11–14.

56. Roy J. Adams, "Industrial Relations in Europe and North America: Some Contemporary Themes," *European Journal of Industrial Relations* 1, no. 1 (1995), p. 50.

57. Margaret Hilton, "Shared Training: Learning from Germany," *Monthly Labor Review* 114 (March 1991), pp. 33–35; Robert J. Gitter, "Job Training in Europe: Lessons from Abroad," *Monthly Labor Review* 115 (April 1992), pp. 25–27.

58. "Europe's Union to Grow by 10," *New York Times,* December 2, 2003, p. C-4; *European Union 2003,* Washington, D.C.: U. S. Printing Office, 2003, pp. 17–19.

59. "Introduction—Special Report," *Daily Labor Report,* June 22, 1990, p. 3.

60. John T. Addison and W. Stanley Siebert, "The Social Charter of the European Community: Evolution and Controversies," *Industrial and Labor Relations Review* 44 (July 1991), pp. 597–623.

61. Trevor Bain and Kim Hester, "Similarities and Differences in a Sample of European Works Council Agreements," *Proceedings of the 52nd Annual Meeting of the Industrial Relations Research Association,* ed. Paula B. Voos (Champaign, Ill.: IRRA, 2000), pp. 45–47.

62. Paul Marginson, "The Eurocompany and Euro Industrial Relations," *European Journal of Industrial Relations* 6, no.

6 (2000), pp. 9–30; Jane Wills, "Great Expectations: Three Years in the Life of a European Works Council," *European Journal of Industrial Relations* 8, no. 1 (2000), pp. 85–107.

63. "A Work in Progress: A Survey of Europe," *The Economist,* October 23, 2000, pp. 3–18.

64. David Metcalf, "Prime Minister Blair's New Labor Industrial Relations Program," *Work in Perspectives* 3, no. 1 (1999), pp. 12–17.

65. Gregory Gall, "Employer Opposition to Union Recognition in Britain," *Proceedings of the 53rd Annual Meeting of the Industrial Relations Research Association,* ed. Paula B. Voos (Champaign, Ill.: IRRA, 2002), p. 243.

66. David Metcalf, "Prime Minister Blair's New Labor Industrial Relations Program," *Work in Perspectives* 3, no. 1 (1999), pp. 12–17.

67. David Soskice, "The German Wage Bargaining System," *Proceedings of the 46th Annual Meeting of the Industrial Relations Research Association,* ed. Paula B. Voos (Madison, Wis.: Industrial Relations Research Association, 1994), p. 350.

68. Kirsten S. Wever, "German Employers' View of Labor Representation," *Proceedings of the 45th Annual Meeting of the Industrial Relations Research Association* (Madison, Wis.: Industrial Relations Research Association, 1992), pp. 109–110.

69. "Collective Bargaining in 2002," *European Industrial Relations Review,* April 2003, pp. 21–24.

70. *Germany* (Washington, D.C.: U.S. Department of Labor, Bureau of International Labor Affairs, 1999), pp. 6–12.

71. "Germany Metal Buckles," *The Economist,* April 1, 2000, pp. 46–48.

72. *Germany* (Washington, D.C.: U.S. Department of Labor, Bureau of International Labor Affairs, 1999), pp. 12–15.

73. John T. Addison, Claus Schnabel, and Joachim Wagner, "On the Determinants of Mandatory Works Councils in Germany," *Industrial Relations* 36 (October 1997), pp. 422–423.

74. *Germany* (Washington, D.C.: U.S. Department of Labor, Bureau of International Labor Affairs, 1999), pp. 14–23.

75. *World Labor Report* 1992 (Geneva: International Labour Office, 1992), p. 57.

76. Peter Galuszka, "Toss Another Match into the Russian Tinderbox: Labor," *Business Week,* June 6, 1994, p. 51.

77. Joseph R. Blasi, "Russian Labor-Management Relations: Some Preliminary Lessons from Newly Privatized Enterprises," *Proceedings of the 47th Annual Meeting of the Industrial Relations Research Association,* ed. Paula B. Voos (Madison, Wis.: Industrial Relations Research Association, 1995), p. 230.

78. Michael Ballot, "Labor Relations in Russia and Eastern Europe," *Labor Law Journal* 46 (March 1995), p. 170.

79. Katharina Bluhm, "Exporting or Abandoning the 'German Model'?: Labour Policies of German Manufacturing Firms in Central Europe," *European Journal of Industrial Relations* 7, no. 2 (July 2001), pp. 153–168.

80. Carola M. Frege, "Transferring Labor Institutions to Emerging Economies: The Case of East Germany," *Industrial Relations* 38 (October 1999), pp. 459–481; Anna Pollert, "Trade Unionism in Transition in Central and Eastern Europe," *European Journal of Industrial Relations* 5, no. 2 (1999), pp. 209–226.

81. Joseph Krislov, "How Does the Japanese Industrial Relations System Differ?" *Labor Law Journal* 40 (June 1989), pp. 338–344.

82. Motohiro Morishima, "Information Sharing and Collective Bargaining in Japan: Effects of Wage Negotiations," *Industrial and Labor Relations Review* 44 (April 1991), pp. 469–482.

83. Motohiro Morishima, "Information Sharing and Firm Performance in Japan," *Industrial Relations* 30 (Winter 1991), pp. 37–57.

84. Kiyoshi Kawahito, "Labor Relations in the Japanese Automobile and Steel Industries," *Journal of Labor Research* 11 (Summer 1990), pp. 232–237.

85. Katsumi Yakabe, *Labor Relations in Japan* (Tokyo: International Society for Educational Information, 1974), pp. 1–14; Hisashi Kawada and Ryuji Komatsu, "Post-War Labor Movements in Japan," in *The International Labor Movement in Transition,* eds. Adolph Strumthal and James G. Scoville (Urbana, Ill.: University of Illinois Press, 1973), pp. 122–148; and Tadashi A. Hanami, "The Multinational Corporation and Japan-

ese Industrial Relations," in *International Labor and Multinational Enterprise*, ed. Duane Kujawa (New York: Praeger Publishers, 1975), pp. 183–185.

86. JIM: Japan Information Network, http://www.jinpapn.org/access/employ/index.html (January 4, 2004).

87. Peter B. Doeringer, Christine Evans-Klock, and David G. Terkla, "Hybrids or Hodgepodge? Workplace Practices of Japanese and Domestic Startups in the United States," *Industrial and Labor Relations Review* 51 (January 1998), pp. 171–177.

88. Krislov, "How Does the Japanese System Differ?" p. 340.

89. JIM: Japan Information Network, http://www.jinpapn.org/access/employ/index.html (January 4, 2004).

90. Glenn Halm and Clinton R. Shiels, "Damage Control: Yen Appreciation and the Japanese Labor Market," *Monthly Labor Review* 111 (November 1988), pp. 3–5.

91. JIM: Japan Information Network, http://www.jinpapn.org/access/employ/index.html (January 4, 2004).

92. *Japan* (Washington, D.C.: U.S. Department of Labor, Bureau of International Labor Affairs, 1996), pp. 10–15.

93. "An Aging Workforce Strains Japan's Traditions," *Business Week*, April 20, 1981, pp. 72–85.

94. Drawn primarily from Mario F. Bognanno, *Korea's Industrial Relations at the Turning Point* (Seoul: Korea Development Institute, 1988), pp. 4–90; Mario F. Bognanno, John W. Budd, and Young-Myon Lee, "Institutional Turmoil and Strike Activity in Korea," *Journal of Industrial Relations* 36 (September 1994), pp. 360–367; *Korea* (Washington, D.C.: U.S. Department of Labor, Bureau of International Labor Affairs, 1998), pp. 8–9; Mario F. Bognanno, Michael L. Bognanno, and Young-Myon Lee, "Incomplete Information and Conversion to a 'No Work—No Pay' Strike Policy: Their Effects on Wage Settlements and Strikes in Korea," *Working Paper*, July 1998, p. 1.

95. *Korea*, Washington D.C.: U.S. Government Printing Office, 2003, pp. 1–19.

96. *Australia*, Washington, D.C.: U.S. Printing Office, 2003, pp. 3–7.

97. Rae Cooper, "Trade Unionism in 2001," *Journal of Industrial Relations* 44, no. 2 (June 2002), p. 257.

98. Diana Kelly, "Trade Unionism in 1994," *Journal of Industrial Relations* 37 (March 1995), pp. 132–139.

99. "The Neighbors Stay Home," *The Economist*, April 12, 1995, p. 36.

100. Brian S. Klass, Michelle Brown, and Herbert G. Heneman III, "The Determinants of Organizations' Usage of Employee Dismissal: Evidence from Australia," *Journal of Labor Research* XIX (Winter 1998) pp. 150–162.

101. Jihi Xia, "Reforming China's Systems of Employment and Labor Relations," *Perspectives on Work* 7, no. 2 (Winter 2004), pp. 28–30.

102. Stephen Frenkel and Sarosh Kuruvilla, "Logic of Action, Globalization, and Changing Employment Relations in China, India, Malaysia, and the Philippines," *Industrial and Labor Relations Review* 55, no. 3 (April 2002), pp. 398–401.

103. Trini Wing-Yue Leung, "Trade Unions and Labor Relations Under Market Socialism in China," *Industrial Relations Between Command and Market: A Comparative Analysis of Eastern Europe and China*, eds. Gerd Chienstock, Paul Thompson, and Franz Traxler (New York: Nova Science, 1997), pp. 2347–280.

104. Xiangquan Zeng, "Changing Employment Relations and Human Resource Management in China," *Perspectives on Work* 7, no. 2 (Winter 2004), pp. 26–27.

105. Jihi Xia, "Reforming China's Systems of Employment and Labor Relations," *Perspectives on Work* 7, no. 2 (Winter 2004), pp. 28–30.

106. Trevor Bain and Chyi-Herng Chang, "Revisiting China and Taiwan," *Perspectives on Work* 7, no. 2 (Winter 2004), pp. 34–35.

Mobile Factory

You are the owner of a small North Carolina factory that makes T-shirts for international distribution. You have observed that your sales have declined by about 10 percent for each of the last 3 years. You believe that the reason is that you are being underpriced by your international competitors even though your market is in the United States and your competitors are required to pay transportation costs from their factories to the United States.

You have been reading several articles about exchange rates and the weakening of the dollar in comparison with many foreign currencies and believe you have come up with a unique solution to your problem. You have surveyed your 50 employees and found that most of them are single and love to travel. Therefore, you have decided to purchase a ship and transfer your machinery and office equipment to the ship. Since you pay employees and sell your goods based on where you dock your ship, you have considerable flexibility on the country in which you conduct business. When the exchange rates change, you would simply move to another location where the exchange rates are more favorable. As an example, 2 years ago, the U.S. dollar was trading for about 90 euros; in early 2004, it required nearly 120 euros to exchange for 100 U.S. dollars. That means that U.S. manufacturers are much more competitive in 2004 than they were in 2002, when the U.S. dollar was stronger internationally.

You have to decide where in the world you would like to dock your ship in order to take advantage of the exchange rates and wage rates of the country where you dock.

Questions

1. Evaluate the exchange rates and wage rates shown in exhibit 14.1 and decide where you should dock your ship for local production.

2. Review the exchange rate and wage rates of 1980, 1990, 1994, and 1998 and determine whether the strategy and decision in 2004 would be the same as in the previous years.

Collective Bargaining Negotiations Exercise: QFM Company and IWU

Learning Objectives

1. To gain an understanding of negotiation preparations, actual negotiations, and the assessment of negotiation outcomes.

2. To develop an appreciation for the psychological interactions and the realism of contract negotiations.

3. To learn to effectively apply bargaining strategies and tactics.

4. To familiarize the participants with the issues in collective bargaining and the difficulty of writing contract language that clearly expresses the intent of both parties.

5. To realize the importance of and problems associated with teamwork (intraorganizational bargaining) within a negotiation situation.

6. To gain an appreciation for the collective bargaining process as a dispute resolution procedure.

Rules of the Negotiations Exercise

1. Each participant will be assigned to either a union or management bargaining team by the instructor. Each team is responsible for determining the appropriate role each member will serve in helping the team to prepare, conduct, and evaluate the results of the contract negotiations.

2. Except for time allotted for negotiating at the bargaining table, the participants must not discuss the exercise with anyone except their assigned team members. The number, schedule, location, and length of formal bargaining meetings will be determined by the instructor. Bargaining between union and management teams should be restricted to scheduled formal bargaining meetings. During scheduled bargaining meetings, either team may call

a **bargaining caucus** for a period lasting no more than 10 minutes to avoid undue use of caucuses as a delaying tactic.

3. The contract being re-negotiated in this exercise applies only to the company's St. Louis, Missouri, plant and the bargaining unit represented by the Industrial Workers Union (IWU) at that plant. Creativity in bargaining is encouraged, but a realistic and pragmatic approach is recommended.

4. Data, materials, and information used for each position or argument on behalf of a proposal should not be falsified. Each party is under a legal duty to bargain in good faith.

5. Each team may have as many meetings *outside* class as are needed and desirable.

6. Team members should follow the instructions of their respective team leaders and represent the interests of their respective parties in a professional and ethical manner.

7. All activities of team members should be directed toward negotiating an agreement that is mutually acceptable and that the parties can live with and prosper under.

Instructions to the Participants

1. Each bargaining team is responsible for its own bargaining preparation. Begin by carefully reading the text material pertaining to the bargaining exercise. Gather background information concerning economic market conditions affecting the furniture making industry and St. Louis, Missouri, area.

2. Each team should identify bargaining subjects or issues that are important to their particular party's interests as well as consider possible subjects that might be raised by the other bargaining party during negotiations. The instructor may establish a minimum and maximum number of issues that can be introduced during the bargaining exercise by each team based upon the amount of time available for face-to-face negotiation meetings during the bargaining exercise. Major issues for negotiations could include:

   - Union security, dues check-off, union shop
   - Wages, job classes, premiums
   - Management's rights
   - Promotions and layoffs (use of seniority)
   - Grievance procedure and arbitration
   - Affirmative action plans
   - Health care insurance costs
   - Pension plans
   - Supplemental unemployment benefits
   - Vacations
   - Holidays
   - Sick leave

- Introduction of new technology
- Length or duration of the contract's term
- Other issues allowed by instructor

3. Upon identifying relevant bargaining subjects to be negotiated, each bargaining team will be responsible for conducting background research into each subject and developing a written bargaining proposal for those subjects your party plans to introduce and possible counter-proposals for subjects your party anticipates the other party is likely to introduce. The party that initially seeks to introduce a subject as part of the bargaining agenda is the party who should present an initial written proposal to the other party covering the subject. At a minimum, each initial bargaining proposal and all final agreed upon contract language should be presented in writing.

4. Based on study and analysis, each team must determine its bargaining strategy and goal priorities.

5. Prior to the first scheduled negotiation session, each team will complete a copy of the Form 1: **Prebargaining Preparation Form** and submit it to the instructor. Information included in Form 1 will identify each team's initial bargaining subjects, each subject's priority to the team, the specific language of the team's initial bargaining proposal regarding each subject, and the outcome the team realistically expects to achieve regarding each of their proposed bargaining subjects. Form 1 contains confidential information and should not be shown to any non-team member other than the instructor. The instructor will make available to participants a Word file copy of Form 1 for their use.

6. The union president and the labor relations director and their respective teams will meet at a time specified by the instructor for the purpose of negotiating a new agreement.

7. At the first meeting, the union as the party who initiated the request to renegotiate the expiring labor agreement will go first in presenting its proposals and explanation of the need for each proposal. Then management will present its initial proposal on any bargaining subjects not raised by the union and/or counterproposals on subjects already introduced by the union and justify each proposal. Each party may wish to include a brief opening statement as part of their initial presentation in an effort to establish a particular tone or atmosphere for the subsequent negotiations or in an effort to highlight or establish certain issues, trends, or expectations that the presenting party believes should guide the parties' negotiations.

8. Actual negotiations will begin after the initial proposals or counter-proposals are exchanged and will continue until a new agreement is negotiated and signed or the present contract expires at the end of the final scheduled bargaining meeting.

9. On completion of the negotiations, each team will submit a written copy of the new labor agreement containing all agreed upon changes in contract language. The labor agreement should be signed by authorized representatives of each bargaining team, signifying the legally binding nature of the contract agreement. The instructor may make other team assignments such as estimating the total annual costs of the new agreement or completion of a **bargaining book**

containing each team's bargaining research, notes, observations, and so on regarding bargaining subjects and the negotiations process.

10. Additional instructions may be given to the participants by the instructor.

Sources of Materials for Preparation

Government publications: U.S. Department of Labor, Bureau of Labor Statistics, *Area Wage Surveys, Employment and Earnings, Handbook of Labor Statistics, Monthly Labor Review, Characteristics of Major Collective Bargaining Agreements.*

U.S. Department of Commerce, *U.S. Industrial Outlook* (published every year).

Binder services of Bureau of National Affairs, Inc. (BNA) and Commerce Clearing House. Especially helpful is the BNA *Collective Bargaining Negotiations and Contracts.*

Business publications: *Business Week* and *The Wall Street Journal.*

Professional labor relations journals: *Dispute Resolution Journal, Employee Relations Law Journal, Industrial and Labor Relations Review, Industrial Relations, Berkeley Journal of Employment and Labor Law, Journal of Collective Negotiations in the Public Sector, Labor Law Journal,* and *Monthly Labor Review.*

Proceedings: Industrial Relations Research Association, Labor Law Developments, National Academy of Arbitrators, and NYU Conference on Labor.

Labor agreements from companies or labor unions, as available.

The Furniture Manufacturing Industry

The furniture industry has undergone significant change over the past decade.[1] The consumer demand for furniture was strong throughout the 1990s as some 76 million "baby boomers" born between 1946 and 1964 reached their prime earning career stage amid strong growth in the general economy. Several important trends in the furniture manufacturing industry have been observed, including a consolidation of the number of firms in the industry through merger and acquisition activity; increased investment in new plants, equipment, and more efficient manufacturing processes and methods; more customization options of mass-produced products and the creation of niche markets (e.g., unstained wood furniture, ready-to-assemble furniture) to better serve consumer preferences; and decreased product delivery lead times.

The U.S. furniture manufacturing industry has been facing significant new global market competition from imported furniture products. Over the past 10 years the U.S. market share of domestic wood household furniture manufacturing firms has declined by approximately one-third, with China accounting for approximately 41 percent and Canada 16 percent of the value of imported goods.[2] Improvements in containerized shipping and packing technologies have lowered transportation costs for importers, and a relatively strong U.S. dollar value and reduced trade barriers for entry into the U.S. market have contributed to the gain in import furniture sales.

Although plants are scattered throughout the United States, two-thirds are located in the Southeast, the Middle Atlantic, and the Great Lakes regions. Because the Pacific Coast has an ample supply of softwood and hardwood, more plants are currently locating there. Manufacturers using plastics and metals rather than wood in their furniture are able to locate closer to their markets and have therefore spread throughout the country.

Products are distributed over fairly wide geographical areas and approximately 72 percent of the output is sold directly to retailers.[3] Brand names and product line identity are important to some of the larger manufacturers, but the demand for high-quality furniture, such as the "Eagle" brand for QFM Company, is basically recession proof.

Furniture manufacturer sales are particularly sensitive to changes in consumer spending patterns since many furniture purchases are capable of being postponed to a later date. Consumer spending on furniture is expected to grow at a rate of 2.1 percent in 2003 and 3.9 percent in 2004.[4] Low mortgage interest rates should encourage continued growth in the housing market, and a weaker U.S. dollar in relation to other foreign currencies should aid U.S. furniture exports.[5] Furniture shipments grew an estimated 5.5 percent in 2002 after suffering a 10 percent decline in 2001.[6] 2003 furniture shipments should rise 5.4% to $24.9 billion, slightly below the record $25.6 billion recorded in 2000. A 4.6% growth rate is forecast for 2004, which would establish a new record of $26.1 billion in furniture shipments.

The QFM Company and the Union

QFM Company began in 1820 in Laconia, New Hampshire, as a family-owned and operated furniture manufacturer. It was headed by Herman Sweeny, one of the early settlers in Laconia. The company grew to thirty employees by 1920, but at that time, Ben Franklin Sweeny, Herman's son, decided to move the firm to St. Louis, Missouri—a location more central to the firm's market. Barely surviving the 1930s depression, QFM was one of the first companies to convert its manufacturing processes to the production of war materials. The company prospered during the war, and afterward, Sweeny decided to expand, sell stock publicly, and focus on producing metal and plastic-laminated furniture. With the production experience it had gained during the war and with its location some distance from the predominantly wood-furniture manufacturers, QFM Company launched a new era for itself in 1946.

By 1970, the St. Louis plant of QFM Company had 1,300 employees and was producing 450 dinette sets, 200 sets of lawn tables and chairs, and 300 bar stools and miscellaneous furniture daily. Furniture sales soared during the 1971 to 1973 furniture boom, raising expectations of continuous growth. QFM's new president, Gerald Brooks, decided that a new, modern plant and more diversity in the product line were necessary to meet the expected demand. Taking into consideration location, material supply, transportation, markets, labor situations, and other factors, Brooks decided to build the new plant in Dallas, Texas. This plant was to specialize in the new product lines, and the St. Louis plant was to concentrate only on dinette sets. In 1972, 200 employees were transferred from St. Louis, and another 200 were hired from the Dallas–Fort Worth area. The Dallas plant started with no union and 400 employees. In 1993 the founder's granddaughter, Bethany Sweeny, became plant manager, and the plant size grew to the current 900-employee non-union workforce. QFM's Dallas employees average at least $1 less per hour than St. Louis employees in comparable jobs, which the company has always attributed to the lower cost of living in the Dallas–Ft. Worth area.

The St. Louis plant continues to produce metal and plastic laminated furniture, mostly for sale to chain retailers (e.g., Wal-Mart, Babcock Home Furnishing, Home Depot), and currently employs 1,010 employees in the bargaining unit represented by the IWU. No new product lines have been added at the St. Louis plant in recent years, and its employment level has remained steady over the past 30 years. The company has invested in modernizing plant equipment and production methods at both the St. Louis and Dallas plants since the mid-1980s. The Dallas plant has started producing a new high-end product line—dinette sets under the Eagle brand name aimed at capturing higher income consumer demand. Consumer response has been positive, and the Dallas plant's future looks very promising. With increasing import competition, the company is investigating the possibility of locating a production facility in China or Mexico, but no final decision has been reached yet on whether to initiate such an expansion. Throughout its history, QFM Company has prided itself on being a progressive employer.

The Industrial Workers United (IWU) first sought to represent QFM employees at the St. Louis plant in 1975. The building of the Dallas plant, increasing employment at the Dallas plant rather than the St. Louis plant, and employee complaints about lower than average area wage rates were all issues in the 1975 representation election campaign at the St. Louis plant. After a heated campaign by both management and the union, NLRB investigations of unfair labor practices, and challenged ballots, the union lost the election by a vote of 497 to 481. Two years later, the union returned and won an NLRB supervised representation election by a vote of 611 to 375. The election campaign was bitter, and the negotiations that followed were even more hostile. After a 6-week strike, QFM and the IWU reached a settlement on the terms of their first labor agreement. There have been nine negotiations since that initial settlement was reached, and no strikes have occurred during that period. The current labor agreement covering bargaining unit employees at the St. Louis plant is close to its expiration date, prompting the Union to notify management requesting the Company renegotiate the existing contract terms which the company has agreed to do. Although the company officials now express a commitment to return to the era when management and labor trusted each other, worked cooperatively, and shared mutual goals and benefits, the union leaders are reacting by waiting to see their deeds. For example, union leaders note that the Company recently announced its intention to increase the employee contribution to health care insurance premium cost by 15 percent to offset an insurance premium cost increase imposed by the insurance carrier on the company. Currently, 75% of bargaining unit members have selected family coverage at an annual premium cost per employee of $2,970, while 25 percent of bargaining unit members have single employee coverage at an annual premium cost of $1,412 per employee. Union members believe the Company could easily afford to absorb this premium cost increase without having to pass it along to bargaining unit members. The upcoming negotiations will determine the extent of the company's commitment to a new era in labor relations at the plant. The union believes it is entering negotiations in a strong position, with 95 percent of the bargaining unit now union members and an improving economic outlook for the company.

REFERENCES

1. Steven H. Bullard and Cynthia D. West, *Furniture Manufacturing and Marketing: Eight Strategic Issues for the 21st Century* (Starkville, Miss.: Forest and Wildlife Research Center, Bulletin FP 227, Mississippi State University, 2002).

2. Albert Schuler and Urs Buehlmann, *Identifying Future Competitive Business Strategies for the U.S. Residential Wood Furniture Industry: Benchmarking and Paradigm Shifts* (Newtown Square, Penn.: USDA Forest Service, 2002); Brian Carroll, "China Imports Surge 33%," *Furniture Today*, November 4, 2002, p. 18; John E. Hilsenrath and Peter Wonacott, "The Economy: Imports Hammer Furniture Makers—Competition from China, Canada Leads to Closings, Price Cuts in U.S. Industry," *Wall Street Journal*, September 20, 2002, p. A2; and Hannah Miller, "Furniture Imports: Opportunity or Threat?" *Wood and Wood Products*, July 2001, pp. 95–100.

3. Schuler and Buehlmann, *Identifying Future Competitive Business Strategies*, p. 11.

4. "Consumer Spending to Drop Slightly," *FDM*, 75 (2), February 2003, p. 25.

5. Brian Collins, "New Home Sales Appear to Be on Rebound After Two Sluggish Months," *National Mortgage News* 27(32), May 5, 2003, p. 6; Kim Kennedy, "Manufacturing to Turn Corner in 2003," *FDM* 75(2), February 2003, p. 32.

6. "2003 Forecast: Slower Growth," *Furniture Today*, January 13, 2003, pp. 8–9.

Form 1: Prebargaining Preparation Form

Each bargaining team must complete both parts A and B of the form. Part A is for the team's own strategic planning and should **not** be revealed to any other bargaining team. Part B contains your team's initial written bargaining proposals to be presented to the other bargaining team with whom you will be negotiating during the first bargaining meeting.

Part A

Bargaining Subject Area	Bargaining Priority (rank in order each subject from 1 to *n*, with 1 being the highest priority subject)	Realistic Expected Bargaining Outcome

Part B: Initial Bargaining Proposals

Instructions: For each initial bargaining proposal or counterproposal that your team intends to introduce as part of the bargaining agenda at the first joint negotiation meeting, include a complete, specific, and clear wording of each bargaining subject proposal.

The (current, but soon to expire) Labor Agreement between Quality Furniture Manufacturing Company (QFM) and Industrial Workers United (IWU), AFL-CIO

This agreement is entered into on _____ by the Quality Furniture Manufacturing Company (QFM), located in St. Louis, Missouri, and Industrial Workers United (IWU). This agreement covers employees at the St. Louis plant only.

Article I—Recognition

The company recognizes the IWU as the sole and exclusive collective bargaining agent in all matters pertaining to rates of pay, wages, hours of employment, and other conditions of employment for all production and maintenance employees at the St. Louis plant, excluding professional employees, storeroom employees, office clerical employees, guards, and supervisors, as defined in the Labor Management Relations Act.

Article II—Union Security

The company agrees not to interfere with the right of employees to join the Union and will not discriminate against employees who are Union members. Employees in the bargaining unit are completely free to participate in the affairs of the Union, provided that such activities do not interfere with their work duties and responsibilities.

While no employee will be required to join the Union as a condition of employment, union dues will be deducted from any bargaining unit employee's pay check, provided proper written notification is given to the Company. At the end of each pay period, the Company will forward the collected dues, minus a 5-percent administrative fee, to the Union.

Article III—Management Rights

All management functions of the enterprise that are not specifically limited by the express language of this agreement are retained by the Company. The functions and rights listed here are examples of the exclusive responsibilities retained by the Company and are not intended as an all-inclusive list: to manage the manufacturing operations and methods of production; to direct the workforce; to decide what work shall be performed in the plant by subcontractors or by employees; to schedule working hours (including overtime work); to hire, promote, demote, and transfer; to suspend, discipline, and discharge for cause; to relieve employees due to lack of work or for other legitimate reasons; to create and enforce reasonable shop rules and regulations; to establish production standards and rates for new or changed jobs; to introduce new and improved methods, materials, equipment, and facilities; to change or eliminate existing methods, materials, equipment, and facilities.

Article IV—No Strike and No Lockout

The company agrees that during the life of this agreement there shall be no lockout of bargaining unit employees. The Union agrees that during the life of this agreement there shall be no strike, work stoppage, slowdown, work refusal, delay of work, refusal to report for work, or boycott.

Article V—Hours of Work

The normal workweek shall consist of eight (8) hours per day, forty (40) hours per week, for a five (5) day week, from Monday to Friday. The starting time shall be made by the Company, and it can be changed by the Company to suit varying conditions of the business. Such changes in working schedules shall be made known to the Union representative in the plant as far in advance as possible. Employees shall be notified by a written bulletin or other communications medium.

Article VI—Grievance and Arbitration Procedures

Grievances arising out of the interpretation and application of the terms of this agreement shall be handled and settled in the following manner:

Step 1: The aggrieved employee and/or shop steward shall discuss the grievance with his or her supervisor.

Step 2: Should the answer provided by the supervisor not produce a satisfactory solution to the grievance, the grievance shall be reduced to writing and shall state the provision of the agreement that has been violated. The department head shall arrange for a meeting of the aggrieved employee, the shop steward, the supervisor, the employee relations supervisor, and himself or herself for the purpose of discussing the grievance. The department head shall provide a written answer to the grievance after the close of the meeting.

Step 3: If a satisfactory conclusion is not reached, the grievance can be referred to the plant manager by the Union. The plant manager shall schedule a meeting to discuss the grievance with the Union. The local Union can bring in a representative of the International Union at this step, and the plant manager can bring in anyone who he or she feels may aid in the resolution of the grievance.

Step 4: If a grievance is appealed to arbitration, the Company and the Union shall attempt to select an arbitrator. If this attempt fails, the Company and/or Union shall ask the Federal Mediation and Conciliation Service to submit a list of seven (7) arbitrators. Each party shall eliminate three (3) names from the list by alternately striking one name and the person whose name remains shall serve as the arbitrator.

The arbitrator shall render a decision in writing that shall be final and binding upon the parties. The arbitrator to whom any grievance is submitted shall have the authority to interpret and apply the provisions of this agreement, and the arbitrator's decision must be in accordance with and based upon the terms of this agreement or of any written amendment thereto. The arbitrator shall have no jurisdiction or authority to add to, subtract from, or modify any of the terms of this agreement.

The Company and local Union shall each pay its own expenses incurred in connection with the arbitration and one-half of the expenses and fees of the arbitrator and the facilities used in the arbitration hearing.

Article VII—Seniority

Seniority as used in this agreement shall be the period of continuous service in the job or plant from the date of the employee's appointment. **Probationary employment** consists of a period of one hundred twenty (120) days of employment.

Layoffs shall be made in the following order:

a. Probationary employees
b. Other employees in order of job seniority

Recall shall be made in the following order:

a. Employees in order of job seniority, given equal job ability
b. Probationary employees

Promotions shall be made on the basis of qualifications, merit, and seniority. Promotions out of the bargaining unit remain management's prerogative.

An employee who quits or is discharged for cause shall lose all seniority rights. If the Company decides to terminate any operation or job and the employees remain on layoff for a period of twelve (12) months, the employees shall be considered to have been terminated for cause at the expiration of said twelve (12)-month period.

Article VIII —Wages and Classifications

Job classifications and a wage schedule setting forth the rates of pay of the various job classifications are included in Schedule A and are hereby made part of this agreement.

If and when the Company creates a new job classification or modifies, alters, amends, or combines existing jobs, or revises the skills and responsibilities of a job, job descriptions will be drawn and a wage rate assigned. The Union shall have a maximum of five (5) working days to examine the job description to determine whether it accurately describes the principal functions and whether the pay range is consistent with established job classification pay ranges.

If the Union takes exception, it can review both factors with the Company. If the issue cannot be resolved, the Union can take the issue through the grievance procedure.

Job classifications are for pay purposes only and do not pertain to whoever might perform the work in that classification—unless modified by the terms of the agreement.

Article IX—Insurance

An employee who has completed ninety (90) days of employment is eligible for enrollment in the company group insurance programs on the monthly premium date for each particular insurance program that next follows the completion of ninety (90) days of employment.

1. **Group Life Insurance** coverage = $20,000
   Accidental Death and Dismemberment coverage = $20,000

2. **Accident and Health Insurance**

Lost income due to a covered condition equals one-half of the employee's weekly pay up to a maximum of $150. It is understood and agreed that the cost of the hospitalization, medical and health insurance, major medical insurance, accident and health and life insurance will be paid 50 percent (50%) by the Company and 50 percent (50%) by the employee, when subscribed to by the employee. It is understood and agreed that in the event that the Company wishes to change carriers, there is no obligation to negotiate with the Union prior to instituting the change.

Employees on medical leave for a period in excess of ninety (90) consecutive days may continue to be covered under the group insurance program after the first ninety (90) days, providing the employee pays the total insurance premium.

Article X—Pension Plan

A pension plan for bargaining unit employees of the company is hereby incorporated as a part of this agreement. The normal monthly retirement benefit for all years of service is $20 per month per year of service.

Article XI—Holidays

All employees, after completing six (6) months of service with the Company, shall be paid eight (8) hours pay for the following holidays:

- New Year's Day
- Independence Day
- Labor Day
- Thanksgiving Day
- Day after Thanksgiving Day
- Christmas Eve Day
- Christmas Day

To be eligible for holiday pay, the employee must have worked the day immediately preceding and following the holiday. Legitimate excuses for absences will be considered.

Article XII—Vacation

Employees shall qualify for vacation with pay in accordance with the following (determined June 1 of each year):

Continuous Service	Vacation with Pay
More than 1 but less than 5 years	1 week
5 years but less than 10 years	2 weeks
10 years but less than 20 years	3 weeks
20 or more years	4 weeks

Vacation pay shall be computed on the basis of each employee's average weekly earnings from June to June. Payment will be made on the work day prior to the vacation period.

Article XIII —Sick Leave

A full-time employee is eligible for sick leave after completing six (6) months service with the Company. An eligible employee will accumulate sick leave at the rate of one-half day per month of service from date of hire. Sick leave will not be carried over from one year (January 1 to December 31) to the next, and it can be used only for personal illness not covered by workers' compensation. The Company retains the right to require a doctor's certificate as proof that an employee's absence was due to a legitimate injury or illness.

Article XIV—Nondiscrimination

The Company and the Union mutually agree not to discriminate in making decisions and determinations concerning hiring, promotion, employment termination, transfer, compensation, and terms or conditions of employment. Both parties agree that all such decisions and determinations will be made without regard to race, color, religion, sex, age, disability not related to job performance, national origin or ancestry, or because an individual is disabled or a Vietnam-era veteran.

Article XV—Complete Agreement

This agreement is complete. It may be amended by mutual agreement in writing. Such amendment may be effective during the term of this agreement and may extend the term of this agreement. This agreement does not operate to include, nor does it obligate the Company to continue in effect, any working condition, benefit or past practice which is not covered or contained in the agreement.

Article XVI—Duration of the Agreement

This agreement shall become effective as of _____, and shall continue in effect until _____. Thereafter, this agreement shall renew itself for yearly periods unless written notice of termination is given by one party to the other not less than sixty (60) nor more than ninety (90) days prior to the expiration of this agreement.

Schedule A: Current Wages and Classifications

Wage Grade	Job Title	Wage Rate
1	Janitor	$7.65
2	General laborer	10.60
3	Materials handler	10.71
4	Packer	9.85
	Machine operator B	13.40
	Utility worker	12.69
	Interplant truck driver	13.50
	Sander	12.69
	Assembler	16.50
5	Welder	14.43
	Machine operator A	16.10
	Electrician B	19.71
	Machinists B	15.71
	Gluer	13.71
6	Mechanic	16.84
	Spray painter	16.84
	Cutoff saw operator	14.84
7	Electrician A	24.86
	Machinists A	21.80
	Inspector	15.86
8	Tool grinder A	16.88
9	Tool and die maker A	17.90
10	Leadperson	20.66

Exhibit 1

QFM Company Balance Sheet, 2003

Assets	
Current Assets:	
Cash	$2,590,105
Notes and accounts receivable	59,890,920
Inventories	75,670,887
Prepaid Expenses	992,037
Total Current Assets	$139,143,949
Fixed Assets:	
Land	$12,062,719
Buildings	30,156,799
Machinery and equipment	23,690,215
Total Fixed Assets	65,909,733
Total Assets	$205,053,682
Liabilities and Stockholders' Investment	
Current Liabilities	
Notes and accounts payable	$19,914,098
Accrued payroll	7,961,395
Taxes (local, state, federal)	59,749,921
Total Current Liabilities	$87,625,414
Stockholders' Investment	
Common stock (common @ $20 per share)	48,251,742
Earned surplus	69,176,526
Total Stockholders' Investment and Earned Surplus	$117,428,268
Total Liabilities and Stockholders' Investment	$205,053,682

Exhibit 2

QFM Company Income Statement

	2002	2003
Net Sales	$238,115,271	$250,021,035
Costs of Goods Sold		
Production (labor, materials, overtime)	$182,314,515	$185,960,805
Administrative	15,806,447	16,280,640
Sales	9,469,799	9,706,544
Other	2,077.494	2,119,044
Total Cost of Goods Sold	$209,668,255	214,067,033
Income before taxes	28,447,016	35,954,002
Taxes (local, state, federal)	7,015,580	6,338,460
Net Income	$21,431,436	29,615,542

Exhibit 3

QFM Company Net Sales and Income

	Net Sales	Net Income
2002	$238,115,271	21,431,436
2003	250,021,035	29,615,542
2004 (estimated)	261,526,337	32,577,096

Exhibit 4

Current Number of QFM Production and Maintenance Employees by Seniority and Plant Location

Years of Seniority	St. Louis	Dallas
Less than 1	10	100
1–2	45	150
3–4	50	90
5–6	120	135
7–10	165	165
11–15	128	84
16–20	190	66
21–25	105	58
26–30	120	45
more than 30	77	7
Total	1,010	900*

*Includes some employees who transferred from the St. Louis plant with seniority.

Exhibit 5

Number of QFM Employees in Each Job Title, by Wage Grade

Wage Grade	Job Title	St. Louis	Dallas
1	Janitor	10	9
2	General laborer	30	32
3	Materials handler	45	48
4	Packer	36	35
	Machine operator B	120	120
	Utility worker	38	20
	Interplant truck driver	16	18
	Sander	40	40
	Assembler	295	319
5	Welder	16	10
	Machine operator A	120	62
	Electrician B	5	7
	Maintenance worker B	11	12
	Gluer	56	40
6	Mechanic	10	8
	Spray painter	43	35
	Cutoff saw operator	25	18
7	Electrician A	15	8
	Maintenance worker A	11	8
	Inspector	26	18
8	Tool grinder A	5	5
9	Tool and die maker A	12	8
10	Lead person	25	20
Total		1,010	900

Exhibit 6

Average Hourly Earnings, Excluding Overtime, for All Manufacturing Employees in Selected Industries

	2002	2003 (Mar.)
Total Manufacturing	$15.29	$15.62
Durable Goods	16.01	16.33
Wood products	12.33	12.51
Furniture and related products	12.62	12.93
Stone, clay, and glass products	15.39	15.52
Primary metal industries	17.68	17.86
Fabricated metal products	14.68	14.97
Machinery	15.93	16.19
Electric equipment and appliances	13.97	14.25
Transportation equipment	20.64	21.07
Miscellaneous manufacturing	12.91	13.22
Nondurable Goods	14.15	14.53
Food manufacturing	12.54	12.70
Textile product mills	10.96	10.98
Apparel	9.10	9.45
Paper and allied products	16.89	17.22
Printing and related support activities	14.93	15.33
Chemicals	17.97	18.33
Petroleum and coal products	23.06	24.17
Plastics and rubber products	13.55	14.00
Leather and allied products	11.01	11.62

SOURCE: Bureau of Labor Statistics, U.S. Department of Labor, "Average Hours and Earnings of Production and Non-supervisory Workers on Private Non-farm Payrolls by Detailed Industry," May 2003 at http://www.bls.gov.

Exhibit 7

Mean Hourly Earnings of Selected Manufacturing Plant Employees in Dallas and St. Louis, 2002

Job Titles	Dallas (Mar.)	St. Louis (June)
Assemblers	$13.91	$18.18
Electrician	20.43	25.93
Production Inspector	11.81	13.49
Machine operator	11.79	15.14
Industrial Machine Repairer	17.31	20.75
Truck driver	16.20	15.49
Stock handler	9.39	11.01
Packer	10.50	10.04
Material handler	13.15	19.18
Forklift operator	15.11	14.31
Janitor	8.15	8.47
Laborer	8.53	11.97

SOURCE: U.S. Department of Labor, Bureau of Labor Statistics, *Dallas–Fort Worth, TX, National Compensation Survey, March 2002* (Washington, D.C.: U.S. Government Printing Office, 1999), pp. 3–5; U.S. Department of Labor, Bureau of Labor Statistics, *St. Louis, MO-IL, National Compensation Survey, June 2002* (Washington, D.C.: U.S. Government Printing Office, 1997), pp. 4–5.

Exhibit 8

Consume Price Index for Urban Wage Earners and Clerical Workers and Percent Changes

Year	Index	Percent Change From Past Year
2001	173.5	2.7
2002	175.9	1.4
2003 (May)	179.4	2.0

SOURCE: Bureau of Labor Statistics, U.S. Department of Labor, "Consumer Price Indexes," May 2003 at http://www.bls.gov.

Exhibit 9

Average Hourly and Weekly Earnings for All Private Workers and for Production Workers

	2001	2002
Hourly Earnings		
Total private	$14.53	$14.95
Manufacturing	14.76	15.29
Furniture and related products	—	12.62
Average Weekly Earnings		
Total private	$493.20	$506.22
Manufacturing	$595.19	$618.87
Furniture and related products	—	494.14
Average Weekly Hours		
Total private	34.0	33.9
Manufacturing	40.3	40.5
Household furniture	—	39.2

SOURCE: Bureau of Labor Statistics, U.S. Department of Labor, "Table B-2: Hours and earnings of production workers or non-supervisory workers on private non-farm payrolls by major industry sector, 1964 to date," and "Table B-15: Average hours and earnings of production workers on private non-farm payrolls by detailed industry," May 2003 at http://www.bls.gov.